Intermediate Microeconomics: An Interactive Approach

Stephen Erfle
Dickinson College

The Quality Instructors Expect.
At Prices Students Can Afford.

Replacing Oligarch Textbooks since 2004

To my children, Dave, Kate, and Vera

I wish to thank Linda Erfle, NWS, AWS, for allowing us to use the image of her painting, *Napa Sunrise*, on the front cover of this book. See more of her work at lindaerfle.net

—*Steve Erfle*

Intermediate Microeconomics: An Interactive Approach

ISBN-13: 978-0-9969962-0-4
ISBN-10: 0-9969962-0-6

Printed in the United States of America by Textbook Media Press.

Contents

PART 2 CONSUMER THEORY

Preface

Anyone undertaking the job of writing an intermediate microeconomics text must first answer the question: Why write a new text when there are excellent texts already available? My answer has nothing to do with topic coverage, but rather with *how* those topics are covered. This text takes an active-learning, geometric approach to the subject by incorporating technology more centrally into the learning experience.

Static figures from the text are supplemented by dynamic counterparts that allow comparative statics analysis via mouse clicks. The interactive Excel files allow student exploration via sliders and click boxes to help students understand how graphic elements relate to one another. These files do not require knowledge of Excel.

The origin of this text can be directly traced to work I did more than 15 years ago, creating Excel materials for Edwin Mansfield's managerial economics text. Due to the success of those materials, Ed Parsons, then economics editor at W. W. Norton & Company, invited me to create materials for Joseph Stiglitz's introductory economics text in 2000. I jumped at this opportunity because I felt that Stiglitz would one day win the Nobel Prize. (He shared the Nobel with George Akerlof and Michael Spence [who taught me microeconomics and who was on my thesis committee while in graduate school] in 2001—you can read about their work in Chapter 21.) I wrote interactive tutorials in Word and Excel that were programmed into Flash. I later learned that those tutorials were the most accessed part of the web resources for Stiglitz's text.

Converting those materials into Flash was a challenge because graphic artists and programmers, unfamiliar with economic concepts, found it difficult to render graphic materials correctly, even when given accurate graphs to reproduce. (The average/marginal relation is perhaps the most common case in point. All economists understand how marginal pulls average, but graphic designers often do not understand this basic point, and inaccurate graphs result.) This experience led me to understand why so many economics texts have incorrect graphics. It also helped me to recognize that my comparative advantage lay in creating interactive graphic materials that could help students learn economics.

I began by working on electronic materials to support existing intermediate microeconomics textbooks for various publishers. But I soon came to believe that the best way to truly add value was to write my own text and to integrate the interactive material as the centerpiece. *Intermediate Microeconomics: An Interactive Approach* is the result.

The overarching premise of *Intermediate Microeconomics: An Interactive Approach* is that microeconomics is most effectively learned in an active-learning, interactive environment. One aspect of that interactivity is that students have access to more than 100 interactive Excel files, identified by the symbol in the text, that allow students to move the graphs using sliders and click boxes. Each of these graphs is "anatomically correct" and able to be moved via student interaction.

Additionally, *Intermediate Microeconomics: An Interactive Approach* has more figures than are typical, and many of the figures involve multiple scenarios of the same basic graph. The text often employs interactive questions that require interpreting these scenarios; questions posed are answered at the bottom of the page.

This geometric orientation does not mean that *Intermediate Microeconomics: An Interactive Approach* is light on algebraic analysis. The geometry is backed up with relevant algebra. More than 500 equations are numbered for easy reference both within and across chapters. And, just like the geometry, the algebra is essentially error-free because it was used to create the graphs. One benefit of this approach is that some of the more intricate or complex algebra (such as Cobb-Douglas cost in Chapters 10 and 11), which in other texts is provided in appendices with warning labels, can be more effectively examined because the essential structure of the algebra is readily visible in geometric relief.

Despite relegating calculus to appendices and endnotes only, *Intermediate Microeconomics: An Interactive Approach* readily could be used in a calculus-enhanced class. For example, Lagrangians are employed in the Chapter 6 Appendix, and lecture notes providing a geometric interpretation of Lagrange multipliers are provided in Chapter 6 of the *Instructor Guide*, which correlates with several Chapter 6 *Workbook* questions.

Flexible Text Organization

Most instructors spend the vast majority of an intermediate microeconomics course focused on the fundamentals and then pick and choose among applications as time permits at the end of the course. As a result, more time, energy, and ink are spent on the core material than on applications.

Intermediate Microeconomics: An Interactive Approach is composed of five parts. The core material is presented in Parts 2–4 (Chapters 3–16), and applications are provided in Part 5 (Chapters 17–22). Because some instructors may wish to explore some of the applications topics in a different order than is presented in the text, prerequisite information for each section is provided next to the section heading. Prerequisite information is also provided in Chapter 16 because some instructors will prefer to interleave the welfare discussion into the earlier parts of the text, rather than have a unified discussion after the various market structures have been discussed.

Even though Excel was heavily employed in writing *Intermediate Microeconomics: An Interactive Approach*, the text is written for traditional instructors who do not wish to teach an "Excel-enhanced" course. Those wishing to teach an Excel-enhanced course might want to bring the present value material from Chapter 19 to the front of the course. That material was written in a layered fashion, and it works quite well inserted in front of Chapter 3. See the schematic of the text denoting section dependencies. The schematic also delineates sections within the core that are optional.

By its very nature, *Intermediate Microeconomics: An Interactive Approach* is built for electronic delivery. Interaction with the Excel figure files that are at the core of the text is most seamlessly accomplished online. For those wishing to use a print textbook, however, one is available for purchase.

Special Features and Ancillaries for Students

Pedagogical and ancillary materials available for student use with this text include:

- The more than 100 interactive Excel files that comprise the core of the text.
- End-of-chapter matching and short-answer questions that provide basic problem-solving scenarios and a quick check on students' understanding of the material. Answers are provided in the Answers Appendix at the end of the text.
- A 34-page *Mathematical Appendix*, available online. This appendix covers three substantive areas: (1) a 14-page review of algebra and geometry, (2) a 13-page primer on basic derivative rules provided from a "user's perspective" for those wishing to incorporate calculus into the class, and (3) a 7-page primer on using Excel in economic modeling. Many of the topics are fleshed out using more than 20 extended examples drawn from portions of the text.
- The *Student Guide to Intermediate Microeconomics: An Interactive Approach*, available online. This guide offers the views of three students *who worked through the text material themselves*. It provides insights regarding where the students got stuck and how they got "unstuck" in the learning process. The *Student Guide* is

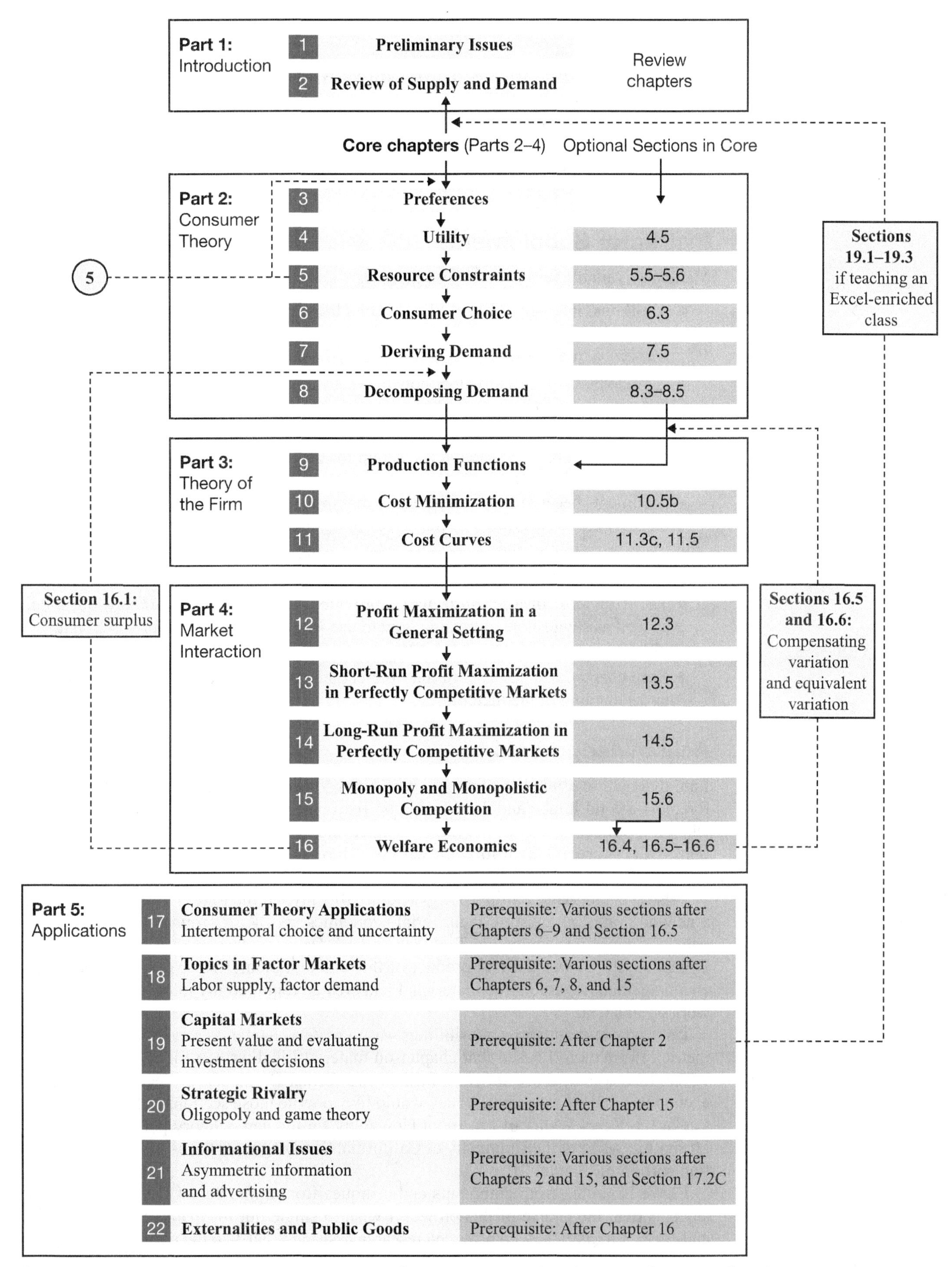

Schematic of Text Organization, Denoting Section Dependencies and Optional Sections

Solid arrows describe proposed flow; dashed arrows suggest alternative flow paths.

provided as a Word document so that students can add their own annotations as they read the text.

- The *Intermediate Microeconomics: An Interactive Approach Workbook*, which provides in-depth problems, a number of which utilize the interactive Excel files that are at the core of the text. These problems are designed to be turned in as homework. Sometimes, the problems build off earlier problems. Problems that are likely to be turned in on different days are placed on different pages. For the same reason, the *Workbook* is delivered single-sided, ready for a three-ring binder.

Instructor Supplements

Materials available for instructor use include:

- Additional interactive Excel files, beyond those provided with the text. These files have built-in scenarios, not available in the student files, which show answers to *Workbook* questions.
- A guide that shows instructors how to create and capture their own scenarios so that they can generate exam questions using the interactive Excel files.
- For each chapter, a Word file that provides screenshots of all textbook figures, together with the scenario Q&As, set up for overhead projection—an exceptionally useful tool when teaching from the text. These chapter files are provided as Word documents because they can be easily manipulated in class, for example, to hide the answers at the bottom of the screen to figures with interactive questions.
- An *Instructor Guide* that provides a quick overview of materials covered in each chapter, along with teaching suggestions.
- The *Workbook Answer Guide*, which provides answers to each *Workbook* question, as well as suggestions regarding how to use *Workbook* questions for additional instruction (and for test purposes).
- Each chapter also has a set of multiple-choice questions for quizzing students' understanding of the material.

Acknowledgments

I am indebted to a number of people who helped bring this project to market. First and foremost are Ed Laube and Tom Doran of Textbook Media Press, who were willing to take on a project of this scope. Mary Monner and Victoria Putman, of Putman Productions, LLC, were a delight to work with on editorial issues; this text is certainly better because of their efforts.

I also wish to thank Philip Young, who in 2012 invited me to join him in coauthoring a new edition of an existing managerial economics text. Keat, Young, and Erfle, *Managerial Economics: Economic Tools for Today's Decision Makers*, 7th edition, Pearson Education, 2013, was the end product of this collaboration. That experience and Phil's encouragement regarding the materials I had created reignited my interest in completing work on this text.

Part of those coauthor responsibilities was to write a chapter on game theory and asymmetric information. I based that chapter on material I had written for this text early on. Rather than rewrite those sections, I asked two former Dickinson College students, now economists in their own right, if they would like to write those sections of this text. I wish to thank J. Kerry Waller of Piedmont University for the game theory portion of Chapter 20 and Jue Wang of the University of California, San Diego, for the asymmetric information portion of Chapter 21.

I have benefited from comments and critiques from a number of Dickinson College students over the course of this project. I wish to single out for thanks Susan Cerniglia and Holly Kirkpatrick, who provided research assistance early in the writing process, and

John Mayers, who was my research assistant this past year. He, together with David Erfle and Jacob Milligan, wrote the *Student Guide* mentioned earlier.

Although I have used many of the *Workbook* questions over the years in intermediate microeconomics and managerial economics classes, I want to single out for thanks the group of 12 students who participated in a semester-long workshop during Spring 2006. These students worked through the text, as well as beta versions of the *Workbook* questions, in a workshop format.

Finally, I want to thank my family. My children—Dave, Kate, and Vera—certainly saw less of me during this process, and it was often in front of a computer screen. My wife, Laura, held it all together and, in addition, offered a keen eye for detail as she read various versions of the manuscript. I wish to thank all of them for helping me see this project through to the end.

About the Author

Stephen Erfle
Photo courtesy of Carl Socolow, Dickinson College.

Dr. Stephen E. Erfle received a BS in mathematics and a BA in economics from the University of California, Davis, and an MA and PhD in economics from Harvard University. During the late 1990s, Dr. Erfle helped found the International Business and Management Department and major at Dickinson College. By 2012, this had become the largest major at Dickinson College. He has also taught in the Economics Department at Dickinson College and in the School of Social Sciences at the University of California, Irvine.

Trained as a microeconomic theorist, Dr. Erfle is an interdisciplinary scholar with published research in a variety of fields, ranging from communications theory, political geography, economics, and economics pedagogy, to the psychology of sports and public health. He is coauthor with Philip Young and Paul Keat of *Managerial Economics: Economic Tools for Today's Decision Makers*, 7th edition, Pearson Education, 2013. His interest in managerial economics stems from a 14-month sabbatical at Seagram Classics Wine Company in the mid-1990s, during which he maintained offices at Sterling Vineyards and at Mumm Cuvée Napa, where the finance and marketing departments of SCWC resided. This sabbatical also provided his introduction to Excel and solidified in his mind the need to integrate Excel into a business curriculum, due to its ubiquity in the business world. As noted in the Preface, that experience also eventually led to this text.

Dr. Erfle has fielded questions from instructors regarding his managerial teaching materials for a number of years, and he is happy to continue that practice with this project. He can be reached at erfle@dickinson.edu.

INTRODUCTION

(I can't get no) satisfaction. (The Rolling Stones, 1965)

You can't always get what you want. (The Rolling Stones, 1969)

Ever wonder why Keith Richards and Mick Jagger of The Rolling Stones focused attention early in their careers on issues of scarcity? Well, scarcity is all around us, and they were only reacting to that. (Of course, Sir Mick was also an economics student at the London School of Economics from 1962–1964. Would he have been as successful without his economics training?)

Economics is the study of resource allocation under conditions of scarcity. Human beings inherently want more. Individuals do not typically stop their quest for more once they have achieved a subsistence level of food and shelter. Similarly, firms want more. Firms are not typically satisfied with their position in the economic system; firms push for more. Of course, exactly what defines "more" varies, but the basic point is that this push for more means that resources are scarce. Scarcity is the key to economics.

Chapters 1 and 2 introduce the basic organization of the text and provide a quick review of material you will have learned in introductory microeconomics. Microeconomics at any level examines the same set of topics; it just does so at a different level of depth and sophistication. Microeconomics is best understood in layers, and you are about to embark on your second layer of study. Before we begin that study, we must remind you what you certainly learned (but may have forgotten) in your first-layer study of microeconomics. In Chapter 1, we lay out some preliminary pieces of the microeconomists' toolkit. In Chapter 2, we focus on the cornerstone model of microeconomics—the supply and demand model—as well as other concepts, such as equilibrium, comparative statics analysis, efficiency, and elasticity, that were covered in your introductory microeconomics text.

Preliminary Issues

CHAPTER 1

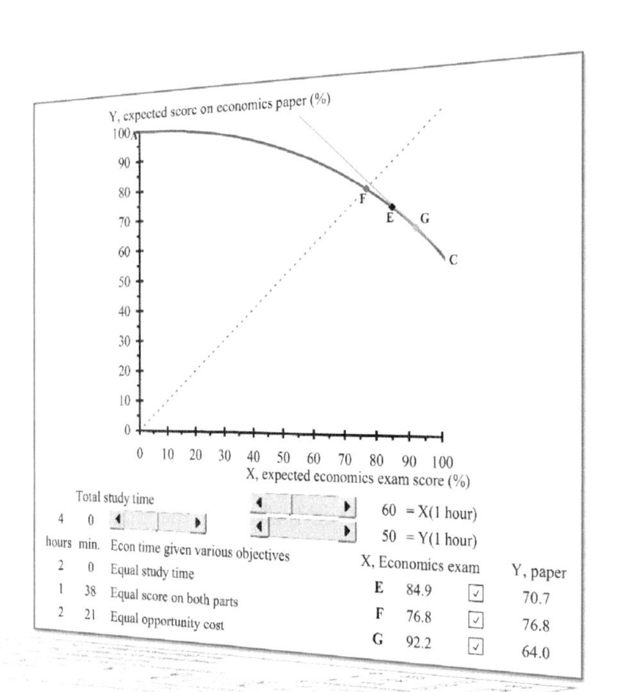

Chapter Outline

Economics is divided into two broad areas of study: microeconomics and macroeconomics. Microeconomics focuses on the actions of individual economic actors in the economic system. Macroeconomics uses a wide-angle lens to examine the economy as a whole. Macroeconomics examines issues such as inflation, unemployment, and economic growth. Since the economy as a whole is composed of individual economic actors, macroeconomists have increasingly begun to examine the microeconomic foundations of macroeconomics.

Consumers, firms, and the government are the three types of economic actors we examine in microeconomics. Our primary focus is on consumers and firms that form the basis for our notions of demand, supply, and the interaction of demand and supply in markets. Consumers purchase goods that firms produce. The government may intervene in various ways (by taxation or direct intervention) and alter the market mechanism set up by the forces of supply and demand.

Chapters 1 and 2 provide a quick review of introductory microeconomics. We also use these chapters to set the agenda for the rest of the text. In this chapter, we describe the scope of microeconomics and examine a number of preliminary issues. In particular, we discuss the role of economic models in microeconomic theory. To demonstrate how to build a model, we create a model that examines how you allocate scarce study time. This model highlights the notion of opportunity cost, one of the other preliminary topics discussed in this chapter. Other preliminary topics include the distinction between real and nominal prices and the distinction between positive and normative analysis. We begin with a discussion of these preliminary issues.

1.1 Some Preliminary Points

Microeconomics focuses on the individual actor embedded in the economic system. This analysis proceeds in a variety of ways, depending on the ultimate goal of the analysis. Some analysis is more theoretically focused, and some is more empirically focused. Microeconomic theory is inherently theoretical. Other areas of microeconomics, such as managerial economics, are driven by empirical data. (This is not to say that theory courses do not benefit from empirical data and that empirical courses do not benefit from a well-developed theory. The point is simply one of focus; empirical analysis takes a back seat to theoretical analysis in this book.) Economic theory is built on a framework of economic models.

Building Models

Economic models are artificial constructs used to describe a more complex reality. By their very nature, models offer a simplified view of the economic phenomenon under consideration. A good economic model strips away the insignificant information and describes the economic phenomenon using a minimalist approach. One of the natural tendencies for a beginning economics student is to try to build too complex of a model. A good model is *parsimonious* (meaning that it provides the simplest explanation possible). Certainly, we can achieve a closer match to reality by adding extra detail, but the price of that closer match is computational complexity and difficulty seeing the implications of the model. The detail involved in a model depends on the use for which the model is being built.

Models are built on assumptions. For example, the model of firm behavior developed in introductory economics (and in this text) is based on the assumption that firms maximize profits. The analysis of perfectly competitive markets via the supply and demand model is based on the assumption that individual consumers and producers have no effect on the market clearing price—they take price as given. Consumers are assumed to try to do the best they can, subject to the constraints they face. One of the tasks for economists is to determine how closely the models developed from assumptions such as these match economic reality.

Often, assumptions are based on numerical values. By changing a numerical value, we can see how critical the assumption is to the results obtained from the model. This is the notion of comparative statics (or sensitivity) analysis that we discuss in greater detail in Chapter 2. The results that are determined within the model are endogenous to the model. These results are based on assumptions that are not determined within, or are exogenous to, the model. When working with numerical values, we call such variables **exogenous variables** and **endogenous variables**.

exogenous variable: An exogenous variable is one whose value is determined outside the economic system (or model) under consideration.

endogenous variable: An endogenous variable is one whose value is determined within the economic system (or model) under consideration.

Students often have difficulty distinguishing between exogenous and endogenous variables in an economic model. Exogenous variables are ones that are taken as given and are not the subject of direct examination within the model. By contrast, endogenous variables are determined within the model. Consider the supply/demand model that will be the focus of Chapter 2. Price and quantity are the endogenous variables in this model. The prices of other goods are some of the exogenous variables in the supply/demand model. Later in this chapter, we examine a model of how you allocate study time across exams. We are interested in knowing how sensitive an average score is to an increase in total time devoted to studying. Study time is the exogenous variable in this model, and average score is the endogenous variable.

Economic models are often mathematical in nature. Two types of mathematical models are typically employed: algebraic and geometric. Geometric models (the use of graphs and figures) are particularly useful because they allow us to summarize the attributes of the model in a more heuristic fashion than we can attain with a verbal, tabular, or algebraic description. Although we do not ignore algebraic models in this text, our primary focus is on attaining a geometric understanding of economic models. We discuss economic modeling at greater length in our extended example in Section 1.2.

Positive versus Normative Analysis

Microeconomic analysis can be used to study both positive and normative issues. **Positive economic analysis** uses economic models to predict or understand the effect of a change in economic circumstance on the economic system. **Normative economic analysis** moves beyond the realm of descriptive and predictive analysis to examine what should be done to achieve a set of goals put forward by policymakers. This distinction between positive and normative issues can be described in a sentence: *Positive examines what is; normative examines what should be.*

positive economic analysis: Positive economic analysis uses economic models to predict or understand the effect of a change in economic circumstance on the economic system.

normative economic analysis: Normative economic analysis moves beyond the realm of descriptive and predictive analysis to examine what should be done to achieve a set of goals put forward by policymakers.

Economists often tackle normative questions, but in doing so, they have no special abilities to determine the set of goals that should be pursued. Economists are well equipped to help achieve a set of goals, but they are not able to set those goals (at least not as economists). The set of goals that society should be pursuing is determined in the sociopolitical system. Economists have no special role in determining which goals should be set, but they can help move the economy in the right direction to achieve these goals. The value judgments involved in setting social goals take us outside the realm of economics. This is one of the reasons economists often disagree.

Any normative analysis should have, at its basis, positive underpinnings. For example, the normative goal of reducing the inequality in the distribution of wealth might be achieved by making the income tax system more progressive or by increasing the estate tax (and, of course, there are other possible policy prescriptions that could be pursued as well). The analysis of these alternatives is a positive economic analysis. Economists would approach such an analysis by examining the trade-offs inherent in each proposed alternative. Such an analysis would include both a qualitative description of likely effects and a quantitative analysis of the magnitude of those effects. Both the qualitative and quantitative analyses are positive in nature. Positive analysis can be used to sharpen the debate about sociopolitical policies by clarifying the trade-offs inherent in various policy options.

Opportunity Cost

Economics is based on scarcity. As a result of scarcity, economic actors inevitably face trade-offs. An individual with a fixed budget can only purchase more of one good by forgoing some purchases of other goods. A firm with fixed resources faced with producing multiple goods can only produce more of one good by producing less of another good (at least if the firm is producing efficiently). An hourly worker who decides to take a day off of work to go skiing forgoes the wages he would receive had he gone to work instead. Each of these represents the notion of **opportunity cost**. Using a resource in one activity means that same resource cannot be used in another activity. Scarcity is the key to opportunity cost.

opportunity cost: The opportunity cost of a resource is the value of that resource in its next-best alternative use. Another term used for opportunity cost is *economic cost*.

Often, we can determine a dollar value for opportunity cost. The worker who decides to go skiing faces an opportunity cost of his time that is represented by the wages foregone. (In addition, this individual faces direct costs of buying lift tickets, as well as transportation cost.) But opportunity cost does not need to be dollar denominated. If you spend income on two goods—apples and bananas—and a pound of apples is twice as expensive as a pound of bananas, then the opportunity cost of a pound of apples is 2 pounds of bananas. Indeed, this opportunity cost does not require market prices. Individuals could engage in barter and achieve an apples-for-bananas opportunity cost ratio via voluntary exchange.[1]

Real versus Nominal Prices

nominal price: The nominal price of a good is the price posted for the good. This price is not adjusted for inflation.

real price: The real price of a good is the nominal price of the good adjusted for inflation.

Placing a dollar value on an opportunity cost requires pricing information. Economists describe two types of price: **nominal price** and **real price**. The nominal price of a good is the price posted for the good. This price is not adjusted for inflation. The real price of a good is the nominal price of the good adjusted for inflation.

inflation: Inflation is the general change in the price level over time. Typically, inflation is calculated using the Consumer Price Index, CPI.

Inflation is the general change in the price level over time. Typically, inflation is calculated using the Consumer Price Index, CPI. Inflation examines what happens to the general price level in an economy. It is one of the central focal points of macroeconomic analysis. Nonetheless, just as macroeconomists benefit from many of the tools, models, and techniques developed by microeconomists, so do microeconomists benefit from understanding macroeconomics issues such as inflation.

The nominal price of a good is what you pay for the good. This is the price you see on the grocery store shelf. As we shall see shortly, in 1980 one dozen large Grade A eggs cost $0.84, and bananas cost $0.34 per pound. In 2014, these same two goods had average prices of $2.02 and $0.60, respectively. All four of these prices are nominal prices.

From these four prices, you can tell which is a better deal on a relative basis in 2014 compared to 1980, using the notion of opportunity cost mentioned earlier. The banana price of eggs in 1980 was 2.47 pounds of bananas = 1 dozen eggs (2.47 = $0.84/$0.34), and in 2014 the banana price of eggs was 2.76 pounds of bananas = 1 dozen eggs (3.37 = $2.02/$0.60). This means that eggs are more expensive relative to bananas in 2014 than in 1980 (since it takes more pounds of bananas to buy a dozen eggs). Much economic analysis could be done with such a fact. But this relative price information leaves begging the question of whether or not one or both of these goods are a better deal in 2014 than they were in 1980. To answer this, we need to know the real prices of the goods; we need to control for inflation.

The vast majority of the models developed in this text are single-period models. For these models, the question of inflation is not relevant because comparisons are not being made over time. When we talk about prices, we typically describe those prices in dollar terms. No explicit mention is made of the purchasing power of the dollar level associated with this price—this is because within the single-period context, the general price level is constant. Microeconomists are interested in the purchasing power provided by the price received. This is a real price. When comparisons are made over time, microeconomists are still interested in the comparison of real purchasing power associated with those prices. As a result, real prices are used in microeconomic analysis. *Whenever you see the term* price *in this text, assume it is a real price.* If the price is a nominal price and a comparison is being made with the real price, then that will be explicitly stated.

To see why we have to adjust prices for inflation when we work across time periods, consider how the nominal price of five products has varied over the 35-year period from 1980–2014. Average price data on an annual basis for electricity, natural gas, gasoline, eggs, and bananas are shown in Table 1.1. Similar data on a variety of other products are readily downloadable from the Bureau of Labor Statistics (BLS) website listed at the bottom of the table. Ignore for now the last two columns in Table 1.1. The first thing you should notice in the data is that, over time, the price of each product tends to rise. The 2014 price is at least 75% higher than the 1980 price for each of the products. This is not, however, surprising if you consider that the general price level has inflated by about 185% over this time period (we explain this in greater detail momentarily). As a result, it is not clear whether each of these goods is becoming a better or a worse deal over time. To understand that, we must adjust for inflation by creating a real price for each of the products.

Inflation is the general change in price level in the economy. The most common measure of inflation is the percentage change in the CPI from year to year. The CPI measures the cost of a "fixed market basket" of goods and compares that cost to the cost of that basket in a base year.[2] This series is calculated on a monthly basis and is available from the website listed at the bottom of Table 1.1. The current series for CPI uses 1982-4 as the "base year." This series is shown in the final column of Table 1.1, and the column just prior to that is an index of medical services over the same time period, also indexed to 1982-4 (ignore the medical series for now). Consider the two numbers in the CPI series in bold, **82.4** from 1980 and **215.3** from 2008 (you will see why we chose 2008 shortly). The 82.4 means that $82.40 in 1980 dollars had the same purchasing power as $100 in 1982-4 dollars. Similarly, $215.30 in 2008 dollars had the same purchasing power as

TABLE 1.1 Comparing Prices over Time

	Nominal Prices					Price Indices	
Year	Electricity, 500 kWh	Utility Gas, 100 Therms	Gasoline (unleaded) per Gallon	Eggs per Dozen	Bananas per Pound	Medical Services Index 1982-4 = 100	CPI 1982-4 = 100
1980	**$30.00**	**$ 40.62**	**$1.25**	**$0.84**	**$0.34**	**74.9**	**82.4**
1981	$34.67	$ 46.69	$1.38	$0.90	$0.36	82.9	90.9
1982	$38.04	$ 55.96	$1.30	$0.87	$0.35	92.5	96.5
1983	$39.13	$ 64.75	$1.24	$0.89	$0.39	100.6	99.6
1984	$40.88	$ 64.73	$1.21	$1.00	$0.36	106.8	103.9
1985	$40.64	$ 63.18	$1.20	$0.80	$0.37	113.5	107.6
1986	$38.29	$ 59.85	$0.93	$0.87	$0.38	122.0	109.6
1987	$39.50	$ 57.82	$0.95	$0.78	$0.36	130.1	113.6
1988	$40.00	$ 58.21	$0.95	$0.79	$0.42	138.6	118.3
1989	$40.92	$ 58.98	$1.02	$1.00	$0.45	149.3	124.0
1990	$41.83	$ 58.90	$1.16	$1.01	$0.46	162.8	130.7
1991	$43.33	$ 59.71	$1.14	$0.99	$0.48	177.0	136.2
1992	$44.04	$ 59.56	$1.13	$0.86	$0.46	190.1	140.3
1993	$45.79	$ 63.47	$1.11	$0.91	$0.44	201.4	144.5
1994	$46.00	$ 64.86	$1.11	$0.86	$0.46	211.0	148.2
1995	$46.79	$ 61.75	$1.15	$0.92	$0.49	220.5	152.4
1996	$47.08	$ 64.60	$1.23	$1.11	$0.49	228.2	156.9
1997	$47.17	$ 68.73	$1.23	$1.06	$0.49	234.6	160.5
1998	$43.42	$ 68.23	$1.06	$1.04	$0.49	242.1	163.0
1999	$43.17	$ 68.53	$1.17	$0.96	$0.49	250.6	166.6
2000	$43.63	$ 80.34	$1.51	$0.91	$0.50	260.8	172.2
2001	$46.17	$ 93.81	$1.46	$0.93	$0.51	272.8	177.1
2002	$45.54	$ 78.53	$1.36	$1.03	$0.51	285.6	179.9
2003	$46.42	$ 96.84	$1.59	$1.24	$0.51	297.1	184.0
2004	$47.17	$104.93	$1.88	$1.34	$0.50	310.1	188.9
2005	$50.00	$125.18	$2.30	$1.22	$0.49	323.2	195.3
2006	$56.17	$128.13	$2.59	$1.31	$0.50	336.2	201.6
2007	$58.33	$126.49	$2.80	$1.68	$0.51	351.1	207.3
2008	**$61.67**	**$144.38**	**$3.27**	**$1.99**	**$0.61**	**364.1**	**215.3**
2009	$63.58	$112.08	$2.35	$1.66	$0.61	375.6	214.5
2010	$63.83	$109.91	$2.79	$1.66	$0.58	388.4	218.1
2011	$64.88	$106.88	$3.53	$1.77	$0.61	400.3	224.9
2012	$64.79	$ 96.55	$3.64	$1.84	$0.60	414.9	229.6
2013	$66.08	$100.88	$3.53	$1.91	$0.60	425.1	233.0
2014	$68.54	$107.89	$3.37	$2.02	$0.60	435.3	236.7

Source: Based on monthly data from BLS: January 1980–December 2014. Nominal prices: http://data.bls.gov/cgi-bin/surveymost?ap. Price indices: http://data.bls.gov/cgi-bin/surveymost?cu.

$100 in 1982-4. To see the inflation that has occurred over these 28 years, simply use these CPI values:

$$\text{28-year inflation} = (CPI_{2008} - CPI_{1980})/CPI_{1980} = CPI_{2008}/CPI_{1980} - 1 = 1.613 \quad \textbf{(1.1)}$$

The 1.613 means that there has been inflation of 161.3% over the 28-year time period, according to the CPI. This is (obviously) not the annual rate but is rather the cumulative inflation over this period. With this information, we can reconsider the question of which goods are becoming better deals over time and which are becoming worse. If the nominal price has increased by less than 161%, then the good has become relatively cheaper; if it has increased by more, then it has become relatively more expensive. Relative prices are what matter to us because relative prices determine relative value (a point that we will explore in detail in Section 5.7).

Real prices hold purchasing power constant, but real prices require one further piece of information: We need to know what year's dollars we are using for our prices. Table 1.2 reproduces the nominal price and CPI information for 1980 and 2008 from Table 1.1. Beneath this information, we have calculated three sets of real prices: one using 1980 dollars, one using 1982-4 dollars, and one using 2008 dollars (formulas for each are provided to the right in each row). Each of these calculations can be thought of as coming from a single formula. Suppose you want to know the real price P, given a nominal price NP in year s, using year t dollars. You would calculate this using the following formula:

$$P_{s,t} = NP_s \cdot CPI_t/CPI_s. \quad \textbf{(1.2)}$$

You should verify for yourself that Equation 1.2 produces each of the six real price equations in Table 1.2. Beneath each set of prices, we have also calculated a percentage

TABLE 1.2 Comparing Nominal Prices with Real Prices

	Nominal Prices from Table 1.1						
Year	Electricity, 500 kWh	Utility Gas, 100 Therms	Gasoline (unleaded) per Gallon	Eggs per Dozen	Bananas per Pound	CPI 1982-4 = 100	
1980	$30.00	$ 40.62	$1.25	$0.84	$0.34	82.4	
2008	$61.67	$144.38	$3.27	$1.99	$0.61	215.3	
%Δ	105.6%	255.5%	162.3%	135.4%	78.3%	161.3%	
	Real Prices Based on the Nominal Price and CPI Information					Which Dollars?	
1980	$30.00	$40.62	$1.25	$0.84	$0.34	= NP	1980
2008	$23.60	$55.25	1.25	$0.76	$0.23	$= NP \cdot CPI_{80}/CPI_{08}$	1980
%Δ	–21.3%	36.0%	0.4%	–9.9%	–31.8%		
1980	$36.41	$49.29	$1.51	$1.02	$0.41	$= NP \cdot 100/CPI_{80}$	1982-4
2008	$28.64	$67.06	$1.52	$0.92	$0.28	$= NP \cdot 100/CPI_{08}$	1982-4
%Δ	–21.3%	36.0%	0.4%	–9.9%	–31.8%		
1980	$78.39	$106.13	$3.25	$2.20	$0.89	$= NP \cdot CPI_{08}/CPI_{80}$	2008
2008	$61.67	$144.38	$3.27	$1.99	$0.61	= NP	2008
%Δ	–21.3%	36.0%	0.4%	–9.9%	–31.8%		

Source: Table 1.1.

change over the period (%Δ = (Price$_{2008}$ – Price$_{1980}$)/Price$_{1980}$, the same formula used for Equation 1.1).

Although the real prices are different, depending on the base year chosen, the way that the real prices change over time does not depend on which base year is chosen. A real price decline is a real price decline, regardless of base year chosen. Indeed, the percentage change in the real price is the same, regardless of base year chosen. Each shows that one of the five products increased by 36% over this period, a second was essentially unchanged over the period (0.4%), and three products had a real price decline, despite having a nominal price increase over this time.

One final way to understand how prices change over time is to chart their progression over time. The most obvious way to do this is to use actual prices (either real or nominal). The problem with this solution is that it is then difficult to see how prices change relative to one another. A simple solution to this problem is to create a price index for each category by simply dividing each price by its initial value and multiplying by 100 so that each index starts at 100. This is done in Chart 1.1A for nominal prices and in Chart 1.1B

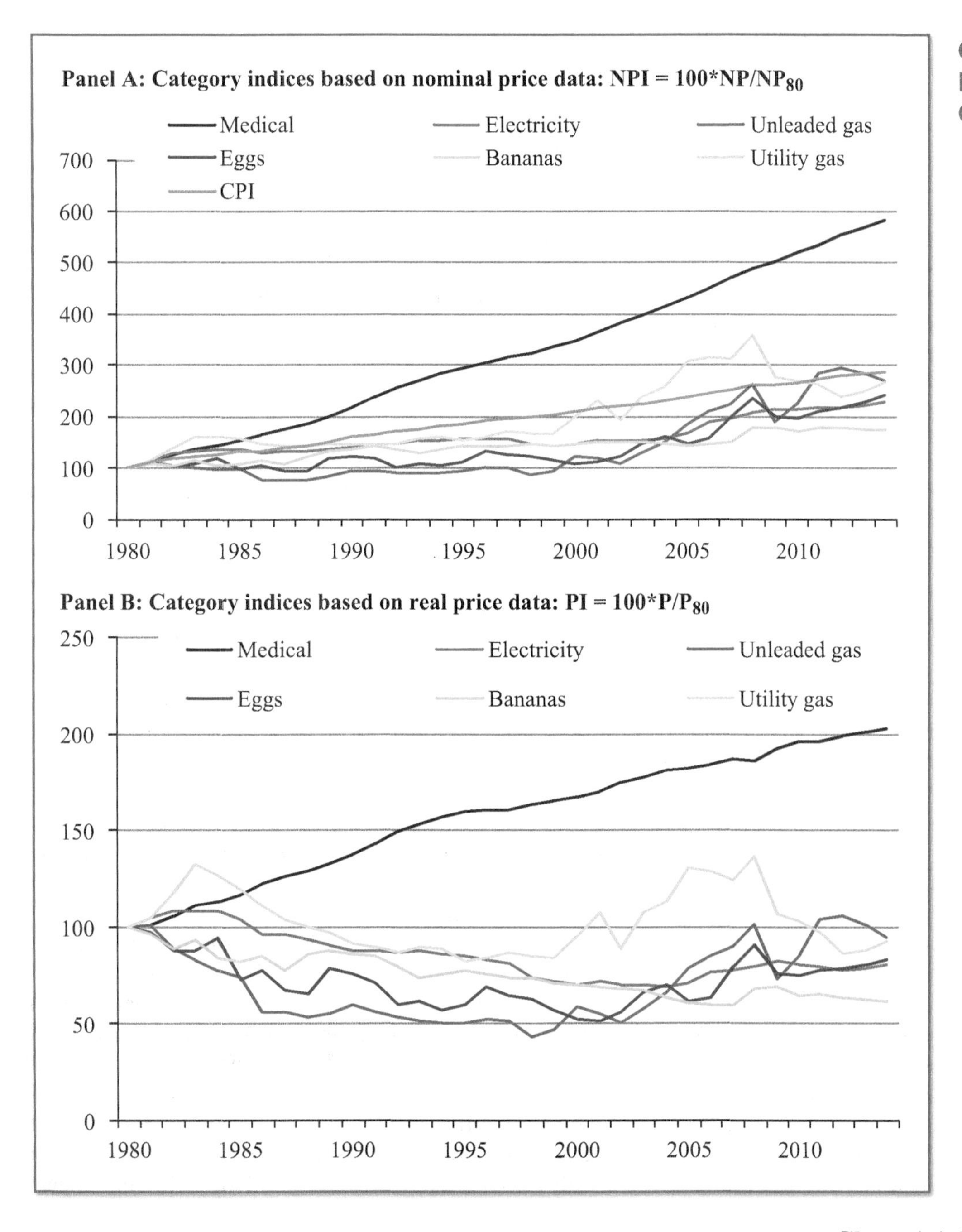

CHART 1.1 Comparing Prices over Time Using Category Indices

for real prices. Included in both panels is the medical services index from Table 1.1 (re-centered to 1980 = 100). Chart 1.1A has one additional series; the thick, green line is the CPI, also re-centered to 1980. Not surprisingly, given the previous discussion, we see that nominal prices trend upward for each product, but in general, real prices trend downward for all but medical and utility (natural) gas (and gasoline for a couple of years). The utility gas peak price in 2008 was the reason 2008t was chosen for Table 1.2. Also unsurprising is how much more quickly medical services have increased in price, relative to the other products. This provides a visual acknowledgement of why medical costs are becoming such an important public policy issue. More surprising, at least to most students, is that gasoline has for much of the past 35 years been quite a bargain (unleaded gasoline is the red curve, and it is below all but eggs [blue] most of the time prior to 2005).

One last reason to show Chart 1.1 is to demonstrate how easy it is to visualize data. Both panels are very easily produced by minor manipulation of Table 1.1. Most students (and many faculty) have more difficulty digesting a table of numbers than a graphical depiction of those numbers. Finally, it is worth noting once again that the vast majority of models developed in this text are single-period models (therefore, we will not have to explicitly calculate real prices in any event).

1.2 Modeling Your Studying Strategy

In economics, we often model an economic situation that is substantially more complex than the model we develop to represent that situation. As noted earlier, that is the value of a model. To focus on modeling itself, we go in the opposite direction in the following example. We are going to provide you with a more complex model than you are likely to have in your mind in answering a simple question you confront regularly in college: How should you allocate scarce study time across classes? Specifically, we wish to examine how you should allocate time if you have two back-to-back exams tomorrow (so you cannot study for the second after you take the first).

Studying for One Exam

Before addressing the question of how to apportion time across classes, it is worthwhile to have a simple model of how you achieve a grade in a single class. Suppose your professor writes hard exams with no give-away questions (this need not be the case, but it simplifies the algebra).[3] If you do not study at all, you get a zero as a result. From past experience, you know that if you study for 1 hour, you will get a 50% score. Unfortunately, studying is "nonlinear" in the sense that you cannot get 100% by devoting 2 hours to studying. To get a perfect score, you require more than 2 hours of study time because the more subtle points on an exam are harder to attain than the more obvious points (after all, not all questions are created equal). Suppose you require 4 hours to get a perfect score on this exam. These three "data points" can be used to help us understand what happens when we devote different amounts of time to studying. These data points are exogenous variables within the model.

One way to use these data points is to graph them and then fit a curve using these observations. *This is a geometric model of studying as a function of study time.* The horizontal axis, t, is time devoted to studying, and the vertical axis, S, is expected percentage correct on the exam. The three data points already identified are the (t, S) points (0, 0), (1, 50), and (4, 100), shown as red diamonds in Figure 1.1A. A curve going through these points is shown in Figure 1.1B. A number of curves could be fit to this data, but the differences between the curves you are likely to draw from this data are small. In particular, you can easily tell from this graph how you are likely to do after 2 or 3 hours of studying. The grid system allows you to see that you are likely to get about a 70% score after 2 hours and an 85% score after 3 hours of studying.

Of course, if your underlying data were different, then different answers would result. Suppose, for example, that you viewed the 50% score at 1 hour as too harsh. Instead, you believe you can get a 55% score with 1 hour of studying, but it still takes 4 hours to get a

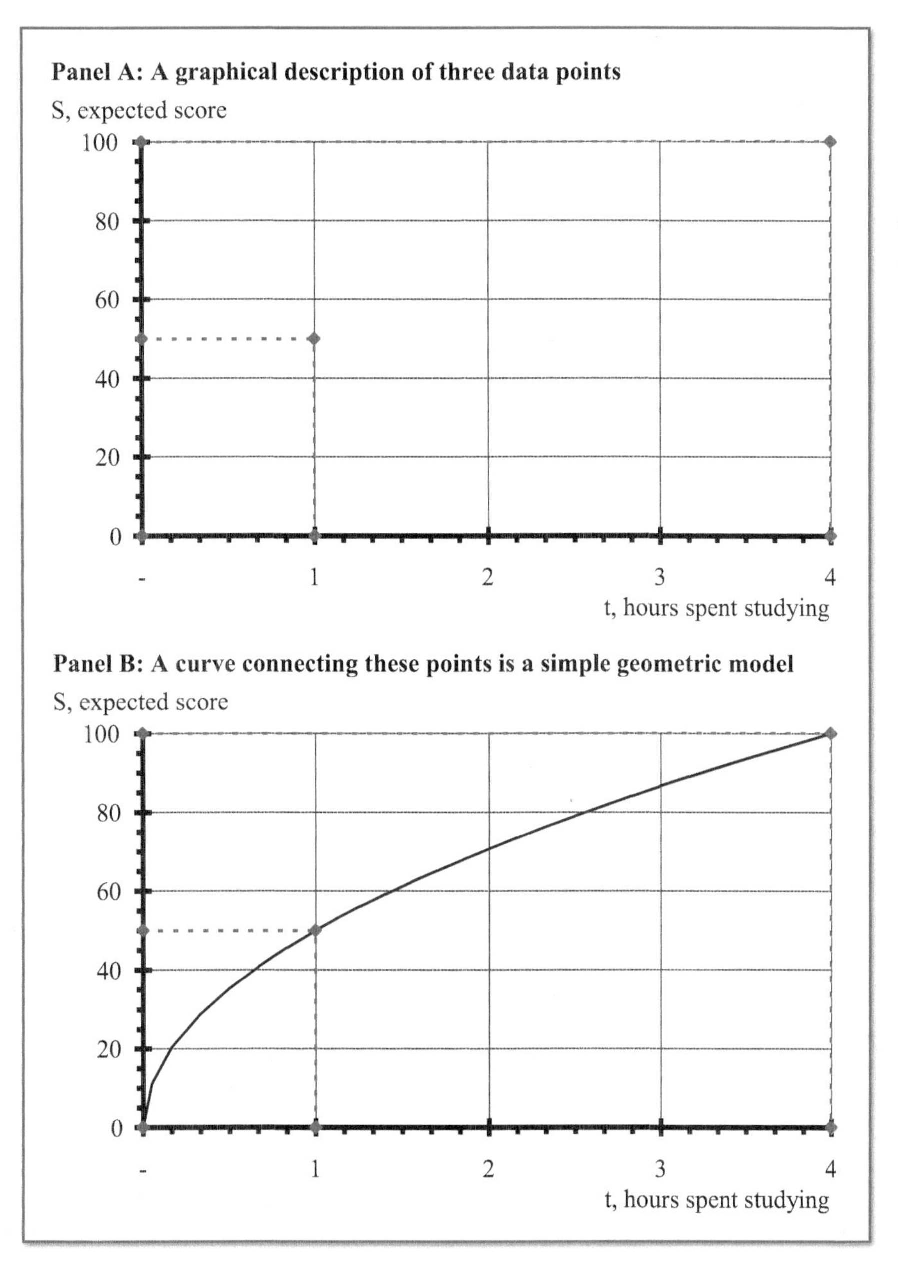

FIGURE 1.1 Modeling Exam Results as a Function of Time Spent Studying

[This icon signifies that there is an Excel file of this figure for dynamic manipulation.]

perfect score. In this event, the graph would look like Figure 1.2, and you are likely to get about a 73% score after 2 hours or a 87% score after 3 hours, based on the grid system (73 is two-thirds of the way between 60 and 80, and 87 is one-third of the way between 80 and 100). As you would expect, incremental hours of studying yield a smaller and smaller increment in total score (the second hour produces an approximate 18% increment to the total, the third hour produces approximately 14%, and the fourth hour produces approximately 13%). And different assumptions will yield different conclusions.

An alternative way to model the relation between score and study time is to consider an algebraic relation that describes the data. As noted earlier, there is no unique way to provide such an algebraic relation. Part of what you will learn in this text is how to choose algebraic relations that produce reasonable results as simply as possible. This is not, however, easy to learn because there are no simple rules that must be followed to achieve a parsimonious algebraic model. This part of economic modeling must be learned by doing (or more explicitly, by seeing what economists do and then by trying to do it yourself).

All of the geometric models we use in the text have algebraic counterparts. Sometimes, we will examine both the algebraic and geometric parts of the model. At other times, we will focus exclusively on the geometric model and relegate the algebraic counterpart to a

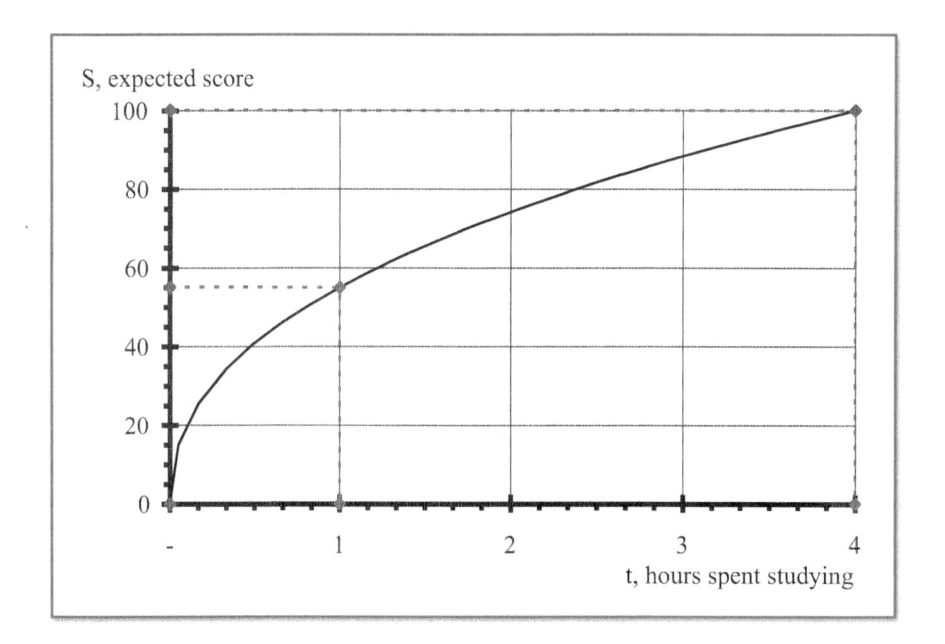

FIGURE 1.2 A Geometric Model Based on a More Nonlinear Study Pattern

footnote (or appendix). In a few instances, we will ignore the algebra completely and rely entirely on the geometry of the model.

The algebraic models of exam score as a function of study time used to create the curves in both Figures 1.1 and 1.2 are power functions. A power function is a function of the form

$y = ax^b$, where a and b are positive constants. **(1.1a)**

The square root and the square function are both examples of power functions.

In the present instance, we will discuss the equation that produced Figure 1.1 and leave the other to a footnote. Recall that the three data points associated with Figure 1.1 are the (t, S) points (0, 0), (1, 50) and (4, 100). A power function such as Equation 1.1a has a wonderful property: If $x = 1$, then $y = a$ regardless of b (since $1^b = 1$ for all $b > 0$). If $y = S$ and $x = t$, then $a = 50$ because we know that 1 hour of studying produces an expected score of 50% right on the exam. The coefficient b is also easy to see in this instance because the data in Figure 1.1 were chosen to make the answer "obvious." We wish to have $S = 100$ when $t = 4$, given $S = 50 \cdot t^b$. Substituting these values for S and t, we see that $100 = 50 \cdot 4^b$. Dividing by 50 on both sides produces $2 = 4^b$. The b that solves this equation is $b = 0.5$ (the square root of 4 is 2). Substituting our information into Equation 1.1a produces the following (most of the time, we will not explicitly write this in both ways):[4]

$$S(t) = 50 \cdot t^{0.5} = 50\sqrt{t} \qquad \textbf{(1.1b)}$$

This square-root function provides an algebraic representation of the data because it passes through each of the three data points in Figure 1.1. This function is not unique, but it does elegantly describe the data; it is parsimonious. We also can confirm that our visual estimate of a 70% score after 2 hours and an 85% score after 3 hours are approximately correct (by simply substituting 2 and 3 into Equation 1.1b, we obtain $S(2) = 70.7$ and $S(3) = 86.6$).

Several points should be made about these models:

1. None of these numbers is certain to be correct. We do not mean to imply that you *will* get these scores based on this much study time. A model cannot always be correct. *Models necessarily abstract from the true situation; at best, they can only provide an approximately correct answer.*
2. We do not mean to imply that the algebraic model is more accurate than its geometric counterpart simply because we provided the algebraic answers to one-tenth of a percent. Indeed, both models would provide the same estimate if we simply

An Aside on Excel

One of the defining features of this textbook (indeed, perhaps *the* defining feature) is that many of the figures within the text have the Excel file that created the figure available from the book's website. A screenshot of the worksheet that created Figures 1.1 and 1.2 is shown as Figure 1.3. The Excel worksheet contains sliders and click boxes such as those shown. By adjusting the sliders and using the click boxes, you can manipulate the file to create your own scenario (and indeed, you can create Figures 1.1 and 1.2 as well).[5] In this instance, one slider allows you to adjust the expected score attained with 1 hour of study (between the bounds of 10% and 90% in 1% increments), and the other allows you to adjust the time required for a perfect exam (from 2 hours to 4 hours in 1-minute increments).

make the graph large enough so that we could distinguish between one-tenth of a percent on the graph. Such detail, of course, would suggest an inappropriate degree of accuracy to our expectations.

3. An algebraic model must be interpreted in the context of the data it is attempting to explain. Note, for example, that if you put the number 9 into Equation 1.1b, you obtain $S(9) = 150$. We do NOT mean to imply that you will get 150% on an exam. *The algebra itself must always be tempered with an understanding of what the algebra is trying to represent.* In this instance, we are representing the percentage correct on an exam; therefore, we know our results are bounded by 0 and 100%, despite the numbers that are mechanistically produced by the algebraic model.

One of the goals of the course is to be able to explain graphical information and to be able to go from a verbal description of a situation to a graphical representation of that information. With that in mind, answer the following question:

Note: *This text has the goal of getting you to interact with the graphs. Questions are numbered by the graphs to which they refer, and not all graphs have questions. (For example, Q3, which follows this "Note," refers to Figure 1.3; do not look for Q1 and*

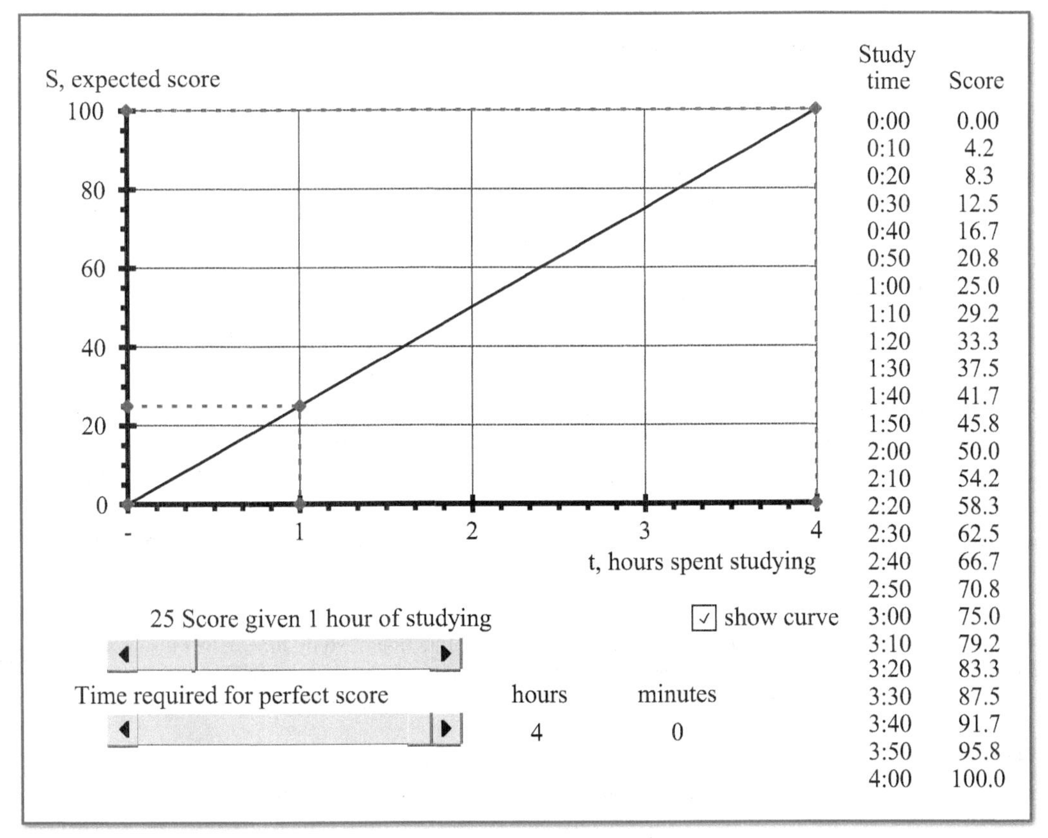

Study time	Score
0:00	0.00
0:10	4.2
0:20	8.3
0:30	12.5
0:40	16.7
0:50	20.8
1:00	25.0
1:10	29.2
1:20	33.3
1:30	37.5
1:40	41.7
1:50	45.8
2:00	50.0
2:10	54.2
2:20	58.3
2:30	62.5
2:40	66.7
2:50	70.8
3:00	75.0
3:10	79.2
3:20	83.3
3:30	87.5
3:40	91.7
3:50	95.8
4:00	100.0

FIGURE 1.3 A Screenshot Showing a Different Scenario Using the File That Created Figures 1.1 and 1.2

Q2—they do not exist. If a question is posed that is not attached to a figure, no number is attached.) Answers are always visible at the bottom of the page in an asterisked footnote attached to the end of a question, scenario, or hint. You will get the most out of your reading if you only look at the footnote after you have formed your own answers to the questions.

Q3. If Figure 1.3 represents how you view studying for an exam in this class, do you view the exam as having hard questions and easy questions?*

You might wonder how this discussion of taking an exam relates to economics. Your exam score as a function of study time (S(t), shown graphically in Figures 1.1–1.3 and algebraically in Equation 1.1b), is most basically a production function (the subject of Chapter 9). The input (or factor of production) is study time, and the output is the score produced. This may sound a bit strange because we typically imagine ourselves as being consumers rather than producers, but this certainly fits the notion of a production function, albeit one in which the good that is produced is not directly sold (unless, of course, you are taking an exam for someone else . . . but that is a different story). The input—study time—is the amount of labor devoted to production. This is exactly the standard image of a short-run production function in Chapter 9. One of the concepts you may remember from introductory microeconomics is the law of diminishing marginal product (also oftentimes called the law of diminishing returns). This is implicit in the convexity of the production function shown in Figures 1.1B and 1.2. Figure 1.3, by contrast, exhibits constant marginal productivity of study time—each hour produces an expected increment of 25%, as indicated by the linearity of the S(t) curve. (One semantic point to note here is that economists have a habit of calling something a "curve" even when it is NOT curved.)

Allocating Scarce Study Time across Classes

The ultimate goal was to consider how we might model the decision to allocate scarce time across classes. To make this specific, suppose you have exams in economics and French tomorrow morning. Unfortunately, this evening you are slated to represent your dorm in the intramural foosball tournament, and you cannot devote as much time as you would like to each class. *This evening you have 2 hours to devote to both classes.* (We realize that this gives very low scores, but this assumption allows us to work with very simple numerical results. It also allows you to attend the foosball tournament.) To simplify the model as much as possible, imagine that you view both exams as being fairly represented by Figure 1.1 and Equation 1.1b. In particular, you can achieve a perfect score on either exam if you devote 4 hours to either class, and you can attain 50% on either exam by devoting 1 hour to that class. Various goals are possible in this situation (since you need not treat both classes equally).

Q. Suppose you wish to do equally well on both exams. What should you do?†

This solution is easy enough to understand that it was posed without reference to a graph. Given equally difficult exams, you would expect to spend the same time studying for each exam. Of course, this solution is not your only option; it is just your preferred one. The set of options can be described using the notion of a **production possibilities frontier (PPF)**. In the present instance, "inputs" refers to the amount of study time available (2 hours), and "technology" is embodied in the production function, which describes how inputs are turned into outputs (i.e., how time studying translates into an expected score on each exam).

production possibilities frontier (PPF): A production possibilities frontier (PPF) represents the set of alternative combinations of goods that a producer can produce, given fixed inputs and technology.

*__Q3 answer__: No, the progression in expected score is a linear function of study time in this instance. The first 25% takes an hour, as does each subsequent 25% correct, according to the graph. This linear graph violates the statement earlier that suggests that you find some questions easier than others (i.e., some points are easier than others to attain on an exam).

†**Q answer:** The answer is straightforward in this instance: You should devote 1 hour to both classes (and get 50% on each exam). These answers (devoting 1 hour to each) are the endogenous variables in this analysis.

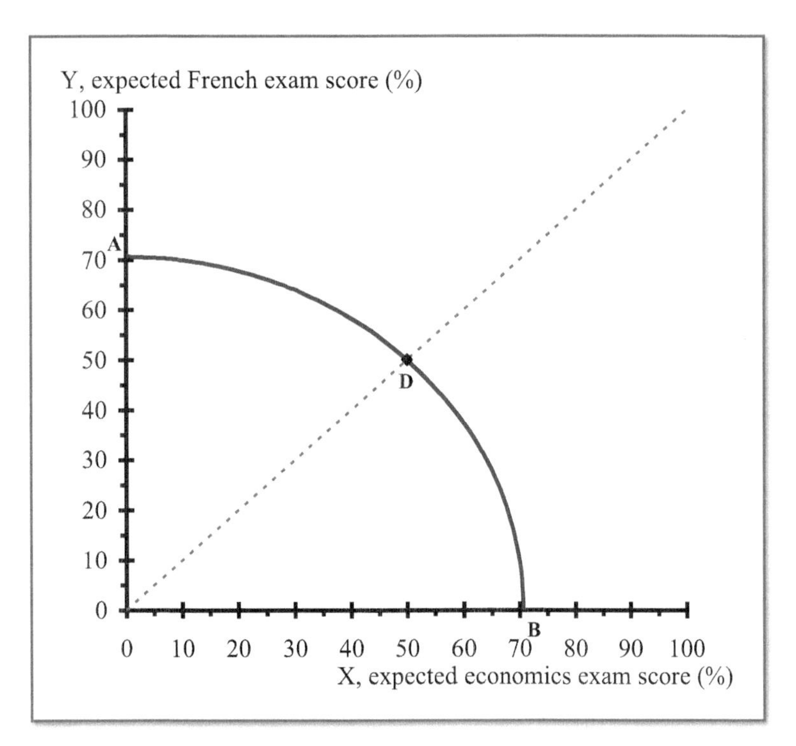

FIGURE 1.4 A Production Possibility Frontier, Given 2 Hours Devoted to Studying

Given equally hard exams, it is not surprising that the PPF in describing this individual's "grade frontier" is symmetric. We learned earlier that if all 2 hours are devoted to one class, you expect about a 70% score in that class and a zero in the other class (S(2) = 70.7, using Equation 1.1b). If you spend 1 hour on each subject, you get 50% on each exam. And if you spend some other fraction on each, then you will be somewhere else along the PPF shown in Figure 1.4. The horizontal axis is the expected economics score, X, and the vertical axis is the expected French score, Y. (We often use the generic letters *X* and *Y* for these axes because it tends to reduce mathematical confusion. When we use these generic letters, it is important to remember which good is on which axis. Put another way: *Label your axes.*) Point **A** represents ignoring economics, and point **B** represents ignoring French. (Throughout this text, a boldfaced letter represents a point on a graph.) The graph also shows a 45° line, since this represents points in "exam score space" associated with equal scores for both exams. **D**, therefore, is a geometric representation of the answer just provided.

Interestingly, unlike the production function in Figures 1.1–1.3, time is hidden in the PPF. But we can easily consider where it is hidden. Total time devoted to studying determines how far out the PPF is in this instance (given that the difficulty of each exam is fixed). And walking along a fixed PPF represents reallocations of time between the two classes. As you walk from **A** to **D** to **B**, you increase the amount of time studying economics and simultaneously decrease the amount of time spent on French (since $t_E + t_F = 2$ along this PPF).[6] The final point to note about the PPF is that the convexity shown (convex downward) is typical for PPFs.[7] This follows from the declining marginal productivity of time devoted to studying a subject embodied in Figure 1.1B and Equation 1.1b. Had we based our analysis on the production function in Figure 1.3 for both subjects, the PPF would have been linear because each production function has a constant marginal product of study time in this instance.

Finding a Better Way to Study

Suppose you start using the Excel files as a study aid in economics and that this increases your productivity by 20% (that is a large percentage, but we want the diagram to show large enough differences that we can easily distinguish between various points in the discussion). This means that the production function in Equation 1.1b only relates to

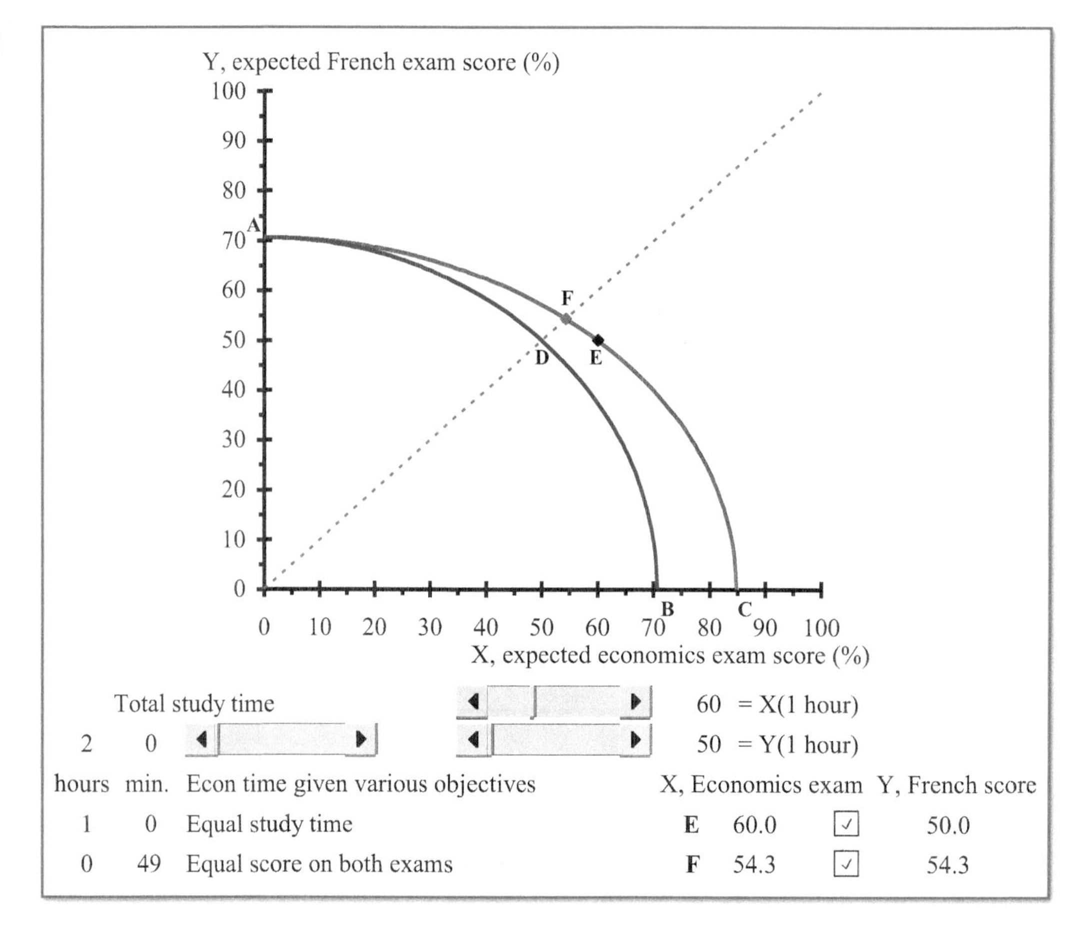

FIGURE 1.5 A Revised PPF Based on Technological Progress

French, but not to economics. The economics score for any given amount of time devoted to economics studying is 20% higher, given technologically aided studying. This is easily modeled algebraically by changing the 50 to a 60 ($60 = 1.2 \cdot 50$). We now have different equations for each class:

$$X = S_{economics}(t_{economics}) = 60 \cdot (t_{economics})^{0.5} \qquad \textbf{(1.2.economics)}$$

$$Y = S_{French}(t_{French}) = 50 \cdot (t_{French})^{0.5} \qquad \textbf{(1.2.French)}$$

Note that this does not change the coefficient $b = 0.5$ in the economics equation. In particular, it no longer takes 4 hours to attain 100% on the economics exam, and 2 hours devoted to economics alone produces an 85% economics score ($84.9 = 60 \cdot 2^{0.5}$).

Q. Use Equation 1.2.economics to determine how long it takes to get a perfect score on the economics exam.*

There are two ways to geometrically visualize the change in economics score. One method is to graph the production function itself (redraw Figure 1.1B to fit the "new" data). This graph would be 20% *higher* for any amount of time devoted to studying (bounded, of course, by 100%).[8] The other method is to incorporate this change into the grade frontier analysis by shifting the PPF. The production functions in Equation 1.2 yield the PPF in Figure 1.5, based on 2 hours of total study time. If all study time is devoted to French, you can attain point **A** with or without the technological progress in economics (since you are not devoting any time to studying economics at **A**, and there has been no "technological progress" in your French study habits). At the opposite end of the spectrum is **C**, a 20% higher score than **B**, as noted earlier. Technological change has shifted the red PPF 20% *to the right* (relative to the initial blue PPF) for any amount of French score. The reason is straightforward: A given French score takes a certain amount of study time. This leaves the

***Q answer:** $100 = 60t^{0.5}$ and solve for t: $t = (100/60)^2 = (5/3)^2 = 25/9 = 2.78$ or 2 hours and 47 minutes.

rest to be devoted to economics, but each minute devoted to economics now produces 20% more correct answers on the exam than were expected prior to the technological change.

Given 2 hours of study time total, you now face a more interesting question. How should you allocate time to take advantage of this increased productivity? The answer depends on your objective function. If you wish to treat both classes equally, then you will simply do better in economics and do the same as before in French. This is point **E** = (60, 50) in Figure 1.5. A more common strategy, at least for many students, is to try to maximize the average score across classes. If this is your goal, then you would be willing to give up a bit of your higher economics score to pump up your French score. By reallocating some study time from economics to French (relative to point **E**), you can move in the direction of greater equality between classes. Equality occurs where the red PPF crosses the dashed 45° line at point **F** = (54.3, 54.3). The amount of study time reallocated in this instance is 11 minutes (so that you should devote 49 minutes to economics and 1 hour and 11 minutes to French).[9]

We can apply the notion of opportunity cost to our discussion of allocating study time across exams. You can only achieve a higher score on one exam by getting a lower score on another exam (given the scenario we have created, in which you have two exams tomorrow and only limited study time available tonight). We achieve this change by reallocating study time from one course to the other. We can use the PPF to describe the opportunity cost of one exam in units of the other exam. The easiest to see, and the one we focus on here, is the opportunity cost of economics in units of French because the opportunity cost of the good on the horizontal axis in units of the good on the vertical axis is the (absolute value of the) slope of the PPF at the point under consideration.

Claim: *The opportunity cost of economics in units of French is the loss in French score for a 1-point increase in economics score. This is the absolute value of the slope of the PPF at the point under consideration.*

Opportunity cost tells us the price of doing better in economics. That price is how much worse we will do in French as a result.

Before we explore a specific example, it is worthwhile to simply consider in general terms what should happen to opportunity cost as we reallocate study time from French to economics. If we are devoting almost the entire available time to French (near **A** in Figures 1.4 and 1.5), then a reallocation of a given amount of time will have a large impact on the economics score at only a small cost to the French score. This is most easily understood by considering the metaphor of harvesting fruit. This is the idea that there is a lot of "low-hanging fruit" on the economics tree, since little time has been devoted to harvesting that tree. Over this range of allocations of resources, the opportunity cost of economics in units of French is small as a result. By contrast, the French tree has no low-hanging fruit because it has already been harvested (i.e., the easy points have already been input into short-term memory). As we increase time devoted to economics and decrease time devoted to French, this will eventually reverse. Eventually, there will be little low-hanging economics fruit and a lot of low-hanging French fruit (near **B** or **C** in Figures 1.4 and 1.5). Over this range of allocations of resources, the opportunity cost of economics in units of French is large. This entire discussion may be summarized by noting that as we walk down the PPF, the opportunity cost of economics in units of French increases.

A slider at the bottom of the worksheet for Figures 1.4–1.7 allows you to allocate time between French and economics as you wish. Figure 1.6 depicts spending 10 minutes studying economics and 1 hour and 50 minutes studying French. The resulting expected score bundle **T** = (24.5, 67.7) is attained by inputting $t_{economics} = 1/6$ and $t_{French} = 11/6$ into the respective production functions, using Equation 1.2. The slope of the PPF at **T** is 0.25. (The slope at a point is the slope of the tangent at that point. This is shown as a light green line.) Put another way, the opportunity cost of a 1% higher economics score is a 1/4% lower French score.[10] It is useful to also consider what this means in terms of getting a higher French score. To get one more point on the French exam, you would have to give up about four points on the economics exam (if you are initially allocating 10 minutes to economics and

FIGURE 1.6 Visualizing Opportunity Cost on a PPF

T represents spending 10 minutes studying economics and 1 hour and 50 minutes studying French. The slope of the PPF is the opportunity cost of a 1% increase in economics score in units of French score. The opportunity cost of economics in units of French at **T** is 0.25.

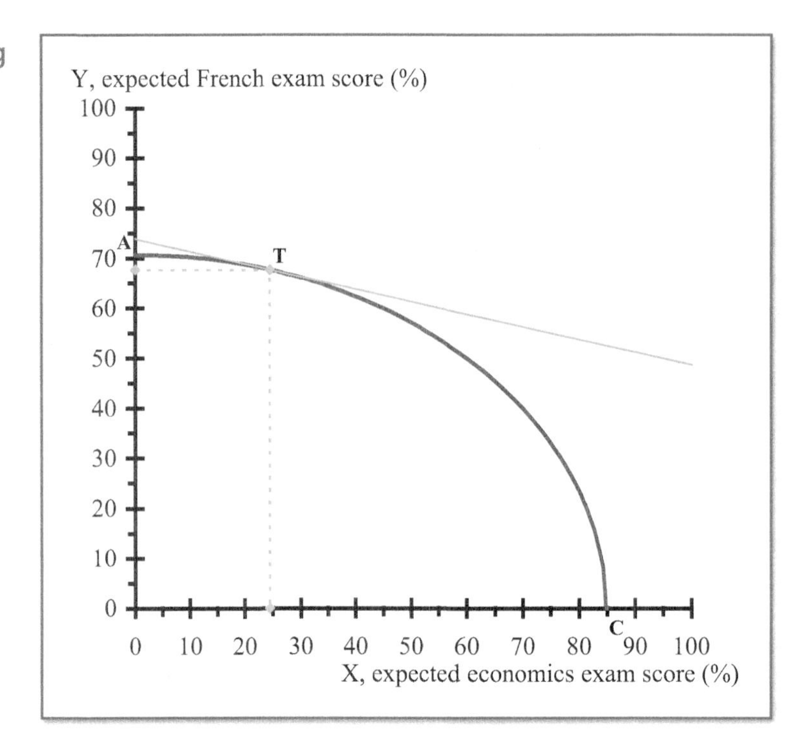

1 hour and 50 minutes to French; i.e., if you are at **T**). This is formally the opportunity cost of French in units of economics (which is 1/slope of the PPF). Both methods of viewing the trade-off suggest that at **T**, economics is a pretty "cheap" deal in units of French.

Allocating Scarce Study Time within a Class

We can use the notion of opportunity cost to model one more strategy often chosen by students given time constraints. To do this, we need to adjust the scenario a bit. Consider, therefore, the night before your final exam in economics. In addition to the exam, you must turn in a short position paper for the class. To simplify this as much as possible, assume that your production function for the exam is still Equation 1.2.economics and that the paper's production function is (the relabeled French production function):

$$Y = S_{paper}(t_{paper}) = 50 \cdot (t_{paper})^{0.5} \qquad \textbf{(1.2.paper)}$$

Suppose the paper and the exam are worth the same portion of your final grade. You have 4 hours to devote to exam preparation and writing the paper. How should you allocate your time?

We adjusted the scenario so that you explicitly would be able to compare different ways of getting a grade in a single class (rather than comparing grades in economics and French). The two initial strategies are shown as points **E** and **F** in Figure 1.7.

Claim: *In this instance, **E** is clearly better than **F**.*

The reason we can make this claim is that the exam and paper are worth equal weight. We can therefore add expected scores to get an expected total, and the goal is to maximize this total by appropriately allocating time between the two tasks.[11] **E** is better than **F** because 155.6 > 153.6. In this instance, you should NOT allocate extra time toward the weaker part of your course (your paper).

In fact, you should take advantage of your strong suit and devote more than 2 hours to studying for the exam. At **E**, the opportunity cost of an extra point on the exam is 0.83 points on the paper (this is the slope of the PPF at **E**).[12] By allocating more time to studying for the exam and less to the paper, the overall score can be increased. The optimal solution in this instance is to allocate time so that **G** is chosen. **G** is the point where the opportunity cost of an extra point on the exam is one point on the paper. Note that the sum of scores at **G** (156.2) exceeds the sum of scores at **E** (albeit by a small amount).

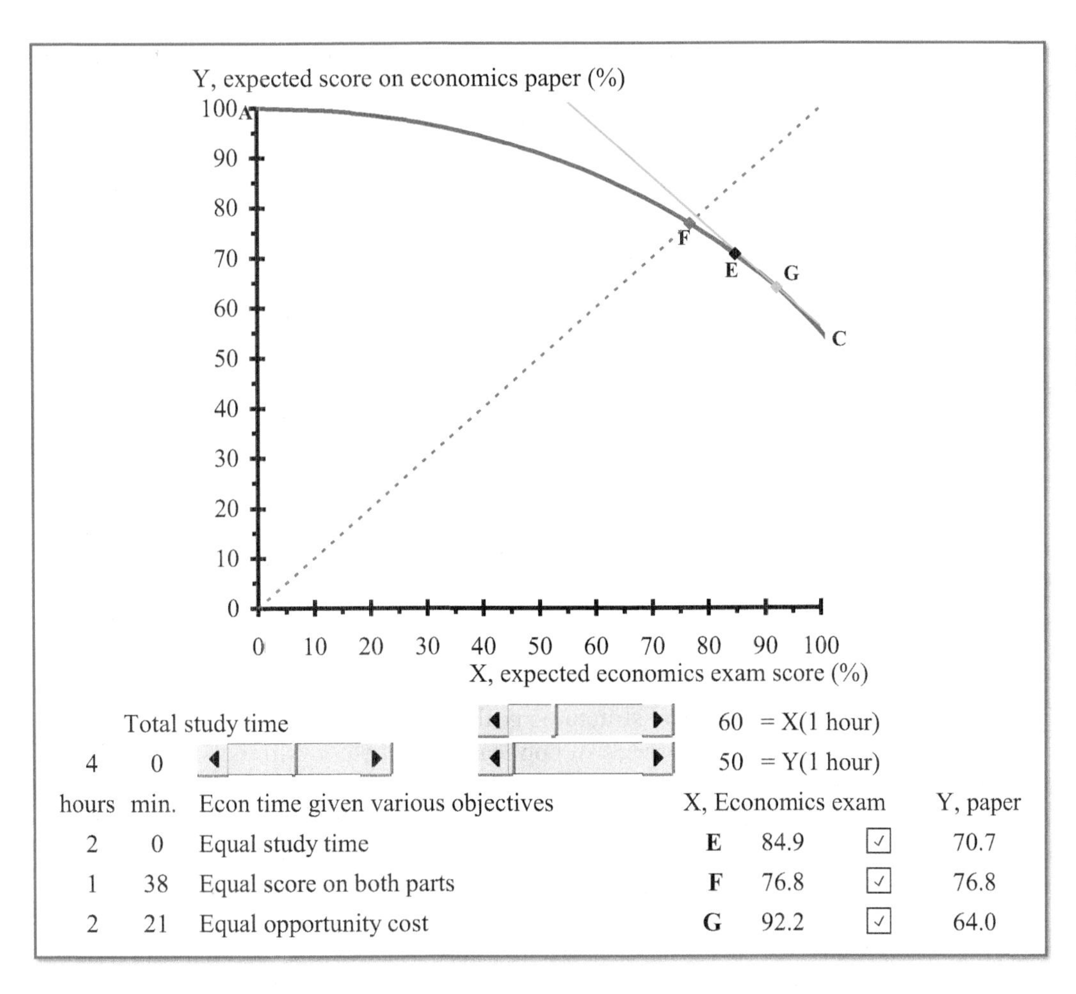

FIGURE 1.7 Allocating 4 Hours between an Economics Exam and an Economics Paper

Assume you have higher productivity for the exam. Compare three notions of equality: (1) Equal time is at **E**, (2) equal score is at **F**, and (3) equal opportunity cost is at **G**.

This is seen geometrically by having the green tangent line at **G** above both **E** and **F** in Figure 1.7. (This tangent line is the equal total score line because the slope at **G** is –1.)

We have devoted considerable discussion to the analysis of allocating study time so as to introduce economic models to you in the context of something with which you are completely familiar. The model itself is not important here; the important point is to see how we developed the model and how we adjusted that model to analyze changed circumstances. Models help economists make more reasoned decisions.

1.3 Unpeeling the Onion: A Roadmap to the Rest of the Text

Since microeconomics is based on a reasonably small number of basic principles that are reworked in various settings, there are a number of ways to teach an intermediate microeconomics class. Textbooks by their very nature are linear, but the linearity of the printed page does not imply that a textbook's order of presentation is necessarily the only way to present or understand this material. This textbook has five major parts. The first is an introduction. The next three parts present the core material that is covered in almost every intermediate microeconomics course. The final part provides applications of the core material. The typical class will not be able to cover all of the topics in the applications chapters and will have to choose among applications based on time constraints as well as faculty and student interest.

Many of the concepts examined in intermediate microeconomics have already been introduced in introductory microeconomics. Microeconomics is best understood in layers, and you are about to embark on your second layer of study. Introductory microeconomics introduced you to the concepts of supply and demand and their interaction via markets. Consumers demand goods, and firms supply goods. You also learned about economic efficiency and how markets might differ in this regard. In Chapter 2, we quickly review these and other major topics covered in your first-layer study of microeconomics.

The core of an intermediate microeconomics class is the more detailed study of consumer behavior and producer behavior, and their interaction via markets. These are the same actors that were the focus of introductory microeconomics; the difference is in the depth with which we analyze these actors. To make new material as concrete as possible, it should be introduced in the most familiar environment possible. This was the rationale for discussing models and for building a model in the context of something that is second nature to virtually all college students: allocating scarce study time across classes. It is also the rationale for presenting consumer theory prior to producer theory. You might have already worked in a firm for a few years, but you have been a consumer since you were very young. Your depth of experience as a consumer far outweighs that of your experience as a producer. Consumer theory is introduced in Part 2, and the theory of the firm is examined in Part 3.

Once we have a detailed understanding of consumer behavior and the behavior of firms, we can put the two together and consider market interaction. Market interaction in Part 4 is a more detailed discussion and extension of the supply/demand interaction discussed in Chapter 2. (Similarly, Part 2 examines the underpinnings of demand, and Part 3 examines the underpinnings of supply.) Part 4 focuses on how this interaction occurs in three market structures: perfect competition, monopoly, and monopolistic competition. The welfare impact of these market structures is also examined in Part 4.

Part 5 of the text consists of a series of applications chapters. Microeconomic theory involves using a small number of powerful tools. These tools can be recast and reused to analyze a wide range of seemingly disparate topics. The most basic example of this is the symbiotic relation between the consumer theory notion of utility and the producer theory notion of production. Either concept can be recast as the other. Indeed, in Section 1.2, we used a production function to describe how you achieve utility (i.e., a higher grade) by studying. The six chapters in Part 5 examine a variety of extensions of the basic models developed in Parts 2–4. These chapters have been written in a modular fashion in order that they may be interleaved into the text at various points, depending on the instructor's preferences. (Of course, in the unlikely event that you are reading this text on your own, you can choose when to attack each of these chapters.) A list of prerequisites provided at the start of each section allows you to quickly understand the intellectual dependencies required to attack this material.

One point in particular should be noted about Chapter 19, "Capital Markets." Each of the other applications chapters has prerequisites ranging from Chapter 3 through Chapter 16. But Chapter 19 does not formally require any of that material, at least for a first reading. Chapter 19 is itself layered because it was written with multiple purposes in mind, one of which is to give you a quick introduction to Excel.

As noted earlier in this chapter, Excel was used to create each of the figures in the text, and you can go to these files to manipulate the diagrams to create your own scenario. Different people learn in different ways, and this text was written with the visual learner in mind. The purpose of these files is *not* to learn Excel but rather to allow you to manipulate diagrams to make them "come alive." You can manipulate the diagrams using sliders and click boxes; you need to have Excel on your computer, but you do not need to know how to use Excel to use these files. *Understanding how to use Excel is not required for anyone using this text.* But this text does leverage Excel's power to create an active learning environment for those who wish to incorporate this tool into their courses. Present-value problems are the natural place to introduce how to use Excel. Chapter 19 can be read prior to any of the core chapters for those wishing to introduce Excel into their study (indeed, Section 19.2 provides this introduction). If approached in this fashion, you should ignore many of the footnotes (which create ties to various parts of the text). Those following this early-reading strategy will find a second quick reading of the chapter late in the course a valuable way to solidify some of the more subtle points in the chapter. The second reading should focus on the footnotes that link this material to other text chapters.

Summary

Economics is the study of resource allocation under conditions of scarcity. Microeconomics examines the behavior of individual economic actors embedded in the economic system. Macroeconomics examines the economic system as a whole. This chapter has reviewed some of the most basic concepts in microeconomics.

The analytical focus in microeconomics is on the individual economic actor: How does the individual or firm make decisions based on the opportunities and constraints that surround them? Microeconomists build economic models to help them understand and predict behavior. They are interested in how individuals and firms decide to allocate resources, given competing uses for those resources. Economic models help us understand the trade-offs inherent in an individual actor's actions.

The opportunity cost of an economic action is driven by scarcity. Opportunity cost is the value of a resource in its next-best alternative use. If you forgo working for an hour to go visit a friend, the opportunity cost of that visit is the wage you would have been paid had you worked instead. The fact that you did not pay out any money to visit your friend simply means you did not incur any direct cost. Nonetheless, you did incur an indirect cost because, by spending the hour with a friend, you could not use that same hour for working. This is the opportunity cost of your action.

Positive economic analysis involves examining the effect of a change in economic circumstance. Normative economic analysis involves moving beyond positive economic analysis to examine issues of social optimality. Such issues necessarily involve value judgments that can only be decided outside the realm of economics. Economists can, however, sharpen the debate over these sociopolitical value judgments by providing more accurate information about the implications of the proposed policy actions. Economists can use positive analysis to help clarify the trade-offs inherent in normative decisions.

Price might be the third or fourth most important word in the microeconomist's lexicon. (The top two are undoubtedly *supply* and *demand*—closely followed by *market*, *cost*, and *price*.) When microeconomists use the term *price*, they mean real price. Real price is price holding purchasing power constant. Most noneconomists would expect that the term *price* means the dollar price of the product (the nominal price). Nominal price and real price coincide if our analysis involves only a single time period. But if our analysis involves multiple time periods, then we need to control for changes in purchasing power that may occur over time; we need to control for inflation. The nominal price does not control for inflation when viewed over time; real price does control for inflation and thereby allows comparisons to occur on a consistent basis across time. We will not typically have to worry about the distinction between real and nominal price because most of our models are single-period models.

The models in the chapters that follow provide geometric descriptions of economic events, often accompanied by their algebraic counterparts. An example of such a model was presented in this chapter to highlight how models are built. This model attempts to describe how you allocate scarce study time across classes. Although the proposed construct is artificial, the model is pushed in a variety of directions to demonstrate the value of economic modeling. The goal is to try to provide a geometric formalization for many of the decisions you already make. It is not to try to get you to change your study habits.

Review Questions

Define the following terms:

economic model	normative economic analysis	inflation
exogenous variable	opportunity cost	production possibilities frontier (PPF)
endogenous variable	nominal price	
positive economic analysis	real price	

Match each of the following terms with its corresponding description:

a. Positive economic analysis	1. An example of an economic model
b. Normative economic analysis	2. Are prices not controlled for inflation
c. Production possibilities frontier	3. Determined outside the economic model
d. Real prices	4. Examines what should be
e. Nominal prices	5. Determined inside the economic model
f. Exogenous variable	6. Examines what is
g. Endogenous variable	7. Are prices controlled for inflation

Provide short answers to the following:

a. What is the relation between nominal price, real price, and inflation?
b. Was the analysis of allocating study time across classes an example of positive or normative modeling?
c. Is the total amount of time devoted to studying for both economics and French an exogenous or endogenous variable in the model presented in the chapter?
d. Suppose that at the allocation of study time that you have chosen, you believe that an extra 1% on economics costs you 1.25% on French. What is the opportunity cost of economics in units of French? What is the opportunity cost of French in units of economics?

Check your answers to the *matching* and *short-answer* exercises in the Answers Appendix at the end of the book.

Notes

1. We examine barter exchanges in detail in Section 3.5 and various notions of cost in Chapters 10 and 11.

2. We examine the measurement of inflation and the problems introduced by using a fixed market basket in Section 8.5.

3. When economists say "suppose," they often are simply introducing an assumption.

4. The more general equation that produces Figure 1.2 is based on **R**, the score after 1 hour (55 in Figure 1.2), and **P**, the amount of time needed for a perfect score (4 in Figure 1.2). The more general function that is a counterpart to Equation 1.1b is:

$$S(t) = R \cdot t^{(\ln(100/R)/\ln(P))}$$

This function passes through the points (0, 0), (1, R) and (P, 100).

5. The quick way to do this is to use the **Scenarios** function in Excel. Specific commands or references in Excel (such as **Scenarios**) are printed in bold in the text. Open the appropriate Excel file (in this instance, the file is called **Ch01.01-07EconFrench**), and click on the appropriate worksheet, using the worksheet tab at the bottom of the screen (in this instance, the worksheet is called **1.1–1.3.Score on one exam**). The **Scenarios** function is in different places in Excel 2003 and 2007. If using Excel 2007 or later, click on **Data, What If Analysis, Scenarios Manager**; if using Excel 2003, click on the **Tools** pulldown menu and select **Scenarios**. Then select the figure you wish to create from the left side of the **Scenarios Manager** menu (in this instance, the choices include 1.1A, 1.1B, 1.2, and 1.3), and click **Show, Close**. The Scenarios function controls the location of the sliders and click boxes in an Excel file and therefore provides a quick way to re-create a specific graph. You can also use the sliders and click boxes to move between figures manually, rather than using the **Scenarios** function.

6. The same can be said of a traditional PPF. Suppose a firm is producing two goods, X and Y, using a fixed amount of labor. The allocation of labor between the two goods is the hidden variable that moves the firm from one (X, Y) output combination to another along its PPF.

7. For a firm, this is based on the ability of a factor of production to be optimally used for the production of a specific good. The easiest example is a farmer who has a given number of acres of land. Some of the land is better (i.e., more productive) at producing rice, and some is better at barley. But if the need arises, the farmer can devote the entire plot of land to rice, or to barley; in each case, this requires some loss of "productivity" (which is illustrated geometrically by the PPF having the convexity shown).

8. Although the graph of this production function is not shown in the text, you can see it by adjusting the sliders on the production function worksheet (**1.1–1.3.Score on one exam** within the Excel file **Ch01.01-07EconFrench**) to 60 and 2 hours 47 minutes (the amount of time to obtain a perfect score derived in footnote at the bottom of page 16). Alternatively, you can use the **Scenarios** function to call up this scenario:

In Excel 2003, click **Tools, Scenarios, GraphOfEquation1.2economics, Show, Close**.

In Excel 2007, click **Data, What If Analysis, Scenarios, GraphOfEquation1.2economics, Show, Close**.

9. You may wonder how we arrived at this distribution of time. It follows easily by setting Equations 1.2.French and 1.2.economics equal to one another. We know that $t_{French} = 2 - t_{economics}$, so we can substitute these values into the equations to obtain (t represents time devoted to economics):

$$50 \cdot (2 - t)^{0.5} = 60 \cdot t^{0.5}$$

Squaring both sides, we obtain: $2 - t = 1.2^2 \cdot t = 1.44 \cdot t$

Solving for t, we obtain: $t = 2/2.44 = 0.82$ or 49 minutes.

10. If you prefer to think of this in terms of discrete changes along the PPF, you model this using the figure file. Start with the Excel file for Figure 1.6; then click the right arrowhead of the time slider (in cell E26) once. This will move the amount of time devoted to economics to 11 minutes. This increases the expected economics score by 1.2 to 25.7, and it decreases the French score by 0.3 to 67.4. Finally, note that 0.3 is one-fourth of 1.2.

11. We could just as easily have calculated the average score. Both methods produce the same conclusion.

12. This slope can easily be seen by adjusting the slider time (in row 26) so that 2:00 is devoted to the exam in the Excel file for Figure 1.7. In this instance, 0.83 results in cell E27 of the worksheet.

A Review of Supply and Demand

CHAPTER 2

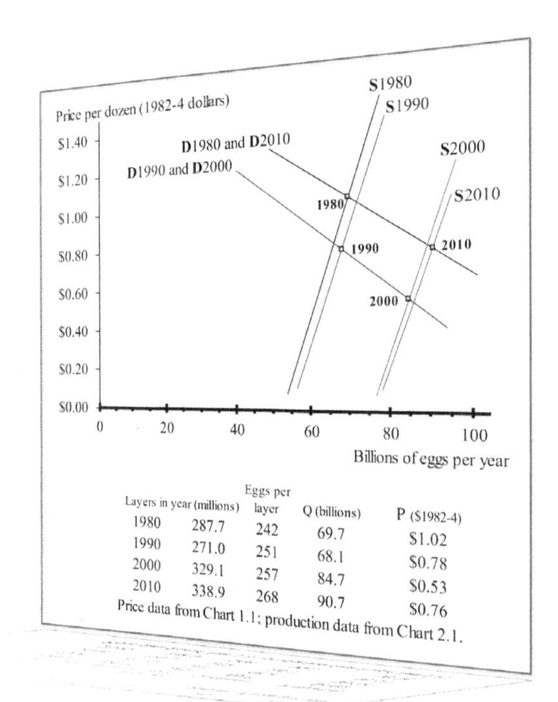

	Layers in year (millions)	Eggs per layer	Q (billions)	P ($1982-4)
1980	287.7	242	69.7	$1.02
1990	271.0	251	68.1	$0.78
2000	329.1	257	84.7	$0.53
2010	338.9	268	90.7	$0.76

Price data from Chart 1.1; production data from Chart 2.1.

Chapter Outline

The centerpiece of microeconomics is the supply and demand model. We spend much of this chapter reviewing the basic attributes of this model, and then the next three parts of the book examine this model in more detail. We begin this detailed study by analyzing consumer choice, the basis for demand, in Part 2. Next, we examine a firm's production and cost functions that are instrumental components of firm supply in Part 3. Part 4 completes the discussion of supply by reintroducing demand into the analysis so that profit-maximizing behavior can be analyzed. Before we begin this in-depth study, we need to review the broad brushstrokes of the supply and demand model developed in introductory microeconomics.

We begin by separately describing demand and supply in Section 2.1. Next, we put supply and demand together in Section 2.2 to examine market interaction. The market equilibrium that results is stable. If jostled out of equilibrium, changing inventory levels provide signals that ultimately return the market to equilibrium. This equilibrium is maintained unless economic circumstances change. If economic circumstances affecting the market change, then a new equilibrium outcome occurs. Section 2.3 examines such comparative statics movements. Section 2.4 investigates responsiveness of supply and demand to changes in price or other economic variables. The measure of responsiveness that economists employ is elasticity. Finally, Section 2.5 examines what happens when the government intervenes to alter the market outcome by imposing price controls. Such price controls void the self-correcting nature of the market and cause market imbalance. Although these imbalances exist because of political expediency, they have unintended consequences that directly oppose the stated goals of the program.

2.1 Supply and Demand

Consumers demand goods that firms supply. Behind that simple statement is a more complex story regarding demand, supply, and the interaction of demand and supply via the market mechanism.

Demand

quantity demanded: The quantity demanded is the amount consumers wish to purchase at a given price.

demand curve: A demand curve describes the quantity consumers wish to purchase for various prices. Often, this is shortened to *demand*.

ceteris paribus: *Ceteris paribus* means all else held equal.

law of downward-sloping demand: The law of downward-sloping demand states that quantity demanded increases as price decreases, *ceteris paribus*. This is also often called the *law of demand*.

The amount that consumers willingly wish to purchase at a given price is called the **quantity demanded** at that price. As we vary price, the quantity demanded varies. If we list these quantities for different prices, we obtain a *demand schedule* (when we write this information in tabular form) or a **demand curve** (when we view this information on a quantity by price graph (x, P)). Demand describes quantity as a function of price, but economists place the independent variable—price—on the vertical axis and the dependent variable—quantity—on the horizontal axis.[1]

A variety of factors determines demand for a product. These factors include the price of the product, but that is only one of the determinants of demand. Other factors include the price of other products (both complements and substitutes), income, and other parameters such as weather and tastes. When these factors are held constant and demand is simply shown as a function of price, we obtain a demand curve. *Holding all else constant* is such an important concept in economic analysis that economists have a special term to describe this statement. The Latin term ***ceteris paribus*** means holding all else equal.

Economists expect that consumers will demand more when the price is lower than they will demand when the price is higher, *ceteris paribus*. When a good becomes a better "deal," it is more highly demanded. Graphically, this means that demand is downward sloping. This is such a pervasive expectation that it is called the **law of downward-sloping demand**. Quantity demanded is inversely related to price. Figure 2.1 provides an example. Suppose you are a budding economist who is also the manager of an airport hotel restaurant, and you have a wine-by-the-glass program, with the per-glass price posted on a chalkboard. (The price is not on a printed menu, so you can freely change the price, and since it is an airport hotel, you have few repeat customers, so they do not know you like to perform economic experiments on them.) Figure 2.1 shows demand for wine by the glass as a function of price charged that you have observed over time.

> **Q1a.** What do you expect to have happen in terms of glasses of wine sold in an evening if you drop the price by $1?
>
> **Q1b.** Does your answer depend on what you are currently charging for a glass of wine?*

You may wonder why we have depicted demand as being linear in Figure 2.1. In general, demand will be nonlinear (curved), but little is gained in the current discussion by modeling demand as nonlinear, and linear functions are easier to analyze. We wish to build models that depict the relation under discussion as simply as possible. The parsimonious solution, therefore, is to stick with linear functions in this instance.

The answer to both Q1a and Q1b is related to the slope of the demand curve, m. The slope of the demand curve is $m = \Delta P/\Delta x$, but Q1a asks what is the change in x for a $1 drop in P (in symbols, what is $\Delta x/\Delta P$ for $\Delta P = -1$)? The answer to Q1a, therefore, is minus the inverse of slope, $-1/m$. When demand is nonlinear, the answer to the second question is decidedly "yes"; the change in demand depends on the price currently being charged because the defining feature of a curve is that the slope changes as we move along the curve.[2]

***Q1 answer:** (a) You expect to sell 20 more glasses for each dollar drop in price. (b) In general, the amount extra sold by dropping the price by a dollar will depend on the starting price, but in this instance, it does not because demand is depicted as being linear.

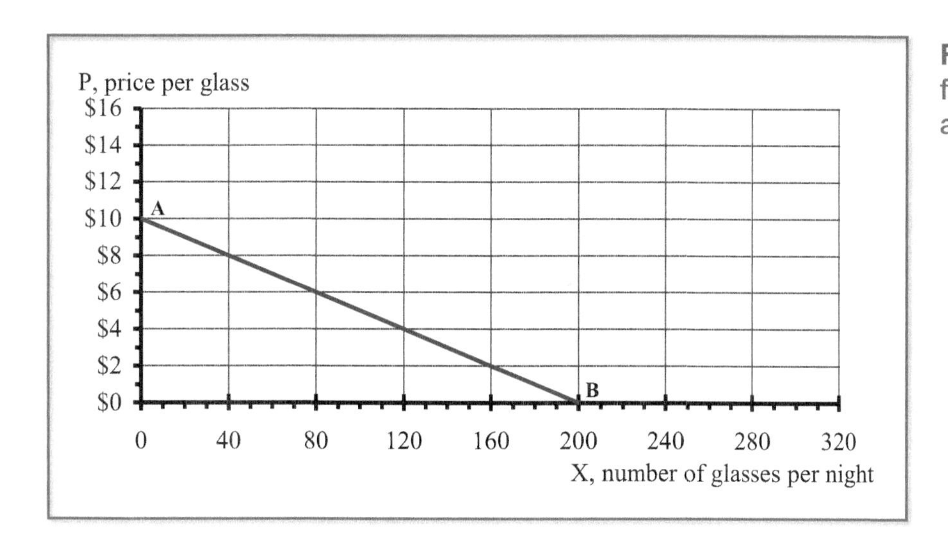

FIGURE 2.1 Demand for Wine by the Glass at a Hotel Restaurant

Shifts in Demand

We do not live in a *ceteris paribus* world. We typically cannot control all but one parameter and allow that one parameter to vary as we would if we were performing a scientific experiment. If a factor that affects demand (other than price) changes, this does not show up as a movement along the demand curve. This shows up as a shift in the demand curve.

One of the most common initial problems students have in introductory microeconomics is distinguishing between a change in quantity demanded and a change in demand. If the price alone changes, there is a *change in quantity demanded.* This is a movement along a fixed demand curve. By contrast, if one of the factors that affect demand (other than the price of the good) changes, then there is a *change in demand.* This is a shift in the demand curve.

A number of factors shift the demand curve. One of the primary determinants of demand is income. The demands for champagne and diamonds are higher during economic booms than during economic downturns; both are considered luxury goods. By contrast, the demands for ground beef and margarine are higher during economic downturns; both are considered inferior goods. Another factor affecting demand is the price of related goods. If the price of tea goes up, the demand for coffee increases; tea and coffee are substitutes. By contrast, if the price of peanut butter goes up, the demand for jelly declines; peanut butter and jelly are complements.

Demand is also affected by tastes. It is difficult to quantify how tastes form and how they change, but this certainly does occur. Consider the fate of pasta and eggs since the 1980s. For much of the 1980s and 1990s, pasta was "in" and eggs were "out" because of the low-fat diets popular at that time. More recently, a reversal of fortunes has occurred due to the rising popularity of the Atkins and South Beach diets, which emphasize protein and avoid carbohydrates. Expectations can also shift demand. One of the interesting side effects of the oil crises was that, during the crises, individuals typically kept their cars closer to full. This exacerbated the market imbalance. Finally, exogenous factors such as weather can affect demand. Coffee-shop owners pray for cold weather, and ice-cream shop owners pray for heat waves.

We can use demand curves to tell economic stories. Consider the wine market in the United States. In the early 1990s, a *60 Minutes* broadcast by Morley Safer, entitled "The French Paradox," caused quite a stir in the wine world. This report (and subsequent widely reported epidemiological evidence) linked moderate wine consumption to lower risk of cardiovascular disease. In short, drinking a glass or two of wine a day is one way to avoid heart attacks. Not surprisingly, this has had quite an effect on demand for wine in the United States. Consider how this might affect the demand curve for wine by the glass faced by the manager of the hotel restaurant described earlier. Certainly, demand

FIGURE 2.2 Hypothetical Increases in Demand for Wine by the Glass (blue is initial; red is final)

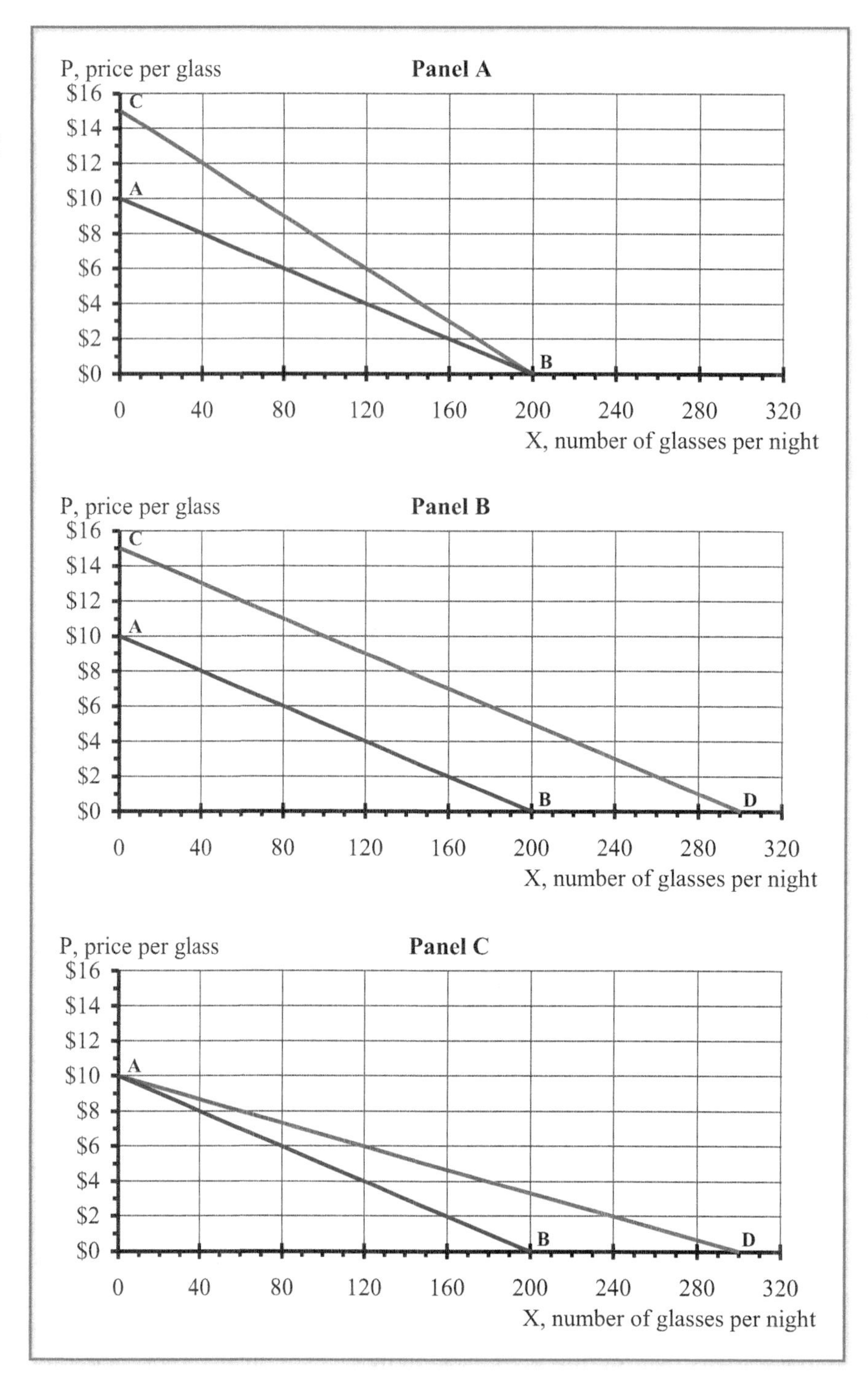

would increase, *ceteris paribus*, because of this report. But how does demand increase? Consider two hypothetical answers (**S**cenarios):

> **S2.i.** Demand increases by 50% for any price, *ceteris paribus*.
>
> **S2.ii.** The price that can be charged to maintain a given number of glasses sold per night increases by 50%, *ceteris paribus*.

Figure 2.2 depicts three increases in demand. Demand prior to the *60 Minutes* broadcast is depicted by the initial blue demand curve (from Figure 2.1); the new demand is red. Two of the panels match the scenarios described in S2.i and S2.ii.

Q2. Which scenario is associated with which panel? (*Hint:* The grid system in each panel may help you with your answer).*

These answers point to the dual way in which demand can be viewed. From a purely mathematical point of view, there is a one-to-one relation between quantity and price because the function is downward sloping. As a result, demand can be viewed from two functional orientations; these might be written D(P) and P(x). The standard way we conceptualize demand is the number of units demanded at a given price, D(P). In this conceptualization, demand is read "outward" for a given price. Scenario 2.i is a verbal description (and Figure 2.2C is a visual presentation) of this orientation. But it is equally valid to ask: What is the value of the *x*th unit of output sold? This is the height of the demand curve when demand is read "upward" for a given quantity, P(x). In this view, the demand curve is a *marginal valuation schedule*; we call this relation *inverse demand* (as we discuss in Chapter 12). If each unit sold is 50% more valuable to the marginal purchaser, then the demand curve has shifted up by 50% (rather than out by 50%). Scenario 2.ii is a verbal description (and Figure 2.2A is a visual presentation) of this orientation. You may have seen this orientation used (perhaps without it being called inverse demand) to describe the welfare concept of *consumer surplus* (which we examine in Chapter 16).

These stories are not numerically accurate (the increase in demand for wine has been somewhat less than 50%, *ceteris paribus*), but they allow you to more easily see the relations described. They were also provided to get you to start thinking more critically about what graphs can say. In introductory microeconomics, we are often satisfied with describing a qualitative relation—demand shifts out; we do not think about how it shifts out or how we might describe that more precisely. We will often be satisfied with qualitative statements here as well, but we will begin to move more forcefully in the direction of understanding quantitative magnitudes as well. We should note, however, that we will not emphasize quantitative estimation from actual data in this text. Such analysis is more the purview of empirically oriented areas of economics, such as managerial economics or econometrics.

Figure 2.2B was provided to make sure you are careful about how you interpret graphs. This panel only shows a 50% change in demand at two points: one when P = \$0 and the other when x = 0. Using the demand orientation (quantity as a function of price), **D** is 50% higher quantity than **B**, given P = \$0. For prices above P = \$0, the percentage increase in quantity is larger than 50%. For example, at P = \$5, the increase in demand is 100% (in moving from $D_{blue}(\$5) = 100$ to $D_{red}(\$5) = 200$). Using the inverse demand orientation (price as a function of quantity), **C** is a 50% higher price than **A**, given x = 0. For quantities greater than zero, the percentage increase in inverse demand is greater than 50%. For example, at x = 100, marginal valuation increases by 100% (in moving from $P_{blue}(100) = \$5$ to $P_{red}(100) = \$10$).

This discussion suggests that a variety of factors can shift demand for a product. When we draw a demand curve, we have returned to the *ceteris paribus* world in which each of these factors is held constant. As we move along a demand curve, we do so holding all else equal. If all else is not held equal, the result is a shift in the demand curve, not a movement along a fixed demand curve.

Supply

The amount that producers willingly wish to sell at a given price is called the **quantity supplied** at that price. As we vary price, the quantity supplied varies. If we connect these

quantity supplied: The quantity supplied is the amount producers wish to sell at a given price.

***Q2 answer:** Figure 2.2A depicts S2.ii because the height of the demand curve increases by 50% at each quantity level. No glasses are sold at a price of \$15 versus \$10 (at **C** vs. **A**); 40 glasses are sold at P = \$12, up from \$8; etc. **CB** is 50% above **AB** in Figure 2.2A. Figure 2.2C depicts S2.i because quantity demanded is 50% greater at each P on **AD** than on **AB**.

supply curve: A supply curve describes the quantity firms wish to sell for various prices. Often, this is shortened to *supply*.

quantities for different prices, we obtain a supply schedule (when we write this information in tabular form) or a **supply curve** (when we view this information on an (x, P) graph). Supply, like demand, describes quantity as a function of price by placing price on the vertical axis and quantity on the horizontal axis.

We expect supply to be upward sloping because when the price of the good is high, firms are willing to employ production processes that are not profitable when the price is low. A simple example is overtime. Suppose you are the manager of a firm. If the price of the good your firm produces increases, it may make sense for you to increase the length of the work shifts to increase production, even if you have to pay workers overtime. And if price continues to increase, it may make sense to add a second or third shift, even if you have to pay higher wages to induce workers to accept swing and graveyard shifts. The same idea applies to other firms and methods of production. When the price of crude oil is high, methods of crude extraction that are not profitable at low prices begin to become profitable. (For example, steam can be injected into a well to increase yield, but this is only cost effective when the price of crude is high.) If the price of a product increases, this acts as a spur to increased investment activity. Plant expansions can occur over time, but this moves us from the short run to the long run—a topic we deal with in greater detail later in this chapter and in Parts 3 and 4.

A typical shape for a market supply curve is a modified "reversed L" shape, shown in Figure 2.3. For output levels below total industry capacity, the supply curve increases modestly (a small price increase induces a large increase in the quantity supplied). In this range of output levels (shaded green in Figure 2.3), excess capacity in the industry exists; some of the capacity may not be as efficient as others, so it will only be utilized at higher prices. Past a point, however, capacity is reached, and extra output is difficult to produce, even for substantial increases in price. This is the part of the curve shaded in red in Figure 2.3.

Many of the points described previously for demand apply equally to supply. We lose little by considering linear supply curves in our initial review of supply. Linear supply works well in both of the ranges discussed earlier; the difference is one of steepness (as you may recall, we have a more formal way to describe steepness using elasticity, a topic we discuss in Section 2.4). We can write supply as S(P), or more formally as $S_x(P)$. As with demand, this function can be conceptualized from two orientations. The standard orientation is quantity as a function of price, but the inverse supply orientation is price required to support a given level of quantity supplied. When we examine both demand and supply at the same time, we must distinguish the inverse demand from the inverse supply, so we would write inverse demand as $P_D(x)$ and inverse supply as $P_S(x)$.

FIGURE 2.3 Supply for a Typical Good

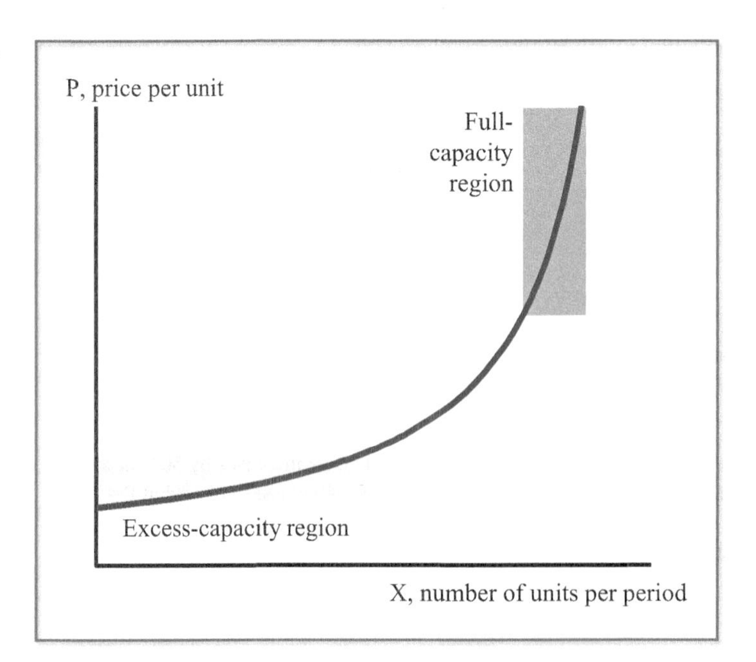

Shifts in Supply

Supply is a function of many factors, and all but price are held constant when we describe supply as a function of price. As we move along a supply curve, we say that the market exhibits a *change in quantity supplied* (as a result of the price change). This move holds all else constant, just as with demand. The exogenous variables that shift the supply curve differ from those affecting the demand curve. These variables include factors that affect the cost of producing the good. Input-cost decreases allow firms to willingly supply a given level of output at a lower price.

If technological progress occurs and allows a firm to produce more output from the same bundle of input resources, supply will expand. Technological change need not be restricted to "high-tech" industries. Consider the lowly egg. Chart 2.1A shows production statistics from 1925–2014. There is a steady increase over time, with a noticeable acceleration during World War II. Annual production almost triples over this period (from 35 billion in 1925 to 97.6 billion in 2014), despite the number of layers (chickens) being approximately constant throughout the period (311 million layers in 1925 and 355 million in 2014). The increase in production occurs due to a dramatic increase in productivity (as measured by average number of eggs per layer). This is shown in Chart 2.1B. Production per layer increases almost every year during the sample and more than doubles over the time period (from 112 eggs per layer in 1925 to 275 in 2014).

The price of goods that are related on a production basis can also affect supply. If the price of hides increases, then this will have an expansive effect on beef producers' willingness to supply beef at a given price because beef and hides are complementary production goods. Conversely, the two main refined petroleum products (on a volume basis) are gasoline and fuel oil (home heating oil and diesel fuel). Gasoline and fuel oil

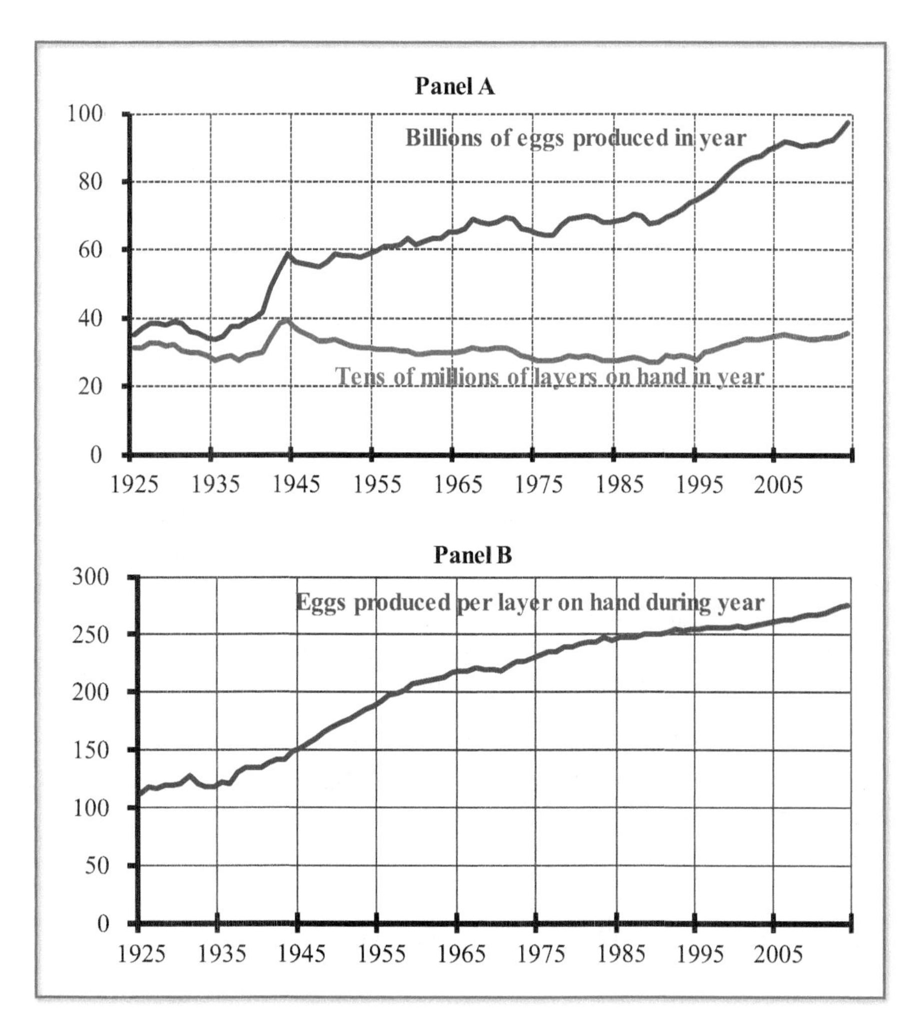

CHART 2.1 Egg Production Statistics, 1925–2014

Source: Data drawn from *Poultry Production and Value Annual Summary and Layers and Egg Production Annual Summary*; Table 2—Eggs: Production, disposition, and value, http://usda.mannlib.cornell.edu/MannUsda/viewDocumentInfo.do?documentID=1509

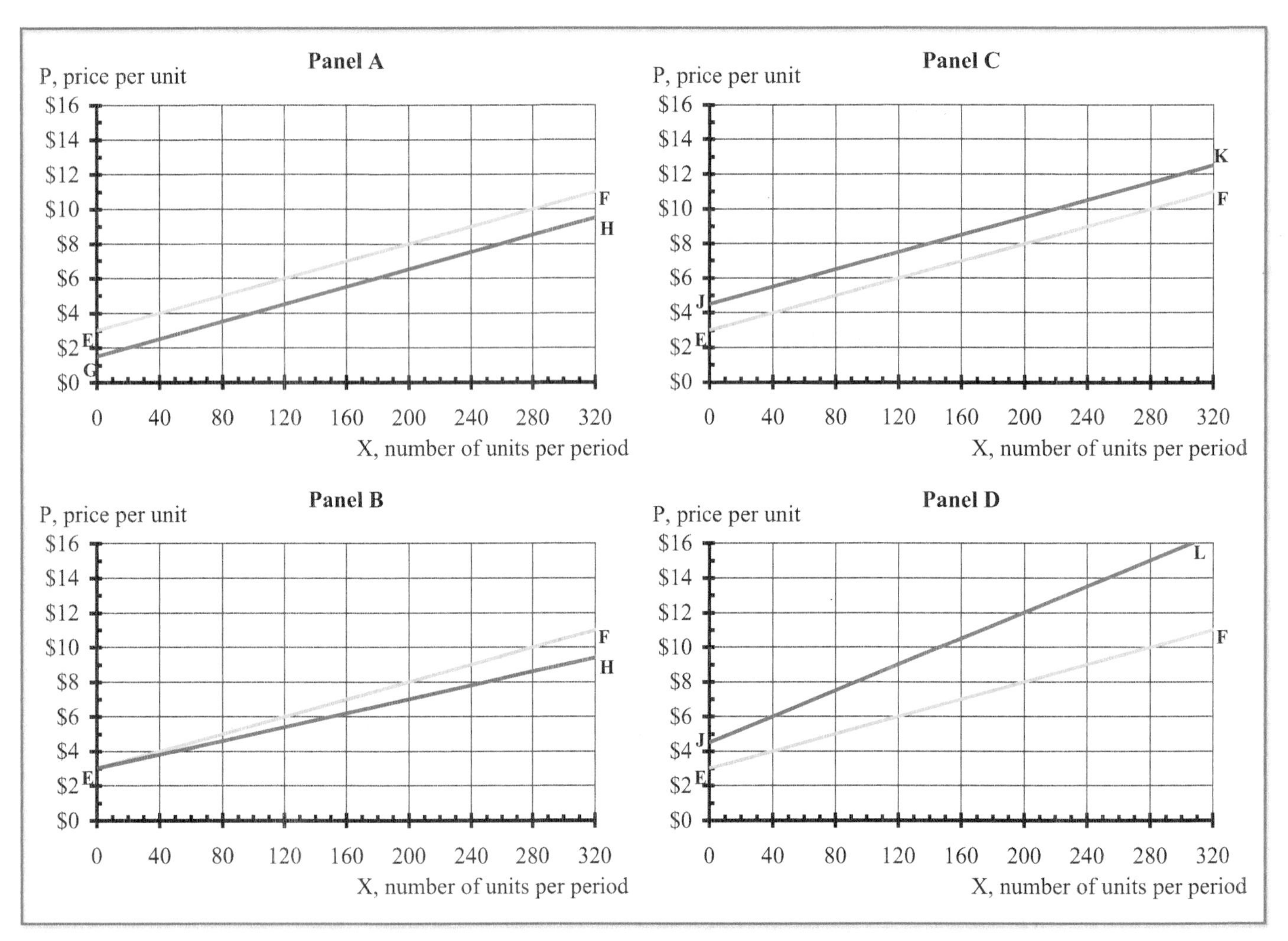

FIGURE 2.4 Four Hypothetical Changes in Supply (blue is initial supply; red is final supply)

are production substitutes. Refiners are able to adjust the mix of refined product produced from a barrel of crude oil and do so over the course of the year. When the price of gasoline is low, a larger percentage of crude is refined as fuel oil, and vice versa.

One final factor that is held constant on a supply curve is the degree of regulatory interference. This interference can come in the form of specific required production processes or levels of taxation (this is discussed in Section 22.1). If taxes increase or if costly new production processes are required, this will increase the cost of production and will therefore reduce the willingness of firms to supply output at a given price. If any of these factors change, then we will see a change in supply, rather than a change in quantity supplied.

We can use a hypothetical market supply curve to further hone your skills at creating economic stories using graphs. The blue initial supply curve labeled **EF** is the same in each panel of Figure 2.4. (Notice that this linear supply curve is a close approximation of the excess-capacity portion of the supply curve in Figure 2.3.) The grid system is provided to help match the panel to the scenario.

Q4. Match Figure 2.4A–2.4D with Scenarios S4.i–S4.iv.

Each of the following four scenarios depicts a change in economic circumstance (exogenous variable) that shifts supply:

S4.i. Technological progress boosts firms' willingness to increase output by 25% at any given price.

S4.ii. An excise tax of $1.50 per unit is imposed on sales.

S4.iii. A 50% tax is imposed on sales of goods in this market.

S4.iv. Cost decreases by \$1.50 per unit due to lower factor prices.*

These scenarios focus on the two orientations we can use to describe supply. Scenario S4.i takes the standard orientation and describes quantity as a function of price, and the other three scenarios take the inverse supply orientation and examine price required to support a given level of supply.

One final point should be made regarding a change in supply: Students often have difficulty verbally distinguishing an expansion in supply and a contraction in supply. Contractions and expansions are viewed using the orientation of quantity as a function of price (not the reverse). Therefore, Figures 2.4A and 2.4B are expansions in supply, and Figures 2.4C and 2.4D are contractions. (The semantic problem arises when students take the reverse orientation and note that a supply contraction means that the price required to support a given level of output increases as a result of the contraction.)

2.2 Market Interaction

The supply/demand intersection is arguably the most famous in all of economics. From a purely mathematical point of view, the intersection of supply and demand provides two pieces of information—a price and a quantity. These are the endogenous variables determined by the supply/demand model. Economists tend to focus on the price at the intersection point, which they call the **market clearing price**. Since both supply and demand are considered a function of price, it is natural to focus on that price where consumer demands are just satisfied by what firms wish to supply. At any other price, there is an imbalance between supply and demand.

When price exceeds the market clearing price, the amount that firms wish to supply exceeds the amount that consumers wish to purchase. This is a situation of **excess supply**. The physical embodiment of excess supply is the buildup of inventories of the product. By contrast, when price is below the market clearing price, the amount consumers wish to purchase exceeds what firms willingly wish to supply. Economists call this state of affairs **excess demand**. The physical embodiment of excess demand is bare shelves and shortage of product. A precursor to both of these signals is a change in inventory level. Inventory levels are drawn down when the market exhibits excess demand, and excess supply causes inventories to build up.

Both excess supply and excess demand signal a need for change. To reduce increased inventories, price should be reduced to spur greater demand and moderate supply. If the reverse is true and inventory levels are below normal or shortages exist, price should increase to reduce demand and increase supply so as to moderate the shortage conditions.

market clearing price: The market clearing price is the price at which supply equals demand. Often, this is called the *equilibrium price*.

excess supply: A market exhibits excess supply at a given price when the amount that firms wish to supply exceeds the amount that consumers wish to purchase.

excess demand: A market exhibits excess demand at a given price when the amount that consumers wish to purchase exceeds the amount that firms wish to supply.

Fact: *Excess demand signals the need to increase the market price, and excess supply signals the need to decrease the market price.*

Both of these signals push in the direction of the market clearing price (and both of these signals only stop pushing in the direction of market clearing if the market clearing price is achieved). Put another way, the market clearing price is the only price at which there is no signal of a need for change. These signals are summarized in Figure 2.5. Excess supply is the difference between supply and demand at this price (in Figure 2.5A,

***Q4 answer:** Figure 2.4A depicts S4.iv because the supply curve shifts down by \$1.50 per unit as a result of the decline in factor costs (**GH** is \$1.50 below **EF** for any output level). Figure 2.4B depicts S4.i because **EH** represents supplying 25% more output at any price than **EF**. The easiest price to see this is at P = \$7; $S_{initial}(\$7) = 160$ along **EF**, but $S_{final}(\$7) = 200$ along **EH**. Figure 2.4C depicts S4.ii because the supply curve shifts up by \$1.50 per unit as a result of the increase in cost induced by the excise tax (**JK** is \$1.50 above **EF** for any output level). Figure 2.4D depicts S4.iii because the supply curve shifts up by 50% for any amount of output due to the 50% tax (**JL** is 50% above **EF** for any output level). This is easiest to see at x = 0, where **J** is 50% higher than **E**, and at x = 200, where $S_{initial}(\$8) = 200$ along **EF**, but $S_{final}(\$12) = 200$ along **JL**.

FIGURE 2.5
Determination of Market Equilibrium

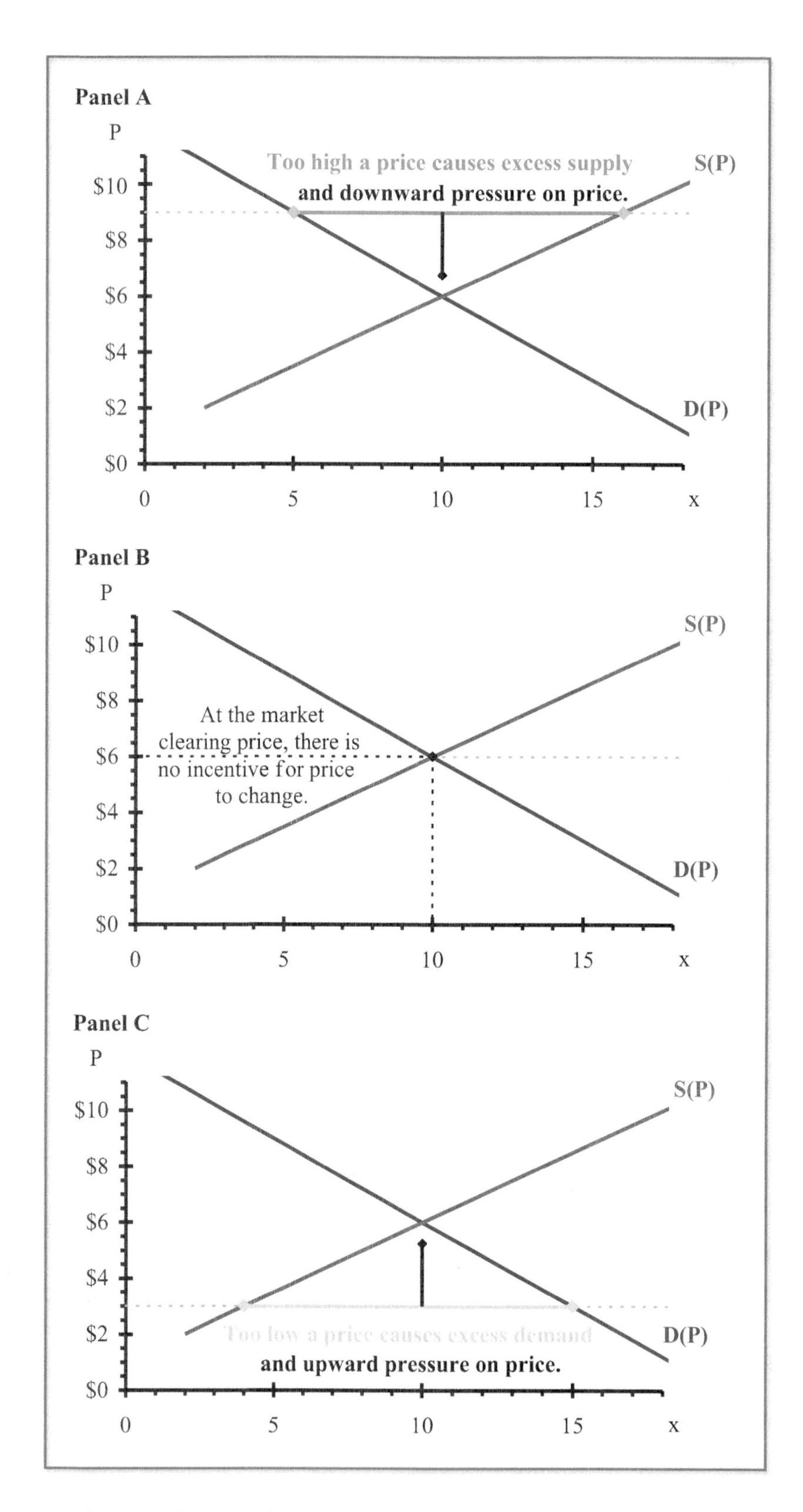

ES($9) = S($9) – D($9) = 16 – 5 = 11). If firms produce these excess units of output, inventories will build up, and this will produce downward pressure on price. The reverse holds true in Figure 2.5C because there is excess demand when price is below the market clearing price. Excess demand is the difference between demand and supply at this price (in Figure 2.5C, ED($3) = D($3) – S($3) = 15 – 4 = 11). This excess demand causes reduced inventories and eventual shortages, and this shortfall causes upward pressure on price. Only in Figure 2.5B are supply and demand balanced. This is a market equilibrium in which there is no signal for change (unless either supply or demand shifts). Consider this from the point of view of inventory level. If demand and supply are balanced, then inventory levels are not increasing or decreasing, and therefore there is no signal that price should change.

Price is an inventory management tool. Suppose you are the manager of the fresh produce section of a grocery store. The quickest way to reduce profits is to have fresh produce spoil. If you are faced with an excess inventory of lettuce that is beginning to wilt, it makes sense to cut the price on the lettuce, rather than maintain the price and sell fewer heads of lettuce before the rest must be thrown out as unsaleable. Conversely, if you notice that you are running out of potatoes and the next shipment will not arrive for two days, it makes sense to raise the price of potatoes to moderate demand and avoid a stock-out situation. (Of course, you cannot follow this strategy if you are running out because you advertised a sale on potatoes and did not correctly estimate demand at the sale price.)

One final problem arises for many students who initially consider the supply/demand nexus. This problem has to do with the tautological nature of the market exchange. Regardless of whether the market is in or out of equilibrium, each market transaction involves a unit sold by a supplier to a demander; at a semantic level, supply always equals demand. But when viewed more critically, we see that this market exchange is only part of the story. If there is excess supply and inventories build up, then demand is the constraining factor in the market interaction. Similarly, if there is excess demand and consumers wish to purchase more than firms are willing to provide, then supply is the constraining factor in the market interaction. In both of these instances, the smaller of the two quantities determines the *actual* number of units exchanged (in the absence of inventory adjustments). One way to think of this is to consider two possible versions of demand and supply—*preferred* and *actual*. *Preferred* demand and *preferred* supply are simply the demand and supply relations we have already discussed. *Actual* demand is the smaller of preferred demand and preferred supply at a given price. This distinction is shown in Figure 2.6.

Actual supply is the smaller of preferred demand and preferred supply at a given price. When price is above the market clearing price, then demand is the constraining factor, and when price is below the market clearing price, then supply is the constraining factor. Only when price is at the market clearing level do *both* actual and preferred supply and demand coincide. At all other prices, there is either unsatisfied supply (when price is too high) or unsatisfied demand (when price is too low).

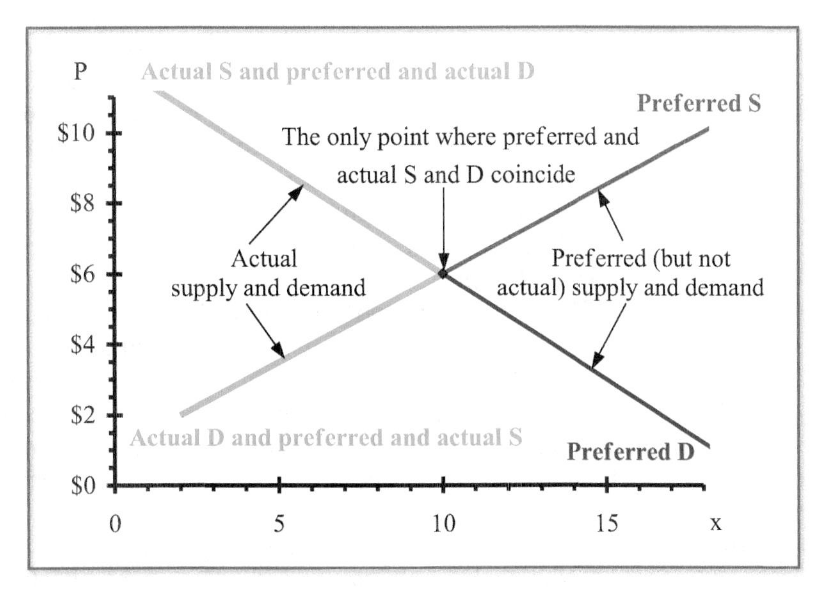

FIGURE 2.6 At a Semantic Level, Supply and Demand Always Are Equal, Since a Market Exchange Involves a Buyer and Seller Interacting

2.3 What Happens When Economic Circumstances Change?

The discussion in Section 2.2 is based on a fixed supply and demand schedule. If supply does not match demand at a given price, then surplus or shortage results. Both conditions induce a price change to correct the imbalance. This disequilibrium adjustment process yields an eventual equilibrium in which supply equals demand at the market clearing price. This equilibrium is a position of stability: Price and quantity are maintained unless something changes to disrupt the equilibrium.

If economic circumstances in a market change, then the equilibrium changes. (Put in more mathematical terms, if an exogenous variable changes, then so do the endogenous variables in the model.) The study of the change in equilibrium in moving from one economic circumstance to another is called **comparative statics analysis**. The term *comparative statics* means the comparison of static situations. Each equilibrium is "static" in the sense that unless economic circumstances change, no change in equilibrium will occur. The term *sensitivity* is used to connote how sensitive the endogenous variables are to a change in an exogenous variable.

comparative statics analysis: Comparative statics analysis involves examining the effect of a change in an exogenous economic variable on various endogenous variables. Economists often call this *sensitivity analysis*.

Comparative statics analysis of the supply/demand model involves examining how market clearing price and quantity change when economic circumstances change. If one of the underlying factors on the demand side of the market changes, then the result is a change in demand, and if one of the underlying factors on the supply side of the market changes, then the result is a change in supply. We noted "laundry lists" of both such sets of exogenous variables in Section 2.1, when we discussed shifts in demand or shifts in supply.

An initial goal is to understand the qualitative change that occurs when demand *or* supply shifts. If both supply and demand simultaneously shift, then definitive relations are more complex than if only one or the other shifts. As a result, we follow economists' typical strategy of analyzing the effect of a shift in one curve to understand the consequences of that shift on the market equilibrium. The magnitude of the change in quantity and price depends on the size of the change in demand or supply *and* on the shape of the curve that does not change. For example, a change in demand affects market clearing price and quantity. The actual change depends on the magnitude of the demand change and on the shape of the supply curve. This occurs for a simple reason: The equilibrium is based on the supply/demand interaction; therefore, the change in equilibrium caused by a change in one curve still requires an understanding of what is happening along the other curve (since the new equilibrium is a movement along that curve).

The initial equilibrium provides a point of reference both in terms of quantity and in terms of price for the new equilibrium. If we draw a horizontal and vertical line through the initial equilibrium, we set up a "shifted" coordinate system based on this initial equilibrium. The light green lines in each panel of Figure 2.7 provide such a shifted coordinate system. The labels I, II, III, and IV represent the quadrants relative to this coordinate system. If the new equilibrium is in the first quadrant, for instance, both price and quantity have increased as a result of the change in economic circumstance.

If demand shifts for fixed supply, then the resulting market equilibrium must be on the initial supply curve. This *forces* the new equilibrium to be in the first or third quadrants because supply is upward sloping. A demand expansion increases both price and quantity, as shown in Figure 2.7A, and a demand contraction decreases both price and quantity, as shown in Figure 2.7B. By contrast, if supply shifts for fixed demand, then the new equilibrium must be in the second or fourth quadrants because demand is downward sloping. A supply expansion increases quantity and decreases price, as shown in Figure 2.7C, and a supply contraction decreases quantity and increases price, as shown in Figure 2.7D. The table at the top of Figure 2.7 summarizes the possible qualitative responses to a supply or a demand shift.

If multiple shifts occur, then we can no longer provide definitive answers for both price and quantity. Nonetheless, we can provide some generalizations. If both supply and demand change, then we can definitively determine the direction of change of either

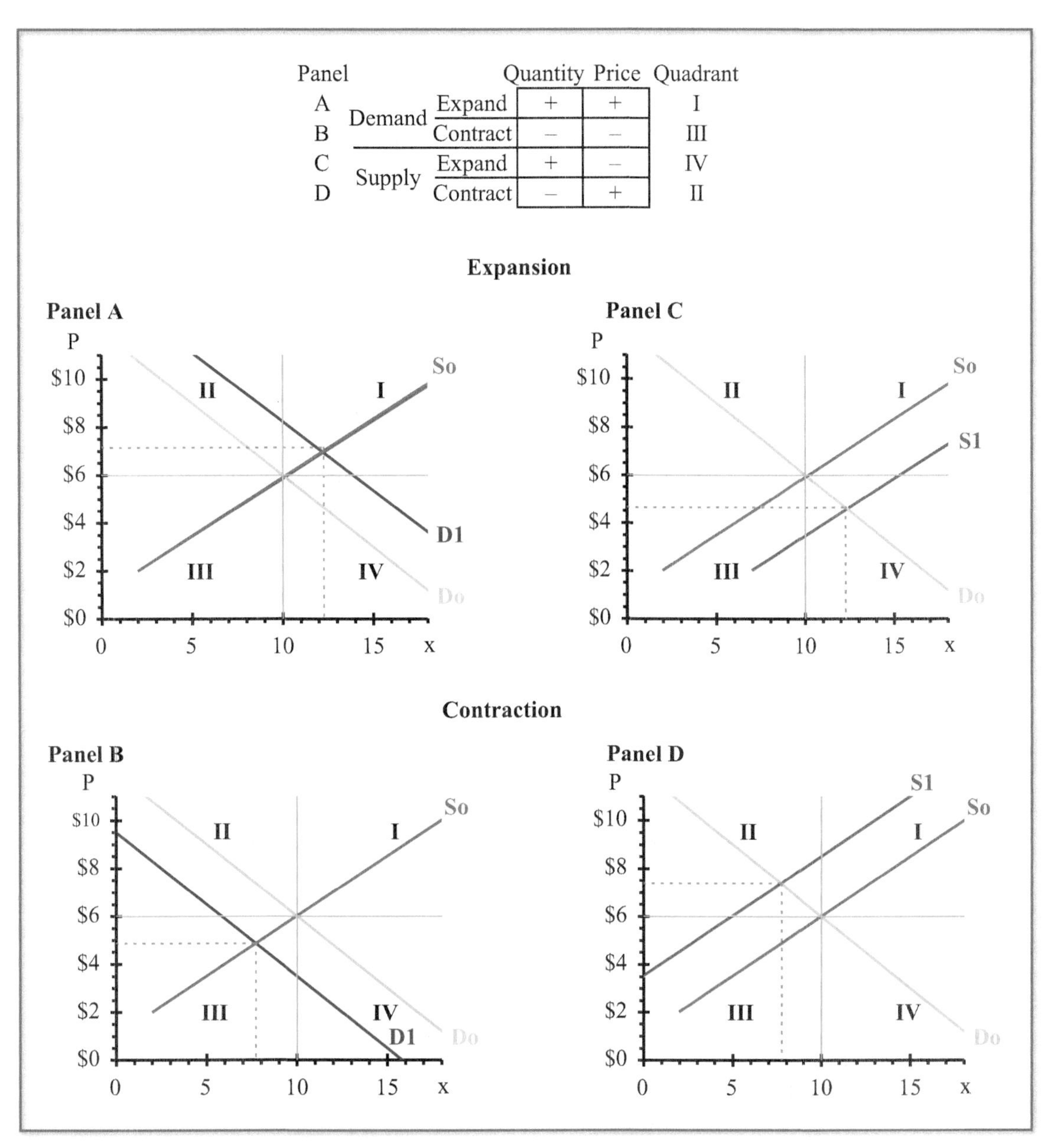

Panel			Quantity	Price	Quadrant
A	Demand	Expand	+	+	I
B		Contract	–	–	III
C	Supply	Expand	+	–	IV
D		Contract	–	+	II

FIGURE 2.7 A Typology of Change

[This icon signifies that there is an Excel file of this figure for dynamic manipulation.]

quantity or price. If supply and demand both expand or both contract, we can determine the net effect on quantity but not price. The reverse holds if one expands and the other contracts. In this event, we can deterministically understand the net effect on price but not on quantity. These results are summarized in Table 2.1. The Excel version of Figure 2.7 allows you to verify the deterministic part of each solution, as well as the ambiguous part. For instance, if you set the demand curve at a modest expansion over the initial demand curve and then vary the size of the supply expansion, you will note that for a "small" supply expansion, price increases; for a moderate supply expansion, price does not change; and for a large supply expansion, price declines. It would be worthwhile to verify the other three relations described in the table with either the file or with pencil and paper.

We can use supply and demand shifts to examine actual markets. Consider once again the incredible, edible egg. As we saw in Chart 1.1B, for much of the 1980s and 1990s, the egg declined in price. Eggs were one of the targets of the "low-fat" diet popular during this time; this certainly led to a decline in demand due to a change in tastes. This shifted back the demand for eggs for a given price. At the same time, we saw in Chart 2.1 that

TABLE 2.1 Direction of Price and Quantity Change, Given Joint Changes in Supply and Demand (based on Figure 2.7)

				Quantity	Price	Quadrants
Demand	Expand	Supply	Expand	+	?	I or IV
			Contract	?	+	I or II
	Contract	Supply	Expand	?	–	III or IV
			Contract	–	?	II or III

? signifies that the change may increase, not change, or decrease.

egg production has become more and more efficient over time. This means that, at a given price, supply increases, *ceteris paribus*. We see in Table 2.1 that if demand contracts and supply expands, the net effect on price is an unambiguous decline, but the effect on quantity is ambiguous. Price and quantity information for 1980, 1990, 2000, and 2010 (reproduced beneath Figure 2.8) provide us with examples of this ambiguity. Figure 2.8 contains a number of simplifying assumptions, but the most obvious are:

1. supply and demand are linear,
2. demand in 1980 and 2010 coincide, and
3. demand in 1990 and 2000 coincide.

The second and third assumptions simplify the discussion, but it need not be the case. For example, if the third assumption is not the case and if demand is flatter than shown, then demand contracts from 1990 to 2000. If demand is steeper than shown, then demand expands between 1990 and 2000. Similar statements could be made about the 1980 and 2010 demand curve, which models the return to higher demand due to high-protein diets.

FIGURE 2.8 Demand and Supply Shifts Consistent with Egg Production and Cost Data (based on data from Charts 1.1 and 2.1, reproduced below)

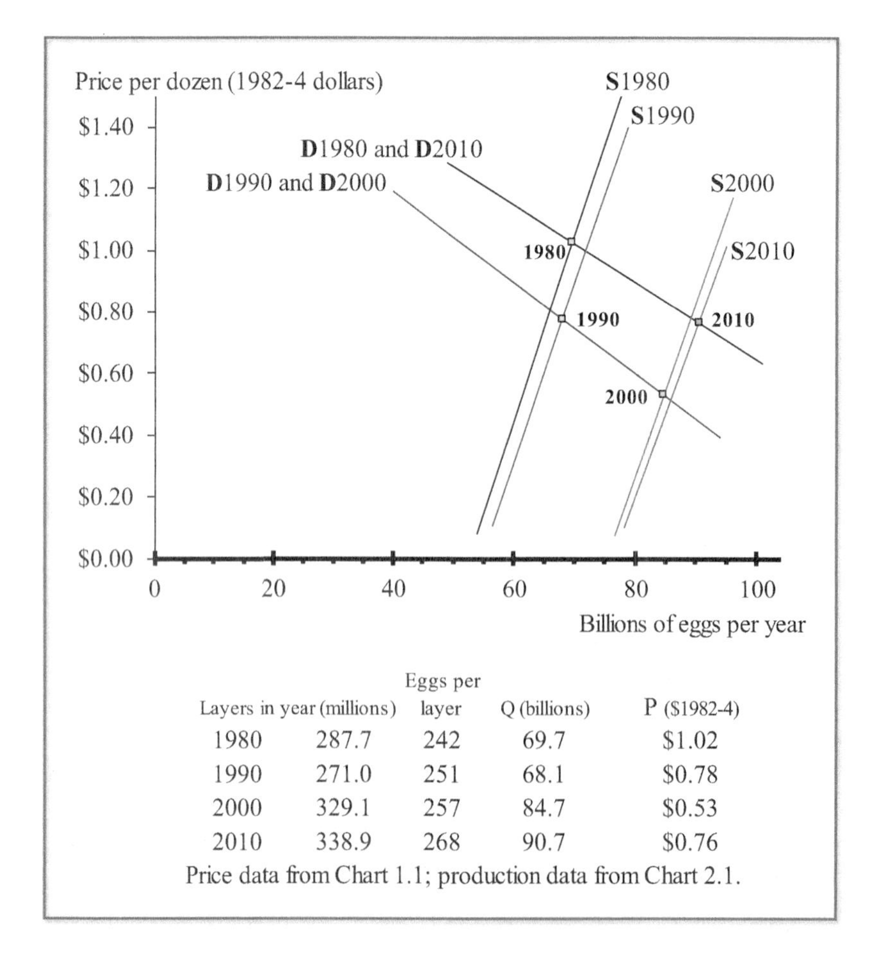

	Layers in year (millions)	Eggs per layer	Q (billions)	P ($1982-4)
1980	287.7	242	69.7	$1.02
1990	271.0	251	68.1	$0.78
2000	329.1	257	84.7	$0.53
2010	338.9	268	90.7	$0.76

Price data from Chart 1.1; production data from Chart 2.1.

Given the decline in demand for eggs due to the popularity of the low-fat diet in moving from 1980 to 1990, the net effect is a decline in quantity for small expansions in supply. Price and quantity both decline. Interestingly, had you only looked at the number of layers (hens) in the year as a proxy for the size of the production process in the year, you would expect supply to contract because the number of layers declined from 287.7 million in 1980 to 271 million in 1990. But, as noted in Chart 2.1B, the productivity per layer increased over this time period. The net effect is an expansion in supply but a decline in quantity demanded and supplied (from 69.7 billion eggs in 1980 to 68.1 billion eggs in 1990). Put in terms of the discussion in Figure 2.7 and Table 2.1, the 1990 market equilibrium is in the third quadrant relative to the 1980 equilibrium. By contrast, the comparison of 1980 and 2000 shows that the 2000 equilibrium is in the fourth quadrant relative to 1980 because price declines and quantity increases. The quantity increase is due to the increase in number of layers producing in 2000 (329.1 million layers relative to 287.7 million in 1980, as noted earlier) and the increase in productivity per layer (from 242 to 257 over this period).

2.4 Elasticity

Economists are interested in knowing more than the direction of change: They are also interested in the magnitude of change. We know that an increase in tax rate will increase price and decrease quantity (and we can model this, using a comparative statics analysis of the supply/demand model). But we would also like to know by how much price will increase and by how much quantity will decrease. Or to take an even simpler example, how much would demand for cigarettes change if price were increased by $1 per pack? Or how much will supply increase if the price of chocolate increases by $1 per pound? Answers such as these can be obtained using *elasticity*. There are a variety of elasticities, but each is based on the same underlying calculation:

$$\text{Elasticity}_{\text{variable}} = \varepsilon_v = \%\Delta\text{quantity}/\%\Delta\text{variable}. \quad \textbf{(2.1a)}$$

ε is the Greek letter *epsilon*. ε_v measures the proportional responsiveness of quantity to a proportional change in a variable that affects quantity. The remaining question, of course, is what do we mean by the term *variable*? The most common variable is price, but other possible variables include (but are not restricted to) other prices, income, and advertising. If we maintain the generic term *variable* and denote variable by V and quantity by Q, then we may rewrite elasticity in a more computationally efficient form (for many purposes):

$$\varepsilon_v = \%\Delta Q/\%\Delta V = (\Delta Q/Q)/(\Delta V/V) = (\Delta Q/\Delta V) \cdot (V/Q). \quad \textbf{(2.1b)}$$

This latter version of the basic formula removes percentages and considers elasticity as a function of slopes (as we will soon see).

Elasticity measures the responsiveness of output to a change in another part of the economic system. There are both elasticities of demand and elasticities of supply. The most common variable to measure output's responsiveness against is price, so price elasticity of demand and price elasticity of supply deserve special attention.

Demand Elasticities

The most common elasticity discussed in microeconomics is the **price elasticity of demand**. When you see elasticity mentioned with no supporting modifiers, assume that the elasticity under consideration is price elasticity of demand. Price elasticity of demand describes moving along a demand curve.

price elasticity of demand: The price elasticity of demand is the percentage change in quantity demanded for a given percentage change in price ($\varepsilon = \%\Delta Q_d/\%\Delta P$).

As noted earlier, price and quantity are inversely related on a demand curve; demand is downward sloping. If we let m denote the slope of the demand for x curve, then m = P/x on the demand curve, where $P = P_x$ (as usual, we avoid subscripts unless they are necessary). We can rewrite price elasticity of demand, ε, using Equation 2.1b, as:

$$\varepsilon = \varepsilon_x = (\Delta x/\Delta P) \cdot (P/x) = (1/(\Delta P/\Delta x)) \cdot (P/x) = (1/m) \cdot (P/x). \quad \textbf{(2.2)}$$

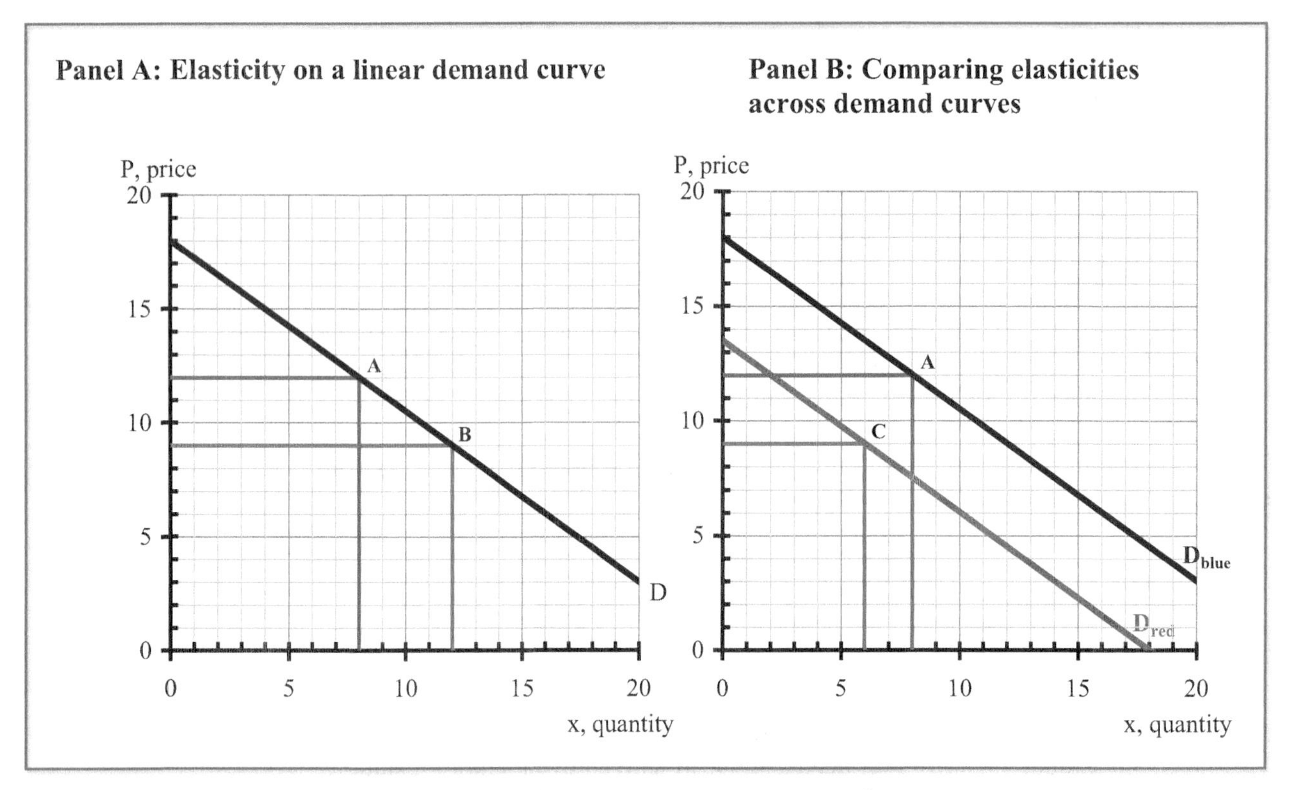

FIGURE 2.9 Comparing Elasticity along and across Linear Demand Curves

Elasticity is inversely related to slope; steeper slope means less elastic demand, and flatter slope means more elastic demand, *ceteris paribus*.

Since $m < 0$, the price elasticity of demand is negative. This may be at odds with what you learned in introductory microeconomics. Many introductory texts (and some intermediate texts as well) treat the price elasticity of demand as a special case and place a minus sign in front of Equation 2.2 so that students are able to work with positive numbers. This is simply a matter of convention, and there is not universal agreement on what should be done. We do not follow this strategy because we wish to provide a unified description of elasticity. Equation 2.2 emanates from Equation 2.1, as do all other elasticities described in this text. Price elasticity will be negative by this definition as a result.

Elasticity is especially easy to calculate when working with linear demand, since slope does not change on a linear demand curve. Elasticity declines as we move down the linear demand curve; price declines and quantity increases so that P/x declines. Consider the demand curve depicted in Figure 2.9A.

Q9a. What is the elasticity of demand at **A** and at **B**?*

Figure 2.9B examines elasticity across demand curves. Both curves have the same slope.

Q9b. How does the elasticity of demand at **A** compare with the elasticity of demand at **C**?†

Elasticity of demand varies by the good under consideration and by the time frame under consideration. We describe how elastic demand is according to the magnitude of elastic-

---

***Q9a answer:** Both elasticities follow easily from Equation 2.2, given $m = -3/4$. $\varepsilon(\mathbf{A}) = (-4/3) \cdot (12/8) = -2$, and $\varepsilon(\mathbf{B}) = (-4/3) \cdot (9/12) = -1$. If you calculated $\varepsilon = -1.4$, you used the arc elasticity formula you learned in introductory microeconomics. This calculation uses the average price, $(P_A + P_B)/2$, and the average quantity, $(x_A + x_B)/2$, rather than either endpoint. Notice that this arc elasticity is between $\varepsilon(\mathbf{A})$ and $\varepsilon(\mathbf{B})$. The arc elasticity is, in some sense, the "average" elasticity on the segment **AB**, but it is not the elasticity at either **A** or **B**.

†Q9b answer: They are the same. We already know from earlier that $\varepsilon(\mathbf{A}) = -2$. The elasticity at **C** is calculated in the same way: $\varepsilon(\mathbf{C}) = (-4/3) \cdot (9/6) = -2$. We will examine why this is the case in a homework problem.

ity: When $|\varepsilon| > 1$, we say that demand is **elastic**; when $|\varepsilon| = 1$, we say that demand has **unitary elasticity**; and when $|\varepsilon| < 1$, we say that demand is **inelastic**. Notice that because of the sign of ε, this is the same as saying: when $\varepsilon < -1$, we say that demand is elastic; when $\varepsilon = -1$, we say that demand has unitary elasticity; and when $\varepsilon > -1$, we say that demand is inelastic.

elastic: When $|\varepsilon| > 1$, we say that demand is elastic.

unitary elasticity: When $|\varepsilon| = 1$, we say that demand has unitary elasticity.

inelastic: When $|\varepsilon| < 1$, we say that demand is inelastic.

One of the most common ways to think about elasticity of demand is to consider how a change in price affects revenue spent on the good. If demand is inelastic, the price change is larger than the quantity change (on a percentage basis). This follows directly from the definition of inelastic: $|\varepsilon| < 1$ only if $|\%\Delta x| < |\%\Delta P|$. This creates a situation where revenue spent on the good increases with an increase in price. More explicitly, if demand is inelastic, an increase in price increases total revenue devoted to purchasing the good.[3] By contrast, if demand is elastic, an increase in price decreases total revenue devoted to purchasing the good. And finally, if demand has unitary elasticity, then an increase in price does not affect total revenue devoted to the good. Symmetric statements could, of course, be made based on a price decrease, rather than a price increase.

Some goods are highly elastic because they have many close substitutes. An example would be Red Delicious apples. Many different varieties of apples typically are available in large grocery stores, and if Red Delicious apples have a 10% price increase, they might have a substantial change in quantity demanded as a result because people can switch to other types of apples or to other kinds of fruit. If demand declines by 35% as a result of the 10% price increase, the price elasticity of demand for Red Delicious apples is $\varepsilon_{\text{Red Delicious apples}} = -3.5 = -35\%/{+10\%}$. By contrast, avocados are much less price elastic because individuals wishing to put them in salads or make guacamole have no close substitutes for avocados. Of course, individuals can decide to put something else on their salads, or they can make bean dip instead of guacamole. Suppose that a 10% increase in price leads to a 10% decline in demand for avocados. The price elasticity of demand for avocados is $\varepsilon_{\text{avocados}} = -1.0 = -10\%/{+10\%}$. Salt is even less price elastic than avocados. Even if the price of salt were to double, the decline in demand would be minimal, on the order of 10%. The price elasticity of demand for salt, based on this information, is $\varepsilon_{\text{salt}} = -0.1 = -10\%/{+100\%}$. Applying the terms from earlier, we would say that demand for Red Delicious apples is elastic, avocados have unitary elasticity, and salt is inelastic.

We typically expect demand to become more elastic over time, as people have the ability to fully adjust to price changes. The standard example of this phenomenon is gasoline. In the short term, if you have to use your car to get to work or to school, there is little you can do to adjust to an increase in the price of gasoline. But over the longer term (i.e., over a time period in which you are able to adjust more fully to the change in price), you may be able to moderate your demand for higher-priced gasoline because you have purchased a more fuel-efficient car or you may have decided to adjust your schedule to ride-share, and so on.

A second demand elasticity involves the responsiveness of demand for one good to a change in the price of another good. The elasticity required for this purpose is called a **cross-price elasticity**. Specifically, suppose we want to know how a change in the price of y affects the demand for good x. The cross-price elasticity, $\varepsilon_{x,y}$, is calculated from Equation 2.1 by replacing the term *variable* with the price of good y, P_y:

cross-price elasticity: A cross-price elasticity examines how a change in the price of one good affects demand for another good.

$$\varepsilon_{x,y} = \%\Delta x/\%\Delta P_y. \quad \textbf{(2.3)}$$

Note: *The order of the subscripts matters;* $\varepsilon_{y,x} = \%\Delta y/\%\Delta P_x$ *is a different cross-price elasticity than* $\varepsilon_{x,y}$*. The first subscript is the quantity, and the second refers to the price. As noted earlier, sometimes price elasticity of demand is called own-price elasticity. This is written as* $\varepsilon_{x,x} = \%\Delta x/\%\Delta P_x$*, and it offers a conceptual counterpoint to cross-price elasticity,* $\varepsilon_{x,y}$*.*

Unlike price elasticity of demand, cross-price elasticity of demand may be positive or negative.[4] When the cross-price elasticity is negative, an increase in the price of one good decreases the demand for the other good ($\varepsilon_{x,y} < 0$ if $\%\Delta x < 0$ when $\%\Delta P_y > 0$). Economists say that y is a **complement** of x in this instance. Lox is a complement of bagels because

complement: If an increase in the price of one good, y, leads to a decrease in demand for the other good, x, then y is a complement of x. In terms of elasticity, y is a complement of x if $\varepsilon_{x,y} < 0$.

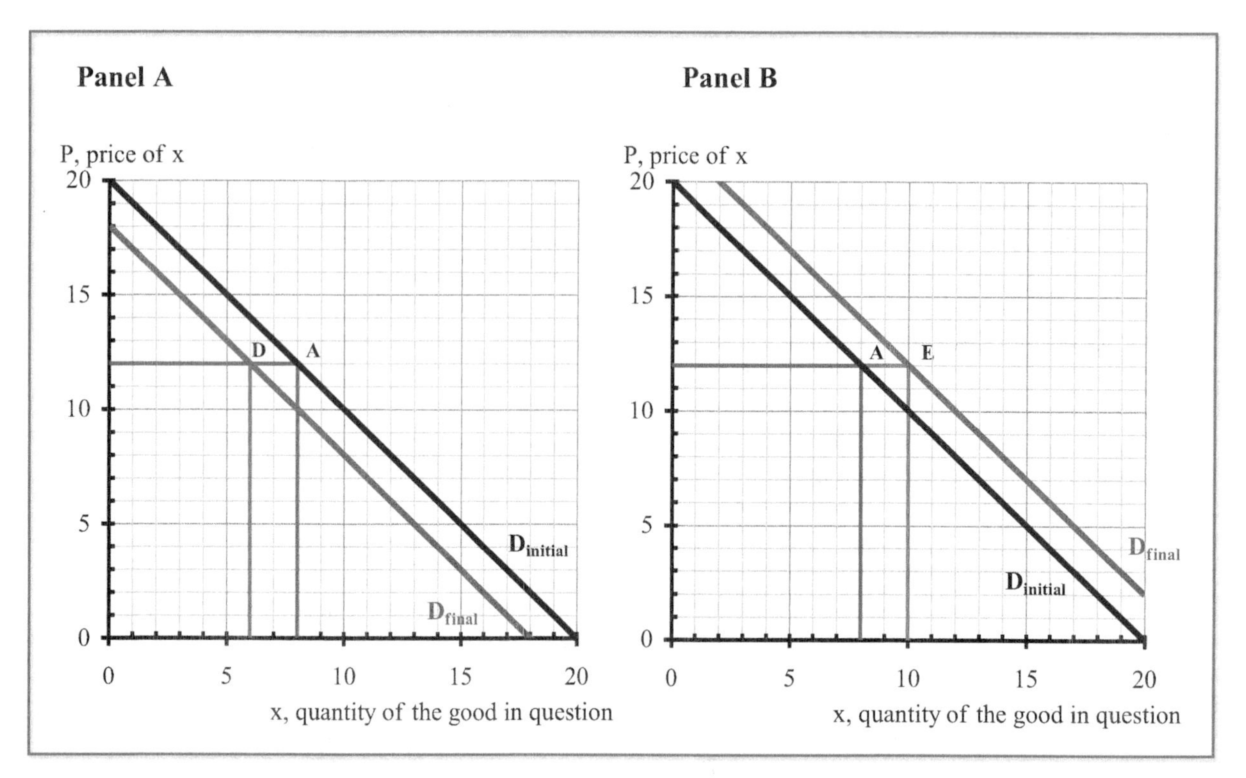

FIGURE 2.10 Demand Shifts from Blue to Red as a Result of Changed Economic Circumstance

an increase in the price of lox is associated with a decrease in demand for bagels. If the reverse is true, the two goods are **substitutes**. Pizza is a substitute for calzones because an increase in the price of pizza is associated with an increase in the demand for calzones. When a change in the price of one good has no effect on demand for the other good, the two goods are said to be **independent**. Pizza is independent of pens because an increase in the price of pizza has no effect on the demand for pens.

substitute: If an increase in the price of one good, y, leads to an increase in demand for the other good, x, then y is a substitute for x. In terms of elasticity, y is a substitute for x if $\varepsilon_{x,y} > 0$.

independent: If an increase in the price of one good, y, has no effect on demand for the other good, x, then y is independent of x. In terms of elasticity, y is independent of x if $\varepsilon_{x,y} = 0$.

normal good: A normal good is a good whose demand increases as income increases. In terms of elasticity, the good is normal if $\eta_x > 0$.

inferior good: An inferior good is a good whose demand decreases as income increases. In terms of elasticity, the good is inferior if $\eta_x < 0$.

The third commonly discussed demand elasticity is *income elasticity* of demand for x, η_x (η is the Greek letter *eta*).[5] This elasticity is calculated in the same way by using income, I, as the variable in Equation 2.1.

$$\eta_x = \%\Delta x / \%\Delta I. \quad \textbf{(2.4)}$$

The typical expectation is that as income increases, demand for the good should increase. Indeed, such goods are called **normal goods**. Not all goods are normal; some goods do better in economic downturns (when real incomes tend to decline). Such goods are called **inferior goods**. Steak is a normal good, and ground beef is an inferior good.

The hypothetical demand curves in Figure 2.10 describe a change in demand caused by a change in an exogenous factor. Two panels are shown, one of which provides a more appropriate representation of each of the scenarios described next. In each panel, the blue initial demand curve passes through point **A** at a price of $12, and the red final demand curve passes through either **D** or **E** at the same price. The final demand curve represents the effect of a change in economic circumstance that shifts demand.

For each scenario, answer the following questions.

Q10a. Is this scenario more accurately described by Figure 2.10A or 2.10B?

Q10b. What is the elasticity associated with this shift in demand? That is, calculate the cross-price or income elasticity implied by this information.

Hint: In the calculations of cross-price elasticity, $\varepsilon_{x,y}$, and income elasticity, η_x, use x = 8 as the base in calculating $\%\Delta x$.

S10.i. The price of tea, P_y, doubles. x is coffee.

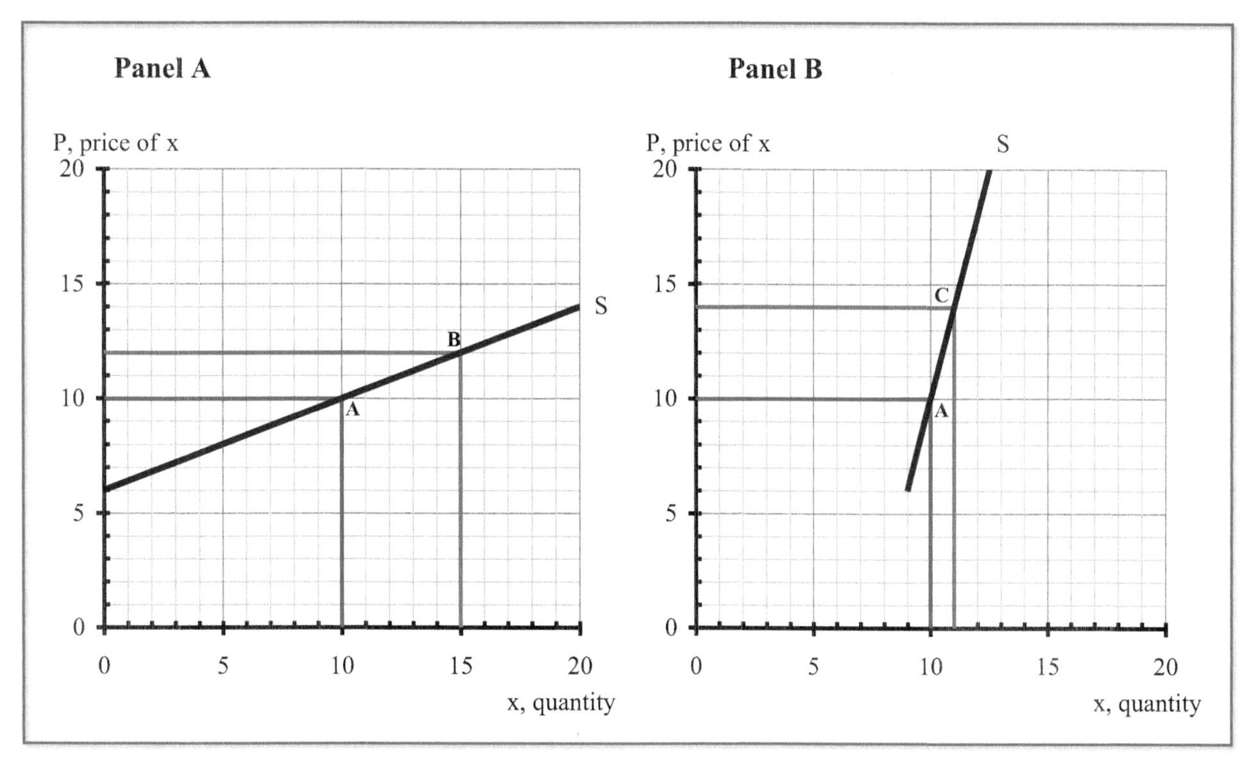

FIGURE 2.11 Elasticity on Two Hypothetical Supply Curves

S10.ii. The price of peanut butter, P_y, increases by 25%. x is jelly.

S10.iii. Average income increases by 50%. x is ground beef.

S10.iv. Average income increases by 10%. x is diamonds.*

Supply Elasticities

The responsiveness of supply to a change in price is the **price elasticity of supply**. Using Equation 2.1, we define elasticity of supply using the supply curve, $S_x(P)$, assuming the slope of the supply curve is m:

price elasticity of supply: The price elasticity of supply is the percentage change in quantity supplied for a given percentage change in price. It is also commonly shortened to *supply elasticity*.

$$\varepsilon_S = (\Delta S_x/\Delta P) \cdot (P/x) = (1/(\Delta P/\Delta S_x)) \cdot (P/S_x) = (1/m) \cdot (P/S_x) \quad \textbf{(2.5)}$$

As noted in Figure 2.3, supply elasticity varies on a typical supply curve. Prior to reaching full capacity, supply is much more elastic than once full capacity is reached. At full capacity, even large changes in price will only produce small changes in supply. At full capacity, supply is highly inelastic. Figure 2.11 provides two hypothetical supply curves (or parts of supply curves).

Q11. Which points have supply elasticities of $\varepsilon_S = 0.25$ and $\varepsilon_S = 2.0$?†

***Q10 answers: (S10.i.)** Tea and coffee are substitutes, so an increase in the price of tea, P_y, increases demand for coffee. Therefore, Figure 2.10B represents scenario S10.i. $\varepsilon_{x,y} = \%\Delta x/\%\Delta P_y = +25\%/+100\% = +0.25$. **(S10.ii.)** Peanut butter and jelly are complements, so an increase in the price of peanut butter, P_y, causes a decline in the demand for jelly, x. Figure 2.10A represents scenario S10.ii. $\varepsilon_{x,y} = \%\Delta x/\%\Delta P_y = -25\%/+25\% = -1.0$. **(S10.iii.)** Ground beef is inferior, so an increase in income leads to a decline in the demand for ground beef, x. Figure 2.10A represents scenario S10.iii. $\eta_x = \%\Delta x/\%\Delta I = -25\%/+50\% = -0.5$. **(S10.iv.)** Diamonds are a normal good (indeed, as we see in Chapter 7, diamonds are a luxury as well), so Figure 2.10B represents scenario S10.iv. $\eta_x = \%\Delta x/\%\Delta I = +25\%/+10\% = +2.5$.

†Q11 answer: Point **A** on Figure 2.11B has a supply elasticity of 0.25 because $\varepsilon_S(\mathbf{A}) = (1/m) \cdot (P/x) = (1/4) \cdot (10/10) = 0.25$. Point **B** on Figure 2.11A has a supply elasticity of 2.0 ($\varepsilon_S(\mathbf{B}) = (1/m) \cdot (P/x) = (5/2) \cdot (12/15) = 2.0$.

FIGURE 2.12
Comparing Long-Run and Short-Run Supply

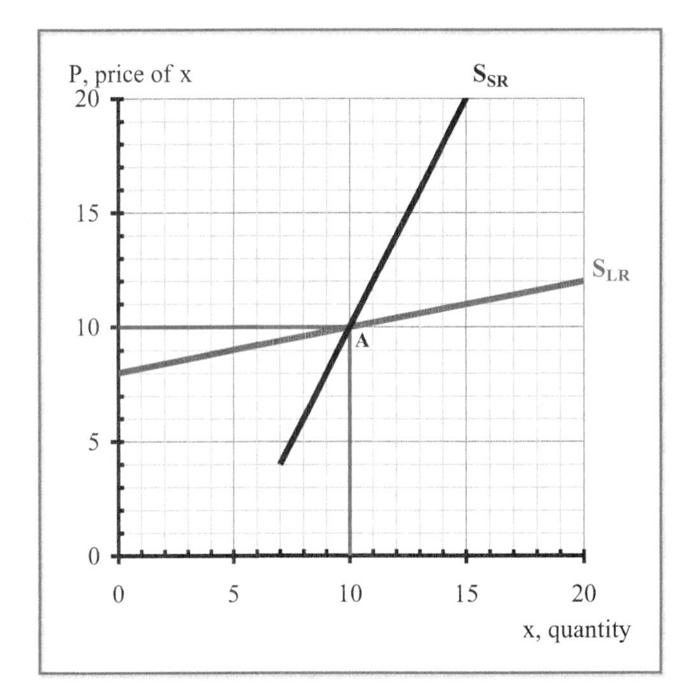

short run: The short run is a time frame over which some factors of production are fixed.

long run: The long run is a time frame over which all factors of production are allowed to vary.

Demand elasticity varies according to time frame, as noted earlier. The same is true of supply elasticity. Indeed, one of the important analytical constructs used to analyze the behavior of firms is to acknowledge that the firm may well act differently in the **short run** versus the **long run**.

The discussion of factors of production typically distinguishes two broad categories of factors (or inputs): capital and labor. Capital means plant and equipment and is assumed to be fixed in the short run. By contrast, labor is allowed to vary in the short run, as well as in the long run. This means that long-run supply is more elastic than short-run supply. Figure 2.12 provides one such example. The short-run elasticity at **A** is $\varepsilon_{S,SR}(\mathbf{A}) = 0.5$, and the long-run elasticity at **A** is $\varepsilon_{S,LR}(\mathbf{A}) = 5$, using Equation 2.5. The long-run elasticity may be more or less than this amount (the Excel file for Figure 2.12 allows you to vary the long-run supply curve). Some capital expansion projects may be completed in a quicker time frame than others. For example, some specialized and complex machinery may have a long lead time for purchase, while other pieces of machinery are essentially "off the rack." This simply means that we can consider different degrees of the "long run" associated with different degrees of flexibility with respect to capital adjustment. The longer the run, the more elastic will be supply, *ceteris paribus*. We examine the short-run/long-run distinction in detail in Chapters 9, 10, 11, and 14.

2.5 Market Intervention

Most markets do not exhibit wide swings in price or quantity—that is, most markets appear stable. This is a result of the self-correcting nature of the supply/demand equilibrium. If the market is jostled out of equilibrium for some reason, it returns once again to equilibrium via the signals of excess supply and excess demand described in Section 2.2. And if the economic circumstances surrounding the market change, the market adjusts to these exogenous shocks by adjusting price and quantity to achieve a new equilibrium. But these adjustments only happen if the market is unfettered—that is, if it is free to adjust at will.

Policymakers sometimes choose to intervene in markets in various ways. The government can impose a variety of mandates on markets that will alter their behavior. Taxes are one form of government intervention (examples of the effect of taxation in a market are shown in Figure 2.4). Although imposing a tax alters the market equilibrium, it does not preclude the use of the market mechanism to achieve that outcome. In contrast, price controls are a form of government intervention that remove the market's ability to adjust freely to disequilibrium.

Policymakers impose price controls in situations where they deem the market-determined price to be too high or too low. Exactly what policymakers consider too high or too low is based on the sociopolitical structure in which the policymakers are embedded. If they deem the price to be too high, they impose a **price ceiling** on the good. If they deem the price to be too low, they impose a **price floor** on the good. Both price ceilings and price floors can cause problems for markets.

price ceiling: A price ceiling is a legally imposed maximum price at which the good can be sold.

In both instances, the market is precluded from adjusting freely. Market disequilibrium can only be maintained by instituting programs directly focused on maintaining the disequilibrium. Such programs include legal prohibitions against resale and selling below the price floor or above the price ceiling, as well as other restrictions aimed at modifying the market to reduce the disequilibrium caused by the price intervention. We begin by examining price ceilings.

price floor: A price floor is a legally imposed minimum price at which the good can be sold.

Price Ceilings

The classic example of a price ceiling is **rent control**, and the poster child for rent control is New York City. Rent control is such a ubiquitous part of New York City culture that books, movies, and television shows often build plotlines around rent-controlled apartments. There are a variety of attributes of rent-controlled markets, but the most obvious attribute (other than price) is the shortage of rent-controlled apartments. New York City has among the lowest apartment vacancy rates in the United States.

rent control: Rent control is a price ceiling applied to rental housing.

We can readily model the effect of rent control, using the supply/demand model. We continue to use linear demand and supply so we can emphasize the salient parts of a price ceiling as simply as possible. The various numerical values have been chosen to simplify the discussion, rather than accurately represent actual conditions in this market. Figure 2.13 depicts the market for apartments in New York City. In the absence of any government intervention, the market would clear at point **E**, with rents of \$2,000 per apartment and 100,000 apartments rented. But the market is not allowed to clear because the city has been under rent control since World War II. Suppose the legally imposed price ceiling is \$1,000 per apartment. This is represented by the green horizontal line at the price of \$1,000 = $\bar{P}$. The market is not allowed to clear because, at this price, individuals wish to rent 140,000 units, **C**, but landlords are only willing to supply 80,000 units, **A**. There is excess demand of 60,000 units at this price, **AC**.

Rent control introduces a variety of inefficiencies. Landlords have little incentive to maintain rental units because the units can be rented "as is," given the artificially low rents. Thus, rent control affects the quality of rental units. Rent control also provides landlords with an incentive to convert rental units into owner-occupied condominiums or into commercial enterprises, which further exacerbates the apartment shortage.

The main winners under rent control are, of course, renters, and the main losers are landlords. But not ALL who wish to rent benefit from rent control; the only ones who

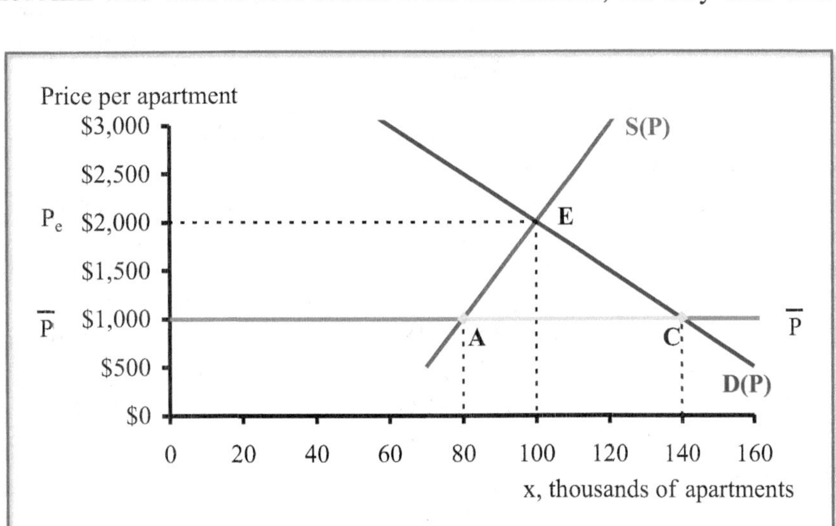

FIGURE 2.13 The Effect of Rent Control

FIGURE 2.14
Subletting Increases Efficiency but Is Often Illegal

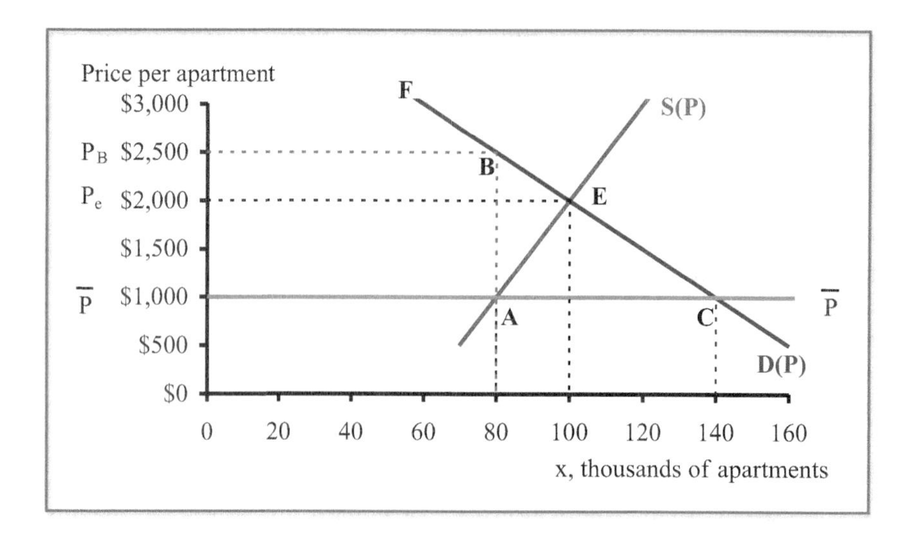

benefit are those who are lucky enough to find a rental unit at the rent-controlled price. And as just noted, the quality of that unit is likely to suffer as a result.

What can we say about those who rent under rent control? Are they the ones who have the highest valuation for the rental units? Unfortunately, the answer is, in general, no. The problem is that rent control makes it illegal to allocate the good according to its value. In terms of the numbers in Figure 2.13, there are 140,000 individuals who value an apartment at $1,000 or more per month. These individuals are graphically depicted as being on the demand curve above **C**. Only 80,000 of these individuals will obtain apartments because actual supply is at **A**. The economically efficient way to allocate these 80,000 apartments is to allocate them to the 80,000 renters who have the highest marginal valuation for a rental unit. These individuals would be willing to pay substantially more than $1,000 for an apartment. In fact, given linear demand, they would be willing to pay at least $2,500 for an apartment (because each 20,000 decline in demand is associated with a $500 increase in marginal valuation along the demand curve from **C** to **E** and beyond). The marginal valuation of the 80,000th renter is shown as point **B** in Figure 2.14. The problem is that there is no reason to believe that apartments will be allocated in this fashion. More likely, they are allocated based on nonmonetary dimensions of interaction (such as simply knowing that a unit is being vacated and being the first in line with a security deposit and first and last month's rent in hand). Being lucky in this way is not the same as having a high marginal valuation—it only guarantees that the renter has a marginal valuation above $1,000.

If an individual who has a value of less than P_B = $2,500 rents for $1,000 in these circumstances, this worsens the economic situation because that individual has displaced an individual who had a value of more than $2,500. Society would be better off if that renter were allowed to privately remarket (i.e., rent) the apartment to an individual who values it more highly, making both better off. To make this specific, suppose an individual at **E** (the 100,000th in terms of declining marginal valuation who has a $2,000 valuation for an apartment) currently rents an apartment for $1,000 but knows a friend, **F**, who would be willing to pay $3,000 to rent an apartment but cannot find one (because none are available due to rent control and because it is illegal to bribe a landlord for an apartment by providing a side-payment). If **E** continues to rent the apartment but sublets to **F** for $2,500, both **E** and **F** are better off. Each receives a $500 net benefit on this transaction because the apartment was only worth $2,000 to **E** ($500 = $2,500 – $2,000), and **F** receives a net benefit of $500 = $3,000 – $2,500. (You may have seen this kind of exchange in introductory microeconomics; it is called a *Pareto improvement*.)[6] **E** and **F** need not split the spoils on a 50/50 basis; the deal can be settled at any price between $2,000 and $3,000, depending on the relative bargaining strengths of the two individuals, and still make both parties better off.

A common response at this point is to say: "Wait, **E** loses out because **E** no longer has a place to stay." True, **E** no longer has an apartment, but **E** did not value that apartment as highly as did **F**; as a result, **arbitrage** opportunities exist. If **E** actually had higher value, then the $2,000 representation of **E**'s marginal valuation was incorrect.

arbitrage: Arbitrage is the process of buying a good at a low price and reselling it at a higher price.

Subletting is a secondary way to bypass the rent-control laws. Money does not go to landlords, but rather to those low-value renters who are willing to sublet. Any individual whose valuation is on the segment **BC** can, at least theoretically, find an individual on the segment above **B** and engage in a mutually beneficial exchange. The net effect is higher rent—indeed, higher rent than under an unfettered market. Perfect arbitrage would allocate all 80,000 units to those who value them most highly (those above **B** on the demand curve). The marginal purchaser (at **B**) will pay $2,500 in this instance, higher than we see under a competitive market, where a price of $2,000 would prevail. Most rent-control laws explicitly make subletting illegal as a result. Those who sublet in this instance are engaging in **black market** activities.

black market: A black market is an illegal market for a good.

In addition to rent-controlled apartments, there are many other examples of price ceilings. They have been broadly applied during a number of wars (World War II, Korean War, and Vietnam War). They have also been imposed on specific markets (such as gasoline) for long periods. Calls for intervention to prevent price gouging occur at various times, and these are informal attempts to impose price ceilings.[7] For example, almost every time a hurricane hits the Gulf Coast, plywood prices increase dramatically, and calls for government investigation result. If lumberyards are precluded from raising prices, they are not able to cover the increased costs involved in having supplies reallocated to stricken areas.

Price Floors

Price floors are imposed in markets where the market-determined price is perceived to be too low. Two common examples of price floors are agricultural price supports and minimum wages. Just as was the case with price ceilings, the presence of a price floor creates an imbalance in the market.

Minimum wage laws attempt to increase the welfare of unskilled laborers by requiring employers to maintain a minimum wage rate for hourly labor. The current minimum wage is $7.25 per hour, but as usual, there are political discussions regarding increasing it. The current minimum wage has been in place since 2009.[8] The effect of the minimum wage can be seen in Figure 2.15. If the minimum wage law is binding on the market for unskilled labor, the market clearing price for unskilled labor is below the minimum wage rate. Suppose, in the absence of a minimum wage, the market for unskilled labor clears at a wage of w_e = $5.50, with L_E laborers employed, at **E**. A minimum wage of $7.25 = $\underline{w}$ is shown as a horizontal line in the figure. Imposing this minimum wage causes unemployment $L_C - L_A$ or **AC**.

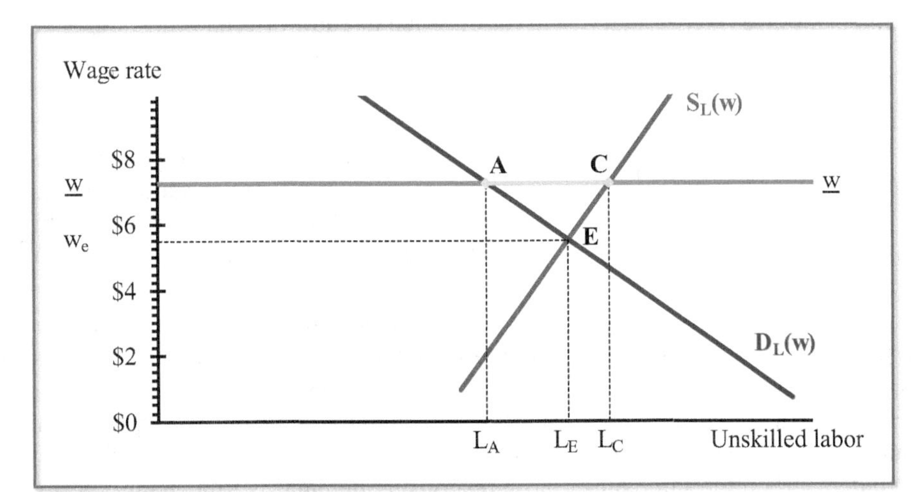

FIGURE 2.15 Imposing a Minimum Wage Law Causes Unemployment

Minimum wage laws are instituted to help the poor, but they only help the poor who are lucky enough to get the jobs. The unemployment caused by the minimum wage comes from two sources: an increase in supply of unskilled laborers looking for work at the higher wage rate and a decrease in demand for those workers by employers. The former is represented by $L_C - L_E$, and the latter is represented by $L_E - L_A$. If we acknowledge that some unskilled laborers have more skills than others, and if employers are able to determine the qualities of workers, then the most unskilled will be the workers who will be unemployed.

A number of agricultural products are subject to programs aimed at propping up the price of those goods with the goal of increasing income for farmers. For some products, such as milk, the government sets a minimum price for which the product can be sold. For other products, the government attempts to alter either supply or demand, with the ultimate goal of increasing the price of the product. Supply is limited by policies such as restrictions on imports or by paying farmers to not plant crops. Demand is increased by direct purchases of surplus supplies. These supply and demand programs are targeted at reducing the imbalance imposed by the price control program.[9] These programs can be analyzed using Figure 2.15 by simply relabeling axes. Formal price controls set a minimum price $\underline{P} > P_e$, the market clearing price. This causes excess supply of **AC**. The magnitude of this disequilibrium is reduced if supply decreases (and therefore shifts **C** back at price $\underline{P}$) or if demand increases (and therefore shifts **A** out at price $\underline{P}$). Both strategies reduce the market imbalance of **AC** induced by the price floor.

Summary

The centerpiece of microeconomics is the supply and demand model. Students can avoid confusion in using this model if they conceptually separate demand from supply before putting them together to examine market interaction.

Demand is the quantity individuals wish to consume as a function of price, holding other parameters fixed. If these fixed parameters vary, then the demand curve shifts. The factors that affect demand include average income level, the prices of other goods (both substitutes and complements), tastes, and other exogenous factors.

Economists make a semantic distinction between change in quantity demanded and change in demand. This semantic distinction underscores the distinction between a movement along, and a shift in, a demand curve. A change in quantity demanded is a movement along a fixed demand curve. This change is the result of a change in price, *ceteris paribus*. A change in demand is a shift in demand caused by changed economic circumstances. A change in the price of peanut butter changes the demand for jelly, *ceteris paribus*. This same distinction is made on the supply side of the market.

Supply is the quantity firms wish to supply as a function of price, holding other parameters fixed. If these fixed parameters vary, then the supply curve shifts. The factors that affect supply include the prices of inputs in the production process, the technology of production, and the prices of production substitutes and complements.

We represent the market interaction of consumers and producers by placing supply and demand on the same diagram. The point where supply and demand intersect represents equilibrium in the market for the good because, at that price, the quantity demanded equals the quantity supplied. At all other prices, an imbalance between supply and demand exists. If the price is too high, the actual amount demanded is less than what firms wish to supply and inventories build up; excess supply exists when price is above the market clearing level. This buildup of surplus inventories signals the need for price to decline to reduce the imbalance. If the price is too low, the amount firms are willing to supply is less than what consumers wish to demand; excess demand exists when price is below the market clearing level. Drawn-down inventories and shortages are signals of the need for price to increase to reduce the market imbalance. When the price is not at the equilibrium level, the market acts as a self-correcting mechanism to return price to equilibrium.

Comparative statics analysis involves examining how the market equilibrium changes due to a change in an exogenous variable. What happens to the supply/demand equilibrium in coffee if, for example, there is a change in the price of tea? Comparative statics analysis of each of the factors that shift demand and shift supply allows us to understand the direction of the change in price and quantity caused by a change in economic circumstances. We can also use elasticity information to examine the magnitude of the change caused by such exogenous shocks.

Elasticity describes the percentage change in quantity for a given percentage change in a variable. The most common "variable" is price. Price elasticity of demand describes how responsive demand is to a change in price, and price elasticity of supply describes how responsive supply is to a change in price. Both price elasticities describe movements along their respective curves. All other elasticities (income, cross-price, etc.) describe how quickly demand or supply shifts for a given percentage change in that variable. These need not be variables in the economic domain. One can calculate, for example, a temperature elasticity of demand for ice cream or coffee. Not surprisingly, the former is positive and the latter is negative.

Markets are self-correcting mechanisms, but markets only work if they are allowed to adjust. Government policymakers sometimes intervene in markets in ways that preclude the market mechanism from adjusting to disequilibrium. One common intervention works by controlling price. Price ceilings are maximum allowable prices for a product. If a price ceiling is set below the market clearing price, then excess demand at the artificially low price results. Price floors cause the opposite problem. If a price floor is set above the market clearing price, then excess supply at the artificially high price results. Shortages and excess inventories cannot be reduced by adjusting price because of government intervention; price cannot be used as an allocation mechanism under price controls.

Market intervention is fraught with unintended consequences. Price ceilings, for example, cause black markets to form, which then sell goods at a price that is even higher than the market clearing price. Rent control is an example of a price ceiling. Minimum wage laws are an example of a price floor. These laws are aimed at improving the economic circumstances of unskilled workers. Minimum wage laws cause unemployment, and that unemployment is disproportionately felt by those the minimum wage laws were meant to help.

Review Questions

Define the following terms:

demand
change in quantity demanded
change in demand
supply
change in quantity supplied
change in supply
ceteris paribus
law of downward-sloping demand (law of demand)
market clearing price
equilibrium price
excess supply
excess demand
comparative statics analysis
price elasticity of demand
elastic demand
unitary elasticity of demand
inelastic demand
cross-price elasticity of demand
complements
substitutes
independent goods
income elasticity
normal goods
inferior goods
price elasticity of supply
supply elasticity
long run versus short run
price controls
price ceiling
price floor
arbitrage
black market

Match the following phrases to best complete the sentences:

a. An increase in price causes
b. An increase in income causes
c. Excess supply causes
d. Given elastic demand, a price decrease causes
e. If a firm is producing near capacity, then
f. Price ceilings cause
g. Given inelastic demand, a price decrease causes

1. a decline in price.
2. short-run supply is inelastic.
3. a decrease in total revenue.
4. a change in quantity demanded.
5. shortages.
6. an increase in total revenue.
7. a change in demand.

Provide short answers to the following:

a. What happens to equilibrium price and quantity if a tax is instituted in a market and supply is perfectly inelastic?
b. What happens to equilibrium price and quantity if a tax is instituted in a market and supply is perfectly elastic?
c. What happens to equilibrium price and quantity if a tax is instituted in a market and demand is perfectly inelastic?
d. What happens to equilibrium price and quantity if a tax is instituted in a market and demand is perfectly elastic?
e. If x and y are substitutes, and the demand for x shifts outward because of a change in the price of y, did the price of y increase or decrease?
f. If x and y are complements, and the demand for x shifts outward because of a change in the price of y, did the price of y increase or decrease?

g. What is the result if a price ceiling is imposed at a price above the market clearing price? Specifically, will excess demand or excess supply result?
h. What is the result if a price ceiling is imposed at a price below the market clearing price? Specifically, will excess demand or excess supply result?
i. What is the result if a price floor is imposed at a price above the market clearing price? Specifically, will excess demand or excess supply result?
j. What is the result if a price floor is imposed at a price below the market clearing price? Specifically, will excess demand or excess supply result?

Check your answers to the *matching* and *short-answer* exercises in the Answers Appendix at the end of the book.

Notes

1. We point this out because you were taught to do the opposite in algebra and geometry. Economists have followed this practice for more than a hundred years, so it is unlikely to change, even though it does not make a lot of sense to those with mathematical sensibilities. A dependent variable is a variable you predict based on one or more independent variables. Quantity is the dependent variable, and quantity demanded is based on independent variables that include price and income.

2. The caveat noted in Chapter 1 still applies: We follow the economists' tradition of calling a line a curve, even though it is linear. We examine the slope of curves in greater detail in Chapter 3.

3. The proof of this assertion is straightforward. Denote the change in price, ΔP, and the associated change in quantity, Δx. In this instance, we have:

Given inelastic demand, $|\varepsilon| < 1$, we have: $|(\Delta x/\Delta P) \cdot (P/x)| < 1$, from Equation 2.1b.
Regrouping, we have: $|P \cdot \Delta x|/|x \cdot \Delta P| < 1$.
Cross-multiplying, we obtain: $|P \cdot \Delta x| < |x \cdot \Delta P|$.

The revenue gained by increasing price, $|x \cdot \Delta P|$, is larger than the revenue lost due to selling fewer units at the higher price, $|P \cdot \Delta x|$. This means that an increase in price increases revenue if demand is inelastic.

Replacing the "<" signs with ">" signs or "=" signs in the above inequalities produces the other two results: Revenue decreases with an increase in price if demand is elastic, and revenue does not change with an increase in price if demand has unitary elasticity.

4. In Chapter 8, we will see what is required to have own-price elasticity of demand be positive. This is the case of a Giffen good.

5. Some authors maintain the use of epsilon in this instance and denote income elasticity as $\varepsilon_{x,\,I}$.

6. A Pareto improvement is a reallocation of resources in which at least one party is better off and no party is worse off. Since both **E** and **F** are better off, this is a Pareto improvement. (We put off the discussion of Pareto efficiency until Chapter 3.) The welfare impact of price controls can be easily examined, using the notions of consumer and producer surplus. This is discussed in Chapter 16.

7. Erfle and McMillan examine this issue in "Media, Political Pressure, and the Firm: The Case of Oil Pricing during the Late 1970s," *Quarterly Journal of Economics*, 105:1, February 1990, pp. 115–134.

8. See http://www.dol.gov/whd/minwage/america.htm for an overview of minimum wage laws.

9. See http://www.ers.usda.gov/topics/farm-economy/farm-commodity-policy.aspx for an overview of agricultural price support policy and programs.

PART 2

CONSUMER THEORY

Because each of us has been actively engaged as a consumer of goods and services from the time we began to earn an allowance as children, it is natural to examine the demand side of the market first. The basis of consumer theory is the individual consumer choice model. Each individual has preferences (likes and dislikes) for goods and services. Different individuals can have different preferences for an individual good or for bundles of goods. For example, Dave may love pepperoni pizza and hate wine, while Kate loves wine but hates pepperoni pizza. Vera may like both of these goods. Once we know an individual's preferences, we can determine how well that individual can do, given his or her economic circumstances. Consumer theory explores the factors that determine consumer choice and how those choices respond to changing circumstances.

Part 2 is devoted to a more complete understanding of how each of us acts as a consumer in a market economy. The consumer choice model boils down to determining which bundle of goods you prefer over all bundles that you can feasibly obtain. To ascertain this, we must be able to identify both what you prefer and what you can feasibly attain. Both sides of the consumer choice model are examined separately before being put together to determine optimal choice.

Chapter 3 focuses on consumer preferences and their geometric representation as indifference curves and preference maps. Chapter 4 connects a useful mathematical construct called utility to preferences and describes how the introductory microeconomics concept of marginal utility is seen in preference maps. Chapter 5 focuses on the other side of the consumer choice model: the consumer's resource constraints. The most obvious constraints are, not surprisingly, the prices of the goods in question and the budget available to devote to those goods. Nonmonetary resource constraints (for example, time constraints) may also be analyzed within the individual consumer model. Chapter 6 brings the two sides of the consumer choice model back together to examine the optimal choice, given the consumer's preferences and constraints. Chapter 7 examines what happens when things change, and Chapter 8 decomposes that change into income and substitution effects.

Preferences

CHAPTER 3

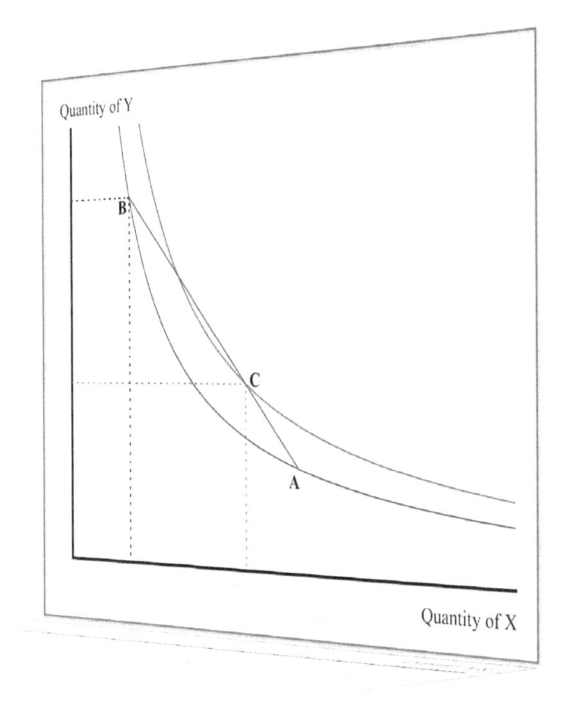

Chapter Outline

The most basic notion about individuals as consuming entities is that they have preferences. Even as a child, before you knew about money or the idea of going to the store to purchase items, you had preferences—you loved green beans and hated squash, for example. Preferences are likes and dislikes, and it is well established in our everyday life that different individuals have different preferences. Two individuals who are offered a free choice between two shopping carts full of goods may well come to different conclusions regarding which they prefer: The vegetarian may prefer the one with lots of fruits and vegetables, while the other individual may be carnivorous and prefer the one with lots of steaks and chops.

This chapter focuses on preferences: an individual's evaluation of goods and services, independent of whether that individual can afford them. Preferences tell us what a consumer likes. Section 3.1 examines the basic properties of preferences. Section 3.2 describes how preferences may be geometrically represented, using indifference curves and indifference maps. Section 3.3 examines commonly analyzed examples of preferences over goods such as perfect substitutes and perfect complements. We also examine what happens when you achieve satiation for one or both goods. The indifference maps of these various situations introduce you to the creation of economic stories dealing with individual consumer behavior. Section 3.4 lays out the requirements for well-behaved preferences and provides a rationale for using them. The chapter concludes with Section 3.5, an analysis of the economics of barter. The barter model highlights how preferences help us understand economic behavior.

3.1 What Does a Consumer Want?

preferences: Preferences are an individual's valuation of goods and services, independent of budget and price.

Since we are interested in individual consumer behavior, we must denote the identity of the consumer. To make this precise and personal, consider your own preferences. For example, given two shopping carts full of goods, you can always answer the question: Which shopping cart do you prefer? This means that you have **preferences** over those bundles of goods.

Consider two bundles of goods, **A** and **B** (the boldface type is meant to signify that this is a bundle of goods, not a single good).[1] Imagine you are offered the choice between two shopping carts, **A** and **B**, filled with different amounts of a number of goods. (You do not have to pay for the shopping carts; the only question is: If offered a choice between the two carts, which would you prefer?) You have preferences if you are able to say one of three things: (1) "I prefer **A** to **B**"; (2) "I prefer **B** to **A**"; or (3) "I am indifferent between **A** and **B**." The symbol "$\succ$" is a shorthand way to say "preferred to" (sometimes, we say "strictly preferred to"), "$\sim$" is a shorthand way to say "indifferent to," and "$\succsim$" is a shorthand way to say "preferred or indifferent to" (sometimes, we say "weakly preferred to").[2] To be specific, suppose you face two small shopping carts: **A** has seven apples and three oranges; **B** has seven oranges and three apples. You may well prefer **A** to **B** but know that your mother would prefer **B** to **A** and that your father would be indifferent between **A** and **B**. In symbols we could state these relations as: $\mathbf{A} \succ_{\text{you}} \mathbf{B}$; $\mathbf{B} \succ_{\text{your mother}} \mathbf{A}$; and $\mathbf{A} \sim_{\text{your father}} \mathbf{B}$ (the subscripts describe whose preferences we are considering). This lack of conformity is not a problem; it simply means that each of you has different preferences over oranges and apples.

We typically assume that preferences have four basic properties: completeness, transitivity, monotonicity, and convexity. The first two are always assumed; the last two are often, but not always, assumed.

complete: Preferences are complete if you are always able to answer the question: Which do you prefer?

transitive: Preferences are transitive if you prefer bundle **A** to **B**, and **B** to **C**, then you must prefer **A** to **C**.

well defined: Preferences are well defined if they are both complete and transitive.

Imagine a pair of shopping carts full of goods. Preferences are **complete** if, once you see what is in each cart, you are always able to answer the question: Which do you prefer? To use symbols: For any two bundles **A** and **B**, either $\mathbf{A} \succ \mathbf{B}$, $\mathbf{B} \succ \mathbf{A}$, or $\mathbf{A} \sim \mathbf{B}$. Completeness is the first basic proposition about preferences. The second property of preferences is **transitivity**. If you prefer bundle **A** to **B**, and **B** to **C**, then you must prefer **A** to **C**. To use symbols: If $\mathbf{A} \succ \mathbf{B}$ and $\mathbf{B} \succ \mathbf{C}$, then $\mathbf{A} \succ \mathbf{C}$.[3] Were this not the case, you would never be able to decide what is best because you would cycle endlessly between alternative bundles. These two properties are required for preferences to be **well defined**.

The final two properties of preferences are monotonicity and convexity. Monotonicity is based on the notion that goods are "goods" rather than "bads." In the grand scheme of things, of course, this is patently false. You can almost certainly name 10 or 20 foods that you actively dislike—you never buy these foods. (An exception would be if you are a *very* good parent who is trying to teach your children the value of brussels sprouts, for example. Economists typically ignore such noble gestures and assume that if you don't like it, you won't buy it.) Put another way, more of a good is preferred to less of that good. Formally, economists call this **monotonicity**. In terms of bundles, if bundle **A** has at least as much of all goods as bundle **B** ($a_i \geq b_i$ for all goods $i = 1, \ldots, n$), then $\mathbf{A} \succsim \mathbf{B}$. Sometimes, monotonicity is called *weak monotonicity* to distinguish it from **strict monotonicity**. Preferences are strictly monotonic if more of a good is better than less of that good. In terms of bundles, if bundle **A** has at least as much of all goods as bundle **B** ($a_i \geq b_i$ for all goods $i = 1, \ldots, n$) and more of at least one good ($a_j > b_j$ for at least one good $j = 1, \ldots, n$), then $\mathbf{A} \succ \mathbf{B}$.

monotonicity: Preferences are monotonic if more of a good is at least as good as less of that good.

strict monotonicity: Preferences are strictly monotonic if more of a good is better than less of that good.

The only difference between these definitions is that if it is found that **A** has at least as much of each good as **B** and more of at least one good, then weak monotonicity *allows* for indifference between **A** and **B**, whereas strict monotonicity *requires* that **A** is strictly preferred to **B**. Geometrically, every point in the first orthant relative to a given bundle is strictly preferred to the given bundle. This includes *all* points on the boundary of this orthant *except* the initial bundle itself. We put off the definition of the final property, *convexity*, until the next section, when we are able to graphically describe preferences.

(Convexity has to do with individuals liking a variety of goods, rather than one good to the exclusion of all others.)

3.2 Representing What a Consumer Wants on a Graph

Preferences form the basis of consumer choice but are rather awkward to work with in practice. For example, finding the most preferred shopping cart among 50 alternatives requires 1,225 pair-wise comparisons. (Shopping cart $\mathbf{S}_1$ must be compared with 49 other carts: $\mathbf{S}_2, \ldots, \mathbf{S}_{50}$; $\mathbf{S}_2$ must be compared with 48 other carts: $\mathbf{S}_3, \ldots, \mathbf{S}_{50}$; and so on. There are $1{,}225 = 50 \cdot 49/2$ comparisons.) As a result, economists have devised algebraic and geometric methods of representing preferences that provide a more computationally efficient solution to the consumer choice problem. We initially focus on the geometric representation of preferences. We examine the algebraic representation of preferences in Chapter 4, when we examine utility functions.

By representing preferences graphically, we can more readily understand what is required to obtain the most preferred bundle. We lose little generality by restricting the discussion to bundles that contain only two goods, x and y. If we are interested in one good in particular, x, the other good, y, can be "all other goods." At other times, we are interested in the interplay between two goods that we expect are related (for example, x is tea and y is a lemon, or x is tea and y is coffee). As a result, we typically restrict our analysis to two goods, x and y.

Preferences over two goods, x and y, are represented using **indifference curves**. An indifference curve represents bundles that provide the same satisfaction for the consumer and between which the consumer is indifferent. Indifference curves also demarcate the boundary between bundles that are better and bundles that are worse than the initial bundle.

indifference curve: An indifference curve represents bundles that provide the same satisfaction for the consumer and between which the consumer is indifferent.

Indifference curves may have many shapes. If both goods are "goods" in the sense that more is better (monotonicity), then indifference curves must be negatively sloped. The reason is simple. Start at a point (x_0, y_0) and ask: What other bundles are indifferent to this bundle? The easiest way to think of this is to: (1) imagine you are the consumer, (2) be specific with regard to the goods in question, and (3) set up a quadrant system based on an initial bundle. Point $\mathbf{C} = (8, 12)$ in Figure 3.1 represents having eight carrot slices and

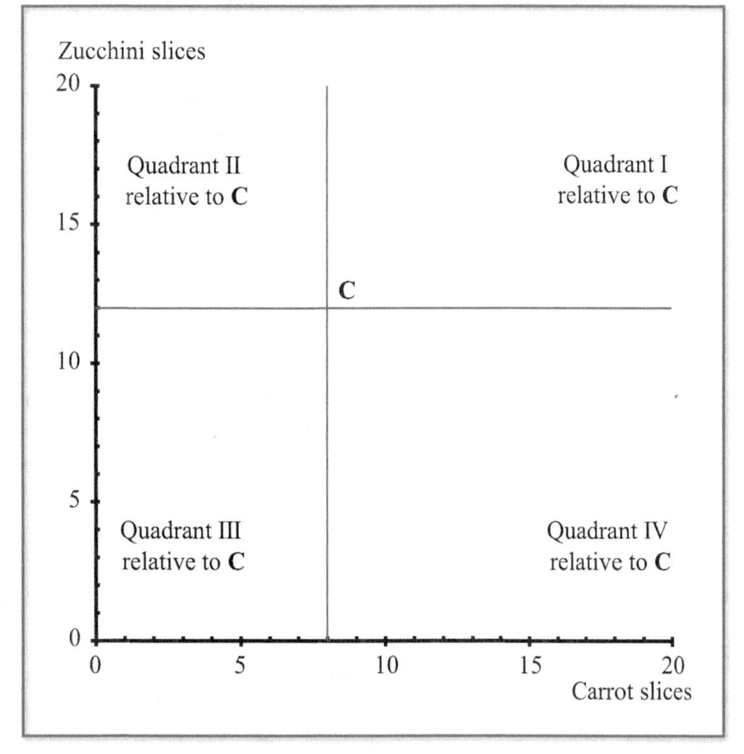

FIGURE 3.1
Comparing Bundles When Both Goods Are "Goods"

twelve zucchini slices. Suppose you have bundle **C** on your plate and, given this bundle, you would like more of each vegetable.

Q1: You are shown other plates with carrots and zucchini, and you like some of them the same as **C**. In which quadrants relative to **C** must those plates "reside"?*

Monotonicity implies that every bundle in quadrant I is preferred to **C**, since there is more of at least one of the vegetables and no less of the other in the entire quadrant. At the same time, **C** is preferred to any bundle in quadrant III. Only in quadrants II and IV are there trade-off possibilities that are necessary to remain indifferent to the initial bundle **C**. In quadrant II, you are getting more zucchini, so you must be willing to give up at least a little bit of carrots, and vice versa in quadrant IV.

From point **C**, consider giving up carrots for zucchini. Suppose you would be willing to give up two carrot slices in exchange for four zucchini slices and end up at point **B** = (6, 16). The rate of exchange between **B** and **C** is two zucchini slices for each carrot slice. Economists have a special term for this rate of exchange along an indifference curve. It is called the **marginal rate of substitution (MRS)**: MRS = $-\Delta y/\Delta x$ along an indifference curve. This represents the rate at which an individual is willing to exchange y for x to remain equally happy as the amount of x and y in the individual's bundle changes.

marginal rate of substitution (MRS): The marginal rate of substitution is defined as MRS = $-\Delta y/\Delta x$ along an indifference curve.

It is worth focusing for a moment on the "–" sign in the definition of the MRS. With few exceptions (and most of those exceptions are discussed in this and the next section), we are concerned with analyzing when both goods are "goods." It is reasonable to assume that consumers only buy goods that they like. We explained in our discussion of Figure 3.1 why the slope of such indifference curves must be negative. We will often wish to talk about bundles where the MRS is larger or smaller than another bundle. The minus sign has been stripped from slope in this instance so that there is no confusion about whether an MRS of 2 is larger than an MRS of 1/2. (Without removing the minus sign, we face the problem that $-1/2 > -2$, even though in magnitude, $2 > 1/2$.) The definition of the MRS just proposed leads to a positive number when both goods are "goods" since the MRS is the negative of the slope of the indifference curve. *The MRS is the rate at which the individual is willing to substitute y for x along an indifference curve.*[4]

The MRS from **B** to **C** is 2: You are willing to exchange two zucchini slices (y) for each carrot slice (x) between **B** and **C**. This is *not* the same as your willingness to exchange carrot slices (x) for one more zucchini slice (y). That rate of exchange is $-\Delta x/\Delta y$ or -1/slope (or 1/MRS). This statement is simply meant as an admonition to ensure that you know which good is on which axis when you calculate the MRS. The MRS is the rate of exchange of the good on the vertical axis for the good on the horizontal axis.[5]

The new bundle, **B** = (6, 16), is indifferent to **C** but is a more zucchini-intensive meal. If you wish to keep a few carrot slices on your plate, and you are asked to give up one of your last six carrot slices, you may well only be willing to do so in exchange for more than two zucchini slices. Suppose that you require three zucchini slices to give up the sixth carrot slice. That means that you are indifferent between point **A** = (5, 19) and **B** = (6, 16) (and **C** as well), and your **A** to **B** MRS is 3.

From **C**, suppose that you would be willing to give up three zucchini slices for three carrot slices. If so, you are indifferent between point **D** = (11, 9) and **C** = (8, 12), and your **C** to **D** MRS is 1. If you wish to keep at least some zucchini slices on your plate, you may well require more than a one for one rate of exchange to be willing to have fewer zucchini slices. From **D**, suppose you would be willing to give up two zucchini slices in exchange for four carrot slices. You are indifferent between the new bundle **E** = (15, 7) and **D** = (11, 9), and your **D** to **E** MRS is 1/2. Finally, if you were at **E**, you might require three carrot slices to give up one of your last seven zucchini slices. If so, you are indifferent between point **E** = (15, 7) and **F** = (18, 6), and your **E** to **F** MRS is 1/3.

***Q1 answer:** Those plates must be in either quadrant II or quadrant IV. If you like both vegetables and if you have more of one vegetable, you must have less of the other if that plate is indifferent to **C**.

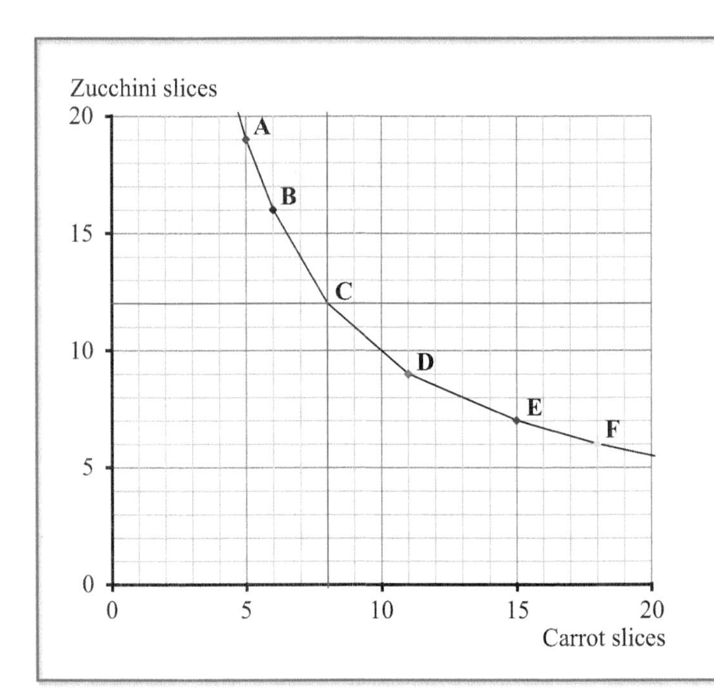

Table for Figure 3.2

Points on an indifference curve	Carrot slices	Zucchini slices	MRS between points
not shown	4	23	
A	5	19	4
B	6	16	3
C	8	12	2
D	11	9	1
E	15	7	1/2
F	18	6	1/3
not shown	22	5	1/4

FIGURE 3.2 Finding Points on the Indifference Curve through Point C

Figure 3.2 and its corresponding table depict the indifference curve containing the six points **A**–**F** (and two others that are outside the range of the graph). All points of indifference are in the second or fourth quadrants, relative to all other points on the indifference curve.

The indifference curve acts as the boundary between two distinct sets of points. The *upper contour set* is the set of bundles that are at least as good or better than the initial bundle. In this instance, these bundles are above and to the right of the indifference curve, together with the indifference curve itself. The *lower contour set* is the set of bundles that are no better than the initial bundle. In this instance, these bundles are below and to the left of the indifference curve, together with the indifference curve itself. The intersection of the upper and lower contour sets is the indifference curve, and this fact provides an alternative way to define an indifference curve.[6]

The indifference curve depicted in Figure 3.2 is made up of a number of line segments. Each segment has a different rate of exchange of zucchini for carrots, as described earlier. Put another way, each segment has a different slope (MRS) based on the indifference-maintaining trade-offs inherent in deciding how many zucchini slices you must receive to accept losing one carrot slice (or how many zucchini slices you would be willing to give up in exchange for one more carrot slice). Discrete changes in the MRS would not be expected unless both goods in question must be consumed in discrete quantities.[7] Both carrot slices and zucchini slices *can* be cut, so it is reasonable to smooth out the curve as shown in Figure 3.3. The smooth curve depicted there goes through each of the points **A**–**F**.

Figure 3.3 focuses on the initial bundle **C** = (8, 12). Two discrete exchanges were described in moving away from **C**. One involved obtaining more zucchini by exchanging in the second quadrant relative to **C**. Point **B** represents obtaining four more zucchini slices in exchange for two fewer carrot slices, an exchange that has an MRS of 2. The other involved obtaining more carrot slices by exchanging in the fourth quadrant relative to **C**. Point **D** represents obtaining three more carrot slices in exchange for three fewer zucchini slices, an exchange that has an MRS of 1. If we were considering *small* exchanges close to **C**, then neither of these rates of exchange would be appropriate. A number between one and two would be more appropriate than either endpoint.

The best answer to the question of the exchange rate near **C** is to find the slope of the indifference curve *at* **C**. **C** has an MRS of 1.5 because the red line that is tangent to the

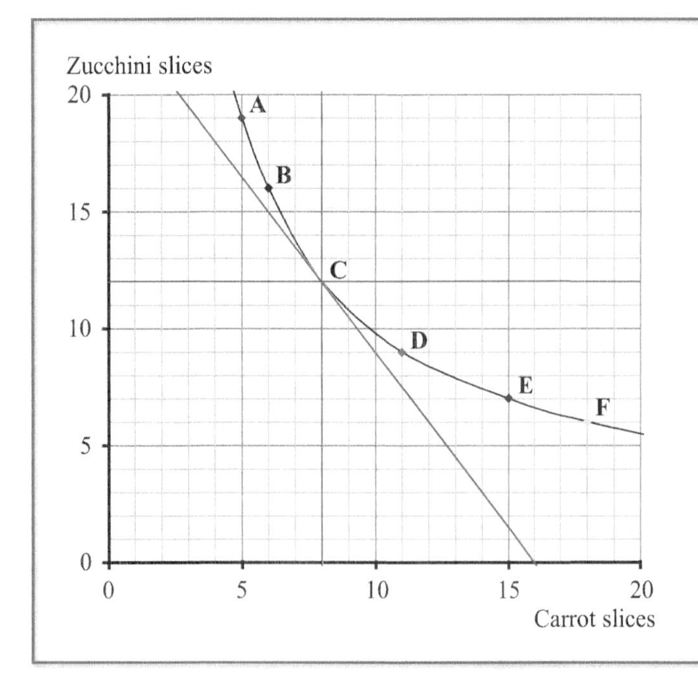

Table for Figure 3.3

Approximate MRS at the point	Points on an indifference curve	Carrot slices	Zucchini slices	MRS between points
	not shown	4	23	
				4
3.5	**A**	5	19	
				3
2.5	**B**	6	16	
				2
1.5	**C**	8	12	
				1
2/3	**D**	11	9	
				1/2
2/5	**E**	15	7	
				1/3
2/7	**F**	18	6	
				1/4
	not shown	22	5	

FIGURE 3.3 A Smooth Indifference Curve through Points A–F

 [This icon signifies that there is an Excel file of this figure for dynamic manipulation.]

indifference curve at **C** has a slope of −1.5. If the curve is a "curve" and we try to calculate slope in the standard fashion (slope = $\Delta y/\Delta x$), there is no unique answer because the slope calculation varies, depending on the size of Δx. Nonetheless, as Δx gets smaller, the calculated slope gets closer and closer to the slope of the tangent line to the curve. The slope of a tangent to a smooth curve is unique; as a result, we say that the slope at **C** is the slope of the tangent line to point **C**.[8] The table provides MRSs for each of the other points in Figure 3.3. The Excel figure for Figure 3.3 allows you to individually examine each of the points **A**–**F**. For each point, you should use the grid in the figure to confirm the MRS values provided in the table. These values are given as fractions to make seeing rise/run easier.

Although you may not have the preferences described earlier for carrots and zucchini, you are likely to feel quite comfortable about the trade-offs described because it is easy to imagine other pairs of goods that exhibit similar trade-offs in your mind. Most consumers like to have some of a lot of goods, rather than a lot of one good to the exclusion of other goods. The well-worn phrase is "*Variety is the spice of life.*" This property is more formally called **convexity**. Although most people have a hazy notion of what is (and is not) convex, it is worthwhile to have a formal geometric definition of convexity: A set is convex if, for any two points in the set, the set of points on the line segment between those two points is also in the set. Ovals are convex; heart and kidney shapes are not. In Figures 3.2 and 3.3, the upper contour set to **C** (the indifference curve through **C** and everything to the right and above that indifference curve) is a convex set.

convexity: A set is convex if, for any two points in the set, the set of points on the line segment between those two points is also in the set.

If both goods are "goods," convexity can be restated in terms of how the MRS varies along the indifference curve. **Preferences are convex** if the MRS declines (slope gets flatter) as x increases along the indifference curve. *Some authors actually describe this as the law of diminishing MRS.* This can be seen both in the graphs and in the MRS numbers in the tables for Figures 3.2 and 3.3. However, if preferences are not monotonic, then convexity cannot be described in terms of declining MRS.

preferences are convex: Preferences are convex if the upper contour set (the set of bundles that is at least as good as a given bundle) is a convex set.

Of course, preferences are not always convex, but examples of nonconvex preferences are the exception, rather than the rule. Most people tend to like more than one food, one drink, one form of recreation, one musical group, and so on. This fact leads to convex preferences for the reasons described in our simple carrots and zucchini example.

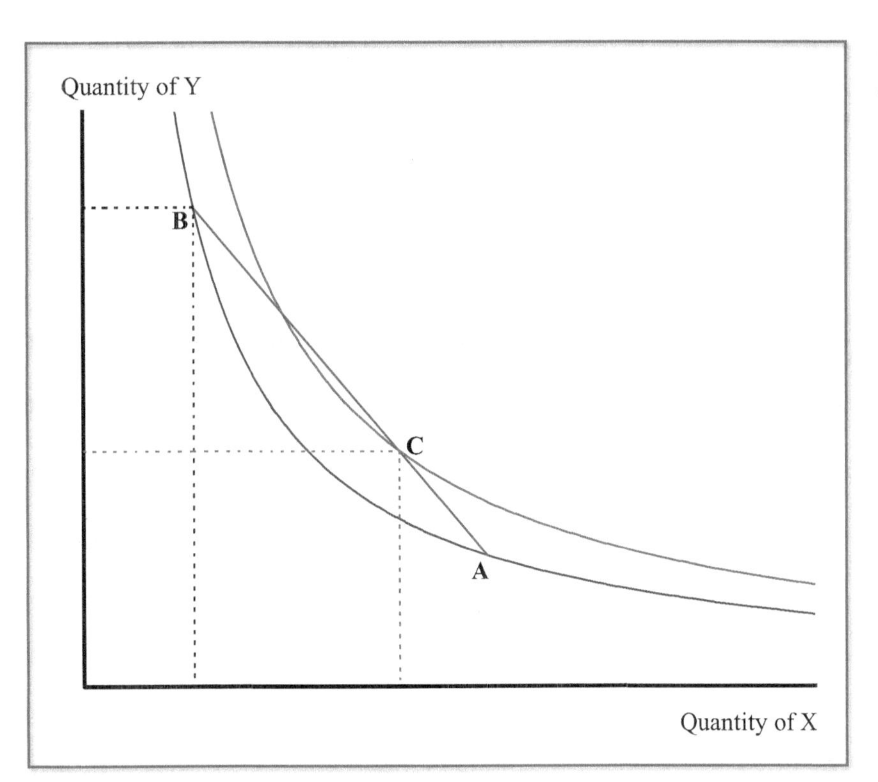

FIGURE 3.4 Strictly Convex Preferences

The graphs also allow us to focus on convexity a bit more clearly by distinguishing two forms of convexity: **strict convexity** and **weak convexity**. Preferences are *strictly convex* if all bundles **C** *between* any two indifferent bundles **A** and **B** are strictly preferred to the endpoints. In symbols, for all **C** between **A** and **B**, **C** ≻ **A** ~ **B**. "Between" in this definition has a very specific meaning. Points between the two bundles are on the line segment connecting the two points. (Mathematicians call such points a "convex combination" or a "weighted average" of the endpoints. The Mathematical Appendix [available in the online version of this text] provides a formal definition of this property.) Point **C** in Figure 3.4 is between indifferent bundles **A** and **B** and is strictly preferred to either endpoint. Preferences are *weakly convex* if all bundles **C** *between* any two indifferent bundles **A** and **B** are weakly preferred (preferred or indifferent) to the endpoints. In symbols, for all **C** between **A** and **B**, **C** ≿ **A** ~ **B**.

strict convexity: Preferences are strictly convex if all bundles **C** *between* any two indifferent bundles **A** and **B** are strictly preferred to the endpoints.

weak convexity: Preferences are weakly convex if all bundles **C** *between* any two indifferent bundles **A** and **B** are weakly preferred (preferred or indifferent) to the endpoints.

Figure 3.2 is weakly convex but not strictly convex. By contrast, Figures 3.3 and 3.4 are both weakly convex and strictly convex. Indifference curves that have linear "parts" cannot be strictly convex. Strict convexity requires indifference curves that continuously "curve."

The definition of strict convexity is most easily understood by looking at Figure 3.4. **A** and **B** are both on the same indifference curve, **A** ~ **B**. Preferences over x and y are strictly convex in this instance because every point on the (red) line segment between **A** and **B** is strictly preferred to the endpoints. **C** is one such point (in fact, it is 30% of the way from **A** to **B**). Every point on the green indifference curve is preferred to every point on the blue indifference curve. The Excel figure for Figure 3.4 allows you to vary the location of point **B**. as well as the location of **C**, along the segment **AB**. In each instance, as long as **C** is not at either endpoint, **C** is strictly preferred to **A** and **B**.

3.3 Using Indifference Curves to Tell Economic Stories

Indifference curves allow a variety of preferences to be depicted over various combinations of goods. We can use indifference curves to tell economic stories. It is worthwhile to briefly examine certain types of preferences and their geometric representations as indifference curves. Once you have mastered these basic mappings of preferences, you will be able to create preference maps to help analyze problems. *Each indifference map in this section includes a number of blue indifference curves. In each case, darker blue indifference curves are preferred to lighter blue curves.* These maps are analogous to topographic maps, where the curves denote different elevations. We begin with two types of preferences that you will probably remember from your introductory microeconomics course: substitutes and complements.

Substitutes and Complements

Two goods are substitutes if you would be willing to use one in place of the other, and they are complements if you like to use the two goods in conjunction with one another. We will make these conceptualizations much more explicit in the next couple of chapters. We start with the polar extremes of these concepts: perfect substitutes and perfect complements. Two goods are **perfect substitutes** if you are willing to trade one good for another at a constant rate. Perfect substitute indifference curves are actually indifference "lines," although economists continue to use the word *curve*. Figure 3.5 depicts three such indifference maps for perfect substitutes. Each panel has a different MRS, and each represents a particular scenario. Your goal is to read the three scenarios and then answer the three questions that follow.

perfect substitutes: Two goods are perfect substitutes if you are willing to trade one good for another at a constant rate.

> **Note:** *Answers are always available in a footnote attached to the end of a question, scenario, or hint. Only look at the footnote after you have formed your own answers to the questions.*

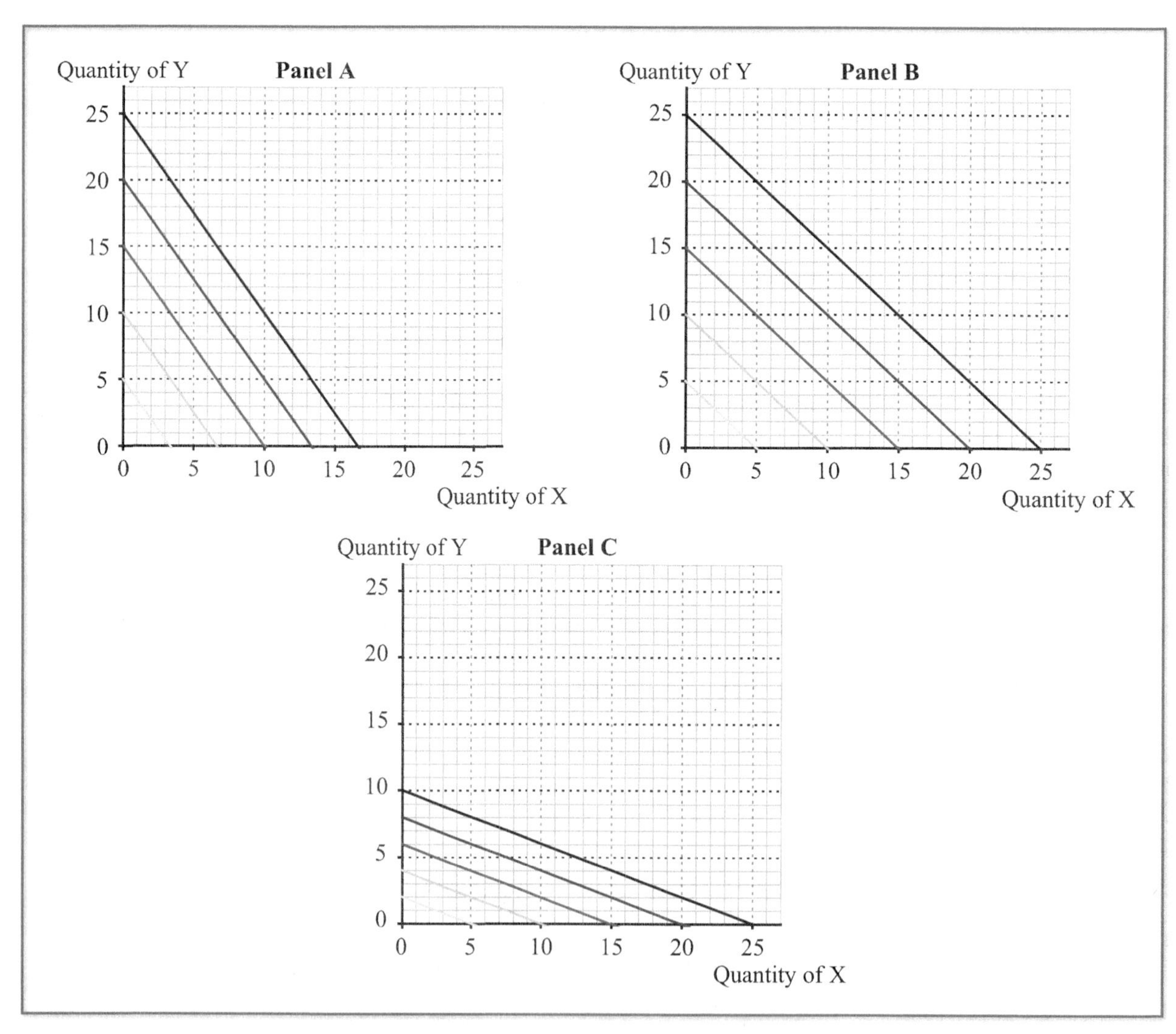

FIGURE 3.5 Perfect Substitutes

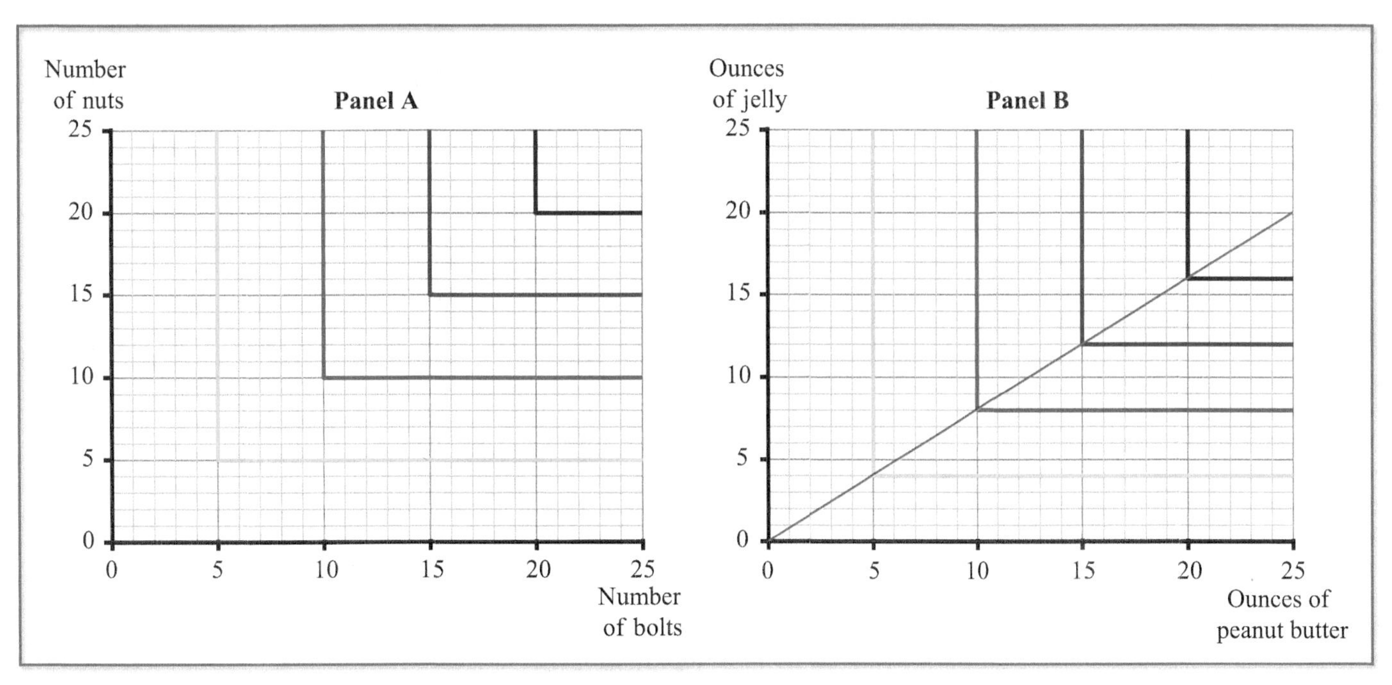

FIGURE 3.6 Perfect Complements

Q5a. Match Figures 3.5A, 3.5B, and 3.5C with Scenarios S5.i, S5.ii, and S5.iii.

Q5b. Delineate which good is x and which good is y.

Q5c. Describe the MRS implicit in this trade-off.

The three scenarios depicted in Figure 3.5 are:

S5.i. Blue pens and black pens, given that neither blue nor black is your favorite color.

S5.ii. Two kinds of raw shrimp, both measured in ounces. One type is peeled, deveined shrimp that are ready to cook; the other type is whole shrimp that have to be prepared for cooking (by removing heads and shells, and by deveining). You have no separate use for the heads and shells that are removed (i.e., you are not in the habit of creating your own fish stock!).

S5.iii. x and y are both standard-denomination U.S. coins (possible choices are penny, nickel, dime, quarter, and half-dollar). You are not a coin collector; you only value each coin for its ability to act as a medium of exchange.*

The polar opposite of perfect substitutes is **perfect complements**—goods that are consumed in fixed proportions. The proportion need not be one to one, as one of the examples in Figure 3.6 shows. Figure 3.6A depicts your preferences over nuts and bolts—if you want to use nuts and bolts as fasteners, you will want to use them in a one-to-one ratio. Extra bolts won't help, and neither will extra nuts.

perfect complements: Two goods are perfect complements if they tend to be consumed in fixed proportions.

By contrast, suppose you are a finicky eater who loves peanut butter and jelly (PB&J) sandwiches. You cannot imagine using either good in anything other than a PB&J sandwich,

***Q5 answer:** Figure 3.5A depicts shrimp, 3.5B depicts pens, and 3.5C depicts coins. You probably came to this in the following way: The only scenario that has a one-for-one trade-off is blue pens and black pens (MRS = 1), so 3.5B is pens. x can be either blue pens or black pens; y is the other color. The MRS in Figure 3.5A is 1.5, and none of the coins listed has a value ratio of three to two, so 3.5A must depict shrimp. Peeled shrimp have higher value, since the heads and shells are already removed. Therefore, x must be peeled shrimp, and y must be whole shrimp. Three ounces of whole shrimp are equal in value to two ounces of peeled shrimp. The MRS in Figure 3.5C is 0.4 (or 2/5), and the only standard U.S. coins that have that value ratio are dimes and quarters. Dimes must be x, and quarters must be y, but from experience, I know that many of you reversed those labels. Doing so means you like 25 quarters the same as 10 dimes!

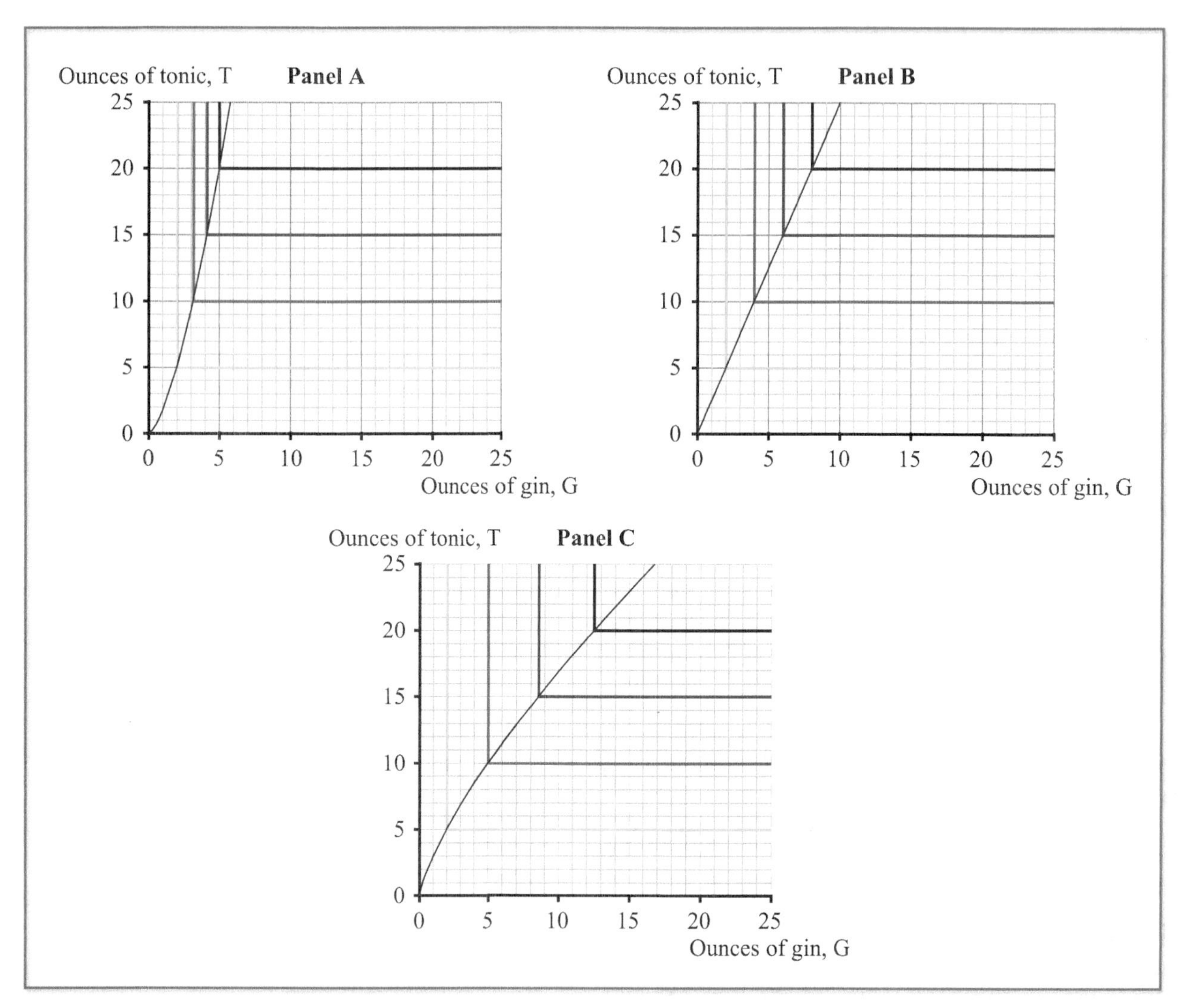

FIGURE 3.7 Mapping the Perfect G&T

and you like your PB&Js "just so." However, you do not like equal parts of PB and J in your sandwiches, as can be seen in Figure 3.6B.

Q6. What is your preferred relative consumption of peanut butter versus jelly implied by the preference map in Figure 3.6B?*

Perfect complement diagrams can become even more creative. Figure 3.7 depicts three preference maps for gin and tonic. Each acknowledges that if you are having a single gin and tonic (G&T) with two ounces of gin, the anatomically correct G&T has two parts gin to five parts tonic because each panel has the vertex of the lowest indifference curve at (2, 5). (If we were to show a third dimension, it would, of course, include one wedge of lime!) Each panel depicts the preferences over G&Ts on a given night for three different types of people. (Also included is a brown curve that depicts the chosen (G, T) bundles in each instance.)

***Q6 answer:** The ratio of peanut butter to jelly depicted in Figure 3.6B can be described either as: "You like to use 25% more peanut butter than jelly," or "You like to use 20% less jelly than peanut butter." If you feel that Figure 3.6B misrepresents your actual peanut butter versus jelly intensity, you can create your own scenario, using the Excel figure for Figure 3.6.

The three types of people may be described as:

S7.i. If I'm going to drink a lot, I want to have each drink stronger so I don't get bloated.

S7.ii. Regardless of how many G&Ts I drink in a night, I want each G&T to be anatomically correct.

S7.iii. If I'm going to drink a lot, I would like to have weaker drinks to moderate my overall alcohol intake.

Answer the following based on these three types of drinkers:

Q7a. Match each panel in Figure 3.7 with type of G&T drinker.

Q7b. To help answer Q7a, find the ratio of tonic to gin that each of the individuals would wish to have poured if they decide to consume 5 ounces of gin in the evening.

You can create your own scenario with more or less moderation using the Excel figure for Figure 3.7.*

Both perfect substitutes and perfect complements are weakly convex and not strictly convex because the indifference curves based on these preferences are composed of line segments. The preference maps depicted thus far in the chapter have also been monotonic (although perfect complements are only weakly monotonic—more of the good that you have too much of does *not* make you better off, but neither does it make you worse off). The same does not always hold, as we will now see.

Satiation and Bliss Points: The Good, the Bad, and the Neutral

Anchovies are a prime example of a good that, past a point, can become a "bad." The world is made up of two kinds of people: those who like anchovies and those who do not. (If you are in the latter group, please suspend your true feelings and bear with this discussion.) Even if you love anchovies, you will admit that too many anchovies on a pizza ruins the pizza. Anchovy lovers may argue over the optimum number of anchovies to have on a pizza, but the simple fact is that anchovies are only good up to a point, and past that point, they become a "bad." The point where a "good" turns into a "bad" is called a **satiation point**. Figure 3.8 depicts preferences over different compositions of an anchovy and mushroom pizza. Anchovies have a satiation point, but mushrooms remain a "good" over the range of mushroom levels shown. The three panels vary according to how important it is to get close to the optimal level of anchovies on the pizza. The Excel figure for Figure 3.8 allows you to graph your own preferences over anchovies and mushrooms on a pizza. If you don't like anchovies at all, set x = 0 and then use the intensity slider to model how much you dislike them.

satiation point: The point where a "good" turns into a "bad" is called a satiation point.

Each panel in Figure 3.8 depicts a satiation point of 13 anchovies per pizza. The red vertical line goes through the horizontal portion of each indifference curve. When more than 13 anchovies are on a pizza, anchovies are a "bad." Once they become a "bad," you require more mushrooms on the pizza to compensate you for having to put up with the extra anchovies. This makes the indifference curves positively sloped to the right of the red line.

Each panel also depicts pizzas (**A**, **B**, and **C**) with different amounts of mushrooms and anchovies. Preferences over these three pizzas vary according to how important it is to get close to the optimal level of anchovies on the pizza. In Figure 3.8A, it is not very important to obtain the optimal level of anchovies, and the extra mushrooms provided by

***Q7 answer:** Figure 3.7A depicts S7.iii, which has a T:G ratio of 4:1 if the individual expects to consume 5 ounces of gin in the evening (and 4 G&Ts). Figure 3.7B depicts S7.ii, which has a T:G ratio of 2.5:1, regardless of how much gin is consumed in the evening (and 2 G&Ts). Figure 3.7C depicts S7.i, which has a T:G ratio of 2:1 if the individual expects to consume 5 ounces of gin in the evening (and 2 G&Ts).

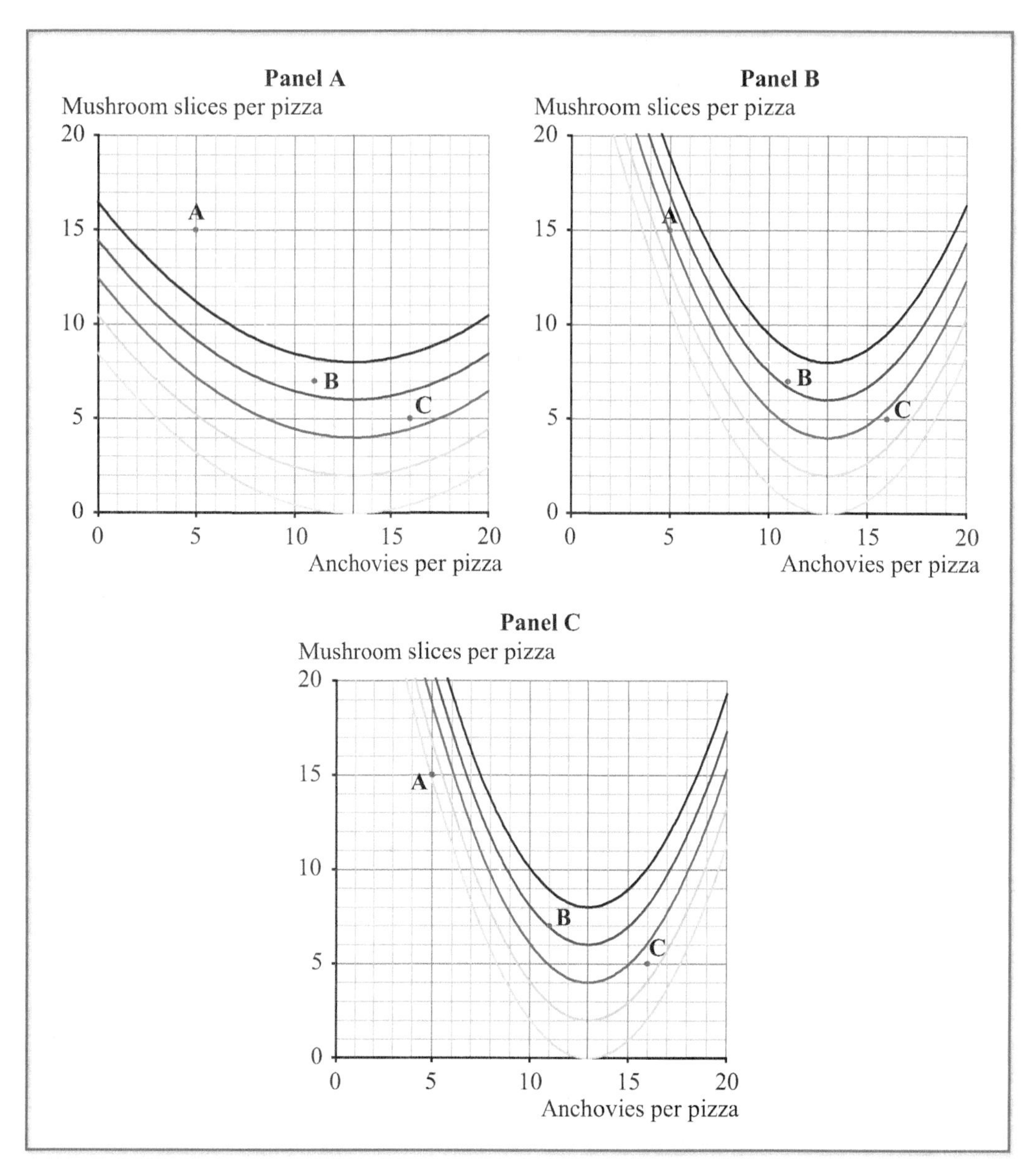

FIGURE 3.8 Convex Preferences with x Satiation

pizza **A** make it the most preferred among the three (**A** ≻ **B** ≻ **C**). In Figure 3.8C, it is very important to obtain the optimal level of anchovies, and pizza **A** becomes the worst among the three (**B** ≻ **C** ≻ **A**). In Figure 3.8B, pizza **A** is the second best of the three (**B** ≻ **A** ≻ **C**).

Of course, there is no reason anchovies have to be on the horizontal axis. If the axes are reversed to model y satiation as in Figure 3.9, it is not surprising that the U-shaped indifference curves rotate 90°.

Note that preferences are convex in Figure 3.8, despite the MRS increasing in magnitude as x increases beyond the satiation point. Once a "good" becomes a "bad," the rule that the MRS must diminish as consumption of the good increases no longer holds. At this point, the MRS passes through zero and becomes negative (slope becomes positive). This often confuses students because they tend to view the diminishing (magnitude of) MRS conclusion (discussed at the end of Section 3.2) as the definition of convexity. (As noted earlier, the actual definition of convexity requires that the set of points at least as good as the indifference curve must be a convex set.) The sets of points above an indifference curve in Figure 3.8 and to the right of an indifference curve in Figure 3.9 are convex sets; hence, the preferences depicted in these figures are convex.

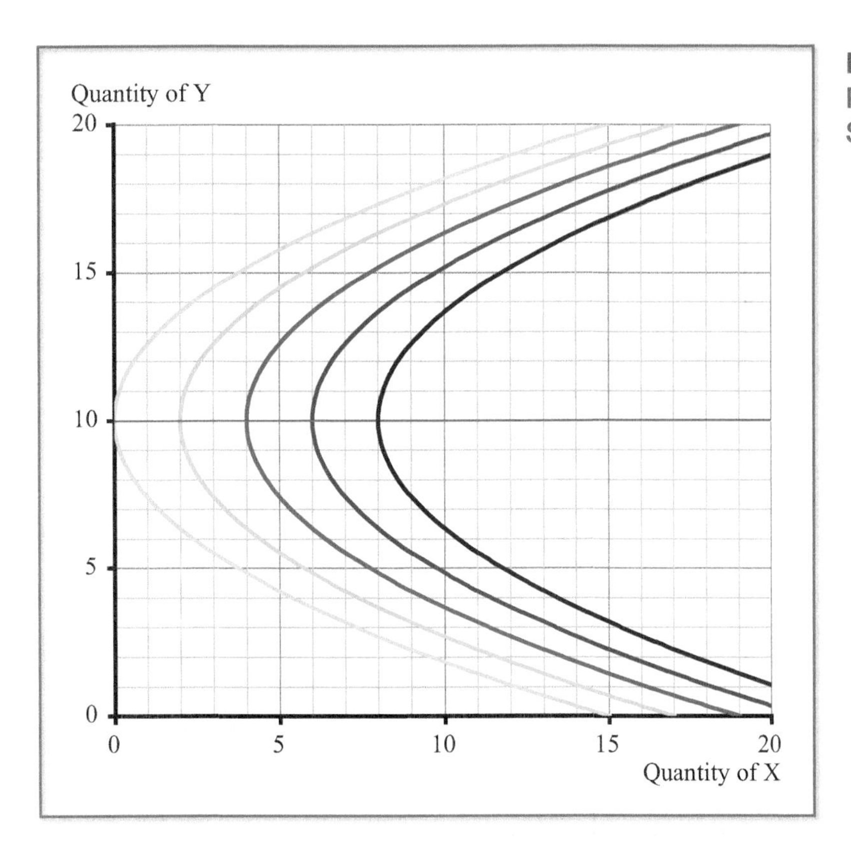

FIGURE 3.9 Convex Preferences with y Satiation

When both goods have a satiation point, there is a consumption bundle that is better than all other bundles near it; this is called a **bliss point**. Figure 3.10 depicts three sets of preferences over the number of pieces of green pepper and mushroom per slice of pizza. Each has a bliss point at (G, M) = (12, 8), and each panel also depicts five points, **A–E**, that represent slices of pizza that are a "distance" of 5 units away from the bliss point. (Recall from the Pythagorean theorem that 3-4-5 is a right triangle; therefore, each of the bundles **A–E** is 5 units away from the bliss point.) The three sets of preferences are:

bliss point: A bliss point occurs at the point of x *and* y satiation.

S10.i. I dislike deviations in mushrooms from the satiation level more than deviations in green peppers.

S10.ii. I dislike deviations in green peppers from the satiation level more than deviations in mushrooms.

S10.iii. I dislike deviations from the satiation level for both toppings equally.

Q10. Match these preferences to the panels in Figure 3.10. In matching panels to preferences, it is useful to describe the preferences over the bundles **A–E** implicit in each preference map.*

The red horizontal and vertical lines through the bliss point in Figure 3.11 set up a quadrant system based on which product is a "good" and which is a "bad." To the right of the red vertical line, x becomes a "bad"; this line is associated with MRS = 0. On the vertical line, x is an **economic neutral** good.

economic neutral: An individual views a good x as an economic neutral if the individual is indifferent between the initial bundle and a new bundle with a bit more or less of x, holding all other goods constant.

Similarly, above the red horizontal line, y becomes a "bad," and on the horizontal line, y is an economic neutral. This line is associated with MRS = ∞ (vertical slope). In quadrants I, II, and IV, at least one of the products is a "bad." Only in quadrant III are both products "goods." Quadrant III is called "the economic region of consumption" because a rational consumer who must pay for a product will typically not purchase more of it once

---

***Q10 answer:** Figure 3.10A depicts preference S10.i. Preferences over the five bundles are **A ≻ B ~ D ≻ C ≻ E**. **A** is best, since there is no deviation from the optimal level of eight mushroom pieces per slice. Figure 3.10B depicts S10.iii, in which **A ~ B ~ C ~ D ~ E**. Figure 3.10C depicts S10.ii. Preferences over the five bundles are **E ≻ C ≻ B ~ D ≻ A**, the opposite of that depicted in Figure 3.8A.

FIGURE 3.10 Plotting a Perfect Slice of Pizza

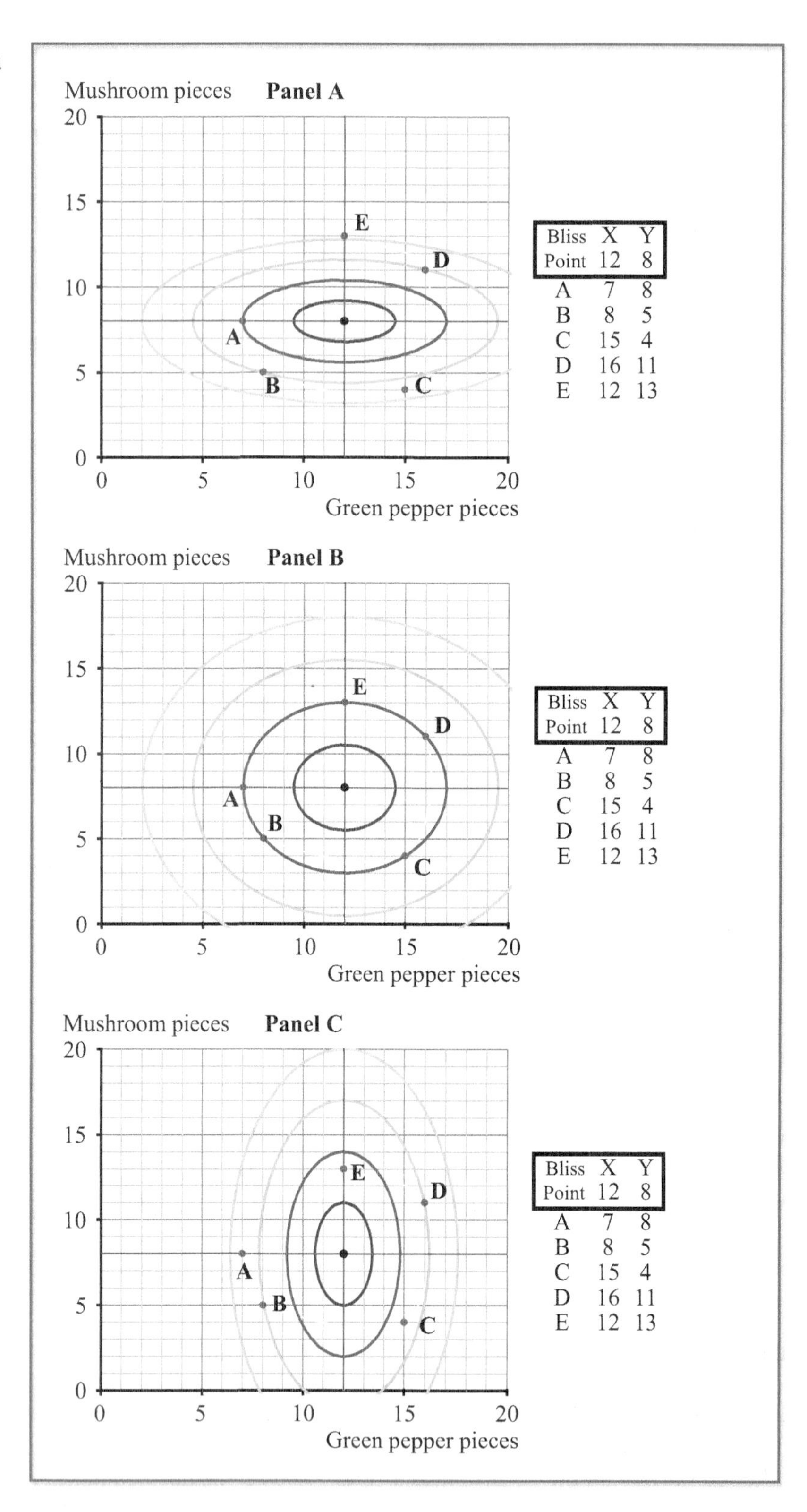

it becomes a "bad." If it is a "bad," the consumer can be made better off by purchasing less of it and the same amount of the other product. This is better for two reasons: (1) The new bundle is preferred to the old, and (2) the new bundle costs less to purchase. The first reason is the focus of this chapter. (We have avoided discussion of the second reason here because preferences are independent of affordability.)

We can talk about the economic region of consumption when only one product becomes a "bad" as well. When x satiation occurs (Figure 3.8), the economic region of consump-

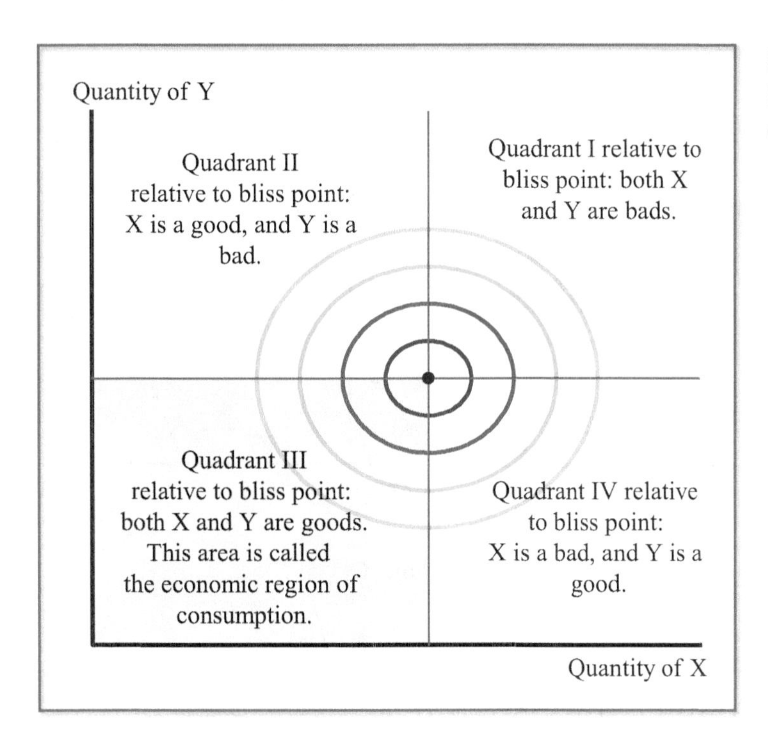
Quantity of Y
Quadrant II
relative to bliss point:
X is a good, and Y is a
bad.
Quadrant I relative to
bliss point: both X
and Y are bads.
Quadrant III
relative to bliss point:
both X and Y are goods.
This area is called
the economic region of
consumption.
Quadrant IV relative
to bliss point:
X is a bad, and Y is a
good.
Quantity of X

FIGURE 3.11 The Economic Region of Consumption

tion is to the left of the red vertical line that describes the bundles where MRS = 0. When y satiation occurs (Figure 3.9), the economic region of consumption is below the red horizontal line that describes the bundles where MRS = ∞. If consumption is restricted to each of these regions, both goods are "goods."

Figures 3.10 and 3.11 implicitly assume independence between each good's satiation level. The satiation level for x is independent of the amount of y being consumed, and vice versa. This need not be the case. The three panels in Figure 3.12 all show a bliss point at (12, 12), but the economic region of consumption for each panel is *not* the quadrant below the horizontal line y = 12 and to the left of the vertical line x = 12; the economic region of consumption is not right-angled beneath and to the left of the bliss point. There is interdependence between products in this instance because the satiation level for each product depends on the amount of the other product consumed.

In Figure 3.12A, an increase in the consumption of one good decreases the amount of the other good that is required before that "good" becomes a "bad." If y = 0, x has a satiation level of 16; x is a "good" for x < 16, and x is a "bad" for x > 16 (for x = 16, x is neither a "good" nor a "bad"; it is an economic neutral). The axis where MRS = 0 (the defining feature of x satiation in Figure 3.8), has rotated so that, as y consumption increases by three, x satiation declines by one. Similarly, y satiation occurs when x = 0 at y = 18, but an x-consumption increase of two leads to a y-satiation decrease of one. Although the trade-offs need not be symmetric, the goods x and y are, in a sense, "competing" in Figure 3.12A.

In Figure 3.12B, an increase in the consumption of one good increases the amount of the other good that is required before that "good" becomes a "bad." When y = 0, x satiation occurs at x = 8, but as y consumption increases by three, x satiation increases by one. Put another way, the slope of the rotated axis where MRS = 0 has a slope of +3 (rather than –3 in Figure 3.12A). When x = 0, y satiation occurs at y = 6, but as x consumption increases by two, y satiation increases by one. In Figure 3.12B, a synergy exists between x and y, albeit not a symmetric synergy. Figure 3.12C also depicts a symmetric synergy between x and y, in which an increase of 4 units of one good increases the satiation level of the other good by 1 unit. The synergy is not as strong as in Figure 3.12B, but it is symmetric. The sliders in the Excel figure for Figure 3.12 allow you to create any level of synergy or competition you wish.

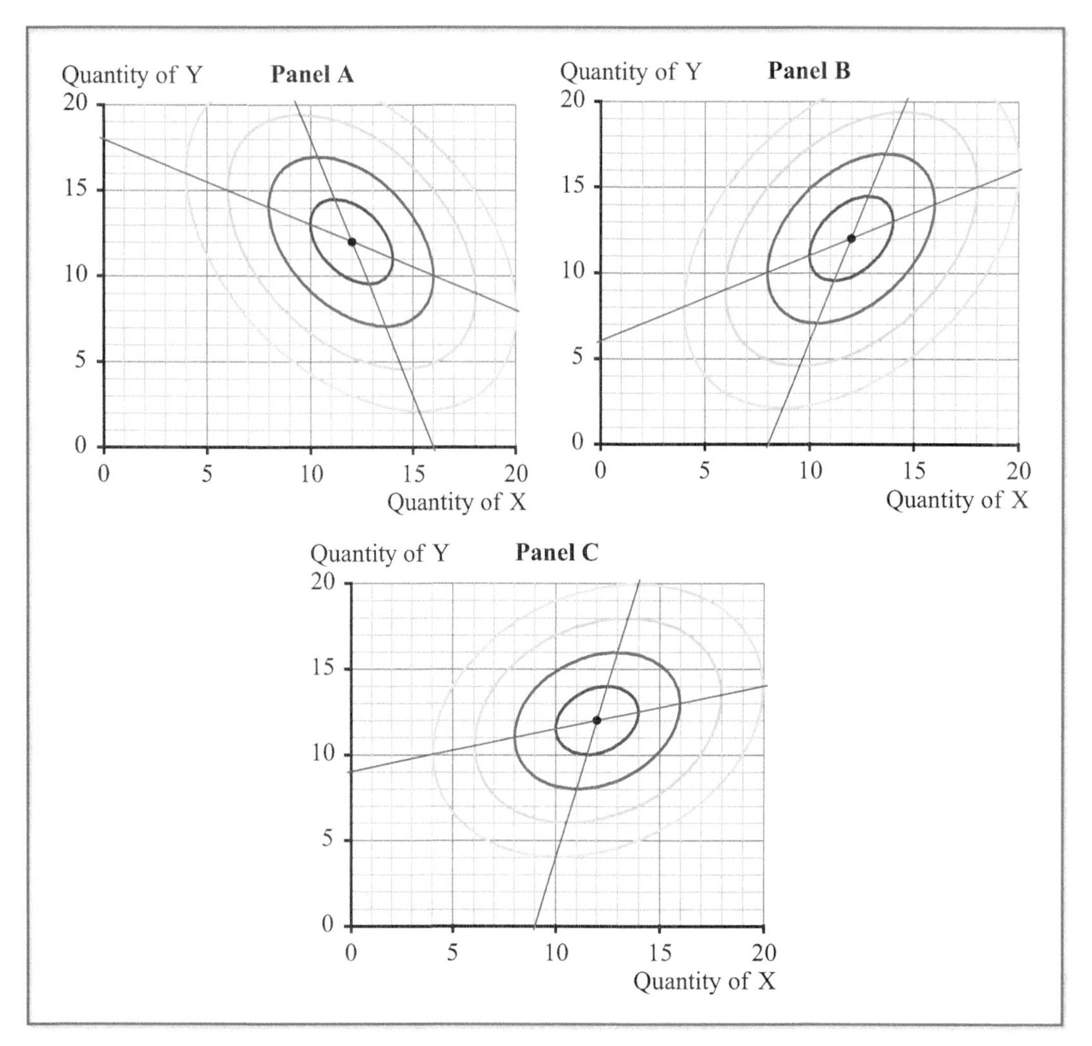

FIGURE 3.12 Bliss Point with Interdependence

Figure 3.13 returns to a discussion of perfect pizzas to highlight the interactivity between goods described in Figure 3.12. The two panels both exhibit the same (x, y) bliss point of (12, 8) but offer dramatically different preferences over the toppings x and y. Consider the following scenarios:

S13.i. I like both mushrooms and anchovies on a pizza up to a point, but I find that the pizza is too bland if there are too many mushrooms for a given amount of anchovies on the pizza and too salty if there are too many anchovies on the pizza for a given amount of mushrooms. My perfect mushroom and anchovy pizza has one-and-a-half times as many mushrooms as anchovies.

S13.ii. I like veggie pizza. In particular, I like green pepper and onion pizza. My optimal pizza has 20 pieces of vegetable per slice, but in this instance, I like 50% more green pepper than onions on the slice. When there are fewer than 20 pieces of vegetable on the slice, I am *roughly* willing to trade green pepper and onions one for one over a range of values of each. For example, consider five slices of pizza, each with 16 total pieces of vegetable per slice (there are between 8 and 12 pieces of green pepper, and the rest of the pieces are onion). I am indifferent between 8 pieces of each and 12 pieces of green pepper and 4 pieces of onion ((8, 8) ~ (12, 4)). I am also indifferent between 9 pieces of green pepper and 7 pieces of onion, and between 11 pieces of green pepper and 5 pieces of onion ((9, 7) ~ (11, 5)). Since my preferences are strictly convex, I prefer the latter two to the former two, but that preference is only *slight*. The fifth slice has 10 pieces of green pepper and 6 pieces of onion.

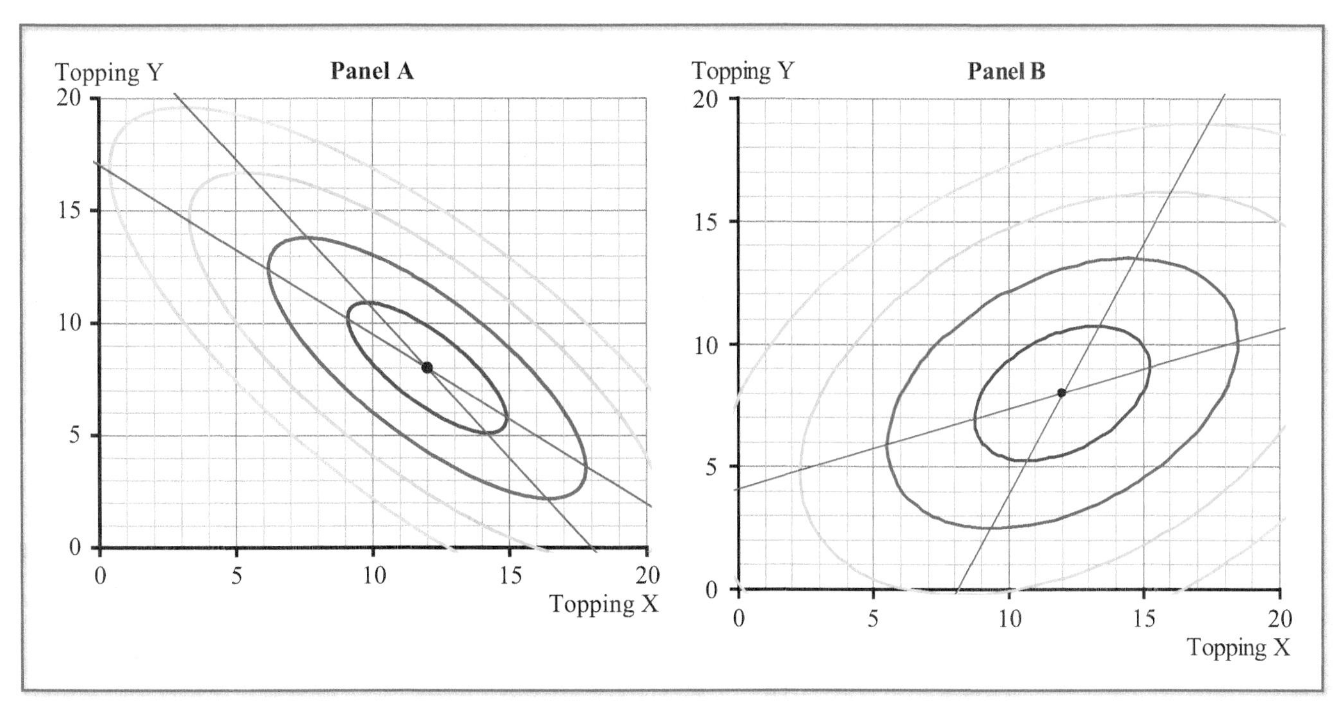

FIGURE 3.13 Plotting Another Perfect Pizza

Use the previous scenarios to answer the following questions.

Q13a. Match Figures 3.13A and 3.13B to Scenarios S13.i and S13.ii.

Q13b. Delineate which topping is x and which is y.

Q13c. Describe the area that represents too much of each topping.

Q13d. Which pair of toppings is more like complements, and which is more like substitutes in the economic region of consumption?*

This section should guide you in creating your own stories about preferences for goods. It takes practice to become comfortable with indifference curves, even though you may feel comfortable about the preferences you are trying to model. Plan to keep a piece of scratch paper available for doodling, and make sure you label your axes. You could also keep the figure files available on your desktop. As you consider your preferences, do not restrict yourself to goods you typically buy in a store. You can also describe preferences over less traditional goods using indifference curves. For example, you could use indifference curves to describe your preferences over various allocations of study time this weekend. Suppose your preferences over hours spent studying economics and French can be described as:

Preferences for studying economics versus French: I dislike studying both economics and French, but I dislike French more than economics. For example, I am indifferent between studying 10 hours of economics and ignoring French, and studying 6 hours of French and ignoring economics. Placing hours spent studying economics on the

***Q13 answer:** Figure 3.13A shows greater substitutability between toppings; therefore, it depicts S13.ii. Since I like 50% more green pepper than onions at my optimum, x is green pepper, and y is onion in Figure 3.13A. Note that the preferences over the slices, $(10, 6) \succ (9, 7) \sim (11, 5) \succ (8, 8) \sim (12, 4)$, can be seen, but the preference is only slight. Bundles above and to the right of the steeper red line have too much green pepper, and bundles above and to the right of the flatter red line have too much onion. Figure 3.13B depicts S13.i; x is mushrooms, and y is anchovies. X and y are more complementary (closer to L-shaped) in the economic region of consumption than in Figure 3.13A. Bundles to the right of the steeper red line are too bland (have too many mushrooms, given the amount of anchovies), and bundles above the flatter red line are too salty (have too many anchovies, given the amount of mushrooms). Note that of the points described in S13.ii, only the points (9, 7) and (10, 6) are in the economic region of consumption in Figure 3.13B.

horizontal axis and hours spent studying French on the vertical axis indicates that (10, 0) ~ (0, 6). I prefer studying some of each, rather than all one or the other: My preferences over studying these two subjects are strictly convex.

Strict convexity requires that if p represents effort devoted to economics and $(1 - p)$ is devoted to French, then I prefer $10 \cdot p$ hours spent on economics and $6 \cdot (1 - p)$ hours spent on French to 10 hours of economics and no French, or 6 hours of French and no economics. This is true for all values of p between 0 and 1. In terms of (E, F) bundles,

$$(10 \cdot p, 6 \cdot (1 - p)) \succ (10, 0) \sim (0, 6) \text{ for all } 0 < p < 1. \quad \textbf{(3.1)}$$

Equation 3.1 provides a formal way of describing the study bundles between the extremes of putting all of your effort into studying economics and all of your effort into studying French. While this is true for every value of p between zero and one, it is worthwhile to consider some specific examples, such as p = 1/3, 1/2, and 2/3. This "p" is the notion of convex combination that was modeled in Figure 3.4 as 30% (p = 0.3). (*Convex combination* is the formal term for being "between" endpoint bundles.)

Graph this using pencil and paper. How much time is devoted to each class when p = 1/3, 1/2, and 2/3? What happens to the total amount of time spent studying as p increases? A solution is suggested in the footnote.*

3.4 Well-Behaved Preferences

well behaved: Preferences are well behaved when they are complete, transitive, monotonic, and convex.

For preferences to be well defined, they must be complete and transitive. Although we described preferences over both "goods" and "bads" in the previous section, we will generally assume that all goods are "goods"; preferences are monotonic. Further, we will often assume that preferences are convex. Preferences are **well behaved** when they are complete, transitive, monotonic, and convex. At times, it is useful to assume the strict versions of monotonicity and convexity, rather than the weak versions. This is done for a number of reasons, some of which will become obvious once we are able to talk about preference maximization in the face of resource constraints in Chapter 6.

The Rationale behind Monotonicity

As we said at the start of the chapter, if you really do not like the good, you will typically decide to not purchase any of it. The (x, y) graph of this result would be quite uninteresting, since either x = 0 or y = 0 in this instance; the problem simplifies to buying only one good. The consumer choice model does allow consumers to not purchase goods; in Chapter 6, we will see exactly under what conditions this occurs. But the most interesting questions involve how to allocate resources across goods that are being consumed in positive quantities to achieve the most preferred allocation, given resource constraints. (Resource constraints are the subject of Chapter 5; we do not discuss them here because it is important to individually focus on preferences and constraints on behavior before putting those two concepts together to talk about optimal choice.)

Even when a product is a "good," it may only be a "good" up to a point. Once satiation occurs, the "good" may become a "bad." In such an instance, we expect consumption to occur at output levels below the satiation point. To do otherwise would imply irrational behavior. Of course, we have all done things that with 20-20 hindsight would be viewed as irrational acts. Although it is instructive to consider what preferences look like in such situations, it should not be the main focus of our analysis because we are interested in modeling typical, rather than atypical, behavior. Most of us do not have continual regret

---

***Solution:** When p = 1/3, you spend 3 hours and 20 minutes on economics and 4 hours on French; when p = 1/2, you spend 5 hours on economics and 3 hours on French; and when p = 2/3, you spend 6 hours and 40 minutes on economics and 2 hours on French. Each of these alternatives is preferred to the endpoints, (10, 0) and (0, 6). The total time devoted to studying increases from 6 hours to 10 hours as p increases from 0 to 1. Two alternative graphs are provided, using the Excel file for Figures 3.10–3.13, one on each worksheet. Click **Data, What If Analysis, Scenarios** in Excel 2007 or **Tools; Scenarios** in Excel 2003; **EconvsFrench; Show; Close** to see this solution on each worksheet.

over our consumption choices (other than, perhaps, to regret not being able to afford *more* choices, which is the issue of resource constraints, the subject of Chapter 5).

A "good" only becomes a "bad" if we cannot freely dispose of unwanted units of the good. That was the implicit assumption behind the L-shaped perfect complements indifference curves in Figures 3.6 and 3.7. The extra bolts, peanut butter, and gin that exist at bundles on the horizontal part of each of these curves provide no extra value to the consumer, but they also do not cause the consumer any harm. As noted earlier, economists call such goods *economic neutrals*. If this were not the case, then the preference maps for each would have to change. (If disposal was costly and storage for future consumption was impossible, then the horizontal lines would have to be upward sloping instead of flat.) And this begs the question of why there are too many units of those goods in the first place. Most basically, when you go to the hardware store looking for nuts and bolts for a project, you are not likely to buy them at other than a 1:1 ratio (indeed, they are often packaged that way). Having anchovies on a pizza is a reasonable example of a "good" that becomes a "bad" because anchovies cannot be freely disposed of; their presence permeates the pizza even if you pick them off. How do you deal with that at the pizza parlor? You simply request that the anchovy pizza not be too "anchovy intensive" when you order.

The Rationale behind Convexity

The discussion in Section 3.2 surrounding Figures 3.2–3.4 laid out the initial rationale for convexity. Individuals typically consume a variety of goods, rather than focus on one good to the exclusion of all others. We now examine other factors that affect the convexity of preferences.

The span of time over which preferences are defined also has an effect on preferences. I might like both wine and beer, but if the time frame under analysis is a single evening, then I am likely to have *concave*, rather than convex, preferences over these two goods.[9] Suppose I am indifferent between the bundle two glasses of wine and no beer and the bundle two glasses of beer and no wine. Both of these options are better than having one glass of each. You should spend a moment with pencil and paper and graph indifference curves consistent with these preferences. A solution is suggested in the endnote.[10]

Over a longer period of time, the reverse is likely to hold. Specifically, consider a time frame of 1 week under the assumption that I like to have one glass of wine or one glass of beer per night. If I am indifferent between the bundle seven glasses of wine and no beer and the bundle seven glasses of beer and no wine for the week, then it is likely the case that bundles between these endpoints will be preferred to either endpoint because I might want to have wine some nights and beer other nights. You are much better off with beer on nights that you are having Mexican or Thai food, and wine on nights that you are having French or Italian food (at least, that is the typical gourmand's view). Although it is interesting to consider the shortened time frames that produce concave results, longer time frames and convex preferences provide a more robust model of consumer behavior.

When preferences are well behaved, indifference curves cannot (with the exception of vertical lines) be upward sloping. Since well-behaved preferences require negatively sloped indifference curves (again, except vertical and horizontal lines), the MRS must be positive, since it is defined as minus slope. The MRS is the *magnitude* of slope and represents the rate at which the individual is willing to exchange y for x.

Perfect substitutes and perfect complements are both well behaved, as are preferences that are between the boundaries of perfect substitutability and no substitutability. In contrast, satiation points and bliss points are excluded when preferences are well behaved.

Strict Monotonicity and Strict Convexity: *Really* Well-Behaved Preferences

Well-behaved preferences require weak convexity and weak monotonicity. If we require strict monotonicity or strict convexity, then this further restricts the types of preferences that have these properties.

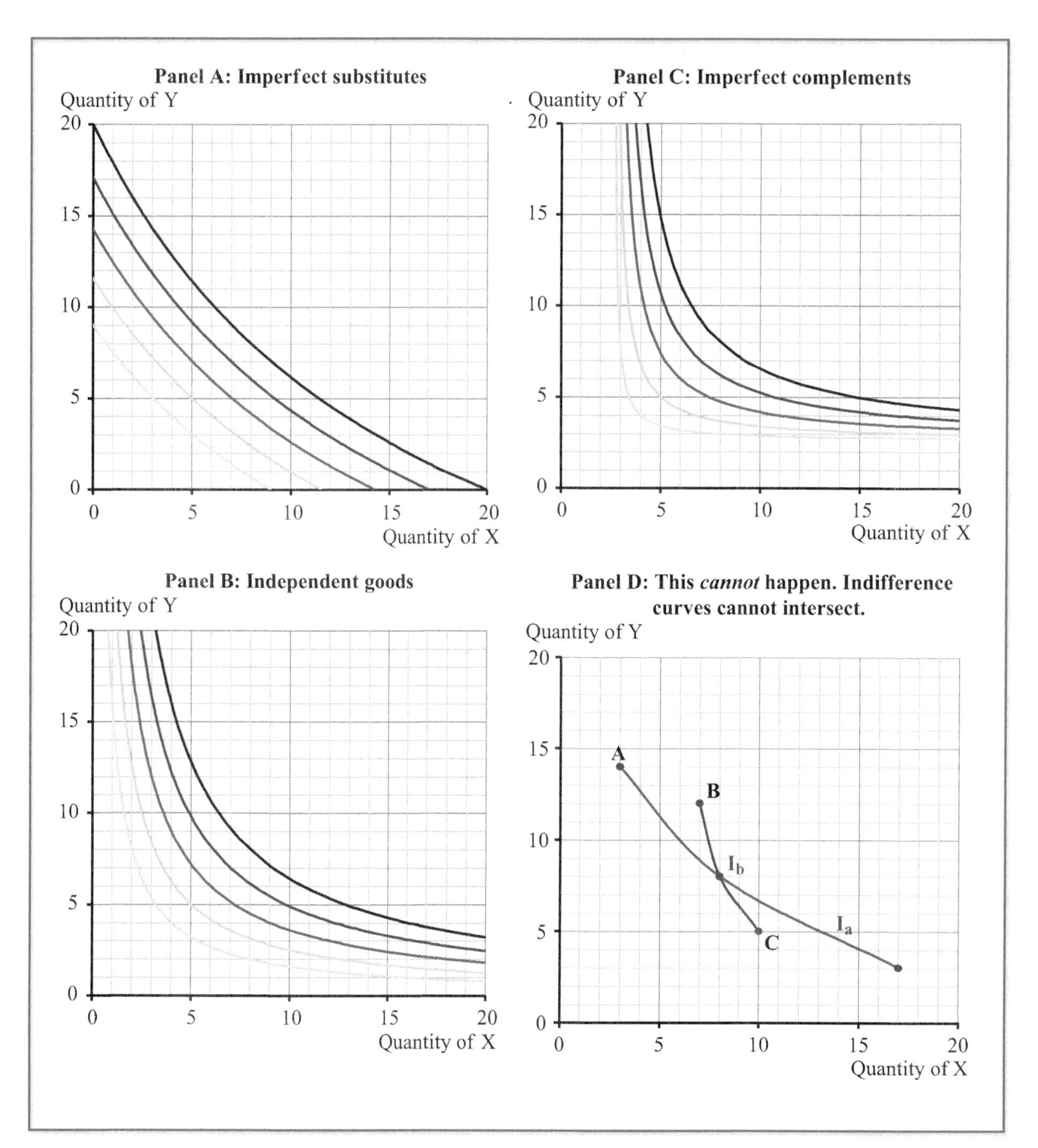

FIGURE 3.14 Well-Behaved Preferences

If we start with well-behaved preferences but replace monotonicity with strict monotonicity, then horizontal and vertical segments are excluded as well. Strict monotonicity requires that if two bundles **B** and **C** are compared, and it is found that **B** has at least as much of each good as **C** and more of at least one good, then it is strictly preferred to **C**. Geometrically, every point in the first quadrant relative to a given bundle (such as **C** in Figure 3.1) is strictly preferred to the given bundle. This includes *all* points on the boundary of this quadrant *except* the initial bundle itself. Strict monotonicity excludes perfect complements.

If we start with well-behaved preferences but replace convexity with strict convexity, then indifference curves must be curves; they cannot have linear segments. This was discussed in the comparison of Figures 3.2 and 3.3. Strict convexity would therefore rule out the endpoints of the substitutability spectrum: perfect complements and perfect substitutes. We saw in Figure 3.13 that curves that are more "curved" in the economic region of consumption are more complementary, and curves that are less curved exhibit greater substitutability in the context of preferences with a bliss point. The same relationship holds in the absence of a bliss point, as Figures 3.14A–3.14C show. Each panel shows indifference curves with unitary MRS (MRS = 1) when there are equal quantities of x and y. Each panel depicts a different degree of substitutability, given really well-behaved preferences.

Since the focus here is on preferences, we have avoided discussion of how changes in price affect an individual's optimal consumption bundle, and we will not be able to describe these changes using the indifference curve map until Chapters 7 and 8. Nonetheless, we can talk about substitutes, complements, and independent goods, using the sign of the cross-price elasticity of demand, as described in Chapter 2 (Equation 2.3). Figure 3.14A depicts preferences over a pair of goods that are imperfect substitutes, while Figure 3.14C depicts preferences over a pair of goods that are imperfect complements. In between, Figure 3.14B depicts goods that are independent. The Excel figure for Figure 3.14 allows you to move between these options and to see preferences that are even more substitutable (closer to linear) or more complementary (closer to L-shaped) than those depicted in Figure 3.14A and 3.14C.

Each of the indifference maps in the chapter share a final, unstated, property. Distinct indifference curves *never* cross. Figure 3.14D shows why. The easiest way to see why distinct indifference curves cannot intersect is to assume they do and derive a contradiction. Start with an indifference curve, I_a, through **A**, and assume an indifference curve, I_b, through a point **B** not on I_a that intersects I_a. Since I_b intersects I_a, there must be a point **C** ~ **B** on the opposite side of I_a from **B**. In both cases, **B** and **C** are not indifferent to **A** (since they are not on I_a). Two possibilities exist: **B** ≻ **A**, and **A** ≻ **B**. If **B** ≻ **A**, then **A** ≻ **C** because **B** and **C** are on opposite sides of I_a. In this instance, transitivity requires **B** ≻ **C**, but this contradicts **B** ~ **C** (since both are on I_b). If, on the other hand, **A** ≻ **B**, then **C** ≻ **A** because **B** and **C** are on opposite sides of I_a. In this instance, transitivity requires **C** ≻ **B**, but this contradicts **B** ~ **C**. Distinct indifference curves cannot intersect because this violates transitivity.

3.5 Applying the Preference Model: A Simple Model of Barter

Although we will put off a discussion of price and budget until Chapter 5, we can examine some of the power of preferences in the face of very simple resource constraints in the context of a **barter** economy.

barter: Barter involves exchanging goods and services without the use of money.

Before you understood money or had an allowance, you probably still traded things with your friends—that is, you knew how to reallocate resources to make yourself better off. When you went to school with a ham and cheese sandwich and your friend had a peanut butter and jelly sandwich, you sometimes traded sandwiches because both of you were better off as a result of the trade. Or after a long evening of trick-or-treating, you may well have spread out your haul on the living-room floor and exchanged candy with your brother, sister, or friend. These are extremely simple examples of reallocating resources via barter. The model of preferences discussed in this chapter allows you to analyze such exchanges. Initially, we do this with two separate diagrams; then we will redo the analysis, using an elegant and powerful tool called the Edgeworth Box.

The model we develop here is admittedly simplistic, but it will give you the flavor of things to come. The following assumptions are sufficient to describe how barter can lead to superior outcomes: Annie and Bob are two friends who go trick-or-treating on Halloween. They only care about chocolate (x) and chewy candy like gummi bears and jelly beans (y). (Since the analysis is fairly complex, we will sometimes revert to x and y as labels, rather than chocolate and gummi bears.) At the end of the evening, they find that Annie has lots of gummis, and Bob has lots of chocolate. They have the following in their bags:

Annie's bag has $(\mathbf{x_A}, \mathbf{y_A}) = \mathbf{(40, 105)}$, while Bob's has $(\mathbf{x_B}, \mathbf{y_B}) = \mathbf{(110, 35)}$.

Economists say that these bundles represent their *initial endowments of resources*.

Both Annie and Bob would like a more balanced haul to take home, so they are certainly going to benefit from trading with each other. To describe their situation more completely, we need to know more about their preferences. It turns out that they have the preferences depicted in Figure 3.14B, although the proof of that assertion can only happen after we have learned about utility functions in Chapter 4.

Assumption 1. Annie and Bob have identical, well-behaved (monotonic and convex) preferences over (x, y) bundles.

Assumption 2. Their MRS at any bundle $(x_0, y_0) = y_0/x_0$. (This means that the slope of their indifference curve at any bundle, (x_0, y_0), is $-y_0/x_0$.)

Assumption 3. They are willing to exchange noninteger quantities of candy if need be. After all, they know that there are lots of M&Ms in a pack; the same goes for gummi bears and Dots. When we say two gummis or two chocolates, we mean two packages (not two pieces, unless they are package-sized pieces).

Assumption 2 is difficult to see in these figures since the grid system has been suppressed to reduce visual clutter. You might find it instructive to go back to Figure 3.14B and use a ruler to verify that Assumption 2 is indeed true.*

Assumption 3 allows us to treat their preferences as continuous rather than discrete. As a result, we can draw an indifference curve through each of their endowment points. This is done in Figure 3.15A and 3.15B.

Annie's MRS of gummis for chocolate is $MRS^A = 2.63$ at her endowment point. She would be willing to give up almost two and two-thirds gummi packages for one package of chocolate. By contrast, Bob's MRS of gummis for chocolate is $MRS^B = 0.32$ at his endowment point. He would be willing to give up less than one-third of a package of gummis for another package of chocolate. Or, viewed in terms of giving up chocolate, he would be better off as long as he gets at least one-third of a pack of gummis. This is not surprising, given how much chocolate Bob already has. Given these MRSs, an exchange of one package of Bob's chocolate in exchange for E packages of Annie's gummis will make both better off as long as $MRS^B = 0.32 < E < 2.63 = MRS^A$. Economists say that such exchanges represent **Pareto superior** reallocations of resources. Exchange will be mutually beneficial as long as the parties do not have equal MRSs. Once Annie and Bob

Pareto superior: A reallocation of resources is Pareto superior to the initial allocation if no one involved is made worse off, and at least one is made better off.

***More about Assumption 2:** It turns out that this particular set of preferences is used a lot in microeconomics. There is an easy geometric way to see what indifference curves look like if MRS(x, y) = y/x. The figure shown in this footnote shows the bundle (6, 9), and the blue indifference curve through this bundle has slope –1.5 and satisfies Assumption 2. The red tangent line is created using a simple geometric trick: Double the x coordinate along the x axis (from 6 to 12), and double the y coordinate along the y axis (from 9 to 18), and connect these endpoints; the result is the red tangent line with the tangent bundle right in the middle. One way to think of this is to imagine flipping the origin bundle out to the point (12, 0), using the x = 6 vertical line as the axis of rotation. The green ray would rotate out to the lower part of the red line (this is what the arrow below the x axis signifies). A symmetric rotation using the y = 9 horizontal line as the axis of rotation would rotate the green ray out to the upper part of the red line (the arrow to the left of the vertical axis shows this rotation).

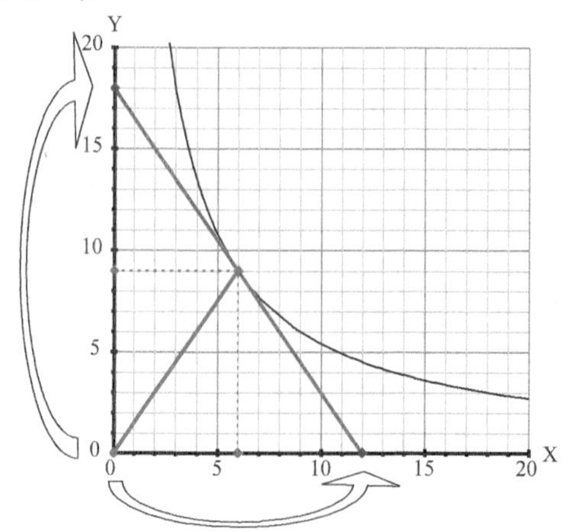

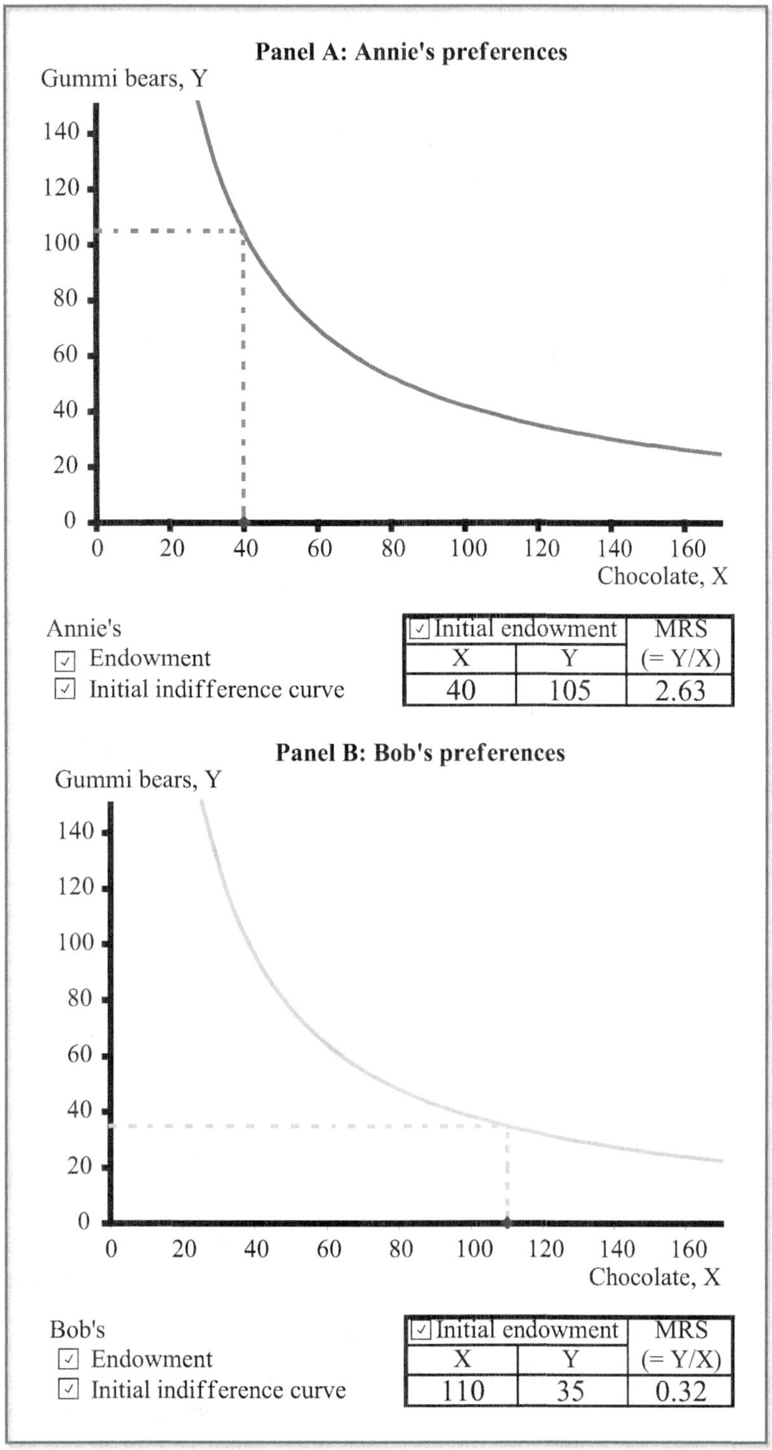

Panel A: Annie's preferences

Annie's
☑ Endowment
☑ Initial indifference curve

☑ Initial endowment		MRS
X	Y	(= Y/X)
40	105	2.63

Panel B: Bob's preferences

Bob's
☑ Endowment
☑ Initial indifference curve

☑ Initial endowment		MRS
X	Y	(= Y/X)
110	35	0.32

FIGURE 3.15 Annie's and Bob's Preferences Prior to Trading on Halloween

have equal MRSs, there is no longer a possibility of mutually beneficial exchange: They cannot *both* be made happier. Economists say that such allocations are **Pareto optimal**. Alternatively, we can define Pareto optimality in terms of Pareto superiority: An allocation is Pareto optimal if there are no Pareto superior reallocations.

Pareto optimal: An allocation of resources is Pareto optimal if there are *no* reallocations of resources in which at least one is made better off and no one involved is made worse off.

Considering these exchanges one package at a time would take a lot longer than Annie and Bob want to devote to this project. As a result, Annie and Bob initially consider a trade of 10 chocolates. Annie would be willing to give up about 26 packs of gummis for 10 chocolates because $\Delta y = \text{slope} \cdot \Delta x$ (recall that $\text{slope} = \Delta y/\Delta x$, so we obtain an approximation of how much y changes on an indifference curve as x changes by multiplying slope times how much x changes). Bob would be willing to exchange about 3 packs of gummis for 10 chocolates for the same reason. A mutually beneficial exchange occurs somewhere between 3 and 26. Each of these numbers is an approximation, since the indifference curves are *curves*. An exact answer for the maximum number of gummi packages Annie would be willing to give up for 10 more chocolates would be based on finding the point on Annie's initial indifference curve associated with 50 chocolates (her initial 40 plus 10 from Bob). As it turns out, (40, 105) ~ (50, 84), so Annie would be willing to give up, at most, 21 gummis for 10 chocolates (21 = 105 – 84). Bob's actual minimum required rate of exchange for 10 chocolates is 3.5 gummis. Reallocations of resources where Bob gives Annie 10 chocolates in exchange for E gummis with $3.5 \leq E \leq 21$ are Pareto superior to the initial allocation. The solid vertical line in each panel of Figure 3.16 represents the set of Pareto superior reallocations in this instance. The purple diagonal line shows one such trade: 10 gummis for 10 chocolates. The green horizontal segment represents the chocolate traded, and the yellow vertical segment represents the gummis traded. The Excel figure for Figure 3.16 allows you to vary each of these values to create your own Pareto superior reallocation.

The 10-for-10 trade is not the end of the story, however, because Annie's and Bob's MRSs are still not equal ($MRS^A = 1.90$ at (50, 95), and $MRS^B = 0.45$ at (100, 45)). The exchange has reduced the gap between their MRSs, but it has not eliminated it. If Annie and Bob continue to exchange gummis for chocolate at a 1:1 rate, they will achieve a Pareto optimal allocation in which each individual has (75, 70). The MRS of this allocation is 0.93.[11] Figure 3.17 provides the Pareto optimal allocation described.

The gummi:chocolate exchange rate of 1:1 was used because it produces a nice, clean equilibrium and because it has the appearance of fairness. (This might be considered fair because both started off with 145 pieces of candy, and both ended with 145 pieces of candy.) Other exchange rates will lead to different Pareto optimal outcomes. We can think of the bargaining game as being one of choosing the rate at which gummis are exchanged for chocolate. The outcome depends on Annie's and Bob's relative bargaining abilities. The Excel figure for Figure 3.17 shows that any exchange rate between 0.55:1 and 1.56:1 will produce a Pareto optimal outcome. Lower exchange rates are associated with Annie being a better bargainer, and higher exchange rates are associated with Bob being a better bargainer.[12]

The previous analysis is tractable but a bit difficult to see because you must move back and forth between two diagrams (and keep track of how the MRS changes in the tables). The Edgeworth Box provides the *same* analysis in a single, elegant diagram. An Edgeworth Box includes information from both individuals by superimposing one individual's information on top of the other's in a way that automatically keeps track of trading between them. As Annie and Bob exchange chocolate and gummis with each other, the total resources in their "economy" remains fixed: There are a total of 150 packages of chocolate and 140 packages of chewy candy (gummis).[13] If we were to create a 150 × 140 box, every point in that box would represent a different allocation of chocolates and gummis for Annie and Bob. If we use Annie's axis as the bottom left of our box and we use the point (150, 140) as the upper right of the box, then this point becomes Bob's origin, with Bob turned "upside down." This is easiest to see (and easiest to draw) by actually turning your book (or notebook) upside down when analyzing or drawing in Bob's information. Figure 3.18 depicts the three allocations described in Figures 3.15–3.17, and the Excel figure for Figure 3.18 allows you to create *any* allocation you wish, using sliders.

The genius of the Edgeworth Box is that Pareto superior and Pareto optimal allocations are quite simple to see, once you include indifference curves. Figure 3.19 depicts the same information provided in Figures 3.15 and 3.16. Focus initially on Figure 3.19A: The indifference curves going through the endowment point create a football-shaped area. This area is the set of allocations that are Pareto superior to the endowment point. A Pareto superior football will exist whenever MRSs are not equal across individuals. It is worth pointing out that putting Bob upside down does *not* change the interpretation of his MRS; his diagram has been turned 180°, a turn that does not affect the orientation of horizontal and vertical axes. Bob's MRS at his endowment point is less than Annie's

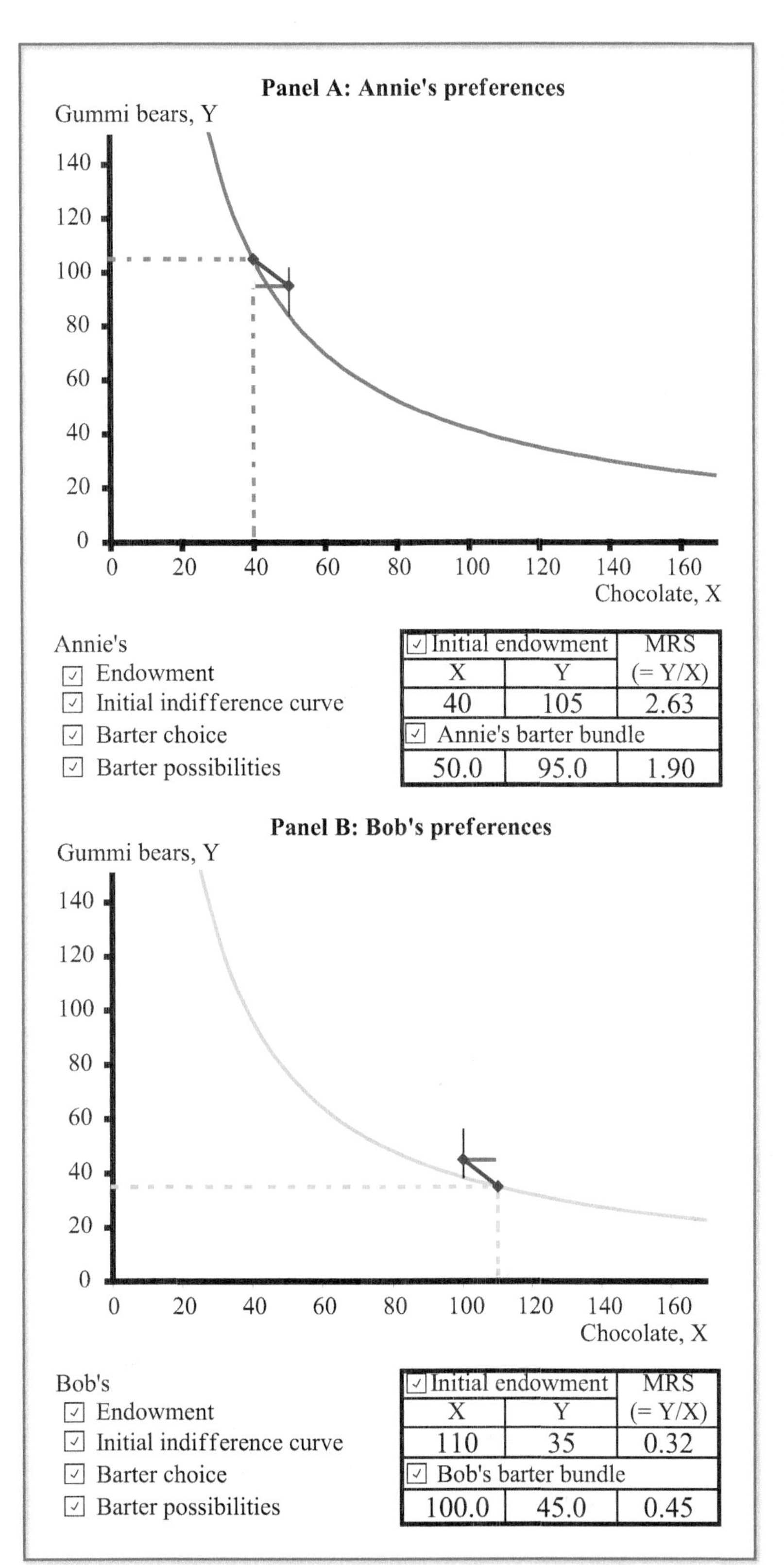

FIGURE 3.16 Annie and Bob after the First Round of Trading

MRS; the slopes of their respective indifference curves at their endowment point reflect this fact. Annie's indifference curve is steeper than Bob's at their endowment point.

The vertical line between their indifference curves in Figure 3.19A represents the set of Pareto superior reallocations where Annie obtains 10 chocolates from Bob. The top point of that line segment represents an allocation in which Annie is the dominant bargainer, since Bob remains indifferent between this bundle and his initial allocation. The bottom

FIGURE 3.17 Annie and Bob Undertaking a Pareto Optimal Trade

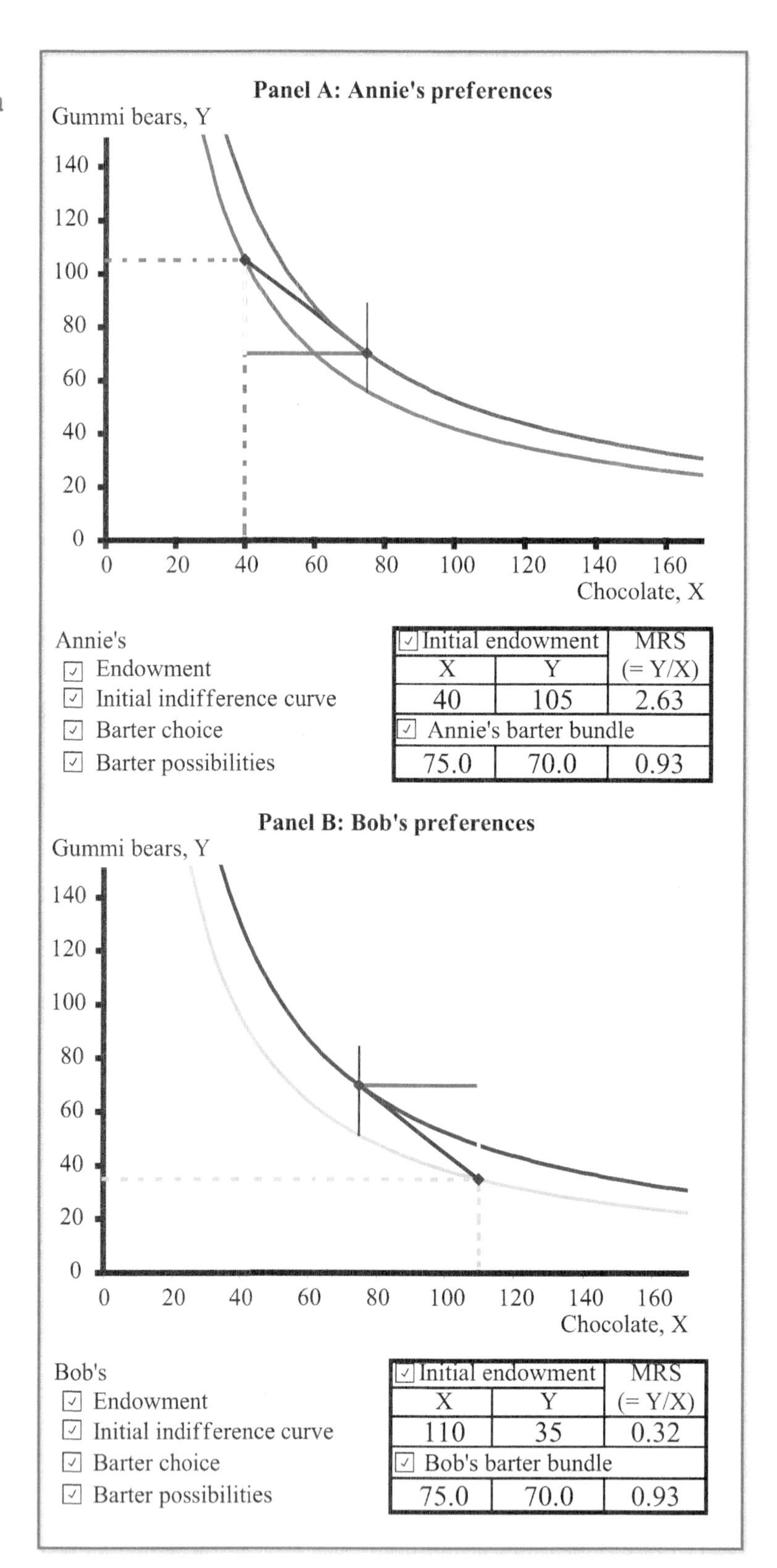

point of that line segment represents an allocation in which Bob is the dominant bargainer, since Annie remains indifferent between this bundle and her initial allocation. The diagonal line between the endowment point and the point in the "middle" of that vertical segment represents the 10:10 trade discussed in Figure 3.16. This is not the end of trading because Annie and Bob do not have equal MRSs at the new allocation. This is easy to see in Figure 3.19B. There is a new, smaller Pareto superior football through the 10:10 trade

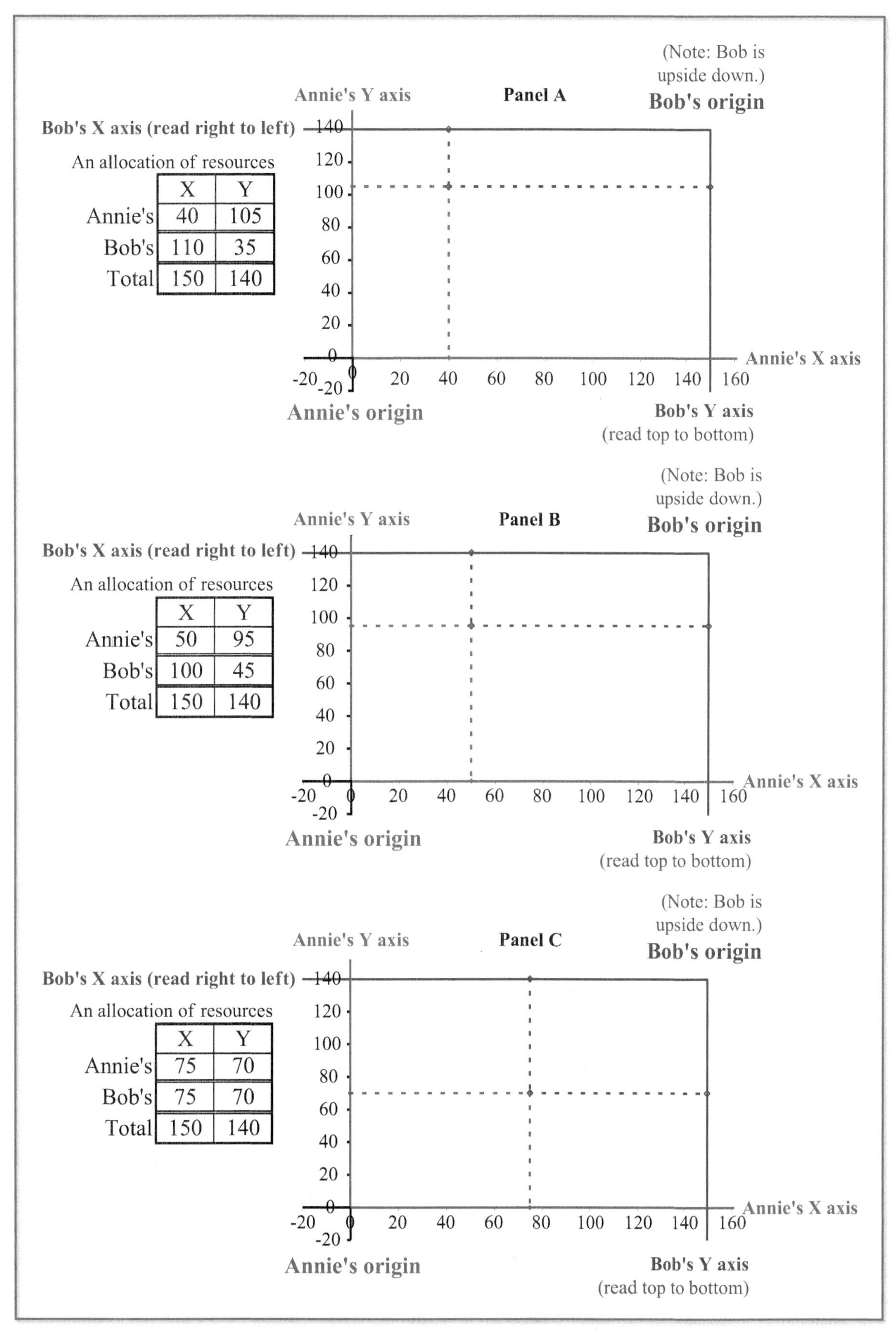

FIGURE 3.18 Every Point in an Edgeworth Box Represents a Possible Allocation of Total Resources

FIGURE 3.19 An Edgeworth Box View of the Initial Trade from Figure 3.16

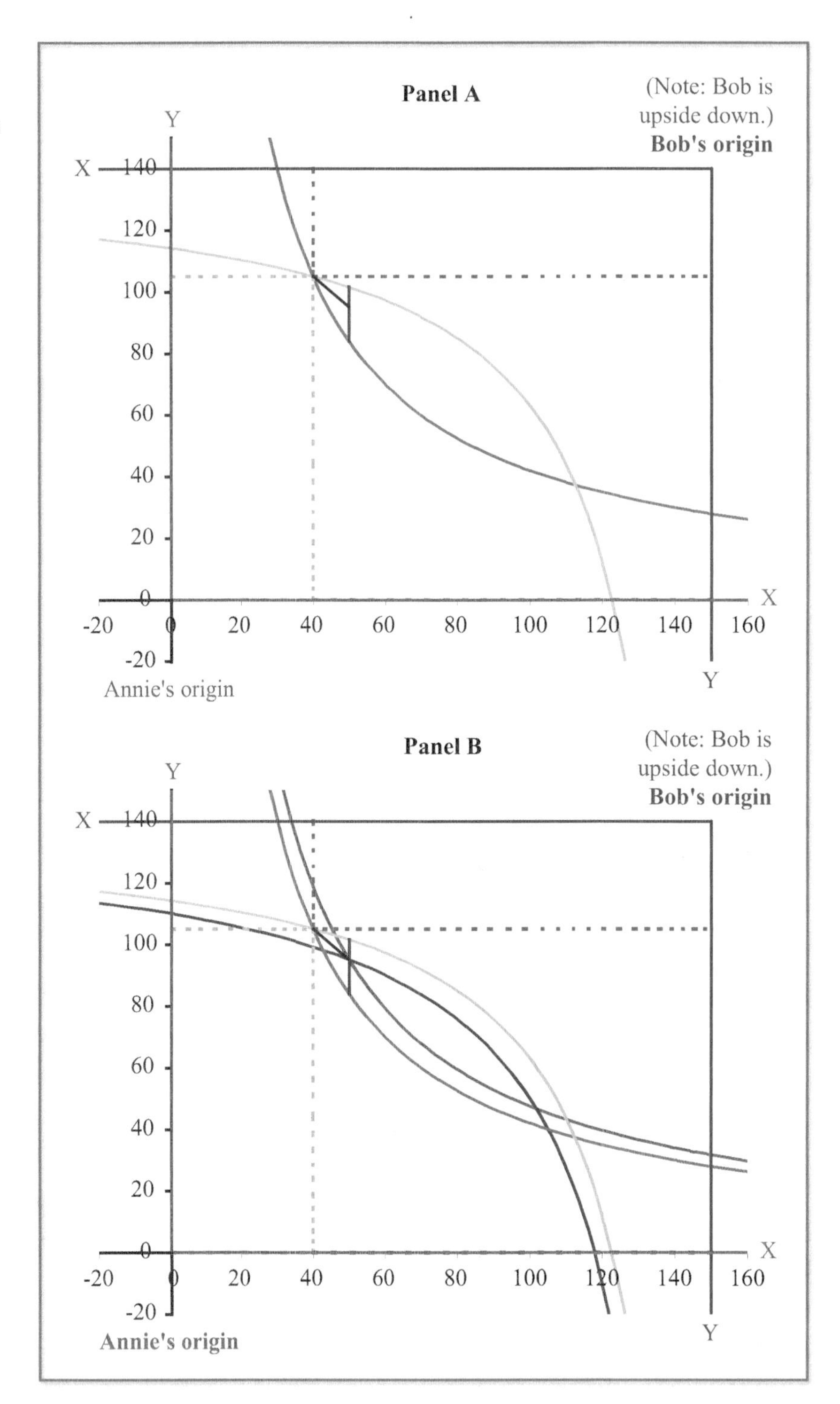

point. Such Pareto superior footballs will exist whenever MRSs are not equal. Trades will continue until a Pareto optimal outcome, a "zero football," is found.

The Pareto optimal solution described in Figure 3.17, in which Annie and Bob trade 35 gummis for 35 chocolates, is shown as Figure 3.20A. The resulting allocation of resources is a Pareto optimum, since $MRS^A = MRS^B$. As previously argued, this is only one of the Pareto optimal allocations achievable, given the initial endowment. The green diagonal line in Figure 3.20B depicts the set of *all* Pareto optimal allocations. (One could alternatively call this the set of all tangencies between indifference curves, points of equal MRS, or "zero footballs" in the Edgeworth Box.) Economists often call the set of Pareto optimal allocations the **contract curve**.

contract curve: The contract curve is the set of all Pareto optimal allocations of resources.

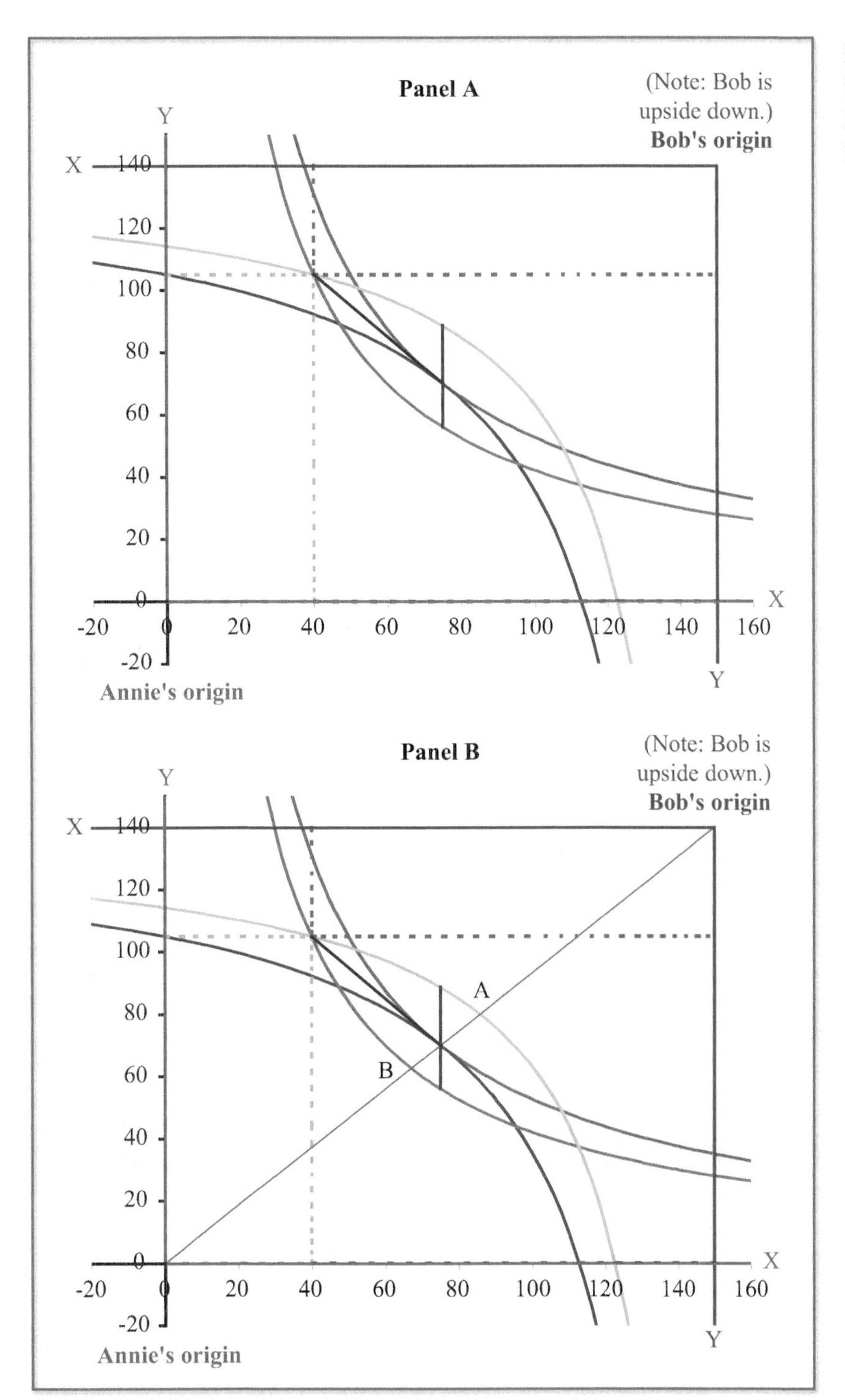

FIGURE 3.20 One Pareto Optimal Exchange in an Edgeworth Box

Not all Pareto optimal allocations are achievable because either Annie or Bob would be better off remaining at their endowment point. In particular, points on the green diagonal below Annie's pink initial indifference curve are Pareto optimal but make Annie worse off (between Annie's origin and point **B**), and points on the diagonal above Bob's light blue initial indifference curve are Pareto optimal but make Bob worse off (between point **A** and Bob's origin). Points on the green Pareto optimal diagonal *inside* the initial Pareto superior football represent the set of possible Pareto optimal reallocations that will ultimately result, given Annie's and Bob's initial bundles (this is the line segment **AB** in Figure 3.20B).

The actual allocation chosen depends on bargaining strength, as discussed earlier. Use the sliders in the Excel figure for Figure 3.20 to model each of the boundary choices (discussed in endnote 12): When Annie is the dominant bargainer, the resulting Pareto optimal reallocation is (85.8, 80.0) for Annie and (64.2, 60.0) for Bob (point **A** in Figure 3.20B); when Bob is the dominant bargainer, the resulting Pareto optimal reallocation is (67.1, 62.6) for Annie and (82.9, 77.4) for Bob (point **B** in Figure 3.20B).

Summary

Preferences form the basis of individuals as consumers of goods and services. Preferences tell us what an individual wants when confronted by a choice among alternatives. When confronted with a choice, you can always say which you prefer: Preferences are complete. Preferences are also transitive: If you prefer bundle **A** to bundle **B** and bundle **B** to bundle **C**, then you prefer **A** to **C**.

Indifference curves provide a geometric representation of preferences for two goods. Indifference curves can take on a variety of shapes, depending on the goods being compared. Indifference maps or preference maps are graphs of a number of indifference curves. Such maps help economists tell economic stories. The rate at which y is traded for x along an indifference curve is called the marginal rate of substitution (MRS). If both goods are "goods," then the MRS is positive, but if one of the goods is a "bad," and the other is a "good," then the MRS is negative. (If both products are "bads," then the MRS is once again positive.) If the MRS changes sign along the indifference curve, then one of the goods has changed from being a "good" to a "bad." We say that satiation occurs at the point where a "good" turns into a "bad." If both goods have a satiation point, then the preferences have a bliss point.

If more is at least as good as less, then preferences are said to be monotonic. If more is preferred to less, then preferences are strictly monotonic. If all bundles between indifferent bundles are at least as good as the endpoint bundles, then we say that preferences are convex. If all bundles between indifferent bundles are better than the endpoint bundles, then we say that preferences are strictly convex. When preferences are complete, transitive, monotonic, and convex, we say that they are well behaved. When preferences are well behaved, indifference curves cannot slope upward (due to monotonicity). As a result, the MRS is positive (or vertical, or zero), and it represents the trade-off between x and y. If monotonicity is replaced by strict monotonicity, then the MRS is strictly positive. If preferences are well behaved, then the MRS cannot increase as x increases (due to convexity). If convexity is replaced by strict convexity, then the MRS is a strictly decreasing function of x.

Preferences allow us to examine the economics of barter. Barter is the exchange of goods or services without the use of money or prices. Barter can be analyzed in a two-goods, two-person economy. Barter will lead to an increase in the economic well-being of at least one party without harming the economic well-being of the other as long as their MRSs are not equal. If MRSs are not equal at the initial allocation of resources, then there are Pareto superior reallocations of resources available. In this instance, voluntary exchange (barter) will lead to a superior solution. This process will continue until there are no Pareto superior reallocations available. The resulting allocation is said to be Pareto optimal. The choice among Pareto optimal allocations is dependent on the bargaining strengths of the parties involved. The process of reallocation leading to a Pareto optimal outcome is easily seen, using a geometric construct called an Edgeworth Box.

Review Questions

Define the following terms:

preferences	marginal rate of substitution (MRS)	really well-behaved preferences
bundle of goods	satiation point	barter
allocation of resources	bliss point	Edgeworth Box
economic "goods"	perfect substitutes	Pareto optimal
economic "bads"	perfect complements	Pareto superior
economic neutrals	well-defined preferences	contract curve
indifference curve	well-behaved preferences	economic region of consumption

Define the following properties of preferences:

completeness	strict monotonicity	weak convexity
transitivity	convexity	
monotonicity	strict convexity	

Match the following phrases:

a. Each good consumed is a "good."
b. The rate the individual is willing to substitute y for x
c. I can freely dispose of goods I do not want.
d. y is valuable relative to x.
e. Variety is the spice of life.
f. x is valuable relative to y.
g. Preferences are monotonic and convex.

1. At worst, the good is an economic neutral.
2. High MRS
3. The MRS diminishes as x increases.
4. Strict monotonicity
5. Low MRS
6. MRS
7. Convexity

Provide short answers to the following:

a. What is the relation between the MRS and the slope of the indifference curve?
b. What must be true if the MRS is negative?
c. What must be true about the MRS in the economic region of consumption?
d. What is true about every point in an Edgeworth Box?
e. Why is a "zero football" Pareto optimal? (Don't ask Tom Brady!)
f. Will individuals ever move from one Pareto optimal allocation to another distinct Pareto optimal allocation via voluntary exchange?

Check your answers to the *matching* and *short-answer* exercises in the Answers Appendix at the end of the book.

Notes

1. If there are n goods, the bundle **A** is composed of a_1 units of good 1, a_2 units of good 2, . . ., a_n units of good n. This is written as the ordered n-tuple $\mathbf{A} = (a_1, a_2, \ldots, a_n)$. Each good can only be consumed in nonnegative quantities; therefore $a_i \geq 0$ for all i. We say that the consumption bundle is in the first *orthant* (*orthant* is the n-dimensional version of *quadrant*). Sometimes $n > 2$; most often, $n = 2$.

2. It is useful to think of the symbols $\succ$, $\sim$, and $\succsim$ as being "like" $>$, $=$, and $\geq$ signs, but they are not the same as these signs (since preferences are defined over bundles of goods and $>$, $=$, and $\geq$ are relations that exist between numbers).

3. An alternative definition of transitivity, involving weakly preferred rather than strictly preferred, is sometimes useful. In this event, preferences are transitive if $\mathbf{A} \succsim \mathbf{B}$, and $\mathbf{B} \succsim \mathbf{C}$, then $\mathbf{A} \succsim \mathbf{C}$.

4. Although the slope is negative, many authors treat slope (and the MRS) as a positive number because the trade-off involved when both goods are "goods" is implicit. This is simply a matter of convention. Beyond the examples provided in the next two sections, goods will, in general, be considered "goods." As a result, the minus sign is implicit in the trade-off between x and y. Just like the discussion of the sign of elasticity of demand in Chapter 2, the sign should not lead to confusion, since it is well understood that demand slopes downward.

5. Some authors make this explicit by denoting the marginal rate of substitution as "$MRS_{y,x}$," but we will omit the subscript "y, x" since, in the two-goods model, MRS will *always* mean how many units of the good on the vertical axis can be exchanged for 1 unit of the good on the horizontal axis.

6. Formally, we could define the following sets: the upper contour set $U(\mathbf{C}) = \{\text{bundles } \mathbf{B} \mid \mathbf{B} \succsim \mathbf{C}\}$; the lower contour set $L(\mathbf{C}) = \{\text{bundles } \mathbf{B} \mid \mathbf{C} \succsim \mathbf{B}\}$. From here, the indifference curve through **C**, $I(\mathbf{C})$ is seen as the intersection of $U(\mathbf{C})$ and $L(\mathbf{C})$, $I(\mathbf{C}) = U(\mathbf{C}) \cap L(\mathbf{C})$, or as $I(\mathbf{C}) = \{\text{bundles } \mathbf{B} \mid \mathbf{B} \sim \mathbf{C}\}$.

7. We typically assume that goods can be consumed in noninteger amounts because little is lost and much is gained from this assumption. We examine discrete goods in Section 5.6. Although this will only become clear once we talk about optimization in Chapter 6, the gain from this assumption is largely due to the simplified mathematics involved if we allow continuous quantities for all goods.

8. Those who know calculus will recognize that the last couple of sentences are the heuristic basis for the concept of derivative. If you don't know calculus, don't be concerned. You will not have to take a derivative to do well in intermediate microeconomics, but you must be able to visualize the slope of a curve, since much of microeconomics is based on marginal analysis and the word *marginal* is synonymous with *slope*. (The word *marginal* is also synonymous with the word *derivative*, but that is not surprising, as the calculus concept of derivative is simply a continuous version of the concept of slope.) Put another way, you already know something about calculus because you know marginal analysis from introductory economics.

9. Preferences are concave if the lower contour set (the set of bundles no better than a given bundle) is a convex set. (See endnote 6.)

10. Preferences would look much like the economics versus French studying example we discussed earlier, with one **important** difference—lighter blue indifference curves in the Excel figure for this result represent more preferred bundles (unlike the rest of the chapter). Graphs of this result are provided, using both worksheets of the Excel file for Figures 3.10–3.13. Click **Data, What If Analysis, Scenarios** in Excel 2007

or **Tools; Scenarios** in Excel 2003; **Concave; Show; Close** to see this solution.

11. Interestingly, the equilibrium MRS need not be the exchange rate of 1.00. More will be said on this topic once we introduce a pricing analysis in Section 7.4.

12. You can use the Excel file for Figure 3.17 to verify that when Annie obtains the entire gains from trade, she is able to obtain 45.8 chocolates from Bob in exchange for 25.0 gummis. The resulting reallocation, (85.8, 80.0) for Annie and (64.2, 60.0) for Bob, is Pareto optimal, since both individuals have the same MRS (of 0.93). At the other end of the bargaining spectrum, Bob obtains the entire gains from trade when he is able to obtain 42.4 gummis from Annie in exchange for 27.1 chocolates. The resulting reallocation, (67.1, 62.6) for Annie and (82.9, 77.4) for Bob, is Pareto optimal, since both individuals have the same MRS (of 0.93). *This is much easier to verify using the Edgeworth Box diagram, so you should redo this once you have read further.*

13. Of course, this analysis ignores the main reason they went out trick-or-treating in the first place! As they eat the candy, they reduce the resources available in their barter economy. For simplicity, we assume that they exhibit a level of willpower rarely seen in children—no eating occurs until they are done trading.

Utility

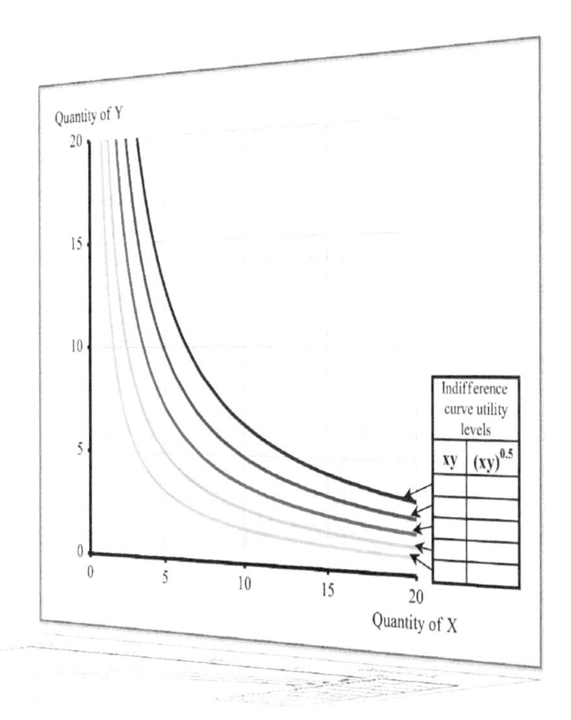

Chapter Outline

Preferences form the basis of consumer choice but are awkward to work with in practice because they require lengthy comparisons of bundles of goods in pairwise fashion. In Chapter 3, we used indifference curves and indifference maps that help simplify consumer choice by describing preferences in a geometric fashion. This chapter provides a symmetric representation of preferences, using an algebraic concept called the utility function. The indifference curves you worked with in Chapter 3 are all based on utility functions. Otherwise, Excel would not have allowed you to move them using sliders. These functions were hidden because the focus was on reading the graphs and telling economic stories using those graphs, rather than on making the graphs.

In this chapter, we focus instead on utility functions and how they algebraically describe preferences. In Section 4.1, we examine how a function can represent preferences and also introduce the notions of utility level and marginal utility. In Section 4.2, we begin to examine actual utility functions, using goods that are perfect substitutes. Perfect substitutes have linear indifference curves, and therefore, their algebraic representation is easy to understand. There is no such thing as *the* utility function that represents preferences; you can only have *a* utility function that represents preferences because there is no unique way to represent preferences with functions. Utility functions are ordinal, not cardinal, and that is the focus of Section 4.3. We then turn to the analysis of specific classes of utility functions. Five classes of utility functions are delineated, four of which were used to develop the figures in Chapter 3. The algebraic and geometric properties of each of the five classes of functions are developed in Section 4.4. The starting point in Section 4.4 is the utility function itself; indifference maps are developed from the utility functions. The chapter concludes in Section 4.5 with a view of the opposite side of the coin: Given preferences, can we find a functional representation of those preferences? That is, must a utility function exist for a given set of preferences?

Before beginning, it is worthwhile to know a bit more about the roadmap for the chapter and what you should "get" out of your first reading. The first time through, you should closely read Sections 4.1, 4.2, 4.3, and 4.5 and skim Section 4.4, which focuses on specific functional forms. We develop much of the economic intuition behind these functions using their graphical representation, but the central focus in Section 4.4 is on the algebra itself. Most students are less comfortable with algebraic analysis than geometric analysis, and as a result, this chapter will likely have less of an intuitive feel than Chapter 3. Consider attacking the chapter in multiple readings; become familiar with what is in the chapter so that you can come back to it for reference as necessary.

Many of the functions described in Section 4.4 are used throughout much of the text. It is not practical to expect you to commit all of the functional relations discussed in Section 4.4 to memory. A more reasonable goal, at least initially, is simply to understand how utility relates to preferences, indifference curves, marginal utility, and the marginal rate of substitution (MRS). It is also useful to know enough about the various functional forms that you can recognize the type of function with which you are dealing. A deeper understanding of this material will come as you begin to apply it to the consumer optimization problem in Chapter 6.

4.1 Representing What a Consumer Wants with Utility Functions

In Chapter 3, we restricted our analysis of preferences to two goods so that we could represent indifference curves using two-dimensional diagrams. Preferences were defined over bundles of goods (or shopping carts full of goods). If there are n distinct goods, then **A** and **B** can be thought of as ordered "n-tuples" $\mathbf{A} = (a_1, a_2, \ldots, a_n)$ and $\mathbf{B} = (b_1, b_2, \ldots, b_n)$, where for each $i = 1, \ldots, n$, $a_i \geq 0$ and $b_i \geq 0$. Put another way, **A** and **B** are contained in the nonnegative orthant (the nonnegative orthant is the n-dimensional analog of the two-dimensional concept of the first quadrant). We introduce utility functions in this more general context because it provides another rationale for **representing** preferences algebraically. Functions involving n variables are much easier to understand than are n-dimensional geometric representations of preferences. Once we provide the algebraic structure for utility functions in a general setting, we return to two-dimensional graphs and functions for the bulk of the chapter. A utility function, U, represents a given set of preferences, $\succ$, if the following holds for any two bundles **A** and **B**: If $\mathbf{A} \succ \mathbf{B}$, then $U(\mathbf{A}) > U(\mathbf{B})$, and if $U(\mathbf{A}) > U(\mathbf{B})$, then $\mathbf{A} \succ \mathbf{B}$. The shorthand way to say this is: U represents $\succ$ when $U(\mathbf{A}) > U(\mathbf{B})$ if and only if $\mathbf{A} \succ \mathbf{B}$. The utility function assigns higher *numbers* to bundles that are preferred to other less-preferred bundles. The **utility level** is the number that is assigned to a given bundle. The numbers representing utility levels are called *utils*.

representing: A utility function, U, represents a given set of preferences, $\succ$, if the following holds for any two bundles **A** and **B**: If $\mathbf{A} \succ \mathbf{B}$, then $U(\mathbf{A}) > U(\mathbf{B})$, and if $U(\mathbf{A}) > U(\mathbf{B})$, then $\mathbf{A} \succ \mathbf{B}$.

utility level: The utility level is the number that is assigned to a given bundle. The numbers representing utility levels are called *utils*.

In introductory microeconomics courses, utility and marginal utility are used to discuss consumer behavior. Typically, *utility* means the utility level "produced" by consuming a given amount of a single good, x, and *marginal utility* is the incremental change in utility from consuming a bit more of that good, Δx. Geometrically, marginal utility is the slope of the (univariate) utility function, $U(x)$. This version of utility and marginal utility can be seen in our multivariate context by considering utility strictly as a function of x and setting the amount of all other goods to zero. A different good y would be analyzed in a symmetric fashion by setting x (among other goods) equal to zero. This implicitly assumes that the different goods under consideration are independent of each other. We examine this assumption later in the chapter. Before jumping into the analysis of actual utility functions, we need a multivariate definition of marginal utility. The **marginal utility** of good *i* at bundle **A**, $MU_i(\mathbf{A})$, is calculated as: $MU_i(\mathbf{A}) = (U(\mathbf{A} + \Delta x_i) - U(\mathbf{A}))/\Delta x_i = \Delta U/\Delta x_i$ for small changes in good *i*, Δx_i. $\mathbf{A} + \Delta x_i = (a_1, \ldots, a_{i-1}, a_i + \Delta x_i, a_{i+1}, \ldots, a_n)$ is the bundle **A** with Δx_i more

marginal utility: The marginal utility of good *i* at bundle **A**, $MU_i(\mathbf{A})$, is calculated as: $MU_i(\mathbf{A}) = (U(\mathbf{A} + \Delta x_i) - U(\mathbf{A}))/\Delta x_i = \Delta U/\Delta x_i$ for small changes in good *i*, Δx_i.

good i (or less if $\Delta x_i < 0$). This is the slope of the utility function in the ith direction at point **A**, *ceteris paribus*.[1] This definition will seem less abstract once we see some examples.

4.2 Representing Perfect Substitutes with Utility Functions

Suppose you like n fruits. These fruits provide you with equal satisfaction, and you consider them perfect substitutes. If n = 2, the indifference map would be the same as Figure 3.5B (straight-line indifference curves with slope of –1). If n = 3, the indifference map would have indifference curves that are planes in three-dimensional space whose vertices are (C, 0, 0), (0, C, 0) and (0, 0, C), where C is the number of pieces of fruit. (Note that economists continue to use the word *curve*, despite it being wrong on two counts: It is a surface, rather than a curve, and it is not curved.) In actuality, it is not the entire plane: It is simply the triangular area of that plane in the nonnegative octant (a three-dimensional orthant). The indifference curve associated with 18 pieces of fruit is shown in Figure 4.1. Other indifference curves in the indifference map could be obtained by changing the number 18, but these indifference curves cannot be shown on the static graph because indifference curves associated with higher utility levels would obscure ones underneath. (The Excel file allows you to vary C. As you do, you can see what the indifference map looks like in a dynamic sense.) When n is greater than three, most people's geometric intuition begins to fail, but the indifference curve associated with having C pieces of fruit would be that part of an n – 1 dimensional hyperplane whose vertices are (C, 0, 0,. . ., 0), . . ., (0,. . ., 0, C, 0,. . ., 0), . . ., (0,. . ., 0, C) in the nonnegative orthant. (The difficulty in conceptualizing this is one of the reasons we typically restrict ourselves to two dimensions when we analyze preferences graphically.)

Interestingly, this is one situation when algebra is more intuitive than geometry! The utility function $U(\mathbf{X}) = U(x_1, \ldots, x_n) = x_1 + \ldots + x_n$ represents these preferences, and the indifference curve associated with C pieces of fruit is simply given by $U(x_1, \ldots, x_n) = C$. This utility function represents the preferences described earlier because $\mathbf{A} \succ \mathbf{B}$ if and only if $U(\mathbf{A}) > U(\mathbf{B})$ (that is to say, if shopping cart A has more pieces of fruit than shopping cart B). The utility level obtained from bundle **A** is simply the number of pieces of fruit in A's shopping cart, and the marginal utility of each of the n fruits is 1 (since adding

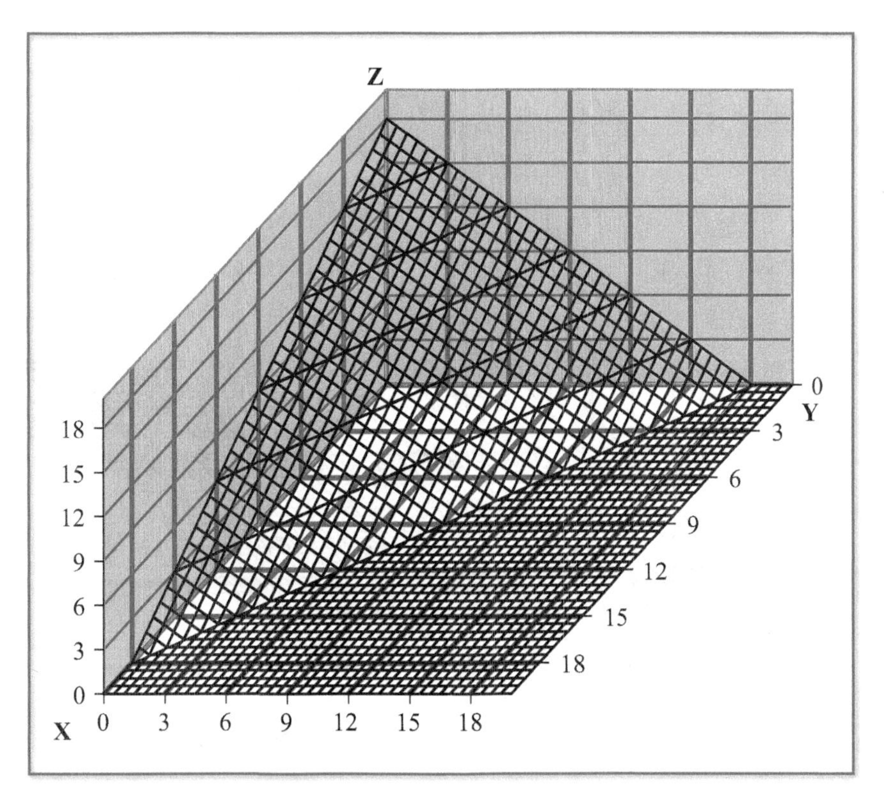

FIGURE 4.1 Graphing Perfect Substitutes

a bit more of fruit i, Δx_i, increases utility by $\Delta U = \Delta x_i$, so $MU_i = \Delta x_i/\Delta x_i = 1$ for each $i = 1, \ldots, n$).

We have just connected the algebraic concept of utility function to the geometric concept of indifference curve. Specifically:

> **Claim:** *If you have a utility function that represents a given set of preferences, you can obtain an indifference curve that represents those preferences by setting the utility function equal to a constant. Indifference maps are obtained by doing this more than once with different constants.*

We can obtain indifference curves easily from a utility function because, if you are indifferent between two bundles, they will have the same utility level. Different constants (utility levels) produce different indifference curves; therefore, we can easily create an indifference map from a utility function.

We saw in Chapter 3 that two goods can be perfect substitutes, even if the individual does not like the goods equally (such as in Figures 3.5A and 3.5C). To continue our fruit example, not all fruit are created equal; most individuals will not consider a 1:1 trade between a grape and a watermelon with indifference. Suppose Dave has dutifully been taught that he should eat fruit. He thinks in portions—grape-sized portions—and he simply likes portions of fruit. Consider three fruits to keep things manageable: grapes, kiwis, and plums. Dave is equally happy with two grapes or one kiwi. He is also equally happy with three grapes or one plum. His indifference "curve" associated with 18 grape-sized portions is the plane whose (G, K, P) vertices are (18, 0, 0), (0, 9, 0), and (0, 0, 6). This is shown in Figure 4.2. A utility function representing these preferences is $U^G(G, K, P) = G + 2K + 3P$, and the indifference curve (plane) in Figure 4.2 is described by setting this utility function equal to 18 ($U^G(G, K, P) = G + 2K + 3P = 18$). (The superscript G reminds us that this utility function measures "grape-sized" portions.)

The coefficient attached to each variable is the marginal utility of each fruit. That is: $MU^G_G = 1$; $MU^G_K = 2$; and $MU^G_P = 3$. (Kiwi's marginal utility is two because one kiwi is worth two grapes, and plum's marginal utility is three because one plum is worth three grapes.)

FIGURE 4.2 Fruit as Perfect Substitutes

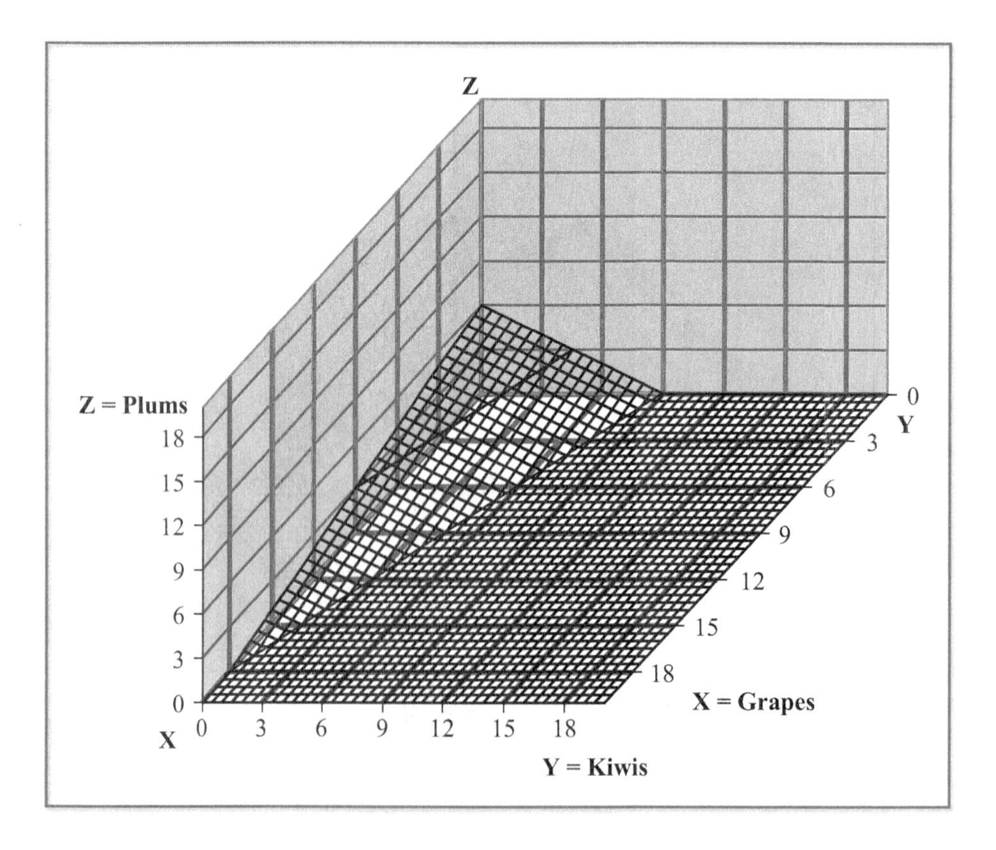

Marginal utility will, in general, be a function, rather than a constant. With perfect substitutes, marginal utility is a constant, regardless of how many units of each good the individual already consumes. Unfortunately, these marginal utilities are not unique because the utility function that represents a given set of preferences is not unique. To see why, return to Dave's fruit example. Consider the following function: $U^K(G, K, P) = 1/2G + K + 3/2P$. This describes the same preferences but measures utility in "kiwi-sized" portions, rather than "grape-sized" portions. If we set this function equal to 9, we end up with the *same* indifference curve as $U^G = 18$. And we could also represent the same indifference curve as $U^P(G, K, P) = 1/3G + 2/3K + P$ if we set $C = 6$.[2] This would describe the same indifference curve, using a utility function metered in "plum-sized" portions.

4.3 Utility Is an Ordinal Concept

The previous example demonstrated that, regardless of what portion size was used as our unit of measurement, each produced the same indifference curve. This results from the mathematical fact that if we multiply both sides of an inequality by the same positive number, then the inequality is maintained (if $x < y$, then $ax < ay$ for any $a > 0$; the number *a* must be positive because the inequality reverses if you multiply both sides by a negative number). The same rule works for equalities (if $x = y$, then $ax = ay$ for any value of a). For example, start with $U^G(G, K, P) = G + 2K + 3P = 18$. Multiply both sides by 1/2 and you obtain $U^K = 1/2G + K + 3/2P = 9$; multiply both sides by 1/3, and you obtain $U^P = 1/3G + 2/3K + P = 6$. The number attached to the utility level is not as important as the relative importance of grapes, kiwis, and plums, and that relation is not affected by such transformations. Indeed, these are simply examples of the following generalization:

> **Claim:** *If you have a utility function that represents a set of preferences as defined earlier, then* any *monotonic transformation of that utility function represents the same set of preferences. A* **monotonic transformation** *is a function, f(x), that preserves order. A function preserves order if whenever $x < y$, then $f(x) < f(y)$.*

monotonic transformation: A monotonic transformation is a function, f(x), that preserves order. A function preserves order if whenever $x < y$, then $f(x) < f(y)$.

There are various ways to check that a function is monotonic. A function is monotonic if $f(x) - f(y)$ has the same sign as $x - y$. A geometric way of saying the same thing is that if f(x) is upward sloping, it is a monotonic transformation.[3] It is helpful to have some examples:

$f(x) = 1/2x$ is monotonic because if $x < y$ then $1/2x < 1/2y$.

$g(x) = 1/2x + a$ is monotonic for any value of a because we can add a constant to both sides of an inequality without changing the inequality.

$h(x) = ax + b$ is monotonic if $a > 0$. If $a < 0$, this is not order preserving because it is a downward-sloping line.

$k(x) = (x - a)^2$ is monotonic for $x \geq a$. If $x < a$, the function is not monotonic. A geometric proof is obtained by recalling that this is the equation for a parabola, which attains a minimum at $x = a$. One can see this algebraically by noting that if $x = a - 1$ and $y = a + 1$, then $x < y$ but $k(x) = k(y) = 1$ (but monotonicity would require $k(x) < k(y)$).

$m(x) = \ln(x)$, where $\ln(x)$ denotes the natural logarithm of x, is monotonic for $x > 0$. The logarithm function is not defined for $x \leq 0$.

$r(x) = x^r$ is monotonic for $r > 0$ and $x \geq 0$.

$s(x) = e^x$ is a monotonic transformation for all x. ($e = 2.718 \ldots$ is the base for natural logarithms.)

Since there is an infinite number of monotonic transformations, there is an infinite number of utility functions that represent the same preferences. Sometimes, economists say that utility functions are "constant up to a monotonic transformation."

The three utility functions U^G, U^K, and U^P all had intuitive appeal, but intuitive appeal is not necessary to represent preferences. After all, utility functions are *artificial* constructs that are used to depict or represent the actual pairwise comparison that defines preferences. We should not expect to be able to plug individuals into utility meters that measure utility levels whenever bundles of goods are placed in front of them. We should expect that the individual will be able to tell us which of two bundles that individual prefers. Therefore, the functions $(U^G)^2$ and $(U^G)^{1/2}$ represent the same preferences as U^G, U^K, and U^P, even though the former have little intuitive appeal.

The important point about utility is that the numbers attached to the indifference curves are not important in defining preferences; the shape of the indifference curves matters, and monotonic transformations have no effect on the shape of indifference curves. All that a monotonic transformation does is to change the utility level associated with that indifference curve. Another way that economists say this is that utility is an **ordinal**, rather than a **cardinal**, concept.

ordinal: A relationship between two distinct numbers is ordinal if the ordering matters. Ordering means which is larger or which is smaller of the two numbers.

cardinal: A relationship between two distinct numbers is cardinal if the magnitude of the difference matters.

Ordinality is concerned with relative size; cardinality is concerned with absolute size. If a utility function provides utility levels of U(**A**) = 100 and U(**B**) = 121, then **B** ≻ **A**, but it is inappropriate to conclude that **B** is 21% better than **A**.[4] The fact that U(**B**) > U(**A**) (the individual is happier with **B** than **A**) is all that matters. How much happier is irrelevant (and unknowable—you would never say, "I'm 21% happier today than yesterday," for example). We could just as easily have taken the square root of U(**A**) and U(**B**). The resulting numbers, 10 and 11, provide the same ordinal information: **B** is still preferred to **A**.

This ambiguity about marginal utility does not filter through to ambiguity about marginal rates of substitution. Before we see why, we have to consider the marginal rate of substitution when we have more than two goods, since it is unclear which is the horizontal axis and which is the vertical axis in this instance. (With the three dimensions pictured, Z is the vertical axis, but we also should be able to talk about the marginal rate of substitution between goods x and y.) It is useful to recall that $MRS_{y,x} = -\Delta y/\Delta x$ along the indifference curve. The MRS is (minus) the slope of the indifference curve. More generally, if we have n goods, then for any two goods i and j the marginal rate of substitution of good j for good i, $MRS_{j,i} = -\Delta x_j/\Delta x_i$, holding all other goods constant along the indifference curve. The $\mathbf{MRS_{j,i}}$, is the rate at which the individual would be willing to exchange good j for good i, *ceteris paribus*. This is just (minus) the slope of the indifference curve in the (x_i, x_j) direction, *ceteris paribus*. In the fruit example: $MRS_{y,x} = MRS_{k,g} = -\Delta k/\Delta g = 1/2$, since you would be willing to give up half of a kiwi for a grape, holding plums constant; $MRS_{z,y} = MRS_{p,k} = -\Delta p/\Delta k = 2/3$, since you would be willing to give up two-thirds of a plum for a kiwi, holding grapes constant; and $MRS_{z,x} = MRS_{p,g} = -\Delta p/\Delta g = 1/3$, since you would be willing to give up one-third of a plum for a grape, holding kiwis constant. Each of these trade-off ratios can be seen in Figure 4.2 as the slopes of the plane when it cuts the (g, k), (k, p), and (p, g) planes. Each of these planes holds the third good constant (at zero in our visual heuristic from Figure 4.2).

$MRS_{j,i}$: $MRS_{j,i} = -\Delta x_j/\Delta x_i$, holding all other goods constant along the indifference curve.

Monotonic changes in the utility function did not change the indifference curve representing a given set of preferences. Therefore, the slopes of the indifference curve in different directions did not change as we changed utility functions. Since MRSs are just (minus) slopes, they did not change either. This is the geometric reason MRSs are not dependent on the specific utility function used to represent a given set of preferences. It is useful to see a second reason why MRSs are not dependent on the specific utility function that represents a given set of preferences because it provides us with an easy method for calculating the MRS if we know the utility function (or more specifically, if we know marginal utilities).

The slope of the indifference curve is $\Delta y/\Delta x$ along the curve, and this is equal to (minus) the ratio of marginal utilities of x and y. Specifically:

> **Claim:** *MRS = $-\Delta y/\Delta x$ along the indifference curve = MU_x/MU_y. This ratio does not depend on the specific function chosen to represent a given set of preferences.*

Chapter 4 Appendix A provides proofs of both assertions. The MRS is the ratio of marginal utilities with the good on the horizontal axis in the numerator and the good on the vertical axis in the denominator (the opposite of slope). More generally, if we have more goods, the marginal rate of substitution of good j for good i is $MRS_{j,i} = -\Delta x_j/\Delta x_i = MU_i/MU_j$

(holding all other goods constant along the indifference curve). As shown in the earlier example, although marginal utility changes as utility changes, the ratio of marginal utilities does not change. That is, the MRS does not depend on the utility function chosen to represent preferences.

4.4 Some Common Utility Functions and Their Algebraic and Geometric Properties

Utility functions representing n perfect substitutes were introduced earlier, but we restricted our geometric representation of perfect substitute indifference curves to three dimensions in Figures 4.1 and 4.2. We used three dimensions in that instance because the planes were easy to visualize. For other types of preferences, we further restrict the analysis to two goods, even though it is possible, in general, to define utility functions over n goods.

For each utility function, it is useful to describe both the marginal utility functions and the MRS. Marginal utilities can be obtained via algebraic manipulation for perfect substitutes, perfect complements, and the first version of both Cobb-Douglas and shifted Cobb-Douglas preferences. The other marginal utilities require calculus. Of course, as we have already shown, once we know MU_x and MU_y, we know the MRS (since it is just the ratio of marginal utilities). Table 4.1 provides utility functions, marginal utilities, and MRSs for five classes of preferences: perfect substitutes, perfect complements, Cobb-Douglas, shifted Cobb-Douglas, and quasilinear. The first four were used in Chapter 3 (albeit the last two were not labeled as such).

Table 4.1 provides multiple functions for each class of preferences, with the final function being the most general form. Do not be put off by the amount of material in Table 4.1; it is provided in tabular form so that you will have a readily available point of reference when you work with utility functions. *You are not expected to be able to digest (or understand) Table 4.1 at this point.* The information in the table will be developed over the next few subsections devoted to each class of preferences.

Perfect Substitutes

As we have already examined perfect substitutes in Section 4.2, we can quickly describe the general form for perfect substitutes:

Utility function	$MU_x(x, y)$	$MU_y(x, y)$	MRS	**(4.1)**
$U(x, y) = ax + by$	a	b	a/b	

The two panels in Figure 4.3 are based on two perfect substitute utility functions. In Figure 4.3A, a = 2 and b = 3; in Figure 4.3B, a = 6 and b = 9, using Equation 4.1. Both panels have MRS = 2/3 (the same as the plum:kiwi substitution ratio, $MRS_{z,y} = MRS_{p,k}$, in Figure 4.2). In both panels, the ratios of marginal utilities are 2/3, but the magnitudes (absolute sizes) of marginal utilities in Figure 4.3B are three times Figure 4.3A's magnitudes. Throughout this section, the green horizontal line segment represents MU_x, and the blue vertical line segment represents MU_y. The lavender diagonal represents MU_x in relation to MU_y and is geometrically constructed by adding both marginal utilities together. We call this diagonal the **MU vector** and denote it as (MU_x, MU_y), since it involves a move of MU_x in the x direction and a move of MU_y in the y direction.[5]

MU vector: The MU vector, (MU_x, MU_y), points in the direction of the maximum rate of change in utility, and the size of the vector represents how quickly this change occurs.

In both panels, the MU vector has a slope of 3/2, signifying that y is 1.5 times as valuable as x to this individual. In Figure 4.3B, however, the magnitudes of MU_x, MU_y, and the MU vector, (MU_x, MU_y) are three times as large because marginal utilities are multiplied by three; utility changes three times faster in Figure 4.3B than in Figure 4.3A. In Figures 4.3A and 4.3B, this slope is –2/3. For smooth curves, the direction of no rate of change is always the furthest away from the direction of maximal change. The MU vector points in the direction of maximal increase in utility. Its opposite, $(-MU_x, -MU_y)$, points in the direction of maximal decrease in utility. The direction of no change is perpendicular to these opposing directions, and the direction of no change is a local description of the

TABLE 4.1 Common Utility Functions

Preference Type	Utility Functions*	$MU_x(x, y)$	$MU_y(x, y)$	MRS
Perfect Substitutes	$U(x, y) = ax + by$	a	b	a/b
Perfect Complements	$U(x, y) = \text{Minimum}(dx, y)$	d if $x < y/d$; 0 if $x \geq y/d$	0 if $y \geq dx$; 1 if $y < dx$	∞ if $x < y/d$; 0 if $x > y/d$; indeterminate when $x = y/d$
	$U(x, y) = \text{Minimum}(x, y/d)$	1 if $x < y/d$; 0 if $x \geq y/d$	0 if $y \geq dx$; $1/d$ if $y < dx$	
	$U(x, y) = \text{Minimum}(ax, by)$	a if $x < by/a$; 0 if $x \geq by/a$	0 if $y \geq ax/b$; b if $y < ax/b$	∞ if $x < by/a$; 0 if $x > by/a$; indeterminate when $x = by/a$
Cobb-Douglas	$U(x, y) = xy$	y	x	y/x
	$U(x, y) = a(xy)^b$	$abx^{(b-1)}y^b$	$abx^by^{(b-1)}$	
	$U(x, y) = x^ry^{(1-r)}$	$r(x/y)^{(r-1)}$	$(1 - r)(x/y)^r$	$(r/(1 - r))(y/x) = (ry)/((1 - r)x)$
	$U(x, y) = ax^cy^d$	$acx^{(c-1)}y^d$	$adx^cy^{(d-1)}$	$(c/d)(y/x) = (cy)/(dx)$
Shifted Cobb-Douglas (defined for $x > a$ and $y > b$); a and b may be postive or negative	$U(x, y) = (x - a)(y - b)$	$y - b$	$x - a$	$(y - b)/(x - a)$
	$U(x, y) = (x - a)^r(y - b)^{(1-r)}$ (for $0 < r < 1$)	$r((y - b)/(x - a))^{(1-r)}$	$(1 - r)((x - a)/(y - b))^r$	$(r/(1 - r))((y - b)/(x - a)) = (r(y - b))/((1 - r)(x - a))$
	$U(x, y) = (x - a)^c(y - b)^d$	$c(x - a)^{(c-1)}(y - b)^d$	$d(x - a)^c(y - b)^{d-1}$	$(c/d)(y - b)/(x - a) = (c(y - b))/(d(x - a))$
Quasilinear	$U(x, y) = ax^r + y$	$arx^{(r-1)}$	1	$arx^{(r-1)}$
	$U(x, y) = a \cdot \ln(x) + y$	a/x	1	a/x
	General quasilinear:† $U(x, y) = f(x) + y$	df/dx	1	df/dx

*a, b, c, and d are positive unless otherwise stated; r is restricted to the range $0 < r < 1$; $x \geq 0$ and $y \geq 0$.

†The general form requires calculus to derive MU_x.

indifference curve (since there is no change in utility along an indifference curve). The MU vector therefore is useful in describing indifference curves:

Claim: *The MU vector is always perpendicular to the indifference curve.*

The *only* difference between the indifference curves in the two panels is the utility level attached to the curves (90 versus 270). This difference is easy to explain, since the utility function in Figure 4.3B is the utility function in Figure 4.3A multiplied by three. This is simply another example of our previous assertion: Two utility functions that only differ by a monotonic transformation represent the same preferences.[6]

Perfect Complements

In Chapter 3, we saw that perfect complements have L-shaped indifference curves. If the vertex of the perfect complements indifference curve has d units of y associated with 1 unit of x, then there are two natural ways to describe this information: The ratio of y:x is d:1, or the ratio is 1:1/d. Put another way, the line describing the set of vertices in this

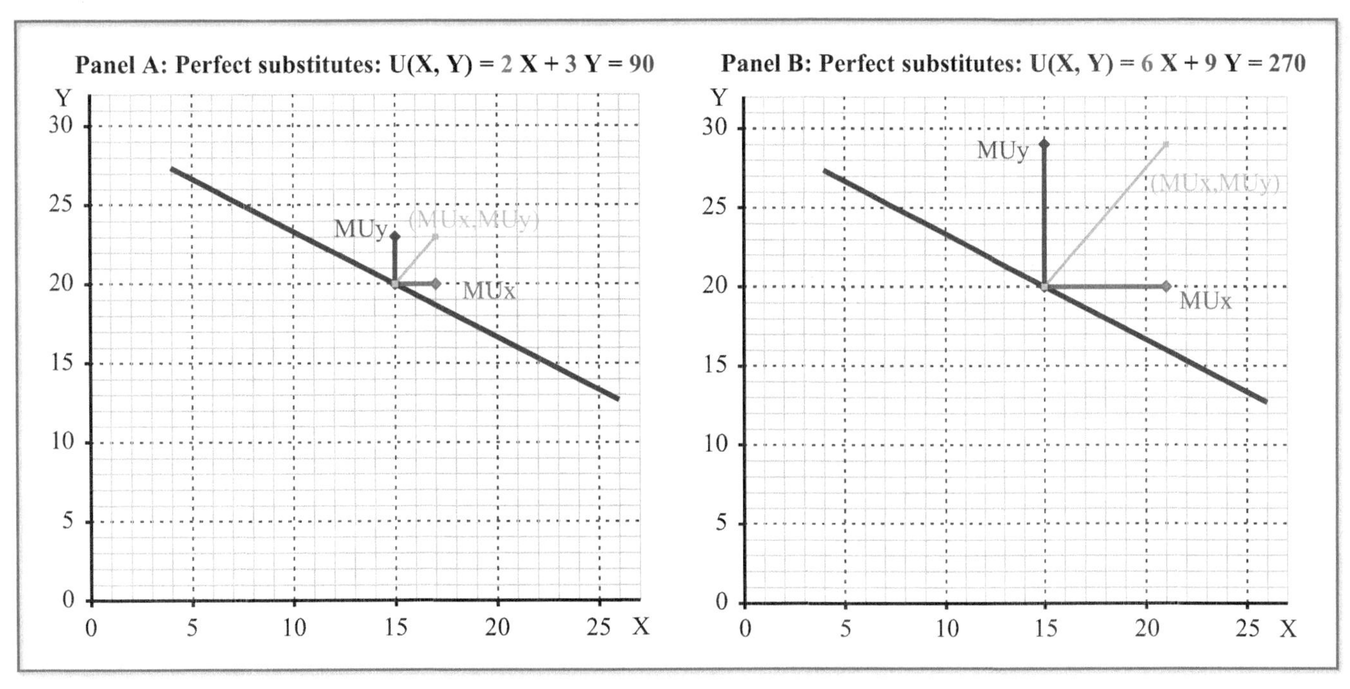

FIGURE 4.3 Two Perfect Substitute Utility Functions

instance is $y = dx$. This forms the basis for the top two perfect complement utility functions described in Table 4.1 and for Figure 3.6.

Utility function	$MU_x(x, y)$	$MU_y(x, y)$	MRS	
$V(x, y) = \text{Minimum}(dx, y)$	d if $x < y/d$;	0 if $y \geq dx$;	∞ if $x < y/d$;	**(4.2a)**
	0 if $x \geq y/d$	1 if $y < dx$	0 if $x > y/d$;	
$U(x, y) = \text{Minimum}(x, y/d)$	1 if $x < y/d$;	0 if $y \geq dx$;	indeterminate	**(4.2b)**
	0 if $x \geq y/d$	$1/d$ if $y < dx$	when $x = y/d$.	

Both equations are provided because neither conforms to most people's intuition. The way to prove that both are correct is to put an actual number in for d (like $d = 1/2$ in Figure 4.4) and choose some points on an indifference curve. For example, choose the indifference curve whose vertex is at the point (10, 5). From here, verify that the bundles (10, 6) and (11, 5) satisfy both Equations 4.2b: $U(x, y) = \text{Minimum}(x, y/d) = U_o$; and 4.2a: $V(x, y) = \text{Minimum}(dx, y) = V_o$, for utility levels U_o or V_o.

Q4. What are the U and V utility levels that are attached to the indifference curve whose vertex is at (10, 5)?*

The map in Figure 4.4 shows indifference curves that are closer together below the red diagonal line $y = x/2$ than above that line. This signifies a steeper increase in utility below the diagonal than above the diagonal. (Those who have gone for hikes and have used topographic maps will recognize that tighter topographic lines meant steeper inclines. The same is true here; the utility incline is steeper if indifference curves are closer together.) This can also be seen in the relative sizes of marginal utilities, a topic to which we now turn.

Each panel in Figure 4.5 focuses on one indifference curve based on Equation 4.2b, $U(x, y) = \text{Minimum}(x, y/d) = 10$ (though the indifference curve could just as easily

***Q4 answer:** The U utility level of this indifference curve is $U_o = 10$, since U utility is equal to the x coordinate of the vertex point. The V utility level is $V_o = 5$ for the same curve, since V utility is the y coordinate of the vertex point.

FIGURE 4.4 Perfect Complements

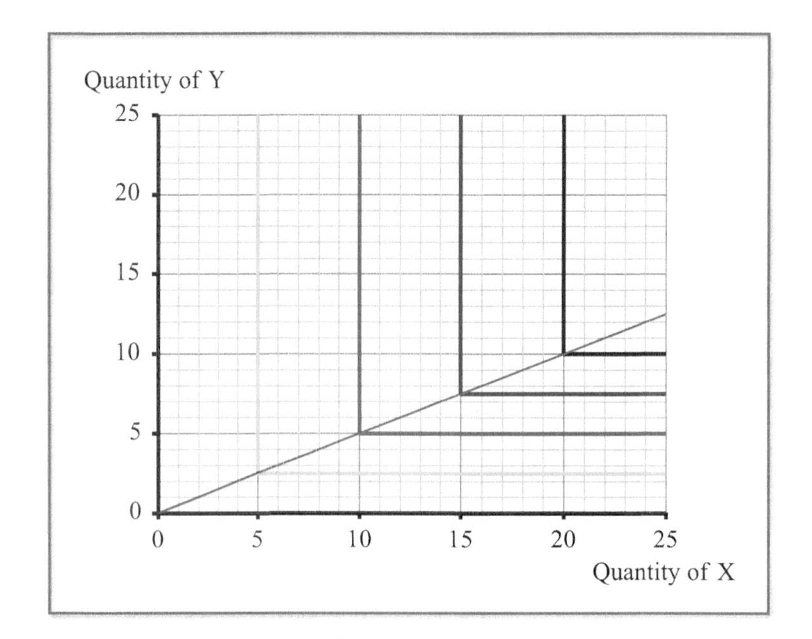

have been obtained from Equation 4.2a as V(x, y) = Minimum(dx, y) = 10d). The gold lines connecting vertices of the L-shaped indifference curves cut the first quadrant into two parts. Above and to the left of the line are bundles where x < y/d (or y > dx). The "constraining" good is x in the sense that U(x, y) = Minimum(x, y/d) = x (or V(x, y) = Minimum(dx, y) = dx). If you increase x, in this instance, utility will rise, while on the other hand, if you increase y, utility will not change. For these bundles, an increase in x increases utility by 1 util of U utility per x, $MU_x = 1$ (and by d utils of V utility per x), while an increase in y has no effect on either utility level, $MU_y = 0$.

The lavender MU vector on the vertical part of the indifference curve in Figure 4.5 depicts this situation. Below and to the right of the gold line, the reverse holds true; y is the "constraining" good, and an increase in x has no effect on utility, $MU_x = 0$, but an increase in y increases utility by 1/d utils of U utility per y, $MU_y = 1/d$ (and by 1 util of V utility per y). The lavender MU vector on the horizontal part of the indifference curve depicts this situation. Along the line y = dx, *both* x and y are constraining, but neither *remain* constraining if they alone increase. Consider x, for example. An increase in x

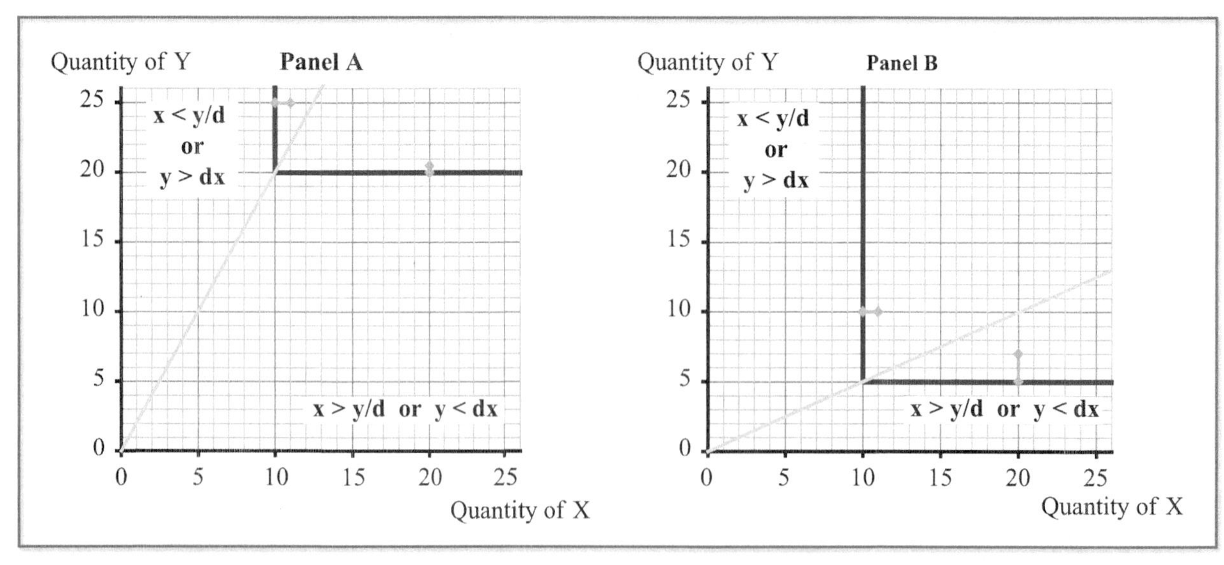

FIGURE 4.5 Marginal Utility on Two Perfect Complement Indifference Curves, U(x, y) = Minimum (x, y/d) = 10

has no effect on utility because y becomes the only constraining factor in this instance (therefore $MU_x = 0$). The reverse holds true for an increase in y. As a result, both marginal utilities are zero for these bundles. These results are summarized as the marginal utilities listed in Table 4.1 and Equation 4.2b. The panels relate to two distinct values of d: d = 1/2, and d = 2.

Q5. Which panel in Figure 4.5 is associated with d = 1/2?*

The relative sizes of MU_x and MU_y in each panel verify which part of the indifference map is steepest. When MU_x is higher than MU_y (as in Figure 4.5A), the next higher indifference curve will be closer in the x direction than in the y direction. If you were to include other indifference curves to create an indifference map for this panel, the vertical segments of the indifference curves would be closer than the horizontal segments (since an increase in x increases utility by more than an increase in y when $MU_x > MU_y$). Conversely, in Figure 4.5B, the indifference map would have closer horizontal segments than vertical segments because $MU_x < MU_y$ (as you can easily verify by looking back at Figure 4.4). The relative size of marginal utilities provides information about where indifference curves will be closer together and where they will be farther apart.

It is worthwhile to consider the MRS for perfect complements. The slopes along the horizontal and vertical segments are clear, but what is the slope at the vertex of an L-shaped indifference curve? There is no unique answer to this question. Recall that slope at a point is defined as the tangent to that point. Unfortunately, there is no tangent to this curve, since this curve is not "smooth."[7] Figure 4.6 graphically depicts this point. The thin pink line in each panel is "tangent" to the curve at the vertex. In Figure 4.6A, the slope is infinite (and the line coincides with the vertical portion of the indifference curve). In Figure 4.6C, the slope is zero (and the line coincides with the horizontal portion of the indifference curve). One solution between these two boundary values is shown in Figure 4.6B, but any slope, m, from $-\infty \leq m \leq 0$ would have worked just as well. The MRS is not well defined at the vertex of L-shaped perfect complement indifference curves.

Cobb-Douglas

We now turn to the workhorse of microeconomic analysis, the Cobb-Douglas (CD) utility function. This function will be revisited on the production side as the Cobb-Douglas production function in Chapter 9. Two versions are described: the equal-weighted version and the general version. As this function is used so heavily for microeconomic analysis, each has its own subsection. Since each CD function involves multiplying x to a power times y to a power, both x and y must be positive if the utility level is positive. In other words, CD indifference curves do not touch either axis (unless U = 0).

Equal-Weighted Cobb-Douglas

The first two CD utility functions in Table 4.1 represent equal-weighted Cobb-Douglas preferences. The first is the simplest CD of all: $U(x, y) = xy$; the second $U(x, y) = a(xy)^b$ looks substantially more complex. Although these functions look quite different, they represent the *same* preferences as long as $a > 0$ and $b > 0$.[8] (The first can be obtained from the second when a = 1 and b = 1. We only reproduce the information on the more general version here.)

Utility function	$MU_x(x, y)$	$MU_y(x, y)$	MRS	
$U(x, y) = a(xy)^b$	$abx^{(b-1)}y^b$	$abx^by^{(b-1)}$	y/x	**(4.3)**

*__Q5 answer:__ Figure 4.5B is associated with d = 1/2. This is seen two ways. First, the gold line y = dx in Figure 4.5A is y = 2x, while in Figure 4.5B, it is y = x/2. Second, the lavender MU vector on the horizontal part of the indifference curve is $(0, MU_y)$. This vector is 1/2 unit long in Figure 4.5A but 2 units long in Figure 4.5B. As noted in Equation 4.2b, $MU_y = 1/d$ when $y < dx$. Both reasons suggest d = 2 in Figure 4.5A and d = 1/2 in Figure 4.5B. The Excel file for Figure 4.5 allows you to vary d between 1/2 and 2.

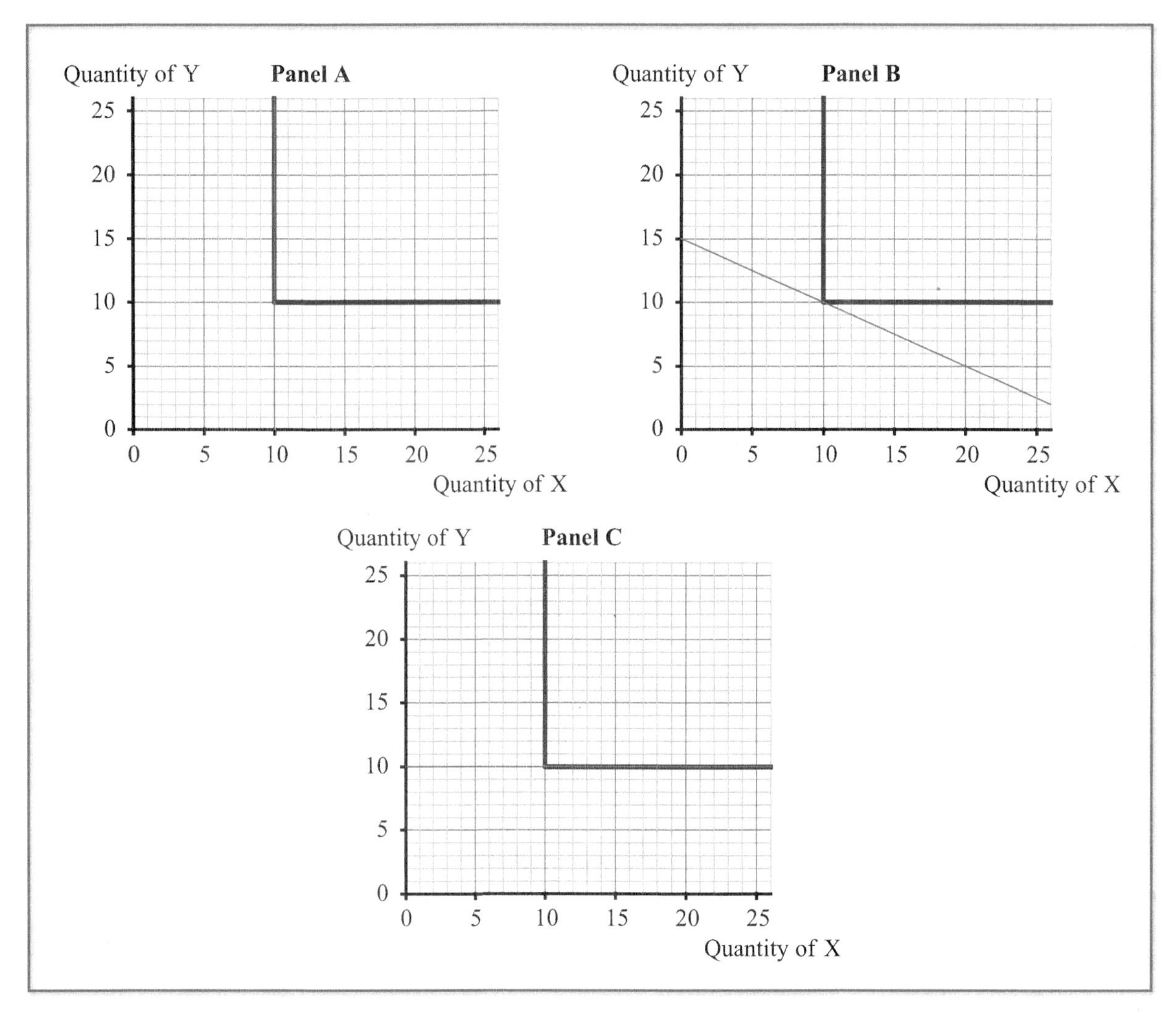

FIGURE 4.6 There Is No MRS at the Vertex of a Perfect Complement Indifference Curve, U(x, y) = Minimum (x, y/d) = 10

Preferences where MRS = y/x formed the basis for the Edgeworth Box barter analysis in Section 3.5, where it was introduced as Assumption 2. Put another way, Annie and Bob had equal-weighted Cobb-Douglas preferences over gummi bears and chocolates (although we did not call them CD preferences at that time).

Geometrically, indifference curves for equal-weighted CD preferences are rectangular hyperbolas whose asymptotes are the horizontal and vertical axes, as shown in Figure 4.7. Since monotonic transformations do not change preferences, the indifference map is the same, regardless of which equal-weighted CD utility function is chosen. The only difference is the utility level attached to each indifference curve. The indifference curves in Figure 4.7 go through the (x, y) bundles with x = y = 4, 5, 6, 7, and 8.

Q7. Fill in the table next to Figure 4.7 for two specific utility functions:

U(x, y) = xy and U(x, y) = $a(xy)^b$, where a = 1 and b = 0.5.*

***Q7 answer:** From lowest to highest indifference curve, the utility levels are 16, 25, 36, 49, and 64 for U(x, y) = xy and 4, 5, 6, 7, and 8 for U(x, y) = $(xy)^{0.5}$. Both results are easy to see, once you think about the functions a bit. The indifference curves go through (x, y) bundles with x = y = n for n = 4, 5, 6, 7, and 8, so U(x, y) = xy utility should be a perfect square of those values, and U(x, y) = $(xy)^{0.5}$ values should match the x = y point on the indifference curve (since $x = (x^2)^{0.5}$). The Excel file for Figure 4.7 allows you to view utility levels of these indifference curves for other equal-weighted CD utility functions by varying a and b in the range $0.5 \le a \le 2.0$ and $0.5 \le b \le 2.0$.

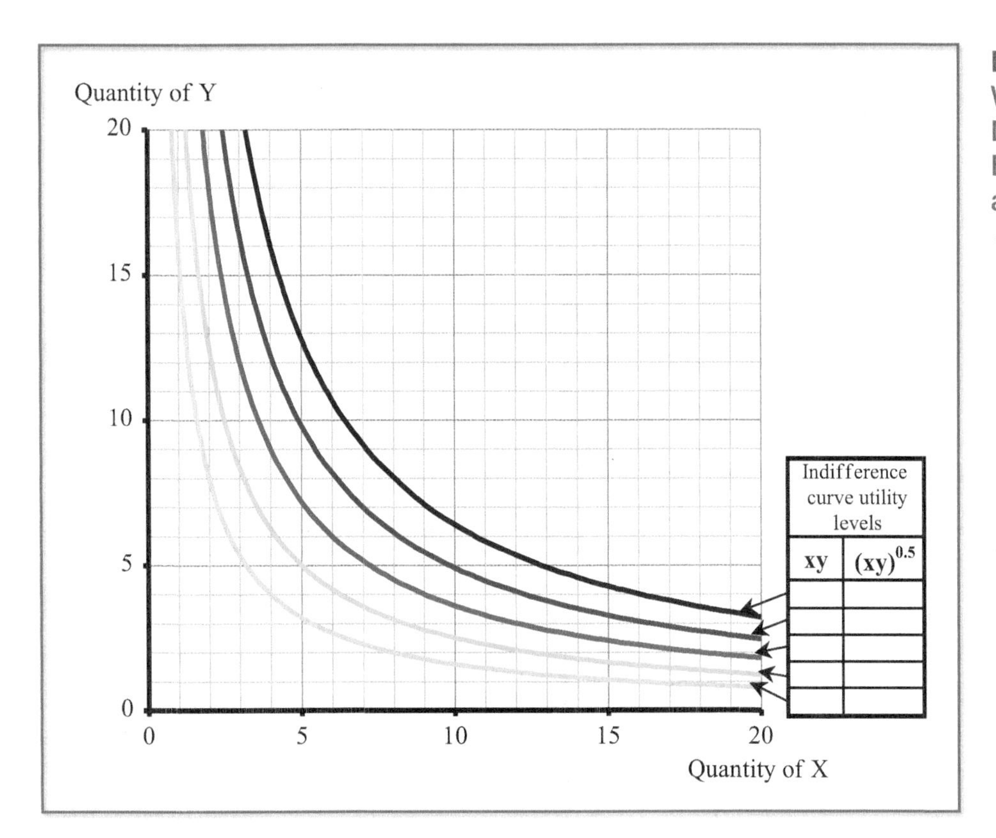

FIGURE 4.7 Equal-Weighted Cobb Douglas Preferences, Based on $U(x, y) = xy$ and $U(x, y) = (xy)^{0.5}$

Figure 4.8 examines the slope of the equal-weighted CD function in more detail.[9] A variety of comparisons may be made with these panels. As discussed earlier, a monotonic transformation of a known utility function that represents a set of preferences changes *only* the utility levels and marginal utilities associated with different bundles. It does not change the indifference map, the MRS, or preferences implicit between those bundles. The final panel is a monotonic transformation of the others; Figures 4.8A–4.8E are based on the simplest form of this function, $U(x, y) = xy$, and Figure 4.8F is based on $U(x, y) = 1/2(xy)^2$.

We focus the bulk of our attention on $U(x, y) = xy$. With this simple form, $MU_x = y$, and $MU_y = x$. MU_x is the horizontal green line segment, and MU_y is the vertical blue line segment. The lavender MU vector combines MU_x and MU_y. It points in the direction of maximum rate of change in utility, and the size of the diagonal represents how quickly this change occurs. Figures 4.8A–4.8C focus on the size of this diagonal as we move along the specific indifference curve $U(x, y) = xy = 25$. This indifference curve is the same as the second lowest indifference curve in Figure 4.7. Note that in Figure 4.7, the indifference curves appear to get closer together the further you stray from the bundle $x = y$ on the indifference curve. Figures 4.8A and 4.8C both have equally sized diagonals (that are simply pointed in different directions), and both of these diagonals are longer than the one depicted in Figure 4.8B. (In fact, Figure 4.8B presents the smallest rate of increase in utility of any point on the indifference curve.)[10] This is another way of saying that equal-weighted CD indifference curves are furthest "apart" along the $x = y$ diagonal.[11]

Figures 4.8A and 4.8D–4.8F have MRS = 4. This is because each of the (x, y) bundles focused on in those panels had $y = 4x$, and the MRS for an equal-weighted CD is y/x. The magnitude of the lavender vector varies in each panel, but each is pointed in the same direction (each vector has a slope of $+1/4$ because MU_x is four times as large as MU_y in each instance). The Excel file for Figure 4.8 allows you to vary a, b, and C over a range of values. As you vary a and b with C fixed, you will see that utility level and marginal utilities change. As long as you do not move the location of the "x slider," however, the MRS will remain fixed, as will the indifference curve (since the indifference curve is defined using C, where $U(x, y) = a(xy)^b = aC^b$; C represents x times y). If you vary C, then the

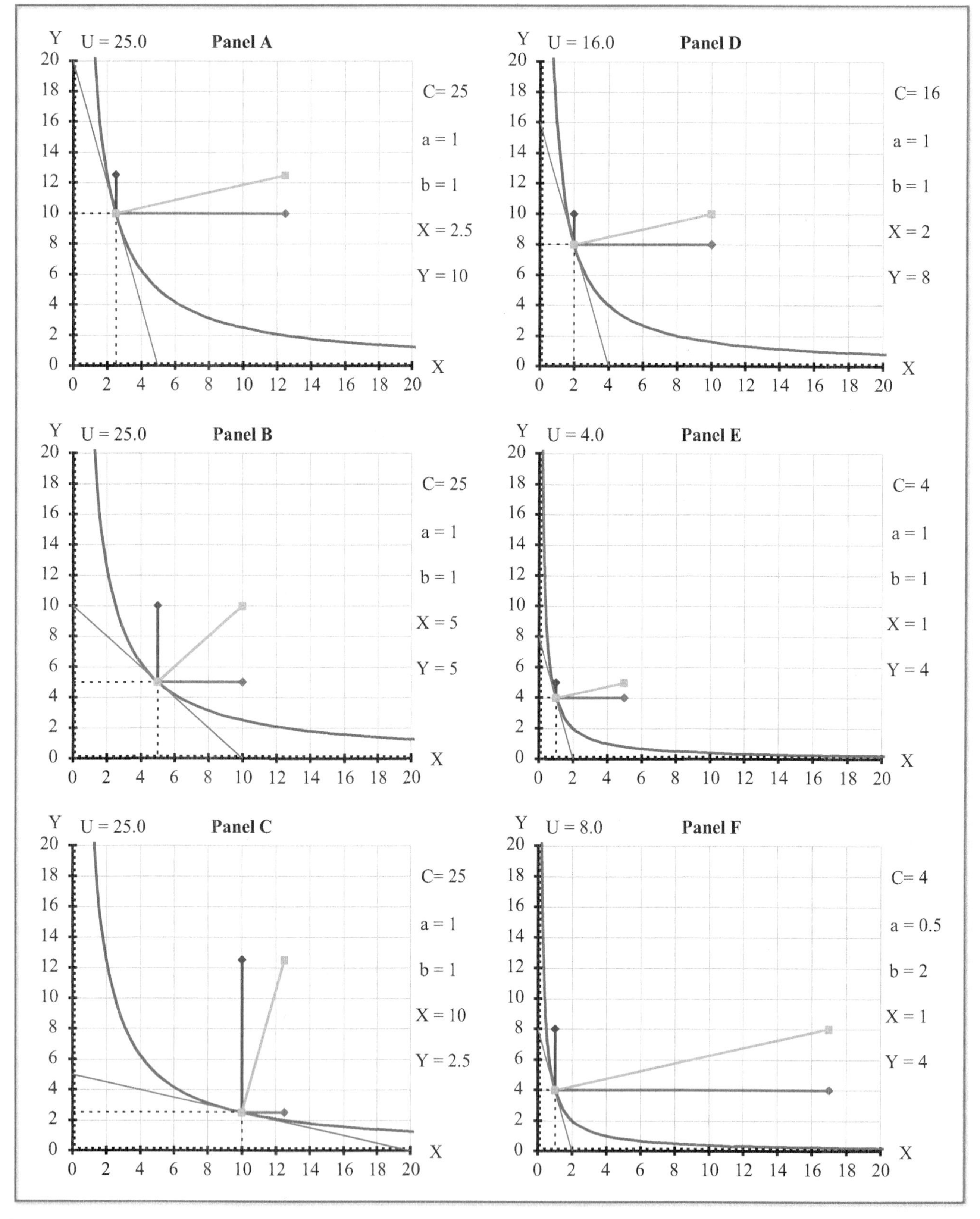

FIGURE 4.8 The Equal-Weighted Cobb-Douglas Utility Function, $U(X,Y) = aX^bY^b = a(XY)^b = aC^b$

indifference curve will change as well, but still the MRS remains fixed. Indeed, the MRS is fixed on any ray through the origin, a point that is easy to show if you move the x slider to a different location and then vary C.

The indifference curve in Figure 4.8F is identical to Figure 4.8E, despite different utility levels in those panels. Utility levels are different because the functional representations of preferences are different. $U(x, y) = xy = 4$ in Figure 4.8E, and $U(x, y) = 1/2(xy)^2 = 8$ in Figure 4.8F. Both utility levels represent the same indifference curve. Due to the function chosen in Figure 4.8F, both marginal utilities are four times as large as in Figure 4.8E. (Verify that the marginal utilities obtained from $U(x, y) = 1/2(xy)^2$ at (1, 4) are four times the marginal utilities obtained from $U(x, y) = xy$ at (1, 4), using the marginal utility information in Equation 4.3.) The parameters a and b in Equation 4.3 affect the utility level and marginal utilities associated with an indifference curve. Despite different utility levels and marginal utilities, both functions have identical indifference maps because the ratio of marginal utilities is not affected by monotonic transformation. In the context of Figures 4.8E and 4.8F, both have MRS = 4. If you vary x along both curves, the same holds true for other bundles as well: The curves are identical; only the numbers of utils associated with each panel varies because the functional representation of those curves varies between panels.

General Cobb-Douglas

There are two versions of the general form Cobb-Douglas (CD) utility function: $U(x, y) = x^r y^{(1-r)}$ and $U(x, y) = ax^c y^d$. These functions are not the same: The first is more restrictive than the second. (In the first, a = 1, and c + d = 1; in the second, the scaling factor a and the sum of the exponents c + d need not equal 1.) Despite this difference, they do represent the same preferences. If we start with the second, we can get to the first by dividing both sides by a and raising both sides to the power $1/(c + d)$. This is a monotonic transformation.[12] The only difference between the indifference maps for these two utility functions is the utility level attached to each indifference curve and marginal utilities at points on the curve. There is no difference in terms of the curve itself, or the MRSs at a given bundle. As a result, we restrict our analysis to the first function because it has greater intuitive appeal.

Utility function	$MU_x(x, y)$	$MU_y(x, y)$	MRS	
$U(x, y) = x^r y^{(1-r)}$	$r(x/y)^{(r-1)}$	$(1 - r)(x/y)^r$	$(r/(1 - r))(y/x)$	**(4.4)**

The only parameter in this utility function is r, the exponent attached to good x. As we vary r, we obtain different preferences. Of course, we have already seen the preferences associated with one value of r, since r = 0.5 brings us back an equal-weighted CD function (recall that the square root function is a monotonic transformation).

Figure 4.9 depicts indifference maps for three values of r shown in two ways.

Q9a. What are the utility levels associated with the five indifference curves in each panel? *Hint:* Look at bundles where x = y on the indifference curves.*

Focus initially on Figures 4.9A–4.9C. Each of these panels shows both the preference map and a gold ray through the origin associated with those bundles where MRS = 1. These are the bundles where the consumer is willing to trade x for y at a 1:1 rate.

Q9b. What is an equation for the ray associated with MRS = 1?†

As r increases, the MRS = 1 ray declines. Put another way, bundles where the individual is willing to trade x for y at a 1:1 rate become more x-intensive as r increases. (Indeed, we will have more to say on this topic once we examine optimization in Chapter 6.)

***Q9a answer:** Regardless of panel, the indifference curves go through the points (4, 4), (5, 5), (6, 6), (7, 7), and (8, 8). Plug these values into $U(x, y) = x^r y^{(1-r)}$ and you will find that utility levels are 4, 5, 6, 7, and 8 for these curves. The answer for the equal-weighted version of this function is the same as noted in Figure 4.7.

†Q9b answer: Set MRS = 1, and solve for y in the equation $(r/(1 - r))(y/x) = 1$. The result is $y = ((1 - r)/r)x$.

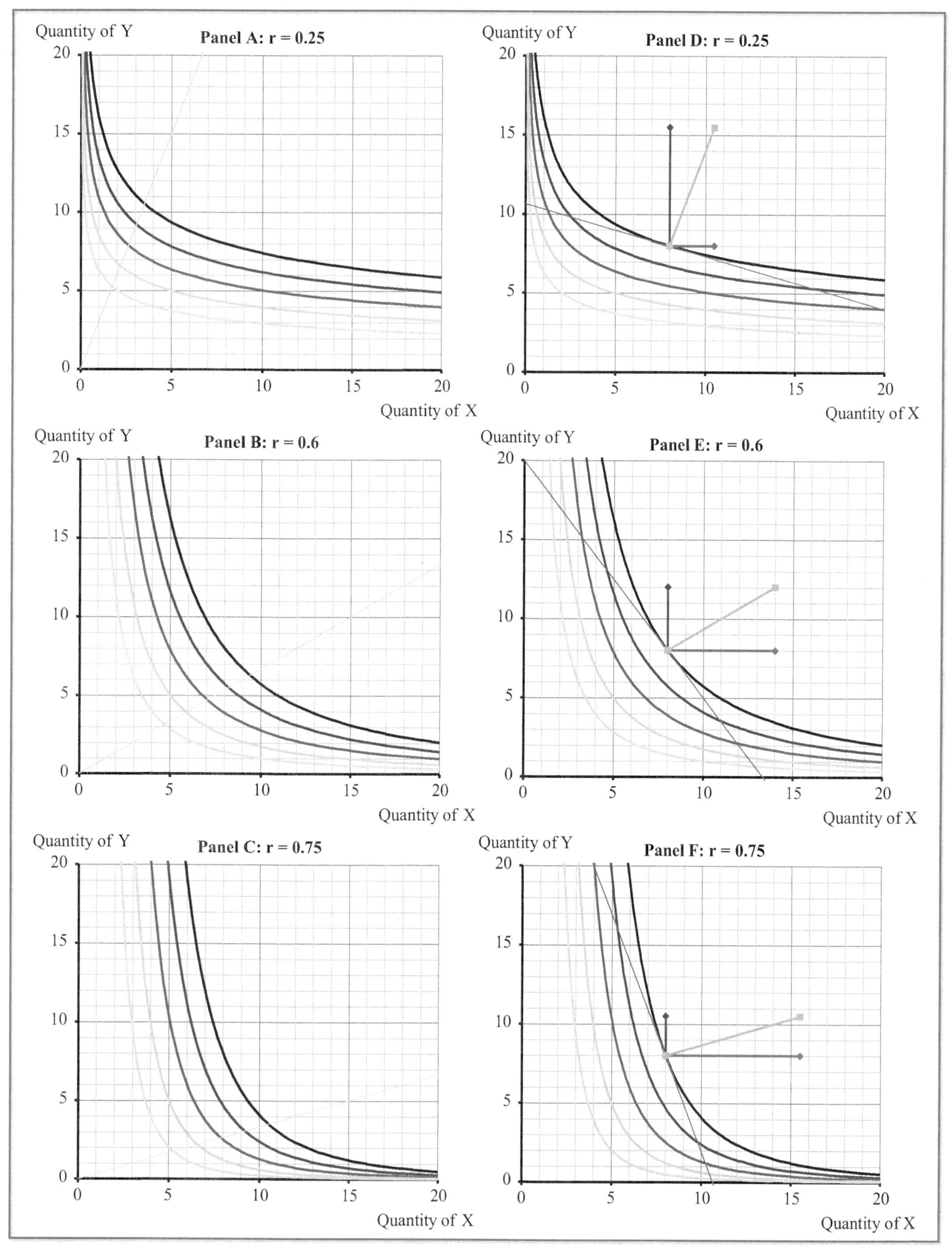

FIGURE 4.9 The General Cobb-Douglas Utility Function, $U(x, y) = x^r y^{(1-r)}$ for Three Values of r

Generally speaking, the smaller the value of r, the tighter and more crowded the indifference map near the y axis; and the larger the value of r, the tighter and more crowded the indifference map near the x axis. As r increases, x becomes more valuable in "producing" utility, *ceteris paribus*.

This is also seen by looking at the magnitudes of $MU_x(8, 8)$ and $MU_y(8, 8)$ in Figures 4.9D–4.9F. The bundle (8, 8) was chosen because it is on the furthest indifference curve and because the indifference curves have been created so that they rotate at x = y bundles. As a result, the bundle (8, 8) is a point on the top indifference curve, regardless of r. The horizontal green line segment depicts $MU_x(8, 8)$, and the vertical blue line segment depicts $MU_y(8, 8)$ in each panel.[13] $MU_x(8, 8)$ increases as r increases (and you can see this more continuously using the Excel file for Figure 4.9 as well). Conversely, $MU_y(8, 8)$ decreases as r increases (or to say the same thing, $MU_y(8, 8)$ increases as the $(1 - r)$ exponent attached to y increases). These combine into a general rule: Larger values for an exponent increase the "value" of that good in "producing" incremental utility, *ceteris paribus*. MRS measures relative valuation in producing utility. The MRS at a given bundle, $MRS(x, y) = (r/(1 - r))(y/x)$, is an increasing function of r. (The MRS(8, 8) is the slope of the pink tangent in Figures 4.9D–4.9F, and is perpendicular to the lavender MU vector, as in earlier figures.) This is increasing in r for two reasons: The numerator increases, and the denominator decreases, and the fraction gets larger as a result of both changes.

With the more general CD utility function, $U(x, y) = ax^cy^d$, the same result holds. An increase in c increases the MRS, *ceteris paribus*, because $MRS(x, y) = (c/d)(y/x)$. The MRS only increases due to the increase in the numerator in this instance, since the exponents are not tied to each other using this variant of the general CD utility function. The MRS is a decreasing function of d, the exponent attached to y for similar reasons. As y becomes more "important" in producing utility, *ceteris paribus*, x becomes less "important"; hence, the MRS—the amount of y the individual is willing to give up to obtain one more x—declines.

Shifted Cobb-Douglas

A more general class of preferences can be mapped by making a small change to the Cobb-Douglas utility function just presented. If you replace x by $(x - a)$ and y by $(y - b)$ in the Cobb-Douglas equations, you obtain the shifted CD equations in Table 4.1. Indifference curves based on these utility functions are "shifted" to the right by a units and up by b units. (If $a < 0$, then the shift is to the left by $|a|$ units, and if $b < 0$, then the shift is down by $|b|$ units.) This is most easily seen using the equal-weighted form: $U(x, y) = (x - a)(y - b)$.

Utility function	$MU_x(x, y)$	$MU_y(x, y)$	MRS	
$U(x, y) = (x - a)(y - b)$	$y - b$	$x - a$	$(y - b)/(x - a)$	**(4.5)**

Figure 4.10 depicts indifference maps for three values of a and b shown in two ways. The indifference curve to focus on in Figure 4.10 is the red indifference curve, $U(x, y) = (x - a)(y - b) = 32$. The blue equal-weighed CD indifference curve, $V(x, y) = xy = 32$, is simply provided for reference. Imagine that the blue and the red indifference curves are associated with different individuals, and therefore, there is no reason to be concerned that the indifference curves cross in some panels (in Chapter 3, we saw that transitivity is violated if indifference curves cross). In Figures 4.10A–4.10C, the red indifference curve is only shown in the first quadrant (based on the black axes) because you cannot consume negative quantities of either good. If you only saw these three panels you may find it difficult to see how the red curve could be obtained from the blue curve. Figures 4.10D–4.10F make the connection clear: The red vertical axis is shifted by a units, and the red horizontal axis is shifted by b units. The red curve is continued in dashed form in the second, third, and fourth quadrants as necessary (whenever at least one of the parameters a or b is negative). The pink segments provide a vector representation of the shift in both the axes and a representative point on the blue curve (the point (4, 8) on the blue curve is

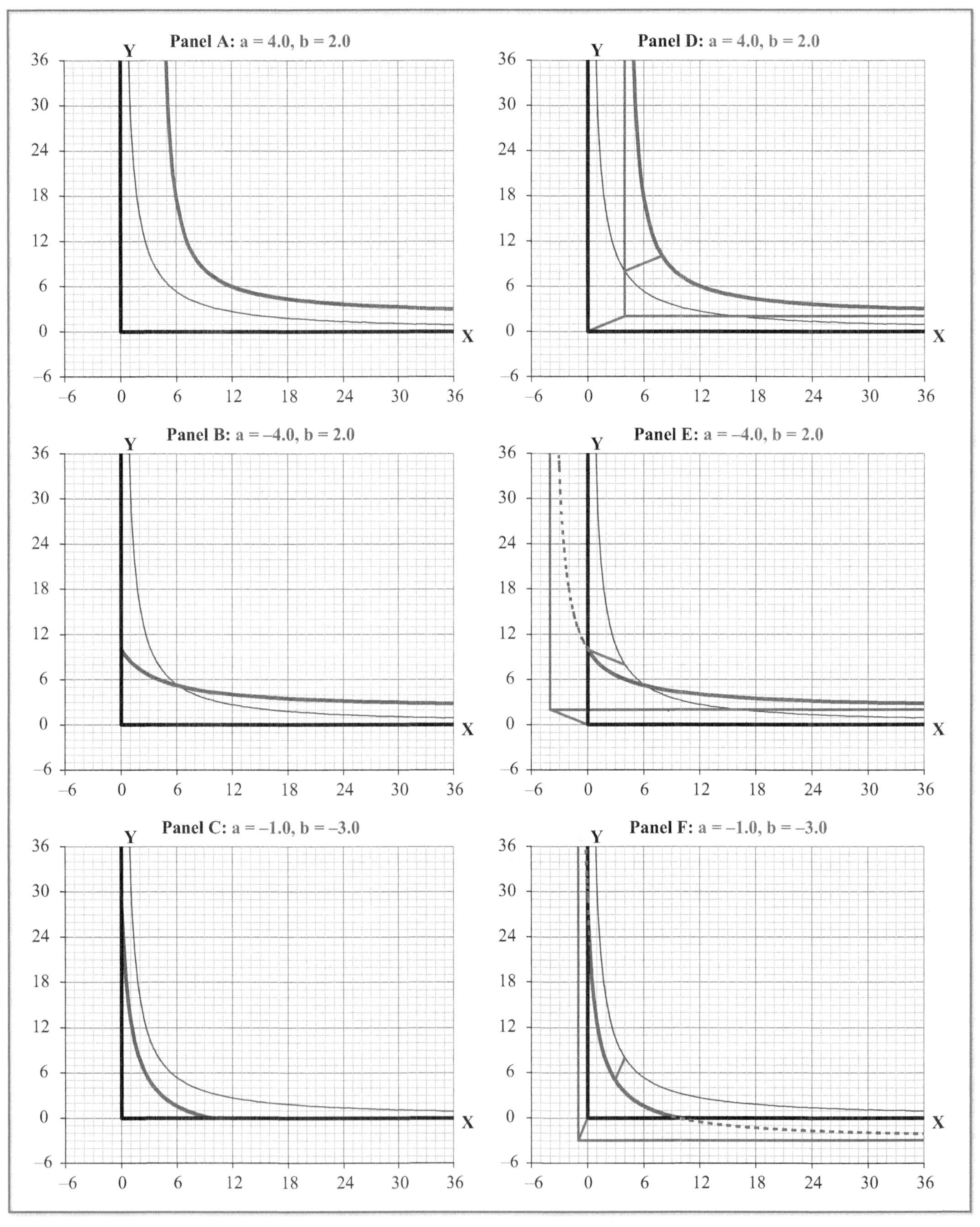

FIGURE 4.10 Examining Shifted Cobb-Douglas Utility, $V(x, y) = xy = 32$ and $U(x, y) = (x - a)(y - b) = 32$)

transformed to the point $(4 + a, 8 + b)$ on the red curve). Both points have MRS = 2. Verify this using the equation for the MRS in Equation 4.5.[14]

The second form of shifted Cobb-Douglas, $U(x, y) = (x - a)^r(y - b)^{(1-r)}$, allows unequal weights on $(x - a)$ and $(y - b)$.

Utility function	$MU_x(x, y)$
$U(x, y) = (x - a)^r(y - b)^{(1-r)}$	$r((x - a)/(y - b))^{(r-1)}$

$MU_y(x, y)$	MRS	
$(1 - r)((x - a)/(y - b))^r$	$(r/(1 - r))((y - b)/(x - a))$	**(4.6)**

Figure 4.11 provides examples of indifference maps using this function. These figures are akin to combining Figures 4.9 and 4.10. Figure 4.9 examined r, the proportional weight that goes to x, in the general form CD, and Figure 4.10 examined the vertical and horizontal axis shift factors, a and b, in the shifted CD function. The three parameters of this model (a, b, and r) produce a wide range of indifference maps. The panels in Figure 4.11 only provide a flavor for the range of preferences that may be modeled using this functional form. It is worthwhile to open the Excel file for Figure 4.11 and examine how changing each of these parameters affects the preference map and marginal utilities. (Try to create "reversed" graphs of each panel, which are symmetric about the 45° line, by adjusting the sliders.) A more complete analysis of the implications of each of the parameters must await the introduction of constraints into the consumer model in Chapter 6.

If $a = b$ and there is equal weighting on $x - a$ and $y - b$, the indifference curves are symmetric about the line $x = y$. Figure 3.14 was created using exactly this functional form: Figure 3.14A had $a = b < 0$; Figure 3.14B had $a = b = 0$; and Figure 3.14C had $a = b > 0$. Using this restriction, you should try to determine the exact values of $a = b$ for Figures 3.14A and 3.14C, using the Excel file for Figure 4.11 (set $r = 0.5$). The answers are in the endnote.[15] If $a \neq b$, there is no longer symmetry along the line $x = y$. (Further, if $r \neq 0.5$, there is not symmetry, even if $a = b$.) However, some of the conclusions we obtained in Chapter 3 still hold: If a and b are negative, the curves are less "curved," and the goods are imperfect substitutes; if both a and b are positive, the curves are more curved, and the goods are imperfect complements. This holds true as r changes.

Quasilinear

The last class of utility functions described in Table 4.1 is called the quasilinear form. The term *quasi* means "almost" or "close to." The general form describes the "almost" linearity: $U(x, y) = f(x) + y$. The quasilinear form is not a linear function of x and y because x enters in a nonlinear fashion (as f(x)), but it is linear in y. (A linear function involves variables that are to the first power with + or – signs between variables. Although the variables in the equal-weighted Cobb-Douglas, $U(x, y) = x \cdot y$, are to the first power, it is nonlinear because there is a multiplication sign between x and y. By contrast, the perfect substitute form, $U(x, y) = ax + by$, is linear in x and y.) This linearity in terms of good y creates a special relationship in the indifference map for every quasilinear utility function, regardless of the specific function f(x) that describes x's contribution to utility. Each indifference curve is parallel to the ones above and below it; the curves are vertical translates of each other.

The two goods x and y each add independent effects to utility: x adds f(x), and y adds y. This independence is perhaps easiest to see by examining the marginal utility of each good in this instance. The two specific examples of quasilinear functions in Table 4.1 (reproduced as Equation 4.7a, $U(x, y) = \alpha x^r + y$, and Equation 4.7b, $U(x, y) = \alpha \ln(x) + y$) and the general form all have marginal utilities that are qualitatively distinct from perfect complements, Cobb-Douglas, and shifted Cobb-Douglas. The marginal utility of good x depends only on x, and the marginal utility of y is constant (indeed, it equals one in each of the examples). By contrast with perfect complements, the CD, and the shifted CD, the marginal utility of one good depends on the level of the other good (and vice versa). This

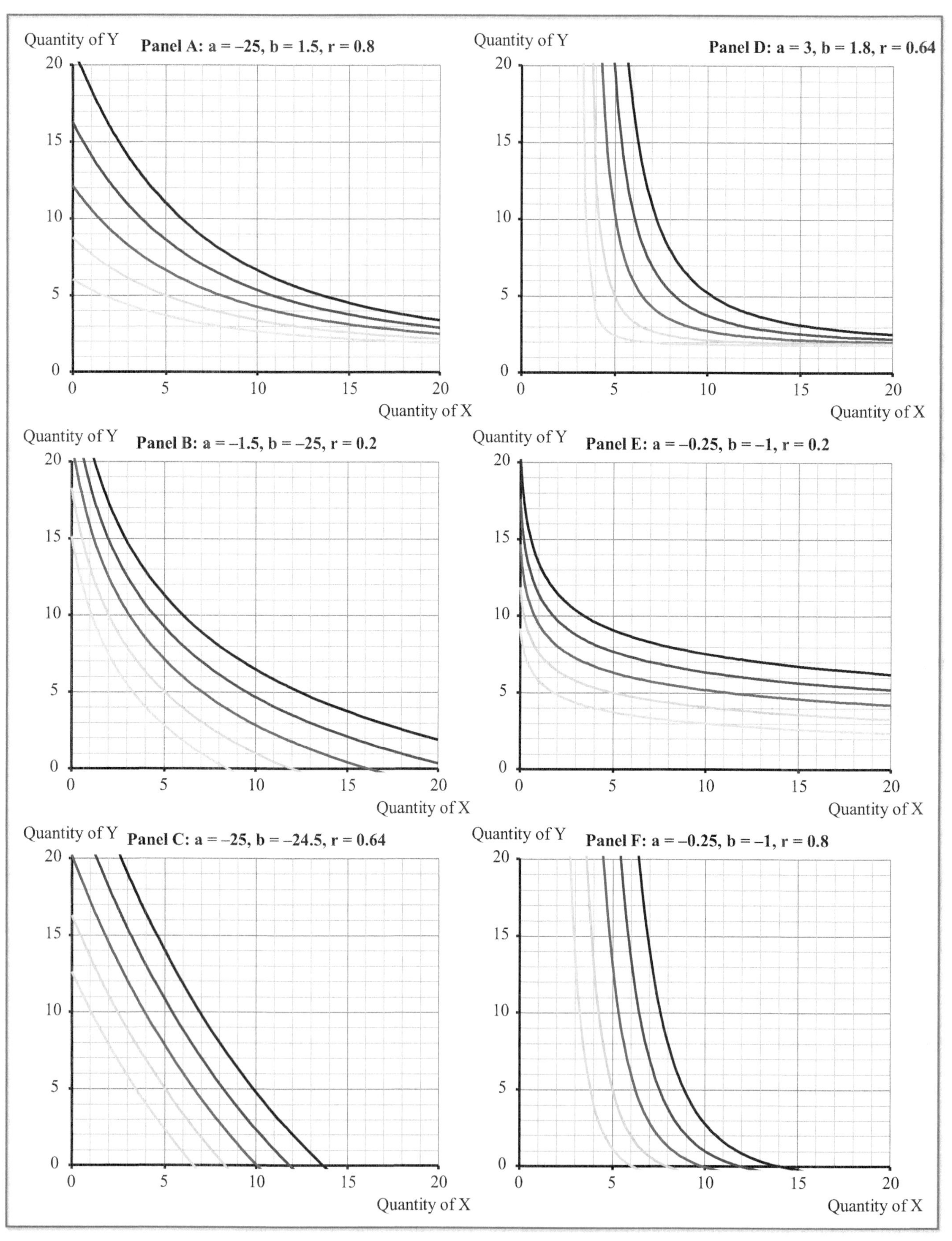

FIGURE 4.11 Shifted Cobb-Douglas Utility, $U(x, y) = (x - a)^r(y - b)^{(1-r)}$ as a, b, and r Vary

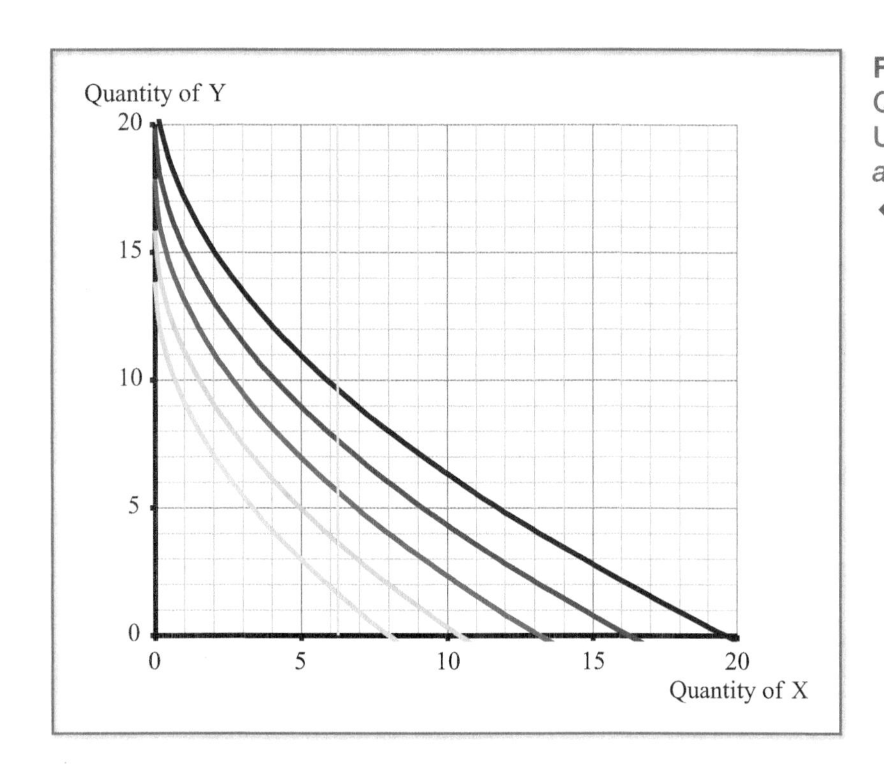

FIGURE 4.12 Quasilinear Utility, $U(x, y) = ax^r + y$ with $a = 5$, $r = 0.5$

filters through to the MRS as well: The MRS depends *only* on the level of x; it does not depend on y for quasilinear functions. By contrast, the MRS depends on the level of both x and y for the other three forms.

Utility function	$MU_x(x, y)$	$MU_y(x, y)$	MRS	
$U(x, y) = ax^r + y$	$arx^{(r-1)}$	1	$arx^{(r-1)}$	**(4.7a)**
$U(x, y) = a\ln(x) + y$	a/x	1	a/x	**(4.7b)**

These algebraic observations about MU and MRS filter through into the graphs of quasilinear functions. Figure 4.12 depicts a specific example based on Equation 4.7a: $U(x, y) = 5x^{0.5} + y$.

Q12a. Use $U(x, y) = 5x^{0.5} + y$ and the graph in Figure 4.12 to estimate the utility levels associated with each of the five indifference curves in the graph. *Hint:* $9^{0.5} = 3$ and $4^{0.5} = 2$.*

Figure 4.12 is not linear but rather quasilinear in a very specific fashion. Each successive indifference curve is 2 units higher than the indifference curve below. Indeed, this is *the* geometric property of quasilinear functions: Once you have one, you obtain others simply by moving the first one up or down. The amount you move it up is the increase in utility level; the amount you move it down would be the decrease in utility level. Since the curve is simply shifted up or down, the MRS is constant for a given x. Put another way, the MRS is constant on vertical lines, one of which is the vertical gold line depicting where MRS = 1 in this graph.

Q12b. Given the utility function depicted in Figure 4.12 and the MRS information in Equation 4.7a, prove that MRS = 1 when x = 6.25.†

***Q12a answer:** The utility levels are 14, 16, 18, 20, and 22. This is easily verified using perfect square x values, such as 1, 4, and 9. For example, the lowest indifference curve goes through the bundle (4, 4), $U(4, 4) = 5 \cdot 4^{0.5} + 4 = 5 \cdot 2 + 4 = 14$. The same value would occur had you used x = 1 instead (since $5 + 9 = 14$).

†Q12b answer: $MRS(x, y) = arx^{(r-1)}$ with a = 5 and r = 0.5. Given this, MRS = 1 if $5/2x^{-0.5} = 1$. Regrouping, $x^{0.5} = 5/2$, or $x = (5/2)^2 = 25/4 = 6.25$.

FIGURE 4.13
Quasilinear Utility, $U(x, y) = a \cdot \ln(x) + y$ with $a = 5$

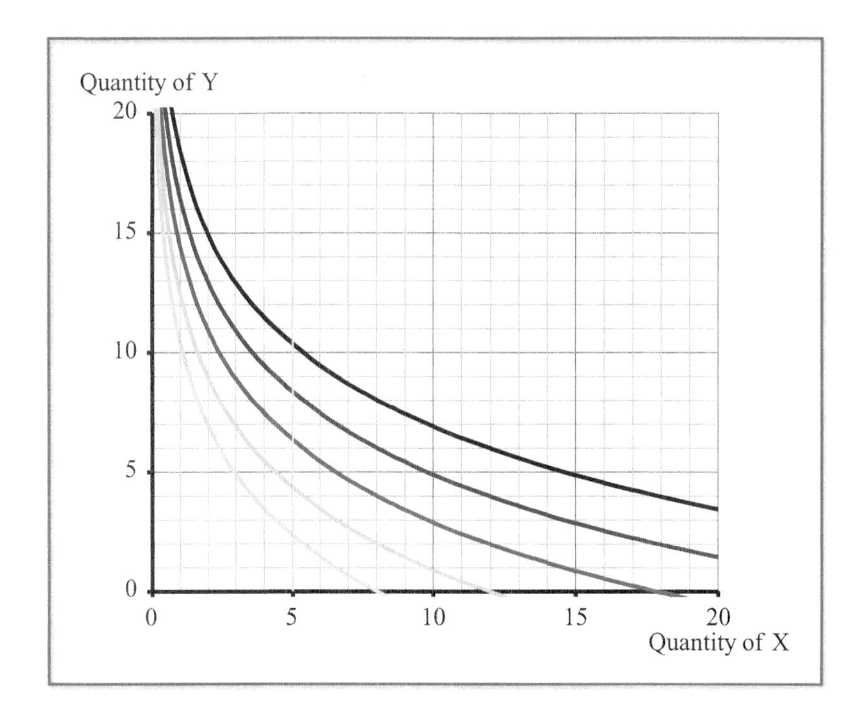

Marginal utilities have been suppressed from Figure 4.12 to reduce clutter, but if you enable them in the Excel version of Figure 4.12 and use the sliders that allow a and r to vary, you will find that MU_y does not change; it always equals one (this is not surprising; it is listed as such in Equation 4.7).

Figure 4.13 depicts a second example of a quasilinear function based on the natural logarithm function, ln(x).[16] The general equation for this form is described in Equation 4.7b. Figure 4.13 depicts the preference map when a = 5: $U(x, y) = 5 \cdot \ln(x) + y$.

> **Q13a.** Use $U(x, y) = 5 \cdot \ln(x) + y$ and the graph in Figure 4.13 to estimate the utility levels associated with each of the five indifference curves in this graph. *Hint:* ln(1) = 0, and ln(5) = 1.6.*

The Excel file for Figure 4.13 allows you to vary the parameter *a* (and it also includes a graph of the function f(x) = ln(x) for your information). The vertical translation property discussed earlier holds here as well; each curve is simply two units of y higher than the one below. Use the gridwork to verify that this is true. Most people's eyes deceive them, and they think that as the slopes get steeper, the curves get closer together. This is an optical illusion; the curves are, indeed, vertical translates of each other.

> **Q13b.** Given $U(x, y) = 5 \cdot \ln(x) + y$ and the MRS information in Equation 4.7b, prove that MRS = 1 when x = 5.†

As with Figure 4.12, marginal utilities have been suppressed to reduce clutter, but the Excel version of Figure 4.13 shows that MU_y is constant, regardless of *a*. This same result would hold for *any* quasilinear function, as the general quasilinear function in Table 4.1 asserts.

The general quasilinear function U(x, y) = f(x) + y is well behaved if the preferences mapped by this function are convex and monotonic. Monotonicity requires that f(x) can-

---

***Q13a answer:** The indifference curves intersect the vertical line x = 5 at about y = 2.4, y = 4.4, y = 6.4, y = 8.4, and y = 10.4. Given ln(5) = 1.6, we have the lowest indifference curve associated with a utility level of 10.4 (because $U(x, y) = 5 \cdot \ln(x) + y = 5 \cdot 1.6 + 2.4 = 8+2.4 = 10.4$). Therefore, the other values are 12.4, 14.4, 16.4, 18.4, and 20.4.

†Q13b answer: The proof of this assertion is even more straightforward than for Figure 4.12. Table 4.1 asserts that when $U(x, y) = a \cdot \ln(x) + y$, MRS = *a*/x. In this instance, *a* = 5, so MRS = 1 when *a* = x, or x = 5. You can see the same result graphically by varying *a* in the Excel version of Figure 4.13. As you do, the vertical gold line associated with MRS = 1 moves so that, in each instance, x = *a*.

not be downward sloping, and strict monotonicity requires that f(x) be upward sloping. Put another way, strict monotonicity requires that f(x) is a monotonic transformation. Convexity requires that f(x) increases at a decreasing rate. Both x^r when $0 < r < 1$ and ln(x) satisfy this requirement, but the convexity requirement cannot be stated more explicitly without the use of calculus.[17]

This section has focused direct attention on five classes of functions used to describe preferences, four of which are examined using multiple utility functions. As a result, you may feel a bit of algebraic overload if this is your first time reading this section. Each of these classes of functions behaves quite differently in the face of price and income changes. The goal of the section is to introduce these forms to you; a deeper understanding of when each is appropriate will await the analysis of Chapters 6–8.

4.5 Must a Utility Function Exist? *OPTIONAL SECTION*

This chapter has focused on algebraic representations of indifference curves. This focus, of course, begs the question of where these functions came from in the first place. Since utility is ordinal, no single utility function represents a given set of preferences. Notwithstanding this problem, the question remains: If you have a set of preferences, can you find a utility function that represents them? If we restrict ourselves to monotonic preferences that have indifference curves, the answer is yes.

Creating a Utility Function from Indifference Curves and the 45° Line[18]

The proof of this assertion is based on the observation that any point **A** = (x_o, y_o) has an indifference curve running through it. Monotonicity requires that the indifference curve must be in the second or fourth quadrants with respect to **A**. This is not a new observation; it is how we started our analysis of indifference curves in Chapter 3 (see the discussion surrounding Figures 3.1 and 3.2). If (x_o, y_o) has $x_o > y_o$, then the bundle is below the 45° line ($x = y$), and if $x_o < y_o$, then the bundle is above the 45° line. In either event, the indifference curve containing **A** must eventually cross the 45° line. If we define the function as the value of x where this occurs, then we have successfully attached a numerical "score" to each bundle that satisfies all of the properties of a utility function. Recall that a utility function *represents* preferences if it associates smaller numbers with less-preferred bundles and larger numbers with more-preferred bundles. Therefore, we have created a utility function to represent an indifference map; all that is required are indifference curves that are monotonic.

Students are sometimes reticent to call this a utility function because it is based on the geometry required by monotonicity rather than an algebraic function. A utility function need not be algebraic; it simply has to connect bundles to numbers in a way that preserves the order of preferences over bundles. The proposed strategy does just that.

Specifically, suppose the bundle **A** = (x_o, y_o) has $x_o > y_o$, then there must be a bundle in the second quadrant relative to (x_o, y_o) that is indifferent to (x_o, y_o) and is on the 45° line. If $x_o < y_o$, that bundle must be in the fourth quadrant relative to (x_o, y_o). Call this bundle (x^*, x^*). Define U(**A**) = $U(x_o, y_o) = x^*$. This is described in Figure 4.14. The top indifference curve in that figure goes through the bundle (20, 5), and that indifference curve crosses the 45° line at x = 13.1.

Q14. What are the utility levels associated with the indifference curves going through the bundles (15, 5), (10, 6), (6, 7), and (3, 8) given this utility function?*

(For your reference, the utility function driving Figure 4.14 is a functional form that has not been discussed in this chapter; it is not quasilinear or the shifted CD. One of the problems at the end of the chapter introduces this functional form to you.)

***Q14 answer:** The utility function U(x, y) is U(15, 5) = 10.6, U(10, 6) = 8.4, U(6, 7) = 6.4 and U(3, 8) = 4.7.

FIGURE 4.14 Creating a Utility Function from Indifference Curves

Define $U(x_0, y_0)$ as the x value on the 45° line where $(x^*, x^*) \sim (x_0, y_0)$. For example, U(20, 5) = 13.1

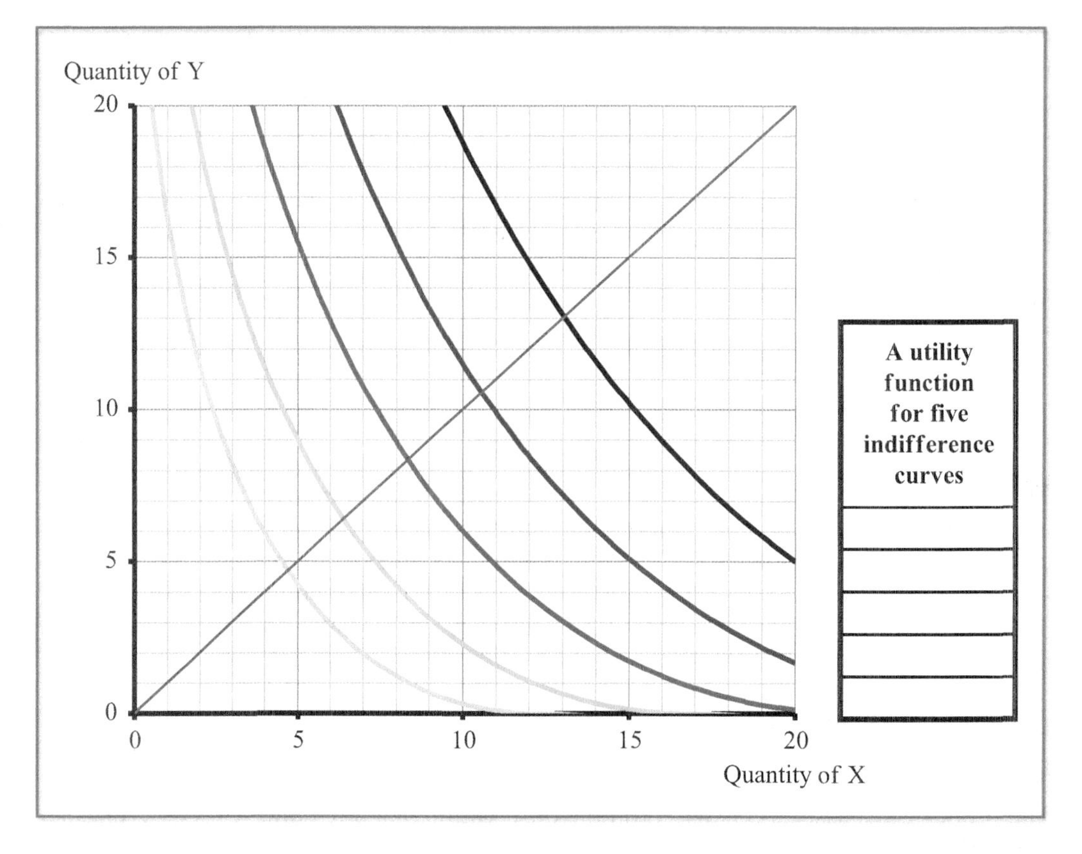

Bracketing Utility

Even if we do not have sufficient information to create a utility function (for example, we do not have an indifference map of the individual's preferences), *we can place bounds on a utility function,* using the methodology proposed for Figure 4.14. In the absence of indifference curves, we can narrow the range of utility level values we would attach to a given bundle by using monotonicity and convexity.

Suppose bundle **A** = (15, 6). This bundle is below the 45° line in Figure 4.15, so there must be a point in the second quadrant relative to **A** that is both on the indifference curve through **A** and on the 45° line. Put another way, all bundles in the first quadrant are better than **A** (with the possible exception of bundles on the border of this quadrant). The *maximum* value that the utility function can attach to bundle **A** is 15, the point on the 45° line associated with the border between the first and second quadrants relative to **A**. The *blue square* at the bundle (15, 15) in Figure 4.15A denotes this maximum.

A *blue square* in Figure 4.15 represents the *upper* bound on the utility level implied by the coordinates of a given bundle. This bound is due to monotonicity.

The maximum would occur if, for example, **A** was on the vertical part of a perfect complement indifference curve with vertex at the bundle (15, 5). **A** dominates all bundles in the third quadrant relative to **A**; therefore, the *minimum* value that the utility function can attach to bundle **A** is 6, the point on the 45° line associated with the border between the second and third quadrants relative to **A**. The *red circle* at the bundle (6, 6) in Figure 4.15A denotes this minimum.

A *red circle* in Figure 4.15 represents the *lower* bound on the utility level implied by the coordinates of a given bundle. This bound is due to monotonicity.

The minimum would occur if, for example, **A** was on the horizontal part of a perfect complement indifference curve with vertex at the bundle (4, 6). Monotonicity has bracketed the utility level associated with bundle **A** to be somewhere between 6 and 15. This is represented on the graph by the *purple segment* on the 45° line between the lower bound of 6 (the red circle) and the upper bound of 15 (the blue square) in Figure 4.15A.

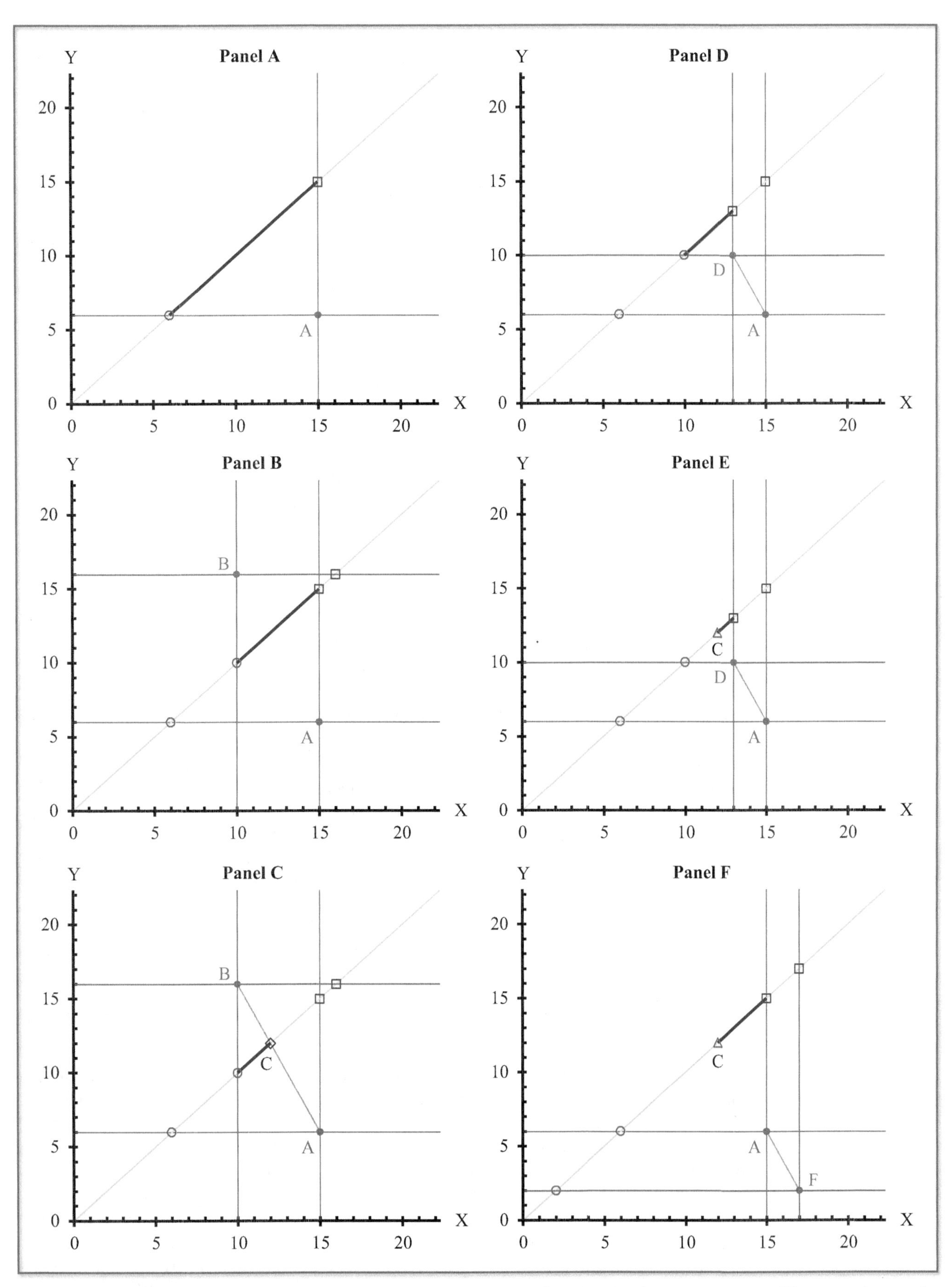

FIGURE 4.15 Bracketing Utility with Monotonicity and Convexity (Monotonicity: □ upper bound, ○ lower bound. Convexity: ◇ upper bound, Δ lower bound.)

The *purple segment* on the 45° line depicts the range of possible utility levels that may be attached to a bundle. The purple segment depicts the range that the utility level has been bracketed to by the known information.

The bottom of the segment is the highest lower bound and the top of the segment is the lowest upper bound implied by the known information. (In Figure 4.15A, the known information is the location of a single bundle.) The other five panels examine what happens when a second indifferent bundle is discovered.

As soon as we find a second bundle, **B**, that is indifferent to **A**, **B** ~ **A**, we can further restrict the range of possible utility levels associated with bundle **A**. Consider bundle **B** = (10, 16) in Figure 4.15B. The blue square represents the upper bound, and the red circle represents the lower bound (as earlier with point **A**). Monotonicity reduces the range of possible utility levels with the discovery of **B** ~ **A** because the lower bound has increased to 10 from 6. The lower bound would be binding (i.e., U(**A**) = 10) if, for example, **A** and **B** were on the same perfect complement indifference curve with vertex at (10, 6). The upper bound remains 15 because **B**'s upper bound is higher than **A**'s (16 > 15). Monotonicity has reduced the range for the utility level associated with bundles **A** ~ **B** to the purple segment between 10 and 15 in Figure 4.15B.

Convexity requires that every bundle between **A** and **B** is at least as good as **A** or **B**. This further reduces the range of possible utility levels, as we see in Figure 4.15C. The *blue diamond* at **C** = (12, 12) is 60% of the way from **A** to **B** along the line segment **AB**.

The *blue diamond* in Figure 4.15 represents an *upper* bound on the utility level implied by convexity. This occurs when the two bundles are on opposite sides of the 45° line.

Since bundle **C** is at least as good as **A** or **B**, convexity has reduced the maximum utility level U(**A**) to 12 from 15. This would be the utility level if **A** and **B** were on the same perfect substitutes indifference curve. (This indifference curve would have MRS = 2.) Convexity plus monotonicity has reduced the range for the utility level associated with bundles **A** ~ **B** to the purple segment between 10 and 12.

Convexity reduced the range of utility levels in Figure 4.15C because **A** and **B** were on opposite sides of the 45° line. Interestingly, convexity will also reduce this range when the two indifferent bundles are on the same side of the 45° line. It does so by increasing the *minimum* possible utility level (rather than decreasing the maximum possible utility level, as in Figure 4.15C). This is the scenario explored in Figures 4.15D–4.15F. Figures 4.15D and 4.15E examine the addition of a second bundle, **D** = (13, 10), in the second quadrant relative to **A**. Since **D** is closer to the 45° line, monotonicity directly reduces the range of possible utility levels associated with bundles **A** ~ **D** to the purple segment from 6 to 15 in Figure 4.15A to 10 to 13 in Figure 4.15D.

Convexity can further reduce the range of possible utility levels attached to **A** ~ **D**. In this instance, convexity increases the lower bound from 10 to 12. The convexity "implied" lower bound is represented by the *red triangle* in Figure 4.15E at point **C** = (12, 12).

The *red triangle* in Figure 4.15 represents a *lower* bound on the utility level implied by convexity. This occurs when the two bundles are on the same side of the 45° line.

Unlike the red circles and blue squares, there is either a red triangle or a blue diamond when there are two indifferent bundles. The determining factor in this instance is whether the two bundles are on opposing sides or on the same side of the 45° line. To understand why the lower bound has increased, imagine that this were not the case. For example, imagine that (11, 11) ~ **A** ~ **D**. Convexity would require that bundles between (11, 11) and **A** are at least as good as (11, 11) or **A**. This would mean that **D** is strictly better than (11, 11) or **A** because there are bundles between (11, 11) and **A** that are in the third quadrant relative to **D**. Further, there are bundles that are on the interior of that quadrant; these bundles include less of both goods. (One such bundle is (12.6, 9), 60% of the way from point **A** = (15, 6) to (11, 11).) Monotonicity requires that **D** would strictly dominate such bundles. Transitivity requires that **D** would strictly dominate the endpoint bundles

((11, 11) and **A**) as well. This contradicts the initial assumption of indifference. Therefore, convexity has increased the lower bound to point **C**. Convexity therefore further reduces the range of possible utility levels associated with bundles **A** ~ **D** to the purple segment from 10 to 13 in Figure 4.15D to 12 to 13 in Figure 4.15E.

This also can be thought of in terms of the MRS between points. Once two indifferent bundles are discovered, an implicit exchange rate between those bundles is created (this is simply $(-)\Delta y/\Delta x$ between the two bundles). Given bundles **A** and **D** in Figure 4.15E, an MRS between **A** and **D** is set up (in this instance, that MRS = 2). "Set up" does not mean that the MRS must equal 2 over the entire range from **A** to **D**. Convexity and monotonicity do imply that, given **A** ~ **D** with **D** in the second quadrant relative to **A**, the MRS at **D** must be at *least* 2, and the MRS at **A** must be at *most* 2. If this was not the case, convexity would have been violated. Therefore, the MRS to the left of **D** along the indifference curve through **A** and **D** must be at least 2 if preferences are convex. (The reverse is also true: Bundles to the right of **A** on the indifference curve can be no larger than the MRS between **A** and **D** if preferences are convex and monotonic.)

Finally, Figure 4.15F shows that a second point reduces the range even if that point is further away from the 45° line than the initial bundle. Suppose point **F** = (17, 2) ~ **A**. The addition of **F** does not reduce the range of utility levels due to monotonicity. However, convexity does cause the range to decrease for the same reason as in Figure 4.15E. Convexity implies that the minimum increases from 6 to 12 because the **A** to **F** MRS = 2 implies that the MRS to the left of **A** along the indifference curve through **A** and **F** must be at least as large as 2. Therefore, convexity reduces the range of possible utility levels associated with bundles **A** ~ **F** to the purple segment from 6 to 15 in Figure 4.15A to 12 to 15 in Figure 4.15F.

The examples in Figures 4.15B–4.15F all use an MRS of 2 between bundles to minimize the complexity of the discussion. The Excel file for Figure 4.15 allows you to relax this assumption by varying the location of both bundles over the range (0, 0) to (20, 20). (The only restriction in the Excel file is that the second point, the pink bundle in the diagram, must be in the second or fourth quadrant relative to the first point, the green bundle in the diagram. If this were not the case, monotonicity would be violated.) The Excel file also allows you to click on and off the various lower and upper bounds associated with monotonicity and convexity, line segments, and shifted axes at each bundle. Together, the controls allow you to explore the bracketing phenomenon discussed earlier in greater detail.

Summary

This chapter describes a second way to represent preferences. Preferences are, at their most basic level, simply pairwise comparisons of bundles of goods: I prefer **A** to **B**; I prefer **B** to **A**; or I am indifferent between **A** and **B**. This makes preferences rather cumbersome to work with in practice. Economists have developed geometric and algebraic methods to make the analysis of consumer choice less cumbersome. Chapter 3 focused, in large part, on a geometric construct called indifference curves that allows you to represent preferences. Chapter 4 provides the symmetric representation, using the algebraic concept of a utility function.

Most of the time, we restrict our analysis to two goods; utility functions and indifference curves can be conceptualized for more than two goods. Sometimes, utility functions are easier to conceptualize than are indifference curves, and as we increase the number of goods under consideration, the algebraic form is often more intuitive. We use goods that are perfect substitutes to motivate these higher dimensional discussions, and we provide a three-dimensional graph of indifference curves in this situation. This introduces a framework for viewing preferences and their algebraic and geometric representation in a more general setting, but we return to the two-goods model for the bulk of our analysis.

We can obtain indifference curves easily from a utility function by setting the utility function equal to a constant. Different constants produce different indifference curves; therefore, we can easily create an indifference map from a utility function.

Unfortunately, utility functions are not uniquely described by a preference map; no single utility function represents a given set of preferences. The problem has to do with the ordinal nature of the preferences themselves.

You can always say which bundle you prefer, but it makes less sense to say by how much you prefer it. Indeed, if you have a utility function that represents a set of preferences, then any monotonic transformation of that utility function represents the same set of preferences.

The bulk of the chapter is devoted to the discussion of five classes of utility functions: (1) perfect substitutes, (2) perfect complements, (3) Cobb-Douglas, (4) shifted Cobb-Douglas, and (5) quasilinear. Since no single utility function represents a given set of preferences, it makes little sense to devote much effort to the notions of utility level and marginal utility, per se. Despite this problem, the ratio of marginal utilities between two goods is *not* affected by the specific function chosen to represent preferences, and the ratio of marginal utilities is equal to the MRS between the two goods. Indifference maps for each of the five classes of functions are not affected by the lack of single utility function; the only thing in the indifference map that is affected are the numbers (utility levels) attached to the indifference curves.

The final section examines the reverse issue. Suppose you have an indifference map that represents a given set of preferences. Can you represent those preferences with a utility function? If the preferences are monotonic, the answer is yes: A geometric solution is proposed that connects a number to a bundle as required by a utility function. A separate analysis shows how monotonicity and convexity can be used to place bounds on such a function, even if you do not have an indifference curve to work with.

Review Questions

Define the following terms:

U represents $\succ$	MU vector	quasilinear utility
utility function	utils	bracketing utility
utility level	Cobb-Douglas utility	
marginal utility	$MRS_{j,i}$	

Define the following properties of functions:

monotonic transformation	ordinal	cardinal

Match the following statements:

a. The vector (MU_x, MU_y) at bundle **A**	1. $MRS_{y,x}$(**A**)
b. $-MU_x$(**A**)/MU_y(**A**)	2. Indifference curves are closer together.
c. MU_x(**A**)/MU_y(**A**)	3. The direction of maximum increase in utility
d. (MU_x, MU_y) at bundle **A** is "larger."	4. Indifference curves are farther apart.
e. (MU_x, MU_y) at bundle **A** is "smaller."	5. The slope of the indifference curve at **A**

Provide short answers to the following:

a. Suppose U(**X**) represents $\succ$. Does 13U(**X**) – 7 represent the same preferences?
b. Suppose U(**X**) represents $\succ$. Does –U(**X**) + 87 represent the same preferences?
c. How would you create an indifference map that represents $\succ$ if you are given a utility function that represents $\succ$?
d. Suppose an indifference map shows that indifference curves intersect the horizontal axis but appear asymptotic to the vertical axis. Could the underlying preference be perfect substitutes, perfect complements, Cobb-Douglas, shifted Cobb-Douglas, or quasilinear?

Check your answers to the *matching* and *short-answer* exercises in the Answers Appendix at the end of the book.

Notes

1. Those who know multivariate calculus will realize that the marginal utility of good i is simply the partial derivative of the utility function in the *i*th direction, $\partial U(\mathbf{A})/\partial x_i$. If you know calculus, you should make it a practice to calculate marginal utilities for yourself, rather than having to depend on having it provided to you.

2. The sliders in the Excel file for Figure 4.2 will not allow you to show U^P, since the sliders do not allow you to set $MU_G = 1/3$ or $MU_K = 2/3$. The **Scenarios** function allows you to bring up U^P and U^G representations of the same indifference curve (click: **Data, What If Analysis, Scenario Manager** in Excel 2007; or **Tools, Scenarios** in Excel 2003; **2 metered in**

(**kiwis,plums), Show, Close**). You can create many other utility functions representing the same preferences with the sliders, as you will soon see.

3. If f(x) is differentiable, then f(x) is monotonic over a range of x values if df/dx > 0 for all x in the range.

4. When we discuss production functions in Part 3, the reverse will be true: Production is cardinal. If you produce 121 desk chairs, then you have produced 21% more than 100 desk chairs. We employ a cardinal utility function when we examine decisions under uncertainty in Chapter 17.

5. Vectors point in a direction and have a certain magnitude. Think of the outer endpoint as an arrowhead (unfortunately, Excel will not allow this to be formatted as such). We used vectors representing Annie's endowment bundle and Bob's endowment bundle in Section 3.5 to build their barter Edgeworth Box. If you have had multivariate calculus, you will recognize that this vector is a gradient; if you have not heard this term before, don't worry: We will not use that term here.

6. The sliders in the Excel version of Figure 4.3 allow you to vary marginal utilities for both goods from –10 to +10 by increments of 0.1. Preferences are not well behaved if marginal utility is negative (since monotonicity is violated), but the sliders allow you to model this situation nonetheless to see the trade-offs inherent in this situation.

7. Mathematically, *smooth* means differentiable. A function is smooth if the limiting ratio of $\Delta y_i/\Delta x_i$ is the same whether Δx approaches zero with $\Delta x_i < 0$ or $\Delta x_i > 0$. This does not hold at the vertex of L-shaped indifference curves, or at the vertices for curves that have connected piecewise linear segments such as Figure 3.2.

8. We can prove this formally using the definition of monotonic transformation because $f(z) = az^b$ is a monotonic function of z if a > 0 and b > 0. The proof of this assertion requires calculus. A function is a monotonic transformation if its derivative is positive: $df/dz = abz^{(b-1)} > 0$ if a > 0 and b > 0. Therefore, both functions represent the same preferences.

9. It may help to review the footnote at the bottom of p. 72 in Chapter 3 (including the graph in the footnote) that describes a geometric trick that helps you to visualize the slope of an equal-weighted CD indifference curve.

10. The proof requires calculus and is proposed as a workbook problem. Nonetheless, you can see the visual "proof" using the Excel file for Figure 4.8. If you move x between 2.5 and 10 along this indifference curve, you find that the magnitude of this diagonal vector is minimized when x = y = 5 (the magnitude of the vector has been calculated in cell E27).

11. To many, it is counterintuitive that indifference curves are farther apart when the MU vector is smaller. Consider the following analogy to topographic maps. If you are hiking and the slope is steep, it does not take that much horizontal distance to increase your elevation 100 feet. If you are hiking and the slope is very shallow, the same 100-foot increase in elevation takes a much greater horizontal distance to achieve. The steepness of slope is the size of the MU vector; the horizontal distance between elevation contours is the distance between indifference curves.

12. In this instance, r = c/(c + d) and 1 – r = d/(c + d). $f(z) = (z/a)^{(1/(c+d))}$ is a monotonic transformation of z as long as a > 0 and c + d > 0. The proof of this assertion requires calculus. A function is a monotonic transformation if its derivative is positive: $df/dz = (1/(a(c + d)))(z/a)^{((1/(c+d))-1)} > 0$ as long as c + d > 0 because $(z/a)^g > 0$ for both positive and negative values of g (so it does not matter from the point of view of sign that the exponent is the ugly-looking term: ((1/(c + d)) – 1)). The sign of df/dz is determined by the sign of 1/(a(c + d)), and this is positive since a > 0, c > 0 and d > 0. Therefore, both functions represent the same preferences.

13. Each of the marginal utilities has been multiplied by 10 for expositional purposes. The actual marginal utilities on the main diagonal (x = y) are $MU_X = r$ and $MU_y = 1 - r$ but these segments are so short that they are difficult to see. The marginal utilities 10r and 10(1 – r) would have resulted had we multiplied the utility function by 10. This is a monotonic transformation so it represents the same preferences. The Excel file for Figure 4.8 allows you to see the actual marginal utilities for the equal-weighted case. Click **Data, What if Analysis, Scenarios** in Excel 2007, or **Tools, Scenarios** in Excel 2003, Figure 4.9, **Actual MUs, Show Close** to see this diagram.

14. The blue MRS(4, 8) = y/x = 8/4 = 2. The red MRS(4 + a, 8 + b) = (y – b)/(x – a) = (8 + b – b)/(4 + a – a) = 8/4 = 2.

15. Figure 3.14A is obtained by setting r = 0.5, a = b = –16, and Figure 3.14C is obtained by setting r = 0.5, a = b = 2.64. (Of course, it is much easier to get close to the correct answer in Figure 3.14A than 3.14C because 3.14A provides reference points where the indifference curves hit the axes.)

16. Two bases are commonly used for logarithms, base 10 and base e (e = 2.718 . . .). These are written $\log_{10}(x)$ and ln(x) (or sometimes $\log_e(x)$). The "n" in ln(x) stands for "natural," ln(x) is called the natural logarithm of x. Although base 10 is more intuitive (since our world is organized around base 10), base e provides cleaner mathematical results, especially for slope. The slope of the function $f(x) = a \cdot \ln(x)$ is a/x while the slope of $g(x) = a \cdot \log_{10}(x)$ is $a \cdot \log_{10}(e)/x$. (The proof requires calculus: take the derivative of each to find slope.) The former slope is certainly cleaner than the latter. As a result, this book will use natural logarithm exclusively.

17. If df/dx > 0, then U is strictly monotonic. If $d^2f/dx^2 < 0$, then U is strictly convex.

18. The analysis in this subsection assumes the existence of nondegenerate indifference curves. See Chapter 4 Appendix B for an example of preferences whose indifference curves are degenerate.

Appendix A

Two Proofs about the MRS

Assertion 1: MRS $= -\Delta y/\Delta x$ along the indifference curve $= MU_x/MU_y$. More generally for goods i and j, $MRS_{j,i} = -\Delta x_j/\Delta x_i = MU_i/MU_j$ (holding all other goods constant along the indifference curve).

Proof 1: If we prove the general formula, then the two-variable case will follow. If **A** and **B** are two bundles of goods where **A** ~ **B** and they only differ in the amounts of goods i and j in their bundles, then one of the two goods must have an incremental increase in utility in moving from **A** to **B**. Suppose this is good i; then the increment to utility from more good i must equal the decrement to utility from the change in good j; otherwise, **A** would not be indifferent to **B**. The increment to utility from good i is $MU_i \cdot (b_i - a_i) = MU_i\Delta x_i$. This must be balanced by the decrement to utility from good j: $MU_j \cdot (b_j - a_j) = MU_j\Delta x_j$.

Thus:	$MU_i(b_i - a_i) + MU_j(b_j - a_j) = MU_i\Delta x_i + MU_j\Delta x_j = 0.$
Rearranging terms, we have:	$MU_i\Delta x_i = -MU_j\Delta x_j.$
Cross-multiplying, we obtain:	$MRS_{j,i} = -\Delta x_j/\Delta x_i = MU_i/MU_j.$
In words,	MRS is the ratio of marginal utilities.

Assertion 2: The MRS does not depend on the specific function chosen to represent a given set of preferences.

Proof 2: The proof of this assertion requires calculus—specifically, the chain rule. Suppose U(**X**) represents preferences, then V(**X**) = f(U(**X**)) as long as f(z) is a monotonic function of z. We have to compare $MRS^U_{j,i}$ with $MRS^V_{j,i}$ to show that the MRS is independent of utility function chosen. Start with V utility:

The chain rule implies:	$MV_i = \partial V(\mathbf{X})/\partial x_i = (df/dU) \cdot (\partial U(\mathbf{X})/\partial x_i).$
Similarly for j,	$MV_j = \partial V(\mathbf{X})/\partial x_j = (df/dU) \cdot (\partial U(\mathbf{X})/\partial x_j).$
As shown in Proof 1,	$MRS^V_{j,i} = MV_i/MV_j.$
Substituting,	$MRS^V_{j,i} = \partial V(\mathbf{X})/\partial x_i/\partial V(\mathbf{X})/\partial x_j.$
So,	$MRS^V_{j,i} = [(df/dU) \cdot (\partial U(\mathbf{X})/\partial x_i)]/[(df/dU) \cdot (\partial U(\mathbf{X})/\partial x_j)].$
The df/dUs cancel, leaving:	$MRS^V_{j,i} = (\partial U(\mathbf{X})/\partial x_i)/(\partial U(\mathbf{X})/\partial x_j) = MRS^U_{j,i}.$
In words,	Both marginal utilities change by the same scaling factor, df/dU; therefore, the ratio does not change.

The choice of utility function has no effect on MRS.

Appendix B

Lexicographic Preferences

Not all preferences can be represented by a utility function, even if the preferences are well behaved (monotonic and convex). The formal requirements for the existence of such a function is beyond the mathematical scope of this text.* It is worthwhile to see an example where a utility function fails to exist. This is the case of **lexicographic** preferences.

lexicographic: Preferences are lexicographic if $A \succ B$ whenever $x_a > x_b$ or if $x_a = x_b$ and $y_a > y_b$.

The Intuition behind Lexicographic Preferences

This function places primary importance on good x. Good y cannot be used to compensate for less good x, regardless of how much y is being offered. No MRS, no matter how large, suffices to maintain indifference. (This is not the same as having y be an economic neutral and hence a vertical indifference curve; in this instance, there is *no* indifference curve.)

These preferences are called lexicographic because this is similar to how a dictionary is organized. The relative placement of two words is based on the relative values of the first letter; if first letters are equal, it is based on the relative values of the second letter; and so on. (Obviously, lexicographic preferences are easily generalized to n goods, but we restrict our discussion to the two-goods case because it allows us to make the case for why no utility function exists here.)

The Problem Lexicographic Preferences Introduce

Consider the indifference curves in this instance: $\mathbf{A} \sim \mathbf{B}$ *only* if $\mathbf{A} = \mathbf{B}$. Indifference curves are "degenerate" because they are points, rather than curves. Each bundle is indifferent only to itself. There are simply "too many" indifference curves in this instance to assign a number to each one as required by a utility function. The exact meaning of "too many" is beyond the scope of this text (since it requires real analysis), but the basic point can be made heuristically.

Suppose $1 = x_a = x_b = x$ (in other words, restrict our analysis to the vertical line $x = 1$). Then $\mathbf{A} \succ \mathbf{B}$ based solely on the amount of y in each bundle. Define $U(\mathbf{C}) = y_c$ in this instance. This represents preferences over the bundles with $x_c = 1$, but this function takes up all numbers (or at least all nonnegative numbers) to do this. We would have to add another number line's worth of numbers for $x = 1.1$ (and 1.01, and 1.001, and . . .). There are not enough numbers to accomplish this task. (Mathematicians say that there are different-sized infinities involved in this situation.)

The problem does not exist when we have indifference curves that are actually curves. (Or more generally, if there are n goods, then this is not a problem as long as the indifference surface is $n - 1$ dimensional (for example, the n good perfect substitute indifference curve is an $n - 1$ dimensional hyperplane, as discussed in Section 4.2).) If that is true, there is only one dimension needed to describe different curves, and a utility function will exist in this instance.

*See Chapter 7 of Varian's graduate microeconomics text (Hal R. Varian, *Microeconomic Analysis*, Third Edition, 1992, W. W. Norton, New York) for the formal requirements.

Resource Constraints

CHAPTER 5

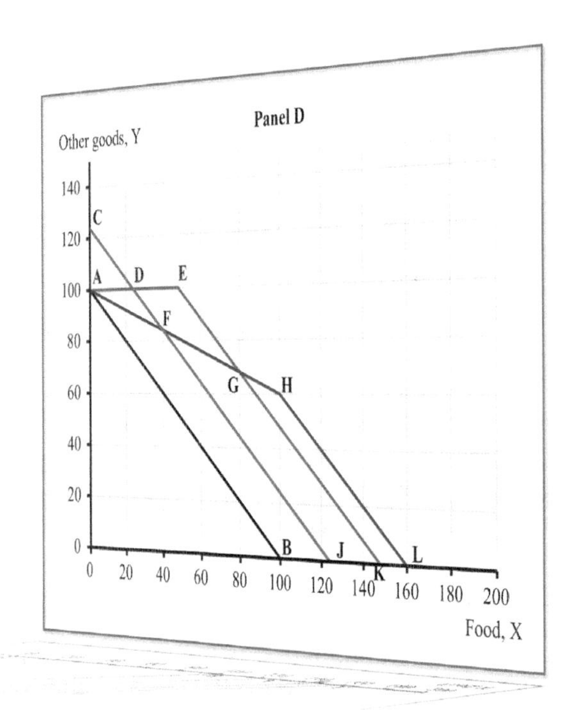

Chapter Outline

Chapters 3 and 4 focused on half of the consumer choice model: What does a consumer like? This chapter focuses on the other half of the model: What can the consumer afford? Or, to put this in a more general context, what are the resource constraints the consumer faces?

In Section 5.1, we provide an initial view of constraints on consumer choice, and we discuss the common mistake of confusing preferences for bundles with the feasibility of affording those bundles. Chapters 3 and 4 focused on the question of preferences; that discussion was predicated on ignoring the question of affordability. Now, we examine the affordability of bundles, while ignoring how attractive those bundles are to the consumer. Section 5.2 describes alternative ways to represent the set of feasible bundles. Different methods are useful in different contexts. Section 5.2 also discusses the notion of a numeraire, which is a good whose price is fixed at $1; the prices of all other goods are measured relative to the numeraire. Section 5.3 examines what happens when price or income changes. Following the economist's strategy of analyzing issues in a *ceteris paribus* fashion, we focus on the effect of changing one parameter at a time, but there is also discussion of what happens when multiple changes occur at once. Section 5.4 describes various applications of the budget constraint model, which allows the analysis of choice among options and introduces conditions that produce nonlinear budget constraints. Section 5.5 expands the discussion from budget constraints to other resource constraints. In contrast to the material in earlier sections, the discussion here examines what happens when consumers face multiple constraints (unlike in Section 5.4, where the consumer faced one constraint but with multiple options). If a good can only be consumed in discrete quantities (one car, not 1.2 cars, for example), then this acts as a constraint (albeit one that we will, in general, ignore in this text). Nonetheless, we examine budget constraints with discrete goods in Section 5.6. Finally, Section 5.7 examines relative prices as a measure of relative market value, using a geometric construct introduced in Chapter 4.

5.1 Avoid Confusing Preferences and Constraints

A common mistake students make is to attempt to analyze preferences and constraints at the same time. This mistake ultimately leads to confusion, rather than clarity. The strategy that economists employ is to analyze each half on its own, making sure to avoid introducing information from the other side. It is worthwhile to point out how this was accomplished in the discussion of preferences. Preferences were defined in terms of choices over bundles of goods that were being offered for consumption. The following is from Section 3.1 (italics added for emphasis):

> . . . Imagine you are offered the choice between two shopping carts, **A** and **B**, filled with different amounts of a number of goods. (*You do not have to pay for the shopping carts*; the only question is: Which do you prefer?)

You were explicitly told to ignore cost. We follow the reverse strategy here. We examine all bundles you can afford, regardless of how much you like or dislike them. Ultimately, we consider which bundles you prefer among those that you can afford. That is exactly what Chapter 6 is all about, but first we must examine constraints in a vacuum.

The most common constraint is the budget constraint. Suppose you have \$20 to spend on a number of items, $\mathbf{X} = (x_1, \ldots, x_n)$, at the store. If you do not have a credit card, checkbook, or your debit card with you (and there is no sales tax), then the following must be true at the checkout:

$$P_1x_1 + P_2x_2 + \ldots + P_nx_n \leq \$20,$$

where P_i is the price of good *i* per unit, and x_i is the number of units of good *i* in the shopping cart. The amount you spend on good *i* is P_ix_i. The bundle you have chosen must satisfy this inequality or else you don't get to leave the store with the bundle. Naturally, you will not always be limited to \$20. If instead of \$20, you have income, I, then the same inequality must hold with \$20 replaced by I. Bundles that satisfy this inequality are **feasible**. Bundles on the boundary of that set are also feasible, since they cost exactly I. These bundles represent the **budget constraint**. Bundles on the budget constraint are said to be **binding**, while feasible bundles not on the budget constraint are **not binding**. Suppose you have \$20 available and are spending \$18 on a bundle. Tightening your budget constraint by a small amount, say by \$0.01, has no effect on the affordability of your bundle. Your budget constraint is not binding on this bundle.

feasible: The set of bundles $(x_1, \ldots, x_n)$ that satisfy the inequality $P_1x_1 + P_2x_2 + \ldots + P_nx_n \leq I$ with each $x_i \geq 0$ is called the set of feasible consumption bundles.

budget constraint: The set of bundles $(x_1, \ldots, x_n)$ that satisfy the equality $P_1x_1 + P_2x_2 + \ldots + P_nx_n = I$ with each $x_i \geq 0$ is called the budget constraint.

binding: A constraint is binding on a given bundle if tightening the constraint by a small amount makes the bundle infeasible.

not binding: A constraint is not binding on a bundle if the bundle remains feasible when the constraint tightens by a small amount.

Geometrically, the budget constraint is a linear function with n vertices—one for each good that is available for purchase. The *j*th vertex would occur if all income were spent on good j; in this event, the vertex is $(x_1, \ldots, x_n) = (0, \ldots, 0, I/P_j, 0, \ldots, 0)$. Bundles in the nonnegative orthant beneath this constraint (closer to the origin) cost less than I and are therefore feasible.[1] The budget constraint is not binding on these bundles.

If we set n = 3, the budget constraint with prices $P_x = \$1.50$, $P_y = \$2$, $P_z = \$1$, and income, I = \$18, then it is described algebraically by $1.5x + 2y + z = 18$ with $x \geq 0$, $y \geq 0$, and $z \geq 0$. Figure 5.1 provides the geometric representation of this budget constraint as the triangle whose x, y, and z vertices are (12, 0, 0), (0, 9, 0), and (0, 0, 18). Put another way, the budget constraint is that part of the $1.5x + 2y + z = 18$ plane that is in the nonnegative octant. Also depicted there is one bundle on the plane: (6, 3, 3). The consumer facing this budget constraint and choosing this bundle will spend \$9 on x, \$6 on y, and \$3 on z.

The budget constraint was introduced with n goods because that is the way you typically go to the store. $P_1x_1 + P_2x_2 + \ldots + P_nx_n$ is how much you spend at the store on $x_1, \ldots, x_n$ units of these n goods (unless they charged sales tax, in which case, that sum

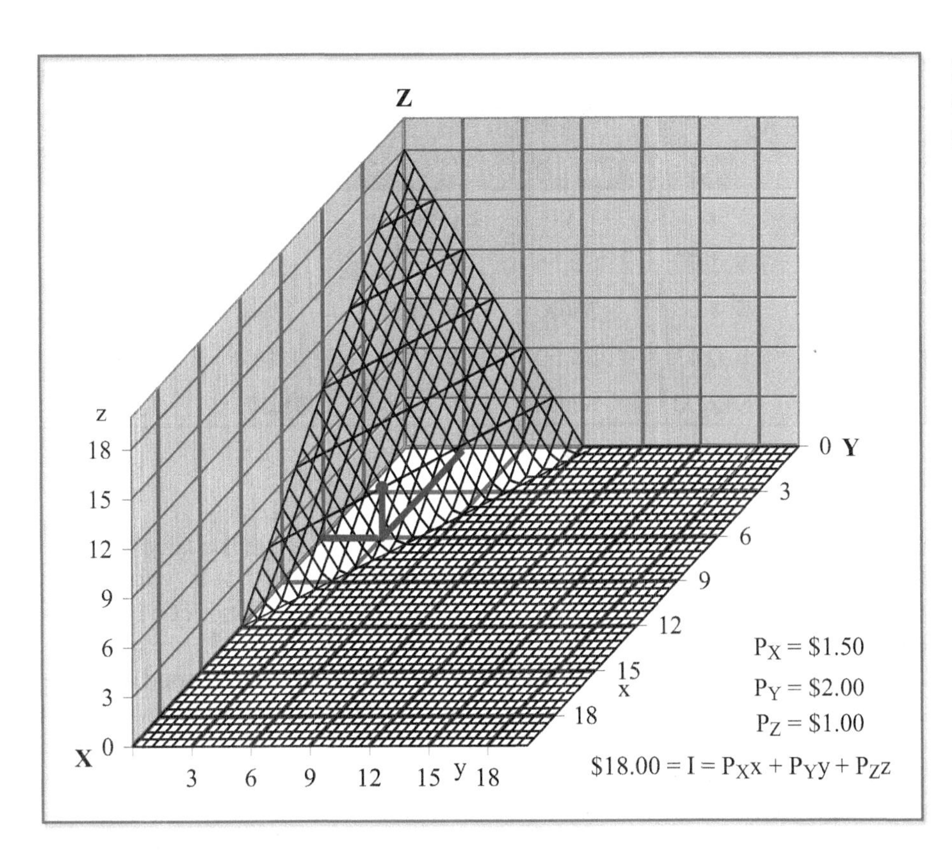

FIGURE 5.1 A Budget Constraint with Three Goods

would be multiplied by (1 + t)). The algebra of the situation is quite intuitive; however, the geometry is decidedly less so as the number of goods increases, and we must be satisfied with $n = 3$ if we wish to show the budget constraint graphically. This should not be surprising: The same discussion occurred in Chapter 4 when we focused on indifference curves associated with n goods that were perfect substitutes. The two graphs, if their sliders are adjusted properly, are *identical*, but their economic interpretation is quite different in the two chapters. In Chapter 4, the planes in Figures 4.1 and 4.2 are perfect substitute indifference curves whose slopes are determined by the ratio of marginal utilities of the goods. Points on an indifference curve certainly could cost different amounts of money; the indifference curve is *not* a budget constraint. In contrast, the plane in Figure 5.1 is a budget constraint whose slopes are determined by the prices of the goods. Points on the budget constraint certainly could be more or less preferred to other points on the budget constraint; the budget constraint is *not* an indifference curve. This conceptual difference, despite geometric similarity, exists because preferences are distinct from budget constraints. Lack of clarity over the distinction often centers on confusing preferences and constraints.

5.2 Alternative Representations of a Budget Constraint

Unfortunately, the algebraic description of the budget constraint is not unique. The budget constraint can be described in terms of an infinite number of equations, not just $P_1x_1 + P_2x_2 + \ldots + P_nx_n = I$. Or, to put this in the context of the budget constraint represented by the triangular surface in Figure 5.1: $1.5x + 2y + z = 18$ does not uniquely describe this area. Suppose all prices and income double; what happens to the budget constraint? The actual shape of the budget constraint will not change, but both sides of the equation for the budget constraint double to $3x + 4y + 2z = 36$. Or, suppose prices and income decrease by a factor of 10. The same thing happens: The geometry remains the same, while the algebra looks different.

Of course, we typically do not have the ability to alter prices or income in such a way. When we go to the store, the prices are marked, and we know how much money is in our

TABLE 5.1 Alternative Ways to Describe the Same Budget Constraint*

Prices Given Different Numeraires				Unitary Income	Another Choice	A General Solution
	x	y	z (shown)			
P_X	**$ 1.00**	$0.75	$ 1.50	1/12	$0.30	$1.5 \cdot r$
P_Y	$ 1.33	**$1.00**	$ 2.00	1/9	$0.40	$2 \cdot r$
P_Z	$ 0.67	$0.50	**$ 1.00**	1/18	$0.20	r
I	$12.00	$9.00	$18.00	**$1.00**	$3.60	$18 \cdot r$

*Each of these scenarios produces a budget constraint whose (x, y, z) vertices are (12, 0, 0), (0, 9, 0), and (0, 0, 18). The bundle (x, y, z) = (6, 3, 3) is on each budget constraint.

pocket. Our budget constraint in this situation is fixed, algebraically and graphically, by the reality we face when walking into the store. Nonetheless, it is worthwhile to consider the implications of alternative algebraic representations of budget constraints. Table 5.1 depicts five such possibilities and a general version as well.

numeraire: A numeraire is a good whose price is fixed at $1.00.

Three of the representations in Table 5.1 are situations where a good acts as a numeraire. A **numeraire** is a good whose price is fixed at $1.00. A numeraire acts as a meter of value; other goods are measured in relation to the numeraire. With z as the numeraire, we see that y is twice as valuable as z, and x is 50% more valuable than z. Had we used y as the numeraire, we would have seen that x is 25% less valuable than y, and z is half as valuable as y. If we had used x as the numeraire, y would be one-third more valuable and z would be one-third less valuable than x. A numeraire acts to define the metric that measures relative value.

The *unitary income* version of the budget constraint is obtained by setting income equal to one and adjusting the prices accordingly. (Clearly, this is not very realistic, but the rationale for doing this will become apparent soon.) The 1 in I = 1 stands for 100%. Given this, the amount spent on good *i*, $P_i x_i$, is the proportion of income devoted to that good, and prices are the fractions of income required to purchase 1 unit of that good. (The prices have been given as fractions so that you can more easily see the proportions of income spent on each good.) The bundle (6, 3, 3) is attained by spending one-half of income on six units of good x ($1/2 = 1/12 \cdot 6$), one-third of income is spent on three units of good y ($1/3 = 1/9 \cdot 3$), and one-sixth of income is spent on three units of good z ($1/6 = 1/18 \cdot 3$). These proportions can also be seen geometrically from the location of the bundle (6, 3, 3) on the budget constraint in Figure 5.1. At the second red line along the x axis, x = 6, and the vertex on the x axis, x = 12, is on the fourth red line. The vertex is attainable if 100% of income is spent on x, so x = 6 represents spending 50% of income on x. Similarly, y = 3 is one-third of the way along the y axis to y's vertex of y = 9. Finally, z = 3 is one-sixth of the way along the z axis toward the vertex of z = 18. (One-sixth of the way is seen as being on the first black diagonal representing the bundles on the budget constraint with z = 3. Subsequent black diagonals are at z = 6, 9, 12, and 15, with the vertex at z = 18.)

There is no intuitive significance of the fifth version of the budget constraint (labeled "Another Choice" in Table 5.1). It is simply one of many alternatives that could be obtained using the sliders in the Excel version of Figure 5.1. More important is the final version in Table 5.1, labeled "A General Solution." Each of the five versions in Table 5.1 could be obtained with different values of r, the scaling factor that is multiplied to each side of the initial budget constraint discussed earlier ($1.5x + 2y + z = 18$).

Q1. What values of r produce each of the columns in Table 5.1?*

*__Q1 answer:__ The values of r for the five columns in Table 5.1 are, from left to right, r = 2/3, r = 1/2, r = 1, r = 1/18, and r = 1/5.

As with the analysis of preferences, we lose little generality by restricting the discussion to bundles that contain only two goods, x and y. Often, we are interested in one good in particular, x. In this instance, y can be thought of as a composite good representing "all other goods," and it makes sense to make y the numeraire. At other times, we are interested in the interplay between two goods that we expect are related. In both situations, two goods are sufficient for our analysis.

The budget constraint with two goods, x and y, is $P_x x + P_y y = I$. If the entire income is spent on good x, I/P_x units can be purchased. Similarly, if the entire income is spent on good y, I/P_y units can be purchased. We can label these border bundles as $\mathbf{A} = (0, I/P_y)$ and $\mathbf{B} = (I/P_x, 0)$. Between these border solutions, a positive portion of income is spent on each good. Figure 5.2A provides an example of such a budget constraint. There is a lot of information packed into this diagram, and knowing only one piece of information allows

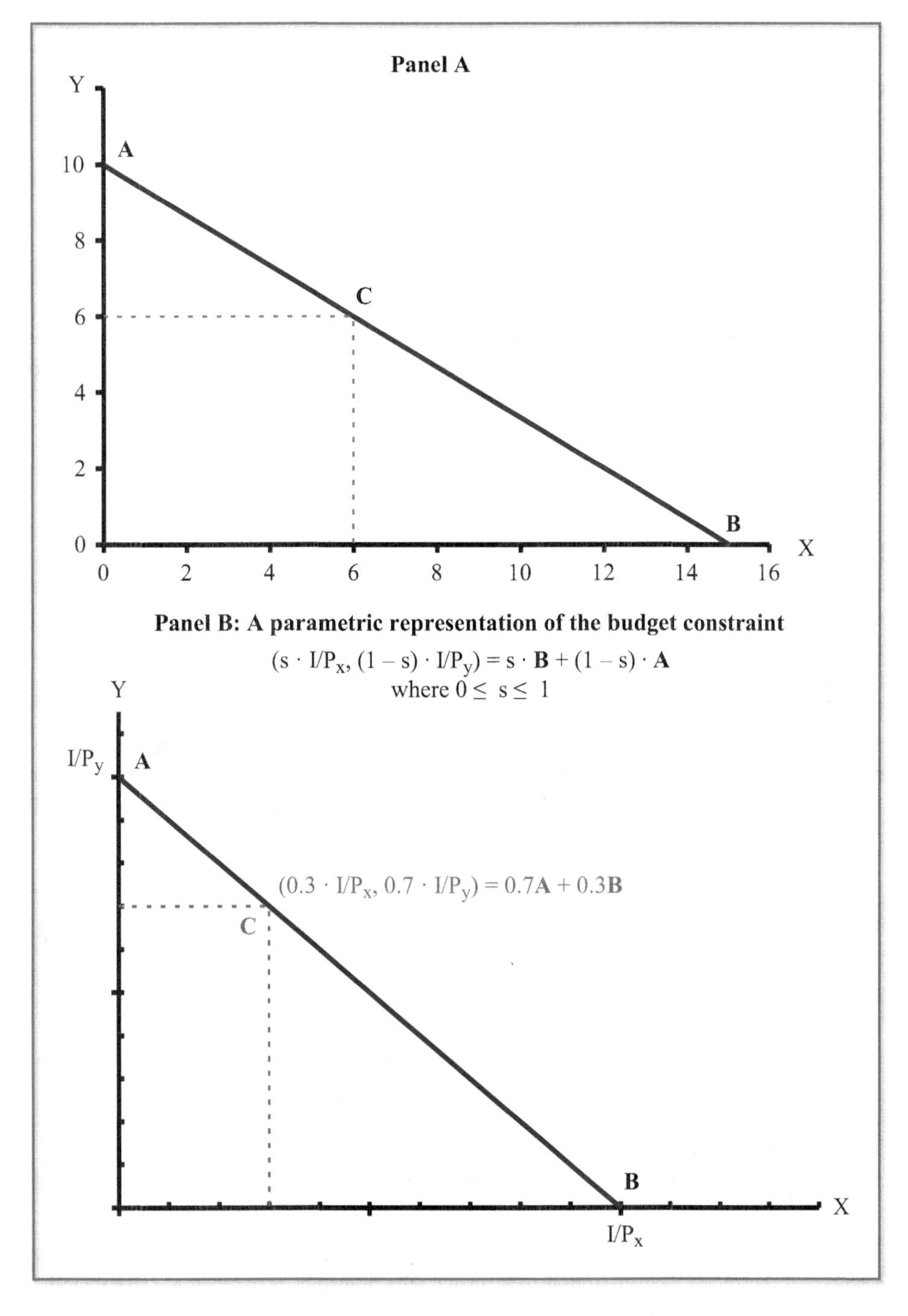

FIGURE 5.2 Deriving Information from a Budget Constraint

you to determine the rest of the information. Suppose, for example, you are given $P_y = 3$ but have no further information. Answer the following:

Q2a. What is the price of x in this situation?

Q2b. How much income does the individual have?

Q2c. Bundle **C** is what percentage of the way from **A** to **B**? (This is the two-dimensional analog of the earlier assertion that the bundle (6, 3, 3) in Figure 5.1 was (1/2, 1/3, 1/6) of the way from each of the vertices.)

Q2d. What percentage of income is spent on good x?

Q2e. How would your answers to Q2a–Q2d change if you had been told that $P_x = 3$, rather than $P_y = 3$?

Q2f. How would your answers to Q2a–Q2d change if you had been told that $I = 3$, rather than $P_y = 3$?*

store method: The store method of representing a budget constraint simply adds the amount spent on each good across goods. The resulting sum is income.

parametric representation: The parametric representation of the budget constraint describes the constraint in terms of the portion of the budget devoted to each good.

Slope-intercept representation: The slope-intercept representation of the budget constraint presents the constraint in $y = m \cdot x + b$ format.

The budget constraint can be described algebraically in a variety of ways. The budget constraint, $P_x x + P_y y = I$, is the equation of a line. This is the most intuitive description of the budget constraint because it describes the amounts that are spent on each of the goods x and y (as noted earlier, $P_x x$ is spent on x, and $P_y y$ is spent on y). We call this the **store method** of describing the budget constraint because this is how we go to the store to purchase goods.

$$P_x x + P_y y = I. \quad \textit{Store representation of the budget constraint} \quad \textbf{(5.1a)}$$

A less common version—the parametric representation—allows you to focus directly on the "percentage of the way" question noted previously. The **parametric** description of the budget constraint **AB**, where **A** represents spending all income on good y and **B** represents spending all income on x, is defined as the set of bundles **C**:

$$\mathbf{C} = (s \cdot I/P_x, (1 - s) \cdot I/P_y)$$
$$\text{or } s \cdot \mathbf{B} + (1 - s) \cdot \mathbf{A} \text{ with } 0 \le s \le 1. \quad \textit{Parametric budget constraint} \quad \textbf{(5.1b)}$$

The parameter, s, represents the proportion of the way from **A** to **B** represented by the bundle **C**. Figure 5.2B shows **C** when s = 0.3; the Excel file for Figure 5.2 allows you to vary s from 0 to 1. As you do, you traverse the line from **A** to **B**.[2] Parametric representations of line segments have already been used in the text (without specifically describing the discussion as being parametrically driven). The most notable instances are in the discussion of convexity (see the discussion of Figure 3.4 and the convexity discussion in the bracketing utility analysis surrounding Figure 4.15).

From a purely *geometric* point of view, the **slope-intercept** form, $y = m \cdot x + b$ (where m is slope and b is the y intercept), is more intuitive than the store form or the parametric form. We can put the budget constraint into slope-intercept form by solving for y. The resulting equation is:

$$y = I/P_y - (P_x/P_y) \cdot x. \quad \textit{Slope-intercept representation of the budget constraint} \quad \textbf{(5.1c)}$$

The y intercept has already been noted; if all income is spent on y, you could purchase $b = I/P_y$ units of y. The slope of the budget constraint is $m = -P_x/P_y$ in Equation 5.1c. This slope can be seen geometrically in two ways with the help of Figure 5.3. The first method is to use the endpoints **A** and **B** and calculate slope between **A** and **B**. For general values of I, P_x, and P_y, we know that $\mathbf{A} = (0, I/P_y)$ and $\mathbf{B} = (I/P_x, 0)$. Slope between bundles **A** and **B** is:

$$\text{Slope} = \Delta y/\Delta x = (y_b - y_a)/(x_b - x_a) = (0 - I/P_y)/(I/P_x - 0) = -P_x/P_y. \quad \textbf{(5.2)}$$

The second method takes a bit longer to show but is, perhaps, a bit more intuitive. Start at a bundle $\mathbf{C} = (x_c, y_c)$ on the budget constraint. Suppose you want to obtain bundle **D** with

***Q2 answer:** With $P_y = 3$, $I = 30$ and $P_x = 2$. If $P_x = 3$, $I = 45$ and $P_y = 4.5$. If $I = 3$, $P_x = 0.2$ and $P_y = 0.3$. In each case, **C** is 40% of the way from **A** to **B**, so that 40% of income is spent on x. The Excel file for Figure 5.2 lets you vary the percentage spent on x from 0 to 100%.

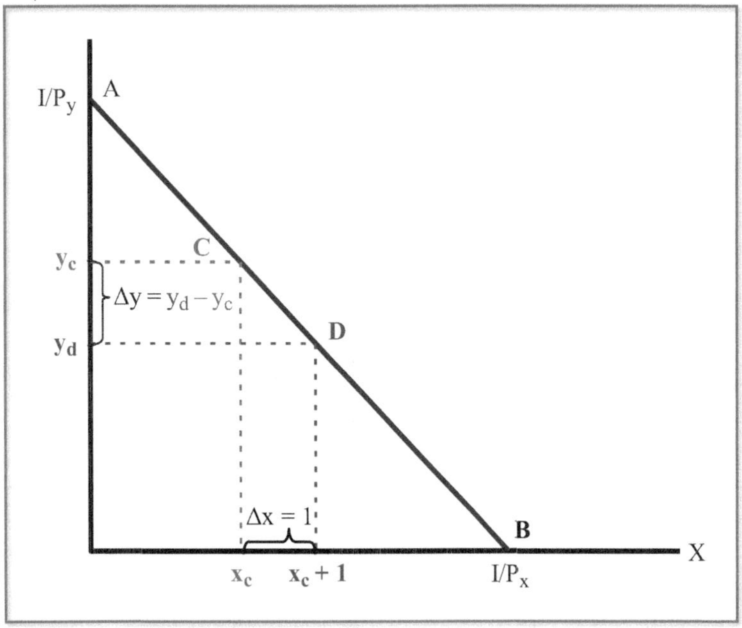

FIGURE 5.3 The Slope of the Budget Constraint

one more unit of x than at **C**. How much y will bundle **D** have if **D** is also on the budget constraint? Put another way, what is the value of y_d in Figure 5.3? If you wish to purchase one unit of good x, you must free up P_x dollars from dollars you previously used to purchase good y. Given a price of P_y dollars per unit of y, you can free up \$1 by purchasing $1/P_y$ fewer *units* of y. To free up $\$P_x$, purchase $P_x \cdot (1/P_y) = P_x/P_y$ fewer units of y than you purchased at **C**. The bundle $\mathbf{D} = (x_c + 1, y_c - P_x/P_y)$ will cost the same as bundle **C**:

$$\text{Cost of } \mathbf{D} = P_x (x_c + 1) + P_y (y_c - P_x/P_y)$$
$$= P_x x_c + \mathbf{P_x} + P_y y_c - \mathbf{P_x} = P_x x_c + P_y y_c = \text{Cost of } \mathbf{C}. \quad \mathbf{(5.3)}$$

The $+ \mathbf{P_x}$ that has been bolded in Equation 5.3 is the cost of the extra unit of x, and the bolded $- \mathbf{P_x}$ is the money saved by purchasing less y. The slope between bundles **C** and **D** is $-P_x/P_y$ because $\Delta y/\Delta x = (-P_x/P_y)/1$.

The slope of the budget constraint describes the rate at which the *market* allows exchange between two goods. As described in Figure 5.3, an extra unit of x can only be obtained on the market by giving up P_x/P_y units of y. This rate is market determined because market prices establish this rate of exchange. It is worth explicitly pointing out that this market-determined rate of exchange is completely *independent* of whether an individual consumer might be willing to make that exchange. The rate at which a particular consumer is willing to make that exchange is her marginal rate of substitution (MRS) at a given bundle, and the MRS is determined by the individual's preferences. As noted in Section 5.1, we avoid consideration of preferences in this chapter to sidestep the common problem that beginning economics students have of conflating preferences and constraints.

5.3 How Do Budget Constraints Change with Changes in Income or Price?

We now turn to how budget constraints change when either income or price changes. As a consumer, you know that you can purchase more with a higher income and fixed prices, or with lower prices and fixed income. It is less clear what happens if more than one of these parameters change at once, but we begin by following the economist's strategy of varying each individually, holding other factors constant (this is the notion of *ceteris paribus*).

Each of the figures in this section has two budget constraints, a red one and a blue one. *The blue is initial, and the red is final.* Rather than focus on actual price or income

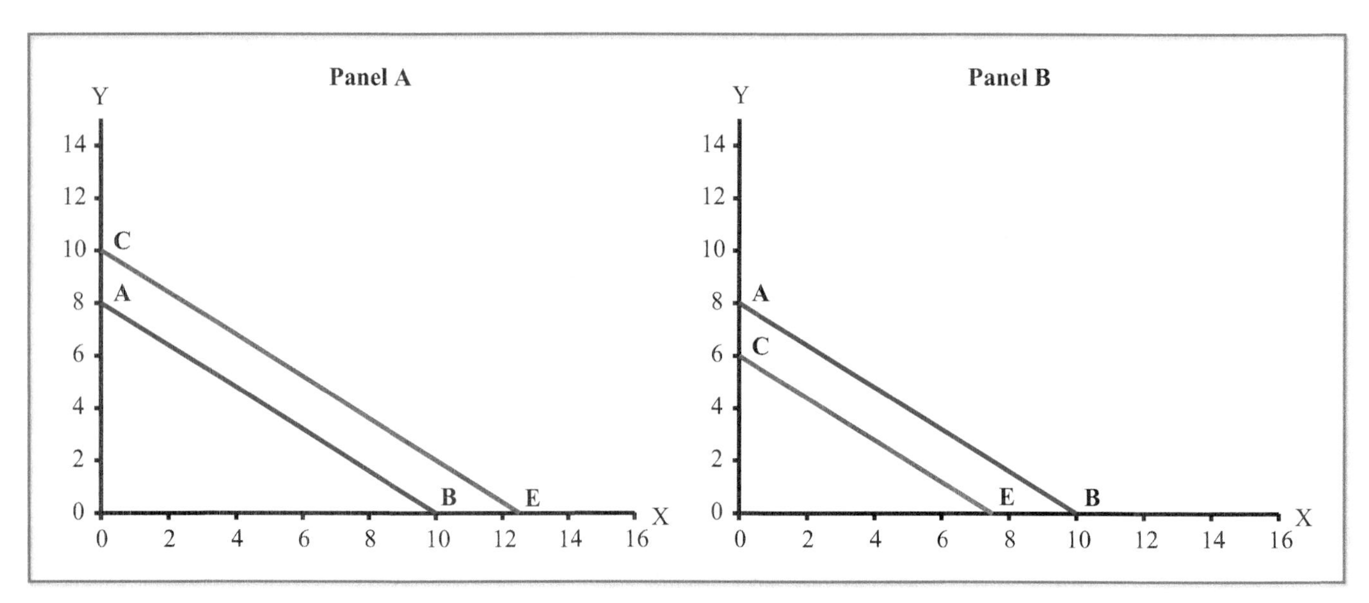

FIGURE 5.4 The Effect of Income Changes on Budget Constraints

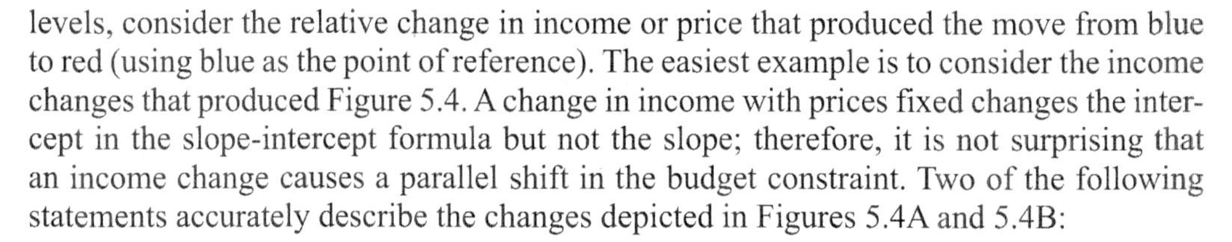
levels, consider the relative change in income or price that produced the move from blue to red (using blue as the point of reference). The easiest example is to consider the income changes that produced Figure 5.4. A change in income with prices fixed changes the intercept in the slope-intercept formula but not the slope; therefore, it is not surprising that an income change causes a parallel shift in the budget constraint. Two of the following statements accurately describe the changes depicted in Figures 5.4A and 5.4B:

S4.i. The move from blue to red represents a 25% decrease in income.

S4.ii. The move from blue to red represents a 20% decrease in income.

S4.iii. The move from blue to red represents a 20% increase in income.

S4.iv. The move from blue to red represents a 25% increase in income.

Q4. Match each panel with one of these four statements.*

A change in the price of x only affects the budget constraint if x is consumed. Since no x is consumed on the vertical axis (x = 0), the budget constraint rotates on the y axis when the price of x changes. Consider the following possible descriptions for the change depicted in each panel of Figure 5.5:

S5.i. The move from blue to red represents a 50% decrease in the price of x.

S5.ii. The move from blue to red represents a 33% decrease in the price of x.

S5.iii. The move from blue to red represents a 50% increase in the price of x.

S5.iv. The move from blue to red represents a 100% increase in the price of x.

Q5. Match each panel with one of these four statements.†

***Q4 answer:** Figure 5.4A is S4.iv, and Figure 5.4B is S4.i. If you believed S4.iii represented Figure 5.A, you used the red income level rather than the blue income level as a point of reference (a move from 8 to 10 is a 20% change, using 10 as the point of reference (2/10), and a 25% change, using 8 as the point of reference (2/8)). The slider in the Excel version of Figure 5.4 allows you to vary the percentage change in income from –50% to +50%.

†Q5 answer: Both panels represent a 50% change in price. Figure 5.5A involves a decrease in price, so the correct statement is S5.i. Figure 5.5B involves an increase in price, so the correct statement is S5.iii. The Excel version of Figure 5.5 allows you to vary the percentage change in price between these two bounds.

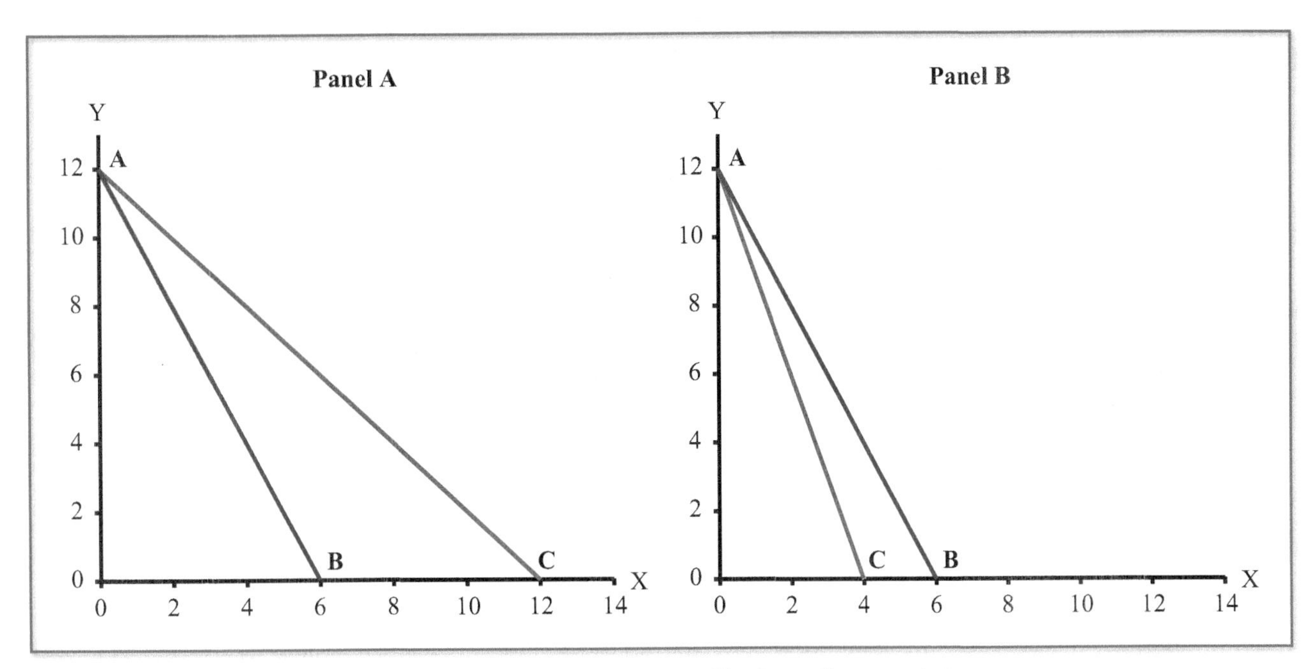

FIGURE 5.5 The Effect of Changes in the Price of x on Budget Constraints

Students are sometimes initially confused by how price changes affect budget constraints because prices changes are inversely related to the size of the feasible set. For fixed income, lower prices mean greater consumption possibilities. In Figure 5.5A, bundles in the triangular area **ABC** were not feasible when the budget constraint was "blue" but are feasible with a 50% reduction in the price of x associated with the "red" budget constraint. Conversely, in Figure 5.5B, bundles in the triangular area **ABC** were feasible when the budget constraint was "blue" but are not feasible with a 50% increase in the price of x associated with the "red" budget constraint.

If the price of y changes for a fixed price of x and income, the budget constraint rotates on the x axis. Not surprisingly, the analysis is symmetric to the previous one provided for the price of x. As a result, you should find it easy to match panels to the following statements for Figure 5.6:

S6.i. The move from blue to red represents a 33% decrease in the price of y.

S6.ii. The move from blue to red represents a 25% decrease in the price of y.

S6.iii. The move from blue to red represents a 33% increase in the price of y.

S6.iv. The move from blue to red represents a 50% increase in the price of y.

Q6. Match each panel with one of these four statements.*

Although both panels in Figure 5.6 involve a change of 3 units in the y intercept as a result of the price change, the percentage change in each is different. This asymmetry occurs because price enters in the denominator of the y intercept, I/P_y. (Contrast this with the income change seen in Figure 5.4: Both panels involve the same numerical change on the vertical axis ($\Delta y = 2$) and the same percentage change in income ($\%\Delta I = 25\%$). This symmetry occurs because income enters in the numerator of the intercept.)

In a two-good model, there are three parameters that define the budget constraint: P_x, P_y, and I. Figures 5.4–5.6 examine how each of these parameters individually impact the set of feasible bundles, holding the other parameters constant. The set of feasible bundles increases if income increases or if either of the prices decreases, *ceteris paribus*. When

***Q6 answer:** Figure 5.6A is S6.ii, and Figure 5.6B is S6.iv.

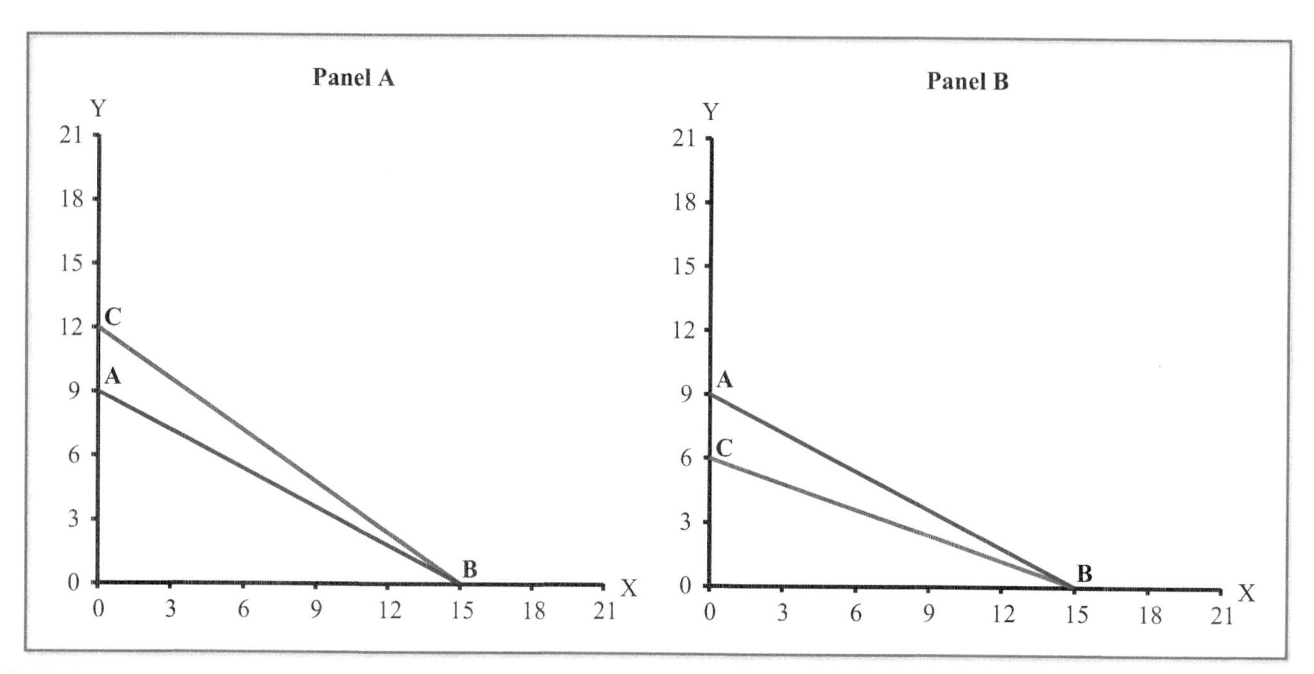

FIGURE 5.6 The Effect of Changes in the Price of y on Budget Constraints

multiple parameters change at once, a more complex picture emerges. Figure 5.7 examines the contours of this picture. Figures 5.7A and 5.7B examine multiple price changes, given fixed income. Consider the following scenario:

S7. Bundles in triangle **DEB** are feasible after prices change (given fixed income), while bundles in triangle **CAD** are no longer feasible after prices change.

Q7. Which of the Figures 5.7A or 5.7B describes this situation?*

Neither budget constraint dominates in Figures 5.7A and 5.7B. Each shows a trade-off between bundles in areas **DEB** versus **CAD**. As income changes, this will continue to hold as long as the percentage change in income is no larger than the percentage change in price. This is shown in Figures 5.7B–5.7D, which all have the same price changes but allow income to vary. A more continuous version can be seen by varying the percentage change in income from –50% to +50% in the Excel file of Figure 5.7.

There will continue to be trade-off areas that are qualitatively similar to **DEB** and **CAD**, as long as the percentage change in income is in the following range:

$$\text{Minimum}(\%\Delta P_x, \%\Delta P_y) < \%\Delta I < \text{Maximum}(\%\Delta P_x, \%\Delta P_y). \quad \textbf{(5.4a)}$$

The proof of this assertion is based on an examination of how the vertices change in this instance. Let $a = \text{Minimum}(\%\Delta P_x, \%\Delta P_y)$, $b = \%\Delta I$, and $c = \text{Maximum}(\%\Delta P_x, \%\Delta P_y)$. Equation 5.4a may be rewritten as

$$a < b < c. \quad \textbf{(5.4b)}$$

Consider the first inequality: $a < b$. Let good i be the good whose price change is the minimum percentage. The budget intercept for good i in this instance is $(1 + b) \cdot I/((1 + a) \cdot P_i) > I/P_i$ since $(1 + b)/(1 + a) > 1$. ($a < b$ means $(1 + a) < (1 + b)$. Dividing both sides by $(1 + a)$ yields $(1 + b)/(1 + a) > 1$.) In words, the budget intercept for good i increases as a result of the multiple changes in price and income. Good i is x in Figure 5.7A and y in Figure 5.7B.

***Q7 answer:** Scenario S7 describes Figure 5.7A. As the price of x declines, more x can be purchased with a given amount of income, and as the price of y increases, less y may be purchased with a given amount of income.

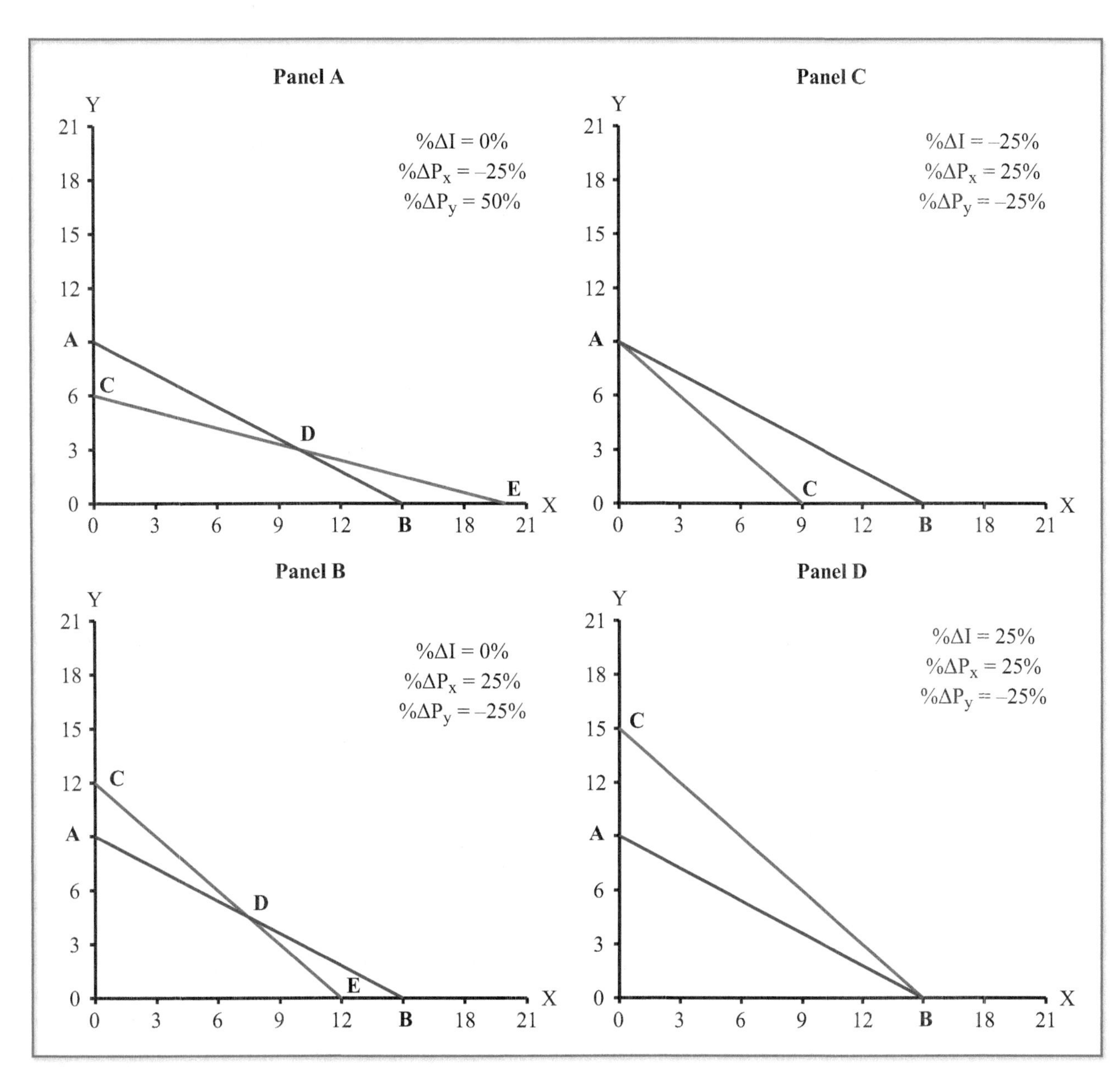

FIGURE 5.7 Changes in Income and Prices

Now consider the second inequality: $b < c$. The budget intercept for good j (whose price change is the maximum percentage) in this instance is $(1 + b) \cdot I/((1 + c) \cdot P_j) < I/P_j$, since, by symmetric reasoning, $(1 + b)/(1 + c) < 1$. In words, the budget intercept for good j decreases as a result of the multiple changes in price and income. Good j is y in Figure 5.7A and x in Figure 5.7B. We have shown that one budget intercept increases and one decreases: This is the same as saying that there are trade-off areas similar to **DEB** and **CAD** in this instance.

Figure 5.7C shows the lower boundary of this inequality, given this specific set of price changes: Minimum($\%\Delta P_x$, $\%\Delta P_y$) = $\%\Delta I$ (both equal –25%). The final budget constraint is completely dominated by the initial budget constraint in this situation. The same holds true if Minimum($\%\Delta P_x$, $\%\Delta P_y$) > $\%\Delta I$. By contrast, Figure 5.7D shows the upper boundary in this inequality, given this specific set of price changes: $\%\Delta I$ = Maximum($\%\Delta P_x$, $\%\Delta P_y$). The final budget constraint now completely dominates the initial budget constraint. The same holds true if $\%\Delta I$ > Maximum($\%\Delta P_x$, $\%\Delta P_y$).

5.4 Applications of Budget Constraint Analysis: Choosing among Constraints

The previous analysis can be used and extended in a variety of ways. Even in the absence of preference information, we can examine choice among options by analyzing budget constraints.

Should You Join a Warehouse Store?

A variety of retail establishments require you to become a member to use the store. Once you become a member (read: "pay a fee"), you obtain goods at discounted prices. Suppose you have $500 per month available with which you can purchase goods. Some of the goods are available at the warehouse store, and some goods are not. Let x denote the goods that are available at the warehouse store and y denote other goods. For simplicity, suppose the price of both x and y is $1 if those goods are purchased in regular stores. (*Both* goods are numeraires in this instance. This allows us to focus more easily on the discount available when goods are purchased in the warehouse store.) The blue budget constraint **AB** in Figure 5.8A depicts purchasing x and y in regular stores. The red budget constraint depicts the budget constraint available if you join the warehouse store. **C** is below **A** because you pay a (monthly) membership fee of **AC** to use the warehouse store.

Q8a. Use the gridlines in Figure 5.8A to determine the discount available in the warehouse store and the monthly membership fee.*

Point **D** in Figure 5.8B depicts the intersection of the two budget constraints.

Q8b. Use this intersection to describe when you would decide to join the warehouse store. *Hint:* The easiest way is to describe your answer in terms of the number of units of the goods you expect to purchase in the warehouse store, x.†

The crossover point occurs at x = 200 because the $50 entry fee is recovered once 200 units of x are purchased in the warehouse store. Each unit of x purchased in the warehouse store saves $0.25 ($0.25 = 25% of the initial price of x, P_x = $1.00), so 200 units of x saves $50. If more x is purchased than that, the warehouse store allows purchases that are not feasible if you do not join. These are the bundles in area **DEB**. Conversely, if fewer than 200 units of x are purchased, there are feasible bundles if you do not join the warehouse store that are not feasible if you join. These are the bundles in area **CAD**. Whether or not you should join depends on how much you plan to use the warehouse store.

Nonlinear Constraints: An Examination of Food-Subsidy Programs

Budget constraints are linear because the market-determined trade-off rate is typically independent of how much of each good is purchased. In terms of the parameters of our simple model, prices are independent of consumption levels of the goods in question. If prices vary based on consumption levels, then the budget constraint will become nonlinear. This is the case with food-subsidy programs targeted to the poor.

Assume an individual has $100 per week to spend on food, x, and other goods, y. As before, let the initial price of both goods equal $1. In the absence of government pro-

---

***Q8a answer:** The red budget line if you join the warehouse has slope –3/4, since it goes through (600, 0) and (200, 300). This implies a discount rate of 25% for goods purchased in the warehouse. (The slope of the warehouse store budget constraint is $P_x^W/P_y = P_x^W/1 = 3/4$. $P_x^W = (1 - d) \cdot P_x$, where d is the percent discount off the retail price of P_x (which equals 1 as discussed earlier). This means that d = 1/4. Extending this budget constraint up to the y intercept implies that **C** = (0, 450). The entry fee **AC** must equal $50 ($500 – $450).

†**Q8b answer:** Join the warehouse store if you plan to purchase more than $200 worth of goods from the store (at 25% discount, the 200 units will cost you $150 [plus the $50 entry fee]); otherwise, do not join the warehouse store.

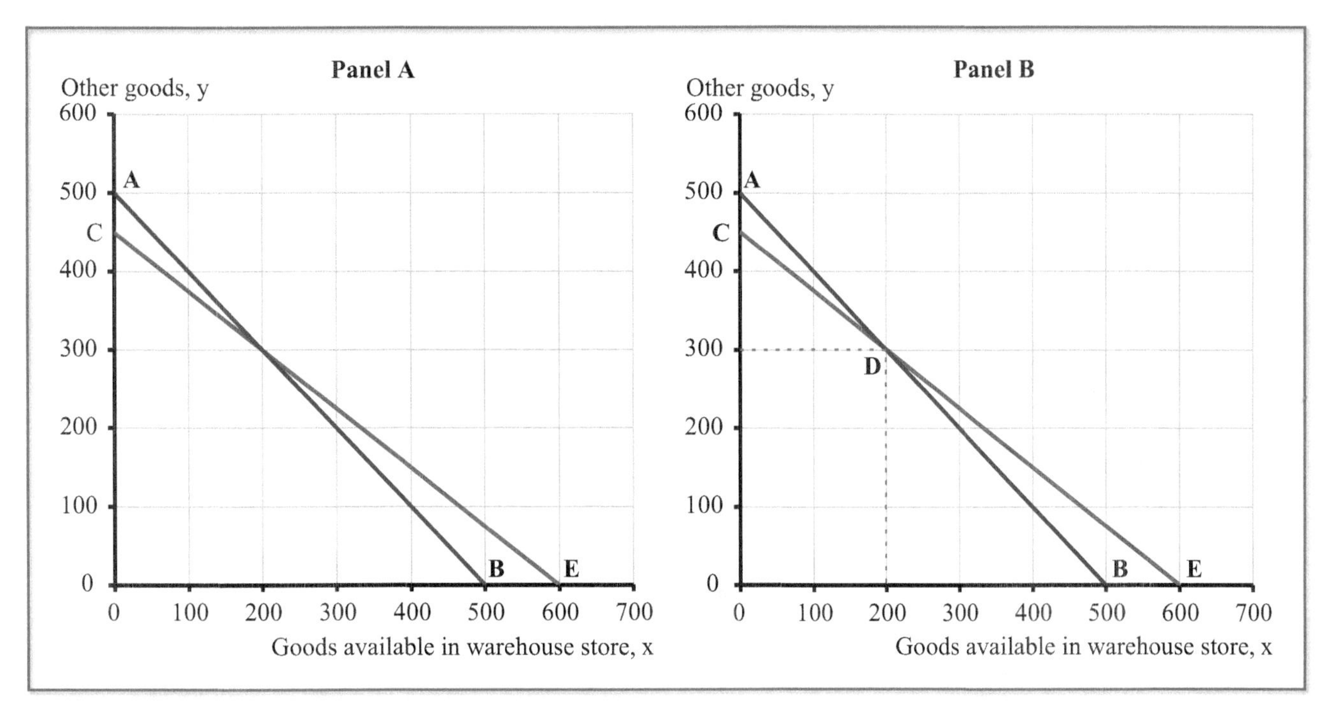

FIGURE 5.8 Should You Join a Warehouse Store?

grams, this individual's budget constraint would be **AB** in Figure 5.9. Consider three possible programs aimed at people in this income bracket:

S9.i. The individual receives R units of free food from a food bank (each unit of food would cost $1 if purchased).

S9.ii. The individual receives $M in cash.

S9.iii. The individual is able to obtain a maximum of T food stamps at a discount rate of d per food stamp. Each food stamp allows the individual to purchase 1 unit of food.

Each panel in Figure 5.9 represents one of these programs.

Q9. Match each panel to its respective program, and provide approximate values for the magnitudes of R, M, T, and d depicted in Figure 5.9.*

Two of the panels in Figure 5.9 depict situations where the price of food depends on how much food is consumed. With the food giveaway depicted in Figure 5.9B, the implicit price of food is $0 for the first 48 units consumed and $1 thereafter. As a result, the budget constraint has slopes of $0 = -P_x/P_y$ along **AE** and $-1 = -P_x/P_y$ along **EK**. With food stamps, the price of food is $(1 - d) = (1 - d) \cdot P_x$ (since the full price of food is $P_x = \$1$) if fewer than T units of food are consumed, since food stamps are sold at a discount of d per unit. In Figure 5.9C, the implicit price of food is $0.40 per unit on the first hundred units of food (along **AH**). If more than 100 units of food are consumed, the price of food is $1 (along **HL**).

Interestingly, you are likely to hear different answers from different people if they are asked which program they would prefer. Their answer depends on how much they

---

***Q9 answer:** Figure 5.9A is the program described in S9.ii. A cash gift of $M increases income and moves out the budget constraint. In Figure 5.9A, the value of this subsidy is length **CA** or **BJ**, since both prices are one. M = $24, although it is not possible to determine an exact value without further information (the numbers were chosen so that the answers later on will be nice and even).

Figure 5.9B is the program described in S9.i, the provision of free food. Specifically, **AE** units of food are provided, and **AE** = R = 48 (although this too is difficult to see exactly).

Figure 5.9C is the program described in S9.iii, the food-stamp program. The total number of stamps available is T = 100, the x coordinate of point **H** in Figure 5.9C. These 100 food stamps are obtained for $40, since there is $60 remaining at point **H**. This represents a 60% discount, d = 0.6.

FIGURE 5.9 Three Food-Subsidy Programs

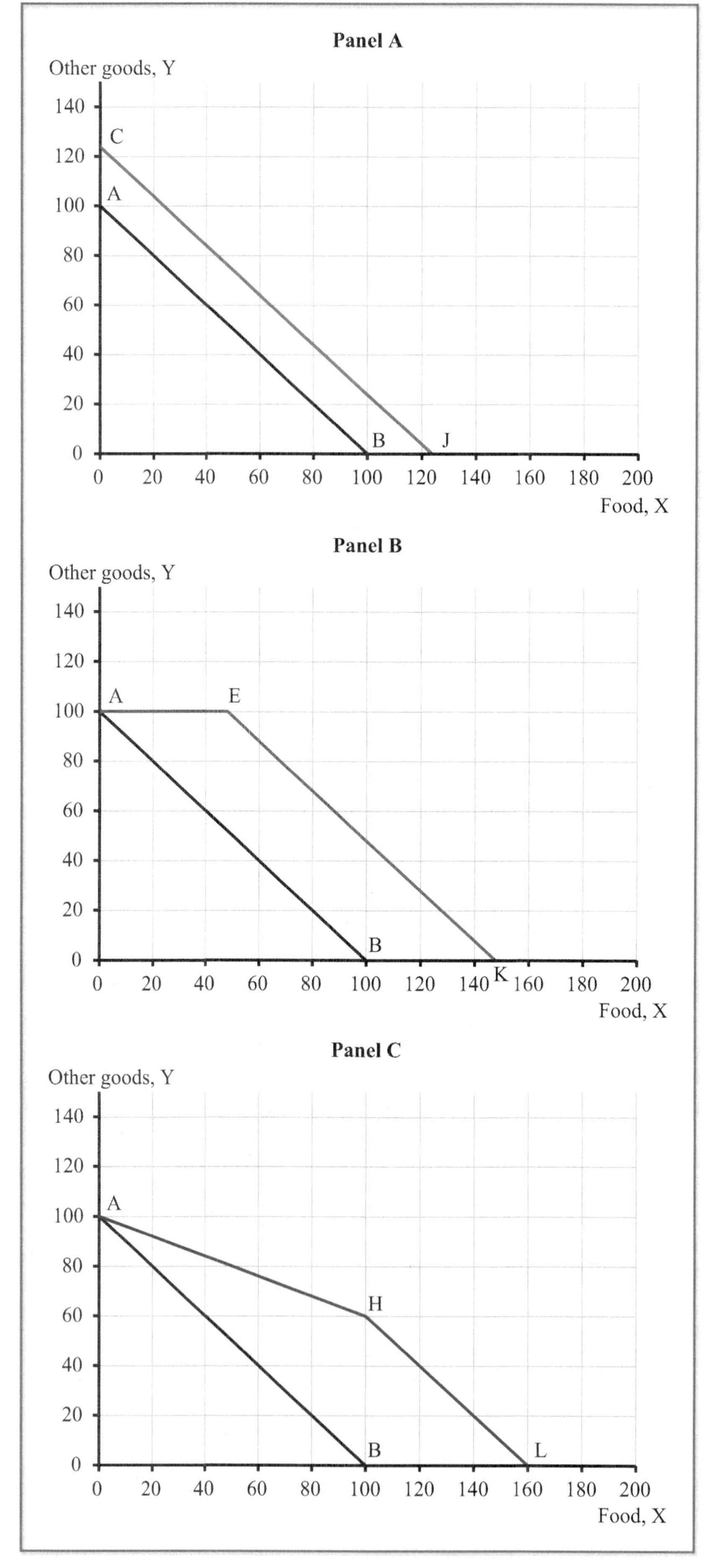

like food. Figure 5.10 examines when each of the programs would be preferred. Figures 5.10A–5.10C provide pairwise comparisons of the programs, and Figure 5.10D shows all three programs together.

Figure 5.10A compares the cash-subsidy program with the free-food program. In this instance, if a particular individual wishes to consume fewer than 24 units of food, he will prefer the cash, since he can obtain bundles in area **CAD** that are not feasible under the free-food plan. Conversely, if an individual wishes to consume more than 24 units of food, the free-food program dominates the cash-subsidy plan because the person can obtain bundles in area **DEKJ** that are not feasible under the cash-subsidy plan. Figure 5.10B examines the choice between the cash-subsidy and food-stamps programs. When a particular individual wishes to consume fewer than 40 units of food, she will prefer the cash-subsidy program, since she can obtain bundles in area **CAF** that are not feasible under the food-stamp plan. Conversely, if an individual wishes to consume more than 40 units of food, the food-stamp plan dominates the cash-subsidy program because

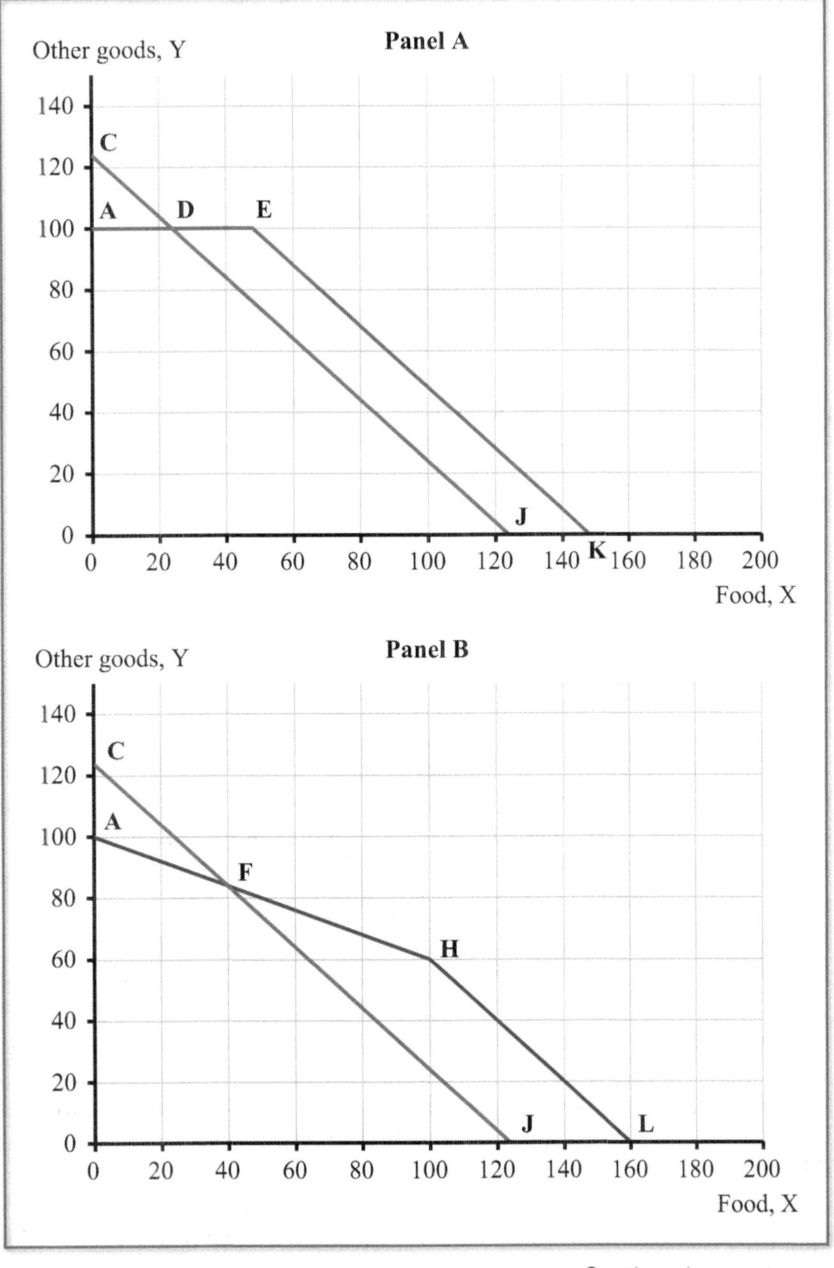

FIGURE 5.10 Comparing Food-Subsidy Programs

Continued on next page

FIGURE 5.10
Continued

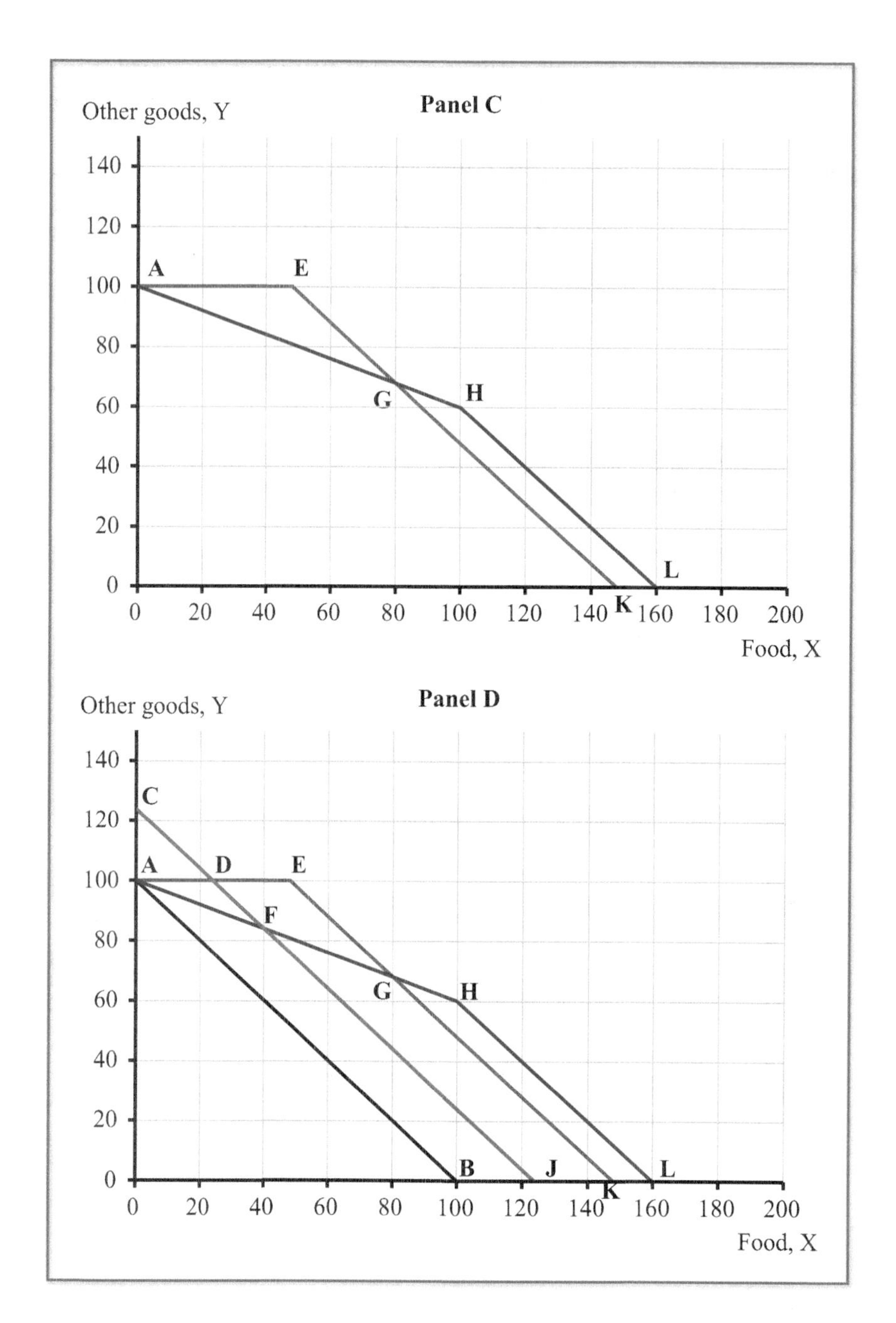

the person can obtain bundles in area **FHLJ** that are not feasible under the cash-subsidy program. Figure 5.10C depicts the choice between free food and food stamps. When a particular individual wishes to consume fewer than 80 units of food, he will prefer the free-food plan, since he can obtain bundles in area **AEG** that are not feasible under the food-stamp plan. Conversely, if an individual wishes to consume more than 80 units of food, the food-stamp plan dominates the free-food plan because the person can obtain bundles in area **GHLK** that are not feasible under the free-food plan.

If you can choose among all three options, your choice will depend on how much food you wish to consume. Figure 5.10D depicts all three programs at once. The cash-subsidy program is preferred if $x < 24$, since bundles in the area **CAD** dominate all other options. For x between $24 < x < 80$, the free-food program dominates, since bundles in the area **DEGF** dominate all other options. Finally, if $x > 80$, the food-stamp program dominates due to area **GHLK**. In Chapter 6, we describe conditions under which each of these options occurs, but for now, it is sufficient to simply acknowledge that, regardless of amount of x consumed, there is a plan that dominates. Two exceptions to this statement exist: If $x = 24$, the cash-subsidy and free-food plans provide the same set of feasible values of y ($y \leq 100$). If $x = 80$, the free-food and food-stamp plans provide the same set of feasible values for y ($y \leq y_G$).

Q10. What is the value of y_G implicit in Figure 5.10D?*

5.5 Other Resource Constraints *OPTIONAL SECTION*

We have focused exclusively on budget constraints thus far in the chapter, but consumers face other constraints as well. Primary among these nonmonetary constraints are time constraints. Perhaps the simplest way to examine how multiple constraints affect consumers is to consider two goods that have both a monetary price and a time "price." Since we have already discussed monetary prices, we will initially focus on time prices.

Figure 5.11A describes the feasible bundles for a consumer who has, at most, 12 hours to spend on two activities at the gym: using the fitness center and playing racquetball. The red line in Figure 5.11A describes the time constraint in this situation; if the individual spends more hours playing racquetball, less time must necessarily be spent in the fitness center. If the only constraint the consumer faced was the time constraint, then she could choose any bundle in area **CEO**. All bundles in the first quadrant on or below the red time constraint are feasible in this instance. This would be the situation if, for example, the individual belongs to a club that sets a fixed fee per month, with no additional fees for usage of specific facilities.

Not all clubs work this way, however. Some charge a fee to join and a separate fee for specific usage. Economists call such a pricing structure a **two-part tariff**. The fee occurs in two parts: the entry fee and the fee for specific usage. The warehouse store analyzed in the previous section is an example of a two-part tariff. In the present context, the entry fee is unimportant, as it occurs regardless of specific quantities consumed. Our focus here is on the second fee—the fee for specific usage. As a result, we assume that the consumer has already paid the entry fee.

two-part tariff: A two-part tariff involves two fees: One part is an entry fee; the other part is a fee for specific usage. Amusement parks often have a two-part tariff structure.

Figure 5.11B introduces a budget constraint for usage of specific facilities. Suppose the blue budget constraint denotes the feasible bundles available when spending $150 per month on these specific activities. Before examining the implications of the time constraint, answer the following:

Q11a. Which activity costs more per hour?

Q11b. What is the cost per hour of using the racquetball court?

Q11c. What is the cost per hour of using the fitness center?†

Suppose you face both the time constraint and the budget constraint. What are the feasible bundles available to you in this instance? Since you must satisfy *both* constraints, your feasible bundles are the intersection of the budget constraint **AB0** and the time constraint **CE0**. You are restricted to the quadrangle **ADE0**. The bundles in triangle **CAD** are too expensive (except on line segment **AD**), and bundles in triangle **DEB** are too time consuming (except on line segment **DE**), given the multiple constraints you face.

Notice that while Figures 5.11B and 5.7B both look quite similar, with the exception of **A** being at (0, 9) in Figure 5.7B rather than (0, 10) in Figure 5.11B, the interpretation and implications obtained from the two diagrams are decidedly different. You should not confuse these two situations. Figure 5.7 examines the change in moving from one budget

---

***Q10 answer:** $y_G = 68$. This can be seen using either equation. The line containing **EGK** is $y = 148 - x$, if $x = 80$, $y = 68$. This requires noting that the line has slope −1 and goes through the bundle (48, 100); thus, the y intercept is 148 (the bundle (0, 148) is *not* feasible under the free-food program, but it does help us describe the line using slope-intercept form). The other solution uses the line through **AFGH**. This line has equation $y = 100 - 0.4 \cdot x$ (the 0.4 is 1 minus the 60% discount). Evaluating this at $x = 80$ yields the same result, $y = 68$.

†Q11 answer: Racquetball is more expensive because you can only purchase 10 hours for $150 versus 15 hours for the fitness center. The hourly rate for using the racquetball court is $15 ($150/10). By contrast, the fitness center costs $10 per hour ($150/15).

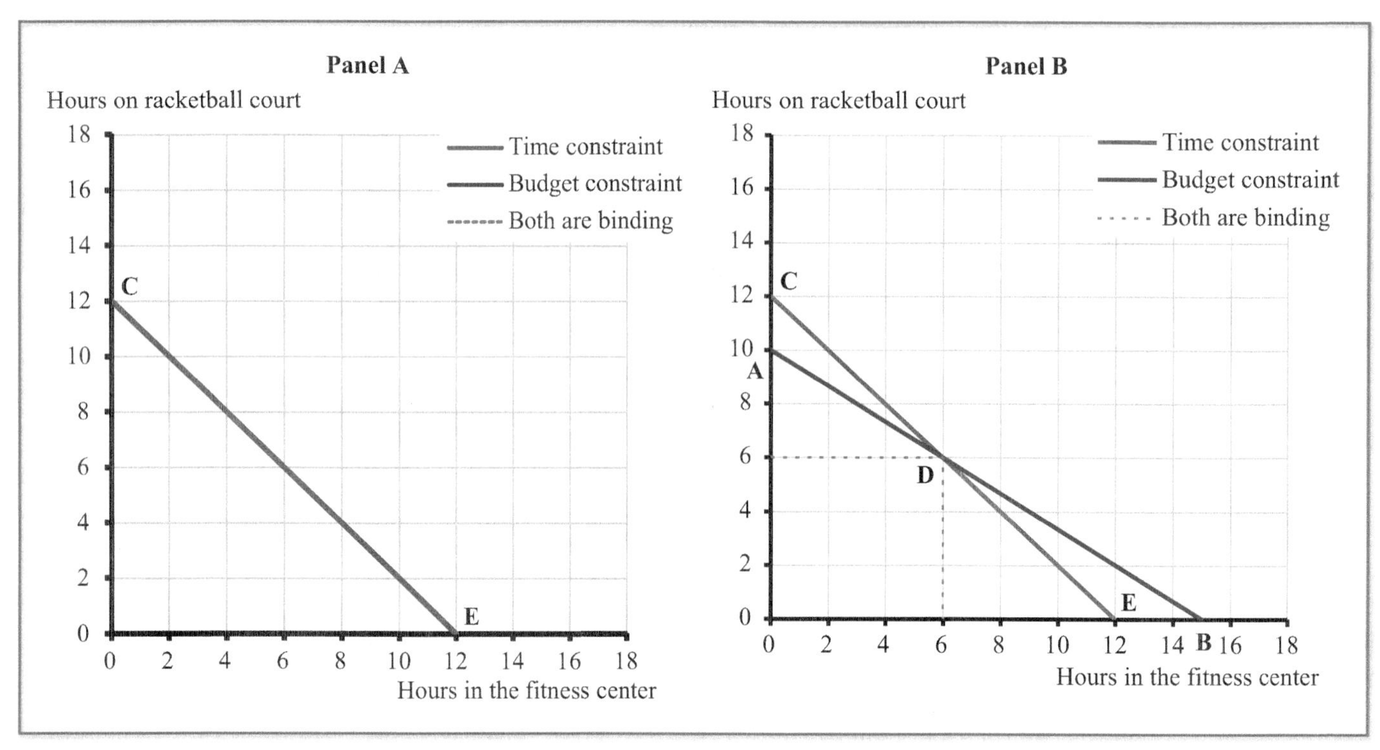

FIGURE 5.11 An Individual Facing Multiple Constraints

constraint to another, while Figure 5.11 examines the addition of a *second* constraint to a fixed budget constraint. If you decide to consume on the segment **AD**, you spend fewer than 12 hours playing racquetball and working out in the fitness center, but you spend \$150 on these activities. Your monetary constraint is binding, but your time constraint is not (except at **D**). Conversely, if you decide to consume on the segment **DE**, you spend 12 hours playing racquetball and working out in the fitness center, but you spend less than \$150 per month on these activities. Your time constraint is binding, but your monetary constraint is not (except at **D**). Only at **D** are both constraints binding.

For a fixed budget constraint, the set of feasible bundles will change as your time constraint changes. Given the budget constraint in Figure 5.11B, the time constraint will always be binding if time available for playing racquetball and working out in the fitness center is fewer than 10 hours per month, and it will never be binding if the time available is more than 15 hours per month. The slider in the Excel version of Figure 5.11 allows you to model these possibilities.

We can formalize the time constraint, using terms that are similar to those used for budget constraints. Let H be the number of hours available to the consumer. As described, each good had a time price of 1 hour ($x + y = 12$ represents the time constraint). More generally, let the "time prices" for x and y be t_x and t_y. These prices represent the amount of time it takes to consume 1 unit of x and 1 unit of y. The time constraint is:

$$t_x \cdot x + t_y \cdot y \leq H \qquad \text{with } x \geq 0 \text{ and } y \geq 0. \qquad \textbf{(5.5)}$$

Figure 5.12 provides six alternative scenarios based on a common good x—rented movies. Suppose the Redbox video kiosk near you charges \$1.50 per movie. For each panel, the red line represents the time constraint. Assume that it takes 2 hours to watch a movie. The total hours available, H, and the time price of good y, t_y, varies in each panel according to how time intensive y is to consume. (Notice that the scales are not the same on the two axes in Figure 5.12.) Since the focus is on the time constraint here, each panel has the same blue budget constraint, whose intercepts are **A** = (0, 15), and **B** = (10, 0).

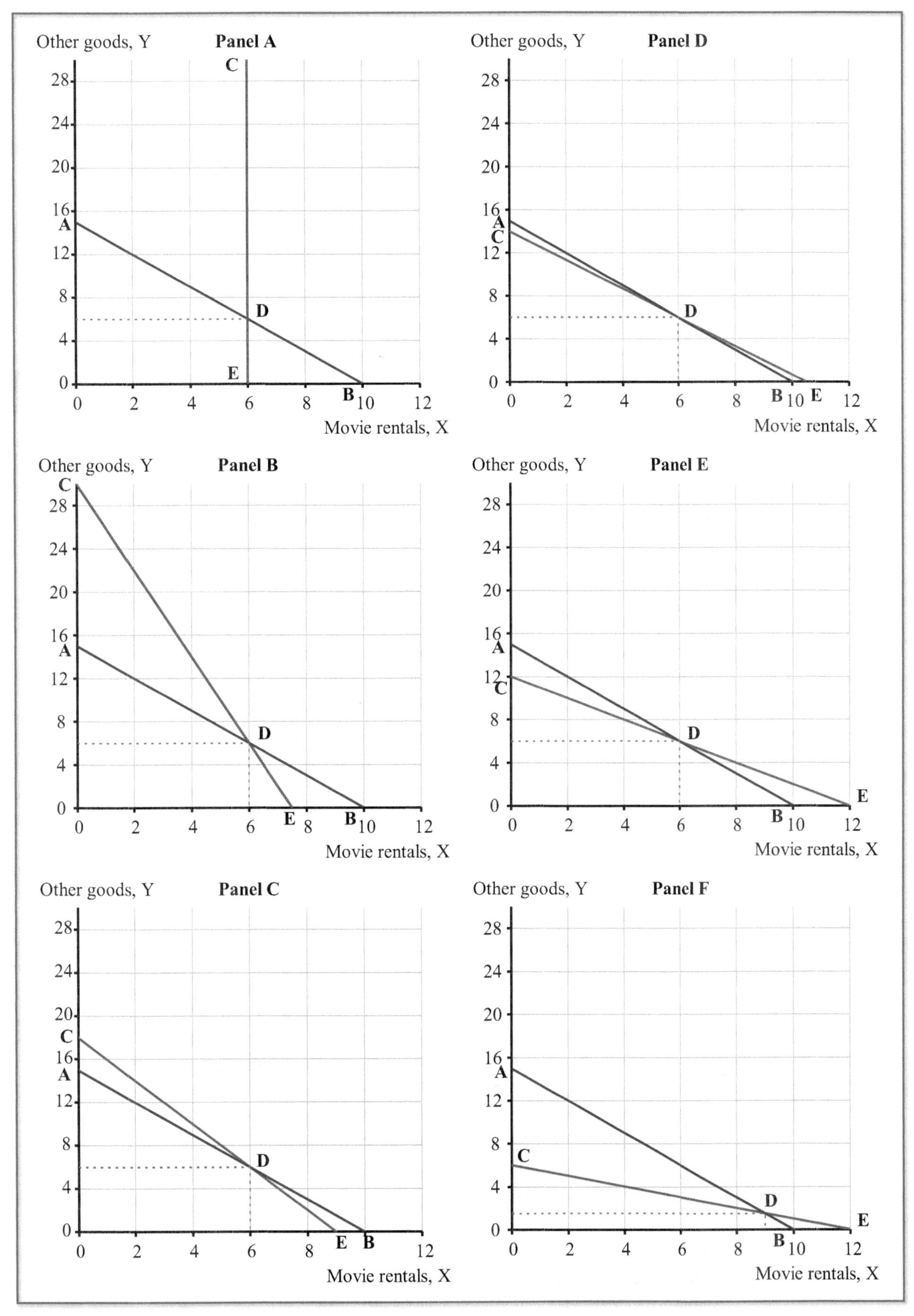

FIGURE 5.12 Time Constraints with Varying Hours and Time Price of y, Given $t_x = 2$; Time Constraint: $t_X \cdot x + t_Y \cdot y \leq H$

Q12a. How much income does the individual have to spend on x and y, and what is the price of y, given P_x = \$1.50?*

For each panel in Figure 5.12, answer the following:

Q12b. What is the time price of y in this panel?

Q12c. How many hours are available with which to consume x and y in this panel?

Q12d. For which panels does the area bounded by **CAD** represent bundles that are too expensive but not too time consuming, given the budget and time constraints shown?

Q12e. For which panels does the area bounded by **DEB** represent bundles that are too expensive but not too time consuming, given the budget and time constraints shown?

Q12f. What is the set of feasible bundles, given both constraints?

This is perhaps easiest to accomplish by filling in the following table:

Panel	t_y	H	Is CAD Too Expensive?	Is DEB Too Expensive?	Feasible Region
5.12A					
5.12B					
5.12C					
5.12D					
5.12E					
5.12F					

A completed table is provided at the end of the chapter. (*Hint:* Time intercept points **C** and **E** are integers except for **E** = (7.5, 0) in Figure 5.12B and **E** = (10.5, 0) in Figure 5.12D. **D** = (6, 6) in Figures 5.12A–5.12E and **D** = (9, 1.5) in Figure 5.12F.)

5.6 Discrete Goods

OPTIONAL SECTION

Throughout this book, we assume that goods can be consumed in continuous quantities. The main reason for this assumption is that it provides a much more elegant solution to optimization problems. Continuous solutions typically will be close to those found by more complex discrete (nonnegative integer) analysis. This will become clear when we examine the consumer's optimal choice problem in Chapter 6. We digress from our focus on continuous goods in this section because discreteness can be viewed as another form of resource constraint. You may have wondered, for example, what it means to rent a noninteger number of movies in the analysis of time constraints in Figure 5.12 (especially if you used the sliders in the Excel file for Figure 5.12 that produced intersection point **D**, where **D**'s x component was not an integer). If goods can only be consumed in discrete quantities, this restricts the consumption set, as you will soon see. We begin with the opposite end of the spectrum, when both goods are discrete.

Suppose both x and y can only be consumed in discrete (nonnegative integer) quantities. Figure 5.13 describes the feasible bundles, given a budget constraint. In each panel, the red line is the budget line. Figures 5.13A–5.13D have the same budget constraint. Suppose I = \$4 in this instance.

Q13. What are the values of P_x and P_y for Figures 5.13A–5.13D?†

***Q12a answer:** I = \$15, and P_y = \$1.00.

†**Q13 answer:** Y is the numeraire in this instance; its price is \$1. Since the budget constraint also goes through the bundle (4, 1), the price of x must equal \$0.75.

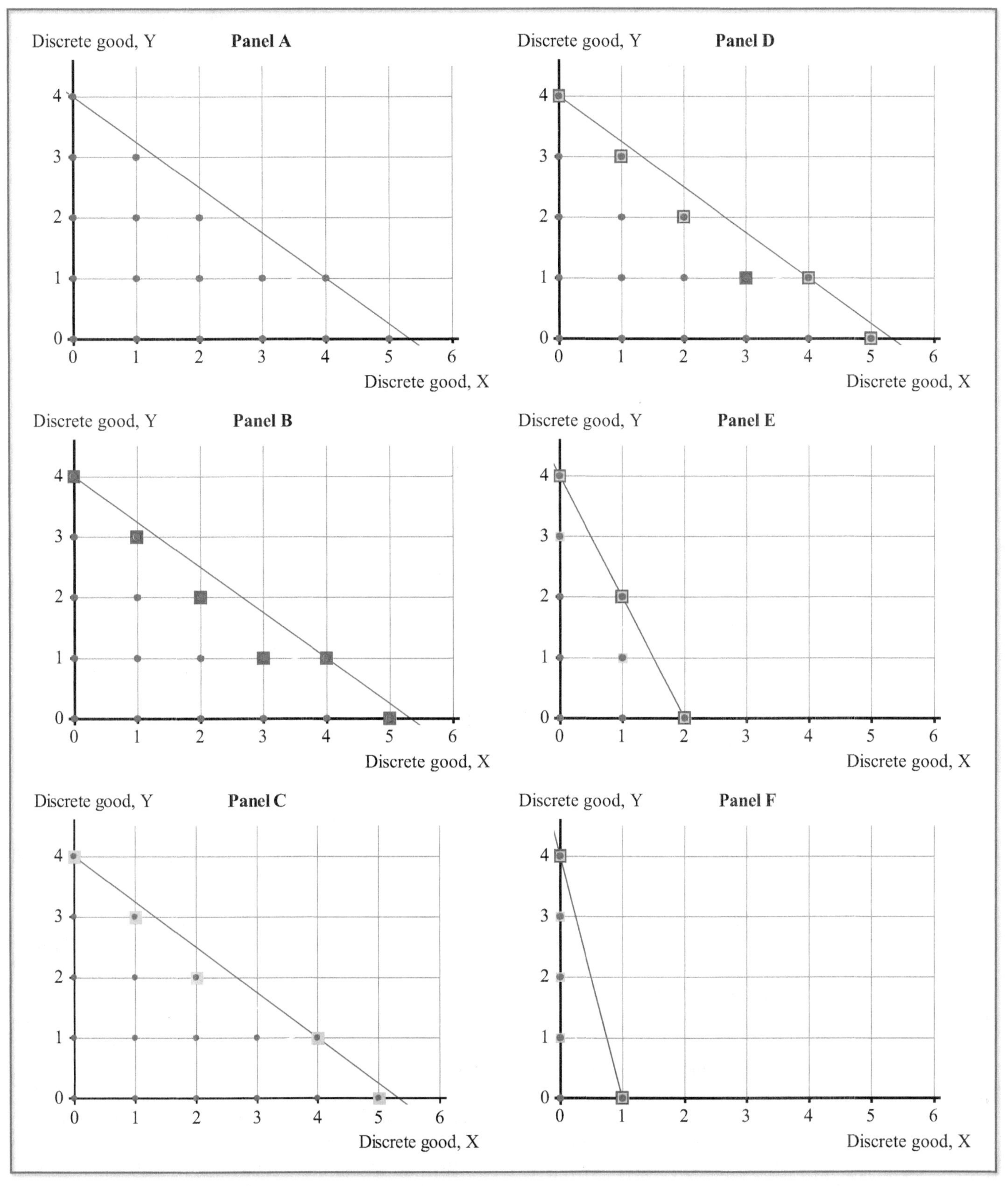

FIGURE 5.13 Feasible Bundles When Both x and y Are Discrete Goods

Key: The green circles represent feasible; the red squares represent binding y, given x; and the blue squares represent binding x, given y.

Figures 5.13A–5.13C introduce three graphical constructs, and Figures 5.13D–5.13F include all three of these constructs on the same graph. (The Excel version of Figure 5.13 allows you to turn on and off these constructs and adjust the price of x.)

The *green circles* in Figure 5.13A represent feasible bundles, given this budget constraint.

Each feasible bundle has integer coordinates and is on or below the budget line.

The red and blue squares represent different versions of the notion of binding in the discrete goods case. Interestingly, when we have discrete goods, we can have a binding constraint and still have money left over. When dealing with discrete goods, a constraint is binding if you cannot buy another unit of that good, since the goods can only be purchased in 1-unit increments.

The six *red squares* in Figure 5.13B represent the most y that can be purchased, given x equals 0, 1, . . ., 5. *Red squares represent the binding level of y, given a level of x.*

Each is the uppermost feasible bundle on that vertical segment (which is why the green circle can be seen in each red square).

The five *blue squares* in Figure 5.13C reverse the orientation by describing the most x that can be purchased, given y equals 0, 1, . . ., 4. *Blue squares represent the binding level of x, given a level of y.*

Each is the rightmost feasible bundle on that horizontal segment (which is why the green circle can be seen in each blue square). Figure 5.13D places both notions of binding on one diagram. Those that are binding in both "directions" show all three colors at one location. This need not be the case. One of the red "binding y, given x" bundles is not also a blue "binding x, given y" bundle. The binding level of y, given x = 3, is (3, 1), but x = 3 is not the binding level of x, given y = 1. One more x can be purchased with the remaining income if y = 1. Since P_y = \$1 and I = \$4, the remaining income in this instance is \$3. Therefore, 4 units of x can be purchased for \$3, since P_x = \$0.75.

The number of red and blue squares is determined by how many units of each good can be purchased if as much income as possible is spent on that good. (We cannot say "all income" because, as discussed earlier, there may be money left over in this situation.) Due to the discrete nature of the goods in this situation, there need not be different numbers of red and blue squares. For general values of I, P_x, and P_y, there will be

Integer(I/P_x) + 1 possible values of x (red squares) and **(5.6a)**

Integer(I/P_y) + 1 possible values of y (blue squares).[3] **(5.6b)**

Whether x or y has more feasible possibilities is determined by which price is smaller. There are more red squares in Figure 5.13D because $P_x < P_y$. The reverse will hold true when $P_x > P_y$, as Figures 5.13E and 5.13F show. These panels depict P_x = \$2 and P_x = \$4, respectively, with P_y and I remaining at their initial levels (of P_y = \$1 and I = \$4).

Suppose only one good is discrete and the other is continuous. In this instance, the analysis maintains some resemblance to that provided when both goods are discrete. The six panels in Figure 5.14 are exactly the same as in Figure 5.13 with one change: Good y is now continuous, rather than discrete. Some interesting distinctions emerge with this one change. For instance, feasible bundles in Figure 5.14A are no longer points on a gridwork system below the budget constraint. Good x is still consumed in discrete quantities, as in Figure 5.13, but y values are "filled in" (along vertical lines) to allow the entire set of y values below the budget line for any given integer value of x. The binding y values for a given value of x (red squares) are now *on* the budget constraint in Figure 5.14B, signifying in each instance that all income is spent. The same is *not* true for binding x values for a given value of y in Figure 5.14C. Since x may only be consumed in discrete quantities, there may well be money left over at "binding x, given y bundles." Indeed, there is *always* money left over at binding bundles (except at the upper end of the half-open, half-closed line segments that represent the set of "binding x, given y bundles" in this situation).

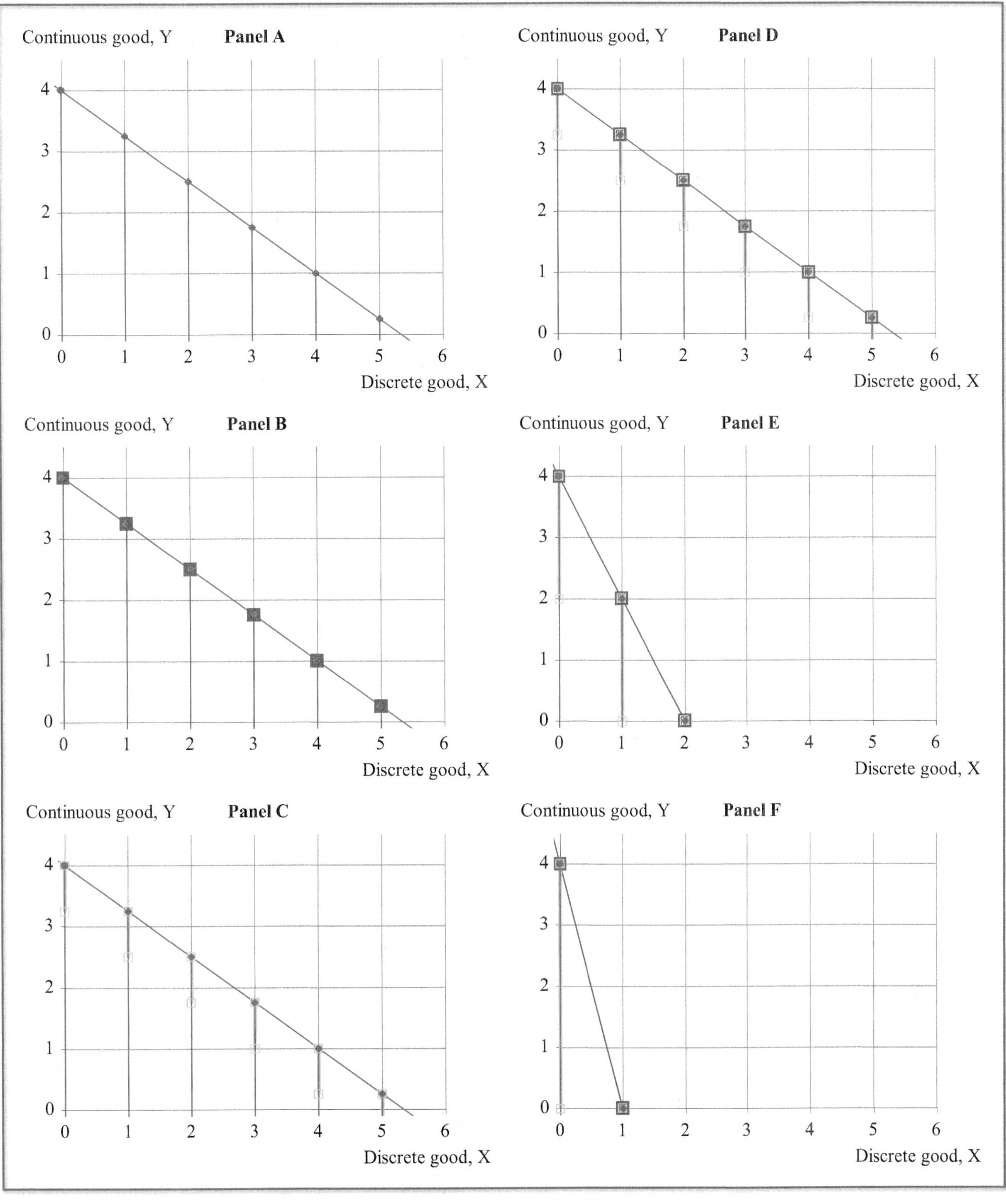

FIGURE 5.14 Feasible Bundles When x Is Discrete and y Is Continuous

Key: The green circles represent feasible; the red squares represent binding y, given x; and the blue squares represent binding x, given y.

Perhaps the easiest way to see this is to think about consuming only good x (by setting y = 0). If you could purchase x in continuous quantities, you would wish to purchase 5.33 units ($5.33 = I/P_x = \$4/\$0.75$), but you must settle for 5 units instead, since x is discrete. These 5 units cost \$3.75 ($\$3.75 = \$0.75 \cdot 5$), so you have \$0.25 of remaining income at this binding bundle (highlighted in blue in Figure 5.14C). The blue line segments representing maximum feasible x for a given value of y are open at the bottom of each segment because this is the level of y at which you are able to purchase one more unit of x. This is perhaps easiest to see at y = 1. For any y > 1, the maximum feasible x is x = 3, but for y = 1, this number jumps to x = 4. The open bottom of each line segment is aligned with the closed upper segment associated with x being 1 unit higher. X values must move in lock-step fashion, one at a time. One final distinction occurs here: Once y is continuous, it no longer makes sense to compare the number of red squares and blue squares that represent the respective binding values of y and x when the other good is held fixed. There are an infinite number of blue bundles, since y may take on an infinite number of feasible values, while x is constrained to take on only, at most, Integer(I/P_x) + 1 feasible integer values.

5.7 Relative Prices Determine Relative Market Value

The statement *relative prices determine relative market value* borders on sounding too simplistic to deserve its own section in a textbook. Of course, relative prices determine relative market value, but relative value is sufficiently important that we focus on it one final time before putting the two sides of the consumer model together in Chapter 6.

The price of a good provides information about how the market views the good. Higher prices mean that the good is more highly valued, and lower prices mean that the good is less highly valued by the market. Economists are careful to note that this is the view of the market, not necessarily of a specific individual. An individual's valuation of two goods is described by that person's marginal utilities for those goods, and the MRS between those goods describes that individual's relative valuation of the goods; both of these topics have been explicitly placed to the sideline in this chapter.

Prices are central to understanding a budget constraint, since prices (together with income) determine the budget constraint's placement. We saw in Section 5.2 that, as long as all prices and income maintain a constant relative relationship, the budget constraint will not vary, despite different algebraic representations of that constraint. This was also pointed out in Table 5.1, where the general solution for the budget constraint in Figure 5.1 was shown to be $(P_x, P_y, P_z, I) = (1.5 \cdot s, 2 \cdot s, s, 18 \cdot s)$ for any s > 0. The ratio between any two of the parameters in this instance is fixed, regardless of the value of the scaling factors, s: All prices and income have maintained a constant relative relation in this instance. If the price ratio between two goods is constant, the market-determined trade-off between the two goods is also constant, even as the prices of those goods vary. This price ratio is called a **relative price**. If r is the relative price, $r = P_x/P_y$, r will be the price of x if y is the numeraire. Figure 5.3 described why the relative price of x and y is the slope of the budget constraint (with a minus sign).

relative price: If r is the relative price, $r = P_x/P_y$, r will be the price of x if y is the numeraire.

price vector: The price vector, (P_x, P_y), points in the direction of maximum increase in cost. Since the components of the price vector are prices, the size of this vector represents how quickly costs increase.

The relative price can be shown using a price version of the MU vector described in Chapter 4. We call this a **price vector**. The price vector, (P_x, P_y), points in the direction of maximum increase in cost. Since the components of the price vector are prices, the size of this vector represents how quickly costs increase. The price vector describes relative price and the slope of budget constraints. This construct is shown in Figure 5.15. Two panels are provided: one with prices $(P_x, P_y) = (2, 3)$ and the other with prices $(P_x, P_y) = (6, 9)$. Income has been adjusted (multiplied by three) so that both budget constraints pass through the bundle (10, 15). The budget constraints are geometrically identical: Both have a y intercept of $y = 65/3 = I/P_y$ and slope of –2/3. The general form of this budget constraint would have $(P_x, P_y, I) = (2 \cdot r, 3 \cdot r, 65 \cdot r)$ for r > 0. Both panels have line segments representing P_x, P_y, and the price vector, (P_x, P_y). (These segments are shown in two locations for reasons that will be described in a moment.) Although P_x, P_y, and (P_x, P_y)

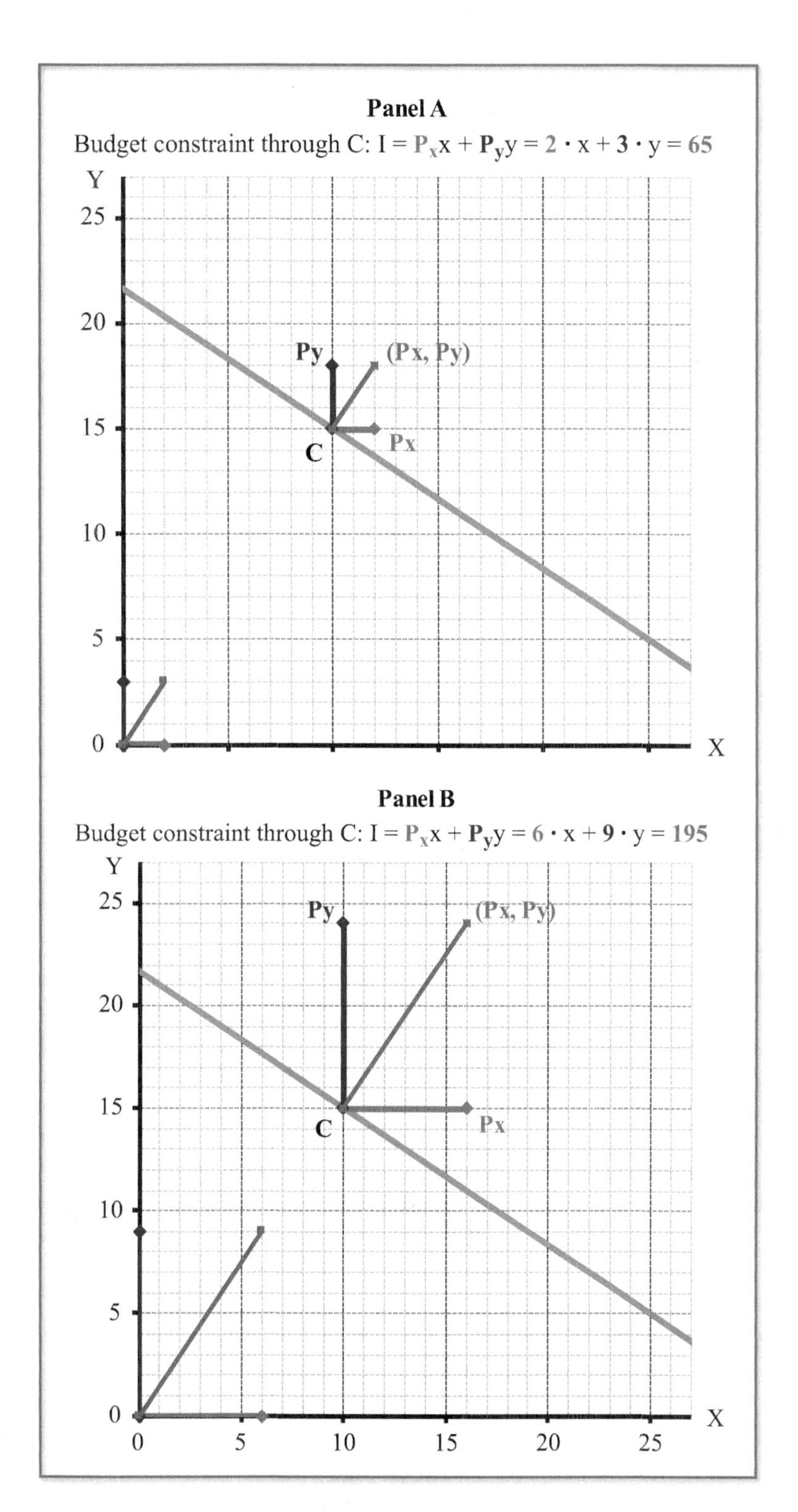

FIGURE 5.15 The Price Vector and Its Relation to the Budget Constraint

vary in size as r varies (r = 1 in Figure 5.15A, and r = 3 in Figure 5.15B), the price vector points in the *same* direction as long as P_x and P_y maintain a 2:3 ratio.[4] Or to say the same thing, the relative value of x to y is 2/3 as long as prices remain in a ratio of 2:3. In both instances, if a budget constraint goes through a given bundle, it must have a slope of –2/3.

Economists often draw the price vector at the origin (with or without the individual component parts P_x and P_y) when working on a problem because it provides a quick reference guide as to the relative value of the two goods provided by the market, and it also allows economists to quickly orient the budget constraint that consumers will face, given these prices. Budget constraints must be perpendicular to the price vector, regardless of income level. The price vector is colored red because it represents the direction of change

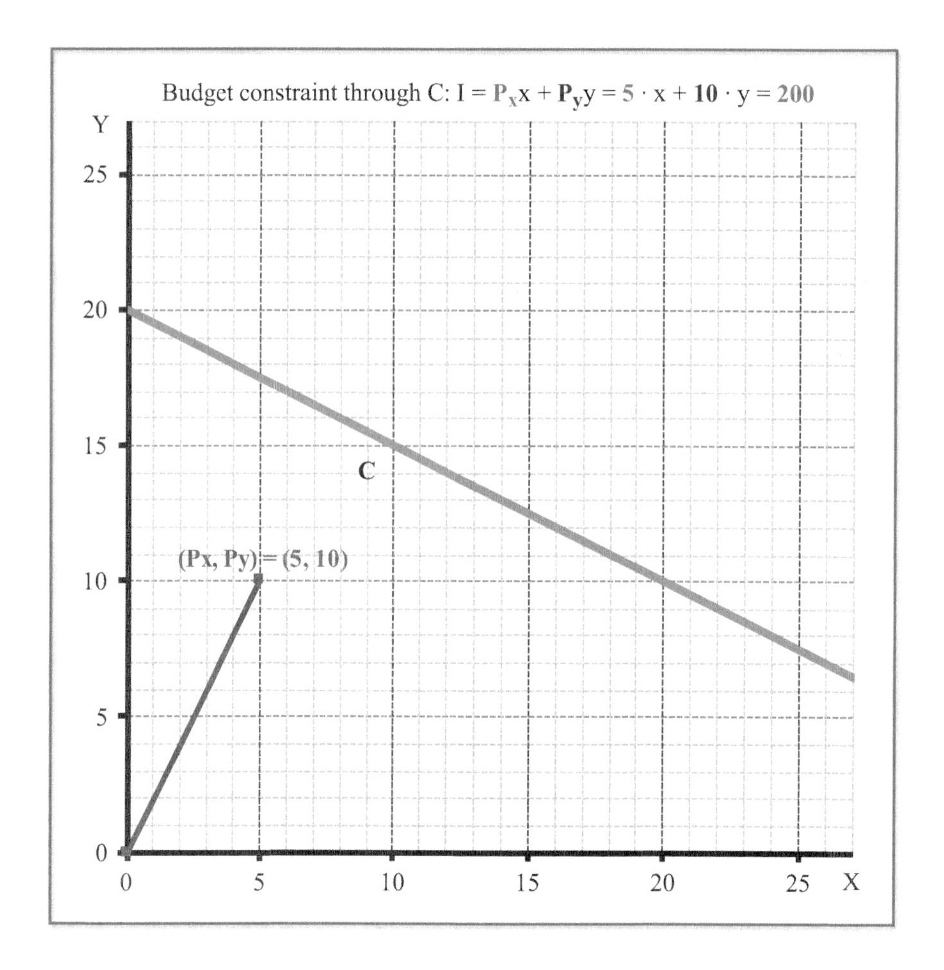

FIGURE 5.16
Economists Read Individual Prices from the Price Vector

that will put you "in the red" (to use an accountant's terminology) the fastest. Figure 5.16 shows how this looks for one budget line. Other budget lines would be higher or lower, given the price ratio, but all would be parallel to the budget line shown (and perpendicular to the price vector (P_x, P_y)). Each will have a slope of $-1/2$ because y is twice as expensive as x, given the prices shown. The price vector does not need to be tied to a specific bundle when describing budget constraints because the price of each good is not dependent on the quantities of each good under consideration (as long as we do not face nonlinear budget constraints). This is in marked contrast to Chapter 4, where the MU vector represented marginal utilities that are dependent on the quantities of each good under consideration.

Summary

Resource constraints are almost as basic a concept as preferences. Individuals, even very young ones, have preferences, but they also have constraints placed on their behavior. The most common of these constraints is the budget constraint. The main focus in this chapter is the affordability of bundles—which bundles are feasible and which are not feasible, given the resource constraints the consumer faces. This discussion of affordability ignores the question of desirability, just as the discussion of desirability in Chapters 3 and 4 ignored the question of affordability.

The individual's budget constraint is based on the prices the consumer faces and the income the consumer has available to purchase those goods. There are a variety of methods, both algebraic and geometric, for describing the budget constraint. If you spend P_ix_i on good *i*, and you plan to buy n goods, then the budget constraint can be described algebraically as $P_1x_1 + P_2x_2 + \ldots + P_nx_n \leq I$. The constraint is not binding if spending is less than I, and the constraint is binding when spending is equal to I. This way of viewing the budget constraint is the most heuristic, since it is how you spend money, but it is not the only possible way to view the budget constraint. Alternative specifications of this inequality are useful for highlighting specific topics. One of these specifications uses the notion of a numeraire—a good whose price is automatically set to 1. All other prices in this conceptualization are relative to the numeraire. A geometric interpretation of relative prices is provided that is analogous to the geometric interpretation of MRS in Chapter 4. The MRS measures an individual's relative valuation of goods. The MRS was shown to be the ratio of marginal utilities. In contrast, the price ratio measures the market's relative valuation of goods. The coordination of these two relative valuations is the subject of Chapter 6.

The budget constraint is a linear function of prices and income. Therefore, it is represented geometrically as a line when there are two goods under consideration, and as a plane when there are three goods. As with preferences, we lose little generality by restricting ourselves to two goods. For fixed prices, an income change moves the budget constraint in a parallel fashion; a higher level of income increases the set of feasible bundles. A change in the price of one good rotates the budget line, using the intercept of the good whose price has not changed as the fulcrum point. Higher prices reduce the set of feasible bundles and rotate the budget constraint toward the origin, and lower prices increase the set of feasible bundles and rotate the budget constraint away from the origin.

When consumers face choices among various budgetary alternatives, budget constraints may be compared to determine which alternative is the best. Two applications of budget constraint analysis are presented; each involves trade-offs so that the best choice depends on the consumer's preferences. Even in the absence of information about preferences, systematic conclusions emerge regarding when one alternative dominates another. For example, a person who is considering whether or not to join a warehouse store is likely to be better off joining a warehouse store if the individual expects to use the store "a lot." The meaning of "a lot" can be described explicitly as a function of the cost to join and the benefit available from joining. Similar conclusions are derived for choosing among food-subsidy programs. Although these examples are quite disparate, their common core involves comparing the trade-offs inherent in various alternatives.

The budget constraint is the most obvious constraint on consumer behavior, but the consumer may face other constraints as well. When a consumer faces multiple constraints, the feasible set is reduced if the additional constraints are binding.

Review Questions

If you did not take the time to fill in the table when you read about time constraints in Section 5.5, take the time to verify the answers provided here.

Table (filled in based on Figure 5.12)

Figure	t_y	H	Is CAD Too Expensive?	Is DEB Too Expensive?	Feasible Region
5.12A	0	12	Yes	No	**ADE0**
5.12B	0.5	15	Yes	No	**ADE0**
5.12C	1.0	18	Yes	No	**ADE0**
5.12D	1.5	21	No	Yes	**CDB0**
5.12E	2.0	24	No	Yes	**CDB0**
5.12F	4.0	24	No	Yes	**CDB0**

Define the following terms:

feasible bundle	store method	relative price
set of feasible bundles	parametric representation	price vector
budget constraint	slope-intercept representation	discrete good
binding constraint	two-part tariff	time price of good x
not binding constraint	numeraire	unitary income budget constraint

Provide alternative algebraic representations of the two-good budget constraint, given income I and prices P_x and P_y:

store method

slope-intercept method

parametric method

Match the statements that follow. What change in price(s) described in the right-hand column causes the budget constraint to shift as described in the left-hand column? (Assume that income is held constant, and if only one price is mentioned, the other price is held constant.)

a. Flatter: y intercept shifts down; x intercept shifts out.	1. P_x decrease *or* P_y increase (or both)
b. Steeper: y intercept shifts up; x intercept shifts in.	2. A decrease in one price
c. A parallel shift outward	3. P_x decrease and P_y increase
d. A parallel shift inward	4. A proportional increase in all prices
e. An outward rotation	5. P_x increase *or* P_y decrease (or both)
f. An inward rotation	6. A proportional decrease in all prices
g. Makes the constraint flatter	7. P_x increase and P_y decrease
h. Makes the constraint steeper	8. An increase in one price

Provide short answers to the following:

a. When all prices and income increase by the same percentage, what happens to the set of feasible bundles?

b. What can cause a single budget constraint to have two different slopes?

For Questions c–g, provide qualitative answers, such as inside, outside, or crossing, and mention whether the new budget line is steeper or flatter than the old.

c. Suppose: $0 < \%\Delta\text{Income} < \%\Delta P_x < \%\Delta P_y$. Explain how the "new" budget constraint relates to the "old" budget constraint.

d. Suppose: $0 < \%\Delta\text{Income} < \%\Delta P_y < \%\Delta P_x$. Explain how the "new" budget constraint relates to the "old" budget constraint.

e. Suppose: $0 > \%\Delta\text{Income} > \%\Delta P_x > \%\Delta P_y$. Explain how the "new" budget constraint relates to the "old" budget constraint.

f. Suppose: $0 > \%\Delta\text{Income} > \%\Delta P_y > \%\Delta P_x$. Explain how the "new" budget constraint relates to the "old" budget constraint.

g. Suppose: $0 < \%\Delta P_x < \%\Delta\text{Income} < \%\Delta P_y$. Explain how the "new" budget constraint relates to the "old" budget constraint.

h. Suppose x is a discrete good and $I/P_x > \text{Integer}(I/P_x)$. What does it mean when an individual consumes $x = \text{Integer}(I/P_x)$ units of x?

Check your answers to the *matching* and *short-answer* exercises in the Answers Appendix at the end of the book.

Notes

1. The nonnegative orthant is the n-dimensional analog of the two-dimensional concept of the first quadrant. Formally, the budget constraint is that part of the $n - 1$ dimensional hyperplane that is in the nonnegative orthant.

2. The n-good parametric version of the budget constraint is the set of bundles: $(s_1 \cdot I/P_1, s_2 \cdot I/P_2, \ldots, s_n \cdot I/P_n)$ subject to conditions: (a) $0 \le s_i \le 1$ for all i, and (b) $s_1 + \ldots + s_n = 1$.

The parameter s_i is the proportion (share) of income spent on good *i*. In the three-dimensional example highlighted in Figure 5.1, the bundle (6,3,3) has $s_x = 1/2$; $s_y = 1/3$; and $s_z = 1/6$. We showed this when we discussed the unitary income version of the budget constraint in Table 5.1.

3. Integer(x) is the integer function. It provides the integer part of any number x. If x = 12.3, Integer(x) = 12; similarly, Integer(12.99) = 12 (not 13—the integer function does *not* round). The formula given, $\text{Integer}(I/P_i) + 1$, is the number of feasible values for good *i* because good *i* can take on all integer values 0, 1, . . ., $\text{Integer}(I/P_i)$.

4. In Chapter 4, the magnitude of the marginal utility vector, (MU_x, MU_y), represented how quickly utility changed as we moved from bundle to bundle. Larger magnitudes meant that utility increased more rapidly. If the bundle changes by $(\Delta x, \Delta y)$, then utility changes by $MU_x \cdot \Delta x + MU_y \cdot \Delta y = \Delta U$. With the budget constraint described in this chapter, the magnitude of the price vector, (P_x, P_y), represents how quickly the income required to purchase a bundle changes as we move from bundle to bundle. Larger magnitudes mean that income must increase more rapidly. If the bundle changes by $(\Delta x, \Delta y)$, then income required to purchase the bundle changes by $P_x \cdot \Delta x + P_y \cdot \Delta y = \Delta I$.

Consumer Choice

CHAPTER 6

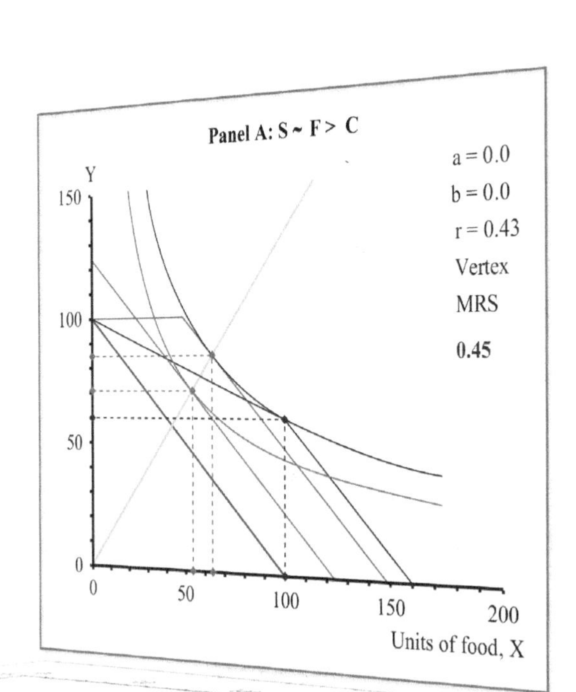

Chapter Outline

The groundwork laid in Chapters 3, 4, and 5 pays quick dividends here. Consumers have preferences for goods and services, but they also face constraints on their behavior. The two sides of the consumer choice problem that have been separately examined are put together in this chapter. We do so in the same *ceteris paribus* fashion used in earlier chapters.To clearly understand what happens when "things" change, we must change one "thing" at a time, holding all other "things" constant. The "things" being discussed here are preferences and constraints.

In this chapter, we show how an individual consumer's optimal choice bundle changes as the parameters that delineate the consumer's preferences change, given a fixed budget constraint. This chapter provides a sensitivity analysis of the optimal outcome to changes in the parameters that are used to represent an individual's preferences. Although each solution to the individual consumer's constrained optimization problem does, indeed, focus on an individual consumer, the goal of this chapter is to see how sensitive those solutions are to the functions used to represent preferences when resources are fixed. In Chapters 7 and 8, we reverse the focus, and allow price and income to change for fixed preferences. Of course, different kinds of preferences produce different responses to price and income change.

Section 6.1 examines the requirements for optimization, using a general function and general constraint. Section 6.2 examines the sensitivity of various parameters used to delineate the utility functions described in Chapter 4 for fixed budget constraint. The goal is to continue to increase the level of familiarity and understanding regarding the utility functions introduced in Chapter 4.

Section 6.3 refines and extends the choice among constraints analysis presented in Section 5.4. We assume well-behaved preferences throughout this text, with few exceptions. (Recall that preferences are well behaved if they are complete, transitive, monotonic, and convex. In Chapter 3, we provided some behavioral rationales for these assumptions, and we placed special emphasis on the notions of monotonicity and convexity because students of microeconomics often view these properties with less familiarity.) When we analyze constrained optimization with preferences that are not well behaved, additional reasons for the assumptions of monotonicity and convexity become apparent. Section 6.4 examines the problems that are introduced when these assumptions are relaxed.

6.1 The Geometry of Optimization

A utility-maximizing individual will choose the point of tangency between that person's indifference curve and budget constraint. This is the simple way of describing the geometry of maximization. Figure 6.1 examines the geometry of optimization for general values of P_x, P_y, and I. Figure 6.1A shows an individual's constrained optimum. Bundle **A** is the best the consumer can do, given the person's budget constraint. **A** has MRS = P_x/P_y, and all income is spent (this is simply another way to say the tangency condition). Three points on a lower indifference curve—**B**, **C**, and **D**—are also shown. These bundles are feasible because they are on or below the (green) budget constraint but are not utility maximizing. Figures 6.1B and 6.1C examine why **A** is superior to **B** and **C**, using the lavender MU vector and red price vector introduced in Chapters 4 and 5. The price vector points in the direction of the most unaffordable bundles; this is the quickest way to get "in the red" (to use accountant's terminology), and the MU vector points in the direction of maximum increase in utility. Each vector is perpendicular to its respective curve: The price vector is perpendicular to the budget constraint, and the MU vector is perpendicular to the indifference curve.

Figure 6.1B highlights the situation faced at points on the budget constraint where too little x is being consumed. The indifference curve through bundle **B** is steeper than the budget constraint: MRS > P_x/P_y. Recall that the MRS measures the individual's relative valuation of the goods, and the price ratio measures the market's relative valuation of the goods. The MRS is the number of units of y the individual is willing to give up to get one more x. The price ratio is the number of units of y that the individual would have to give up to get one more x (because the individual is already on a budget constraint and must stay within the budget constraint as consumption is readjusted). MRS > P_x/P_y means that the individual's relative valuation of x for y exceeds the market's relative valuation of x for y.

Numbers have been removed from the axes of all figures in Section 6.1 to focus on the general optimization problem. Though we cannot talk about the absolute size of the MRS or price ratio, P_x/P_y, the relative size of these relative valuations is provided for specific bundles in each of Figures 6.1B–6.1D. For example, MRS = 4.9 · P_x/P_y at bundle **B** in Figure 6.1B states that the MRS(**B**) is nearly five times larger than the price ratio: The consumer values x relative to y more highly than the market at that bundle. Therefore, it makes sense for the consumer to reallocate consumption along the budget constraint toward a more x-intensive consumption bundle (the blue allocation arrow points in the direction of **C**). The reverse holds true at **C** in Figure 6.1C: MRS(**C**) = 0.2 · P_x/P_y. MRS < P_x/P_y implies that the market's valuation of one more unit of x (in units of y) is *more* than the individual is willing to give up to get one more x. It makes sense for this individual to reverse course and reallocate consumption along the budget constraint toward a more y-intensive consumption bundle (the blue allocation arrow points in the direction of **B**). From either side, such reallocations will continue to increase the consumer's utility as long as MRS ≠ P_x/P_y. The benefit of reallocating ends only when MRS = P_x/P_y. This occurs at bundle **A** in Figures 6.1A and 6.1D. In Figure 6.1D, we see this in three interrelated ways. Visually, we see the tangency shown in Figure 6.1A. We also note that MRS = 1.0 · P_x/P_y at **A**. Finally, we also see it in the price vector and MU vector pointing in the same direction.

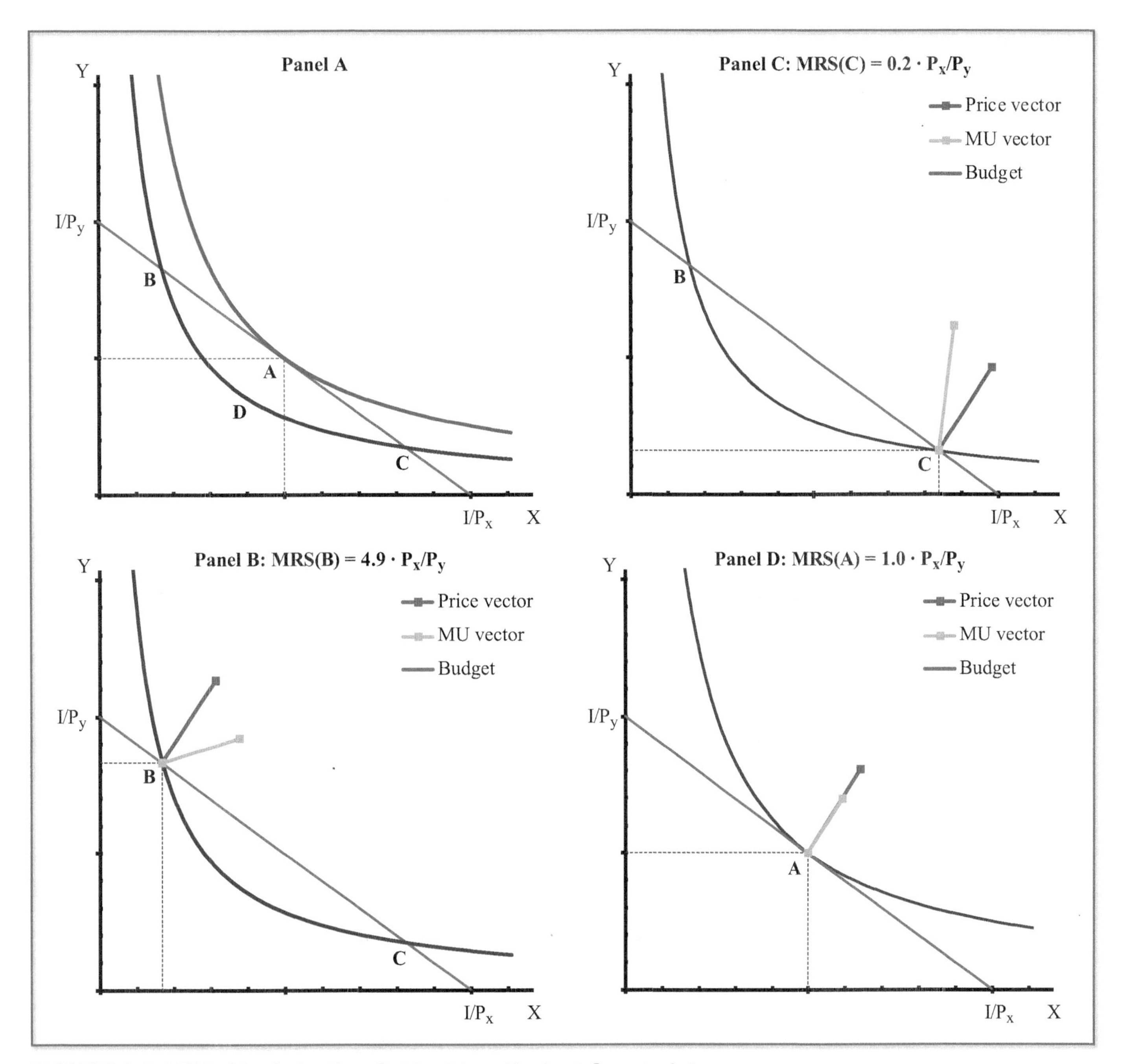

FIGURE 6.1 Utility Maximization Subject to a Budget Constraint

Before leaving this analysis, it is worthwhile to explicitly understand why bundle **D** in Figure 6.1A is also suboptimal, despite having MRS = P_x/P_y. The answer is straightforward: There are bundles that are preferred to **D** and that are still affordable (every bundle in the crescent **BDCA** above the indifference curve through **BDC** satisfies this joint condition). Optimality in the world of scarcity requires that the MRS equals the price ratio *and* that all income should be spent. If you achieve one of these two conditions without the other, you can do better.

The tangency condition is *the* hallmark of the constrained optimization problem. As a result, it is worthwhile to examine it in greater detail. The first point to note is that a tangency can *only* occur if the curve is smooth. If the curve is not smooth, then it is not clear what "tangency" actually signifies. This is, perhaps, best exemplified by perfect complements. The discussion of Figure 4.6 showed that an infinite number of lines are "tangent" to the vertex of the L-shaped perfect complement indifference curve. In this

FIGURE 6.2 Constrained Optimization without Smooth Indifference Curves

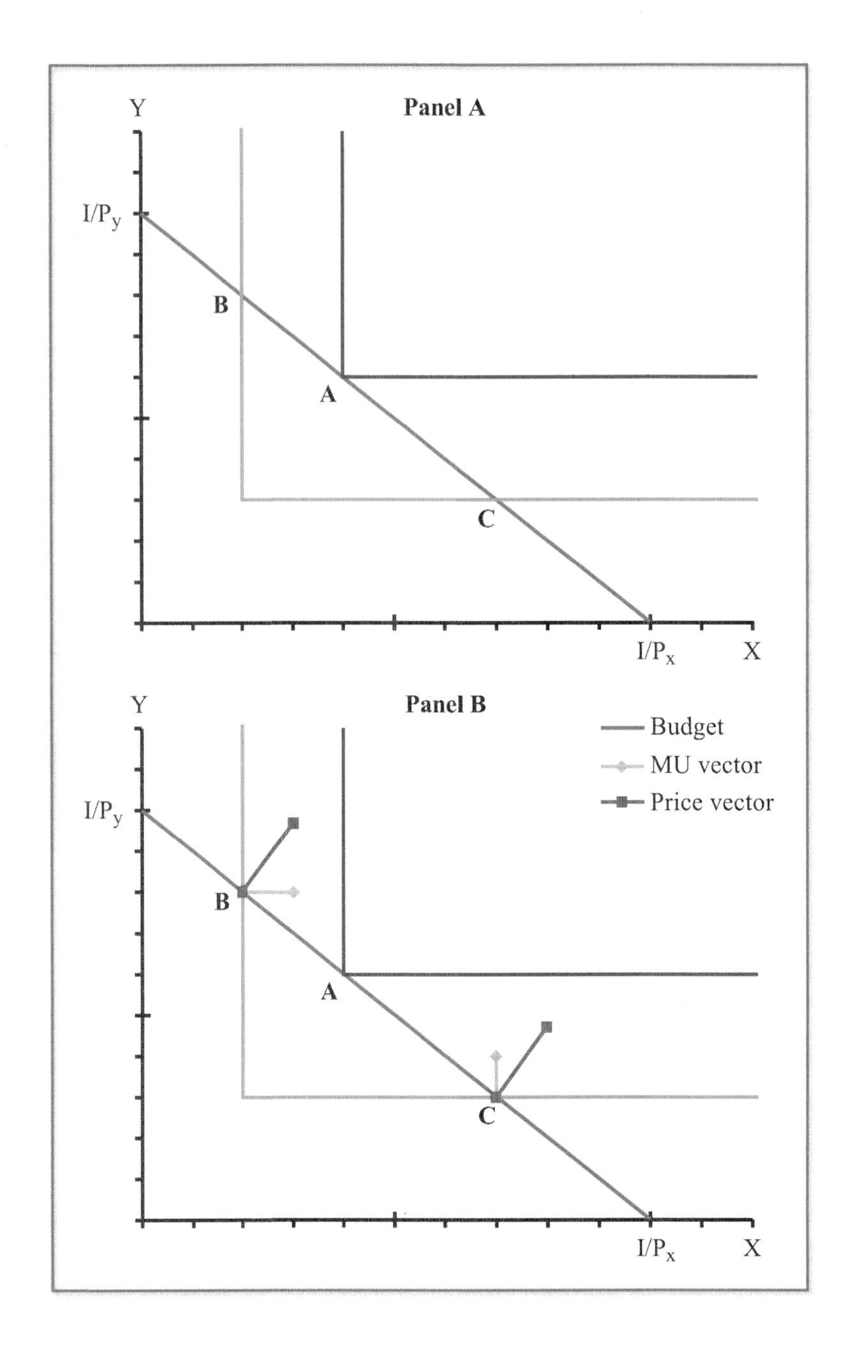

instance, the highest indifference curve does not coincide with more than one point on the budget constraint. If it did, one of two things must be true: Either (1) one of the prices is zero (so the budget constraint is either vertical or horizontal) or (2) there are preferred bundles that are still affordable. Figure 6.2 depicts the second situation. The bundles **B** and **C** in Figure 6.2A cost the same as **A** but **A** $\succ$ **B** ~ **C**; bundle **A** is feasible and better than **B** or **C**. Figure 6.2B includes price vectors and MU vectors similar to those used in Figure 6.1. The vectors at point **B** are oriented in the same way as the vectors at point **B** in Figure 6.1B. In both instances, the lavender MU vector is flatter than the price vector; the MRS is steeper than the price ratio (indeed, the MRS is infinite at **B** in Figure 6.2), and therefore, more x should be purchased along the budget constraint. Conversely, the vectors at point **C** are oriented in the same way as the vectors at point **C** in Figure 6.1C. In both instances, the lavender MU vector is steeper; the MRS is flatter than the price ratio (indeed, the MRS is zero at **C** in Figure 6.2), and therefore, more y should be purchased along the budget constraint.[1]

It is useful to focus explicitly on what the MU vector and the price vector signify. When the MU vector and price vector point in the same direction, equilibrium is established.

Claim: *When the MU vector and price vector point in different directions, their relative orientation tells us the direction to reallocate.*

Specifically, note that the lavender MU vector points toward more x (relative to the price vector) at bundle **B** in Figures 6.1B and 6.2B, and the lavender MU vector points toward more y (relative to the price vector) at **C** in Figures 6.1C and 6.2B.

Figures 6.1 and 6.2 involve interior solutions to the optimization problem. An **interior** bundle is a bundle that contains positive quantities of all goods. By contrast, if a consumption bundle does not have positive quantities of all goods, it is on the boundary of the consumption set. A bundle on the **boundary** of the consumption set contains at least one good that is not consumed. (Alternatively, we say that consumption of that good is zero.) *Any interior solution will be a point of tangency, given smooth indifference curves.* In the absence of smooth indifference curves, the interior solution cannot cross over the budget constraint so that there are indifferent bundles that cost less than the given income level. This would lead to affordable bundles in the first quadrant (relative to that bundle) that are strictly preferred to the initial bundle. The crossed-over bundle cannot be the constrained optimum.

interior: An interior bundle is a bundle that contains positive quantities of all goods.

boundary: A bundle on the boundary of the consumption set contains at least one good that is not consumed. (Alternatively, we say that consumption of that good is zero.)

The tangency condition is tremendously powerful. It says that all consumers act the same! Of course, they do not have the same preferences, or income for that matter, and even if they did have the same income, they would not necessarily purchase the same bundle of goods. But as long as two consumers have smooth, well-behaved preferences and purchase positive quantities of both goods, their *marginal* behavior is identical. Consider Bob and Linda, both of whom purchase some beer and some wine. Bob is predominantly a beer drinker, but he occasionally drinks wine, and Linda is the reverse. Bob's shopping cart will be beer intensive, and Linda's will be wine intensive, but at the margin, they have identical willingness to trade wine for beer. They will have identical MRSs of beer for wine. The reason is simple: Both are utility maximizing only when $MRS^B = MRS^L = P_x/P_y$ (assuming they have well-defined MRSs). The only restriction required to make their MRSs equal is that they face common prices for the two goods (by shopping at the same stores, for instance).

The tangency condition is related to how your introductory microeconomics class described individual behavior. Introductory microeconomics classes typically describe individual consumer behavior through a sequential examination of a consumer's purchasing. The utility-maximizing consumer spends initial dollars on the good that provides the highest marginal utility per dollar spent before purchasing other goods, based on the same rule, until all income is exhausted. Assuming that the consumer can buy each good in continuous quantities, all goods purchased at this point will have equal marginal utility per dollar spent. A dollar more spent on any good should produce the same incremental utility. If not, the consumer can be made better off by reallocating toward that good that has the higher marginal utility per dollar spent and away from the good that has lower marginal utility per dollar spent. Some economists say that there must be equal "bang for the buck" across goods. Good *i*'s bang for the buck (or marginal utility per dollar spent) is simply MU_i/P_i. Suppose the consumer consumes both x and y. Then:

$MU_x/P_x = MU_y/P_y$ at the optimal bundle. Cross-multiply and obtain:

$MU_x/MU_y = P_x/P_y$. Chapter 4 Appendix A shows that $MU_x/MU_y = MRS$; therefore,

$MRS = P_x/P_y$ at the utility-maximizing consumption bundle.

The two conditions are identical: Having *equal "bang for the buck" across goods* is the same as saying that *the MRS equals the price ratio*. Either one can be derived from the other; both describe how an individual's relative valuation of goods must match the market's evaluation of the relative value of the goods.

The difference between the two conceptualizations is that the MRS makes a more direct relative comparison, since it removes the ambiguity created by the ordinality of utility discussed in Section 4.3. As shown in Chapter 4 Appendix A, the MRS is independent of the specific utility function chosen to represents preferences; taking the ratio of marginal utilities removes the scaling factor induced by monotonic transformation. (This problem does not arise in introductory microeconomics classes because the ordinal nature of utility is not typically discussed in introductory texts.)

When indifference curves are smooth and a tangency does not occur on the interior of a budget constraint, there will no longer be an interior solution to the constrained optimization problem. Instead, the optimum will occur at a point where the quantity of at least one of the goods is zero (in a two-good model, one must be zero). An optimum such as this is called a *boundary solution* (as opposed to an *interior solution*). The general solution to the consumer optimization problem must include both interior and boundary solutions. In a two-good model, the general solution to the constrained optimization problem (assuming well-behaved preferences with smooth indifference curves) is:[2]

Claim: *If an individual with well-behaved preferences and smooth indifference curves faces the constrained optimization problem:*

Maximize $U(x, y)$ subject to $P_x x + P_y y \leq I$. **(6.1-Problem)**

The following must hold at a constrained optimal solution:

(A) All income must be spent; $P_x x + P_y y = I$; and **(6.1A)**

(B) *One* of the following three conditions must hold:

(i) $MRS_{y,x} = P_x/P_y$ if $x > 0$ and $y > 0$, or **(6.1Bi)**

(ii) $MRS_{y,x} \leq P_x/P_y$ if $x = 0$ and $y = I/P_y$, or **(6.1Bii)**

(iii) $MRS_{y,x} \geq P_x/P_y$ if $y = 0$ and $x = I/P_x$. **(6.1Biii)**

The Chapter 6 Appendix provides a calculus-based analysis of this assertion. Equation 6.1A is required by monotonicity. Equation 6.1Bi is the interior solution described earlier and depicted in Figure 6.1. Equation 6.1Bii is depicted in Figures 6.3A and 6.3C. Equation 6.1Biii is depicted in Figures 6.3B and 6.3D. Also included in Figure 6.3 is a yellow line that depicts the bundles where $MRS = P_x/P_y$. These would be points of tangency between indifference curves and the budget constraint if income were to change with no change in prices. In each instance depicted in Figure 6.3, the yellow line does not intersect the budget constraint on the interior of the budget constraint **AB**. Each panel depicts a boundary solution to the constrained optimization problem.

Figures 6.3A and 6.3B have equality between the MRS and the price ratio; tangency exists at point **A** in Figure 6.3A and point **B** in Figure 6.3B. This can also be seen by the coincidence of the MU vector and price vector in these panels and by having the yellow $MRS = P_x/P_y$ line pass through the optimal bundle in each of these panels. The relative orientation of the MU vector and price vector at **A** in Figure 6.3C is similar to bundle **C** in Figures 6.1C and 6.2B. In Figures 6.1 and 6.2, this orientation indicated a decreased consumption of x and an increased consumption of y to increase utility. This cannot occur in Figure 6.3C because x is already at the minimum value possible at **A** (x = 0 along the vertical axis). Similarly, the relative orientation of the MU vector and price vector at **B** in Figure 6.3D is similar to bundle **B** in Figures 6.1B and 6.2B. In Figures 6.1 and 6.2, the message provided by this orientation was to increase consumption of x and decrease consumption of y to increase utility. This cannot occur in Figure 6.3D because y is already at the minimum value possible at **B** (y = 0 along the horizontal axis).

The boundary solutions depicted in Figure 6.3 are based on indifference curves that do not curve "much," just as required by the imperfect substitutes indifference curves that were initially examined in the discussion of Figure 3.14. As a result, it is not surprising that perfect substitutes lead to corner solutions as well. Perfect substitutes, however, will *always* lead to corner solutions, unless $MRS = P_x/P_y$. Figure 6.4 shows the three possibilities. Figure 6.4A depicts $MRS < P_x/P_y$. In this instance, **A** is the constrained optimum, and the lavender MU vector points toward even greater consumption of y and less of x; this option is precluded because x consumption is already at zero. Figure 6.4C depicts the reverse situation. Figure 6.4B depicts the razor-edge solution of $MRS = P_x/P_y$. In this

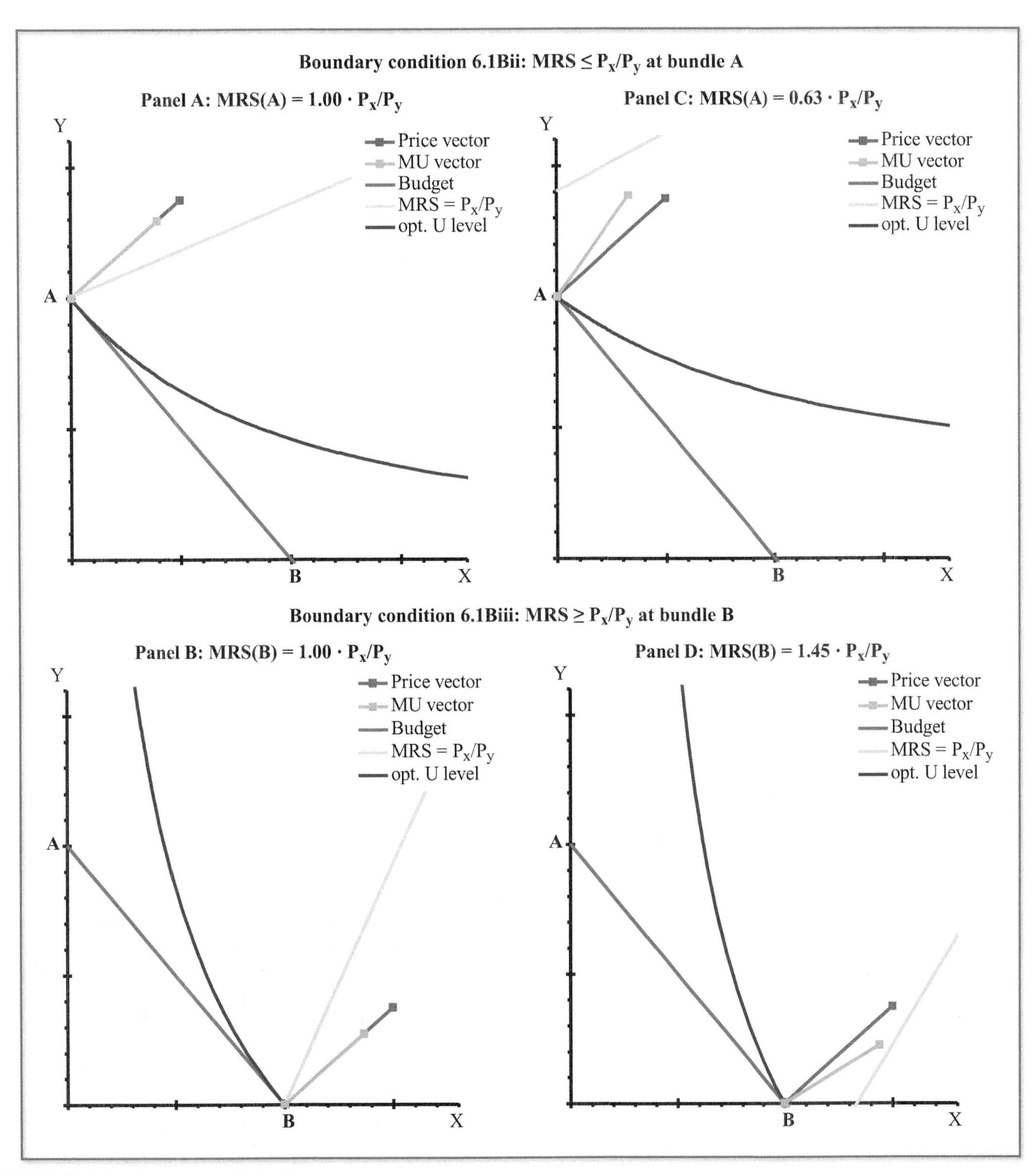

FIGURE 6.3 Boundary Solutions

instance, the utility-maximizing indifference curve *coincides* with the budget constraint **AB** (and the MU vector and price vector point in the same direction). Every bundle on **AB** achieves the same utility level, each is equally satisfactory, and no bundle dominates in this situation.

When two goods are perfect substitutes, there are multiple optimal bundles where the MRS coincides with price ratio. The reason this was described as a "razor-edge" solution is that the solution switches from spending all of the budget on x to all of the budget on y as the price ratio jostles out of equality with the MRS. If indifference curves have some curvature, a small change in price ratio does not have such a dramatic change in optimal

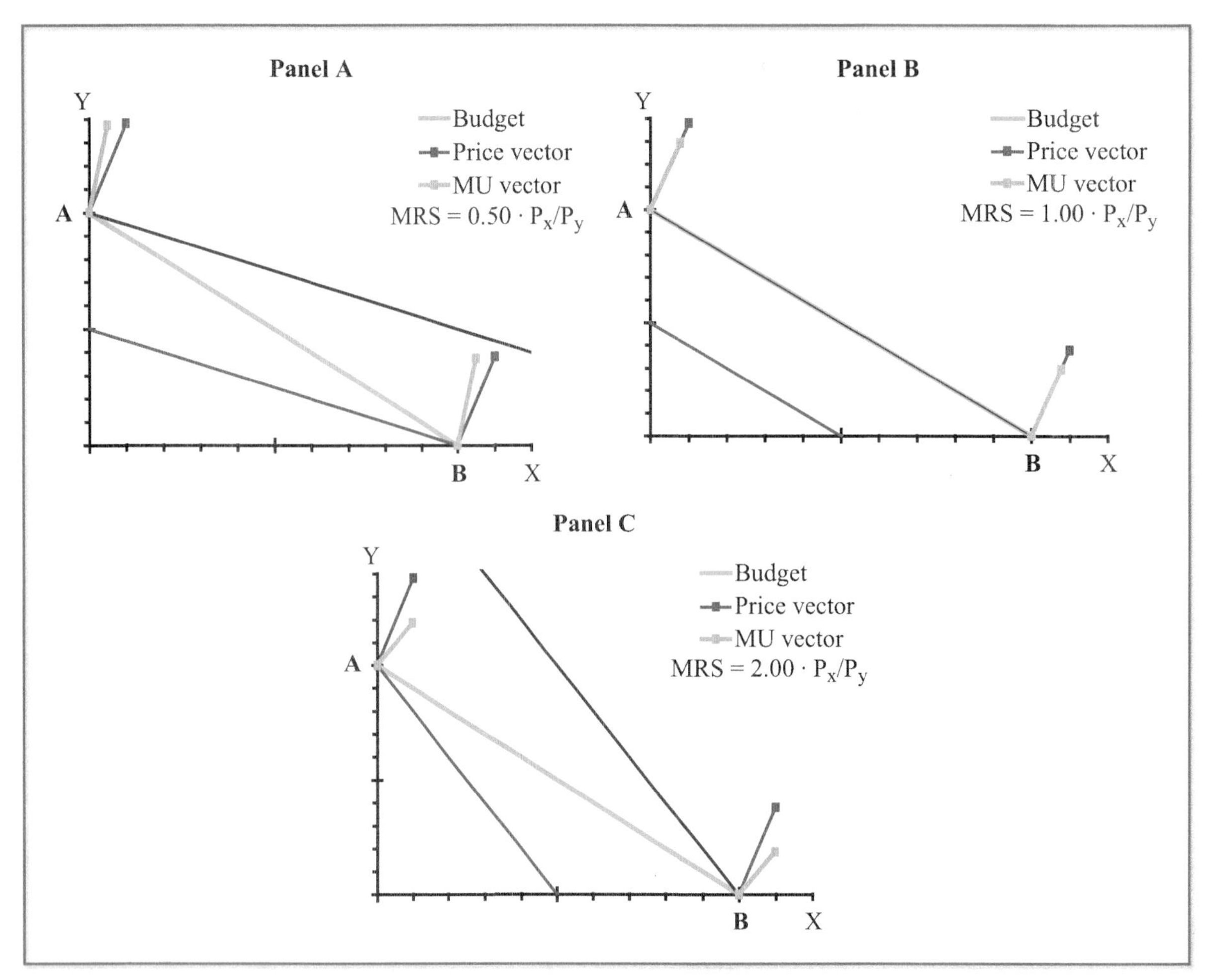

FIGURE 6.4 Constrained Optimization with Perfect Substitute Preferences

consumption bundle—the smaller the curvature, the greater the change. With no curve, the change is all or nothing as a result of an even miniscule change in price ratio.

In the discussion of well-behaved preferences in Chapter 3, we noted that if convexity is replaced by strict convexity, then indifference curves must be "curves." With smooth, well-behaved preferences that are strictly convex, *a* constrained optimum will be *the* constrained optimum. If a bundle is found that satisfies the constrained optimum conditions described in Equation 6.1, it will be the only such bundle found because the tangency between an (indifference) curve and a (budget) line is a single point.

6.2 The Algebra of Optimization

In Section 6.1, we focused on the geometry of optimization for a general budget constraint. As long as preferences are well behaved and smooth, optimization requires tangency between the indifference curve and budget constraint if both goods are consumed, or a border solution in which only one good is consumed. This is the answer embodied in Equation 6.1. In this section, we examine the algebra of optimization for a fixed budget constraint and how the optimal bundle varies as the parameters of the underlying utility function vary. In Chapters 7 and 8, we reverse course and allow price and income to vary, and obtain demand as a function of prices and income (for fixed utility functions).

unitary budget constraint: A unitary budget constraint is obtained by setting all prices and income equal to one.

Since the present focus is on the parameters used to describe utility functions, we use the same budget constraint for each constrained optimization in this section: $P_x = \$1$, $P_y = \$1$, and $I = \$1$. In this instance, the budget constraint is simply the line segment from (0, 1) to (1, 0). This is called a unitary budget constraint. A **unitary budget constraint** is obtained by setting all prices and income equal to one.

A variety of benefits can be obtained from using a unitary budget constraint, as you will soon see. The analysis does not appreciably change when we assume alternative numerical values for prices and income, and the interpretation is more complex in this instance. In Section 5.2, we noted that the bundle (x, y) has an easy interpretation, given the unitary income version of the budget constraint: $P_x x$ is the proportion of income spent on x, and $P_y y$ is the proportion of income spent on y. In this section, we also assume $P_x = P_y = \$1$, so the constraint simplifies even further. If (x, y) is on this budget constraint, then $(x, y) = (x, 1 - x)$. In this interpretation, x is the proportion of income spent on good x (the rest, $1 - x$, is the proportion of income spent on y).

The solution of each problem can be obtained algebraically, given the MRS information in Table 4.1. We begin with the general Cobb-Douglas utility function because the results are particularly elegant.

Cobb-Douglas

Equation 6.1 describes the general solution to the constrained optimization problem. For Cobb-Douglas (CD) preferences, the only relevant MRS condition is Equation 6.1Bi, $MRS = P_x/P_y$, because CD preferences require positive quantities of each good as long as income is greater than zero (since indifference curves do not touch the axes for CD preferences). There are two alternative specifications for the general CD form delineated in Table 4.1, but we argued in the discussion surrounding Equation 4.4 that the relative exponent version is more parsimonious because all that really matters is the relative size of the exponents due to the ordinality of utility (the absolute size only determines the utility levels associated with indifference curves). That version is: $U(x, y) = x^r \cdot y^{(1-r)}$ with $0 < r < 1$. The MRS for this utility function is: $MRS = (r/(1 - r)) \cdot (y/x)$. Given $P_x = 1$, $P_y = 1$, and $I = 1$, Equation 6.1A and 6.1Bi may be rewritten as:

$$1 = x + y. \quad \textbf{(6.2a)}$$

$$(r/(1 - r)) \cdot (y/x) = P_x/P_y = 1. \quad \textbf{(6.2b)}$$

Solving for y in Equation 6.2b, we obtain:

$$y = ((1 - r)/r) \cdot x. \quad \textbf{(6.2c)}$$

Substituting this into Equation 6.2a, we obtain:

$$1 = x + ((1 - r)/r) \cdot x. \quad \textbf{(6.2d)}$$

Simplifying this equation (by finding a common denominator and solving for x), we obtain two useful final results:

Demand for x $\quad x = r$, and **(6.3a)**

Demand for y $\quad y = 1 - r$. **(6.3b)**

Figure 6.5 depicts Equation 6.3 for three values of r; the Excel version of Figure 6.5 allows you to vary r from 0.20 to 0.80. The CD result is particularly straightforward: *The percent of income spent on each good is determined by the relative size of the CD exponents.* (Recall that the version of the CD used is the one in which the exponents sum to 1. Therefore, each exponent can be thought of as being a relative weight. As noted earlier, given unitary income and prices, the resulting coordinates of the demanded bundle, $(r, 1 - r)$, can be thought of as the proportion of income spent on each good.) These are points on the individual's demand curves for x and y (since we typically think of demand as being quantity demanded as a function of price of the good, holding all other prices and income constant). When $r = 0.2$, 20% of income is spent on x, and 80% is spent on y, or to say the same thing, the utility-maximizing bundle is 20% of the way from **A** to **B** in Figure 6.5A. As discussed in Chapter 4, $(r, 1 - r)$ is the parametric representation of being 100r% of the way from **A** to **B** on the budget constraint. (The axes in Figure 6.5 have 10 tick marks between the origin and the budget intercept to make percentages easy to see.) With $r = 0.4$, the tangency occurs 40% of the way from **A** to **B**. Each panel also includes

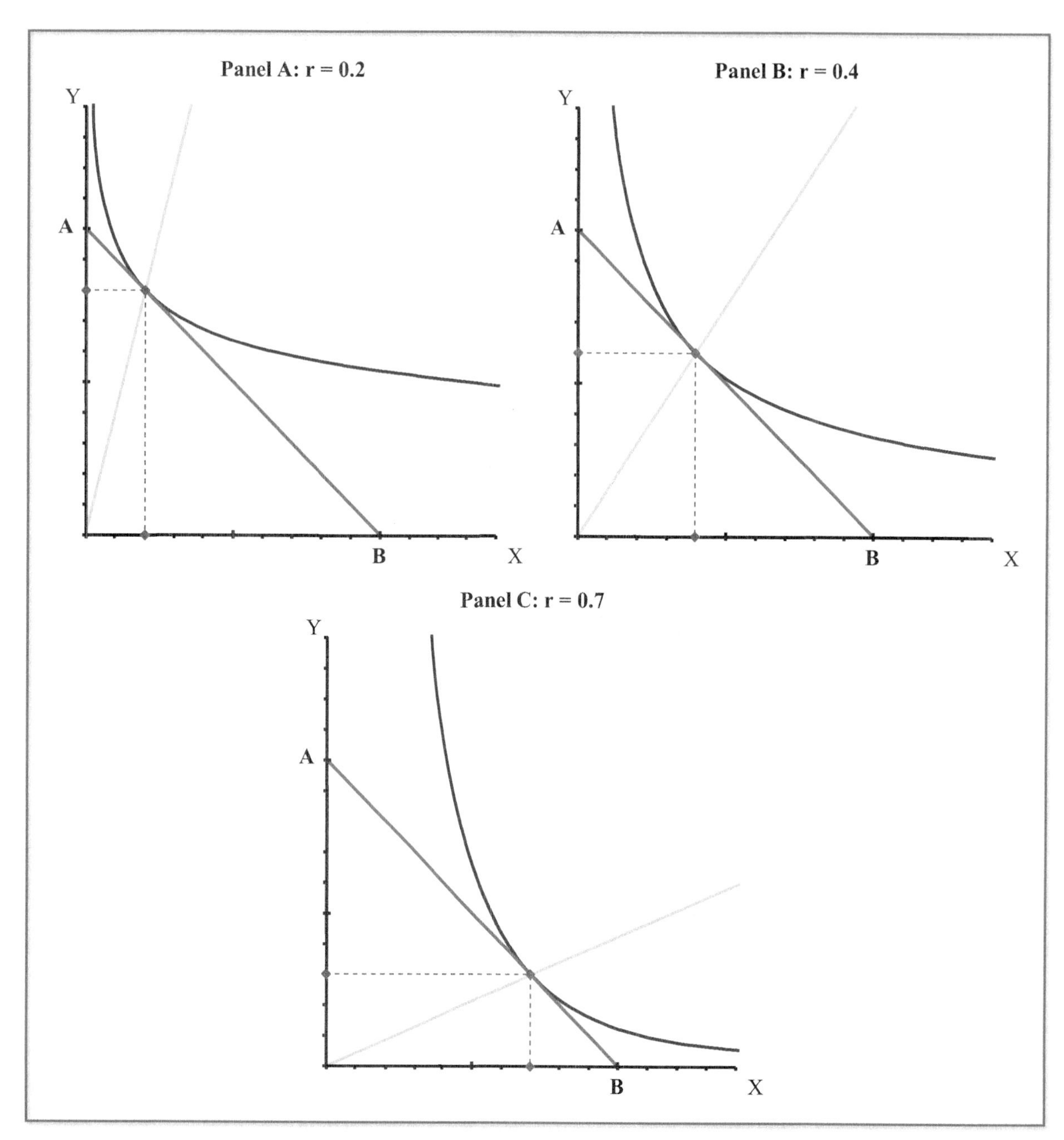

FIGURE 6.5 General Cobb-Douglas Utility, $U(x, y) = x^r \cdot y^{(1-r)}$, for three values of r

a yellow line depicting the set of bundles where MRS = 1. In each panel, this line goes through the optimal bundle and through the origin, signifying that the ratio of x to y would not change as income changes, as long as the price ratio does not change. We examine the properties of CD preferences further in Chapters 7 and 8.

Shifted Cobb-Douglas

Three parameters control the shifted CD utility function given in Equation 4.6, $U(x, y) = (x - a)^r \cdot (y - b)^{(1-r)}$: a is the vertical axis shift; b is the horizontal axis shift; and r is the relative CD exponent. The MRS for this utility function is given by: $MRS = (r/(1 - r)) \cdot ((y - b)/(x - a))$. As noted in the Chapter 4 discussion of the shifted CD utility function, if a and b are less than zero, the goods are imperfect substitutes, and if a and b are greater than zero, they are imperfect complements. When one is positive and the other is negative, a more complex picture of the substitute/complement issue emerges (in Chapter 8).

We initially set r = 0.5 (an equal weighting on both x and y) so that we can focus on the shift factors a and b. We further assume a = b with $a < 0$ to streamline the analysis. An equal-weighted shifted CD with equal shift factors to both axes will necessarily be tangent to the budget constraint with $P_x/P_y = 1$ along the 45° line. Thus, it is not surprising that the optimal bundle in this situation is **C** = (0.5, 0.5). This can be shown as follows:

$$\text{MRS}(x, y) = (r/(1 - r)) \cdot ((y - b)/(x - a)), \text{ or} \quad \textbf{(6.4a)}$$

$$\text{MRS}(x, y) = (y - a)/(x - a), \text{ given that } a = b \text{ and } r = 0.5. \quad \textbf{(6.4b)}$$

MRS = P_x/P_y at the optimum as required by Equation 6.1Bi. Therefore, in the context of symmetric shifted CD, MRS(x, y) = $P_x/P_y = 1$ implies that:

$$y - a = x - a \text{ or } x = y \text{ at the optimum.} \quad \textbf{(6.4c)}$$

Since x + y = 1, both must equal 0.5. This tangency is shown in Figures 6.6A–6.6C. Also included in each panel is the yellow MRS = 1 line that (given r = 0.5 and a = b) must be the 45° ray through the origin: y = x. This ray intersects the budget constraint and the indifference curve at bundle **C**.

More interesting is the MRS at the boundaries of the budget constraint in this instance. Bundle **A** = (0, 1) and **B** = (1, 0), so we have the following MRSs at bundles **A** and **B**:

$$\text{MRS}(\mathbf{A}) = (r/(1 - r)) \cdot ((1 - b)/(-a)), \text{ or} \quad \textbf{(6.5a)}$$

$$\text{MRS}(\mathbf{A}) = (a - 1)/a > 1, \text{ given that } a = b < 0 \text{ and } r = 0.5; \text{ and} \quad \textbf{(6.5b)}$$

$$\text{MRS}(\mathbf{B}) = (r/(1 - r)) \cdot ((-b)/(1 - a)), \text{ or} \quad \textbf{(6.5c)}$$

$$\text{MRS}(\mathbf{B}) = a/(a - 1) < 1, \text{ given that } a = b < 0 \text{ and } r = 0.5. \quad \textbf{(6.5d)}$$

Figures 6.6A–6.6C examine these symmetric shifted CD boundary MRSs for three values of a; the Excel version of Figure 6.6 allows you to vary a and b from –10 to 0 to understand alternative versions of imperfect substitutes (to keep this equal weighted, you must vary both a and b by the same amount). When a = –0.2, the boundary MRSs using Equations 6.5b and 6.5d are MRS(**A**) = 6 and MRS(**B**) = 1/6.

These MRSs can be interpreted using the conditions delineated in Equation 6.1B. Focus initially on bundle **A** in Figure 6.6A. Equation 6.1Bii states that **A** is the constrained optimum if all income is spent and MRS(**A**) ≤ P_x/P_y. **A** will remain on the budget constraint if I and P_y remain fixed. Increasing the price of x rotates the budget constraint inward, using **A** as the fulcrum point. As this occurs, the optimal bundle **C** will necessarily adjust, but the optimal bundle will remain an interior solution, x > 0, as long as $P_x < 6$ (since MRS(**A**) = 6 > P_x), and **A** is the boundary solution if $P_x \geq 6$.

Conversely, Equation 6.1Biii states that **B** will remain the constrained optimum as long as all income is spent and MRS(**B**) ≥ P_x/P_y. **B** will remain on the budget constraint if the price of x and income remain fixed. Increasing the price of y rotates the budget constraint inward, using **B** as the fulcrum point. As this occurs, the optimal bundle **C** will necessarily adjust, but the optimal bundle will remain an interior solution, y > 0, as long as $P_y < 6$ (since $1/P_y > 1/6$ = MRS(**B**) if $P_y < 6$), and **B** is the boundary solution if $P_y \geq 6$. Not surprisingly, the solution is symmetric (since a = b and r = 0.5). Figures 6.6B and 6.6C describe closer substitutes by setting a = b = –1 and –5. What do the resulting MRSs signify? Consider the following:

S6.i. Purchase only y if P_x increases by more than 200%, *ceteris paribus*, and only x if P_y increases by more than 200%, *ceteris paribus*.

S6.ii. Purchase only y if P_x increases by more than 100%, *ceteris paribus*, and only x if P_y increases by more than 100%, *ceteris paribus*.

S6.iii. Purchase only y if P_x increases by more than 20%, *ceteris paribus*, and only x if P_y increases by more than 20%, *ceteris paribus*.

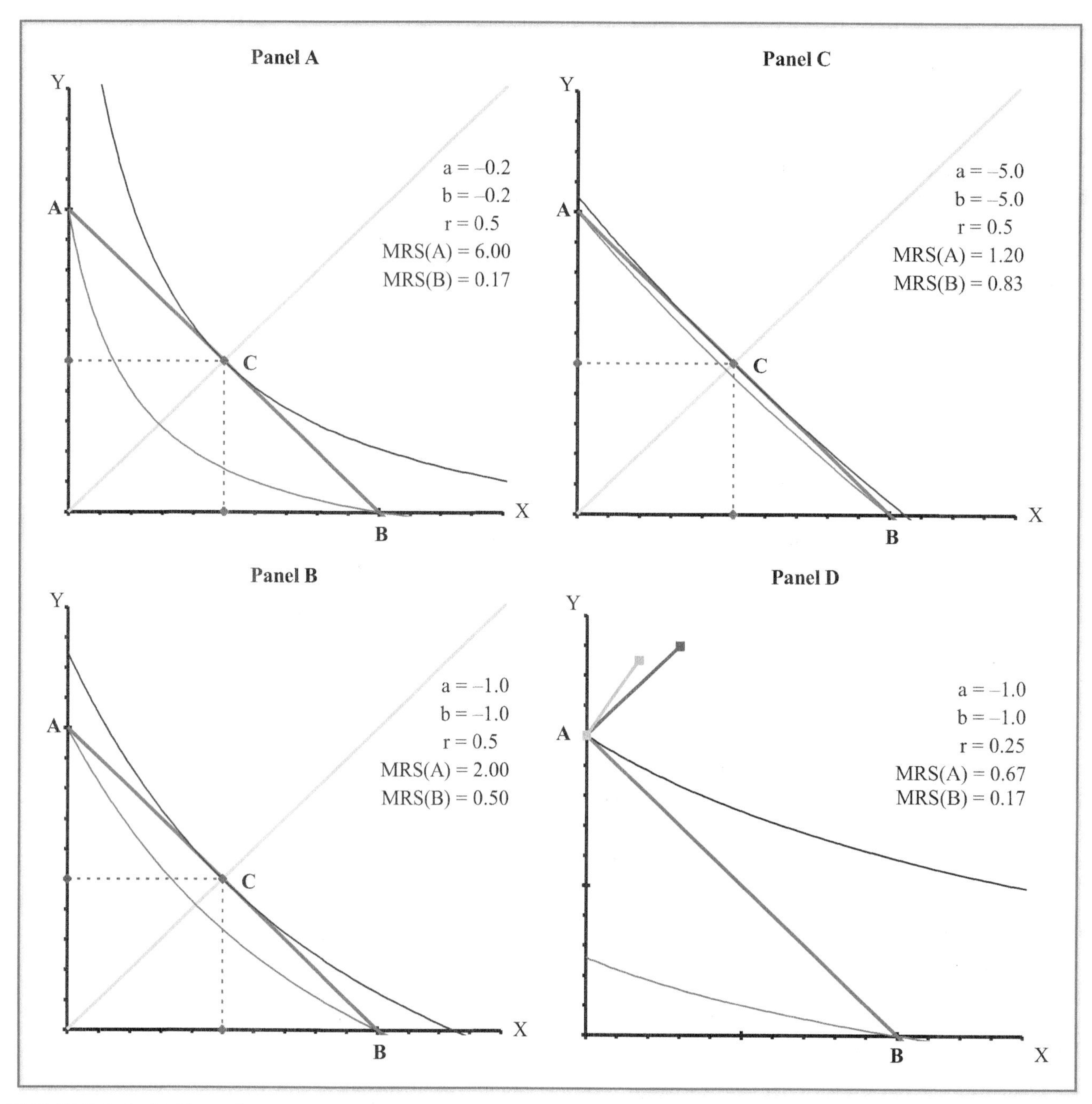

FIGURE 6.6 Shifted Cobb-Douglas Utility, $U(x, y) = (x - a)^r \cdot (y - b)^{(1-r)}$

S6.iv. Purchase only y if P_x increases by more than 120%, *ceteris paribus*, and only x if P_y increases by more than 120%, *ceteris paribus*.

Q6. Which statement accurately describes Figure 6.6B, and which describes 6.6C?*

Figure 6.6D examines the boundary solutions more directly, using the unitary budget constraint rather than through analyzing price changes. Consider the shifted CD utility function with $a = b = -1$ and $r = 0.25$. (Figure 6.6D has the same a and b as Figure 6.6B,

*__Q6 answer:__ S6.ii describes Figure 6.6B, and S6.iii describes Figure 6.6C. If you thought S6.i describes 6.6B, you are misusing the concept of percentage *change*. A price increase from 1 to 2 is a 100% change.

but the exponents on the terms $(x - a)$ and $(y - b)$ are no longer symmetric.) Our task is to find the bundle that satisfies MRS = P_x/P_y and all income is spent. The unitary budget constraint implies $y = 1 - x$. Further, $r/(1 - r) = 1/3$ when $r = 1/4$. Substituting this information into Equation 6.4a yields:

$$\begin{aligned} MRS(x, y) &= (r/(1 - r)) \cdot ((y - b)/(x - a)) \\ &= (1/3) \cdot ((1 - x) + 1)/(x + 1) = (2 - x)/(3 \cdot x + 3). \end{aligned} \quad \textbf{(6.6a)}$$

Setting this equal to the price ratio ($P_x/P_y = 1$) and cross-multiplying yields:

$$2 - x = 3 \cdot x + 3. \quad \textbf{(6.6b)}$$

Solving for x, we obtain:

$$x = -1/4. \quad \textbf{(6.6c)}$$

This is the solution required by Equation 6.1Bi, but x cannot take on negative values; therefore $x = 0$ will be the constrained optimum. (Convexity ensures that if MRS = 1 when x is negative, then MRS ≤ 1 when $x = 0$. The MRS declines as x increases along an indifference curve, as discussed in Chapter 3.) This may be checked by calculating the MRS(**A**), using Equation 6.5a. This yields:

$$MRS(\mathbf{A}) = (1/3) \cdot ((1 + 1)/1) = 2/3. \quad \textbf{(6.6d)}$$

As expected, **A** is the constrained optimum because MRS(**A**) < P_x/P_y. This is confirmed visually as well. The relative orientation of the MU vector and price vector at **A** are the same as in Figure 6.3C. Less x should be consumed ($x = -1/4$ according to Equation 6.6c), but it is already at its minimum allowable level since $x = 0$.

Buying Cabernet Versus Merlot

The shifted CD function can help explain fairly sophisticated behavior. If you know any wine connoisseurs, you might ask them if the following is a reasonable description of their behavior. They may differ in their degree of substitutability, but in all likelihood, they will be able to provide you with similar answers to the following three questions about their consumption of merlot (M) versus cabernet sauvignon (CS). Assume that we are talking about everyday bottles of wine, not first-growth Bordeaux or Napa Valley cult bottlings at $250 a bottle.

Wine (Q1): If the price of cabernet is the same as merlot, what percentage of your cabernet/merlot budget will you devote to cabernet, and what percentage will you devote to merlot?

Wine (Q2): How much higher must the price of merlot be before you decide to purchase cabernet exclusively? (For this question, assume that the price of cabernet does not change.)

Wine (Q3): How much higher must the price of cabernet be before you decide to purchase merlot exclusively? (For this question, assume that the price of merlot does not change.)

Think of the answers to questions 2 and 3 in terms of price ratios. The answer to Q2 will be P_m/P_{cs}, and the answer to Q3 will be P_{cs}/P_m. For example, Steve would say:

Wine (Steve, A1): Sixty percent of my budget would go to cabernet, and 40% would go to merlot when $P_{cs}/P_m = 1$.

Wine (Steve, A2): If $P_m/P_{cs} = 5/3$, I will switch to purchasing only cabernet. This ratio says that if the price of merlot increases by more than 2/3 (67%), I will buy cabernet exclusively.

Wine (Steve, A3): If $P_{cs}/P_m = 2$, I will switch to purchasing only merlot. If the price of cabernet doubles, I will switch to merlot exclusively.

This can be modeled using the shifted CD form. Let merlot be the x axis and cabernet be the y axis. Steve's answers can be *algebraically* described as:

(A1): MRS(0.4, 0.6) = 1 at the (M, CS) bundle (0.4, 0.6).

(A2): $MRS(0, 1) = P_m/P_{cs} = 5/3$.

(A3): $MRS(1, 0) = P_m/P_{cs} = 1/(P_{cs}/P_m) = 1/2$.

Using Equation 6.4a, these answers can be rewritten as:

$$(r/(1 - r)) \cdot ((0.6 - b)/(0.4 - a)) = 1. \quad \textbf{(6.7a)}$$

$$(r/(1 - r)) \cdot ((1 - b)/(0 - a)) = 5/3. \quad \textbf{(6.7b)}$$

$$(r/(1 - r)) \cdot ((0 - b)/(1 - a)) = 1/2. \quad \textbf{(6.7c)}$$

Three equations in three unknowns can be solved for *a*, b, and r. This can be done in a number of ways. (One is provided in the endnote.[3]) The solution obtained is:

$$a = -1, b = -1.5, \text{ and } r = 0.4. \quad \textbf{(6.8)}$$

Figure 6.7A depicts indifference curves based on Steve's preferences defined by answers A1–A3. It is worth explicitly confirming that each of Steve's answers to questions 1–3 is accurately depicted in Figure 6.7A. In his first answer, Steve states that he would spend 60% of his cabernet/merlot budget on cabernet and 40% on merlot when cabernet and merlot are equally expensive. The diagram depicts imperfect substitutes, with cabernet being preferred to merlot overall, despite having MRS = 1 at the constrained optimal bundle **C**. The coefficient r tells us this algebraically, while the geometric way to see this is to examine the indifference curve associated with bundle **C**, which is 40% of the way from **A** (100% cabernet) to **B** (100% merlot). In his second answer, Steve states that he will purchase cabernet exclusively if merlot's price increases by more than two-thirds for a fixed price of cabernet. As noted in Figure 6.7A, MRS(**A**) = 1.67, so if $P_m/P_{cs} > 5/3$, $P_m/P_{cs} >$ MRS(**A**), and **A** will be the constrained optimal bundle, according to the condition required by Equation 6.1Bii. In his third answer, Steve states that the price of caber-

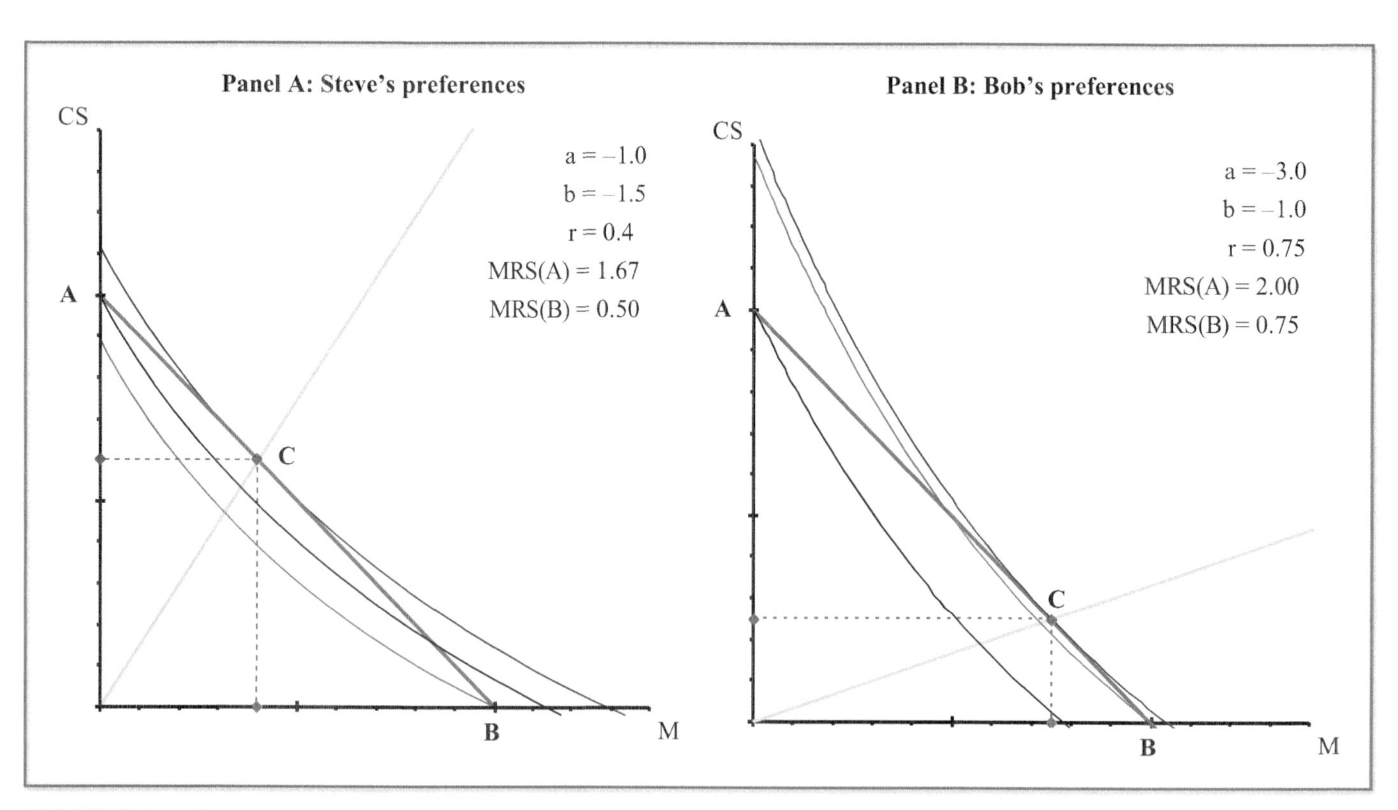

FIGURE 6.7 Preferences for Cabernet Sauvignon versus Merlot, Based on $U(x, y) = (x - a)^r \cdot (y - b)^{(1-r)}$

net would have to double for a fixed price of merlot before he would move to exclusively purchasing merlot. As noted in Figure 6.7A, MRS(**B**) = 0.5, so if the price of cabernet at least doubles for a fixed price of merlot, then $P_m/P_{cs} \leq 1/2$, so MRS(**B**) $\geq P_m/P_{cs}$, and **B** will be the constrained optimal bundle, as required by Equation 6.1Biii.

We can obtain further information from Figure 6.7A as well. Note that having equal prices implies that every bundle on budget constraint **AB** will have the same number of bottles. Suppose you were offered bundle **C** or two other possibilities: **D** involves 20% more bottles than **C**, but all of them are cabernet; and **E** involves 30% more bottles than **C**, but all of them are merlot. (**D** and **E** are not shown on Figure 6.7A, but you should be able to place them on the graph, based on the information given.)

Q7a. Provide a rank ordering of **C**, **D**, and **E**, based on the preferences depicted in Figure 6.7A.*

The diagram also includes a yellow ray associated with bundles where MRS = 1. This ray suggests that, as income changes, Steve will maintain the 40:60 ratio of merlot to cabernet, assuming that the prices of cabernet and merlot remain equal.

Of course, not all wine lovers are the same: Figure 6.7B depicts Bob's preferences.

Q7b. Provide answers to Wine Q1–Q3, based on Bob's preferences.†

The focus thus far in our analysis of the shifted CD has been when a and b are both negative. When $a \geq 0$, indifference curves never touch the vertical (x = 0) axis. When $b \geq 0$, indifference curves never touch the horizontal (y = 0) axis. (Indeed, as stated in Table 4.1, the shifted CD function is constrained beyond the standard restriction that the bundle be in the first quadrant. The shifted CD function is only defined for $x > a$ and $y > b$.) When one is positive and the other is negative, indifference curves intersect only one axis, and when both are positive, indifference curves are imperfect complements. Use the Excel file for Figures 6.5–6.8 (the shifted CD), and make sure you can produce examples of each of these assertions.

Before leaving the shifted CD function, it is worthwhile to see how each parameter affects the location of the constrained optimum, *ceteris paribus*. Each parameter in the shifted CD function has been adjusted so that the constrained optimum occurs at one of two bundles: **C** = (0.35, 0.65) and **D** = (0.65, 0.35) in Figure 6.8. Figures 6.8A–6.8C have constrained optima at **C**, and Figures 6.8D–6.8F have constrained optima at **D**.

Figures 6.8A and 6.8D allow a to vary (with b and r set to their neutral positions of zero and 0.5). Figures 6.8B and 6.8E allow b to vary (with a and r set to their neutral positions). Figures 6.8C and 6.8F allow r to vary. Since Figure 6.5 already examined how to obtain bundles **C** and **D** with a and b set to zero (by setting r = 0.35 and 0.65), these two panels examine changing r when a and b are not zero. In this instance, both are set to –1.[4] The following conclusions can be made, based on these panels: First, increasing a increases the proportion of x in the constrained optimum, *ceteris paribus*. Second, decreasing b increases the proportion of x in the constrained optimum, *ceteris paribus*. Third, increasing r increases the proportion of x in the constrained optimum, *ceteris paribus*.

Perfect Substitutes

Both ends of the substitutability spectrum have easy algebraic solutions to the constrained optimization problem. The earlier discussion of Figure 6.4 already provided the geometric solution for perfect substitutes for general values of prices and income. Since perfect

---

***Q7a answer: D ≻ C ≻ E**, despite **E** having the most bottles. Each tick mark is 10%. The indifference curve through **C** intersects the cabernet axis at about 12% above **A** and the merlot axis at about 32% to the right of **B**. Therefore, **D** is better than **C**, but **C** is better than **E**.

†Q7b answer: (A1) Bob would spend 75% on merlot and 25% on cabernet when $P_{cs}/P_m = 1$. **(A2)** If $P_m/P_{cs} = 2$, Bob will switch to purchasing only cabernet. This ratio says that if the price of merlot doubles, Bob will buy cabernet exclusively. **(A3)** If $P_{cs}/P_m = 4/3$, Bob will switch to purchasing only merlot. If the price of cabernet increases by one-third, Bob will switch to merlot exclusively.

FIGURE 6.8 Sensitivity Analysis of the Shifted CD Function, $U(x, y) = (x - a)^r \cdot (y - b)^{(1-r)}$

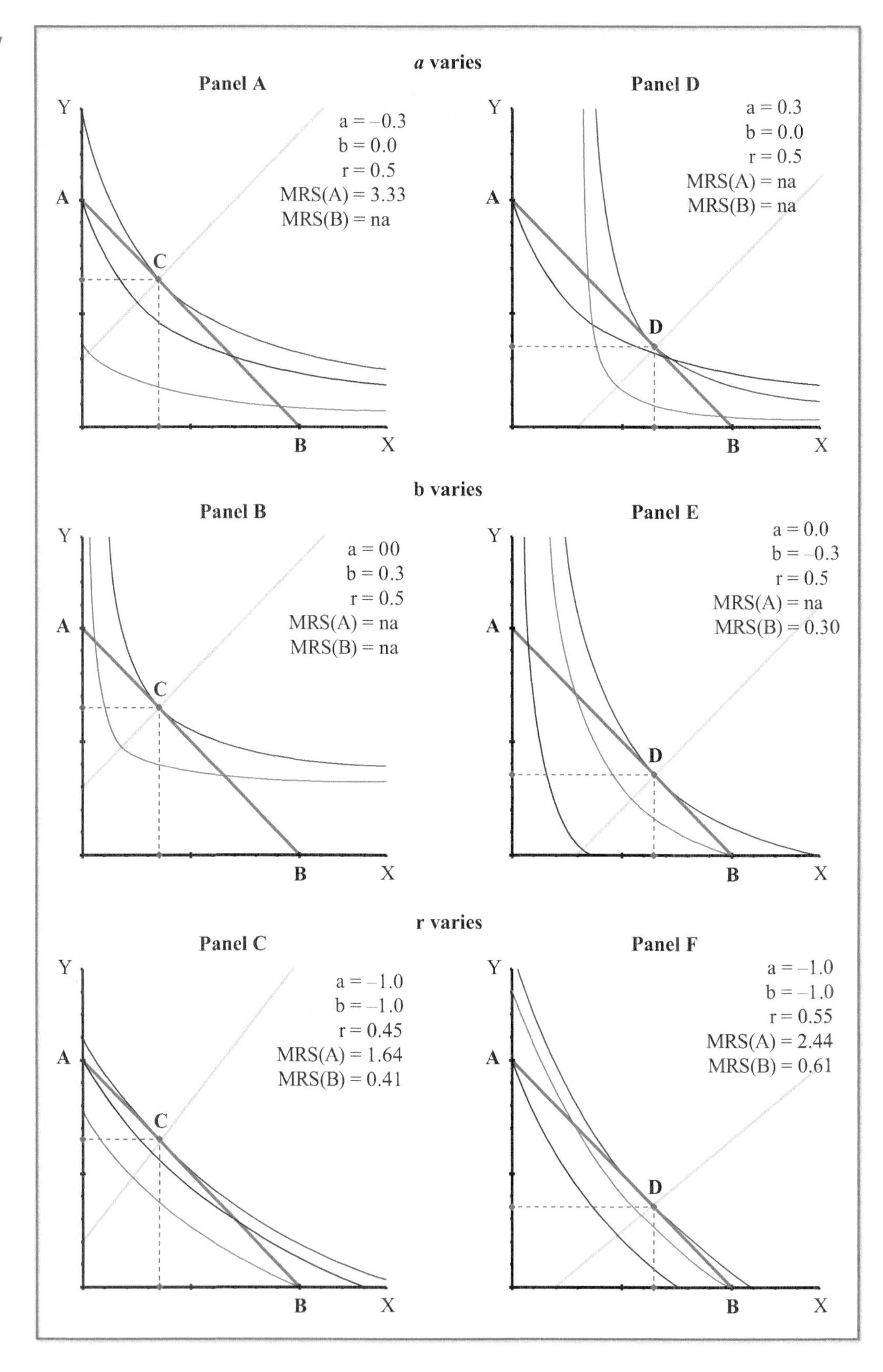

substitutes have constant MRS = *a*/b, based on $U(x, y) = a \cdot x + b \cdot y$, the rule obtained there is algebraically described as:

$$x = 0 \text{ and } y = I/P_y \text{ if MRS} = a/b < P_x/P_y. \quad \textbf{(6.9a)}$$

(Bundle **A** in Figure 6.4A; spend all income on y if $a/P_x < b/P_y$.)

$0 \leq x \leq I/P_x$ and $y = (I - P_x x)/P_y$ if $MRS = a/b = P_x/P_y$. **(6.9b)**

(Segment **AB** in Figure 6.4B; buy anywhere on budget constraint if $a/P_x = b/P_y$.)

$x = I/P_x$ and $y = 0$ if $MRS = a/b > P_x/P_y$. **(6.9c)**

(Bundle **B** in Figure 6.4C; spend all income on x if $a/P_x > b/P_y$.)

A unitary budget constraint further simplifies these equations, since $P_x/P_y = 1$ and $I/P_x = 1$. In this instance, buy only y ($y = 1$) if $b > a$, buy only x ($x = 1$) if $a > b$, and buy anywhere on the budget constraint, $(s, 1 - s)$ for $0 \leq s \leq 1$, when $a = b$.

Perfect Complements

As shown in Figure 6.2, the constrained optimum for perfect complements must occur at a vertex of the perfect complements indifference curve. Multiple algebraic representations of perfect complements utility functions are provided in Table 4.1; the main one used in that discussion was Equation 4.2b, $U(x, y) = \text{Minimum}(x, y/d)$. In this interpretation, the x value of the vertex bundle meters utility level. The vertex of each indifference curve is on the ray

$$y = d \cdot x. \quad \textbf{(6.10)}$$

Given $P_x = P_y = I = 1$, the budget constraint is $1 = x + y$. Substituting Equation 6.10 into the budget constraint and solving for x yields:

$$x = 1/(1 + d). \quad \textbf{(6.11a)}$$

Another way to look at this is to start from the solution bundle, $(x, 1 - x)$, and ask: What is the value of d associated with this bundle? This can be obtained by solving Equation 6.11a for d:

$$d = (1/x) - 1. \quad \textbf{(6.11b)}$$

(This could also have been obtained by taking Equation 6.10 and solving for d. This yields: $d = y/x$, but $(x, y) = (x, 1 - x)$ in this instance, so $y/x = (1 - x)/x = (1/x) - 1$.)

The solution for perfect complements described in Equation 6.11 is shown for two values of d in Figure 6.9. We see in general that the proportion of income spent on x decreases as d increases (since each unit of x requires d units of y).

Quasilinear

The implication of the quasilinear property (quasilinear indifference curves are vertical translates) is not readily apparent without examining income changes. As a result, the bulk of the analysis of quasilinear functions, $U(x, y) = f(x) + y$, must be put off until later chapters. Nonetheless, it is worthwhile varying the parameter(s) that define each quasilinear function to become more comfortable with how each parameter affects the constrained optimal outcome. Two distinct functions were delineated in Table 4.1. One involved exponents; the other involved logarithms. Both must be analyzed separately.

The first quasilinear function discussed in Chapter 4 was Equation 4.7a, $U(x, y) = a \cdot x^r + y$ (with $0 < r < 1$). This function is controlled by two parameters, a and r. The MRS for this utility function is: $MRS = a \cdot r \cdot x^{(r-1)}$. The hallmark of quasilinear functions is the absence of y in the MRS. The MRS is entirely determined by the amount of x consumed. (This is why quasilinear indifference curves are vertical translates of one another.) This makes it particularly easy to derive the optimal bundle in this situation. The tangency condition requires $MRS = P_x/P_y$. (Notice that even though y is not in the MRS, P_y is still in the price ratio.) Given a unitary budget constraint, $MRS = P_x/P_y$ becomes:

$$a \cdot r \cdot x^{(r-1)} = 1. \quad \textbf{(6.12a)}$$

Solving for x, we obtain:

$$x = (1/(a \cdot r))^{(1/(r-1))} = (a \cdot r)^{(-1/(r-1))} = (a \cdot r)^{(1/(1-r))}. \quad \textbf{(6.12b)}$$

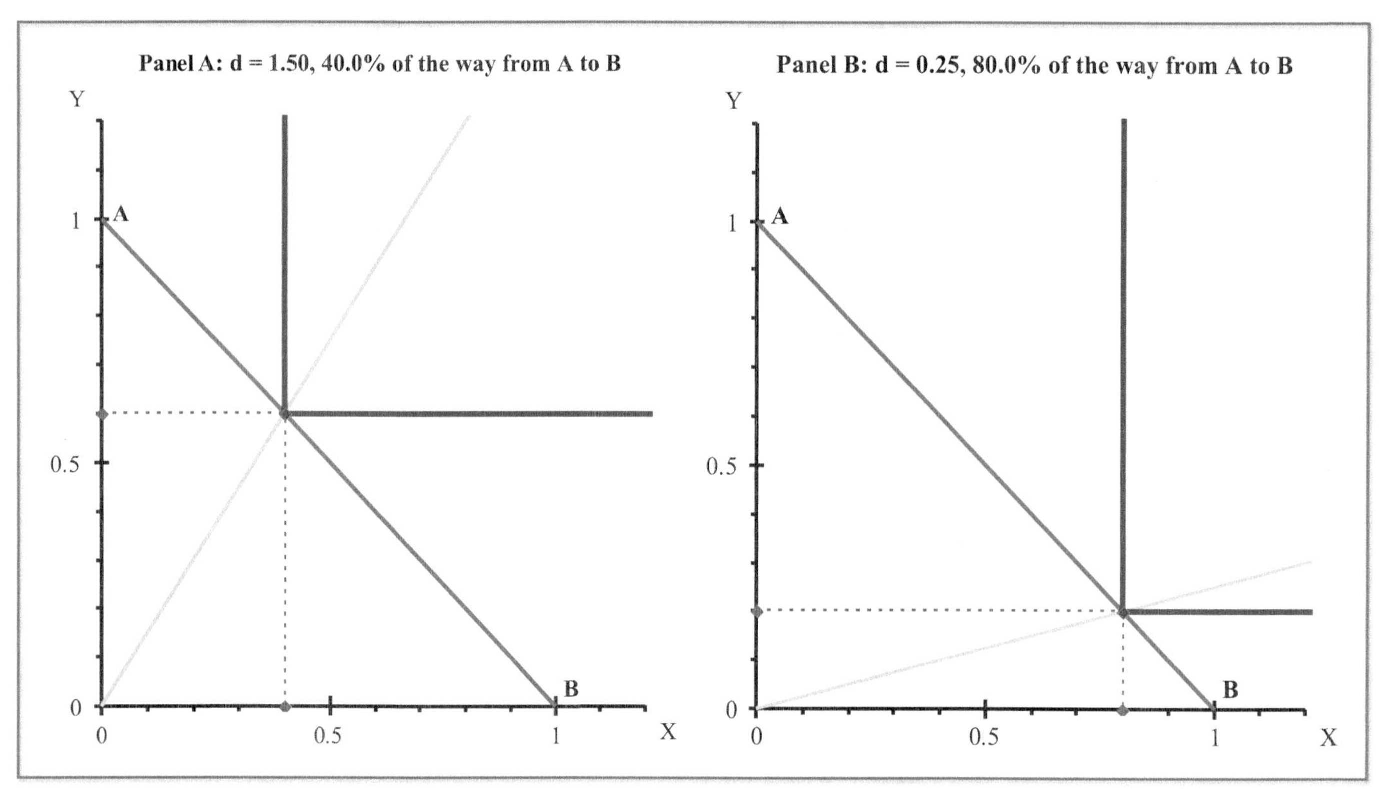

FIGURE 6.9 Perfect Complements Constrained Optimization Based on U(x, y) = Minimum (x, y/d)

This is, admittedly, not a very intuitive-looking equation. As a result, it is worthwhile to simply find the optimal x for a value of a and r. Since r is bounded by zero and 1, it seems reasonable to try r = 0.5. The parameter a is a scaling factor in other utility functions described in Chapter 4; thus, $a = 1$ is a reasonable place to start. In this instance, the optimal x = 0.25 ($x = 1/2^{(1/(1/2))} = 1/2^2 = 1/4$). This is the solution depicted in Figure 6.10E. Figures 6.10A–6.10C vary a with r = 1/2. As long as r = 1/2, the exponent $(1/(1 - r)) = 2$, so x is simply $(a/2)^2$. Figures 6.10D–6.10F vary r for $a = 1$. These panels provide the following general conclusions: First, the optimal x increases as a and r increase. Second, as seen in Figure 6.10C, when a is large enough, the optimal condition becomes MRS ≥ 1, rather than MRS = 1 (so, for example, in Figure 6.10C, MRS(**B**) = 1.1 = 2.2 · 0.5). This is the boundary condition in Equation 6.1Biii that produces **B** as the optimal bundle. (The same conclusion would be obtained for r in Figures 6.10E and 6.10F, if a was based on $a = 2$, rather than $a = 1$. In that instance (not shown), MRS(**B**) = 1.0, and MRS(**B**) = 1.5 in those adjusted panels.)

Q10. Given r = 0.5, what is the largest value of a where the chosen bundle has MRS = 1?*

In the quasilinear context, the boundary condition in Equation 6.1Biii can be thought of as simply being based on the value of x where MRS = P_x/P_y. Only the budget constraint of the constrained optimization process contains y, so the only question in determining whether the chosen x is an interior solution or a boundary solution is whether the optimal x is affordable. In Figures 6.10A, 6.10B, and 6.10D–6.10F, the optimal x is affordable. In Figure 6.10C, it is not, and the individual must be satisfied with the constrained boundary optimum **B**.

***Q10 answer:** This would happen at $a = 2.0$. Anytime $a \cdot r > 1$, then MRS > 1, and the unrestricted optimal x in Equation 6.12b would be larger than 1; the unitary budget constraint restricts x ≤ 1. You can check this using the Excel version of Figure 6.10.

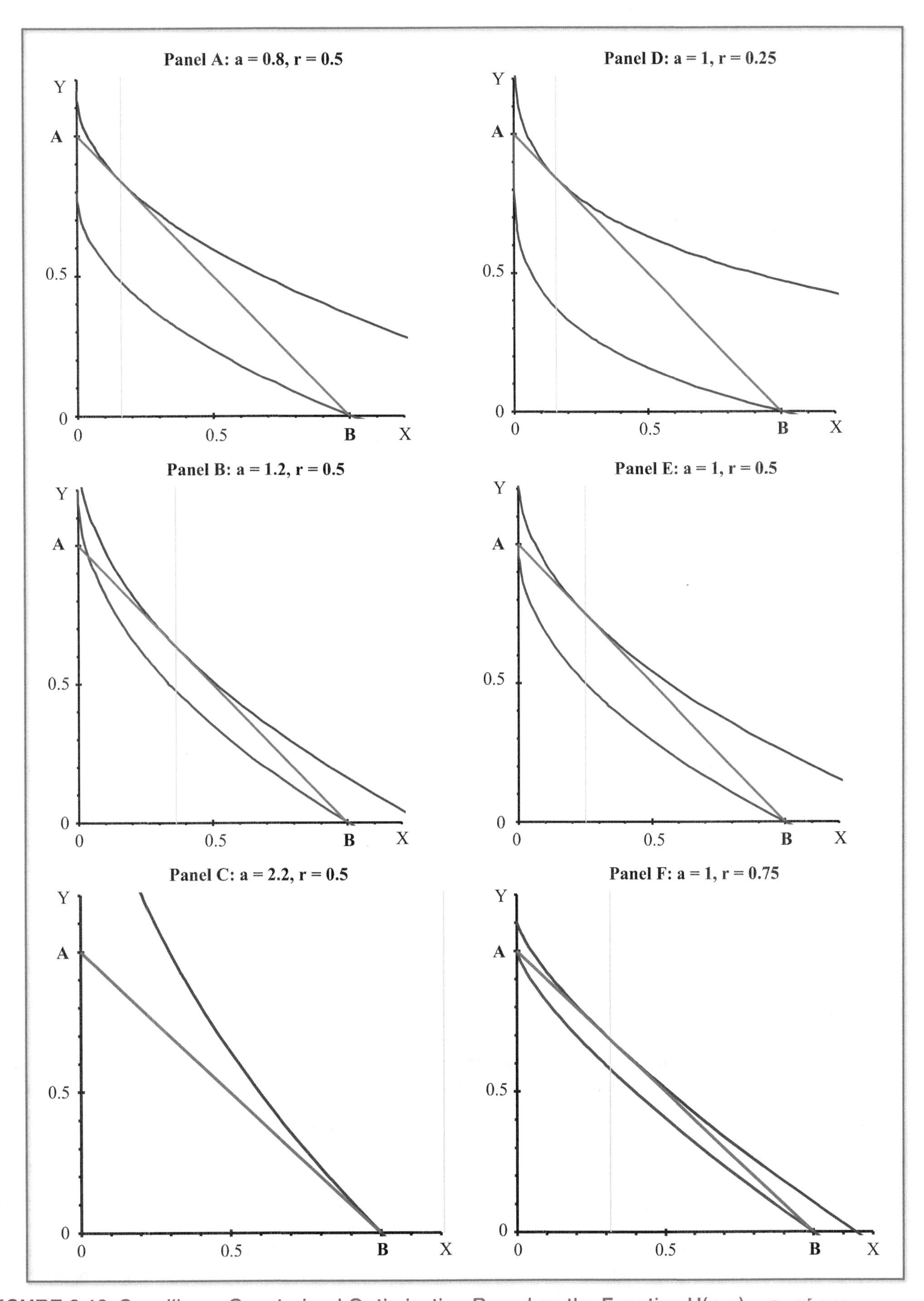

FIGURE 6.10 Quasilinear Constrained Optimization Based on the Function $U(x, y) = a \cdot x^r + y$

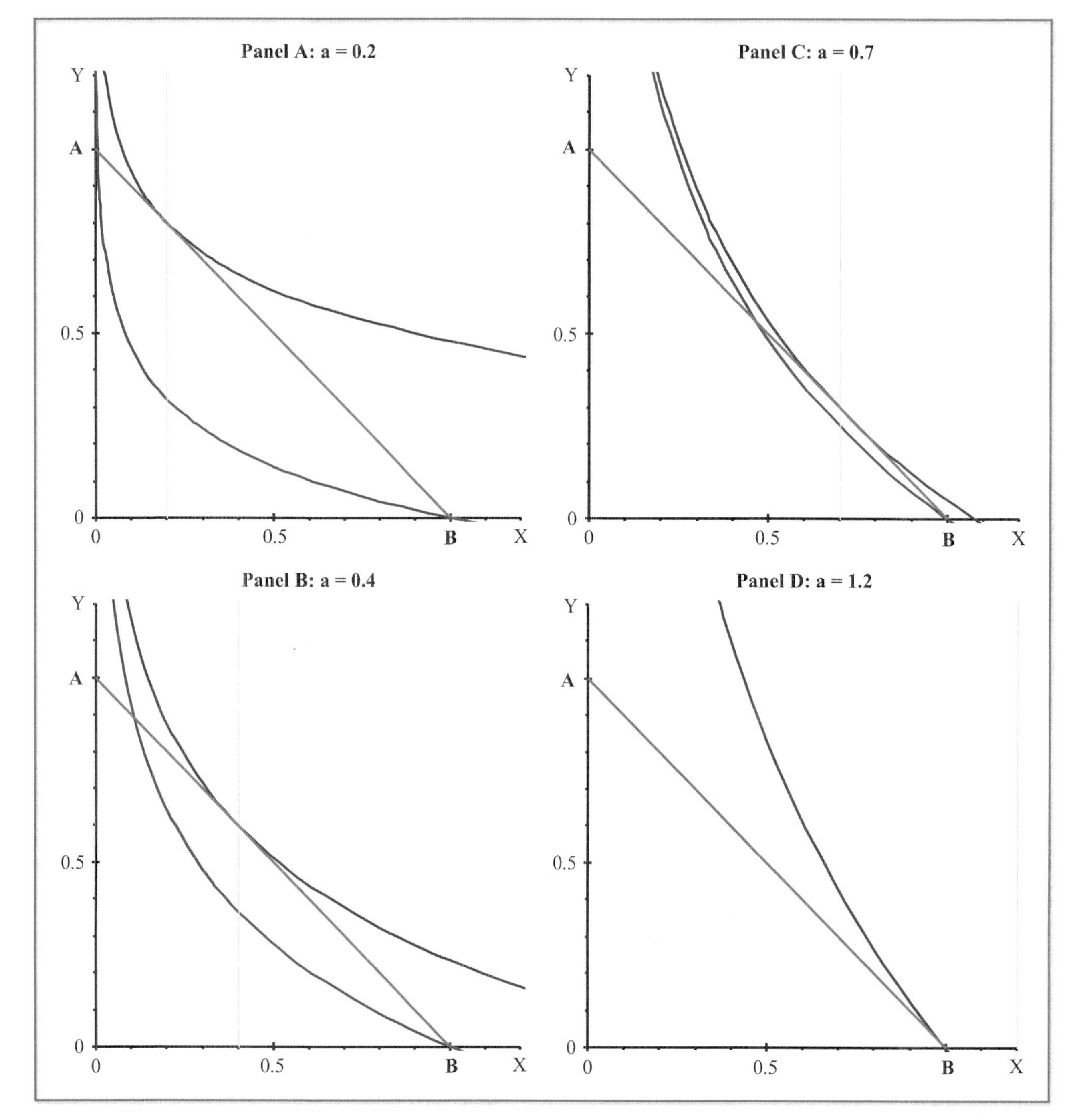

FIGURE 6.11 Quasilinear Constrained Optimization Based on the Utility Function $U(x, y) = a \cdot \ln(x) + y$

The second quasilinear function discussed in Chapter 4, $U(x, y) = a \cdot \ln(x) + y$ (Equation 4.7b), is controlled by the scaling parameter a. The MRS for this utility function is $MRS = a/x$.

Given a unitary budget constraint, $MRS = P_x/P_y$ becomes:

$$x = a. \tag{6.13}$$

The demand for x is given by the size of the parameter a. The solution described in Equation 6.13 is shown for four values of a in Figure 6.11. As a increases from 0.2 to 0.4 to 0.7, the optimal x increases by the same amount in Figures 6.11A–6.11C. Figure 6.11D shows that, just as with the quasilinear function analyzed in Figure 6.10, if a is large enough, the optimal condition becomes the boundary condition in Equation 6.1Biii:

MRS ≥ 1, rather than MRS = 1. (Given the unitary budget constraint assumed here, this occurs when $a \geq 1$.)

This takes us full circle in a way: a is the proportion of income spent on x in this instance, just as r is the proportion of income spent on x in the general Cobb-Douglas (CD) form in Equation 6.3. The difference between these functions, however, is profound and is easily seen by comparing the yellow MRS = 1 lines in Figures 6.5 and 6.11. These lines are rays through the origin in Figure 6.5 and vertical lines in Figure 6.11. Were income to change for fixed prices, the CD form would adjust consumption of both x and y so that the same proportionate relation is maintained, given unchanged prices. In contrast, the amount spent on x would remain constant, and all adjustments in consumption would come from changes in y if income were to change for fixed price, given quasilinear preferences. A second distinction between the two forms is that the quasilinear functions can have boundary solutions, and the general CD cannot.[5] This geometric observation is tied to the numeric restrictions placed on r in the CD function and a in the quasilinear form. $0 < r < 1$ and $a > 0$ are the respective restrictions. Since $a > 0$, $a \geq 1$ is allowed for quasilinear; it just signifies a boundary solution to the constrained optimization problem with unitary budget constraint.

6.3 Choosing among Alternatives: Food-Subsidy Programs Revisited *OPTIONAL SECTION*

We can use the constrained optimization methodology developed in this chapter to further refine the choice among constraints presented in Section 5.4. The warehouse store and food-subsidy examples described there can both benefit from further analysis based on the preferences of the individual who is faced with the choice among alternatives. As the warehouse store example is qualitatively the same as the food-subsidy example with one of the choices removed, we focus on the food-subsidy example.

The three low-income subsidy programs examined were (1) a direct cash giveaway, (2) a direct food giveaway, and (3) a food-stamp program that allows the individual to purchase a certain amount of food at reduced prices. These programs were described as:

Cash: The individual receives \$M in cash.

Free food: The individual receives R units of free food from a food bank (each unit of food would cost \$1 if purchased).

Food stamps: The individual is able to obtain a maximum of T food stamps at a discount rate of d per food stamp. Each food stamp allows the individual to purchase 1 unit of food.

We use the same numerical values as in Chapter 5 for \$M, R, T, and d for the majority of our analysis in this section. (These values are: M = \$24, R = 48, T = 100, and d = 0.6.) In Chapter 5, we concluded that the choice of program depends on how much food, x, you wish to consume. *To streamline the discussion, we can talk about the programs as C (cash), F (free food), and S (food stamps).* C is preferred if $x < 24$, F is preferred for x between $24 < x < 80$, and S is preferred if $x > 80$. If you choose to consume x = 24 (and y = 100), C ~ F, and if x = 80 (and y = 68), F ~ S.

The question we examine here is: When would you choose a given value of x? The answer, of course, depends on your preferences. You will choose x so that utility is maximized, subject to the choices you have available to you. This answer is clarified in Figures 6.12–6.14, using two distinct utility functions: perfect complements and shifted CD. The programs are color-coded, using the same scheme as in Chapter 5. **Green depicts the cash-subsidy program, red depicts the free-food program,** and **blue depicts the food-stamp program.**

Given perfect complement preferences, each possible value of x (and the corresponding y value) would be chosen as the optimal bundle, given different values of d, the parameter that delineates the number of units of x per unit of y associated with perfect

FIGURE 6.12 Choosing among Food-Subsidy Programs, Given Perfect Complement Preferences, U(x, y) = Minimum(x, y/d)

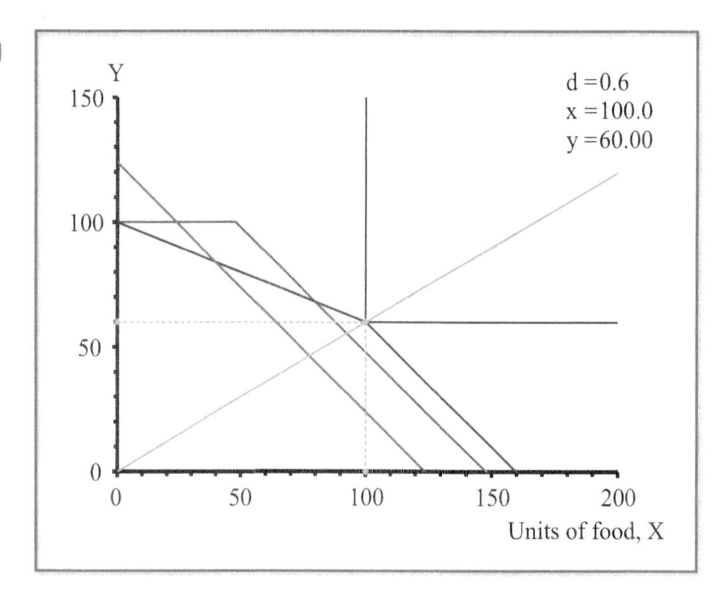

complement preferences. (Note that the parameter d listed in Figure 6.12 is a different d from the discount rate previously used to describe the food-stamp program.) As discussed earlier, vertex bundles are efficient and are described by Equation 6.10: $y = d \cdot x$. The results from Section 5.4's discussion of feasible bundles and the choice among alternatives (described two paragraphs ago) may be obtained as constrained optimal solutions for an individual with perfect complement preferences, based on the value of d used to define the perfect complements preferences in Equation 4.2b. As d changes, so will the preferred program. Each of the three programs dominates for different values of d.

Fact: C (cash) is preferred if $d > 4.17 = 100/24$. If $d < 4.17$, then either F (free food) or S (food stamps) is preferred. Figure 6.12 shows one such situation: $d = 0.6$.

Q12. What is the rank ordering of C, F, and S in Figure 6.12? For what values of d does S dominate? For what values of d does F dominate? For what value of d is C indifferent to F? For what value of d is F indifferent to S?*

At some level, the use of perfect complements in this instance is an oversimplification because it is unlikely that an individual would view food and all other goods as perfect complements. Perfect complement preferences provide a crisp solution to the question of when you will choose cash subsidy, free food, or food stamps. More likely, however, the consumer would have smooth, well-behaved, strictly convex, strictly monotonic preferences over food and other goods, rather than strict, L-shaped, "I need to consume food and other goods in a precise ratio; I don't want more food without more of other goods and vice versa" preferences that are implicit in perfect complements. The shifted CD functional form provides a great deal of flexibility, while maintaining strict convexity and strict monotonicity.

Figure 6.13 shows each of the six possible rank orderings of three choices. (Each panel is labeled with the rank ordering, but > signs are used in the panels, rather than ≻, because of limitations in Excel.) The best program is the one with the highest indifference curve. If two programs are liked equally well, one of the indifference curves will disappear: The two programs will be associated with the same level of utility. The panels allow each curve to be on top twice (most preferred), in the middle twice, and on the bottom twice (least preferred). The first four rank orderings (Figures 6.13A–6.13D) are produced from the same axis-shifted CD function ($a = -6$, and $b = 30$) by varying the parameter r. The

*__Q12 answer:__ S ≻ F ≻ C. The rank ordering in this instance can be seen by the order in which the three budget constraints intersect the lavender ray $y = d \cdot x$, since the vertices of all perfect complement indifference curves are on this ray. S (food stamps) is preferred if $d < 0.85 = 68/80$, and F (free food) is preferred for d between $0.85 < d < 4.17$. C ~ F for $d = 4.17$, and F ~ S for $d = 0.85$.

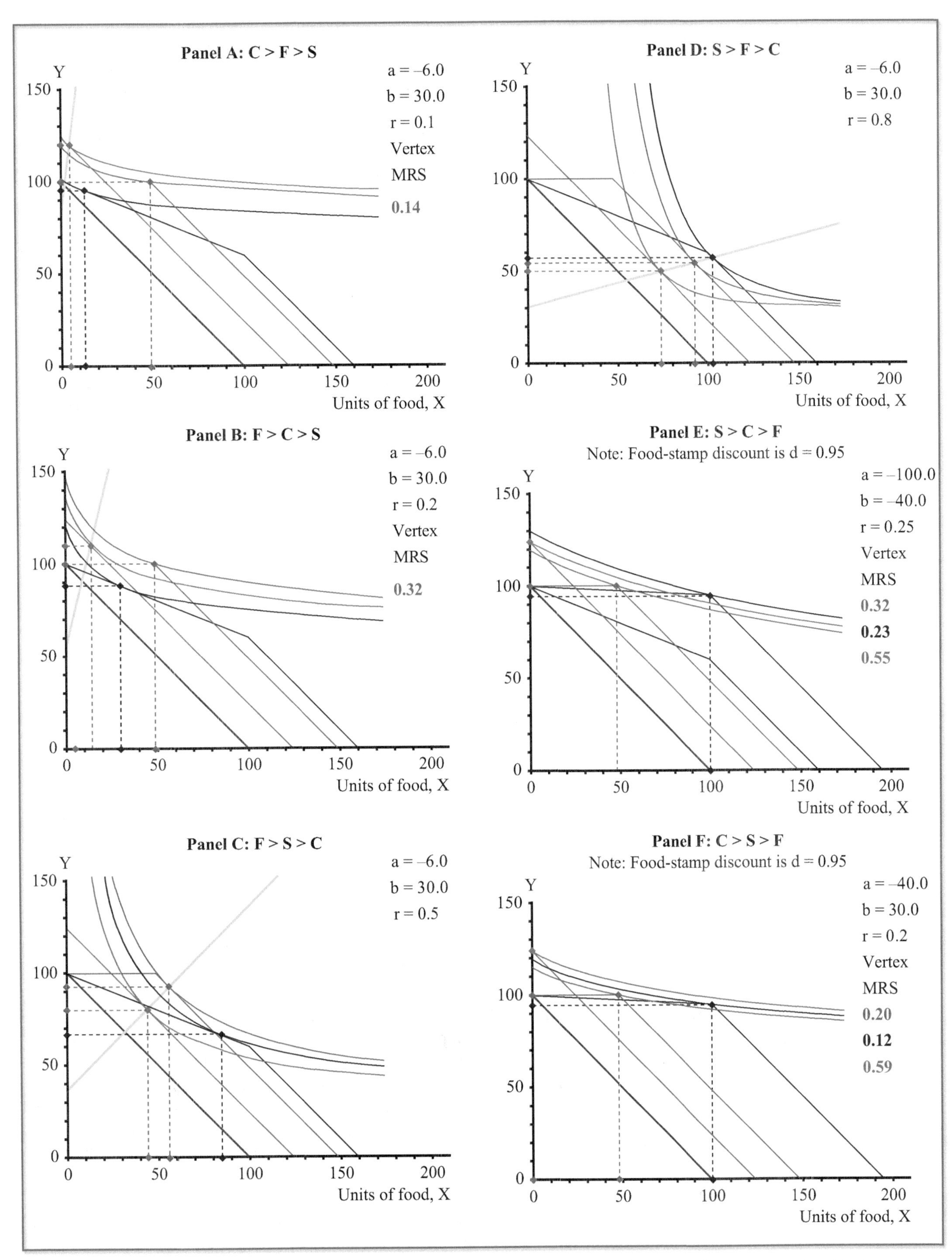

FIGURE 6.13 Choosing among Food-Subsidy Programs, Based on Shifted Cobb-Douglas Preferences

last two rank orderings (Figures 6.13E and 6.13F) require further adjustments to create; the reason for this will be clarified shortly. (*In Figure 6.13, indifference curves and bundle markers are color-coded to match the three programs.* ***Green is cash, red is free food,*** *and* ***blue is food stamps.***)

Figures 6.13A–6.13D are obtained by varying r, the coefficient denoting the relative importance of x—food. As r increases, the cash subsidy become less preferred, as does the free-food program. Eventually, the food-stamp program will win out over the other two because when a "lot" of food is preferred, there is more left over for other goods with the food-stamp program.

The MRS of the optimal bundle changes under both the free-food and food-stamp programs as we increase r in these panels. With nonlinear budget constraints, the optimal bundle may rotate on an internal vertex of the budget constraint. (With standard linear budget constraints, this can only happen at the boundary of the consumption set.) In Figures 6.13A and 6.13B, MRS(48, 100) < 1. Under these conditions, the bundle (48, 100) is the optimal bundle, given the free-food program, because an extra unit of food is worth MRS(48, 100) (0.14 or 0.32) to the individual but has a real resource cost of 1 unit of y (given $P_x = P_y = 1$ for purchased food). Since MRS < P_x/P_y, less x should be purchased. But, less x is *free* (under this program). Therefore, the constrained optimum for this policy choice (free food) is the vertex bundle, (48, 100).

A similar condition exists for the food-stamp program. If $1 - d < \text{MRS}(100, 100 \cdot d) < 1$, then $(100, 100 \cdot d)$ is the constrained optimum, given the food-stamp program. At this point, additional food has a higher cost (1) than its value to the individual (MRS(100, 60)), and less food has a lower cost (1 – d) than its value to the individual (MRS(100, 60)).This is not shown in Figures 6.13A–6.13D. In Figures 6.13A–6.13C, the MRS for the optimal bundle under the food-stamp program is along the upper blue segment, where slope is –(1 – d). In Figure 6.13D, the optimal bundle under the food-stamp program is along the lower blue segment, where slope is –1. This signifies that somewhere between r = 0.5 and r = 0.8, the optimal bundle under the food-stamp program will rotate on the vertex (100, 60) if *a* = –6 and b = 30.

Four of the six possible rank orderings of three options are covered by varying r for fixed *a* and b. Two other rank orderings—S ≻ C ≻ F and C ≻ S ≻ F (or blue ≻ green ≻ red and green ≻ blue ≻ red)—remain uncovered. These two orderings require the free-food program to be considered the worst option (the red indifference curve should be on the bottom). You should use the Excel version of Figure 6.13 and vary *a*, b, and r to see if you can obtain examples of either of these rank orderings. Inevitably, you will fail at this task because these rank orderings *cannot* be obtained from the programs, based on the numerical values for $M, R, T, and d shown in Figures 6.13A–6.13D.

Claim: *Any set of preferences that satisfies these rankings must necessarily violate convexity.*

The easiest way to prove this is to take the limiting case of convex preferences—perfect substitutes—and take the limiting case for cash versus food subsidy (green versus blue) of indifference between the two. This occurs only if the indifference curve goes through the bundles (0, 124) and (100, 60), which are the cash-subsidy y-intercept and the food-stamp vertex discussed in the last paragraph. The slope of the line containing these vertices is –0.64 = (124 – 60)/(0 – 100). This line intersects the horizontal part of the free-food program, y = 100, at x = 37.5 (solve for x, using y = 100 and $y = 124 - 0.64 \cdot x$). Given strict convexity, any bundle along this line *must* dominate either end bundle.[6] In particular, the optimal free-food bundle (48, 100) must dominate both (0, 124) and (100, 60). The only way to get the (free food) red indifference curve behind the (food stamps) blue and the (cash) green curves is to either tuck the red vertex back behind the line between the green intercept and the blue vertex (in this instance, R < 37.5 units of free food would work) or to move either the blue vertex out or the green vertex up so that the line segment no longer intersects the red nonlinear budget constraint. The strategy followed in Figures 6.13E and 6.13F is to move the blue vertex out.

One adjustment is made in the food-stamp policy in Figures 6.13E and 6.13F: The discount rate, d, is increased from 60% to 95%. A 95% discount means that you are able to purchase $100 worth of food for $5. This rotates the blue food-stamp vertex up to (100, 95) and creates enough "room" so that red indifference curves can be tucked underneath the green and blue ones, as required by the two remaining rank orderings. Both of these panels provide vertex solutions for all three programs, but by moving the free-food vertex in (giving less than $48 in free food), internal solutions can be obtained for the cash-subsidy and food-stamp constrained optima.

Figure 6.13 focused on strict preference rank orderings between programs. This need not be the case: An individual might be indifferent between two or more of the alternatives. Figure 6.14 examines this situation. Figure 6.14A depicts an individual who is indifferent between free food and food stamps, given CD preferences (not shifted CD) with r = 0.43. When r < 0.43, free food would be preferred, and when r > 0.43, food stamps would be preferred (you could check this with the Excel version of Figure 6.14). The food-stamp optimum occurs at the vertex bundle because MRS(100, 60) = 0.45 > 0.40 = 1 – d. Figure 6.14B shows that this need not be the case. The optimal bundles in Figure 6.14B are **F** = (69, 79) on the free-food budget constraint and **S** = (97.5, 61) on the food-stamp budget constraint. Both bundles provide the individual with the same satisfaction (**F** ~ **S**), but they do so in a very different fashion. **S** is a much more food-intensive consumption bundle than **F** because the individual faces a much lower cost of food under the food-stamp program than the free-food program. (The relative costs are $1 per unit of food under the free-food program, since food consumption at **F** exceeds R = 48 units, and 1 – d = $0.40 per unit of food under the food-stamp program, since food consumption under food stamps at **S** is less than 100 = T.)

One way to describe the amount of x and y in a bundle is to consider the number of units of y per unit of x consumed, or the "y-intensity" of the consumption bundle. The y-intensity of bundle **F** is 1.14 (1.14 = 79/69), and the y-intensity of bundle **S** is 0.63 (0.63 = 61/97.5). Although the individual is indifferent between the two programs, once a program is selected, the person would choose dramatically different optimal bundles to achieve the optimal outcome. The choice is predicated on the relative price of food and other goods in this instance, and this price ratio depends on the program chosen. When food is cheaper, more will be consumed.

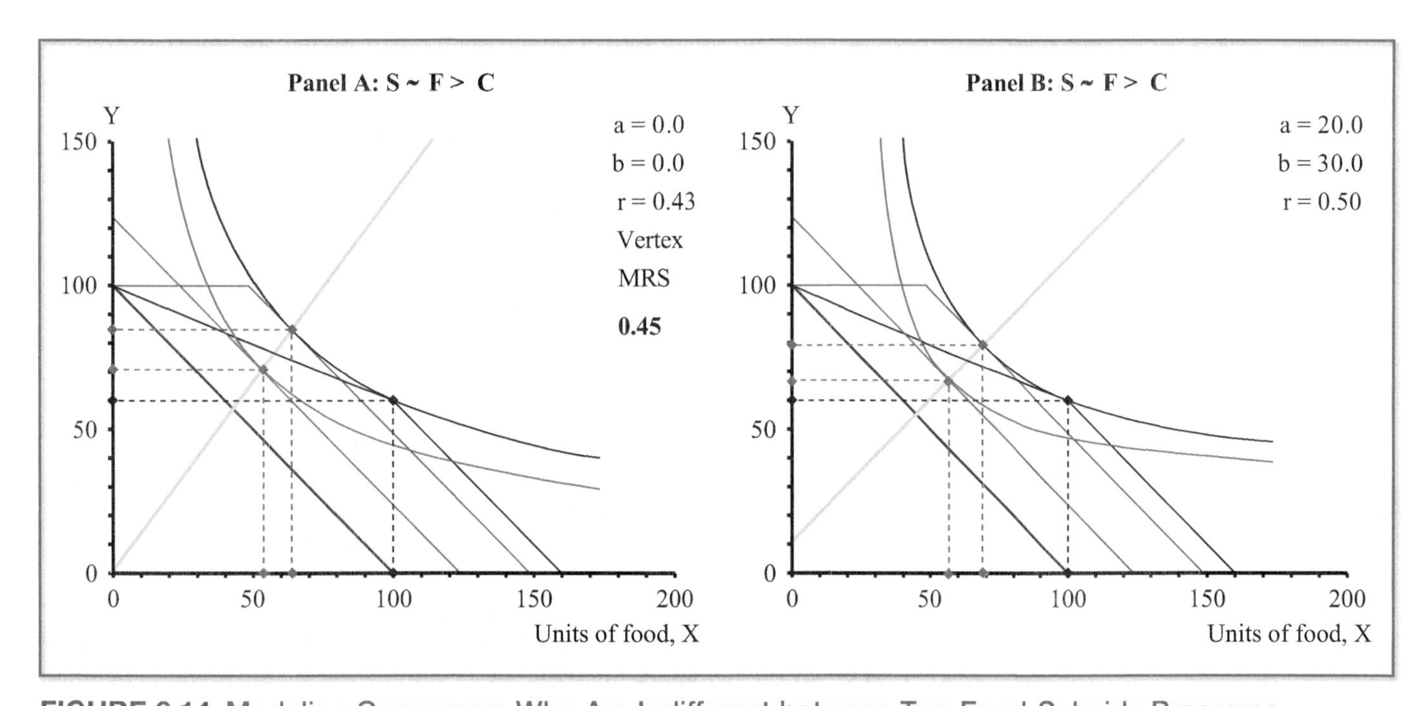

FIGURE 6.14 Modeling Consumers Who Are Indifferent between Two Food-Subsidy Programs

The optimal bundle with y-intensity of 0.85 is (80, 68) in Figure 6.14 and represents that level of x for which the free-food program provides exactly as much remaining income, y, as the food-stamp program. Put another way, (80, 68) is the intersection of the red and blue constraints. Both programs have $68 remaining if 80 units of food are consumed. This bundle will *never* be chosen by an individual with smooth preferences. The problem is that the slopes of the two budget constraints passing through this bundle are different. A smooth curve cannot accomplish both trade-off rates at one point because the slopes from both sides are different. There is no unique slope at the point. (This is similar to the discussion we had regarding Figure 4.6 that examined the slope at the vertex of a perfect complement indifference curve. And if we had a person with perfect complement preferences with $y = 0.85 \cdot x$ as vertex bundles, then that person would, indeed, choose this bundle and be indifferent between the two programs.)

6.4 On the Importance of Being Well Behaved

Two of the assumptions of well-behaved preferences—monotonicity and convexity—affect the geometry of optimization described in this chapter. Monotonicity has already been discussed in Section 6.1; it is behind the first condition required for constrained optimization: All income is spent. Were this not the case, then the optimization would not be a *constrained* optimization. For example, if an individual has bliss-point preferences for two goods and enough money to purchase those goods with money left over, the person would not purchase more just to move out to the budget constraint. The budget constraint would not be binding. We are unlikely to live in a world of bliss points, at least as long as we allow more goods to be added to the analysis. For example, most people have enough money to buy all the salt and pepper they desire, with money left over; a bliss point can be achieved in this two-dimensional world. As soon as we add a third good and call it "all other goods," however, we move beyond a bliss-point analysis, since it is unlikely that an individual can be satiated over all the goods the person wishes to consume. Most people live in a world of scarcity; they would like to have more of at least some goods than they can afford. This produces individuals who find their budget constraint binding, even if the good that makes it binding is the "amount of money in the bank." Monotonicity simply takes us to the edge of the feasible region of consumption and onto the budget constraint.

More interesting is what happens when preferences are nonconvex. Suppose that Figure 6.15A represents an indifference curve over two goods, x and y. Preferences over these two goods are nonconvex, as shown. Since the focus is on the general shape of the indifference curves in this instance, rather than specific slopes or values (or indeed, the function that created these preferences), numbers have been removed from axes, just as in Section 6.1. Immediate difficulties arise due to nonconvexity. The optimality condition described in Equation 6.1 (MRS = price ratio, and all income is spent at an interior solution) holds at bundle **B** in Figure 6.15B, since **B** is an interior bundle that is on the indifference curve and is tangent to the budget constraint. Unfortunately, **B** represents a relative *minimum*, rather than a maximum in this instance. To see this, move slightly away from **B** in either direction along the budget constraint and note that utility *increases*, rather than decreases, as would be the case if preferences were convex. This bundle is *locally* the worst you can do; all nearby affordable bundles along the budget constraint are better than **B**.

Equally problematic from an analytic viewpoint is the possibility of multiple local maximums that are not contiguous to each other. If an indifference curve has linear segments, then there may be multiple local contiguous maximums. (For example, as noted earlier, the entire budget constraint is the set of local maximums if the goods are perfect substitutes and $MRS = P_x/P_y$.) This situation is different; the local maximums are discrete distances from each other, and they are separated by a local minimum. Figure 6.15C depicts two such local maximums, **A** and **C**. These are local maximums because a slight move away from either bundle along the budget constraint yields a worse outcome than the local maximums. The bundles are dramatically different in terms of their x:y intensity. In the instance shown, **C** is the constrained optimum because the indifference curve

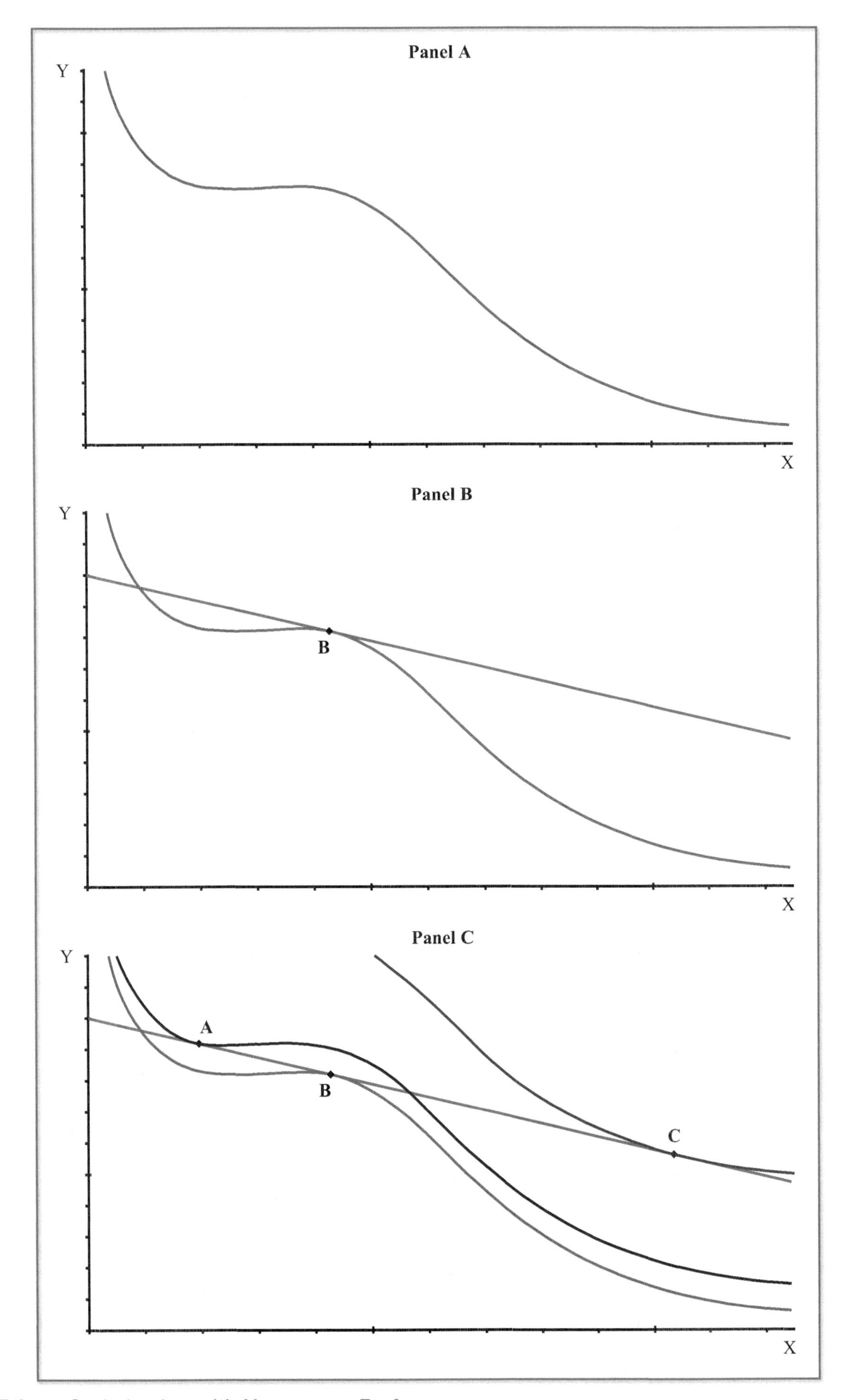

FIGURE 6.15 Optimization with Nonconvex Preferences

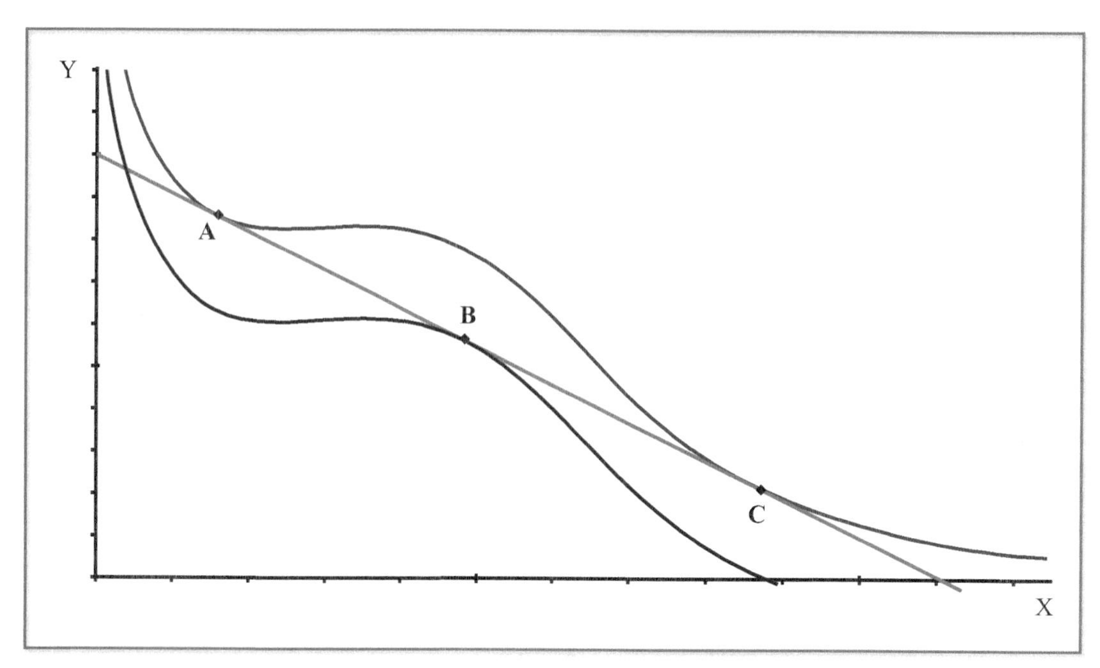

FIGURE 6.16 Multiple Constrained Optimal Bundles with Nonconvex Preferences

through **C** is better than the one through **A**. In this instance, **C** is the unique "best" option because **C** ≻ **A**. This need not be the case. By simply redrawing the budget constraint, we can obtain two *indifferent* bundles that are dramatically different in terms of their x:y intensity.

This situation is shown in Figure 6.16. As in Figure 6.15, there are two local maximums and one local minimum along the budget constraint. In this instance, **A** ~ **C** ≻ **B**. The consumer faced with this situation would have no preference for **A** over **C** but would prefer either of these bundles to bundle **B** between **A** and **C**. Both **A** and **C** provide equal utility for the fixed budget constraint.

You should not confuse the multiple distinct indifferent *equilibriums* (at **A** and **C**) in this situation with the multiple distinct indifferent *options* shown in Figure 6.14 (at **F** and **S**). In the present context, these disparate indifferent bundles share the same common relative prices and income—that is, the bundles share a single budget constraint. In the food-subsidy program discussion, the bundles are constrained optimal bundles for two distinct programs. Each bundle has a different slope and intercept, and each faces a different budget constraint. Disparate indifferent outcomes in the former situation are reasonable because the individual faces different marginal signals under each program. In contrast, disparate indifferent outcomes in the face of a single budget constraint suggest behavior that is counter to our intuition.

Economists believe that such disparate behavior is not a common occurrence and that convex preferences produce results that are much more in line with observed behavior. As discussed in Chapter 3, nonconvex behavior may occur (indeed, we argued there that if the time frame under consideration is small and storage is not possible, one might expect concave preferences for certain pairs of goods), but this is the exception rather than the rule. Convex preferences are assumed unless otherwise specified. We often assume the more stringent version of strict convexity rather than weak convexity because perfect substitutes lead to similarly extreme behavior that may be avoided if we assume that indifference curves are, indeed, curves. As discussed at the end of Section 6.1, it also allows us the analytical certainty of knowing that if we find *a* solution to the constrained optimum problem, it will be *the* solution to the problem. A strictly convex curve can only be tangent to a line at a single point; this point is the solution to the constrained optimum problem. The multiple alternatives, such as **A** and **C** in Figures 6.15 and 6.16, are avoided, as are entire line segment solutions, such as the entire budget constraint described in the discussion of perfect substitutes in Figure 6.4.

Summary

Tangency, tangency, tangency—not much more needs to be said. Well, perhaps a bit more should be said. An individual consumer with well-behaved preferences will choose a bundle on that person's budget constraint where the MRS equals the price ratio. When equality does not hold, the direction of the inequality tells us the direction of reallocation that will increase utility while still satisfying the budget constraint. If the MRS exceeds the price ratio, then reallocating consumption toward more x and less y will increase utility, and if the MRS is less than the price ratio, then reallocating toward less x and more y will increase utility. Equality of the MRS and price ratio need not hold at corner or boundary solutions.

Constrained optimization is examined for each of the classes of utility function analyzed in Chapter 4. This is done for fixed budget constraint in this chapter; in Chapters 7 and 8, we reverse this process and examine how the constrained optimum changes as the budget constraint changes. Special attention was paid to the shifted Cobb-Douglas functional form, since it allows us to model a very broad range of preferences. This form is used to reexamine the choice of food-subsidy programs first introduced in Chapter 5 and to examine red wine consumption.

Finally, we examine the problems that arise when preferences are not well behaved. When preferences are not monotonic, the budget constraint may not be binding. When preferences are nonconvex, the solutions obtained by setting the MRS equal to the price ratio may lead to minimums, as well as multiple spatially, distinct maximums. This should not create significant uneasiness because there are behavioral reasons to expect that preferences are monotonic and convex. These reasons are discussed both in Chapter 3 and in this chapter.

Review Questions

Define the following terms:

interior solution | boundary solution | unitary budget constraint

Match the following statements:

a. MU vector is steeper than price vector.
b. MU vector is flatter than price vector.
c. MU and price vectors are equally steep.
d. MRS > P_x/P_y at the constrained equilibrium.
e. MRS < P_x/P_y at the constrained equilibrium.

1. MRS = P_x/P_y at the constrained equilibrium.
2. Buy more x if possible.
3. Constrained optimum must have y = 0.
4. Buy more y if possible.
5. Constrained optimum must have x = 0.

Provide short answers to the following:

a. Why do economists say that all consumers have the same marginal behavior?
b. What is required at a constrained optimum if indifference curves are not smooth?
c. Why is MRS equal to price ratio not a sufficient requirement for the constrained optimum?
d. An individual has CD preferences in which the exponent attached to x is three times as large as the exponent attached to y. If the individual behaves optimally, what proportion of income will be devoted to purchasing x?
e. Suppose that you are consuming at bundle **A** on your budget constraint (where both x and y are greater than zero), and you face a price vector of (1, 1) and an MU vector at **A** of (1, 2). Should you allocate more spending to x and less to y, or vice versa?
f. Suppose that you are consuming at bundle **A** on your budget constraint (where both x and y are greater than zero), and you face a price vector of (1, 1) and an MU vector at **A** of (2, 1). Should you allocate more spending to x and less to y, or vice versa?
g. Suppose that you are consuming at bundle **A** on your budget constraint (where both x and y are greater than zero), and you face a price vector of (1, 1) and an MU vector at **A** of (2, 2). Should you allocate more spending to x and less to y, or vice versa?

Check your answers to the *matching* and *short-answer* exercises in the Answers Appendix at the end of the book.

Notes

1. The difference between Figure 6.1 and Figure 6.2, of course, is that it is impossible to uniquely describe the slope at point **A** in Figure 6.2; therefore, one cannot show a panel similar to Figure 6.1D for point **A** in Figure 6.2.

2. The general solution with n goods requires that for any two goods, *i* and j, the following must hold at the constrained optimum, assuming well-behaved preferences with smooth indifference curves: All income must be spent and either $MRS_{j,i} = -\Delta x_j/\Delta x_i = MU_i/MU_j = P_i/P_j$ if $x_i > 0$ and $x_j > 0$, or $MRS_{j,i} = -\Delta x_j/\Delta x_i = MU_i/MU_j \geq P_i/P_j$ if $x_i > 0$ and $x_j = 0$.

3. Unfortunately, this is not a very clean piece of algebra to solve, but if you are careful, you can do it. Each of the three equations has the same term $r/(1-r)$, so r may be removed by solving for $r/(1-r)$ in each equation. This yields:

(A1) $r/(1-r) = (0.4 - a)/(0.6 - b) = (2 - 5 \cdot a)/(3 - 5 \cdot b)$.

(A2) $r/(1-r) = (5/3) \cdot (0 - a)/(1 - b) = 5 \cdot a/(3 \cdot b - 3)$.

(A3) $r/(1-r) = 1/2 \cdot (1 - a)/(0 - b) = (a - 1)/(2 \cdot b)$.

Setting A1 = A2 and cross-multiplying yields:

(B1) $(2 - 5 \cdot a) \cdot (3 \cdot b - 3) = 5 \cdot a \cdot (3 - 5 \cdot b)$.

Expanding and regrouping, we obtain:
$5 \cdot a \cdot (3 - 3 \cdot b) - 5 \cdot a \cdot (3 - 5 \cdot b) = 6 - 6 \cdot b$;
regrouping, this becomes $10 \cdot a \cdot b = 6 - 6 \cdot b$.

Solving for *a*:

(B2) $a = (3 - 3 \cdot b)/(5 \cdot b)$.

Setting A2 = A3 and cross-multiplying yields:

(C1) $10 \cdot a \cdot b = (3 \cdot b - 3) \cdot (a - 1)$.

Expanding and regrouping, we obtain:
$7 \cdot a \cdot b + 3 \cdot a = 3 - 3 \cdot b$.

Solving for *a*:

(C2) $a = (3 - 3 \cdot b)/(3 + 7 \cdot b)$.

Setting B2 = C2 and cross-multiplying, we obtain:
$3 + 7 \cdot b = 5 \cdot b$.
Therefore, $b = -3/2 = -1.5$.

Substituting into either B2 or C2 yields: $a = -1.0$.

Substituting *a* and b into either A1, A2, or A3 and regrouping yields: $r = 0.4$.

4. It is easy to see why $a = b = -1$ and $r = 0.45$ produces an optimum at **C**. Start with bundle **C** and $a = b = -1$; then derive r as follows. Tangency requires: $MRS(\mathbf{C}) = 1.65 \cdot r/(1.35 \cdot (1 - r)) = 1$. Cross-multiply to obtain: $1.65 \cdot r = 1.35 \cdot (1 - r)$. Solve for r by regrouping: $3 \cdot r = 1.35$, or $r = 0.45$. A symmetric calculation derives an optimum at **D** by setting $r = 0.55$.

5. You should not confuse the general CD with the shifted CD. We spent a good deal of time showing that the shifted CD can have boundary solutions as long as the axis shift factors *a* and b are negative.

6. This argument is similar to the one used when we discussed bracketing utility in Figure 4.15.

Appendix

The Mathematics of Constrained Optimization

Equation 6.1 describes the solution to the consumer's constrained optimization problem. Separate solutions are provided on the interior (Equation 6.1Bi) and the boundary (6.1Bii and 6.1Biii) of the consumption set. The mathematical proof of the boundary conditions requires the use of the Kuhn-Tucker optimization technique. This technique allows for inequality constraints as well as equality constraints, but it is beyond the scope of this text. For a formal exposition of Kuhn-Tucker, see any advanced microeconomics text or mathematical economics text.[1]

The geometric description of the boundary solution is provided within the text. The geometric solution of the boundary optimum keys off the idea that if the constrained optimum occurs outside the first quadrant, then either $x < 0$ or $y < 0$. If $x < 0$, then the best that can be achieved is $x = 0$, and all income is spent on y. At this bundle, $MRS(0, I/P_y) \leq P_x/P_y$, due to convexity of well-behaved indifference curves (Equation 6.1Bii). If $y < 0$, then the best that can be achieved is $y = 0$, and all income is spent on x. At this bundle, $MRS(I/P_x, 0) \geq P_x/P_y$ due to convexity of well-behaved indifference curves (Equation 6.1Biii). We can therefore restrict our discussion to why the budget constraint condition (Equation 6.1A) and the $MRS = P_x/P_y$ condition (Equation 6.1Bi) hold at the optimal bundle.

In this appendix, we examine constrained optimization using two techniques. These methods are also discussed in a more general context in the Mathematical Appendix (available in the online version of this text). Both methods produce the same results, but they attack the problem in very different fashions. The first method is the *substitution method*, and the second is the *Lagrangian method*. Both methods start from the presumption that the constraint is binding. The reason for this presumption in the consumer context is that we assume preferences are well behaved; in particular, we assume that preferences are monotonic. If an individual believes that more is better, then that person will never choose to consume below the budget constraint. Doing so suggests that there are no better bundles available with income left over; that is, the individual must be at a bliss point. But preferences that include a bliss point are not well behaved, according to the definition of "well behaved" in Section 3.4. Therefore, the constrained optimal solution described as Equation 6.1 holds at the consumer optimum.

The Substitution Method

The substitution method for solving a constrained optimization problem is to substitute the constraint function into the objective function, thereby reducing the dimensionality of the problem. (Although this sounds abstract, it is quite straightforward: The typical utility function is two-dimensional [goods x and y], and the constraint is the budget constraint. By folding the budget constraint into the objective function, we turn a two-variable constrained optimization problem into a one-variable unconstrained optimization problem.)

The general budget constraint is:

$$P_x x + P_y y = I. \qquad \textbf{(6A.1)}$$

Solving for y in Equation 6A.1, we obtain the slope-intercept form:

$$y(x) = I/P_y - (P_x/P_y) \cdot x. \qquad \textbf{(6A.2)}$$

Substituting this into a general utility function, we obtain:

$$U(x) = U(x, y(x)). \qquad \textbf{(6A.3)}$$

This utility function is univariate. We can maximize utility by taking the derivative and setting it equal to zero (using the chain rule):

$$0 = dU/dx = \partial U/\partial x + (\partial U/\partial y) \cdot dy/dx = MU_x + MU_y \cdot dy/dx. \qquad \textbf{(6A.4)}$$

From Equation 6A.2, we know that $dy/dx = -(P_x/P_y)$, so we can rewrite Equation 6A.4 as:

$$MU_x = MU_y \cdot (P_x/P_y). \quad \textbf{(6A.5)}$$

Dividing through by the marginal utility of y, we obtain:

$$MU_x/MU_y = P_x/P_y. \quad \textbf{(6A.6)}$$

Chapter 4 Appendix A shows that $MRS = MU_x/MU_y$, so 6A.6 becomes:

$$MRS = P_x/P_y. \quad \textbf{(6A.7)}$$

Therefore, we have shown the MRS = price ratio condition, Equation 6.Bi.

Cobb-Douglas Solved by the Substitution Method Let's see how this method works for two specific examples. The first examines optimization, given equal-weighted Cobb-Douglas (CD) preferences and known prices and income. Then we examine the general CD solution, given general prices and income.

Example 1: Suppose the consumer faces utility function $U(x, y) = x \cdot y$, has income \$60, and faces prices of \$2 for x and \$3 for y. How much x and y would the individual consume?

Substitution Solution 1: The budget constraint, $60 = 2 \cdot x + 3 \cdot y$, can be rewritten in slope-intercept form as:

$$y = 20 - 2/3 \cdot x. \quad \textbf{(6A.8)}$$

Substituting this into the utility function produces utility as a function of x alone:

$$U(x) = x \cdot (20 - 2/3 \cdot x) = 20 \cdot x - 2/3 \cdot x^2. \quad \textbf{(6A.9)}$$

Taking the derivative and setting it equal to zero, we obtain:

$$0 = 20 - 4/3 \cdot x. \quad \textbf{(6A.10a)}$$

Solving for x, we obtain:

$$x = 15. \quad \textbf{(6A.10b)}$$

Substituting Equation 6A.10a into the budget constraint (Equation 6A.8), we obtain:

$$y = 20 - 2/3 \cdot 15 = 10. \quad \textbf{(6A.10c)}$$

The consumer maximizes utility by choosing the bundle (x, y) = (15, 10).

Example 2: Suppose the consumer faces utility function $U(x, y) = x^r \cdot y^{(1-r)}$, has income I, and faces prices of P_x for x and P_y for y. How much x and y would the individual consume?

Substitution Solution 2: Substituting the constraint function (Equation 6A.2) into the objective function U(x, y), we obtain:

$$U(x) = x^r \cdot (I/P_y - (P_x/P_y) \cdot x)^{(1-r)}. \quad \textbf{(6A.11)}$$

Although Equation 6A.11 looks complex, it is a univariate function that has a special form: It includes both the objective function and the constraint function in a single equation. By solving for one of the variables in the constraint function and substituting that equation into the objective function, we have rewritten the objective function in a way that incorporates the constraint. This is an unconstrained univariate function. We can easily find the optimal level of x by taking the derivative of this unconstrained function, setting it equal to zero, and then solving for x. (The mathematics is a bit ugly but quite doable if care is taken. This derivative uses the chain rule, power rule, and product rule.)

$$dU/dx = x^r \cdot (1-r) \cdot (I/P_y - (P_x/P_y) \cdot x)^{-r} \cdot (-P_x/P_y) + r \cdot x^{(r-1)} \cdot (I/P_y - (P_x/P_y) \cdot x)^{(1-r)} = 0. \quad \textbf{(6A.12)}$$

This is most easily simplified by substituting y from Equation 6A.2 back into Equation 6A.12. This produces the following:

$$x^r \cdot (1-r) \cdot (y)^{-r} \cdot (-P_x/P_y) + r \cdot x^{(r-1)} \cdot (y)^{(1-r)} = 0. \quad \textbf{(6A.13)}$$

We remove the minus sign by bringing the first term to the other side of the equation:

$$r \cdot x^{(r-1)} \cdot (y)^{(1-r)} = x^r \cdot (1 - r) \cdot (y)^{-r} \cdot (P_x/P_y). \qquad \textbf{(6A.14)}$$

Multiplying both sides by $(y/x)^r/(1 - r)$, we obtain upon simplification:

$$(r/(1 - r)) \cdot (y/x) = P_x/P_y. \qquad \textbf{(6A.15)}$$

The left-hand side is simply the MRS as described in Equation 4.4 and Table 4.1.

Equations 6A.15 and 6A.1 describe the two conditions required for optimization, given the interior solutions described in Equation 6.1.We could stop here, but it is worthwhile to go one step further and use these equations to derive demands for x and y, given CD preferences. By regrouping Equation 6A.15, we obtain:

$$P_y y = ((1 - r)/r) \cdot (P_x x) \qquad \textbf{(6A.16a)}$$

Plugging Equation 6A.16a into the budget constraint and regrouping, we obtain:

$$I = P_x x + ((1 - r)/r) \cdot (P_x x) = (r \cdot P_x + (1 - r) \cdot P_x) \cdot x/r = P_x x/r. \qquad \textbf{(6A.16b)}$$

Solving for x, we obtain:

Demand for x: $$x(P_x, P_y, I) = r \cdot I/P_x. \qquad \textbf{(6A.17a)}$$

Substituting Equation 6A.17a into Equation 6A.16a and solving for y, we obtain:[2]

Demand for y: $$y(P_x, P_y, I) = (1 - r) \cdot I/P_y. \qquad \textbf{(6A.17b)}$$

These demand functions are elegant generalizations of the unitary income result from Equations 6.3a and 6.3b. (We will see these demand functions once again as Equations 7.3a and 7.3b.)

The substitution method can also be used with more than one constraint. Each constraint that is folded into the objective function reduces the dimensionality of the problem by one dimension. For example, if the objective function has three variables but there are two constraints, then substituting the two constraint functions into the objective function reduces the dimensionality of the problem to one. If it is difficult to solve for one of the variables in the constraint function, the Lagrange method provides a more elegant method of solving the same problem.

The Lagrange Method

The Lagrange method rewrites the objective function and the constraint function as a single equation called a *Lagrangian.* Interestingly, the Lagrange method works in the opposite direction from the substitution method because the Lagrange method increases the dimensionality of the problem by one dimension for each constraint. Although this sounds like it would make the problem more complex, in actuality, this makes it less complex.

The Lagrange method requires that the constraint function be written in a form that equals zero. For example, the budget constraint is rewritten as: $I - P_x x - P_y y = 0$. The left-hand side becomes part of the Lagrangian equation once it is multiplied by the *Lagrange multiplier*, λ (lambda). The Lagrangian is typically written as a script L ($\mathcal{L}$), and it includes the objective function's variables, together with the Lagrange multiplier (or multipliers, if there are multiple constraint functions under consideration).

The Lagrangian for the general utility maximization problem is therefore:

$$\mathcal{L}(x, y, \lambda) = U(x, y) + \lambda \cdot (I - P_x x - P_y y). \qquad \textbf{(6A.18)}$$

The Lagrangian is a function of three variables. The optimum of a function occurs at the point where the derivative is zero. With multiple variables, multiple partial derivatives must simultaneously equal zero.

Claim: *By taking the partial derivative of the Lagrangian with respect to each of the three variables and setting them equal to zero, we obtain the maximum of the objective function subject to the constraint.*

At one level, this sounds surprising, since $\mathcal{L}$ is not the objective function U. But at the optimum point, it is! The reason why this is true is straightforward: The optimum occurs when $\partial\mathcal{L}/\partial\lambda = 0$, but that restriction is simply the constraint function. If the constraint function equals zero, the Lagrangian is the objective function.

The three first-order conditions (FOCs) are therefore:

$$\partial\mathcal{L}/\partial x = 0 \quad \text{or} \quad \partial U/\partial x - \lambda \cdot P_x = 0 \quad \text{or} \quad MU_x = \lambda \cdot P_x. \tag{6A.19a}$$

$$\partial\mathcal{L}/\partial y = 0 \quad \text{or} \quad \partial U/\partial y - \lambda \cdot P_y = 0 \quad \text{or} \quad MU_y = \lambda \cdot P_y. \tag{6A.19b}$$

$$\partial\mathcal{L}/\partial\lambda = 0 \quad \text{or} \quad I - P_x x - P_y y = 0 \quad \text{or} \quad P_x x + P_y y = I. \tag{6A.19c}$$

If a = b and c = d, then a/c = b/d. Applying this algebraic identity to the first two FOCs, we obtain:

$$MRS = MU_x/MU_y = P_x/P_y \tag{6A.20}$$

because the λs in the numerator and denominator cancel each other. The Lagrangian's FOCs provide exactly the same information as the substitution method. Both produce the dual requirements for constrained optimum: Budget constraint is binding (Equation 6A.1 or 6A.19c), and the MRS equals price ratio (Equation 6A.7 or 6A.20).

Cobb-Douglas Solved by the Lagrange Method

It is worthwhile to work through the Lagrangian for both of the examples discussed earlier because it allows you to see the strengths and weaknesses of each method. Since the problems are the same in both instances, they will not be restated here.

Lagrangian Solution 1: Set up the Lagrangian as the objective function plus λ times the constraint function.

$$\mathcal{L}(x, y, \lambda) = x \cdot y + \lambda \cdot (60 - 2 \cdot x - 3 \cdot y). \tag{6A.21}$$

The first-order conditions are:

$$\partial\mathcal{L}/\partial x = 0 \quad \text{or} \quad y = 2 \cdot \lambda. \tag{6A.22a}$$

$$\partial\mathcal{L}/\partial y = 0 \quad \text{or} \quad x = 3 \cdot \lambda. \tag{6A.22b}$$

$$\partial\mathcal{L}/\partial\lambda = 0 \quad \text{or} \quad 60 = 2 \cdot x + 3 \cdot y. \tag{6A.22c}$$

Taking the ratio of the two first-order conditions, we obtain:

$$y/x = 2/3. \tag{6A.23a}$$

This is MRS = price ratio. Solving for y, we obtain:

$$y = 2/3 \cdot x. \tag{6A.23b}$$

Substituting into the budget equation (Equation 6A.22c), we obtain:

$$60 = 2 \cdot x + 3 \cdot 2/3 \cdot x = 4 \cdot x. \tag{6A.23c}$$

Solving for x, we obtain:

$$x = 15. \tag{6A.23d}$$

Substituting x = 15 into either Equation 6A.23b or the budget Equation 6A.22c, we obtain:

$$y = 10. \tag{6A.23e}$$

The consumer maximizes utility by choosing the bundle (x, y) = (15, 10).

Lagrangian Solution 2: Set up the Lagrangian as the objective function plus λ times the constraint function.

$$\mathcal{L}(x, y, \lambda) = x^r \cdot y^{(1-r)} + \lambda \cdot (I - P_x x - P_y y). \tag{6A.24}$$

The first-order conditions are (upon simplification):

$\partial \mathcal{L}/\partial x = 0$ or $r \cdot x^{(r-1)} \cdot y^{(1-r)} = \lambda \cdot P_x$. **(6A.25a)**

$\partial \mathcal{L}/\partial y = 0$ or $(1 - r) \cdot x^r \cdot y^{(-r)} = \lambda \cdot P_y$. **(6A.25b)**

$\partial \mathcal{L}/\partial \lambda = 0$ or $P_x x + P_y y = I$. **(6A.25c)**

Taking the ratio of the first two first-order conditions, we obtain the same CD result as Equation 6A.15:

$$r \cdot x^{(r-1)} \cdot y^{(1-r)}/((1 - r) \cdot x^r \cdot y^{(-r)}) = (r/(1 - r)) \cdot (y/x) = MRS^{CD} = P_x/P_y. \quad \textbf{(6A.26)}$$

From here, we could obtain demands for x and y in the same way they were derived in Equations 6A.16 and 6A.17.

Although the Lagrangian method looks more complex, the algebra is often simpler. (In particular, many students think that Equations 6A.24–6A.26 are easier to navigate than are Equations 6A.11–6A.15. The Lagrangian method requires more variables and equations, but each piece is simpler than the more complex univariate mathematics involved in the substitution method.) Both constrained optimization methods produce the same result. The choice is much like choosing between a sledgehammer and a rock pick. Both will break up rocks, but one is more elegant than the other.

An added bonus from using a Lagrangian is that the Lagrange multiplier has a useful economic interpretation. The Lagrange multiplier, λ, is the change in the objective function for a 1-unit relaxation in the constraint. In the context of the consumer optimization problem we have been discussing, it is the marginal utility of income. This is easily seen by solving for λ, using Equations 6A.19a and 6A.19b, which produces the following:

$$MU_x/P_x = \lambda = MU_y/P_y. \quad \textbf{(6A.27)}$$

The Lagrange multiplier λ equals the marginal utility of income because an extra dollar spent on any good must provide the same incremental utility. MU_i/P_i is simply the incremental utility achieved by spending an extra dollar on good *i* (since a dollar spent on good *i* purchases $1/P_i$ units of that good). As noted in your introductory microeconomics text, this must be equal across goods for the consumer to be maximizing utility. Unstated in that discussion (not surprisingly) is that it also equals the magnitude of the Lagrange multiplier.

Appendix Notes

1. An excellent exposition is found in Chapter 12 of *Using Mathematics in Economic Analysis* by Peter Hess, Prentice Hall, 2002.

2. Demand for y takes a couple of steps to derive. Substituting Equation 6A.17a into Equation 6A.16a yields:

$$P_y y = ((1 - r)/r) \cdot (P_x \cdot (r \cdot I/P_x)) = ((1 - r)/r) \cdot (r \cdot I) = (1 - r) \cdot I.$$

Dividing by P_y on both sides yields Equation 6A.17b.

CHAPTER 7

Deriving Demand

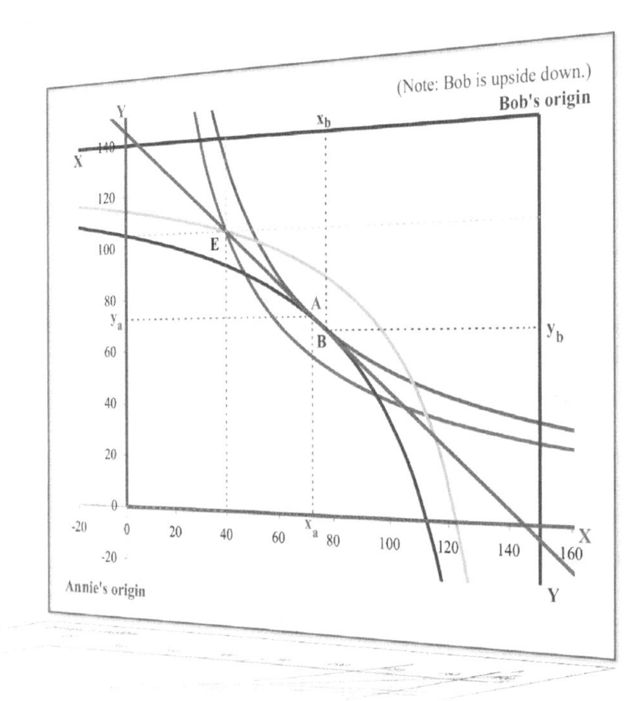

Chapter Outline

In this chapter, we allow price to vary and map out what happens to the tangency conditions required by the constrained optimum. This can be viewed from a variety of perspectives; each has its own purpose. We explore those perspectives in this chapter, with our primary focus on the own-price perspective, since it allows us to understand how demand is created from preferences. Although we examined how changes in the price of x and y affect the budget constraint in Chapter 5, we focus solely on changes in the price of x in this chapter. (This allows us to tie consumption choices to the demand for x later in this chapter.)

In Section 7.1, we examine how the constrained optimal consumption bundle changes in response to price changes. A change in the price of x causes a change in the budget constraint and, hence, a change in optimal bundle. These changes can be viewed as movements along the demand curve for x and shifts in the demand curve for y (since demand for y changes without the price of y changing). Section 7.2 uses the consumption diagram as the starting point for creating individual demand for x as a function of the price of x. This is done for general preference maps to focus on the geometry of the derivation. Section 7.3 uses an algebraic analysis to derive individual demand functions from specific utility functions. Demand is seen to be a multivariate function of prices, income, and the parameters that describe each specific utility function. A demand curve is simply a univariate function of the good's own price, holding all other factors fixed. Section 7.4 revisits economic efficiency in the face of exchange by reexamining the Edgeworth Box analysis of Section 3.5. The analysis in Chapter 3 focused on good-for-good barter exchanges; this chapter's Edgeworth Box analysis examines how markets can achieve efficient outcomes via the signals provided by the price system. Section 7.5 uses the demand information obtained in Section 7.3 to revisit the choice among options analysis first introduced in Section 5.4. This is done, in part, to introduce you to a powerful tool you have been passively using throughout this text. To this point, Excel has been in the background, since you have only been asked to use sliders and check boxes to manipulate graphs; all of the calculation has been done for you (and has been hidden from view). This section introduces you to doing calculations within Excel to simplify economic modeling. Excel is, most basically, a large calculator that allows you to perform comparative statics analysis with ease. Section 7.6 uses the algebraic results derived in Section 7.3 but focuses on income change, rather than price change. Income changes shift demand curves, but the effects of income changes can be described in other ways, as will be shown.

7.1 How Optimal Bundles Change with Price Changes: The Price Consumption Curve

We saw in Chapter 6 that the tangency between the individual's budget constraint and indifference curve is the key to the constrained maximization problem. Although the major focus in Chapter 6 was on preferences for a fixed budget constraint, we did examine some instances of the effect of a price change on the constrained optimum. In particular, we examined price adjustments that turn an interior optimum into a boundary optimum for shifted Cobb-Douglas (CD) preferences in the discussion of Figures 6.6 and 6.7. In this section, we focus more directly on price changes and how the tangency required by constrained optimization adjusts to changes in price.

A change in the price of x rotates the budget constraint, using the y intercept, $(0, I/P_y)$, as a fulcrum. As the budget constraint rotates, the optimal bundle necessarily adjusts; the constrained optimal bundle changes as the price of x changes. As a result, the individual's demand for both x *and* y may change. To depict the range of possible outcomes in this situation, the six panels in Figure 7.1 are based on three shifted CD utility functions (signs for *a*, the vertical shift factor, are listed). Panels are paired side by side: Figures 7.1A and 7.1D are based on the same utility function (as are Figures 7.1B and 7.1E, and Figures 7.1C and 7.1F). In each panel, the blue budget constraint depicts an initial set of prices and income. Preferences have been chosen so that the optimal blue bundle represents spending 50% on each good; the point of tangency is midway between **A** and **B** on the blue budget constraint. Since the price of x is changing, measuring percentages of income is easier to do on the vertical axis (since the price of y does not change). As at the beginning of Chapter 6, we have removed numbers from both axes—except for 0.5 halfway up the vertical axis toward bundle **A**. There are 20 tick marks between the origin and bundle **A**, and each tick mark on the vertical axis represents 5% of income spent on y.

Consider the following scenarios (each price change is relative to the blue budget constraint):

S1.i. The red budget constraint represents a doubling of the price of x. The quantity of x demanded decreases by less than 50% because of a 5% increase in the percentage of income spent on x.

S1.ii. The red budget constraint represents a doubling of the price of x. The quantity of x demanded decreases by more than 50% because of a 5% decrease in the percentage of income spent on x.

S1.iii. The red budget constraint represents a doubling of the price of x. The quantity of x demanded decreases by less than 50% because of a 20% increase in the percentage of income spent on x.

S1.iv. The red budget constraint represents a doubling of the price of x. The quantity of x demanded decreases by more than 50% because of a 10% decrease in the percentage of income spent on x.

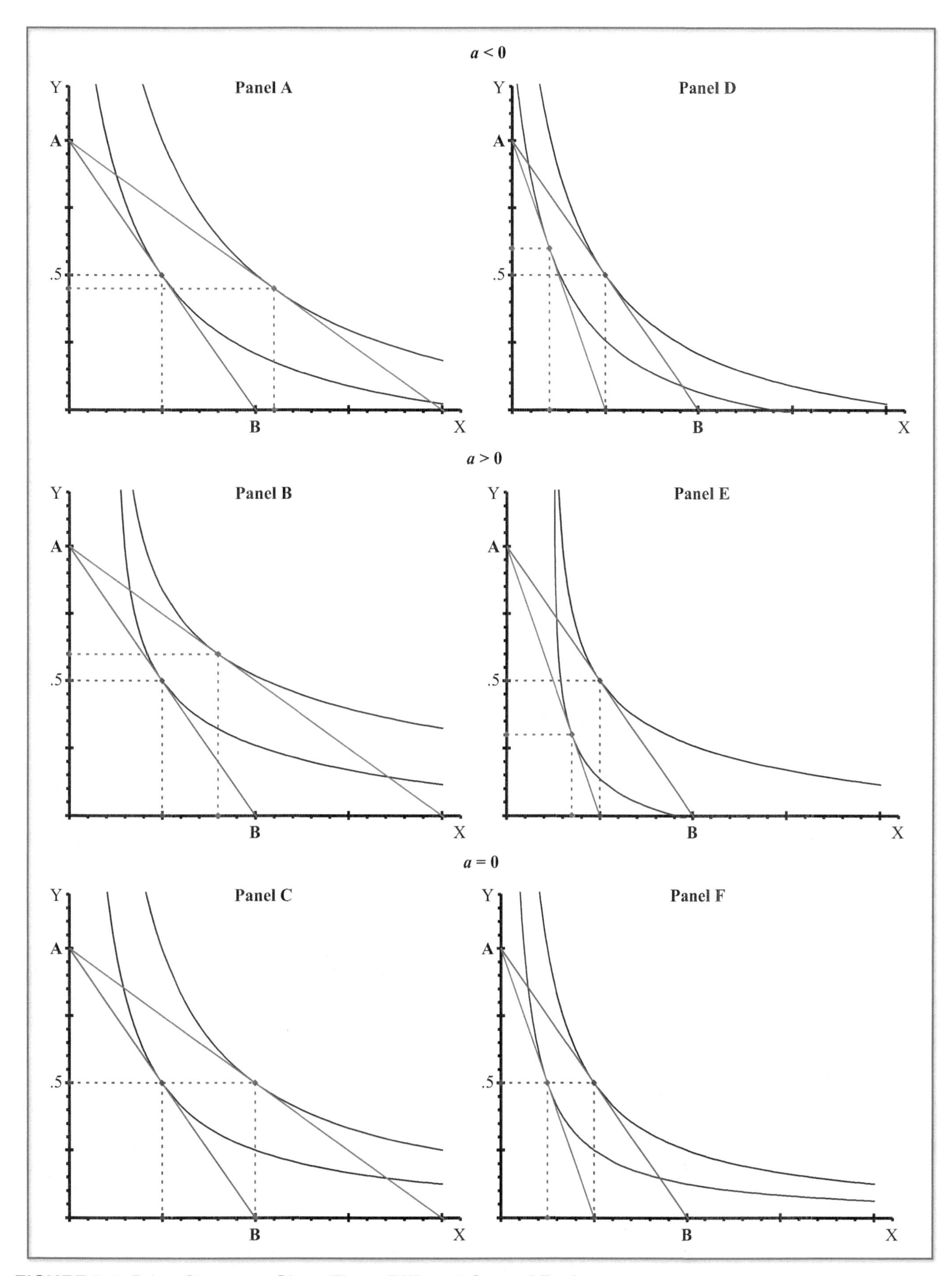

FIGURE 7.1 Price Changes, Given Three Different Sets of Preferences, Based on Shifted Cobb-Douglas Utility Functions

S1.v. The red budget constraint represents a halving of the price of x. The quantity of x demanded more than doubles because of a 5% increase in the percentage of income spent on x.

S1.vi. The red budget constraint represents a halving of the price of x. The quantity of x demanded less than doubles because of a 5% decrease in the percentage of income spent on x.

S1.vii. The red budget constraint represents a halving of the price of x. The quantity of x demanded more than doubles because of a 20% increase in the percentage of income spent on x.

S1.viii. The red budget constraint represents a halving of the price of x. The quantity of x demanded less than doubles because of a 10% decrease in the percentage of income spent on x.

Q1a. Which scenario accurately represents the changes depicted in Figures 7.1A, 7.1B, 7.1D, and 7.1E?*

Q1a takes an "own-price" orientation, since it examines the change in optimal bundle strictly in terms of the effect of a change in price of x on spending on x. Of course, in a two-good model, we just as easily could have described the changes in terms of the good whose price has not changed, y. Indeed, we suggested earlier that the easiest way to examine the change is to look at what happens to the good whose price has not changed, since the "income yardstick" does not change on the y axis but it does on the x axis as the price of x changes.[1]

Figures 7.1C and 7.1F depict no change in y consumption as the price of x changes. In Chapter 2, we said that two such goods were independent. Independent goods are defined using Equation 2.3 in terms of cross-price elasticity, rather than actual change in quantity of the "other" good. Two goods are independent if the cross-price elasticity is zero. Similarly, two goods are substitutes if the cross-price elasticity is positive, and two goods are complements if the cross-price elasticity is negative. Based on these definitions, answer two questions for Figures 7.1A, 7.1B, 7.1D, and 7.1E:

Q1b. For which panels are x and y substitutes, and for which panels are x and y complements?

Q1c. What is the cross-price elasticity, $\varepsilon_{y,x} = \%\Delta y/\%\Delta P_x$, implied by the change in constrained optima in each panel?†

consumption diagram: The consumption diagram is consumption bundle space, (x, y).

demand diagram: A demand diagram is a diagram whose axes are the quantity of a good on the horizontal axis and the price of that good on the vertical axis.

The analysis based on Q1a takes an "own-price" orientation, while Q1b and Q1c take a "cross-price" orientation of the same preferences. These are both different ways of viewing the effect of a price change within the consumption diagram. The **consumption diagram** is consumption bundle space (x, y). Budget constraints and indifference curves are represented in the consumption diagram. We have used consumption diagrams since Chapter 3, but only in this chapter is it necessary to give them a formal name to distinguish them from demand diagrams. A **demand diagram** is a diagram whose axes are the quantity of a good on the horizontal axis and the price of that good on the vertical axis. (We do not discuss demand diagrams until Section 7.2. The definition is provided here to distinguish the two diagrams that form the basis for our analysis in this chapter.)

***Q1a answer:** S1.v is depicted in Figure 7.1A; S1.viii is depicted in Figure7.1B; S1.iv is depicted in Figure 7.1D; and S1.iii is depicted in Figure 7.1E. These statements are easier to see by focusing on what happens to y. In Figure 7.1D, the percentage devoted to y goes from 50% to 60%, so the percentage devoted to x must decline by 10%. The actual quantity declines by 60%, due to the combined effect of the price doubling and the reallocation of income toward increased y consumption.

†Q1b and Q1c answers: The cross-price elasticity is positive in Figures 7.1A and 7.1D; therefore, they are substitutes: $\varepsilon_{y,x} = \%\Delta y/\%\Delta P_x = -5\%/-50\% = +0.1$ in Figure 7.1A, and $\varepsilon_{y,x} = +10\%/+100\% = +0.1$ in Figure 7.1D. Figures 7.1B and 7.1E are complements because the cross-price elasticities are negative: $\varepsilon_{y,x} = +10\%/-50\% = -0.2$ in Figure 7.1B, and $\varepsilon_{y,x} = 20\%/+100\% = -0.2$ in Figure 7.1C.

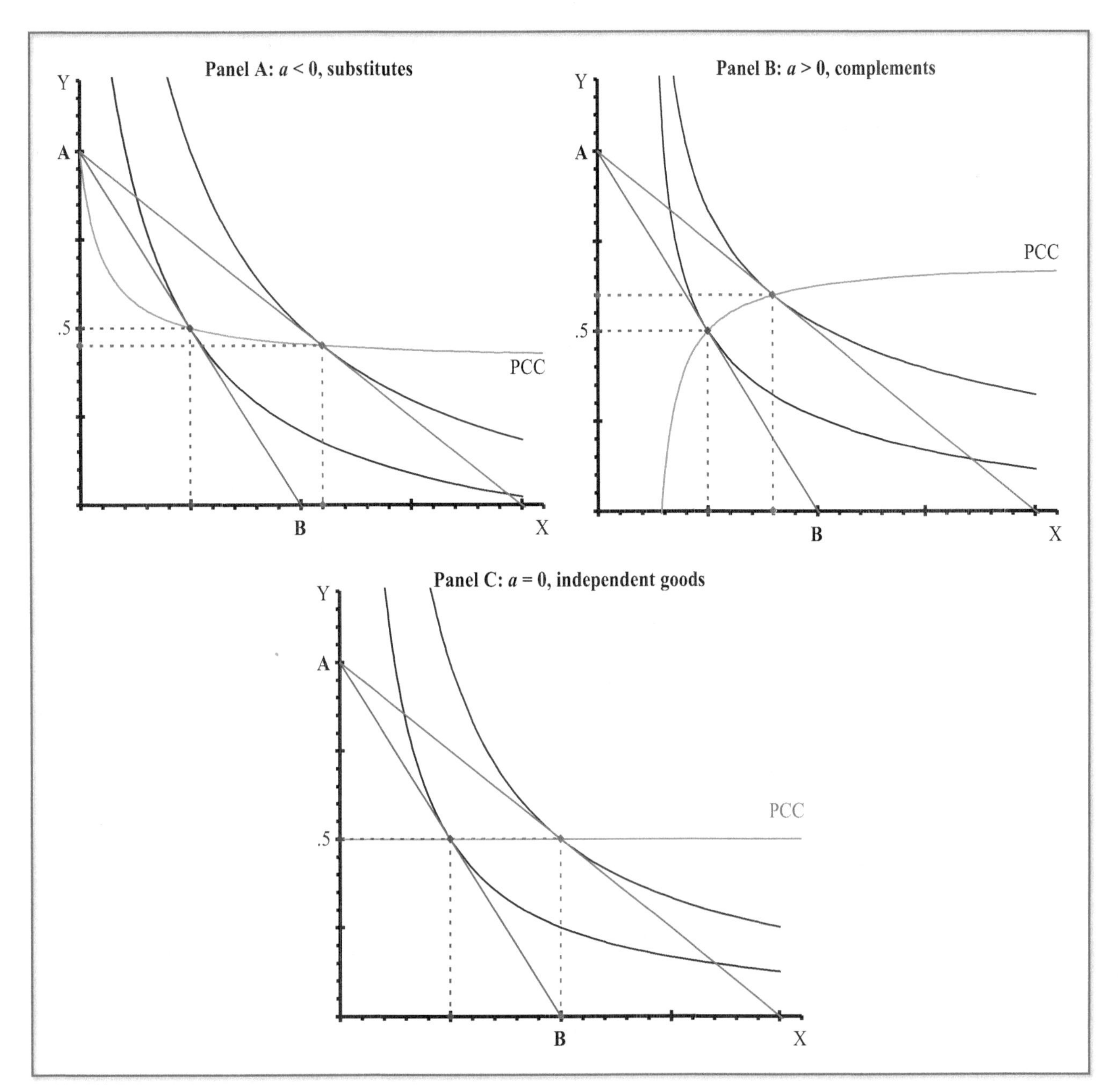

FIGURE 7.2 Price Consumption Curves for Shifted Cobb-Douglas

The final way to examine how the optimal choices change is to take a "bundle" orientation. The bundle orientation incorporates information from both individual orientations. This is most easily accomplished by connecting optimal bundles as price changes in the consumption diagram. (The Excel file for Figure 7.2 is particularly useful here because you can do this dynamically with the slider.) In the absence of a dynamic diagram, you can show the set of optimal bundles using a curve called the **price consumption curve (PCC)**. The PCC is the set of consumption bundle tangencies for different prices of x. (There is not universal agreement on the name for this curve; some authors use the terms *price expansion path* or *price offer curve*. We use the word *consumption* rather than the words *offer* or *expansion* to highlight that this curve describes bundles in the consumption diagram.) Note that there are two PCCs in a two-good model: $PCC(P_x)$ and $PCC(P_y)$. Since we hold the price of y fixed throughout this chapter, when we refer to the PCC, we mean $PCC(P_x)$.

price consumption curve (PCC): The price consumption curve is the set of utility-maximizing consumption bundles associated with different prices for a good.

Figure 7.2 shows price consumption curves for the three sets of preferences depicted in Figure 7.1. The PCC is a downward-sloping function of x in Figure 7.2A, an upward-sloping function of x in Figure 7.2B, and a horizontal function of x in Figure 7.2C. Since x increases as P_x decreases, a downward-sloping PCC implies that the goods are substitutes, an upward-sloping PCC implies that the goods are complements, and a horizontal PCC implies that the goods are independent. Recall that substitutes and complements are defined in terms of cross-price effects, even though they are often conceptualized in terms of changes in one good causing change in another good. Although that may align more closely with a layperson's understanding of these terms, economists describe these concepts in terms of the effect of a change in price of one good on the demand for another good.

When two goods are perfect substitutes, indifference curves are straight lines. As discussed in Chapter 6, the resulting constrained optimal bundles are always boundary solutions unless the marginal rate of substitution (MRS) equals the price ratio. In that instance, the demand for x is indeterminate. As stated by Equation 6.9, for high prices of x, the boundary solution is on the y axis, and for low prices of x, the boundary solution is on the x axis. Figure 7.3 depicts this situation. In the present diagram, the red line is the budget constraint, the blue line is the indifference curve, and the green curve is the PCC. *To highlight how the PCC is built, the PCC is only shown up to the budget constraint in each panel.* Figure 7.3A depicts a "high" price for x. The utility-maximizing indifference curve given these prices is **AB**, and this level of utility is affordable at **A** (**A** satisfies Equation 6.1Bii). **A** is a point on the price consumption curve. **A** remains the PCC chosen bundle until the price ratio P_x/P_y = MRS is achieved in Figure 7.3B. In this instance, the indifference curve, budget constraint, and the PCC coincide. Interestingly, the individual is no better off in Figure 7.3B than in Figure 7.3A, despite facing a lower price of x: Both figures achieve a utility-maximizing utility level associated with the indifference curve **AB**. The only difference is that in Figure 7.3B, there are multiple affordable ways to achieve

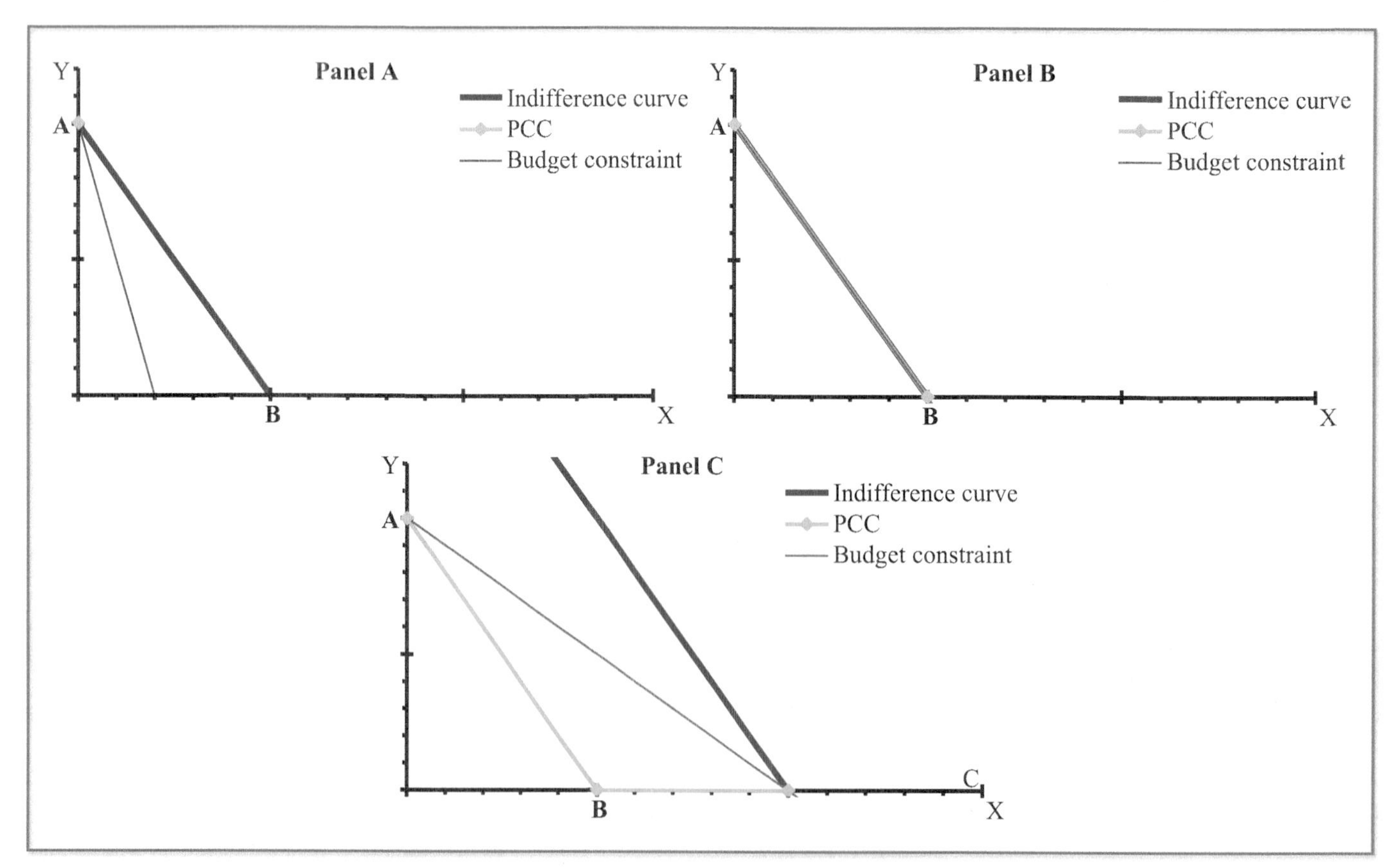

FIGURE 7.3 Price Consumption Curve for Perfect Substitutes

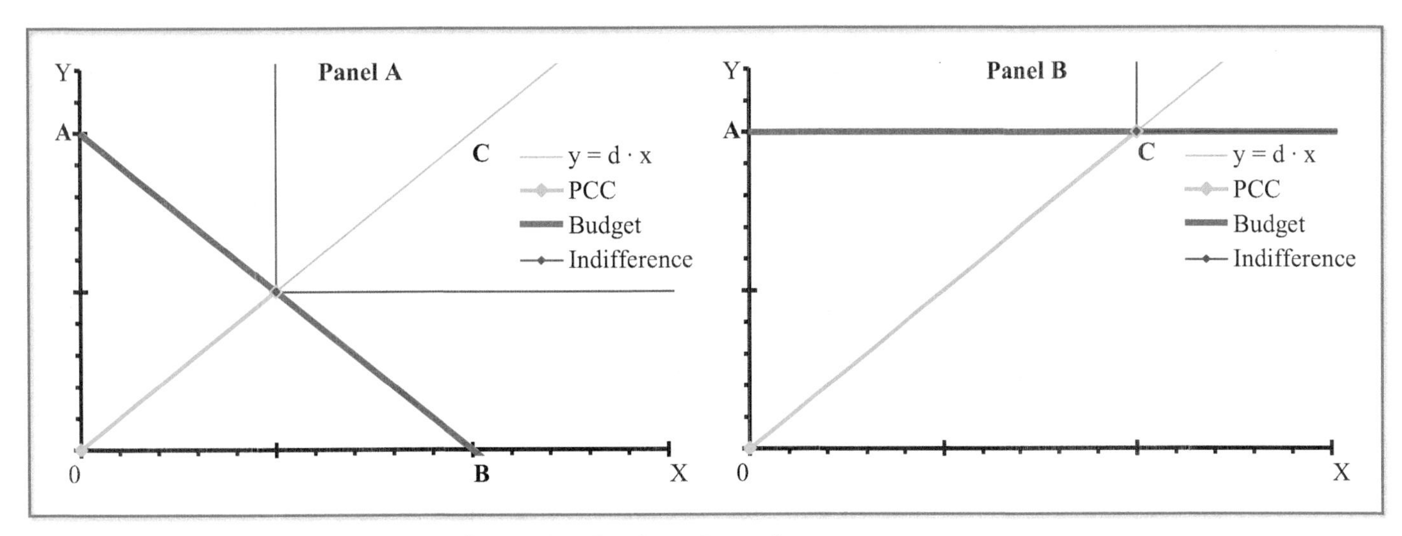

FIGURE 7.4 Price Consumption Curve for Perfect Complements

this utility level (the entire segment **AB** satisfies Equation 6.1Bi), while in Figure 7.3A, the only affordable way to achieve this utility level is to consume at **A**. Figure 7.3C depicts a lower price of x than Figure 7.3B (in this instance, 50% lower). The utility-maximizing consumption bundle is now the intersection of the budget constraint with the x axis (these constrained optimums satisfy Equation 6.1Biii). The PCC for perfect substitutes is **ABC** in Figure 7.3C, although **C** would require an even lower price of x before it became feasible. Notice that the general orientation of the perfect substitutes PCC is downward sloping, just like the imperfect substitutes PCC depicted in Figure 7.2A.

At the opposite end of the substitutability spectrum, perfect complements require fixed proportions be consumed: d units of y are consumed per unit of x (according to the utility function, U(x, y) = Minimum(x, y/d), used in Chapters 4 and 6). The indifference curves are L-shaped, with vertices on the ray y = d · x. These vertices are also constrained optimal bundles, given the appropriate budget constraint (as described in Figure 6.2). Figure 7.4 depicts the situation. The lavender ray is the set of efficient consumption choices. As long as the price of x is positive, some income is spent on each good. In Figure 7.4A, for instance, about half is spent on each good (since the vertex bundle on budget constraint **AB** appears to be approximately midway between **A** and **B**). As prices vary, the proportion spent on each good will vary. If the price of x is $0, all income is spent on y, I/P_y units of y are purchased, and $x = y/d = I/(d \cdot P_y)$ units of x are consumed. This is bundle **C** = $(I/(d \cdot P_y), I/P_y)$ in Figure 7.4B. The PCC for perfect complements is the line segment **0C** in Figure 7.4B. (The other limiting case for price is to have a very high price of x. In this instance, the constrained optimal bundle will be on the lavender ray close to the origin, and most of the income will be spent on x. In the Excel file for Figure 7.4, the highest allowable price of x creates a situation where 10% of income is spent on y, and 90% is spent on x; see this by moving the price slider all of the way to the right.) The general orientation of the perfect complements PCC is upward sloping, just like the imperfect complements PCC depicted in Figure 7.2B.

7.2 Deriving Individual Demand from Optimal Bundles: The Geometry of Optimization

Perhaps the most important use of the price consumption curve is that it acts as a springboard to derive the individual's demand for x. *Demand* is one of the two most important words in microeconomics; therefore, it is worthwhile to examine a more precise definition of an individual's demand for x. In introductory economics, you learned that demand is the number of units demanded for a given price. Typically, this is described as a market demand, rather than an individual demand, although you may not have noticed this distinction at the time. We held constant a number of factors to reach this definition (the notion of *ceteris paribus* is central to understanding demand). Indeed, the factors that are held constant provide the laundry list of those factors that cause a demand curve to shift. One of the problems introductory students typically have is discerning the difference between a movement along a demand curve and a shift in a demand curve. Varying the price of the good causes a movement along the demand curve; if the good is x, then changing the price of x involves moving along the demand curve for x. Economists say that this is a change in quantity demanded. Primary among those factors being held constant as we move along a demand curve are the prices of other goods and income.[2] If either of these changes, then demand will shift.

individual's demand for a good: An individual's demand for a good shows how much of the good the individual willingly consumes at various prices of the good, *ceteris paribus*. This term is often shortened to (most commonly) *individual demand*, *demand curve*, and *demand*.

In the present context, we are explicitly interested in an individual's demand for a good. An **individual's demand for a good** shows how much of the good the individual willingly consumes at various prices of the good, *ceteris paribus*. Individual demand is easy to discern from the consumption diagram. If you are interested in demand for x, simply examine what happens to the x coordinate of the optimal (x, y) bundle as the price of x changes. If you graph the x coordinate against the price of x, you have drawn an individual's demand for x as a function of the price of x. This is done in a demand diagram, in (x, P_x) space, as opposed to a consumption diagram in (x, y) space, so the vertical axis is the price of x (rather than the quantity of y).[3] The two graphs share a common x axis; therefore, we can easily transfer the optimal x value from one graph to the other by

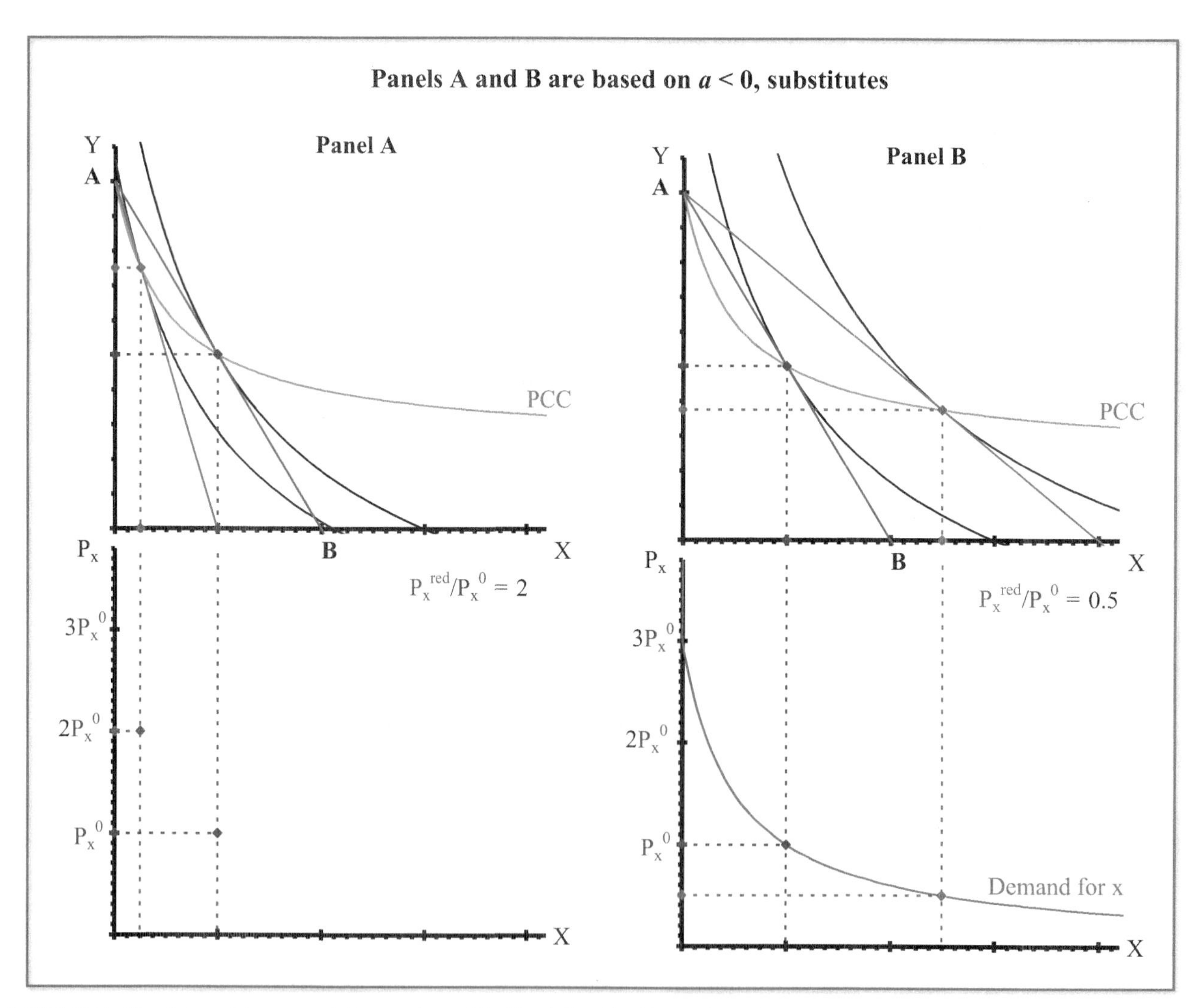

FIGURE 7.5 Deriving Demand Based on Shifted Cobb-Douglas Preferences

vertically aligning the graphs and dropping vertical lines. Figure 7.5 shows the vertical stacking of a consumption graph on top and a demand graph on the bottom. (A common mistake students make is to ignore this vertical stacking and put the diagrams side by side in their notebook. Much is lost in doing this; here is a place to waste a bit of paper in your notebook.)

Figure 7.5 derives demand for two shifted CD preferences. The first, shown in Figures 7.5A and 7.5B, involves imperfect substitutes. The second, shown in Figures 7.5C and 7.5D, involves imperfect complements. (The equal-weighted CD described in Figure 7.2C is not shown here, but you can create this for yourself from the Excel file for Figure 7.5, using the scenario "Equal CD.") As in Section 7.1, we avoid actual prices and income in this section to describe the general relations between optimal bundles and points on the demand curve. To fix relative prices, consider the blue budget constraint **AB** to be the base price of x, $P_x^{blue} = P_x^0$. Other prices of x are then simply relative to this price. For example, the red budget constraint in Figure 7.5A depicts twice as high a price, $P_x^{red}/P_x^{blue} = 2$, because the x intercept is midway between 0 and **B** along the x axis. Figure 7.5A suppresses the demand curve to focus on how individual points on the demand curve are created. The x value from the optimal bundle in the upper diagram is dropped down to the second graph to create the x coordinate of the demand curve (these are the dashed vertical blue and red lines). The vertical axis coordinate is determined by the price associated with that point on the PCC (in Figure 7.5A, $P_x^{red} = 2 \cdot P_x^0$; in Figure 7.5B, $P_x^{red} = 1/2 \cdot P_x^0$). The dashed horizontal lines at these heights in the lower diagram depict these prices. The slider allows you

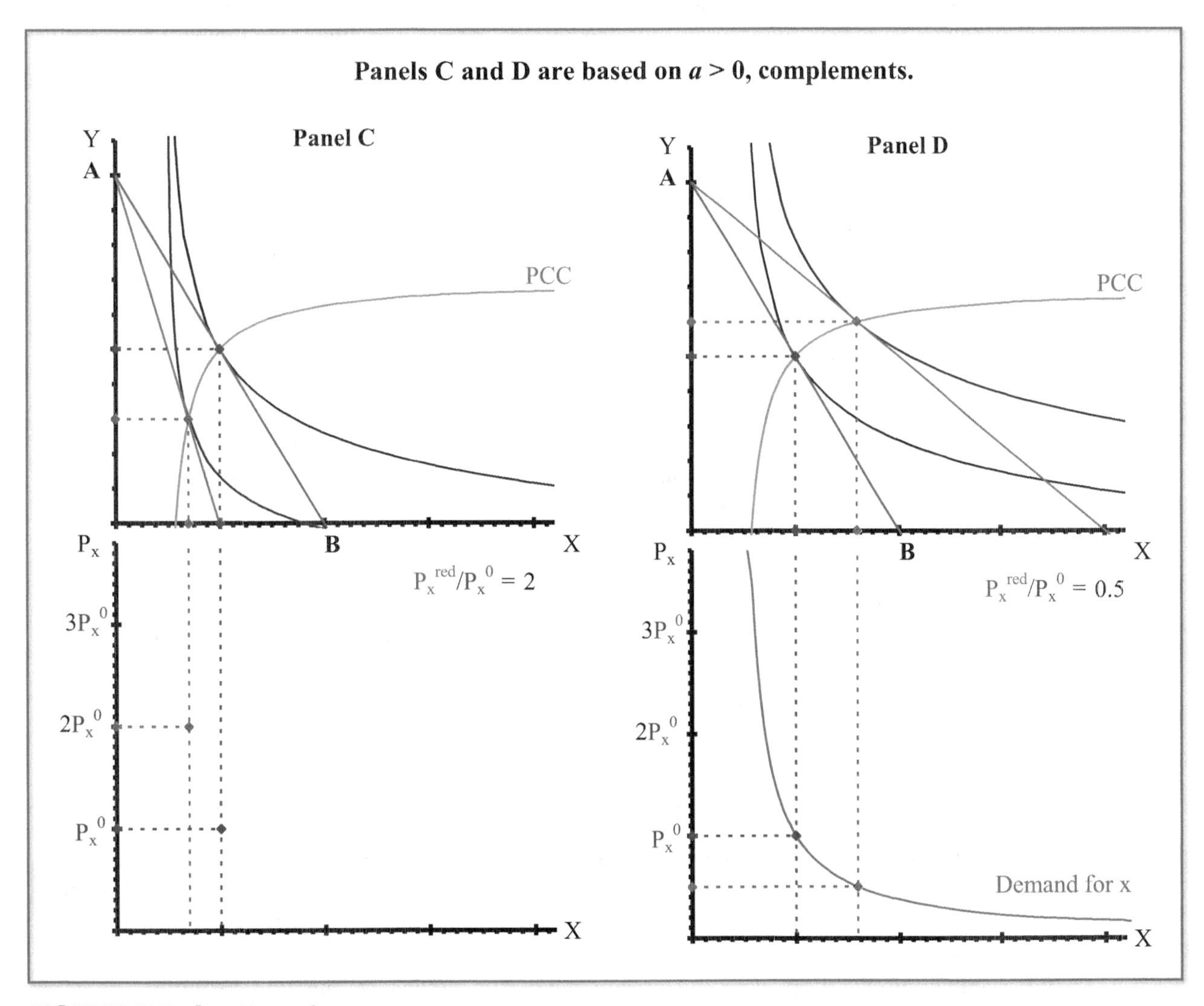

FIGURE 7.5 Continued

to vary red's price from 0.2 to 6 times P_x^0, although the vertical axis is truncated at 3.8 times P_x^0 (tick marks on the vertical axis in the lower graph are 0.1 times P_x^0).

As you would expect, the individual demand curve mapped out as price varies differs, based on the individual's preferences. In Figure 7.5B, the demand for x is zero if red's price is three times P_x^0. This is shown in the PCC in the upper diagram as well: The PCC approaches **A** with a slope of three times the slope of the blue budget constraint (this ratio is not visible, but it can be seen by using the slider).[4] If the price differential P_x/P_y is too high, demand for x is zero because y is an imperfect substitute for x (this is exactly what happened with merlot in Figure 6.7).[5]

By contrast, Figures 7.5C and 7.5D depict imperfect complements. In Figure 7.5D, demand for y is zero when P_x^{red} is more than 3.5 times P_x^0. In this instance, all income is spent on x. (This is visible in the Excel figure by setting $P_x^{red} = 3.5 \cdot P_x^0$ and noting that the budget constraint intersects the x axis at the same point where the PCC intersects the x axis.) This occurs because the vertical intercept shift factor *a* is positive for Figures 7.5C and 7.5D (although the value has been suppressed to create the diagrams as general solutions, rather than being tied to a specific shifted CD utility function). You may have noticed that there is a slight kink in the demand curve at $3.5 \cdot P_x^0$ in Figure 7.5D. The reason is straightforward. For prices of x below $3.5 \cdot P_x^0$, the tangency condition holds on the interior of the consumption set (where some income is spent on each good). For prices of x above $3.5 \cdot P_x^0$, a border solution exists along the x axis, as noted earlier. (Indeed, given the specific functional form shown, any price above $4 \cdot P_x^0$ has a feasible budget set in which preferences are not defined for any of the feasible bundles. These are x values below *a*, the axis shift factor. This can be seen in the Excel figure for Figure 7.5 by noting that the red indifference curve is vertical and intersects the red budget constraint on the x axis when $P_x^{red} = 4 \cdot P_x^0$.) Different values of shifted CD *a*, b, and r would lead to qualitatively similar but numerically different results. When *a* is positive, there will be some prices for x where the set of feasible bundles is completely outside the set of bundles over which the utility function is defined.[6]

An individual's demand for x can be derived from the geometric information provided in the consumption diagram. The demand curve described earlier maps out optimal choices of x as the price of x varies, holding all other prices and income constant. The PCC that was the focus of Section 7.1 also holds all other prices and income fixed. In many ways, both curves contain the same information; the difference is that the PCC focuses on consumption bundles and places price in the background (price information is embedded in the location of the budget constraint), while the demand curve takes the orientation of price of x and quantity of x and places information about y in the background (y can be derived from x as $y = I/P_y - (P_x/P_y) \cdot x$ due to the budget constraint). The difference between the PCC and demand is, in large part, one of orientation. If you wish to take the broad view of how consumption changes, then the PCC provides more germane information, since the PCC in the consumption diagram is in (x, y) space, but if you want to focus on x alone, the demand orientation provides a more direct view of how x is affected by a change in its price, since the demand curve is in (x, P_x) space.

7.3 Deriving Individual Demand: The Algebra of Optimization

In Chapter 6, we examined the algebra of optimization for a unitary budget constraint to focus on the parameters that delineate the various classes of utility function laid out in Table 4.1. The strategy here is to provide much the same analysis for a general budget constraint. We use the same two-part requirement for optimization described in Equation 6.1 (one part is that all income is spent; the other relates the MRS to price ratio). Algebraically, demand is a multivariate function, but the way we talk about demand is as a univariate function, $x(P_x)$. As a result, we derive the general functional solutions here but graph those solutions for fixed (albeit sometimes general) values of income and the price of y. In Section 7.5, we allow income to vary for fixed prices.

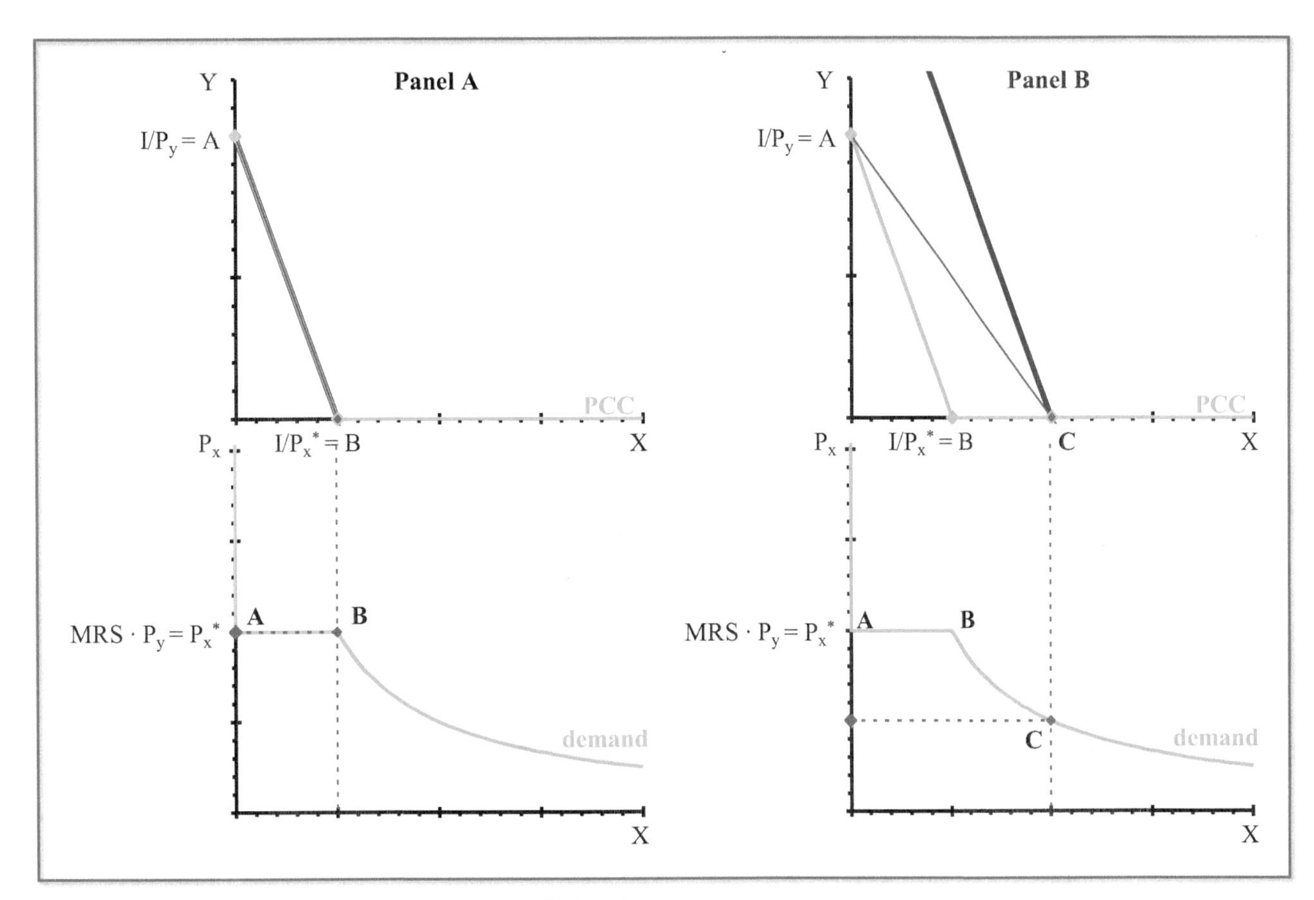

FIGURE 7.6 Deriving Demand for Perfect Substitutes

Perfect Substitutes

As noted in the discussion of Figure 7.3, Equation 6.9 derived the algebra for perfect substitutes for general prices and income. The demand curve in this situation is particularly interesting. Perfect substitutes are entirely defined by the MRS (the trade-off rate between x and y), and the MRS is a constant for perfect substitutes. For a fixed price of y, P_y, there will be some price of x, P_x*, such that MRS = P_x^*/P_y. Demand is indeterminate at $P_x^* = MRS \cdot P_y$; somewhere between 0% and 100% of income will be spent on x, and the rest will be spent on y. For prices above P_x*, demand for x is zero, since bundle **A** in the upper diagram is the constrained optimum. For prices below P_x*, all income will be spent on x, and I/Px will be consumed. Figure 7.6 depicts demand in this situation. Figure 7.6A depicts the "razor's edge" price, P_x*, where demand is somewhere between 0% (**A**) and 100% (**B**) of income spent on x (this is the flat part of the demand curve **AB** in the lower diagram). Figure 7.6B depicts a lower price; indeed, the price has been cut in half from P_x*. In this instance, **C** = $(I/(0.5 \cdot P_x^*), 0.5 \cdot P_x^*)$; twice as much x is consumed as at bundle **B**.

Perfect Complements

Bundles that are efficient, given perfect complement preferences represented by the function U(x, y) = Minimum(x, y/d), must satisfy $y = d \cdot x$, as discussed in Section 6.2. Substituting this into the budget constraint $I = P_x x + P_y y$ and solving for x, we obtain:

Demand for x: $$x(P_x, P_y, I) = I/(P_x + d \cdot P_y). \quad \textbf{(7.1a)}$$

Substituting this back into the efficiency condition produces:

Demand for y: $$y(P_x, P_y, I) = d \cdot I/(P_x + d \cdot P_y). \quad \textbf{(7.1b)}$$

You may recall demand for x, given a unitary budget constraint in Equation 6.11a, was $x = 1/(1 + d)$. This equation is a special case within Equation 7.1a: Demand in a specific

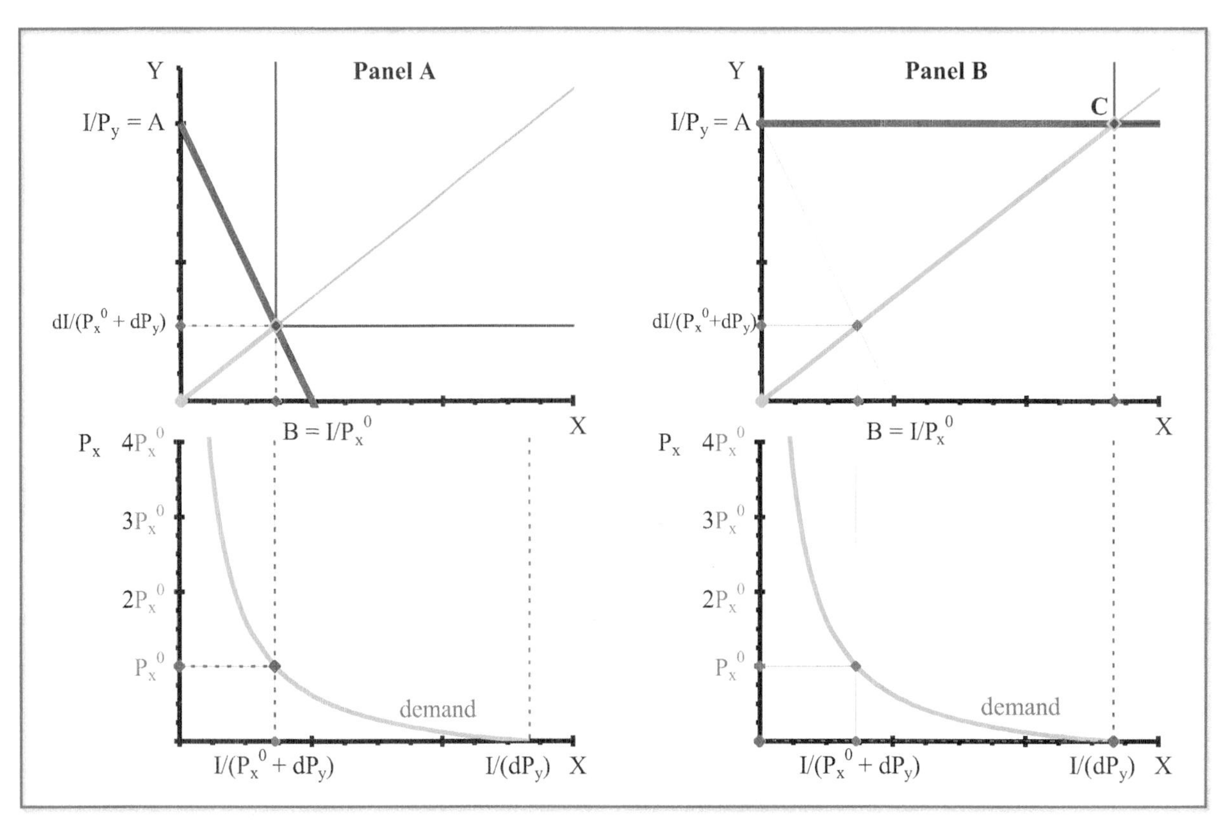

FIGURE 7.7 Deriving Demand for Perfect Complements: U(x, y) = Minimum(x, y/d)

case can be obtained from the general demand function by plugging in the values for P_x, P_y, and I (which all equal one for a unitary budget constraint). Demand for x is shown for a general price P_x^0 in Figure 7.7A and for $P_x = 0$ in Figure 7.7B.

It is instructive to compare demand for x in Figures 7.6B and 7.7B. These two demand curves are polar opposites on the substitutability scale, and their graphs are quite reasonable in light of this fact. Perfect substitutes have zero demand if the price becomes too high, and demand is unbounded when the price is very low. By contrast, demand given perfect complements is finite when the price of x is zero, and quantity of x demanded is positive for all prices of x, no matter how high. With perfect complements, x must be consumed with y in fixed proportions, regardless of the specific prices of each.

Cobb-Douglas

As noted in Chapter 6, the constrained optimum for CD preferences is an interior solution. Equation 6.1Bi requires MRS = P_x/P_y at interior solutions, so $r/(1 - r) \cdot (y/x) = P_x/P_y$, given the CD utility function $U(x, y) = x^r \cdot y^{(1-r)}$ according to the MRS information in Table 4.1. The general budget constraint is $I = P_x x + P_y y$. By regrouping the MRS condition, we obtain:

$$P_y y = ((1 - r)/r) \cdot (P_x x). \quad \textbf{(7.2a)}$$

Plugging Equation 7.2a into the budget constraint and regrouping, we obtain:

$$I = P_x x + ((1 - r)/r \cdot P_x x) = (r \cdot P_x + (1 - r) \cdot P_x) \cdot x/r = P_x x/r. \quad \textbf{(7.2b)}$$

Solving for x, we obtain:

Demand for x: $$x(P_x, P_y, I) = r \cdot I/P_x. \quad \textbf{(7.3a)}$$

Substituting Equation 7.3a into Equation 7.2a and solving for y, we obtain:[7]

Demand for y: $$y(P_x, P_y, I) = (1 - r) \cdot I/P_y. \quad \textbf{(7.3b)}$$

These demand functions are elegant generalizations of the unitary income result from Equations 6.3a and 6.3b. Since $P_x x$ is the amount spent on x, and $P_y y$ is the amount spent on y, we can obtain these quantities by multiplying the demand functions by P_x and P_y. This yields:

Spending on x: $$P_x x = r \cdot I. \quad \textbf{(7.4a)}$$

Spending on y: $$P_y y = (1 - r) \cdot I. \quad \textbf{(7.4b)}$$

Spending on each good is a constant percentage of income, given CD preferences, and the percentage of income spent on each good is determined by the relative size of the exponents attached to each good.

Consider the CD demand for y in Equation 7.3b. Notice that there is no P_x in the demand for y; therefore, a change in the price of x has no effect on demand for y. The two goods are independent in this instance, just as shown in Figures 7.1C and 7.1F and by the PCC in Figure 7.2C.[8] These figures are based on an equal-weighted CD. The only change if r is different from 0.5 would be the percentage of income spent on x and y; in each case, the PCC will be horizontal because there is no cross-price effect for CD preferences. The individual spends a constant percentage of income on each good when preferences are CD. Were you to adjust the price of x using Figures 6.5A, 6.5B, and 6.5C, the resulting constrained optimum would continue to have the same y coordinate; 80%, 60%, and 30% is spent on y, and 20%, 40%, and 70% is spent on x in the three panels, regardless of price. A separate graph is not provided here because it is easy to check this with the shifted CD file used to create Figure 7.8 (by setting $a = b = 0$).

CD functions are easy to work with. Suppose you know that the proportion of income spent on two goods is relatively constant. Then you could model this using the CD functional form, and you could expand this beyond two goods as well. For example, suppose you know that you typically spend 10% of your mad money on paperback books (B), 30% on movies (M), 40% on fine dining (D), 15% on junk food (J), and 5% on other goods (G). You can represent your preferences over these goods, using the CD utility function:

$$U(B, M, D, J, G) = B^{0.1} \cdot M^{0.3} \cdot D^{0.4} \cdot J^{0.15} \cdot G^{0.05}.$$

Shifted Cobb-Douglas

As shown in Chapter 6, the shifted CD function, $U(x, y) = (x - a)^r \cdot (y - b)^{(1-r)}$, can produce boundary solutions, but the way we determine whether the constrained optimum is indeed a boundary or interior solution is to treat the optimization as if it were an interior solution and then make sure the resulting bundle is in the first quadrant. (This is the strategy used to examine Figure 6.6D; see the discussion at Equations 6.6a–6.6d.[9]) The MRS equals price ratio condition in Equation 6.1Bi implies:

$$(r/(1 - r)) \cdot ((y - b)/(x - a)) = P_x/P_y. \quad \textbf{(7.5a)}$$

As before, solve for $P_y y$ by cross-multiplying to obtain:

$$P_y y = ((1 - r)/r) \cdot P_x x - ((1 - r)/r) \cdot P_x \cdot a + P_y \cdot b. \quad \textbf{(7.5b)}$$

Plug Equation 7.5b into the budget constraint to obtain:

$$\begin{aligned} I &= P_x x + ((1 - r)/r) \cdot P_x x - ((1 - r)/r) \cdot P_x \cdot a + P_y \cdot b \\ &= P_x x/r - ((1 - r)/r) \cdot P_x \cdot a + P_y \cdot b. \end{aligned} \quad \textbf{(7.5c)}$$

Solving for x in Equation 7.5c, we obtain:

$$x(P_x, P_y, I) = (r \cdot I + (1 - r) \cdot P_x \cdot a - r \cdot P_y \cdot b)/P_x. \quad \textbf{(7.6a)}$$

Demand for x: $$x(P_x, P_y, I) = r \cdot I/P_x + (1 - r) \cdot a - r \cdot b \cdot P_y/P_x. \quad \textbf{(7.6b)}$$

$$x(P_x, P_y, I) = CD_x + x_{\text{vertical shift}} - x_{\text{horizontal shift}}. \quad \textbf{(7.6c)}$$

Symmetrically, we obtain demand for y by substituting Equation 7.6a into Equation 7.5b and solving for y:[10]

$$y(P_x, P_y, I) = ((1 - r) \cdot I - (1 - r) \cdot P_x \cdot a + r \cdot P_y \cdot b)/P_y. \quad \textbf{(7.6d)}$$

Demand for y:

$$y(P_x, P_y, I) = (1 - r) \cdot I/P_y - (1 - r) \cdot a \cdot P_x/P_y + r \cdot b. \quad \textbf{(7.6e)}$$

$$y(P_x, P_y, I) = CD_y - y_{\text{vertical shift}} + y_{\text{horizontal shift}}. \quad \textbf{(7.6f)}$$

Both demand functions are provided in three different ways. The first is the most direct algebraic derivation, the second pulls apart the three separate terms, and the third labels these terms. Shifted CD demand is CD demand adjusted for both vertical and horizontal axis shifts. As described in Chapter 4 (Table 4.1 and Figure 4.10), x is only defined for $x > a$, and y is only defined for $y > b$. Good x can only have a boundary solution on the y axis ($x = 0$) if $a < 0$ because only in this instance will indifference curves cross the vertical axis. The constrained optimum will be an interior solution as long as $0 < x < I/P_x$, where x is the solution to Equation 7.6a. If x is an interior solution, y will be as well (since (x, y) is on the budget constraint where x and y are defined by Equations 7.6a and 7.6d).

The condition $a < 0$ is necessary but not sufficient to obtain a boundary solution on the vertical axis. A vertical axis boundary solution will occur if $x(P_x, P_y, I) \leq 0$ in Equation 7.6a. Once the price of x is high enough, $x(P_x, P_y, I) \leq 0$. For fixed r, I, b, and $a < 0$, the numerator in the fraction in Equation 7.6a will be negative once P_x is large enough (since $(1 - r) \cdot P_x \cdot a < 0$ will eventually overtake in magnitude the other two terms in the numerator). The lowest price of x where **A** will be the constrained optimum (Equation 6.1Bii) is the price, P_x^{min}, where $x(P_x, P_y, I) = 0$ in Equation 7.6a. Solving for P_x in this equation, we obtain:[11]

$$P_x^{min} = (r/(1 - r)) \cdot (b \cdot P_y - I)/a. \quad \textit{Lowest } P_x \textit{ where all income is spent on y.} \quad \textbf{(7.7)}$$

When $P_x \geq P_x^{min}$, demand for x will be zero, and a boundary-constrained optimum will hold in which all income is spent on y.

The condition $b < 0$ is necessary but not sufficient to obtain a boundary solution on the horizontal axis. We can obtain the highest price of x where the constrained optimum would be on the horizontal axis, P_x^{max}, either by setting $x(P_x, P_y, I) = I/P_x$ in Equation 7.6a or by setting $y(P_x, P_y, I) = 0$ in Equation 7.6d. Solving for P_x using either equation yields:

$$P_x^{max} = (I/a) - (r/(1 - r)) \cdot b \cdot P_y/a. \quad \textit{Highest } P_x \textit{ where all income is spent on x.} \quad \textbf{(7.8)}$$

When $P_x \leq P_x^{max}$, demand for y will be zero, and a boundary-constrained optimum will hold in which all income is spent on x.

The solution to this constrained-optimization problem is a function of six parameters, three that define the constraint: P_x, P_y, I, and three that define preferences: a, b, and r. Two of these parameters are held fixed in the Excel file for Figure 7.8 ($I = 10$, and $P_y = 1$); the others can be adjusted using four sliders. Figure 7.8 shows one set of preferences based on shifted CD preferences ($a = -20$, $b = -5$, and $r = 0.75$) for two prices $P_x^{red} = 1$ and $P_x^{blue} = 0.25$. Since both $a < 0$ and $b < 0$, we can obtain solutions for both boundary Equations 7.7 and 7.8. As shown in Figure 7.8, $P_x^{min} = 2.25$, and $P_x^{max} = 0.25$. Both can be seen in the upper and lower diagrams. You obtain a tangency at **A** in the consumption diagram when the P_x slider is set equal to 2.25. In the demand diagram, this is associated with the point on the demand curve (0, 2.25). The constrained optimum is on the horizontal axis in the consumption diagram when $P_x = 0.25$; the blue budget constraint is tangent to the blue indifference curve at bundle **B** = (40, 0) in the consumption diagram and at the point (40, 0.25) on the demand curve in Figure 7.8.

The demand for y shown in Equation 7.6e provides the answer for why we were able to describe substitutes or complements based solely on the sign of the parameter a in Figures 7.1 and 7.2. The only part of the demand for y that is based on the price of x is the vertical axis shift factor, $-(1 - r) \cdot a \cdot P_x/P_y$ in Equation 7.6e. With all parameters except P_x constant, what happens as P_x varies? The answer depends on the sign of a since the rest

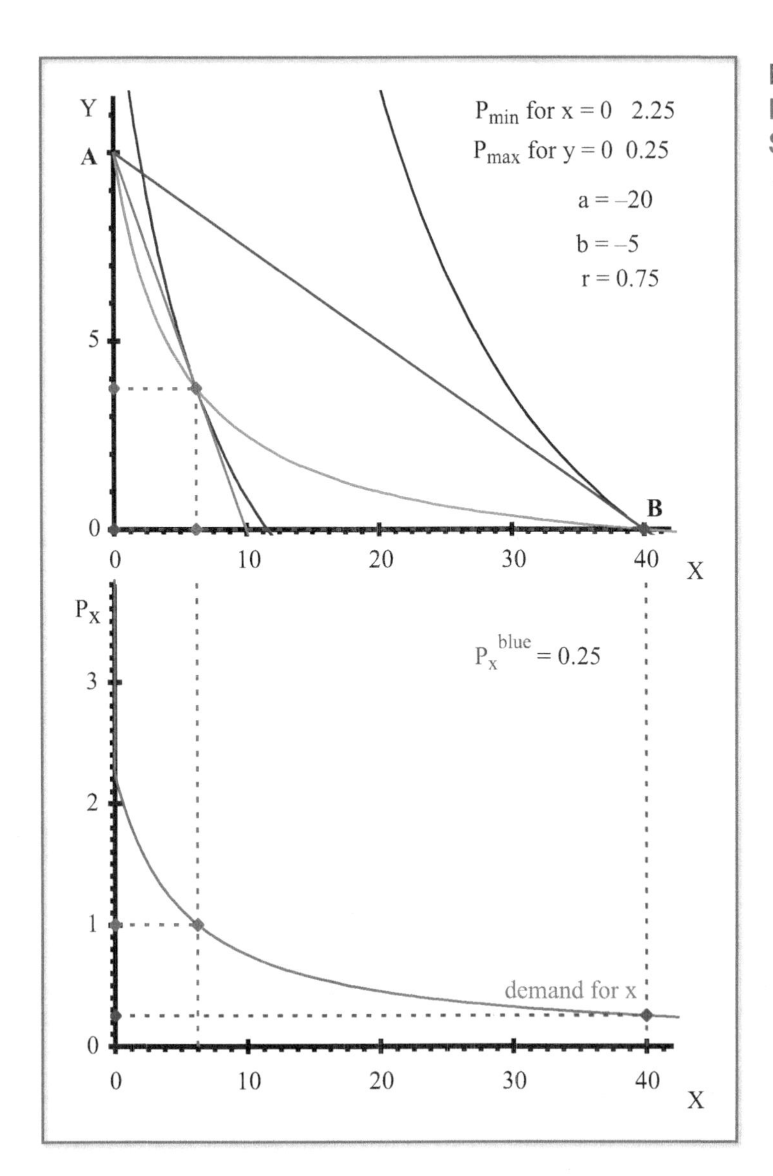

FIGURE 7.8 Individual Demand Based on Shifted CD Preferences

of the term is unambiguously negative (because $-(1 - r) < 0$, $P_x > 0$, and $P_y > 0$). If $a < 0$, an increase in P_x increases y, as in Figures 7.1A, 7.1D, 7.2A, and 7.8; if $a > 0$, an increase in P_x decreases y, as in Figure 7.1B, 7.1E, and 7.2B; and if $a = 0$, an increase in P_x has no effect on y, as in Figure 7.1C, 7.1F, and 7.2C. For shifted CD, the sign of a determines the sign of the cross-price elasticity of demand $\varepsilon_{y,x} = \%\Delta y/\%\Delta P_x$.[12]

Quasilinear

The first quasilinear function discussed in Chapter 4, $U(x, y) = a \cdot x^r + y$ (with $0 < r < 1$), is controlled by two parameters, a and r. The MRS for this utility function is: $MRS = a \cdot r \cdot x^{(r-1)}$; therefore, the tangency condition becomes:

$$a \cdot r \cdot x^{(r-1)} = P_x/P_y. \quad \textbf{(7.9)}$$

Solving for x, we obtain:

Demand for x: $$x(P_x, P_y, I) = (a \cdot r \cdot P_y/P_x)^{(1/(1-r))}. \quad \textbf{(7.10a)}$$

Substituting Equation 7.10a into the budget constraint and solving for y, we obtain upon simplification:

Demand for y: $$y(P_x, P_y, I) = I/P_y - P_x/P_y \cdot (a \cdot r \cdot P_y/P_x)^{(1/(1-r))}. \quad \textbf{(7.10b)}$$

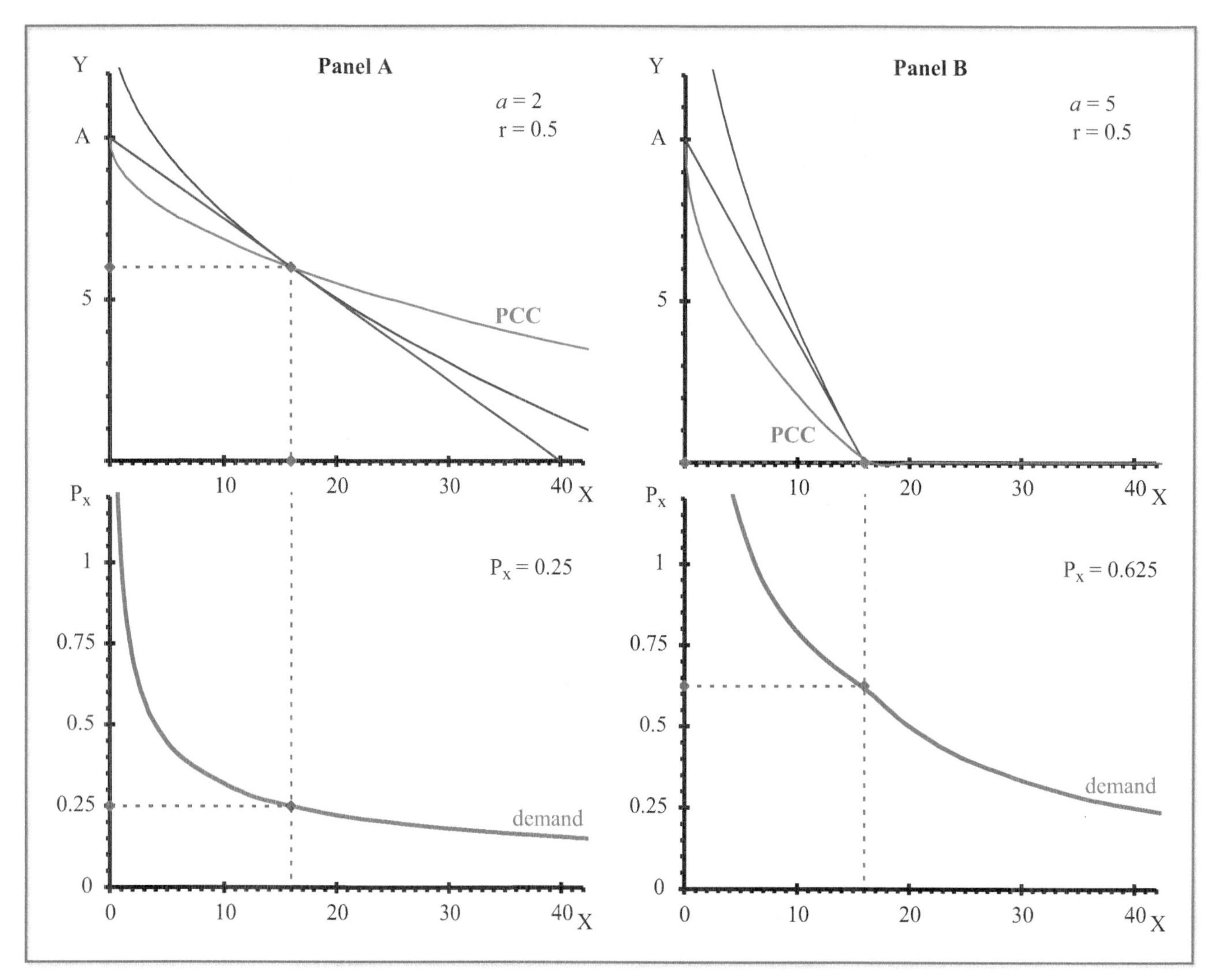

FIGURE 7.9 Demand Based on Quasilinear Preferences: $U(x, y) = a \cdot x^r + y$

Figure 7.9 provides two examples based on this quasilinear function. Each assumes $I = 10$ and $P_y = 1$, as before. Figure 7.9A uses $a = 2$ and $r = 0.5$, since $a \cdot r \cdot P_y = 1$ and $1/(1 - r) = 2$ in this instance. Demand for x reduces to $1/P_x^2$ according to Equation 7.10a (when $P_x = 0.25$, demand for x is 16, and when $P_x = 1$, demand for x is 1). The price consumption curve in both Figures 7.9a and 7.9b shows that x and y are substitutes in this situation, since the PCC is downward sloping. Figure 7.9B depicts preferences similar to the shifted CD preferences shown in Figure 7.8, in which for low enough price of x, x becomes the sole good consumed. In Figure 7.9B, the price of x at which this occurs is $P_x = 0.625$, as can be seen by setting Equation 7.10a equal to I/P_x and solving for P_x (just as with Equation 7.8).[13] The imperfect substitute preferences shift from an interior optimum to a boundary optimum at this price. As a result, the demand curve is not smooth at (16, 0.625). For prices of x above 0.625, some income is spent on y as well as x; for prices below 0.625, income is only spent on x, given the preferences depicted in Figure 7.9B.[14]

The second quasilinear function discussed in Chapter 4, $U(x, y) = a \cdot \ln(x) + y$, is controlled by the parameter a. The MRS for this utility function is: $MRS = a/x$. Equation 6.1Bi requiring $MRS = P_x/P_y$ implies:

Demand for x: $$x(P_x, P_y, I) = a \cdot P_y/P_x. \quad \textbf{(7.11a)}$$

Substituting Equation 7.11a into the budget constraint and solving for y, we obtain:

Demand for y: $$y(P_x, P_y, I) = I/P_y - a. \quad \textbf{(7.11b)}$$

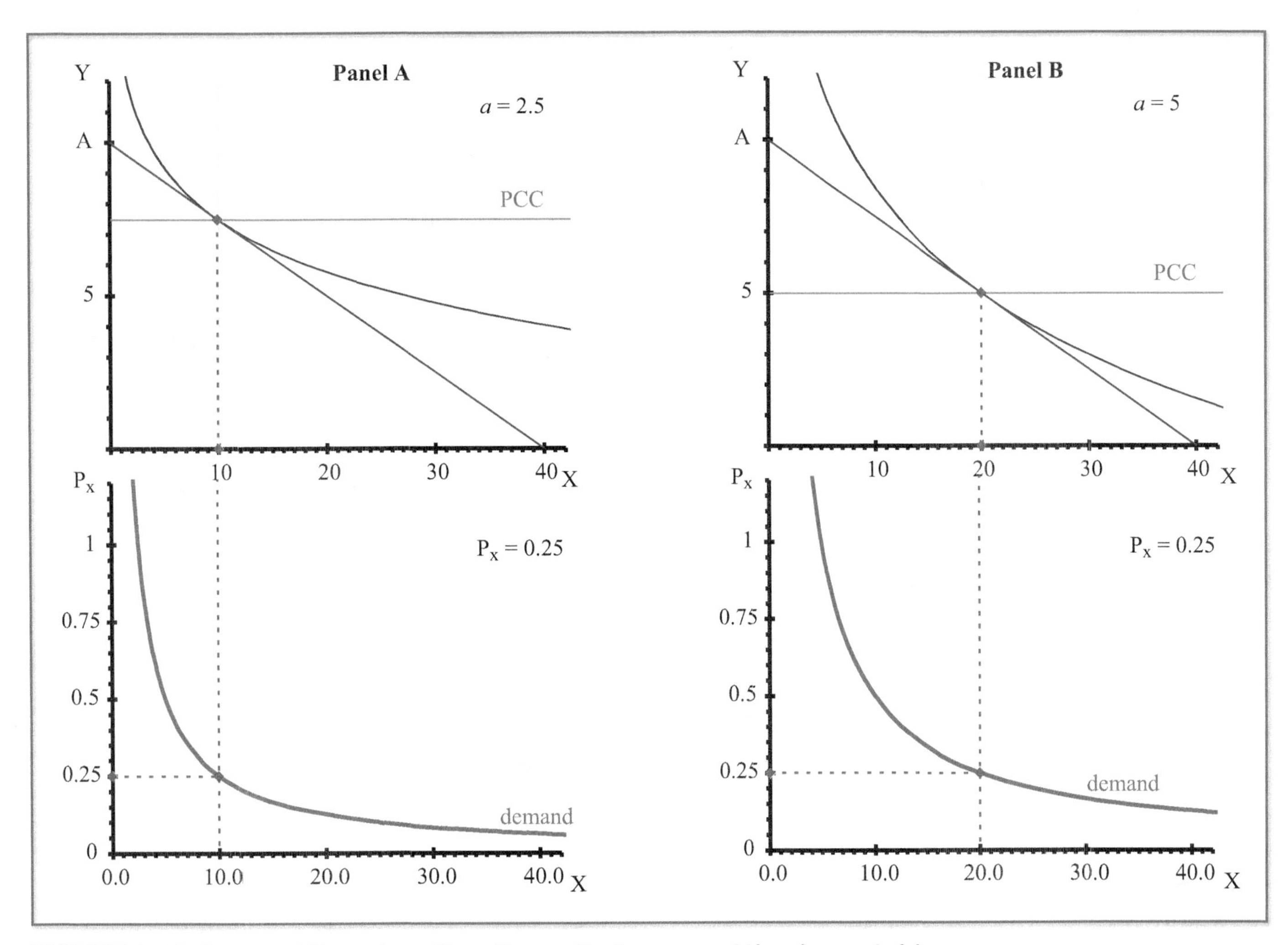

FIGURE 7.10 Demand Based on Quasilinear Preferences: $U(x, y) = a \cdot \ln(x) + y$

For fixed a, I, and P_y, demand for y is fixed. The price of x has no effect on demand for y; they are independent goods (this is clear from the horizontal PCC in Figure 7.10). As long as $a < I/P_y$, the constrained optimum will remain an interior solution, since both x and y are greater than zero in Equations 7.11a and 7.11b. If $a \geq I/P_y$ then all income is spent on x, and demand for x is no longer as shown in Equation 7.11a but is constrained to $x = I/P_x$. This is because $a \geq I/P_y$ implies $a \cdot P_y \geq I$, so that the demanded bundle in Equation 7.11a will not be affordable (except in the border situation of $a = I/P_y$—in which case, all income is still spent on x). Figure 7.10 provides demand curves for two values of a, both of which produce interior solutions. In each, the percentage of income spent on each good is constant (25% and 75%, respectively) in Figure 7.10A and 50% each in Figure 7.10B. The a slider allows you to vary the percentage of income spent on x from zero to 100% by varying a from 0 to 10. When $a > 10$, an Equation 6.1Biii boundary solution exists in which all income is spent on x, regardless of the price of x.

Demand for x is independent of income for quasilinear functions (as long as the optimum is an interior solution). This is seen by the absence of income in both quasilinear demand for x functions (Equations 7.10a and 7.11a). Compare this with each of the other demand functions derived in Section 7.3; as a general rule, they are a function of income. This is simply the algebraic realization of the relationship described as early as Chapter 4, when we first introduced quasilinear utility functions. *The way to most easily conceptualize demand based on quasilinear preferences is to think of demand for x being fulfilled "first"; then demand for y is filled in as income allows.* This will be seen even more explicitly in Section 7.6, when we examine income changes.

Nonconvex Preferences

Before turning to an application of demand, it is worthwhile to examine nonconvex preferences in the face of price changes. We use the same preferences shown in Section 6.4, and we follow the strategy used there (and earlier in this chapter) of removing numbers from axes to focus attention on general attributes, rather than specific values. Figure 7.11 combines results of Figures 6.15 and 6.16. The blue budget constraint depicts the information from Figure 6.15, and the gold budget constraint relates to Figure 6.16.

Six bundles, **A** through **F**, are shown in Figure 7.11. Bundles **A** and **C** are local maximums, given the blue budget constraint. **C** is on the PCC in this instance, and the x coordinate of this point is mapped to point **C** on the demand curve in the lower diagram. **A** is a point of minor confusion here, since it is a local optimum, but it is not a point on the demand curve, since **C** is better and is on the same budget constraint. **B** has the problem discussed in Section 6.4: It satisfies the optimality condition required by Equation 6.1 but is locally the worst you can do on the blue budget constraint. A larger problem occurs when the consumer faces the gold budget constraint. In this instance, **D** and **F** are both indifferent optimums: Both points are on the PCC, and both points are on the demand curve. These two points on the demand curve are at the *same* price, but the quantity of x demanded at **F** is more than five times as large as at **D**. And unlike perfect substitute demand in Figure 7.6, the points between **D** and **F** are *not* on the demand curve (indeed, as discussed in Section 6.4, bundle **E** is the worst you can do on the budget constraint between **D** and **F**, despite satisfying Equation 6.1). The demand curve has two segments with a jump discontinuity at a single price. At that price, one of the demand points is more than five times as large as the other. For prices of x above this price, the PCC moves to the southwest from bundle **D**, and for prices below this price, the PCC moves to the northeast from **F**. The behavior implied by Figure 7.11 does not mesh with observed behavior: People do not, in general, make such widely disparate and seemingly inconsistent choices.

FIGURE 7.11 Price Consumption Curve and Demand, Given Nonconvex Preferences

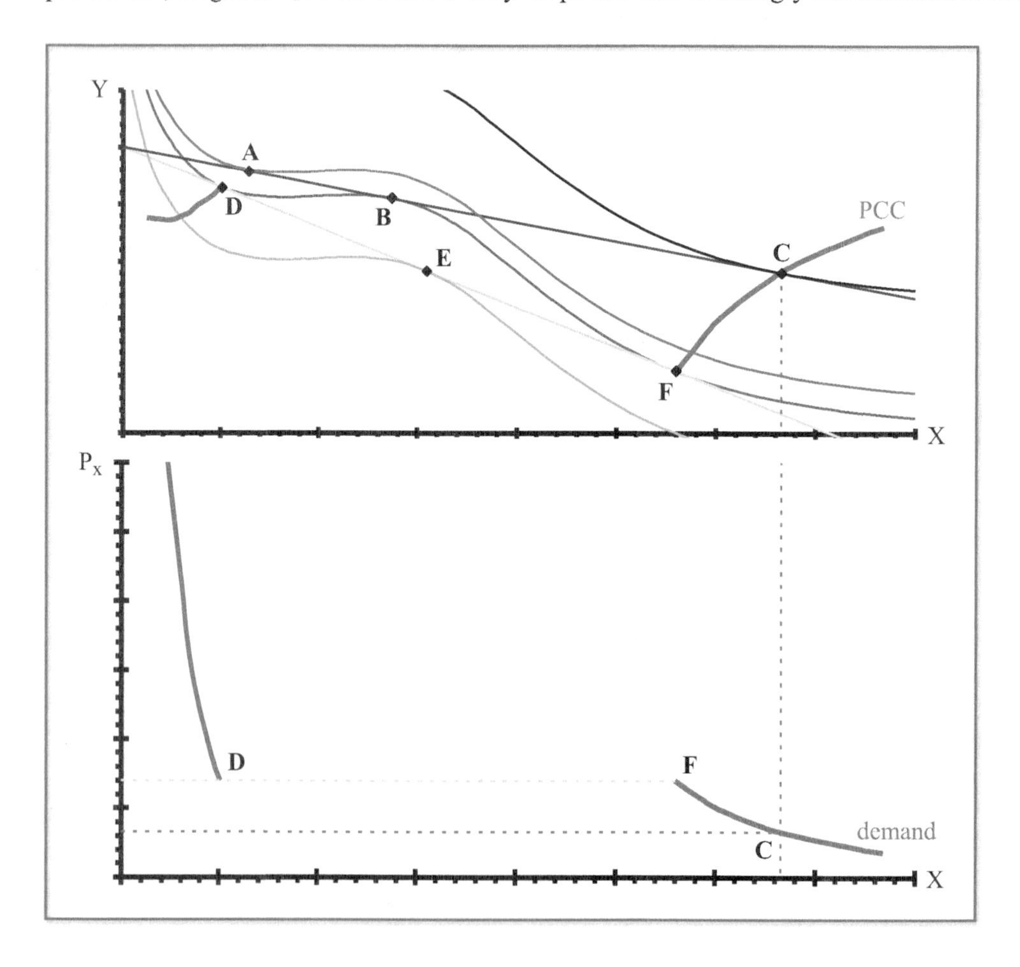

Convexity leads to much more reasonable behavior, as discussed previously; convexity is assumed unless otherwise stated.

7.4 Price Efficiency: Market Exchange in an Edgeworth Box

The Edgeworth Box analysis originally put forward in the context of barter in Section 3.5 can be expanded to describe individuals trading with each other via a market system, using prices of goods as a measure of value. You have worked through a significant amount of material since you read Section 3.5, and none of it has involved the kind of direct comparison across individuals that the Edgeworth Box was created to accomplish. You may wish to review the figures in Section 3.5 to refresh your memory about how the Edgeworth Box is constructed and about the basic properties of Edgeworth Boxes (the Price Edgeworth Box Excel file includes the barter box worksheets so that barter and price models are easily compared). We do not spend time on the basics of Edgeworth Box construction here, but we quickly recount the main conclusion obtained in Chapter 3.

Even in the absence of money and a price system to act as a medium of exchange and measure of value, individuals find it advantageous to exchange goods with each other (barter) as long as MRSs are not equal across individuals. Pareto superior reallocations of resources exist whenever MRSs are not equal across individuals. We use the same basic assumptions about preferences and resource constraints here to be able to directly compare the price and barter solutions.

To consider constrained optimization, we need to know about both preferences and constraints. Constraints within an exchange economy are provided by total resources available to the individuals in the economy. Annie ($\mathbf{E_a}$) and Bob ($\mathbf{E_b}$) have endowments of chocolate (x), and gummis (y) given by: $\mathbf{E_a} = (x_a^e, y_a^e) = (40, 105)$, and $\mathbf{E_b} = (x_b^e, y_b^e) = (110, 35)$. At the time the Edgeworth Box was introduced, we had not talked about utility functions, we had not used the term *Cobb-Douglas preferences*, and we had not described CD preferences in any detail. Nonetheless, both individuals had equal-weighted CD preferences. (Assumption 2 stated that $MRS(x_0, y_0) = y_0/x_0$ for any bundle (x_0, y_0), the equal-weighted CD result. By now, this assumption should seem pretty simple; back in Chapter 3, it was probably a bit of a stretch.)

Both Annie and Bob have an equal number of pieces of candy, but Annie has a very gummi-intensive bundle, and Bob has a very chocolate-intensive bundle. Each one trades with the other until their MRSs are equal. A variety of Pareto optimal outcomes are possible from this starting point (indeed, any barter exchange rate between 0.55:1 and 1.56:1 will produce a Pareto optimal outcome in this instance). Section 3.5 used a 1:1 barter exchange rate because the analysis was created to be as streamlined as possible. Given this 1:1 exchange rate and a starting point in which both have the same number of pieces of candy, a Pareto optimum occurs when each trades 35 units of the good they have more of for 35 units of the other good. Both individuals end up with half the candy, as shown in Figures 3.17 and 3.20. This solution is Pareto optimal, since the MRS is equal for each individual ($MRS_A(75, 70) = MRS_B(75, 70) = 0.93 = 70/75$).

An Edgeworth Box can also be used to show exchanges involving the purchase of goods. This is, perhaps, a bit more artificial than the barter analysis, since if there really are only two individuals and two goods, then it is probably not necessary to impose a price system on the analysis. (After all, we were able to completely describe two people exchanging one good for another without a price system in the barter analysis of Section 3.5.) Most of the time, we do not see people using barter as a medium of exchange, so it is useful to consider a price version of the Edgeworth Box analysis. The reason we do not see barter used more often is that barter requires putting people together who have goods or services they wish to exchange. Finding individuals who have what you want and who want something you have is difficult to do. More-complex exchanges can be accomplished if we consider each good to be worth a certain amount of money (i.e., each good has a price at which that good could be bought or sold). Then we can describe the value of each endowment in terms of the value of that person's endowment bundle. If the endowment bundle is $\mathbf{E} = (x^e, y^e)$, then the value of the endowment is $V(\mathbf{E}) = P_x x^e + P_y y^e$. This can be thought of as the "income" for the individual. This produces the following budget constraints for Annie and Bob:

$$\text{Annie's budget constraint:} \quad V_a(\mathbf{E_a}) = 40 \cdot P_x + 105 \cdot P_y = P_x x + P_y y. \tag{7.12a}$$

$$\text{Bob's budget constraint:} \quad V_b(\mathbf{E_b}) = 110 \cdot P_x + 35 \cdot P_y = P_x x + P_y y. \tag{7.12b}$$

The left-hand side of each budget constraint looks a bit unusual because each is the value of the endowment point. The endowment bundle is always affordable for each individual: Annie can always afford $\mathbf{E_a} = (40, 105)$, while Bob can always afford $\mathbf{E_b} = (110, 35)$. The budget constraint rotates on the endowment point as either price changes.

The only outstanding question is "What are the prices for x and y?" As discussed in Section 5.2, we are able to fix the budget constraint by setting one of the prices or incomes equal to a specific value. As a result, treat gummis as the numeraire, $P_y = 1$. Since a 1:1 exchange rate was used in Section 3.5, a useful starting point is to imagine that both x and y have the same price. $MRS = P_x/P_y$ in this instance is particularly easy, since $MRS = y/x$, and $P_x/P_y = 1$, so $x = y$. Under these circumstances, both Annie and Bob demand 72.5 units of each good ($72.5 = V_a(\mathbf{E_a})/2 = V_b(\mathbf{E_b})/2 = 145/2$). This is the situation depicted in Figure 7.12. *Notice that the line through the endowment point represents the budget constraint for both individuals.* For example, points to the northwest of **E** along the budget constraint represent Annie selling chocolate and buying gummis, *and* they also represent Bob selling gummis and buying chocolate. Prove this to yourself by turning your book upside down to look at the budget constraint from Bob's perspective (in this instance, the budget line has a y intercept of 145 and a slope of –1).

The initial set of prices does not clear either of the markets. Annie's optimal choice, given her endowment $\mathbf{E_a}$ and $P_x = P_y = 1$, is **A**, and Bob's optimal choice, given his endowment $\mathbf{E_b}$ and $P_x = P_y = 1$, is **B**. (Recall that every point in an Edgeworth Box is an allocation of resources, so that $\mathbf{E_a} = \mathbf{E_b} = \mathbf{E}$ in the Edgeworth Box.) Annie's demanded bundle **A** does not match Bob's demanded bundle **B** within the box; thus, *their joint*

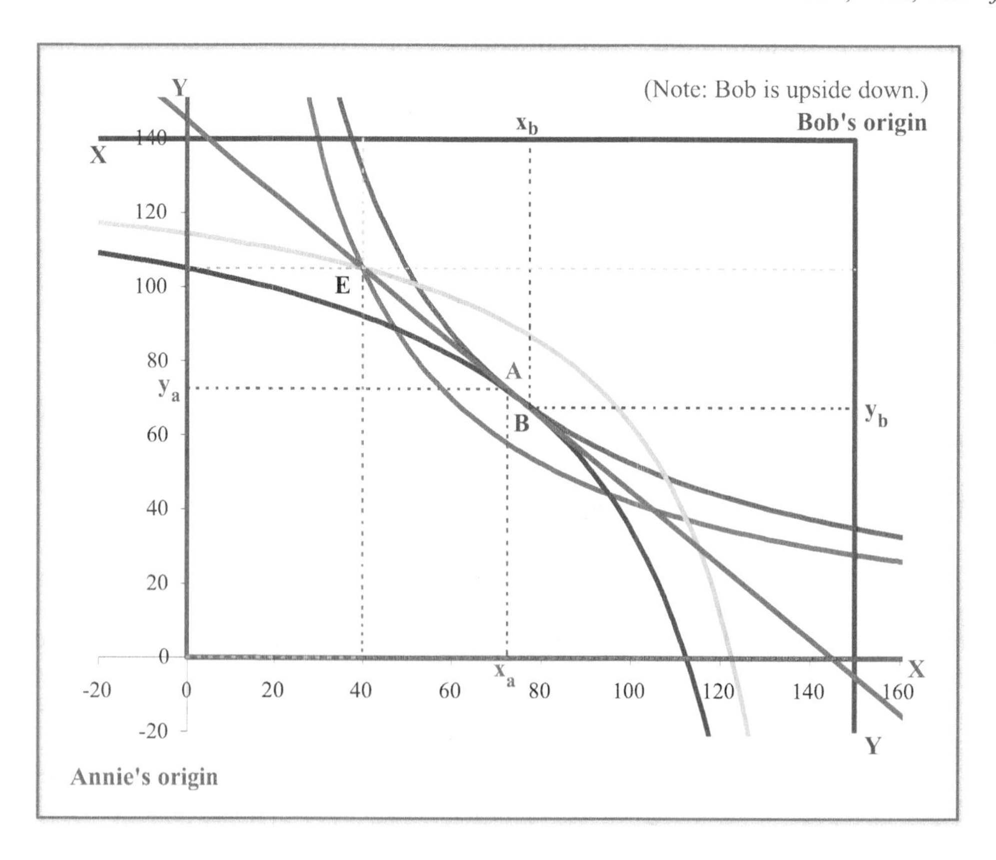

FIGURE 7.12 A Pricing Edgeworth Box: Initial Round of Pricing Consistent with Figure 3.20

In this instance, $P_x = P_y$.

demands are not a possible allocation of resources within this two-person economy. This is easiest to see by looking at each good separately.

Consider chocolate, x, first. Total demand for chocolate is 145 (145 = 72.5 + 72.5), but total supply is 150 (150 = 40 + 110); therefore, there is excess supply of chocolate. This is seen by adding x_a and x_b on the horizontal axis and comparing it with the total length of the box (the supply of chocolate). The units from $x_a = 72.5$ on Annie's horizontal axis to $x_b = 72.5$ on Bob's horizontal axis represent demand for all but 5 of the 150 units of available supply. The excess supply of chocolate is the horizontal distance between bundles **A** and **B** (between x = 72.5 and 77.5 *when measured along Annie's x axis*). Neither person demands these 5 units of chocolate.

The opposite occurs for gummis. Total demand for gummis is 145 (145 = 72.5 + 72.5) despite total supply of 140 (140 = 105 + 35). The units from $y_a = 72.5$ on Annie's vertical axis to $y_b = 72.5$ on Bob's vertical axis represent a double demand for 5 units of y. The excess demand for gummis is the vertical distance between bundles **A** and **B** (put on a single axis, these are the units from y = 67.5 to 72.5 *on Annie's y axis*). Both people demand these 5 units of gummis.

Excess demand in a market causes the price of the good to increase (gasoline lines, for instance). Excess supply in a market causes a buildup in inventories and puts downward pressure on price. Therefore, there is downward pressure on the price of chocolate and upward pressure on the price of gummis. Rather than examine individual price movements, consider what happens to the price ratio, P_x/P_y, as a result of these pressures. Downward pressure on the numerator and upward pressure on the denominator of a fraction cause the fraction to decline; P_x/P_y will decline. This process will continue until both markets clear.

The equilibrium price ratio will have no excess supply or excess demand. We use the equilibrium between total supply and total demand in each market to determine the equilibrium price ratio. Demand is based on MRS = P_x/P_y for each individual; therefore, the following equations hold for Annie and Bob:

$y_a = (P_x/P_y) \cdot x_a$ at Annie's optimal bundle. **(7.13a)**

$y_b = (P_x/P_y) \cdot x_b$ at Bob's optimal bundle. **(7.13b)**

Substituting Equation 7.13a into Equation 7.12a and dividing both sides by $2 \cdot P_x$, we obtain Annie's demand for x as a function of price ratio (after simplification):

$x_a = 20 + (105/2)/(P_x/P_y)$. **(7.14a)**

Similarly, from Equations 7.12b and 7.13b, we obtain from Bob's demand for x as a function of price ratio (after simplification):

$x_b = 55 + (35/2)/(P_x/P_y)$. **(7.14b)**

Adding Equations 7.14a and 7.14b together, we obtain aggregate demand for x as a function of price ratio:

$x_a + x_b = 75 + 70/(P_x/P_y)$. **(7.15a)**

At the equilibrium price ratio, demand equals supply in both markets. In particular, in equilibrium, the market for chocolate requires that $x_a + x_b = 150$. Substitute this into Equation 7.15a to obtain:

$150 = 75 + 70/(P_x/P_y)$. **(7.15b)**

Solving for P_x/P_y, we obtain the equilibrium price ratio:

$P_x/P_y = 70/75 = 14/15$. **(7.15c)**

As expected, the equilibrium price ratio declines from its initial value of $P_x/P_y = 1$, due to excess supply of x and excess demand for y. We use the equilibrium price ratio to determine Annie and Bob's constrained optimal bundles. Annie's x_a is obtained by substituting

Equation 7.15c back into Equation 7.14a, and her y_a is obtained by substituting this result into Equation 7.13a. This produces Annie's constrained optimal bundle, $\mathbf{C_a}$:

$$(x_a^c, y_a^c) = (76.25, 71.17). \tag{7.16a}$$

Bob's constrained optimum can be obtained in symmetric fashion using Equations 7.15c, 7.14b, and 7.13b. An easier solution is to recall that, in equilibrium, supply equals demand in each market (this only works if you have done your mathematics correctly; you can use this as a check on your work). Bob's constrained optimum bundle based on market clearing prices is $\mathbf{C_b}$:

$$(x_b^c, y_b^c) = (73.75, 68.83). \tag{7.16b}$$

Even though Annie and Bob start off with the same number of pieces of candy, market clearing prices lead to a Pareto optimal solution in which Annie is better off than Bob (since she has more of both goods). The reason this result occurs is straightforward: Annie's endowment is gummi intensive, and gummis are in shorter supply. Given equal-weighted CD preferences, the resulting equilibrium will necessarily place a higher price on gummis than chocolate, making her endowment bundle more valuable than that of Bob's.

It is worth noting that $MRS = y/x = P_x/P_y = 14/15$ for both individuals, based on these bundles. This is the solution depicted in Figure 7.13. Both Annie and Bob start at their individual endowment bundle, **E**, and then exchange y for x at the rate $P_x/P_y = 14/15$ along their personal budget constraint to achieve the constrained optimal bundle, **C**. The Excel file for Figure 7.13 allows you to see the dynamics of adjustment to the equilibrium price ratio. As you examine the dynamics of adjustment using this file, note that the budget constraint rotates on the endowment point as the price ratio changes.

The bundle obtained is a Pareto optimum, since $MRS_A = MRS_B$. The MRSs are equal because they both are equal to the equilibrium price ratio, P_x/P_y (in this instance, $14/15 = 0.93$). Interestingly, the same ratio holds for *all* Pareto optimal bundles, given the assumption of equal-weighted CD preferences and total resource endowment of (150, 140). All Pareto optimal outcomes in this instance are along the diagonal from Annie's origin to Bob's; all bundles along this ray have $MRS = 14/15$, since that is the ratio of y to x along this ray. (The last two problems in Workbook Chapter 3 asked you to examine this issue.)

FIGURE 7.13 A Pricing Edgeworth Box: Market Clearing Prices Consistent with Equal-Weighted CD Preferences (and endowments as shown)

$P_x = (14/15) \cdot P_y$

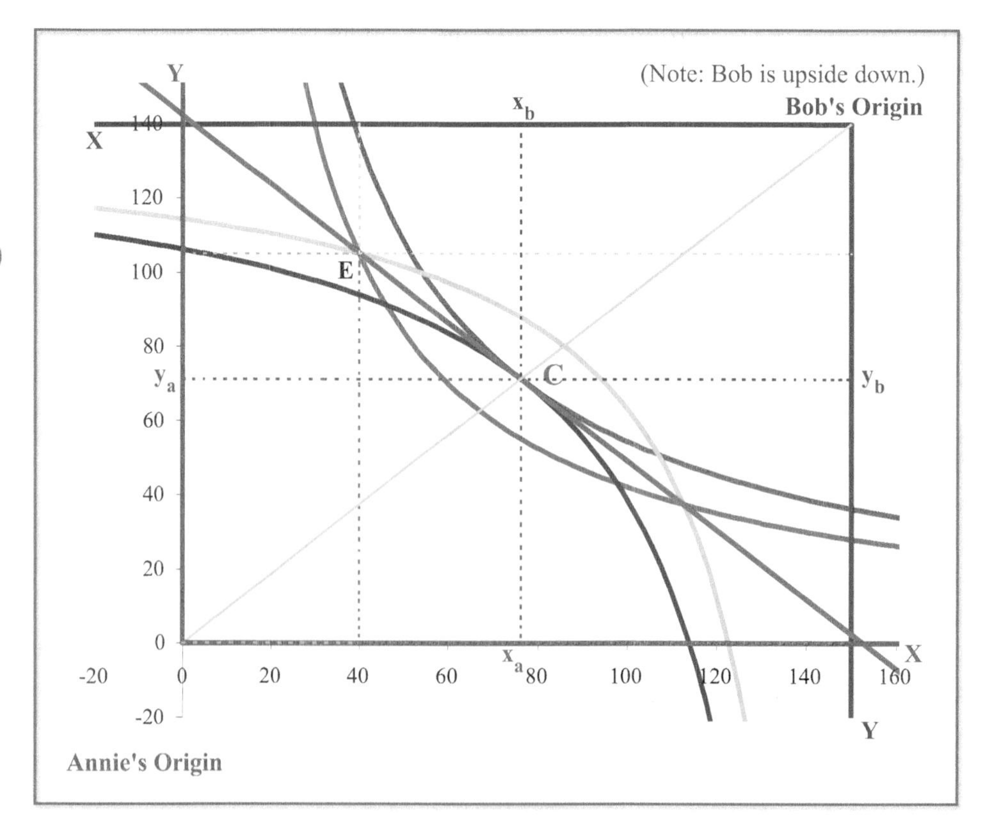

This provides an interesting counterpoint between the two solutions. Barter can, in theory, produce any of the Pareto optimal outcomes along the contract curve inside the Pareto superior "football" (line segment **AB** in Figure 3.20B). The location along **AB** depends on the barter exchange rate used between Annie and Bob. (As noted earlier, using the Excel file for Figure 3.20, we can show that this exchange rate is bounded by 0.55:1 and 1.56:1.) Outcomes closer to **A** occur if the barter exchange rate is closer to 0.55:1, in which event Annie is the dominant bargainer. Outcomes closer to **B** occur if the barter exchange rate is closer to 1.56:1, in which event Bob is the dominant bargainer. By contrast, the price system produces a single Pareto optimal outcome **C**, shown in Figure 7.13. **C** is unique among the Pareto optimal bundles on line segment **AB** in having a barter exchange rate that matches the Pareto optimal MRS. Both of these rates match the price ratio.[15]

7.5 Choice among Constraints Revisited: Getting a "Power Assist" from Excel *OPTIONAL SECTION*

You have at your disposal a very powerful tool that will assist you in economic analysis, and that tool is Excel. The third section of the Mathematical Appendix (available in the online version of this text) includes a short discussion of Excel, and that discussion goes into greater detail than this section. This very simplified introduction to Excel is provided in the context of helping to solve a problem you might be asked to solve for homework. You can obtain a solution without Excel, but it is much more tedious to do.

The present analysis revisits whether Steve should go to Washington, DC, to buy wine. This question was initially examined as Workbook Problem 6 in Chapter 5. This problem is formally equivalent to the choice among constraints analysis in Section 5.4 that examined whether you should join a warehouse store. We can use the demand information derived in Section 7.3 to further refine the analysis of choice among constraints.

The question of whether Steve should go to Washington, DC, to buy wine at a discount depends critically on how important wine is in his consumption mix. But that was not formally discussed in Chapter 5 because the focus there was on describing resource constraints. We make three basic assumptions about Steve's constraints:[16]

1. Steve has \$1,000 in disposable income to spend on wine, x, and other goods, y.
2. If he buys in Pennsylvania, the price of a bottle of wine is \$20. If he buys in Washington, DC, the price of wine is \$10. The price of y is \$1.
3. It costs Steve \$200 to go to Washington, DC.

Based on this, Steve has two potential budget constraints:

$$1{,}000 = 20 \cdot x + y \quad \text{if he stays in Pennsylvania, and} \qquad \textbf{(7.17)}$$

$$800 = 10 \cdot x + y \quad \text{if he goes to Washington, DC.} \qquad \textbf{(7.18)}$$

These budget constraints intersect at the bundle $(x, y) = (20, 600) = \mathbf{D}$. (This is easily obtained by solving for y in Equation 7.18 and substituting the result into Equation 7.17 to obtain $200 = 10 \cdot x$; therefore, $x = 20$.)

The method used in Chapter 5 to decide whether or not to go to DC was to simply decide how many bottles of wine Steve would purchase. If he plans to purchase more than 20 bottles of wine, he should go to DC, and if he plans to purchase fewer than 20 bottles of wine, he should stay in Pennsylvania.

Suppose Steve has Cobb-Douglas preferences over x and y: $\mathbf{U(x, y) = x^r \cdot y^{(1-r)}}$. We should be able to determine when Steve should go to DC, based upon the magnitude of r, the coefficient attached to wine. Clearly, the larger is r, the more likely Steve is to go to DC (recall from Equation 7.4a that *r is the proportion of income devoted to wine*). Steve's demand for x, based on Equation 7.3a, is $\mathbf{x(P_x, P_y, I) = r \cdot I/P_x}$. In this instance, the values of I and P_x depend on whether Steve goes to DC or stays in Pennsylvania.

When $r = 0.25$, Steve would choose the intersection bundle **D** upon going to DC because $20 = 0.25 \cdot \$800/\$10$. But he would have been better off to stay home, as we see

FIGURE 7.14 Steve Should Stay in Pennsylvania (based on $r = 0.25$ or $U(x, y) = x^{0.25} \cdot y^{0.75}$)

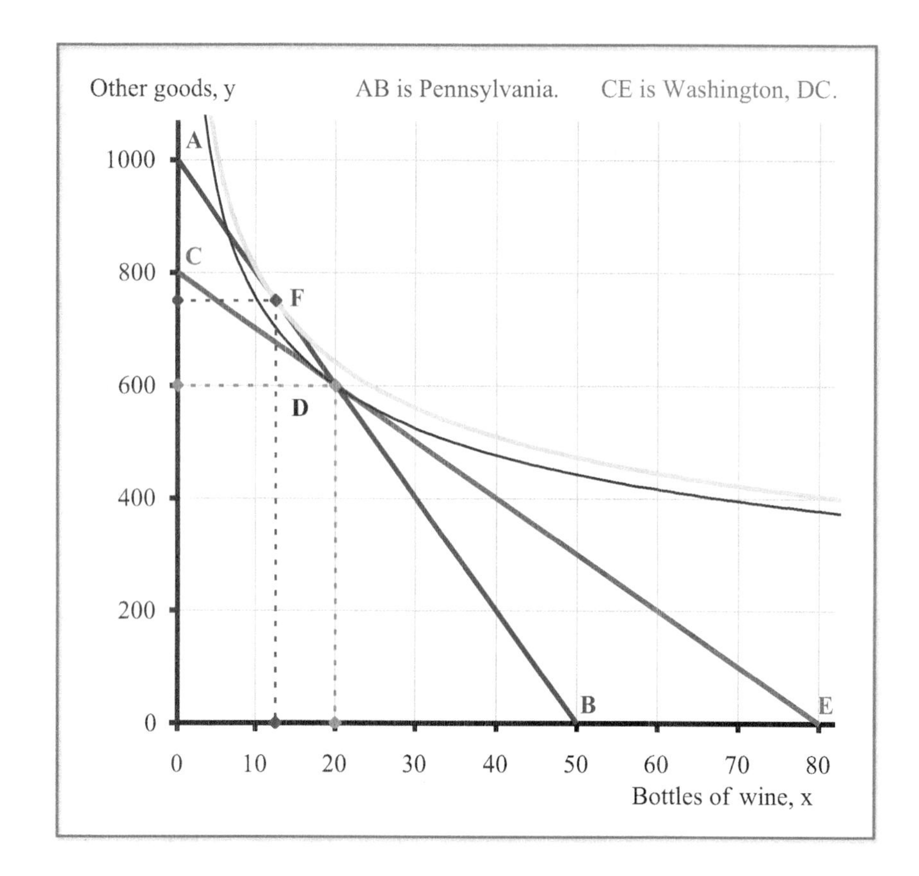

in Figure 7.14. With $r = 1/4$, Steve would demand **F** = (12.5, 750) if he stays in Pennsylvania (bundle **F** satisfies demand Equations 7.3a and 7.3b, given $I = \$1{,}000$, and $P_x = \$20$). This achieves a higher utility level because **F** is a tangency on **AD**; **F** is not a feasible consumption bundle if Steve goes to DC.

By contrast, when $r = 0.4$, Steve would choose the intersection bundle **D** if he stays in Pennsylvania (since $20 = 0.4 \cdot \$1{,}000/\$20$), but he would be better off by going to DC, as we see in Figure 7.15. With $r = 0.4$, Steve would demand **G** = (32, 480) if he goes to DC (bundle **G** satisfies demand Equations 7.3a and 7.3b, given $I = \$800$ and $P_x = \$10$). This achieves a higher utility level because **G** is a tangency on **DE**; **G** is not a feasible consumption bundle if Steve stays in Pennsylvania.

These figures provide us with two clear boundaries on Steve's behavior: When $r \leq 1/4$, Steve should stay in Pennsylvania because the Pennsylvania (constrained optimum) tangency along **AD** dominates the tangency along **CD** that he would get if he were to travel to Washington, DC. If he spends less than one-fourth of his discretionary income on wine, Steve should stay in Pennsylvania. Similarly, when $r \geq 0.4$, Steve should go to DC because the tangency along **DE** that he would obtain if he were to go to Washington, DC, dominates his Pennsylvania tangency along **DB**. If he spends more than 40% of his discretionary income on wine, he should go to DC.

The question remains: What happens when $1/4 < r < 0.4$? When r is between these two bounds, Steve will achieve tangencies under each option that are not feasible under the other option. In particular, his Pennsylvania tangency would be along **AD**, and his DC tangency would be along **DE**. The closer r is to 1/4, the more likely it is that Steve should stay in Pennsylvania, and the closer it is to 0.4, the more likely it is that he should go to DC to buy wine.

Just like the food-subsidy analysis in Section 6.3, there will be a value of r that produces indifferent tangent bundles along **AD** and **DE**; call this value of r, r*. If Steve's r is greater than r*, he should go to DC, and if his r is less than r*, he should remain in Pennsylvania. You could zero in on the value of r* where this occurs, using the demand

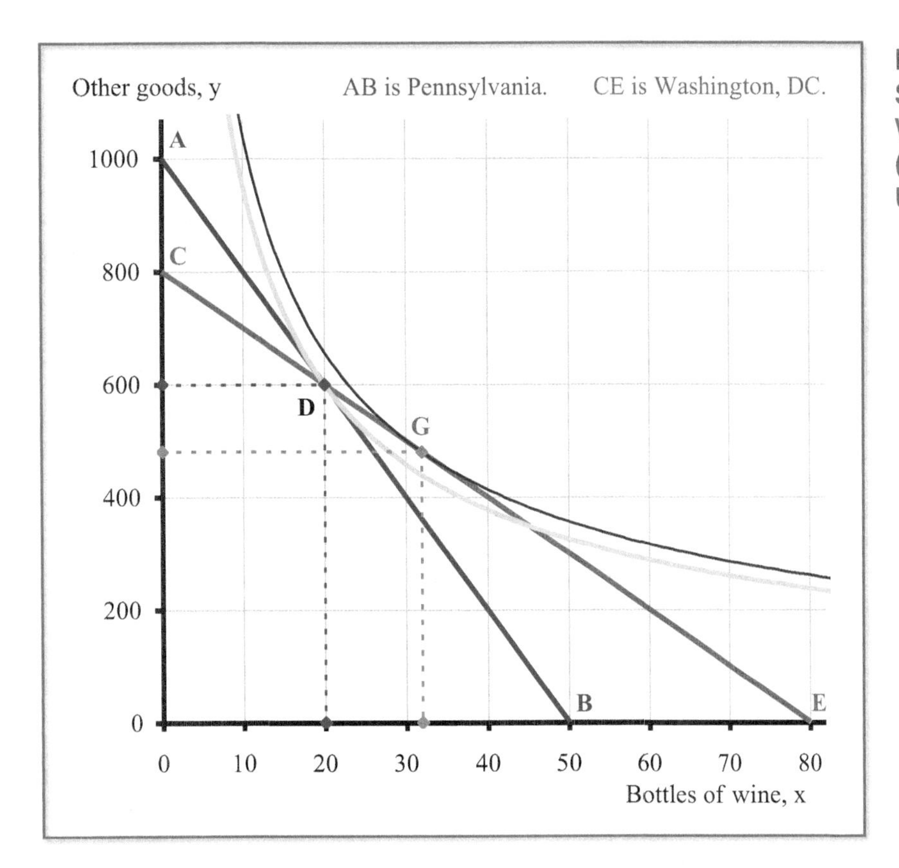

FIGURE 7.15 Steve Should Go to Washington, DC (based on r = 0.4 or $U(x, y) = x^{0.4} \cdot y^{0.6}$)

Equations 7.3a and 7.3b and the utility function to determine which option achieves a higher utility level. A better solution is to simply let Excel help you figure this out.

Table 7.1 has two parts. The upper part has numbers (and labels), and the lower part has numbers and equations. Both depict an actual Excel file you should open and use. *Cells within an Excel file are labeled according to their row and column location (rows are numbers and columns are letters).* The seven yellow cells have numbers from the problem typed into the cell; this is the data for the problem. For example, the number 200 typed into cell F1 represents the cost of going to DC. These seven pieces of data are used to create the other numbers in the spreadsheet (via the equations shown in the lower part of Table 7.1).

Before we see how those numbers are created, let's see what they say. The key cells are G3 and G4, which are the constrained maximum utility levels achieved by staying in Pennsylvania or by going to DC when r = 0.4 (from cell B1). Steve is better off going to DC since, as we argued earlier, his chosen bundle in this instance (x, y) = (E4, F4) = (32, 480) = **G** in Figure 7.15 dominates what he could attain were he to stay in Pennsylvania. (In Pennsylvania, he demands (x, y) = (E3, F3) = (20, 600) = **D**.) In terms of utility, U(**G**) > U(**D**), as seen by G4 > G3. This is exactly the scenario shown in Figure 7.15.

Each number in a white cell is calculated from the data in the yellow cells. For example, cell B4 shows that Steve's disposable income if he goes to DC is $800, since $200 must be subtracted from the gross income of $1,000 that is available if he stays in Pennsylvania. If you go to the Excel file for Table 7.1, cell B4 looks like it has 800 typed into the cell, but if you click on cell B4, you will see instead the equation =B3-F1 in the "Formula Bar" just next to the f_x above the column letters. (This is the equation for disposable income if Steve goes to DC. It equals Pennsylvania income less the cost of going to DC.) For ease of reference, these equations are shown in the lower part of Table 7.1.

Demand for x in Equation 7.3a, $r \cdot I/P_x$, is entered in Excel in cells E3 and E4. Demand for y in Equation 7.3b, $(1 - r) \cdot I/P_y$, is similarly entered in cells F3 and F4. Cobb-Douglas utility is calculated in G3 and G4 as $x^r \cdot y^{(1-r)}$. Once the seven equations have been entered

TABLE 7.1 Steve's Excel Sheet Evaluating a Choice among Constraints

This is what the Excel worksheet looks like that helps answer whether Steve should go to Washington, DC, or stay in Pennsylvania to buy wine.

	A	B	C	D	E	F	G	H
1	r =	0.4			cost going to DC =	200		
2		I	Px	Py	demand for x	demand for y	CD utility level, U	
3	PA	1000	20	1	20	600	153.9227268	PA
4	DC	800	10	1	32	480	162.4818045	DC
5						Upa-Udc =	-8.559077729	

The yellow cells are numbers that have been entered based on information in the problem. The other numbers in the upper part of the table are based on the equations shown in the lower part of the table. To type an equation, use an equals sign and then refer to a cell, type a number, or type a mathematical operator. For example, in cell B4, you want disposable income if going to DC. This is equal to total income less the cost of going to DC, so you would type =B3-F1.

	A	B	C	D	E	F	G	H
1	r =	0.4			cost going to DC =	200		
2		I	Px	Py	demand for x	demand for y	CD Utility level, U	
3	PA	1000	20	1	=B1*B3/C3	=(1-B1)*B3/D3	=E3^B1*F3^(1-B1)	PA
4	DC	=B3-F1	10	1	=B1*B4/C4	=(1-B1)*B4/D4	=E4^B1*F4^(1-B1)	DC
5						Upa-Udc=	=G3-G4	

in cells B4 and E3:G4 (the colon is the easy way to describe a block of cells), the r = 0.25 scenario depicted in Figure 7.14 can be obtained by changing the number in cell B1. The result is Table 7.2. Notice that changing one of the yellow cells automatically changes any calculations using that cell. In particular, changing B1 from 0.4 to 0.25 changes *every* calculated number *except* disposable income from going to DC (the 800 in Cell B4). This shows you some of the power of Excel; it does repetitive calculations very easily (and with less chance of making mistakes). As expected, based on the discussion of Figure 7.14, when r = 0.25, the DC constrained optimal bundle is **D**, just as the Pennsylvania optimal bundle was **D** when r = 0.4. This is seen by comparing cells E3:F3 in Table 7.1 with cells E4:F4 in Table 7.2.

The final equation (in cell G5) simply calculates the difference between the utility levels achieved in Pennsylvania and in DC. When this is greater than zero, Steve should not go to DC, and when this is less than zero, he should go to DC. This difference is provided to show you a *very* powerful tool in Excel's toolkit called *Goal Seek*.

Goal Seek is a function built into Excel that allows you to adjust the scenario to fit specifications you define. *We know that sounds abstract, but here is how it works.* You

TABLE 7.2 Steve's Choices with r = 0.25

	A	B	C	D	E	F	G	H
1	r =	0.25			cost going to DC =	200		
2		I	Px	Py	demand for x	demand for y	CD utility level, U	
3	PA	1000	20	1	12.5	750	269.478084	PA
4	DC	800	10	1	20	600	256.3722038	DC
5						Upa-Udc =	13.10588013	

have already defined a goal: You have been asked to determine the value r, such that going to DC and staying in Pennsylvania are equally useful; that is, you wish to find the value of r such that utility in G3 equals utility in G4. There are three ways to do this:

1. Without Excel, you could zero in on the value of r*, using the demand Equations 7.3a and 7.3b, and the utility function to determine which option achieves a higher utility level; then adjust your next guess accordingly.
2. With Excel, you could simply try values of r and adjust your next guess accordingly. (This is a semi-automated version of A.)
3. With Goal Seek, you let Excel find the solution.

Option 3 is faster than Options 1 or 2. Here are the steps you must follow to use Goal Seek:

1. Click on cell G5 with your mouse.
2. Click **Data, What If Analysis, Goal Seek** in Excel 2007 (or **Tools, Goal Seek** in Excel 2003). The **Goal Seek Popup Menu** will appear (see Exhibit 7.1). G5 is already located in the **Set cell** part of that menu.
3. Click on **To value** area in that menu. Type in 0. (You want there to be no difference between DC and PA utility levels, so set G5 to zero.)
4. Click on **By changing cell** area in that menu. Type B1. (Alternatively, you may click on cell B1, both methods do the same thing. If you click on B1, it appears as $B$1.)
5. Click **OK.**
6. Click **OK.**

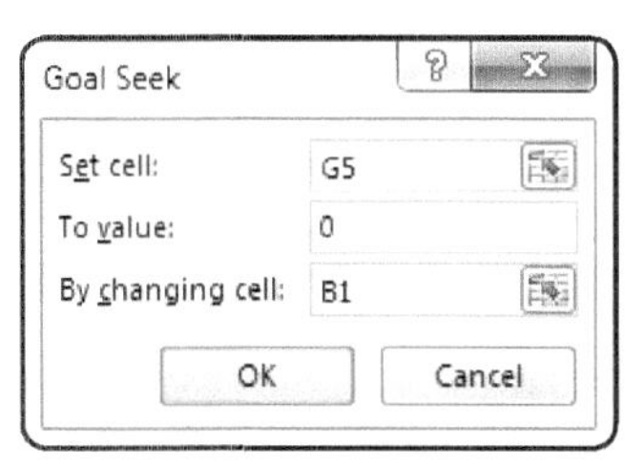

EXHIBIT 7.1 The Goal Seek Popup Menu

These steps produce Table 7.3. Table 7.3 tells us that r* = .3219 produces outcomes in which going to DC and staying in Pennsylvania produce two bundles that Steve finds equally interesting.[17] Of course, these bundles have quite different levels of consumption of x and y. You can see this result graphically in Figure 7.16.

Figure 7.16 was produced by the same process as Table 7.3; Goal Seek was imposed on the difference between utility levels achieved under the two outcomes. The resulting figure has the thin, red, DC indifference curve superimposed on the broad, light-blue, Pennsylvania indifference curve. Dashed lines denote the locations of the *two* optimal bundles at **P** and **W**. Neither bundle can be afforded under the other option; this diagram is formally the same as those shown in Figure 6.14, when an individual was indifferent between two food-subsidy programs. Here, Steve is indifferent between going to DC and staying in Pennsylvania to buy wine.

You could have gotten very close to this solution using the r slider on the Excel worksheet (the top slider shown in the Figure 7.14-16 worksheet). The arrowhead of this slider allows you to change r in increments of 0.001. As a result, you could have zeroed in on this result visually by adjusting the r slider and watching the resulting indifference curves.

Excel can do much more than this, and there are even more-elegant ways to do what has been shown. What was shown here, however, is a useful starting point because it shows some of the power of Excel and also how to use Goal Seek, a search tool built into Excel that allows you to quickly answer a variety of questions that economists typically ask.

	A	B	C	D	E	F	G	H
1	r =	0.3219			cost going to DC =	200		
2		I	Px	Py	demand for x	demand for y	CD utility level, U	
3	PA	1000	20	1	16.09639523	678.0720954	203.3708865	PA
4	DC	800	10	1	25.75423236	542.4576764	203.3708597	DC
5						Upa-Udc =	2.68305E-05	

TABLE 7.3 The Cobb-Douglas r Where Steve Is Indifferent between PA and DC, Obtained by Goal Seek

FIGURE 7.16 Steve Is Indifferent between Pennsylvania and Washington, DC (based on r = 0.3219 or $U(x, y) = x^{0.3219} \cdot y^{0.6781}$)

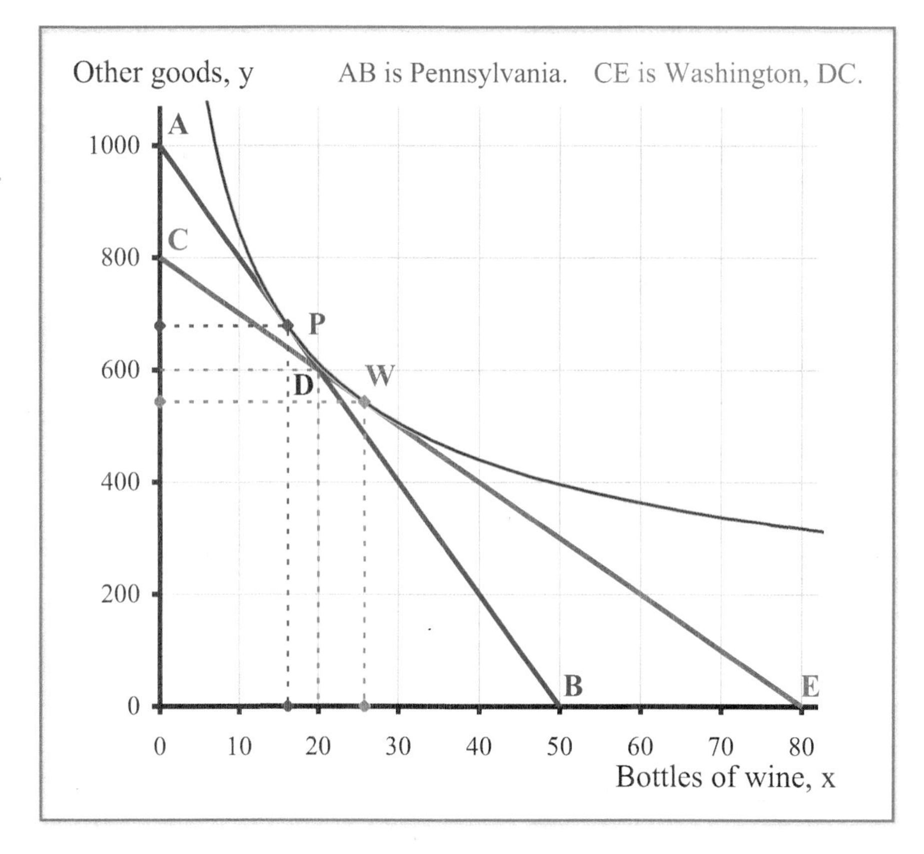

7.6. Mapping Income Changes: Income Consumption Curves and Engel Curves

When economists speak of demand, they typically focus on demand as a function of price, but as noted at the beginning of Section 7.3, demand is also a function of income. The graphical depiction of demand presented there is as a function of price, holding other prices and income fixed. In this section, we hold prices fixed and examine what happens to demand as income changes.

Economists have a number of terms to describe how demand changes as income changes. We begin by providing formal definitions of six terms that are attached to income changes. These definitions are based on the size of the income elasticity of demand, η (eta) (initially defined as Equation 2.4 and reproduced here):

$$\eta = \%\Delta x/\%\Delta I = (\Delta x/\Delta I)/(I/x) = ((I/x)/(\Delta I/\Delta x)). \quad \textbf{(7.19)}$$

Income elasticity is written in a variety of ways in Equation 7.19. The rightmost version is especially useful because it has a geometric interpretation that we explore a little later.

- A good is a **luxury** if $\eta > 1$. An increasing percentage of income is spent on the good as income increases.
- A good has **unitary income elasticity** if $\eta = 1$. A constant percentage of income is spent on the good.
- A good is a **necessity** if $\eta < 1$. A decreasing percentage of income is spent on the good as income increases.
- A good is **independent of income** if $\eta = 0$. Demand is independent of income.
- A good is **inferior** if $\eta < 0$. Demand for the good decreases as income increases.
- A good is **normal** if $\eta > 0$. Demand for the good increases as income increases.

These definitions may be viewed as creating two partitions of the income elasticity number line, as shown in "Equation" 7.20:[18]

luxury: A good is a luxury if $\eta > 1$. An increasing percentage of income is spent on the good as income increases.

unitary income elasticity: A good has unitary income elasticity if $\eta = 1$. A constant percentage of income is spent on the good.

necessity: A good is a necessity if $\eta < 1$. A decreasing percentage of income is spent on the good as income increases.

independent of income: A good is independent of income if $\eta = 0$. Demand is independent of income.

inferior: A good is inferior if $\eta < 0$. Demand for the good decreases as income increases.

normal: A good is normal if $\eta > 0$. Demand for the good increases as income increases.

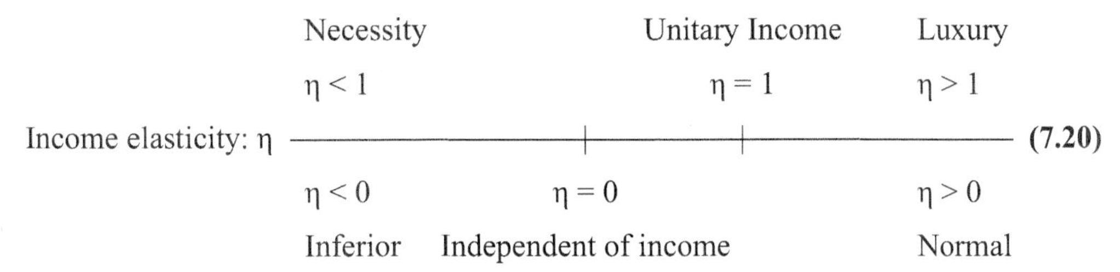

You may not have seen the $\eta = 0$ and $\eta = 1$ definitions, but the other four terms are commonly discussed in introductory microeconomics courses. (You may be used to seeing a definition that does not use income elasticity. The second sentence in each definition is an alternative definition that avoids using income elasticity.) The number line in Equation 7.20 makes it easy to see that, if a good is independent of income or if it is inferior, it is also a necessity (since if $\eta \leq 0$, it is also less than one). Similarly, a normal good may be a necessity, a good with unitary income elasticity, or a luxury.

We can describe the effect of an income change on x as a *shift* in demand for fixed prices of x and y. We can also examine the effect of income changes in the consumption diagram, using the income analog to the PCC, the **income consumption curve (ICC)**. The ICC is the set of consumption bundle tangencies for different incomes. (As with the PCC, there is not universal agreement on the name for this curve; some authors use the term *income expansion path* or *income offer curve*. We use *consumption* rather than *offer* or *expansion* to highlight that this curve describes consumption bundles (x, y).)

income consumption curve (ICC): The income consumption curve is the set of utility-maximizing consumption bundles associated with different levels of income (for fixed prices).

Economists also have an income analog to the demand curve for income changes. This curve is called an Engel curve. An **Engel curve** maps optimal levels of a good as a function of income. Just like price of x for the demand curve, income is placed on the vertical axis for the Engel curve.

Engel curve: An Engel curve maps optimal levels of a good as a function of income.

We have already examined income consumption curves in previous chapters (without calling it by that name). A pedagogical tool used in many of the figures in Chapters 4 and 6 included a yellow line in which the MRS was a constant (sometimes, that constant was 1; at other times, it was a general value P_x/P_y). These lines are the ICC for interior solutions, since MRS = P_x/P_y is required by interior constrained optimal solutions of the maximization problem (Equation 6.1Bi). Figures 6.5–6.11 include these yellow lines for each of the functional forms we have used in the text.

In general, we have seen that these constant MRS lines are (1) linear and (2) upward sloping in all cases except quasilinear—in which case, they are vertical. The graphs provided examples of each of the types of goods just defined except inferior goods. Indeed, the shifted CD form provides examples of the first three, as shown in Figure 7.17, and each of these is also normal. Figure 7.18 shows the fourth, using quasilinear preferences, and Figure 7.19 provides an example of preferences over an inferior good x. (The last two have separate figure numbers, since they are based on different functional forms.) Each panel has three graphs arranged in a vertical stack. This is not commonly done, and it is only done here so that you can see how the three graphs are tied to each other via a common x axis. The upper graph is in consumption space (x, y), and the lower graph is in demand space (x, P_x), just as in Section 7.3. The middle graph maps out an Engel curve: x consumption as a function of income. This is the new curve in each panel, and this is also the focus of much of our current attention. These graphs are shown together because a number of aspects of each consumption graph are common. For example, in each consumption graph, the red income level is below the blue income level, and only interior constrained optimal solutions are shown. This allows us to obtain some quick conclusions as we compare across graphs.

Before we turn to the direct description of the effect of income on demand for x via the Engel curve, it is worthwhile to examine some other general conclusions that we can obtain from upper and lower graphs. An increase in income (budget going from red to blue in the upper graph) *shifts demand* (in the lower graph) *out*, as long as $\eta > 0$ in Figure 7.17; has no effect on demand if $\eta = 0$, as in Figure 7.18; and *shifts demand in* if $\eta < 0$, as in Figure 7.19. Each ICC must eventually pass through the origin because the budget

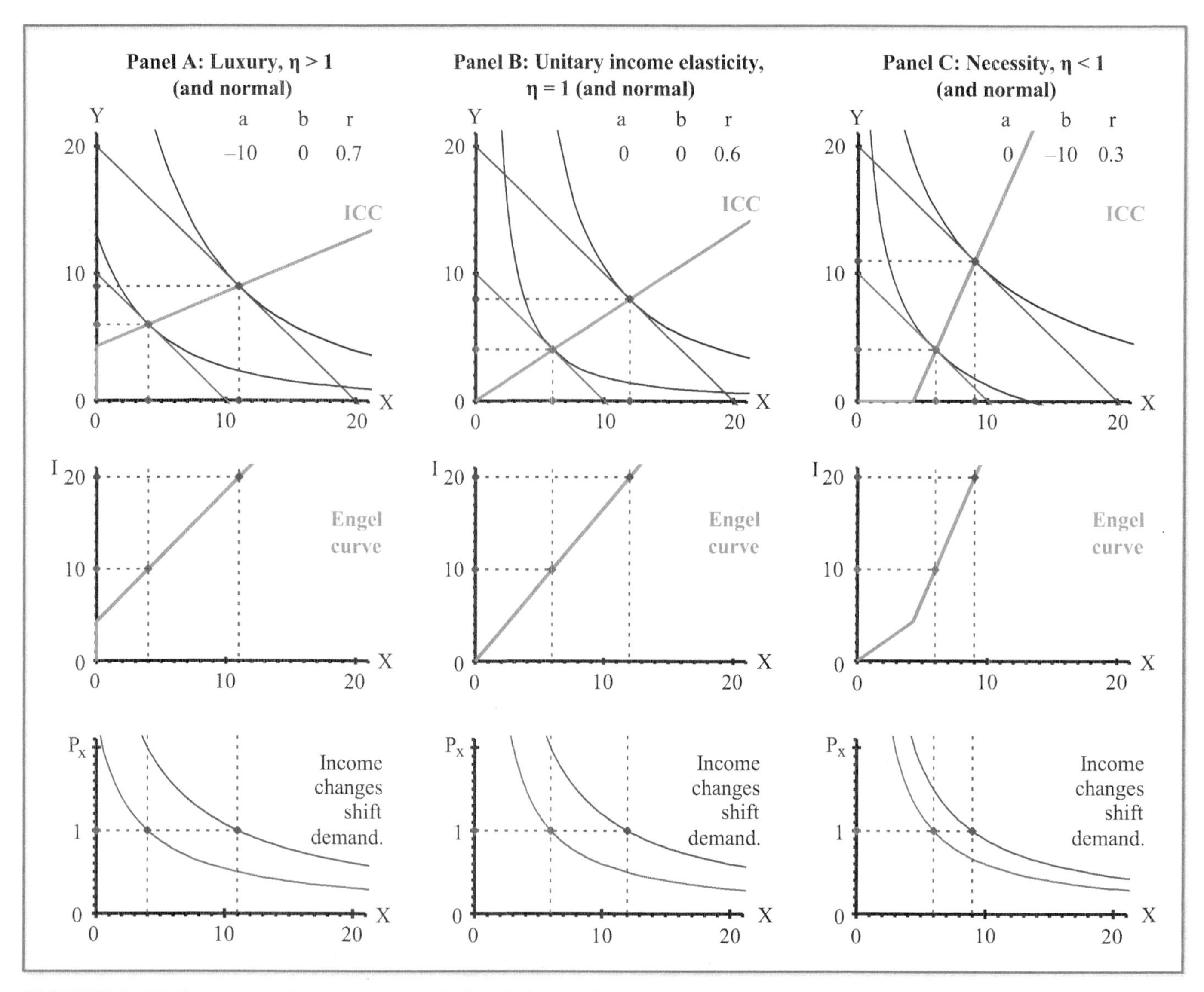

FIGURE 7.17 Income Changes with Shifted Cobb-Douglas Preferences (for income levels above the Engel curve kink)

constraint shrinks to the origin as income approaches zero (as long as both prices are positive). In each of the five panels except Figure 7.17B, the MRS = P_x/P_y set of bundles in the upper diagram does not go through the origin. As a result, in each of these panels, when income is low enough, the constrained optimum will be a boundary solution. These are the green segments of the ICC on the vertical axis in Figure 7.17A, and the horizontal axis in Figures 7.17C, 7.18, and 7.19. This shift from an interior solution to a boundary solution as income decreases leads to kinks in both the ICC and the Engel curve at this income level.

As the Engel curve in Figure 7.19 shows, an Engel curve need not be made up of linear segments. The linearity in the other examples shown is because the functional forms we have focused on in this text are simple enough that the MRS is constant along lines. Linear Engel curves are easily analyzed using the rightmost version of Equation 7.19: $\eta = ((I/x)/(\Delta I/\Delta x))$. The denominator, $\Delta I/\Delta x$, is the slope of the Engel curve, and the numerator, I/x, is the slope of the chord connecting the origin to a point on that curve (since slope is rise over run, and the chord connects the points (0, 0) and (x, I) so $\text{slope}_{\text{chord}} = I/x$). If the Engel curve is flatter than the chord, then $\eta > 1$:

$$\eta = ((I/x)/(\Delta I/\Delta x)) = (\text{slope}_{\text{chord}}/\text{slope}_{\text{Engel}}) > 1, \text{ if } \text{slope}_{\text{Engel}} < \text{slope}_{\text{chord}}. \quad (7.21)$$

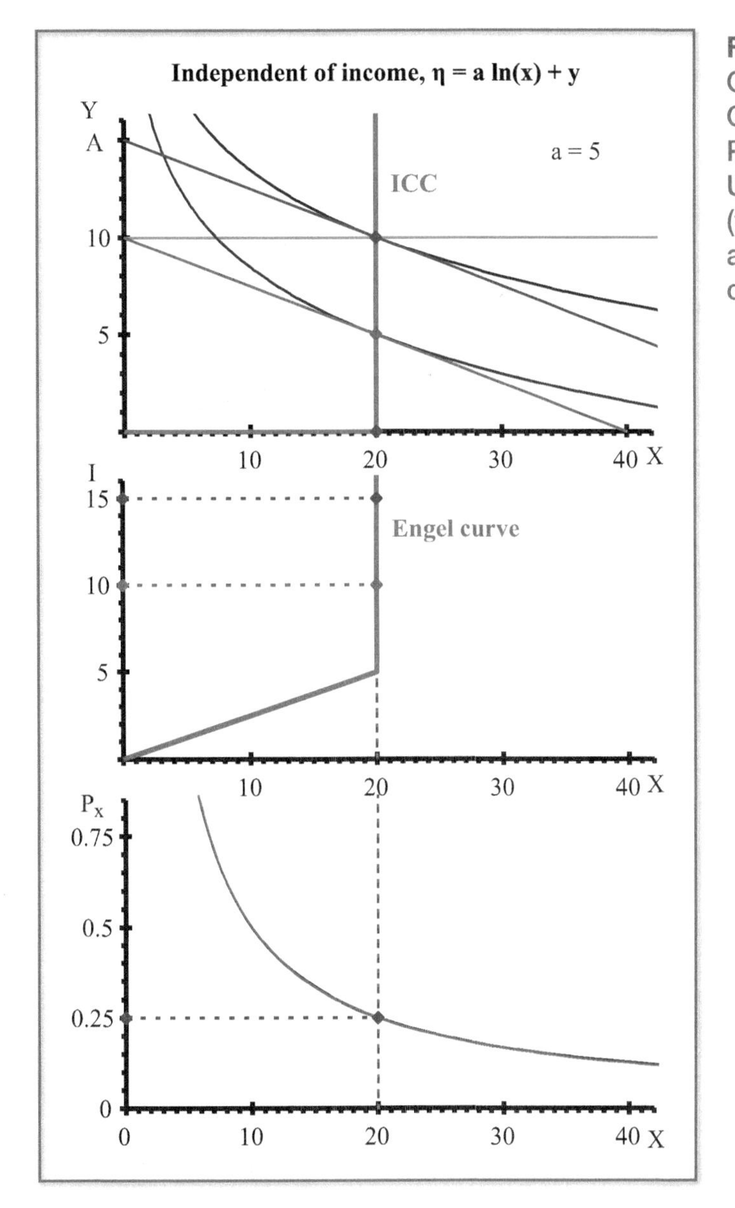

FIGURE 7.18 Income Changes with Quasilinear Preferences: $U(x, y) = a \cdot \ln(x) + y$ (for income levels above the Engel curve kink)

This is the situation shown in Figure 7.17A. Similarly, $\eta < 1$ if the Engel curve is steeper than the chord:

$$\eta = ((I/x)/(\Delta I/\Delta x)) = (\text{slope}_{\text{chord}}/\text{slope}_{\text{Engel}}) < 1, \text{ if slope}_{\text{Engel}} > \text{slope}_{\text{chord}}. \quad \textbf{(7.22)}$$

This is shown in Figure 7.17C.[19]

If the Engel curve is a line through the origin, it implies that x (and y) have unitary income elasticity (since $\text{slope}_{\text{Engel}} = \text{slope}_{\text{chord}}$ at all points on the Engel curve). Consumption of x and y increases proportionately with increases in income if the Engel curve is a line through the origin. This is the same as saying that both goods have unitary income elasticity. Cobb-Douglas preferences have constant unitary income elasticity, of course. We have known this for a while now; certainly, since we discussed Equation 7.4 earlier in this chapter. The same holds true for perfect substitutes and perfect complements, as can be seen by an examination of Equations 6.9 and 7.1.[20] X also has unitary income elasticity for the boundary-constrained optimum shown in Figures 7.17C, 7.18, and 7.19. For low income levels, all income is spent on x; as a result, η_x must equal one over this range of income. Once income has increased enough that the constrained optimum is an interior optimum, income elasticity need no longer remain unitary. In Figure 7.17C, $0 < \eta < 1$; in Figure 7.18, $\eta = 0$; and in Figure 7.19, $\eta < 0$.

FIGURE 7.19
Preferences with x as an Inferior Good (for income levels above the Engel curve kink)

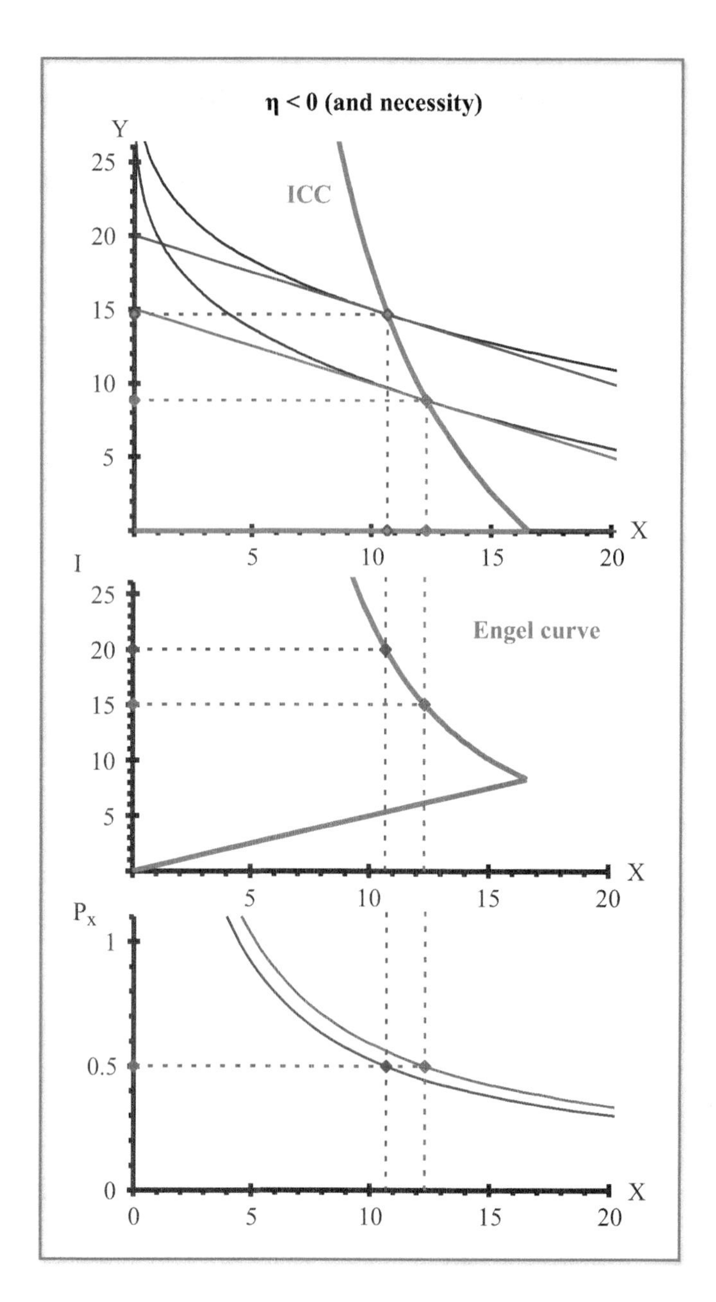

The sign of the slope of the ICC curve determines the sign of the income elasticity of demand. If the ICC is upward sloping, the good is normal (Figure 7.17); if the ICC is vertical, the income elasticity is zero (Figure 7.18); and if the ICC is downward sloping, the good is inferior and the income elasticity is negative (Figure 7.19).

In the two-good model, the income elasticity can also be seen indirectly in the consumption diagram, using the slope of the chord connecting the origin and a point on the ICC. As income increases, the constrained optimum moves outward from the origin along the ICC. By examining how the slope of the chord connecting the origin and points on the ICC changes as we move outward along the ICC, we can see whether consumption is becoming more or less x intensive. In Figure 7.17A, consumption becomes more x intensive, since the slope of the chord declines; x is a luxury, and y is a necessity. In Figure 7.17B, there is no change in x intensity, since the ray and chord coincide in this instance, regardless of income level. In Figures 7.17C, 7.18, and 7.19, the slope of the chord increases, moving away from the origin (once interior optimums are chosen). This implies that y intensity increases as income increases and that x intensity decreases as income increases for these goods; x is a necessity, and y is a luxury. Notice that, in each instance, if one good is a luxury, the other must be a necessity. The reason is straightforward: In a two-good world, a given percentage increase in income cannot lead to a more-than-proportionate increase in consumption of both goods, since this would require more income than is available. Further, a less-than-proportionate increase in both goods would mean that some income is left over—an outcome that would not occur in the presence of monotonic preferences. If one good is a luxury, the other must be a necessity. (Chapter 7 Appendix C provides a mathematical proof of this assertion.)

Summary

This chapter has focused on how individual demand is derived from preferences. As the price of a good changes, an individual adjusts consumption of goods to achieve the best outcome possible under the new, altered circumstances. This can be viewed directly in the consumption diagram used in the last four chapters, using the price consumption curve. A second way to view consumption behavior is to take a cross-price orientation and examine the issue of substitutes and complements. A third way to view consumption behavior is to take an own-price orientation and examine demand as a function of price.

Individual demand for a good is derived from the consumption diagram by mapping how the x coordinate of the optimal bundle changes as the price of x changes. The demand curve can be most easily seen by vertically stacking the consumption diagram and the demand diagram, since they share a common x axis.

Demand can also be derived algebraically, as the solution to the constrained optimization problem set up in Equation 6.1. The algebraic solution obtained there is a function of prices and income, as well as the parameters that are used to define each specific utility function. If the "other" price, income, and all the utility function parameters are held constant, then the demand curve can be seen as a univariate function of price. If both prices and all the utility function parameters are held constant, then the Engel curve can be seen as a univariate function of income. This is the symmetric notion to the more common concept of the demand curve, which holds "other" prices and income, as well as all the utility function parameters, constant. Price varies along a demand curve; income varies along an Engel curve.

Two applications of demand analysis are examined in this chapter; both use Cobb-Douglas preferences. Both applications revisit topics examined earlier in the text. The Edgeworth Box analysis is an outgrowth of the barter version of this analysis from Chapter 3, and the analysis of choice among options is a topic first examined in Chapter 5.

The results obtained from the Edgeworth Box analysis using prices are an interesting counterpoint to the results obtained in the barter version of exchange. The Pareto optimal solution obtained via barter need not match the Pareto optimal solution obtained via the price system. The price system forces a solution in which each individual's MRS matches the price ratio. Barter can lead to Pareto optimal solutions in which the barter exchange rate need not match the common MRS.

We can describe the optimal choice among options, using the underlying preferences of the individual rather than that individual's constraint set. We began this discussion in Section 6.3 in the context of food-subsidy programs, but we refined that analysis in this chapter based on demand functions. We also introduced you to using Excel to perform simple, repetitive calculations. Excel not only minimizes the mistakes you are likely to make when doing a series of calculations, but it also allows you to quickly determine when two options are equally valuable. This kind of break-even analysis is used in a number of settings in economics. For example, "how much does a firm have to produce to break even?" is exactly the same kind of question.

Review Questions

Define the following terms:

consumption diagram
demand diagram
price consumption curve
individual demand
demand curve
demand
luxury
unitary income elasticity
necessity
normal
independent of income
inferior
income consumption curve
Engel curve

Match the following phrases:

a. Demand increases more rapidly than income.
b. Demand increases less rapidly than income.
c. Demand increases as income increases.
d. Demand decreases as income increases.
e. The PCC is upward sloping.
f. The PCC is downward sloping.
g. The ICC is vertical.
h. The PCC is horizontal.
i. The ICC is a ray through the origin.

1. Demand is independent of income.
2. Normal
3. y is independent of x.
4. Necessity
5. Income elasticity is unitary.
6. Luxury
7. y is a substitute for x.
8. y is a complement of x.
9. Inferior

Provide short answers to the following:

a. What happens to demand if, at a given price of x, the constrained optimal tangency bundle is in the second quadrant (where x is negative and y is positive)?
b. What happens to demand if, at a given price of x, the constrained optimal tangency bundle is in the fourth quadrant (where x is positive and y is negative)?
c. What happens to demand as we move along an Engel curve?
d. Why does the demand curve for perfect substitute preferences have a horizontal segment?
e. Why is the PCC for perfect complement preferences a line segment?
f. Is it possible for a good to be both a luxury and inferior at the same time?
g. Is it possible for a good to be both a necessity and inferior at the same time?
h. Is it possible for a good to be both a necessity and normal at the same time?

Check your answers to the *matching* and *short-answer* exercises in the Answers Appendix at the end of the book.

Notes

1. By "income yardstick," we mean how much of a good can be purchased for a given percentage of income. This number changes on the x axis as the price of x changes; therefore, the income yardstick on this axis varies, but on the y axis, it does not because the price of y does not change in this analysis.

2. Preferences are also assumed fixed in this view. Since the discussion is typically market demand, we cannot talk about preferences as a monolithic concept. Individuals are allowed to have different preferences, and those preferences are assumed to be fixed. If they change—for example, if the Atkins diet causes a movement away from bread, rice, and potatoes—then this is reflected in shifts in demand for these goods.

3. If you are mathematically inclined, you may be puzzled by the orientation of a demand curve, since the independent variable in describing demand is price, and it is on the vertical axis. In math classes, you were taught to place the independent variable on the horizontal axis and the dependent variable on the vertical axis. Mathematicians write $y = f(x)$: x is the independent variable, and y depends on x via the function f. We do not follow mathematicians on this score because economists have been graphing this backward for more than a century now. As a result, we follow our earlier backward economists and put price on the vertical axis. An important benefit of this backward arrangement is that it allows the vertical stacking of two graphs that share a common x axis. This graphical device is central to this section of the text.

4. A different result occurs for the imperfect substitute preferences in Figure 7.2A. In this instance, the blue price would have to be six times the blue price to have $x = 0$. The focus in Figure 7.5 is on deriving the demand curve from the preference map, so an imperfect substitute utility function with less curved PCC was chosen to highlight this issue.

5. It is worthwhile recalling that this entire discussion is based on the price of y being held constant; the price differential causing demand for x to decline to zero is the price differential between x and y. The P_x^{red}/P_x^{blue} ratio has been discussed here simply as a way of talking about changes in the price of x without having to put dollar values on price.

6. It is easy to see that this would be the case. Suppose $a > 0$. If $P_x > I/a$, then $I/P_x < a$. The right-hand side of the inequality is the lower bound on bundles over which the shifted CD is defined (see Table 4.1); the left-hand side of the inequality is the amount of x that could be purchased if all income is spent on x.

7. Demand for y takes a couple of steps to derive. Plugging Equation 7.3a into Equation 7.2a yields:

$$P_y y = ((1 - r)/r) \cdot (P_x \cdot (r \cdot I/P_x)) = ((1 - r)/r) \cdot (r \cdot I) = (1 - r) \cdot I.$$

Dividing both sides by P_y yields 7.3b.

8. The same conclusion holds true regarding the effect of changes in the price of y on the demand for x, as can be seen in Equation 7.3a.

9. There are more-elegant mathematical methods to accomplish this task. The Lagrangian and substitution techniques discussed in the Chapter 6 Appendix are more elegant than Equation 6.1 but are based on equality constraints. As a result, the solution obtained must be checked to make sure $x \geq 0$, and $y \geq 0$, as just suggested. The Kuhn-Tucker method allows optimization subject to inequality constraints, but this technique is beyond the scope of this book. For a discussion of Kuhn-Tucker, see

Chapter 27 of Varian's advanced microeconomics text (Hal R. Varian, *Microeconomic Analysis*, 3d ed., 1992, W. W. Norton, New York).

10. Demand for y takes a few steps to derive. Plugging Equation 7.6a into Equation 7.5b yields:

$$P_y y = ((1 - r)/r) \cdot P_x \cdot [(r \cdot I + (1 - r) \cdot P_x \cdot a - r \cdot P_y \cdot b)/P_x] - ((1 - r)/r) \cdot P_x \cdot a + P_y \cdot b.$$

Simplifying:

$$P_y y = ((1 - r)/r) \cdot [(r \cdot I + (1 - r) \cdot P_x \cdot a - r \cdot P_y \cdot b)] - ((1 - r)/r) \cdot P_x \cdot a + P_y \cdot b.$$

Simplifying again:

$$P_y y = (1 - r) \cdot I - (1 - r) \cdot P_x \cdot a + r \cdot P_y \cdot b.$$

Dividing by P_y on both sides yields Equation 7.6d.

11. An alternative way to have obtained this would be to set $y(P_x, P_y, I) = I/P_y$ in Equation 7.6d (demand for x is zero if all income is spent on y) and solve for P_x. This works because x and y are on the budget constraint. You may be wondering whether $b \cdot P_y - I < 0$ as would be required, given $a < 0$. This is necessarily true because $b < I/P_y$ in order to have the y intercept feasible (recall from Table 4.1 that the function is only defined for $x > a$ and $y > b$). This provides a general solution to the boundary MRS discussed in Figure 7.5B and in Q2 about merlot prices for Figure 6.7.

12. We have not talked about changes in the price of y here, but consider the effect of a change in price of y on demand for x. The sign of b determines the sign of the cross-price elasticity of demand, $\varepsilon_{x,y} = \%\Delta x/\%\Delta P_y$. The results are symmetric to those described for a. Notice that these two cross-price elasticities need not be the same. They measure different concepts.

13. In Figure 7.10B, this occurs when, $I/P_x = (P_y \cdot a \cdot r/P_x)^{(1/(1-r))}$ with $I = 10$, $P_y = 1$, $a = 5$ and $r = 0.5$. Substituting these values into the equation yields $10/P_x = (2.5/P_x)^2$. Solving for P_x obtains $P_x = 2.5^2/10 = 0.625$.

14. This is similar to what happened at the point on the demand curve $(I/(3.5 \cdot P_x^0), 3.5 \cdot P_x^0)$ in Figure 7.5D, and at point (40, 0.25) on the demand curve in Figure 7.8. In each instance, this demarks the boundary between spending all income on one good and spending some income on each good.

15. The barter analysis presented in Section 3.5 ignored one important question in achieving the Pareto optimal outcomes from **A** to **B** in Figure 3.20. The question has to do with why an individual would choose to continue trading when such trades make the individual worse off in the barter solution. Consider, for example, Annie in the 35-for-35 barter exchange described in Section 3.5. This leads Annie to the Pareto optimal bundle (75, 70), but why would Annie trade past the bundle (72.5, 72.5) that is also achievable, given a 1:1 barter exchange rate, and is preferred to (75, 70)? One answer to this question is to imagine the trades as being offered in "chunks," rather than incrementally. A 35-for-35 trade is certainly better than doing nothing and remaining at **E**. But both individuals would prefer a different outcome in this instance: Annie would prefer to trade 32.5 gummis for 32.5 chocolates, and Bob would prefer to trade 37.5 chocolates for 37.5 gummis; this is why we might imagine that they both can agree to trade 35 gummis for 35 chocolates.

Similar arguments could be made for each barter exchange rate; some, however, are harder to justify. For example, consider the "Annie takes all" rate of 0.55:1 that produces bundle **A**. Use the price slider and set $P_x = 0.55$, the same rate as the barter exchange rate. The disequilibrium solution shown in this situation suggests that Bob would choose to exchange 22.9 chocolates for 12.5 gummis, rather than move all of the way to bundle **A**. Annie would have to be a *very* good bargainer to make Bob willing to make twice as large a trade (45.8 chocolates for 25 gummis) that leaves Bob indifferent to **E** rather than stop at any intermediate exchange. (By strict convexity, each intermediate bundle is preferred to the endpoints.) Section 20.6 examines the basics of bargaining.

16. Two of these numbers are different from those used in Chapter 5. In Chapter 5, the Washington, DC, price was $15 and a cost of going to DC of $100 (numbers that more accurately reflect price differences in these two locations). We have adjusted the numbers so that the analysis is easier to discuss and visualize. The Excel file for Figure 7.14 allows you to examine other versions as well.

17. Do not be bothered by the number of digits being shown (and by the fact that utilities are not equal, once you go out five decimal places). You can clean that up with Excel, but it was not cleaned up here so that you can see what the "raw" Excel output looks like. Goal Seek's search routine looks for an answer that is "close enough" to an exact answer.

18. Economists do not universally agree on these definitions. Some economists restrict necessities to those goods with income elasticity between 0 and 1.

19. Chapter 7 Appendix A examines the general conditions under which shifted Cobb-Douglas preferences lead to x being a luxury, unitary income elasticity, or a necessity.

20. Chapter 7 Appendix B provides a mathematical description of what is required to have preferences in which each good maintains unitary income elasticity, regardless of price ratio.

Appendix A:

Luxuries and Necessities with Shifted CD Preferences

This appendix derives conditions under which x is a luxury or a necessity, given shifted CD preferences. We have seen that shifted CD preferences have linear ICCs. We also have seen geometrically from Figure 7.17 that one of the three conditions holds:

1. If the ICC intersects the positive part of the y axis, then x is a luxury and y is a necessity (as in Figure 7.17A);
2. If the ICC intersects the x and y axes at the origin, then x and y both have unitary income elasticity (as in Figure 7.17B); and
3. If the ICC intersects the positive part of the x axis, then y is a luxury and x is a necessity (as in Figure 7.17C).

One way to examine when each of these conditions will occur is to ask: What is the value of y along the ICC when demand for x is zero? If the value of y is positive, then condition 1 holds; if the value of y is zero, then condition 2 holds; and if the value of y is negative, then condition 3 holds. From the demand for x, Equation7.6b, we know that x = 0 if:

$$r \cdot I/P_x = r \cdot b \cdot P_y/P_x - (1 - r) \cdot a. \qquad \textbf{(7A.1a)}$$

Solving for I, we obtain the income required for demand for x to be zero:

$$I = b \cdot P_y - ((1 - r)/r) \cdot a \cdot P_x. \qquad \textbf{(7A.1b)}$$

Substituting this value of income in place of I in the demand for y (Equation 7.6e), we obtain:

$$y = (1 - r) \cdot [b \cdot P_y - ((1 - r)/r) \cdot a \cdot P_x]/P_y - (1 - r) \cdot a \cdot P_x/P_y + r \cdot b. \qquad \textbf{(7A.2a)}$$

Simplifying, we obtain:

$$y = b - ((1 - r)/r) \cdot (a \cdot P_x/P_y). \qquad \textbf{(7A.2b)}$$

The sign of y is the same as the sign of $r \cdot P_y y$, so we can multiply both sides of Equation 7A.2b by $r \cdot P_y$ to obtain:

$$r \cdot P_y \cdot y = r \cdot b \cdot P_y - (1 - r) \cdot a \cdot P_x. \qquad \textbf{(7A.2c)}$$

Since r, P_x, and P_y are all positive, the sign of the difference in Equation 7A.2c depends on the signs and relative magnitudes of the intercept shift factors *a* and b. The sign of y may be restated as:

y is positive if	$r \cdot b \cdot P_y > (1 - r) \cdot a \cdot P_x$.	This is condition 1.	**(7A.3a)**
y is zero if	$r \cdot b \cdot P_y = (1 - r) \cdot a \cdot P_x$.	This is condition 2.	**(7A.3b)**
y is negative if	$r \cdot b \cdot P_y < (1 - r) \cdot a \cdot P_x$.	This is condition 3.	**(7A.3c)**

The conditions required by Equation 7A.3 depend on the values of five parameters: the intercept shift factors *a* and b, the relative intensity factor r, and the prices of x and y. The Excel file for Figure 7.17 allows you to manipulate *a*, b, and r and see the resulting ICC. (The ICC in the Excel file is based on the simplifying assumption that $P_x = P_y$.) We can further reduce the dimensionality of the problem if we assume that nonzero intercept shift factors are equal to one another. In this event, the previous conditions may be summarized in tabular form (see Table 7A.1). It would be worthwhile to verify the assertions in Table 7A.1 graphically, using the Excel file for Figure 7.17.

TABLE 7A.1 Parameter Conditions Required for Luxuries and Necessities with Shifted CD Preferences

This table assumes that if $P_x = P_y$ and given		$a = b > 0$	$a = 0$	$a = b < 0$
Then,	1. x is a luxury and y is a necessity if	r > 0.5	b > 0	r < 0.5
	2. x and y have unitary income elasticity if	r = 0.5	b = 0	r = 0.5
	3. x is a necessity and y is a luxury if	r < 0.5	b < 0	r > 0.5

Appendix B:

Homogeneous and Homothetic Functions

A function $f(\mathbf{X})$ is **homogeneous of degree k** if

$$f(t \cdot \mathbf{X}) = t^k \cdot f(\mathbf{X}). \quad \textbf{(7B.1a)}$$

homogeneous of degree k: A function $f(\mathbf{X})$ is homogeneous of degree k if $f(t \cdot \mathbf{X}) = t^k \cdot f(\mathbf{X})$.

Given $\mathbf{X} = (x_1, \ldots, x_n)$ and $t \cdot \mathbf{X} = (t \cdot x_1, \ldots, t \cdot x_n)$, Equation 7B.1a may be rewritten as:

$$f(t \cdot x_1, \ldots, t \cdot x_n) = t^k \cdot f(x_1, \ldots, x_n). \quad \textbf{(7B.1b)}$$

A function $g(\mathbf{X})$ is **homothetic** if it is a positive monotonic transformation of a homogeneous function.

homothetic: A function $g(\mathbf{X})$ is homothetic if it is a positive monotonic transformation of a homogeneous function.

Homogeneous and homothetic functions have a number of useful properties. As a general statement, homogeneous functions have cardinality and therefore are used in producer theory, due to the cardinality implicit in production functions. Homothetic functions are ordinal generalizations of homogeneous functions that are commonly encountered in consumer theory because utility functions are ordinal. (Utility functions that only differ by monotonic transformation represent the same preferences for reasons discussed at length in Section 4.3.) Any function that is homogeneous is also homothetic, but the reverse is not true.

The Geometry of Homothetic Functions

Homothetic functions (and hence homogeneous functions as well) have a *proportional expansion property*.

Claim: *The slope of the level sets of the function is constant on rays through the origin.*

In the context of consumer theory, this means that income expansion paths are rays through the origin for preferences that are homothetic. The ray through the origin and bundle $\mathbf{X}$ is described by the set of bundles $\mathbf{Y} = t \cdot \mathbf{X}$ with $t \geq 0$. We can show that the "j, i" slope of the level set is constant on a ray through the origin by differentiating with respect to x_i and x_j, and taking the ratio of these partial derivatives to obtain $MRS_{j,i}$.

Let $g(\mathbf{X})$ be homothetic, then $g(\mathbf{X}) = h(f(\mathbf{X}))$, where $h(f)$ is a monotonic increasing function and $f(\mathbf{X})$ is homogeneous of degree k. Differentiate g at the bundle $\mathbf{Y} = t \cdot \mathbf{X}$ with respect to x_i:

$$\partial g(\mathbf{Y})/\partial x_i = \partial g(t \cdot \mathbf{X})/\partial x_i. \quad \textbf{(7B.2a)}$$

$$\partial g(\mathbf{Y})/\partial x_i = (dh/df) \cdot (\partial f(t \cdot \mathbf{X})/\partial x_i). \quad \textbf{(7B.2b)}$$

But we know that $f(t \cdot \mathbf{X}) = t^k \cdot f(\mathbf{X})$ because f is homogeneous of degree k. The derivative of the right-hand side with respect to x_i is therefore:

$$\partial g(\mathbf{Y})/\partial x_i = (dh/df) \cdot (\partial(t^k \cdot f(\mathbf{X}))/\partial x_i). \quad \textbf{(7B.2c)}$$

The product rule applied to $t^k \cdot f(\mathbf{X})$ implies that Equation 7B.2c simplifies to:

$$\partial g(\mathbf{Y})/\partial x_i = (dh/df) \cdot t^k \cdot (\partial f(\mathbf{X})/\partial x_i). \quad \textbf{(7B.2d)}$$

The partial with respect to x_j is obtained by replacing *i* with j in Equation 7B.2d:

$$\partial g(\mathbf{Y})/\partial x_j = (dh/df) \cdot t^k \cdot (\partial f(\mathbf{X})/\partial x_j). \quad \textbf{(7B.3)}$$

If $g(\mathbf{X})$ represents a utility function, the ratio of partial derivatives is MRS evaluated at the point under consideration. Suppose $\mathbf{Y} = t \cdot \mathbf{X}$; then we can use Equations 7B.2d and 7B.3 to show that MRS is constant on rays through the origin:

$$MRS_{j,i}(\mathbf{Y}) = [\partial g(\mathbf{Y})/\partial x_i]/[\partial g(\mathbf{Y})/\partial x_j].$$

$$MRS_{j,i}(\mathbf{Y}) = [(dh/df) \cdot t^k \cdot (\partial f(\mathbf{X})/\partial x_i)]/[(dh/df) \cdot t^k \cdot (\partial f(\mathbf{X})/\partial x_j)].$$

$$MRS_{j,i}(\mathbf{Y}) = [\partial f(\mathbf{X})/\partial x_i]/[\partial f(\mathbf{X})/\partial x_j].$$

$$MRS_{j,i}(\mathbf{Y}) = MRS_{j,i}(\mathbf{X}) \text{ whenever } \mathbf{Y} = t \cdot \mathbf{X}. \quad \textbf{(7B.4)}$$

Since this is true for *any* **X**, Equation 7B.4 states that MRS is constant on *any* ray through the origin.

The ICC is the set of tangencies between indifference curve and budget constraint for different levels of income. If preferences are represented by a homothetic utility function, we see that the ICC will be a ray through the origin because MRS = P_x/P_y and Equation 7B.4 states that MRS is constant on each ray through the origin.

Another implication of homothetic functions is that if U(**X**) represents the individual's preferences, and if U is homothetic, then $\mathbf{X} \succ \mathbf{Y}$ if and only if $t \cdot \mathbf{X} \succ t \cdot \mathbf{Y}$. The reasoning is straightforward: If U(**X**) represents $\succ$, and $\mathbf{X} \succ \mathbf{Y}$, then $U(\mathbf{X}) > U(\mathbf{Y})$. But this implies that a "t" expansion or contraction of bundle **X** also is preferred to the same contraction or expansion of the **Y** bundle: $t \cdot \mathbf{X} \succ t \cdot \mathbf{Y}$ because $U(t \cdot \mathbf{X}) = t^k \cdot U(\mathbf{X}) > t^k \cdot U(\mathbf{Y}) = U(t \cdot \mathbf{Y})$. This is sometimes described as the proportional expansion property of homothetic functions. Imagine you are positioned at the center of a balloon. As the balloon is blown up, the surface of the balloon gets farther and farther away from you, but the slope of the balloon's surface in any given direction does not change. That is proportional expansion.

Examples

Homogeneous of degree:	**1**	**2**	**k**
f(x, y) =	$x^r \cdot y^{1-r}$	$x \cdot y$	$x^a \cdot y^{k-a}$ for $0 < a < k$.
	$\min(a \cdot x, b \cdot y)$	$\min((a \cdot x)^2, (b \cdot y)^2)$	$\min((a \cdot x)^k, (b \cdot y)^k)$.
	$a \cdot x + b \cdot y$	$(a \cdot x + b \cdot y)^2$	$(a \cdot x + b \cdot y)^k$.

Each should be readily recognizable as CD, perfect complements, and perfect substitutes. Each of the previous functions can be made homothetic but not homogeneous by applying a monotonic transformation of the function f. The function remains homothetic but is no longer homogeneous if the monotonic transformation adds a constant, or by taking logarithms, for example. Thus, $g(x, y) = r \cdot \ln(x) + (1 - r) \cdot \ln(y)$ is homothetic but not homogeneous. The level sets obtained from this function (indifference curves) are identical to those obtained from $f(x, y) = x^r \cdot y^{1-r}$, but the numerical values attached to those curves are related via the monotonic transformation $g(f) = \ln(f)$.

Appendix C:

Proof That Not All Goods Can Be Luxuries

This appendix derives an elegant equation that can be used to prove that not all goods can be luxuries. Without loss of generality, we can work within a two-good model. Within a two-good model, we wish to examine the reason why, if x is a luxury, then y must be a necessity. As noted at the end of Section 7.6, this result is based on consuming along the budget constraint.

A utility-maximizing consumer will consume on the budget constraint (as long as preferences are monotonic):

$$P_x x + P_y y = I. \quad \textbf{(7C.1)}$$

Differentiating the budget constraint with respect to income produces the following:

$$P_x \cdot dx/dI + P_y \cdot dy/dI = 1. \quad \textbf{(7C.2)}$$

This simply says that a consumer will continue to spend all of personal income by altering consumption of x and y so that the incremental income is spent. Multiply the first term by $(I \cdot x)/(I \cdot x)$ and the second term by $(I \cdot y)/(I \cdot y)$ and regroup to obtain:

$$(P_x x/I) \cdot ((dx/dI) \cdot (I/x)) + (P_y y/I) \cdot ((dy/dI) \cdot (I/y)) = 1. \quad \textbf{(7C.3a)}$$

Both terms have two components. The first component is the proportion of income spent on the good (for x and y), and the second is the income elasticities of demand (for x and y). If we denote shares of income devoted to each good by $s_x = P_x x/I$ and $s_y = P_y y/I$, and income elasticities by $\eta_x = (dx/dI) \cdot (I/x)$ and $\eta_y = (dy/dI) \cdot (I/y)$, then we can rewrite Equation 7C.3a as:

$$s_x \cdot \eta_x + s_y \cdot \eta_y = 1. \quad \textbf{(7C.3b)}$$

Since all income is spent, we know that the sum of the shares of income spent on x and y will be 100%. Put another way, $s_x + s_y = 1$. (This is easily obtained by dividing both sides of the budget constraint, Equation 7C.1 by I.) We may therefore rewrite 7C.3b as:

$$s_x \cdot \eta_x + (1 - s_x) \cdot \eta_y = 1. \quad \textbf{(7C.3c)}$$

Equation 7C.3c implies that if one good has unitary income elasticity, then so does the other. Assume that this is not the case. In this event, one of the goods must be a luxury (because otherwise, not all income will be spent). Without loss of generality, suppose x is a luxury, $\eta_x > 1$. Equation 7C.3c says that the number 1 is a weighted average or convex combination of η_x and η_y. A weighted average must be between the boundary numbers η_x and η_y. This assertion is easy to prove. The share spent on y cannot equal zero (since then $s_x = 1$ and $s_x \cdot \eta_x = \eta_x = 1$), so $s_x < 1$. We may therefore solve for η_y in Equation 7C.3c by regrouping and dividing by $1 - s_x$ to obtain:

$$\eta_y = (1 - s_x \cdot \eta_x)/(1 - s_x). \quad \textbf{(7C.4a)}$$

Given $\eta_x > 1$, we wish to show that $\eta_y < 1$. Subtracting 1 from each side of Equation 7C.4a and creating a common denominator for the fraction, we obtain:

$$\begin{aligned}
\eta_y - 1 &= (1 - s_x \cdot \eta_x)/(1 - s_x) - (1 - s_x)/(1 - s_x). \\
&= ((1 - s_x \cdot \eta_x) - (1 - s_x))/(1 - s_x). \\
&= [s_x \cdot (1 - \eta_x)]/(1 - s_x). \quad \textbf{(7C.4b)} \\
&= [+ \cdot (-)]/(+) < 0.
\end{aligned}$$

If $\eta_y - 1 < 0$ then $\eta_y < 1$.

Given $\eta_x > 1$, Equation 7C.3c therefore implies:

$$\eta_x > 1 > \eta_y. \tag{7C.5}$$

Equation 7C.5 says that if x is a luxury, then y must be a necessity. We saw an example of this result in Chapter 7 Appendix A and in Figure 7.17. When x was a luxury, y was a necessity (in Figure 7.17A), and when x was a necessity, y was a luxury (in Figure 7.17C).

The equation that provides us with this result is Equation 7C.3b. This equation states that a convex combination of income elasticities always equals one. This may be generalized to n goods:

$$1 = s_1 \cdot \eta_1 + \ldots + s_n \cdot \eta_n. \tag{7C.6}$$

If all but one of these goods are a luxury, then the last must be a necessity. Similarly, if we assume that preferences are well behaved, then if all but one of the goods are a necessity, then the last must be a luxury. Each of these results is based on the notion that the consumer will remain on the budget constraint as income changes.

Decomposing Demand

CHAPTER 8

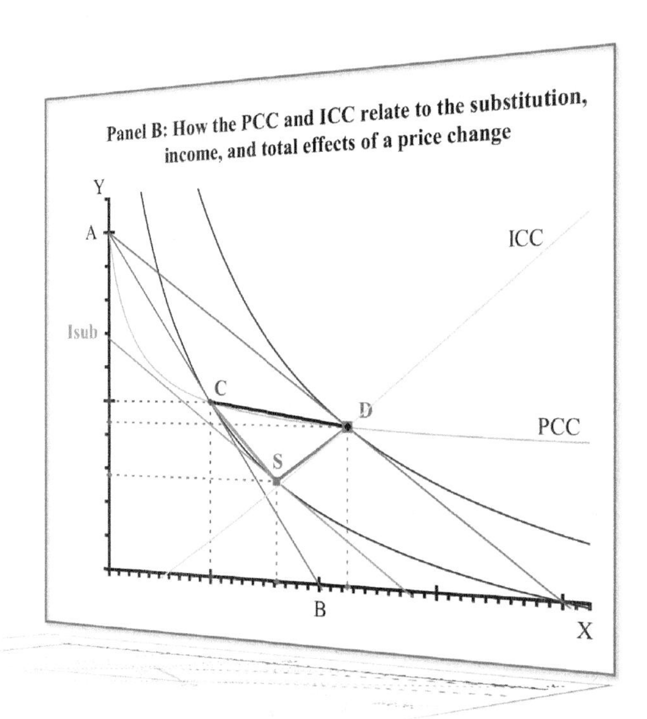

Chapter Outline

In this chapter, we take a second look at the effect of a change in price on quantity demanded. We do this using both the consumption diagram and the demand diagram to sharpen our focus and provide further detail to our understanding of consumer behavior. As in Chapter 7, we concentrate on changes in the price of x.

Our initial focus is on the consumption diagram. Section 8.1 lays out the geometric underpinnings of demand decomposition. The total effect of a price change is composed of two distinct components: the substitution effect of the price change and the income effect of the price change. Both of these effects can be seen using the indifference curve analysis of a price change started in Chapter 7. Section 8.2 examines these effects from the same three perspectives used in Chapter 7: the bundle view, the own-price view, and the cross-price view. The own-price view allows us to analyze the law of downward-sloping demand, and the cross-price view allows us to examine the requirements for substitutes and complements. These views allow us to complete a typology of goods according to the orientation of the optimal bundles on the indifference curve map as prices change. Section 8.3 presents algebraic representations of this decomposition, based on specific utility functions, and Section 8.4 translates this decomposition into demand space. Two demand concepts are distinguished in this section: Hicksian demand and Marshallian demand. Finally, Section 8.5 presents an algebraic structure that allows economists to examine demand decomposition in a more general setting in which the specific utility function that represents preferences is unknown. This structure is called the Slutsky equation. We conclude with two policy applications: (1) the substitution bias inherent in the Consumer Price Index and (2) how you might structure a low-income energy assistance program in the face of a fuel-oil price spike.

8.1 The Substitution and Income Effect of a Price Change

When the price of a good changes, the consumer adjusts optimal purchasing behavior, as described in Chapter 7. The adjustment occurs along the consumer's price consumption curve (PCC) when viewed in the consumption diagram and along the consumer's demand curve when viewed from a demand diagram. We initially focus on movements caused by changes in price in the consumption diagram. The move from an initial point of tangency to a final point of tangency as a result of a price change is called the total effect of the price change. The **total effect** of a price change is the change in consumption of both x and y induced by a change in price. The total effect of a price change is seen as the move from one point on the PCC to another point on the PCC. This move was the focus of Section 7.1.

total effect: The total effect of a price change is the change in consumption of both x and y induced by a change in price.

There are two distinct and conceptually separate aspects to the adjustment in x and y caused by this price change. One adjustment involves the consumer changing purchasing so that personal marginal rate of substitution (MRS) matches the new market signals. The other adjustment involves the consumer modifying purchasing in response to the change in purchasing power induced by the change in price. The first effect is called the substitution effect of the price change, and the second is called the income effect of the price change. The **substitution effect** of a price change is the part of the total effect that is due to the individual adjusting consumption in response to changing relative prices of both goods induced by a price change. The **income effect** of a price change is that part of the total effect that is due to the individual adjusting consumption in response to the changing purchasing power induced by the price change. **Purchasing power** is the ability to generate utility through the purchase of goods. As the price of x changes, the price ratio P_x/P_y changes as well—and this change in price ratio induces a change in the relative value of x versus y because one good has become relatively less expensive because of the price change. (If the price of x declines, x has become relatively less expensive. If the price of x increases, y has become relatively less expensive.)

substitution effect: The substitution effect of a price change is the part of the total effect that is due to the individual adjusting consumption in response to changing relative prices of both goods induced by a price change.

income effect: The income effect of a price change is that part of the total effect that is due to the individual adjusting consumption in response to the changing purchasing power induced by the price change.

purchasing power: Purchasing power is the ability to generate utility through the purchase of goods.

Purchasing the same bundle is not necessary to have the same purchasing power. Instead, *having the same purchasing power requires being able to purchase bundles that achieve the same utility level.*[1] An example from Chapter 6 should make this distinction clear. Figure 6.14 examined the choice between three food-subsidy programs—two of which dominated given preferences shown. In both panels of Figure 6.14, free food and food stamps produced the same utility level—but they did so in dramatically different fashions. (As you may recall, the food-stamp solution produced a more food-intensive outcome because the effective price of food was lower under a food-stamps program than under a free-food program at the chosen bundles.) Both programs exhibited the same purchasing power because the consumer was able to achieve the same level of satisfaction under both programs, despite doing so in quite a different manner under each program. The utility-maximizing bundle under each program was not feasible under the other program.

In the present context, an increase in price reduces purchasing power because the initial optimal bundle is no longer affordable. A reduction in price increases purchasing power because the initial bundle is now dominated by other affordable bundles. The initial optimal bundle is no longer on the boundary of the feasible set; the budget constraint is no longer binding at the initial bundle.

The sum of the substitution and income effects is the total effect of the price change. These effects are often discussed in introductory courses but are rarely shown graphically because introductory courses typically do not devote sufficient time to indifference curve analysis to make graphical analysis of these effects possible. This pulling apart of the total effect of a price change into two conceptually distinct component parts—the substitution effect of a price change and the income effect of a price change—is often called **demand decomposition**.

demand decomposition: The total effect of a price change on demand is decomposed into the substitution effect and the income effect of a price change.

The three effects are shown in Figure 8.1 for one specific set of preferences (based on shifted Cobb-Douglas [CD] preferences with $a < 0$ and $b < 0$). Specific values are not shown, and numbers have been suppressed from axes to focus attention on the general attributes of these effects. As in Chapters 5 and 7, blue budget constraints and indifference curves represent the initial situation, and red budget constraints and indifference curves represent the final situation. Figures 8.1A–8.1C represent a 50% decrease in the price of x in moving from blue to red, and Figures 8.1D–8.1F represent a 150% increase in the price of x in moving from blue to red.[2] The total effect of the price change is shown as the move from **C** to **D** in Figures 8.1C and 8.1F (this is the black "arrow" pointing from **C** to **D**). The total effect can be geometrically viewed as the sum of the substitution and income effects. The substitution effect should be conceptually examined first, since it is viewed as a move from the initial bundle to an intermediate substitution bundle, while the income effect is viewed as a move from the intermediate bundle to the final bundle. Each of these moves is discussed in turn.

The substitution effect of a price change occurs because when a single price changes, all other prices change relative to that price. If the price of x decreases (as in Figures 8.1A–8.1C), then x becomes less expensive, *and* simultaneously, y becomes relatively more expensive, even though the price of y *does not change*. If P_y was $2, it remains $2. There is a larger gap, however, between the price of x and the price of y, making y seem "more expensive." A consumer interested in receiving the best "bang for the buck" will substitute x for y in this instance.[3] If the price of x increases (as in Figures 8.1D–8.1F), the reverse holds true: x becomes more expensive, and in a relative sense, y becomes cheaper. A consumer interested in receiving the best "bang for the buck" will substitute y for x. In *both* instances, this substitution will occur as long as the individual's willingness to trade y for x (the individual's MRS at that point on the initial indifference curve) does not match the new price ratio. Whenever this inequality occurs, one good remains a better deal on a relative basis in producing incremental utility per dollar spent. Both a price decrease and a price increase are seen as movements along the initial indifference curve to a point where the MRS equals the new price ratio. The substitution effect asks, how substitutable are x and y in achieving utility? The answer can be represented in the consumption diagram as the movement from the initial bundle **C** to the substitution bundle **S** (this is the green arrow pointing from **C** to **S** in Figures 8.1A, 8.1C, 8.1D, and 8.1F).

Claim: *The substitution effect is represented as a roll (movement) along the initial indifference curve to the new price ratio.*

For a price decrease, this roll is to the southeast (Figure 8.1A), and for a price increase, this roll is to the northwest (Figure 8.1D). The substitution effect is that part of the price change that is simply a response to an altered relative market valuation of x and y implied by a change in the price of one good.

The income effect of a price change acknowledges that when a price changes, so does real purchasing power. Most readily, this is seen as the triangle of bundles between the red and blue budget constraints that is now attainable (for a price decrease in Figures 8.1A–8.1C) or that is no longer attainable (for a price increase in Figures 8.1D–8.1F).[4] Unfortunately, this triangular description of the change in purchasing power has both an income and a substitution effect embedded in it, since the price ratio changes on the two downward-sloping edges of the triangle, where the (interior) constrained optimum tangencies occur. We just discussed how to remove the substitution effect while holding the individual's purchasing power constant by rolling along the initial indifference curve from **C** to **S**. The income effect asks, how much is the change in price "worth" in terms of income change? Put another way, how "far apart" are the indifference curves attained in the initial and the final situation? The answer can be represented in the consumption diagram as the movement from the substitution point **S** to the final point **D** (this is the pink arrow pointing from **S** to **D** in Figures 8.1B, 8.1C, 8.1E, and 8.1F).

Claim: *The income effect is represented as a jump from the initial indifference curve to the final indifference curve at the new price ratio.*

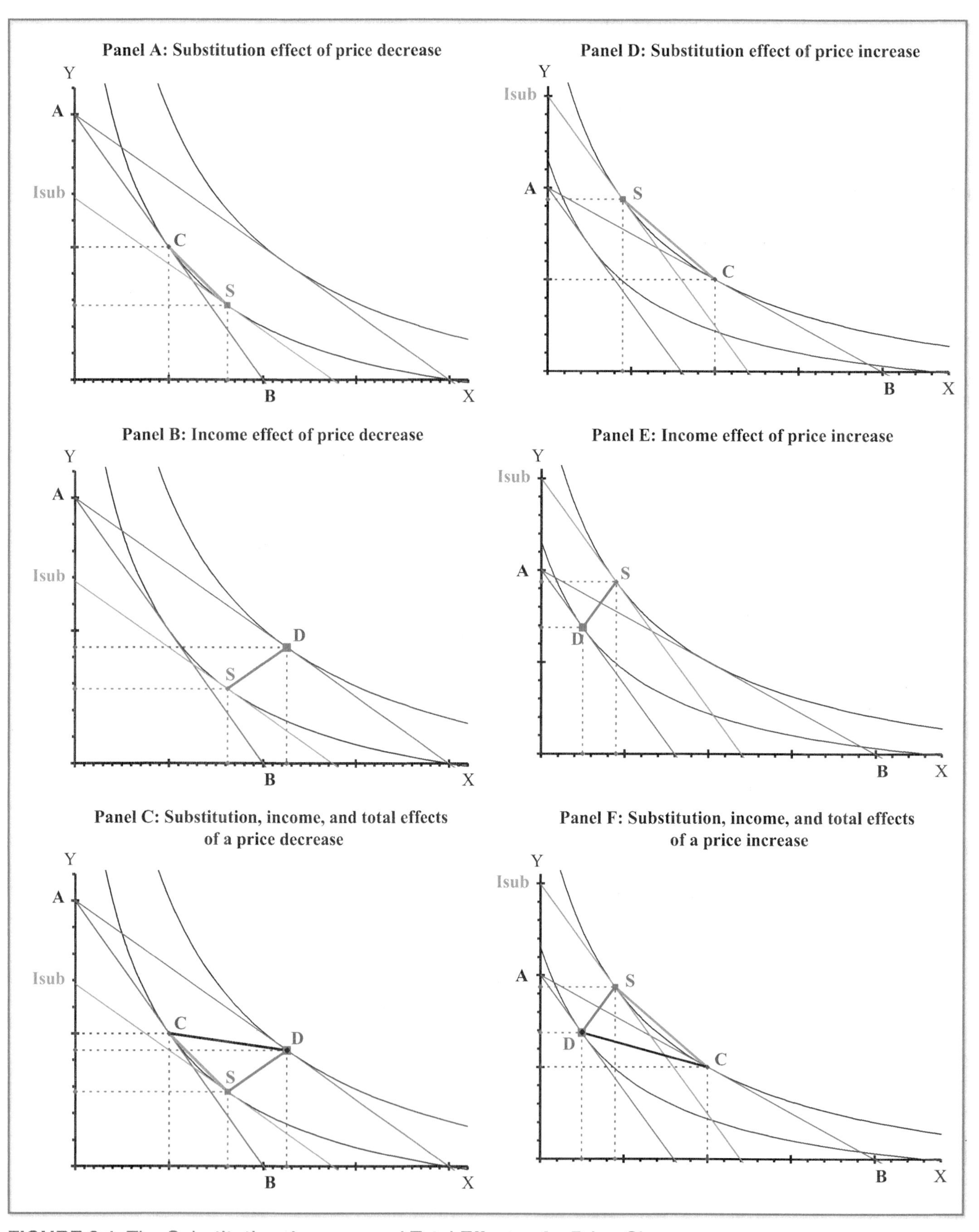

FIGURE 8.1 The Substitution, Income, and Total Effects of a Price Change

For a price decrease, the income effect is positive (since **D** is on a higher indifference curve than **S**). For a price increase, the income effect is negative (since **D** is on a lower indifference curve than **S**).

A dollar value for the size of the income effect can be obtained by comparing income levels used to support bundles **D** and **S**. Assume, for simplicity, that y is the numeraire: $P_y = 1$. In this instance, the y-axis intercept of a budget constraint represents income ($I/P_y = I$ when $P_y = 1$), so the dollar size of the income effect of a decrease in the price of x is $\mathbf{A} - \mathbf{I_{sub}}$, where **A** and $\mathbf{I_{sub}}$ are the y-intercept bundles in Figure 8.1A–8.1C.[5] An income of A achieves the final utility level, given final prices (at tangent bundle **D**), while an income of I_{sub} achieves the initial utility level at minimum expenditure, given final prices (at tangent bundle **S** = (x_s, y_s)). More generally, the income required to support the substitution bundle, I_{sub}, can be derived as:

$$I_{sub} = P_x^{final} \cdot x_s + P_y \cdot y_s. \tag{8.1}$$

The difference between the two income levels is the "value" of the lower price. The reverse holds true for a price increase. The "cost" of the price increase to the consumer is how much worse off the consumer is with the higher price that produces the final (red) utility level at **D** in Figures 8.1D–8.1F than when the consumer faced the initial lower price. An income of I_{sub} would have been required to maintain the (blue) initial utility level in the face of the higher final price (at substitution bundle **S**). Since A is available, the cost is the difference $\mathbf{I_{sub}} - \mathbf{A}$.[6]

The total effect is the sum of the substitution effect that rolls along the initial indifference curve to the new price ratio, and the income effect that moves from the initial indifference curve to the final indifference curve. In Figures 8.1C and 8.1F, this is seen graphically as (the colors are those used in figures; typically, the text will not maintain this color scheme):

$$\overrightarrow{\mathbf{CD}} = \overrightarrow{\mathbf{CS}} + \overrightarrow{\mathbf{SD}}. \tag{8.2}$$

The **Total** effect = the **Substitution** effect + the **Income** effect.

The arrows (or more accurately, vectors) for each effect set up a triangle in consumption space where each vertex is a bundle (initial bundle **C**, substitution bundle **S**, and final bundle **D**), and each side represents one of the three effects with directional arrows attached to the sides (from **C** to **S** for substitution, **S** to **D** for income, and **C** to **D** for total). This demand decomposition triangle is depicted in Figure 8.2A for a price decrease.

Figure 8.2B adds one final dimension to Figure 8.1C by explicitly showing the price consumption curve (PCC) and income consumption curve (ICC) associated with this price decrease. As noted earlier, the PCC passes through all points connecting initial and final consumption bundles, since that is how the PCC was created. Therefore, both endpoints of the total effect are on the PCC. Each ICC maps out how consumption changes as income changes for fixed prices. Since this is a diagram of price change, we must decide whether the ICC for initial or final prices should be shown. To highlight the income effect, the ICC for final prices is shown, since both the substitution bundle and the final bundle are based on final prices; therefore, both endpoints of the income effect are on the ICC. As you vary the price of x, **D** will move along a fixed PCC, and the ICC will shift as **D** and **S** adjust to reflect altered prices (this is most easily seen using the price slider in the Excel version of Figure 8.2). The PCC and ICC form two sides of the demand decomposition triangle.

8.2 Three Views of Demand Decomposition

The demand decomposition described in Section 8.1 is useful for analyzing a variety of topics. Discussion of one of the most important of these topics—the welfare impact of a price change—is largely postponed until Chapter 16. The decomposition is immediately useful for two purposes: (1) It clarifies how to recognize substitutes and complements,

FIGURE 8.2
The Demand Decomposition Triangle

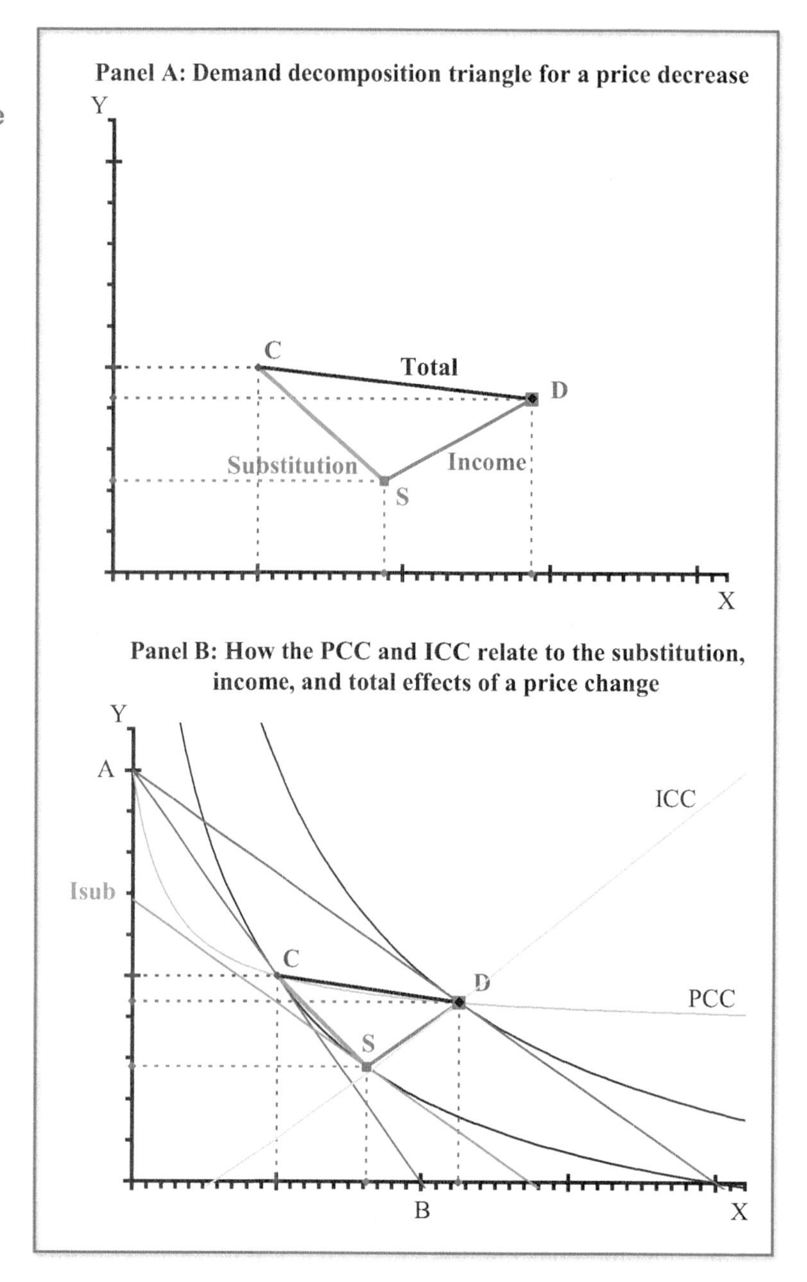

and (2) it helps verify the law of demand. Both of these topics require a different view of the decomposition shown previously.

The substitution, income, and total effects of a price change can be viewed from three orientations: the bundle view, the own-price view, and the cross-price view. These orientations are much the same as those described in Section 7.1 in examining the (un-decomposed) effect of a price change (see, in particular, the discussion of Figures 7.1 and 7.2). The bundle view examines the effect on both goods of a change in price of one good. This was the view in the previous section. The other two views simply examine the effects one good at a time.

The Own-Price View and the Law of Downward-Sloping Demand

One of the most universal laws of economics is that demand is downward sloping. The substitution and income effects of a price change provide independent rationales for that assertion. This is most sharply focused by taking an own-price view of demand decomposition. The own-price view examines how the consumption of x changes as the price of x changes. Figure 8.3 shows the three effects on x consumption as horizontal arrows

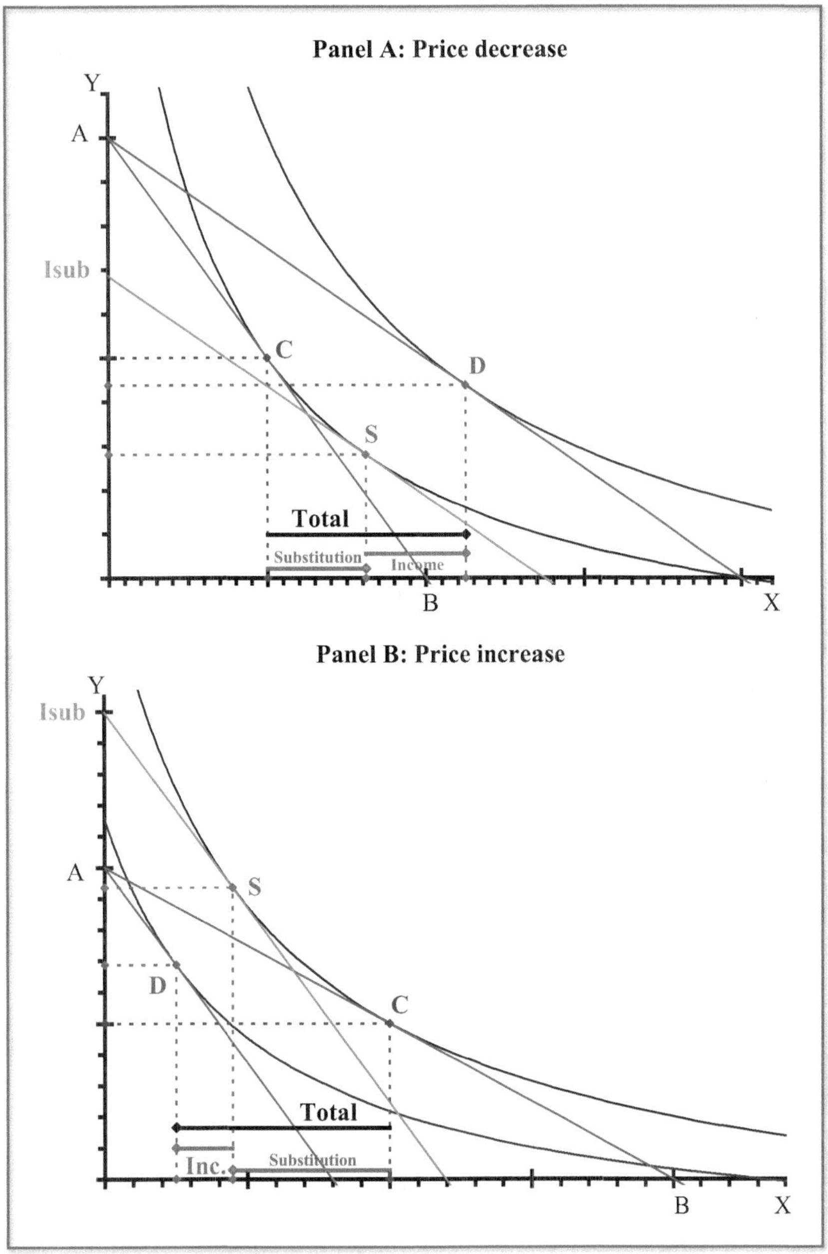

FIGURE 8.3 The Own-Price View of Demand Decomposition

for the x components of each of the three effects. Figure 8.3A examines a price decrease, and Figure 8.3B examines a price increase. In both figures, it is immediately apparent that the substitution and income arrows point in the same direction. For a price decrease, both effects point toward an increase in demand, and for a price increase, both effects point toward a decrease in demand. If this were always the case, then the law of downward-sloping demand would be assured. Unfortunately, it is not quite that simple.

As long as preferences are smooth and well behaved (convex and monotonic), the own-price substitution effect will always move in opposition to the price of the good. The reason is straightforward: As discussed in Section 3.2, the MRS declines as x increases along the indifference curve. The roll along the indifference curve required by the substitution effect necessarily brings us to a point of greater x consumption if the price of x declines and smaller x consumption if the price of x increases (since the MRS = P_x^{final}/P_y at the substitution point). This may be restated as:

Claim: *The substitution effect requires an unambiguously inverse relation between the price of a good and the quantity of that good demanded.*

The only caveat to this claim is that the substitution effect may be zero if the indifference curve is not smooth at the initial optimal consumption bundle. The most obvious example of such preferences is perfect complements. As discussed in Chapters 4 and 6, especially Figures 4.6 and 6.2A, the efficient consumption bundle, given perfect complements preferences, is at the vertex of the L-shaped indifference curve (as long as both prices are greater than zero). Any price ratio produces the same efficient bundle on a given indifference curve. Put another way, there is *no* substitution effect if the goods are perfect complements.

The sign of the own-price income effect depends on the sign of the income elasticity of demand for the good, η_x. If the good is normal, then $\eta_x > 0$, and the sign of the own-price income effect is the same as the sign of the own-price substitution effect. This is the situation depicted in Figures 8.1 and 8.2. This is the typical situation. Quasilinear preferences are the only atypical preferences discussed in Chapter 4, and as discussed in Section 7.6, $\eta_x = 0$ in this instance. The own-price demand decomposition when x is inferior is shown in Figure 8.4 (these preferences were initially analyzed in Figure 7.19). In this instance, the total effect of the price decrease is smaller than the substitution effect because the extra purchasing power provided by a lower price leads to a reduced interest in the inferior good x. The income effect of the price decrease is to reduce demand for x (as shown by the pink income effect arrow pointing leftward in Figure 8.4). Nonetheless, the net effect of a price decrease is to increase demand for x in Figure 8.4; demand is downward sloping for this inferior good x. If demand for x and the price of x are inversely related, we say that x is an **ordinary good**.

ordinary good: A good is an ordinary good if its demand is downward sloping.

At a theoretical level, this need not be the case. If the tangent bundle **D** in Figure 8.4 had a smaller x value than the x value at bundle **C**, demand would be upward sloping. This would require a "super inferior" good—a good in which the own-price income effect opposes *and* dominates the own-price substitution effect. Only in that event could we have the theoretical possibility of a Giffen good. A **Giffen good** is a good with a positively sloped demand curve. As a practical reality, a Giffen good is indeed rare; Giffen's analysis was based on demand for potatoes during the Irish potato famine in the 19th cen-

Giffen good: A Giffen good is a good with a positively sloped demand curve.

FIGURE 8.4 Demand Decomposition When x Is an Inferior Good

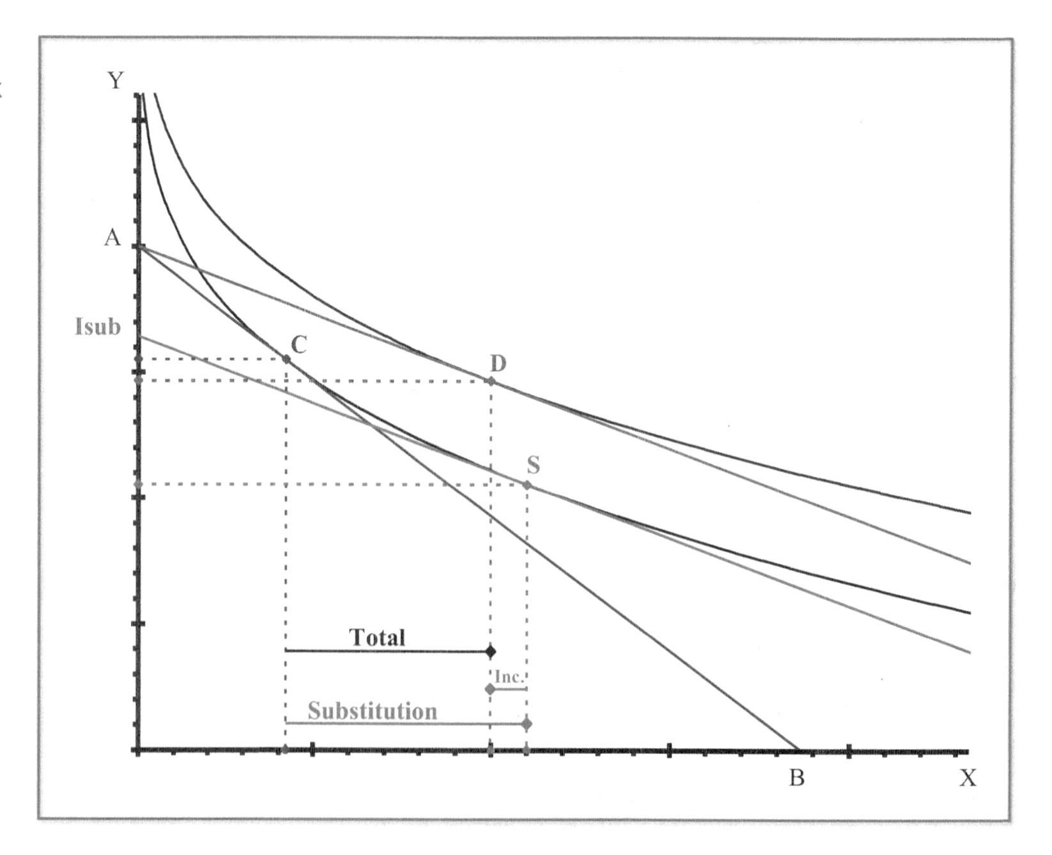

tury.[7] This should be thought of as more of a theoretical curiosity than a practical reality. Nonetheless, the demand decomposition allows us to see what is required for a good to be a Giffen good.

The Cross-Price View and the Determination of Substitutes and Complements

The cross-price view examines the effect on the "other" good, the one whose price is not changing. In our discussion, this is y; y is a substitute or complement of x, based on the cross-price elasticity of demand for y ($\varepsilon_{y,x} = \%\Delta y/\%\Delta P_x$). If the cross-price elasticity of demand for y is positive, then y is a substitute for x, and if the cross-price elasticity is negative, y is a complement of x.

Substitutes are easy to distinguish from complements by using a cross-price view. Symmetric to the own-price analysis, the cross-price effects are shown as vertical arrows for the y components of each of the three effects in Figure 8.5. Both Figures 8.5A and 8.5B depict a price decrease, but the Excel file for Figure 8.5 allows symmetric analysis of price increases. The common element to both Figures 8.5A and 8.5B is that the cross-price substitution and income arrows oppose each other. This will be true as long as y is a normal good. The reason is simple: For a price decrease, the cross-price substitution effect is unambiguously negative, since y is becoming more expensive on a relative basis (or, at most, zero in the case of perfect complements). By contrast, there is a positive income effect of a price decrease as long as the good is normal, since purchasing power has increased because of the price decrease. If y is a normal good, the net effect depends on the relative size of the two opposing cross-price effects.

> **Claim:** *y is a substitute for x if the cross-price substitution effect dominates, y is a complement of x if the cross-price income effect dominates, and y is independent of x if the cross-price income and substitution effects are the same magnitude (and cancel each other).*

Figure 8.5A depicts the first situation, and Figure 8.5B depicts the second. When the two effects are equal in magnitude and oppose each other, the goods are independent. (This occurs when $a = 0$ in the shifted CD form, as can be seen in Equation 7.6e. Although the independent goods scenario is not shown, it can easily be obtained, using the substitutability slider in the Excel file for Figure 8.5.)

A Typology of Goods

The current discussion can be generalized to provide a typology of outcomes to a price decrease based on the location of the final bundle on the final budget constraint. This is shown in Figure 8.6A. In this diagram, the final bundle must be tangent to the red budget constraint somewhere between bundles **E** and **L** (**E** and **L** are jointly located on the final budget constraint and on the initial indifference curve). Any point on the interior of segment **EL** provides a theoretical point of tangency, given well-behaved preferences. By now, you should be able to sketch a representative indifference curve for various possible locations along this curve. The only restrictions you should follow are convexity and monotonicity; make sure that the curves continue to curve and remain downward sloping. And, of course, they cannot intersect the blue indifference curve.

The typology is based on the quadrant systems set up from the initial bundle **C** and the substitution bundle **S**. Consider first the system set up by **C**. If the tangent bundle is to the left of **C** on the budget constraint (along **EF**), demand will be upward sloping, and x is a Giffen good because the own-price income effect is negative and dominates the own-price substitution effect. If the tangent bundle is to the right of **C** on the budget constraint (along **FL**), x is an ordinary good. If the tangent bundle is above **C** on the budget constraint (along **EH**), demand for y has increased, and y is a complement of x. The reverse holds true below **C** on the budget constraint (along **HL**), and y is a substitute for x. The quadrant

FIGURE 8.5 Demand Decomposition of a Price Decrease: The Cross-Price View

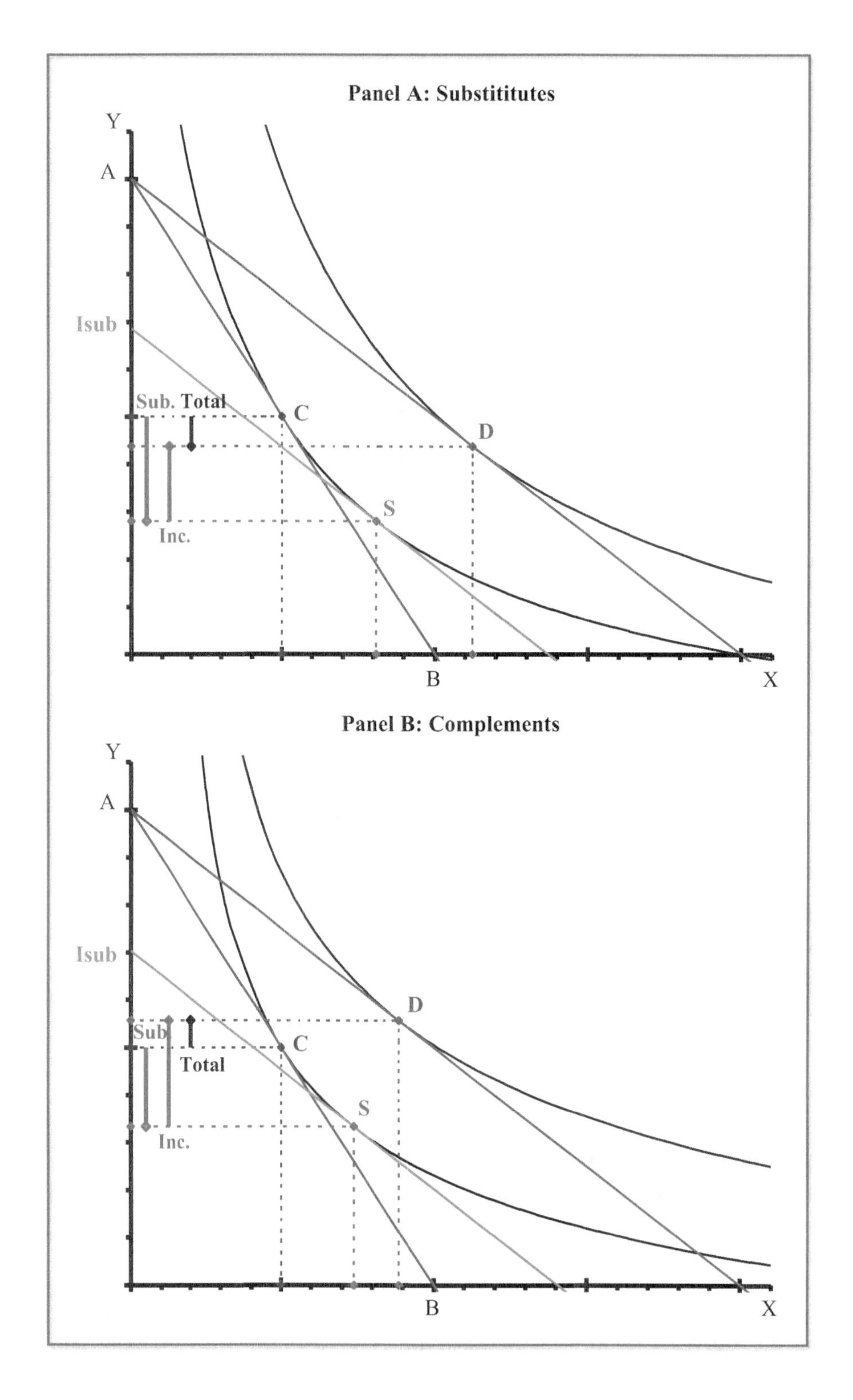

system based on the substitution bundle **S** sets up the income typology discussed in Section 7.6 (see especially the income elasticity number line described in Equation 7.20). The key to this system is not simply bundles **G** and **K** but also bundle **J**. At point **J**, both goods have unitary income elasticity. If the tangent bundle is to the left of **J** on the budget constraint, the proportion of income spent on y is increasing, and the proportion spent on x is decreasing: x is a necessity and y is a luxury, and the reverse holds true to the right of **J**. Similarly, if the tangent bundle is to the left of **G** on the budget constraint, an increase in income decreases consumption of x: x is inferior. To the right the reverse is true. If the tangency is on **GL**, x is normal. Finally, **K** marks the boundary point at which y changes

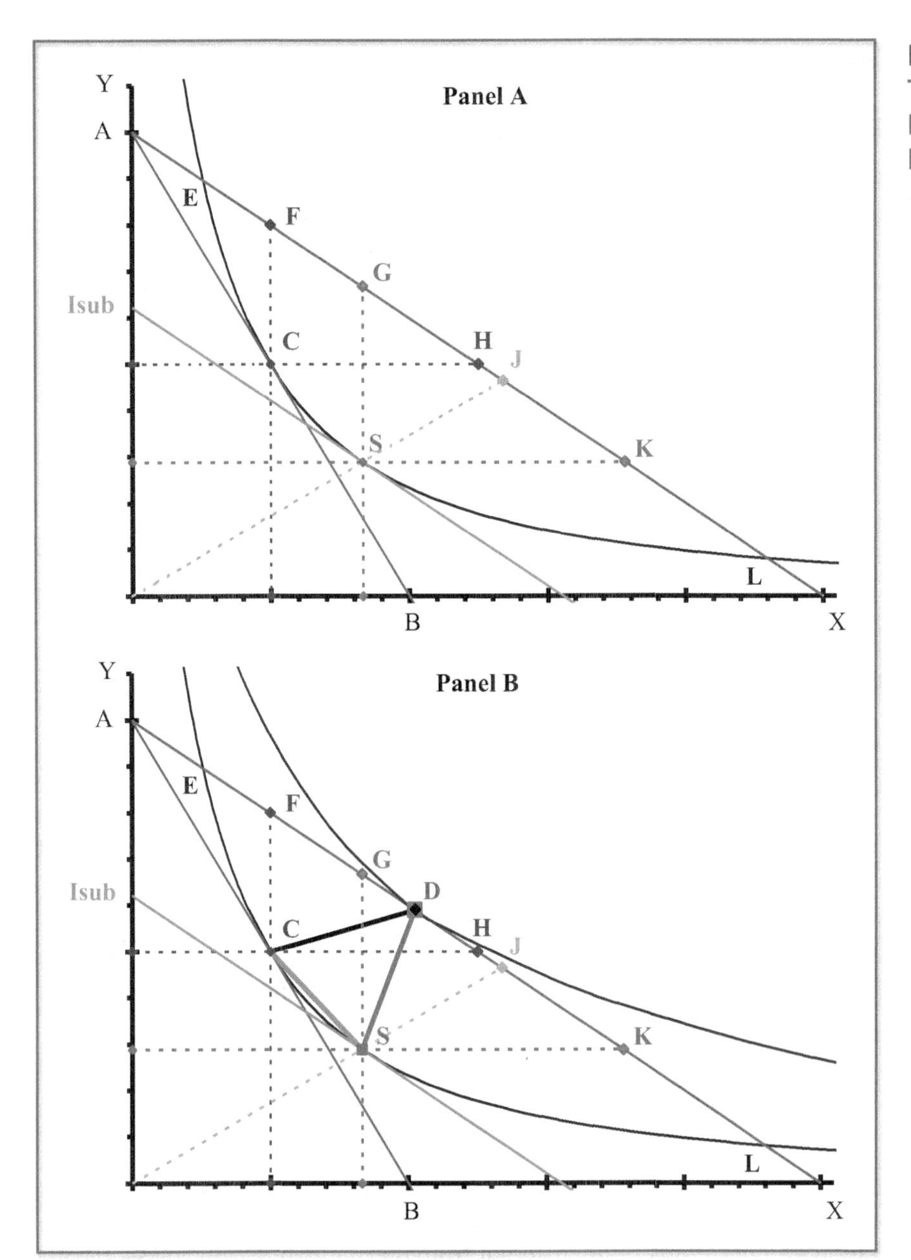

FIGURE 8.6 A Typology of Goods Based on a Price Decrease

from being a normal good to being an inferior good. These relations are summarized in Table 8.1. Figure 8.6B introduces one possible tangency point **D** and includes the bundle demand decomposition arrows associated with this final bundle. The bottom part of Table 8.1 describes x and y based on this typology. Sliders in the Excel file for Figure 8.6 allow you to move **D** to any bundle along **EL** and to vary the size of the price decrease.

8.3 Demand Decomposition for Some Specific Utility Functions *OPTIONAL SECTION*

We already have obtained algebraic solutions for the total effect of a price change in Chapter 7. The initial and final bundles, **C** and **D**, are points on the PCC. In the present context, all we need do to obtain an algebraic solution for demand decomposition is to determine the location of the substitution bundle **S** = (x_s, y_s). The substitution bundle can be obtained by minimizing expenditure on goods x and y, while maintaining a given utility level. The general solution to this minimization problem must include both interior and boundary solutions (similar to utility maximization problem discussed in Section 6.1).[8]

TABLE 8.1 A Typology of Goods Based on Figure 8.6

Location of final tangency on the red budget constraint		
Northwest of point (toward **E**)		Southeast of point (toward **L**)
x Giffen	**F**	x Ordinary
x Inferior	**G**	x Normal
y Complement of x	**H**	y Substitute for x
x Necessity, y Luxury	**J**	x Luxury, Y Necessity
y Normal	**K**	y Inferior
At point:		
G	x has zero income elasticity.	
H	y is independent of x.	
J	x and y have unitary income elasticity.	
K	y has zero income elasticity.	
Suppose the optimal bundle is at **D** in Figure 8.6B. The following can be concluded (if **D** is between **G** and **H**):		
At **D**	x is ordinary, normal, and a necessity. y is a complement of x, a luxury, and normal.	

Claim: *If an individual with well-behaved preferences and smooth indifference curves faces the constrained optimization problem:*

$$\text{Minimize} \quad P_x x + P_y y \quad \text{subject to} \quad U(x, y) = U_0. \qquad \textbf{(8.3–Problem)}$$

The following must hold at a constrained optimal solution:

(A) The optimal bundle $\mathbf{S} = (x_s, y_s)$ must satisfy $U(\mathbf{S}) = U_0$; and **(8.3A)**

(B) *One* of the following three conditions must hold:

(i) $MRS_{y,x} = P_x/P_y$ if $x_s > 0$ and $y_s > 0$; or **(8.3Bi)**

(ii) $MRS_{y,x} \leq P_x/P_y$ if $x_s = 0$ and $y_s > 0$; or **(8.3Bii)**

(iii) $MRS_{y,x} \geq P_x/P_y$ if $x_s > 0$ and $y_s = 0$. **(8.3Biii)**

The utility maximization problem in Equation 6.1 obtains bundles **C** and **D**, and the expenditure minimization problem in Equation 8.3 obtains bundle **S**. These two optimization problems look quite different from one another. Nonetheless, the solutions to these two problems exhibit a surprising degree of similarity. Part A in each equation is different (in the utility-maximization problem, condition A was spend all income; here, it is maintain utility level U_0), but Part B in both equations is identical across equations. Equation 8.3Bi is the interior solution described earlier; Equation 8.3Bii is the y-axis boundary solution, and Equation 8.3Biii is the x-axis boundary solution. The interior solution has been the focus of our discussion thus far (and will continue to remain the focus of our attention); boundary answers follow the same reasoning put forward in Section 6.1 and are not repeated here. The similarity between the solutions to the two optimization problems is not a coincidence: The two problems are related (indeed, economists have a term for their relation—the two problems are called *duals* of one another).[9]

Cobb-Douglas

Consider the general CD utility function, $U(x, y) = x^r \cdot y^{(1-r)}$. The substitution bundle S can be obtained by solving two equations in two unknowns:

$x^r \cdot y^{(1-r)} = U_0$ utility level is constant (Part A), and **(8.4a)**

$(r/(1-r)) \cdot (y/x) = P_x/P_y$ the MRS equals price ratio (Part Bi). **(8.4b)**

Solving for y, using Equation 8.4b, we obtain:

$$y = ((1 - r)/r) \cdot (P_x/P_y) \cdot x. \qquad \textbf{(8.4c)}$$

Substituting Equation 8.4c into Equation 8.4a and solving for x, we obtain the x coordinate of the substitution bundle:

$$x_s = U_0 \cdot ((r/(1 - r)) \cdot (P_y/P_x))^{(1-r)}. \qquad \textbf{(8.5a)}$$

Substituting this back into Equation 8.4a and simplifying yields the y coordinate of the substitution bundle:

$$y_s = U_0 \cdot (((1 - r)/r) \cdot (P_x/P_y))^r. \qquad \textbf{(8.5b)}$$

You can check your mathematics here in two ways: (1) Substitute Equations 8.5a and 8.5b back into the utility function, and make sure that this bundle achieves utility level U_0; and (2) substitute Equations 8.5a and 8.5b back into Equation 8.4b, and make sure that this bundle has the MRS equal to the price ratio (the mathematics here is a bit messy, but both results do work out in the end). We will have more to say about the x and y values produced by Equations 8.5a and 8.5b in the next section.

Given the complexity of the CD solution, the shifted CD solution is not shown here. (Of course, you have already seen the results in many of the figures in this chapter, and the algebra for the shifted CD solution is described in the Chapter 8 Appendix.)

Perfect Complements

Perfect complement preferences have an interesting and simple demand decomposition. Regardless of the magnitude of the price increase or price decrease, the roll along the indifference curve to the substitution bundle **S** leaves you at the initial bundle **C**. The total effect of a price change is due entirely to the income effect for perfect complements. Figure 8.7 depicts this situation. Regardless of price change, bundle **C** = **S**; there is no substitution effect for perfect complements (since the substitution effect measures substitutability, there is no substitutability with perfect complements). Therefore, the total effect (from **C** to **D**) coincides with the income effect (from **S** to **D**); as a result, it is shown as a pink arrow with a thin, black centerline and a black "arrowhead" at **D**.

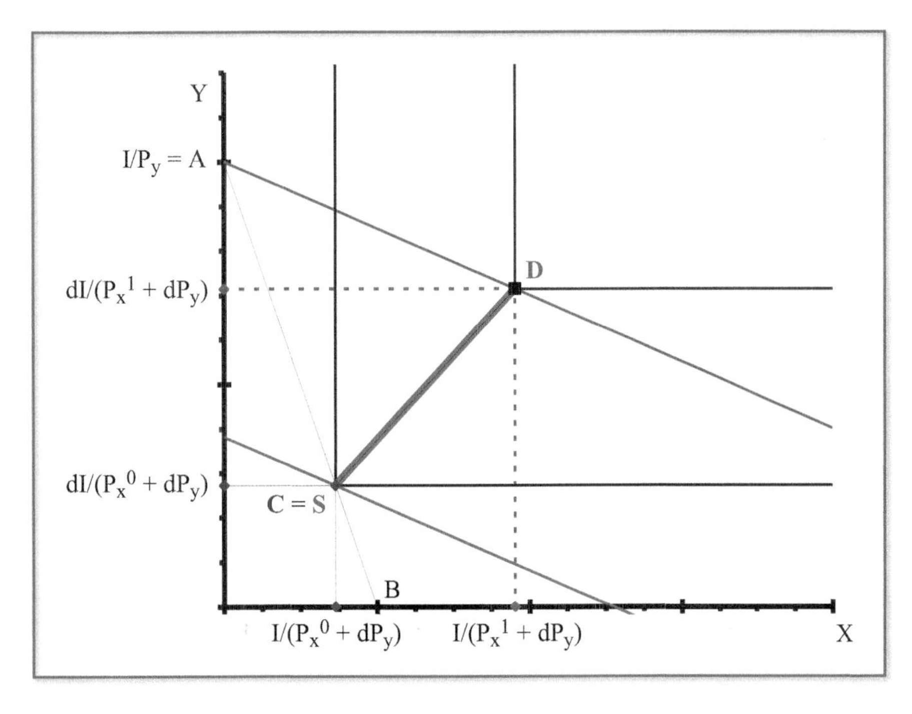

FIGURE 8.7 Demand Decomposition for Perfect Complements

Perfect Substitutes

Demand decomposition for perfect substitute preferences depends on the location of the starting and ending price ratio relative to the MRS (which is constant for perfect substitutes). If both are greater than the MRS, then the price change has *no* effect on consumption; consumption remains at bundle **A** (Equation 8.3Bii). If both price ratios are below the MRS, then the effect of the price change is solely an income effect, since both optimal bundles are on the x axis in this instance. No substitution of y for x occurs, since x is preferred to y for all price ratios below the MRS (Equation 8.3Biii). Only when the price ratios straddle the MRS is there a nonzero substitution and income effect. Two situations are possible: $P_x^0/P_y > MRS > P_x^1/P_y$, and $P_x^0/P_y < MRS < P_x^1/P_y$. (Figure 8.8A depicts the former, and Figure 8.8B depicts the latter.) Since both budget constraints, indifference curves, and the demand decomposition effects are linear in this instance, colors have been altered from earlier figures, and some lines have been widened to allow you to see when one line coincides with another. Also, the bundles **C**, **S**, and **D** are shown as large, open circles at the appropriate locations. These circles are always on the boundary of the consumption set for reasons discussed earlier. (*Note:* The caveat to the boundary solution is that the entire budget constraint is optimal if the price ratio equals the MRS [see Figure 6.4B and Equation 6.9].) Figure 8.8A depicts a price decrease; the substitution effect moves the individual from the y axis to the x axis along the initial indifference curve (**C** to **S**), and the income effect moves out to the new indifference curve along the

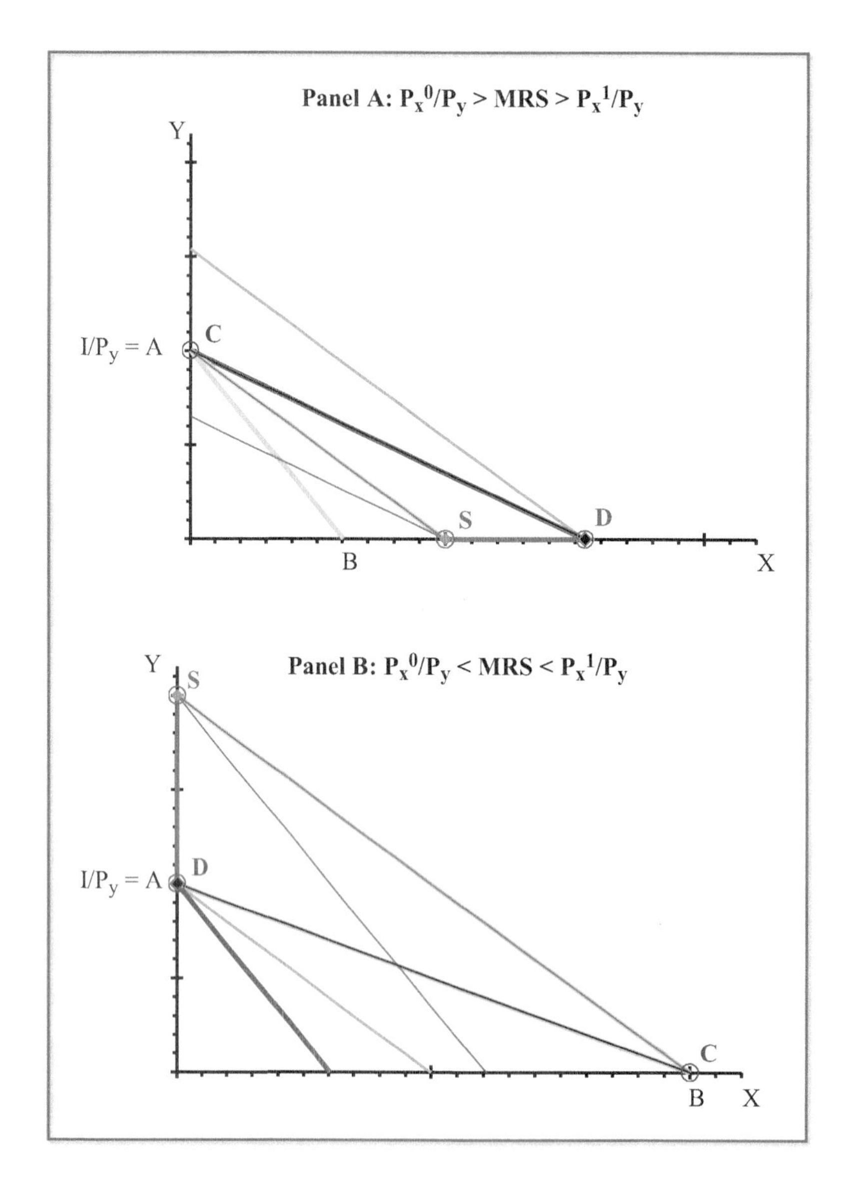

FIGURE 8.8 Demand Decomposition for Perfect Substitutes

x axis (**S** to **D**). The total effect is seen as a move along the final budget constraint in this instance (from **C** to **D**). The reverse holds true in Figure 8.8B. The substitution effect moves from the x axis to the y axis along the initial indifference curve, the income effect moves down the y axis, and the total effect moves along the initial budget constraint. In both instances, the substitution effect of moving across the razor's edge price ratio (equal to the MRS) causes the substitution bundle to move to the "opposite" boundary from the initial bundle on the initial indifference curve; the substitution effect and the initial indifference curve coincide in both Figures 8.8A and 8.8B.

Quasilinear

Demand decomposition with quasilinear preferences is particularly simple. As long as there is enough income so that initial and final constrained optimums and the substitution bundle are interior to the consumption set, the entire own-price effect will be the substitution effect. Put another way, the substitution and final bundles will be vertically aligned as long as demand for x is quasilinear, or **S** and **D** will be vertically aligned as long as both are interior constrained optimums. The reason is straightforward and can be seen both in the geometry used to introduce quasilinear preferences in Chapter 4 and in the algebra of the demand functions derived in Equations 7.10 and 7.11. The MRS only depends on x; it does not depend on income. Demand for x is independent of income; therefore, the ICC is vertical for quasilinear functions. Figure 8.9 depicts demand decomposition when the price of x doubles for one of the quasilinear utility functions introduced in Chapter 4, $U(x, y) = a \cdot \ln(x) + y$. As shown in Figure 7.10, the PCC for this utility function is horizontal; as a result, the substitution/income/total triangle is a right triangle. This need not be the case for quasilinear preferences; the PCC need not be horizontal, but the ICC must be vertical for interior optimal solutions to the respective constrained optimization problems if preferences are quasilinear. This implies that the income effect will be entirely borne on y consumption. As argued in Chapter 7, the way to most easily conceptualize demand based on quasilinear preferences is to think of demand for x being fulfilled "first," and then demand for y is "filled in" as income allows. Once demand for x is fulfilled, all extra income is spent on y.

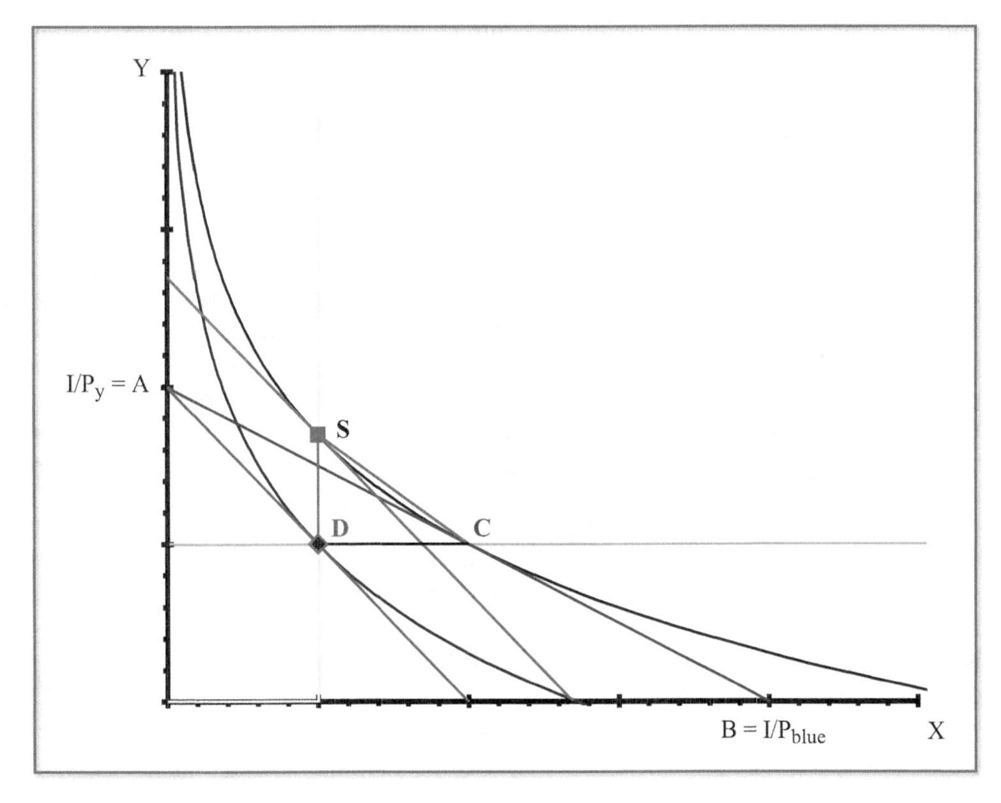

FIGURE 8.9 Demand Decomposition for Quasilinear Preferences, $U(x, y) = a \cdot \ln(x) + y$

8.4. Decomposing a Demand Curve: Hicksian versus Marshallian Demand *OPTIONAL SECTION*

Just as we can decompose the total effect of a price change into its component parts, so can we decompose a demand curve into its component parts. The individual demand curve derived in Chapter 7 includes both income and substitution components. This is easy to see if you remember that, as we walk down the individual's demand curve, the consumer is becoming better off. The demand curve holds income constant, but as price declines, purchasing power increases. This increase in purchasing power derived from the price decrease *is* the income component of demand.

The previous discussion of demand decomposition has been based on the consumption diagram; demand for both x and y has been examined as price changes. The starting point for the current discussion is the own-price view of demand decomposition described in Section 8.2 that provided two separate rationales for the law of downward-sloping demand. If we translate the substitution effect and the total effect of the own-price demand decomposition into a demand diagram, we obtain two separate but interrelated demand concepts: Marshallian demand and Hicksian demand. **Marshallian demand** is demand for a good as a function of its price, holding all other prices and income constant. By contrast, Hicksian demand holds utility constant. **Hicksian demand** is demand for a good as a function of its price, holding all other prices and utility constant.

Marshallian demand: Marshallian demand is demand for a good as a function of its price, holding all other prices and income constant.

Hicksian demand: Hicksian demand is demand for a good as a function of its price, holding all other prices and utility constant.

Marshallian demand has already been examined at length in Sections 7.2 and 7.3; Marshallian demand is simply the formal name for individual demand. When the type of individual demand curve is not specified, it is undoubtedly Marshallian. The term *Marshallian* is typically used only when Hicksian demand is also being discussed. Marshallian demand holds income constant and allows utility to vary as price varies. Hicksian demand does exactly the opposite. Hicksian demand holds utility constant, and it does so by adjusting income to maintain the same purchasing power in the face of price changes. *Hicksian demand is sometimes called "income-compensated demand" because income is compensated (adjusted) to maintain utility.* Using this terminology, we could call Marshallian demand "utility-compensated demand" because utility is compensated (adjusted) to maintain income. (At some level, this utility adjustment sounds simplistic and trivial because the demand curves we typically imagine when we consider our own consumption behavior hold income constant. By contrast, income adjustments sound complex and obscure, since we do not live in a world that typically compensates income to maintain utility.)

Hicksian demand holds utility constant, and as a result, a utility level is required to talk about Hicksian demand (just like an income level is required to talk about Marshallian demand). Figure 8.10A shows the Hicksian demand curve associated with a utility level of U_0. The substitution effect of a price change holds utility constant as required by Hicksian demand; therefore, the Hicksian demand curve is geometrically mapped by dropping the x coordinate of the substitution bundle **S** into (x, P_x) space as the price of x changes. The Hicksian demand curve is mapped by rolling along the indifference curve to the new price ratio and dropping the x coordinate to the lower diagram. Figure 8.10A depicts the price of x declining by 50% in moving from bundle **C** = (x_c, y_c) to bundle **S** = (x_s, y_s) in the consumption diagram, and by a move from **C** = (x_c, P_x^0) to **S** = (x_s, $0.5 \cdot P_x^0$) in the demand diagram. Hicksian demand is algebraically derived by solving the constrained optimization problem set out in Equation 8.3.

Figure 8.10B introduces the Marshallian demand curve back into the analysis. As shown in Chapter 7, Marshallian demand maps how the constrained optimal level of x changes as the price of x changes. Bundles **C** and **D** in the consumption diagram are mapped to demand points **C** and **D** on the Marshallian demand curve. The (red) price of x is 50% of the initial (blue) price of x, so point **D** on Marshallian demand is (x_d, $0.5 \cdot P_x^0$). As discussed earlier, Marshallian demand includes both a substitution effect (from **C** to **S**) and an income effect (from **S** to **D**). This can be depicted using both the own-price view of the consumption diagram analyzed in Section 8.2 and by moving from point **C** to point

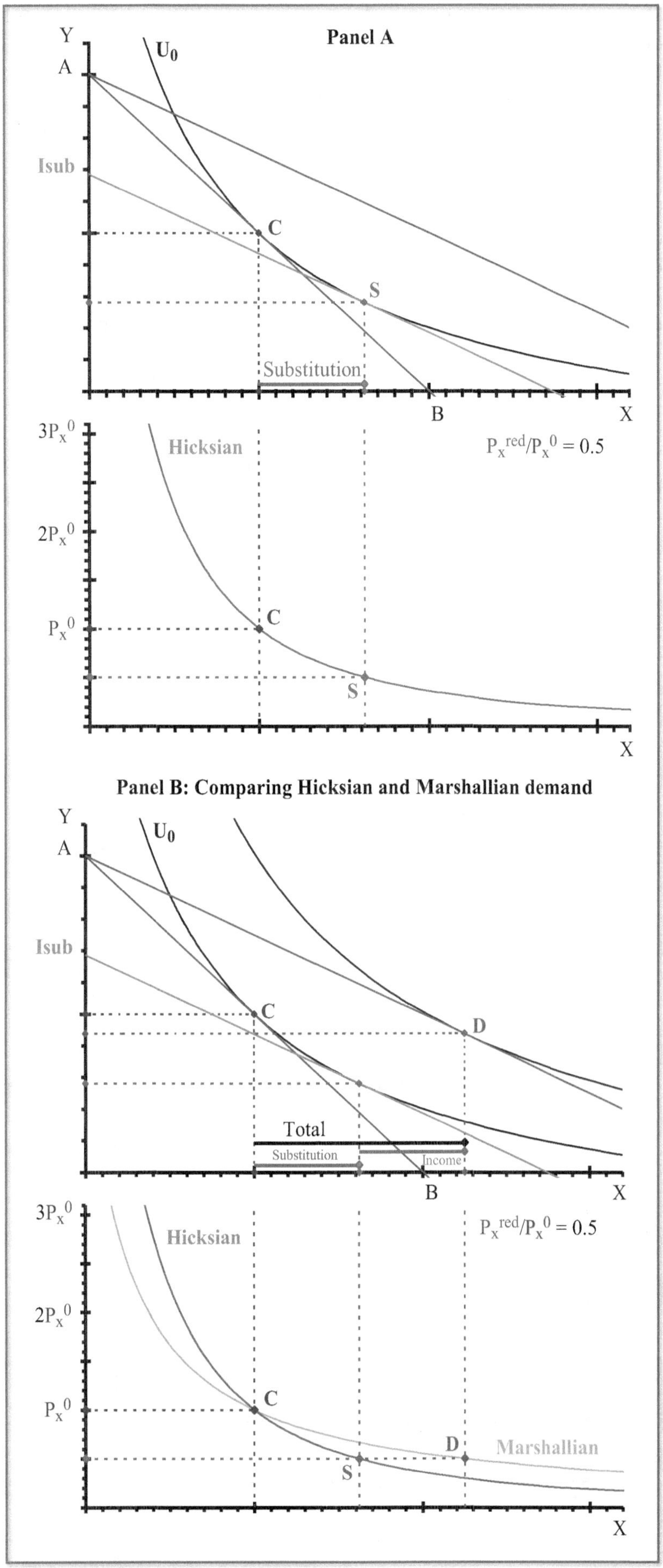

FIGURE 8.10 Hicksian versus Marshallian Demand

Panel A

Panel B: Comparing Hicksian and Marshallian demand

D on the (Marshallian) demand curve (by way of the substitution point **S** on the Hicksian demand curve). Marshallian demand is composed of two parts: (1) a substitution effect that represents how the individual adjusts to take advantage of the new price ratio for fixed purchasing power and (2) an income effect that represents the impact of the change in price on purchasing power. Hicksian demand describes the substitution component of the response.

Hicksian demand appears steeper than Marshallian demand in Figure 8.10B. This will be true as long as x is a normal good because Marshallian demand includes an income effect as well as a substitution effect. For a price decrease, the income effect increases demand for a normal good; Marshallian demand increases by more than Hicksian demand for a price decrease. Conversely, for a price increase, the substitution effect decreases demand for x, and the income effect also decreases demand for x as long as x is normal because purchasing power is reduced by a price increase. For a price increase, Marshallian demand declines by more than Hicksian as long as the good is normal. For both price increases and price decreases, Marshallian is flatter than Hicksian because, if the good is normal, the income effect reinforces the substitution effect embodied in Hicksian demand.

When x is inferior, the reverse situation occurs: Marshallian demand is steeper than Hicksian demand because the own-price substitution and income effects now work in opposition to each other, as depicted in Figure 8.4. Figure 8.11 shows the orientation of Hicksian and Marshallian demands when x is an inferior good. The final possibility occurs when x is neither normal nor inferior. This occurs if x has zero income elasticity, a possibility associated with quasilinear preferences. In this instance, Hicksian and Marshallian demand for x coincide because the own-price substitution and total effects

FIGURE 8.11 Hicksian versus Marshallian Demand: The Case of an Inferior Good

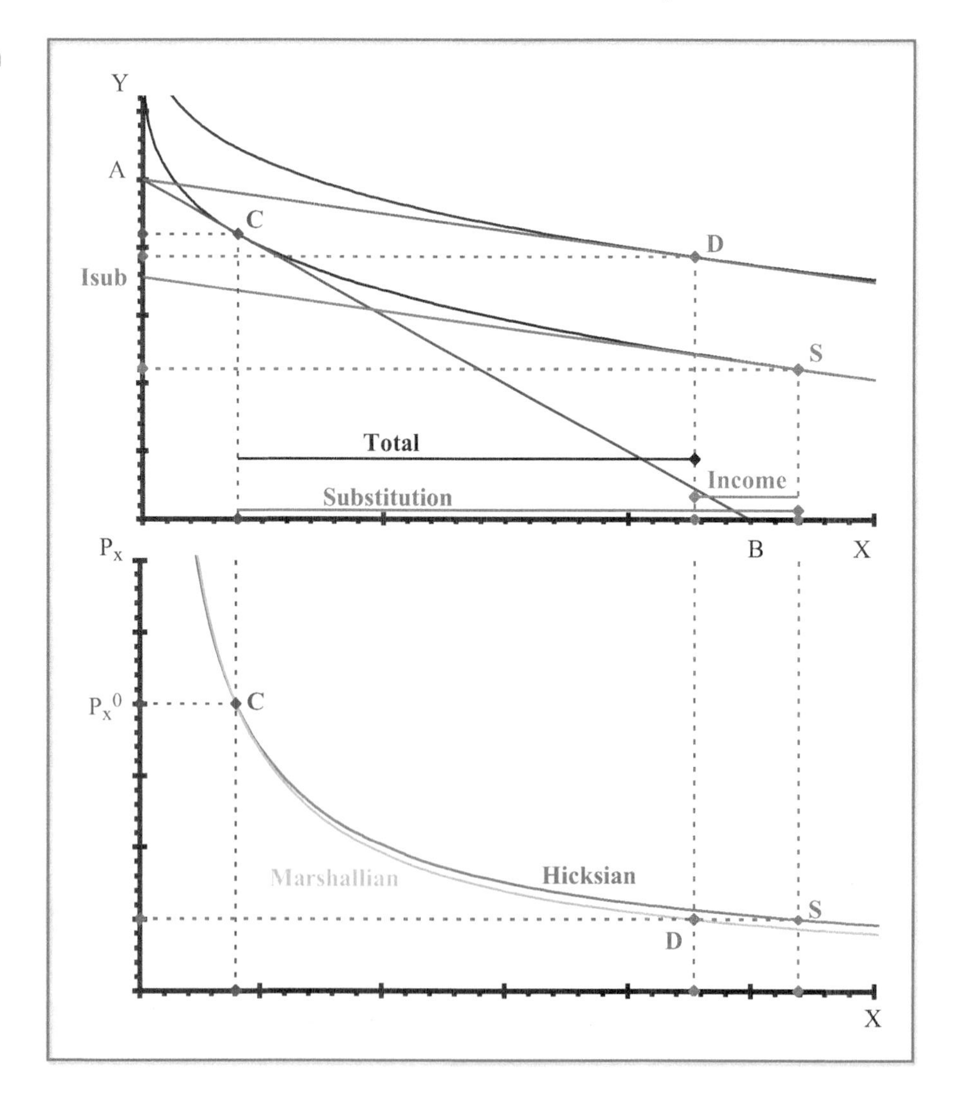

coincide in Figure 8.9 (since there is no own-price income effect for quasilinear preferences). As a result, the demands for x depicted back in Figure 7.9 are both Hicksian and Marshallian.

It is worth considering why Hicksian and Marshallian demand intersect at point **C** in the demand diagrams depicted in Figures 8.10 and 8.11. Both demand curves are depicted as univariate functions of price of x, and both hold other parameters fixed. In particular, the Marshallian demand curve holds income fixed (at $I = A \cdot P_y$, where A is the y coordinate of y intercept bundle **A**), and Hicksian demand holds utility fixed at utility level U_0. But how is U_0 defined? U_0 is the utility-maximizing utility level achieved, given initial prices P_x^0, P_y, and income I. This utility level is achieved at the tangency bundle **C** in the consumption diagram, and the x coordinate of this bundle is the point (x_c, P_x^0) on the Marshallian demand curve. This is also on the Hicksian demand curve because bundle **C** in the consumption diagram is the expenditure-minimizing way of achieving utility level U_0, given initial prices. It is the point on the indifference curve U_0 associated with $MRS = P_x^0/P_y$. Put another way, bundle **C** in the consumption diagram satisfies Equation 8.3, given prices P_x^0 and P_y. (This is perhaps easiest to see using the Excel version of Figure 8.10 by adjusting the slider so that $P_x^{red} = P_x^0$. The resulting diagram has the red and blue budget constraints tucked underneath the green substitution budget constraint.) This may be stated algebraically as the following identity:[10]

$$x(P_x^0; P_y, I) \equiv x_h(P_x^0; P_y, U_0), \text{ where } U_0 = U(x(P_x^0; P_y, I), y(P_x^0; P_y, I)) = U(\mathbf{C}). \quad \textbf{(8.6)}$$

Hicksian and Marshallian demand only intersect at this point because the utility level achieved, given the initial budget constraint, is the utility level being held fixed in the Hicksian demand function.

The equality between Hicksian and Marshallian demand at price P_x^0 appears reasonable geometrically but is less apparent upon inspection of the demand functions involved for a specific utility function. Consider the Hicksian and Marshallian demands for the general CD function derived in Equations 7.3 and 8.5:

Utility function	**(7.3a-b) Marshallian demands**	**(8.5a) Hicksian demand for x**
$U(x, y) = x^r \cdot y^{(1-r)}$.	$x = r \cdot I/P_x$ $y = (1 - r) \cdot I/P_y$.	$x_h = U_0 \cdot ((r/(1 - r)) \cdot (P_y/P_x))^{(1-r)}$.

It is rather surprising that Equation 8.6 is true, given how different Marshallian demand for x (Equation 7.3a) and Hicksian demand for x (Equation 8.5a) appear. Nonetheless, we can show that they are equal in a few steps. Evaluating utility at initial prices yields utility level U_0. This can be accomplished by substituting Equations 7.3a and 7.3b (Marshallian demands for x and y), evaluated at prices P_x^0, P_y, and income I, into the utility function:

$$U_0 = U(\mathbf{C}) = (r \cdot I/P_x^0)^r \cdot ((1 - r) \cdot I/P_y)^{(1-r)} = I \cdot (r/P_x^0)^r \cdot ((1 - r)/P_y)^{(1-r)}. \quad \textbf{(8.7)}$$

Substitute utility level U_0 (Equation 8.7) into Equation 8.5a (Hicksian demand for x), evaluated at prices P_x^0, P_y, and utility level U_0, to obtain:

$$x_h(P_x^0; P_y, U_0) = I \cdot (r/P_x^0)^r \cdot ((1 - r)/P_y)^{(1-r)} \cdot ((r/(1 - r)) \cdot (P_y/P_x^0))^{(1-r)}. \quad \textbf{(8.8a)}$$

Regrouping, we have:

$$x_h(P_x^0; P_y, U_0) = I \cdot (r/P_x^0)^r \cdot ((1 - r)/P_y)^{(1-r)} \cdot (P_y/(1 - r))^{(1-r)} \cdot (r/P_x^0)^{(1-r)}. \quad \textbf{(8.8b)}$$

Canceling and simplifying, we obtain Marshallian demand for x, evaluated at prices P_x^0, P_y, and income I, as expected from Equation 8.6:

$$x_h(P_x^0; P_y, U_0) = r \cdot I/P_x^0 = x(P_x^0; P_y, I). \quad \textbf{(8.8c)}$$

Hicksian demand is not directly observable from market behavior because it is based solely on the substitution effect. Hicksian demand answers the conceptual question: How much x will an individual purchase at different prices to maintain a certain utility level? The answer, of course, depends on the utility level that we wish to have the individual maintain (just as the Marshallian answer depends on the income level the individual wishes to devote to consuming x and y). The Marshallian demand function would shift if income changed (as shown in Section 7.6), and the Hicksian demand function would shift if utility changed.

Each demand curve is simply a univariate description of a larger multivariate phenomenon. Utility maximization produced x and y as multivariate functions of prices and income in Section 7.3. These functions were geometrically described as univariate Marshallian demand functions (and as univariate Engel curves in Section 7.6).[11] The expenditure minimization described in Section 8.3 produced multivariate functions of prices and utility. We obtain univariate Hicksian demand functions by holding utility and the other price constant. Two examples of these shifts in demand are apparent in Figure 8.10B. Consider bundle **S** in the consumption diagram. This is a point on the Hicksian demand curve associated with utility level U_0, and on a Marshallian demand curve associated with income of I_{sub}. The change in income shifts Marshallian demand, as shown in Section 7.6. (The Marshallian demand associated with income level I_{sub} is not shown in Figure 8.10B, but it would pass through bundle **S**.) By contrast, bundle **D** is on the Marshallian demand curve associated with income level I and on a Hicksian demand curve associated with utility level U(**D**) (rather than $U_0 = U(\mathbf{C})$). (The Hicksian demand associated with utility level U(**D**) is not shown in Figure 8.10B, but it would pass through bundle **D**.)

The most important reason for understanding Hicksian demand will only become apparent in Chapter 16, when we examine welfare economics. In the present context, Hicksian demand is useful in providing independent confirmation that demand is indeed downward sloping, a subject we first examined using the own-price view of demand decomposition in the consumption diagram. We now turn to an algebraic analysis that provides further insight into demand decomposition.

8.5 The Slutsky Equation: The Algebra of Approximation

OPTIONAL SECTION

Slutsky equation: The algebraic structure used to describe demand decomposition is called the Slutsky equation.

Thus far, the majority of the analysis of demand decomposition has focused on the geometry of decomposition. The algebraic discussion in Section 8.3 described the constrained optimization problem embodied in the substitution effect and solutions to that problem for specific classes of utility functions. The **Slutsky equation** is an algebraic structure that allows economists to examine demand decomposition in the more general setting in which we do not know the specific utility function that represents preferences. The Slutsky equation is an outgrowth of Equation 8.2, or more specifically, it is an outgrowth of the own-price part of Equation 8.2.

Since Hicksian demand is unobservable, how can it be obtained from observable demand functions? Hicksian demand can be obtained from Marshallian demand because Marshallian demand *is* observable—both in terms of how Marshallian demand changes as price changes, and how Marshallian demand changes as income changes. The total effect of a change in the price of x on the demand for x is decomposed as:

$$\begin{aligned} &\text{Total Effect} &&= \text{Substitution Effect} &&+ \text{Income Effect.} \\ &\Delta x_{total} &&= \Delta x_{substitution} &&+ \Delta x_{income}. \\ &\Delta x_{Marshallian} &&= \Delta x_{Hicksian} &&+ \Delta x_{income}. \end{aligned} \quad \textbf{(8.9)}$$

Equation 8.9 restates Equation 8.2, using an own-price orientation and the Hicksian and Marshallian demand concepts described in the last section. If we know the consumer's underlying preferences, we can, in theory, derive Hicksian and Marshallian demands for x from the constrained optimization problems described in Equations 6.1 and 8.3. In the absence of specific information about preferences, we can still approximate the Hicksian adjustment from observable demand behavior.

Consider an increase in the price of x. If x is normal, the income effect is negative. The change in income required to maintain utility is $\Delta I = I_{sub} - I$, where I_{sub} is defined by Equation 8.1. Since utility is not held constant as price increases, *purchasing power declines by* ΔI. The own-price income effect is the change in x consumption that occurs due to a change in income. This can be written as:

$$\Delta x_{income} = -\Delta I \cdot (\Delta x/\Delta I) \qquad \textbf{(8.10a)}$$

The term $\Delta x/\Delta I$ describes the responsiveness of demand to a change in income. Is this Marshallian or Hicksian demand? The answer is Marshallian (since it is a function of income).

Claim: *For small changes in price of x,* ΔP_x*, the change in income required to maintain utility,* ΔI*, is approximated by* $x \cdot \Delta P_x$*. This is written as* $x \cdot \Delta P_x \doteq \Delta I$*.*

The dot over the equals sign means "approximately equal to."[12] The income effect on x therefore may be approximated by:

$$\Delta x_{income} \doteq -(x \cdot \Delta P_x) \cdot (\Delta x/\Delta I). \qquad \textbf{(8.10b)}$$

By substituting Equation 8.10b into Equation 8.9, we obtain the Slutsky equation:

$$\Delta x_{total} \doteq \Delta x_{substitution} - (x \cdot \Delta P_x) \cdot (\Delta x/\Delta I). \qquad \textbf{(8.11a)}$$

$$\Delta x_{Marshallian} \doteq \Delta x_{Hicksian} - (x \cdot \Delta P_x) \cdot (\Delta x/\Delta I). \qquad \textit{Absolute-change Slutsky}$$

The Slutsky equation described in Equation 8.11a examines change in demand in absolute terms. An alternative version examines change in relative terms:

$$\Delta x_{total}/\Delta P_x \doteq \Delta x_{substitution}/\Delta P_x - x \cdot (\Delta x/\Delta I). \qquad \textbf{(8.11b)}$$

$$\Delta x_{Marshallian}/\Delta P_x \doteq \Delta x_{Hicksian}/\Delta P_x - x \cdot (\Delta x/\Delta I). \qquad \textit{Relative-change Slutsky}$$

Common misconceptions about the relative-change Slutsky equation described in Equation 8.11b are that the $\Delta x/\Delta P_x$ terms denote slopes of the respective demand curves and that $\Delta x/\Delta I$ is the slope of the Engel curve. Recall that slope is rise/run. These are not slopes; they are inverses of slopes of these respective curves.[13]

One final version of the Slutsky equation examines these changes in terms of elasticity of demand. The general form of an elasticity equation is $\varepsilon_f = \%\Delta x/\%\Delta f = (\Delta x/\Delta f) \cdot (f/x)$, where f is a "factor" that affects demand (such as own-price, cross-price, or income). As a result, if we multiply both sides of Equation 8.11b by P_x/x, we obtain (upon simplification and noting that the share of income spent on x is $s_x = P_x x/I$):

$$\varepsilon_x^{Marshallian} \doteq \varepsilon_x^{Hicksian} - s_x \cdot \eta_x. \qquad \textit{Elasticity Slutsky} \qquad \textbf{(8.11c)}$$

The Slutsky equation describes the total effect of a price change as the sum of two effects: the substitution effect and the income effect. We still use the word *sum*, despite the minus sign in each version of Equation 8.11. The minus sign is predicated on the inverse relation between purchasing power and price change described earlier.

Consider the signs of each part of the right-hand side of Equation 8.11c. For smooth indifference curves, $\varepsilon_x^{Hicksian}$ is unambiguously negative, and s_x is a positive number bounded by 0 and 1. Therefore, the only part of the right-hand side of the Slutsky equation with an ambiguous sign is the income elasticity of demand for x, η_x.

As stated in Section 8.2, demand can be upward sloping ($\varepsilon_x^{Marshallian} > 0$) only if x is an inferior good, $\eta_x < 0$. The Slutsky equation shows why this is the case.[14] Indeed, the Slutsky equation allows us to say even more: The Marshallian demand elasticity is positive (Giffen good) only if x is inferior and if $|s_x \cdot \eta_x| > |\varepsilon_x^{Hicksian}|$. This is more likely to occur: The smaller the substitution elasticity of demand, the more inferior is the good (larger magnitude η_x) and the more important the good is to the consumer (in terms of the proportion of the budget devoted to the good). Put in these terms, we can begin to understand why potatoes in Ireland during the Irish potato famine may provide an example of a Giffen good. Potatoes were a staple of the Irish peasant diet (large s_x) for which there may have been few readily available consumption substitutes (small $|\varepsilon_x^{Hicksian}|$). Only with increased income could peasants afford more expensive alternative nutrition sources (negative η_x).

FIGURE 8.12 A Budget Constraint That Maintains a Fixed Basket of Goods

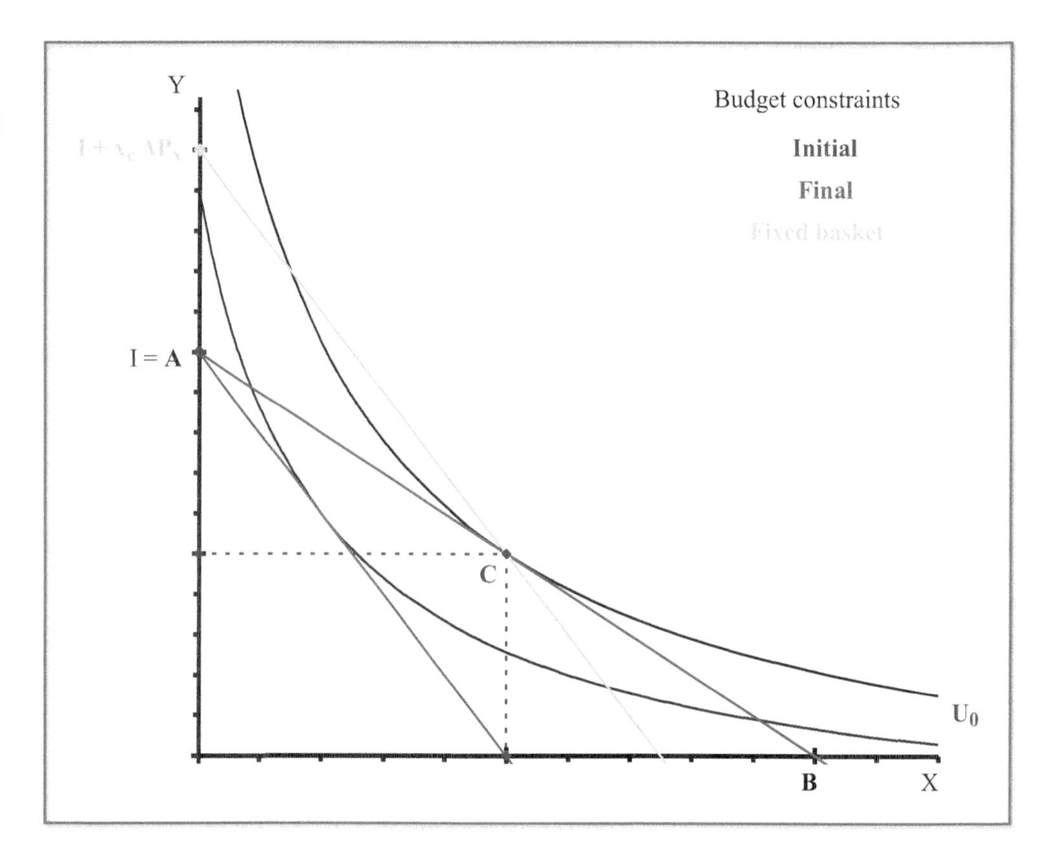

Each of the versions of the Slutsky equation could be rearranged to describe the unobservable substitution effect as a function of observable demand effects. Perhaps the most interesting version is based on the elasticity Slutsky:

$$\varepsilon_x^{\text{Hicksian}} \doteq \varepsilon_x^{\text{Marshallian}} + s_x \cdot \eta_x. \tag{8.12}$$

This equation tells us how to estimate Hicksian demand elasticity from observable share of income spent on the good, as well as price and income elasticities.

The approximation inherent in the Slutsky equation occurs because the required compensation to maintain utility in the face of a price change is given by $\Delta I \doteq x \cdot \Delta P_x$ (or more explicitly, $\Delta I \doteq x_c \cdot \Delta P_x$), rather than the exact value for ΔI obtained using Equation 8.1. This was initially discussed in deriving Equation 8.10b as an approximation of the exact income effect on x, described in Equation 8.10a. It is instructive to consider the budget constraint produced by the approximation. If $x_c \cdot \Delta P_x$ is added to the initial income level of I, then the initial bundle will *always* be affordable. The budget constraint with final prices and income level $I + x_c \cdot \Delta P_x$ rotates on the initial bundle **C** in Figure 8.12 as the price of x changes. The reason for this is straightforward:

$$\begin{aligned} I + x_c \cdot \Delta P_x &= I + x_c \cdot (P_x^{\text{final}} - P_x^0) = (P_x^0 x_c + P_y y_c) + x_c \cdot (P_x^{\text{final}} - P_x^0) \\ &= P_x^{\text{final}} x_c + P_y y_c. \end{aligned} \tag{8.13}$$

Bundle **C** is always affordable, since $x \cdot \Delta P_x$ provides just enough extra income to allow the initial bundle to still be consumed. Put another way, income is adjusted so that the fixed market basket **C** is maintained as a feasible bundle. In effect, income is adjusted so that the budget constraint rotates on the fixed market basket **C**.

Consumer Price Indices and the Substitution Bias

indexing: A program is indexed to a fixed market basket if the level of payments provided by the program is adjusted to maintain the affordability of that market basket.

The approximation inherent in the calculation of compensation required to maintain a fixed bundle is more than a theoretical curiosity. Government assistance programs often **index** their payments based on a fixed market basket of goods. A program is indexed to a fixed market basket if the level of payments provided by the program is adjusted to maintain the affordability of that market basket.

The most common example of such an index is the Consumer Price Index (CPI). The CPI is calculated based on a fixed market basket (bundle) of goods. The CPI attempts to measure the cost of living for the "average" individual. Changes in the CPI measure how the cost of purchasing that basket of goods changes, relative to a base time period.

When a fixed market basket is used and the price of a good in the basket changes, then the resulting change in assistance payment will have the effect of *overcompensating* for the price change because the index does not take into consideration the substitution effect of the price change. Interestingly, this occurs regardless of the direction of the price change. Figure 8.13 depicts both a price increase and a price decrease in separate panels. A change in price induces a change in optimal bundle, due to the substitution effect. If the initial bundle is always affordable, it will only be the constrained optimum if no prices

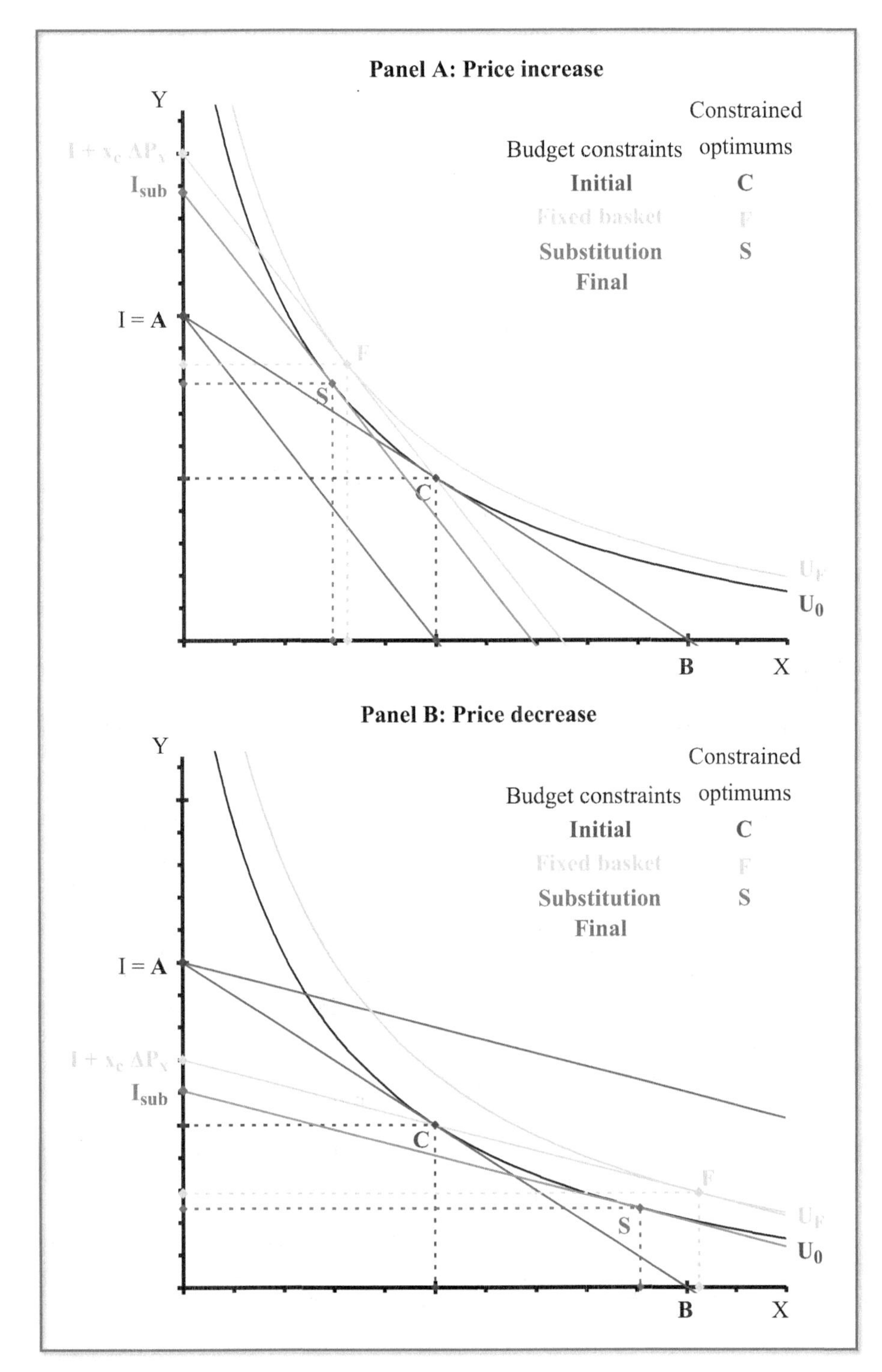

FIGURE 8.13 The Substitution Bias of a Price Change

change (or if all prices change in proportion so that the price ratio does not change from its initial level). As long as the price ratio changes, the individual will substitute one good for another to maximize bang for the buck. This occurs at point **F** in both Figures 8.13A and 8.13B at a utility level of $U_F > U_0$. Economists call this the **substitution bias**. The (theoretically appropriate) level of compensation that allows utility to be maintained at U_0, given the price changes depicted in Figures 8.13A and 8.13B, is denoted I_{sub} in each figure. This level of income maintains purchasing power, rather than initial bundle.[15] In both instances, I_{sub} is less than $I + x_c \cdot \Delta P_x$ because the fixed-basket level of compensation ignores the value of substituting in the direction of the good that is now less expensive; the fixed-basket calculation ignores the substitution effect.

substitution bias: The compensation required to maintain a fixed market basket overstates the true cost of living because it does not control for the substitution that occurs when relative prices change. This overstatement is called the substitution bias.

The differences between the theoretically appropriate compensation level in Equation 8.1 and the approximation in Equation 8.13 appear large in Figure 8.13 because the price changes shown are large and the amount spent on the good is large (in both Figures 8.13A and 8.13B, 50% of income is devoted to x consumption at bundle **C**). Typically, prices do not change that dramatically, and individuals do not devote 50% of their income to a single good. Nonetheless, the bias introduced by using a fixed basket when calculating the CPI does lead to significant overstatement of the rate of inflation based on the CPI. Research suggests that the substitution bias results in an approximate 0.4% bias in the inflation rate. This has significant budgetary implications, both in terms of increased government expenditures and in decreased tax revenues, since marginal tax-rate boundaries are also indexed (on the order of tens of billions of dollars per year).[16]

Responding to a Fuel-Oil Price Spike

Suppose you are in charge of low-income energy assistance in Boston, and you face a price spike in the market for home heating oil (HHO). Consider an individual with $10,000 in income who paid $1,500 for HHO last year. Numbers have been chosen so answers are easy to see; the actual amount paid for HHO would likely be lower (but the diagram would be less clear in this instance). With information about the individual's utility function, we can be more precise about the size of the substitution bias. Assume that this individual has CD preferences over home heating oil, x, and other goods, y, and that the initial price of both of these goods is unitary. The initial consumption bundle is therefore **C** = (1500, 8500). Suppose the price of HHO doubles, but the price of all other goods does not change. How large of a subsidy should you provide if you wish this individual to be able to maintain the standard of living experienced the previous year?

The fixed-market-basket solution is to give the individual $1,500 ($\$1{,}500 = 1{,}500 \cdot \$1 = x_c \cdot \Delta P_x$). This allows the individual to maintain the initial bundle in the face of the price spike. Of course, in this instance, rather than choosing to stay at this bundle, the individual will naturally take some of the money and spend it on other goods, instead of on home heating oil. Indeed, with CD preferences given by $U(x, y) = x^{0.15} \cdot y^{0.85}$, we would expect spending on y to increase from $8,500 to $9,775 ($\$9{,}775 = 0.85 \cdot \$11{,}500$), since an individual will spend 15% of income on x ($1,725) and 85% of income on y, given these preferences, according to Equations 7.4a and 7.4b. This is the solution depicted in Figure 8.14 by bundle **F** = (862.5, 9775) because 862.5 = $1725/$2.

As argued earlier, $1,500 overcompensates the individual because it ignores the substitution effect (as a result, $U_F > U_0$ in Figure 8.14). Hicksian demands for x and y associated with general CD preferences, Equations 8.5a and 8.5b, evaluated at $P_x = \$2$, $P_y = \$1$, and $U_0 = 6552.7$ ($6552.7 = 1500^{0.15} \cdot 8500^{0.85}$), become:

$$x_s = U_0 \cdot ((r/(1 - r)) \cdot (P_y/P_x))^{(1-r)} = 6552.7 \cdot ((0.15/0.85) \cdot (1/2))^{0.85} = 832.2. \quad \textbf{(8.14a)}$$

$$y_s = U_0 \cdot (((1 - r)/r) \cdot (P_x/P_y))^{r} = 6552.7 \cdot ((0.85/0.15) \cdot (2))^{0.15} = 9{,}431.3. \quad \textbf{(8.14b)}$$

This is the bundle **S** = (832.2, 9431.3) in Figure 8.14. An income of $11,096 is required to support this bundle (using Equation 8.1). Since the individual starts with $10,000, the actual required subsidy is $1,096 ($11,096 – $10,000).

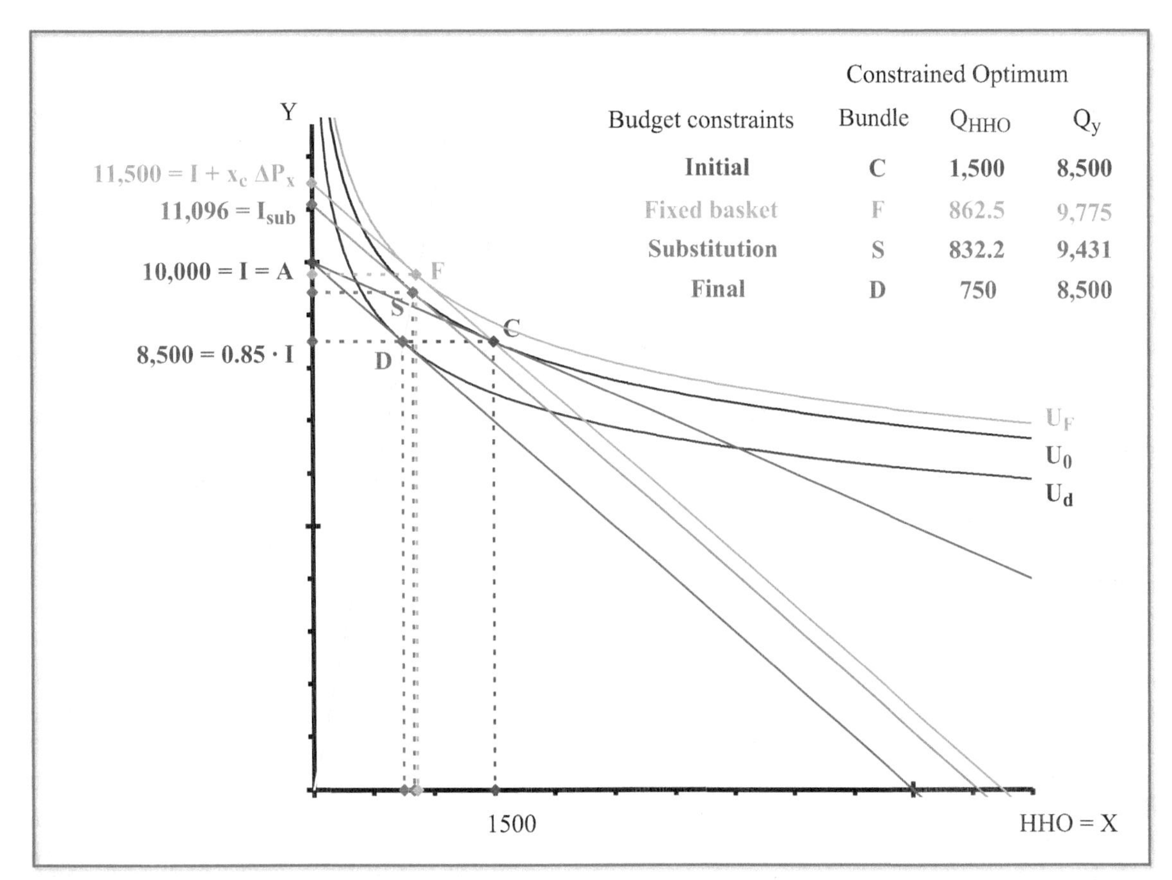

FIGURE 8.14 Low-Income Assistance with a Home Heating Oil Price Spike

$U(x, y) = x^{0.15} \cdot y^{0.85}$. Initial P_{HHO} = \$1; Final P_{HHO} = \$2; P_y = \$1; I = \$10,000.

In the absence of any subsidy, the individual consumes at **D**, which maintains y consumption (since y is independent of x, given CD preferences) and cuts HHO consumption in half because of the doubling in price. Each of the three bundles associated with the final price of HHO (**D**, **S**, and **F**) are on the yellow, P_x = \$2, ICC. As expected, the required subsidy $\Delta I = I_{sub} - I$ is less than the fixed-market-basket estimate $\Delta I = x \cdot \Delta P_x$.

It is easy to tie these two examples to each other to examine the notion of substitution bias in greater detail. Suppose that bundle **C** in Figure 8.14 represents the fixed market bundle used for calculating the CPI. In this instance, a doubling of price of HHO leads to a 15% increase in the CPI (15% = \$1,500/\$10,000). The substitution bias in this instance would be just over 4%, since the required subsidy to maintain the individual's standard of living is 10.96% (10.96% = \$1,096/\$10,000).

A bias of 4% is a much larger substitution bias than the 0.4% bias discussed earlier. The reason the bias is larger is that this example is atypical; price spikes of 100% for a product comprising 15% of a budget are not typical. The Excel version of Figure 8.14 allows you to vary the size of the price spike; as you would expect, the smaller the price spike, the smaller the bias. As mentioned previously, the numbers were chosen so that the various bundles would be easily distinguished on the graph. An alternative scenario has been built into the Excel file for Figure 8.14 so you can see what happens if 5% of income is spent on HHO (r = 0.05), rather than 15%. The qualitative results are the same; the numerical differences are, of course, much smaller in this instance. The difference between the two subsidies is \$147 when r = 0.05, rather than \$404 when r = 0.15. In percentage terms, the substitution bias is then approximately 1.5% in this instance.

Summary

Indifference curve analysis allows us to visually examine the substitution and income effects of a price change. Separating the total effect of a price change into these component parts is called demand decomposition. The substitution effect of a price change holds purchasing power constant but adjusts consumption to take advantage of changes in relative prices induced by the price change. The substitution effect is seen as a roll along the initial indifference curve to the final price ratio. By contrast, the income effect of the price change examines the change in purchasing power induced by the price change. The income effect is seen as the jump from the initial indifference curve to the final indifference curve induced by the change in purchasing power created by the change in price. Any change in price creates both effects, and the magnitude of each effect is the subject of this chapter.

Demand decomposition can be viewed from three orientations in the consumption diagram. The bundle view describes the effect on both goods of a change in price of one good. The other two views examine the effect of a price change one good at a time. The own-price view examines the effect on the good whose price has changed. This view allows economists to examine the law of demand (that demand is downward sloping), using two independent rationales. By contrast, the cross-price view examines the effect on the "other" good. This view allows a quick determination of whether the two goods are substitutes, complements, or independent. Goods are substitutes if the cross-price substitution effect dominates the income effect; if the reverse holds true, the goods are complements. If the two cross-price effects cancel each other, the goods are independent. The own-price and cross-price views allow us to complete a typology of goods according to the orientation of the initial, substitution, and final bundles on the indifference curve map as prices change.

The substitution bundle is algebraically obtained by solving a constrained optimization problem whose solution is similar to the utility maximization problem examined in Chapter 6. Algebraic solutions are obtained for specific utility functions.

The own-price view of demand decomposition is the starting point for a second analysis of how demand is derived from the consumption diagram. Two interrelated demand concepts are introduced, only one of which is actually new. Marshallian demand is the full name for the demand curve derived in Chapter 7. This demand curve describes the total effect of a price change; Marshallian demand includes both an income and a substitution effect. By contrast, Hicksian demand is a function of price while maintaining constant purchasing power; Hicksian demand includes only a substitution effect.

Hicksian demand is not directly observable but can be derived from observable behavior. The Slutsky equation describes the interrelation between Hicksian and Marshallian demand and provides an algebraic structure that allows economists to examine demand decomposition when no specific utility function is given. The chapter concludes with an analysis of two policy applications: (1) the substitution bias inherent in the Consumer Price Index and (2) how you might structure a low-income energy assistance program in the face of a fuel-oil price spike.

Review Questions

Define the following terms:

total effect	demand decomposition	Hicksian demand
income effect	ordinary good	Slutsky equation
substitution effect	Giffen good	indexing
purchasing power	Marshallian demand	substitution bias

Match the terms on the right with the statements on the left:

a. The substitution effect holds ______ fixed.	1. Utility
b. The income effect holds ________ fixed.	2. Complements
c. The total effect holds ________ fixed.	3. Income
d. Purchasing power holds _______ fixed.	4. Purchasing power
e. An indexed program holds ______ fixed.	5. An ordinary good
f. The substitution effect dominates the income effect.	6. A market basket
g. The income effect dominates the substitution effect.	7. A Giffen good
h. _________ is necessarily also an inferior good.	8. Substitutes
i. _________ need not be a normal good.	9. Prices

Provide short answers to the following:

a. What is the size of the substitution effect for perfect complement preferences?
b. What are the three views of demand decomposition discussed in Section 8.2?
c. What is the magnitude of the income effect for quasilinear preferences?
d. What is the approximate size of the substitution bias inherent in the CPI? In particular, what percentage overstatement of the rate of inflation is attributed to the substitution bias?
e. Use the elasticity Slutsky equation to describe what is required for demand to be upward sloping.
f. Why is Hicksian demand typically steeper than Marshallian demand?
g. What is required to have Hicksian demand flatter than Marshallian demand?

Check your answers to the *matching* and *short-answer* exercises in the Answers Appendix at the end of the book.

Notes

1. There is not universal agreement on this terminology. Some authors say that individuals have the same purchasing power if they can purchase the same bundle. The definition used in this text holds utility, rather than bundle, constant (for constant purchasing power) because this definition allows a more elegant welfare analysis in Chapter 16. We will examine this distinction further in Section 8.5.

2. The blue (initial) budget constraints look different in Figures 8.1A–8.1C and in Figures 8.1D–8.1F, but they are, in fact, the same in all panels in Figure 8.1. To show the effects as clearly as possible, the axes have been adjusted so that Figures 8.1A–8.1C have a larger x axis and smaller y axis than Figures 8.1D–8.1F. The Excel file for Figure 8.1 allows you to view all six panels (as well as the movement of red's price of x between 0.4 and 3.0 times blue's price of x) on one graph. Figures 8.1A–8.1C depict $P_x^{red} = 0.5 \cdot P_x^{blue}$, and Figures 8.1D–8.1F depict $P_x^{red} = 2.5 \cdot P_x^{blue}$.

3. The reference to "bang for the buck" is based on the notion that marginal utility per dollar spent should be equal across goods at an efficient consumption bundle. As discussed in Section 6.1, equal bang for the buck across goods provides an alternative (but equivalent) rule for optimization to the MRS equals price ratio rule followed in the text and set forth in Equation 6.1. The arguments in Section 6.1 are similar to those proposed here, but differ in one key aspect: In Section 6.1, the goal was to maximize utility for fixed budget constraint. The search for bundle **S** in the present context examines the most efficient way to obtain a fixed utility level. Effectively, the present optimization is to minimize the expenditure required to "produce" a given utility level, rather than to maximize utility for fixed budget constraint. Both optimizations require the same slope condition: $MRS = P_x/P_y$.

4. These triangles were discussed at length in Figure 5.5.

5. If the price of y is not 1 the y-intercept values could still be used; the only difference is that the intercept values would have to be multiplied by P_y to obtain the dollar value of the income effect. Both bundles **A** and $\mathbf{I_{sub}}$ can be viewed as income levels A and I_{sub} as well as bundles; following the convention used in the text, the bundle is boldfaced, and the income level is not boldfaced.

6. Chapter 16 expands on this discussion of the cost or benefit of a price change.

7. We will have more to say about this example in Section 8.5.

8. The optimization methods described in the Chapter 6 Appendix can be used to obtain this result.

9. A discussion of duality is beyond the mathematical scope of this text. For an elegant discussion of duality, see William J. Baumol, *Economic Theory and Operations Analysis*, 4th edition, Prentice-Hall, 1977.

10. The semicolon in each function is a shorthand way of stating that the factors to the right of the semicolon are being held constant. The equation is read as "Marshallian demand for x at price P_x^0, *given* price P_y and income level I, is identically equal to Hicksian demand for x at price P_x^0, *given* price P_y and utility level U_0." Dynamically, this simply states that bundle **C** = **S** in both diagrams when $P_x = P_x^0$. The ≡ symbol is read: "identically equal to."

11. Algebraically, the univariate demand curves are denoted by having the semicolon after P_x; for example, $x(P_x; P_y, I)$ is Marshallian demand. Conceptually, the multivariate phenomenon would simply be $x(P_x, P_y, I)$, where the commas denote that each of the three variables are allowed to vary. Were we to evaluate this function for different income levels for fixed prices, the result would be an Engel curve.

12. The proof is straightforward. Define $\mathbf{S} = (x_c + \Delta x, y_c + \Delta y)$. Then $I_{sub} - I$ may be written as $\Delta I = [(P_x^{final} \cdot (x_c + \Delta x) + P_y \cdot (y_c + \Delta y)) - (P_x^0 x_c + P_y y_c)]$. Regrouping and canceling terms produces: $\Delta I = \Delta P_x \cdot x_c + P_x^{final} \cdot \Delta x + P_y \cdot \Delta y$. Since **S** ~ **C**, Δx and Δy have opposite signs. If the changes in x and y are small, then $\Delta y/\Delta x$ approximates the slope at **S**, but the slope at x must equal $-P_x/P_y$, since MRS = price ratio at the constrained optimum, according to Equation 8.3Bi. Therefore, for small changes in price, the final two terms approximately cancel each other, and we are left with the first term as an approximation of the change in income required to maintain utility. We shorten this to $x \cdot \Delta P_x$ by dropping the subscript "c".

13. The calculus-based version of the Slutsky equation is, of course, related to Equation 8.11b. The Δ signs need only be replaced by partial derivative symbols: $\partial x_{Marshallian}/\partial P_x = \partial x_{Hicksian}/\partial P_x - x_c \cdot (\partial x/\partial I)$. In the derivative version of the Slutsky equation, the ≐ symbol from Equation 8.11b is replaced by an = symbol. Given the infinitesimal change required by calculus, the approximation of change in income provided

by $x_c \cdot \Delta P_x$ equals the actual change in income described by $I_{sub} - I$.

14. For a price increase the signs of the right-hand-side terms are:

$$\varepsilon_x^{Hicksian} - s_x \cdot \eta_x$$
$$(-) \quad -(+) \cdot (?).$$

The net effect of these terms is positive *only if* the income elasticity of demand for x is negative.

15. As mentioned at the start of this chapter, there is not universal agreement on the definition of *purchasing power*. The discussion here should make clear the difference between the two definitions. When purchasing power is defined in terms of the ability to maintain a fixed bundle of goods, the result is an increase in standard of living as prices change, rather than the maintenance of the standard of living due to the substitution bias.

16. A Google search of the words *substitution bias CPI* produces a variety of reports on this topic. See, for example, the newsletters from the Federal Reserve Bank of San Francisco Economic Letter No. 97-16 and 99-05 (at www.frbsf.org/econrsrch/wklyltr/el97-16.html). The magnitude of the bias is difficult to estimate. Economists estimate that the substitution bias overstates the rate of inflation between 0.4% and 1.5%. This bias forms the theoretical basis for calls to use "chained CPI" in policy discussions.

Appendix:

Expenditure Minimization with Shifted Cobb-Douglas Preferences

The substitution bundle for shifted CD preferences is obtained by solving Equation 8.3, given shifted CD preferences. As with the utility-maximization discussion in Chapter 6, the solution to the expenditure-minimization problem proceeds by assuming equality between the MRS and the price ratio, and then adjusts accordingly if one of the resulting demands is negative. In the utility-maximization problem, this adjustment occurs along the budget line, but in the present context, the adjustment occurs along the indifference curve. (Note that the expenditure-minimization problem is analogous to cost minimization subject to a production constraint, a topic that we examine in Chapter 10.)

Expenditure minimization requires two conditions: one is that the bundle is on the indifference curve, and the other is that MRS = P_x/P_y. Equation 4.6 summarizes utility and MRS information for shifted CD preferences. The indifference curve requirement may be written as:

$$U_0 = (x - a)^r \cdot (y - b)^{(1-r)}. \quad \textbf{(8A.1)}$$

The MRS condition is:

$$(r/(1 - r)) \cdot ((y - b)/(x - a)) = P_x/P_y. \quad \textbf{(8A.2)}$$

Two equations with two unknowns (x and y) may be solved by algebraic methods. One method is to solve for one variable in terms of the other in both equations and then set these two equations equal to one another. If we solve for y in Equation 8A.1, we obtain:

$$y = (U_0/(x - a)^r)^{(1/(1-r))} + b. \quad \textbf{(8A.3)}$$

Similarly, solving for y in Equation 8A.2 yields:

$$y = (P_x/P_y) \cdot (x - a) \cdot (1 - r)/r + b. \quad \textbf{(8A.4)}$$

Setting Equation 8A.3 equal to Equation 8A.4 and solving for x, we obtain (since this is messy, some intermediate steps are included here):

$$(U_0)^{(1/(1-r))} \cdot (x - a)^{(r/(r-1))} = (P_x/P_y) \cdot (x - a) \cdot (1 - r)/r. \quad \textbf{(8A.5a)}$$

$$(U_0)^{(1/(1-r))} \cdot (P_y/P_x) \cdot (r/(1 - r)) = (x - a)^{(1/(1-r))}. \quad \textbf{(8A.5b)}$$

From here, solving for x is simply a matter of raising both sides to the (1 – r) power and adding *a* to both sides to obtain the expenditure-minimizing level of x:

$$x_s = U_0 \cdot ((P_y/P_x) \cdot (r/(1 - r)))^{(1-r)} + a. \quad \textbf{(8A.6a)}$$

Substituting this back into Equation 8A.4 and simplifying, we obtain the expenditure-minimizing level of y:

$$y_s = U_0 \cdot ((P_x/P_y) \cdot ((1 - r)/r))^r + b. \quad \textbf{(8A.6b)}$$

(We should note that the solutions for x and y are symmetric. If you start with x in Equation 8A.6a and replace x with y, y with x, r with (1 – r), and *a* with b throughout, you will obtain Equation 8A.6b.)

Equations 8A.6a and 8A.6b satisfy the two conditions required by Equation 8.3. In particular, substituting these equations into the right-hand side of Equation 8A.1 produces the left-hand side of Equation 8A.1 (and the same goes for Equation 8A.2). Indeed, it is worth checking both conditions whenever complex answers result to make sure that algebraic mistakes have not been made. The x and y values in Equation 8A.6 describe the expenditure-minimizing substitution bundle. That is, the substitution bundle **S** = (x_s, y_s) in the figures within the chapter is obtained, given shifted CD preferences, using x_s from Equation 8A.6a and y_s from Equation 8A.6b. The only caveat to this statement is that x_s

and y_s must both be in the first quadrant. In particular, if either Equations 8A.6a or 8A.6b produces negative numbers, the substitution bundle must be recalculated.

Suppose Equation 8A.6a produces an $x < 0$. In this instance, $x = 0$ must hold, *and* Equation 8A.1 must also hold. Equation 8A.1 may be rewritten in this instance as:

$$U_0 = (-a)^r \cdot (y - b)^{(1-r)} \qquad \text{given } x = 0. \qquad \textbf{(8A.7a)}$$

To find the y coordinate of the bundle on the y axis associated with a utility level of U_0, we must solve for y in Equation 8A.7a. The result is:

$$y_s = (U_0/(-a)^r)^{(1/(1-r))} + b. \qquad \text{given } x = 0. \qquad \textbf{(8A.7b)}$$

This produces a substitution bundle of **S** $= (0, y_s)$, where y_s is from Equation 8A.7b. This bundle satisfies the expenditure-minimization problem in Equation 8.3, using Equation 8.3Bii (the inequality is ensured because shifted CD preferences are strictly convex and monotonic; the MRS declines as x increases from a negative number to zero). A substitution bundle such as this will be along the y axis, like bundle **A** in Figure 6.3A and Figure 6.3C.

Suppose instead that Equation 8A.6b produces a $y < 0$. In this instance, $y = 0$ must hold, *and* Equation 8A.1 must also hold. Equation 8A.1 may be rewritten in this instance as:

$$U_0 = (x - a)^r \cdot (-b)^{(1-r)} \qquad \text{given } y = 0. \qquad \textbf{(8A.8a)}$$

To find the x coordinate of the bundle on the x axis associated with a utility level of U_0, we must solve for x in Equation 8A.8a. The result is:

$$x_s = (U_0/(-b)^{(1-r)})^{(1/r)} + a. \qquad \text{given } y = 0. \qquad \textbf{(8A.8b)}$$

This produces a substitution bundle of **S** $= (x_s, 0)$, where x_s is from Equation 8A.8b. This bundle satisfies the expenditure-minimization problem in Equation 8.3, using Equation 8.3Biii (the inequality is ensured because shifted CD preferences are strictly convex and monotonic; the MRS increases as x decreases [as y moves from a negative number to zero]). A substitution bundle such as this will be along the x axis, like bundle **B** in Figure 6.3B and Figure 6.3D.

To summarize: The expenditure-minimizing bundle will be (x_s, y_s), where x_s and y_s are obtained from Equations 6A.6a and 6A.6b as long as both are non-negative. If Equation 6A.6a produces a negative value of x, then expenditure minimization occurs on the y axis, with the y coordinate provided by Equation 6A.7b. If Equation 6A.6b produces a negative value of y, then expenditure minimization occurs on the x axis, with the x coordinate provided by Equation 6A.8b.

PART 3

THEORY OF THE FIRM

Part 3 examines the theory of the firm, and Part 4 puts together consumers and firms to examine market interaction. We typically assume that firms wish to maximize profits, the difference between total revenues and total costs. To create revenues, firms must sell goods, and to sell goods, they must first produce the goods, using inputs in the production process, or buy the goods from another producer. In either event, the firm incurs costs. The end goal of maximizing profits can only be achieved by taking appropriate steps at each point in this chain. Or, to use another metaphor, there are many layers to the "onion" representing profit-maximizing behavior; we will spend a few chapters unpeeling the onion, layer by layer.

Understanding profit-maximizing behavior requires examining how a firm's revenue compares to that firm's costs. Revenues are sales: If x_0 units of x are being sold at a price of P_x per unit, then $P_x x_0$ is revenue to the firm from the sale of the x_0 units. (In Part 2, the consumer saw $P_x x_0$ as the cost of purchasing x_0 units of x.) Revenues depend both on the number of units sold and the price per unit. Since the relation between quantity sold and price requires demand information, the discussion of revenue will not occur until we reintroduce consumers into the analysis in Chapter 12 at the start of Part 4. The other determinant of profits is cost. Chapter 11 examines cost in a general setting—cost as a function of output produced. Chapter 10 examines the more restricted question: How can a firm minimize the cost of producing a given level of output? An understanding of cost-minimizing behavior requires that we understand the cost of factors of production, as well as how those factors of production get put together to create output. Chapter 9 begins this journey by examining production.

The time spent on consumer theory in Part 2 will pay dividends in this part of the course. Many consumer theory concepts have direct analogs on the producer side. This is especially true in Chapters 9 and 10. (Chapter 9 has analogs in Chapters 3 and 4, while Chapter 10 has analogs in Chapters 5, 6, 7, and 8). The similarities are striking, but care must be taken to understand the differences between the consumer side and the producer side.

Production Functions

CHAPTER 9

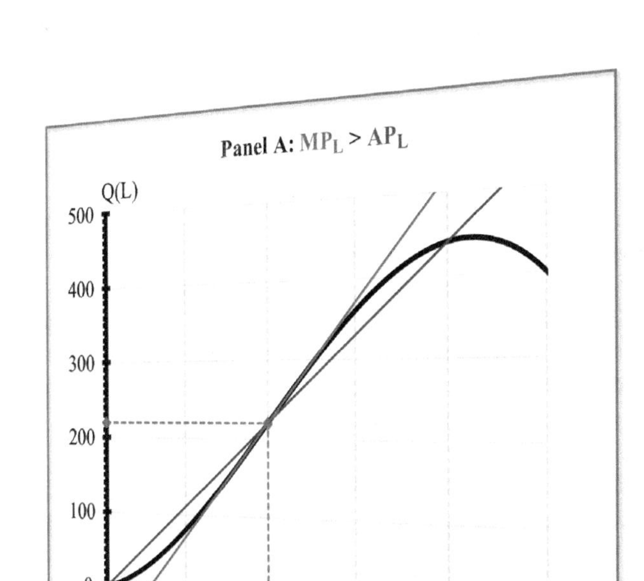

Chapter Outline

Firms produce goods using factors of production, which include land, labor, capital, and materials. The way that firms put together inputs to produce outputs depends on what is technologically feasible. Some outputs may be produced from a given bundle of inputs and a given state of technology, while other outputs may simply not be feasible. The production function summarizes what is feasible. Specifically, a production function describes the maximum amount of output that can be produced from a given bundle of inputs. This is analogous to the concept of a utility function, which formed the analytical backbone of consumer theory.

The links between consumer-side concepts and producer-side concepts are the focus of Section 9.1. One main difference distinguishes the two sides, and that is the concept of cardinality. Cardinality means that magnitude matters; production is cardinal, and this makes producer theory more concrete. (The most difficult aspect of consumer theory for most students to understand is the ordinality of utility functions; this distinction makes a number of producer-side concepts easier to grasp.) Section 9.2 examines the concepts of marginal and average productivity, as well as the relation between these notions of productivity. Both concepts examine productivity in a *ceteris paribus* fashion. The law of diminishing marginal product is also examined in Section 9.2. Section 9.3 examines three production functions that describe production processes with different degrees of input factor substitutability. These functions range from perfect-input-substitutability linear production to no-input-substitutability perfect-complement production. Cobb-Douglas (CD) production provides a middle ground in terms of input substitutability. Each of these functions has a consumer theory analog, but each must be considered in light of the cardinality that is the hallmark of production functions. Section 9.4 examines the question of what happens to output when all inputs increase by the same proportion. This is the notion of returns to scale. Three types of returns to scale are delineated: (1) decreasing returns to scale, (2) constant returns to scale, and (3) increasing returns to scale. The production functions examined in Section 9.3 are reexamined in light of the notion of returns to scale. Finally, a cubic production function is examined that allows economists to model increasing, constant, and decreasing returns to scale with a single production function. This form provides the basis for the discussion of marginal versus average product in Section 9.2. As a result, Section 9.4 concludes with a direct comparison of returns to scale with average and marginal productivity.

9.1 Producer Theory as Consumer Theory with Cardinality

Many of the geometric and algebraic constructs used to analyze consumer behavior in Part 2 can be remolded and reused on the producer side. In some ways, the producer calculus is harder because the end game of profit maximization can only be understood by bringing consumers back into the analysis, since profits require revenue, and revenue requires demand. In other ways, the producer calculus is easier than the consumer calculus, despite the lack of formal experience most students have as members of firms. (Students have been consumers since they were very small, but many have been formal members of the "other side" only in summer jobs.) Producer theory is easier because it is cardinal, rather than ordinal, in nature.

Perhaps the hardest thing to understand about consumer theory is the ordinality of utility functions (discussed in Section 4.3). The concept of utility is ethereal. Order matters but not numerical differences, at least not with regard to utility.[1] By contrast, production is a *cardinal concept.* If you once produced 20 gallons of apple cider, and you now produce 160 gallons of apple cider, you now produce 8 times as much cider (and 140 gallons more as well). Each of these numbers has cardinal meaning (20 gallons, 160 gallons, 8 times as much, 140 gallons more), and each of these magnitudes matters. There is a physical reality about the difference in production that is not matched on the consumer side: You can typically count the goods produced, but you cannot count in a cardinal sense the utility "produced" in the process of consumption.

The starting point for our analysis of firm behavior is to examine firms as producers of goods and services. Firms use inputs or factors of production to produce outputs. An **input** is a resource used in the production process. Another common term for an input is a *factor of production.* Typically, inputs are described using the broad categorical labels of land, labor, capital, and raw materials. While land, labor, and raw materials are reasonably self-evident, *capital* is a term that economists use in enough different ways that it should be more formally defined in this context. If an input is itself an output, it is called **capital** or a **capital good**. Capital goods are goods that are used to produce other goods. Buildings and machines are examples of capital goods. We can define inputs much more narrowly than the four-way classification (distinguishing, for example, different types of labor or raw material), but we often move in the opposite direction and work within a two-input model (just as we restricted our analysis to two goods when we discussed preferences).

input: An input is a resource used in the production process. Another common term for an input is a *factor of production.*

capital or capital good: If an input is itself an output, it is called capital or a capital good. Capital goods are goods that are used to produce other goods.

When we talk about inputs in the production process, as well as outputs of that process, we think in terms of *flows* rather than *stocks*. If we are considering the hourly output as a function of inputs, then output is output per hour, and inputs are number of units of each input per hour. The easiest way to understand this distinction is in the context of capital. The number of units of capital employed in the production process is not the number of machines, but the number of machine hours. Other inputs are also measured in flow terms. We typically omit the reference to time period when we talk about inputs and outputs, and simply refer to both without the explicit reference to "per unit of time."

The technology of production determines the way that inputs are combined to create output. Quite simply, some outcomes are not technologically possible for a given bundle of inputs, while others are possible. To take a simple example, suppose you have a bushel of apples and an apple press, and your goal is to make apple cider. The apples are raw material, the apple press is capital, and your labor is the labor input. In this instance, you might be able to obtain three gallons of apple cider from the bushel of apples. Three gallons are feasible, but four gallons are not technologically possible; there simply is not enough liquid in one bushel of apples to obtain that much cider. Obviously, many firms have production processes that are substantially more complex than our example of pressing cider, but the common element remains: For a given bundle of inputs in the production process, some outputs are possible, and others are not. A **production function** summarizes the relation that exists between a given bundle of inputs and the maximum amount of output that can be produced from those inputs. A production function is based on a given state of technology. Mathematically, we write this as $Q = Q(\mathbf{F}) = Q(f_1, f_2, \ldots, f_n)$, given n factors of production, or more commonly, $Q = Q(L, K)$, where L is labor and K is capital. Sometimes, it is convenient to fix all factors of production except one and talk about production as a univariate function, such as $Q = Q(L)$.

production function: A production function summarizes the relation that exists between a given bundle of inputs and the maximum amount of output that can be produced from those inputs. A production function is based on a given state of technology.

Production functions are the producer-side analog to the utility function. Inputs are "consumed" by the firm in the production process, just as utility is "produced" by consumers as they consume goods. As with utility functions, we can describe production functions both geometrically and algebraically. Cardinality makes production functions easier to conceptualize; the output of a production function typically has a physicality not shared by the output of a utility function. Utility is ordinal in nature, but by contrast, a production function has cardinality. If you have produced 1.25 gallons of apple cider, you can measure this and note that it is, indeed, 1 quart (0.25 gallons) more than 1 gallon.

A production function takes technology as given and fixed. If technological change occurs, then the production function changes.

Claim: *If you have* **a** *production function that represents a given state of technology, then you have* **the** *production function that represents that state of technology.*

Exactly the opposite held true about utility functions, as shown in Section 4.3; two utility functions that only differ by a monotonic transformation represent the *same* preferences.[2] This distinction is also based on the cardinality/ordinality difference between the producer and consumer sides.

Many of the concepts used to analyze utility functions have producer-side analogs. The **marginal product of factor i at input bundle F, $MP_i(\mathbf{F})$**, for small changes in input i, Δf_i, is calculated as: $MP_i(\mathbf{F}) = (Q(\mathbf{F} + \Delta f_i) - Q(\mathbf{F}))/\Delta f_i = \Delta Q/\Delta f_i$. This is also sometimes called the *marginal physical product of factor i*. $\mathbf{F} + \Delta f_i = (f_1, \ldots, f_{i-1}, f_i + \Delta f_i, f_{i+1}, \ldots, f_n)$ is the input bundle **F** with Δf_i more input i (or less if $\Delta f_i < 0$). Marginal product tells us how valuable an input is in incremental production of the good. Marginal product is a rate of change.

marginal product of factor i at input bundle F, $MP_i(\mathbf{F})$: The marginal product of factor i at input bundle **F**, $MP_i(\mathbf{F})$ for small changes in input i, Δf_i, is calculated as $MP_i(\mathbf{F}) = (Q(\mathbf{F} + \Delta f_i) - Q(\mathbf{F}))/\Delta f_i = \Delta Q/\Delta f_i$. This is also sometimes called the *marginal physical product of factor i*.

Claim: *Marginal product is the slope of the production function in the ith direction at point **F**, ceteris paribus, just like marginal utility is the slope of utility.*[3]

An **isoquant** maps out the set of input bundles that produce the same level of output. This is analogous to an indifference curve. An isoquant is obtained by setting the production function equal to a constant ($Q_0 = Q(L, K)$) for the two-input case. Different levels of output yield different isoquants. Although this has already been noted, it is worth reemphasizing that the numbers attached to the isoquants *mean* something that is absent in examining the numbers attached to indifference curves. The number of utils attached to an indifference curve can be conceptualized but cannot be counted in a cardinal sense. Output produced can be counted. An **isoquant map** is a graphical display of multiple isoquants. This is analogous to an indifference map, or preference map. The **marginal rate of technical substitution, $MRTS_{j,i} = -\Delta f_j/\Delta f_i$**, holding all other factors of production constant along the isoquant. The MRTS is the rate at which one input can be substituted for another input without affecting output level; the MRTS is minus the slope of the isoquant in the (f_i, f_j) direction. Most of the time, we will work with the two-input Q(L, K) model;

isoquant: An isoquant maps out the set of input bundles that produce the same level of output.

isoquant map: An isoquant map is a graphical display of multiple isoquants.

marginal rate of technical substitution, $MRTS_{j,i} = -\Delta f_j/\Delta f_i$: The marginal rate of technical substitution, $MRTS_{j,i} = -\Delta f_j/\Delta f_i$, holding all other factors of production constant along the isoquant.

in this instance, the subscripts are omitted, and the MRTS = $-\Delta K/\Delta L$ along the isoquant. The MRTS is the producer-side analog of the marginal rate of substitution (MRS); some authors actually call both concepts MRS. The T (for technical) is added in this text to remind you that the two concepts are distinct.

The relation between MRTS and marginal products is the same as between MRS and marginal utilities:

$$MRTS = MP_L/MP_K \text{ in the two-input } Q(L, K) \text{ context.} \quad \textbf{(9.1a)}$$

In the n-input case, the slope in the input i, input j direction along the isoquant is given by:

$$MRTS_{j,i} = MP_i/MP_j. \quad \textbf{(9.1b)}$$

The proof is identical to the proof in Chapter 4 Appendix A that MRS = MU_x/MU_y. All that must be done is to replace the utility function by the production function, and outputs x_i and x_j by input factors of production f_i and f_j. We have explicitly noted the difference between the consumer-side and the producer-side analogs of each concept created by the cardinal/ordinal difference. It should be noted that the ordinality of utility does not affect the MRS (as shown in Chapter 4 Appendix A). The MRS *and* the MRTS are both cardinal concepts that describe substitutability.

There are a number of other producer-side analogs to concepts we initially examined on the consumer side, but they have to do with various cost concepts. Before analyzing cost of production, it is appropriate to examine how we represent production. As a result, the cost discussion will be put off until Chapter 10, just as we initially separated notions of preferences and their geometric and algebraic representation in Chapters 3 and 4 from constraints on those preferences (which we initially examined in Chapter 5).

9.2 The Relation between Total, Marginal, and Average Product

If all factors of production save one are held constant, then production is a function of that single factor. When there is only one factor of production that varies, the production function is often called a total product curve. A **total product curve** is the maximum quantity produced as a function of a single factor of production, holding all other factors of production fixed. A total product curve is simply a univariate production function, *ceteris paribus* (where all other inputs, as well as technology, are held constant).

total product curve: A total product curve is the maximum quantity produced as a function of a single factor of production, holding all other factors of production fixed.

The analysis in this section is conceptually appropriate for any factor of production, but we use labor as the variable factor of production. As a result, we write the total product curve as Q = Q(L) = TP(L). In Section 9.3, we extend the analysis to production functions with more than one variable input.

Total Product versus Marginal Product

A total product curve often conforms to a common shape. Given fixed plant, property, and equipment, initial units of labor should be increasingly productive (since there is less stopping and starting of machines if there are more workers available to use the available machines). This is seen in a total product curve that is initially convex upward; the total product curve is initially increasing in slope in (L, Q) space. Over this range of units of labor, each extra unit of labor increases output by more than the last unit of labor; the marginal product of labor is an increasing function of labor. Past a point, the reverse must be true. Once plant capacity has been reached (and all the jobs are covered), additional workers should have diminishing productivity. Additional units of labor may continue to increase output, but output increases at a decreasing rate; the marginal product of labor is a declining function of labor. Over this range of output, the total product curve is convex downward. Past some point, adding additional workers may even cause aggregate output to decline (as workers get in each other's way). In this event, the total product curve will have a negative slope, and the marginal product of labor is negative.

Figure 9.1 shows a graph consistent with this analysis. Before considering Figures 9.1B–9.1E, examine Figure 9.1A. It shows the total product curve without including tangent lines to the curve. For L between zero and about 20, the TP curve is convex upward (like a bowl). When L is larger than about 20, the TP curve is convex downward (like a dome). When L is larger than about 42, the TP curve is negatively sloped. In terms of the productivity discussed earlier, productivity increases up to about L = 20 and decreases once L is larger than 20. For L larger than about 42, productivity becomes negative. The geometric interpretation of the graph is more important at this juncture than the algebraic analysis, which is shown in the endnote.[4]

The interpretation of the graph is based on marginal product being the slope of the total product curve. Figures 9.1B–9.1E examine this slope at various values of L. As with the discussion of the MRS as slope of the indifference curve in Chapter 3 (see Figure 3.3), the most accurate description of slope is the slope of the tangent line. As a result, the red line in Figures 9.1B–9.1E is tangent to the total product curve at the value of L specified in the figure. For example, L = 0 in Figure 9.1B and shows that the initial marginal product of labor is 3 (since $3 = \Delta TP/\Delta L = 150/50$). Figure 9.1C shows that the estimate of about 42 is accurate as the point of maximum total product. Total product is maximized when marginal product is zero (it is left as a workbook problem to prove that total product is maximized at 42.36). Figure 9.1D shows one of two levels of labor where the marginal product of labor is 10 (a slope that is easy to visualize, given the gridwork size in the figure).

The point where a curve changes concavity is called a *point of inflection*. It is difficult to see visually that this occurs exactly at L = 20, but this is easy to prove algebraically.[5] (You should be able to see this in a rough sense, using the tangent line in the upper diagram of Figure 9.1E. The table in the Excel version of Figure 9.1 allows you to see MP_L (slope) to the nearest 0.01 units for L. A slider allows you to vary L and see what happens to the tangent line as a result. Moving the slider and watching for the steepest tangent line quickly gets you close to L = 20 without use of the table.) The point of inflection is the point of maximum marginal productivity of labor. We see in Figure 9.1E that $MP_L(20) = 15$ is the maximum marginal product of labor. This figure includes a marginal product curve in a second graph beneath the total product graph and a table of values. To conserve on space, the $MP_L(L)$ curve is only shown once, but it is appropriate to consider how the slope of the TP(L) curve at various points depicted in Figures 9.1B–9.1D tie to this curve.

The eventual concavity of the total product curve occurs for every univariate production process because, eventually, the fixed factors of production become "fully utilized," no matter how plentiful those fixed factors initially appear. Adding more and more of one factor of production, while holding all other factors fixed, inevitably and inexorably leads to the eventual decline in the marginal product of that factor of production. This is called the law of diminishing marginal product. The **law of diminishing marginal product** states that as more and more of a factor of production is used, with all other factors and technology held constant, there must eventually be a decline in the incremental output produced by extra units of the variable factor of production. Put another way, given a fixed production process and fixed factors of production, there must exist a level of employment for the variable factor of production beyond which the marginal product of that factor declines.[6]

law of diminishing marginal product: The law of diminishing marginal product states that as more and more of a factor of production is used, with all other factors and technology held constant, there must eventually be a decline in the incremental output produced by extra units of the variable factor of production.

Interestingly, the law of diminishing marginal product is another concept that has a consumer-side analog. You may recall that your introductory microeconomics text described a "law of diminishing marginal utility (or returns)" on the consumer side that helped clarify the consumer utility maximization problem. The law stated that as individuals consume more and more of a good, their marginal utility for the good declines. We did not mention this "law" during our discussion of consumer theory because we focused on MRS (the ratio of marginal utilities), rather than marginal utility itself.[7] We did so because *no* behavioral weight should be placed on an individual marginal utility; the "law of diminishing marginal utility" does not make economic sense, due to the ordinal nature

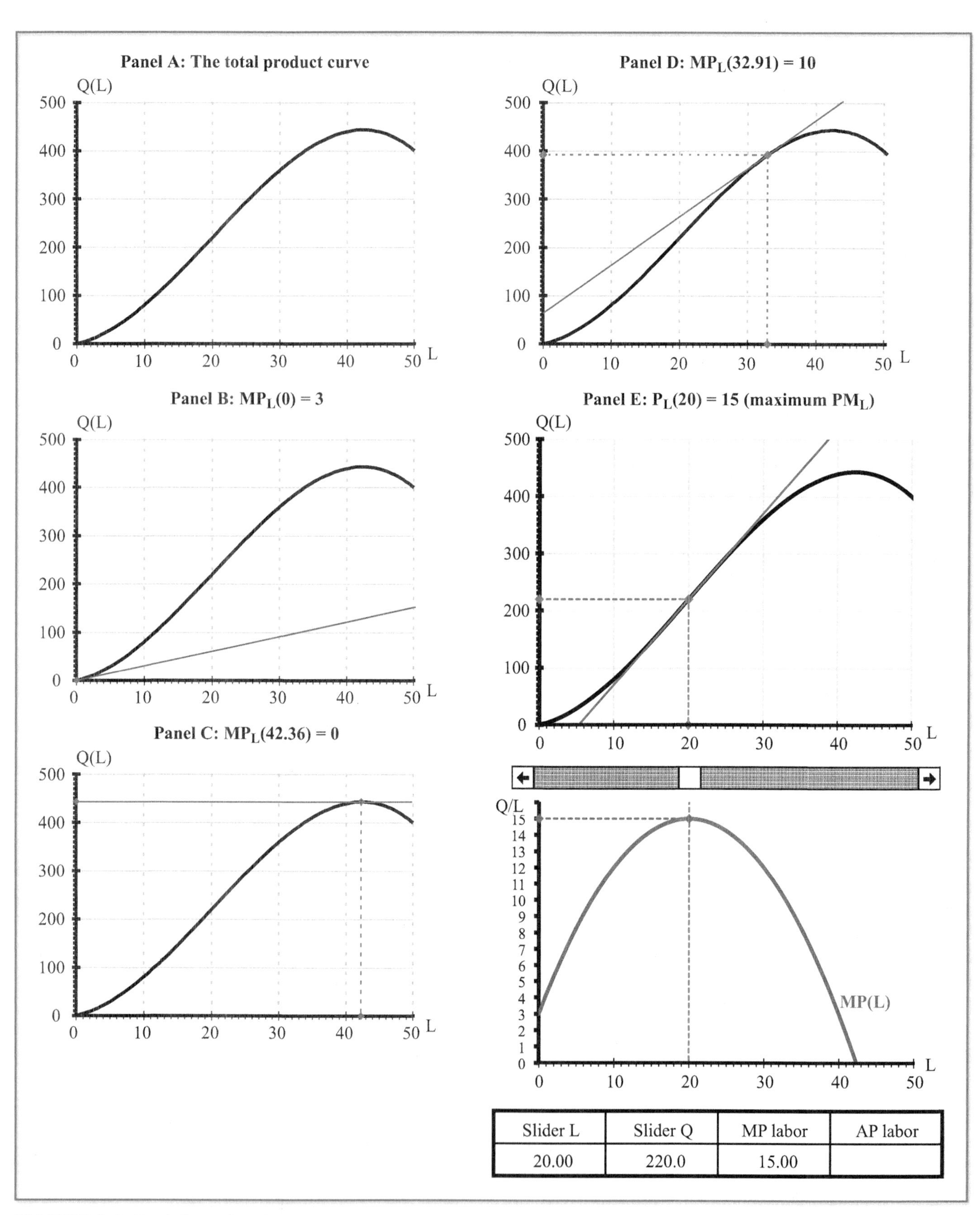

Slider L	Slider Q	MP labor	AP labor
20.00	220.0	15.00	

FIGURE 9.1 Deriving Marginal Product

of utility.[8] This "law" is used as a "white lie" by introductory textbook authors to simplify the presentation of the consumer's optimization problem in the absence of indifference curves. Despite the lack of behavioral content to the consumer-side "law," the producer-side law has a strong theoretical underpinning, due to the cardinality of production. As Dick Cheney said to Prince Bandar of Saudi Arabia, "You can take it to the bank."

Total Product versus Average Product

There are really two versions or answers to the question: How productive is a factor of production? The first answer is provided by marginal productivity, which we just discussed. The second answer is based on the notion of average productivity. The **average product of labor** is defined as $AP_L(L) = TP(L)/L$. It is total output divided by the amount of labor used and tells us the average number of units of output produced per unit of labor, given that other factors of production are held fixed. Labor is not unique here, and similar definitions could be given for any factor of production. Notice that average productivity is predicated on a given and fixed level of other factors. If those levels change, then so would average productivity. This is not surprising; labor will have greater average productivity if laborers have access to more capital in the production process. (Of course, the same can be said for marginal productivity.)

average product of labor: The average product of labor is defined as $AP_L(L) = TP(L)/L$. It tells us the average number of units of output produced per unit of labor.

An average value for a point on a curve can be derived using a simple geometric trick. The *slope* of the chord connecting the origin to a point on the total product curve is the average product of that point.[9] This is shown for a variety of values of labor in Figure 9.2. The slope of the blue chord connecting the origin to a point on the TP(L) curve is the average product of that level of labor. Figure 9.2A depicts a very easy version of the blue chord; the blue chord has slope of 10, since it passes through (0, 0) and (50, 500). This chord intersects the total product curve at about L = 16 and L = 44 (44 is easier to see than 16, since the pink (L, Q) marker is shown for this value; exact values could be obtained using the slider). Figure 9.2B depicts the situation at L = 0. At a formal level, there is no such thing as the average product at L = 0, since this requires dividing by zero. Nonetheless, we can examine the slope of the chord for small values of L (L = 0.05 can be seen using the slider). The limit of these slopes is a slope of 3; $AP_L(0) = 3$.[10] The blue chord in Figure 9.2C has a slope of 8 (400/50), and it intersects the total product curve at L = 10 and L = 50. Figure 9.2D depicts a useful heuristic device for finding the point of maximum average product. Think of the origin as the hinge of a hardcover book. If you open the front cover and then let it fall back, the place where it comes to rest and just touches the total product curve is the point of maximum average product. Consider the blue tangent line in Figure 9.2D as the front cover; it is tangent at L = 30 at a slope of $AP_L(30) = 12$ (12 = 360/30).

Marginal Product versus Average Product

Average and marginal productivity have been examined separately in Figures 9.1 and 9.2 to focus individual attention on each concept. Although they are distinct concepts, they are nonetheless intimately related, as Figure 9.3 shows. You may have noted that we used the word *tangent* rather than *chord* in the last paragraph when discussing Figure 9.2D; this is because L = 30 represents a point where both average and marginal productivity concepts achieve the same outcome: The tangent is the chord (MP = AP) at the point of maximum average productivity. The other place where both productivity concepts are equal is at L = 0 (as a comparison of Figures 9.1B and 9.2B shows). At other values of L, one function or the other is larger. Figures 9.3A and 9.3B show the two possibilities. The orientation of MP_L and AP_L is seen both in terms of the slopes of the red (MP tangent) and blue (AP chord) lines in the upper diagrams, and in the orientation of the AP_L and MP_L points on their respective curves in the lower diagrams. In Figure 9.3A, marginal product exceeds average product, and as a result, average product is increasing. When the marginal product of labor exceeds the average product of labor, then an increase in labor will pull up the average. The reverse holds true in Figure 9.3B. When average product exceeds

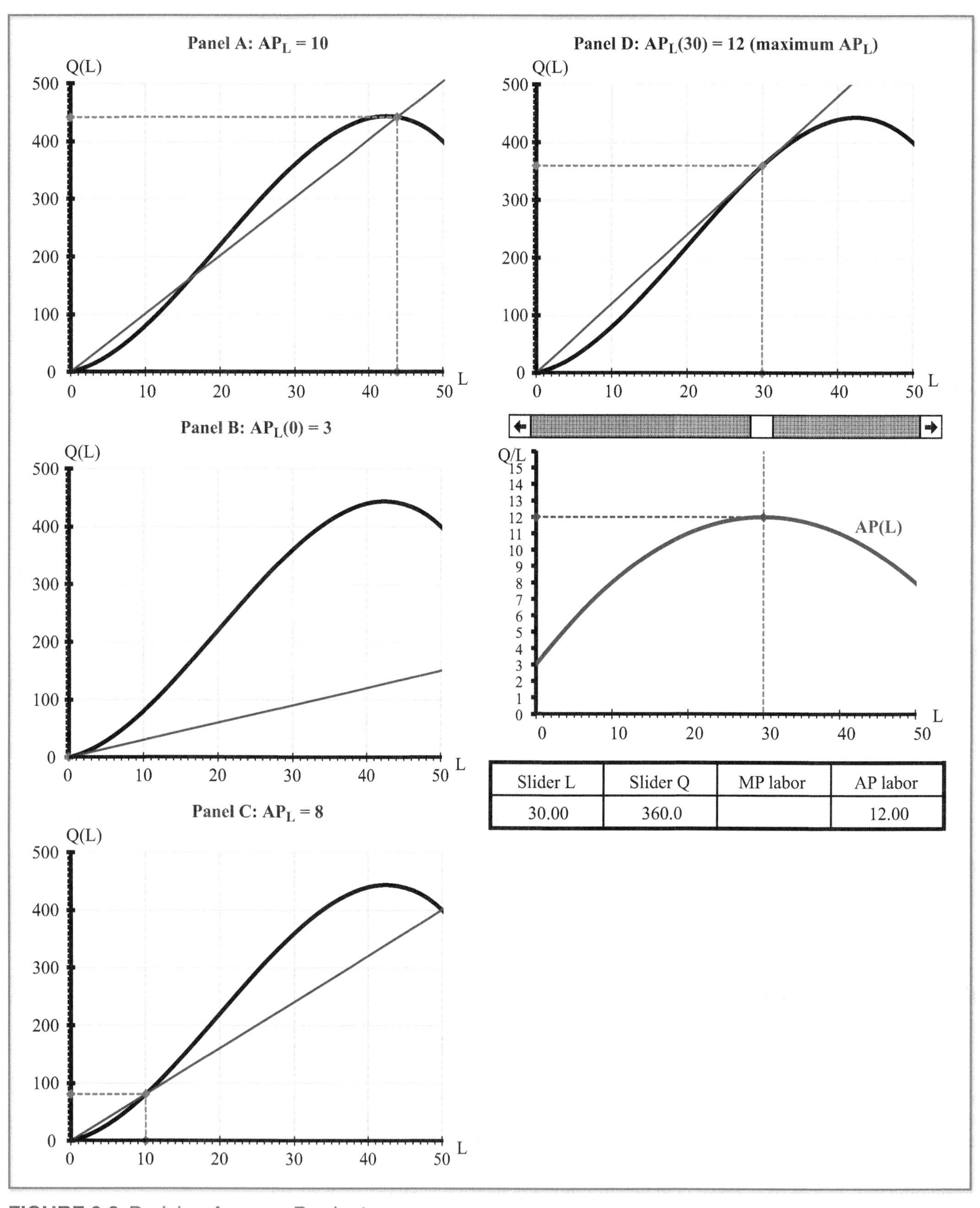

Slider L	Slider Q	MP labor	AP labor
30.00	360.0		12.00

FIGURE 9.2 Deriving Average Product

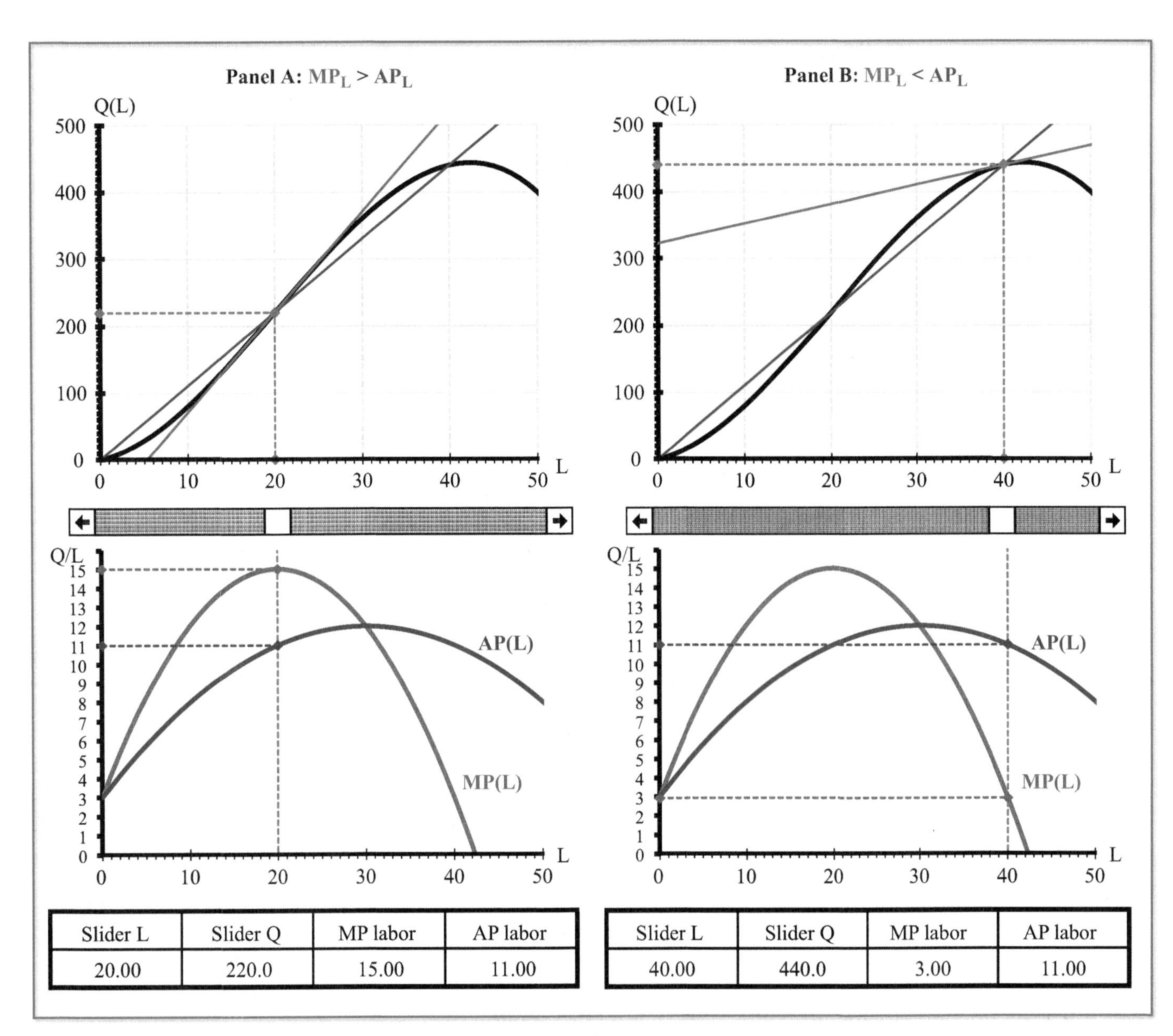

FIGURE 9.3 Comparing Average and Marginal Product

marginal product, an increase in labor pulls down the average product. Average product is maximized when average equals marginal. More generally, the following must always hold between average and marginal:

Claim: *Marginal pulls average up or down, depending on whether marginal is above or below average.*

On Batting Averages and GPAs

The relation between average and marginal will always hold; the relative size of average and marginal *always* determines whether the average is increasing or decreasing. If marginal exceeds average, then average is increasing. If average exceeds marginal, then average is decreasing. Although you may not have considered this before, you almost certainly have already figured this out based on your real-world experiences.

If you follow baseball, you have noticed that an individual's batting average does not change by much from day to day, but it always changes in the direction of what happened in the previous game. For example, suppose you are following a player who has a 0.300 batting average. If the player has 2 hits in 5 at bats, his average will increase to, say 0.302.

Put in the context of marginal pulling average: 2 for 5 on the day is a (marginal) 0.400 day; marginal exceeds average, so average increases. Had the reverse held true—for example, if the player had had a 0-for-5 day—his average would have declined to, say, 0.295.

If you do not follow baseball, you still have seen this phenomenon, since you undoubtedly follow your own GPA. Suppose you have a 3.00 GPA. You can only increase your GPA by having a (marginal) semester that exceeds 3.00. Conversely, you will only decrease your GPA by having a (marginal) semester that is worse than a 3.00. Both of these examples conform to the standard relation that exists between marginal and average: Marginal pulls average up or down, depending on whether it is above or below average.

Marginal shows more variability than average—that is, average moves more "slowly" than marginal—and the "speed" with which average moves gets slower (or movements are smaller) as the base on which the average is calculated becomes larger. In the context of the previous examples, this means that a player has an easier time increasing his single-season batting average by 0.020 points earlier in the season than later in the season. It also means that a second-semester college freshman has a much easier time increasing personal GPA by 0.2 than a second-semester senior.

Table 9.1 shows this point both for batting averages and for GPAs. Both have the same underlying assumptions (to simplify matters as much as possible): Both have a starting average of 0.300 (or 3.00), and both have a marginal "observation" of 0.400 (or 4.00). The average adjusts over time as new information is introduced. In the batting example, the new information is provided every time the player goes up to bat (but this is examined on a cumulative basis at the end of a day in which the player went to bat 5 times). A 0.400 day produces a 0.020-point bump if it is very early in the season (if you have only been at bat 20 times prior to that day), but produces a 0.001-point bump if the player is closing in on 400 at bats for the season. A similar point is made with GPA adjustments. The calculations assume that each semester has the same number of course credits (so each semester can be treated as a single observation). A 4.0 marginal semester on top of a first-semester freshman year GPA of 3.00 causes the end-of-freshman year GPA to increase to 3.50. Had the same marginal semester occurred in the second semester of the senior year, the adjustment in GPA would be 0.125, rather than 0.50. Of course, the same holds true for marginal semesters below average. For a given starting GPA, a really bad semester will have a larger effect on GPA if it occurs early in the college career, rather than later in the college career. Because the average is spread out over a larger number of semesters, the damage caused by a bad (marginal) semester is spread out over a larger base.

TABLE 9.1 Examining How Averages Adjust to the Introduction of New Information

How Batting Averages Adjust to a 2-for-5 Day at Different Points in the Season								
At bats prior to current day	n_0	20	45	70	95	195	295	395
Start-of-day batting average	A_0	0.300	0.300	0.300	0.300	0.300	0.300	0.300
At bats for the day	b_1	5	5	5	5	5	5	5
Hits for the day	h_1	2	2	2	2	2	2	2
Batting average for the day (marginal)	$m_1 = h_1/b_1$	0.400	0.400	0.400	0.400	0.400	0.400	0.400
Total at bats through the day	$n_1 = n_0 + b_1$	25	50	75	100	200	300	400
End-of-day batting average	$(A_0n_0 + m_1b_1)/n_1$	0.320	0.310	0.307	0.305	0.303	0.302	0.301
How GPA Adjusts to a 4.00 Semester at Different Points in a College Career								
Semesters already completed	n_0	1	2	3	4	5	6	7
GPA	A_0	3.00	3.00	3.00	3.00	3.00	3.00	3.00
Current-semester GPA (marginal)	m_1	4.00	4.00	4.00	4.00	4.00	4.00	4.00
End-of-semester GPA	$(A_0n_0 + m_1)/(n_0 + 1)$	3.50	3.33	3.25	3.20	3.167	3.143	3.125

9.3 Production Functions and Their Geometric Representation as Isoquants

While there are solid reasons to examine production functions in a univariate context, the most robust analysis of production functions occurs in the context of multiple variable inputs. In this section, we expand our analysis to a two-input model (to provide a graphical representation of the model). As with the consumer side, restricting our analysis to two inputs does not materially affect our ability to obtain meaningful results. We typically work with labor and capital as the two inputs, and we put labor on the horizontal axis, so the production function is algebraically described as Q = Q(L, K). We highlight three functions, familiar from Chapter 4, in this section: perfect complements, perfect substitutes, and CD. These functions represent both ends and the middle of the input substitutability spectrum.

No Input Substitutability: Leontief Production

If technology suggests that inputs need to be used in a certain ratio, then the production process is a fixed-proportion production process. The inputs in this case are perfect complements to one another. Suppose it takes *a* units of labor and b units of capital to produce 1 unit of output (and less of either input means that less than 1 unit of output is produced). Suppose further that if you have more than *a* units of labor but only b units of capital, you can still produce only 1 unit of output. Finally, if you have *a* units of labor and more than b units of capital, you can still produce only 1 unit of output. We could write the production function representing this process as:

$$Q(L, K) = \text{Minimum}(L/a, K/b). \quad \textbf{(9.2a)}$$

Fixed-proportion production functions form the basis for input-output analysis, an area of study for which Wassily Leontief won the Nobel Prize in Economics. Such production functions are often called **Leontief** production functions.

Leontief: A production function is Leontief if it exhibits fixed proportions.

To give a simple example, suppose the task under consideration is part of a larger production process that puts together bicycles. Consider the job of attaching the wheels. To put one wheel together requires one worker and two wrenches (*a* = 1, b = 2). If you have only one worker, more than two wrenches does not increase productivity, and if you have two wrenches, more than one worker does not increase productivity. Of course, each additional worker and two wrenches increases output by 1 unit in this example. Figure 9.4 shows an isoquant map associated with this production process. If you consider

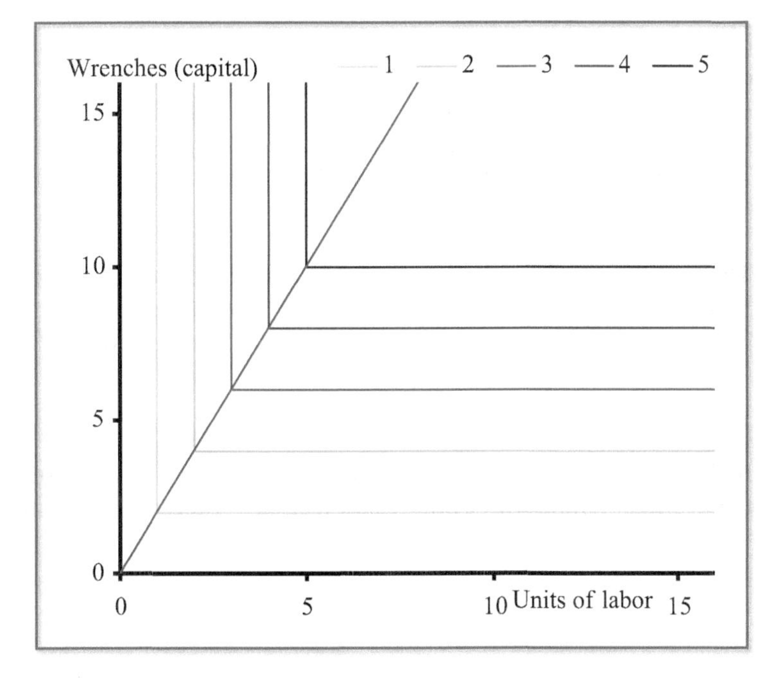

FIGURE 9.4 Fixed-Proportion (Leontief) Isoquant Map

a different production process, you might wish to change a or b to match the new job described by the process.

The output of the production process need not be one when L = 1 and K = 2 in this instance. Suppose you attach 10 wheels per hour. Then the hourly production function is just as shown in Figure 9.4, but the quantities attached to each isoquant are measured in 10s of wheels attached per hour. You could accomplish the same thing in two other ways: You could adjust the time period under consideration (from 1 hour to 1/10th of an hour), or you could simply adjust the production function as:

$$Q(L, K) = c \cdot \text{Minimum}(L/a, K/b). \quad \textbf{(9.2b)}$$

The parameter c is a scaling factor that describes how many units are produced per unit of time.[11] In the previous example, c = 10. A common mistake in this instance is to simply say, "Wait a second, if (L, K) = (1, 2) represents producing 10 fastened wheels, why wouldn't (2, 2) represent producing 20 fastened wheels, since the worker just takes 2 hours with the two wrenches?" The problem with this logic is that it ignores the time dimensionality of capital in this instance; recall that inputs are measured as flows. The 2 is really 2 wrench hours—or more specifically, two wrenches used for 1 hour each. To take advantage of the additional hour of labor, you would need 2 more wrench hours as well; you would need the input bundle (2, 4) rather than (2, 2).

Many pieces of machinery exhibit fixed proportions, or at least very close to fixed proportions. The choice of machine, of course, affects the production function. For example, suppose we used ratchets rather than wrenches in the previous example. A worker would still require two ratchets, but the worker might be able to increase the speed of production so that, perhaps, $c_{ratchet} = 15$, as opposed to $c_{wrench} = 10$ in Equation 9.2b. Each of these functions represents a different production function (unlike on the consumer side, where $U(x, y) = 10 \cdot \text{Minimum}(x, y/2)$, and $V(x, y) = 15 \cdot \text{Minimum}(x, y/2)$ represent the same perfect complements preferences, since they are monotonic transformations of each other).

Perfectly Substitutable Production Processes: Linear Production

At the opposite end of the substitutability spectrum are perfect substitutes. It is difficult to imagine a perfectly substitutable production process using broad categories such as capital and labor, since producing even basic goods with manual labor requires the use of rudimentary tools (capital), and even highly automated production processes require at least *some* labor to make sure the process is working smoothly.

If we consider production processes more narrowly, then it is easier to construct examples of perfect substitutes in production. Consider, for example, the production of framing lumber (8-foot-long two-by-fours) from logs in a lumber mill. Fir and spruce are two commonly used woods for framing lumber, and a 12-inch-diameter, 9-foot-long log of either type of tree would act as perfectly substitutable raw material inputs in the production of framing lumber. Suppose that such a log produces, on average, 10 two-by-fours. Then 1,000 two-by-fours would be produced, using the following input materials bundles:

$$1000 = Q(F, S) = 10 \cdot F + 10 \cdot S. \quad \textbf{(9.3a)}$$

This is an isoquant from the perfect-substitute production function $Q(F, S) = 10 \cdot F + 10 \cdot S$. More generally, suppose that the average fir log produces a different number of two-by-fours than the average spruce log. The isoquant associated with 1,000 two-by-fours would then be described as:

$$1000 = Q(F, S) = b \cdot F + a \cdot S. \quad \textbf{(9.3b)}$$

In this conceptualization, b is the average number of two-by-fours from a fir log, and a is the average number of two-by-fours from a spruce log. Examine Figure 9.5 and answer three questions:

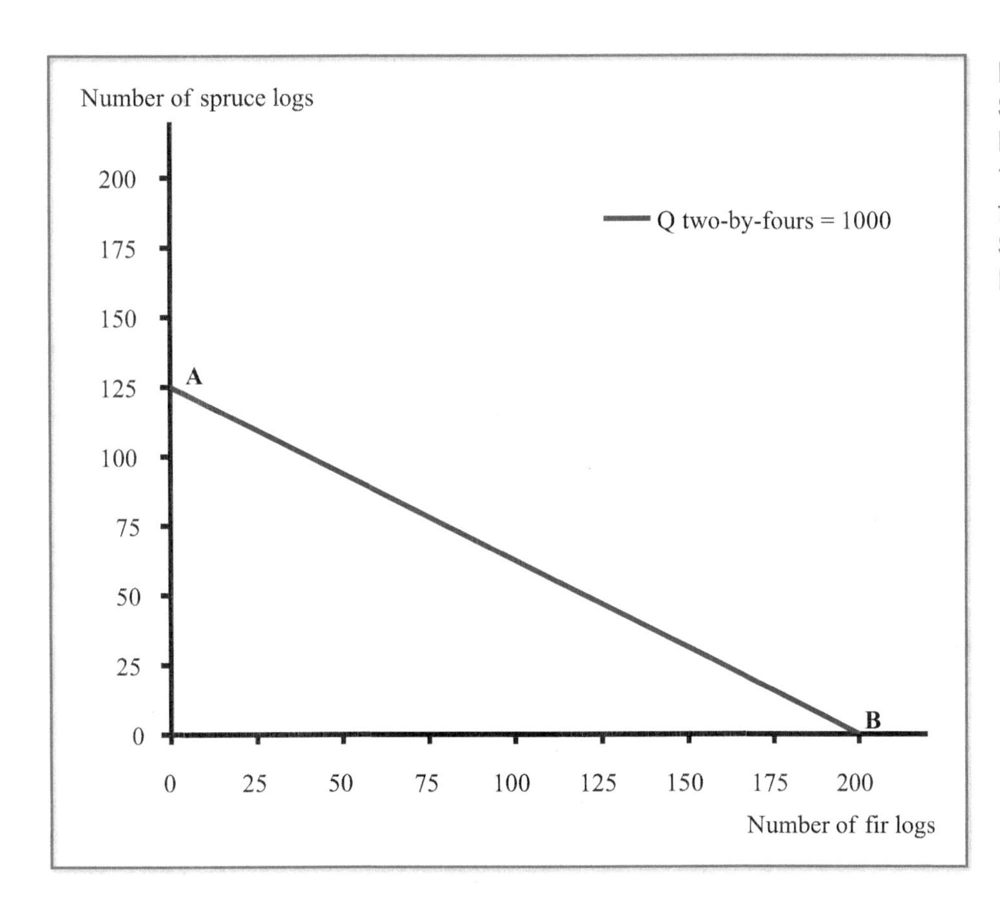

FIGURE 9.5 Perfect Substitutability in Production: Producing 1,000 Two-by-Fours from Two Alternative Sources of Raw Materials

Q5a. What are the values of *a* and b implicit in Figure 9.5?

Q5b. What are the values of the marginal product of fir and the marginal product of spruce implicit in Figure 9.5?

Q5c. What is the MRTS in this instance?*

Some Input Substitutability, Cobb-Douglas Production

Between the extremes of no-input-substitutability Leontief production and perfect-substitutability linear production is the intermediate case of "some" input substitutability. Labor can be substituted for capital, and so there are multiple ways to produce the good, using different quantities of capital and labor (unlike Leontief), but the rate at which that substitution occurs is not constant as you move along the isoquant (as is the case for perfect substitutes). Capital is more readily substituted for labor if the input bundle is capital intensive to begin with, *ceteris paribus*. This means that the MRTS is larger when K/L is larger. Conversely, labor is more readily substituted for capital if the input bundle is more labor intensive to begin with, *ceteris paribus*. This means that the MRTS is smaller as K/L is smaller. Put another way, the MRTS declines as we "walk" down an isoquant; isoquants are convex (just as indifference curves are convex). The degree of substitutability is determined by the technological opportunities available for producing the specific good

***Q5 answer:** Fir produces an average of 5 two-by-fours per log, and spruce produces an average of 8 two-by-fours per log. This is obtained by looking at the fir and spruce intercepts: $1000 = 200 \cdot b$ implies that $b = 5$, and $1000 = 125 \cdot a$ implies that $a = 8$. $MP_F = 5$, $MP_S = 8$, and $MRTS = MP_F/MP_S = 5/8 = 0.625$. (These results can be calculated directly or by using Table 4.1.)

in question. Some goods have a greater range of flexibility than others. A function that provides a middle-ground level of flexibility is the CD production function:

CD production function $Q(L, K) = a \cdot L^r \cdot K^{(1-r)}$. **(9.4a)**

Marginal products $MP_L(L, K) = a \cdot r \cdot (K/L)^{(1-r)}$. **(9.4b)**

$MP_K(L, K) = a \cdot (1 - r) \cdot (L/K)^r$. **(9.4c)**

MRTS: $MRTS = (r/(1 - r)) \cdot (K/L)$. **(9.4d)**

It is worth noting that, as expected, the MRTS declines as we walk down the isoquant according to Equation 9.4d (since K/L declines as L increases along the isoquant).

The only change from the CD utility function discussed in Section 4.4 and described in Figure 4.9 is the parameter a in Equation 9.4a. This parameter should be thought of as a scaling factor. The easiest way to see this is to consider how many units of output are produced when $L = K = 1$ (the input bundle (1, 1) is chosen because $1^r \cdot 1^{(1-r)} = 1$, regardless of the value of r). If the answer is 4 units of output are produced in this instance, then $a = 4$. And, of course, if inputs double to (2, 2), output would also double to eight, and so on. This is the situation depicted in Figure 9.6A for $r = 0.6$. Of course, if the input bundle (1, 1) produces a different amount of output, the numbers attached to the isoquant map for each isoquant change. (For example, the difference between Figures 9.6A and 9.6B is that $a = 1$ in Figure 9.6B, rather than $a = 4$ in Figure 9.6A. As a result, output levels attached to isoquants in Figure 9.6B are four times smaller than in Figure 9.6A.)

MP vector, (MP_L, MP_K): The MP vector, (MP_L, MP_K), points in the direction of the maximum rate of change in production, and the size of the vector represents how quickly this change occurs.

Both Figures 9.6A and 9.6B include MP_L, MP_K, and the MP vector at the input bundle (5, 5), which is analogous to the MU vector at (8, 8) in Figure 4.9. The **MP vector, (MP_L, MP_K)**, points in the direction of the maximum rate of change in production, and the size of the vector represents how quickly this change occurs. The MP vector is always perpendicular to the isoquant. This relation is the same as on the consumer side, where the MU vector is always perpendicular to the indifference curve. (Both vectors depict the direction of maximal change; the direction of no change is necessarily perpendicular to the direction of maximal change, and the slope of the isoquant [indifference curve] locally describes direction of no change.) Both Figures 9.6A and 9.6B also include a yellow MRTS = 1 line as a reference. Above the yellow line, MRTS > 1, and below the line, MRTS < 1. Larger values of r are associated with isoquants that are more tightly clustered to the labor axis (and hence, the yellow MRTS = 1 and the lavender MP vector tilt more toward the labor axis). Smaller values of r are more tightly clustered to the capital axis (and hence, the MRTS = 1 line and the MP vector tilt more toward the capital axis). In both Figures 9.6A and 9.6B, the marginal product of labor is larger than the marginal product of capital since $r > 0.5$. This appears as isoquants that are steeper in the labor direction than in the capital direction along the main diagonal. ($K/L = 1$ along the main diagonal, so the marginal products in Equations 9.4b and 9.4c simplify to $MP_L = a \cdot r$ and $MP_K = a \cdot (1 - r)$. Given $r = 0.6$ in Figure 9.6, $MP_L = 0.6 \cdot a$, and $MP_K = 0.4 \cdot a$ along the main diagonal.)

An alternative way of visualizing this production function is to use a three-dimensional graph. Figure 9.7 depicts the production function shown in Figure 9.6B. The input bundle (5, 5) is the point of intersection of the red L = K line, with the curve associated with 5 units of output. You should be able to see that, starting from this point, the hill is steeper in the L direction than in the K direction. If this is still difficult to visualize, you should go to the Excel version of Figure 9.7 and adjust r to see how the production hill changes as r changes (r is allowed to vary from 0.2 to 0.8 in the Excel file). When you do this, notice that as the hill shifts due to variations in r, the points on the main diagonal do not vary; when $L = K$, then $Q = L^r \cdot K^{(1-r)} = L$, regardless of r.

The marginal product of labor can be seen in Figure 9.7 as the slope of the production function where the hill is sliced so that capital is held fixed. The easiest slice of the production function holding capital fixed to visualize is the curve on the border of the graph (where K = 10). This is the curve to the *left* of the red main diagonal connecting the (L, K, Q) point (0, 10, 0) at the far left of the figure to the point (10, 10, 10) at the top of the figure. The equation for this total product curve is:

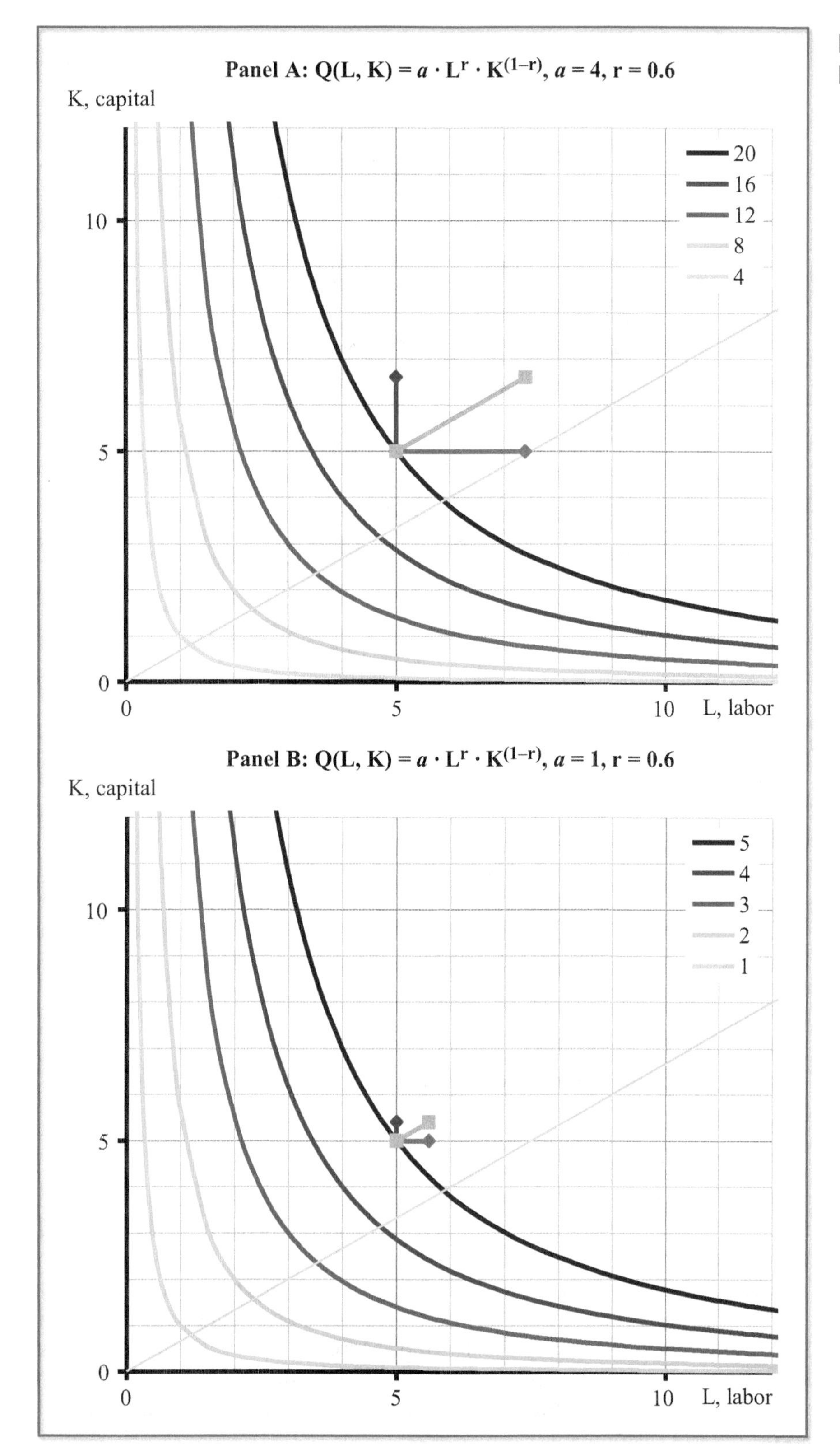

FIGURE 9.6 Cobb-Douglas Production

$Q(L) = TP(L) = Q(L, 10) = 10^{0.4} \cdot L^{0.6}$. **(9.5a)**

The marginal product of labor is algebraically given as Equation 9.4b with $a = 1$, $r = 0.6$, and $K = 10$:

$MP_L(L) = 0.6 \cdot (10/L)^{0.4}$. **(9.5b)**

Other total product of labor curves are seen by following a gridline associated with a given amount of capital, K_o, from its starting place on the capital axis at point $(0, K_o, 0)$

FIGURE 9.7 Cobb-Douglas Production—Three-Dimensional View of Figure 9.6B: $Q(L, K) = L^{0.6} \cdot K^{0.4}$

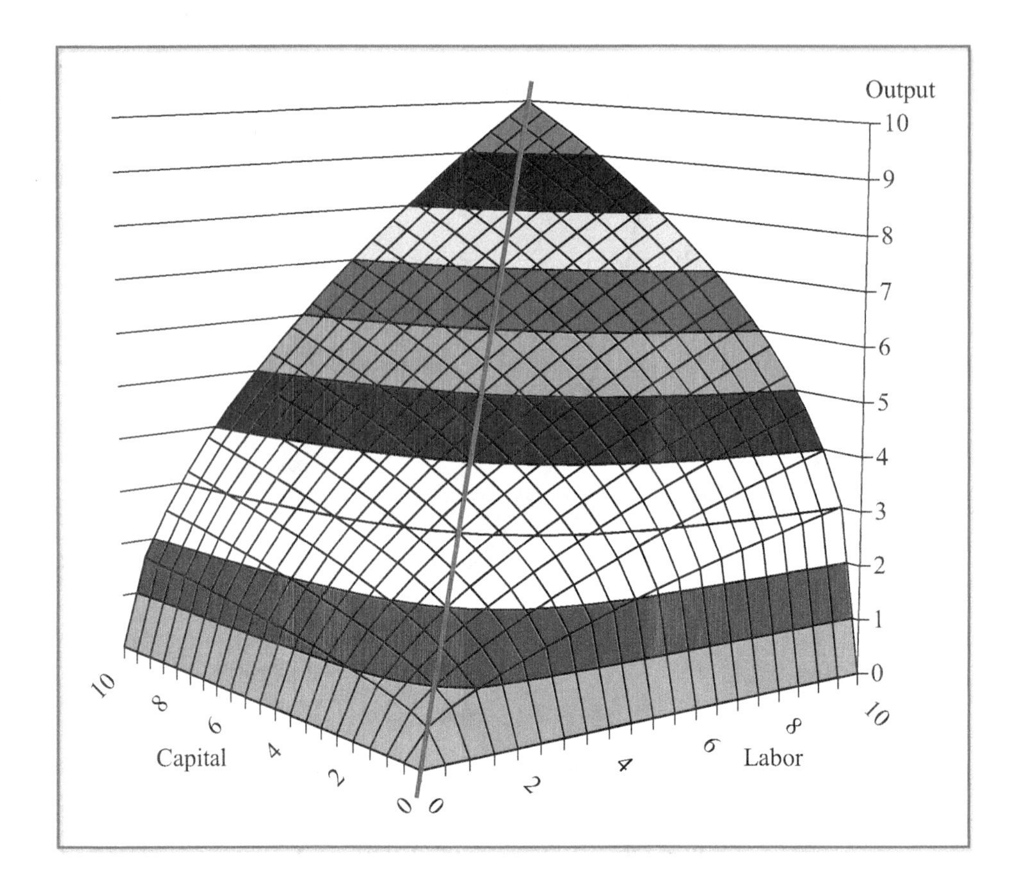

northeast along the $K = K_o$ gridline (20 gridlines are shown in each direction in Figure 9.7, based on a grid system of $\Delta L = 0.5$ and $\Delta K = 0.5$).

Similarly, the marginal product of capital is seen as the slope of the total product of capital curve. As with labor, the easiest total product of capital curve to see is the border of the graph (where L = 10). This is the curve to the *right* of the red diagonal connecting the (L, K, Q) point (10, 0, 0) at the far right of the figure to the point (10, 10, 10) at the top of the figure. The equation for this total product curve is:

$$Q(K) = TP(K) = Q(10, K) = 10^{0.6} \cdot K^{0.4}. \quad \textbf{(9.6a)}$$

The marginal product of capital is algebraically given as Equation 9.4c with $a = 1$, $r = 0.6$, and $L = 10$:

$$MP_K(K) = 0.4 \cdot (10/K)^{0.6}. \quad \textbf{(9.6b)}$$

Other total product of capital curves are seen by following a gridline associated with a given amount of labor, L_o, from its starting place on the labor axis at point (L_o, 0, 0) northwest along the $L = L_o$ gridline.

Figure 9.7 shows that each of the total product curves exhibits diminishing marginal product for all levels of output. The marginal product functions in Equations 9.5b and 9.6b show this algebraically for $r = 0.6$. More generally, Equation 9.4b implies that as long as $r < 1$, the marginal product of labor is a declining function of labor. And as long as $r > 0$, then $1 - r < 1$, and the marginal product of capital is a declining function of capital, according to Equation 9.4c.

9.4 Returns to Scale

What happens when all factors of production vary in a proportionate fashion? For example, if all inputs double, will output necessarily double as well? For certain types of production processes, the answer is yes, but for other processes, the answer is no. Questions of this sort examine the concept of *returns to scale*. Three types of returns to scale are delineated: (1) If an increase of s% in all factors of production causes a less than s%

increase in output, the production process exhibits **decreasing returns to scale (DRTS)**. Sometimes, DRTS processes are said to exhibit *diseconomies of scale*. If an increase of s% in all factors of production causes an s% increase in output, the production process exhibits **constant returns to scale (CRTS)**. If an increase of s% in all factors of production causes a more than s% increase in output, the production process exhibits **increasing returns to scale (IRTS)**. Sometimes, IRTS processes are said to exhibit *economies of scale*.

decreasing returns to scale (DRTS): If an increase of s% in all factors of production causes a less than s% increase in output, the production process exhibits decreasing returns to scale.

constant returns to scale (CRTS): If an increase of s% in all factors of production causes an s% increase in output, the production process exhibits constant returns to scale.

increasing returns to scale (IRTS): If an increase of s% in all factors of production causes a more than s% increase in output, the production process exhibits increasing returns to scale.

Constant returns to scale seems quite comfortable: Doubling inputs should double output, since you can simply replicate the existing production process; the second plant should always be able to achieve the same productive outcome as the first. Increasing returns may occur because of technological opportunities that become available with larger-scale production (for example, a robotic welder is not feasible for smaller-scale production but is for larger-scale production). Also, some processes are simply not as efficient at small scale as they are at large scale. Steel is not produced 1 pound at a time for a reason; small-scale production is simply not as efficient as large-scale production on a cost basis because of economies of scale involved in heating the materials used to create steel. The most common reason for diseconomies of scale has to do with inefficiencies inherent in large-scale organizations. Informational problems become more important the larger the scale of the organization, and these problems may create a situation where the large-scale organization cannot act with the same flexibility as a number of smaller organizations.

Students often confuse the concepts of returns to scale and marginal productivity. Marginal product is a *ceteris paribus* concept (all factors save one are held constant), while returns to scale varies all factors of production. The geometric interpretation of returns to scale is very specific and very different from the geometric interpretation of marginal product. As discussed in Section 9.2, marginal product involves holding all but one factor of production constant; in the two-input (L, K) model, MP_L is obtained by examining production along a horizontal line (holding capital fixed), and MP_K is obtained by examining production along a vertical line (holding labor fixed) in (L, K) space. By contrast, returns to scale *requires* all factors to vary and to vary in a specific way. A proportionate change in all factors of production is geometrically interpreted as a movement along a ray through the origin. Figure 9.8 depicts one such ray, based on an initial input factor bundle $\mathbf{F_0} = (10, 5)$. The parametric representation of the ray through $\mathbf{F_0}$ is simply $(10 \cdot t, 5 \cdot t)$ for nonnegative values of t. One such t is depicted in Figure 9.8, where t = 1.5; this produces a final factor bundle $\mathbf{F_1} = (15, 7.5)$. Returns to scale is determined by the output produced from these two

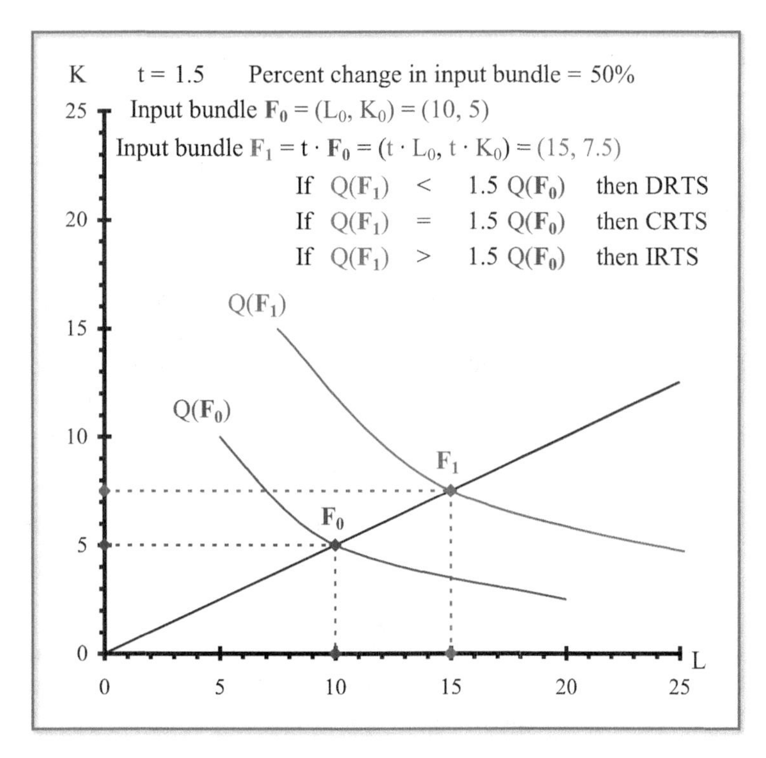

FIGURE 9.8 Examining the Concept of Returns to Scale

input bundles. Is $Q(\mathbf{F}_1)$ less than, equal to, or larger than 50% larger than $Q(\mathbf{F}_0)$? The answer determines returns to scale, but without specific information about the production function, we cannot answer this question. With the production function, we can provide an answer.

Returns to Scale with CD Production

Each of the production functions discussed in the last section exhibited CRTS. It is worthwhile to prove this assertion because it shows how to test for returns to scale. Consider the CD function from Equation 9.4a. Let $\mathbf{F}_0 = (L_0, K_0)$ be an initial input factor bundle that produces Q_0 units of output, where Q_0 is defined as:

$$Q_0 = Q(\mathbf{F}_0) = Q(L_0, K_0) = a \cdot L_0^r \cdot K_0^{(1-r)}. \quad \textbf{(9.7a)}$$

Consider a new input bundle $\mathbf{F}_1$ that involves using s% more of all factors. We can describe the new input bundle as $t = (1 + s/100)$ times the initial bundle; $\mathbf{F}_1 = t \cdot \mathbf{F}_0 = (t \cdot L_0, t \cdot K_0)$. As argued earlier, as we vary t, we map out bundles on the ray through the origin that includes bundle $\mathbf{F}_0$ ($\mathbf{F}_0$ occurs when $t = 1$). What is the value of $Q(\mathbf{F}_1)$? The answer is straightforward:

$$Q(\mathbf{F}_1) = Q(t \cdot L_0, t \cdot K_0) = a \cdot (t \cdot L_0)^r \cdot (t \cdot K_0)^{(1-r)} = a \cdot t^r \cdot L_0^r \cdot t^{(1-r)} \cdot K_0^{(1-r)}. \quad \textbf{(9.7b)}$$

Regrouping, we see that this simplifies to:

$$Q(\mathbf{F}_1) = a \cdot t^{(r+(1-r))} \cdot L_0^r \cdot K_0^{(1-r)} = a \cdot t \cdot L_0^r \cdot K_0^{(1-r)} = t \cdot (a \cdot L_0^r \cdot K_0^{(1-r)}) = t \cdot Q_0. \quad \textbf{(9.7c)}$$

Equation 9.7c shows that an increase in all inputs by a factor of t increases output by a factor of t. This defines constant returns to scale. The same strategy could be used to show that the perfect-complements and perfect-substitutes production functions defined in Equations 9.2 and 9.3 both exhibit CRTS.

An easy adjustment to these functions would provide either decreasing returns or increasing returns. If any of these functions are raised to the power d, where $d < 1$, then the resulting function exhibits decreasing returns, and if $d > 1$, then the resulting function exhibits increasing returns. The general Cobb-Douglas function is a case in point. Consider the production function:

General CD function	$Q(L, K) = a \cdot L^b \cdot K^c$.	**(9.8a)**
Marginal products	$MP_L(L, K) = a \cdot b \cdot L^{(b-1)} \cdot K^c$.	**(9.8b)**
	$MP_K(L, K) = a \cdot c \cdot L^b \cdot K^{(c-1)}$.	**(9.8c)**
MRTS:	$MRTS = (b/c) \cdot (K/L)$.	**(9.8d)**

This function exhibits CRTS if $b + c = 1$ (since then $c = 1 - b$, and Equations 9.8a–9.8d become Equations 9.4a–9.4d). To determine the returns to scale of Equation 9.8a, apply the analysis used to determine returns to scale in Equation 9.7. In this instance, the following would hold:

$$Q(\mathbf{F}_1) = Q(t \cdot L_0, t \cdot K_0) = a \cdot (t \cdot L_0)^b \cdot (t \cdot K_0)^c = t^{(b+c)} \cdot Q(\mathbf{F}_0). \quad \textbf{(9.9)}$$

Since $\mathbf{F}_1$ represents an s% increase in all factors of production, $s > 0$, and $t = (1 + s/100) > 1$. If a number larger than one is raised to a power, the resulting quantity is larger than the initial number, depending on the size of the exponent $b + c$ relative to 1. Equation 9.9 therefore suggests the following rule, given the general CD production function in Equation 9.8a:[12]

The CD production function exhibits DRTS if $b + c < 1$ since $t^{(b+c)} < t$. **(9.10a)**

The CD production function exhibits CRTS if $b + c = 1$ since $t^{(b+c)} = t$. **(9.10b)**

The CD production function exhibits IRTS if $b + c > 1$ since $t^{(b+c)} > t$. **(9.10c)**

For CD production functions, the type of returns to scale is determined by the sum of the exponents attached to the inputs. Figures 9.6 and 9.7 depict CRTS. Figure 9.9 focuses on returns to scale using an equal-weighted CD production function. Each panel maintains "Q bands" that are 1 unit wide, and the three-dimensional views to the right are tilted

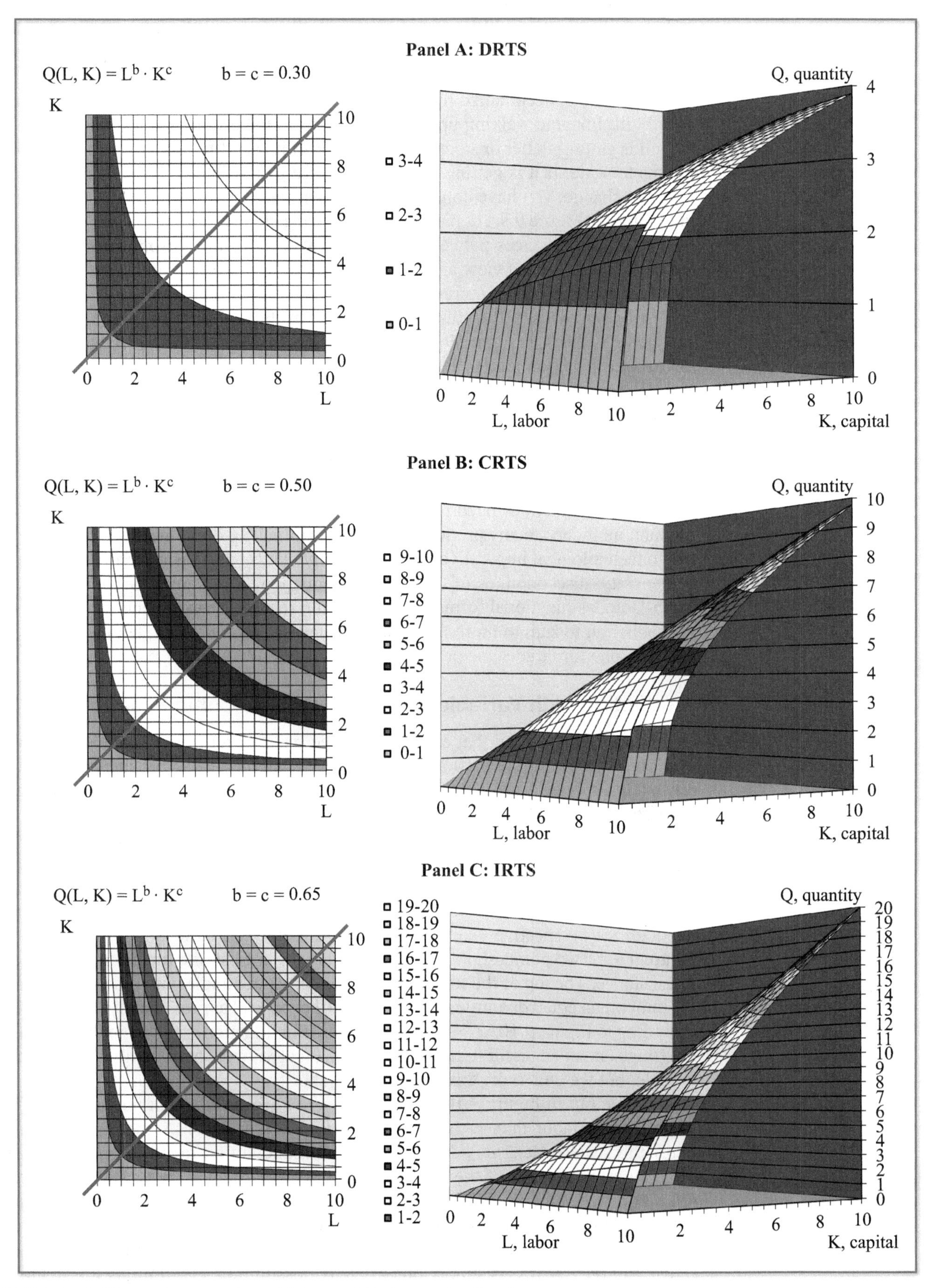

FIGURE 9.9 A Three-Dimensional View of Returns to Scale

so that the production hill is viewed from a shallow angle.[13] Each panel also includes an overhead view to the left.[14] The red 45° line in the overhead panel is roughly the line of sight for the edge of the three-dimensional hill.

The way to conceptualize returns to scale is to think of the production function as an actual hill. Imagine walking up the hill away from the origin on a ray. Consider whether the hill is getting flatter or steeper as you walk. If it is getting flatter, you have decreasing returns to scale; if it is getting steeper, you have increasing returns to scale; if the slope does not change, you have constant returns to scale. You can see each of these situations in Figure 9.9. Figure 9.9A depicts DRTS, since the slope is getting flatter; this can be seen both as longer distances between Q bands as you move away from the origin along the red ray in the overhead view and by the convex downward edge in the three-dimensional view. Greater and greater increments of labor and capital are required for each successive unit of output. This is the situation described by Equation 9.10a, since the sum of the exponents is $0.6 < 1$. Figure 9.9B depicts CRTS, since the slope is constant ($b + c = 1$, as required by Equation 9.10b). Figure 9.9C depicts IRTS, since the slope along a ray increases; the edge is convex upward in the three-dimensional view. IRTS implies that a smaller and smaller proportional increase in inputs is required to obtain a 1-unit increase in output; isoquants are getting closer together as we move away from the origin along any ray through the origin. The sum of the exponents in this instance is 1.3, as required by Equation 9.10c.

Production functions need not maintain one type of returns to scale over all levels of production. Indeed, many production processes initially exhibit increasing returns to scale due to technological imperatives, but eventually exhibit decreasing returns to scale due to bureaucratic diseconomies of large-scale production. This cannot be modeled using the Cobb-Douglas functional form, since this would require the exponents attached to factors of production to sum to more than one for small-scale production, but eventually sum to less than one for large-scale production.

Production with Variable Returns to Scale: Cubic Production

One production function that exhibits all three types of returns to scale is the cubic production function. Figure 9.10 shows a specific example of this production function. We rely exclusively on a geometric analysis of this production function, rather than resort to the algebra that lies beneath the graphics. The algebra in this case is complex, and little is gained beyond what can be gleaned from the graphical analysis. The algebraic details of this function are left to the Chapter 9 Appendix.

Figures 9.10A, 9.10B, and 9.10C examine the same function from different perspectives. The overhead and three-dimensional view are similar to those used in Figure 9.9, although the perspective taken for the three-dimensional view is not as "shallow" as in Figure 9.9.[15] Two points should be immediately clear. First, the function is asymmetric in this instance. The top of the function occurs at an input bundle with more labor than capital, rather than equal quantities of each input (the top is at approximately $(L, K) = (40, 32)$, according to Figure 9.10A). Second, the production function gets steeper before it flattens out (this is most apparent in the three-dimensional view). This roughly describes returns to scale, but we will make this more explicit shortly.

The blue ray in Figure 9.10A depicts $K = 0.95 \cdot L$ (production points on this ray are slightly more labor than capital intensive, $k = K/L = 0.95$). As shown in Figure 9.8, returns to scale is determined by examining production on rays through the origin; the blue ray is simply one of the possible rays.[16] This particular ray was chosen because it roughly matches the production hill outline shown in the three-dimensional view; this is not immediately obvious, but we show why this is the case shortly. (When setting up a surface diagram in Excel, you can rotate the surface in a variety of directions; the view shown in Figure 9.10C is simply one of many possibilities.) Examining the "bandwidth" of the 50-unit-wide Q bands in Figure 9.10A along the blue line suggests that this production function initially exhibits increasing returns to scale (since the bands initially get

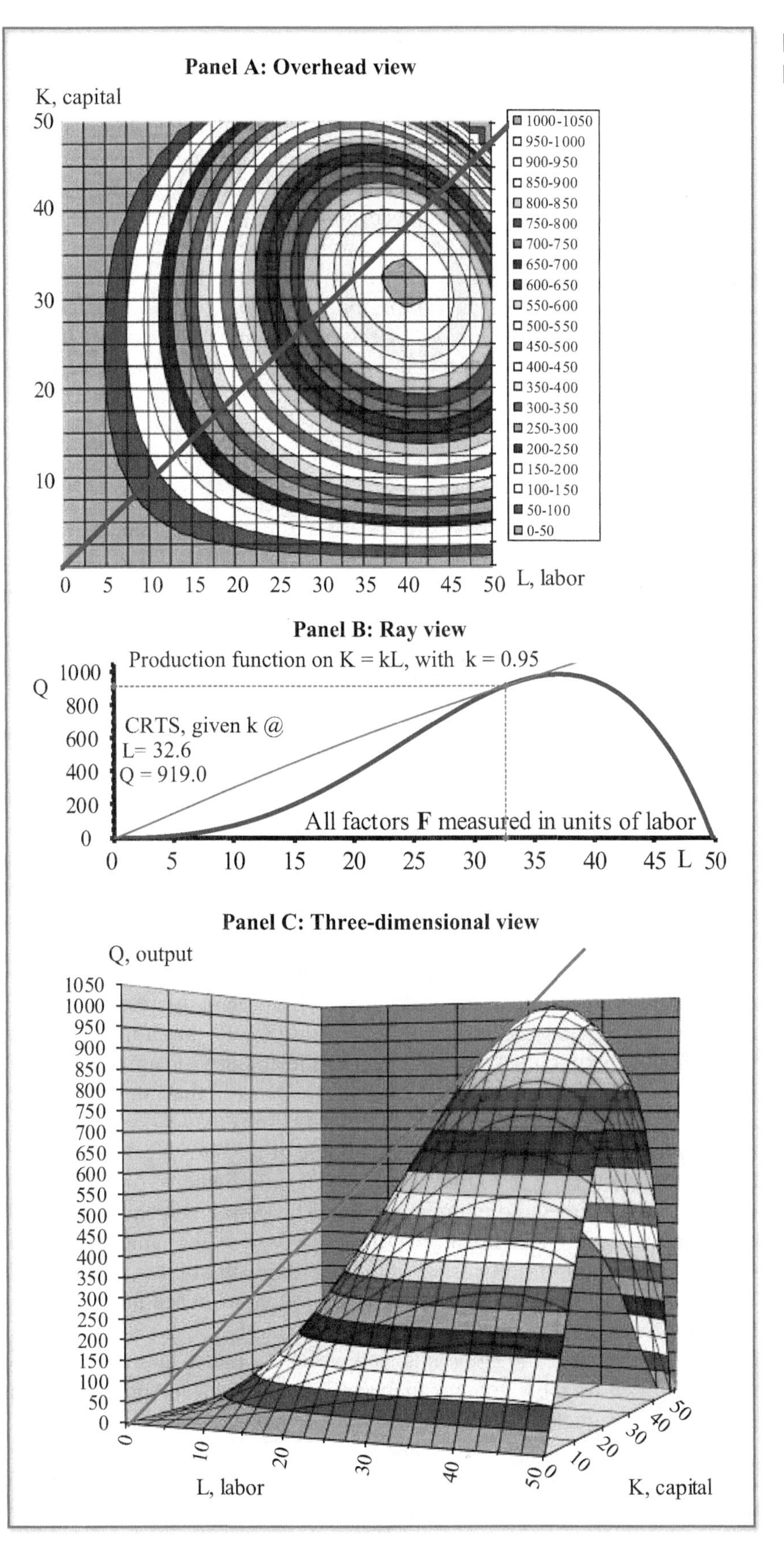

Panel A: Overhead view
K, capital
50
40
30
20
10
0 5 10 15 20 25 30 35 40 45 50 L, labor
1000-1050
950-1000
900-950
850-900
800-850
750-800
700-750
650-700
600-650
550-600
500-550
450-500
400-450
350-400
300-350
250-300
200-250
150-200
100-150
50-100
0-50
Panel B: Ray view
Production function on K = kL, with k = 0.95
Q
1000
800
600
400
200
0
CRTS, given k @
L= 32.6
Q = 919.0
All factors F measured in units of labor
0 5 10 15 20 25 30 35 40 45 L 50
Panel C: Three-dimensional view
Q, output
1050
1000
950
900
850
800
750
700
650
600
550
500
450
400
350
300
250
200
150
100
50
0
0 10 20 30 40 50
L, labor
0 10 20 30 40 50
K, capital

FIGURE 9.10 A Cubic Production Function

closer and closer together), but eventually, the reverse holds true, once L (and K = 0.95 · L) become "large enough." Figure 9.10B examines the question of what is "large enough" in greater detail.

Figure 9.10B maps output as a function of labor along the blue ray. The blue curve in Figure 9.10B is the production function evaluated along the blue ray in Figure 9.10A. This is graphed as a function of labor, but unlike the total product curves in Figures 9.1–9.3, capital varies as labor varies (according to the equation K = 0.95 · L).[17] Interestingly, this curve describes returns to scale just as the total product curve in Figure 9.1 describes marginal and average product. The reason is straightforward: *Although the horizontal axis in Figure 9.10B is marked off in units of labor, it actually represents all factors of production varying in proportion.* Effectively, labor acts as a proxy for all factors of production in this instance. With this in mind, consider the following equation (F represents all factors of production varying in proportion along a ray):

$$\%\Delta Q/\%\Delta F = (\Delta Q/Q)/(\Delta F/F). \qquad \textbf{(9.11a)}$$

$$\%\Delta Q/\%\Delta F = (\Delta Q/\Delta F)/(Q/F). \qquad \textbf{(9.11b)}$$

The magnitude of the left-hand side determines returns to scale. If this is larger than one, then we have increasing returns to scale, since a given percentage increase in all factors of production (the denominator) leads to a larger percentage increase in output (the numerator). Now focus on the right-hand side of Equation 9.11b. Both terms are geometrically recognizable in Figure 9.10B: ΔQ/ΔF is the slope of the production function (since L is a proxy for all factors), and Q/F is the slope of the chord connecting the origin and a point on the curve. Therefore, Equation 9.11b may be rewritten as:

$$\%\Delta Q/\%\Delta F = \text{slope}_{\text{production function}}/\text{slope}_{\text{chord connecting origin to point on the curve}} \qquad \textbf{(9.11c)}$$

In terms of the specific curve depicted in Figure 9.10B, for all L < 32.6 and K = 0.95 · L, the slope of the function is steeper than the slope of the chord.[18] For L < 32.6 and K = 0.95 · L, the numerator exceeds the denominator of Equation 9.11c, so the fraction is greater than one; as a result, over this range of input usage along the ray K = 0.95 · L, there is IRTS. For L > 32.6 and K = 0.95 · L, the reverse holds true, and there is DRTS. At L = 32.6 and K = 0.95 · L, there is CRTS.

The purple tangent to the blue production function in Figure 9.10B represents the point where the production process changes from being increasing returns to decreasing returns to scale. This occurs at L = 32.6 and Q = 919, but a more complete description would include explicit acknowledgment of the amount of capital at this point on the ray K = 0.95 · L. CRTS production occurs at (L, K, Q) = (32.6, 31.0, 919); all three coordinates are perhaps easiest to see (approximately) using the overhead view. The blue K = 0.95 · L ray intersects L = 32.5 at K = 31 in the middle of the blue-green Q = 900–950 production band in Figure 9.10A. In Figure 9.10B, the K coordinate is, of course, hidden, since the horizontal axis is metered in units of labor. The purple tangent in Figure 9.10B is reproduced in the three-dimensional view Figure 9.10C as the tangent line going from point (0, 0, 0) at the bottom-left corner to the approximate point (L, K, Q) = (32.6, 31, 919). This bundle is difficult to tie down exactly, but you can see the Q height of 900–950 as being approximately correct, and if you follow the L = 32.5 total product as a function of capital curve up from the labor axis, you will see it is also approximately correct. (Actual numbers based on the algebraic analysis in the Chapter 9 Appendix are provided in the Excel file for Figures 9.10 and 9.11 for any k value chosen.)

The visual rule discussed earlier regarding CD production functions to determine returns to scale was that if the production hill was convex downward, the function exhibited DRTS (Figure 9.9A), and if the hill was convex upward, the function exhibited IRTS (Figure 9.9C). We see from the ray view in Figure 9.10B and from the three-dimensional view in Figure 9.10C that when returns to scale vary, the picture is a bit more complex. Students often believe that the point of inflection in Figure 9.10B (which occurs at approximately L = 25 and K = 0.95 · L) is the point of CRTS because it is the point where concavity changes from convex upward to convex downward. This is not the case, as

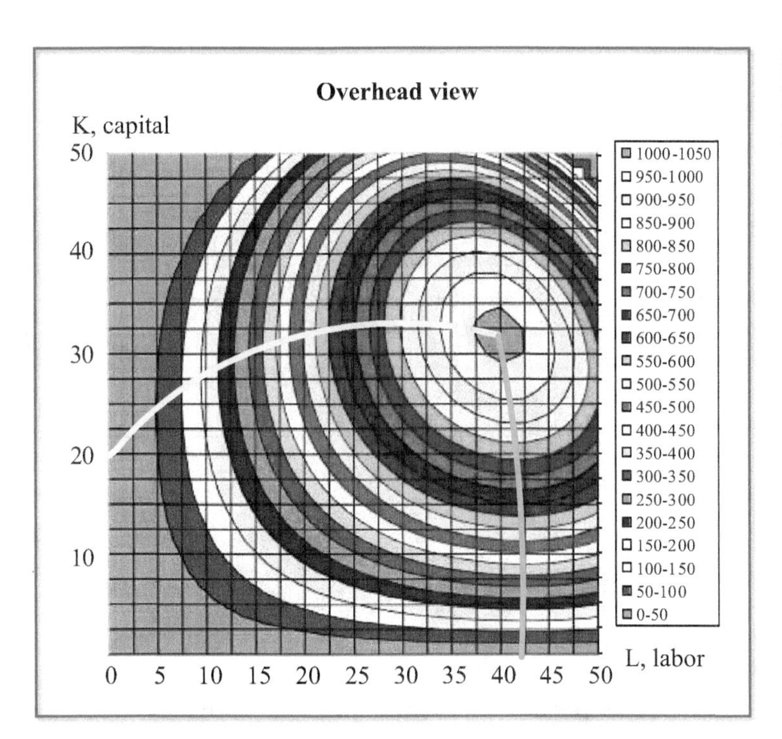

FIGURE 9.11 The Economic Region of Production

we proved earlier in the discussion surrounding Equation 9.11. It is also inappropriate to consider this point as being the maximum MP_L, since the concept of marginal product of labor holds capital fixed, and as we have already stated, capital is not fixed along the ray $K = 0.95 \cdot L$. The point of inflection is more accurately viewed as the point of maximum *factor* productivity, where *factor* means adjusting all factors at once, according to the rule implicit in being on the ray (in this instance, $K = k \cdot L = 0.95 \cdot L$). Different values of k lead to different points of inflection, as well as different $(L, K, Q) = (L, k \cdot L, Q(L, k \cdot L))$ points associated with CRTS, as you can readily verify by adjusting k in the Excel version of Figures 9.10 and 9.11.

The cubic production function depicted in Figure 9.10 describes input bundles where at least one of the two inputs has negative marginal productivity. This creates a situation where using less of that input and the same amount of the other input produces more output. Since inputs are costly to obtain, production does not occur at such input bundles. Economic production only occurs where both factors have positive marginal productivity. Figure 9.11 depicts the economic region of production, using the overhead view of the production function: The **economic region of production** is the set of input bundles where each input has positive marginal productivity.

economic region of production: The economic region of production is the set of input bundles where each input has positive marginal productivity.

The economic region of production occurs below the yellow curve and to the left of the green curve in Figure 9.11. The yellow curve depicts the set of input bundles where the marginal product of capital is zero, and the green curve depicts the set of input bundles where the marginal product of labor is zero. Since $MRTS = MP_L/MP_K$ according to Equation 9.1, the curves can be restated in terms of the MRTS. The MRTS is vertical on the yellow curve (when $MP_K = 0$) and horizontal ($MRTS = 0$) on the green curve (when $MP_L = 0$). This is the producer-side analog to the economic region of consumption described in Figure 3.11.

The cubic production function described in Figures 9.10 and 9.11 formed the basis for the total product of labor function examined in Section 9.2. As shown in the Chapter 9 Appendix, when this production function is evaluated at $K = 10$, the result is the total product curve depicted in Figures 9.1–9.3. (Algebraically, the total product curve, TP(L), is embedded as part of the cubic production function, Q(L, K), given $K = 10$, so that $Q(L; 10) = TP(L)$. The 10 after the semicolon signifies that capital is fixed at $K = 10$.) This total product curve is shown as an embedded part of the cubic production function to clarify how total product curves differ from the "univariate" production function depicted

FIGURE 9.12 A Total Product Curve Embedded in a Cubic Production Function: Figures 9.1–9.3 in the Context of Figure 9.10

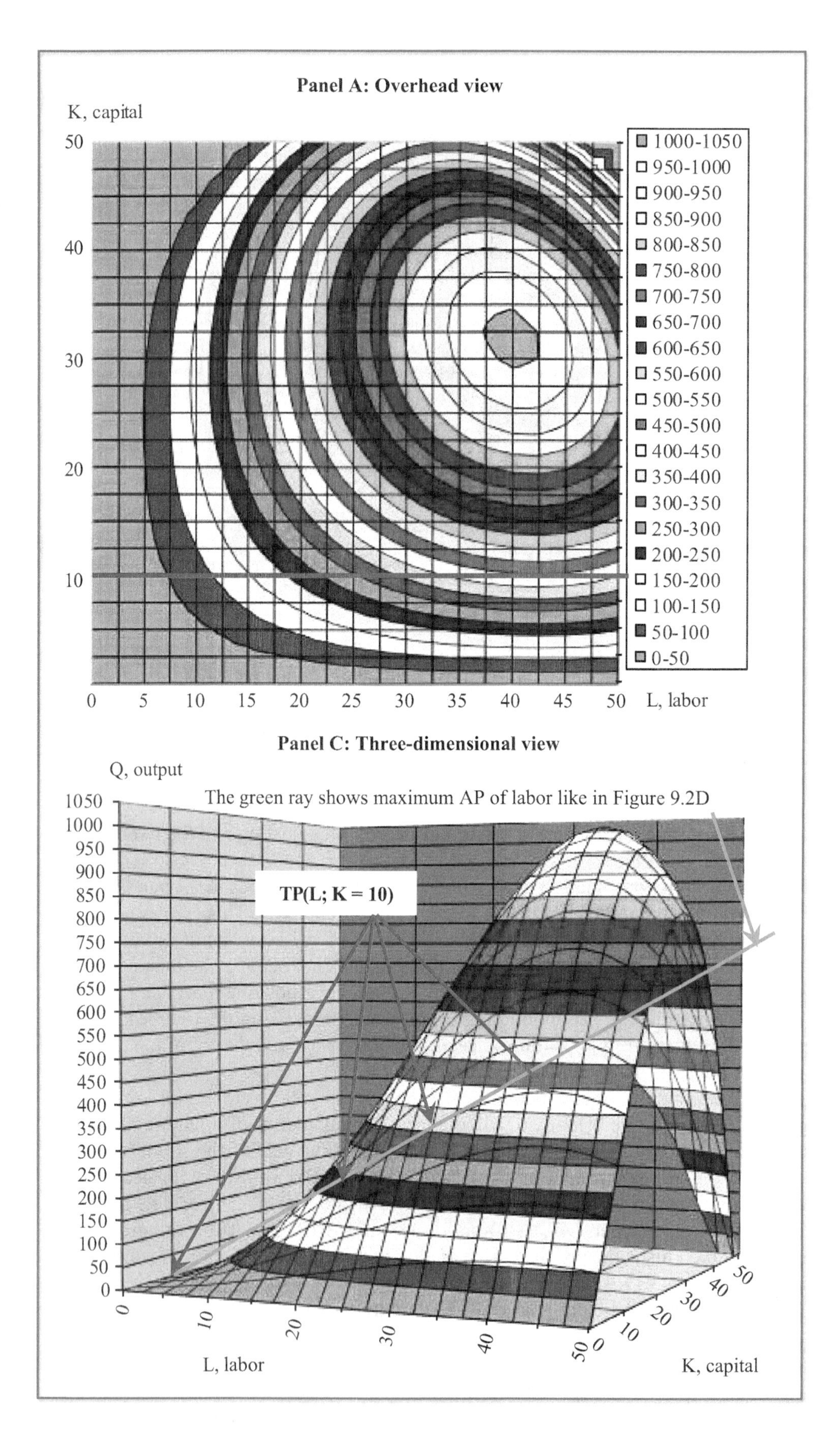

in Figure 9.10B. As argued earlier, Figure 9.10B depicts output on the ray $K = 0.95 \cdot L$ in (L, K) space, while the total product curve in Figures 9.1–9.3 depicts output on the horizontal line K = 10 in (L, K) space. The latter is shown in Figure 9.12. The two panels in Figure 9.12 are labeled 9.12A and 9.12C, since they strictly mirror the same panels in Figure 9.10. Panel B is omitted in Figure 9.12 because that panel does *not* hold capital fixed. The overhead view in Figure 9.12A shows a horizontal red line at K = 10. Input bundles along the red line produce different levels of output as labor varies (with K fixed). The total product curve mapped out as labor varies is shown in Figures 9.1–9.3, and as the K = 10 curve highlighted in Figure 9.12C. Looking back at Figure 9.1C, we see that maximum output on this curve (of Q = 443.6) occurs at L = 42.36. Obviously, we cannot be that precise in the three-dimensional graph, but the curve highlighted in Figure 9.12C does achieve its maximum at about L = 42.5—at which point, output is slightly less than 450 (toward the upper edge of the white 400–450 band in the three-dimensional view). The right-most red arrow in Figure 9.12C points to this (L, K, Q) bundle.

One of the outcomes of the analysis of the cubic total product curve in Section 9.2 was that the point of maximum marginal product occurs at L = 20 in Figure 9.1E, and maximum average product occurs at L = 30 in Figure 9.2D. At L = 30, $MP_L = AP_L$ in Figure 9.3. This can also be seen in the context of the three-dimensional diagram shown in Figure 9.12C and is explicitly shown here to reemphasize the difference between marginal and average productivity and returns to scale. Figure 9.12 embeds Figure 9.2D in a three-dimensional context. The left-most arrow in this figure points at the "origin" of the total product curve highlighted in Figure 9.12C. The "origin" at (L, K, Q) = (0, 10, 0) is shifted over to K = 10 because a TP(L) curve holds capital fixed at 10. The green line emanating from this point is tangent to the total product curve at the point (L, K, Q) = (30, 10, 360) in Figure 9.12C (at the point of the third arrow from the left). This is *exactly* the same tangency shown in Figure 9.2D as the blue chord emanating from the (L, Q) origin of (0, 0) and tangent to the point (L, Q) = (30, 360). The slope of a tangent to the total product curve represents marginal product, and the slope of the chord represents average product. In this instance, $MP_L = AP_L = 12$ at L = 30 in both Figures 9.2D and 9.12C (because 12 = 360/30). The green line tangency in Figure 9.12C holds capital fixed and determines the point of maximum average product of labor (given fixed capital). The point of maximum MP_L (given K = 10) occurs at L = 20 in Figure 9.1E and at (L, K, Q) = (20, 10, 220) in Figure 9.12C (at the point of the second arrow from the left). At this point, $MP_L = 15$ (as we know from Figure 9.1E). By contrast, the purple tangent lines in Figures 9.10B and 9.10C hold capital intensity fixed (at K/L = 0.95) but explicitly require both inputs to vary in proportion with one another. This line determines the point of constant returns to scale, (L, K, Q) = (32.6, 31, 919), as described earlier, at which point maximum AP of input usage is 20.4, as shown in the Chapter 9 Appendix.

Summary

This chapter examines the most basic function of a firm—the firm as a producer of goods. Although this is the first chapter dealing with producers rather than consumers, much of the material has a familiar feel because many of the analytical tools developed on the consumer side can be used with modification on the producer side as well. In many ways, the producer-side analysis is easier to conceptualize because production is a cardinal concept (you can count the number of chairs produced and know that 200 is twice as many chairs as 100). In contrast, utility is an ordinal concept (achieving a utility level of 200 does mean that you are happier than when you achieve a utility level of 100, but it does not mean that you are twice as happy). Magnitude differences make sense when talking about production, and this difference makes many production-side concepts much more concrete.

The way that inputs get put together to produce output is based on what is technologically feasible. Technology is assumed to be given and fixed when we discuss production functions. Production functions describe the maximum amount of output that can be produced from a given bundle of inputs. If technological progress occurs, then the production function must change. Production functions are the producer-side analog to the consumer-side notion of utility functions. Inputs in the production process (factors of production) are typically described in broad terms, such as labor, raw materials, and capital, but narrower definitions are also possible and are useful in certain instances to examine specific topics. If we restrict our analysis to two factors of production, then we can describe production using isoquant maps (the producer-side analog of indifference maps).

Marginal product describes the productivity of an input in producing output. Due to the cardinality of production, marginal product is also cardinal. If we examine productivity one factor at a time, holding all other factors and technology fixed, then eventually, that factor must exhibit diminishing marginal productivity. Average productivity is also examined in a *ceteris paribus* fashion. Average and marginal product are tied to each other by a simple rule: Marginal pulls average up or down, depending on whether it is above or below average. This rule holds for marginal and average product, as well as for any other situation where an average adjusts to new (marginal) information. We see this same relation in Chapter 11, when we examine average versus marginal cost.

The degree of input substitutability is based on the production process under consideration. Certain processes must be done in one and only one way; in this situation, there is no input substitutability, and isoquants are L-shaped, just like perfect-complement indifference curves. This type of production is often described as Leontief production. At the opposite end of the spectrum is perfect substitutability; the isoquants are linear in this instance. An intermediate degree of substitutability is provided by Cobb-Douglas production functions. Each of these functions has, of course, been the focus when we examined consumer behavior, but in the producer context, these functions are easier to conceptualize because of the cardinality of production.

The notions of marginal and average product are predicated on examining factors of production one factor at a time. Such analysis is common in economics and is described using the term *ceteris paribus*. By contrast, returns to scale examines how production varies if all factors of production are allowed to vary at once. Specifically, returns to scale examines the consequence of a proportionate change in all factors of production. If output increases in the same proportion as inputs, then the process exhibits constant returns to scale. If output increases more than proportionately, then there are economies of scale in production (or increasing returns to scale). If output increases less than proportionately, then there are diseconomies of scale (or decreasing returns to scale). There are a variety of reasons why returns to scale may vary. The production of a good need not always exhibit one type of returns to scale or another. Indeed, many production processes may initially exhibit increasing returns to scale for small-scale production, then a range of output at constant returns to scale, followed by diseconomies of large-scale production.

Review Questions

Define the following terms:

cardinality	isoquant map	average product of an input
factors of production	Leontief production function	economic region of production
capital goods	decreasing returns to scale (DRTS)	law of diminishing marginal product
production function	increasing returns to scale (IRTS)	marginal rate of technical substitution (MRTS)
marginal product	constant returns to scale (CRTS)	
isoquant	total product curve	

Match the following production terms and phrases with their consumer theory counterparts:

a. Production function	1. Ordinality
b. Isoquant	2. MRS
c. Cardinality	3. Economic region of consumption
d. Marginal product	4. Indifference curve
e. MRTS	5. MU vector
f. Isoquant map	6. Marginal utility
g. Economic region of production	7. Perfect complements
h. MP vector	8. Utility function
i. Leontief production	9. Preference map

Provide short answers to the following:

a. What is the single most important difference between an isoquant and an indifference curve?

b. Is it possible for a production process to exhibit the law of diminishing marginal product with respect to all factors of production and at the same time exhibit increasing returns to scale?

c. Describe the typical shape of a total product curve. What is the significance of the convexity on different segments of this curve? What happens at the point of inflection?
d. Why is it difficult to imagine a perfectly substitutable production process, using broad categories of inputs, such as labor and capital?
e. What is required for a Cobb-Douglas production function to exhibit increasing returns to scale?
f. What happens to average when marginal is above average?

Use the following production function for Questions g–i. Suppose a production process is described by:

$Q(L, K) = (c \cdot \text{Minimum}(L/a, K/b))^d$ for a, b, c, and $d > 0$.

g. What further restriction(s) should be placed on the parameters a, b, c, and d if the production process in g exhibits increasing returns to scale?
h. Describe the amount of substitutability implicit in this production process.
i. If the production process exhibits increasing returns to scale, what does the isoquant map associated with this process look like? Describe both the general shape of this map and the location of two isoquants—one that produces twice as many units of output as the other.

Use the following production function for Questions j–l. Suppose a production process is described by:

$Q(L, K) = (a \cdot L + b \cdot K)^c$ for a, b, and $c > 0$.

j. What further restriction(s) should be placed on the parameters a, b, and c if the production process exhibits decreasing returns to scale?
k. Describe the amount of substitutability implicit in this production process.
l. If the production process exhibits decreasing returns to scale, what does the isoquant map associated with this process look like? Describe both the general shape of this map and the location of two isoquants—one that produces twice as many units of output as the other.

m. How is the marginal product vector at a given production point related to the isoquant associated with that production point?

Check your answers to the *matching* and *short-answer* exercises in the Answers Appendix at the end of the book.

Notes

1. If an individual attains 160 utils worth of utility from bundle **A** and 20 utils worth of utility from bundle **B**, then we conclude that the individual prefers bundle **A** to bundle **B**, but we *do not* conclude that bundle **A** is eight times as good as **B**. Utility is *ordinal* because it describes ordering between competing bundles, but it is not cardinal because it does not describe how much better one is than the other.

2. A quick example should suffice to remind you of the basic point: $U(x, y) = (x \cdot y)^{0.5}$ and $V(x, y) = (x \cdot y)^2$ both represent the same preferences (equal-weighted CD), since they are monotonic transformations of each other. The only difference in indifference curves associated with the two utility functions is the utility level associated with a given indifference curve. (For example, the indifference curve through (2, 2) has $U(2, 2) = 2$ while $V(2, 2) = 16$. Both indifference curves through this bundle are the same set of points; the only difference is the U or V util number attached to the curve.)

3. As with marginal utility, marginal product of input i is simply the partial derivative of the production function in the ith direction, $MP_i(\mathbf{F}) = \partial Q(\mathbf{F})/\partial f_i$.

4. The easiest way to obtain this general shape is to use a cubic function. Figure 9.1 is based on the function $TP(L) = 3 \cdot L + 0.6 \cdot L^2 - 0.01 \cdot L^3$. Marginal product of labor is $MP_L(L) = dTP(L)/dL = 3 + 1.2 \cdot L - 0.03 \cdot L^2$, and average product of labor is $AP_L(L) = TP(L)/L = 3 + 0.6 \cdot L - 0.01 \cdot L^2$. This univariate function is part of a larger production function that is discussed later in Chapter 9 (and in the Chapter 9 Appendix).

5. The point of inflection occurs where $dMP_L(L)/dL = 0$. $dMP_L(L)/dL = 1.2 - 0.06 \cdot L$; this equals zero when $L = 20$.

6. There is not universal agreement on the terminology for this law. Some authors call this the "law of diminishing returns" or the "law of diminishing marginal returns." We avoid use of the word *returns* in the present context to avoid confusing the eventual decline in the marginal product with the eventual decline in returns to scale. Returns to scale is discussed in Section 9.4.

7. We did get close to this "law" in Section 6.1 when we described the introductory microeconomics "story" of sequential purchasing of goods according to diminishing bang for the buck that leads to the optimization rule $MU_x/P_x = MU_y/P_y$.

8. The example from Figure 4.7 makes this point easily; $U(x, y) = (x \cdot y)^{0.5}$ and $V(x, y) = (x \cdot y)^2$ both represent the same preferences but have dramatically different marginal utilities: $MU_x^U(x, y) = 0.5 \cdot (y/x)^{0.5}$ and $MU_x^V(x, y) = 2 \cdot x \cdot y^2$ according to Table 4.1 (or by taking the partial derivative of utility with respect to x). The first function exhibits diminishing marginal utility as x increases, holding y fixed, while the second exhibits

increasing marginal utility as x increases, holding y fixed; nonetheless, both functions represent the same preferences.

9. This same geometric trick is used to visualize average cost in Chapter 11.

10. And it is easy to see why $AP_L(0) = 3$, given the average product function described in endnote 4. Evaluate $AP_L(L) = 3 + 0.6 \cdot L - 0.01 \cdot L^2$ at $L = 0$ yields $AP_L(0) = 3$.

11. If $a \neq 1$, then the meaning of c should be adjusted. The input bundle $(L, K) = (1, b/a)$ is at the vertex of the Leontief isoquant associated with output level Q_1. Using Equation 9.2b, $Q_1 = Q(1, b/a) = c \cdot \text{Minimum}(1/a, (b/a)/b) = c/a$, so $c = a \cdot Q_1$.

12. This can be stated more elegantly by noting that the CD production function is homogeneous of degree b + c. (Homogeneous functions are discussed in Chapter 7 Appendix B.) If the production function is homogeneous of degree k, it exhibits CRTS if $k = 1$, DRTS if $k < 1$, and IRTS if $k > 1$.

13. Q bands are different-colored bands that Excel provides with surface graphs. Think of each boundary between colors as an isoquant. Contiguous color boundaries share a common number; this is the production level of the isoquant.

14. There are two idiosyncrasies to Excel's surface-plotting capabilities that should be noted. First, with the overhead view, the vertical axis is labeled to the right rather than to the left (as is usual). Second, the three-dimensional view shows a "kink" near the bottom of the graph (near the point (0, 0, 0) in the lower left corner of each graph). A more accurate graph would maintain the curve smoothly down to the point, but Excel does not do this. These limitations are mentioned so that you do not focus undue attention on these idiosyncrasies of Excel.

15. Excel's overhead view shows isoquants close to the top of the hill as almost polygons and toward the bottom as being scalloped (near $L = K = 47.5$). Both of these depictions are not accurate but simply point to another idiosyncrasy of Excel's three-dimensional view. More accurate three-dimensional graphs could be obtained but at the expense of having a tighter grid system showing in the graph (or by having no grid system showing).

16. The Excel version of Figure 9.10 allows you to vary capital intensity (k in the equation $K = k \cdot L$) from 0.4 to 2.5 and view the results both in terms of Figures 9.10A and 9.10B.

17. The Chapter 9 Appendix shows that, as a result, the curve depicted in Figure 9.10B is actually a quartic function of labor. By contrast, any univariate total product curve (as a function of either labor or capital) is a cubic function of that variable *because the other factor of production is held constant.*

18. This geometric analysis is strictly analogous to the discussion of Figure 9.3A earlier in this chapter that examined the relation between MP_L and AP_L. The important difference between the two analyses is that for the discussion of MP_L versus AP_L, K was fixed. In the present context, K varies as L varies, according to the equation $K = 0.95 \cdot L$. This is also similar to the geometric discussion of income elasticity in Section 7.6.

Appendix:

A Primer on the Cubic Production Function

The cubic production function is a particularly useful functional form because it allows varying returns to scale, as well as varying marginal productivity. Unfortunately, it is a bit cumbersome to work with algebraically, relative to Cobb-Douglas, and as a result, the text treatment of this form in Chapter 9 was graphical in nature. This appendix provides the algebraic counterpart to the graphical treatment in the chapter.

The function is defined by five parameters *a*–e, all of which are nonnegative. The function is:

$$Q(L, K) = a \cdot K \cdot L + b \cdot L^2 \cdot K + c \cdot L \cdot K^2 - d \cdot L^3 \cdot K - e \cdot L \cdot K^3 \quad \textbf{(9A.1)}$$

Note that there are minus signs in front of the cubic terms, d and e. This means that production will eventually decline as either labor or capital increases with the other factor held fixed, *ceteris paribus*, because the cubic terms will eventually dominate the quadratic and linear terms.

Short-Run Versions of Cubic Production

For fixed capital, the total product function is a cubic function of labor (since K, K^2, and K^3 are all fixed in this instance). A similar statement can be made for fixed labor; the total product of capital function is then a cubic function of capital. Each of these functions may be considered a univariate version of Equation 9A.1 by simply using the semicolon convention common in describing mathematical functions (variables to the right of the semicolon are considered fixed, and variables to the left are variable). The total product of labor curve is thus written as TP(L) = Q(L; K), while the total product of capital curve is TP(K) = Q(K; L). These univariate functions form the basis for the average and marginal product functions discussed in Chapter 9 (the focus in Section 9.2 is on the TP(L) function).

Average product of labor is obtained by dividing by L, and the average product of capital is obtained by dividing by K:

$$AP_L(L; K) = a \cdot K + b \cdot L \cdot K + c \cdot K^2 - d \cdot L^2 \cdot K - e \cdot K^3 \quad \textbf{(9A.2a)}$$

$$AP_K(K; L) = a \cdot L + b \cdot L^2 + c \cdot L \cdot K - d \cdot L^3 - e \cdot L \cdot K^2 \quad \textbf{(9A.2b)}$$

Each average product function is a quadratic function of the factor that varies because the cubic terms are cubic in the fixed factor of production.

Marginal products are similarly obtained by taking the partial derivatives of the production function in the labor and capital direction:

$$MP_L(L; K) = a \cdot K + 2 \cdot b \cdot L \cdot K + c \cdot K^2 - 3 \cdot d \cdot L^2 \cdot K - e \cdot K^3 \quad \textbf{(9A.3a)}$$

$$MP_K(K; L) = a \cdot L + b \cdot L^2 + 2 \cdot c \cdot L \cdot K - d \cdot L^3 - 3 \cdot e \cdot L \cdot K^2 \quad \textbf{(9A.3b)}$$

As with the average product functions, the marginal product functions are quadratic functions of the factor that varies. These marginal products are reproduced in the Excel file for the cubic production functions in Figures 9.10–9.12. These figures are based on $a = 0.28$, $b = 0.06$, $c = 0.007$, $d = 0.001$, and $e = 0.0005$. But as noted in the discussion surrounding Figure 9.12, the cubic production function is also the basis for the total product analysis in Section 9.2.

As noted in endnote 4 of Chapter 9, the total product curve in Figures 9.1–9.3 is $TP(L) = 3 \cdot L + 0.6 \cdot L^2 - 0.01 \cdot L^3$. The average product and marginal product functions based on this total product function are: $AP_L(L) = TP(L)/L = 3 + 0.6 \cdot L - 0.01 \cdot L^2$ and $MP_L(L) = dTP(L)/dL = 3 + 1.2 \cdot L - 0.03 \cdot L^2$. These functions can be obtained from Equations 9A.1, 9A.2a, and 9A.3a, using the parameter values *a*–e listed earlier, assuming $K = 10$.

The economic region of production in Figure 9.11 is obtained from the marginal product equations. The green curve describes the set of L values, where $MP_L = 0$ for different levels of K. This varies in a nonlinear fashion, based on the amount of capital employed. The yellow curve describes the set of K values, where $MP_K = 0$ for different levels of L. This varies in a nonlinear fashion, based on the amount of labor employed. Both marginal products are zero at the top of the production hill. We can determine using **Goal Seek** that the top of the production hill occurs at (L, K, Q) = (40.0, 31.9, 1013.8), quite close to the visually estimated top of the hill at the intersection of the green and yellow MP = 0 curves at (40, 32) in Figure 9.11.

Returns to Scale, Given Cubic Production

Returns to scale is examined by varying both capital and labor. The CD production function has a simple returns-to-scale result based on the size of the sum of the exponents to the CD production function. The cubic production function is more complex because it has varying returns to scale.

Returns-to-scale issues are examined using a ray through the origin. Different rays depict different degrees of capital intensity, k. The three views shown in Figure 9.10 depict an expansion path along the ray $K = 0.95 \cdot L$. This is only one possible ray, and the Excel file allows you to vary k in $K = k \cdot L$ over the range $0.4 \leq k \leq 2.5$. If $k \cdot L$ replaces K in Equation 9A.1, the resulting equation is a quartic function of labor. This function is:

$$Q(L) = a \cdot k \cdot L^2 + [b \cdot k + c \cdot k^2] \cdot L^3 - [d \cdot k + e \cdot k^3] \cdot L^4$$
$$= f \cdot L^2 + g \cdot L^3 - h \cdot L^4 \quad \textbf{(9A.4a)}$$

The second version of this function describes the relation using $f = a \cdot k$, $g = b \cdot k + c \cdot k^2$, and $h = (d \cdot k + e \cdot k^3)$ to ease discussion. The average product along the ray is:

$$AP(L; K = k \cdot L) = f \cdot L + g \cdot L^2 - h \cdot L^3 \quad \textbf{(9A.4b)}$$

The marginal product along the ray is:

$$MP(L; K = k \cdot L) = 2 \cdot f \cdot L + 3 \cdot g \cdot L^2 - 4 \cdot h \cdot L^3 \quad \textbf{(9A.4c)}$$

Equations 9A.4b and 9A.4c are both metered in units of labor along the ray $K = k \cdot L$. To describe both as slopes along the ray, we must recall that a 1-unit increase in L means a k-unit increase in K or a movement of $(1 + k^2)^{0.5}$ along the ray (using the Pythagorean theorem). The steepness of both the average product chord and the marginal product tangent are therefore AP and MP in Equations 9A.4b and 9A.4c, divided by $(1 + k^2)^{0.5}$, the horizontal distance associated with a 1-unit change in L and a concurrent k-unit change in K.

Average product along the ray is maximized when AP = MP. This is the point of CRTS, as argued in the discussion surrounding Figure 9.10B. If Equation 9A.4b is set equal to Equation 9A.4c, and both sides are multiplied by 1/L, we obtain:

$$f + 2 \cdot g \cdot L - 3 \cdot h \cdot L^2 = 0. \quad \textbf{(9A.5)}$$

The L that satisfies Equation 9A.5 exhibits CRTS. This may be obtained using the quadratic formula. The labor value for which the cubic production function exhibits CRTS, given $K = k \cdot L$, occurs when:

$$L = (g + (g^2 + 3 \cdot f \cdot h)^{0.5})/(3 \cdot h). \quad \textbf{(9A.6)}$$

The calculations are complex enough that it is worth using Excel in this instance. The Excel file for Appendix 9 is provided for your convenience. The cubic production function in Chapter 9, based on coefficients listed earlier, are listed together with capital intensity k in cells A1:A6 in the Excel file. Given $a = 0.28$, $b = 0.06$, $c = 0.007$, $d = 0.001$, $e = 0.0005$, and $k = 0.95$, we obtain $f = 0.266$, $g = 0.06332$, and $h = 0.00138$ in cells C1:C3, using the definitions of f, g, and h in Equation 9A.4a. Substituting these values into Equation 9A.6, we obtain L = 32.6 in cell C5 (and shown in Figure 9.10B). Given $K = 0.95 \cdot L$, we have K = 31.0 in cell C6, and given these values for L and K, we have Q = 919.0 in cell C7 (and shown in Figure 9.10B). These values are quite close to the visual values of $(L, K, Q) = (32.5, 31, 920)$ described in the discussion of Figure 9.10. Along the ray $K = 0.95 \cdot L$, the production function exhibits increasing returns up to $L = 32.6$ and decreasing returns thereafter.

The average product of this CRTS production point is 20.4, as noted in cell D1 of the Excel file for Figure 9.10 (and shown in cell G6 of the Excel file for the Chapter 9 Appendix). This number may be obtained in a variety of ways from the previous information. The most direct calculation is simply $20.4 = 919/(32.6^2 + 31^2)^{0.5}$. This is calculated in cell G6 of the Excel file for Appendix 9 (the denominator of the fraction is the distance from the origin to the production point along the $K = k \cdot L$ ray). Two alternative calculations would produce the same result. Since AP = MP at this output level, we could use either AP or MP using Equation 9A.4b or 9A.4c to obtain AP = MP = 28.2, metered in units of labor. This number must be divided by $(1 + k^2)^{0.5}$ (equal to 1.38 for $k = 0.95$), as noted in the discussion after Equation 9A.4c, to obtain $AP_F = 28.2/1.38 = 20.4$ on the ray $K = 0.95 \cdot L$.

Cost Minimization

CHAPTER 10

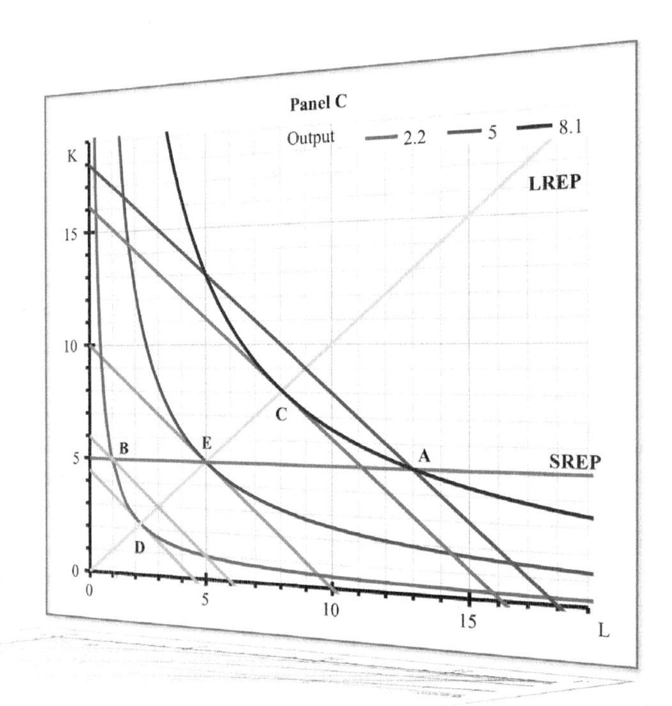

Chapter Outline

We examine costs of production in two related ways in Chapters 10 and 11. In Chapter 10, we examine costs directly based on inputs used to produce output; that is, we examine cost based on isoquant maps. In Chapter 11, we examine cost in an indirect fashion by describing cost as a function of output. This indirect method incorporates the more direct analysis based on isoquants and isocost lines that forms the core of Chapter 10, but it does so with that analysis kept in the background. The cost curves developed in Chapter 11 form the basis for profit-maximizing decisions by the firm. Before we proceed to these cost curves, we turn to the more restricted analysis of how a firm produces a given level of output at minimum cost.

We continue to uncover concepts from the consumer side that may be retooled and reused in our analysis of firm behavior. The chapter begins by examining isocost lines—the set of input bundles that cost the firm the same amount of money to purchase. This is analogous to budget constraints. Just as in Chapter 5, it is important to distinguish between the cost of a given bundle of inputs and what those inputs can produce. Section 10.2 examines the geometric requirements for cost minimization—producing a given level of output at minimum production cost. The tangency result that forms the basis of the consumer optimization problem resurfaces on the producer side. This result is also described in terms of marginal productivity per dollar spent on inputs. Section 10.3 examines the algebraic requirements for cost minimization, which are formally the same as those derived on the consumer side in Chapter 8. The optimization problem is then examined for perfect substitutes, perfect complements, and Cobb-Douglas (CD) production functions. Section 10.4 relaxes the requirement that a specific level of output be produced. An expansion path of input bundles that produce different levels of output at minimum cost can be mapped out. This expansion path is similar to the income consumption curve derived in Section 7.6 on the consumer side. Finally, Section 10.5 examines the importance of time frames in the analysis of production decisions. Firms may be restricted in their ability to adjust certain parts of their operations in the short run. This affects how firms respond to market signals suggesting that they either increase or decrease production levels.

10.1 Isocost Lines versus Budget Constraints

isocost line: An isocost line is the set of input bundles that cost the same amount of money.

If we assume that inputs can be purchased at fixed prices per unit, then the set of input bundles that cost the same amount of money is a linear function of input prices and input quantities. We call this an **isocost line**. When there are n factors of production, each would have a price of P_i per unit. As described in Chapter 9, each input is measured as a flow, and therefore, the price of each input is the rental rate per unit of time.[1] In this event, the isocost line associated with a cost of C_0 dollars is:

$$C_0 = P_1 \cdot f_1 + \ldots + P_n \cdot f_n, \text{ where } f_i \text{ is the quantity of input factor i purchased.} \quad \textbf{(10.1)}$$

This is the producer-side analog to the consumer-side concept of a budget constraint.

Two important differences distinguish budget constraints from isocost lines. First and most obvious is the difference between outputs and inputs. In the present context, P_i is the price of input factor i, rather than the price of good i, and f_i is the quantity of input factor i purchased, rather than the quantity of good i purchased. A more subtle difference relates to the flexibility that a firm faces with regard to spending on inputs. Firms do not view an input resource constraint with the same degree of "finality" as consumers view their budget constraint. The end game for the firm is profit maximization, but profit maximization requires determining the correct level of output to produce, given cost and demand conditions. Costs must be compared against revenues to determine profits, and the formal discussion of choosing the profit-maximizing level of output is put off until Part 4. In the absence of this formal discussion, it is nonetheless clear that a firm should have flexibility in deciding how many dollars to devote to purchasing inputs, since profits will increase as cost increases, so long as revenue increases by more than cost.

We typically work with the two broad categories of inputs—capital and labor. By restricting the analysis to two inputs, we are able to obtain simple geometric insights using isocost lines.[2] We typically think of each input as a homogeneous input, rather than as a specific type of labor or a specific type of machine. As a result,

We will often talk about the price of labor per unit of time as the wage rate w, $\boldsymbol{w = P_L}$*, and price of capital per unit of time as the rental rate of a unit of capital, r,* $\boldsymbol{r = P_K}$.

An isocost line associated with spending C_0 dollars on labor and capital in this instance can be written in three ways, just as the budget constraint was described in three ways in Section 5.2:

Spending method:	$C_0 = w \cdot L + r \cdot K.$	**(10.2a)**
Slope-intercept method:	$K = C_0/r - (w/r) \cdot L.$	**(10.2b)**
Parametric method:	$(s \cdot C_0/w, (1 - s) \cdot C_0/r) = s \cdot \mathbf{B} + (1 - s) \cdot \mathbf{A}$, with $0 \le s \le 1$.	**(10.2c)**

The spending method is akin to the store method of describing the budget constraint; it is perhaps the most intuitive way to look at spending on inputs. Equation 10.2b is useful for geometric analysis: The intercept, C_0/r, is the number of units of capital that can be purchased if all C_0 dollars are spent on capital, and the slope, $-w/r$, describes the relative valuation of the two inputs determined by the market. In Equation 10.2c, bundles **A** and **B** represent devoting all of C_0 to either capital, $\mathbf{A} = (0, C_0/r)$, or labor, $\mathbf{B} = (C_0/w, 0)$. Intermediate bundles represent spending some on each good; in Equation 10.2c, s is the proportion of spending devoted to labor, and 1 – s is the proportion of spending devoted

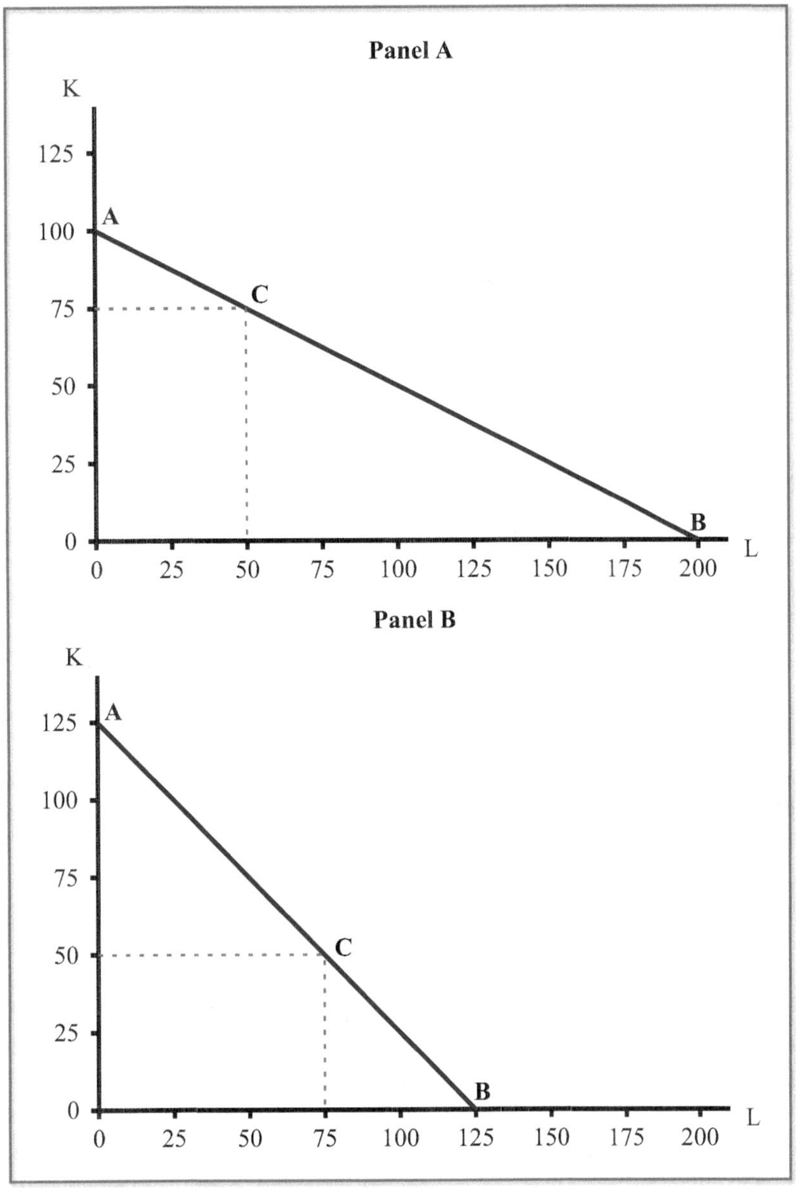

FIGURE 10.1 Deriving Information from an Isocost Line, Given $C_0 = \$1,000$

to capital. This parametric method is useful when considering how to allocate spending across factors of production.

Figure 10.1 provides two examples of isocost lines, both based on spending $1,000 on labor and capital. Based on Figures 10.1A and 10.1B, answer the following three questions:

> **Q1a.** What are the prices of capital and labor implicit in Figures 10.1A and 10.1B?
>
> **Q1b.** What percentage of cost is devoted to labor at input bundle **C** in Figures 10.1A and 10.1B?
>
> **Q1c.** What is the marginal rate of technical substitution (MRTS) implicit at bundles on the isocost line in Figures 10.1A and 10.1B?*

***Q1 answer:** In Figure 10.1A, w = $5, r = $10, and the percentage of cost devoted to labor at bundle **C** is 25% (50/200). In Figure 10.1B, w = $8, r = $8, and the percentage of cost devoted to labor at bundle **C** is 60% (75/125). The answer to Q1c in both Figures 10.1A and 10.1B is: The MRTS varies on an isocost line; as a result, there is no single answer to this question. If you answered MRTS = 0.5 in Figure 10.1A and MRTS = 1 in Figure 10.1B, you are confusing the factor price ratio with the relative valuation of labor and capital provided by the MRTS.

FIGURE 10.2 Using the Input Price Vector to Orient Isocost Lines

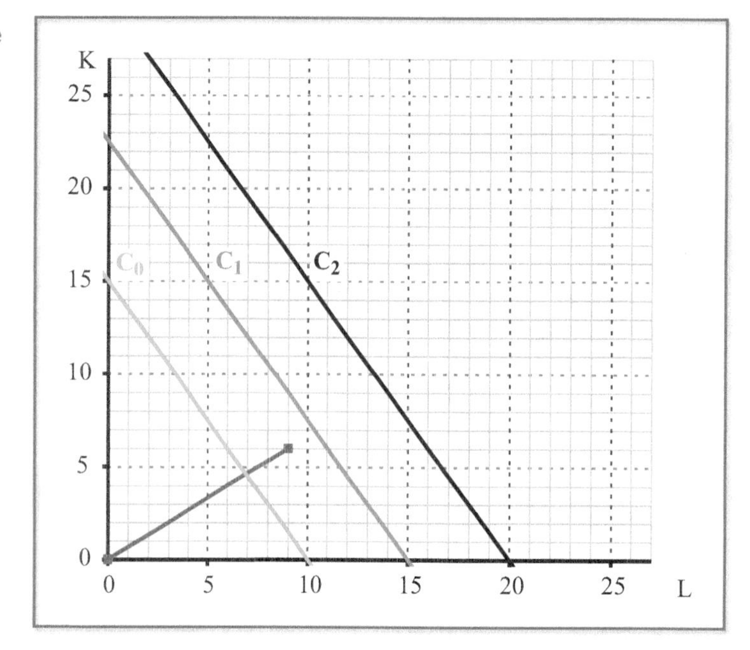

It is worthwhile to focus on Q1c before we continue. Q1c has no answer because isocost lines are distinct concepts from isoquants. Isoquants describe factor trade-offs inherent in the technology of production; the MRTS at a given input bundle describes the substitutability of capital for labor at that input bundle. The MRTS describes technological trade-offs that are inherently independent of the market-determined trade-off between factors of production that is summarized by the factor price ratio. This is the producer-side analog to the discussion in Section 5.1 that admonished you to avoid confusing preferences and constraints. In both contexts, it is important to maintain a conceptual distance between the two types of trade-offs. The MRS (marginal rate of substitution) describes trade-offs between goods, and the MRTS describes trade-offs between inputs in the production process. Both of these trade-offs are independent of the cost of the goods on the consumer side (represented by the output price ratio) and the cost of the inputs on the producer side (represented by the input price ratio). In this section, we ignore the technological trade-offs examined in Chapter 9 to explicitly focus on the other side of the coin. To do this, we must examine the cost of factors of production.

The factor price ratio is readily depicted using the *input price vector* (from (0, 0) to (w, r)). This same geometric construct was used in Section 5.7 to describe the (output) price ratio in Figure 5.17. Economists often draw the relative price vector at the origin, rather than on a budget constraint. In some ways, it is even more appropriate to use the origin in the producer context because there are multiple isocost lines, as opposed to a single budget constraint. Each isocost line will be perpendicular to the relative (input or factor) price vector. Different levels of cost are simply described by different green isocost lines. Each has a slope of $-w/r$ (the slope of the line in Equation 10.2b) and is perpendicular to the red input price vector (w, r) in Figure 10.2. Three isocost lines—labeled C_0, C_1, and C_2—are shown in Figure 10.2. These have been created to support the input bundles (0, 15), (5, 15), and (10, 15), respectively. Based on this information, answer the following:

Q2. What are w, r, C_0, C_1, and C_2 in Figure 10.2?*

***Q2 answer:** The wage rate w = \$9, and the rental rate on capital r = \$6 (the wage rate w and the rental rate on capital r are the coordinates of the red input price vector (9, 6)). Given these factor prices, Equation 10.2a implies that the cost levels associated with the isocost lines are $C_0 = \$90$ $(90 = 9 \cdot 0 + 6 \cdot 15)$, $C_1 = \$135$ $(135 = 9 \cdot 5 + 6 \cdot 15)$, and $C_2 = \$180$ $(180 = 9 \cdot 10 + 6 \cdot 15)$.

10.2 Producing a Given Level of Output at Minimum Cost

For any given level of revenue, lower cost will produce higher profits. Revenue is price times quantity (number of units sold). Because price varies with quantity along a demand curve, total revenue (TR) can be thought of as a function of quantity. Given this, a subsidiary goal to profit maximization, and the one we examine in this chapter, is to minimize the cost of producing whatever output level is under consideration.

> **Claim:** *A profit-maximizing firm necessarily minimizes the total cost of producing whatever level of output it produces.*

The reason is straightforward: profit is $\pi = TR(Q) - TC(Q)$, where TC(Q) is the total cost of producing Q units of output. TR is constant for fixed quantity, Q_0. Therefore, minimizing the cost of producing Q_0 units of output maximizes profit, given that production level. Cost minimization is a more general concept than profit maximization; any profit-maximizing outcome will necessarily be cost minimizing. But not all cost-minimizing outcomes will be profit maximizing; the firm may be minimizing the cost of producing the wrong level of output. The Venn diagram in Exhibit 10.1 shows the nesting of these possible outcomes. The determination of how much to produce—the determination of the profit-maximizing output level—is put off until Part 4.

We have already examined the consumer-side analog to cost minimization in Chapter 8. Cost minimization puts the technological possibilities of production functions together with market-determined constraints of isocost lines in a way that mirrors expenditure minimization, subject to maintaining a given utility level. (This expenditure-minimization problem describes the substitution bundle in the context of demand decomposition in Section 8.3.) If both factors of production are used, then the rule is straightforward:

MRTS = w/r at the cost-minimizing (L, K) bundle. **(10.3a)**

This result is depicted in Figure 10.3A. Cost is minimized when the red input price vector and the lavender marginal product (MP) vector point in the same direction. (Recall that the input price vector is perpendicular to the isocost line, and the MP vector is perpendicular to the isoquant.) When this does not occur, the orientation of the MP vector relative to the input price vector tells us in which direction to reallocate resources. When the isoquant is steeper than the isocost line, the MP vector points toward using more L and less K along the isoquant (relative to the input price vector); a less capital-intensive production process reduces costs (since K/L will decline). This may be restated as:

MRTS > w/r implies using more L and less K on the isoquant to reduce cost. **(10.3b)**

This is the situation depicted in Figure 10.3B. By contrast, at points on the isoquant where the isocost line is steeper than the isoquant, the MP vector points toward using more K

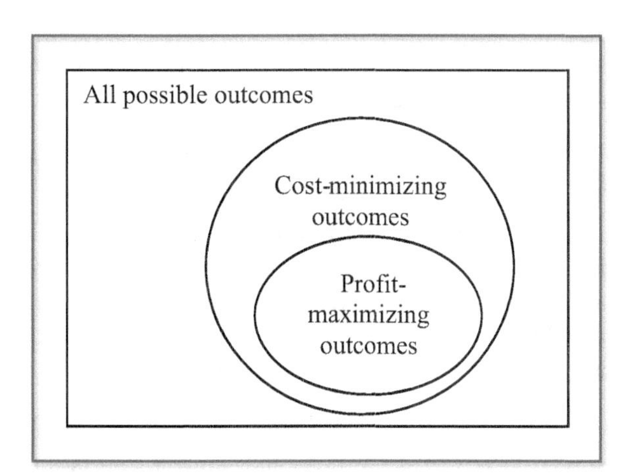

EXHIBIT 10.1 The Relation between Profit Maximization and Cost Minimization

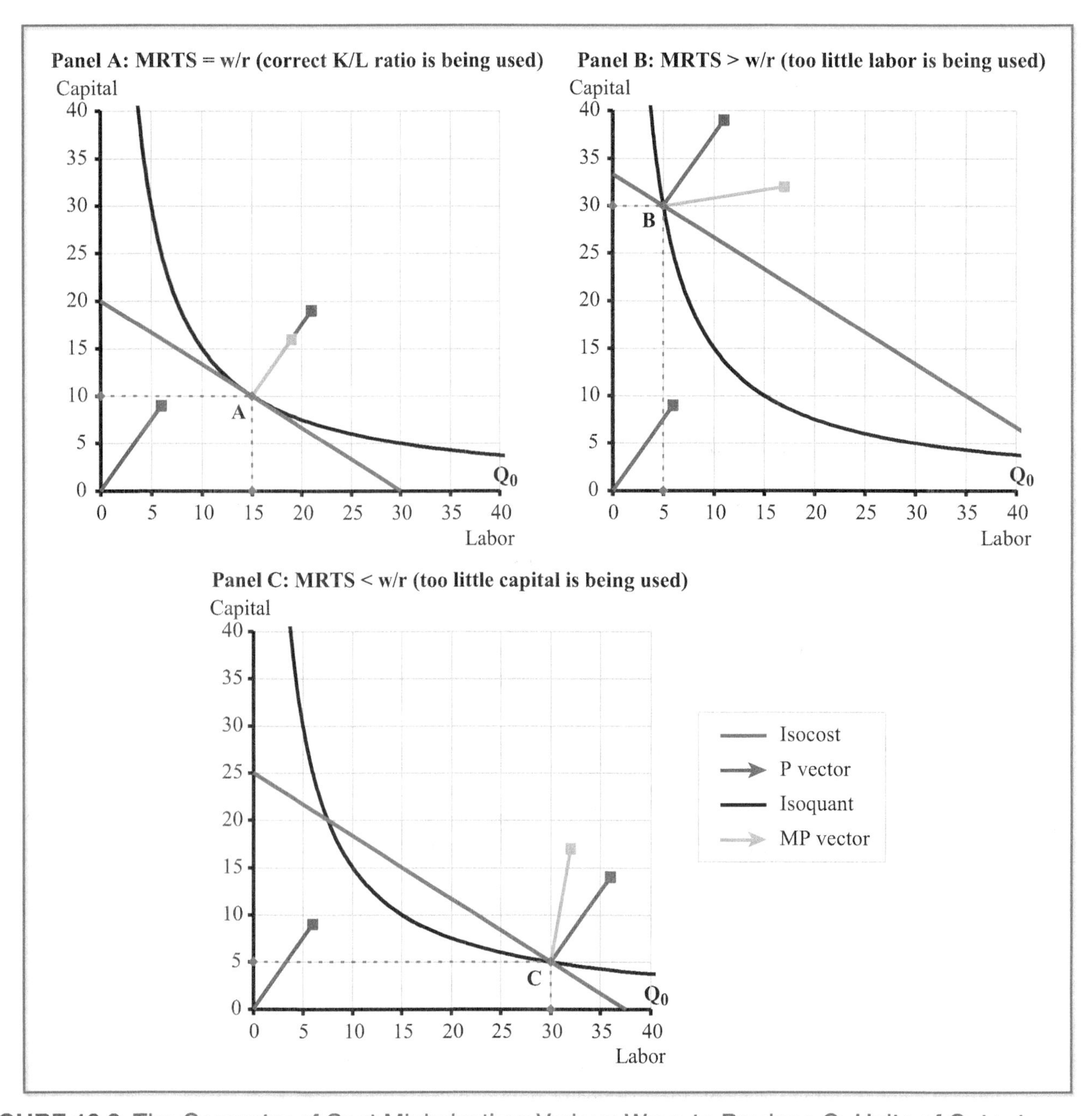

FIGURE 10.3 The Geometry of Cost Minimization: Various Ways to Produce Q_0 Units of Output

at the expense of less L along the isoquant; a more capital-intensive production process reduces costs (since K/L will increase). This may be restated as:

MRTS < w/r implies using more K and less L on the isoquant to reduce cost. **(10.3c)**

This is the situation depicted in Figure 10.3C.[3]

An alternative specification of Equation 10.3 provides a more direct heuristic rule regarding cost-minimizing behavior. The rule is based on the relation between the MRTS and marginal products described in Equation 9.1a: MRTS = MP_L/MP_K. Using this relation and Equation 10.3, we find upon cross multiplication that if both factors of production are being used:

$MP_L/w = MP_K/r$ at the cost-minimizing (L, K) bundle. **(10.4a)**

$MP_L/w > MP_K/r$ implies using more L and less K on the isoquant to reduce cost. **(10.4b)**

$MP_L/w < MP_K/r$ implies using more K and less L on the isoquant to reduce cost. **(10.4c)**

Each side of the equality in Equation10.4a describes the extra output produced by spending an incremental dollar on that factor of production. (If labor costs w per unit, then \$1 spent on labor purchases 1/w units of labor. Each unit of labor has marginal productivity of MP_L, so 1/w units of labor produces an extra MP_L/w units of output.) Equation 10.4 allows us to restate the cost-minimizing rule as:

Claim: *Factors of production are used so that they produce an equal increase in output per dollar spent on each factor of production.* MP_i/P_i *must be equal across factors being used in the production process.*

This is the producer-side analog to the "equal-bang-for-the-buck" across goods rule that forms the centerpiece of introductory microeconomic textbook discussions of consumer utility maximization (this rule was discussed in Section 6.1).[4] Equations 10.3 and 10.4 provide equally valid heuristic descriptions of a firm as a cost-minimizing producer of a given quantity of output.

10.3 The Algebra behind Cost Minimization

The discussion in Section 10.2 was predicated on an interior solution to the cost-minimization problem. As shown through Equation 10.3a, the cost-minimizing input bundle is the point of tangency between an isocost line and the Q_0 isoquant. Equation 10.4a shows that it is also the input bundle on the Q_0 isoquant where each factor of production has the same marginal product per dollar spent. The general solution to this minimization problem must include both interior and boundary solutions (analogous to the expenditure-minimization problem described in Section 8.3). It should not be surprising then to find that the general solution to the cost-minimization problem has a familiar feel.

Claim: *If a firm wishes to minimize the cost of producing a given level of output* Q_0, *using labor, L, and capital, K, whose prices are w and r, respectively:*

Minimize $w \cdot L + r \cdot K$ subject to $Q(L, K) = Q_0$. **(10.5–Problem)**

The following must hold at a constrained optimal solution:

(A) The optimal bundle $\mathbf{F} = (L_f, K_f)$ must satisfy $Q(\mathbf{F}) = Q_0$, and **(10.5A)**

(B) *One* of three conditions must hold:

(i) $MRTS = w/r$ if $L_f > 0$ and $K_f > 0$; or **(10.5Bi)**

(ii) $MRTS \le w/r$ if $L_f = 0$ and $K_f > 0$; or **(10.5Bii)**

(iii) $MRTS \ge w/r$ if $L_f > 0$ and $K_f = 0$. **(10.5Biii)**

The conditions in Equations 10.5Bi–10.5Biii can be recast in terms of marginal products (just as Equation 10.3 was recast as Equation 10.4 earlier). These versions simply use the same equation numbering but use a prime symbol (′) in the equation to denote the MP version:

(B′) *One* of three conditions must hold:

(i) $MP_L/w = MP_K/r$ if $L_f > 0$ and $K_f > 0$; or **(10.5B′i)**

(ii) $MP_L/w \le MP_K/r$ if $L_f = 0$ and $K_f > 0$; or **(10.5B′ii)**

(iii) $MP_L/w \ge MP_K/r$ if $L_f > 0$ and $K_f = 0$. **(10.5B′iii)**

Equation 10.5 is based on (L, K) but is equally valid if labor and capital are replaced by other factors of production.

The optimization problem can also be examined for more general production functions. In the n factor case, the following must hold at the cost-minimizing production bundle:

Claim: *If a firm wishes to minimize the cost of producing a given level of output* Q_0, *using factors* $\mathbf{F} = (f_1, f_2, \ldots, f_n)$, *whose prices are* $P_1, \ldots, P_n$, *respectively:*

Minimize $P_1 \cdot f_1 + \ldots + P_n \cdot f_n$ subject to $Q(\mathbf{F}) = Q_0$. **(10.6–Problem)**

The following must hold at a constrained optimal solution:

(A) The optimal bundle **F** must satisfy $Q(\mathbf{F}) = Q_0$; and **(10.6A)**

(B) *One* of two conditions must hold:

(i) $MRTS_{j,i} = P_i/P_j$ if $f_i > 0$ and $f_j > 0$; or **(10.6Bi)**

(ii) $MRTS_{j,i} \geq P_i/P_j$ if $f_i > 0$ and $f_j = 0$. **(10.6Bii)**

This more general version can also be described in terms of marginal productivity as:

(B′) *One* of two conditions must hold:

(i) $MP_i/P_i = MP_j/P_j$ if $f_i > 0$ and $f_j > 0$; or **(10.6B′i)**

(ii) $MP_i/P_i \geq MP_j/P_j$ if $f_i > 0$ and $f_j = 0$. **(10.6B′ii)**

Although the graphic depiction of Equation 10.6 at a point in n-dimensional input space is difficult for most to conceptualize, the algebra is particularly easy to interpret.

A general rule: If factors are used in positive quantities in producing a good at minimum cost, they must have equal marginal productivity per dollar spent at the input point under consideration (Equation 10.6Bi), and any factors *not* used in production must *not* have a higher productivity per dollar spent than those used in production (Equation 10.6B′ii).

The proof is similar to that used to prove the expenditure-minimization rule in Equation 8.3. All that must be done is to replace the utility function by the production function, outputs x_i and x_j by input factors of production f_i and f_j, and output prices by input prices.

Now that we have discussed general solutions to the cost-minimization problem, it is worthwhile to consider why we worry about boundary conditions on the production side. The need for boundary solutions becomes clear by viewing factors of productions in a narrow sense. For example, there are a variety of methods available to weld metal. The least capital-intensive method of welding involves using a person with a welding torch, and the most capital-intensive method involves using robotic welders. A welding torch and a robotic welder are both examples of capital goods that can be used to join pieces of metal, but the robotic welder would not be cost effective for the small-scale jobs typified by a local welding shop. Conversely, complete reliance on manual welders would not be cost effective for the large-scale operations at an automobile assembly plant. The typical welding shop will have $MP_t/P_t > MP_r/P_r$ (where the t stands for welding torch and the r stands for robotic welder), and consequently, $t > 0$ and $r = 0$ (Equation 10.6B′ii). At the auto assembly plant, $MP_t/P_t = MP_r/P_r$, since the plant will employ both robotic welders and individuals with torches (Equation 10.6B′i). It may also be the case that the plant has fully automated the welding function so that $t = 0$ and $r > 0$; in this instance, the plant may have $MP_t/P_t < MP_r/P_r$ (Equation 10.6B′ii). If we consider a continuum of plant sizes that require welding operations, there will be some size below which robotic welders are simply not cost effective. Beyond that size level, robotic welders would be employed.

Equations 10.5 and 10.6 allow us to examine cost minimization for specific production functions. Each of the production functions examined in Section 9.3 can be used to obtain cost-minimizing input usage, given that production process.

Cost Minimization with Perfect Substitutes

As discussed in Chapter 9, it is unrealistic to expect broad categories of inputs such as capital and labor to be perfect substitutes in production. More narrowly defined production substitutes are easier to imagine. Consider once again the two-by-four production function described in Equation 9.3b: $Q(F, S) = a \cdot F + b \cdot S$, where F is the number of fir logs and S is the number of spruce logs. It is worthwhile to rewrite this production function explicitly, using marginal products:

$$Q(F, S) = MP_f \cdot F + MP_s \cdot S. \qquad \textbf{(10.7)}$$

Suppose the prices of inputs are P_f and P_s. The cost-minimizing production bundle with perfect substitutes will always be on the boundary of input space (just as the substitution bundle with perfect substitutes in consumption in Figure 8.8 will always be on the boundary of consumption space). Two possibilities exist: Use only fir and use only spruce. The required input bundle that uses fir exclusively is $(F, S) = (Q_0/MP_f, 0)$, and the required input bundle that uses spruce exclusively is $(F, S) = (0, Q_0/MP_s)$. The costs of these two alternatives are $P_f \cdot Q_0/MP_f$ and $P_s \cdot Q_0/MP_s$. The least costly of these two alternatives may be written as:

$$C_0 = \text{Minimum}(P_f \cdot Q_0/MP_f, P_s \cdot Q_0/MP_s) = Q_0 \cdot \text{Minimum}(P_f/MP_f, P_s/MP_s). \quad \textbf{(10.8)}$$

Interestingly, Equation 10.8 is directly visible as an application of Equation 10.6B′ii. Equation 10.6B′ii tells the firm to use the factor of production that has the highest marginal productivity per dollar spent. If MP_i/P_i is larger than MP_j/P_j, then P_i/MP_i is smaller than P_j/MP_j, as required by Equation 10.8.

Figure 10.4 revisits the production of 1,000 two-by-fours using fir and spruce logs initially shown in Figure 9.5. Both Figures 10.4A and 10.4B assume that the price of a spruce log is $P_s = \$10$. The blue line **AB** is the isoquant, and the green isocost line does not support production of 1,000 two-by-fours. Answer Q4a–Q4c for both Figures 10.4A and 10.4B; also answer Q4d, which has the same answer in both Figures 10.4A and 10.4B:

> **Q4a.** What is the price of a fir log implicit in each figure?
>
> **Q4b.** Which input bundle will produce 1,000 two-by-fours at minimum cost, given these cost and production conditions?
>
> **Q4c.** How much will the logs required to produce 1,000 two-by-fours cost in this situation? Put another way, what is C_{1000}?
>
> **Q4d.** For what price of fir logs will the entire isoquant **AB** be cost minimizing, given $P_s = \$10$? What happens above and below that price of fir? How does your answer relate to Q4b?*

Cost Minimization with Leontief Production

The cost-minimizing production bundle will be at the vertex of the L-shaped Leontief isoquant, regardless of factor prices. The reason has already been put forward on the consumer side in the discussion of Figure 6.2. Given the general Leontief production function described by Equation 9.2b, $Q(L, K) = c \cdot \text{Minimum}(L/a, K/b)$, the vertex of each isoquant will be on the line $K = (b/a) \cdot L$. In this instance, the vertex of the Q_0 isoquant is described as:

$$Q_0 = c \cdot \text{Minimum}(L/a, K/b) = c \cdot \text{Minimum}(L/a, (b/a) \cdot L/b) = c \cdot L/a. \quad \textbf{(10.9a)}$$

Solving for L, we obtain the amount of L required to produce Q_0 units of output at minimum cost, L_0:

$$L_0 = a \cdot Q_0/c. \quad \textbf{(10.9b)}$$

Substituting Equation10.9b into the equation $K = (b/a) \cdot L$, we obtain the amount of K required to produce Q_0 units of output at minimum cost, K_0:

$$K_0 = b \cdot Q_0/c. \quad \textbf{(10.9c)}$$

The expenditure required to support the (L, K) bundle described in Equations 10.9b and 10.9c is:

$$C_0 = w \cdot L_0 + r \cdot K_0 = w \cdot a \cdot Q_0/c + r \cdot b \cdot Q_0/c = (w \cdot a + r \cdot b) \cdot Q_0/c. \quad \textbf{(10.10)}$$

***Q4 answer:** In Figure 10.4A, $P_f = \$7.50$ ($P_f/P_s = P_f/\$10 = 0.75$), choose **A** at a cost of $C_{1000} = \$1{,}250$. In Figure 10.4B, $P_f = \$5.00$ ($P_f/P_s = P_f/\$10 = 0.50$), choose **B** at a cost of $C_{1000} = \$1{,}000$. In both figures, the razor's-edge price for fir, given a price of spruce of \$10 per log, is $P_f = \$6.25$. For prices of fir above \$6.25, use only spruce (as in Figure 10.4A), and for prices of fir below \$6.25, use only fir (as in Figure 10.4B).

FIGURE 10.4 Cost Minimization with Perfect Substitute Production

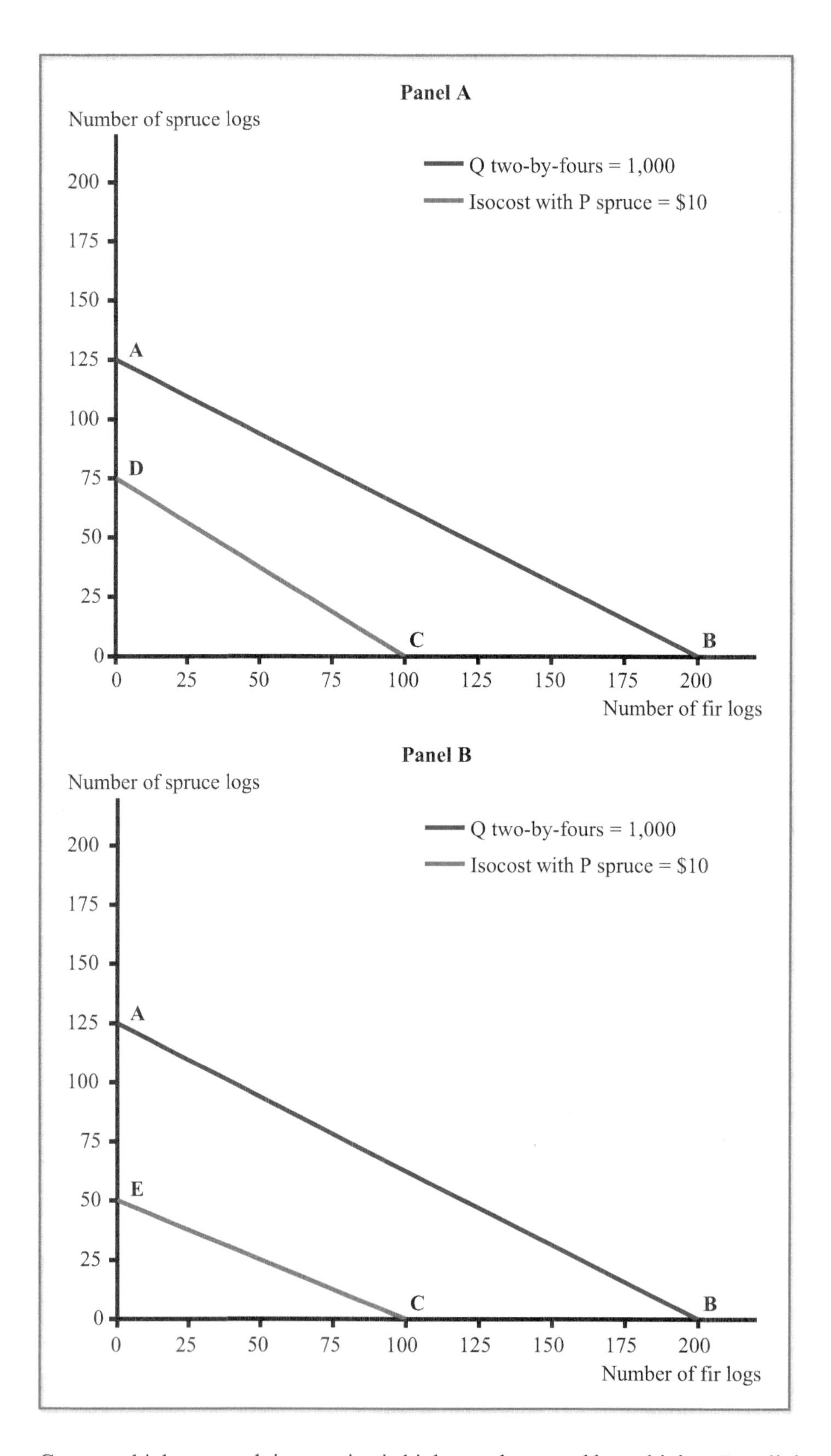

Costs are higher as each input price is higher and as a and b are higher. Recall that a and b represent the number of units of labor and capital required to produce c units of output. The cost of producing a given level of output is also inversely related to the scaling factor c. Figure 10.5 depicts one such Leontief technology isoquant and a representative isocost line. The isoquant shown produces 80 units of output and has $a = 3$; the isocost line is associated with spending $40 on labor and capital. Given this, answer the following:

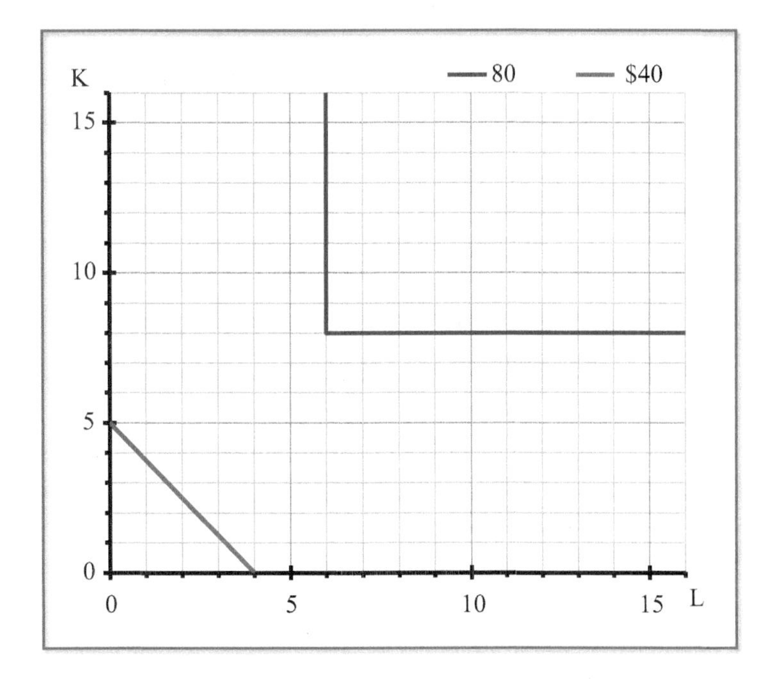

FIGURE 10.5 Cost Minimization with Leontief Production: $Q(L, K) = c \cdot \text{Minimum}(L/a, K/b)$

Q5a. What are the prices of labor and capital in this instance?

Q5b. Given $a = 3$, what are b and c, consistent with the isoquant shown?

Q5c. What level of cost supports this production level?*

Cost increases linearly with quantity in the previous examples. This is seen easily in Equations 10.8 and 10.10 because both functions are proportional to Q_0. If $Q_1 = 2 \cdot Q_0$, then the cost required to support production doubles, using both equations. This is in accord with our discussion in Section 9.4, where we showed that both of these production functions exhibit constant returns to scale (CRTS). The same is not true with the general CD production function, as we have shown in our discussion of Equations 9.8–9.10.

Cost Minimization with Cobb-Douglas Production

The first condition required for cost minimization (Equation 10.5A) is that the input bundle produces Q_0 units of output:

$$Q_0 = a \cdot L^b \cdot K^c. \qquad \textbf{(10.11a)}$$

The CD production function will have its cost-minimizing input bundle on the interior of the input set, just as the CD utility function always has interior solutions to the utility-maximization problem. Therefore, the Cobb-Douglas MRTS described in Equation 9.8 can be substituted into Equation 10.5Bi:

$$(b/c) \cdot (K/L) = w/r. \qquad \textbf{(10.11b)}$$

Solving for K in Equation 10.11b, we obtain:

$$K = (c/b) \cdot (w/r) \cdot L = ((w \cdot c)/(r \cdot b)) \cdot L. \qquad \textbf{(10.11c)}$$

Substituting Equation10.11c into Equation10.11a, we obtain quantity as a function of labor:

$$Q_0 = a \cdot L^b \cdot K^c = a \cdot L^b \cdot (((w \cdot c)/(r \cdot b)) \cdot L)^c = a \cdot ((w \cdot c)/(r \cdot b))^c \cdot L^{(b+c)}. \qquad \textbf{(10.11d)}$$

***Q5 answer:** Given that \$40 spent on inputs will purchase 4 units of labor, w = \$10. Similarly, r = \$8. The vertex of the isoquant is at $(L, K) = (6, 8)$, so given $a = 3$, $b = 4$ (since $K = (b/a) \cdot L$). The isoquant is $Q_0 = 80$, so Equation 10.9a implies: $80 = Q_0 = c \cdot \text{Minimum}(L/a, K/b) = c \cdot \text{Minimum}(6/3, 8/4) = 2 \cdot c$ implies $c = 40$. The cost to produce this output level is $C_0 = (w \cdot a + r \cdot b) \cdot Q_0/c = (\$10 \cdot 3 + \$8 \cdot 4) \cdot 80/40 = \$124$, according to Equation 10.10. This can be checked manually, as $C_0 = w \cdot L + r \cdot K = \$10 \cdot 6 + \$8 \cdot 8 = \$124$.

Solving for L, we obtain labor required to produce Q_0 units of output in a cost-minimizing fashion, L_0, as a function of CD parameters a, b, and c; factor prices w and r; and output level:

$$L_0 = ((Q_0/a) \cdot ((r \cdot b)/(w \cdot c))^c)^{(1/(b+c))}. \quad \textbf{(10.12a)}$$

Substituting Equation 10.12a back into Equation 10.11c gives us the capital required to produce Q_0 units of output in a cost-minimizing fashion, K_0, as a function of CD parameters a, b, and c; factor prices w and r; and output level:

$$K_0 = ((Q_0/a) \cdot ((w \cdot c)/(r \cdot b))^b)^{(1/(b+c))}. \quad \textbf{(10.12b)}$$

Note: *Equations 10.12a and 10.12b are derived factor demands for the labor and capital required to produce Q_0 units of output at minimum cost.*[5]

The cost of producing Q_0 units of output in this instance is obtained by calculating C_0 with Equation 10.2a by using the derived factor demands obtained in Equations10.12a and 10.12b. This yields cost as a function of output, parameters of the CD production function, and factor prices:

$$C_0 = w \cdot L_0 + r \cdot K_0 = Q_0^{(1/(b+c))} \cdot [a^{(-1/(b+c))} \cdot w^{(b/(b+c))} \cdot r^{(c/(b+c))} \cdot ((b/c)^{(c/(b+c))} + (c/b)^{(b/(b+c))})]. \quad \textbf{(10.13a)}$$

$$C = \mathbf{Q^{(1/(b+c))}} \cdot H(w, r, a, b, c). \quad \textbf{(10.13b)}$$

Equation 10.13a is, admittedly, fairly complicated, but it can be simplified by writing all but the first term as H(w, r, a, b, c), as shown in Equation 10.13b. This allows us to focus on the boldfaced first term shown in the equation: $Q_0^{(1/(b+c))}$.

Unlike the cost functions in Equations 10.8 and 10.10, Equation 10.13 is not, in general, a linear function of quantity, Q. Cost, however, responds just as you would expect in light of the returns-to-scale results described in Equation 9.10. If $(b + c) > 1$, then the production function exhibits increasing returns to scale (IRTS). With IRTS, costs increase less than proportionately with quantity increases (if $Q_1 = t \cdot Q_0$, then $C(Q_1) < t \cdot C(Q_0)$, since $(1/(b + c)) < 1$ and $t^{(1/(b+c))} < t$ for any number $t > 1$). When $(b + c) = 1$, the production function exhibits CRTS, and costs increase proportionately with quantity, according to Equation 10.13. When $(b + c) < 1$, the production function exhibits decreasing returns to scale (DRTS), and costs increase more than proportionately with increases in output (since $(1/(b + c)) > 1$ in this instance).[6]

The cost and derived demand equations for the Cobb-Douglas production function (Equations 10.12 and 10.13) are more complex than many of their counterparts on the consumer side because the exponents are not restricted to sum to one on the producer side, due to returns to scale.[7] Nonetheless, the same elegant results provided by CD utility functions are visible here (after a bit of algebraic manipulation). In particular, cost-minimizing production requires that the relative size of the exponents in the CD production function indicates relative spending on the goods. The discussion surrounding Equations 7.4 and 7.5 suggested a symmetric result on the consumer side. The relative size of the exponents in the general CD function determines spending on each good. We can see this on the producer side, using Equations 10.12 and 10.13. In particular, we can show that the following holds at the cost-minimizing production point:[8]

$$\text{Proportion of spending on labor} = w \cdot L_0/C_0 = b/(b + c). \quad \textbf{(10.14a)}$$

$$\text{Proportion of spending on capital} = r \cdot K_0/C_0 = c/(b + c). \quad \textbf{(10.14b)}$$

The fraction b/(b + c) is the relative size of the exponent attached to labor, and c/(b + c) is the relative size of the exponent attached to capital; these relative sizes determine the proportion of cost devoted to each input required to achieve cost-minimizing production. Figure 10.6 depicts this situation.

Figures 10.6A–10.6F are based on a 3 × 2 comparison. Three sets of relative input prices and two production functions are shown. All of the figures depict producing 15 units of output, using a CD production function, with 60% of the weight on labor and

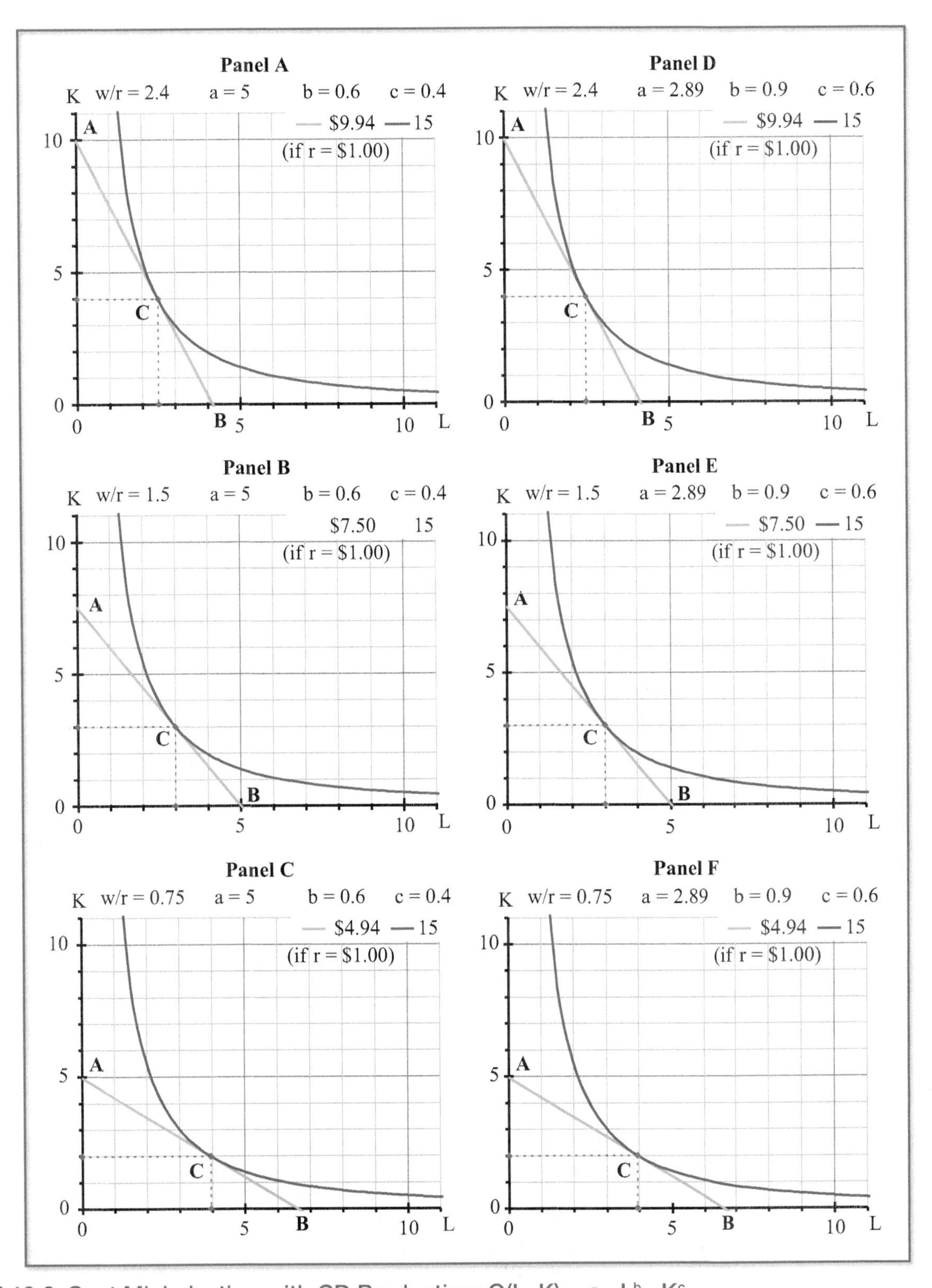

FIGURE 10.6 Cost Minimization with CD Production: $Q(L, K) = a \cdot L^b \cdot K^c$

40% of the weight on capital ($b/(b + c) = 0.6$ and $c/(b + c) = 0.4$). Figures 10.6A–10.6C depict a CRTS production function (since $b + c = 1$), and Figures 10.6D–10.6F depict an IRTS production function (since $b + c > 1$). Both production functions can have the same $Q_0 = 15$ isoquant in this instance by appropriately adjusting the scaling factor a for the two production functions ($a = 5$ in Figures 10.6A–10.6C, and $a = 2.89$ in Figures 10.6D–10.6F). Figures are paired (Figures 10.6A with 10.6D, etc.) according to the factor price ratio depicted in each situation. The capital/labor ratio chosen in each figure depends entirely on the relative size of the exponents and the factor price ratio according to Equation 10.11b, MRTS = (b/c) · (K/L) = w/r. In all of the figures, b/c = 1.5, so it should not be surprising that K = L in Figures 10.6B and 10.6E (since w/r = 1.5 for these figures).

The cost-minimizing production point in each case involves devoting 60% of cost to labor in Figures 10.6A–10.6F in accord with Equation 10.14a (b/(b + c) = 0.6). The numbers are not whole numbers in each instance, but price ratios have been chosen so that the 60:40 split is clear in each graph. Capital is assumed to be a numeraire in this instance, so the dollar cost level is seen as the K intercept in each figure. K_c in Figures 10.6A and 10.6D is approximately 4/10 of the capital intercept of **A** (9.94 ≐ 10) for C_0. In Figures 10.6B and 10.6E, L_c is 3/5 of C_0 (using the labor axis intercept of **B** at (5, 0)). In Figures 10.6C and 10.6F, K_c is approximately 2/5 of the capital intercept of **A** (4.94 ≐ 5) for C_0. Regardless of price ratio, **C** is 60% of the way from **A** to **B** on **AB** (since b/(b + c) = 0.6).

10.4 Producing Different Levels of Output at Minimum Cost

expansion path: An expansion path depicts the set of cost-minimizing input bundles as output varies for fixed factor prices.

The results derived thus far are based on a fixed level of output. As output changes, the cost-minimizing input bundle changes, but the same marginal condition holds at the new constrained optimum; the cost-minimizing solution maintains the point of tangency between isoquant and isocost line, as described in Equation 10.5. The formal term for this set of points is the **expansion path**. This is akin to the income consumption curve (ICC) in consumption space described in Section 7.6 because the isocost lines in this instance maintain a slope of –w/r, regardless of how much capital or labor is purchased (just as the budget constraint maintains its slope of $-P_x/P_y$ as income changes; indeed, some authors call the ICC an expansion path).

The expansion path for perfect substitutes is simply one axis or the other, depending on which axis has a larger MP_i/P_i ratio. This is true unless both marginal products per dollar spent are equal (or to say the same thing, $MRTS_{j,i} = P_i/P_j$). In this event, the expansion path includes all (f_i, f_j) bundles, since both factors have equal productivity per dollar spent.

The expansion path for Leontief production is the line connecting the vertices of the L-shaped isoquants. Given the general Leontief production function described by Equation 9.2b, Q(L, K) = c · Minimum(L/*a*, K/b), the vertex of each isoquant will be on the line K = (b/*a*) · L.

For the general Cobb-Douglas production function, $Q = a \cdot L^b \cdot K^c$, the expansion path is the ray through the origin. Capital intensity, K/L, is seen to be K/L = (c/b) · (w/r), according to Equation 10.11c. As expected, the cost-minimizing production process will be more capital intensive, the larger the relative importance of capital relative to labor in the CD production process. The relative importance of capital to labor is measured by c/b. Similarly, the cost-minimizing production process will be more capital intensive, the larger the relative factor price ratio w/r.

If c/b and w/r do not vary, then the expansion path will not vary, even as the production function varies. Figure 10.7 provides an example of this fact. Figures 10.7A–10.7C have w/r = 3/4 and c/b = 2/3. As a result, each figure has cost-minimizing capital intensity of K/L = (c/b) · (w/r) = 1/2; the gold expansion path in each figure is K = 1/2 · L. Figure 10.7A is based on the CRTS production function and factor prices from Figure 10.6C. Figure 10.7B is based on the IRTS production function and factor prices from Figure 10.6F. Figure 10.7C provides a DRTS production function that maintains c/b and w/r.[9] Figures 10.7A–10.7C have the (light blue) $Q_0 = 15$ isoquant go through the input bundle (3, 3) by an appropriate adjustment in the scaling factor *a*; each figure depicts cost-minimizing production of 15 units of output at **C** at a cost of \$4.94 (given w = \$0.75 and r = \$1.00).[10] Each figure also depicts a second (dark blue) isoquant associated with a doubling of output to $Q_1 = 30$. The cost-minimizing production point on the Q_1 isoquant is labeled **D** in each figure. The cost of this input bundle is listed in each figure. We see that doubling output at **D** costs twice as much as **C** if production exhibits CRTS (Figure 10.7A). Costs

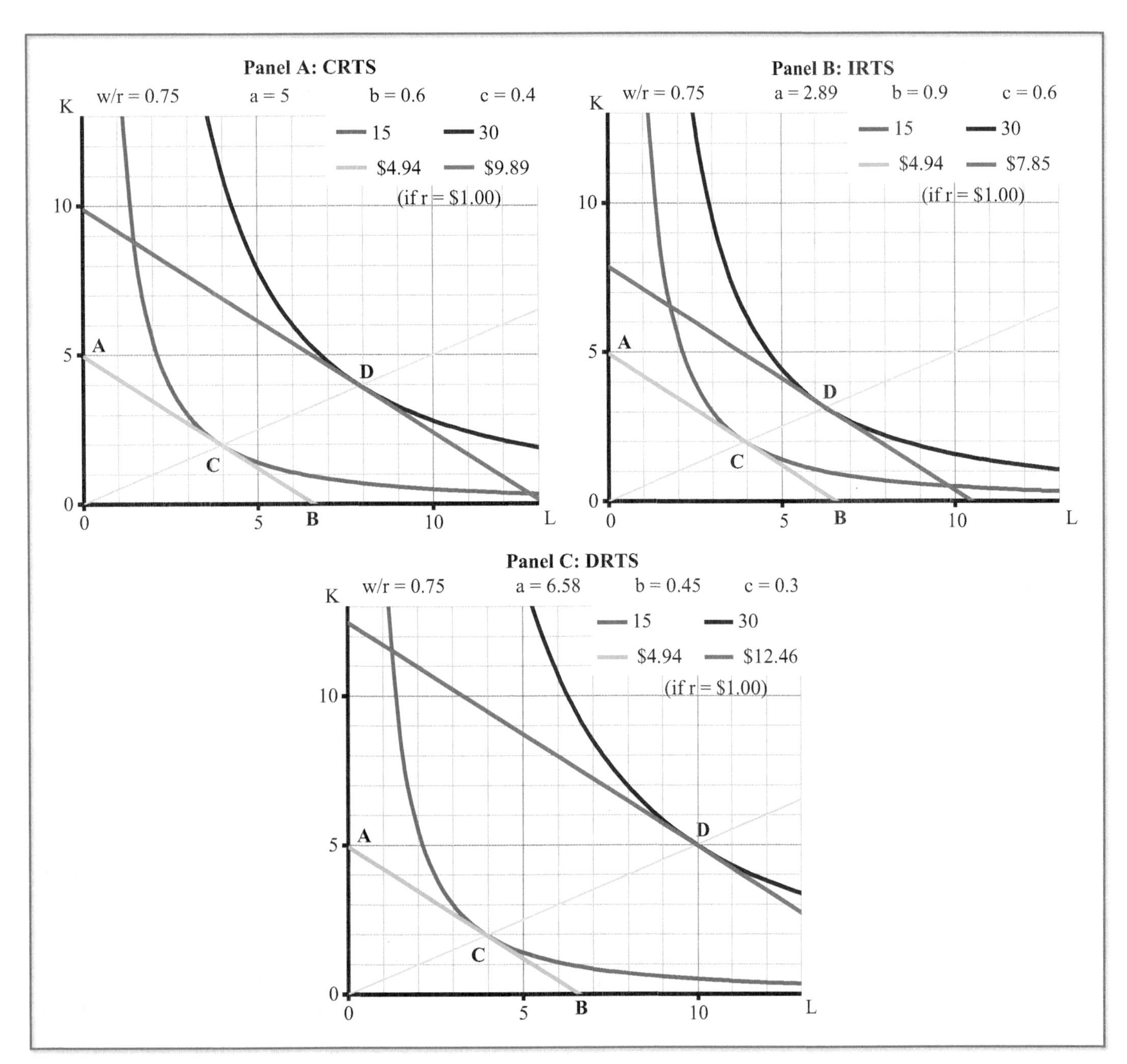

FIGURE 10.7 An Expansion Path for Cobb-Douglas Production: $Q(L, K) = a \cdot L^b \cdot K^c$

are less than double if production exhibits IRTS (Figure 10.7B), and they are more than double if production exhibits DRTS (Figure 10.7C).

Figures 10.7A–10.7C include the dollar cost required to support each production level, but we can also describe how much costs change using Equation 10.13. The parameters *a*, b, c, w, and r are constant for Figures 10.7A–10.7C; the only distinguishing feature in moving from the lower isoquant to the upper isoquant is that $Q_1 = 2Q_0$. Therefore, the only change in Equation 10.13 as a result of the output change is the magnitude of that change; doubling output should increase costs by a factor of $2^{(1/(b+c))}$, according Equation 10.13. In Figure 10.7A, b + c = 1, so we see algebraically why costs double in this panel. By contrast in Figure 10.7B, costs increase by 59% as a result of the move from bundle **C** to **D**. In the context of Equation 10.13, this is seen as $1.59 = 2^{(1/(b+c))} = 2^{(1/1.5)} = 2^{2/3}$. Similarly, costs increase by 152% as a result of the move from bundle **C** to **D** when faced with the DRTS production function in Figure 10.7C. In this instance, b + c = 0.75, so $2.52 = 2^{(1/0.75)} = 2^{4/3}$.

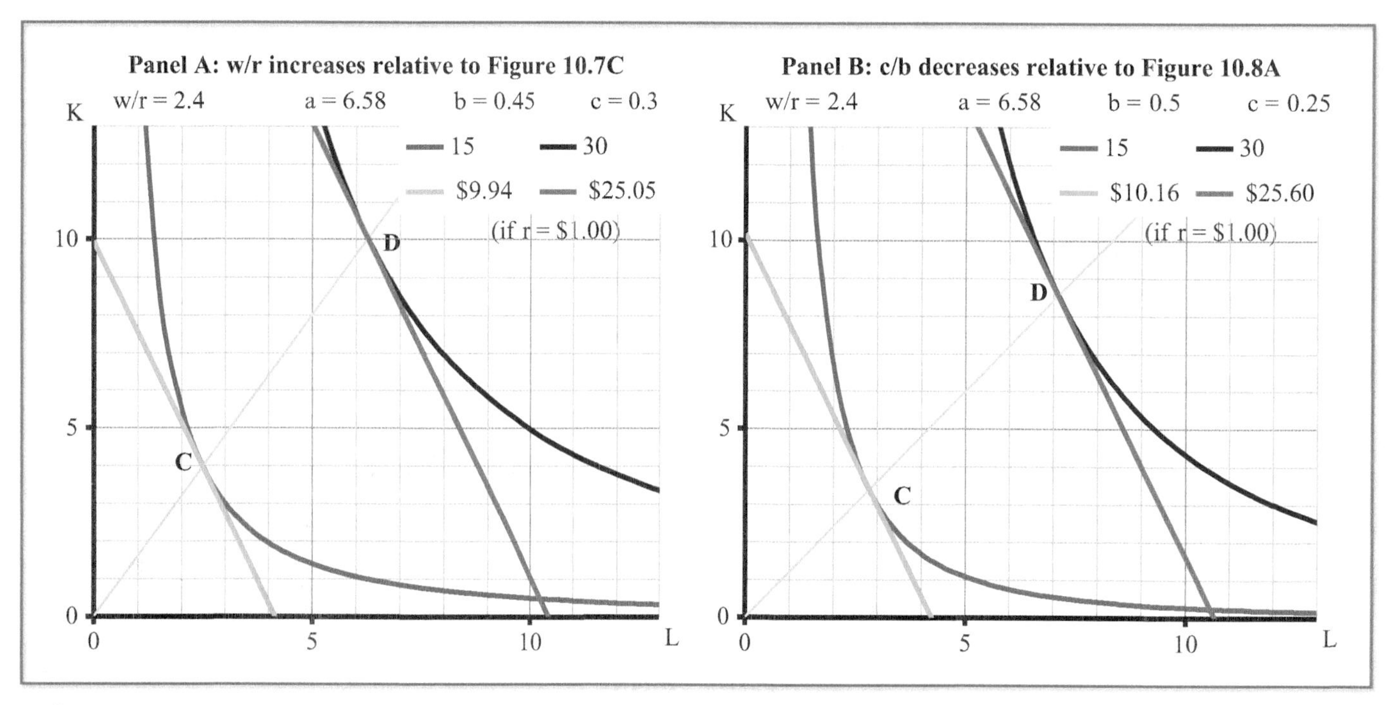

FIGURE 10.8
Expansion Paths for Cobb-Douglas Production: $Q(L, K) = a \cdot L^b \cdot K^c$

As the input price ratio changes, so will the expansion path, *ceteris paribus*. Figure 10.8A starts with the DRTS production function in Figure 10.7C but adjusts the input price ratio to w/r = 2.4 (as in Figures 10.6A and 10.6D). The expansion path in this instance is $K = (c/b) \cdot (w/r) \cdot L = (2/3) \cdot (2.4) \cdot L = 1.6 \cdot L$, according to Equation 10.11c. Notice that although costs are initially different in this circumstance, $C_0 = \$9.94$ at **C** (when w = \$2.40 and r = \$1.00), the cost increase required to double output remains 152% in moving to **D** (2.52 = \$25.05/\$9.94). Indeed, as long as b + c = 0.75, a doubling of output will increase costs by 152%, according to Equation 10.13. This is true as long as the sum of b and c remains constant—even if b and c change values, as shown in Figure 10.8B. Figure 10.8B holds w/r = 2.4 and b + c = 0.75 (as in Figure 10.8A), but b increases to b = 0.5 and c decreases to c = 0.25. The ratio c/b therefore declines to 0.5 (rather than 2/3 in Figure 10.8A). The expansion path using Equation 10.11c adjusts to this change by becoming less capital intensive as a result: $K = (c/b) \cdot (w/r) \cdot L = (1/2) \cdot (2.4) \cdot L = 1.2 \cdot L$, which is shown by the gold ray in Figure 10.8B. As in Figures 10.8A and 10.7C, the cost increase required to double output remains 152% in moving from **C** to **D**, since b + c = 0.75 (2.52 = \$25.60/\$10.16). One final difference contained in Figure 10.8B is that **C** and **D** are input bundles, where two-thirds of spending is devoted to labor (b/(b + c) = 2/3) and one-third of spending is on capital (c/(b + c) = 1/3), rather than a 60%/40% split (using Equations 10.14a and 10.14b). This is a result of b and c changing in relative size in Figure 10.8B.

Each of the expansion paths discussed thus far has been a ray through the origin.[11] This need not be true; an example is the discussion of robotic welders from the start of Section 10.3. When the scale of production is sufficiently small, certain capital-intensive production processes are not as cost effective as less capital-intensive methods of production. For small output levels, derived demand for robotic welders is zero. Therefore, the expansion path is no longer a ray through the origin of an input space that includes robotic welders and welding torches as separate types of capital. A quick glance back at the ICC curves for shifted CD utility functions in Figure 7.17 (and MRS = 1 yellow lines in Chapter 4 versions of the shifted CD) suggests that this form could model this situation.

The cubic production function that formed the basis for much of Section 9.4 provides a geometric example of a production function whose expansion path is nonlinear. Figure 10.9 provides two expansion paths, based on two input price ratios. Both Figures 10.9A and 10.9B are overhead views of this production function. Each figure also includes two

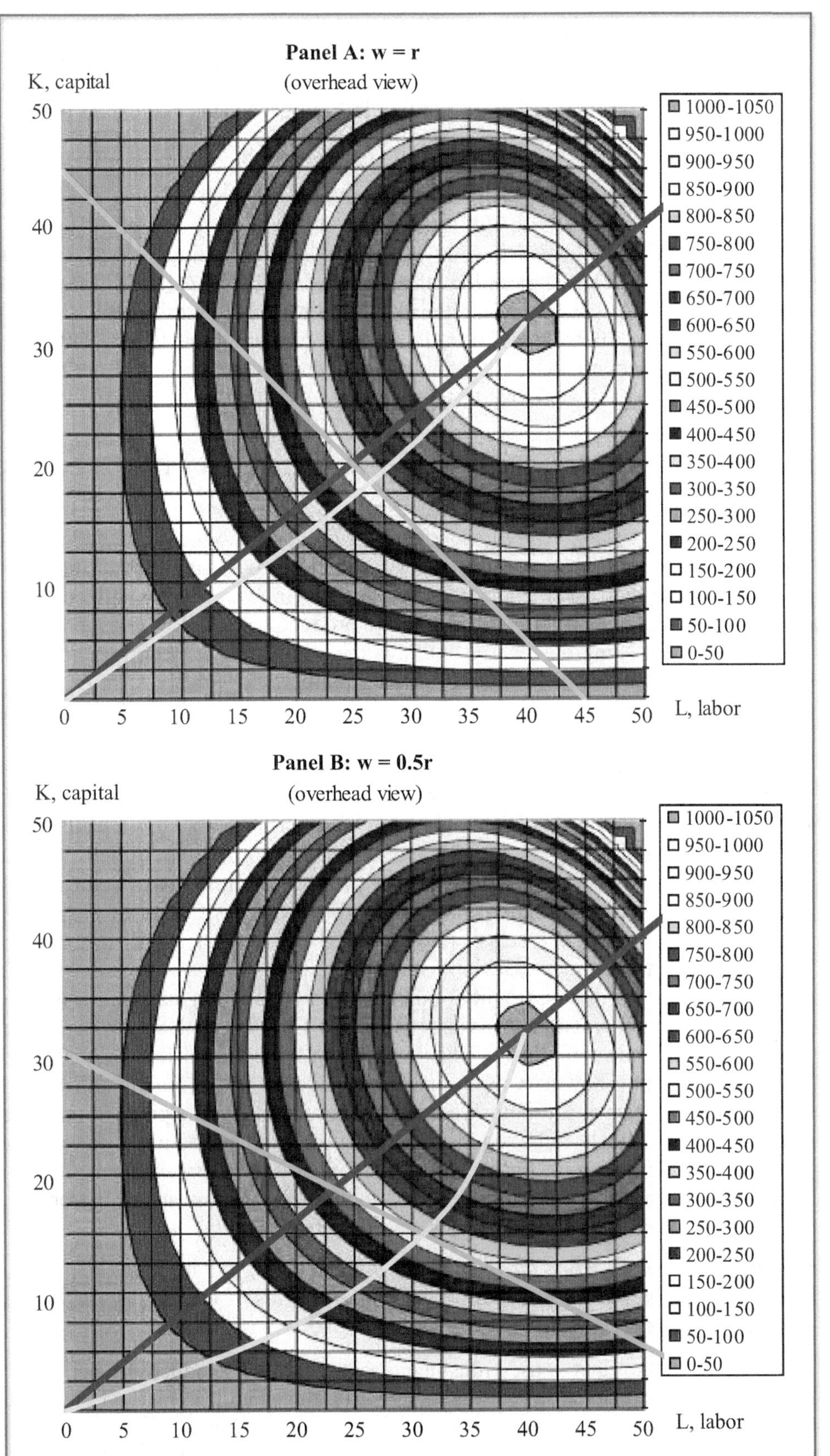

FIGURE 10.9
Expansion Paths with Cubic Production

lines and a curve. The blue line in both figures depicts the ray $K = 0.80 \cdot L$, a ray that passes through the top of the production hill (this occurs at (L, K) = (40.0, 31.9)). The green isocost line in Figure 10.9A is associated with spending $45 on labor and capital, given w = r = $1.00. The green isocost line in Figure 10.9B is associated with spending $31 on labor and capital, given w = $0.50 and r = $1.00. Each isocost line supports production of 550 units of output at minimum cost, given these cost conditions. The points of tangency between the isocost line and the isoquant $Q_0 = 550$ occur at approximately (L, K) = (26.5, 18.5) in Figure 10.9A and at (31.2, 15) in Figure 10.9B. (This isoquant is the boundary between the yellow (500–550) band and the medium blue (550–600) band.) There are points on each expansion path, and each occurs at a capital/labor ratio that differs from K/L = k = 0.80, the K/L ratio associated with the top of the hill. (K/L = 0.70 at $Q_0 = 550$ in Figure 10.9A, and K/L = 0.48 at $Q_0 = 550$ in Figure 10.9B.) Other points on each expansion path are depicted using the gold curve, and a slider in the Excel file for Figure 10.9 allows you vary cost to see these various points of tangency.[12]

10.5 On the Importance of Time Frame in Producer Theory

The analysis thus far in this chapter has assumed that the firm has complete freedom in determining how much to use of each factor of production. One of the hallmarks of production processes is that some aspects of a production process are easier to adjust than are others. Over the short term, plant, property, and equipment are largely fixed, while labor and materials can more readily be adjusted to produce more or less output. For example, a firm can use existing machinery but have the employees work longer hours or add a second shift of workers if it wishes to increase output. Conversely, the firm can move to a restricted workweek if a decrease in output is required. The firm finds it impractical, however, or even impossible to quickly expand or contract property, plant, and machinery as a way of adjusting output in the short run. The **short run** is the time period in which the firm is unable to vary some of its inputs. That is, some inputs are fixed in the short run. By contrast, the **long run** is the time frame in which the firm is able to vary all of its inputs. The expansion paths discussed in Section 10.4 are more accurately described as long-run expansion paths because both factors of production (in the two-factor model) were allowed to vary. The **long-run expansion path (LREP)** is the set of cost-minimizing input bundles for different levels of output and fixed factor prices. All factors of production vary along a long-run expansion path.

short run: The short run is the time period in which the firm is unable to vary some of its inputs.

long run: The long run is the time frame in which the firm is able to vary all of its inputs.

long-run expansion path (LREP): The long-run expansion path is the set of cost-minimizing input bundles for different levels of output and fixed factor prices.

If we increase the dimensionality of the model, we could talk in terms of different levels of the long run. For example, assume in the short run that both arc welders and robotic welders are in fixed supply in a production facility. It may be easier to adjust the number of arc welding units, however, in response to changes in output than to adjust more complex machinery, such as a robotic welder. The more complex the piece of machinery, the more lead time is likely to be required to adjust the stock of the input. Put another way, the more complex the piece of machinery, the longer is the short run.

If some factors of production are fixed, output changes must result from adjusting those factors of production that may be varied in the short run.

> **Claim:** *If more than one factor of production is variable in the short run, then the optimization described in Section 10.3 must hold for each variable factor to minimize the short-run cost of production.*

Each variable factor that is used must have equal marginal productivity per dollar spent, as required by Equation 10.6. As output changes, the expansion path will look like ones shown in Section 10.4, assuming that the figure is based solely on variable factors of production. This is one way to view a short-run expansion path. The **short-run expansion path (SREP)** is the set of cost-minimizing input bundles for different levels of output and fixed factor prices, given some fixed factors of production. Once fixed *and* variable factors of production are included in the graph of the production function, the SREP is not based on the tangency between the isoquant and isocost line because tangency is not

short-run expansion path (SREP): The short-run expansion path is the set of cost-minimizing input bundles for different levels of output and fixed factor prices, given some fixed factors of production.

required when comparing fixed and variable factors of production. Put another way, *fixed* factors need not satisfy Equations 10.5 and 10.6 in the short run. If a factor is fixed, the marginal productivity per dollar spent on that factor may be more or less than that spent on variable factors. We will be able to see this shortly, when we analyze short-run optimization in the two-input case.

As in previous chapters, we typically model the short-run/long-run distinction with only two inputs. Economists model this differential ability in an (L, K) model by saying that in the short run, capital is fixed. The only way to increase output in this instance is to increase labor; output is a function of labor in the short run. This is why we described the univariate production function as a function of labor in Section 9.2. We defined such a production function as a total product curve. The TP(L) curve from Section 9.2 was embedded as part of the production hill in Section 9.4 (compare Figure 9.1A and Figure 9.12) because the total product curve is the short-run production function. In this instance, there is no flexibility regarding how to produce extra output; if you have fixed capital, the only way to produce extra output is to use extra labor (and this only produces extra output so long as the marginal product of labor is positive). The short-run expansion path is simply a horizontal line in (L, K) space, since K is held constant. This was also shown three-dimensionally for CD production in Figure 9.7 as that slice of the production hill that keeps capital fixed (the slice of Figure 9.7 where $K = 10$ forms the basis for Equation 9.5a).

Figure 10.10 examines the relation between the long-run expansion path and the short-run expansion path. To simplify matters as much as possible, we assume that each input costs \$1 ($w = r = \$1$) and that the production function is the equal-weighted CRTS CD production function, $Q(L, K) = (L \cdot K)^{0.5}$. Isoquant output levels with this production function are simply the value of L and K where the isoquant crosses the 45° line. Three isoquants are shown: $Q = 2.2$, 5.0, and 8.1. Given an equal-weighted CD production function and equal factor prices, the LREP is simply the main diagonal, $L = K$ (according to Equation 10.11c), as shown in Figure 10.10A. Based on Figure 10.10A, determine the long-run cost of producing each of these levels of output:

Q10a. What are the long-run costs associated with producing at **D**, **E**, and **C**? (Fill in the upper of the two rows in the table shown in Figure 10.10B.)*

To move from a long-run analysis to a short-run analysis, we must know how much of the fixed factor of production the firm has available to it in the short run. One way to determine this is to examine the firm's expectations regarding future production; another way to proceed is to simply assume a given level of capital stock, K_0, in the short run.

A hypothetical short-run assumption: *Suppose that the firm expects to produce 5 units of output per unit of time and that it does not expect relative input prices to change over time.*

Cost-minimizing production of 5 units of output occurs at input bundle **E** in Figure 10.10. Therefore, the firm invests in 5 units of capital. This investment decision is a long-run decision. Once this decision is made, the firm is now embedded in a short run. Short-run changes in output can only occur by adjusting labor; the short-run expansion path is the horizontal line at $K_0 = 5$ in Figure 10.10B, based on the short-run production function $TP(L) = (5 \cdot L)^{0.5}$. In this short run, 5 units of labor are required to produce 5 units of output (because you have 5 units of capital), but if you want to produce 8.1 units of output, you must use 13 units of labor, and if you want to produce 2.2 units of output, you can do so with 1 unit of labor. Costs, in this instance, are easy to calculate (since input bundles **A** and **B** are approximately integer solutions). **A** = (13, 5), so production at **A** is $Q(\mathbf{A}) = (13 \cdot 5)^{0.5} = 65^{0.5} \doteq 8.1$; and **B** = (1, 5), so production at **B** is $Q(\mathbf{B}) = 5^{0.5} \doteq 2.2$.

***Q10a answer:** This is easily seen as $w \cdot L + r \cdot K$ at each point. Given unitary prices for both factors, the answers are $C(\mathbf{D}) = C_{2.2}^{LR} = \$4.40$, $C(\mathbf{E}) = C_5^{LR} = \$10$, and $C(\mathbf{C}) = C_{8.1}^{LR} = \$16.20$. These costs can also be seen as the intercept on either axis (since $w = r = \$1$). This could also be obtained from Equation 10.13, noting that when $w = r = 1$, $a = 1$, $c/b = 1$, and $c + b = 1$, then $C_{LR} = 2 \cdot Q$.

FIGURE 10.10 Short-Run versus Long-Run Expansion Paths, Given $Q = (L \cdot K)^{0.5}$ and $w = r = \$1$

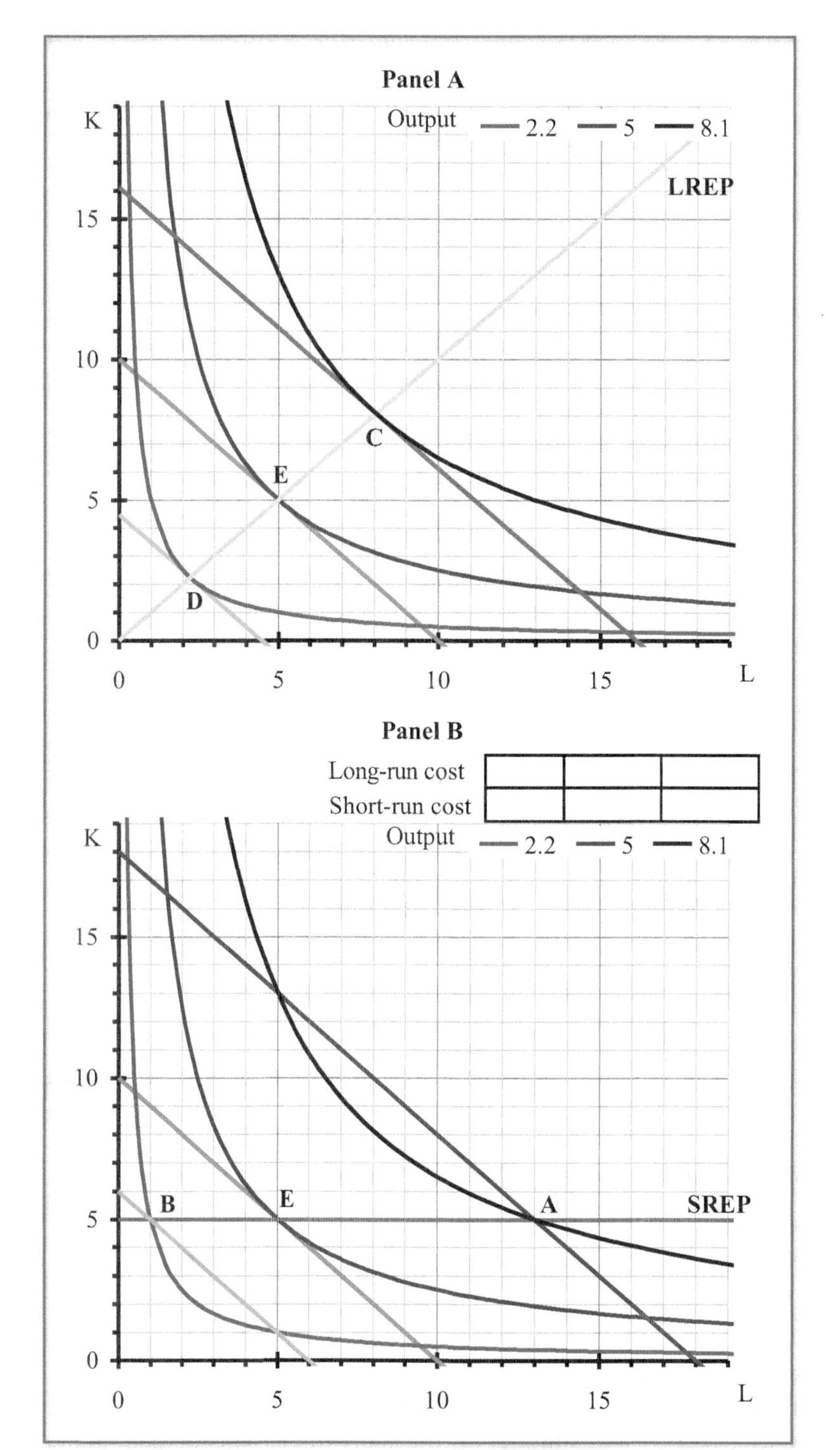

Q10b. What are the short-run costs associated with producing at **B**, **E**, or **A**? (Fill in the lower of the two rows in the table shown in Figure 10.10B.)*

Figure 10.10C shows both time frames in the same figure. Bundle **E** depicts production at a point of tangency between the isoquant and the isocost line. This is a point where $MP_K/r = MP_L/w$ (or in terms of slopes of isoquant and isocost, MRTS = w/r). But once we have chosen our plant size (that is, once we have decided to use $K_0 = 5$), this equality

---

***Q10b answer:** Since w = r = \$1, costs are calculated by adding the L and K values of each bundle. C(**B**) = $C_{2.2}^{SR}$ = \$6, C(**E**) = C_5^{SR} = \$10, and C(**A**) = $C_{8.1}^{SR}$ = \$18. Exact long-run cost values can be obtained from the Excel file for Figure 10.10, and the output level can also be adjusted from Q = 1 to Q = 9 in increments of 0.1 unit.

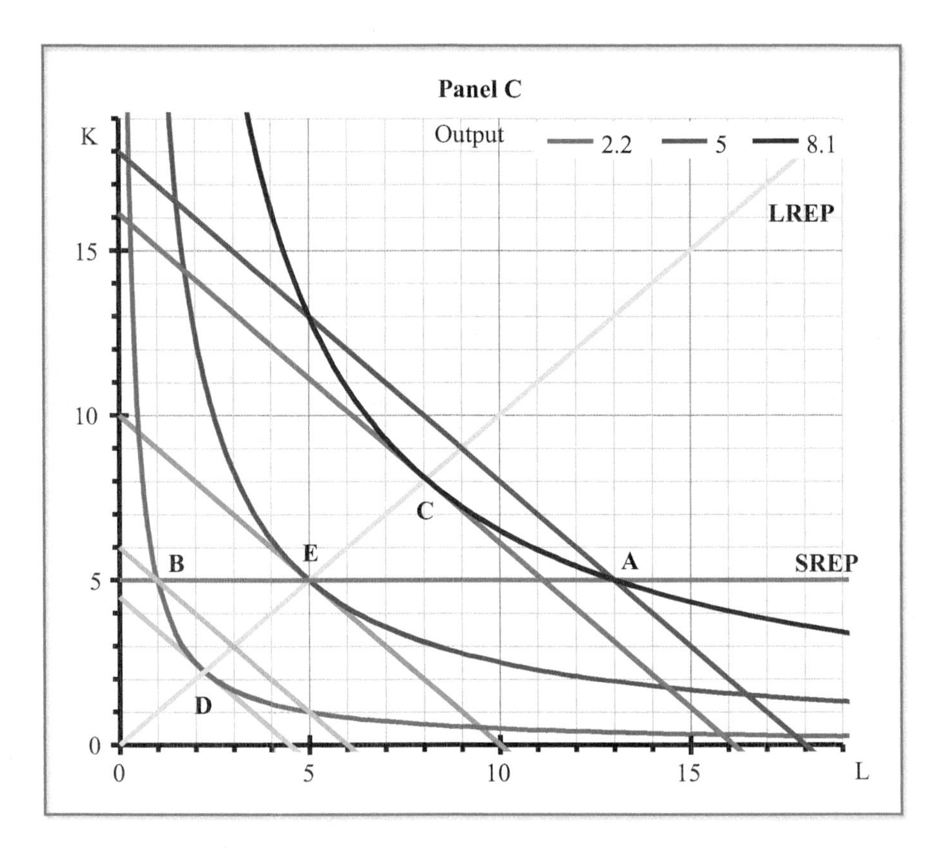

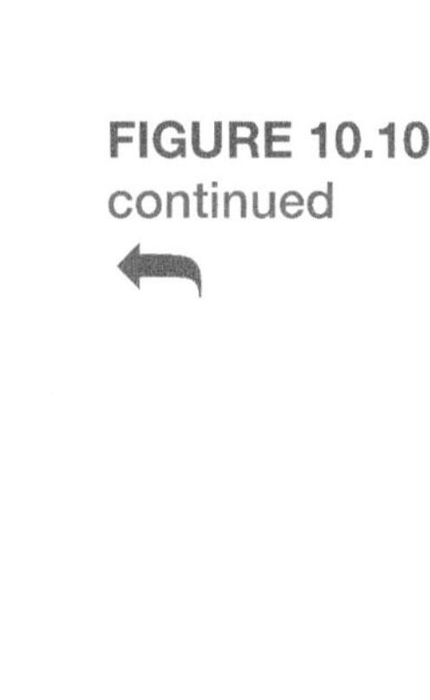
FIGURE 10.10
continued

is *irrelevant*. Certainly, some level of output will be cost minimizing (in the sense that each factor has equal MP_i/P_i), but the fact remains that the only way to expand or contract output is to adjust labor. If you wish to produce more than 5 units of output, such as Q = 8.1, you would like to produce at input bundle **C**, which requires 8.1 units of capital. Unfortunately, you do not have more than 5 units of capital available, so you must expand employment of labor from 5 to 13 to increase output from 5 to 8.1. There is a cost to this restriction (beyond the cost of the inputs themselves): *Short-run costs are always at least as high as, or higher than, long-run costs.* We see this extra cost as the difference between the isocost line through **A** and **C**. **A** costs about \$1.80 more than **C**, according to estimates based on the graph (\$1.80 = \$18.00 – \$16.20). Similarly, **B** is more expensive than **D** at producing Q = 2.2. The extra cost in this instance is about \$1.60, the difference between the isocost lines through **D** and **B** (\$1.60 = \$6.00 – \$4.40). Both of these differences can be seen as either the vertical or horizontal distance between respective isocost lines because w = r = \$1.

While a short-run expansion in output is reasonably straightforward to conceptualize, students often have trouble with short-run contractions in output. It is easy to understand that a plant may become too small if you suddenly wish to produce more than you have typically produced. The only solution is to increase labor, since capital cannot increase in the short run. However, why can't you just leave some of your plant unused if you wish to contract output in the short run? Students often examine Figure 10.10C and suggest the following analysis:

> Five units of capital are available in the short run, but cost-minimizing production only requires the use of 2.2 units of capital and 2.2 units of labor at input bundle **D** (at a cost of \$4.40). Therefore, I will only use 2.2 units of capital.

The problem with this analysis is that it ignores the fixed nature of capital in the short run. If you follow this strategy, you still must pay for the 2.8 units of capital that are left unused in the short run. These units of capital are part of the firm's short-run capital stock; the firm must pay rent on its capital stock, regardless of usage in the short run.

Claim: *As long as the fixed factor has positive marginal productivity in the short run, it should be utilized in the production process.*

By producing at **D** in the short run, you incur an extra \$1.20 in labor costs above what you would use had you produced 2.2 units of output using **B** instead. **D** costs a total of \$5 from capital and \$2.20 from labor, and **B** costs \$5 from capital and \$1 from labor. Both options produce 2.2 units of output (as long as you keep the remaining 2.8 units of capital you have already paid for that remain unused by producing at **D**).

Focus once again on input bundle **A** in Figure 10.10C. At this bundle, MRTS < w/r, or $MP_L/w < MP_K/r$. This violates the requirements for cost minimization in Equations 10.5 and 10.6, but as we said at the beginning of this section, the tangency condition (or equal marginal product per dollar spent) is irrelevant when we compare a fixed factor to a variable factor. The reverse inequality holds at bundle **B** but is also irrelevant, due to the fixed nature of capital in the short run. In the short run, these inequalities provide the firm with no actionable information, since no short-run capital changes are possible, given fixed capital. But if the new output level is maintained for a period of time, then this same inequality provides information regarding the direction the firm should move as it considers further capital investment.

In Figure 10.10C, if bundle **A** becomes the new "typical" level of production, then the inequality $MP_L/w < MP_K/r$ signals increased usage of capital and decreased usage of labor. This investment moves the firm from **A** to **C**. Conversely, if **B** becomes the new "typical" production point, then the inequality $MP_L/w > MP_K/r$ suggests that capital employment should be reduced and labor employment should be increased. This investment moves the firm from **B** to **D**. Both of these investment decisions are long run in nature. Both of these investments would move the firm to another short run at a new level of capital. Each of these new levels of capital would define a new horizontal SREP.

Short-Run Cost Minimization with CD Production *OPTIONAL SECTION*

The analysis of CD production in Section 10.3 produced algebraic descriptions of points on the long-run expansion path as a function of quantity produced, together with the parameters of the CD function (a, b, and c) and factor prices w and r in Equation 10.12. The cost of the long-run input bundle is described using Equation 10.13. We now turn to the short-run analog to these equations to be able to compare short-run cost to long-run cost.

Starting from the production function in Equation 10.11a for fixed $K = K_0$, solve for L to obtain labor required to produce Q units of output in the short run:

$$L = ((Q/a) \cdot (K_0)^{-c})^{(1/b)}. \quad \textbf{(10.15)}$$

This is the short-run analog to Equation 10.12a. By substituting Equation 10.15 back into Equation 10.2a, we obtain the short-run cost as a function of output, capital stock K_0, the parameters of the CD production function, and factor prices:

$$C_{SR} = r \cdot K_0 + Q^{(1/b)} \cdot [w \cdot (K_0^{-c}/a)^{(1/b)}]. \quad \textbf{(10.16a)}$$

$$C_{SR} = F(r, K_0) + \mathbf{Q^{(1/b)}} \cdot G(w, a, b, c, K_0). \quad \textbf{(10.16b)}$$

The first version of this equation is the short-run analog of Equation 10.13a, while the second version is analogous to Equation 10.13b. The function F in Equation 10.16b is fixed cost, and G acts as a scaling factor for the variable cost component. This short-run cost equation can be used to verify the cost levels derived in Figure 10.10B.

Before leaving our analysis of CD production, it is worthwhile to compare short-run costs with long-run costs, using Equations 10.13 and 10.16. We have seen graphically in Figure 10.10C that short-run costs are, in general, larger than long-run costs. This is a reasonable proposition: The long run provides the firm with alternatives that are not available in the short run, and some of those options may lower costs. We can also show this algebraically. Figure 10.10 assumed input prices, w = r = \$1, and CD production function, $a = 1$, b = c = 0.5. Short-run cost and long-run cost therefore simplify to:

Long-run cost: $C_{LR} = 2 \cdot Q$ (from Equation 10.13). **(10.17a)**

Short-run cost: $C_{SR} = K_0 + Q^2/K_0$ (from Equation 10.16). **(10.17b)**

The difference between these two costs is a quadratic equation in Q:

$$C_{SR} - C_{LR} = K_0 + Q^2/K_0 - 2 \cdot Q. \quad \textbf{(10.17c)}$$

If short-run costs are always greater than or equal to long-run costs, then this difference should always be greater than or equal to zero. The quantity of output where Equation 10.17c equals zero is given by the quadratic formula as:[13]

$$Q = (2 \pm (4 - 4 \cdot K_0/K_0)^{0.5})/(2/K_0) = K_0. \quad \textbf{(10.18)}$$

As expected, for this output level, $C_{SR} - C_{LR} = 0$ (which is found by substituting $Q = K_0$ into Equation 10.17c and simplifying). Equation 10.17c is a quadratic equation with a positive quadratic coefficient ($1/K_0 > 0$); therefore, all other values of Q will have $C_{SR} - C_{LR} > 0$ (since Equation 10.17c is a parabola with bottom at $Q = K_0$). As expected, based on Figure 10.10, short-run costs are greater than or equal to long-run costs, and $C_{SR} = C_{LR}$ when $Q = K_0 = 5$.

Short-Run Cost Minimization with Cubic Production

Cobb-Douglas production requires all inputs to maintain positive marginal productivity. As a result, capital will always be fully utilized in the short run, even for small levels of output, as discussed earlier in our comparison of producing at **D** versus **B** in Figure 10.10C. This need not be the case, as we demonstrate using the cubic production function utilized earlier in this chapter and in Chapter 9.

Figure 10.11 continues the analysis of Figure 10.9, which examined the production of 550 units of output at minimum cost, given different w/r ratios. In the present context, the isocost line has a slope of (–)10; w = 10 · r. The tangent to Q = 550 isoquant occurs

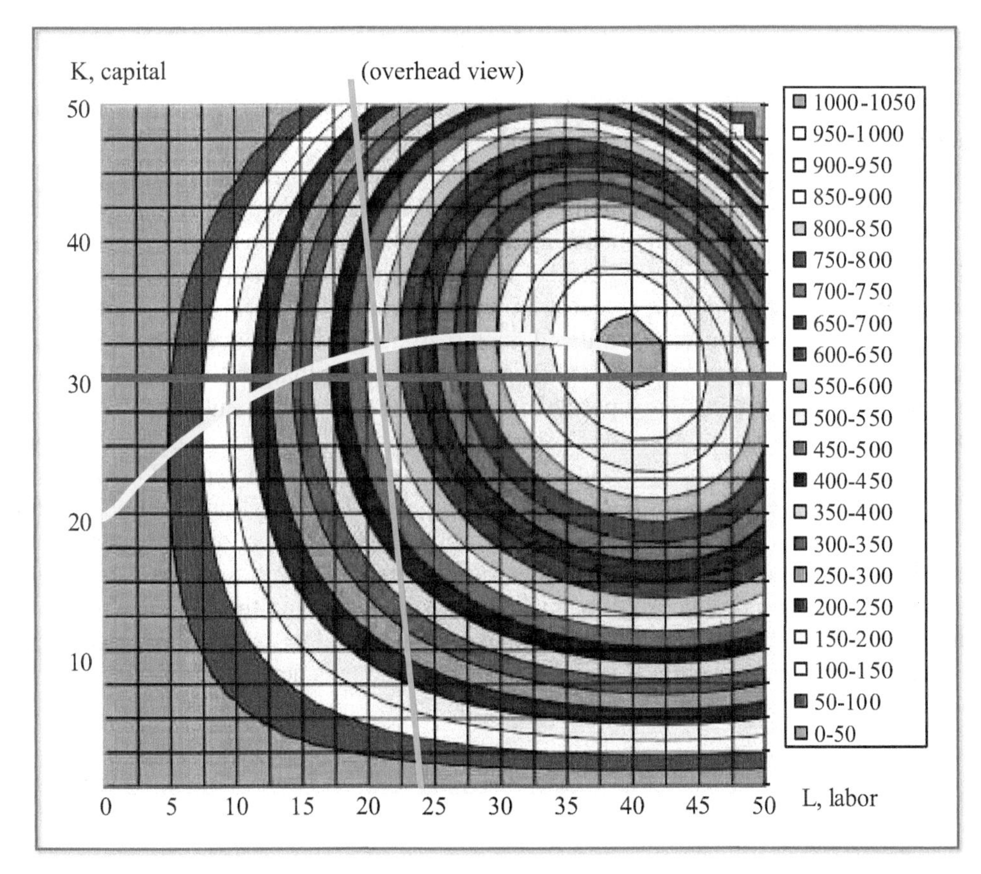

FIGURE 10.11 Capital Utilization on a Short-Run Expansion Path: The Case for Idle Capital in the Short Run ($w = 10 \cdot r$; $K_0 = 30$)

at (21.2, 30). If the firm fixes capital at $K_0 = 30$, the SREP is the red horizontal line shown. Also included is the yellow $MP_K = 0$ curve introduced in Figure 9.11 (and used to provide bounds on the economic region of production). Suppose the firm is embedded in the short run with $K_0 = 30$ as shown, and it wishes to produce a small level of output, such as $Q = 100$. In this instance, the firm would reduce costs by leaving 3.66 of the 30 units of capital idle because the input bundle (7.456, 26.34) produces 100 units of output cheaper than using all 30 units of capital. When $K > 26.34$ on the $Q = 100$ isoquant, the marginal product of capital is negative; output can only be maintained in this instance when more capital is used by increasing the amount of labor used, as well. (For instance, $Q(7.456, 30) = 96.58$. In this instance, labor must be increased by 0.147 if $K = 30$ is used because (7.603, 30) produces $Q = 100$ units of output.) Put another way, the slope of the isoquant becomes positive above the yellow $MP_K = 0$ curve. To force complete usage of $K_0 = 30$ in this instance creates extra labor costs, and it is better to leave some capital unused. (This is true even though the 3.66 units of idle capital must still be paid for in the short run.) The SREP in this instance should be modified for output levels below about $Q = 285$ (the output level where the red SREP intersects the yellow $MP_K = 0$ curve). In this instance, although the firm has 30 units of capital stock (and must pay for that capital stock in the short run), it should utilize that stock along the yellow $MP_K = 0$ curve.

Summary

The firm's ultimate goal of profit maximization can only be obtained if the firm produces goods at minimum cost. Cost minimization is a necessary but not sufficient condition for profit maximization and must be analyzed by combining the technological information provided by production functions with the market-based information provided by factor prices. The technological information in Chapter 9 examined various aspects of production and productivity, using isoquants in much the same way that Chapters 3 and 4 focused on consumer preferences and the representation of those preferences as utility functions and indifference curves. This chapter begins by examining isocost lines, the producer-side analog to the budget constraint.

Initially, isocost lines are examined in the absence of production information, just as budget constraints are examined in the absence of preference information in Chapter 5. Isocost lines are like budget constraints, but they differ in one important respect: Typically, the firm has greater flexibility in spending on inputs than consumers have flexibility in spending on goods. Firms must balance revenues against costs to generate profits. Revenues are constant for a given level of production. Therefore, the firm does not typically view the input choice question as "How much can be produced for a certain level of cost?" This is what the firm might ask if it felt resource constrained in some absolute sense. Rather, the firm is more likely to view the question as "If we want to produce a given level of output, how can we do that at minimum cost?" This means finding the lowest isocost line that supports a given isoquant. (The contrast with the consumer maximization problem should be clear. The main consumer question is "How can I maximize utility subject to a budget constraint?" The main question on the consumer side is thus how to achieve the highest indifference curve, given a fixed budget constraint.)

The answer to the firm's cost-minimization problem is to find the point of tangency between the isocost and isoquant. There are two heuristic interpretations of this point of tangency: (1) It can be viewed as making sure that the firm's willingness to substitute factors of production matches the market's relative valuation of those factors of production, and (2) it can also be viewed as making sure that all factors of production have equal marginal productivity per dollar spent at the cost-minimizing production point. The formal algebraic solution to the problem must also include boundary conditions. These conditions suggest that if a firm is producing a given level of output in a cost-minimizing fashion and a factor of production is not utilized, then that factor cannot have higher marginal productivity per dollar spent than the marginal productivity per dollar spent on factors that are utilized.

Cost-minimizing input choice is examined for perfect substitutes, perfect complements (Leontief), cubic, and Cobb-Douglas (CD) production functions. The input choices for each of these production functions mirror the consumer-side expenditure-minimization problem examined in Chapter 8. In particular, the CD solution maintains the hallmark CD result: The proportion of spending on each factor of production is determined by the relative size of the CD exponents.

Costs are inversely related to returns to scale. Costs increase less than proportionately with output changes if the production process exhibits increasing returns to scale. Costs increase proportionately with output changes if production processes exhibit constant returns to scale. And costs increase more rapidly than output if the production process exhibits decreasing returns to scale.

Expansion paths examine how inputs should change in response to output changes if the firm wishes to minimize cost. Expansion paths differ according to the time frame under consideration. In the long run, all factors of production are allowed to vary, and the expansion path is the set of tangencies of isoquant and isocost lines. In the short run, some factors of production are fixed. In this instance, the tangency condition no longer holds when fixed factors of production are viewed against factors that are allowed to vary in the short run.

Review Questions

Define the following terms:

isocost line	long run	long-run expansion path
expansion path	short-run expansion path	input price vector
short run		

Match the concepts from producer theory with the corresponding concepts from consumer theory:

a. Isocost line	1. $MRS = P_x/P_y$
b. Equal bang for the buck	2. Income consumption curve
c. Cost minimization	3. Budget constraint
d. Long-run expansion path	4. Expenditure minimization

Provide short answers to the following:

a. What is the relation between profit-maximizing behavior and cost-minimizing behavior?

b. What is the single most important difference between an isocost line and a budget constraint?

c. What is the geometric difference between a short-run expansion path and a long-run expansion path?

d. Suppose $MRTS_{K,L} > P_L/P_K$ with $L_0 > 0$ and $K_0 > 0$. Is it possible that (L_0, K_0) is a point on the long-run expansion path?

e. Suppose $MRTS_{K,L} > P_L/P_K$ with $L_0 > 0$ and $K_0 > 0$. Is it possible that (L_0, K_0) is a point on the short-run expansion path?

f. Suppose $MRTS_{K,L} > P_L/P_K$ with $L_0 > 0$ and $K_0 > 0$. If the firm wishes to maintain production at $Q_0 = Q(L_0, K_0)$ and can vary all factors of production, what should it do?

g. Answer questions d–f again, replacing the first inequality with $MRTS_{K,L} = P_L/P_K$.

h. Answer questions d–f again, replacing the first inequality with $MRTS_{K,L} < P_L/P_K$.

i. Suppose a firm facing CD production technology is embedded in a short run with a fixed amount of capital stock. Should it *ever* allow some of its capital to remain idle? Provide a one-sentence defense of your answer.

j. Suppose a firm facing cubic production technology is embedded in a short run with a fixed amount of capital stock. Should it *ever* allow some of its capital to remain idle? Provide a one-sentence defense of your answer.

k. Suppose you face a CRTS Cobb-Douglas production function and you find that two-thirds of your budget is devoted to labor and one-third is devoted to capital in the long run. If your production process is $Q(L, K) = a \cdot L^b \cdot K^c$, provide values for a, b, and c, as appropriate given this information. Provide explicit values for a, b, and c if possible.

l. Suppose you face a Cobb-Douglas production function, and you find that two-thirds of your budget is devoted to labor and one-third is devoted to capital in the long run. If your production process is $Q(L, K) = a \cdot L^b \cdot K^c$, provide values for a, b, and c, as appropriate given this information. Provide explicit values for a, b, and c if possible.

Check your answers to the *matching* and *short-answer* exercises in the Answers Appendix at the end of the book.

Notes

1. For raw materials, the input price is the price per unit. The distinguishing feature here is that raw materials (such as spruce logs) are consumed in the production process in the sense that they no longer exist once they are used (the logs have been turned into two-by-fours). Inputs such as labor and capital are not consumed in the same sense in the process of production because each has a useful life that extends beyond the specific time period. We think of such longer-lived assets as being rented in this instance.

2. With n inputs the isocost line is an $n - 1$ dimensional hyperplane in input space—the three-input analog is a plane in (f_1, f_2, f_3) space. Different levels of cost are associated with different planes, just as different levels of income are associated with different budget constraints in the Excel file for Figure 5.1.

3. Figures 10.3A, 10.3B, and 10.3C are qualitatively similar to those in Figure 6.1. The difference is instructive, however. Figure 6.1 allows utility to vary for fixed budget constraint, while Figure 10.3 allows expenditure to vary for fixed quantity produced. The marginal conditions involved are the same for both optimization processes, but the objective of one optimization process is the constraint in the other, and vice versa. This is another example of the concept of *duality* mentioned in the discussion of Equation 8.3.

4. We did not focus on this consumer-side rule in Chapter 6 because of the ordinality of utility functions. (The optimization rule that formed the basis of Section 6.1 used MRS because MRS is independent of this ordinality problem, as discussed in Chapter 4.) The same problem does not apply to the producer side, due to the cardinality of production functions described in Chapter 9.

5. Some authors call this "conditional factor demand" because this is a demand for a factor of production that is conditional on the firm producing Q_0 units of output in a cost-minimizing fashion. Equations 10.12a and 10.12b are generalizations of the CD substitution-bundle results derived in Equations 8.5a and 8.5b. Starting with Equations 10.12a and 10.12b, make the following substitutions: $L = x$, $K = y$, $Q_0 = U_0$, $a = 1$, $r = P_y$, $w = P_x$, $b = r$, $c = 1 - r$ (so $b + c = 1$). Once you make these substitutions, Equation 10.12a becomes Equation 8.5a, and Equation 10.12b becomes Equation 8.5b. As described at the beginning of this section, the optimization described by Equation 10.5 is identical to that provided by Equation 8.3. Equation 8.5 is the general consumer-side CD result based on the optimization described in Equation 8.3, but it is less general than the general CD production function (since a is not necessarily equal to 1 and $b + c$ is not restricted to 1, as in Equation 8.5). The restrictions on the consumer side are justified because utility is ordinal. Once these restrictions are placed on Equation 10.12, it simplifies to Equation 8.5.

6. This result can be stated in terms of the degree of homogeneity of the production function. As noted in the discussion of returns to scale in Section 9.4, if the production function is homogeneous of degree k, the returns to scale are determined by whether k is less than, equal to, or greater than 1. For CD production, $k = b + c$, so the cost function increases by $1/k$. This implies a less-than-proportionate increase in cost if $k > 1$ (IRTS), a proportionate increase in cost if $k = 1$ (CRTS), and a more-than-proportionate increase in cost if $k < 1$ (DRTS). (See Chapter 7 Appendix B for further discussion of homogeneous functions.)

7. The ordinality of the consumer side allowed us to restrict our analysis to $b + c = 1$ without loss of generality. The cardinality that is the hallmark of the producer side requires us to examine the CD production function in its more general form, where $b + c$ is not restricted to sum to one.

8. The mathematics here is a bit ugly but manageable:

$$w \cdot L_0/C_0 = ((Q_0/a)^{(1/(b+c))} \cdot w^{(b/(b+c))} \cdot r^{(c/(b+c))} \cdot (b/c)^{(c/(b+c))})/ ((Q_0/a)^{(1/(b+c))} \cdot w^{(b/(b+c))} \cdot r^{(c/(b+c))} \cdot ((b/c)^{(c/(b+c)} + (c/b)^{(b/(b+c))})).$$

This simplifies to $(b/c)^{(c/(b+c)}/((b/c)^{(c/(b+c)} + (c/b)^{(b/(b+c))})$. Multiplying numerator and denominator of this fraction by $c^{(c/(b+c)} \cdot b^{(b/(b+c)}$ produces $b/(b + c)$, the result in Equation 10.14a. Equation 10.14b is obtained in similar fashion.

9. If you still feel uncomfortable about returns to scale, then you should revisit the discussion of Figure 9.9.

10. Do not be bothered by the low wage rate; recall that we can define the time period however we wish. Seventy-five cents per minute is $45 per hour. Alternatively, you could multiply w and r by a common factor such as 10 to obtain an hourly wage of $7.50 and an hourly rental rate on capital of $10; the only change in this instance would be that the light green isocost line would represent $49.40 rather than $4.94.

11. If this is true for any price ratio, then the production function must be either homogeneous or homothetic. These concepts are discussed in Chapter 7 Appendix B.

12. This production function is algebraically examined in the Chapter 9 Appendix. Due to the complexity of the cubic production function, each marginal product is a mixture of cubic, quadratic, and linear terms in L and K. Since $MRTS = MP_L/MP_K$, the expansion path is seen to be a much more complex function of L and K than those examined algebraically in this chapter.

13. The quadratic formula states that $A \cdot x^2 + B \cdot x + C = 0$ for $x = (-B \pm (B^2 - 4 \cdot A \cdot C)^{0.5})/(2 \cdot A)$. In Equation 10.17c, $A = 1/K_0$, $B = -2$, and $C = K_0$.

Cost Curves

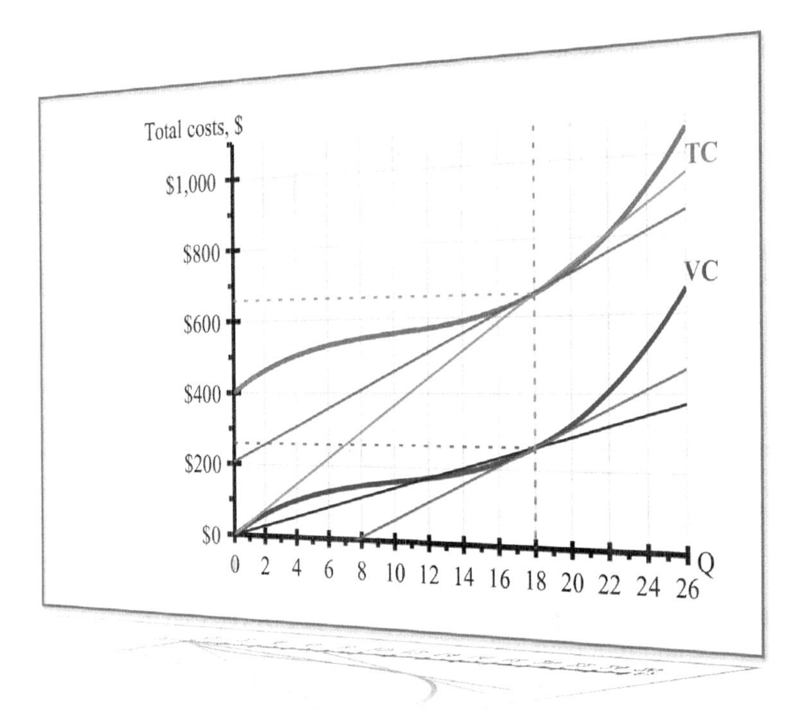

Chapter Outline

The cost analysis in Chapter 10 links the cost of factors of production with how the factors are combined to produce goods. Cost minimization is based on a comparison of the relative value of factors of production in producing the good and the relative market valuation of those factors. The more direct analysis based on isoquants and isocost lines that forms the core of Chapter 10 is indirectly used in this chapter, where we examine cost as a function of output. The cost curves developed in this chapter form the basis for profit-maximizing decisions by the firm.

Cost is used in a variety of settings and in a variety of disciplines, so it is important to delineate how the economist's notion of cost differs from others. To an economist, opportunity cost is of preeminent importance. Other cost concepts examined in Section 11.1 include accounting cost; implicit and explicit cost; fixed, variable, and total cost; and sunk cost. Section 11.2 examines the geometry of short-run cost functions. Costs can be analyzed on both a total and a per-unit basis, just as production functions can be analyzed on a total and a per-unit (of input) basis. Of the seven cost functions examined, three are total, and four are per unit. The notion of "average versus marginal" that first surfaced in the discussion of average versus marginal productivity in Chapter 9 reemerges in this chapter. Section 11.3 shifts the analysis from short-run to long-run cost. The relation between short-run cost and long-run cost that was first examined in Section 10.5 is reexamined in the context of cost as a function of output. Section 11.4 examines the algebra that ties together cubic cost functions; cubic cost functions are the simplest functions that depict the changing productivity we often observe in production processes. The chapter concludes with a second analysis of cost of production, given Cobb-Douglas technology. The Cobb-Douglas total cost results derived in Chapter 10 form the basis for the long- and short-run cost functions presented in Section 11.5.

11.1 Various Notions of Cost

opportunity cost: The opportunity cost of a resource is the value of that resource in its next best alternative use.

To an economist, the overarching concept that must be applied when considering all types of cost is the notion of opportunity cost. The **opportunity cost** of a resource is the value of that resource in its next best alternative use. Another term used for opportunity cost is *economic cost*. Resources are scarce and can only be applied to one task at a time. Suppose you have two part-time jobs during the summer. If you work an hour at the fast-food restaurant, you cannot work that same hour at the convenience store. The opportunity cost of each job is the value forgone by not being able to do the other one. Similarly, the opportunity cost of deciding to hang out with friends for an hour when you could have worked is the hour's wages you gave up by hanging out with your friends. Consider a second example: Suppose you own both halves of a duplex; you live on one side, and you rent out the other. Suppose that the current tenant decides to leave, and your mother-in-law moves into the vacant unit so she can save on rent and be closer to the grandkids. The opportunity cost of this move is the rent forgone by not being able to rent to other renters once your mother-in-law moves in. (Indeed, in this event, the opportunity cost is much, much higher, but you would need to be "Married with Children" to really understand!)

For many of the resources used in the production process, the market price of that input acts as its opportunity cost. Recall from our discussion at the start of Section 10.1 that this price is a rental rate per unit of time. For labor, this price is a wage rate; for capital, it is the rental rate on a unit of capital; and for land, it is the rental rate per unit of land. Raw materials prices are the price per unit of the raw material.

explicit costs: Explicit costs are out-of-pocket expenses.

implicit costs: Implicit costs are costs that are not explicitly paid out but are nonetheless incurred.

Not all costs, however, have a price tag attached to them. It is important to distinguish between explicit and implicit costs. **Explicit costs** are out-of-pocket expenses. Wages paid, raw material purchases, and rent paid on property that is being leased are examples of explicit costs. Explicit costs tend to be easier to quantify than implicit costs. **Implicit costs** are costs that are not explicitly paid out but are nonetheless incurred. Implicit costs are inherent in the notion of opportunity cost. Suppose you give up a \$40K-a-year job to start your own company. At the end of the year, you are ecstatic because you have broken even and indeed had an accounting net income of \$25K for the year. An economist would not look at this as making an economic profit because it ignores the opportunity cost of your own labor in determining net income. From an economist's point of view, the accounting profit of \$25K in net income must be balanced against what you lost by giving up your job; this is the value of your labor in its next best alternative use. An economist would restate this as the accounting profit of \$25K less the implicit cost of \$40K, or an economic loss of \$15K due to the opportunity cost of your labor. Since the foregone wages are only implicit in this instance, they are somewhat harder to quantify. This does not mean that they should be ignored.

Consider once again starting your own company. Suppose you use your own savings to help fund this start-up. If these funds would have earned you \$5K in income had you invested elsewhere (with another start-up operation or a money market fund, for example), then the \$5K in foregone income is another implicit cost that should be considered when determining the profitability of the start-up.

accounting costs: Accounting costs are the costs reported by accountants on financial reports.

These examples of explicit versus implicit costs point to one difference between an accountant's and an economist's perspective. Interestingly, while accountants and economists both discuss "cost," they have different definitions of what comprises cost. As a broad brushstroke, accountants view costs in a historical context, while economists use the notion of opportunity cost to examine the current context. **Accounting costs** are the costs reported by accountants on financial reports. These costs include actual expenses and depreciation, following established rules (in the United States, these rules are called the Generally Accepted Accounting Principles [GAAP]). Financial accountants describe past performance for external audiences—most notably, investors—in quarterly and annual reports, and for tax purposes.

Suppose you are an appliance manufacturer who uses an integrated circuit chip as part of the production process. Three months ago, you purchased 5,000 units at $10 per unit, and you are working through this inventory as you produce appliances. You find that you can now purchase the same chip for $8 per unit, due to changes that have occurred in the integrated chip market. How should you value your remaining inventory of chips in this instance? Accountants would use the historic price of $10 as their point of reference; economists would use the $8 current price as their point of reference. Economists determine value by using the next best alternative use for the factor, and if that factor can now be bought or sold for $8 per unit, that is more relevant than what the factor originally cost. Managerial accountants attempt to bridge the gap between the financial accountant's need to provide reliable information for external audiences and the business manager's need to obtain reliable information for making decisions.

Opportunity costs comprise total cost and can be further classified according to the short-run/long-run distinction described in Section 10.5 as either fixed cost or variable cost. **Fixed cost (FC)** is the opportunity cost that accrues to factors of production that are fixed in the short run. **Variable cost (VC)** is the opportunity cost that accrues to factors of production that are allowed to vary in the short run. **Total cost (TC)** is the sum of fixed and variable cost. Since fixed cost accrues to factors that do not change in the short run, they are themselves fixed. More explicitly stated: Fixed cost does not vary as output produced varies. By contrast, variable cost varies as output varies, since output changes by adjusting the usage of variable factors of production.

fixed cost (FC): Fixed cost is the opportunity cost that accrues to factors of production that are fixed in the short run.

variable cost (VC): Variable cost is the opportunity cost that accrues to factors of production that are allowed to vary in the short run.

total cost (TC): Total cost is the sum of fixed and variable cost.

One type of cost is not included in an economist's decision calculus. If a cost has already occurred but its opportunity cost is zero, then it should not be included, even though it is a readily visible explicit cost. Economists call such costs sunk costs. A **sunk cost** is a cost that has already occurred and cannot be recovered. The defining feature of a sunk cost is the inability to recover the cost; the next best alternative use has zero value. An important example of a sunk cost is an option to purchase a factor of production (as long as the option does not allow resale). Consider the following example, which examines options for crude oil.

sunk cost: A sunk cost is a cost that has already occurred and cannot be recovered.

Suppose you are a crude-oil refiner, and you wish to reduce the risk you face in the crude-oil market because of rising prices. One solution is to purchase an options contract to purchase crude oil at a fixed price in the future. An **options contract** gives the purchaser the ability to purchase a product at a given date in the future for a fixed price. This price is called the *exercise price* or *strike price*. The price of an option depends on the time remaining before the option expires, the exercise price, the volatility in the price of the product being traded, and interest rates.[1] Consider the following scenario:

options contract: An options contract gives the purchaser the ability to purchase a product at a given date in the future for a fixed price.

1. The current open-market price of crude oil is $40/bbl (per barrel).
2. An options contract to purchase crude at an exercise price of $40/bbl 3 months from now costs $1.50/bbl.

The total price per barrel in this instance would be $41.50/bbl. Assume you purchase an options contract for 1,000 barrels at a cost of $1,500. Three months from now, the open-market price of crude is $41/bbl. You wish to purchase 1,000 barrels of oil. Should you exercise your contract or let it expire? The answer in this instance is you should exercise your contract and purchase the 1,000 barrels at $40/bbl, rather than purchase the barrels on the open market at $41/bbl. The appropriate comparison ignores the sunk cost of $1,500, since this cost is not recoverable. The decision is not to purchase 1,000 barrels of oil at $41,500 or $41,000, but to purchase at $40,000 or $41,000. The $1,500 has already been spent (regardless of whether you exercise the option or let it expire) and should therefore have no effect on the current decision. In this instance, you should exercise the contract whenever the open-market price is higher than the exercise price, and you should let it expire when the reverse holds true.

The same logic applies to other types of options as well. When firms are considering where to locate a plant, they often purchase an option on a piece of land. The option provides them the right to purchase the land at a given price, as long as the sale occurs within a fixed period of time. If another piece of land becomes available prior to exercising the option, the cost of the option should have no bearing on the choice between the two pieces of property. The option cost has already occurred and is not recoverable. Of course, if the decision being considered is whether or not to purchase the option, then the option cost has *not* already occurred, and it should be considered as part of the decision-making process. The truisms "Let bygones be bygones" and the business version "Don't throw good money after bad" attempt to get at this point.

A final important concept necessary to understand costs relates to the units used to discuss them. Broadly speaking, costs can be described in two ways—total cost and per-unit cost. To take a simple example, suppose it costs $1,500 to produce 1,000 two-by-fours. This can be described as $1,500 in total cost and as a per-unit cost of $1.50. Both of these methodologies have their uses. The total cost version tends to provide the greatest intuition, at least initially. The per-unit cost version is more useful for decision making. Both can be viewed from either a short-run or long-run perspective.

Opening a Take-Out Pizza Shop

To put the cost notions just discussed in perspective, consider the decision to open a take-out pizza shop near a college campus. Suppose that Steve is considering giving up his $24K-per-year job as an assistant manager of a retail store to open a take-out pizza shop. He faces various decisions regarding how he should proceed and these decisions relate to various factors of production:

- *Location*—A storefront suitable for the shop is currently available. Steve has talked to the owner of the property, and the owner is offering an option to rent the property on a month-to-month basis for $1,200 per month. This option is good for 30 days and costs $700.
- *Equipment*—A local restaurant supply company is willing to lease pizza ovens, refrigeration units, preparation tables, and miscellaneous utensils to Steve. This equipment rents for $800 per month, with a one-time setup fee of $1,000.
- *Utilities*—Steve estimates that telephone, gas, and electric will cost $300 per month. The hookup fees for these utilities are an additional $200.
- *Advertising*—The local newspaper has a special deal for new businesses that provides $1,000 worth of advertising per month (based on the paper's normal rates) for $500 per month. To qualify, you must agree to purchase the advertising every month that you are open in the first year. The shop's phone number is listed in the Yellow Pages as part of the monthly telephone fee, but a quarter-page Yellow Pages advertisement costs $600. This lump-sum fee occurs on an annual basis when the new edition of the Yellow Pages is published.
- *Ingredients*—Steve estimates that cheese, toppings, tomato sauce, spices, and flour will cost $2.50 per pizza.
- *Packaging*—Generic pizza boxes are available from a cardboard fabricator for $1 per box. These boxes can be purchased in any quantity. Personalized boxes (with logo, address, and phone number) are available for $1.50 per box but must be purchased in minimum lots of 5,000 boxes.
- *Labor*—Steve plans to run the shop himself, and he plans to pay himself out of the profits from the business. He figures that he will need to hire a part-time worker for peak hours on Friday and Saturday evenings. The part-time worker would cost him $400 per month.

Suppose that Steve moves forward with his plan by taking out the option on the storefront and pays rent. He obtains the equipment and utilities, and takes advantage of the special newspaper advertising deal, as well as the quarter-page advertisement in the Yellow Pages. He decides to use the generic pizza boxes, hires the part-time worker, and begins making pizzas. How should he view each of the costs he has incurred? Are they fixed, variable, or sunk? Implicit or explicit? How would your answer change if Steve had made other choices for advertising and packaging? (Try to work through each part before reading the analysis in the next few paragraphs.)

Steve has incurred a variety of costs in this instance. Consider first which of the costs are fixed and which are variable. All of the costs except ingredients and packaging are fixed in nature because each is independent of the number of pizzas made. The ovens must be on and rent must be paid, whether one or a thousand pizzas are made. Some of these costs, however, are fixed, while others are sunk. The \$700 option to rent the storefront is the most obvious sunk cost. Once it is made, it should have no bearing on further decisions because it has already occurred, and it is not recoverable. Similarly, the \$1,000 equipment setup fee, the \$200 utilities hookup fee, and the \$600 Yellow Pages advertising fee are sunk costs because their opportunity cost is zero—each has no alternative use. If Steve decides to go out of business, he cannot recover any of these fees. The phone company may allow a business that has been in place for some time and is stable to spread out the \$600 cost of the advertisement over 12 months at \$50 per month. In this case, the \$600 would not be sunk at the beginning of the year, and the Yellow Pages advertisement would be considered a fixed—not sunk—cost.

The packaging is a variable cost: It varies as output varies. The same would not be true, at least as a startup, had Steve decided to use the personalized boxes instead. It is true that the price quoted is a per-unit price, but the minimum lot size is 5,000 boxes. Suppose that Steve had decided to pursue this course of action, instead of buying boxes in smaller lots as needed. The purchase would have cost Steve \$7,500, and if Steve went out of business at a point when he had 3,000 boxes left, the remaining boxes would have no recovery cost (other than for recycling purposes). The problem in this instance is that the personalized boxes cannot be resold or used by another pizza shop; the value of the boxes in their next best alternative use is zero (or at most, the salvage value of the cardboard). The personalized boxes are more expensive on several scores: They cost more on a per-unit basis, they must be purchased in larger lot sizes, *and* they have no resale value. (If you look around at independent pizza shops near your college, it should not be surprising that most use generic boxes.) As we have seen, much of the cost involved in producing takeout pizza is fixed in nature, and the only variable costs of production in this instance are \$3.50 per pizza on a per-unit basis (\$2.50 for ingredients and \$1.00 for packaging).

All costs are explicit save one in this instance. Steve planned to run the shop himself and pay himself out of the profits from the business. His labor is an implicit cost because his labor services have a next best alternative use. Steve gave up a \$24K-per-year job to undertake the start-up. An economist would include in the cost calculation Steve's implicit labor cost of \$2,000 per month when determining the costs inherent in running the shop.

11.2 The Geometry of Short-Run Cost Functions

Short-run cost functions can be viewed from two orientations: total cost and per-unit cost. (Each orientation requires its own diagram, but the diagrams are tied to each other, just as total product and marginal product requires two diagrams that are tied to each other via a common horizontal axis.) Short-run total costs are comprised of two components—fixed cost and variable cost:

$$TC = FC + VC. \qquad \textbf{(11.1a)}$$

Before we discuss these cost functions, it is worth quickly mentioning their shorthand references. The complete name for *total cost* is *short-run total cost (STC)*, *fixed cost* is *short-run total fixed cost (SFC)*, and the complete name for *variable cost* is *short-run total variable cost (SVC)*. The "short run" is omitted unless we are discussing both short-run and long-run costs together (and any discussion of long-run costs will explicitly state that the costs are long run). Similarly, each of the per-unit cost functions will have prefaces (average or marginal) attached to their name that signify that the cost function being examined is a per-unit cost function. Unless otherwise stated, we can omit both prefaces and assume that variable cost is short-run total variable cost and fixed cost is short-run total fixed cost. We begin with the total cost orientation, since it ties directly to the production and cost-minimization discussion of Chapters 9 and 10.

Total Costs

Variable cost varies as output varies, and therefore, variable cost may be written as VC(Q). When there are multiple variable input factors, the contribution of each should be included in determining variable cost. As discussed in Section 10.5, these variable factors should be used in a cost-minimizing fashion to produce a given level of output—that is, production should be on the short-run expansion path (SREP). In the take-out pizza example in Section 11.1, production was Leontief in ingredients and packaging.[2] A pizza requires one "unit" of ingredients and one box; ingredients cost \$2.50/pizza, and packaging is \$1.00/pizza, so $VC(Q) = \$3.50 \cdot Q$.

In the two-input (L, K) model, variable costs are labor costs, and labor costs vary, depending on how much output we wish to produce and the wage rate. Figure 11.1A describes a total product curve, $Q = TP(L)$. For reasons described in Section 9.2, labor initially has increasing marginal productivity, but past the point of inflection, it exhibits decreasing marginal productivity. The variable cost of producing Q units of output is:

$$VC(Q) = w \cdot L(Q). \tag{11.1b}$$

L(Q) is the amount of labor necessary to produce Q units of output, given K_0 units of capital. L(Q) is the inverse of the total product curve. The second line beneath the horizontal axis in Figure 11.1A simply takes L and multiplies by w; in this instance, $w = \$100$ (think of this as a daily wage rate). These numbers are variable cost. Variable cost as a function of output, VC(Q) in Figure 11.1B, is simply the total product curve rotated 90° with the vertical axis relabeled as variable cost in dollars, rather than units of labor. (Because w is denominated in dollars per unit of labor and L is denominated in units of labor, $(\$/L) \cdot L = \$$, $w \cdot L = VC$ is measured in dollars.)

The variable cost curve in Figure 11.1B is based on a specific wage rate; a different wage rate leads to a different variable cost curve. The total product curve in Figure 11.1A is fixed because (1) it describes technological possibilities that are not affected by factor prices, and (2) capital is fixed. The Excel file for Figure 11.1 allows you to vary the wage rate from \$1 to \$100 in \$1 increments to see this change dynamically. While the position of the cost curve in Figure 11.1B changes as the wage rate changes, its shape does not change. The two graphs are always direct inverses so that, for example, the output level where the point of inflection occurs remains the same in both Figures 11.1A and 11.1B (at $Q = 10$). Only the units on the vertical axis of the variable cost graph change as w changes. For example, if $w = \$10$, then the vertical axis labels in Figure 11.1B are in increments of \$10, rather than \$100, and if $w = \$1$, then the vertical axis labels are in increments of \$1.

The changing convexity of the variable cost curve is a direct result of the changing convexity of the total product curve on which it is based. Although the horizontal axis in Figure 11.1A is related to the vertical axis in Figure 11.1B (via $VC = w \cdot L$), the easiest way to talk about both graphs is to talk in terms of quantity (the vertical axis in Figure 11.1A and the horizontal axis in Figure 11.1B). For Q between 0 and 10, the TP curve is convex upward, and consequently, the VC curve is convex downward over the same range. For Q larger than 10, the reverse holds true: TP is convex downward, and consequently, VC is convex upward.

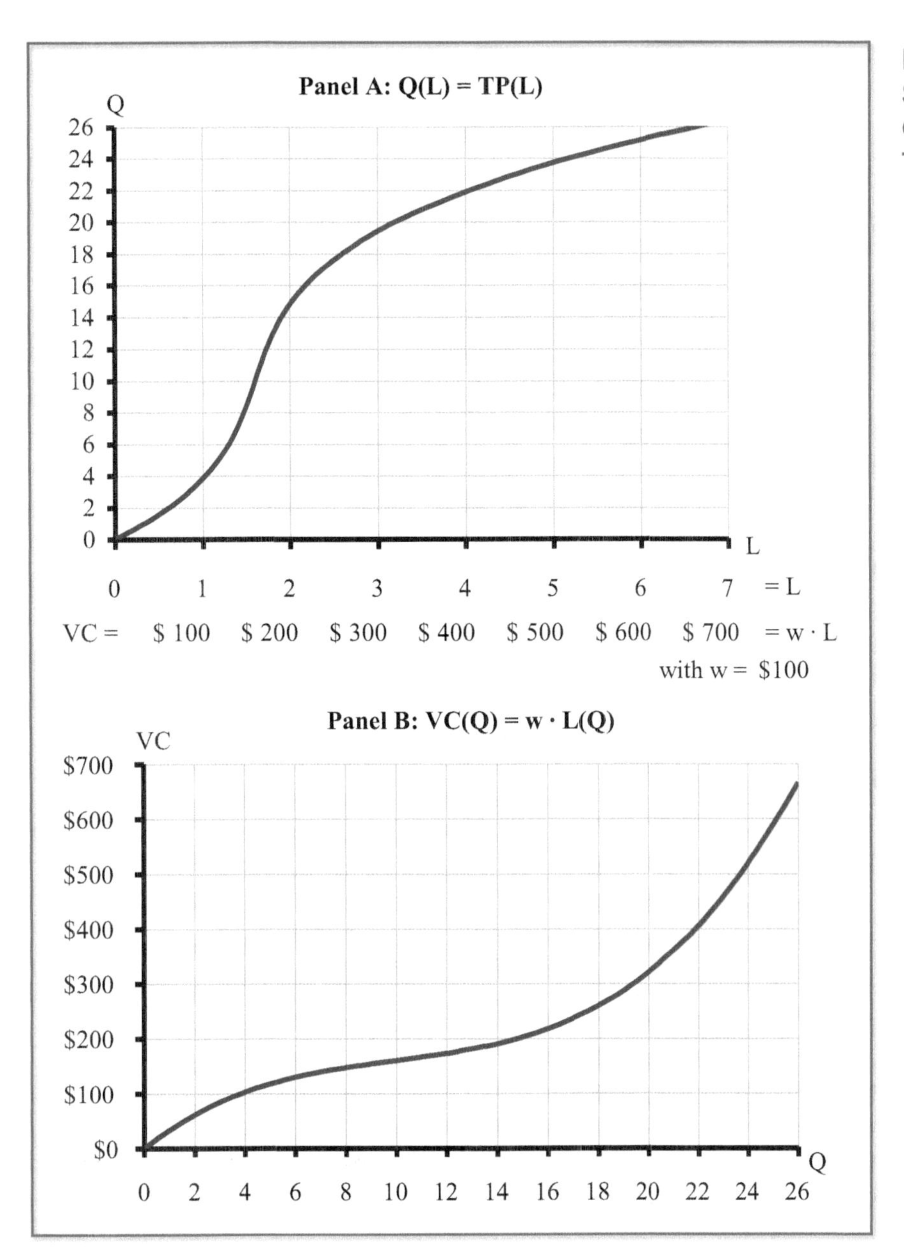

FIGURE 11.1 Deriving Short-Run Variable Cost from Short-Run Total Product

Q1a: How would either Figures 11.1A or 11.1B change if w = $10 rather than $100?

Q1b: Would a change in wage alter the quantity where the point of inflection occurs in Figure 11.1B?*

When working with multiple fixed components in the short run, total fixed cost is simply the sum of the individual fixed costs. In the pizza example, the monthly fixed cost is the sum of rent, equipment rental, utilities, newspaper advertising, and labor.

Q. What is the monthly total fixed cost in the pizza example from Section 11.1?†

***Q1 answer:** There would be no change to Figure 11.1A because a change in factor prices would not affect short-run production. Figure 11.1B would look the same if you reduce each number on the vertical axis by a power of 10 (i.e., the range for VC is from $0 to $70). The quantity of the point of inflection would not change because it is determined by the output level having the maximum MP_L in Figure 11.1A.

†Q answer: Total monthly fixed cost is $5,200 = $1,200 + $800 + $300 + $500 + $400 + $2,000. The most difficult of these costs to see is the $2,000 opportunity cost of Steve's time.

FIGURE 11.2 Short-Run Total Cost Curves

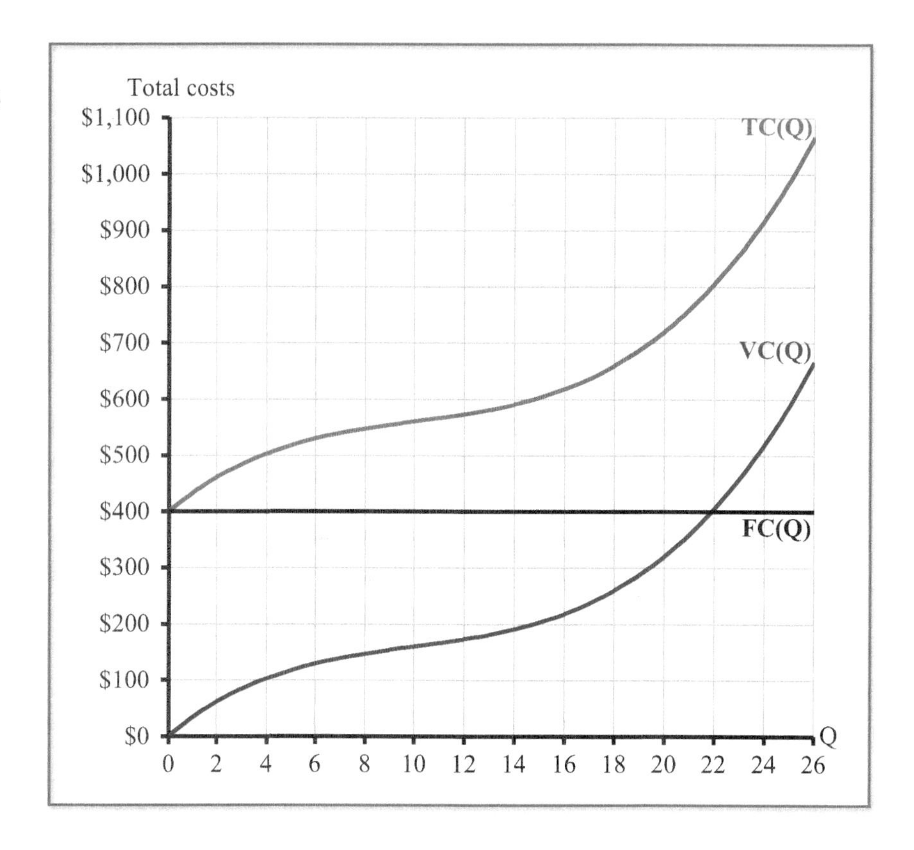

In the two-input (L, K) model, fixed costs per unit of time are:

$$FC(Q) = r \cdot K_0. \quad \textbf{(11.1c)}$$

The rental rate on capital is r, and the firm employs K_0 units of capital in the short run. Even though fixed cost is formally written as a function of quantity, its fixed nature makes it, in reality, independent of quantity. This cost is incurred regardless of the number of units of output produced. The only way to avoid this cost in the short run is to go out of business. Fixed cost is the horizontal line at a height of $FC(Q) = r \cdot K_0 = \$400$ in Figure 11.2. Once we have VC(Q) and FC(Q), TC(Q) is easily seen as their sum, according to Equation 11.1a. The green short-run total cost curve, TC(Q), is simply the variable cost curve translated up by fixed cost.

Per-Unit Costs

marginal cost (MC): Marginal cost is the incremental cost of producing one more unit of output.

The per-unit counterparts to the total cost curves just discussed are more useful for decision-making purposes. The most important of these curves is marginal cost. **Marginal cost (MC)** is the incremental cost of producing one more unit of output. This is more formally described as a *short-run marginal cost (SMC) curve*, but as discussed earlier, we usually drop the short-run S. As with other "marginal" concepts in the text, this is calculated as a slope, but the question is: the slope of what? In this instance, there are two equally valid answers: Marginal cost is the slope of the variable cost curve and the slope of the total cost curve. Incremental cost can be measured using either curve. This is not surprising in light of the relation that holds between variable cost and total cost described in Equation 11.1a and Figure 11.2; these two curves differ by a constant amount (FC). Algebraically, $MC(Q) = \Delta TC(Q)/\Delta Q = \Delta VC(Q)/\Delta Q$ for small changes in quantity, ΔQ.[3] Marginal cost is shown at two levels of output in Figure 11.3. Both Figures 11.3A and 11.3B depict two diagrams tied by a common horizontal axis. The upper diagram in each reproduces the TC(Q) and VC(Q) curves from Figure 11.2 and adds a red line tangent to both curves at a given output level. The first thing to note about both figures is that the tangent lines are parallel; this will always be the case, since TC(Q) is simply a vertical translate of VC(Q).[4]

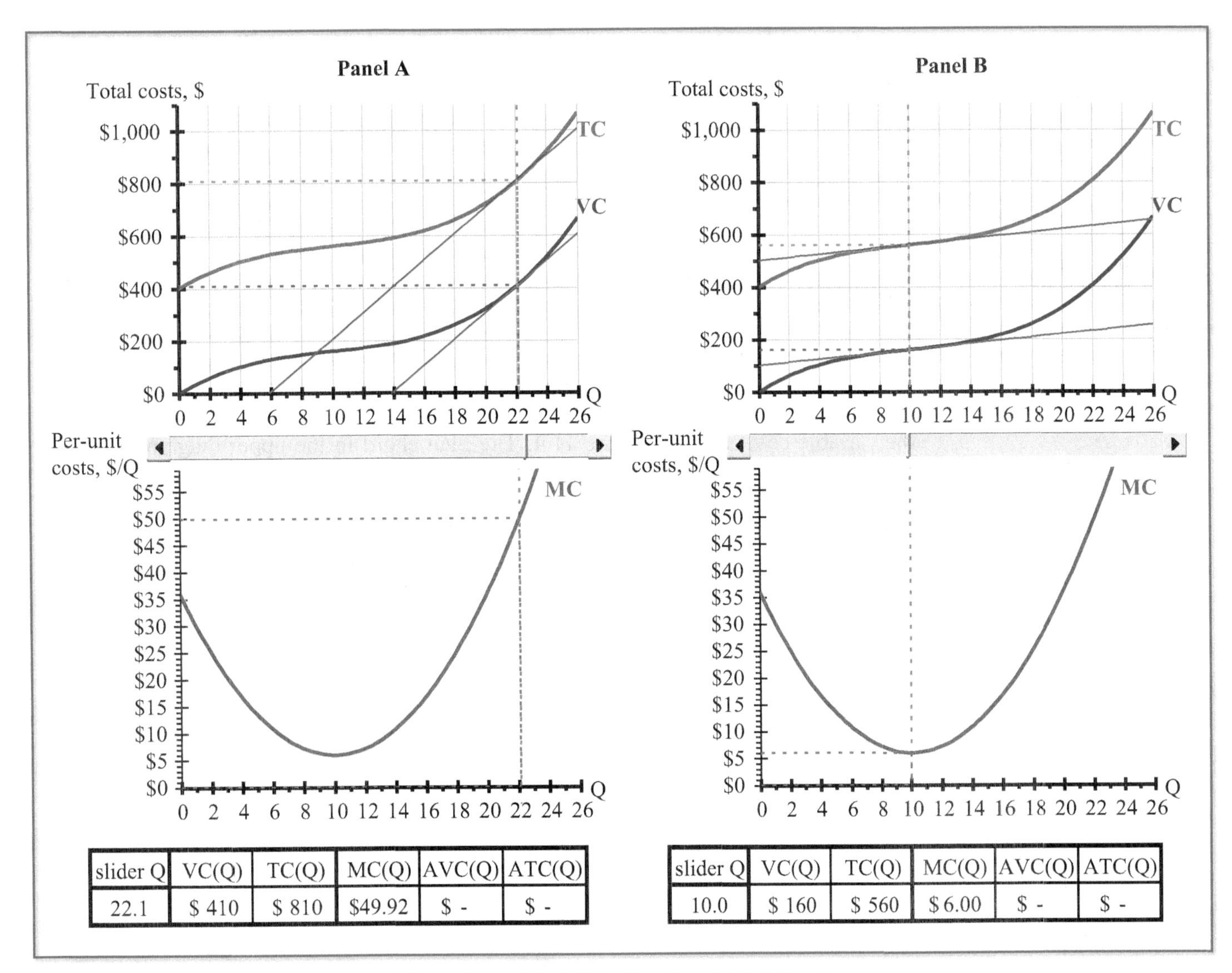

FIGURE 11.3 Deriving Marginal Cost from Variable Cost or Total Cost

The output level in Figure 11.3A was chosen so that the slope could be calculated using the grid system in the upper diagram. Verify that marginal cost is approximately $50 per unit by calculating the slope of either of the red tangent lines. Figure 11.3B depicts the point where marginal cost achieves its minimum. As described in Figure 11.1, Q = 10 is the point of minimum marginal cost *and* the point of maximum marginal product of labor. Of course, if we had chosen a different level of capital, then the short-run production function would change, and the output level that achieves maximum marginal product of labor and minimum marginal cost would also change. A larger level of capital (i.e., a short run with $K_1 > K_0$) would typically be associated with a total product curve in which a larger amount of labor is required before labor achieves its maximum productivity and, hence, a larger amount of output before achieving minimum marginal cost.

This tie between labor productivity and marginal cost can be seen in Figure 11.1. For output levels below Q = 10 (to the left of the vertical line at Q = 10 in Figure 11.1B), marginal cost is decreasing, since the marginal product of labor is increasing (below the horizontal line at Q = 10 in Figure 11.1A), and for output levels above Q =10, marginal cost is increasing because the marginal product of labor is decreasing. The output level associated with maximum marginal productivity is also the minimum marginal cost level of output because both are associated with the point of inflection that occurs at the same output level for both curves (as argued previously).

average total cost (ATC): Average total cost is total cost divided by quantity, ATC(Q) = TC(Q)/Q.

average variable cost (AVC): Average variable cost is variable cost divided by quantity, AVC(Q) = VC(Q)/Q.

average fixed cost (AFC): Average fixed cost is fixed cost divided by quantity, AFC(Q) = FC(Q)/Q.

In addition to marginal cost, the other three per-unit curves are "average" versions of each of the three total cost curves, TC(Q), VC(Q), and FC(Q). As discussed earlier, the more formal preface S for "short-run" is implicit in each definition. **Average total cost (ATC)** is total cost divided by quantity, ATC(Q) = TC(Q)/Q. **Average variable cost (AVC)** is variable cost divided by quantity, AVC(Q) = VC(Q)/Q. **Average fixed cost (AFC)** is fixed cost divided by quantity, AFC(Q) = FC(Q)/Q. The relation between these three curves can be seen algebraically by dividing both sides of Equation 11.1a (TC = FC + VC) by Q to obtain:

$$ATC(Q) = AFC(Q) + AVC(Q). \quad \textbf{(11.2)}$$

We use the same geometric trick to examine the concept of average cost as we used to examine average productivity in Figure 9.2. *The slope of the chord connecting the origin to any point on a cost curve is the average cost for that level of output.*

Average variable cost is the slope of the chord connecting the origin to points on the variable cost curve in Figure 11.4. The blue chord in the upper diagram of Figure 11.4A has a slope of 16 (it passes through the point (25, \$400); the slope of this chord is 16 = 400/25). The blue chord passes through the variable cost curve at Q = 10 and Q = 20; this corresponds to AVC(10) = \$16 and AVC(20) = \$16 in the lower diagram. The point of minimum average variable cost is found by finding the chord that is tangent to the VC(Q) curve. This occurs at approximately (15, \$200) in the upper diagram. (In Chapter 9, you

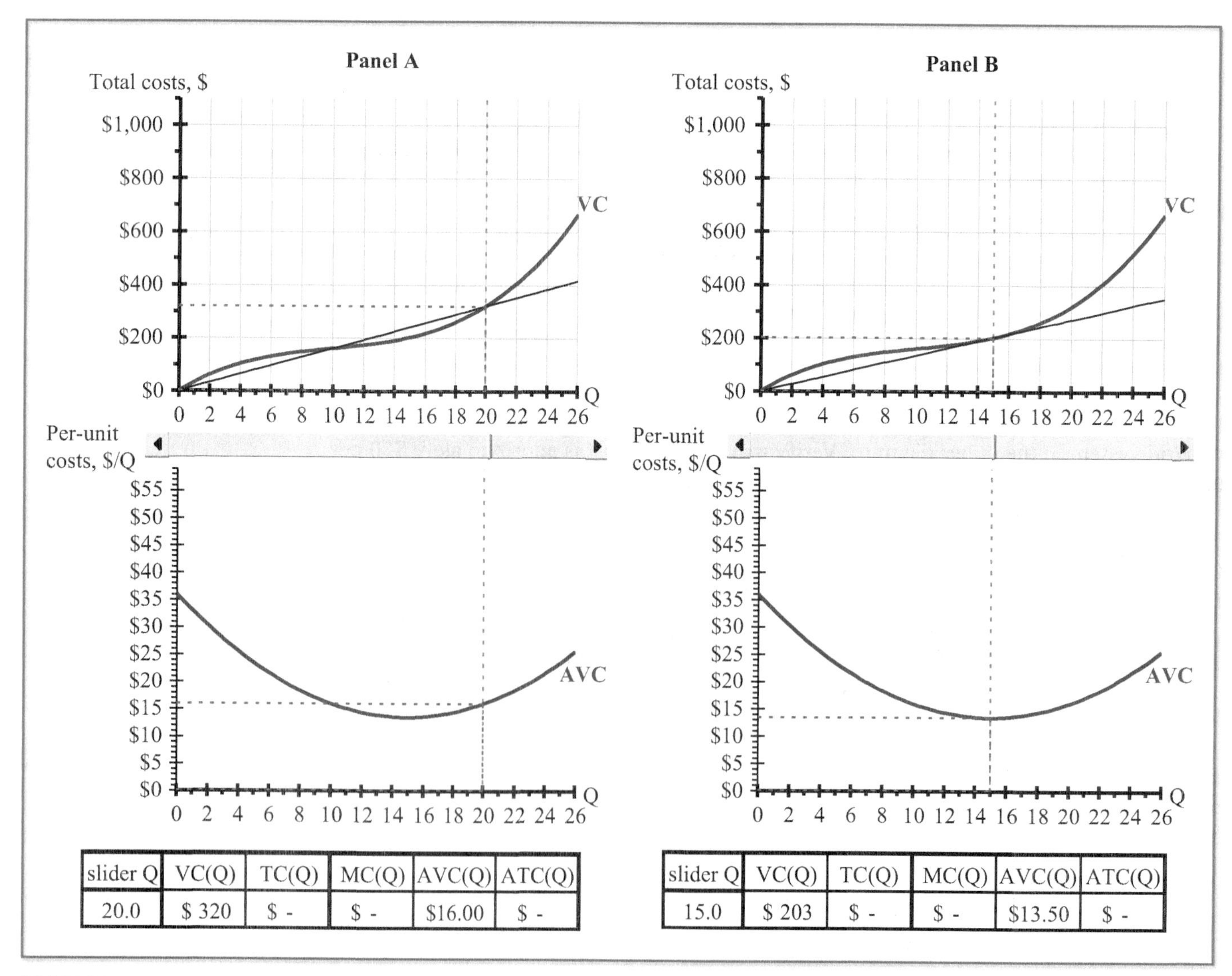

slider Q	VC(Q)	TC(Q)	MC(Q)	AVC(Q)	ATC(Q)
20.0	\$ 320	\$ -	\$ -	\$16.00	\$ -

slider Q	VC(Q)	TC(Q)	MC(Q)	AVC(Q)	ATC(Q)
15.0	\$ 203	\$ -	\$ -	\$13.50	\$ -

FIGURE 11.4 Deriving Average Variable Cost from Variable Cost

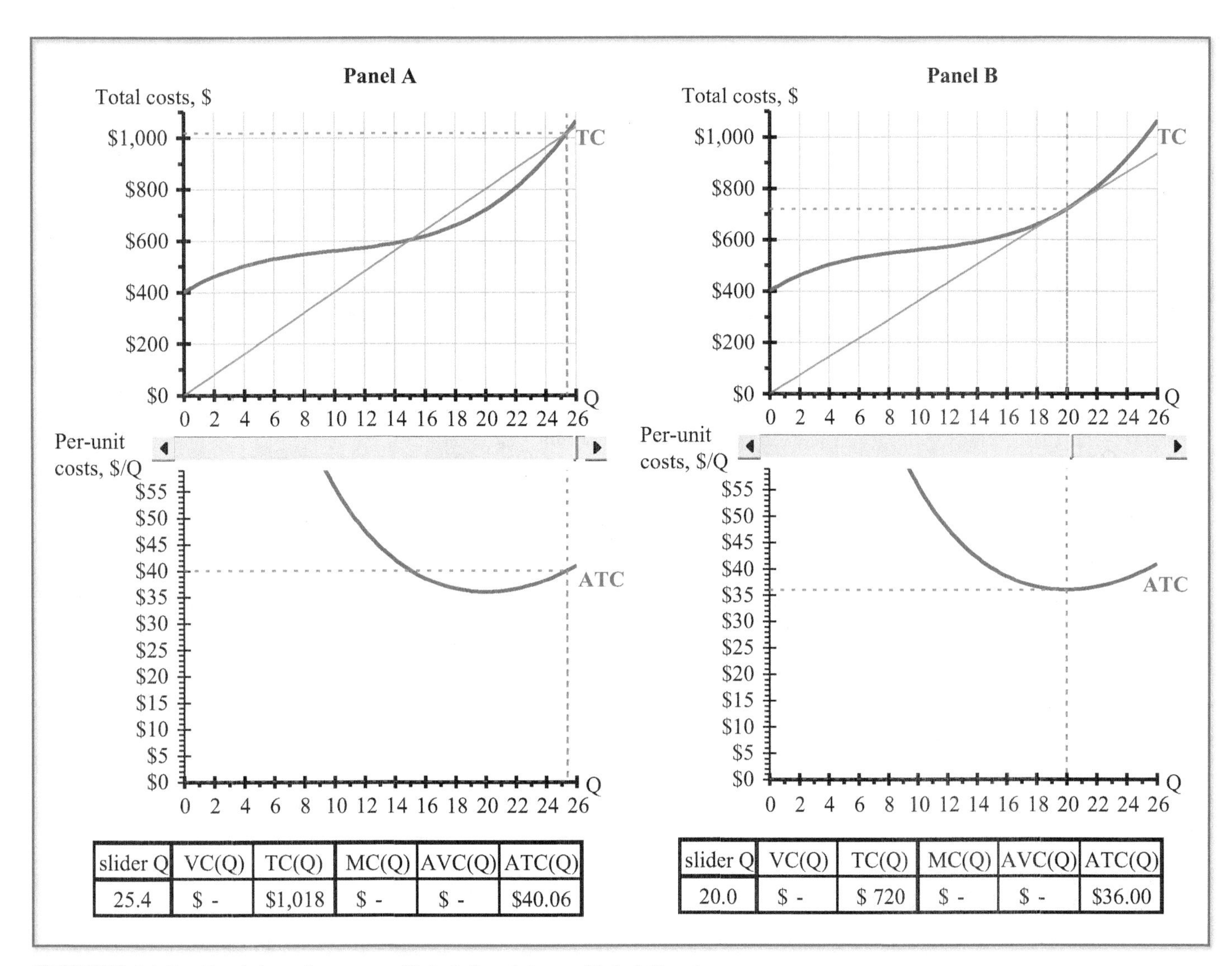

slider Q	VC(Q)	TC(Q)	MC(Q)	AVC(Q)	ATC(Q)
25.4	$ -	$1,018	$ -	$ -	$40.06

slider Q	VC(Q)	TC(Q)	MC(Q)	AVC(Q)	ATC(Q)
20.0	$ -	$ 720	$ -	$ -	$36.00

FIGURE 11.5 Deriving Average Total Cost from Total Cost

were asked to think of the horizontal axis as the hinge of a hardcover book. The minimum occurs at the output level where you have just opened the book far enough that you "kiss" the curve [at Q = 15].) Not surprisingly, Q = 15 is also the point of maximum average product of labor in Figure 11.1A.

Average total cost is the slope of the chord connecting the origin to points on the total cost curve in Figure 11.5. The green chord in the upper diagram of Figure 11.5A has slope 40 (40 = 800/20), and it intersects the total cost curve at about Q = 25.4 and Q = 15. These output levels correspond to the two points on the ATC(Q) curve in the lower diagram, where ATC(Q) = $40. Figure 11.5B shows the point of minimum average total cost at (20, $720) in the upper diagram. This is the point of tangency between the total cost curve and the chord that just "kisses" the TC(Q) curve. In the lower diagram, this is the point of minimum average total cost; this occurs at Q = 20 and ATC(20) = $36 ($36 = $720/20).

In addition to these associations between the TC and ATC curves and between the VC and AVC curves, there is also a relation between marginal and average. Figure 11.6 examines the points of minimum average variable and average total cost. These are also points for which marginal equals average. The common theme in both Figures 11.6A and 11.6B is that at this output level, the slope of the line tangent to the curve (marginal) equals the slope of the chord (average).This is shown in the upper diagrams in Figures 11.6A and 11.6B, which resemble the upper diagrams in Figures 11.4B and 11.5B, except that the blue and green chords and red tangent line overlap, and consequently, the chord cannot be seen. If you use the Excel file for Figure 11.6 and adjust Q, the average chord disappears

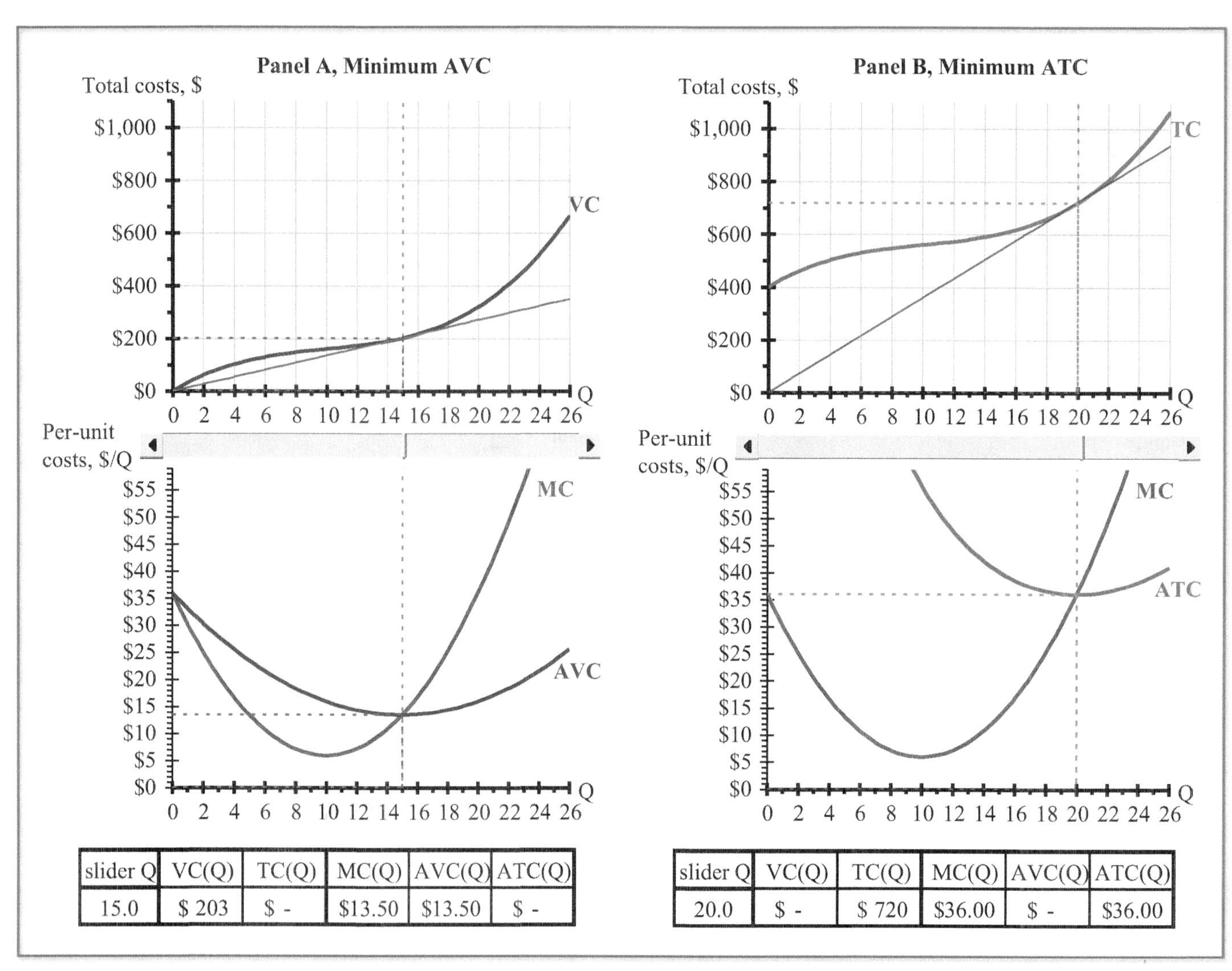

slider Q	VC(Q)	TC(Q)	MC(Q)	AVC(Q)	ATC(Q)
15.0	$ 203	$ -	$13.50	$13.50	$ -

slider Q	VC(Q)	TC(Q)	MC(Q)	AVC(Q)	ATC(Q)
20.0	$ -	$ 720	$36.00	$ -	$36.00

FIGURE 11.6 Comparing Marginal Cost to Average Cost

and reappears as you move away from these output levels. *Average always equals marginal at the minimum of average, regardless of whether it is average variable or average total cost.* Chapter 9 outlined a similar relation between average and marginal productivity; we can tell whether average is increasing or decreasing at a given output level by finding out where marginal is in relation to average. The same rule applies here as in Chapter 9:

Claim: *Marginal pulls average up or down, depending on whether it is above or below average.*

(If this still feels uncomfortable, reread the discussion in Section 9.2 regarding batting averages and GPAs.)

Figure 11.7 combines all of the elements described in Figures 11.3–11.6. An output level was chosen, $Q = 18$, such that $ATC > MC > AVC$. This ordering is clear in the lower diagram of Figure 11.7 (and in the accompanying table), but it is worthwhile to examine the slopes of the chords and tangents to TC(18) and VC(18) so that we can verify the ordering of per-unit costs. The red tangents (MC) are parallel (as required because TC is a vertical translate of VC). At this output level, the tangent is steeper than the blue VC(18) chord but flatter than the green TC(18) chord. This is geometric proof that $AVC(18) < MC(18) < ATC(18)$.

For simplicity, one per-unit cost function has been omitted thus far in our discussion. Average fixed cost is FC/Q, or by regrouping Equation 11.2, $AFC(Q) = ATC(Q) - AVC(Q)$. This is shown for $Q = 10$ in Figure 11.8, with total fixed cost equal to $400. AFC(Q) in

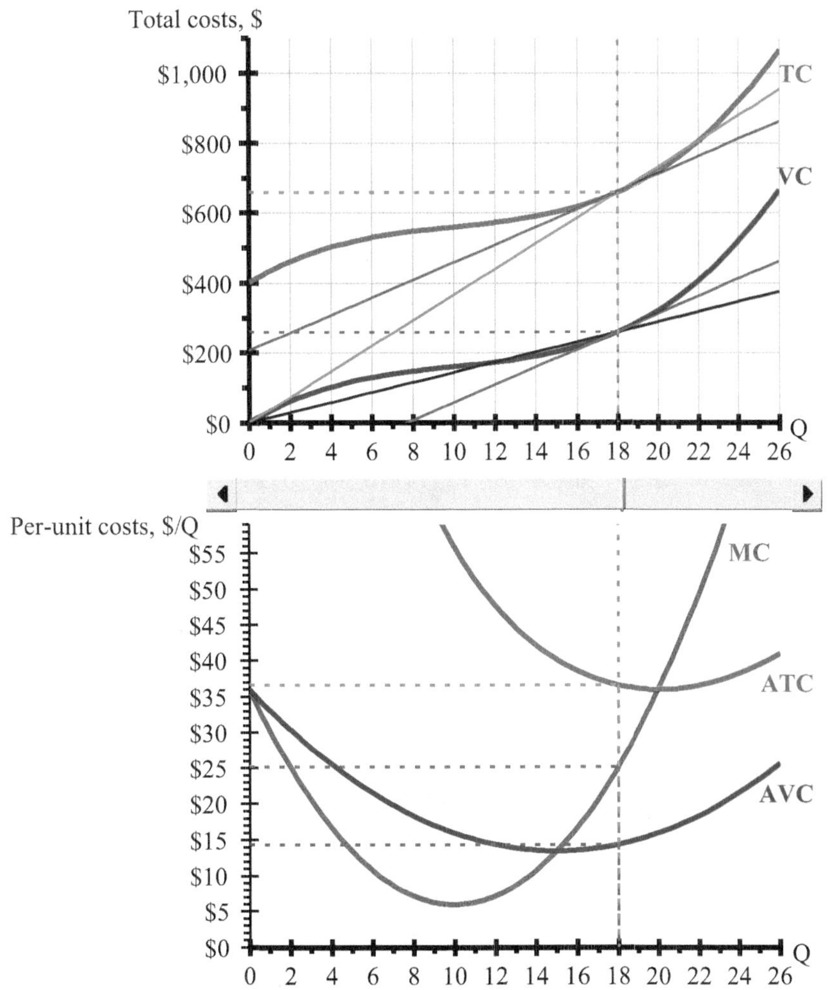

slider Q	VC(Q)	TC(Q)	MC(Q)	AVC(Q)	ATC(Q)
18.0	$ 259	$ 659	$25.20	$14.40	$36.62

FIGURE 11.7
Comparing AVC, ATC, and MC

Figure 11.8 can be derived in two ways. It is most directly the red rectangular hyperbola (AFC = FC/Q), but it is also the difference between ATC and AVC at any quantity level. The vertical red line segment from the Q axis to AFC and the vertical lavender line segment from AVC to ATC are the same length for any Q (and that length is FC/Q). Given Q = 10, both line segments are $40 long. When Q = 20, both are $20, and so on. In effect, the AFC curve provides no new information (since it is already included in earlier per-unit figures as ATC – AVC). As a result, economists often omit AFC from graphs of per-unit cost curves.

Before leaving the discussion of short-run cost functions, we must review what is being held constant in the short run. Most obviously, fixed costs are held constant, but these costs are constant because fixed factors of production are held constant in the short run. Indeed, we defined the short run as the time frame in which some factors of production are held fixed. And, of course, technology is held fixed in the short run; a given bundle of inputs produces a certain amount of output, and this does not change in the short run.

Short-run cost curves are based on fixed-factor prices. If these prices change in the short run, then the short-run cost curves will shift. The easiest way to see this is to imagine all factor prices doubling. This would double the cost of producing any level of output because fixed cost and variable cost both double in this instance. Since capital is fixed,

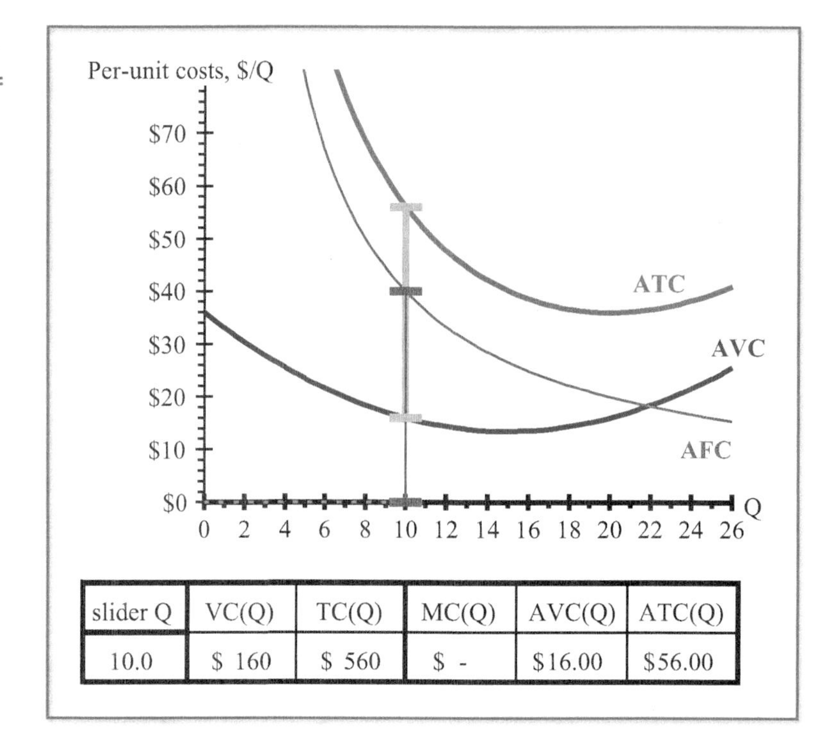

slider Q	VC(Q)	TC(Q)	MC(Q)	AVC(Q)	ATC(Q)
10.0	$ 160	$ 560	$ -	$16.00	$56.00

FIGURE 11.8 Average Fixed Cost as AFC(Q)= ATC(Q) – AVC(Q)

Therefore, economists typically do not show AFC.

the short-run expansion path does not change. The only change is the cost of achieving that production level. Suppose instead that only variable factor prices double, but that fixed-factor prices do not change. How would this change short-run cost curves? Consider each of the three total cost curves and each of the four per-unit curves, and try to answer what will happen to each before reading the answer in the next paragraph.

Variable cost and average variable cost would double for all output levels. This can be seen using the Excel file for Figure 11.1; change w = $50 to w = $100 and the variable costs in Figure 11.1B double for the fixed total product curve in Figure 11.1A. Since the price and quantity of fixed factors do not change, neither does fixed cost or average fixed cost. Because variable cost doubles, marginal cost doubles as well (since marginal cost is the slope of variable cost, and doubling variable cost doubles the slope of the VC curve at any point). Total cost and average total cost increase, but they do not double (since fixed cost remains fixed).

11.3 Long-Run Cost Curves

As we discussed in Chapter 10, if the firm is able to adjust all factors of production, it is able to produce output at lower cost than if it cannot. We saw this directly in the comparison of the long-run expansion path (LREP) with the short-run expansion path (SREP) in Figure 10.10. The cost curves examined in Section 11.2 are based on the short-run expansion path: Short-run cost curves hold capital fixed (or more generally, all fixed factors are fixed). Different levels of capital lead to different short-run cost curves, so each short-run cost curve is based on a fixed capital stock. We now turn to an analysis of cost curves that are appropriate to long-run decision making.

long-run total cost curve, LTC(Q): The long-run total cost curve, LTC(Q), is the curve relating the total cost of production to the level of output produced when all factors of production are allowed to vary.

long-run average cost curve, LAC(Q): The long-run average cost curve, LAC(Q), is the curve relating the average cost of production to the level of output produced when all factors of production are allowed to vary.

In the long run, there are no fixed factors of production; therefore, there are no fixed costs in the long run, and *all* costs are variable. This reduces the number of cost curves that need to be considered to three: (1) long-run total cost (LTC), (2) long-run average cost (LAC), and (3) long-run marginal cost (LMC). The **long-run total cost curve, LTC(Q)**, is the curve relating the total cost of production to the level of output produced when all factors of production are allowed to vary. The LTC curve is the representation in (Q, $) space of the cost associated with points on the LREP (just as STC(Q) in Section 11.2 is the representation in (Q, $) space of the total cost associated with points on the SREP). The **long-run average cost curve, LAC(Q)**, is the curve relating the average cost of production to the level of output produced when all factors of production are allowed to vary. The **long-run marginal cost curve, LMC(Q)**, is the curve relating the incremental cost of production to the level of output produced when all factors of production are allowed to vary. Note that we do not have to call LAC by the longer name LATC, since there are no fixed costs, and therefore, there is nothing to distinguish between average total cost and average variable cost.

long-run marginal cost curve, LMC(Q): The long-run marginal cost curve, LMC(Q), is the curve relating the incremental cost of production to the level of output produced when all factors of production are allowed to vary.

We initially focus on LTC and LAC, since both are based on short-run total cost curves and average total cost curves in a common fashion. Both are envelopes of their respective short-run curves. For every quantity, there are multiple short-run total cost curves. For each output level, one of these curves provides the least-expensive option. An **envelope** is a curve drawn by connecting these least-cost points for all quantities. An envelope is most easily seen geometrically.

envelope: An envelope is a curve drawn by connecting least-cost points for all quantities.

LTC and LAC: The Geometry of Envelopes

Suppose that there are only two plant sizes available: small and large. The small plant produces a smaller amount of goods cheaper than a large plant, and vice versa. This is the situation depicted in Figure 11.9. Figure 11.9A provides the total cost analysis, while Figure 11.9B provides the per-unit cost analysis. The large plant is the short-run cost function that formed the basis for Section 11.2 (note in particular that $FC_{large} = \$400$ in Figure 11.9A), while the small plant produces output using much less capital (although we cannot determine this with precision from the graph, in this instance, $FC_{small} = \$32$). When output is less than about 8.5, the small plant produces output more cheaply than the large plant. You would choose the small plant if you expect to produce fewer than 8.5 units, and

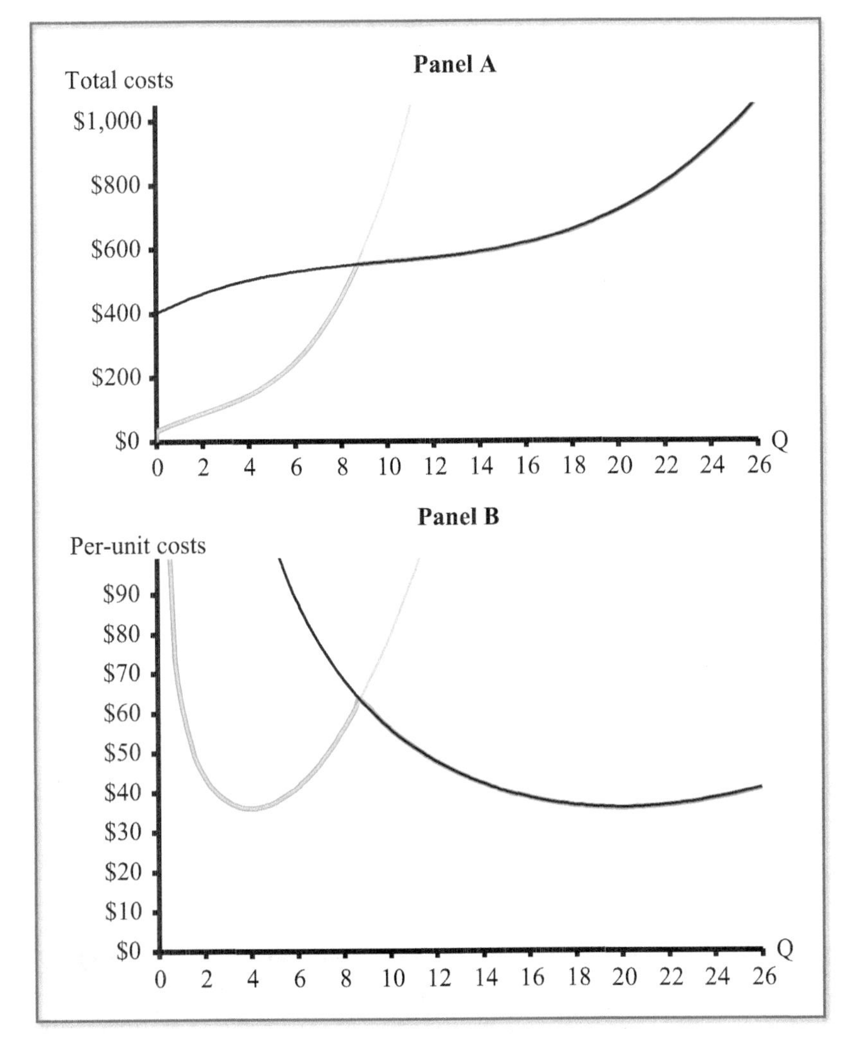

FIGURE 11.9 Long-Run Costs with Two Plant Sizes

you would choose the large plant if you expect to produce more than 8.5 units per time period. These choices produce the green LTC and LAC curves as the envelope of the blue STC and SATC curves.

The orientation of the two STC curves in Figure 11.9A accords with the expectation of fixed versus variable components of cost discussed in the previous paragraph. The small plant has smaller fixed cost and larger variable cost than the large plant. The relative size of the fixed component is seen in the vertical axis intercept for the two curves; as noted earlier, $FC_{small} = \$32 < \$400 = FC_{large}$. We argued that a smaller plant size would likely achieve a point of maximum labor productivity (point of inflection) at a smaller output level than a larger plant size. The point of inflection for the large plant size is at Q = 10; it turns out that the point of inflection for the small plant occurs at Q = 2, although the only thing that is clear from Figure 11.9 alone is that the quantity where this occurs is "small." Further, the variable cost curve is steeper for the small plant than for the large plant. These facts suggest that the small plant will be more labor intensive (or variable factor intensive) than the large plant, which will therefore be more capital intensive at producing the same level of output.

Suppose, now, that a third plant size is considered—one that is in between the small and large plants. The long-run curve with three available plant sizes is shown in Figure 11.10. Given these three plants, if output is expected to be less than about 7, the small plant would be chosen; if output is expected to be between 7 and 15, the medium plant would be chosen; and if output is expected to be larger than 15, the large plant would be chosen. The long-run total cost and long-run average cost curves are the envelope of short-run curves, just as with two available plant sizes. The only difference is that now there is an additional "scallop" to the curve, caused by the introduction of a new plant size.

FIGURE 11.10 Long-Run Costs with Three Plant Sizes

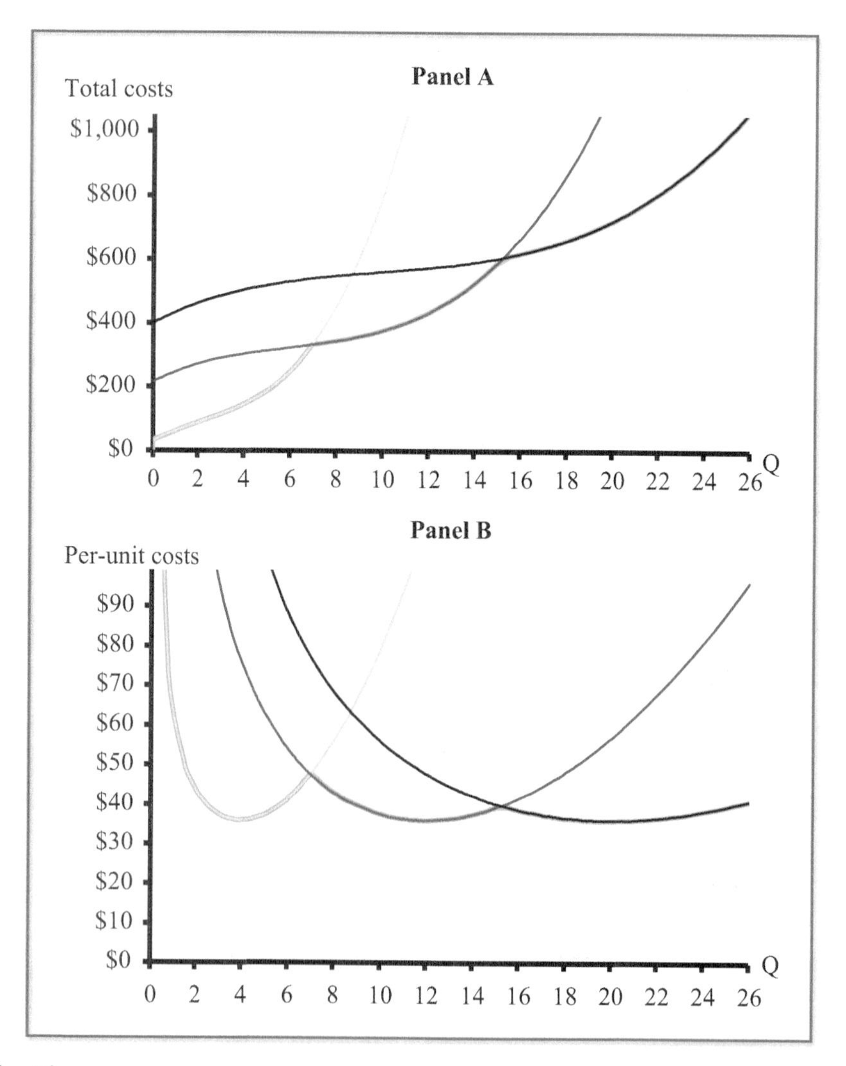

If we assume that we can create a variety of plant sizes, then we can "fill in" more sizes to create a smooth (not scalloped), continuous, long-run total cost and long-run average cost curve. This continuum of plant sizes is implicit in the production functions we examined in Chapters 9 and 10 (since K was continuous), and it is implicit in the smooth LREP discussed in Figure 10.10.[5] Figure 11.11 depicts how different plant sizes might fill in with intermediate-sized plants to those that existed in Figure 11.10. Now, five plant sizes are explicitly shown; each plant produces a different level of output at the same minimum short-run average total cost of production. The plants produce 4, 8, 12, 16, and 20 units of output at a minimum average total cost of $36 per unit. And more plants could be added in between each of these as well. The wide, light-blue LTC curve shown in Figure 11.11A is a straight line with a slope of $36. It is the envelope of an assumed continuum of plants that each produces different levels of output at minimum total cost. Similarly, the wide, light-blue LAC curve in Figure 11.11B is a horizontal line at a cost of $36/unit.

The envelope is a useful way to view long-run cost because each long-run choice returns us to a short-run situation. The long-run decision is the decision of which plant size to choose, and that is based on expected output. The envelope reminds us that this is actually a series of short runs. Different capital levels will be chosen, depending on what the firm expects to produce in the future. Once a capital size is chosen, the firm returns to a short run because the capital stock has been determined. A useful way to view this relation is to say:

The long run is the envelope of potential short runs.

The linearity of the LTC curve in Figure 11.11A is the result of a constant returns to scale (CRTS) production technology. In the present context, the easiest way to consider

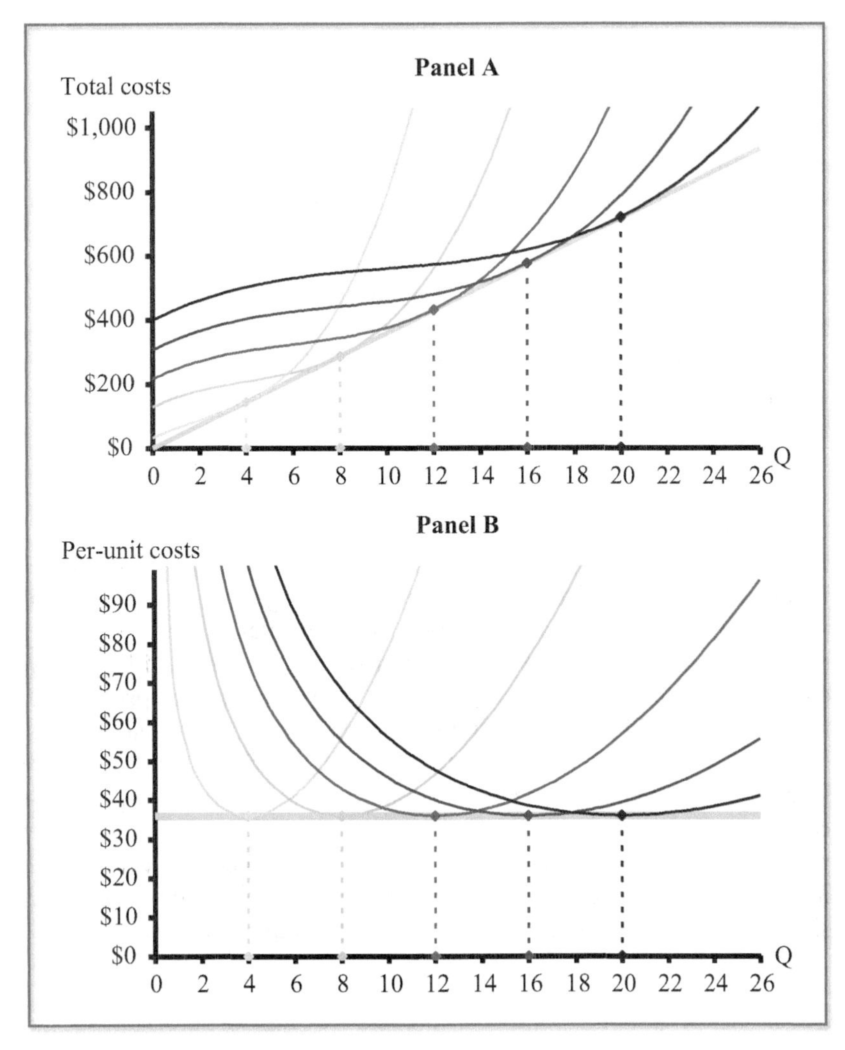

FIGURE 11.11 Long-Run Costs as the Envelope of Short-Run Costs with a Continuum of Plant Sizes: Constant Returns to Scale (CRTS)

returns to scale is to consider the cost of doubling output. With CRTS, doubling output doubles cost, but it only doubles cost in the long run because, in the short-run, capital cannot change. Indeed, in the short run, costs more than double.

We cannot examine returns to scale with a short-run cost function because the short-run cost function does not allow all factors to vary as required by the definition of returns to scale. We can, however, answer a different question in the short run:

Does a proportionate increase in output require a less-than-proportionate, proportionate, or more-than-proportionate increase in cost?

This question is answered according to whether the SATC is downward sloping, flat, or upward sloping at the output level under consideration. The proof of this assertion is straightforward. Consider the ratio of proportional change in cost to proportional change in output:

$$\%\Delta STC(Q)/\%\Delta Q = (\Delta STC(Q)/STC(Q))/(\Delta Q/Q). \quad \textbf{(11.3a)}$$

The left-hand side is less than one if costs increase less than proportionately with output changes, and it is greater than one if the reverse holds true. Regrouping the terms on the right-hand side of Equation 11.3a, we obtain:

$$\%\Delta STC(Q)/\%\Delta Q = [\Delta STC(Q)/\Delta Q]/[STC(Q)/Q]. \quad \textbf{(11.3b)}$$

The first bracketed term (the numerator) of the right-hand side of Equation 11.3b is SMC(Q), and the second bracketed term (the denominator) is SATC(Q). Therefore, Equation 11.3b simplifies to:

$$\%\Delta STC(Q)/\%\Delta Q = SMC(Q)/SATC(Q). \quad \textbf{(11.3c)}$$

We see from Equation 11.3c that costs increase less than proportionately with output change if $SMC(Q) < SATC(Q)$ (so the change in cost to change in output ratio is less than one). This occurs for output levels below the minimum average total cost level of output. Similarly, costs increase more than proportionately with output changes when output is larger than the minimum average total cost level of output. This restates the relation between average and marginal discussed in Sections 9.2 and 11.1 (marginal pulls average up or down, depending on whether marginal is above or below average). A quick reflection on the meaning of average total cost verifies this result. Total cost increases less than proportionately if average total cost is declining (since total cost is average total cost times quantity; if there is a proportional increase in quantity but a decline in average total cost, then the product [of average total cost and quantity] is a less-than-proportional increase in total cost).

As discussed in Chapter 9, long-run production processes often exhibit increasing returns to scale for small levels of output and decreasing returns for large-scale production. If we assume a continuum of plant sizes (as we did for Figure 11.11), then we obtain smooth, long-run total cost and long-run average cost curves in this situation. Figure 11.12 shows a long-run total cost and long-run average cost curve consistent with this scenario. Also included are four short-run plant sizes; each short run is labeled in the graph according to the output level where there is tangency between the short-run and long-run curves. For example, K2 is the plant size that produces 2 units of output at minimum cost, K4 produces 4 units of output at minimum cost, etc.[6] The short-run curves holding capital fixed are denoted $STC(Q; K_i)$ or $SATC(Q; K_i)$, where "i" is the output level where tangency between short- and long-run curves occurs (capital after the semi-colon means that capital is fixed). The economic interpretation of the tangency is that this plant size produces this level of output at minimum cost. The Excel file for Figure 11.12 includes larger versions of each diagram because fixed-cost differences for each of the short-run total cost curves are difficult to see in this instance.

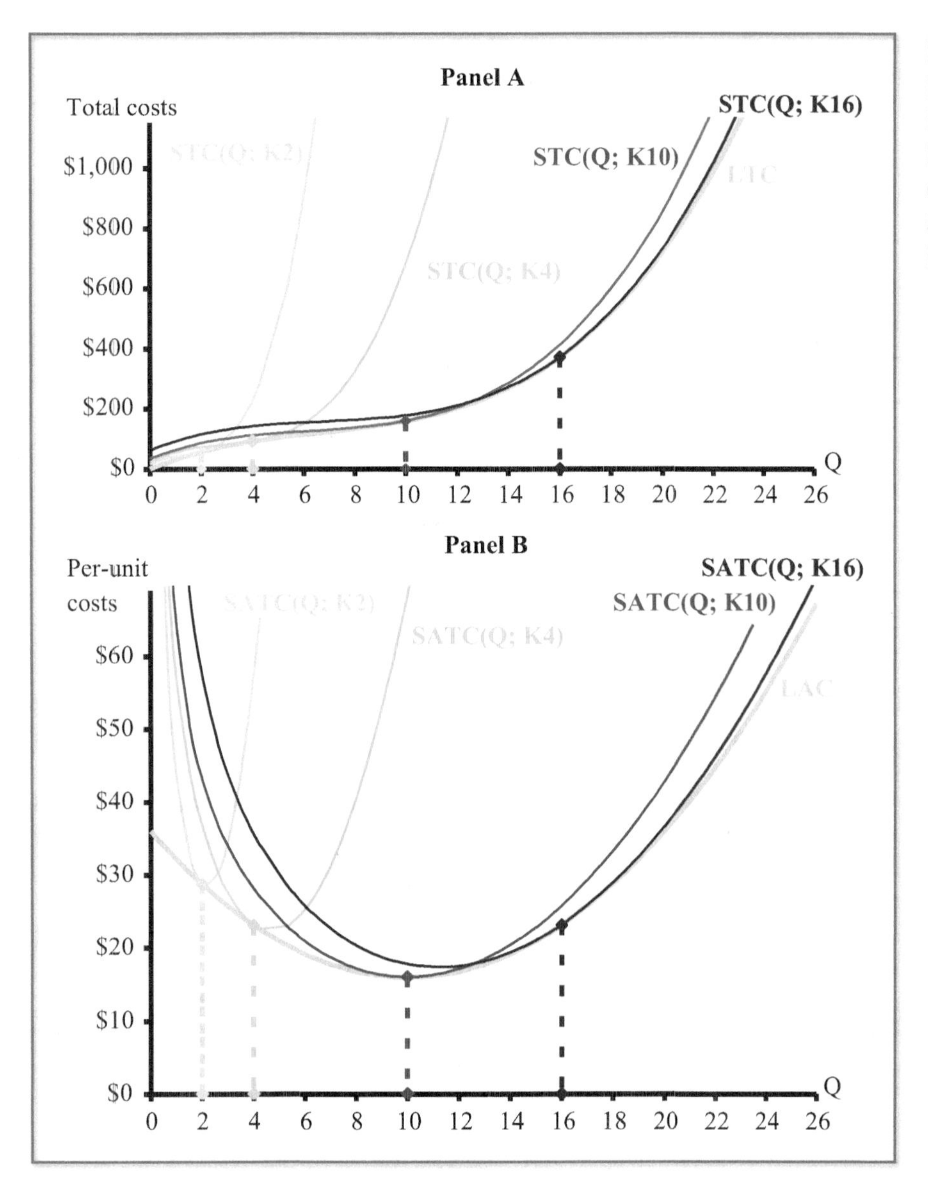

FIGURE 11.12 Long-Run Costs as the Envelope of Short-Run Costs with a Continuum of Plant Sizes: Economies and Diseconomies of Scale

The Geometry of Long-Run Marginal Cost (LMC)

The long-run marginal cost curve is the slope of the long-run total cost curve. Long-run marginal cost (LMC) can be derived from short-run cost functions, but *LMC is not the envelope of SMCs* (unlike LTC and LAC). As we will see, these two methods of deriving LMC are interrelated.

When production exhibits constant returns to scale, the long-run total cost curve is linear; therefore, long-run marginal cost is flat. Figure 11.11B can depict this situation if one change is made: LAC should be relabeled LMC. If LTC is linear, the slope of the chord and the slope of the tangent are the same. Both have a slope of $36 in Figure 11.11A; therefore, LAC(Q) = LMC(Q) = $36 in Figure 11.11B.

In contrast, when returns to scale vary, long-run total cost has the upward-sloping "S" shape shown in Figure 11.12A. LTC has a shape similar to SVC, so long-run marginal cost looks much like an SMC curve (just as LAC looks much like SAVC). Therefore, LMC and LAC are U-shaped, and just as with the short run, LMC = LAC at minimum LAC. This is shown in Figure 11.13. *Although the curves in both diagrams have the same shape as those in Figure 11.6A, they have entirely different conceptual meanings.* The

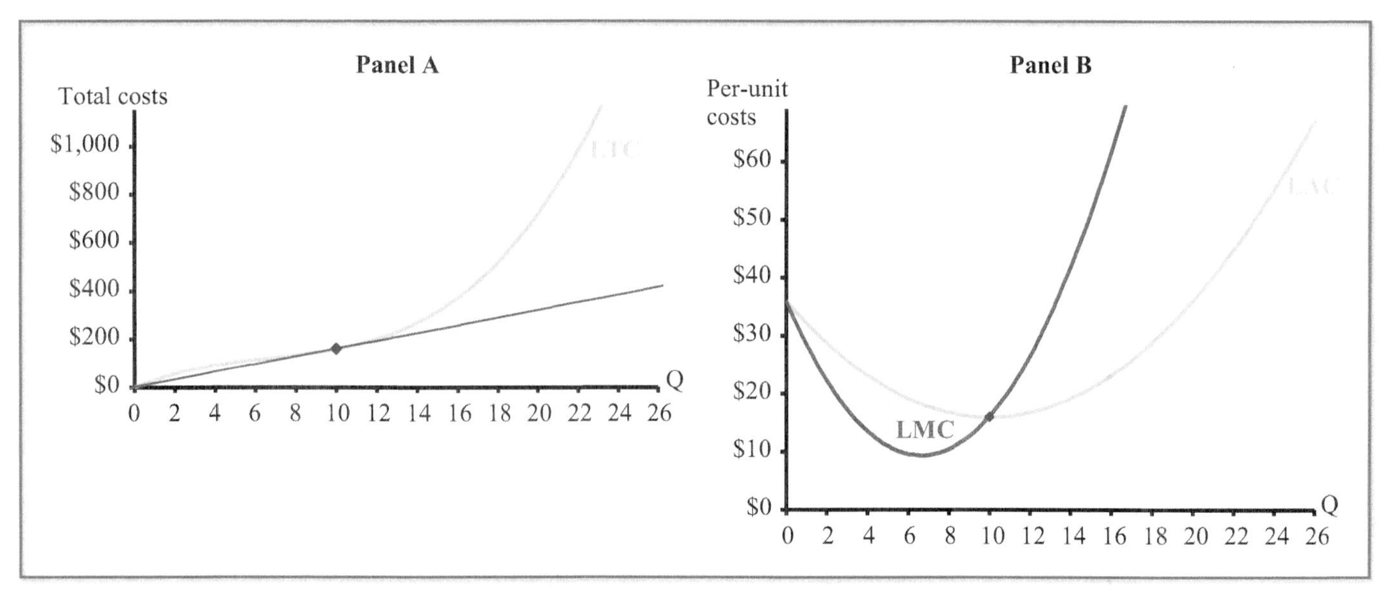

FIGURE 11.13 Long-Run Marginal Cost (LMC) as Slope of Long-Run Total Cost (LTC)

shape of SVC(Q) in the upper diagram in Figure 11.6A is due to varying labor productivity, given fixed capital. More specifically, the shape of SVC(Q) is determined by the cost of producing each level of output, using the short-run expansion path in Figure 10.10. The shape of LTC(Q) in Figure 11.13A is due to varying returns to scale (that occurs as all factors of production vary). Long-run average cost equals long-run marginal cost at minimum long-run average cost. Also like the short run, the slope of the minimum sloping chord to the LTC curve equals the slope of the tangent to that curve at that point. This occurs at the blue diamond tangency point (Q, $) = (10, $160) in Figure 11.13A; therefore, LAC(10) = LMC(10) = $16 in Figure 11.13B.

Suppose you wish to produce Q* units of output at minimum long-run cost. In this instance, you would be on the LTC curve at the point Q = Q*. Since LTC is the envelope of short-run curves, there must be a short-run plant size, K*, that produces this output level; LTC(Q*) = STC(Q*; K*). Dividing by Q*, we obtain:

$$LAC(Q^*) = SATC(Q^*; K^*). \quad \textbf{(11.4a)}$$

This is seen geometrically by the coincidence of LAC and different SATCs at Q* = 2, 4, 10, and 16, given plant sizes K2, K4, K10, and K16 in Figure 11.12B. We actually know more, since the LTC curve is tangent to each of the STC curves at these output levels in Figure 11.12A. Tangency at this point means that the slope of each curve is the same, and slope is marginal cost. Therefore, we may formally state this as:

$$LMC(Q^*) = SMC(Q^*; K^*). \quad \textbf{(11.4b)}$$

Long-run marginal cost is seen as the short-run marginal cost associated with the capital stock that produces that output level at minimum cost.

Long-run average cost is equal to the associated short-run average total cost (Equation 11.4a), and long-run marginal cost is equal to the associated short-run marginal cost (Equation 11.4b). Short- and long-run costs are seen to be pair-wise equal; average equals average and marginal equals marginal, according to Equations 11.4a and 11.4b.

The pair-wise equality between short-run and long-run marginal cost from Equation 11.4b is seen in Figure 11.14 for two output levels, Q* = 4 and Q* = 16 (the Q* = 16 versions of Equations 11.4a and 11.4b are explicitly noted on Figure 11.14).

The tangency between LTC and STC at these output levels in Figure 11.14A represents the coincidence of LAC and SATC at these output levels in Figure 11.14B. (This tangency in Figure 11.14A and coincidence in Figure 11.14B are geometric representations of Equation 11.4a.) The point (4, SMC(4; K4)) = (4, $13.60) on the gold SMC(Q; K4) curve equals

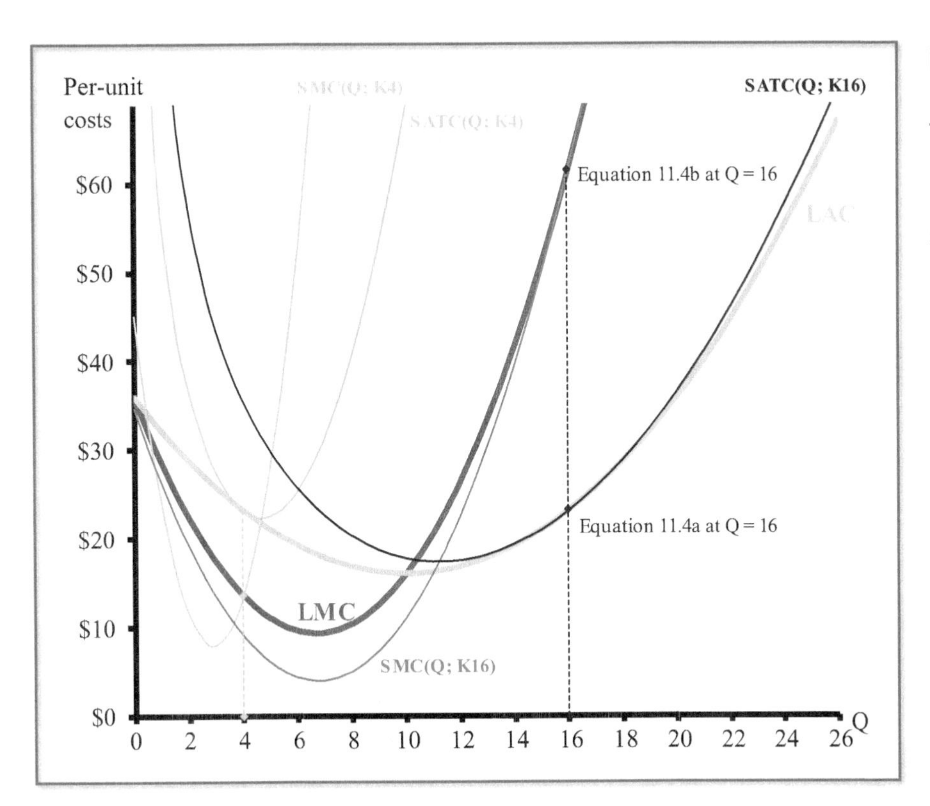

FIGURE 11.14 Long-Run Marginal Cost from Short-Run Per-Unit Costs

LMC is *not* the envelope of SMCs.

LMC(4), according to Equation 11.4b, and the point (16, SMC(16; K16)) = (16, $61.60) on the orange SMC(Q; K16) curve equals LMC(16), according to Equation 11.4b.[7] This shows how LMC can be constructed from short-run per-unit cost curves.

Students commonly believe that a given plant size must be run at minimum average cost to be producing at a point on the long-run cost function. The following example shows that this belief is false. Consider the K16 plant size that produces 16 units of output at minimum average cost of $23.20 per unit in Figure 11.14. Marginal cost in this instance is substantially higher ($61.60 as stated previously), and therefore producing a smaller level of output reduces average cost, given this short-run production process. Minimum SATC(Q; K16) occurs at Q =11, and SATC(11; K16) = SMC(11; K16) = $17.38. This plant produces 16 units of output at minimum cost, but it produces 11 units of output even more cheaply (on the basis of ATC comparisons). Of course, there is a plant size, K11, that would produce 11 units of output even more cheaply than the K16 plant; this plant size would be between K10 and K16 in size (assuming a continuum of plant sizes). Similarly, the K4 plant size produces output at lower average cost if Q = 4.67 units are produced than if 4 units are produced.

The belief that a given plant size must be run at minimum average cost to be producing at a point on the long-run cost function is unfounded. The plants that produce 4 and 16 units in the most cost-effective manner are, in a more global sense, not producing at least cost. The same is true for other plant sizes as well, and it will continue to be true if the production point under consideration is *not* a point of minimum long-run average cost.

Equations 11.4a and 11.4b require pair-wise equalities at minimum-cost production of a given level of output. *But these pair-wise equalities are also equal to each other when Q* is an output level that produces output at minimum long-run average cost.* This can be stated algebraically as:

$$\text{SATC}(Q^*; K^*) = \text{minimum LAC}(Q^*) = \text{LMC}(Q^*) = \text{SMC}(Q^*; K^*). \qquad \textbf{(11.5)}$$

The first equality in Equation 11.5 is required by Equation 11.4a, and the third is required by Equation 11.4b. The second is the relation that exists between average and marginal, discussed in Chapters 9 and 11: Average equals marginal only at maximums or minimums of average. In Chapter 9, marginal product passes through the maximum of average

FIGURE 11.15 Minimum LAC: The Point Where LAC = LMC = SMC = SATC

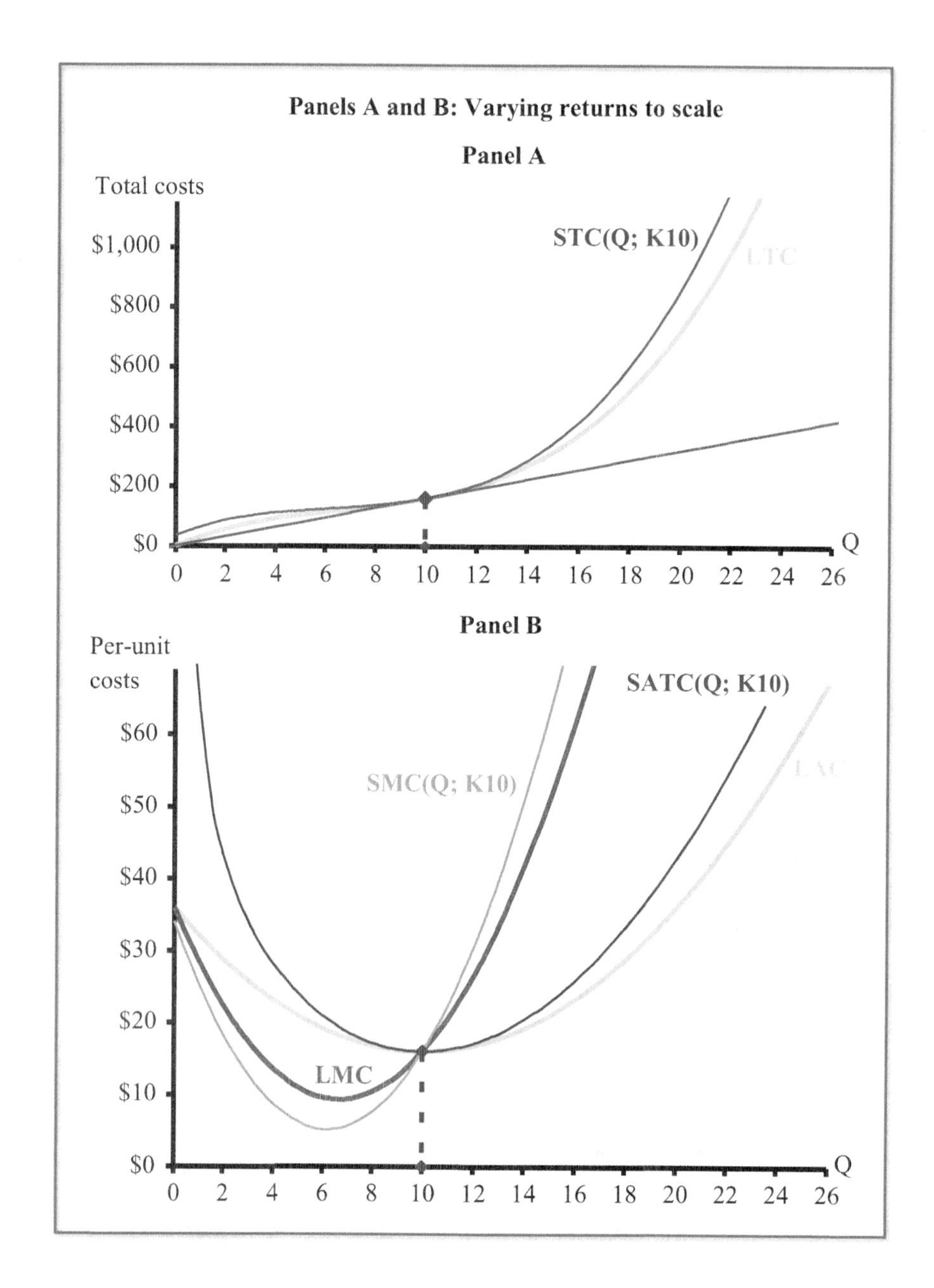

product (as explicitly shown in Figure 9.3); in this chapter, marginal cost passes through the minimum of average cost (as shown in Figures 11.6 and 11.13). The coincidence of these four cost curves shown in Figure 11.15B is based on the varying returns to scale, U-shaped, long-run average cost curve examined in Figures 11.12–11.14. With the varying returns to scale (the cost structure shown in Figures 11.15A and 11.15B), Equation 11.5 holds at a single, long-run, average cost-minimizing output level—in this event, Q* = 10.

If the production function exhibited constant returns to scale (as in Figures 11.9–11.11), then *each* point on the LAC(Q) curve would be associated with a plant size for which Equation 11.5 would hold. The reason is straightforward: If LAC is flat, then LAC(Q) = LMC(Q) for every output level. The center equality in Equation 11.5 holds for all output levels, while the first and third equalities hold at each output level for the plant size that produces that output at minimum cost, according to Equations 11.4a and 11.4b. This is shown in Figures 11.15C and 11.15D. These figures show five output levels (Q* = 4, 8, 12, 16, and 20) where Equation 11.5 holds, although the same condition holds at other output levels as well (if the capital stock is appropriately adjusted).

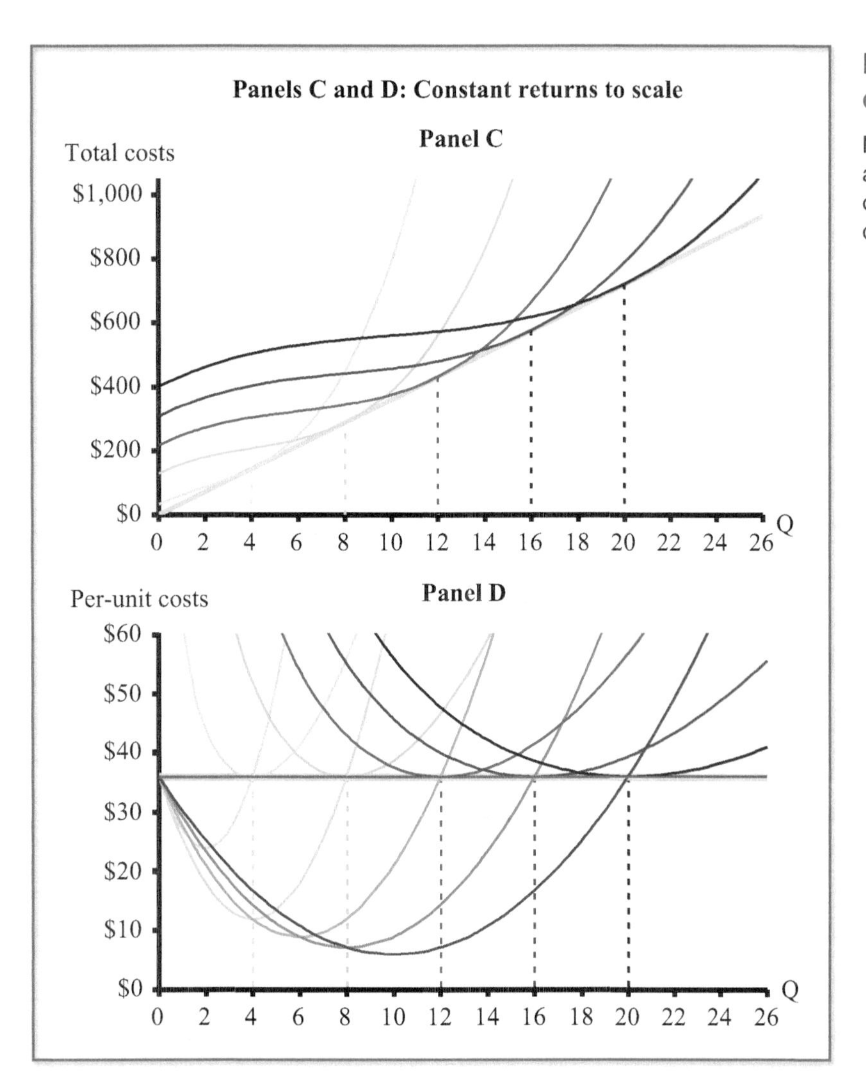

FIGURE 11.15
continued

Key: STC and SATC curves are different gradations of blue; SMC curves are different gradations of gold.

Long-Run Cost with Discrete Plant Sizes *OPTIONAL SECTION*

When production can only be accomplished with discrete plant sizes, the LTC and LAC curves are scalloped, as described in Figures 11.9 and 11.10. Most basically, long-run marginal cost is the slope of long-run total cost, as described in Figure 11.13, and therefore, the long-run marginal cost curve would have jump discontinuities at the output levels where the lowest cost method of production switches from one size plant to the next. For production levels just below this critical level of output, the smaller plant size is utilized, and LMC equals the SMC for the smaller plant. For production levels just above this output, the larger plant size is utilized, and LMC equals the SMC for the larger plant. Both of these marginal costs are different from each other because the two STC curves have different slopes at the point of intersection. This is what causes the LTC curve to be scalloped in Figures 11.9 and 11.10. At other output levels, the LTC, LMC, and LAC equal the short-run curves that minimize production cost for that output level.

The cost curves with discrete plant sizes depend, of course, on the plant sizes that are available. Figure 11.16 shows LAC(Q) and LMC(Q), given four plant sizes—K2, K4, K10, and K16—for the variable returns process depicted in Figures 11.12–11.15A and 11.15B. Figure 11.17 shows the same per-unit cost curves for the five discrete plant sizes used to depict Figures 11.9–11.11 and Figures 11.15C and 11.15D. Both figures exhibit jump discontinuities at crossover output levels as expected. The Excel files for Figures 11.16 and 11.17 allow you to view the LTC curves for both production processes, but these LTC curves are scalloped as expected, based on Figures 11.9 and 11.10. The scalloping of LTC causes scalloping of LAC and jumps in LMC for the reason discussed earlier.

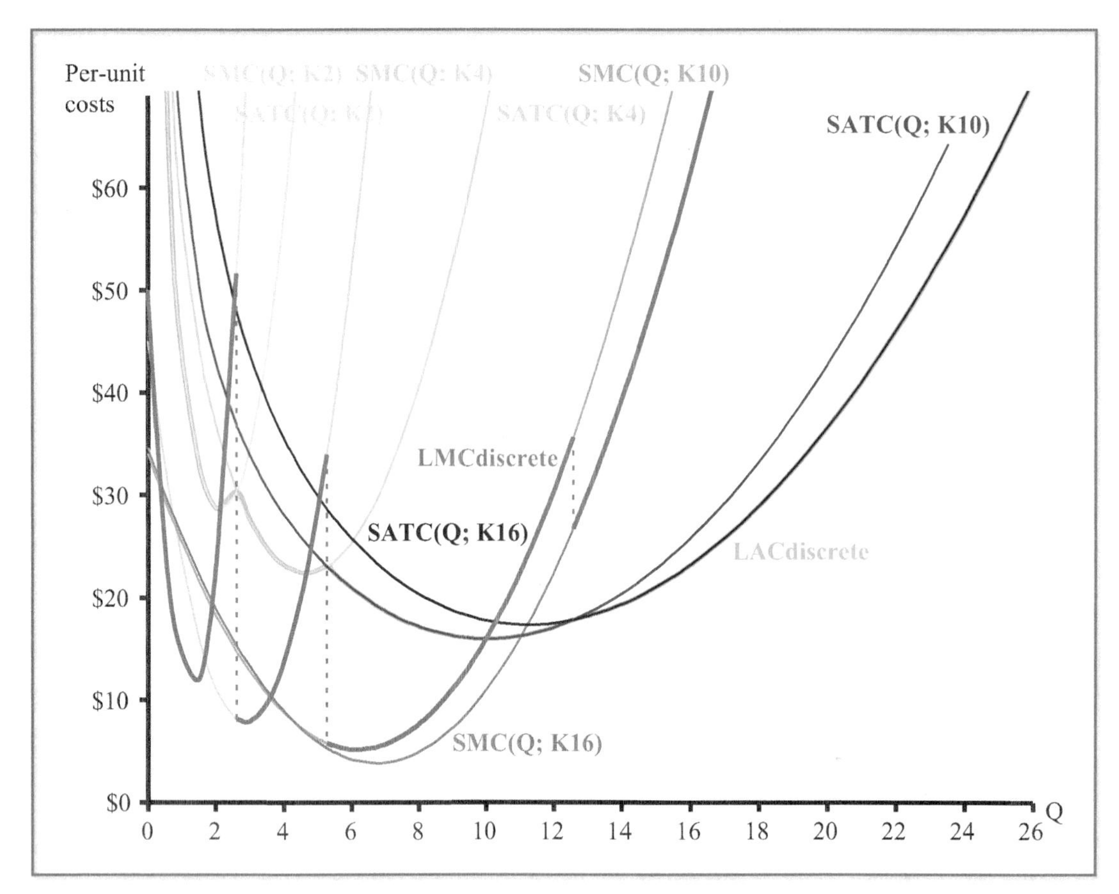

FIGURE 11.16 Long-Run Marginal Cost with Discrete Plant Sizes and Varying Returns to Scale

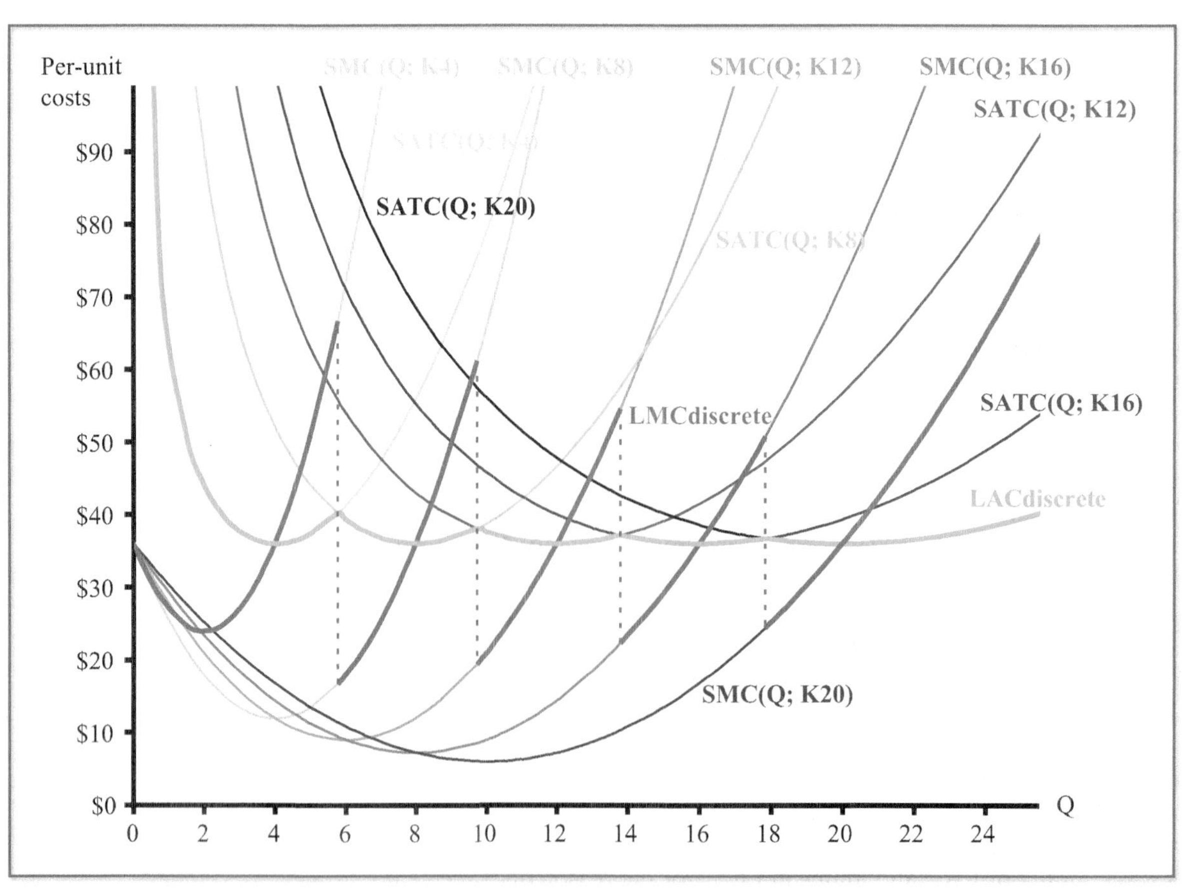

FIGURE 11.17 Long-Run Marginal Cost with Discrete Plant Sizes and Constant Returns to Scale

11.4 The Algebra of Cubic Cost Functions

The cost curves depicted thus far in this chapter are based on the cubic functional form. Cost functions need not be cubic, but this form offers the simplest algebraic means of describing a total or variable cost curve that is first convex downward and then convex upward. As described in Section 11.2, a typical short-run cost curve exhibits this changing convexity due to changing marginal productivity of the variable factors of production. Initial increasing marginal productivity is eventually replaced by declining marginal productivity, due to the law of diminishing marginal product. In Section 11.3, we argued that the long-run total cost curve may also have this shape, due to varying returns to scale. This would occur if initial increasing returns to scale are eventually replaced by decreasing returns to large-scale production.

Both short-run and long-run cost curves may be depicted algebraically, using the cubic functional form. We focus on the seven short-run curves delineated in Section 11.2 because, as argued earlier, in the discussion of Figure 11.12, LTC, LAC, and LMC curves based on varying returns to scale are *geometrically* identical to SVC, SAVC, and SMC. The general form of the cubic total cost function is:

$TC(Q) = a + b \cdot Q - c \cdot Q^2 + d \cdot Q^3$, where a, b, c, and d are positive numbers. **(11.6a)**

Before continuing, we should note a couple of points. First, there is a minus sign in front of the quadratic term c and plus signs in front of the linear and cubic terms. This is what produces U-shaped average and marginal cost curves. Second, we explicitly stated at the start of the paragraph that we would focus on short-run costs. As a result, the "S" is implicit for each of the cost functions in Equations 11.6a–11.6g. Third, this is the short run because parameter a represents fixed cost.

$FC(Q) = a$, given the total cost function in Equation 11.6a. **(11.6b)**

Each of the other five short-run cost functions (VC, ATC, AVC, AFC, MC) is obtained by algebraic manipulation of Equation 11.6a.

Since a is fixed cost, and total cost is variable cost plus fixed cost (Equation 11.1a), the rest of Equation 11.6a is variable cost.

$VC(Q) = b \cdot Q - c \cdot Q^2 + d \cdot Q^3$, given the total cost function in Equation 11.6a. **(11.6c)**

The short-run average cost functions are obtained by dividing each function by Q.

$ATC(Q) = a/Q + b - c \cdot Q + d \cdot Q^2$. **(11.6d)**

$AFC(Q) = a/Q$. **(11.6e)**

$AVC(Q) = b - c \cdot Q + d \cdot Q^2$. **(11.6f)**

As expected, $TC(Q) = FC(Q) + VC(Q)$ and $ATC(Q) = AFC(Q) + AVC(Q)$.

Marginal cost is the slope of the total cost and variable cost curves. Given the total cost curve in Equation 11.6a or the variable cost curve in Equation 11.6c, marginal cost is given by:

$MC(Q) = b - 2 \cdot c \cdot Q + 3 \cdot d \cdot Q^2$. **(11.6g)**

Equation 11.6g describes the slope of total cost and variable cost, and can be found by taking the derivative of either TC(Q) or VC(Q) in Equations 11.6a or 11.6c. If you have not seen calculus before, then this is simply a fact that can be used whenever you have a cubic cost function.

Claim: *You can obtain marginal cost from a cubic cost function by applying Rules 1 and 2 to the total cost function:*

Rule 1—Drop the fixed cost component a; this only shifts total cost up or down, but does not change slope at a given output level.

Rule 2—The linear, quadratic, and cubic terms (b, c, and d) become the constant, linear, and quadratic coefficients, once they are multiplied by 1, 2, and 3.

This simple "cookbook" method will always provide you with marginal cost.[8]

AVC and MC in Equations 11.6f and 11.6g have been placed next to each other so that it is easy to see the similarity between these functions. MC looks like AVC, except that the last two terms are multiplied by 2 and 3 (using Rule 2 in the previous "cookbook" method).

Each of the U-shaped per-unit cost curves attains a minimum value. Two of the three minimum values are easy to obtain. Minimum marginal cost occurs at:[9]

$$Q_{minMC} = c/(3 \cdot d). \quad \textbf{(11.7a)}$$

Minimum AVC may be obtained algebraically using the fact that MC = minimum AVC (as shown in Figure 11.6A). Using Equations 11.6f and 11.6g we obtain upon simplification:

$$Q_{minAVC} = c/(2 \cdot d). \quad \textbf{(11.7b)}$$

Comparing Equations 11.7a and 11.7b, we see that when costs are cubic, minimum MC occurs at two-thirds the output of minimum AVC. This is a helpful fact for graphing these two per-unit cost functions.

Unfortunately, if you follow the same strategy to find minimum average total cost (ATC), you obtain a cubic equation. The general solution of cubic equations is beyond the scope of this text. However, we can find a numerical solution, once we know *a*, b, c, and d, by comparing ATC(Q) and MC(Q) for different values of Q. (When ATC(Q) > MC(Q) at the given Q, increase Q; when ATC(Q) < MC(Q) at a given Q, decrease Q.) This will quickly produce as close of a numerical solution as necessary.[10] (And of course, problems produced for exams will often have clean solutions that need little numerical approximation. Once you know *a*, b, c, and d, set ATC(Q) = MC(Q), and look to see if an "easy" solution is visible—it often is, and it gets easier to see the more often you look for it.)

It is worthwhile to apply this to a specific cubic cost function. Consider, for instance, the cost function used to produce each of the figures in Section 11.2. We derived each of the minimum values graphically; we now confirm these answers algebraically. The cost function used is:

$$TC(Q) = 400 + 36 \cdot Q - 3 \cdot Q^2 + 0.1 \cdot Q^3. \quad \textbf{(11.8a)}$$

Focus on the U-shaped per-unit cost curves.

$$ATC(Q) = 400/Q + 36 - 3 \cdot Q + 0.1 \cdot Q^2. \quad \textbf{(11.8b)}$$

$$AVC(Q) = 36 - 3 \cdot Q + 0.1 \cdot Q^2. \quad \textbf{(11.8c)}$$

$$MC(Q) = 36 - 6 \cdot Q + 0.3 \cdot Q^2. \quad \textbf{(11.8d)}$$

The similarity between AVC and MC just described applies with numbers in place of parameters (as you would expect). Applying Equations 11.7a and 11.7b to this cost function, we see that minimum marginal cost and average variable cost occur at:

$$Q_{minMC} = c/(3 \cdot d) = 3/(3 \cdot 0.1) = 10. \quad \textbf{(11.9a)}$$

$$Q_{minAVC} = c/(2 \cdot d) = 3/(2 \cdot 0.1) = 15. \quad \textbf{(11.9b)}$$

Note that, as expected, minimum MC occurs at two-thirds the output level of minimum AVC.

As stated earlier, the general solution for minimum ATC(Q) requires the solution of a cubic equation. The strategy suggested in the last paragraph provides the following (by equating ATC to MC):

$$400/Q + 36 - 3 \cdot Q + 0.1 \cdot Q^2 = 36 - 6 \cdot Q + 0.3 \cdot Q^2. \quad \textbf{(11.9c)}$$

Combining common terms and putting all terms on one side of the equality yields:

$$0.2 \cdot Q^2 - 3 \cdot Q - 400/Q = 0. \quad \textbf{(11.9d)}$$

Multiplying by 5Q, we obtain:

$$Q^3 - 15 \cdot Q^2 - 2000 = 0. \quad \textbf{(11.9e)}$$

TABLE 11.1 Using Excel to Find Minimum ATC, Given Cubic Cost

Panel A: ATC versus MC for an initial value of output

	A	B	C	D
1	Q	ATC(Q) (Equation 11.8b)	MC(Q) (Equation 11.8d)	ATC-MC
2	15	40.16666667	13.5	26.6666667
3	Row 2 Equations	=400/A2+36-3*A2+0.1*A2^2	=36-6*A2+0.3*A2^2	=B2-C2

Panel B: Minimum ATC—a numerical solution achieved by Goal Seek

	A	B	C	D
1	Q	ATC(Q) (Equation 11.8b)	MC(Q) (Equation 11.8d)	ATC-MC
2	19.99999981	36	35.99999886	1.14E-06
3	Row 2 Equations	=400/A2+36-3*A2+0.1*A2^2	=36-6*A2+0.3*A2^2	=B2-C2

Panel C: Minimum ATC—an exact solution obtained by typing 20 in cell A2

	A	B	C	D
1	Q	ATC(Q) (Equation 11.8b)	MC(Q) (Equation 11.8d)	ATC-MC
2	20	36	36	0
3	Row 2 Equations	=400/A2+36-3*A2+0.1*A2^2	=36-6*A2+0.3*A2^2	=B2-C2

This equation (or its precursors, Equations 11.9c and11.9d) can be checked for values of Q to determine the minimum ATC quantity level. Any Q chosen must, of course, be larger than that found in Equation 11.9b, since $Q_{minAVC} < Q_{minATC}$. Substituting Q values larger than Q = 15 will quickly produce Q = 20 as a solution. This search can be done manually or by programming the equations into Excel and using the **Goal Seek** function (described in Section 7.5) to obtain the answer. If checking manually, it is worthwhile to work from Equation 11.9c, rather than the cubic equation in Equation 11.9e, since the information provided by the relative sizes of ATC(Q) and MC(Q) tells us whether to increase or decrease Q in the next iteration of our search. The directional change rule is based on the relation that governs the relative size of marginal and average cost discussed earlier: *When ATC(Q) > MC(Q) at a given Q, increase Q; when ATC(Q) < MC(Q) at a given Q, decrease Q.* Not surprisingly, the answers obtained in Equation 11.9 mirror those obtained graphically in Section 11.2.

Table 11.1 shows the Excel version of this search. Table 11.1A sets out the equations for ATC and MC from Equations11.8b and 11.8d in cells B2 and C2, based on the quantity in cell A2 (the equations in these cells are shown beneath in cells B3 and C3). Table 11.1B shows the results of a **Goal Seek** on cell D2 by changing cell A2. (Click on cell D2, click **Data, What If Analysis, Goal Seek** in Excel 2007 (or **Tools, Goal Seek** in Excel 2003). Put 0 (zero) in the **To value** area and A2 in the **By changing cell** area, click **OK, OK.**) The result is Q=19.99999981, a number that is *very* close to 20. You may wonder why 20 was not obtained as the solution in this instance. **Goal Seek** is a numerical search routine that stops when an answer "close enough" to the goal is achieved. As you can see in cell D2, ATC and MC are not equal, but they are within 0.00000116 of each other! Table 11.1C depicts the solution obtained by putting the value Q = 20 in cell A2. In this instance, the answer is exact.

Interpreting and Restricting Cubic Cost Parameters

The cubic cost curves described in Equations 11.6a–11.6g change as *a*, b, c, and d vary. Two of these parameters, *a* and b, have easily seen intuitive meanings: *a* is fixed cost as noted earlier, and b is the initial level of marginal cost and average variable cost (according to Equations 11.6b, 11.6f, and 11.6g). If either of these parameters changes, you should be able to work through what happens to the various cost curves. The other parameters are less intuitive but have readily understood interpretations. Larger values of c will make the s shape of the cost curve more pronounced over the middle range of outputs, and larger values of d will make the cost curve steeper for large values of output. Changing the value of these parameters may lead to cubic functions that no longer represent a total cost curve because the shape is no longer a valid representation of cost as a function of output. A further restriction must be placed on the parameters b, c, and d to assure that the resulting function represents a possible cost curve.

The initial restriction on these parameters is that each must be positive. A restriction on the shape of the total cost curve is that it must be upward sloping (because it must be more expensive to produce more output than less output); put another way, marginal cost must be positive. Marginal cost in Equation 11.6g is greater than zero when the following holds:

$$c^2 < 3 \cdot b \cdot d. \tag{11.10}$$

This restriction may appear a bit strange but it has an easy explanation. Marginal cost is a quadratic function of quantity, Q. Because we do not want MC(Q) = 0, the quadratic equation should have no solutions (you may recall from algebra that a quadratic equation can have zero, one, or two solutions).[11] A quick check of the total cost function described in Equation 11.8a confirms this condition ($3^2 = 9 < 3 \cdot 36 \cdot 0.1 = 10.8$).

When you create your own cubic cost functions, you will quickly know if you violate the inequality in Equation 11.10: Your total and variable cost curves will have a downward-sloping segment (or the slope will be zero at a point), and marginal cost will have output levels where it is less than zero (or zero). It would be worthwhile to spend some time adjusting parameters *a*–d to see what happens to the various cost curves, using the Excel file for the Chapter 11 Appendix.

11.5 Cobb-Douglas Cost Functions *OPTIONAL SECTION*

Cost functions based on the Cobb-Douglas production function $Q(L, K) = a \cdot L^b \cdot K^c$ have already been derived in Chapter 10. The long-run total cost function is derived as Equation 10.13a, and the short-run total cost function is Equation 10.16a, but they are reproduced here as Equations 11.11a and 11.12a to provide a more unified exposition. Each of the other cost curves discussed in Chapter 11 can be obtained from these two functions. Much can be gleaned from this section by focusing on the figures, rather than worrying about the algebra. In many cases, the second version of equations in this section shows the functional relation without the algebraic detail. Even without working through the algebra, it is worth opening the Excel file that produced all of the figures in this section and manipulating *a*, b, c, w, and r to see what happens to each of the cost curves as a result.

The long-run total cost function is:

$$LTC(Q) = Q^{(1/(b+c))} \cdot [a^{(-1/(b+c))} \cdot w^{(b/(b+c))} \cdot r^{(c/(b+c))} \cdot ((b/c)^{(c/(b+c)} + (c/b)^{(b/(b+c))})]. \tag{11.11a}$$

$$LTC(Q) = \mathbf{Q}^{(1/(b+c))} \cdot H(w, r, a, b, c). \tag{11.11b}$$

H is the shorthand term for the function in the brackets [ ] in Equation 11.11a. The "a" version is the actual cost equation; the "b" version shows the functional form implicit in the equation (LTC is a power function of quantity, Q). From here, the average cost function is easily obtained by dividing by Q:

$$LAC(Q) = \mathbf{Q}^{((1/(b+c))-1)} \cdot H(w, r, a, b, c). \tag{11.11c}$$

The long-run marginal cost function associated with this cost curve is:[12]

$$LMC(Q) = \mathbf{Q}^{((1/(b+c))-1)} \cdot H(w, r, a, b, c)/(b + c). \tag{11.11d}$$

The short-run cost function associated with having K_0 units of capital from Equation 10.16 is (in each case, we provide two versions of each equation to highlight the functional relation that connects quantity to cost):

$$STC(Q; K_0) = r \cdot K_0 + Q^{(1/b)} \cdot [w \cdot (K_0^{-c}/a)^{(1/b)}].$$

$$STC(Q; K_0) = F(r, K_0) + \mathbf{Q}^{(1/b)} \cdot G(w, a, b, c, K_0). \quad \textbf{(11.12a)}$$

Short-run total cost is easily decomposed into fixed and variable components:

$$SFC(Q; K_0) = r \cdot K_0.$$

$$SFC(Q; K_0) = F(r, K_0). \quad \textbf{(11.12b)}$$

$$SVC(Q; K_0) = Q^{(1/b)} \cdot [w \cdot (K_0^{-c}/a)^{(1/b)}].$$

$$SVC(Q; K_0) = \mathbf{Q}^{(1/b)} \cdot G(w, a, b, c, K_0). \quad \textbf{(11.12c)}$$

From here, each of the average cost functions (SATC, SAVC, and SAFC) is obtained by dividing each of the respective total functions by Q:

$$SATC(Q; K_0) = r \cdot K_0/Q + Q^{((1/b)-1)} \cdot [w \cdot (K_0^{-c}/a)^{(1/b)}].$$

$$SATC(Q; K_0) = SAFC + SAVC. \quad \textbf{(11.12d)}$$

$$SAFC(Q; K_0) = r \cdot K_0/Q.$$

$$SAFC(Q; K_0) = F(r, K_0)/Q. \quad \textbf{(11.12e)}$$

$$SAVC(Q; K_0) = Q^{((1/b)-1)} \cdot [w \cdot (K_0^{-c}/a)^{(1/b)}].$$

$$SAVC(Q; K_0) = \mathbf{Q}^{((1/b)-1)} \cdot G(w, a, b, c, K_0). \quad \textbf{(11.12f)}$$

Finally, short-run marginal cost is:

$$SMC(Q; K_0) = (1/b) \cdot Q^{((1/b)-1)} \cdot [w \cdot (K_0^{-c}/a)^{(1/b)}].$$

$$SMC(Q; K_0) = \mathbf{Q}^{((1/b)-1)} \cdot G(w, a, b, c, K_0)/b. \quad \textbf{(11.12g)}$$

The total cost functions were further examined, based on specific values of the parameters used to produce Figure 10.10; $a = 1$, $b = c = 0.5$, and $w = r = 1$. These values of a, b, c, w, and r produce the quadratic short-run total cost function and the linear long-run total cost function described in Equations 10.17a and 10.17b, reproduced here as Equations 11.13a and 11.13b.

LR cost: $LTC(Q) = 2 \cdot Q$ from Equation 11.11a. **(11.13a)**

SR cost: $STC(Q; K_0) = K_0 + Q^2/K_0$ from Equation 11.12a. **(11.13b)**

These cost functions are depicted in Figure 11.18A (the parameter values are listed to the left of Figure 11.18B). The long-run cost curves are shown together with short-run cost curves associated with four different plant sizes ($K_i = 0.5$, 1, 2, and 3). Due to the complexity of Figure 11.18B, only LAC, LMC, SATC, and SMC are shown. The result proven at Equation 10.18 based on these cost functions is that $STC(Q; K_0) \geq LTC(Q)$, and they are only equal when $Q = K_0$. This result is seen both in Figure 11.18A as the tangency of each of the short-run total cost curves with the long-run total cost curve, and in Figure 11.18B by the convergence of SMC, SATC, and LAC = LMC at Q = 0.5, 1, 2, and 3 (according to Equation 11.5). Per-unit costs are minimized at a cost of 2 per unit according to Equation 11.13a and by the height of LAC in Figure 11.18B.

The general total and per-unit Cobb-Douglas cost equations in Equations 11.11 and 11.12 are complex, but beneath the complexity are some readily apparent patterns. To understand these patterns, it is necessary to distinguish between two aspects of a curve: the basic *shape* of a curve and its *placement*. By *shape*, we mean: What is the functional form inherent in the function? How does cost relate to quantity? Is the curve convex upward, convex downward, or does it change convexity? By *placement*, we mean the graph's location horizontally and vertically on the graph. The vertical placement is the height of cost; the horizontal placement is how stretched out is the curve. Think of a curve drawn on a clear, elastic surface above a fixed piece of graph paper. If you fix the horizontal axis and pull upward on the top of the piece of elastic, the shape of the curve will not change, but its vertical placement relative to the fixed graph paper will change.

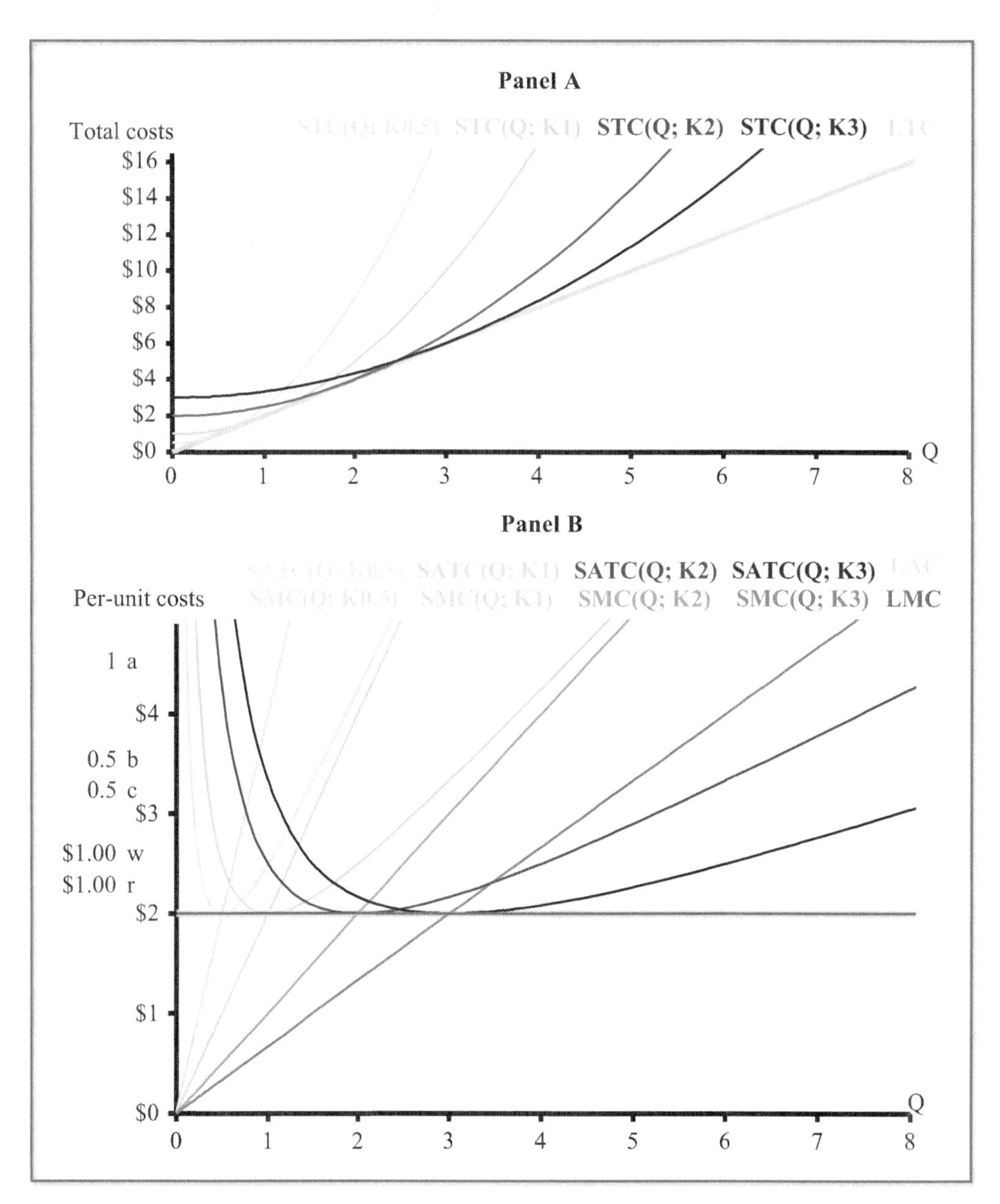

FIGURE 11.18 Cobb-Douglas Cost Function

Constant returns to scale (CRTS): Linear long run, quadratic short run

Similarly, if you fix the vertical axis and pull the right edge to the right, the shape of the curve will not change, but its horizontal placement will change. Finally, if you pull both horizontally and vertically at the same time, the shape does not change, but its horizontal and vertical placement does. For example, the various STC curves in Figure 11.18A are the same shape and can be obtained from each other by horizontal and vertical pulls, while the SATC and SMC curves in Figure 11.18 are also the same shape as each other but require horizontal pulls only.

Focus initially on the long-run cost functions in Equation 11.11. The shapes of the three long-run cost functions are determined entirely by the magnitude of b + c. Basically, the long-run total cost function in Equation 11.11b is a power function of Q, where the exponent attached to Q is 1/(b + c). As discussed in Section 9.4, returns to scale are determined by the magnitude of b + c. When b + c = 1, we have constant returns to scale and consequently linear long-run cost functions, as discussed in Section 11.3. (This is why long-run cost is linear in Equation 11.13a when b = c = 0.5.) We see the same result algebraically in Equations 11.11c and 11.11d (LAC = LMC = H(w, r, *a*, b, c) because

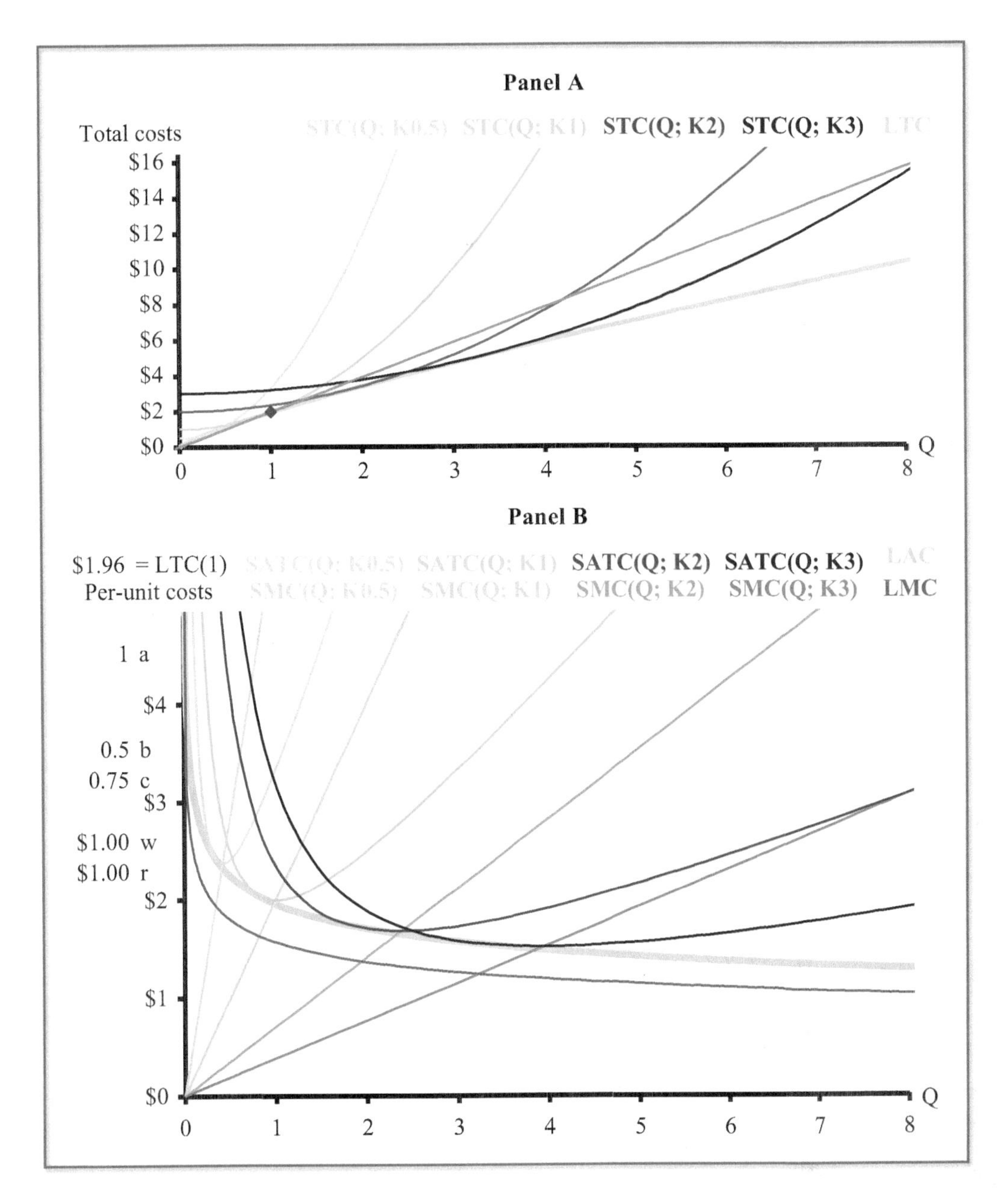

FIGURE 11.19 Cobb-Douglas Cost Function

Increasing returns to scale (IRTS): Convex downward long run, quadratic short run

b + c = 1 implies 1/(b + c) – 1 = 0 and $Q^0 = 1$ for any Q). For instance, H(w, r, *a*, b, c) = 2, given these values of *a*, b, c, w, and r; therefore, LAC and LMC are flat at a height of 2 in Figure 11.18B.

When b + c > 1, we have increasing returns to scale. An example of increasing returns to scale (IRTS) is shown in Figure 11.19, which differs from Figure 11.18 in only two respects: In Figure 11.19A, c = 0.75, and a green ray has been added to represent LTC(1). The blue diamond at (1, LTC(1)) is on the long-run total cost curve, but it does *not* coincide with that curve unless production exhibits constant returns to scale, as was true in Figure 11.18. In the absence of CRTS, the line is provided to make the curvature of the LTC curve more obvious. In this instance, LTC is convex downward because its shape is a power function, where the power is less than one (1/(b + c) = 4/5 < 1). In Figure 11.19B, both LAC and LMC are declining functions of Q because they are power functions, where the power is less than zero (1/(b + c) – 1 = –1/5 < 0).

The reverse holds true in Figure 11.20A, where c = 0.25 (and b remains at b = 0.5), so the Cobb-Douglas production function exhibits decreasing returns to scale. LTC is

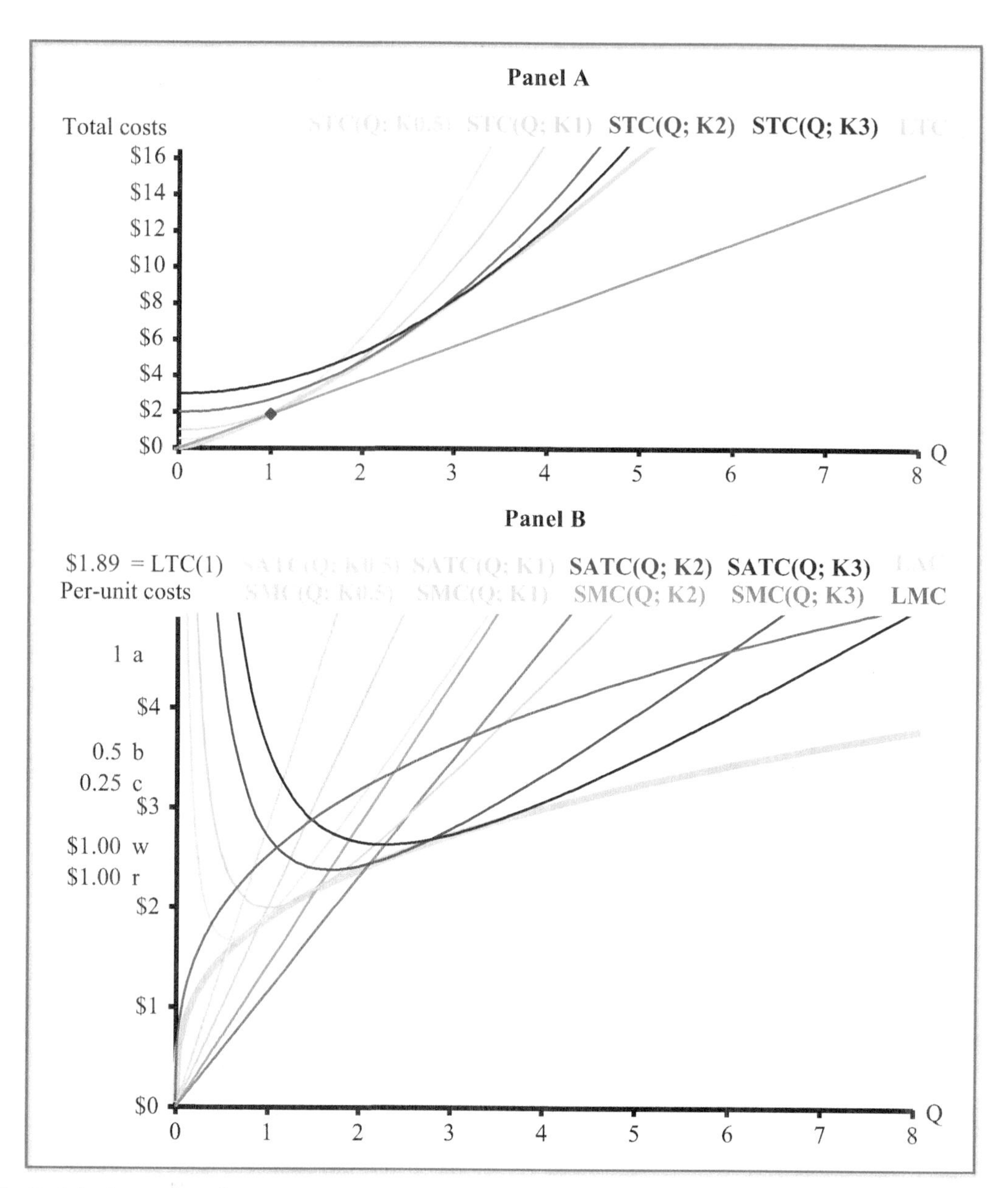

FIGURE 11.20 Cobb-Douglas Cost Function

Decreasing returns to scale (DRTS): Convex upward long run, quadratic short run

convex upward, given decreasing returns to scale (DRTS), because its shape is a power function, where the power is greater than one ($1/(b + c) = 4/3 > 1$). In Figure 11.20B, LAC and LMC are increasing functions of Q because they are power functions, where the power is greater than zero ($1/(b + c) - 1 = 1/3 > 0$).

The relative orientation of average and marginal holds in this instance as well: Marginal below average implies average is declining (in Figure 11.19), and marginal above average implies average is increasing (in Figure 11.20). This is confirmed algebraically by a quick examination of Equations 11.11c and 11.11d. The only difference between LAC and LMC is the $(b + c)$ in the denominator of LMC. The two functions have the same shape; they only differ by their relative placement. When $b + c < 1$, $1/(b + c) > 1$, and so LMC > LAC. (Think of LMC as being "stretched" upward relative to LAC in Figure 11.20.) The reverse holds true when $b + c > 1$, $1/(b + c) < 1$, so LMC < LAC. (Think of LAC as being "stretched" upward relative to LMC in Figure 11.19.)

Each of the short-run total cost functions in Figures 11.18–11.20 is quadratic in nature. This may not be obvious in the Panel A's in each figure, but the Panel B's show this in another way: Each short-run marginal cost curve is linear. This will be the case only if total cost is quadratic.[13] The power of the STC power function is determined by the magnitude of b (or more specifically, by 1/b). Each STC function in Figures 11.18–11.20 is quadratic because b = 0.5 in each figure; therefore, SMC and SAVC are linear functions of quantity in Equations 11.12f and 11.12g (since 1/b – 1 = 1 if b = 0.5). Average variable cost has been omitted from these figures, but it differs only in placement from marginal cost because SMC = SAVC/b, using Equations 11.12f and 11.12g. This is analogous to the relation between LAC and LMC discussed in the previous paragraph with one difference. The parameter b must be less than one for the production function to satisfy the law of diminishing marginal product, as discussed in Section 9.3; therefore, 1/b > 1, and hence, SMC > SAVC.[14]

When b ≠ 0.5, the short-run total cost functions will no longer be quadratic, and hence, marginal and average variable cost functions will no longer be linear. To focus attention on the shape of these short-run functions, c is adjusted in Figures 11.21 and 11.22 to maintain CRTS (b + c = 1). If b < 0.5, then 1/b > 2, and 1/b – 1 > 1, which leads the short-run marginal cost curve to be convex upward (the power of the SMC power function is greater than one).

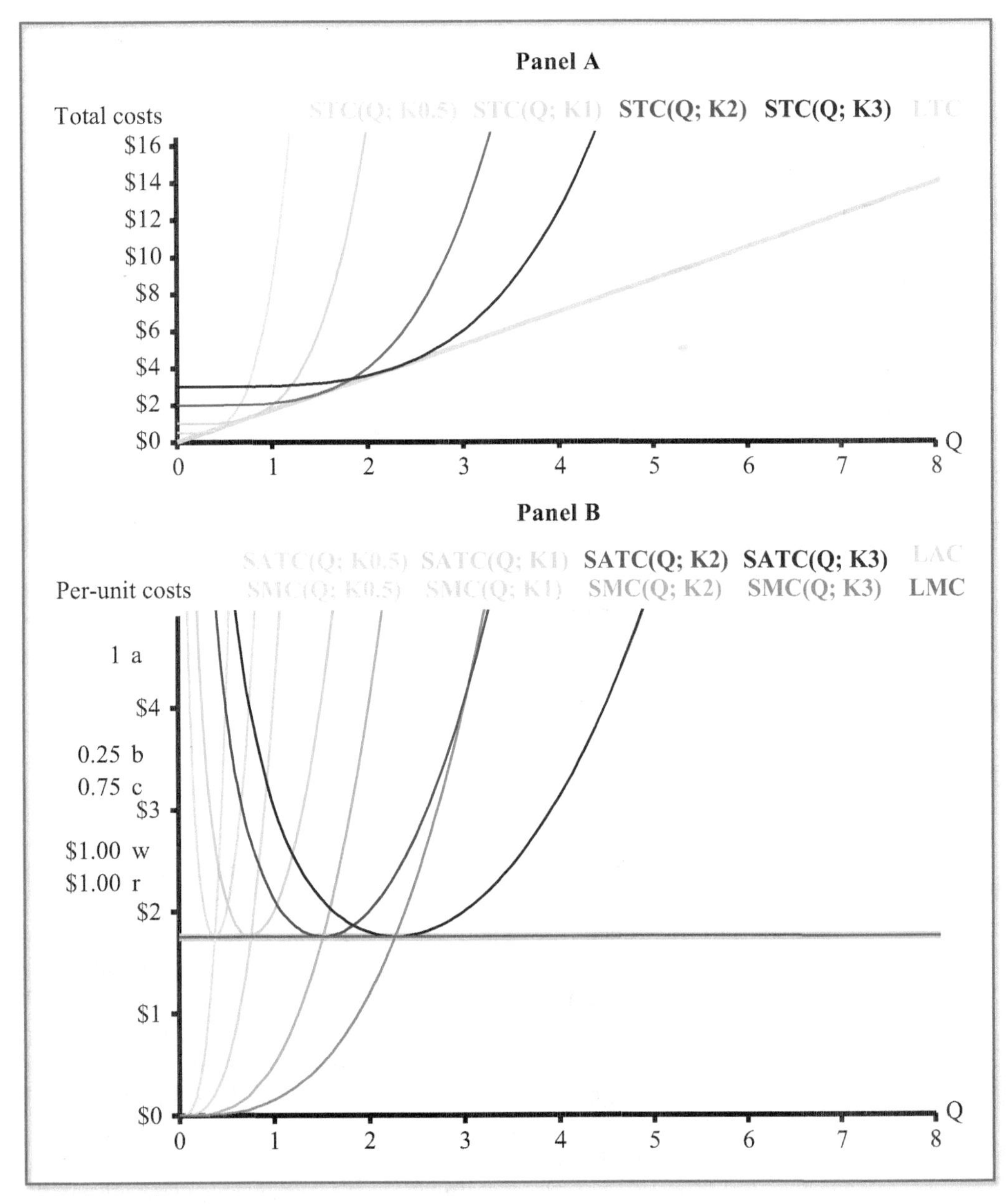

FIGURE 11.21 Cobb-Douglas Cost Function

CRTS: Linear long run, quartic short run

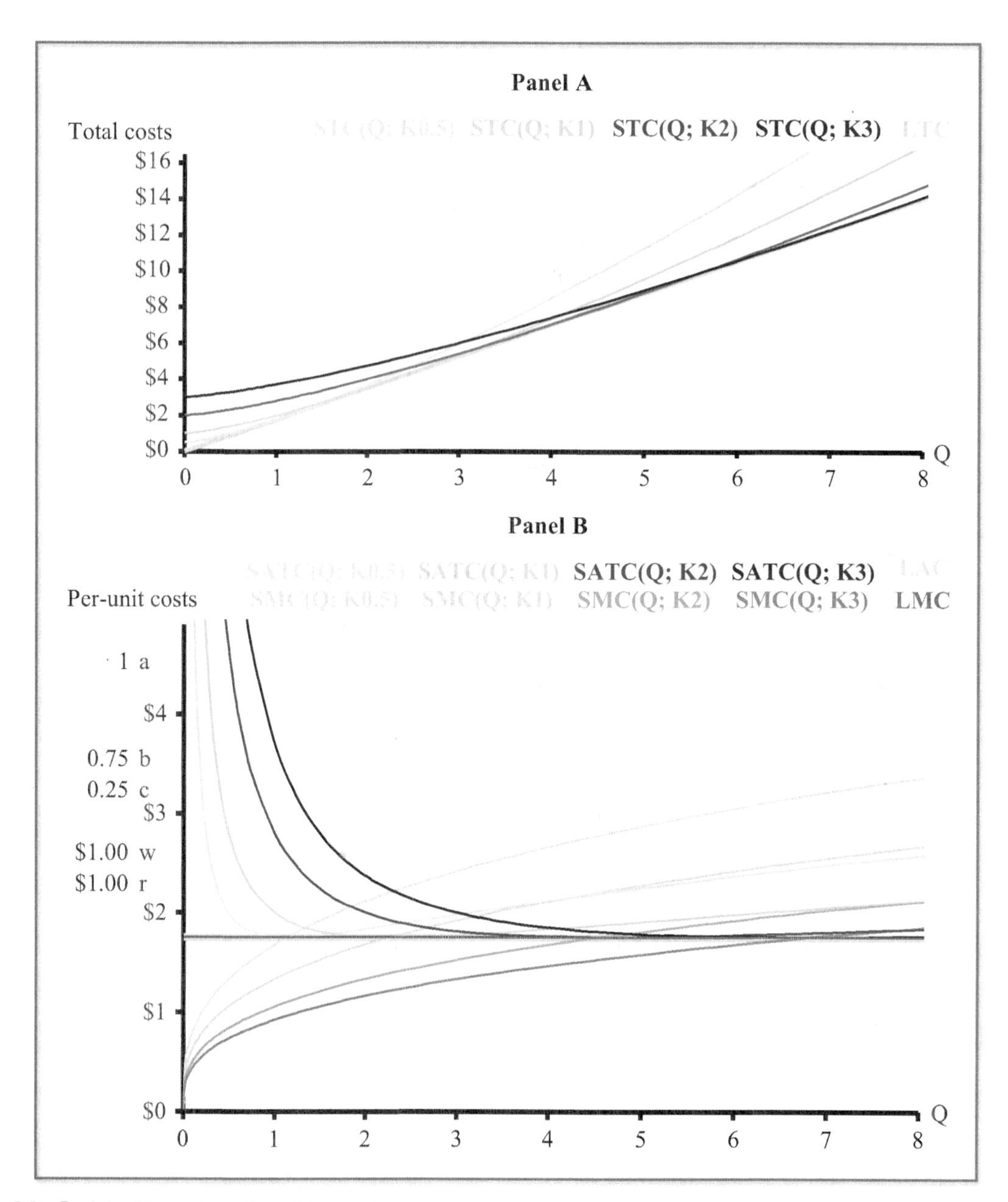

FIGURE 11.22 Cobb-Douglas Cost Function

CRTS: Linear long run; short run is a function of $Q^{4/3}$

This is depicted in Figure 11.21 for b = 0.25. In this instance, 1/b = 4, and STC is a quartic function of Q, and SMC is a cubic function of Q. The convexity of short-run marginal cost reverses if b > 0.5, since 1/b < 2 and 1/b – 1 < 1. STC remains convex upward, since 1/b > 1; STC must be convex upward for a linear LTC curve to be the envelope of STCs, but SMC is now convex downward (since its power is less than one). This is depicted in Figure 11.22 for b = 0.75, so 1/b = 4/3, and STC is a function of Q raised to the 4/3 power. SMC is now a function of $Q^{1/3}$; the cube root function. To examine what happens as b increases (and c decreases to maintain b + c = 1), look from Figure 11.21 to Figure 11.18 to Figure 11.22. For fixed capital, the cost-minimizing output level increases as b increases.

The focus thus far has been on the parameters b and c, the exponents attached to labor and capital in the CD production function. The other parameters have the effect on cost expected. Three parameters remain to be considered: *a*, w, and r. The parameter *a* is a scaling factor in the CD production function; thus far in the discussion, we have set *a* = 1. If *a* increases, then more output can be produced from a given amount of capital and labor.

TABLE 11.2 Cost Curves Based on the Cobb-Douglas Production Function $Q(L, K) = a \cdot L^b \cdot K^c$

Shape and Orientation of Long-Run Cobb-Douglas Cost Curves				
Condition	**Figure**	**RTS**	**Shape of LTC**	**LAC and LMC**
$b + c < 1$	11.20	DRTS	Convex upward	Increasing in Q, LMC > LAC
$b + c = 1$	11.18	CRTS	Linear	Constant in Q, LMC = LAC
$b + c > 1$	11.19	IRTS	Convex downward	Decreasing in Q, LMC < LAC

Shape and Orientation of Short-Run Cobb-Douglas Cost Curves				
Condition	**Figure**	**Shape of SVC and STC**	**Shape of SMC and SVC**	**Orientation**
$0 < b < 0.5$	11.21	Power function greater than quadratic	More than linear in Q	SMC > SAVC
$b = 0.5$	11.18–11.20	Quadratic cost function	Linear in Q	
$0.5 < b < 1$	11.22	Power function less than quadratic	Less than linear in Q	

Change Parameter	**Effect of an Increase in This Parameter**
Productivity factor, *a*	Decreases all short- and long-run cost curves
Wage rate, w	Increases SVC, STC, SAVC, SATC, SMC, and all long-run cost curves; does not change SFC or SAFC
Capital cost, r	Increases SFC, STC, SAFC, SATC, and all long-run cost curves; does not change SVC, SAVC, or SMC

Put another way, the cost of producing a fixed amount of output declines. An increase in wage rate increases variable costs of production: Marginal cost rotates upward but has no effect on fixed cost. By contrast, an increase in the rental rate on capital increases fixed cost but has no effect on variable cost. Each of these conclusions is most easily seen by using the sliders in the Excel file for Figures 11.18–11.22. The results described in this section about Cobb-Douglas cost functions are summarized in Table 11.2.

Summary

Cost of production is a direct outgrowth of production technology. The direct linkage between inputs used to produce output and the cost of those inputs is the subject of Chapter 10. The focus there is on the cost-minimizing input mix for producing a given level of output. The connection between input choice and output cost is most directly seen in this chapter in the geometric analysis that begins and ends the chapter. Between these geometric bookends, the analysis examines cost as a function of output. The cost functions derived in this chapter form the basis for profit-maximizing decisions by firms.

Various notions of cost are examined and compared in Section 11.1. Opportunity cost—the cost of a resource in its next best alternative use—forms the basis for economic analysis of cost. Economic cost is distinguished from accounting cost, as are explicit versus implicit cost and fixed versus variable cost. Sunk cost—a cost that has already occurred and that cannot be recovered—is also distinguished as a separate notion of cost.

Cost curves show cost as a function of output. Output is the horizontal axis for cost diagrams, but the vertical axis can be one of two things: total dollars spent or dollars spent per unit of output. The two versions of cost curves are, of course, related, and that relation forms the basis for much of the analysis in the chapter.

Short-run total cost is the sum of fixed and variable cost. Dividing each of these three cost functions by quantity gives us their per-unit counterparts: average total cost, average fixed cost, and average variable cost. Marginal cost, the final short-run per-unit cost function, is, arguably, the most important, as we will soon see. Marginal cost is the incremental cost of production. How much does an extra unit of output cost? The slope of the total cost or the variable cost function provides an answer to this question.

Marginal cost has the same relation to each of the average cost curves that marginal product has to average product in Chapter 9. When marginal is below average, average is declining, and when marginal is above average, average is increasing. Marginal cost equals average cost at minimum average cost. This is true for both average variable cost and for average total cost.

Often, the short-run total cost curve is initially convex downward, due to an initial range of increasing marginal productivity for variable factors of production. The convexity eventually changes, and the cost curve becomes convex upward, due to the law of diminishing marginal product. Total cost curves that have this upward-sloping "S" shape produce U-shaped average variable, average total, and marginal cost curves. Although it is not necessary to model cost curves using cubic equations, this is the simplest functional form that produces these results.

Long-run costs have no fixed component because, in the long run, there are no fixed factors of production. Therefore, there are only three long-run cost curves, as opposed to seven short-run cost curves. Long-run total cost is the sole long-run total cost curve, and long-run average and long-run marginal cost are per-unit cost curves.

In the long run, firms have extra options available that they do not have in the short run; for example, they can change plant size in response to market signals. As a result, long-run costs are always less than or equal to short-run costs. Indeed, one way to conceptualize long-run costs is that the long run is the best (lowest cost) of each possible short run. Formally, long-run total cost is the envelope of short-run total cost curves, and long-run average cost is the envelope of short-run average total cost. The same is not true for long-run marginal cost.

Long-run cost functions based on constant returns to scale production technologies have linear long-run total cost and flat long-run average and marginal cost. Another common shape for long-run total cost is similar to the upward-sloping "S" shape of a short-run variable cost function. The interpretation of these two visually similar functions is, however, entirely different. Short-run variable cost has this shape due to increasing and then decreasing marginal productivity of variable factors of production. By contrast, the long-run total cost curve has this shape due to initial economies of scale in the production process, which are eventually replaced by diseconomies of large-scale production.

The chapter concludes with an analysis of cost curves based on Cobb-Douglas production technology. As noted in Chapter 9, Cobb-Douglas production functions do not have varying returns to scale, and factors of production have diminishing marginal product over the entire range of usage of the factors of production. Therefore, short-run total cost curves deriving from Cobb-Douglas technology are convex upward, and long-run total cost curves may be convex upward (if the production process exhibits decreasing returns to scale), linear (if the production process exhibits constant returns to scale), or upward sloping but convex downward (if the production process exhibits increasing returns to scale). But the Cobb-Douglas production function will not have varying returns to scale without further modification of the function.

Review Questions

Define the following terms:

opportunity cost	total cost (TC)	average fixed cost (AFC)
economic cost	sunk cost	long-run total cost curve, LTC(Q)
explicit cost	options contract	long-run marginal cost curve, LMC(Q)
implicit cost	per-unit costs	long-run average cost curve, LAC(Q)
accounting cost	marginal cost (MC)	the geometric concept of an *envelope*
fixed cost (FC)	average total cost (ATC)	
variable cost (VC)	average variable cost (AVC)	

Match the following phrases:

a. Average fixed cost plus average variable cost	1. $\Delta VC(Q)/\Delta Q$
b. Fixed cost	2. $VC(Q) + FC(Q)$
c. Explicit cost plus implicit cost	3. Minimum average total cost
d. Marginal cost equals average variable cost	4. $Q \cdot (ATC(Q) - AVC(Q))$
e. Average fixed cost at output level Q	5. Economic cost
f. Total cost at output level Q	6. $ATC(Q) - AVC(Q)$
g. Marginal cost	7. Minimum average variable cost
h. Marginal cost equals average total cost	8. $ATC(Q)$

Provide short answers to the following:

a. If at a given output level, you know that marginal cost is more than average variable cost, what happens to average variable cost as output expands by a small amount?

b. If at a given output level, you know that marginal cost is less than average total cost, what happens to average total cost as output expands by a small amount?

c. Why are there seven short-run cost curves but only three long-run cost curves?
d. If average variable cost is declining at a given output level, is it possible that average total cost is increasing at that same output level?
e. If average variable cost is increasing at a given output level, is it possible that average total cost is declining at that same output level?
f. If both average variable cost and average total cost are declining at a given output level, what is true about marginal cost at that output level? (Must it also be declining?)
g. If both average variable cost and average total cost are increasing at a given output level, what is true about marginal cost at that output level? (Must it also be increasing?)
h. What is the geometric relation between short-run total cost curves for various plant sizes and the long-run total cost curve for this firm?
i. What is the geometric relation between short-run average total cost curves for various plant sizes and the long-run average cost curve for this firm?

Check your answers to the *matching* and *short-answer* exercises in the Answers Appendix at the end of the book.

Notes

1. There are excellent educational materials on the Chicago Board Options Exchange website. Go to http://www.cboe.com/

2. Had the example been of an "eat-in" pizza shop, the production function would no longer be Leontief because eat-in pizzas do not require a box. Of course, an "eat-in" shop would have been more complex to examine, due to the extra costs involved in such an operation.

3. As with marginal utility and marginal product, marginal cost is more formally defined using derivatives. In this instance, $MC(Q) = dTC(Q)/dQ = dVC(Q)/dQ$. These two derivatives are equal because TC and VC only differ by a constant, FC, and the derivative of a constant is zero.

4. You have seen an analogous piece of geometry in the consumer context when we discussed quasilinear preferences. The defining geometric feature of quasilinear preferences was that indifference curves were vertical translates of each other. As a result, the slope of the indifference curve (MRS) depended only on how much x was being consumed (rather than how much x *and* y was consumed). The same result holds here: The slopes of TC(Q) and VC(Q) are the same for any level of output and only depend on the level of Q under consideration.

5. If only discrete plant sizes were possible, then the production function would have more of the look of the discrete goods utility function described in Section 5.6. Suppose, for example, that capital is discrete and labor is continuous. Then the production function would be defined on horizontal lines in (L, K) space, where each horizontal line is an available plant size.

6.The K_i numbers do not represent cardinal differences between capital stock. K4 is not twice the size of K2, and K16 is not four times the size of K4. This is also seen in Figure 11.9. We knew that the small plant produced Q = 4 at minimum cost, and the large plant produced Q = 20 at the same minimum average total cost, despite FC_{small} = \$32 not being one-fifth the size of FC_{large} = \$400.

7. Exact values for the various cost functions require the actual cost functions. The algebraic functions are unimportant here; the figures allow you to see these as approximate values.

8. To understand why this is true requires a basic understanding of derivatives. This understanding is not necessary to do well in intermediate microeconomics (just as it was unnecessary to explain why the marginal utilities in Table 4.1 were what they were).

9. The proof in this instance requires calculus. Set $dMC(Q)/dQ = 0$ and solve for Q.

10. This is a perfect place to use Excel's **Goal Seek** function, discussed in Section 7.5. If you put labels in A1:D1 and a sample value of Q in cell A2, and the ATC and MC equations in B2 and C2, then you can place the difference in D2 and **Goal Seek** by setting D2 to zero by changing A2. An example of this is provided in Table 11.1. The Chapter 11 Appendix discusses graphing cubic cost functions using Excel.

11. As noted in the Mathematical Appendix (available in the online version of this text), the quadratic formula states that the equation $A \cdot x^2 + B \cdot x + C = 0$ has solutions $x = (-B \pm (B^2 - 4 \cdot A \cdot C)^{0.5})/(2 \cdot A)$. In Equation 11.6g, $A = 3 \cdot d$, $B = -2 \cdot c$, and $C = b$. Two solutions occur when the part under the square root (the part raised to the 0.5 power) is positive; there is one solution when the square root is zero. To have no solution, the part under the square root must be negative, a condition that simplifies to Equation 11.10.

12. As above, marginal cost is the derivative of total cost. If you know calculus make sure you can derive this yourself. If not, do not worry; marginal cost will be given for any total cost function used.

13. The proof of this assertion is simple if you know calculus. A derivative reduces the power of the function by one, so if you end up with a function to the first power (linear), then you must have started with a function that was to the second power.

14. We need not focus on the functional form of the SATC function. This function will necessarily include a 1/Q component due to the inclusion of fixed cost in the short run. For large values of output, SAFC becomes negligible, and SATC closely tracks SAVC. Indeed, mathematicians say that SATC is asymptotic to SAVC for large Q; as Q approaches zero, SATC is asymptotic to the vertical axis.

Appendix:

Using Excel to Graph Cubic Cost Functions

This appendix is most effectively read if you have the Excel file for this appendix open as you read and if you enter equations described into the cells suggested on the **DoItYourself** worksheet. The cubic cost curves derived in Section 11.4 are readily graphed, using Excel. This appendix focuses on the per-unit cost curves derived in that section, but the methods discussed here could just as easily produce a total cost graph. They also could be used to provide graphs of the Cobb-Douglas cost functions discussed in Section 11.5. This appendix assumes some familiarity with basic Excel functions, such as using absolute versus relative referencing, dragging equations, and using **Goal Seek**. (These topics are discussed in the Mathematical Appendix [available in the online version of this text] and in Chapter 19, but they are considered here as well.)

The discussion in this appendix relates to the Excel spreadsheet shown in Table 11A.1. Panel A in Table 11A.1 provides the actual Excel spreadsheet, and Panel B provides equations for seven "critical cells" (highlighted in yellow). If care is taken in entering the equations in these cells, then the equations can be dragged to create the entire spreadsheet. (Note that column widths in Panel B differ from Panel A to accommodate the size of each equation.) The blue cells have equations entered into them via dragging from above. Finally, the six green cells represent the data used to produce the graphs. Panel A includes two graphs in E1:I21. The first graph depicts the raw output, and the second provides a more finished presentation.

Consider the total cost function:

$$TC(Q) = 9800 + 760 \cdot Q - 12 \cdot Q^2 + 0.1 \cdot Q^3. \tag{11A.1}$$

Rather than typing numbers into equations (as you would do, for example, if you were entering Equations 11.8a–11.8d), it is more effective to place the cubic total cost parameters *a*, b, c, and d from Equation 11.6a in a data area at the top of the file and then use those parameters in building the equations (Equation 11.6a is reproduced in cell C1:D1). Place the values for *a*–d in cells A1:A4.

It is worthwhile to build a bit of flexibility into the file. If you are not familiar with the cost function under consideration, for example, it is worth having a parameter that provides the change in quantity between Q values so that the size of the graph can be easily adjusted (cell A5). The size of the quantity runner (in A8:A18) is readily adjusted in this instance by changing A5. We use dQ = 10 in the present instance because each of the minimums of MC, AVC, and ATC are captured over the range 0–100.

To build the quantity runner in this instance, simply start at Q = 0 (type the number 0 in cell A8). In cell A9, type the equation =A8+$A$5 (the $ signs fix the reference). Drag this from A9 to A18 by moving to the lower right corner of the cell and press down on the mouse once the crossed arrows turn into a + sign; then drag to A18. The number 100 will appear in cell A18. Click on cell A18, and the equation in that cell should be =A17+$A$5 (the lack of a dollar sign in the first term in the equation means that A8 has turned into A17, but A5 has remained fixed because cell A9 has been dragged to cell A18).

The per-unit cost equations can be entered using one equation for each per-unit cost function in cells B8, C8, and D9. Equations 11.6g, 11.6f, and 11.6d in the text are noted in cells B6:D6 for ease of reference. For example, marginal cost from Equation 11.6g is:

$$MC(Q) = b - 2 \cdot c \cdot Q + 3 \cdot d \cdot Q^2. \tag{11A.2a}$$

This is entered in cell B8 as:

=$A$2-2*$A$3*A8+3*$A$4*A8^2 **(11A.2b)**

Notice that each equation uses $ signs in front of the letter and number reference to each of the parameters b–d (A2:A4), but no $ signs in front of the letter or number reference to Q (A8). This means that when this equation is dragged to B18, the quantity values will change, but the coefficient values for b–d will remain fixed. Notice also that you

TABLE 11A.1 Cubic Per-Unit Costs in Excel

Panel A: Spreadsheet for cubic per-unit costs (see Panel B for formula key)

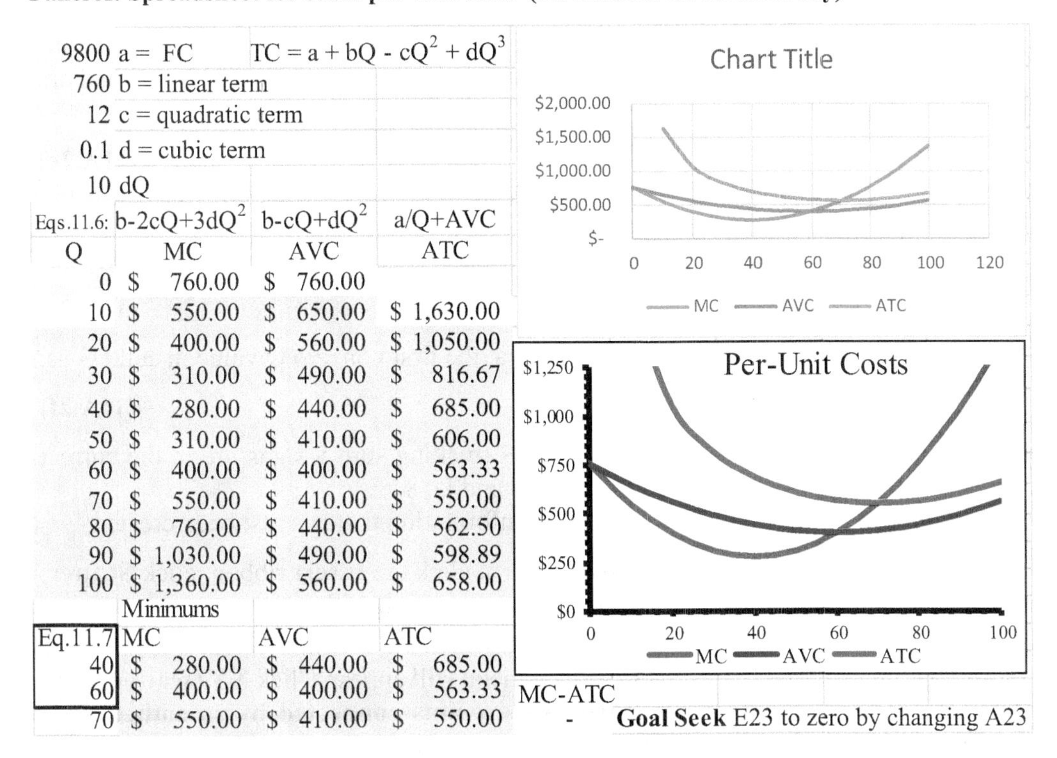

9800 a = FC	TC = a + bQ - cQ² + dQ³		
760 b = linear term			
12 c = quadratic term			
0.1 d = cubic term			
10 dQ			
Eqs.11.6:	b-2cQ+3dQ²	b-cQ+dQ²	a/Q+AVC
Q	MC	AVC	ATC
0	$ 760.00	$ 760.00	
10	$ 550.00	$ 650.00	$ 1,630.00
20	$ 400.00	$ 560.00	$ 1,050.00
30	$ 310.00	$ 490.00	$ 816.67
40	$ 280.00	$ 440.00	$ 685.00
50	$ 310.00	$ 410.00	$ 606.00
60	$ 400.00	$ 400.00	$ 563.33
70	$ 550.00	$ 410.00	$ 550.00
80	$ 760.00	$ 440.00	$ 562.50
90	$ 1,030.00	$ 490.00	$ 598.89
100	$ 1,360.00	$ 560.00	$ 658.00
	Minimums		
Eq.11.7	MC	AVC	ATC
40	$ 280.00	$ 440.00	$ 685.00
60	$ 400.00	$ 400.00	$ 563.33
70	$ 550.00	$ 410.00	$ 550.00

MC-ATC -
Goal Seek E23 to zero by changing A23

Panel B: Formulas for the (yellow) critical cells in Panel A

	A	B	C	D	E
1	9800 a = FC		Eq. 11.6a. TC(Q) = a + bQ - cQ² + dQ³		# of cells
2	760 b = linear term		Green cells require data entry.		6
3	12 c = quadratic term		Yellow cells require inputting critical equations.		7
4	0.1 d = cubic term		Blue cells with borders require dragging critical equa		47
5	10 ΔQ (size of the quantity runner)				
6	Eqs.11.6g,f,d:	MC(Q) = b-2cQ+3dQ²	AVC(Q) = b-cQ+dQ²	ATC(Q)=a/Q+AVC(Q)	
7	Q	MC	AVC	ATC	
8	0	=$A$2-2*$A$3*A8+3*$A$4*A8^2	=$A$2-$A$3*A8+$A$4*A8^2		
9	=A8+$A$5			=$A$1/A9+C9	
10					
11					
12					
13					
14					
15					
16					
17					
18					
19		Minimums			
20	Eq.11.7	MC	AVC	ATC	
21	=A3/(3*A4)				
22	=A3/(2*A4)				MC-ATC
23	100	**Goal Seek** MC-ATC (E23) to zero by changing Q (A23) to obtain minimum ATC.			=B23-D23

should not add spaces when entering equations in Excel. (If you are using the Excel file and click on this cell on the main worksheet, this equation is also shown in the **Formula Bar** [above the C|D column header to the right of ***fx***], since this shows the equation in the active cell.)

It is worth remembering that the minus sign in front of the linear term in marginal cost is because total cost was defined with a minus sign in front of the quadratic term $c \cdot Q^2$. This is simply the convention chosen for the text. Had we assumed a plus sign in front of this term, then c in cell A3 would have to be entered with a minus sign. Both conventions would have produced the same result (but the equations in B8 and C8 would have used a plus sign in front of the linear term [and the equations in cells A21 and A22 would both have led with a minus sign]).

The other two per-unit cost curves are entered in the same way. The specific equations for AVC in cell C8 and ATC in D9 are shown in those respective cells in Panel B and are reproduced here:

$$AVC(Q) = b - c \cdot Q + d \cdot Q^2. \quad \textbf{(11A.2c)}$$

This is entered in cell C8 as:

```
=$A$2-*$A$3*A8+*$A$4*A8^2
```
(11A.2d)

$$ATC(Q) = a/Q + AVC(Q). \quad \textbf{(11A.2e)}$$

ATC is not defined at Q = 0; therefore, we start at the first nonzero Q value in cell D9 as:

```
=$A$1/A9+C9
```
(11A.2f)

Once these equations are entered in C8 and D9 (making sure $ signs are in the correct positions), the equations can be dragged to C18 and D18.

The graph is readily obtained from the cost information that has just been created:

If using Excel 2007, highlight A7:D18 and then click the **Insert** ribbon, click **Scatter**, then click **Scatter with Smooth Lines**. The upper graph will appear.

If using Excel 2003, highlight A7:D18 and then click the **Chart Wizard** icon on the **Standard** toolbar. The Chart Wizard popup menu will appear. Click **XY (scatter)** from the Chart type menu and **Scatter with data points connected by smoothed lines without markers** from the Chart subtype menu. Click **Finish**, and the upper graph will appear.

The lower graph simply cleans up the preliminary version by adjusting axes, changing the color and width of curves, and adjusting the background and borders of the graph. Each of these tasks is easily accomplished by clicking on various parts of the graph.

The final part of Table 11A.1, in rows 21–23, obtains minimum values of each function. As noted in the text, two of these values are readily derived from the parameters of the total cost function. In particular, marginal cost is minimized when $Q = c/(3 \cdot d)$, and average variable cost is minimized when $Q = c/(2 \cdot d)$, according to Equations 11.7a and 11.7b. These equations are entered into cells A21 and A22, using the coefficients for c and d from cells A3 and A4. MC, AVC, and ATC are copied from an earlier row and pasted into cells B21:D21 and then dragged to B23:D23 to obtain values of each function at these output levels. Note that MC = AVC at minimum AVC, according to cells B22 and C22 (as expected).

This same strategy is used to find minimum ATC, as discussed in Table 11.1 in the chapter. A number is placed in cell A23 (since **Goal Seek** cannot work on an equation). The actual value is not important, as it simply provides a starting point for Excel's search process. (Recall that you reach **Goal Seek** by clicking **Data, What If Analysis, Goal Seek** in Excel 2007, or **Tools, Goal Seek** in Excel 2003.) The difference between ATC and MC is calculated in cell E23. Minimum ATC is found by Goal Seeking on cell E23 to zero by changing A23. The result is shown in the table: As expected, ATC = MC = $550 when Q = 70. The minimum value for each of the three curves is visually confirmed on the graph (but the quantity and dollar values cannot be seen with the same degree of accuracy in a graph). In this instance, the minimum MC, AVC, and ATC answers derived in rows 21–23 are also seen in rows 12, 14, and 15 because Q = 40, 60, and 70 in those rows.

PART 4

MARKET INTERACTION

Part 4 examines how the consumer information from Part 2 is combined with the producer information from Part 3 to determine a market outcome. We typically assume that firms wish to maximize profits, the difference between total revenue and total cost. The analysis in Part 3 focused, in large part, on the cost side of the profit calculation. Revenues depend both on the number of units sold and the price per unit. Since the relation between quantity sold and price requires demand information, the discussion of revenue was postponed until Part 4, where we reintroduce consumers into the analysis.

The profit-maximizing decision rule is the focus of Chapter 12. This rule holds, regardless of market structure; as a result, it is examined in a general setting. Of course, different markets have different market structures. Some goods are produced by many firms, which each produce a very small portion of total output; in other markets, one or a very small number of firms dominate the market. Perfectly competitive markets are markets where each individual firm and each individual consumer is "small," relative to the size of the market. Perfect competition is the starting point for most economic analysis, and it is examined in Chapters 13 and 14. Chapter 13 focuses on short-run profit maximization in perfectly competitive markets, and Chapter 14 examines perfect competition in the long run. Chapter 15 examines the opposite end of the spectrum—monopoly—as well as a third market structure: monopolistic competition that blends aspects of both monopoly and competition (as the name suggests). Chapter 16 concludes Part 4 with a discussion of the welfare impact of these market structures.

Profit Maximization in a General Setting

CHAPTER 12

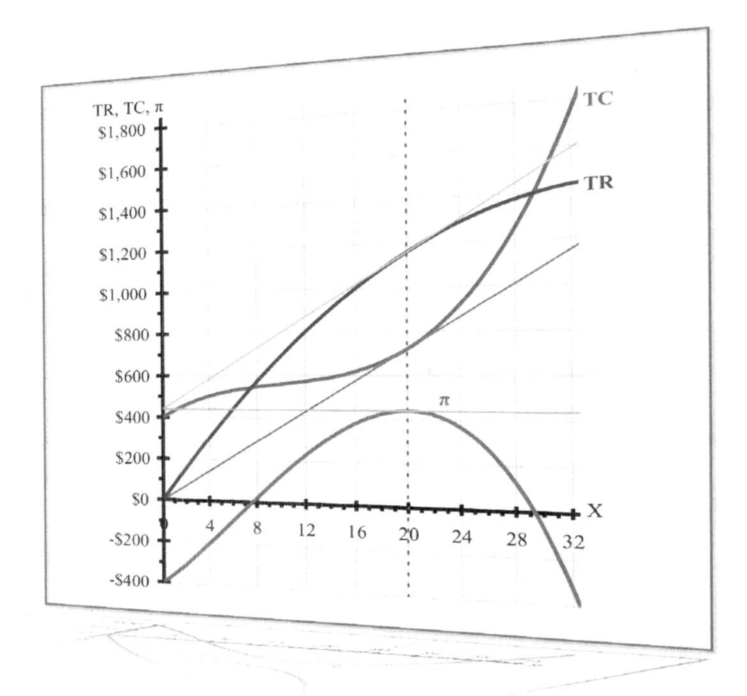

Chapter Outline

Just as an individual compares marginal value and marginal cost of goods to maximize utility, so must a firm compare the marginal benefit it obtains from producing a good with the marginal cost of producing that good to maximize profits. This chapter examines the marginal trade-offs that together allow a firm to achieve the best outcome it can, given the constraints it faces in the market. The rule identified in this chapter applies to any firm, regardless of market structure, as the firm attempts to achieve maximum profits. As we further define the market by imposing specific market structures on the firm (for example, in Chapters 13 and 14, we assume that the firm is embedded in a competitive industry, and in Chapter 15, we examine monopoly and monopolistic competition), the end results of the profit-maximization process appear different. In each case, the results are based on the same underlying profit-maximizing decision rule; that rule is the focus of this chapter.

In Chapter 12, we reintroduce consumers to the analysis. Market demand is the horizontal sum of individual demand curves. That result is delineated in Section 12.1. As we add consumers, we must be careful to recognize that, at different prices, different numbers of consumers are actively engaged in the market. Lower prices attract more consumers to the market. In the end, we model market demand, using smooth demand curves. Consumers demand goods based on the perceived value of those goods, but firms value the same goods based on the revenue that those goods can generate. Section 12.2 examines the relation between demand and revenue. More specifically, we examine the relation between demand, revenue, marginal revenue, and elasticity for a firm facing linear demand. In Section 12.3, we provide a symmetric analysis for a nonlinear demand function, the constant elasticity demand function. Section 12.4 lays out the comparison of revenue versus cost that forms the basis for profit maximization. The firm's ultimate goal is profit maximization; therefore, the firm's ultimate decision is to decide how much to produce. The profit-maximizing firm will increase production as long as the marginal revenue generated by the increased output exceeds the marginal cost of producing those units of output. Conversely, if the firm is producing at a point where incremental cost exceeds incremental revenue, then profits will increase by reducing production. Simply put, the profit-maximizing producer chooses that level of output where marginal revenue equals marginal cost.

12.1 Market Demand

Market demand is simply the sum of individual consumer demand curves. A simple example of this has already been seen in Chapter 7, where a two-person "economy" was analyzed via the Edgeworth Box. Of course, a two-person economy is an artificial construct; nonetheless, the same notion holds when we increase the number from two to many individuals. To make this specific, suppose there are n individuals who consume the good x at a price of P. Market demand at this price, X(P), is:

$$X(P) = x_1(P) + \ldots + x_n(P). \tag{12.1}$$

The capital X denotes the market, and the lowercase x_i for $i = 1, \ldots, n$, is individual i's demand. Economists call this a "horizontal sum," since individual demands are summed for a common price to obtain market demand at that price.

If each individual has the same demand, then the market demand is simply a stretched-out version of the individual demand. If each individual demands x(P), and there are n individuals in the market, then market demand in this situation is simply:

$$X(P) = n \cdot x(P). \tag{12.2a}$$

Market demand in this instance is a stretched-out version of individual demand because market demand is n times as far out at any given price; in terms of slope, if the slope of individual demand at price P is denoted m(P), then the slope of market demand, M(P), is:[1]

$$M(P) = m(P)/n. \tag{12.2b}$$

If different individuals have different demands, then the geometry of the situation is easier to see than the algebra. As a result, we start with the geometry.

The Geometry of Market Demand

Suppose we start with n individuals, each with a linear demand for x. Each demand curve can be described in terms of its P intercept and slope. These individuals can be numbered so that the one who has the highest P intercept is Individual 1, the one with the next highest is Individual 2, the next highest is Individual 3, and so on. To make this explicit, consider two assumptions about slope and intercept for each individual:

Assumption 1.1. Each individual's demand curve has a slope of –1.

Assumption 1.2. Each individual's price intercept is half that of the next highest individual's price intercept; thus, for example, Individual 1's intercept is $P_1^{max} = \$128$, $P_2^{max} = \$64$, $P_3^{max} = \$32$, and so on.

The first assumption is relatively innocuous; it simply says that each individual in the market would buy one more unit for every dollar price decrease faced. There is no reason to expect that the second assumption matches with an actual market, but it allows us to consider n different individuals without worrying about how large n is. (Further, if $n \leq 8$, then each individual's intercept is an integer, since $128 = 2^7$.) These intercepts are the highest price at which the individual is *"in the market."* At this price, this individual's demand is zero, but for any price lower than this price, the individual will purchase positive quantities of the good.

Figure 12.1 depicts demand by the first three individuals, as well as market demand (where the first six individuals' demands have been incorporated into the market demand curve). In Figure 12.1A, only two individuals are in the market at a price of \$48, and in Figure 12.1B, four individuals are in the market at a price of \$8. Market demand is constructed by horizontally summing individual demand curves. On segment **AB**, only Individual 1 is in the market (all others have demand of zero, since the price is above each individual's P intercept); on segment **BC**, two individuals are in the market; on segment **CD**, three individuals are in the market; and so on. In Figure 12.1A, Individual 1 has demand of 80, and Individual 2 has demand of 16; all other individuals have demand of zero at this price. Market demand is therefore 96, an amount that is marked off using the individual demands of 80 + 16 in the market demand diagram. You can also think of the demand curves being "added" to each other horizontally to obtain this result. Individual 1's demand point (the diamond at **G** = (80, \$48)) is on a line that extends through **AB** beyond **B**. The rest (**GH**) represents demand by Individual 2 of 16 units at this price. The **AG** part of market demand represents demand by Individual 1, and the segment **BH** represents adding Individual 2's demand to that of Individual 1's.

Figure 12.1B depicts a price of \$8 and market demand at point **E**. Answer the following questions, based on Figure 12.1B:

> **Q1a.** What is the demand by the fourth individual (whose individual demand curve is not shown) at a price of \$8?
>
> **Q1b.** What is the slope of the demand curve on the segment **DE**?
>
> **Q1c.** What is the slope of the demand curve on the segment **EF**?
>
> **Q1d.** Why do your answers to Q1b and Q1c differ?*

We see from our example in Figure 12.1 that if each individual has a slope of –1 and if there are k individuals in the market at this price, then the slope of market demand is –1/k. The reasoning is straightforward: Each of the k individuals in the market demand one more unit as price declines by \$1; demand increases by k. As a result, the slope of market demand is $M = \Delta P/\Delta X = -1/k$, according to Equation 12.2b. The only thing that would change if each individual had a slope of m instead of –1 is that the market demand when k individuals are in the market would be $M = m/k$, rather than $-1/k$.

Figure 12.2 examines what happens if individuals have different slopes of their demand curves, as well as different intercepts. To focus on slope differences, we restrict our analysis to two individuals, 1 and 2. Their individual demands are summed horizontally to obtain market demand. For prices above \$40, only Individual 2 is in the market (along segment **AB**), and for prices below \$40, both are in the market (along segment **BC**). Market demand has a kink at P = \$40 (at point **B**). Figure 12.2 depicts demand at a price of \$30. Individual 1 demands $x_1(\$30)$ = **EF** = 20 units, while Individual 2 demands $x_2(\$30)$ = **DE** = 35 units, for a total market demand of X(\$30) = **DF** = 55 units of output.

The slope of market demand is related to the slope of the individual demand curves, but that relation is a bit more complicated if individuals have different slopes. In Figure 12.2, Individual 1 has slope $m_1 = -1/2$, and Individual 2 has slope $m_2 = -2$. By construction, it is clear that market demand has a slope of –2 above P = \$40 (on **AB**) and a slope of –2/5

***Q1 answer:** At a price of \$8, demand by the fourth individual is 8. This can be seen in the difference between market demand of 208 and the sum of the first three individuals' demands (of 120, 56, and 24). This can also be seen based on the fourth individual's P intercept of \$16 and slope of –1. The slope on **DE** is –1/4, since there are four consumers in the market for prices above \$8, and the slope on **EF** is –1/5, since there are five consumers in the market for prices below \$8. These slopes differ because \$8 is the price at which we go from having four to five people in the market. You can verify these results, using the Excel file for Figure 12.1, by dropping price to \$7 and by raising price to \$9.

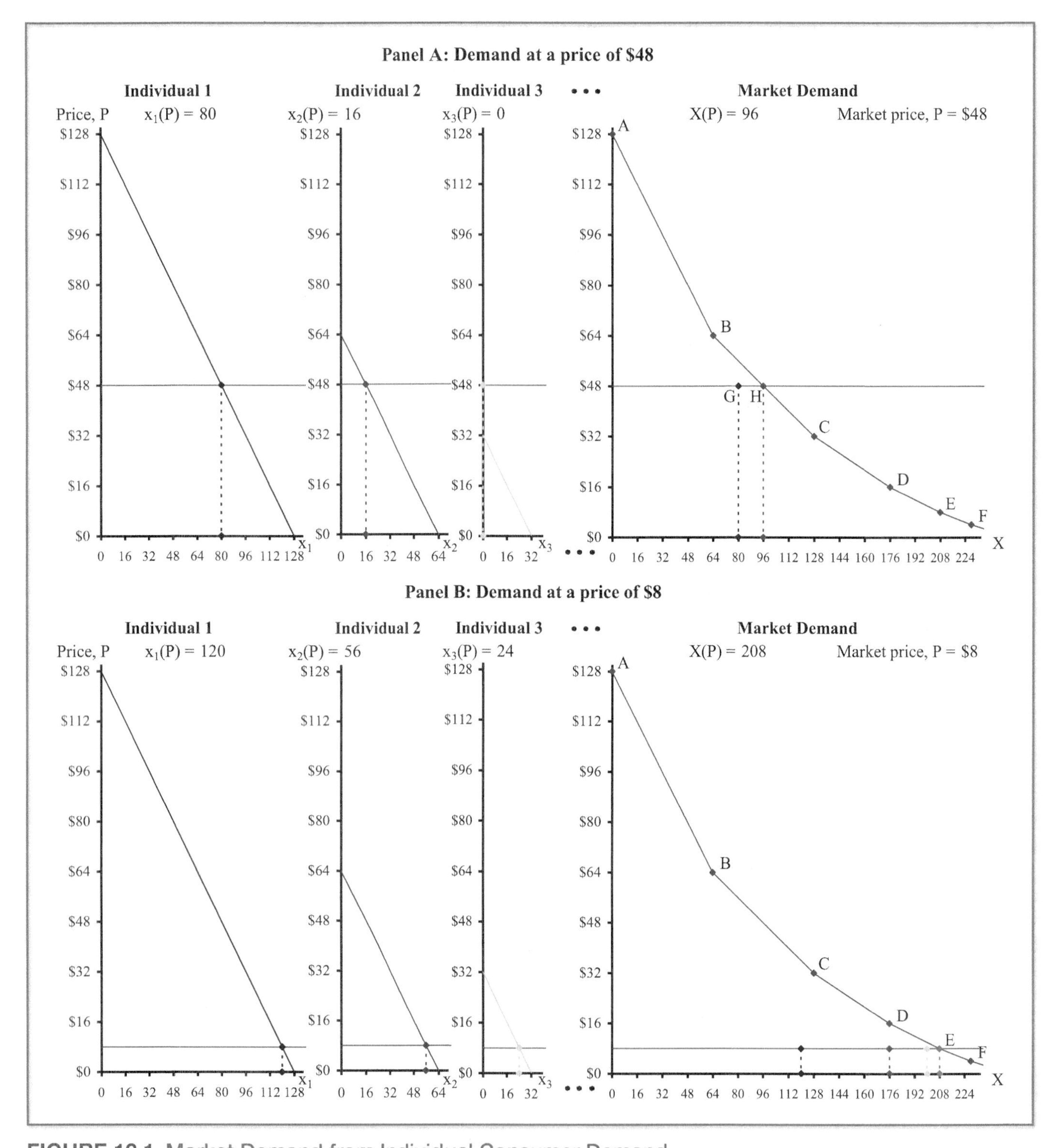

FIGURE 12.1 Market Demand from Individual Consumer Demand

Each individual's demand has the same slope.

below P = \$40 (because $\Delta P/\Delta x = -40/100 = -2/5$ from **B** to **C**). The **AB** slope is the same as Individual 2's slope, since Individual 2 is the only one in the market at prices above \$40. The **BC** slope on the market demand curve is obtained from the individual slopes as:

$$M_{BC} = 1/((1/m_1) + (1/m_2)) = 1/((1/(-1/2)) + (1/(-2)))$$
$$= 1/(-2 - 1/2) = -1/(5/2) = -2/5. \qquad \textbf{(12.3a)}$$

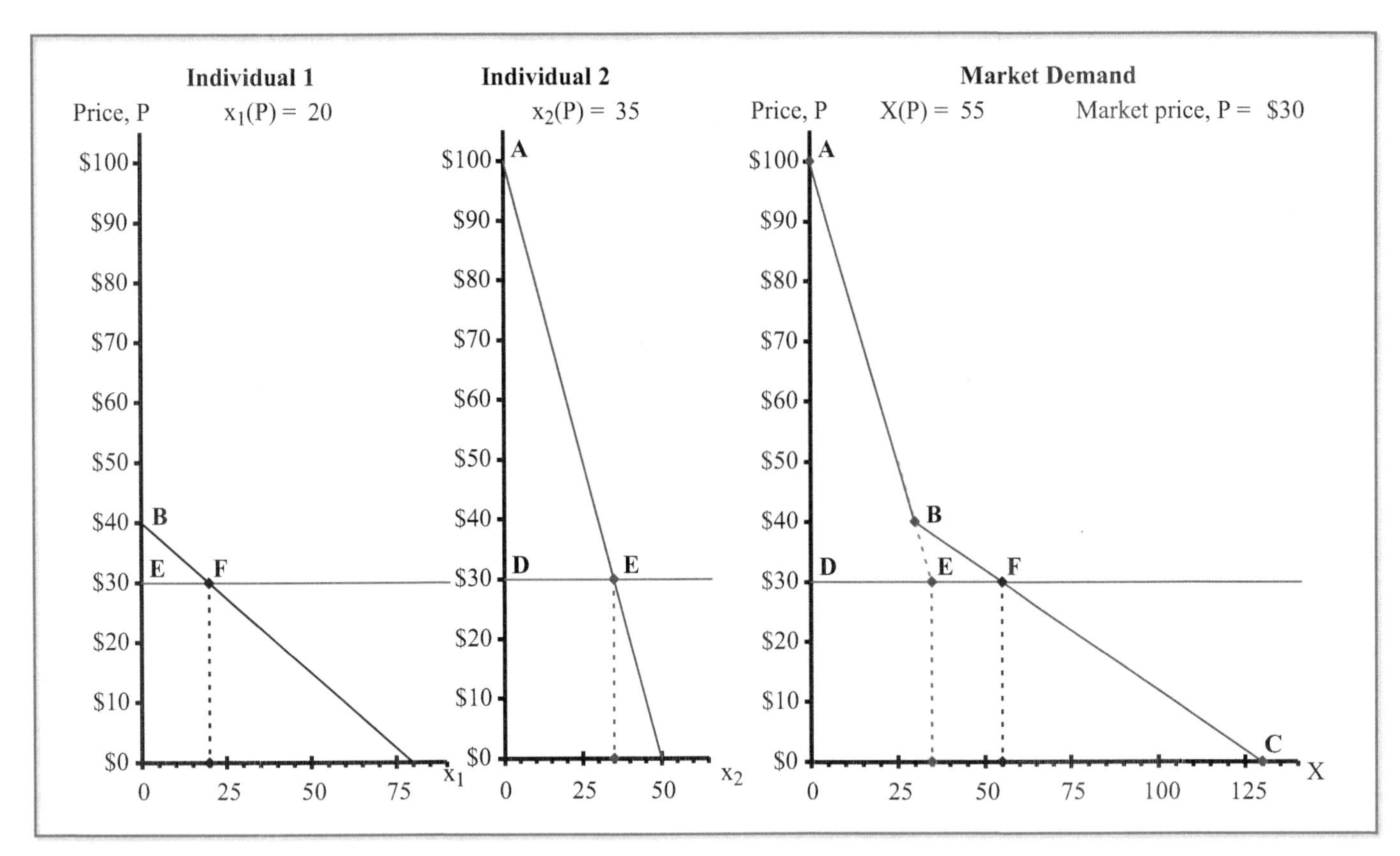

FIGURE 12.2 Market Demand from Individual Consumer Demand

Each individual's demand has a different slope.

More generally, the relation between the slope of market demand, M, and the slopes of the n individuals who are in the market at a given price, m_i, where i = 1, . . ., n, is given by:

$$M = 1/((1/m_1) + \ldots + (1/m_n)). \qquad \textbf{(12.3b)}$$

The multiplicity of reciprocals in this equation is disconcerting to look at but easy to understand if you simply consider how individuals react to a \$1 price decrease. Suppose, for example, that Individuals 1–4 have the following behavior in the face of a \$1 price decrease: Individual 1 consumes one more unit, Individual 2 consumes two more units, Individual 3 consumes three more units, and Individual 4 consumes four more units. If the market consists of these four individuals, then a \$1 price decrease leads to a 10-unit increase in demand (10 = 1 + 2 + 3 + 4). But the slope is simply $m = \Delta P/\Delta x$, so a \$1 price decrease is the same as –1 in the numerator of each fraction that calculates the individual's slope (where the denominator is the number of unit consumption increase). In our example: $m_1 = -1$; $m_2 = -1/2$; $m_3 = -1/3$; and $m_4 = -1/4$, with a market slope of $M = -1/10$. This is seen from Equation 12.3b as:

$$M = 1/((1/-1) + (1/(-1/2)) + (1/(-1/3)) + (1/(-1/4)))$$
$$= -1/(1 + 2 + 3 + 4) = -1/10. \qquad \textbf{(12.3c)}$$

The Algebra of Market Demand

Market demand is the horizontal sum of individual demand curves, according to Equation 12.1. We have worked through several examples of how we accomplish this horizontal summation from a geometric point of view. It remains to show how we accomplish the same task algebraically. The focus thus far has been on linear demand (to keep the mathematics simple), and we continue to use linear demand in this instance. Indeed, we approach the algebraic solution by examining the demand equations that form the basis for Figure 12.2.

The slope-intercept form of the demand equation is the most intuitive from a purely geometric perspective, but it is not *truly* a demand equation. The problem is that this equation describes price as a function of quantity, P(Q), but demand is quantity as a function of price, Q(P). Since demand is downward sloping, one relation may be obtained from the other by simply inverting the function. The slope-intercept version is formally called inverse demand. An **inverse demand curve** describes price as a function of quantity. This is also sometimes called an *inverse demand function* or a *marginal valuation schedule*.

inverse demand curve: An inverse demand curve describes price as a function of quantity.

Inverse demand curves are heavily used in welfare economics, a topic that is discussed at length in Chapter 16. Just like demand curves, inverse demand curves come in two varieties—individual and market. In the individual case, the price provided by P(Q) is the answer to the question: What is the marginal valuation of the *Q*th unit of output by the individual? In the market demand case, the price provided by P(Q) is the answer to the question: What is the marginal valuation of the *Q*th unit of output by the market as a whole (regardless of who purchases the *Q*th unit)? Demand curves and inverse demand curves should be thought of as two sides of the same coin, since they describe the same information from different orientations.

The inverse demand curves for Individuals 1 and 2 in Figure 12.2 are:

$$P(x_1) = 40 - 0.5 \cdot x_1. \quad \textbf{(12.4a)}$$

$$P(x_2) = 100 - 2 \cdot x_2. \quad \textbf{(12.4b)}$$

If we solve for x in each of these equations (that is, if we *invert* inverse demand), we obtain each individual's demand as a function of price:

$$x_1(P) = 80 - 2 \cdot P. \quad \textbf{(12.5a)}$$

$$x_2(P) = 50 - 0.5 \cdot P. \quad \textbf{(12.5b)}$$

If you look at the demand curves for Individuals 1 and 2 "sideways," you can see Equations 12.5a and 12.5b in Figure 12.2 (although, of course, we are not taught to look at graphs this way).[2] From here, market demand, based on Equation 12.1, is:

$$X(P) = x_1(P) + x_2(P) = (80 - 2 \cdot P) + (50 - 0.5 \cdot P) = 130 - 2.5 \cdot P. \quad \textbf{(12.6a)}$$

There is one problem with Equation 12.6a: It only works for $P \le 40$. Consider, for example, P = \$50. Equation 12.6a suggests that X(\$50) = 5, but Figure 12.2 shows that X(\$50) = 25. When the price exceeds 40, then Individual 1 drops from the market, and market demand reverts to Individual 2's demand. A complete version of market demand would be:

$X(P) = 0$	for $P \ge 100$	(above **A** in Figure 12.2).	
$X(P) = 50 - 0.5 \cdot P$	for $100 \ge P \ge 40$	(on **AB** in Figure 12.2).	**(12.6b)**
$X(P) = 130 - 2.5 \cdot P$	for $40 \ge P \ge 0$	(on **BC** in Figure 12.2).	

This can be rewritten as inverse demand to see slope and intercept in their standard form:

$P(X) = 100 - 2 \cdot X$	for $0 \le X \le 30$	(on **AB** in Figure 12.2).	
$P(X) = 52 - 0.4 \cdot X$	for $30 \le X \le 130$	(on **BC** in Figure 12.2).	**(12.6c)**
$P(X) = 0$	for $130 \le X$	(to right of **B** in Figure 12.2).	

Our earlier geometric analysis is confirmed by the algebraic analysis in Equation 12.6c. The slope on **AB** is –2, and the slope on **BC** is –0.4, using inverse demand in Equation 12.6c. Equation 12.3a also calculated a slope on **BC** of –2/5 = –0.4, using the reciprocal of sum of reciprocal slopes formula put forward in that equation.

Smoothing Out the Kinks in Market Demand

Demand curves derived in Chapter 7 often had kinks at price levels associated with boundary optimums. We have just seen that kinks can also occur as we horizontally add individual demand curves; as price declines, more individuals enter the market. *As we*

Price, P	Individuals in Market	For Prices P′ within $2 of P = $50	Slope of Market Demand		
			Decimal	*Fraction*	X(P)
$50	25	$52 > P′ > $50	0.04	1/25	650
	26	$50 > P′ > $48	0.0384615	1/26	

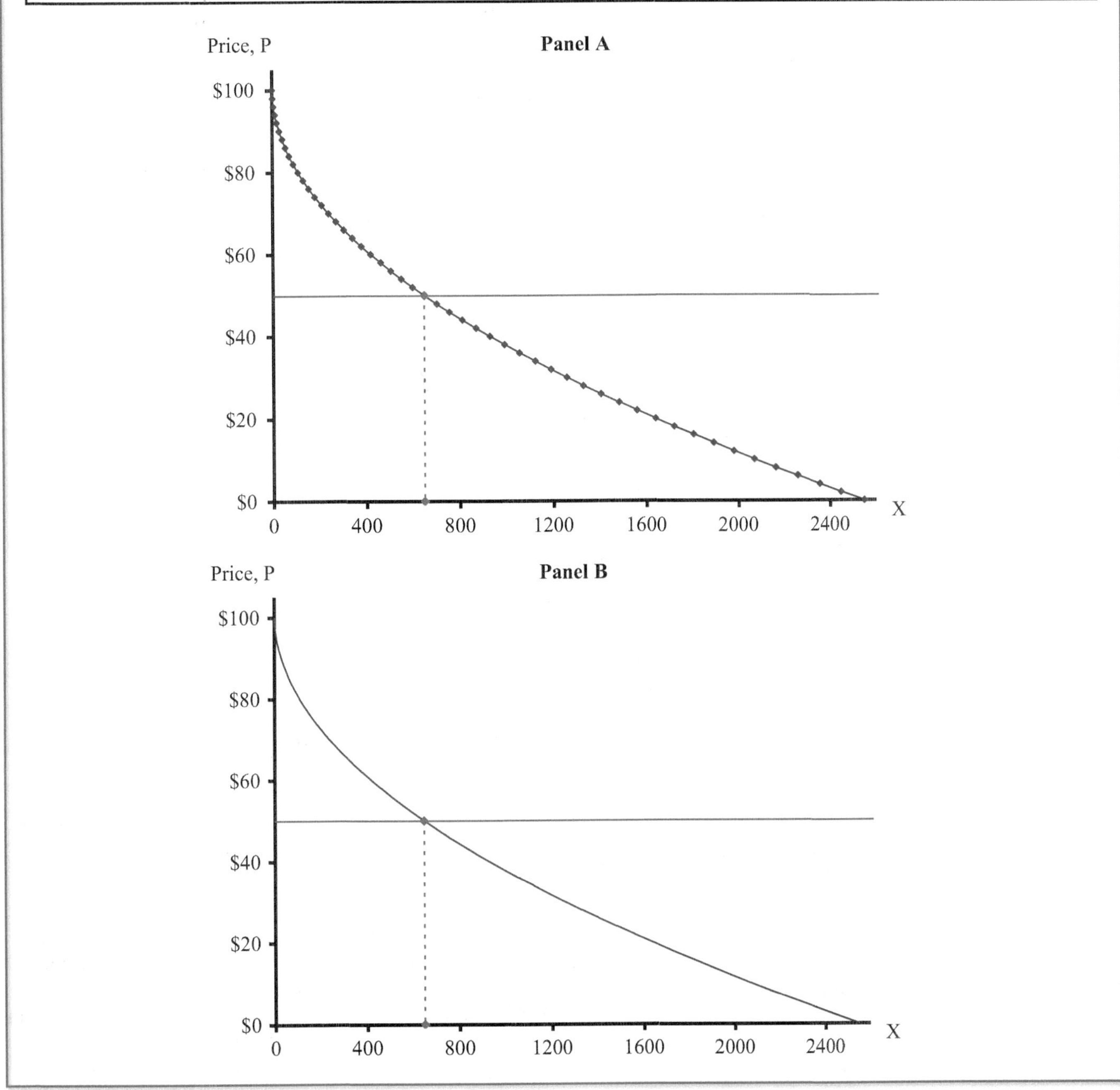

FIGURE 12.3 Market Demand Based on 50 Individuals with One Individual Each Whose P Intercept on the Demand Curve Is at 2, 4, . . ., 100

Each individual's demand has a slope of −1.

add more individuals to the market, the kinks will, for all intents and purposes, disappear. The easiest way to see this is to examine one final horizontal sum of individual demand curves in Figure 12.3.

Consider a market composed of 50 individuals, ordered as in Figure 12.1 according to the height of their price intercept. These individuals' demand curves can be described by the following two assumptions:

Assumption 3.1. Each individual's demand curve has slope of –1.

Assumption 3.2. Each individual's price intercept is \$2 less than that of the next highest individual's price intercept; thus, for example, Individual 1's intercept is $P_1^{max} = \$100$; $P_2^{max} = \$98$; $P_3^{max} = \$96$, and so on.

Assumption 3.1 is the same as Assumption 1.1. Assumption 3.2 is based on a linear decline in intercept, rather than a geometric decline implicit in Assumption 1.2. Market demand based on these assumptions is shown in Figure 12.3. Also shown is a price of \$50, a price for which half of the individuals are in the market, and half are not. Figure 12.3A has diamonds at each kink; the diamonds are removed in Figure 12.3B to depict a "curve" without the kink (Q, P) points shown. Market demand is actually a series of 50 connected line segments, where the *k*th line segment has slope 1/k. Despite its actual piecewise linear shape, the curve is, for all intents and purposes, a smooth demand curve.[3]

We will typically work with market demand curves that are smooth. This makes the algebraic solutions simpler because it is easier to work with a single function than with a series of functions that apply over-restricted values of price and quantity (such as was the case for the market demand or inverse demand in Equations 12.6b and 12.6c, whose graphic representation is Figure 12.2). Indeed, we will often go even further and assume that market demand is linear, since the mathematics then is particularly easy, and little is lost by assuming that this is the case.

12.2 Demand and Revenue

Demands for goods are based on consumers' perceived value of those goods. The money consumers spend on goods represents a cost to consumers, but from the firm's perspective, these consumer demands are valuable because they produce revenue. Regardless of market structure, a firm views the demand for its product in terms of the revenues that the demand it faces can produce.

Unless the firm is a monopolist, it does not face the entire market demand for a product; it shares the market with other firms. As a result, in a general setting, the firm's perceived demand is predicated on what it expects other firms to do in response to its actions. Much of the analysis of oligopoly markets centers on modeling how one firm acts, based on the expected reaction of its interdependent rivals to its actions. We examine these issues in Chapter 20; we do not focus on those interdependencies here. Instead, we simply assume that a firm is able to determine, at a conceptual level, the demand curve it faces.

Individual demand is a multivariate function of prices and income, but an individual demand curve is represented on a two-dimensional graph, holding all but the price of the product constant. Market demand is similarly a multivariate function of prices and income (or more accurately, a distribution of income), but we typically assume that all factors affecting demand, except the price of the product, are held constant so that we can describe market demand in (X, P) space. Similarly, the demand curve faced by a firm, x(P), holds all but the price of the product constant so that it may also be described in a two-dimensional fashion. In this section, we restrict our analysis to linear demand to focus on the general relation between demand, revenue, marginal revenue, and elasticity.

Demand, Total Revenue, and Elasticity

Suppose a firm faces the linear inverse demand curve:

$$P(x) = b - m \cdot x. \qquad \textbf{(12.7a)}$$

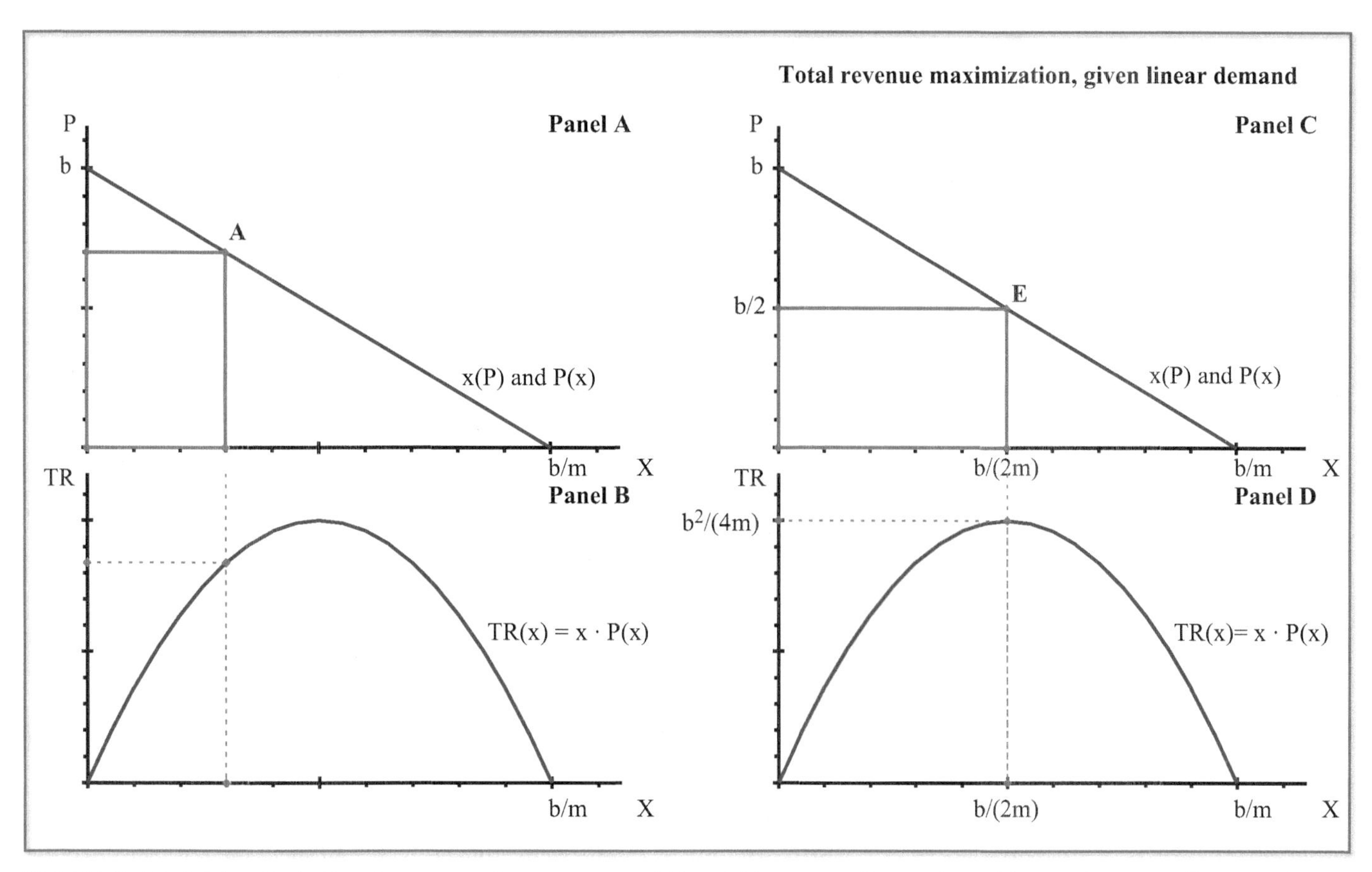

FIGURE 12.4 The Relation between Demand and Total Revenue (Based on Linear Inverse Demand: $P(x) = b - m \cdot x$)

Price b is the price at which the firm is first able to sell the good (or just not able to sell the good). As price decreases by \$1 from there, the firm sells 1/m more units of output. (This may seem counterintuitive, but recall that the slope is $-m = \Delta P/\Delta x$; the question in the last sentence asks: What is the value of $\Delta x/\Delta P$ when $\Delta P = -1$? The answer is 1/m.) This implies that the x intercept, when $P = 0$, occurs at $x = b/m$, as shown in Figure 12.4, which depicts the linear demand relation for general values of b and m.

If demand is linear, then total revenue is quadratic in quantity. Total revenue is simply price times quantity, so total revenue as a function of quantity is:

$$TR(x) = P(x) \cdot x = b \cdot x - m \cdot x^2. \quad \textbf{(12.7b)}$$

Since the quadratic coefficient is negative (–m), total revenue is a parabola pointed downward (dome shaped). The absence of a constant term in Equation12.7b signifies that the parabola passes through (Q, \$) = (0, \$0); total revenue is zero when no units are sold. Figures 12.4A–12.4D all show total revenue. In the (per-unit) Figures 12.4A and 12.4C, total revenue is the size of the pink rectangle from (0, 0) to (x, P(x)) on the demand curve. In the (total) Figures 12.4B and 12.4D, total revenue is the height of the total revenue hill at that output level. Figures 12.4A and 12.4B represent an output level where increasing output increases revenue, and Figures 12.4C and 12.4D represent the total revenue-maximizing level of output.

Given linear demand, total revenue will *always* be maximized halfway down the demand curve at $(x, P) = (b/(2 \cdot m), b/2)$. It is easy to show that this is the point of unitary elasticity of demand.[4] Recall that one of the methods of calculating elasticity described in Chapter 2 is Equation 2.2, which relates elasticity and slope, $\varepsilon_x = (1/\text{slope}) \cdot (P/Q)$. Given this, we see that total revenue is maximized when demand has unitary elasticity:

$$\varepsilon_x = (1/\text{slope}) \cdot (P/Q) = (1/(-m)) \cdot ((b/2)/(b/(2 \cdot m)) = (-1/m) \cdot m = -1. \quad \textbf{(12.8a)}$$

FIGURE 12.5 How Elasticity Varies along a Linear Demand Curve

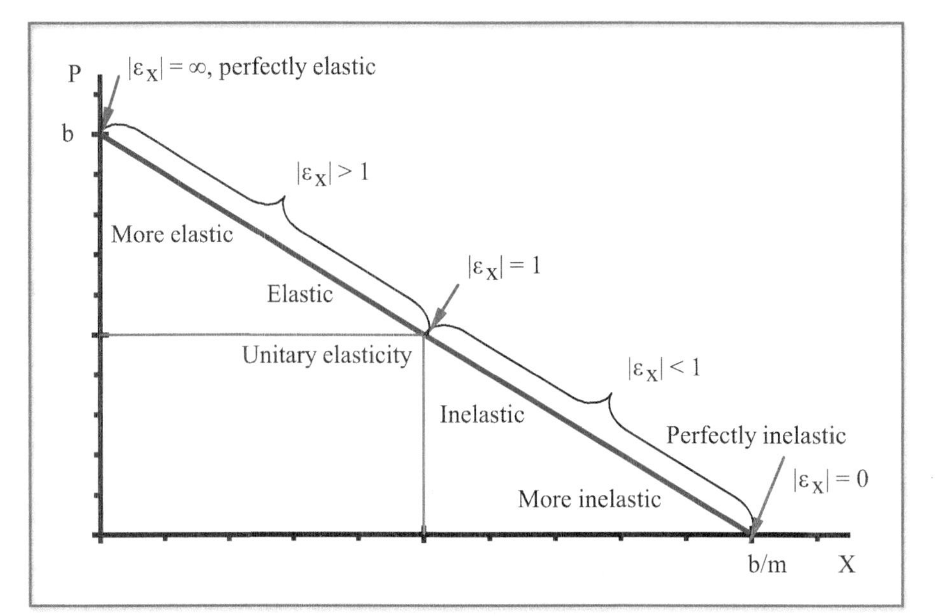

Often, you will see own-price elasticity of demand discussed in terms of absolute values, in which case the minus sign is implied; unitary elasticity is also described as $|\varepsilon_x| = 1$. In this view, own-price elasticity is thought of in terms of magnitude.[5] More generally, we see that at any point on the demand curve, elasticity is given by:

$$\varepsilon_x = (1/(-m)) \cdot ((b - m \cdot x)/x) = 1 - (b/m)/x \text{ for any x in the range } 0 \leq x \leq b/m. \quad \textbf{(12.8b)}$$

We see from Equation 12.8b that elasticity declines as x increases along a linear demand curve. When $x = 0$ (at the P intercept point (0, b)), demand is infinitely elastic. It remains elastic as long as $x < b/(2 \cdot m)$, since $\varepsilon_x < -1$ (or to say the same thing in a more intuitive fashion, $|\varepsilon_x| > 1$). Demand is inelastic when $x > b/(2 \cdot m)$, since $\varepsilon_x > -1$ (or to say the same thing in a more intuitive fashion, $|\varepsilon_x| < 1$). Finally, demand is perfectly inelastic, $\varepsilon_x = 0$, when $x = b/m$ (since $P = 0$ in this instance).[6] These conclusions are perhaps best visualized along the demand curve itself. As a result, Figure 12.4C has been reproduced as Figure 12.5 with elasticity information delineated on the graph.

Demand and Marginal Revenue

An alternative way to examine how revenue changes as we change output is to ask: What revenue is gained and what revenue is lost as more output is sold? For a firm facing a downward-sloping demand curve, an increase in units sold creates revenue on those incremental units, but at the cost of having to reduce the price on all units sold (since demand is downward sloping). We can see this graphically by altering Figure 12.4A to consider a change in quantity sold.

Suppose we start with sales of x_0, and we end with sales of $x_1 > x_0$ units sold. This change can be thought of in terms of the three rectangles in Figure 12.6. Initially, total revenue is P_0x_0 or area **A** + **B**, but the output increase causes total revenue to become P_1x_1 or area **B** + **C**. The increase in output ($\Delta x = x_1 - x_0$) increases revenue by $P \cdot \Delta x$ (area **C**) at a cost of the reduced price ($\Delta P = P_1 - P_0$) on all units sold, given by $x \cdot \Delta P$ (area **A**); the change in total revenue is $P \cdot \Delta x + x \cdot \Delta P$ (the sign of the second term is negative since $\Delta P < 0$ when $\Delta x > 0$). In terms of areas, ΔTR = area **C** – **A**. Since demand is elastic in this range of output, area **C** > area **A**, so the change in total revenue is positive. Had x_0 been at a point on the inelastic part of the demand curve, then the opposite would be true.

The change in total revenue is the difference between area **C** and area **A** in Figure 12.6. These rectangles have different lengths and widths, but we can construct a new rectangle, **A′**, that has an area of **A** but is Δx units wide. If **A′** is subtracted from **C**, then the remainder is a geometric representation of the change in total revenue caused by a change in

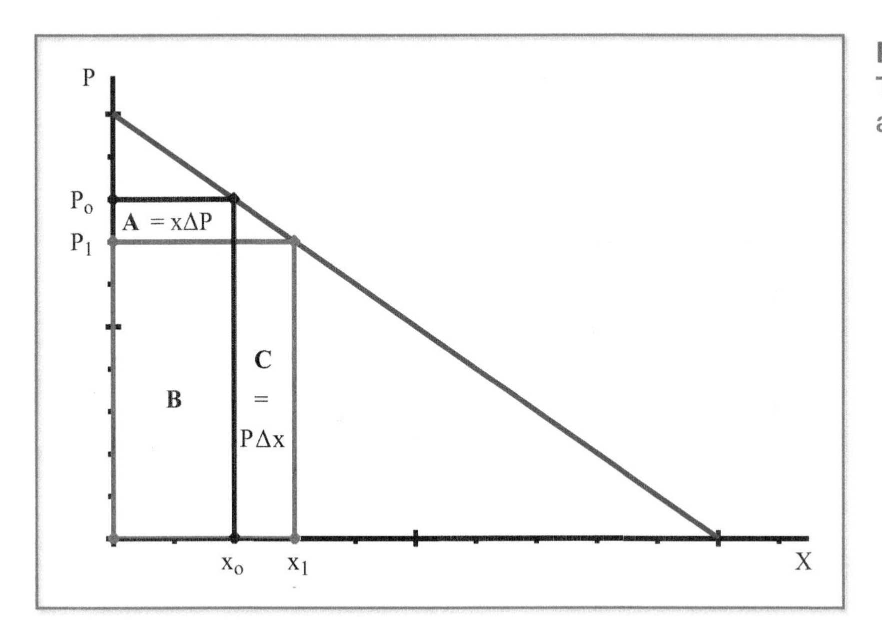

FIGURE 12.6 How Total Revenue Changes as Quantity Changes

sales of Δx units. This is shown in Figure 12.7A as area **D**; area **D** represents the change in total revenue produced by increasing production by Δx, ΔTR = area **D**. If we let the height of rectangle **D** be denoted by d, then

$$\Delta TR = d \cdot \Delta x. \qquad \textbf{(12.9a)}$$

We can use this description of change in total revenue to obtain estimated marginal revenue. **Estimated marginal revenue (MR_e)** is calculated as the rate of change in revenue for a discrete change in output. Algebraically, this is given by:

estimated marginal revenue (MR_e): Estimated marginal revenue is calculated as the rate of change in revenue for a discrete change in output.

$$MR_e = \Delta TR/\Delta x = (P_1x_1 - P_0x_0)/(x_1 - x_0).$$

Given the change in total revenue in Equation 12.9a, we obtain a geometric description of MR_e by dividing both sides of Equation 12.9a by Δx:

$$MR_e = \Delta TR/\Delta x = d. \qquad \textbf{(12.9b)}$$

The height of the rectangle **D** is an approximate value of marginal revenue. This is estimated, since it is based on a discrete change in output, Δx. Actual marginal revenue is the slope of total revenue (just as all of the other "marginals" in the text are the slopes of their respective "totals"). We examine the geometry and algebra of marginal revenue momentarily, but Figure 12.7B provides a preview of the result. The downward-sloping green line is marginal revenue. The dynamic version of this figure allows you to vary the size of the change in output, Δx. As you do, you will note that marginal revenue passes through the line separating area **A′** and area **D** at its midpoint in each instance; two examples are shown in Figures 12.7B and 12.7C.

Total Revenue, Marginal Revenue, and Elasticity

The total revenue diagram provides an alternative view of the relation between the two versions of marginal revenue. Figure 12.8 shows both a per-unit diagram and a total diagram of these relations. The change in x used in estimating marginal revenue may take on an infinite number of values; therefore, there is no unique value of MR_e.[7] MR_e is the slope of the red chord connecting points (x_0, TR(x_0)) and (x_1, TR(x_1)) on the total revenue hill, according to the definition of MR_e (since slope of the chord is ΔTR/Δx). MR_e is calculated over an interval, and its value is quite close to the actual marginal revenue for the midpoint of that interval (this is why the green marginal revenue curve appears to intersect the line separating **A′** and **D** halfway between x_0 and x_1 in Figures 12.7B and 12.7C). **Marginal revenue (MR)** at a given output level is the slope of total revenue at that output level.

marginal revenue (MR): Marginal revenue at a given output level is the slope of total revenue at that output level.

FIGURE 12.7 Deriving Marginal Revenue from Demand

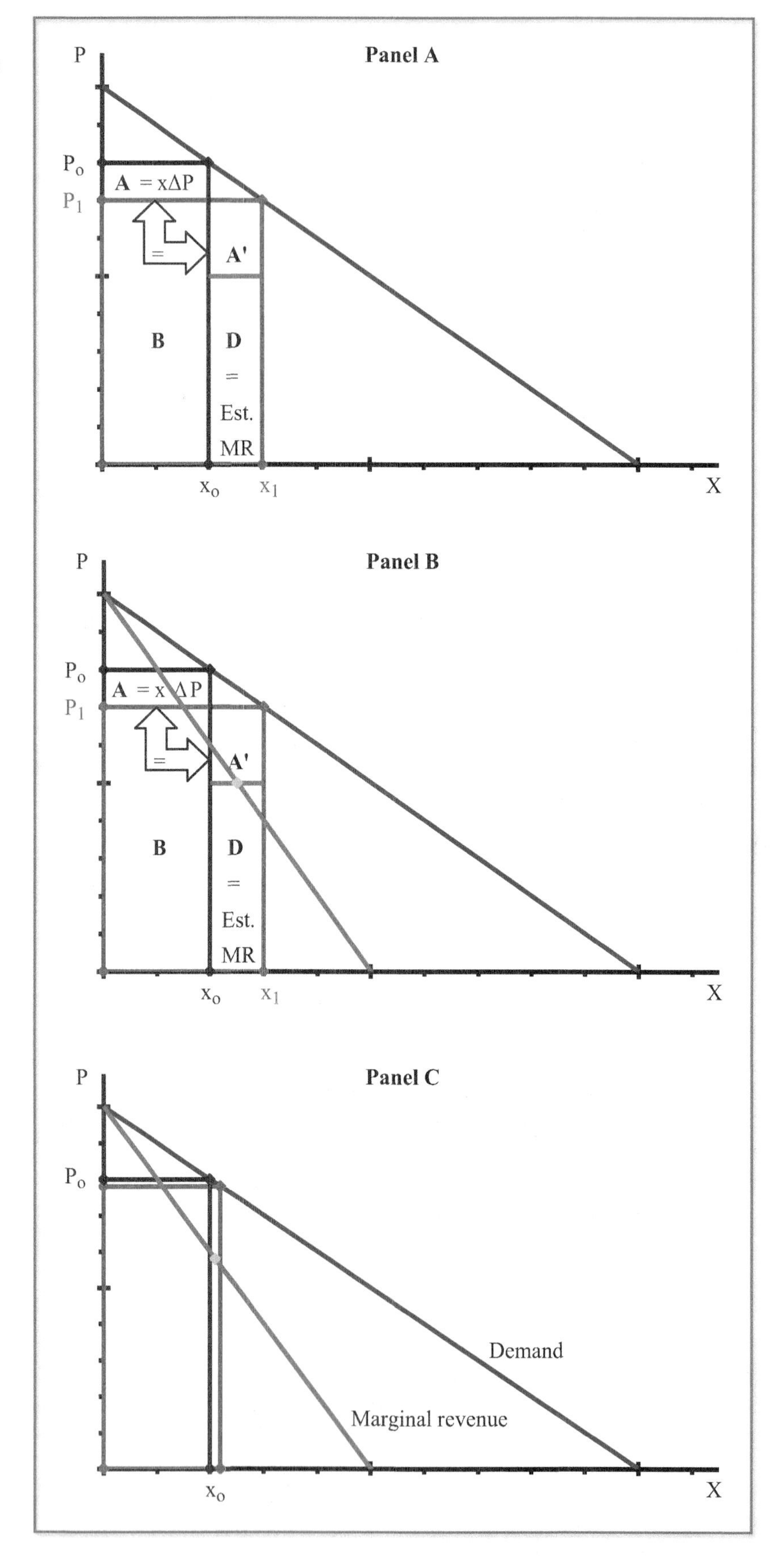

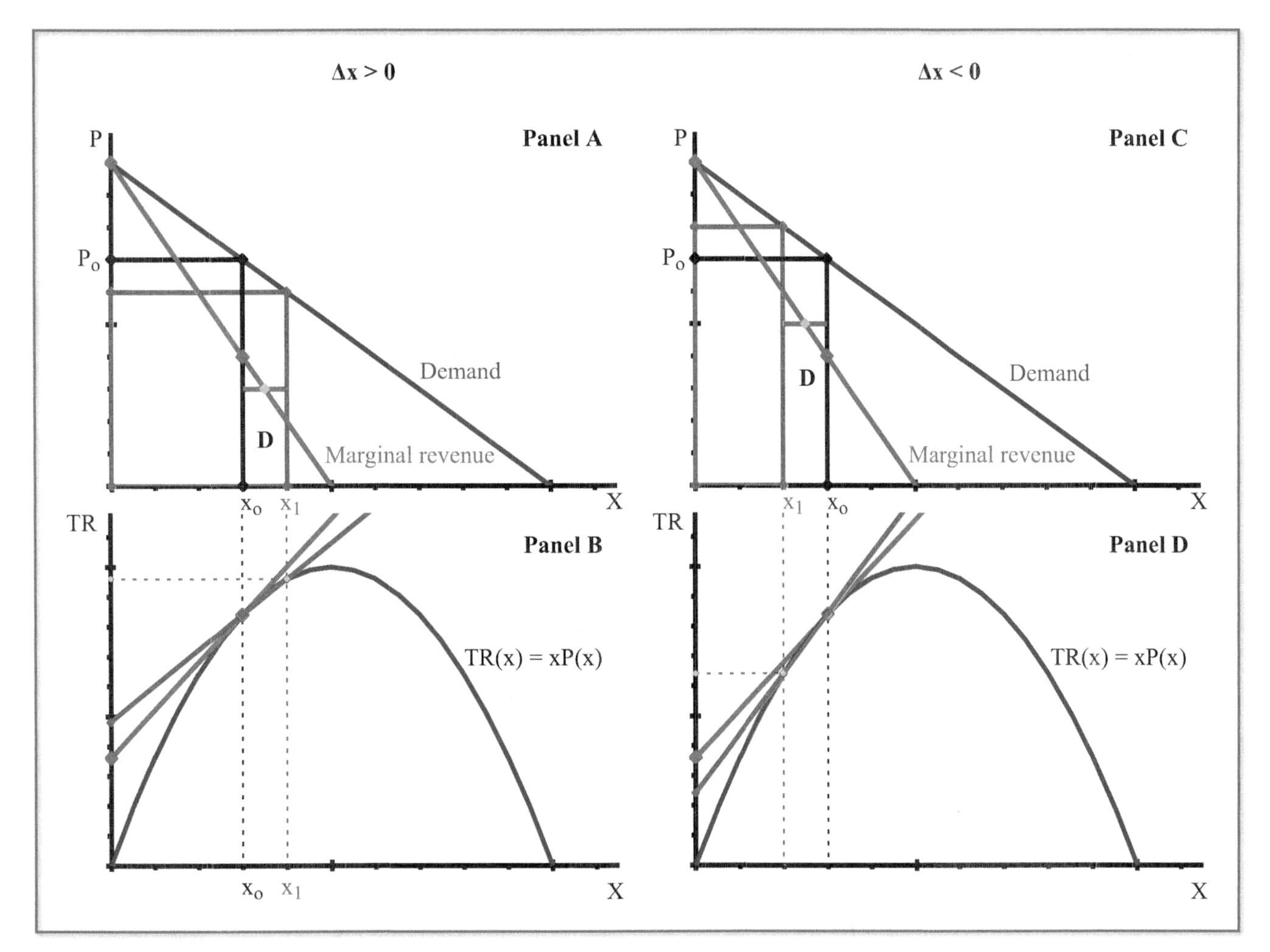

FIGURE 12.8 Deriving Marginal Revenue from Total Revenue

Figure 12.8 depicts MR_e versus actual MR for two values of Δx, one positive and one negative. Figures 12.8A and 12.8B depict a positive Δx; MR_e is less than actual MR. This is seen in two ways. The height of the rectangle **D** is $d = MR_e$ from Equation 12.9b. In Figure 12.8A, $MR_e < MR(x_0)$, as measured by the green MR curve. In Figure 12.8B, the same comparison is seen because the slope of the red chord (MR_e) is smaller than the slope of the green tangent to total revenue at x_0 ($MR(x_0)$). The reverse holds true when $\Delta x < 0$, according to Figures 12.8C and 12.8D. The height of rectangle **D** is higher than $MR(x_0)$ in Figure 12.8C, and the red chord is steeper than the green tangent in Figure 12.8D ($MR_e > MR(x_0)$). The Excel file for Figure 12.8 allows you to vary the magnitude of Δx between these bounds; as you do this, you will find that as Δx gets closer and closer to zero, MR_e gets closer and closer to actual MR.

We can calculate MR algebraically, given linear demand. Given $x_1 = x_0 + \Delta x$, and total revenue in Equation 12.7b, we obtain:

$$\Delta TR = TR(x_1) - TR(x_0).$$

$$\Delta TR = b \cdot (x_0 + \Delta x) - m \cdot (x_0 + \Delta x)^2 - (b \cdot x_0 - m \cdot x_0^2). \quad \textbf{(12.10a)}$$

$$\Delta TR = b \cdot \Delta x - 2 \cdot m \cdot x_0 \cdot \Delta x - m \cdot \Delta x^2.$$

Dividing by Δx, we obtain MR_e, given linear demand:

$$MR_e = \Delta TR/\Delta x = b - 2 \cdot m \cdot x_0 - m \cdot \Delta x. \quad \textbf{(12.10b)}$$

FIGURE 12.9 Negative Marginal Revenue

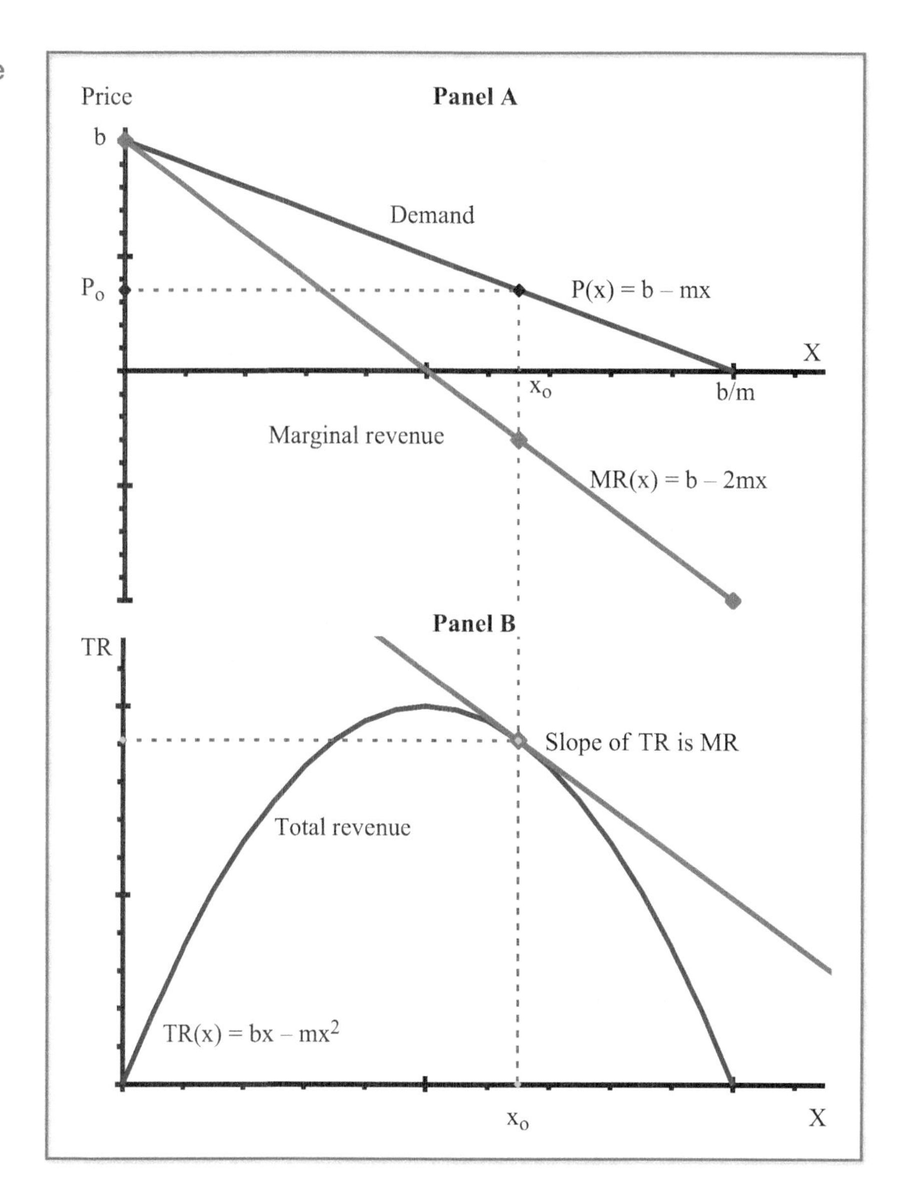

Actual MR is the limiting value of MR_e as Δx approaches zero (look at this using the Excel file for Figure 12.8). As Δx approaches zero, MR_e becomes actual MR, since the last term, $-m \cdot \Delta x$, tends to zero as Δx tends to zero. This leaves MR *at* output level x_0:

$$MR(x_0) = b - 2 \cdot m \cdot x_0. \quad \textbf{(12.11)}$$

The result is easy to remember: If you begin with linear inverse demand $P(x) = b - m \cdot x$, then MR is given by $MR(x) = b - 2 \cdot m \cdot x$. *MR has the same P intercept and twice the slope as inverse demand.* (This rule is often given in introductory microeconomics textbooks, so it may seem familiar.[8])

A comparison of Equations 12.10b and 12.11 confirms the geometric discussion surrounding Figure 12.8. When $\Delta x > 0$, $MR_e < MR(x_0)$, since $-m \cdot \Delta x < 0$ (algebraically confirming the fact that the red chord in Figure 12.8B is flatter than the green tangent). And when $x_1 < x_0$, so that $\Delta x < 0$, $MR_e > MR(x_0)$, since $-m \cdot \Delta x > 0$ (algebraically confirming the fact that the red chord in Figure 12.8D is steeper than the green tangent).

MR is related to elasticity. MR is positive if an increase in output increases total revenue. This occurs when demand is elastic (and area **C** > area **A** in Figure 12.6). MR is equal to zero when demand is unitary (and area **C** = area **A** in Figure 12.6). We saw that demand has unitary elasticity, given linear demand at $x = b/(2 \cdot m)$ in Figure 12.5, and this output level maximizes total revenue in Figures 12.4C and 12.4D. This same result is easily derived from Equation 12.11 by setting $MR(x) = 0$ and solving for x (at the top of the hill $MR(x) = 0$). Finally, when MR is negative, an increase in output decreases total revenue. This occurs when demand is inelastic (and area **C** < area **A** in Figure 12.6).

We restrict the demand diagram to the positive quadrant, since negative prices or quantities do not make economic sense, but MR is negative whenever demand is inelastic. Figure 12.9 depicts a situation where MR is negative. In the Excel file for this figure, the slider allows you to vary x across the entire range of output to tie the two diagrams together.

We see that demand, elasticity, total revenue, and marginal revenue are intimately related. These relations have been derived based on an assumption of linear demand.

But, of course, demand need not be linear; linear demand was chosen because it is particularly simple to work with from an algebraic and geometric point of view. We now turn to a nonlinear functional form that is also particularly easy to work with—constant elasticity demand.

12.3 Constant Elasticity Demand *OPTIONAL SECTION*

We saw in Figure 12.5 that demand varies along the linear demand curve, taking on the entire range of values of elasticity—from perfectly elastic ($\varepsilon_x = -\infty$) to perfectly inelastic ($\varepsilon_x = 0$). At the opposite end of the spectrum of elasticity movements, we find the constant elasticity demand function:

$$x(P) = a \cdot P^{-b}. \qquad \textbf{(12.12a)}$$

For demand to be downward sloping, P's exponent must be less than zero. Therefore, the minus sign is provided, and $b > 0$ (so that $-b < 0$). The parameter, a, is a scaling factor that determines the magnitude of demand, and the exponent, $-b$, is the price elasticity of demand, $-b = \varepsilon_x$. Of course, it should not be at all obvious that $-b$ is the price elasticity of demand; proving this assertion requires calculus.[9] We have already seen an example of a constant elasticity demand function in Part 2 of the text: Cobb-Douglas preferences produce demand curves that have constant unitary elasticity of demand (Equation 7.3a, for example, can be rewritten as $x(P_x, P_y, I) = r \cdot I/P_x = a \cdot P^{-b}$ by setting $a = r \cdot I$, $P = P_x$, and $b = 1$).[10]

We may obtain total revenue in this instance in the same way we obtained total revenue based on linear demand: Multiply inverse demand times quantity. Inverse demand is obtained by solving for P in Equation 12.12a:

$$P(x) = (1/a)^{(-1/b)} \cdot x^{(-1/b)} = a^{(1/b)} \cdot x^{(-1/b)} = K \cdot x^{(-1/b)}. \qquad \textbf{(12.12b)}$$

Total revenue is then $P(x) \cdot x$, or:

$$TR(x) = x \cdot a^{(1/b)} \cdot x^{(-1/b)} = K \cdot x^{(1-(1/b))}. \qquad \textbf{(12.12c)}$$

As shown in the Chapter 12 Appendix, marginal revenue in this instance is:

$$MR(x) = (1 - (1/b)) \cdot a^{(1/b)} \cdot x^{(-1/b)} = (1 - (1/b)) \cdot K \cdot x^{(-1/b)}. \qquad \textbf{(12.12d)}$$

When the constant elasticity demand function has unitary elasticity, $MR = 0$ (since $1 - (1/b) = 0$ if $|\varepsilon_x| = b = 1$). In this instance, a constant amount is spent on the good; this is the Cobb-Douglas result described in Equation 7.4. When the constant elasticity demand function is inelastic, marginal revenue is negative, and total revenue is a declining function of output (since $1 - (1/b) < 0$ in Equations 12.12c and 12.12d if $|\varepsilon_x| = b < 1$). Finally, when the constant elasticity demand function is elastic, total revenue is an increasing function of output, and marginal revenue is positive (since $1 - (1/b) > 0$ in Equations 12.12c and 12.12d if $|\varepsilon_x| = b > 1$).

The relation between inverse demand and marginal revenue described by Equations 12.12b and 12.12d is instructive. MR is proportional to inverse demand (the factor of proportionality is $1 - (1/b)$). When demand is elastic, MR is a fraction of inverse demand (since $0 < 1-(1/b) < 1$ if $b > 1$). Figure 12.10 depicts two examples: $b = 2$ and $b = 4$. When $b = 2$ in Figure 12.10A, marginal revenue (the green curve) is half the height of inverse demand (the blue curve) for every output level. In Figure 12.10B, $b = 4$, and marginal

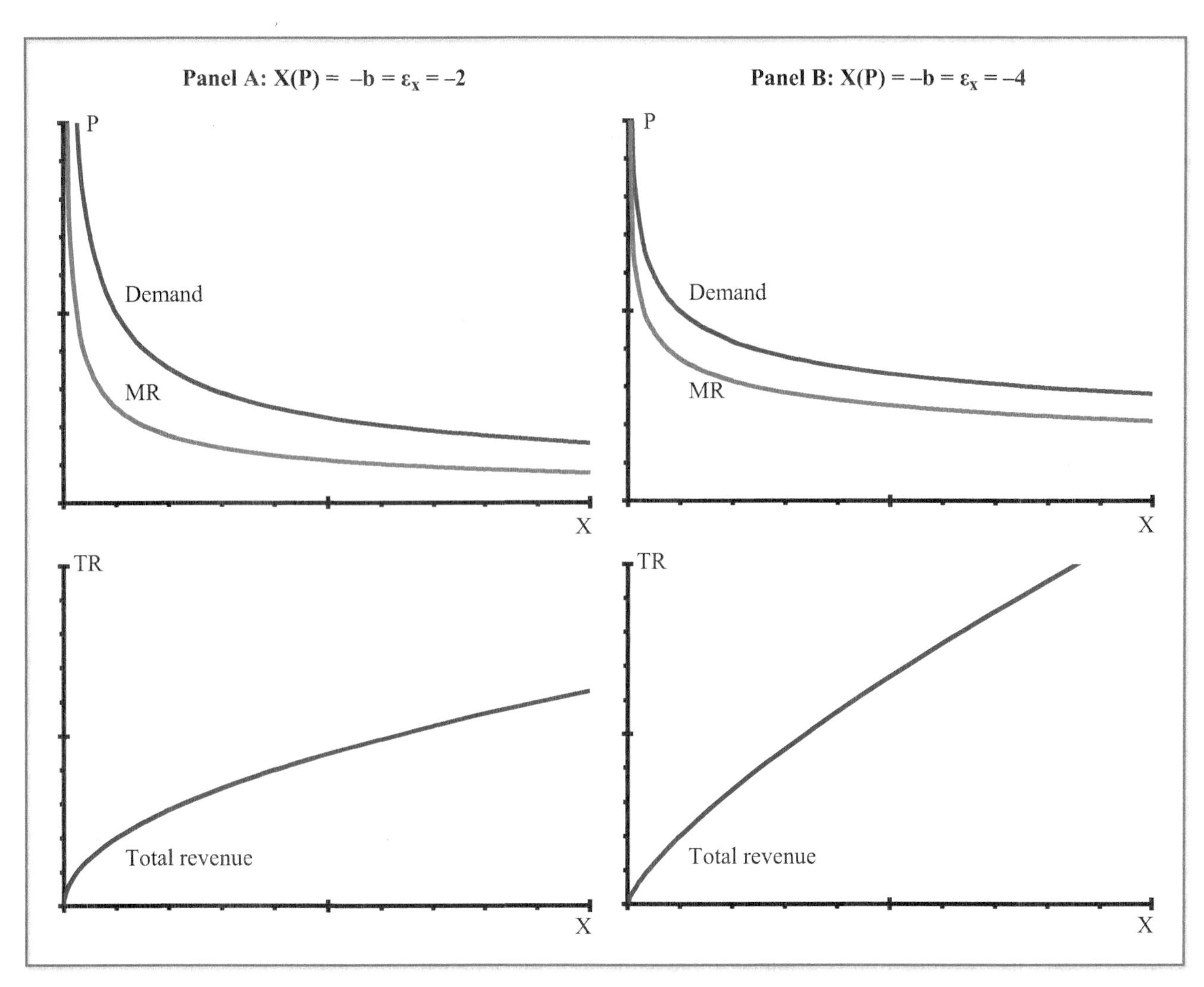

FIGURE 12.10 Demand, Marginal Revenue, and Total Revenue, Given a Constant Elasticity Demand Function, $X(P) = a \cdot P^{-b}$

revenue is three-fourths the height of inverse demand for every level of output. The lower graphs in Figures 12.10A and 12.10B depict total revenue in this situation. Total revenue is a square-root function in Figure 12.10A (since $1 - (1/b) = 1/2$). In Figure 12.10B, total revenue is "closer" to linear: It is a power function of x, where the power is three-fourths. If demand is even more elastic, then total revenue would be even closer to linear, since the exponent in Equation 12.12c would be closer to one. Conversely, if demand is even closer to unitary elasticity, then total revenue would more closely resemble a horizontal line, since the exponent in Equation 12.12c would be closer to zero. (Cobb-Douglas is the limiting case here; total revenue is constant in this instance, as discussed earlier.)

12.4 Determining the Profit-Maximizing Level of Output

We have now separately examined revenue and cost, the two sides of the profit equation:

$$\pi(x) = TR(x) - TC(x). \qquad \textbf{(12.13)}$$

The most basic question for a profit-maximizing firm is to determine the optimal level of production, given cost and demand conditions. As discussed in Section 10.2, any profit-maximizing outcome necessarily will be cost minimizing as well, but the reverse is not necessarily true: Not all cost-minimizing outcomes are profit maximizing. The firm may be producing the wrong level of output. We begin our discussion of output determination by comparing profit-maximizing production, given two different demand scenarios.

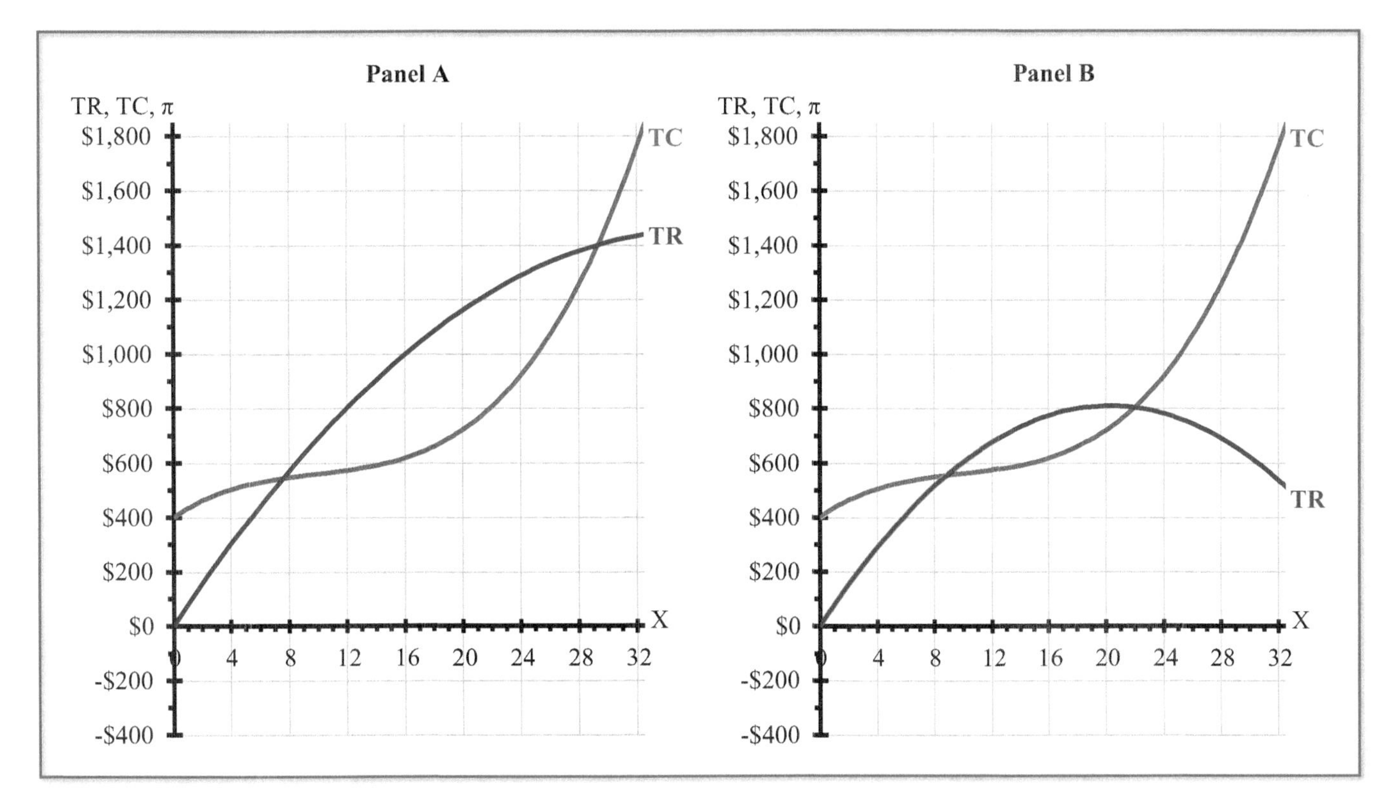

FIGURE 12.11 Deriving Profits from Total Revenue and Total Cost

The Geometry of Profit Maximization

Figures 12.11A and 12.11B depict total revenue and total cost functions. They are based on the following three facts:

1. The total cost functions are the same in both figures.
2. The total revenue hills are based on two distinct linear demand functions.
3. The P intercept of the demand curve that was implicitly used to create the total revenue hill is the same for both figures.[11]

Given these three facts, answer the following question.

Q11a. Which panel has a flatter demand curve—Figure 12.11A or 12.11B?*

A simple numerical example makes this point: If two demand curves have the same price intercept, the one that has a slope that is half the size of the other (in magnitude) has twice the demand at any price (as long as that price is lower than the price intercept). Or put in terms of a quantity orientation, the demand curve with half the slope will support a higher price for any output level, so total revenue is higher for a given quantity if demand is more expansive.

The geometric relation between revenue, cost, and profit is straightforward, given Equation 12.13. Answer the following questions for both Figures 12.11A and 12.11B. Your answers can only be approximate, since total revenue and total cost functions have not been algebraically delineated.

Q11b. For what output levels are profits zero?

Q11c. What are profits at $x = 0$ and $x = 32$?

***Q11a answer:** Figure 12.11A is flatter than 12.11B. Given $P(x) = b - m \cdot x$, the total revenue hill achieves a maximum at $b/(2 \cdot m)$, as seen in Figure 12.4B. Since b is assumed to be equal across figures, slope m must be smaller in Figure 12.11A because the top of the hill occurs at a larger output in that figure.

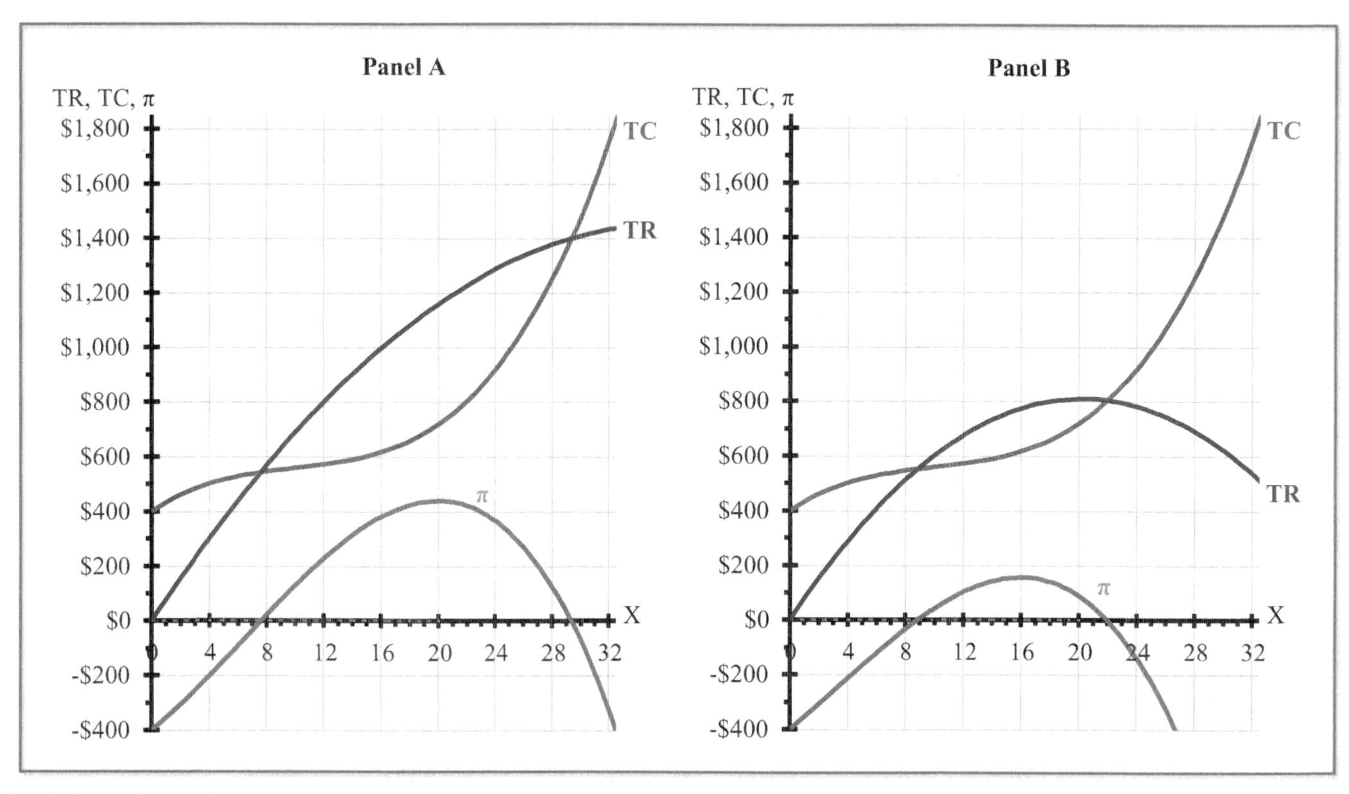

FIGURE 12.12 Profits Are the Difference between Total Revenue and Total Cost

Q11d. What output level is profit maximizing?

Q11e. What are profits in this instance?*

For a given total cost function and total revenue function, profit is simply the difference between total revenue and total cost. At each output level, profit is simply the vertical difference between these two curves. Profits are positive when total revenue is higher than total cost, and they are negative when the reverse holds true. Figure 12.12 depicts profits for both of the scenarios shown in Figure 12.11.

The answers to Q11b–Q11e are confirmed by the green profit function in Figure 12.12. Note in particular that a firm's profit-maximizing level of output depends on the demand the firm faces; profits are maximized at $x = 20$ in Figure 12.12A and at $x = 16$ in Figure 12.12B. Profits are maximized when the vertical distance between TR(x) and TC(x) is as large as possible; the top of the profit hill occurs at the same level of output where the vertical difference between total revenue and total cost is as large as possible (and the height of that hill is the vertical difference between TR and TC).

A Profit-Maximizing Firm Sets MR = MC

Given smooth total revenue and total cost curves, the vertical distance between total revenue and total cost is maximized when the slopes of the two curves are equal. Both of these slopes already have been examined extensively: The slope of total cost is marginal cost (Section 11.2), and the slope of total revenue is marginal revenue (Section 12.2). So the profit-maximizing condition can be restated as:

Claim: *A profit-maximizing firm will choose an output level where marginal revenue equals marginal cost.*

***Q11b–Q11e answer:** For Figure 12.11A, $\pi = 0$ at about $Q = 7$ and $Q = 29.5$; $\pi(0) = -\$400$ and $\pi(32) = -\$300$; profits are maximized at about $Q = 20$, and profits there are about \$450. For Figure 12.11B, $\pi = 0$ at about $Q = 9$ and $Q = 22$; $\pi(0) = -\$400$ and $\pi(32) = -\$1{,}200$; profits are maximized at about $Q = 16$, and profits there are about \$150.

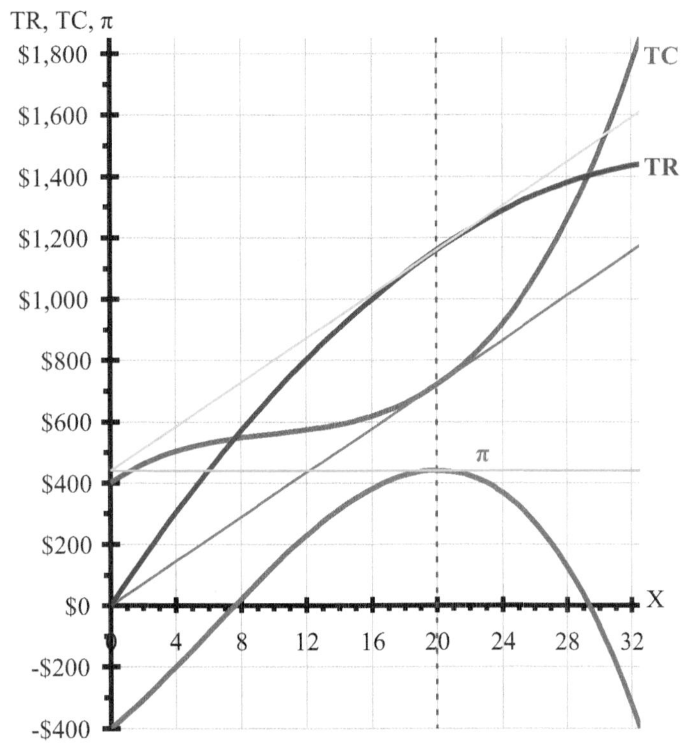

FIGURE 12.13 Profits Are Maximized When MR(x) = MC(x)

slider X	TR(X)	TC(X)	π(X)	MR(X)	MC(X)
19.9	$1,156	$716	$439.96	$36.22	$35.40

slider X	TR(X)	TC(X)	π(X)	MR(X)	MC(X)
20.0	$1,160	$720	$440.00	$36.00	$36.00

slider X	TR(X)	TC(X)	π(X)	MR(X)	MC(X)
20.1	$1,164	$724	$439.96	$35.78	$36.60

The geometric proof of this assertion not only provides information about what happens at the profit-maximizing output level but also about what happens when an output level is chosen that is not profit maximizing.

The slopes of total revenue and total cost are easier to see if tangent lines are provided for each curve. Figure 12.13 reproduces the TR, TC, and profit information from Figure 12.12A and includes tangent lines at output level x = 20. Also included is a table providing actual numerical values for the various functions in this instance (focus initially on the graph). The color of each tangent line is a light version of its respective total curve. Visually, MR = MC at this output level, since the slope of the light blue tangent line is parallel to the pink tangent line. At this same output level, the top of the profit hill is achieved, since the slope of the light green tangent to the profit hill, marginal profit, is zero. **Marginal profit (Mπ(x))** is the slope of the profit hill. Algebraically, marginal profit is calculated as $M\pi(x) = MR(x) - MC(x)$. Marginal profit describes the incremental profit from producing a bit more output.[12] We see algebraically why marginal profit is zero when marginal revenue equals marginal cost.

marginal profit (Mπ(x)): Marginal profit is the slope of the profit hill.

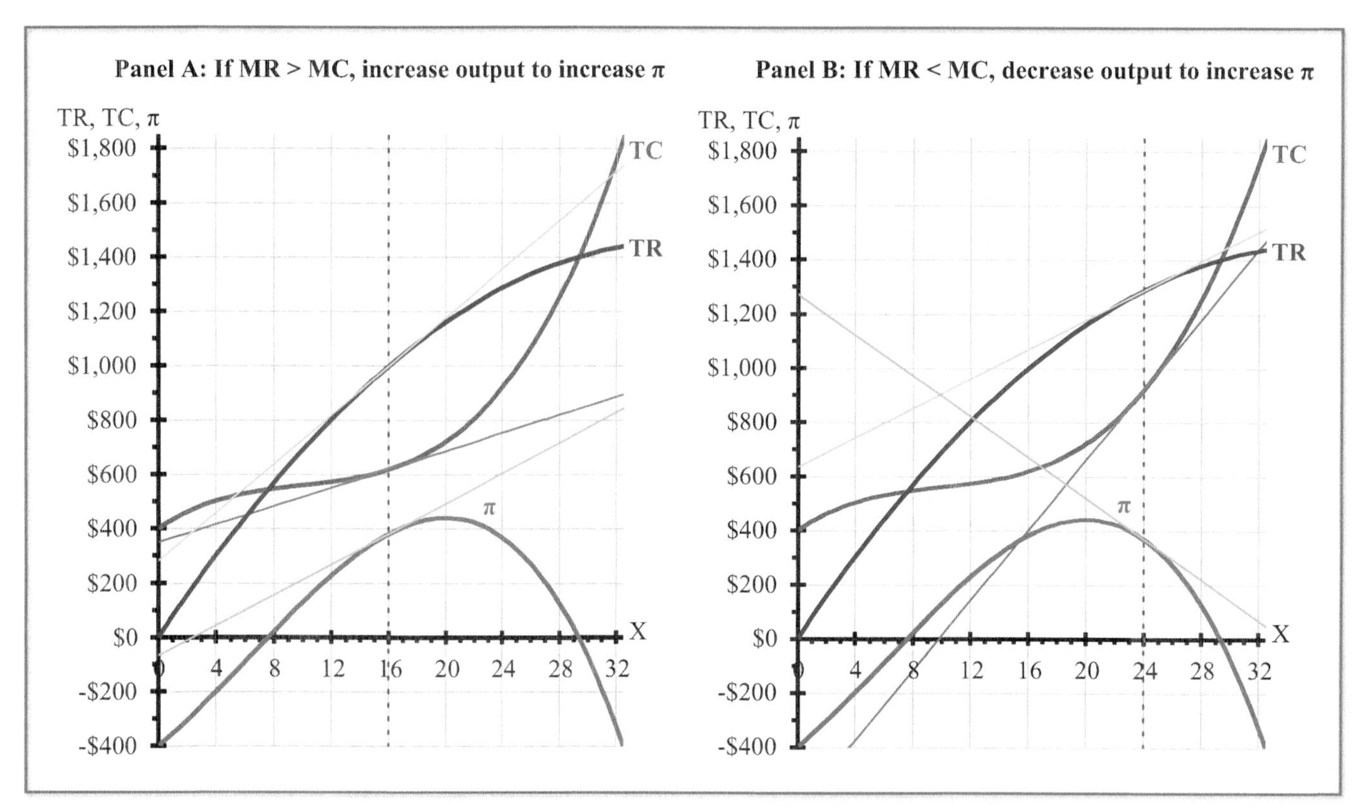

FIGURE 12.14 The Output Response When MR ≠ MC

Since the top of the profit hill is flat, small changes in output near the optimum produce only small changes in profits. A move of 0.1 units in output, for example, leads to a decline in profits of \$0.04, according to the table beneath Figure 12.13. The output level x = 20.0 is, indeed, profit maximizing in this instance, according to the table. At this output level, π = \$440 (which is close to the visual guess of \$450 provided for Q11e). At 19.9 and 20.1 units of output, profits decline to \$439.96. This is seen in terms of marginal revenue and marginal cost as well; at x = 19.9, MR > MC, and at x = 20.1, MR < MC. In both instances, profits increase by changing quantity. At x = 20.0, MR = MC, and no further increases in profits are possible, based on changing quantity.

If marginal profit is positive, then an increase in output will increase profits. We saw this on a small scale in the tabular information in Figure 12.13, but the differences in slope were small enough so as to be geometrically imperceptible. Figure 12.14 depicts output levels further from the optimum to provide a visual description of what happens when output is too low or too high. In Figure 12.14A, x = 16, and revenue is increasing faster than costs. Put another way, MR(16) > MC(16), since the blue tangent is steeper than the pink tangent. This implies that Mn > 0; the green tangent is upward sloping. In short, when incremental revenue exceeds incremental cost, output should be expanded to increase profits.[13] The reverse holds true when costs are increasing faster than revenue. In Figure 12.14B, x = 24, and revenue is increasing slower than costs. Put another way, MR(24) < MC(24), since the blue tangent is flatter than the pink tangent. This implies that Mn < 0; the green tangent is downward sloping. In short, when incremental cost exceeds incremental revenue, output should be reduced to increase profits.

The Algebra of Profit Maximization

The geometric analysis thus far in this section is based on a cubic cost function and a quadratic total revenue function (or to say the same thing, a linear demand function). If we have algebraic representations of cost and demand, we can determine the profit-maximizing output level by algebraic manipulation. To show how this works, we use the cost and demand curves that describe the profit-maximizing outcome in Figure 12.13.

Challenge question: *Before looking at Equations 12.15 and 12.16 for the answers, try to derive the equations for TR(x), π(x), MR(x), and MC(x), based on inverse demand and total cost functions in Equations 12.14a and 12.14b.*

Hint: Section 12.2 describes how TR and MR are obtained from linear demand, and Section 11.4 describes how to obtain MC from a cubic cost function.

Inverse demand in this situation is:

$$P(x) = 80 - 1.1 \cdot x. \qquad \textbf{(12.14a)}$$

The cost function is the same one examined in Sections 11.2 and 11.4. Total cost from Equation 11.8a is reproduced here as Equation 12.14b:

$$TC(x) = 400 + 36 \cdot x - 3 \cdot x^2 + 0.1 \cdot x^3. \qquad \textbf{(12.14b)}$$

Total revenue in this situation is given by:

$$TR(x) = 80 \cdot x - 1.1 \cdot x^2. \qquad \textbf{(12.15a)}$$

The profit function is total revenue minus total cost, based on Equations 12.15a and 12.14b:

$$\begin{aligned}\pi(x) &= 80 \cdot x - 1.1 \cdot x^2 - (400 + 36 \cdot x - 3 \cdot x^2 + 0.1 \cdot x^3)\\ &= -0.1 \cdot x^3 + 1.9 \cdot x^2 + 44 \cdot x - 400. \qquad \textbf{(12.15b)}\end{aligned}$$

The profit function is cubic with a negative lead coefficient (–0.1); therefore, the profit hill shown in Figures 12.13 and 12.15 is reasonable (for large enough values of x, profits must be negative).

Marginal revenue follows the "same intercept, twice the slope of inverse demand" rule described in Equation 12.11. In this instance, we have:

$$MR(x) = 80 - 2.2 \cdot x. \qquad \textbf{(12.16a)}$$

Marginal cost follows the rule described in Equation 11.6g.

$$MC(x) = 36 - 6 \cdot x + 0.3 \cdot x^2. \qquad \textbf{(12.16b)}$$

Profits are maximized when MR = MC. Given these marginal revenue and marginal cost functions, the profit-maximizing output level must satisfy:

$$80 - 2.2 \cdot x = 36 - 6 \cdot x + 0.3 \cdot x^2. \qquad \textbf{(12.17a)}$$

Regrouping, we obtain:

$$0 = 0.3 \cdot x^2 - 3.8 \cdot x - 44. \qquad \textbf{(12.17b)}$$

The quadratic formula leads to two possible solutions: x = –22/3, and x = 20.[14] The only one of these possible solutions in the positive range of output is x = 20, an answer that algebraically confirms the geometric solution shown in Figure 12.13. Substituting x = 20 into Equation 12.15b yields π(20) = $440, as expected.

Note that the same result could be obtained by setting the marginal profit equation equal to zero. From Equations 12.16a and 12.16b, this condition requires:

$$0 = M\pi(x) = MR(x) - MC(x) \text{ if } 0 = -0.3 \cdot x^2 + 3.8 \cdot x + 44. \qquad \textbf{(12.17c)}$$

The ultimate result is the same because this equation is formally the same as Equation 12.17b. (This is not surprising when you note that the condition 0 = *a* – b is the same as saying *a* = b.)

Some Implications of MR = MC

The profit-maximizing rule of MR = MC holds, regardless of market structure. It is hard to overemphasize the importance of this rule. This rule is applied in a variety of contexts, and it has a number of implications, some of which we examine in later chapters. Nonetheless, some important implications can be drawn immediately from this rule.

MR = MC holds for other dimensions beyond the price/quantity locus. Up to this point, we have described demand simply as a function of price, holding all other economic parameters fixed. But what if, for example, the firm's demand curve is affected by advertising? In this instance, to maximize profits, the firm should set MR = MC along the multiple dimensions on which the firm competes. Specifically, the firm should increase advertising as long as the incremental revenue derived from an additional dollar of advertising exceeds the incremental cost of that advertising. The firm faces two decisions in this instance: setting advertising and setting price/quantity. These joint decisions each follow the rule that incremental revenue must be compared against incremental cost to maximize profits—and this must occur across decision variables available to the firm for the firm to maximize profits. Although we do not focus on the multivariate decision calculus here, it is worthwhile to know that the same marginal decision rule applies for each dimension on which a firm competes.[15]

Another implication of MR = MC is that the profit-maximizing firm will always produce on the elastic section of its demand curve ($|\varepsilon| > 1$ in Figure 12.5). The reason for this assertion is straightforward: Marginal cost is always positive; therefore, MR = MC occurs on the positive range of the marginal revenue curve. We saw in Figure 12.7C that MR > 0 implies that demand is elastic at this production point.

The profit-maximizing firm need only compare marginal revenue with marginal cost to determine how it should proceed. As noted earlier, this result is both simple to understand and powerful to apply. One of the more surprising results derived from this rule is that the amount of fixed cost paid has no effect on the optimal output choice for a firm wishing to maximize profits. Once the firm determines how much capital (plant, property, and equipment) to use, it is required to pay for that capital (or more accurately, rent it), regardless of short-run output level chosen. A given plant size will have the same variable cost function, regardless of the size of fixed cost. Imagine that capital becomes cheaper after you have made your capital choice (because interest rates, for example, decline). This causes fixed cost to decline, and hence, the short-run total cost function will shift down. But this change has no effect on variable cost or marginal cost. It also has *no effect* on the profit-maximizing output level.[16]

Each of the figures in this section has been based on a cubic cost function, with fixed cost of $400. Initially, we focused on two linear demand functions (in Figures 12.11 and 12.12). In Figures 12.13 and 12.14, we examined profit-maximizing output determination for the more expansive of these two demand functions. We determined geometrically that the profit-maximizing output level was Q* = 20 and we confirmed this algebraically using Equation 12.17. These results are independent of the size of fixed cost. Figure 12.15 depicts this point. Fixed cost has declined from $400 to $200 but none of the marginal functions change as a result of this change. In particular, MR(20) = MC(20) = $36 and $M\pi(20) = 0$. The only difference is profits increase by $200 since total cost has declined by $200 (with no change in marginal cost).

Finally, the total revenue functions in this section have been based on linear demand functions. This functional form was chosen because it allows for an easy algebraic solution, as we have just seen. In Section 12.3, we examined an alternative nonlinear form that is also easily tractable from an algebraic point of view: the constant elasticity demand function, $x(P) = a \cdot P^{-b}$. This function is controlled by two parameters: a is the scaling factor, and b is the magnitude of the price elasticity of demand.

Suppose that we wish to determine the appropriate scaling factor so that Q* = 20 is profit maximizing when b = 2 (elasticity of demand is –2), given the variable cost function used in Figures 12.11–12.15. We know from the table in Figure 12.13 (and by evaluating MC(20) in Equation 12.16b) that MC(20) = $36. Therefore, given marginal revenue in Equation 12.12d, MR(20) = MC(20) requires:

$$MR(20) = (1 - (1/b)) \cdot a^{(1/b)} \cdot 20^{(-1/b)} = (1/2) \cdot a^{(1/2)} \cdot 20^{(-1/2)} = 36. \quad \textbf{(12.18a)}$$

Solving for a using Equation 12.18a, we obtain:

$$a = (72 \cdot 20^{(1/2)})^2 = 72^2 \cdot 20 = 103{,}680. \quad \textbf{(12.18b)}$$

The profit-maximizing outcome, given this constant elasticity demand function, is shown in Figure 12.16. Fixed cost has been increased to $500 to make the graph clearer.[17] The same

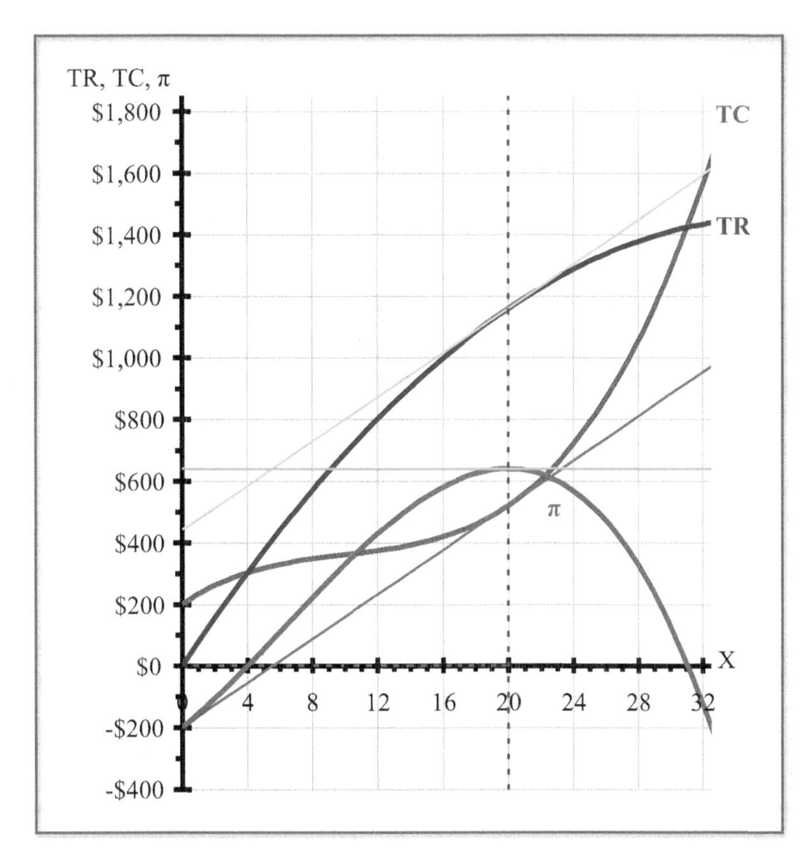

FIGURE 12.15 Changes in Fixed Cost Do Not Affect the Profit-Maximizing Level of Output (compare with Figure 12.13)

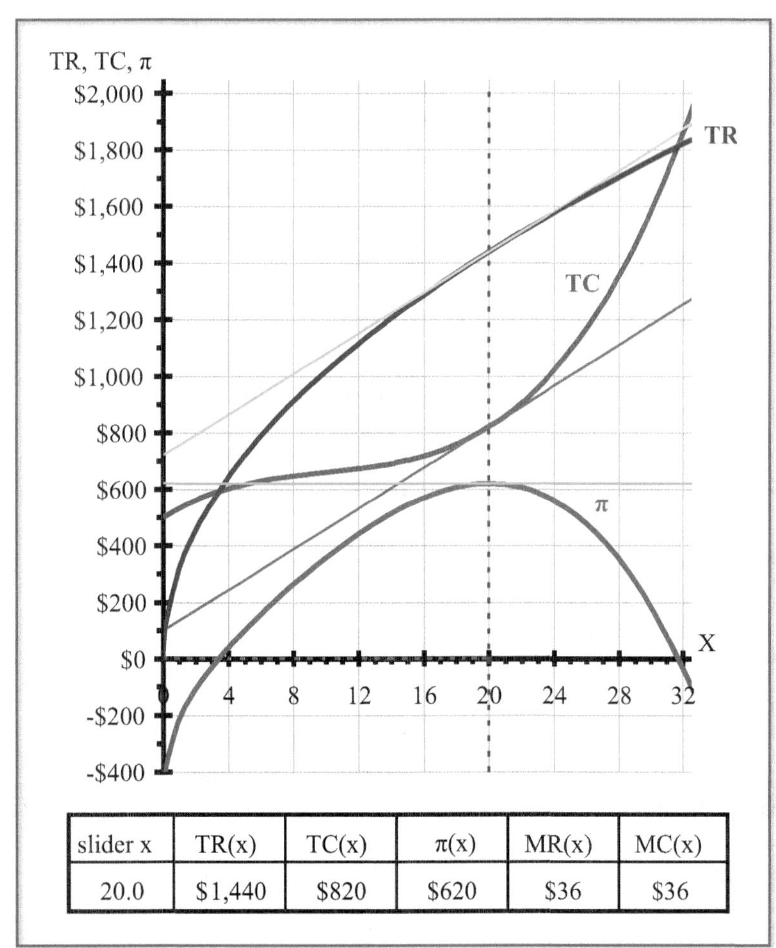

slider x	TR(x)	TC(x)	π(x)	MR(x)	MC(x)
20.0	$1,440	$820	$620	$36	$36

FIGURE 12.16 Profit Maximization with Constant Elasticity Demand

$x(P) = 103680P^{-2}$, and $TC(x) = 500 + 36x - 3x^2 + 0.1x^3$

requirement for profit maximization holds in this instance: Marginal revenue equals marginal cost to maximize profits (as seen by the parallel tangent lines to TR and TC at $x = 20$ and by the horizontal tangent to $\pi(x)$ at $x = 20$). The Excel file for Figure 12.16 allows you to vary the price elasticity of demand between $-2.50 \leq -b \leq -1.95$. As you do, you see that optimal output varies, just as was the case when linear demand varied in Figure 12.12; more expansive demand leads to a larger optimal output, just as with linear demand.

Summary

The discussion of market interaction requires that the consumer analysis from Part 2 be combined with the theory of the firm discussion from Part 3. We begin by describing how we obtain market demand from individual demand. Most basically, market demand is the horizontal sum of individual demand curves. Care must be taken when calculating this sum algebraically, since different numbers of consumers are likely to be in the market at different prices.

Although market demand will likely have kinks at points where a new consumer enters the market, we need not work with "kinked" curves as a practical matter because as the number of individuals involved in the market increases, the kinks tend to smooth out. Working with a single smooth demand function is preferable to working with piecewise smooth kinked curves because the algebra is much simpler, and the smooth curve closely approximates the kinked curve.

From the firm's perspective, consumer demands are valuable because they produce revenue. Regardless of market structure, a firm views the demand for its product in terms of the revenues that its demand can produce. Market demand describes how the market as a whole demands the good. Unless an individual firm controls the entire market—that is, the firm is a monopolist in this market—the individual firm will not face the entire market demand. We are not interested in how a firm determines its demand curve; that discussion is postponed until later. We simply assume that a firm is able to determine, at a conceptual level, the demand curve it faces. To focus on the profit-maximizing output decision, we often assume that the firm faces linear demand.

In large part, this chapter is devoted to a very simple rule, but the rule is so important that it is examined from a number of perspectives: *A profit-maximizing firm will choose that output level where marginal revenue equals marginal cost.* When this does not occur, the direction of the imbalance between marginal revenue and marginal cost tells the firm whether to increase output or decrease output to increase profits. When marginal revenue exceeds marginal cost, the firm should increase output, and when marginal cost exceeds marginal revenue, the firm should decrease output to increase profits.

The bulk of the analysis in the chapter used linear demand curves to examine the relation between demand, revenue, marginal revenue, elasticity, and profits. The results derived using this simple functional form are not tied to that functional form. The easiest proof of this assertion is to simply note that the main result, MR = MC, is derived as a geometric result—not as an algebraic result. The specific output level where MR = MC is, of course, dependent on the underlying algebra behind the total revenue and total cost functions, but the geometry of that solution is qualitatively independent of the algebra. Nonetheless, one nonlinear demand curve is introduced that also allows for easy algebraic analysis: the constant elasticity demand function.

Review Questions

Define the following terms:

market demand	estimated marginal revenue	marginal profits
inverse demand curve	marginal revenue	constant elasticity demand
marginal valuation schedule		

Match the following statements:

a. Inverse demand	1. Demand is inelastic.
b. An increase in output increases revenue.	2. Marginal valuation schedule
c. An increase in output decreases revenue.	3. Decrease output to maximize profits.
d. If $MR > MC$, what should a firm do?	4. Demand is elastic.
e. If $MR < MC$, what should a firm do?	5. Increase output to maximize profits.

Provide short answers to the following:

a. Why is it reasonable to think of market demand as being smooth, rather than kinked?
b. What is the difference between demand and inverse demand?

c. What is the relation between inverse demand and marginal revenue, given linear demand?
d. What is the relation between inverse demand and marginal revenue, given constant elasticity demand?
e. When are marginal profits equal to zero?
f. What is the golden rule of profit maximization?
g. Why will a profit-maximizing firm always produce on the elastic portion of its demand curve?

Check your answers to the *matching* and *short-answer* exercises in the Answers Appendix at the end of the book.

Notes

1. The proof requires calculus. Differentiating Equation 12.2a, we have $dX/dP = n \cdot dx/dP$. But slope of market demand is $M(P) = dP/dX$, and individual demand is $m(P) = dP/dx$, so inverting both sides of the initial equation yields:
$M(P) = dP/dX = (1/n) \cdot dP/dx = m(P)/n$.

2. Individual 1's x intercept is 80, and relative to that axis, the "slope" is –2 (go in 80 and up 40 to get to point **B**). Individual 2's x intercept is 50, and relative to that axis, the "slope" is –1/2 (go in 50 and up 100 to get to point **A**).

3. Indeed, in this instance, the function

$$X(P) = (51 - P/2) \cdot (50 - P/2)$$

contains each kinked (X, P) point in Figure 12.3. A quick check verifies that this works for

$$P = \$50: X(50) = 26 \cdot 25 = 650,$$

as shown in Figure 12.3. The proof that this function represents market demand in this instance is based on the algebraic fact that the sum of $0 + 1 + \ldots + (n - 1) = n \cdot (n - 1)/2$, but the proof is left as a workbook problem.

4. The formal proof requires calculus. Set the derivative of Equation 12.7b to zero and solve for x.

5. As noted in Section 2.4, some authors go even further and define own-price elasticity with a minus sign in the equation so that own-price elasticity is positive. We do *not* do this to have the unified definition of elasticity provided by Equation 2.1: $\varepsilon_{x,?} = \%\Delta x/\%\Delta ?$, where "?" is any factor that might affect x. (Those factors include own-price, the prices of other goods, income, advertising, etc.)

6. These same relations are seen in the slope form of the elasticity equation $\varepsilon_x = (1/\text{slope}) \cdot (P/Q)$. Along a linear demand curve, the slope is constant and P declines as Q increases, so P/Q declines and $|\varepsilon_x|$ declines as well.

7. Astute students sometimes note that $\Delta x = 1$ seems a natural choice for incremental change in quantity. This is the heuristic value we intuitively gravitate toward because it is how marginal revenue is introduced in introductory microeconomics texts.

8. If you have not had calculus before but understood the discussion in the last paragraph about how MR_e tends to MR as Δx tends to zero, then you have just digested your first formal calculus-style proof!

9. This is easy to see using calculus: $\varepsilon_x = dx/dP \cdot (P/x)$, but $dx/dP = -b \cdot a \cdot P^{(-b-1)}$ so $\varepsilon_x = dx/dP \cdot (P/x) =$
$-b \cdot a \cdot P^{(-b-1)} \cdot (P/x) = -b \cdot (a \cdot P^{-b})/x = -b$. The Chapter 12 Appendix provides a detailed analysis of this demand function.

10. Both quasilinear preferences examined in Part 2 produced demands for x that are constant elasticity demand functions. Interestingly, however, in this instance, the demands for y are not constant elasticity, given these preferences. See, in particular, Equations 7.10 and 7.11.

11. This is not immediately obvious without an intimate knowledge of how the total revenue hill is constructed. The second and third facts imply that the slope of the total revenue hill is the same at the origin in both figures. The reason is clear from Equation 12.11: Evaluating marginal revenue at x = 0, we obtain MR(0) = b; the slope of both total revenue hills at x = 0 is the same for both figures.

12. The proof that $M\pi(x) = MR(x) - MC(x)$ is straightforward but requires calculus. Given $\pi(x) = TR(x) - TC(x)$, the derivative is marginal profit:

$$M\pi(x) = d\pi(x)/dx = d(TR(x) - TC(x))/dx$$
$$= dTR(x)/dx - dTC(x)/dx = MR(x) - MC(x).$$

13. If you are geometrically inclined, you should note that the slope of the green tangent ($M\pi$) is the difference in the slope of the blue tangent and the red tangent. This can be seen by noting that the red and blue tangents intersect at the same quantity level at which the green tangent line intersects the x axis. (In Figure 12.14A, this occurs at approximately x = 2.5, so $M\pi(16) = \Delta\pi/\Delta x \doteq 380/13.5 = 28.15$, quite close to its actual value of \$28.00, as can be seen using the Excel version of Figure 12.14.)

14. The quadratic formula requires

$$x = (3.8 \pm ((-3.8)^2 - 4 \cdot (0.3) \cdot (-44))^{0.5}/(2 \cdot (0.3))$$
$$= (3.8 \pm 8.2)/0.6.$$

This yields solutions: $x = -4.4/0.6 = -22/3$, and $x = 12/0.6 = 20$.

15. By applying this decision rule across multiple decision variables, we obtain the Dorfman-Steiner optimal advertising result described in Chapter 21.

16. Of course, if the lower fixed cost is due to a smaller plant, then profit-maximizing output would change because marginal cost would change. As discussed in Chapter 11, different plant sizes produce different variable cost functions. In this instance, profit-maximizing output would decline, since the variable factors of production must be used more intensively when the fixed factors are smaller. Variable cost is higher when fixed cost is smaller.

17. We have just seen that changes in fixed cost have no effect on the profit-maximizing output level in this instance. It turns out that if FC = \$400, then TC(20) = π(20) = \$720, and the resulting graph has a coincidental intersection of total cost and profit hill at the top of the profit hill. Rather than cause confusion over this *coincidence*, fixed cost was increased so that the solution appears similar to Figure 12.13.

Appendix:

A Primer on the Constant Elasticity Demand Function

Equation 12.12a is a specific example of a general class of demand functions that have constant elasticity. That equation had constant price elasticity of demand, but we can more generally describe demand as a function of own price, the prices of complements and substitutes, and income (as well as other variables), using a functional form in which all elasticities are constant.

If demand is a linear function of these parameters, we could write demand as:

$$x = a - b \cdot P_{own} - c \cdot P_{comp} + d \cdot P_{sub} + e \cdot I. \qquad \textit{Linear demand} \qquad \textbf{(12A.1)}$$

Each of the coefficients a through d is positive, and e is positive if x is a normal good. The various elasticities of demand *are not constant* in this instance because they depend on the values of each of the prices, as well as income. (This is easy to see if you recall the general formula for elasticity as $\varepsilon_v = \%\Delta x/\%\Delta V = (\Delta x/\Delta V) \cdot (V/x) = (1/\text{slope}) \cdot (V/x)$. Slope is constant in each direction, given linear demand, but as the value of V varies, so does x; therefore, so does the "V" elasticity.) We examined this in the case of own-price elasticity in Section 12.2, especially in the discussion of Figure 12.5.

If, instead, demand is a product of various parameters raised to powers, then the result is a constant elasticity demand (CED) function. The elasticities are the powers, as we shall soon see. Consider the function:

$$x = a \cdot P_{own}^{-b} \cdot P_{comp}^{-c} \cdot P_{sub}^{d} \cdot I^{e}. \qquad \textit{CED} \qquad \textbf{(12A.2)}$$

Own-price elasticity of demand is calculated by taking the partial derivative with respect to own price:

$$\varepsilon_{own} = \%\Delta x/\%\Delta P_{own} = (\Delta x/\Delta P_{own}) \cdot (P_{own}/x) = (\partial x/\partial P_{own}) \cdot (P_{own}/x).$$

$$\varepsilon_{own} = (-b \cdot a \cdot P_{own}^{-b-1} \cdot P_{comp}^{-c} \cdot P_{sub}^{d} \cdot I^{e}) \cdot (P_{own}/x). \qquad \textbf{(12A.3own)}$$

$$\varepsilon_{own} = -b \cdot (a \cdot P_{own}^{-b} \cdot P_{comp}^{-c} \cdot P_{sub}^{d} \cdot I^{e})/x = -b.$$

Symmetric calculations produce cross-price and income elasticities (upon simplification):

$$\varepsilon_{comp} = -c. \qquad \textbf{(12A.3comp.)}$$

$$\varepsilon_{sub} = d. \qquad \textbf{(12A.3sub.)}$$

$$\eta = \varepsilon_{Income} = e. \qquad \textbf{(12A.3inc.)}$$

If e is positive, then x is a normal good, and if e is negative, it is an inferior good.

An alternative algebraic form of describing CED functions is based on transforming the demand function using logarithms. Start with the demand function in Equation 12A.2 and take the natural logarithm of both sides (we denote the natural log function by ln(x)). Upon simplification, we obtain (see the Mathematical Appendix [available in the online version of this text] for a review of the basic properties of logarithms):

$$\ln(x) = A - b \cdot \ln(P_{own}) - c \cdot \ln(P_{comp}) + d \cdot \ln(P_{sub}) + e \cdot \ln(I). \qquad \textbf{(12A.4)}$$

Log-log form of CED

In Equation 12A.4, $A = \ln(a)$. The log-log form of CED is useful because it is linear in logarithms, and each coefficient, except the intercept, is an elasticity. Empirical estimation of elasticities based on CED is easily accomplished, using econometric techniques that are beyond the scope of this text, using Equation 12A.4.

Constant elasticity demand functions have an interesting relationship between inverse demand and marginal revenue. Marginal revenue is a constant fraction of inverse demand if demand is CED. This is detailed in Equation 12.12 and in Figure 12.10, based on the

CED function: $x = a \cdot P^{-b}$. The same point holds for the more general CED function described in Equation 12A.2. Inverse demand solves for P_{own} to obtain:

$$P_{own}(x) = [(1/(a \cdot P_{comp}^{-c} \cdot P_{sub}^{d} \cdot I^{e}))^{(-1/b)}] \cdot x^{(-1/b)} \quad \textbf{(12A.5)}$$
$$= K \cdot x^{(-1/b)}, \text{ where } K = a^{(1/b)} \cdot P_{comp}^{(-c/b)} \cdot P_{sub}^{(d/b)} \cdot I^{(e/b)}.$$

Total revenue is then $P_{own}(x) \cdot x$, or:

$$TR(x) = x \cdot [a^{(1/b)} \cdot P_{comp}^{(-c/b)} \cdot P_{sub}^{(d/b)} \cdot I^{(e/b)}] \cdot x^{(-1/b)} \quad \textbf{(12A.6)}$$
$$= K \cdot x^{(1-(1/b))}.$$

Marginal revenue is the derivative of total revenue, which in this instance, is:

$$MR(x) = (1 - (1/b)) \cdot [a^{(1/b)} \cdot P_{comp}^{(-c/b)} \cdot P_{sub}^{(d/b)} \cdot I^{(e/b)}] \cdot x^{(-1/b)}. \quad \textbf{(12A.7)}$$
$$= (1 - (1/b)) \cdot K \cdot x^{(-1/b)} = (1 - (1/b)) \cdot P_{own}(x).$$

Equation 12A.7 shows that marginal revenue is a constant proportion of inverse demand. The constant of proportionality is $(1 - (1/b))$. Figure 12.10 shows that, for example, if $b = 2$, then marginal revenue is half of inverse demand, but if $b = 4$, then marginal revenue is three-fourths of inverse demand.

Short-Run Profit Maximization in Perfectly Competitive Markets

CHAPTER 13

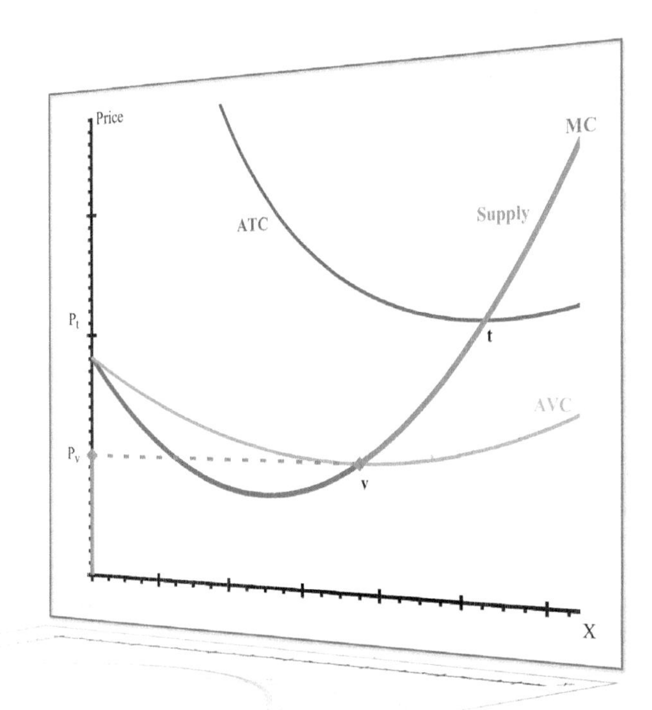

Chapter Outline

The analysis in Chapter 12 assumed a "general" market structure to focus on the profit-maximizing decision rule. In this chapter, we impose the most important basic market structure—perfect competition—on this analysis to see how individual firms and the market as a whole interact to determine the market clearing outcome. This chapter provides only half of the answer because it focuses on the short-run behavior of firms in competitive markets. In Chapter 14, we examine how firms move from the short run to the long run in a competitive market setting.

The typical starting point for understanding market behavior is to assume that the market is competitive. Although the requirements for perfect competition are not strictly adhered to in a wide range of markets, it is worthwhile to study perfect competition carefully because all other market structures are measured against this competitive ideal.

The assumptions that define perfectly competitive markets are the focus of Section 13.1. Firms in a competitive market face a perfectly elastic demand for their output. As a result, marginal revenue equals price, unlike in a market setting, where the firm has some price-making ability. The coincidence of price and marginal revenue means that the profit-maximizing decision rule from Chapter 12 can be recast in an even simpler form: P = MC. The implication of this result is examined in Section 13.2. Section 13.3 further refines this analysis by examining two caveats to the P = MC decision rule. This section concludes with a formal description of the firm's supply curve in a competitive market. The supply curve is a function that relates market price to how much output the firm wishes to supply. Section 13.4 puts together individual supply curves to determine market supply as a function of price. This section begins by analyzing why firms might exhibit different levels of profitability in competitive markets in the short run. From here, in a symmetric analysis to that presented in Section 12.1 on the demand side, market supply is seen as the horizontal sum of individual supply curves. Section 13.5 describes a special case of the analysis presented earlier in the chapter by focusing attention on quadratic cost functions. These cost functions are particularly easy to use, since they produce linear marginal cost and, hence, linear supply curves for individual firms.

13.1 Perfectly Competitive Markets

Perfect competition is the typical starting place for economists examining market structures. Four tenets define a perfectly competitive market:

1. *There are a large number of buyers and sellers.* Each buyer and seller is insignificant, relative to the size of the market. As a result, no single buyer or seller has appreciable market power; any individual actor's action has only a negligible effect on market price or market quantity.
2. *The product under consideration is homogeneous.* Consumers cannot tell a difference between the offerings of various producers.
3. *There is free entry and exit in the market.* Established producers do not have access to proprietary methods of production (such as patents) that put entrants at an economic disadvantage, relative to existing firms. Similarly, there is an active secondhand market for factors of production so that a firm faces minimal loss should it decide to exit the industry. Consumers can also switch between suppliers costlessly.
4. *There is perfect information about relevant aspects of this and related markets.* Consumers know their preferences and the quality of the products they are interested in consuming, as well as the prices charged for those products. Producers know the technology of production, the prices of factors of production, and the price at which they are able to sell their product.

Although few markets adhere strictly to all four of these tenets, many markets deviate only slightly from one or more of them. Many agricultural products (such as corn, wheat, etc.) closely adhere to the perfectly competitive norm. A variety of other goods traded on commodities markets (such as gold, silver, etc.) also satisfy the requirements of perfect competition.

The word *competition* has a very different connotation to the layperson (noneconomist) than to the economist. The layperson views competition as *rivalry*. An economist describes competition when there is atomistic behavior in which no firm can affect another firm's situation. By contrast, rivalry involves interdependence among actors—for example, how does Coke react to Pepsi, or how does Microsoft react to Apple? These markets are not competitive using the previous criteria; in particular, each of these players is "large," relative to the size of their market. Both of these markets are more aptly described as oligopolistic, rather than competitive. We examine such interdependent behavior in Chapter 20.

short-run perfectly competitive equilibrium: The short-run perfectly competitive equilibrium is the (Q, P) combination for which market demand and short-run market supply are equal.

market clearing price: The market clearing price is the price at which supply equals demand. This is often also called the *market price*.

Economists describe perfectly competitive markets in a variety of ways, but the essence of each description includes the idea that economic actors cannot individually affect the market outcome. By economic actors, we mean individual consumers and producers.

The market outcome is simply the intersection of market supply with market demand. Economists call this outcome the short-run perfectly competitive equilibrium. The **short-run perfectly competitive equilibrium** is the (Q, P) combination for which market demand and short-run market supply are equal. Since both the market demand curve and the market supply curve describe quantity as a function of price, we typically describe the market equilibrium in terms of the market clearing price (rather than the market clearing quantity). The **market clearing price** is the price at which supply equals demand. This is often also called the *market price*. Market demand was described in Section 12.1; (short-run) market supply will be more explicitly defined in Section 13.4. It is based on the symmetric notion from the production side; market supply is simply the horizontal sum of individual firm supply curves. Market supply describes what the market as a whole is willing to supply at different prices. As in Chapter 12, we often describe market supply as being linear to simplify the analytics and allow us to focus on other more salient issues.

If an individual firm is small relative to the size of the market, then it cannot individually affect the market outcome. Any activity that the individual firm undertakes will be insignificant when viewed from a lens focused on the market as a whole. If an individual firm tries to increase the price it receives, it will find that demand is zero. Conversely, the firm can sell as much as it can possibly produce without having to lower its price. The firm is small, relative to the size of the market; therefore, its actions have no effect on the market. Put another way, an individual firm takes price as given; economists often say that an individual firm is a **price taker** in competitive markets because it can buy or sell as little or as much as it wishes without affecting the prevailing market price. Similarly, an individual consumer views price as given and beyond that individual's control.

price taker: An economic actor is a price taker if it can buy or sell as much or as little as it wishes without affecting the market price of the product.

Economic actors take price as fixed and given. Economists sometimes say that price is an exogenous variable in this situation. Although we focus here on the firm as a price taker, the same idea applies to consumers: Consumers are price takers if they cannot affect the market price by their actions. When you go to the grocery store to buy bananas, you can buy as much or as little as you want at the going market (posted) price. You do *not*, in general, ask the clerk if you can get a better deal. You are a price taker at the grocery store; you take the posted prices on the shelves as given and fixed. Price is exogenously determined by the grocery store in this conceptualization of price taking.

The Demand Curve Facing an Individual Firm

What does being a price taker imply about the demand curve perceived by the firm? The firm views demand as being flat at the going market price. For higher prices, the firm cannot sell any of its output, and it can sell as much as it wishes at the going market price; there is simply no need for the firm to reduce price to attract further demand. If a firm faces a flat demand for its product, then its demand is perfectly elastic.

The distinction between the individual firm and the market is most easily seen by examining a specific market, so consider the market for vine-ripened tomatoes. The demand curve perceived by an individual firm (farmer), dd, is shown in Figure 13.1A, based on the market supply, S, and demand, D, intersection at the short-run perfectly competitive equilibrium point **A** = (85,000,000, $9.00) in Figure 13.1B. The individual farmer can sell as much or as little as the farmer wishes at the going market price of $9/bushel.

This farmer's contribution to the overall crop of vine-ripened tomatoes is so small, relative to market supply, that any actions by this farmer will not affect the going market price. This is most easily seen by noting the difference in units of measurement on the horizontal axis in each panel (thousands of bushels versus millions of bushels). Put another way, this farmer faces perfectly elastic demand at a price of $9/bushel.

Q1a. Suppose a tornado wipes out a farmer's crop. What does this do to the market?*

Q1b. Suppose a hurricane touches down and wipes out the southern New Jersey tomato crop. What does this do to the market?†

We have not specifically delineated how the farmer determines how much to supply in this instance; indeed, that is the subject of much of this chapter. The number of acres that the farmer wishes to devote to growing tomatoes is determined by comparing the expected trade-offs inherent in growing other crops on the land. Once that decision is made, the

*__Q1a answer:__ The market is not affected by the loss of an individual firm's product. The effect on market supply is negligible, so the market remains as in Figure 13.1.

†__Q1b answer:__ Many firms are affected, so supply shifts back, and the market clearing price increases as shown in Figure 13.2.

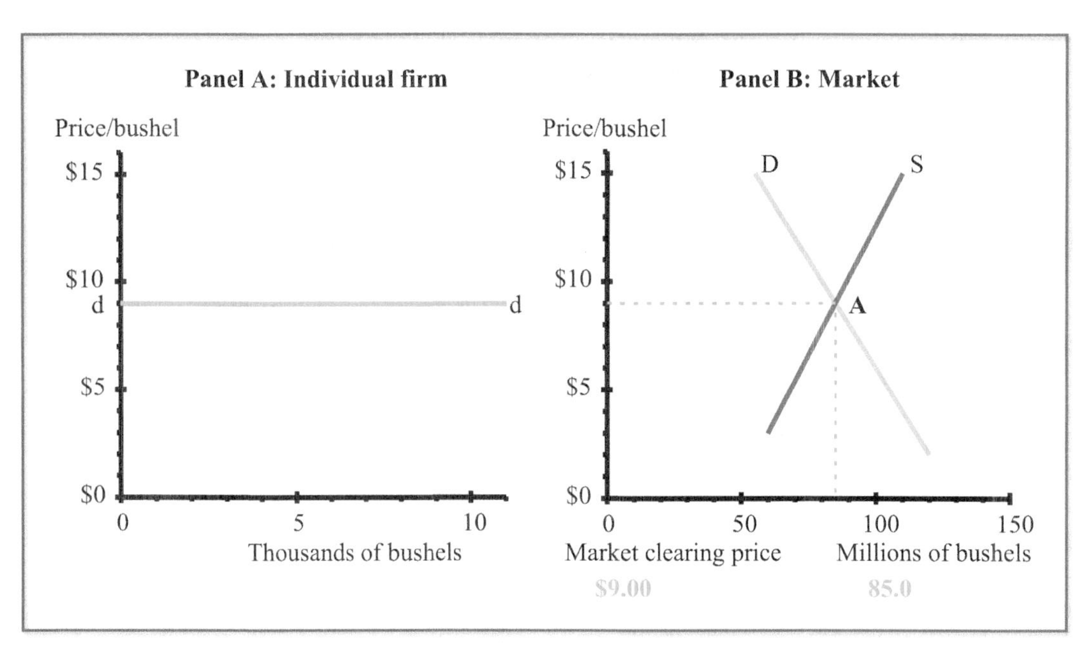

FIGURE 13.1 How an Individual Firm Is Embedded in a Perfectly Competitive Market: The Market for Vine-Ripened Tomatoes

ultimate yield from those acres is, of course, dependent on growing conditions that prevail until harvest time. Suppose that a hailstorm wipes out the farmer's tomato crop. What effect will this have on the market for tomatoes? As long as the storm was a localized phenomenon, there will be no effect on the market for tomatoes. Ten thousand bushels more or less will not significantly affect a supply/demand equilibrium at 85,000,000 bushels. The shift in market supply, S, due to this loss in the individual farmer's supply is imperceptible; therefore, the intersection point **A** does not appreciably change due to the hailstorm. This is why demand faced by the farmer, dd, is flat at the market clearing price of $9.

The effect would be different if severe weather adversely affects crops more generally. Suppose that a larger weather event, such as a hurricane, reduces yield along much of the eastern seaboard. This scenario is depicted in Figure 13.2.[1] Market supply would shift from S to S′ and create a new equilibrium at **A′**. The market clearing price would increase from $9 to $11.40, and individual farmers would perceive a new perfectly elastic demand curve, d′d′, at that price.

Confusion often surrounds the notion that an individual firm faces a flat demand, while market demand is downward sloping. To understand this distinction, it is useful to examine another market in which this might be the case.

Consider the market for firewood in the northeastern United States. How does this market conform to the tenets of a perfectly competitive market? Consumers are individual homeowners who have fireplaces and who wish to use the fireplaces for heating and ambiance; certainly, there are many consumers in this market. Similarly, in a given community, there are likely to be a number of producers offering firewood for sale. You may not have considered this market in the past, but if you live in a part of the country where many homes have fireplaces, a quick check of the "for sale" advertisements in the local newspaper or on *craigslist* will confirm that a variety of sellers is available. The second tenet is product homogeneity. Perhaps if you are a true firewood aficionado, you will have a preference for split hickory, oak, or maple, but many individual users would not likely be able to tell one wood type from another. Consumers want the BTUs and the ambiance provided by the burning log but are not likely to be concerned with the type of wood they are burning. The third tenet is free entry and exit. Free entry and exit does not mean that entry is costless; it just means that it is not differentially costly. Anyone with a

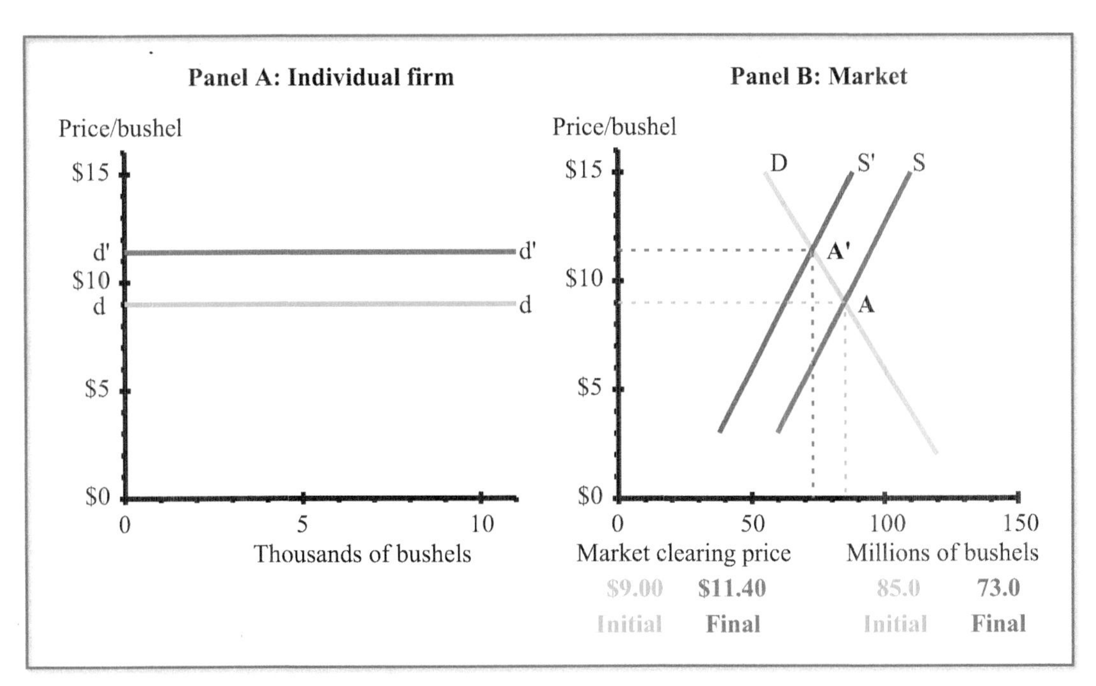

FIGURE 13.2 The Effect of Widespread Adverse Weather Conditions in a Competitive Market: The Market for Vine-Ripened Tomatoes

chainsaw and a pickup truck can get into this market. Of course, it helps to own land, but it is also possible to obtain the right to log on public lands or to clear someone else's land. Access is not restricted due to patents or other restrictive hurdles that must be overcome to enter this market. Finally, information is perfect: Buyers and sellers know all relevant information. In this context, the question is: How hidden is information about the cord of firewood? The answer is: not very hidden. Advertisements typically provide price and phone numbers—not much more is required.

Suppose that you own 100 acres of hardwood forest from which you harvest trees that you turn into cut and split firewood. The going market price in your area is $150 per cord. You are only one of a large number of individual producers of firewood. If you currently produce (and sell) 20 cords per week, you could cut your production to zero or double it to 40 cords per week, and you would still have no effect on the prevailing market price of $150 per cord. Put another way, your actions would have no effect on the market-determined price.

An individual producer has no effect on the market price of a product in a perfectly competitive market; nonetheless, all producers cumulatively determine price (in conjunction with all consumers). So, the market outcome would change if *all* producers decided to double their production; in that event, the increased production could only be supported by a lower market price. An increase in market supply would create a new equilibrium at a higher output and lower price. (This occurs due to a shift in the market supply curve and a movement down a market demand curve.) You should be able to work through this process using the Excel file for Figures 13.1and 13.2. (Of course, the prices on the vertical axis and quantities would have to be adjusted, but the qualitative relationship can easily be described using this file.)

This distinction between perception and actuality is worth considering. Market demand is the sum of individual consumer demand curves, not individual firm demand curves. As noted in Section 12.2, unless the firm is a monopolist, the firm views the demand it faces as some part of market demand. In perfectly competitive markets, an individual firm views market demand as so much larger than what it can possibly supply that it is not able to perceive a downward slope to its demand curve.

What Is Marginal Revenue in Perfect Competition?

If no action by an individual firm can change the price at which it can sell its goods, then marginal revenue is this price. Marginal revenue asks: What is the incremental revenue obtained by selling a bit more output, $MR = \Delta TR/\Delta x$? The "bit more" that is used for heuristic purposes is $\Delta x = 1$. Selling one more unit of output produces P more revenue in perfect competition.

$$MR(x) = P \text{ for all values of x produced by the firm.} \quad \textbf{(13.1)}$$

This is in stark contrast to when the firm faces downward-sloping demand. In Chapter 12, we saw that, in general, $MR(x) < P(x)$, where $P(x)$ is the inverse demand curve facing the firm. $P(x)$ in this incarnation is the price that supports x units of output; in general, we saw that this price was a declining function of output. The reason $MR(x) = P$ in perfect competition is straightforward, when examined from the perspective of how $MR(x) < P(x)$ was derived in Section 12.2. In perfect competition, the demand curve faced by the firm is horizontal; therefore, area **A** $= x \cdot \Delta P = 0$ in Figure 12.7 (since $\Delta P = 0$). Therefore, area **A′** = 0 and area **C** = area **D** in Figure 12.7B. Incremental revenue is area **C** – area **A**, but area **A** = 0, so incremental revenue is ΔTR = area **C** $= P \cdot \Delta x$, and marginal revenue, $MR = \Delta TR/\Delta x = P \cdot \Delta x/\Delta x = P$, is a constant, just as in Equation 13.1.

13.2 Profit Maximization under Perfect Competition

In Chapter 12, we saw that the general requirement for profit maximization is that output is set so that marginal revenue equals marginal cost, $MR = MC$. We have just seen that in perfectly competitive markets, marginal revenue is not dependent on output; rather, it is only dependent on the market price. This creates a profit-maximizing decision rule that is especially simple in competitive markets.

P = MC as a Special Case of MR = MC

Marginal revenue is the slope of the total revenue hill. In the perfectly competitive setting, the "hill" is not actually a hill but a constant sloped incline that increases by P per unit of output; that is, the total revenue curve is a ray through the origin with slope P. Figure 13.3 shows this hill and its per-unit counterpart—a horizontal line at a price of \$65, since $P = MR$ = slope of TR is constant on rays through the origin. (Exact values are suppressed so that we can examine the qualitative relationships involved in output determination.)

The total cost curve has the typical upward-sloping S shape described in Chapter 11. As a result, marginal cost varies along the total cost curve. Profit maximization requires that $MR = MC$. In this instance, setting $MR = MC$ involves finding an output level where marginal cost equals the going market price. This is given algebraically by finding the output x where:

$$\underset{\textbf{Perfect}\uparrow\textbf{competition}}{P = MR(x)} \quad \underset{\textbf{Profit}\uparrow\textbf{maximization}}{= MC(x).} \quad \textbf{(13.2)}$$

This simple chain of equalities shows how the general profit-maximizing rule of $MR = MC$ turns into the special case $P = MC$ rule, due to the introduction of perfect competition. In Figure 13.3, $P = \$65$ and $MC(24) = \$65$, so the profit-maximizing firm will set $x = 24$ and obtain profits of approximately \$640. Put another way, *the point A = (24, \$65) on the firm's marginal cost curve is a point on the firm's supply curve.*

A Competitive Firm Supplies along Its Marginal Cost Curve

Figure 13.3 shows one point on the firm's supply curve, **A**. That point is determined by setting $P = MC$, according to Equation 13.2. As price changes, the total revenue hill rotates up or down, depending on whether the change is an increase or decrease in price in the upper (total) diagram of Figure 13.3. Simultaneously, the demand curve faced by

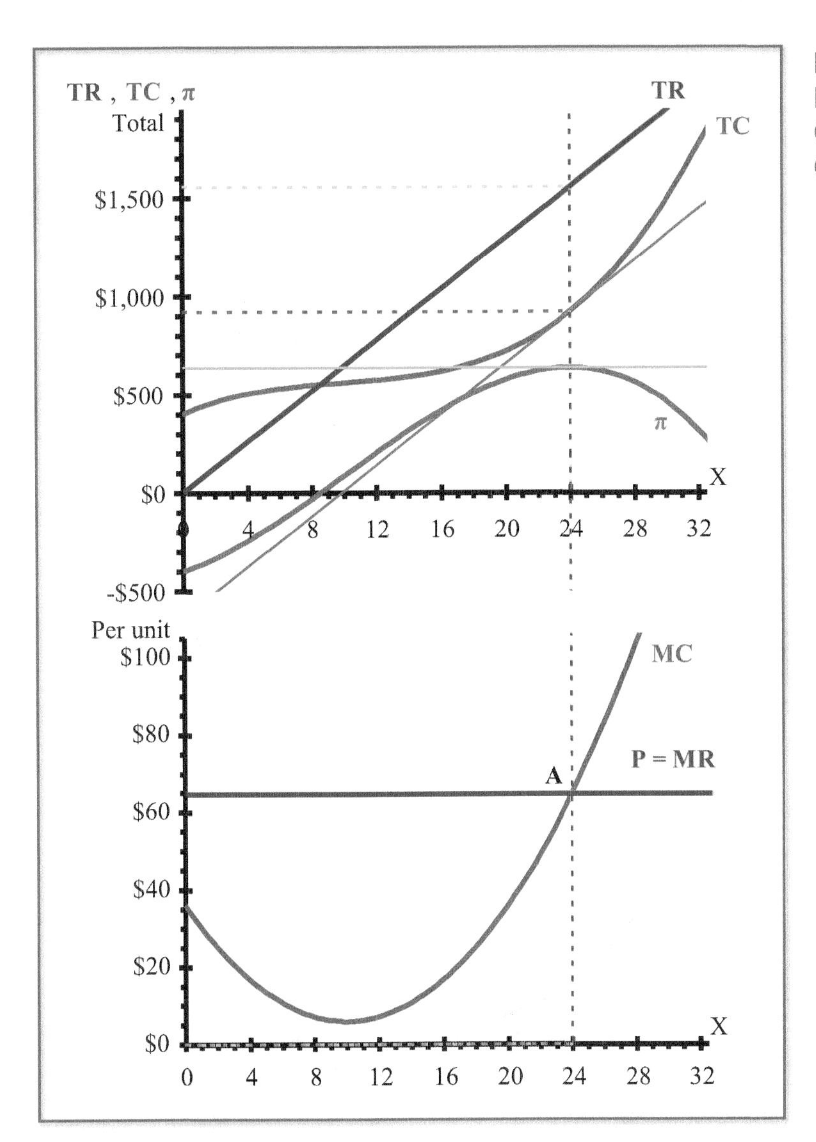

FIGURE 13.3 Profit-Maximizing Output, Given Perfect Competition

the firm, P = MR, shifts up or down, and output level where P = MR = MC moves out or in along the fixed marginal cost curve in the lower (per-unit) diagram. The marginal cost curve acts to determine the profit-maximizing level of output in this setting. *As price changes, the profit-maximizing output level is obtained by "walking" along the marginal cost curve.*

The supply curve takes a price orientation. The supply curve answers the question: How many units are supplied at a given *price*? By contrast, the marginal cost curve takes a quantity orientation. Marginal cost answers the question: What is the incremental cost of the *x*th unit of output? As we have just seen, both answers can be obtained from the marginal cost curve.[2]

To this point, the profit-maximizing output has occurred at a point where profits are positive, since TR > TC at the profit-maximizing level of output in each figure in Chapter 12 and in Figure 13.3. This need not be the case, as we see in Figure 13.4. At a price of \$25, profits are maximized at x = 18, a point where P = MR = MC. But revenues do not cover cost in this instance, so profits are negative. Indeed, we see that profits are approximately a loss of \$200 in this instance. At this price, no output level allows the firm to cover its cost, but profits are maximized when losses are minimized, and this occurs at x = 18.

Students often consider negative profits as being unreasonable; no firm likes to lose money. Why should the firm stand for such a situation? The answer is that the firm does not have a choice, at least not in the short run. Given the market conditions it faces, the best the firm can do is to produce at a loss because it will have to pay its fixed costs

FIGURE 13.4 Loss Minimization versus Profit Maximization

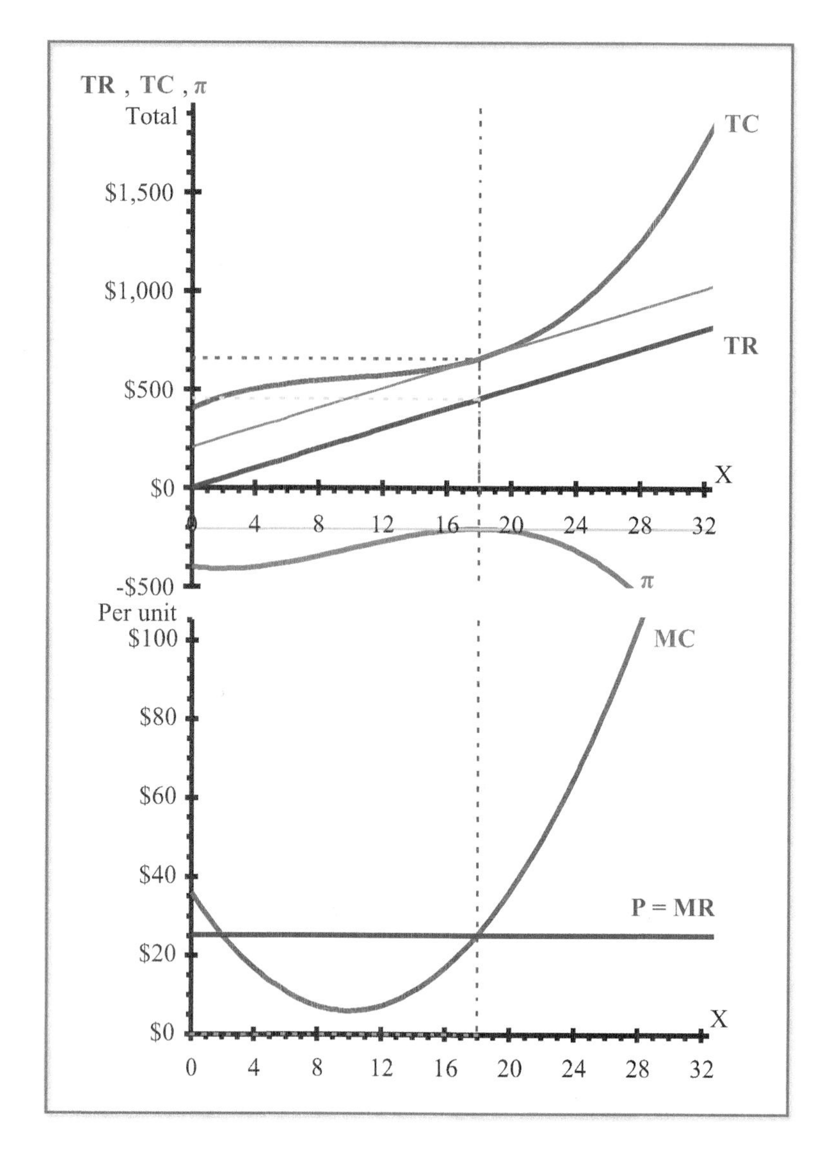

whether it produces or not. In Figure 13.4, the firm faces the choice of not producing in the short run and losing $400, or producing 18 units of output and losing $200. The profit-maximizing firm will minimize losses, since losses are simply negative profits. Although it does not sound as appealing as profit maximization, loss minimization *is* profit maximization for the firm.

13.3 Two Caveats to Marginal Cost as Supply

If a firm is embedded in a perfectly competitive market and produces output, then that firm supplies along its marginal cost curve to maximize profits. Students often restate this as: "The marginal cost curve is the firm's supply curve in a competitive market." Unfortunately, this is not completely accurate. This statement must be adjusted in two ways because not all of the marginal cost curve provides a profit-maximizing solution to output determination. One adjustment has to do with distinguishing "the best a firm can do" from "the worst a firm can do." The other adjustment has to do with when it is preferable to shut down in the short run.

Distinguishing Maximums and Minimums

For a range of prices, there are two output levels where P = MC. For example, in Figure 13.4, P = MC = $25 at x = 2 and x = 18. The earlier discussion ignored the x = 2 solution and argued that x = 18 is profit maximizing, since it is loss minimizing in the short run. As it turns out, x = 2 is locally the worst the firm could do, given cost and price information provided in Figure 13.4. That is, x = 2 is a profit minimum, and x = 18 is a profit maximum. This is most easily understood by examining a figure that allows us to focus directly on best- versus worst-case scenarios.

Given U-shaped marginal cost curves, there are a range of prices for which P = MC(x) at two output levels x. For any price, P, in the range MC(0) > P > $MC_{minimum}$, there are two output levels where P = MC(x). Figure 13.5 depicts a typical upward-sloping, S-shaped, total cost curve with fixed cost of $50 (ignore for the time being the table beneath the figure). The total revenue hill in the upper diagram has a slope of $20, so a firm embedded in this industry will face a perfectly elastic demand curve at a price of $20; this is shown in the lower diagram as the horizontal line P = MR. MR = MC is required for

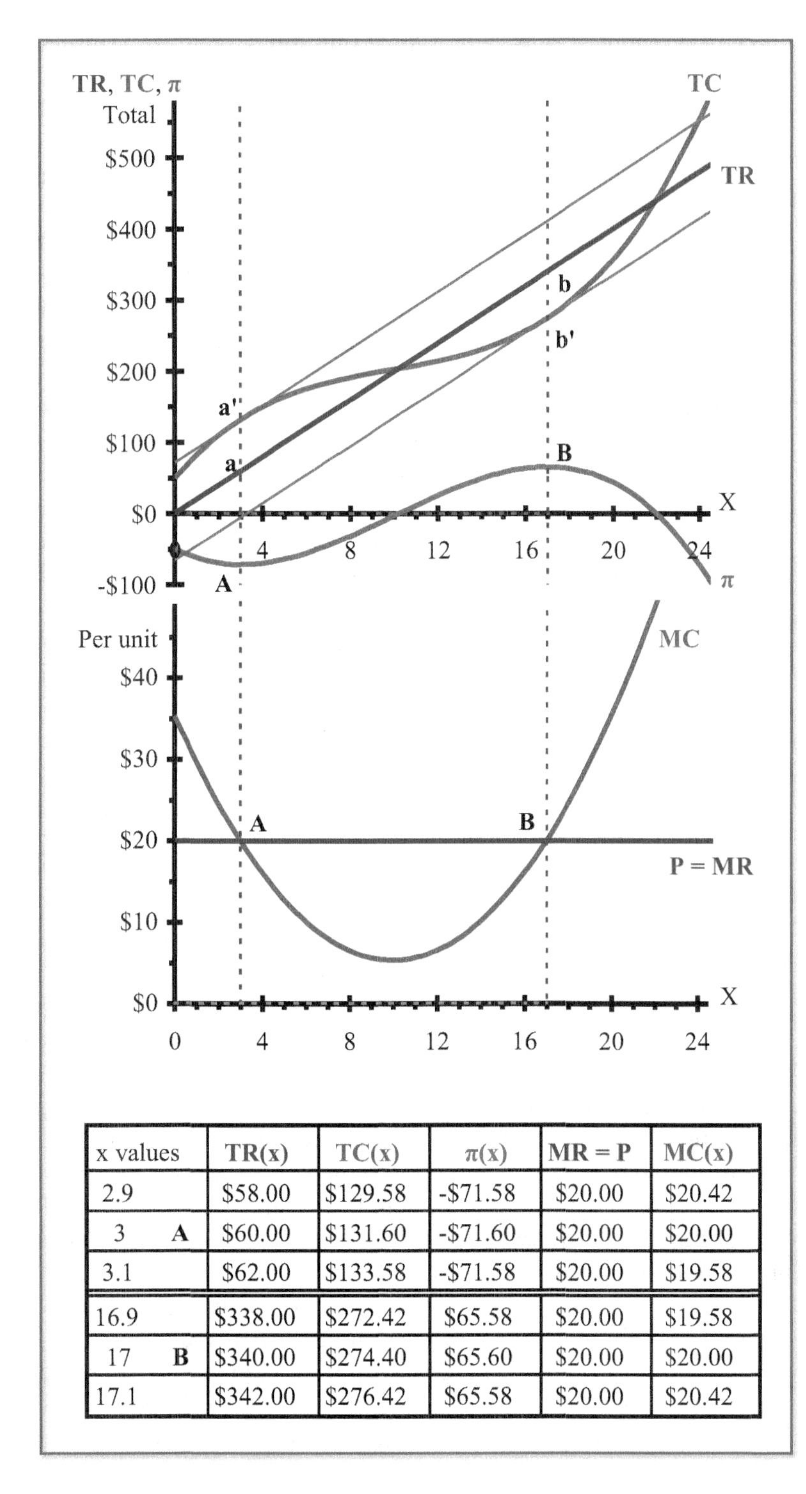

x values		TR(x)	TC(x)	π(x)	MR = P	MC(x)
2.9		$58.00	$129.58	-$71.58	$20.00	$20.42
3	A	$60.00	$131.60	-$71.60	$20.00	$20.00
3.1		$62.00	$133.58	-$71.58	$20.00	$19.58
16.9		$338.00	$272.42	$65.58	$20.00	$19.58
17	B	$340.00	$274.40	$65.60	$20.00	$20.00
17.1		$342.00	$276.42	$65.58	$20.00	$20.42

FIGURE 13.5 Profit Maximization versus Profit Minimization

profit maximization. Two possible solutions are seen in the lower diagram of Figure 13.5, since $MC(0) = \$35 > P = \$20 > \$5 = MC_{minimum}$. These two possible solutions are points **A** = (3, \$20) and **B** = (17, \$20).

Visually, the green profit curve in the upper diagram shows that **A** is a profit minimum, while **B** is a profit maximum. The reason why one is a minimum and one is a maximum is straightforward: Since $\pi(x) = TR(x) - TC(x)$, we see that $\pi(3) = \mathbf{a} - \mathbf{a'} < 0$ and $\pi(17) = \mathbf{b} - \mathbf{b'} > 0$ in the upper diagram.

Claim: *Both **A** and **B** represent output levels where there is locally a maximum difference between the two curves, but in the first case, this is the point where cost is locally the largest difference above revenue, and in the second case, it is the point where revenue is the largest difference above cost.*

The minimum at **A** is only a local minimum because if output is large enough, costs will inevitably overtake revenue, due to the law of diminishing marginal product. For example, at x = 24, losses are the same as at x = 3, and for x > 24, losses are larger than at **A**.

Consider changing output from x = 3 in either direction; both changes produce an increase in profits. As you increase output from x = 3, the incremental revenue exceeds the incremental cost because P = MR > MC to the right of x = 3 in the per-unit diagram of Figure 13.5. Therefore, incremental profits, $M\pi = MR - MC$, increase. Conversely, if you reduce output from x = 3, you avoid incremental costs that are higher than the incremental revenues you lose on those units, and again, incremental profits increase. This can be seen in the table associated with Figure 13.5, which describes profits at **A** and **B**, as well as ±0.1 units on either side of **A** and **B**. For both 0.1 unit movements away from **A**, profits increase by \$0.02. **A** therefore represents a local profit minimum.

The reverse holds true at **B**. Small movements away from **B** in either direction decrease profits, as seen by the profit information in the table accompanying Figure 13.5. The Excel file for Figure 13.5 allows you to adjust the size of the change in output. As you do, you will find that further moves away from either output level lead to larger changes in profits.

We can see the loss in profitability that accrues from not producing at **B**, using the graphs and tabular information provided in Figure 13.5. To view this loss graphically, we must examine larger changes in output from **B** than the ±0.1 unit changes described in the table. Figure 13.6 examines the loss due to production that is too small and too large. Profit at a point like x = 13 is the height **D** in the upper diagram of Figure 13.6A, and the loss in profits from producing 13 rather than 17 units is **CD** in the upper diagram. This same loss in profits is seen in the lower (per-unit) diagram as the "triangular" area **BCD**. The area under the marginal cost curve is the incremental cost of producing those units, and the area under the marginal revenue curve is the incremental revenue generated by those units.[3] Since incremental revenue exceeds the incremental cost on the units from 13 to 17, it makes sense to increase output from 13 to 17. If this is not done, the loss in profits is "triangle" **BCD**. Similarly, if we consider the production of too much output, such as x = 22 in Figure 13.6B, we see the loss due to overproduction as length **CD** in the upper diagram and as "triangle" **BCD** in the lower diagram. The reasoning is the same: The incremental units from 17 to 22 cost the area under the marginal cost curve from **B** to **D** to produce, and the incremental revenue on those units is the area under the marginal revenue curve from **B** to **C**. Since incremental cost exceeds incremental revenue, the extra production should not be undertaken; if it is undertaken, a loss of **BCD** results. The Excel file for Figure 13.6 allows you to vary the production point x and see the resulting loss in profits due to over- or under-production.

Although the numbers would change if we examined different market clearing prices, the same qualitative relation would hold. When marginal cost is declining, the point where P = MC represents a local profit minimum, and when marginal cost is increasing, the point where P = MC represents a local profit maximum. A geometric justification has just been given; a formal mathematical proof of this assertion requires calculus.[4]

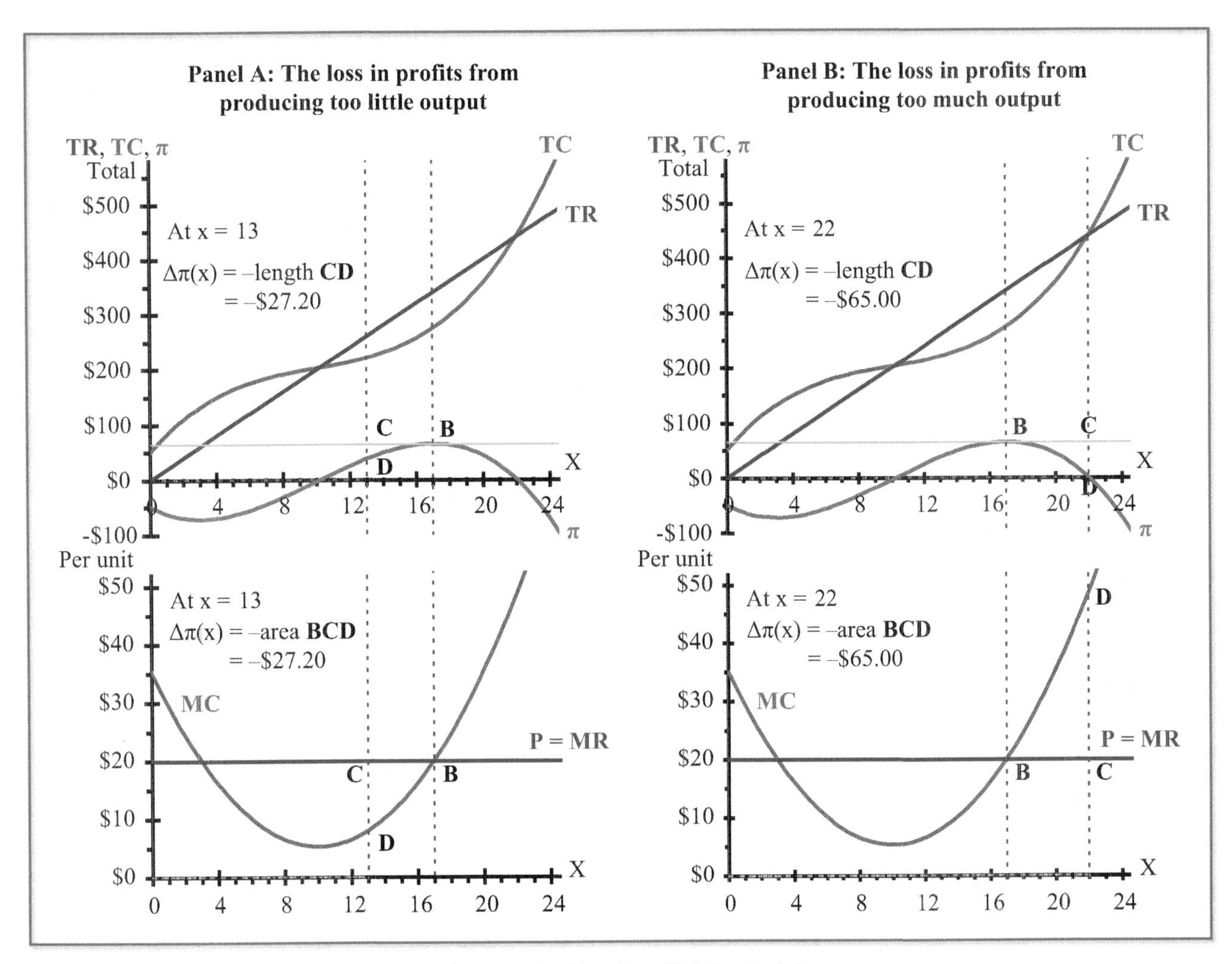

FIGURE 13.6 What Happens When Output Is Not Profit Maximizing

We can use the distinction between profit maximums and minimums to sharpen our description of the supply curve for a firm embedded in a perfectly competitive industry. The first caveat can be stated as:

Claim: *A profit-maximizing firm in a competitive industry will choose an output level, x, where P = MC(x) on the positively sloped part of its marginal cost curve.*

Put another way, the firm's supply curve is restricted to the positively sloped part of its marginal cost curve.

The Shutdown Decision

Although all points on the positively sloped part of the marginal cost curve represent local profit-maximizing solutions for various prices, there are a range of prices for which it is better to shut down instead of continuing to produce. The problem in this instance is that some prices are so low that variable costs are not covered. As a result, producing at the point where P = MC on the positively sloped part of the marginal cost curve produces a loss that is greater than simply shutting down and incurring a loss of fixed cost.

It is important to distinguish between *shutdown* and *exit* to understand this discussion. If a firm decides to produce no output in the short run, economists say the firm has decided to **shut down**. When a firm shuts down, it still must pay its fixed costs. If a firm decides to leave the market and sell its capital stock, it is said to **exit** the market. Once the firm exits the market, it no longer has fixed assets, and therefore it no longer has fixed

shut down: If a firm decides to produce no output in the short run, economists say the firm has decided to shut down. When a firm shuts down, it still must pay its fixed costs.

exit: If a firm decides to leave the market and sell its capital stock, it is said to exit the market. Once the firm exits the market, it no longer has fixed assets, and therefore, it no longer has fixed costs.

costs. *Shutting down is a short-run decision, and exiting is a long-run decision.* We postpone the formal discussion of *exit* until Chapter 14.

If the profit-maximizing level of profits is negative, then it may make sense to shut down, rather than produce at a loss. In Figure 13.4, we saw that the firm should produce because the loss from producing a positive level of output is smaller than the loss in fixed cost that occurs if the firm decides to shut down in the short run. This is because price in Figure 13.4 covers average variable cost and indeed covers part of fixed cost as well. The variable cost curve was not shown in that figure, but the dollar amounts involved were a loss of $200 when producing 18 units of output and a loss of $400 if the firm decides to shut down. Because $200 of the $400 fixed cost are covered in this situation, it made sense to produce at a loss in the short run because that production creates revenue that covers variable cost, as well as part of fixed cost. The same result is not always true, as we see in Figure 13.7. When price is low enough, it does not cover variable costs of production. At a price of $10 per unit, P = MC at x = 13 on the positively sloped part of the marginal cost curve, as required for profit maximization. Profits in this instance are a loss of $467.60, according to the table. A better solution is to shut down and incur the fixed cost loss of $400.

FIGURE 13.7 Price So Low That the Firm Should Shut Down in the Short Run

Produce and lose **A – C = Areas I + II**; shut down and lose **A – B = Area I = FC.**

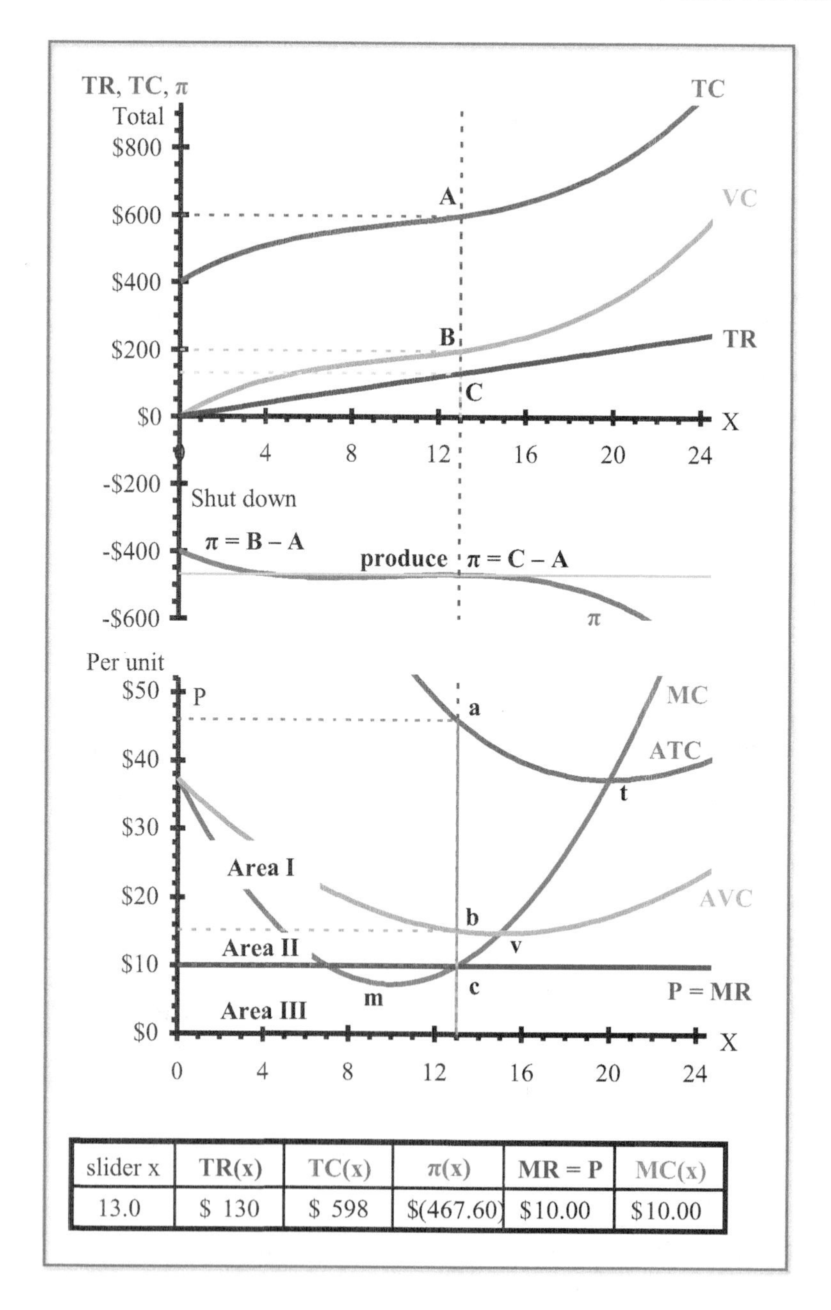

slider x	TR(x)	TC(x)	π(x)	MR = P	MC(x)
13.0	$ 130	$ 598	$(467.60)	$10.00	$10.00

The choice between x = 0 and x = 13 can be seen in a number of ways in Figure 13.7. Consider first the top half of the upper (total) diagram. At x = 13, total cost exceeds total revenue by **A** – **C**; put another way, $\pi(13) = \mathbf{C} - \mathbf{A}$. If the firm shuts down and produces at x = 0, then it incurs a loss of \$400 (the point (0, \$400) on the total cost curve). But this is the same as a loss of **A** – **B**, since FC = TC(x) – VC(x). Producing at x = 13 yields extra losses of **B** – **C** over fixed cost losses of **A** – **B**. A second way to see that the firm should shut down is to note that for no output level (other than x = 0) is the total revenue ray above the variable cost curve. This would be required for variable costs to be covered by production. The green profit function provides a third way to see the comparison, using the upper (total) diagram. The profit function is negative for all output levels, so the profit curve is below the x axis. The profit function starts at the shutdown point of (0, –\$400), initially declines to the local minimum at x = 7, and then rises to the local maximum at x = 13. The tangent line at x = 13 shows graphically that losses in this instance are approximately \$470 (when read off of the negative part of the vertical axis). This meshes closely with the tabular value of $\pi(13) = -\$467.60$.

The same information can be seen in the per-unit diagram of Figure 13.7. Average total and variable cost curves are included, and three rectangular areas are labeled **Area I**, **Area II**, and **Area III**. The points with lowercase letters **a**, **b**, and **c** are the per-unit counterparts of points **A**, **B**, and **C** in the upper diagram. The total revenue of producing 13 units of output and selling it at \$10 per unit is \$130, or the rectangle whose opposing vertices are **0** and **c**. In terms of areas in the lower diagram,

$$TR(13) = P \cdot x = \$10 \cdot 13 = \textbf{Area III}. \qquad \textbf{(13.3a)}$$

(This is the height **C** in the upper diagram.) The total cost of producing 13 units of output is the height **A** in the upper diagram; in the lower diagram, this is seen as the rectangle whose opposing vertices are **0** and **a**:

$$TC(13) = ATC(13) \cdot 13 = \textbf{Area I} + \textbf{Area II} + \textbf{Area III}. \qquad \textbf{(13.3b)}$$

(This is the height **A** in the upper diagram.) The profit generated by producing 13 units of output is the difference between Equations 13.3a and 13.3b:

$$\begin{aligned} \pi(13) &= TR(13) - TC(13) = (P - ATC(13)) \cdot 13 = (\mathbf{c} - \mathbf{a}) \cdot 13 \\ &= -\textbf{Area I} - \textbf{Area II}. \qquad \textbf{(13.3c)} \end{aligned}$$

(This is the same as the length **C** – **A** in the upper diagram.)

By contrast, profit from shutting down is a loss of fixed cost. As noted earlier, fixed cost can be seen as the difference between total and variable cost (length **A** – **B** in the upper diagram). In the per-unit context, this can be seen as:

$$\pi(0) = -FC = -(ATC(x) - AVC(x)) \cdot x = -(\mathbf{a} - \mathbf{b}) \cdot 13 = -\textbf{Area I}. \qquad \textbf{(13.3d)}$$

By producing at x = 13, the firm incurs an extra loss of **Area II** = (**b** – **c**) · 13 in the lower diagram and length **B** – **C** in the upper diagram. Both quantities represent the part of variable cost *not* covered by revenue due to price below average variable cost; they therefore also represent the extra loss the firm incurs if it decides to produce at x = 13, rather than shut down in the short run.

Although different numbers would result at different prices, the same qualitative relation would hold for any price below minimum average variable cost. The minimum points on each of the three per-unit curves are labeled **m**, **v**, and **t**. For any price $P < AVC_{minimum} = P_v$, the firm would be better off to shut down. Conversely, if price P is in the range $ATC_{minimum} = P_t > P > P_v$, then the short-run profit-maximizing firm will produce at an output level where P = MC(x) on the positively sloped part of the marginal cost curve. By doing this, the firm will cover all of its variable costs of production, as well as some portion of fixed cost. Therefore, the firm will minimize short-run losses by producing at P = MC and thereby maximize short-run profits.

FIGURE 13.8 The Short-Run Supply Curve for a Firm in a Competitive Market

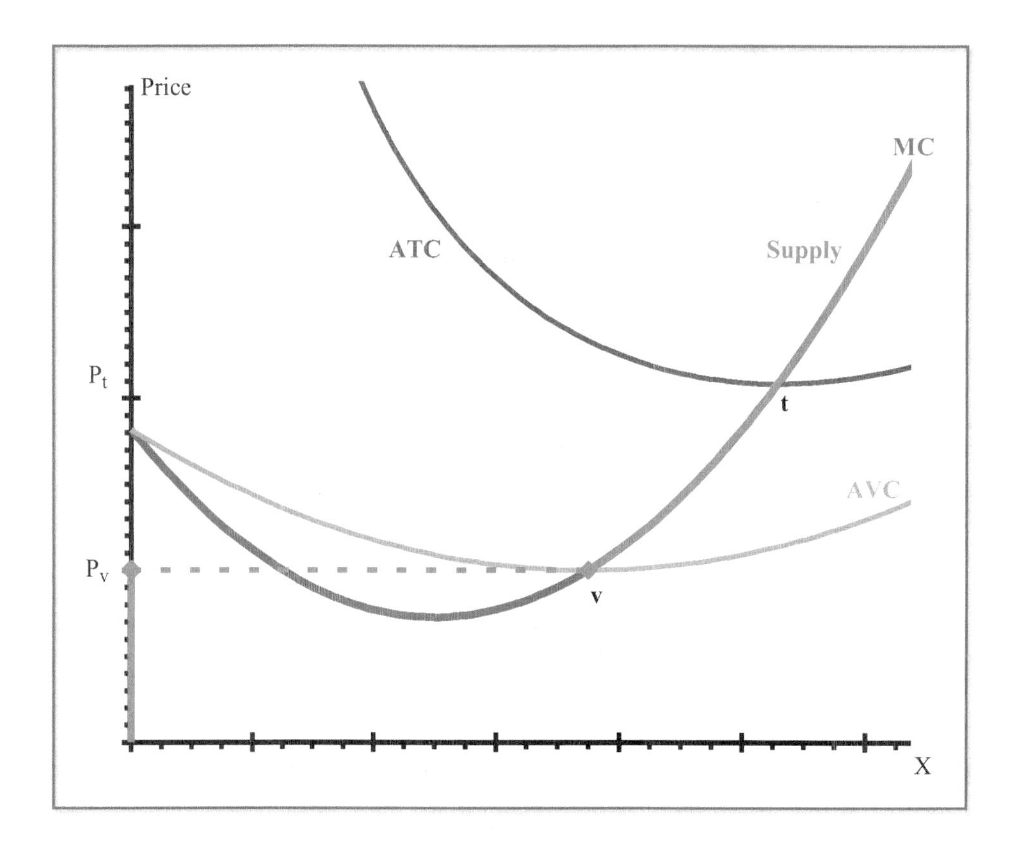

The profit-maximizing decision of the firm can therefore be restated as the following:

Claim: *A profit-maximizing firm in a competitive industry will choose an output level, x, where P = MC(x) on the positively sloped part of its marginal cost curve above minimum average variable cost. If price is below minimum average variable cost, then the firm will shut down in the short run.*

firm's supply curve, s(P): The firm's supply curve, s(P), is the positively sloped part of its marginal cost curve above minimum average variable cost. For prices below minimum average variable cost, the firm shuts down and supplies no output in the short run.

These profit-maximizing production decisions provide us with the firm's supply curve as a function of price, s(P). The **firm's supply curve, s(P),** is the positively sloped part of its marginal cost curve above minimum average variable cost. For prices below minimum average variable cost, the firm shuts down and supplies no output in the short run. The supply curve can be graphically described as a two-part curve. For prices below P_v, x = 0 is supplied; this is shown as a line on the vertical axis below P_v. For prices above P_v, the supply curve coincides with the positively sloped part of the marginal cost curve. This is shown in Figure 13.8. The two parts of the firm's (green) supply curve are connected with a dashed line at the price $P = P_v$.

The supply curve in Figure 13.8 can be thought of in terms of the short-run profits that result at different points along the supply curve. Four alternatives are clearly possible for an individual firm. First, the firm faces a loss of fixed cost by shutting down (along the x = 0 segment) for prices below P_v. Second, for prices between P_v and P_t, the firm produces at a loss, but a loss that is smaller than the loss incurred were the firm to shut down. Third, at a price of P_t, the firm earns zero economic profit. Finally, for prices above P_t, the firm earns a positive economic profit. All of these possibilities exist in the short run. The ultimate outcome depends entirely on something over which the competitive firm has no control: the market clearing price.

13.4 The Market Supply Curve

In Section 13.1, we used the idea of a market supply curve to examine the demand curve facing a firm, but we did not formally describe how we would obtain such a market supply curve. The discussion thus far in this chapter has a "chicken and egg" aspect to it, since we need a market supply curve to formally derive an individual firm supply curve (because the intersection of market supply and market demand gave us price, which forms the firm's perfectly elastic demand curve), but that individual firm supply curve is required to create the market supply curve. We are now in a position to complete the circle and formally describe how market supply is derived from individual firm supply.

At its most basic level, market supply is derived in the same way as market demand in Section 12.1. **Market supply** is the horizontal sum of individual firm supply curves. This is a "horizontal sum," since each individual firm's quantity supplied at a given price is added to all other individual firms' quantities supplied at that price to determine market supply at that price, S(P).

market supply: Market supply is the horizontal sum of individual firm supply curves.

$$S(P) = s_1(P) + \ldots + s_m(P), \text{ where there are m firms in the market.} \quad \textbf{(13.4)}$$

If all firms have the same supply curve, then market supply is simply a stretched-out version of individual supply. Since the reasoning is the same as when n individuals have identical demand, it is not pursued here (see the discussion surrounding Equations 12.2a and 12.2b).[5]

More interesting is the question of whether individual firms in a competitive market can have different supply curves in the short run. This is the question to which we now turn our attention.

Can $\pi = -FC$, $-FC < \pi < 0$, $\pi = 0$, and $\pi > 0$ Occur for a Single Price?

The discussion surrounding Figure 13.8 argues that each of the four possible short-run profit outcomes ($\pi = -FC$, $-FC < \pi < 0$, $\pi = 0$, and $\pi > 0$) can exist for a single firm, based upon different prices. The question we address here is: Is the reverse possible as well? That is, can each of the four profit possibilities occur for a single price? The answer is yes, and the reason this can happen is that firms may have access to different-sized plants in the short run.

Output is produced using fixed and variable factors of production. If a firm has higher fixed factors of production, then it will have lower variable factors of production. The easiest way to show this is to use a cost function in which only two parameters vary: the amount of fixed cost and the vertical location of the variable and marginal cost curves. This is accomplished by using a cubic cost function where the quadratic and cubic coefficients, c and d, are fixed. Consider the cubic cost function:

$$TC(x) = a + b \cdot x - 3 \cdot x^2 + 0.1 \cdot x^3. \quad \textbf{(13.5)}$$

From Equations 11.7 and 11.7b, the output levels that achieve minimum MC and AVC are $MC_{minimum} = c/(3 \cdot d) = 3/(3 \cdot 0.1) = 10$, and $AVC_{minimum} = c/(2 \cdot d) = 3/(2 \cdot 0.1) = 15$. The placement of AVC and MC on the vertical axis is determined by the linear coefficient, b. Indeed, an easy way to describe b is to note that b is the vertical intercept of each curve ($b = MC(0) = AVC(0)$), according to Equations 11.6f and 11.6g. Given fixed c and d, the output level where ATC is minimized is based entirely on the size of fixed cost, *a*. As fixed cost increases, the output level where ATC = MC increases.[6]

Higher fixed cost would be associated with lower variable cost, so larger values of *a* (FC) would be associated with smaller values of b (VC). Figure 13.9 depicts all five potential profitability outcomes by varying FC and VC. The panels are ordered from smallest VC to largest VC, and hence, largest FC to smallest FC. In each panel, P = MR = \$50. Figure 13.9A depicts positive profits, and all other panels depict zero or negative profits. Figure 13.9B depicts zero economic profit, and Figure 13.9C depicts producing at a loss but preferring that loss to shutting down because the firm would incur a larger loss in that event. Figure 13.9D depicts P = minimum AVC, a situation where the same loss can be attained in two ways: The firm can produce at $x = 0$ and lose FC of \$250, or it can produce at $x = 15$ and incur a loss of \$250, since $P \cdot 15$ just covers the variable cost of producing those 15 units of output ($VC(15) = 15 \cdot AVC(15)$). For all outcomes other than Figure 13.9D (for P ≠ minimum AVC), a single output level will dominate in terms of profitability. Figure 13.9E depicts shutting down and incurring a loss of FC = \$200, rather than producing at $x = 13$ and incurring a loss of \$267 (the larger loss would occur, since price does not cover average variable cost of production in this instance).

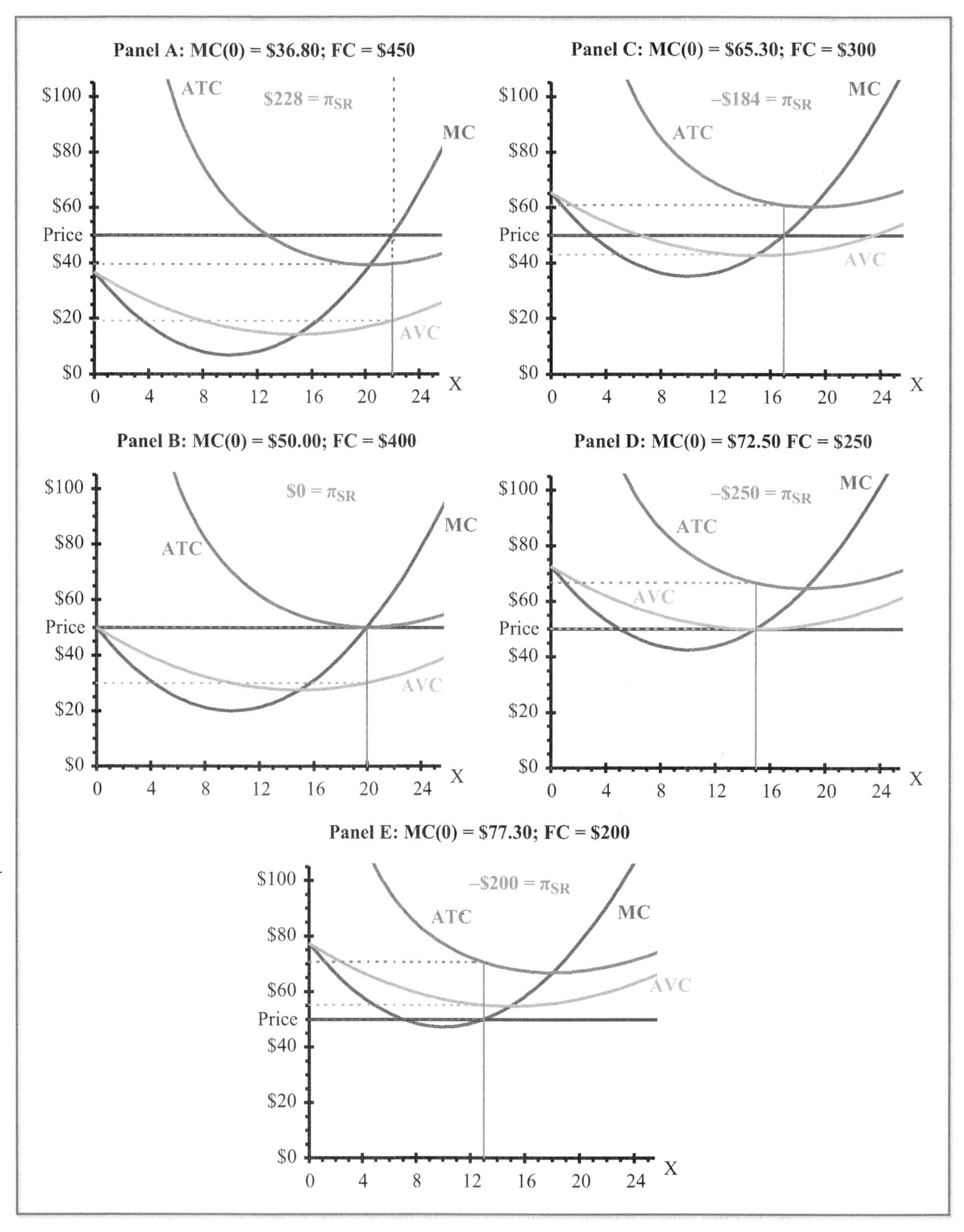

FIGURE 13.9 Per-Unit Cost Functions Based on $TC(x) = FC + MC(0) \cdot x - 3 \cdot x^2 + 0.1 \cdot x^3$

We might conclude from the progression of panels in Figure 13.9 that higher fixed cost and lower variable cost will unambiguously increase profits. This is not necessarily true; it depends on how expensive it is to reduce variable cost (in terms of fixed cost). Compare, for example, Figures 13.9A and 13.9B. The reduction in MC(0) of $13.20 ($13.20 = $50 – $36.80) is based on an increase in fixed cost of $50 (from $400 to $450).

Had this instead cost an extra \$300 in fixed cost, then the \$228 profit would turn into a \$22 loss (\$300 is \$250 more than \$50 extra, so profits would be –\$22 = \$228 – \$250), and the revised Figure 13.9A would qualitatively "look like" Figure 13.9C. Note that a change in fixed cost in Figure 13.9A would have *no* effect on profit-maximizing quantity, since the hypothetical being discussed is how much it costs to reduce variable cost by \$13.20. If that reduction in variable cost is achieved, then MC in Figure 13.9A would not be affected by the magnitude of fixed cost; therefore, P = MC would continue to occur at x = 22 in Figure 13.9A, regardless of whether profits are positive, negative, or zero. The only scenarios in Figure 13.9 that we could not generate by varying fixed cost in Figure 13.9A are those shown in Figures 13.9D and 13.9E. The reason is straightforward: Given fixed quadratic and cubic coefficients, minimum average variable cost occurs at x = 15, as shown earlier. Since P = MC at x = 22 in Figure 13.9A, we cannot cause an $x \leq 15$ intersection of P and MC to occur, as required by Figures 13.9D and 13.9E. (The Excel file for Figure 13.9 allows you to vary fixed cost and MC(0), as well as price, so you can create your own scenario.)

One part of the analysis in Figure 13.9 remains unrealistic, in light of our discussion of production functions in Chapter 9 and cost functions in Chapter 11. To simplify the presentation, we assumed that the quadratic and cubic coefficients of the total cost function in Equation 13.5 were fixed across the panels in Figure 13.9. As noted earlier, this allows the marginal cost and average variable cost curves in each panel to simply float up or down, depending on the size of b, the linear coefficient. In Chapter 9, however, we argued that small plants typically achieve maximum productivity at small levels of output, while large plants do so at large levels of output. This was described jointly in terms of the point of inflection of the total product curve, as well as the point of inflection of the variable cost curve in Figure 11.1. Larger plants typically achieve maximum marginal product and minimum marginal cost at larger levels of output. This is contrary to the assumptions that form the basis for Figure 13.9—namely, that c and d are fixed and independent of fixed cost changes. We now turn to a set of short-run cost curves that incorporate this into their analysis. We use these curves to describe market supply in the face of heterogeneous plant sizes.

Market Supply from Individual Firm Supply

As we saw in the discussion of long-run costs in Section 11.3, when different-sized plants achieve maximum marginal productivity at different output levels, then the various marginal cost curves achieve their minimum at different output levels. Figure 13.10 depicts four firms, labeled A–D, each with different capital stocks and, hence, different short-run cost curves.[7] If the market is made up of these four firms, then the market supply curve is as shown in the right-most diagram. At different prices, a different number of firms is actively producing in the market. At a very low price (for example at P = \$12), only Firm D produces output (because $AVC^{d}_{minimum}$ is \$11.53), and as price increases, other firms move from a short-run shutdown mode to producing output. A market clearing price of \$17.36 was chosen so that each of the four profit possibilities can be seen in Figure 13.10.[8]

At the market clearing price of \$17.36, we see that Firms B, C, and D produce output because \$17.36 > $AVC_{minimum}$ for each of these firms. In contrast, Firm A chooses to shut down at this price because \$17.36 < \$20.78 = $AVC^{a}_{minimum}$. Firm A is thus similar to Figure 13.9E. The next largest plant is controlled by Firm B. Firm B produces on its short-run supply curve at P = MC(4.32). At x = 4.32, there are losses, but those losses are smaller than would occur had Firm B decided to shut down ($\pi_b(4.32) = -\$22.71 > -\$23.60 = \pi_b(0) = -FC_b$). Firm B is qualitatively similar to Figure 13.9C, although the market price is quite close to $AVC^{b}_{minimum}$ (so that it almost looks like Figure 13.9D).

The next largest firm in terms of fixed cost is Firm C, but interestingly, this firm is more profitable than the largest firm, Firm D. This is an example that confirms the discussion that compared Figures 13.9A and 13.9B earlier. There is a trade-off between fixed and variable factors of production; Firm D has lower variable costs, but they are only marginally lower. The price tag for this lower variable cost is that the fixed cost of Firm D is substantially larger than the fixed cost of Firm C.[9] As a result, Firm C is qualitatively the

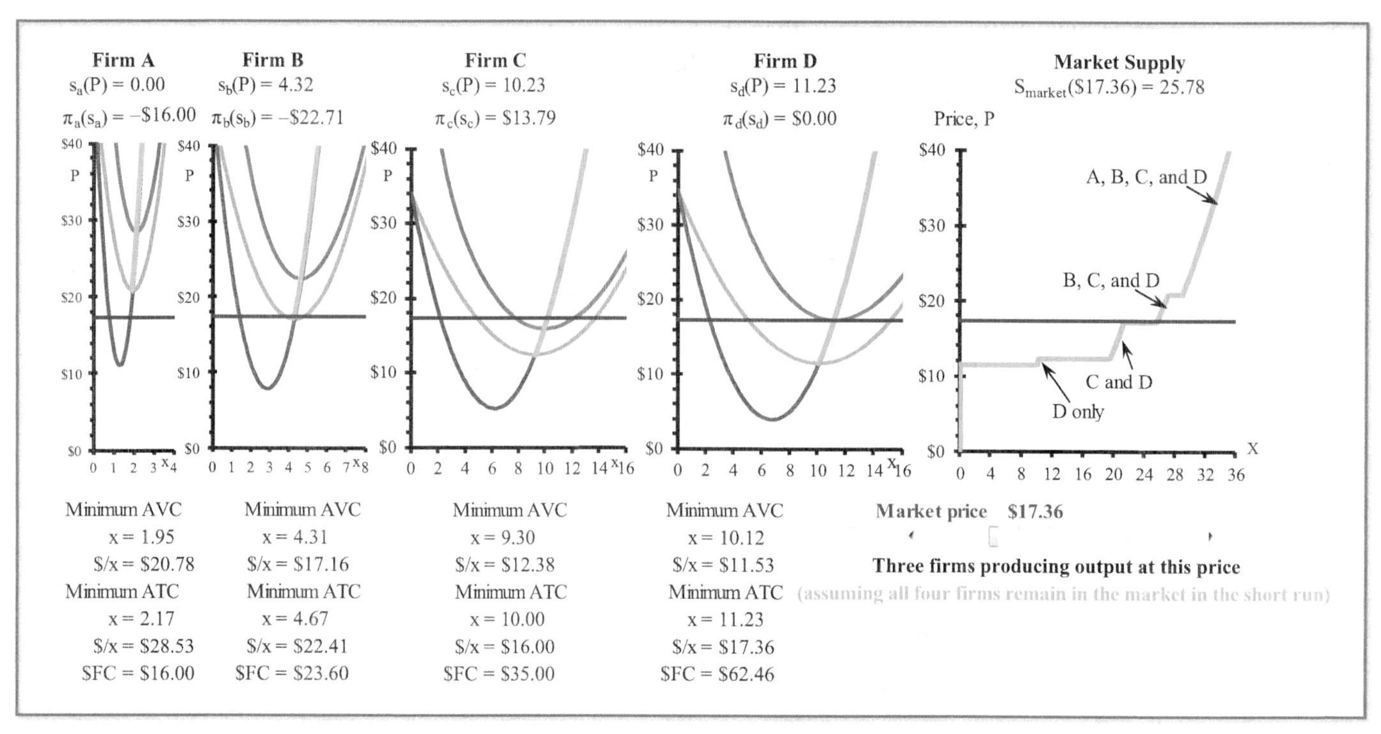

FIGURE 13.10 Market Supply as the Horizontal Sum of Individual Firm Supply Curves

The nonzero portion of individual firm supply is the green portion of MC for each firm.

same as Figure 13.9A, and Firm D is qualitatively the same as Figure 13.9B. As should be clear by now, the market clearing price was chosen so that Firm D would have zero economic profit.

Filling in Market Supply

Were these the only four firms in the industry, then it would not be appropriate to consider the industry competitive, since each firm would be "large," relative to the size of the market. In this event, it would not make sense to add across firms to obtain market supply, since each of the individual supply curves is predicated on that firm facing a perfectly elastic demand for its output. Nonetheless, if we were to add across firms, the "market supply curve" should have dashed horizontal segments, just as the individual firm supply curves have dashed horizontal segments from $x = 0$ to x_{minAVC} in Figure 13.8. These dashed segments occur as firms move from the shutdown mode to producing output to cover at least part of the firm's fixed cost of production.

The industry supply curve is not shown with such dashed segments for two reasons. The first point has to do with discrete plant sizes. As shown in the discussions of production functions in Chapter 9, cost minimization in Chapter 10, and long-run cost functions in Section 11.3, we typically expect production processes to come in a continuum of potential plant sizes. We expect that firms can adjust plant size in the long run to more closely match production process with projected output. Of course, the present analysis is a short-run analysis, and the supply scenario just described is one of only four plant sizes. The most practical reason for only four plant sizes is the lack of horizontal space on the printed page. Theoretically, it is reasonable to assume that more than four plant sizes are available in an industry characterized by a large number of firms. As we introduce other plant sizes, we see a more expansive industry supply curve with small, discrete, horizontal jumps at a number of P = minimum AVC price levels. When viewed from the macro perspective, such a market supply curve could, for practical purposes, be considered smooth, just as market demand is imagined to be smooth, despite the "kinks" discussed in Section 12.1.

Even if there were only a discrete number of plant sizes available, we should consider the horizontal parts filled in if the market is perfectly competitive and if there are a number of firms of each size. Suppose, for instance, that instead of four firms A, B, C, and D, we have 400 firms—100 each of A, B, C, and D. The only change in Figure 13.10 in this instance is to change the units on the horizontal axis of the market supply curve from units to hundreds of units. The market supply at a price of $17.36 is then 25.78 hundreds of units or 2,578 units. Each of the 100 B, C, and D firms produce 4.32, 10.23, and 11.23 units, respectively, and each A firm shuts down in the short run, since $17.36 < $20.78.

Suppose instead that the market supply/market demand intersection occurs on one of the horizontal segments of market supply. Figure 13.11 depicts this situation. Market demand at P = $20.78 = $AVC^{a}_{minimum}$, and market demand at this price is 28.06 hundred units, midway along the horizontal part of market supply from (27.09, $20.78) to (29.03, $20.78).[10] This output level can be supported by all of the B, C, and D firms producing along their individual supply curves and half of the A firms producing at x = 0 and the other half producing at x = 1.95. (This is why the market equilibrium is labeled as B, C, D, and "1/2" A.) Other output levels could be similarly obtained by adjusting the number of A firms that are shut down versus producing at minimum AVC, both of which are equally profitable alternatives for A-style firms. This fills in the horizontal points of the market supply curve.

Before leaving this discussion, we should mention that these cost curves need not achieve minimum average total cost at different $/x levels. Figures 13.10 and 13.11 show four types of firms, with each achieving minimum average total cost at a different $/x level. This is due to reasons that will only unfold completely in the long-run discussion in Chapter 14. Nonetheless, it is worth reemphasizing that these are the *same* four short-run cost curves that formed the envelope analysis of long-run costs with varying returns to scale in Figures 11.12–11.14 and 11.16. Had the analysis instead been based on a constant returns to scale technology, then each of the average total cost curves would achieve minimum average total cost at the same $/x level as seen in Figures 11.11, 11.15C, and 11.15D. The shutdown price level would still depend on plant size, but if one firm had positive profits at a given market price, then all firms would as well (as long as they were using a production process that is on the long-run expansion path for some level of output). These issues are considered in greater detail when we examine the short-run/long-run distinction in Chapter 14.

13.5 A Special Case: Market Supply with Quadratic Costs

OPTIONAL SECTION

The discussion of market demand in Section 12.1 focuses on linear demand curves to simplify the analysis. The same simplification is theoretically justified on the supply side if firms face quadratic short-run total cost functions. The Cobb-Douglas (CD) cost functions described in Section 11.5 provide one example of short-run total cost functions that are quadratic (although this is not a requirement of cost functions based on CD technology, as a comparison of Figures 11.18–11.22 shows). Each of the quadratic cost functions in Figures 11.18–11.20 has marginal cost and average variable cost as rays through the origin, as compared with the nonquadratic CD cost functions depicted in Figures 11.21–11.22.

Quadratic cost functions need not have marginal cost and average variable cost as rays through the origin. The quadratic CD cost function is a special case of the more general quadratic cost function described next. Before we examine market supply in this instance, we must provide a short primer on quadratic cost functions. Happily, such functions are much simpler to work with than cubic cost functions (examined in Section 11.4), although they suffer from an inability to describe the increasing marginal productivity and then the decreasing marginal productivity that give rise to U-shaped marginal cost curves.

A Primer on Quadratic Cost Functions

Consider the general form short-run quadratic total cost function:

$$TC(x) = a + b \cdot x + c \cdot x^2, \text{ where } a > 0,\ b \geq 0 \text{ and } c > 0. \quad \textbf{(13.6a)}$$

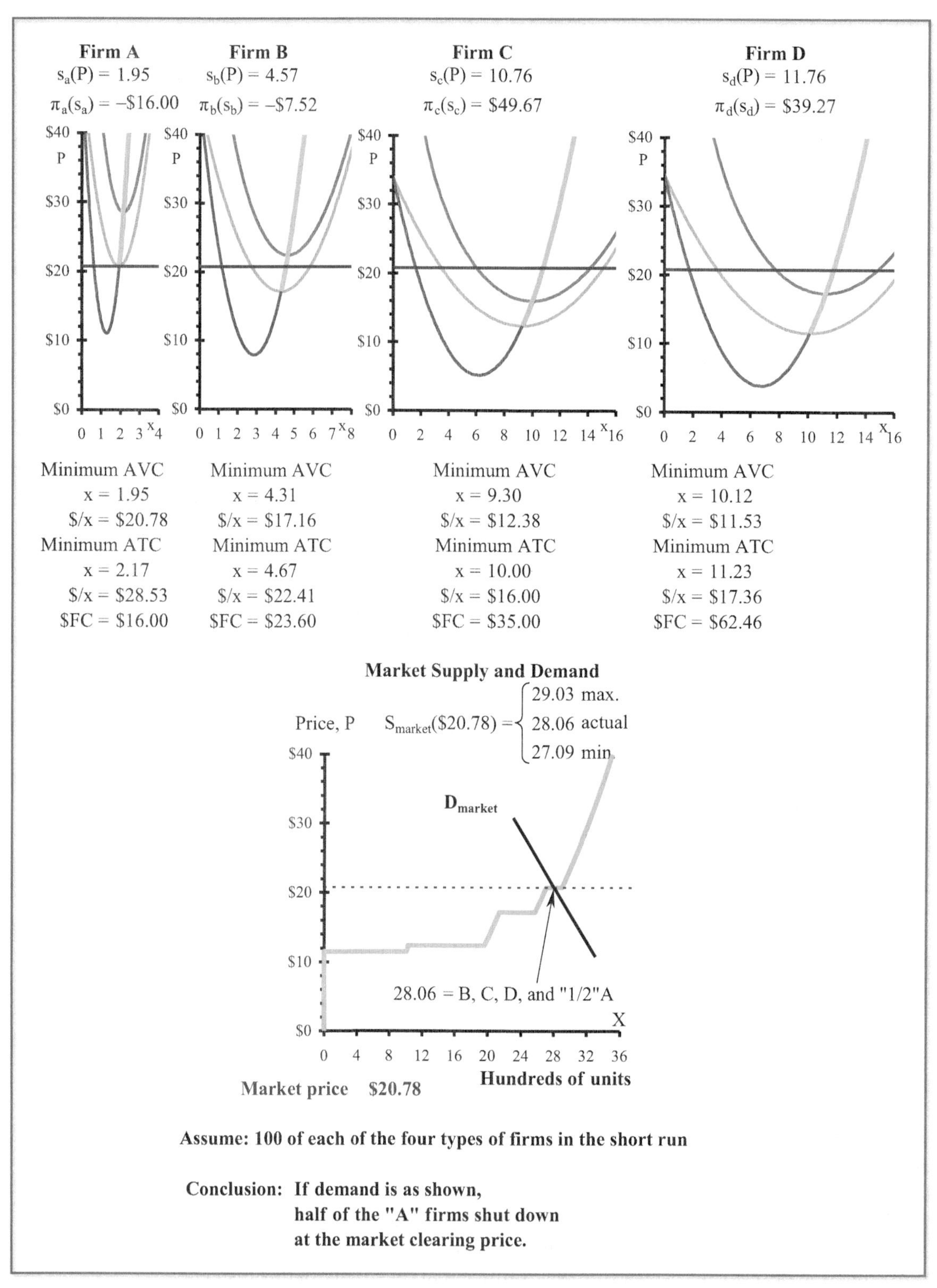

FIGURE 13.11 Market Supply and Market Demand Interact to Set the Market Clearing Price

The nonzero portion of individual firm supply is the green portion of MC for each firm.

Note first that none of the coefficients are negative (unlike the cubic total cost function in Equation 11.6a, which has a negative quadratic term). The first term, a, is fixed cost, just as with its cubic counterpart:

$$FC(x) = a, \text{ given the total cost function in Equation 13.6a.} \quad \textbf{(13.6b)}$$

As a result, the rest of the total cost function represents variable cost:

$$VC(x) = b \cdot x + c \cdot x^2, \text{ given the total cost function in Equation 13.6a.} \quad \textbf{(13.6c)}$$

Each of the short-run average cost functions is obtained by dividing each of Equations 13.6a–13.6c by x:

$$ATC(x) = a/x + b + c \cdot x. \quad \textbf{(13.6d)}$$

$$AFC(x) = a/x. \quad \textbf{(13.6e)}$$

$$AVC(x) = b + c \cdot x. \quad \textbf{(13.6f)}$$

Marginal cost is the slope of the total cost and variable cost curves. Given the total cost curve in Equation 13.6a or the variable cost curve in Equation 13.6c, marginal cost is given by:

$$MC(x) = b + 2 \cdot c \cdot x. \quad \textbf{(13.6g)}$$

As with the discussion of cubic cost functions in Equations 11.6a–11.6g, the only function requiring further discussion is marginal cost. The same rule is followed as in Chapter 11 to turn total cost into marginal cost; the only difference here is that you do not have to worry about the cubic term, since it is not present! The cookbook method for finding marginal cost from a quadratic cost function is to apply Rules 1 and 2 to the total cost function:

Rule 1: Drop the fixed cost component, *a*; this only shifts TC up or down, but does not change slope at a given output level.

Rule 2: The linear and quadratic coefficients (b and c) become the constant and linear coefficients, once they are multiplied by 1 and 2.

This simple cookbook method will always provide you with marginal cost. For those who wish to see the graph of these cost functions, look ahead to Figure 13.12. The present discussion, however, initially focuses on the algebra of the situation, since the geometry is particularly simple, compared to the cubic cost functions that we have been using since Chapter 9.

MC and AVC in Equations 11.6f and 11.6g have been placed next to each other, so it is easy to see the similarity between these functions. MC looks like AVC except that the last term is multiplied by 2 (using Rule 2 in the cookbook method). Both cost curves are linear, but marginal cost increases twice as quickly as variable cost.[11] The coefficient c represents the rate of increase in average variable cost per unit of output (and $2 \cdot c$ is the increase in marginal cost per unit of output). Both MC and AVC start from the same point on the vertical axis of the per-unit diagram, since, just as in the cubic form, $b = MC(0) = AVC(0)$.

As always, average total cost and average variable cost only differ by average fixed cost. Average fixed cost is still a rectangular hyperbola, so ATC is asymptotic to AVC. This simply means that for large values of output, although the average total cost curve remains a curve, it becomes closer and closer to the linear function AVC.

Another benefit of the quadratic over cubic form is the ease in finding the output level where average total cost is minimized. As always, MC = ATC at minimum ATC, so we use Equations 13.6d and 13.6g to obtain the average total cost-maximizing output level:

$$a/x + b + c \cdot x = b + 2 \cdot c \cdot x. \quad \textbf{(13.7a)}$$

Solving for x, we obtain:

$$x_{minATC} = (a/c)^{0.5}. \quad \textbf{(13.7b)}$$

(With cubic cost functions, such a simple, closed-form solution was not possible. The simplest way to find minimum ATC for cubic functions is to use **Goal Seek** in Excel, as described in Section 11.4.)

FIGURE 13.12 The Geometry of Quadratic Cost Curves: $TC(x) = a + b \cdot x + c \cdot x^2$

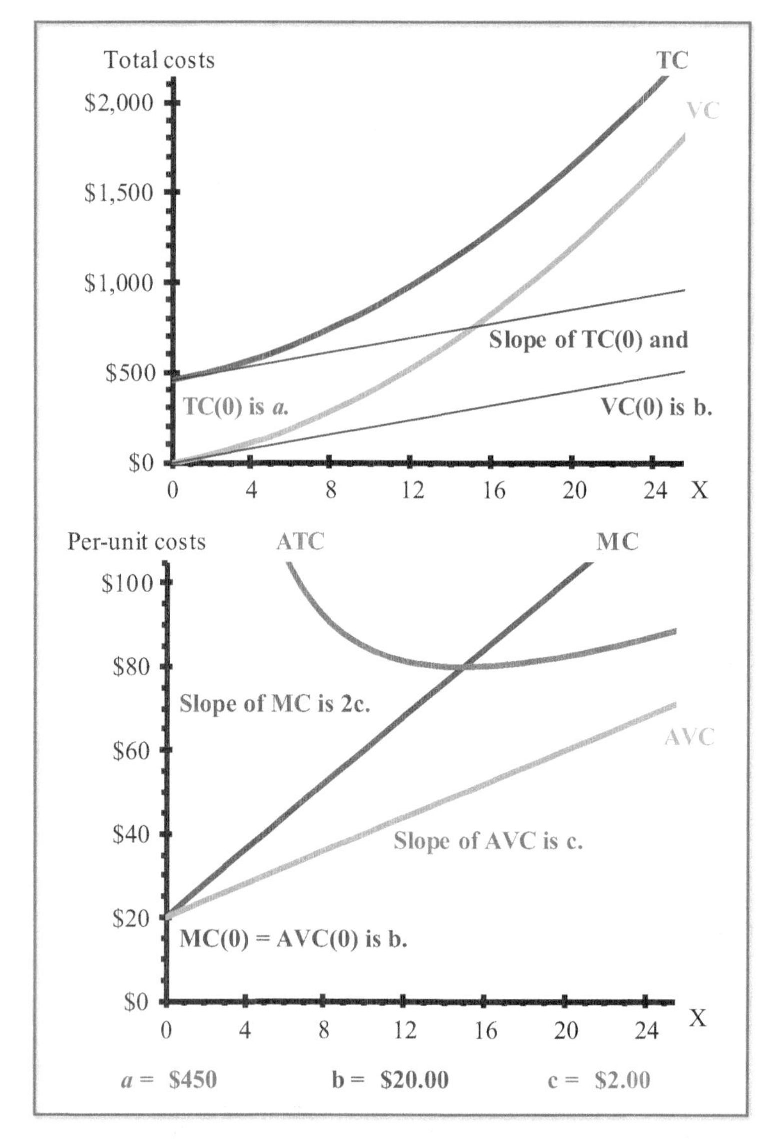

Minimum average total cost is an increasing function of fixed cost, a, and a decreasing function of the increase in average variable cost per unit of output, c. Interestingly, it is *not* a function of the linear term, b. Of course, the $/x value of the average total cost-minimizing production level is a function of b (as well as a and c):

$$ATC(x_{minATC}) = MC(x_{minATC}) = b + 2 \cdot c \cdot (a/c)^{0.5} = b + 2 \cdot (a \cdot c)^{0.5}. \qquad \textbf{(13.7c)}$$

This chain of equalities points out that the easy way to calculate minimum ATC is to use MC, since they are equal; MC is a linear function and is therefore easier to simplify than a function involving a 1/x term.

The simplified algebraic conclusions are supported by a simplified geometric analysis, given quadratic cost functions. As noted earlier, the CD cost analysis in Section 11.5 had a number of quadratic cost functions, but they were all special cases of the functions just described because each had b = 0. If you look back at those figures, you will note that total cost curves are initially flat (and consequently, the marginal cost curves emanate from the origin). The more general quadratic cost curves are shown in Figure 13.12. AVC and MC both emanate from the same point on the vertical axis, and MC is twice as steep as AVC.

Q12. Based on the information provided regarding Figure 13.12, what is the output level that minimizes average total cost?*

***Q12 answer:** Average total cost is minimized when x = 15. This is seen by applying Equation 13.7b: $x = (a/c)^{0.5} = (450/2)^{0.5} = 225^{0.5} = 15$.

Supply with Quadratic Cost Functions

Notice that $x = 0$ is the point of minimum average variable cost, unlike the cubic case, where $x > 0$ at minimum AVC (according to Equation 11.7b). This means in particular that *there will be no jump discontinuity in the firm supply curve, given quadratic costs at the shutdown output level.* The firm should shut down whenever $P < b = MC(0) = AVC(0)$, but unlike the cubic cost analysis just presented, this does not lead to two output levels when P = minimum AVC (in the cubic cost case, $x = 0$, and $x = c/(2 \cdot d)$, using Equation 11.7b and shown in Figure 13.9D).

The firm should produce along the entire MC(x) curve, given quadratic costs. The reason is straightforward: If $P = MC(x)$ for $x > 0$, then $MC(x) > AVC(x)$. Average variable cost is below marginal cost for all output levels greater than zero.

If all firms are the same, then market supply is easily obtained. Geometrically, if we have two identical firms, then the market supply curve will have the same P intercept and twice as much x for a given P, or put in terms of slope, half the slope. With N firms, the market supply will have the same P intercept and 1/N times the slope. Algebraically, we derive this result by putting marginal cost into a price orientation (just as we put demand into inverse demand orientation in Section 12.1 to derive market demand). Since a competitive market sets $P = MC$, we have $P = b + 2 \cdot c \cdot x$ from Equation 13.6g. Firm supply, s(P), is obtained by solving for supply x in the previous equation (the lowercase x and s remind us that this is individual firm supply):

$$s(P) = -b/(2 \cdot c) + 1/(2 \cdot c) \cdot P. \quad \textbf{(13.8a)}$$

Given N identical firms, market supply, S(P), is simply $N \cdot s(P)$:

$$S(P) = N \cdot s(P) = -N \cdot b/(2 \cdot c) + N/(2 \cdot c) \cdot P. \quad \textbf{(13.8b)}$$

To see that this is the same answer we described geometrically earlier, simply solve for P in Equation 13.8b, letting $S(P) = X$.

$$P = b + (2 \cdot c/N) \cdot X. \quad \textbf{(13.8c)}$$

As noted previously, if there are N identical quadratic cost firms, then the market supply curve has the same P intercept as marginal cost and has 1/N times the slope.

Differences in the fixed cost/variable cost structure of a firm can lead to differences in profitability. This can be modeled with quadratic costs by considering how increasing fixed cost, *a*, should affect the parameters that define variable cost. Variable cost is described by parameters b and c in Equation 13.6c. Variable cost is smaller as b and c are smaller. Therefore, an increase in *a* should be associated with smaller values of b and/or c. Figure 13.13 depicts four firms that satisfy this requirement. Fixed cost increases by \$10 in moving from Firm A to Firm B, and by another \$9.98 from Firm B to Firm C, and by \$10.02 in moving to Firm D. This increase in fixed factors of production reduces the need for variable factors of production and, hence, variable cost. This is modeled in two ways. The initial level of marginal cost, $b = MC(0) = AVC(0)$, declines from firm to firm (but by a decreasing amount). At the same time, the increase in AVC (and MC) declines by 20% from firm to firm. (This does not show up visually across diagrams because, to conserve space, the horizontal scales are not the same across firms.) Specific coefficient values for each cost curve are provided beneath the diagrams in Figure 13.13. Firm supply for each firm is the entire marginal cost curve (unlike in Figure 13.10, the light-green supply curve covers the entire red marginal cost curve in each diagram).

The market clearing price chosen in Figure 13.13—\$19.76—allows each of the four profit outcomes described earlier. Firm C has zero profit at this price, since this is the value of minimum average total cost for this firm. (Profit would be \$0.02 off if we used FC = \$30, rather than \$29.98; therefore, this minor adjustment was made to fixed cost for Firm C.) Firm A should shut down because this price is below minimum AVC (of \$21). Firm B produces in the short run, despite producing at a loss because more than \$7 of the \$20 fixed cost is recovered by producing $x = 2.98$ units of output. Firm D depicts short-run profits, since $ATC(x) < P$ at $P = MC(x)$.

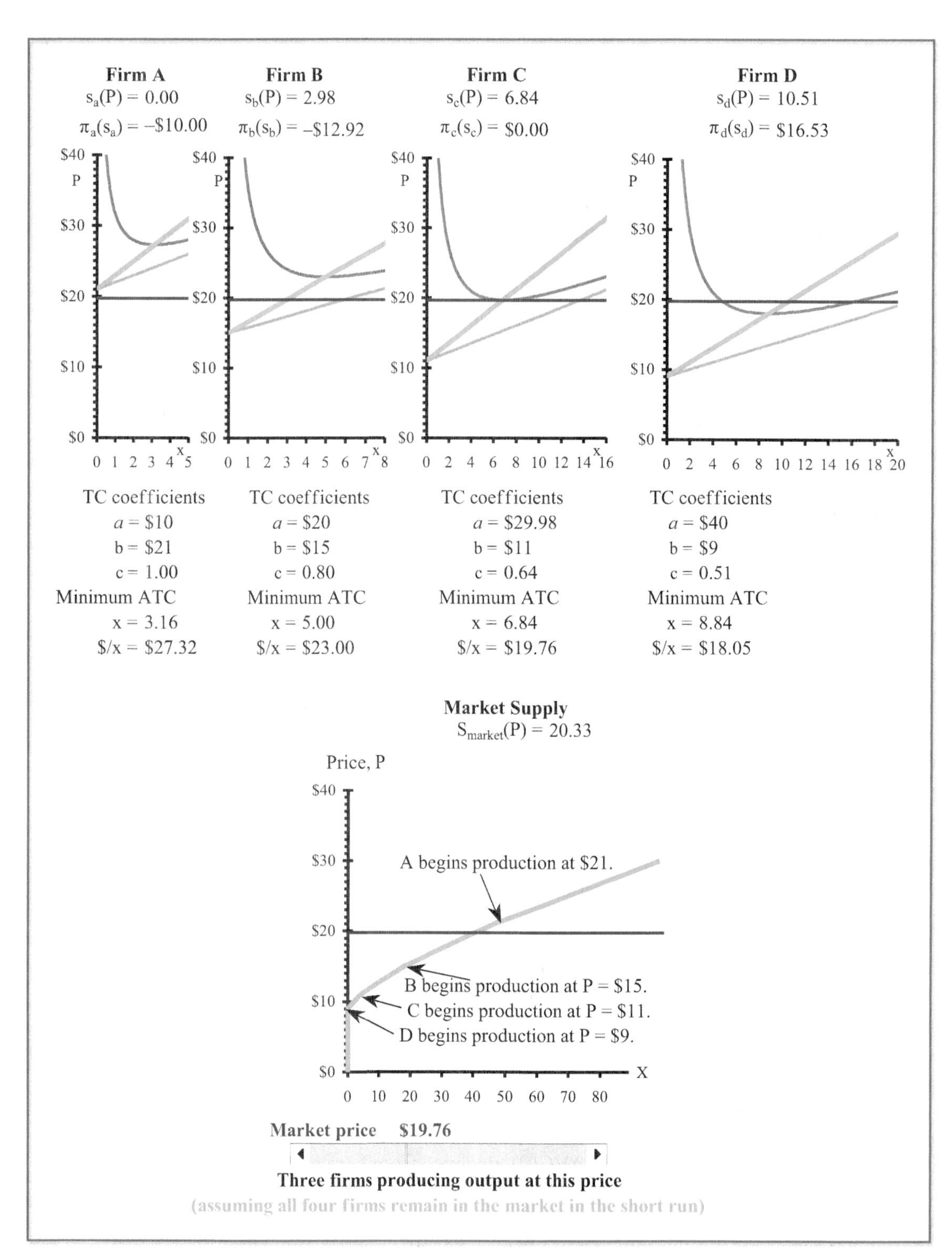

FIGURE 13.13 Market Supply Based on Quadratic Total Cost Functions: $TC(x) = a + b \cdot x + c \cdot x^2$

Given these individual firm supply curves, market supply is a piecewise linear function, much like those described in Section 12.1 (except, of course, supply is upward sloping). To find the market supply curve, you must follow the same strategy followed in Section 12.1: Each part must be put into s(P) format, and these are added to one another, based on how many firms are in the market at a given price, using Equation 13.4. And just like in Section 12.1, as more firms are incorporated into the analysis, the kinks should smooth out, and we can model market supply using a smooth curve.

Summary

One of the primary models in microeconomics is the model of perfect competition. Competitive markets are markets in which consumers and producers cannot affect the market outcome by their individual actions. More specifically, both consumers and producers take the market clearing price as fixed and given; both are price takers. Perfect competition also assumes that consumers and producers do not view the output produced by different producers as different; the product under discussion is homogeneous. Perfect competition also assumes perfect information and free entry and exit. When these conditions hold, a single market clearing price will prevail in the market. How that price is determined is the subject of this chapter.

The market demand side of the supply/demand model is derived in Chapter 12, based on the consumer analysis in Part 2 of the text. The perfectly competitive market supply curve is the horizontal sum of individual firm supply curves. An individual firm supply curve is based on the firm's cost curves derived in Part 3 of the text, together with demand information provided in a very simple way—via the market clearing price.

All consumers and firms view the market clearing price as fixed and given. In this setting, an individual firm views the demand curve for its product as a horizontal line at the market clearing price; demand is perfectly elastic from the perspective of an individual firm. Given this, the marginal revenue attained from any unit is the market clearing price as well; unlike a firm that has some price-making ability, a price taker will view P = MR. As a result, in perfect competition, the profit-maximizing firm will set P = MC, since the profit-maximizing condition MR = MC can be restated as P = MC. Put another way, the firm supplies along its marginal cost curve.

There are two qualifications or caveats to the statement that the firm supplies along its marginal cost curve. One qualification examines which part of the marginal cost curve produces a profit maximum and which produces a profit minimum. Profit is maximized when marginal cost is equal to marginal revenue on the upward-sloping part of the marginal cost curve. The downward-sloping part of marginal cost gives the opposite result: It produces a level of output that is locally the worst that the firm can do. When marginal cost approaches price from below (i.e., marginal cost is increasing), incremental units produce greater incremental revenue than incremental cost, and as a result, incremental profits are positive.

The second qualification examines when it is preferable to shut down rather than produce in the short run. Shutting down does not imply that the firm is leaving the market; it just means that the firm is not producing in the current period. The firm still must cover its fixed costs in the short run, whether or not it produces any output. The firm chooses to shut down rather than produce if the output where P = MC on the positively sloped part of the marginal cost curve does not cover variable costs of production. This occurs when price is less than minimum average variable cost. In this instance, producing output creates greater losses than shutting down because price is so low that variable costs of production cannot be fully covered.

These two caveats produce a complete description of the firm's supply curve in a competitive market. The firm produces no output as long as price is below minimum average variable cost. When price is above minimum average variable cost, the firm produces on the positively sloped part of its marginal cost curve. This supply decision results in an outcome that always maximizes profits, even when those profits are less than zero.

Firms in a competitive market are atomistic, but they are not identical to one another. Even though they are small, relative to the size of the market, they may well have different plant sizes in the short run. This leads to the possibility that some firms may choose to shut down in the short run, while others produce at a loss, and others produce at a profit. This may occur at a given point in time and at a single market clearing price. The difference has to do with the cost structure of various firms in the market in the short run.

The market supply curve is the horizontal sum of a large number of individual firm supply curves. This curve appears somewhat disjointed when viewed from a microscopic perspective. When viewed from the lens of the market as a whole, however, it should appear smooth. The same problem occurs on the demand side of the market. On the demand side, modeling market demand with linear functions does little harm. The same is true on the supply side, especially if some firms in the industry face quadratic cost conditions. Quadratic total cost curves produce linear marginal cost and individual firm supply curves.

Review Questions

Define the following terms:

perfectly competitive market
short-run perfectly competitive equilibrium
market clearing price
price taker
shutdown
exit
firm's supply curve, s(P)
market supply

Match the following statements:

a. No firm can alter the market price.
b. Demand curve facing a competitive firm
c. $P = MC$.
d. $P = MC$ with MC declining.
e. Price, P, is between $AVC_{minimum}$ and $ATC_{minimum}$.

1. MR = MC in competitive markets.
2. Firm has short-run losses smaller than fixed costs.
3. Perfectly elastic
4. Price taker
5. Profit minimum

Provide short answers to the following:

a. What is the general rule required for profit maximization? How does this relate to the specific rule faced by a firm in a competitive market?
b. Describe explicitly the relation between a firm's competitive supply curve and its marginal cost curve.
c. What is the relation between individual firm supply and market supply in a competitive market?
d. If a firm faces a quadratic cost function, what shape is marginal cost?
e. What are the four tenets that define a perfectly competitive market?

Check your answers to the *matching* and *short-answer* exercises in the Answers Appendix at the end of the book.

Notes

1. If you do not think this would happen in the tomato market, then consider what happens to the market for orange juice each time a hurricane or hard freeze hits the Florida orange groves. Still not convinced? Watch the movie *Trading Places*.

2. We saw a similar distinction in our discussion of demand curves. Demand takes a price orientation (how many units are demanded at a given price?), and inverse demand takes a quantity orientation (what is the marginal value of the *Q*th unit?), but both answers are derived from the demand curve. Indeed, both are simply different ways of describing the demand relationship.

3. A formal proof of the cost assertion requires integral calculus. If you have not studied integral calculus, then the following will be new; nonetheless, some intuition is possible in this situation. Integrals are used much less in microeconomics than derivatives, but they are basically the "opposite" of a derivative. Indeed, some calculus texts call them anti-derivatives. From a geometric perspective, integrals allow us to calculate areas. The integral of marginal cost is change in total cost (or to say the same thing, change in variable cost) on those units. This is the incremental cost on those units.

$$\int_a^b MC(x)dx = \int_a^b (dTC(x)/dx)\,dx = TC(b) - TC(a)$$

This integral has the same solution if TC(x) is replaced by VC(x) because marginal cost may be based on either curve. (As discussed in Section 11.2, marginal cost is equally well defined as $MC(x) = dVC(x)/dx$.)

4. Since $\pi(x) = TR(x) - TC(x)$, extreme values of profits require that marginal profits equal zero:

$$M\pi(x) = d\pi/dx = 0 = MR(x) - MC(x).$$

Mathematically, this is called a first-order condition, FOC. As discussed in the Mathematical Appendix (available in the online version of this text), the way to distinguish local minimums from local maximums using calculus is to examine the second-order condition at the output level where the FOC holds. If $d^2\pi/dx^2 < 0$ at the output level where the FOC holds, then this output level is a maximum. If $d^2\pi/dx^2 > 0$ at the output level where the FOC holds, then this output level is a minimum. Applying this rule, we find:

$d^2\pi/dx^2 = -dMC(x)/dx$, since $dMR(x)/dx = 0$ in perfect competition.

Given this, profits are maximized if MC(x) is increasing, and they are minimized if MC(x) is decreasing.

5. Marginal cost typically is described as a quadratic function; the individual firm's supply curve is the positively sloped part of MC above minimum AVC (as noted earlier). A natural tendency is simply to say that supply from two identical firms is simply $2 \cdot MC$. This is true geometrically, but it is not, in general, easy to describe supply algebraically because it involves inverting a quadratic function. (As Equation 13.4 makes clear, we obtain market supply by summing supply curves for a common price.) The workbook problems and the discussion in Section 13.5 provide examples of market supply curves that are easy to derive algebraically.

6. This assertion can be proven in a couple of steps. ATC is minimized when ATC(x) = MC(x). Given the cubic cost in Equation 13.5, we have $ATC(x) = a/x + b - 3 \cdot x + 0.1 \cdot x^2$, and $MC(x) = b - 6 \cdot x + 0.3 \cdot x^2$. Setting these equal to each other and regrouping, we obtain $0.2 \cdot x^2 - 3 \cdot x = a/x$. Multiplying both sides by $5 \cdot x$, we obtain $x^3 - 15 \cdot x^2 = 5 \cdot a$. It is not immediately obvious that the value of x that solves this cubic equation is an increasing function of *a*. Nonetheless, we can see this by noting that as *a* increases, so does $5 \cdot a$ (the right-hand side of the last equation). Therefore we wish to know for what values of x the left-hand side is increasing in x. let $F(x) = x^3 - 15 \cdot x^2$, then $dF/dx = 3 \cdot x^2 - 30 \cdot x = 3 \cdot x \cdot (x - 10)$, and $dF/dx > 0$ as long as $x > 10$. But $x_{minATC} > x_{minAVC} = 15$ so $x > 10$ is assured. Therefore, if fixed cost *a* increases so does the short-run average total cost-minimizing output level.

7. These are the four short-run cost curves that formed the envelope analysis of long-run costs with varying returns to scale in Figures 11.12–11.14 and 11.16.

8. This market clearing price is based on a market demand/market supply intersection. Since we wish to focus on the supply curve here, we have omitted the market demand curve in this instance. The solution shown is based on the (X, P) point (25.78, \$17.36) being on the market demand curve.

9. There is no single way to quantify either of these ideas, but notice that the ratio of minimum AVCs across C and D shows that minimum AVC is 7% lower for D than for C (0.93 = \$11.53/\$12.38) but this reduction is based on a 78% increase in fixed cost (1.78 = \$62.46/\$35).

10. Figure 13.11, as well as later figures in the text that compare multiple individual firms together with market information based on individual firm information, share a common price axis. As a result, they are theoretically tied side-by-side to one another, just as was shown in Figure 13.10. Nonetheless, we now are showing the market graph beneath the individual firm graphs to allow larger display of the various graphical elements in the figure.

11. This should not surprise you. It is the same rule you saw in Chapter 12 when discussing the relation between linear inverse demand and marginal revenue, where marginal revenue was the same intercept and twice the slope as inverse demand (compare Equations 12.7a and 12.11). Another interpretation for inverse demand is as an average revenue function, AR(x), because TR(x) = P(x) · x means that AR(x) = TR(x)/x = P(x).

Long-Run Profit Maximization in Perfectly Competitive Markets

CHAPTER 14

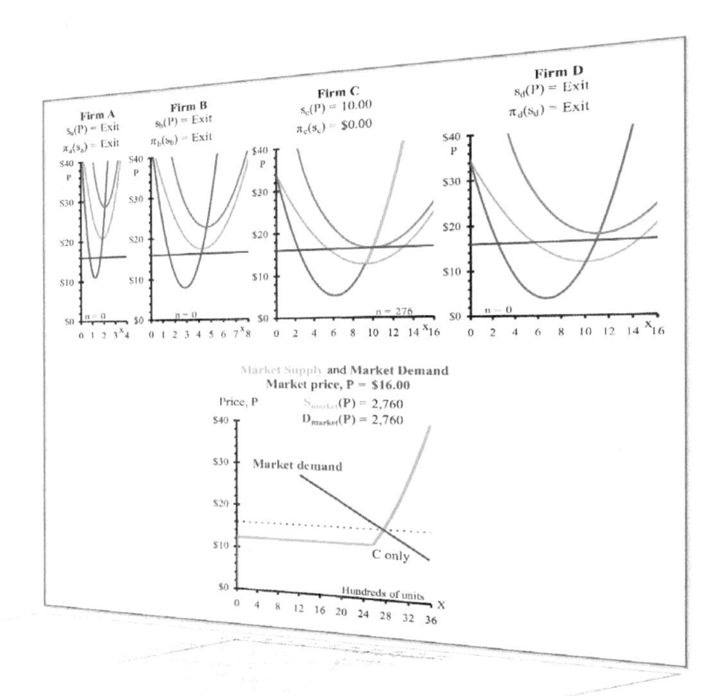

Chapter Outline

The short-run analysis in Chapter 13 assumed that a fixed number of firms each faced a situation where some of its factors of production were fixed. A firm can decide to shut down in the short run, but it is not able to avoid its fixed costs by shutting down; there is an opportunity cost associated with fixed factors of production, regardless of production level. As discussed in Section 13.3, shutting down is a short-run decision. This chapter examines entry, exit (the long-run concept that is often confused with shutting down), and how entry and exit lead to a long-run competitive equilibrium. Long-run equilibrium is based on fixed demand. A final notion of long-run response is how the long-run equilibrium changes as demand changes.

Section 14.1 describes the key distinguishing attribute of long-run analysis. Long-run analysis is based on being able to adjust factors of production that are fixed in the short run. In particular, existing firms can adjust plant size, or they can exit the industry. New firms can decide to enter an industry in response to the short-run profit signals provided by firms already within the industry. Sections 14.2 and 14.3 describe what is required for a short-run competitive equilibrium to also be a long-run equilibrium. Entry and exit lead to a situation in which all firms earn zero profits. Section 14.2 examines the long-run equilibration process in the context of varying returns production technology. Section 14.3 focuses on the equilibration process in the context of constant returns to scale production. Both of these analyses are predicated on fixed market demand. As market demand changes, so will the long-run equilibrium. Section 14.4 examines this long-run adjustment to changes in demand. The relation between long-run equilibrium price and quantity for different levels of demand is called the long-run supply curve. The orientation of this curve is a function of how factor costs change as demand for those factors changes. Three possibilities exist: Factor costs could remain constant, they could increase, or they could decrease in the face of an increase in demand for those factors. Each of these situations is theoretically possible, although as a practical matter, the first two possibilities occur with greater frequency.

14.1 The Key to Long-Run Analysis Is Entry and Exit

When prices are high and firms in a competitive market are profitable, existing firms can expect entry by other firms. When prices are low and firms in the market are struggling to cover costs, we would not expect outsiders to enter the market. Indeed, we would expect firms to exit the market. These decisions, which are qualitatively different from the firm's short-run decisions discussed in Chapter 13, are capital investment decisions.

Firms are notoriously secretive about how well they are doing (and how they are "doing it"), and as a result, it may be difficult for an outsider to know whether firms are earning positive or negative profits in a given setting. It may also be difficult for different producers to know how well they are doing, relative to other firms in the market. These informational issues are not considered in the perfectly competitive model, but they offer one rationale for why we might see disparate activity by firms in the short run. As we move from the short run to the long run, disparate activity dissipates as firms adjust to profit or loss signals and fine-tune their process in response to those signals.

How firms respond to market signals differs in the short and the long run. In the short run, firms adjust variable factors of production to maximize profit by setting marginal revenue equal to short-run marginal cost. In the long run, the same rule holds, but marginal cost is now long-run marginal cost (LMC). Long-run marginal cost is obtained by adjusting all factors of production, since in the long run, all factors are variable. In particular, in the two-input model, the firm is able to adjust capital as well as labor to achieve the lowest-cost method of producing a given level of output. The output level chosen maximizes profits by setting marginal revenue equal to long-run marginal cost.

If a price-taking firm views the price of the product as constant at P^* for the foreseeable future, then a firm considering the capital investment decision involved in entering the market will choose a plant size k^*, where the output level x^* satisfies $P^* = LMC(x^*) = SMC(x^*; k^*)$, as described in Equation 11.4b. This output level will have $LAC(x^*) = SATC(x^*; k^*)$ according to Equation 11.4a. The resulting profit would be $\pi_{max}(x^*) = (P^* - LAC(x^*)) \cdot x^*$.

To undertake the capital investment of k^*, $\pi_{max}(x^*) \geq 0$. The reason is straightforward: If $\pi_{max}(x^*) < 0$, then $P^* < LAC(x^*)$, and cost is not covered, so the potential entrant will invest elsewhere because the market will not support a competitive return on investment. However, $\pi_{max}(x^*) \geq 0$ implies that $P^* \geq LAC(x^*)$, and the firm covers the opportunity cost of its investment. This suggests that a firm that is expecting price to remain fixed will invest along the long-run marginal cost curve at or above minimum long-run average cost (LAC). If price is below minimum LAC, the firm would instead invest elsewhere. The green curve in Figure 14.1 depicts optimal production scale as a function of price in this instance. Each point on the LMC curve is associated with a short-run capital stock that produces that output level at minimum cost. In Section 11.3, the capital stock associated with a given level of cost-minimizing production was labeled according to the level of output produced at minimum cost. Using the terminology of that section, a plant of size K10 or larger is required in this instance, since minimum LAC occurs at $x = 10$. In terms of short-run and long-run cost curves, Equation 11.5 requires that $SATC(x; K10) = \text{minimum } LAC(x) = LMC(x) = SMC(x; K10)$ at $x = 10$, as shown in Figure 11.15B.

Figure 14.1 may look like it is based on a different condition than the one that describes short-run profit-maximizing behavior (summarized in Figure 13.8), but it is actually the same condition. Consider the two conditions:

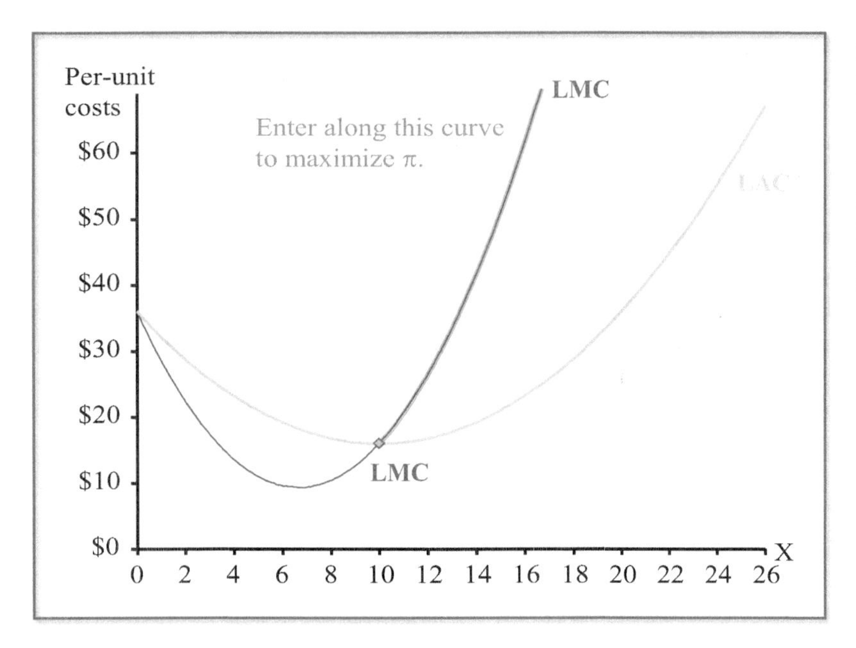

FIGURE 14.1 A Potential Entrant's Profit-Maximizing Entry Decision

If the entrant expects price to remain constant, it should supply along LMC as long as $P \geq LAC_{minimum}$.

- The short-run condition is to produce along the upward-sloping part of the short-run marginal cost curve as long as $P \geq AVC_{minimum}$. When price is at least this high, all variable cost of production is covered, and anything left over helps cover fixed cost and profit (see Figure 13.8).
- The long-run condition is to produce along the upward-sloping part of the long-run marginal cost curve as long as $P \geq LAC_{minimum}$ (Figure 14.1).

A firm considering the investment has no fixed cost, so all cost is variable. Therefore, an investment will be made only if all variable cost (which in this case is all cost) is covered by the prevailing market price. The short-run and long-run conditions only appear different if you view LAC as LATC (which it is). The short-run and long-run conditions appear the same if you view LAC as LAVC (which it *also* is). As discussed in Section 11.3, there is no distinction in the long run between fixed and variable components: All components are variable, and therefore, variable cost is total cost in the long run. The difference between the two conditions is that the short-run condition describes the *shutdown/produce* choice, and the long-run condition describes the *do not enter/enter* choice.

Short-run losses do not necessarily mean that the firm will shut down in the short run. As shown in Section 13.3, it pays to produce at a loss in the short run, as long as that loss is less than the loss in fixed cost. The loss of fixed cost is a lower bound on profits in the short run, since the firm can always simply pay its fixed cost and decide to shut down in the short run. The decision to exit is a different one; exit involves selling the assets and leaving the industry. If there is an active secondhand market for the capital used in the industry (as there is in perfect competition, according to the free-entry and free-exit assumption), then a firm will consider exit whenever revenues generated in the production process do not meet the opportunity cost of that asset. (Recall that opportunity cost is the value of a resource in the next best alternative use.)

If a firm in a competitive market is currently earning negative profits (i.e., losses), then it will consider exiting the industry unless it expects market conditions to change in the future. A firm expects to earn a normal rate of return on its assets. If it does not obtain a normal return, it can reallocate those assets to other competitive uses. In most settings, such reallocations are not costless (despite the perfectly competitive assumption to the contrary); as a result, we should not expect *immediate* exit whenever profits are less than zero. Nonetheless, negative profits in the short run offer a primary signal that exit may follow in the long run. Conversely, if a firm attains positive short-run profits in a competitive market environment, it should not expect that happy condition to persist.

normal profits: A firm earns normal profits when total revenue and total cost coincide.

Positive profits are a signal to outsiders considering entry that entry is worthwhile. Only when profits are zero is there no signal for change to occur. Economists often call zero profits normal profits. A firm earns **normal profits** when total revenue and total cost coincide. Total cost includes all relevant opportunity costs, as described in Chapter 11. In this instance, profits are zero.

All firms would *like* to earn supra-normal profits (i.e., positive profits) over the long term. Most firms, however, are not able to achieve positive profits on more than a transitory basis. This is simply another way of saying that there is a competitive market for capital. Firms continually search for profitable opportunities, but such opportunities are rarely sheltered so that the profits maintain over the long run. Beginning economics students often reject undertaking a zero-profit opportunity. But zero profit to an economist means that the firm is doing as well as can be expected. A firm earning zero profit is covering the opportunity cost of the investment; it is earning a *normal* return on its investment in this instance.

As we initially noted in Chapter 11, each long-run decision returns us to a short run (this is the conceptual basis for long-run costs as the envelope of short-run costs). Once a capital investment is made, the firm has fixed capital stock until another capital investment decision is made. The profits or losses that are generated are short-run profits or losses. These short-run profits or losses are also *signals* of future change in a perfectly competitive market. We now turn to how those signals nudge us toward a long-run outcome where further change is unwarranted.

14.2 Long-Run Competitive Equilibrium

Entry and exit cause the short-run supply curve to change over time. These changes continue until there are no longer signals that future change should continue. That is, entry and exit will continue in a perfectly competitive market until an equilibrium is achieved where there are no signals that change should continue. Such an outcome is called a long-run perfectly competitive equilibrium. A **long-run perfectly competitive equilibrium** exists if market supply equals market demand, and firms have no incentive to enter or exit the industry.

long-run perfectly competitive equilibrium: A long-run perfectly competitive equilibrium exists if market supply equals market demand, and firms have no incentive to enter or exit the industry.

Operationally, *three conditions* are required for long-run competitive equilibrium:

Condition 1: The market is in short-run equilibrium, meaning that market supply equals market demand at the market clearing price of P*.

Condition 2: Each firm in the market is earning zero economic profit at this price.

Condition 3: $P^* = LAC_{minimum}$.

If all three conditions hold true, a long-run equilibrium is assured.

One of the tenets of perfectly competitive markets is that an individual firm's actions will have no effect on the market outcome. If an individual firm decides to exit the market or to shut down but remain in the market in the short run, this will have no effect on the market clearing price (or the effect will be so small that it is unobservable). For the market outcome to change, a number of firms must adjust their behavior. As this occurs via entry and exit, the number of firms in the industry will adjust in response to the profit signals provided by the short run.

The Geometry of Long-Run Adjustment

The starting point for our move toward long-run competitive equilibrium is the short-run market equilibrium described by Figure 13.10, which had a market clearing price of $17.36. To have this diagram simulate a competitive market, it is useful to employ the heuristic device described in Section 13.4 of assuming that the market has 400 firms, with 100 firms of each of the four styles, A, B, C, and D. At a price of $17.36, each of the 100 A-style firms should shut down in the short run, and each of the other firms should produce output on its supply curve. Figure 14.2 replicates the information provided in Figure 13.10 with two exceptions: (1) Each of the A firms decides to exit the market, and (2) the

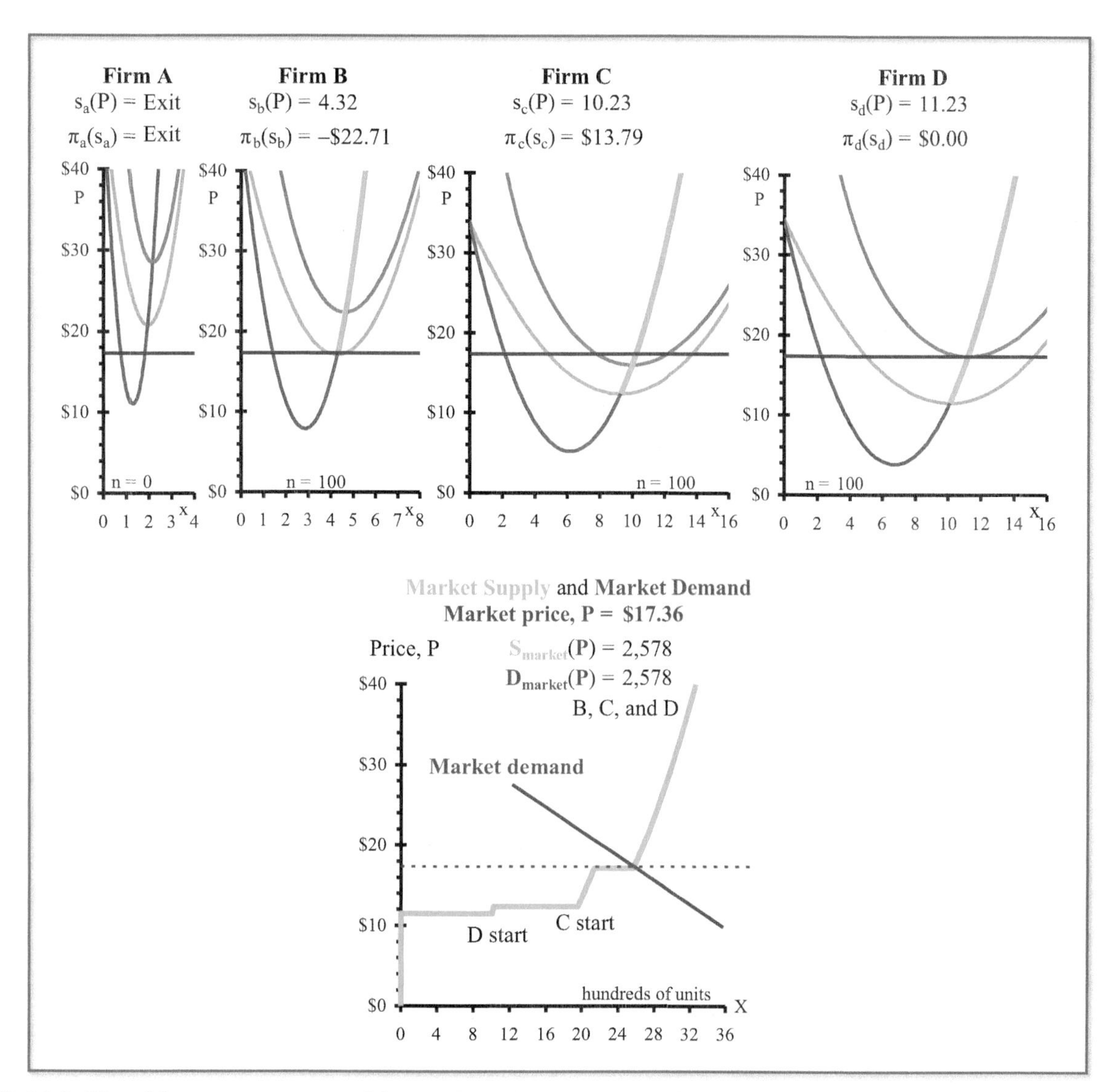

FIGURE 14.2 The Movement toward Long-Run Equilibrium: Shutdown Turns into Exit

market demand curve is now explicitly provided. Minimum AVC and ATC information is the same as in Figure 13.10 and is not reproduced in Figure 14.2.

The short-run equilibrium in Figure 14.2 is the same as in Figure 13.10, despite 100 firms leaving the market. Notice that there is no longer a fourth "flat" part to the market supply curve at this price because the 100 A-style firms have left the market (and hence, the green short-run supply curve has been removed from the left-most graph). The reason these firms had no effect on the short-run equilibrium in this instance is because none of the firms added production to the market at this price; each viewed the short-run situation of shutting down the plant as preferable to producing below minimum AVC. The same qualitative result would hold as long as $P < AVC^{a}_{minimum} = \$20.78$. By exiting the market, the A-style firms can avoid fixed cost charges in the future; at the same time, they do not affect aggregate production, since they were already producing $x = 0$ in the short run.

The next weakest firms in the market at this price are B-style firms. Although they are covering all of their variable costs of production, they are only covering a small portion of their fixed component. At the price of \$17.36, they cover \$0.89 of their fixed cost of \$23.60 (since B-style firms maximize profits in this instance by producing $s_b(\$17.36) = 4.32$ and earn a short-run profit of $\pi_b(s_b) = -\$22.71$, which is \$0.89 better than they would receive were they to shut down in the short run). These firms are therefore the most likely to exit the market and invest elsewhere. If all 100 of the B-style firms exit the market, the short-run equilibrium changes (unlike what happened when A-style firms left the market). At

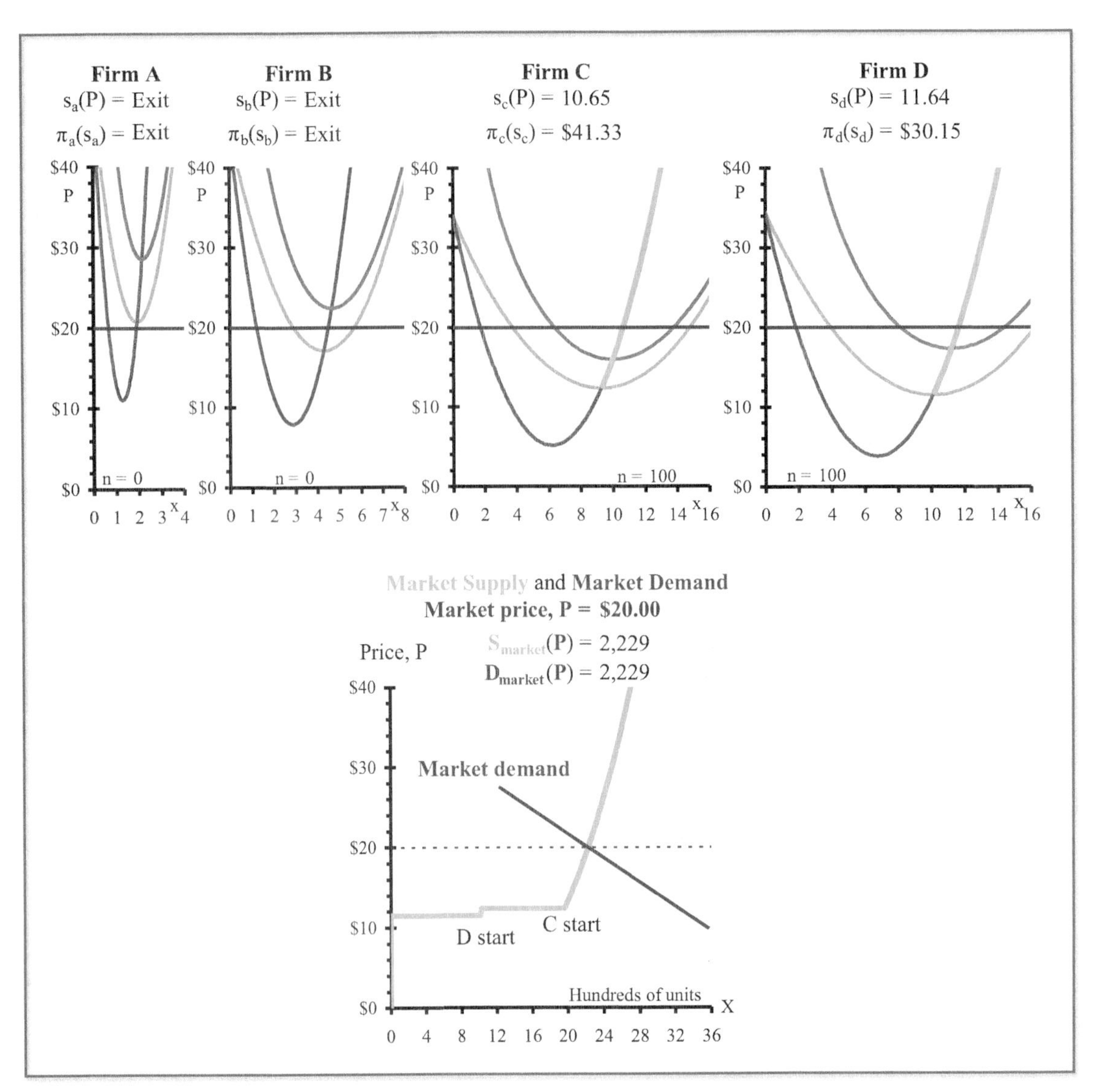

FIGURE 14.3 The Movement toward Long-Run Equilibrium: Firms with Short-Run Losses Exit

a price of $17.36, there is excess demand in the market of 432 units (432 = 100 · 4.32). The market clearing price therefore increases to the level where supply equals demand. Figure 14.3 depicts the new equilibrium at P = $20. The loss of the 100 B-style firms has shifted the upper portion of the supply curve back (because the upper portion of the supply curve only contains 100 C-style and 100 D-style firms) and thereby increased the market clearing price. The increase in price increases the profit-maximizing production levels and profits for the remaining firms. At this price, 200 firms remain, each producing positive profits. These short-run profits are a signal for potential entrants to enter this market.

If the market price is not expected to change, then an entering firm will produce along its LMC curve as long as LMC is above minimum LAC, as described in Figure 14.1. At a price of $20, we can compare the two remaining firm styles, C and D, with the profit-maximizing style embodied by producing at P = $20 = LMC. The comparison is easiest to see by putting the cost curves for C- and D-style firms together with the LAC and LMC curves that they were used to create (via the long-run envelope described in Section 11.3). This is shown in Figure 14.4. At a price of $20, three possible profit-maximizing production levels are highlighted via three green boxed diamonds on the line P = $20 at the points where individual firm demand P = MR intersects each associated marginal cost curve. The existing firms are profit maximizing in a short-run sense; the output levels

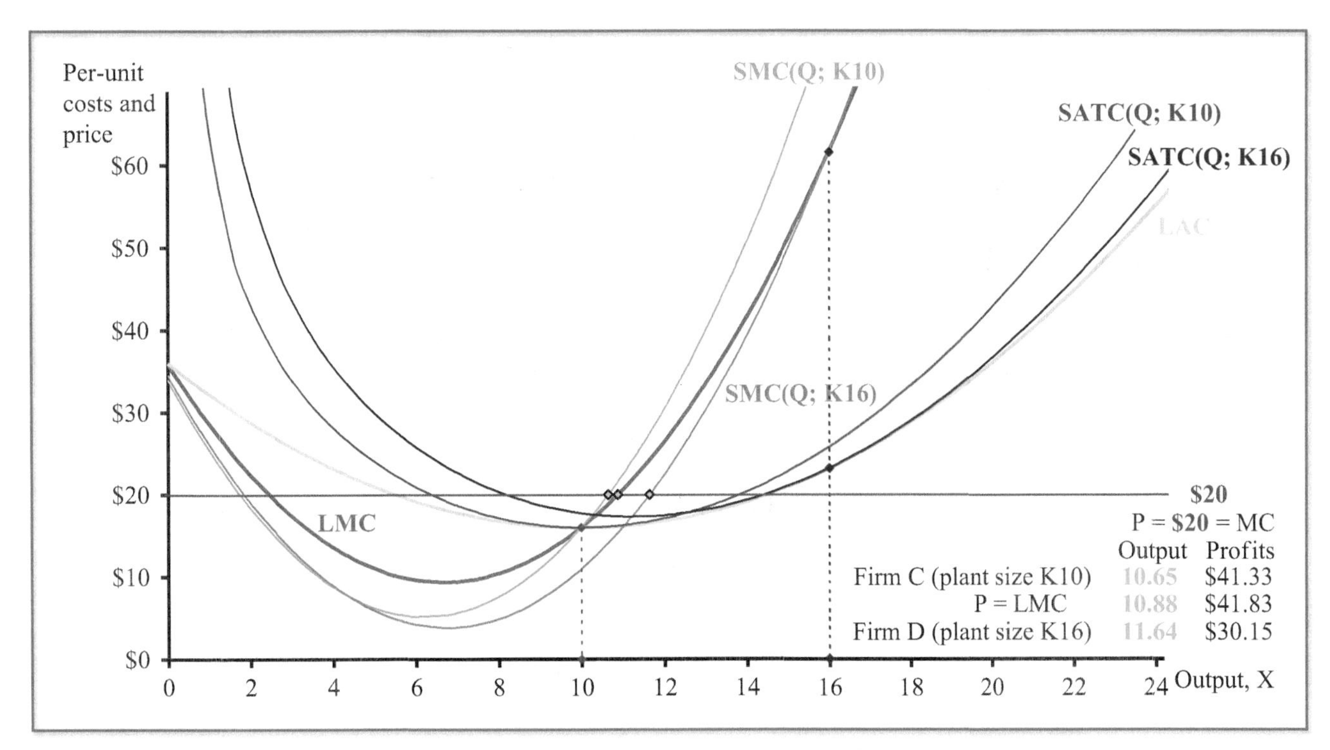

FIGURE 14.4 Comparing Existing Plants to Adding a New Plant, Given Fixed Price

x = 10.65 and x = 11.64 produce the highest profit possible, given the capital stock K10 and K16. Both profit levels are lower than exist using a plant size between these two firm sizes. Long-run profits are maximized, given the price of $20, if a plant size of K10.88 is chosen (10.88 is that level of capital that produces a short-run average total cost curve tangent to LAC(10.88)). (This new short-run cost curve is not shown for reasons that will be explained shortly.) Profits are higher than either existing plant in this instance: $\pi_{SR;K10.88}(10.88, \$20) = \$41.83 > \pi_c(10.65, \$20) = \$41.33 > \pi_d(11.64, \$20) = \$30.15$.

The previous discussion suggests that a potential entrant would best be served by entering with a K10.88 plant size, given a market clearing price of $20. Individual firm entry will have a negligible effect on the market clearing price, but the entry of a number of firms will shift the short-run supply curve out and create a new short-run equilibrium at a price below $20. In this event, the K10.88 plant size is no longer optimal; a somewhat smaller plant would be the most profitable investment in this case, since $20 > P = LMC(x') for x' < 10.88. As price continues to decline, equilibrium plant size will continue to decrease; the end result is a plant size of K10, as we will soon see.

Return now to the two firm styles, C and D, for which we have short-run cost curves. Suppose that a number of new C-style firms enter the market. As they do, the market clearing price will begin to decline as the short-run supply curve shifts out. As the market clearing price declines, so does the profit-maximizing output level for both C- and D-style firms. Profits also decline for both styles of firms. Once enough firms enter, it is easy to see that, eventually, D-style firms will lose money since C-style entry will remain profitable for prices below $17.36 (the price in Figure 14.2 for which $\pi_d = 0$). Figure 14.5 depicts one such short run. Relative to the short run shown in Figure 14.3, 57 C-style firms have entered the market. Price has declined from $20 to $16.50 as a result of this entry. Each of the C-style firms operates at a profit of $\pi_c(10.09, \$16.50) = \$5.02$, but each of the D-style firms operates at a loss of $\pi_d(11.08, \$16.50) = -\$9.63$.

The profit signals described in Figure 14.5 suggest that two things should happen: First, more C-style firms should enter the market, since such firms appear profitable. Second, D-style firms should exit the market, since they are no longer profitable. D-style firms will become more and more unprofitable as more C-style firms enter the market, since the market clearing price will continue to be driven lower in this instance. Ultimately, D-style

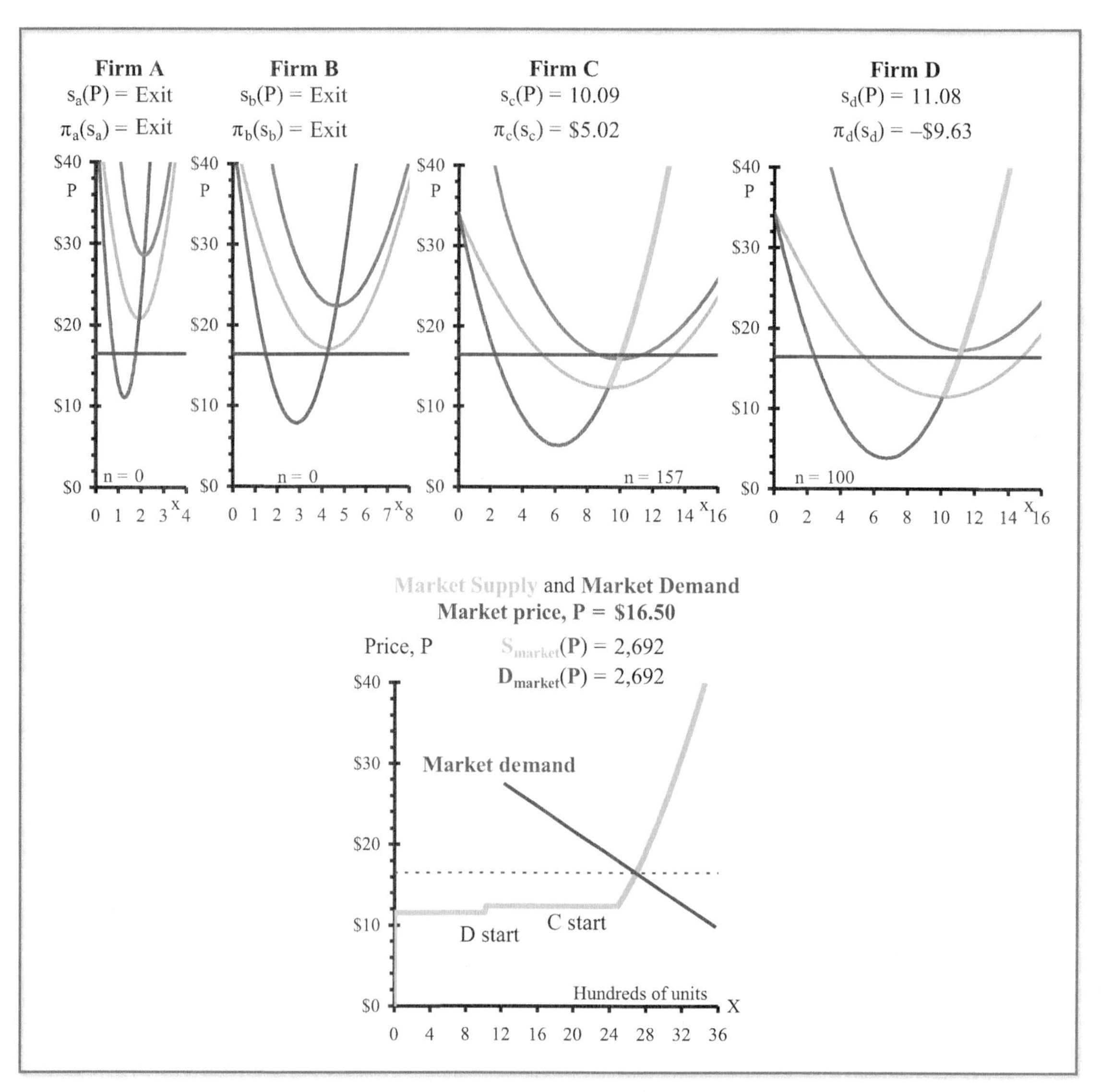

FIGURE 14.5 The Movement toward Long-Run Equilibrium: The Most Profitable Plant Size Becomes More Common

firms will decide to exit the market to obtain a normal return on their capital. C-style entry will continue as long as existing C-style firms remain profitable.

This process of entry and exit will continue until profits are zero for all firms in the market. Given the demand and cost conditions shown in Figure 14.5, this will occur when there are 276 C-style firms in the industry. The solution shown in Figure 14.6 is a long-run competitive equilibrium because it satisfies the *three conditions* required of long-run equilibria. $S_{market}(P^*) = n \cdot s_c(P^*) = 276 \cdot 10.00 = 2{,}760 = D_{market}(P^*)$ at $P^* = \$16$, so *Condition 1* is satisfied. Each of the 276 C-style firms in the market earns zero profit in this instance, $\pi_c(s_c(P^*)) = \$0.00$, so *Condition 2* holds. And, according to Figure 14.4, we see that $P^* = SMC_c(x^*) = SATC_c(x^*) = LAC(x^*) = LMC(x^*)$. But this only holds at minimum LAC, according to Equation 11.5, so *Condition 3* holds as well.

The Algebra of Long-Run Equilibrium

We could derive this result algebraically, given either the long-run cost curve or the short-run cost curve associated with the efficient scale plant size. The equation for long-run cost used to graph Figures 14.2–14.6 (as well as cost curves in Chapter 11) is:

$$LTC(x) = 36 \cdot x - 4 \cdot x^2 + 0.2 \cdot x^3. \quad \textbf{(14.1)}$$

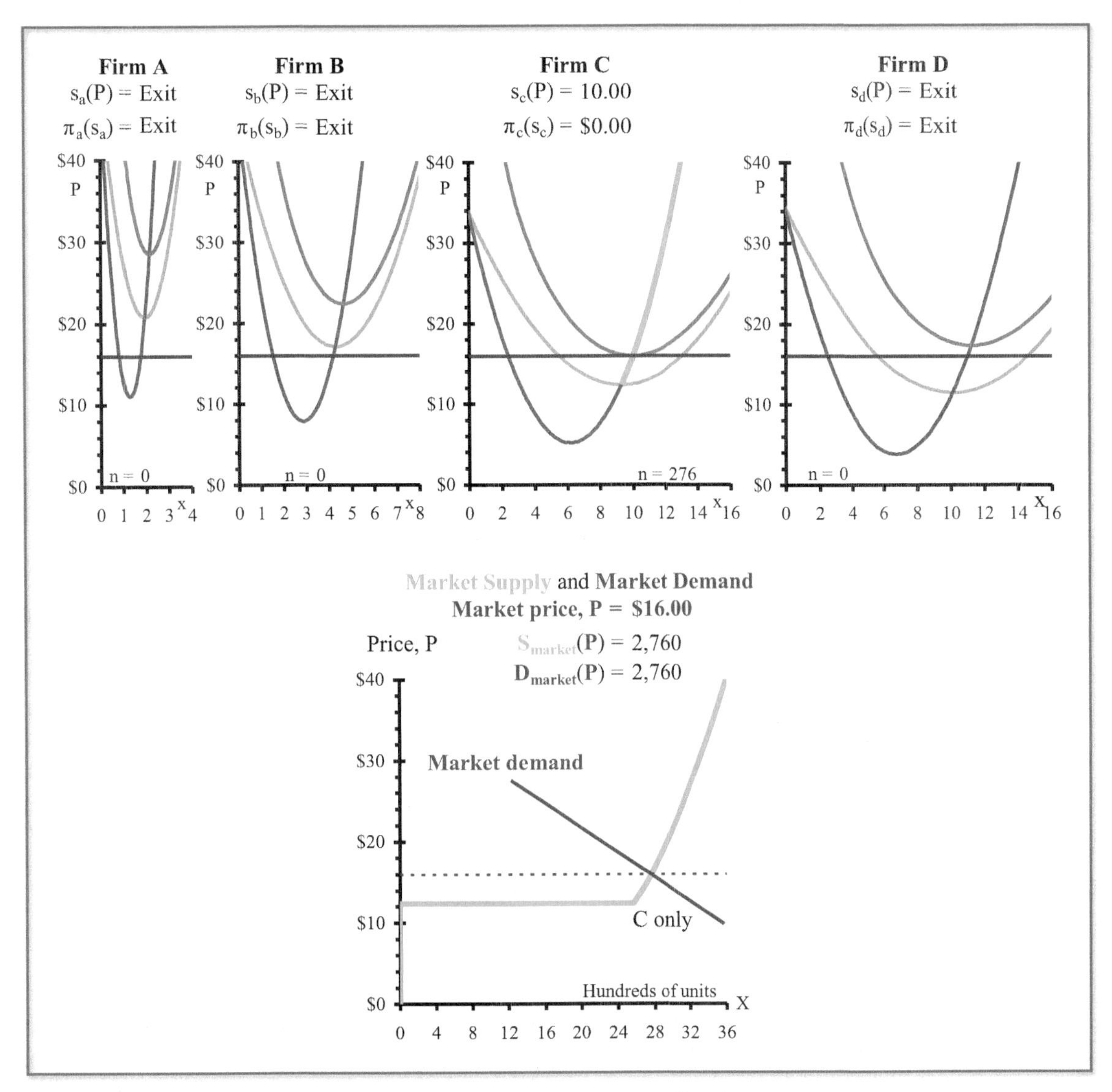

FIGURE 14.6 Long-Run Equilibrium with Varying Returns to Scale

The equation of short-run total cost for C-style firms is:

$$STC(x) = 35 + 34 \cdot x - 4.65 \cdot x^2 + 0.25 \cdot x^3. \quad \textbf{(14.2)}$$

Typically, we would not know both cost curves, but either provides us with the long-run equilibrium output level produced by each firm. As discussed in Section 11.3, the point of minimum LAC has SATC = SMC = LMC = LAC, according to Equation 11.5. This is the long-run equilibrium production point, given a competitive market. Since we typically do not have both, we will separately derive each result and then note that both methods produce the same answer.

The point of minimum long-run average cost is the point where LAC = LMC. Given Equation 14.1, we therefore require:

$$36 - 4 \cdot x + 0.2 \cdot x^2 = 36 - 8 \cdot x + 0.6 \cdot x^2. \quad \textbf{(14.3a)}$$

Regrouping, we have:

$$0 = 0.4 \cdot x^2 - 4 \cdot x. \quad \textbf{(14.3b)}$$

This has possible solutions x = 0 and x = 10. When x = 0, LAC(0) = LMC(0) = 36, and when x = 10, LAC(10) = LMC(10) = 16; therefore, x = 10 is minimum LAC.

The point of minimum short-run average total cost occurs when SATC = SMC. Given Equation 14.2, we therefore require:

$$35/x + 34 - 4.65 \cdot x + 0.25 \cdot x^2 = 34 - 9.3 \cdot x + 0.75 \cdot x^2. \quad \textbf{(14.4a)}$$

Regrouping, we have:

$$0 = 0.5 \cdot x^2 - 4.65 \cdot x - 35/x. \quad \textbf{(14.4b)}$$

Multiplying by x, we obtain a cubic equation in x:

$$0 = 0.5 \cdot x^3 - 4.65 \cdot x^2 - 35. \quad \textbf{(14.4c)}$$

As noted in Section 11.4, this is most easily solved using **Goal Seek** (see the discussion surrounding Table 11.1). Not surprisingly, x = 10 satisfies Equation 14.4c (substituting x = 10 into Equation 14.4c produces 500 – 465 – 35 = 0). Evaluating SATC and SMC at x = 10 produces SATC(10) = SMC(10) = 16, the same answer obtained using the LTC curve. The coincidence of all four curves at minimum LAC is algebraically noted in Equation 11.5 and is shown geometrically at x = 10 in Figures 11.15A and 11.15B and in Figure 14.4 (for C-style (K10-sized) firms).

We have modeled a long-run equilibration process in which individual firms decide to remain with their existing capital stock or to exit the market. We have also described entry as occurring by "outsiders" to the market. This is simply a heuristic device that allows us to describe how firms adjust in moving toward competitive equilibrium. We could just as easily have described firms within the industry adjusting their plant size in response to changes in the market clearing price. In moving from Figure 14.5 to Figure 14.6, for example, suppose that the 100 D-style firms are able to adjust their capital stock from K16 to K10 to produce output at a lower per-unit cost, rather than shut down, and that 19 new C-style firms undertake *de novo* entry. The end result would be the same: 276 C-style firms would each earn a normal profit by producing 10 units of output at a long-run equilibrium price of P* = $16 in this instance.

Suppose that the technology of production of a good is subject to variable returns to scale, such that general U-shaped LAC and LMC curves result. If the market for the good is perfectly competitive, then the long-run equilibrium will have a number of firms, each of which produces the same amount of output. Each firm will produce at minimum long-run average cost. If we call this point (x*, P*), then P* = LAC(x*) = LMC(x*). If market demand is D(P*), then the number of firms in the market in long-run equilibrium is n, where n satisfies:

$$n = D(P^*)/x^*. \quad \textbf{(14.5)}$$

Given U-shaped, long-run, per-unit cost curves, a unique plant size dominates in the long run because only one plant size produces goods at minimum long-run average cost. We say that this plant size represents an **efficient scale of production**.

efficient scale of production: A short-run production process is produced at an efficient scale of production if this plant size is associated with minimum long-run average cost.

As discussed in Section 9.4, the point of maximum average productivity is the output level where the production process turns from exhibiting increasing returns to scale to exhibiting decreasing returns to scale. This is the point where production exhibits constant returns to scale (CRTS). This is analogous to the short-run discussion that tied average and marginal productivity to average and marginal cost, using short-run total product and variable cost curves in Figure 11.1. In the short-run context, this analysis concludes that short-run average variable cost is minimized at the output level where short-run average factor productivity is maximized. The same analysis applies to long-run cost curves, except that now the productivity notion is one of returns to scale, rather than productivity of a single factor of production. In the long-run context, this analysis concludes that long-run average cost is minimized at the output level where production exhibits maximum long-run average productivity (which is also the point at which production exhibits CRTS). We now turn to an analysis of long-run equilibrium where the production process exhibits CRTS over a range of outputs.

14.3 A Special Case: Long-Run Competitive Equilibrium with CRTS

OPTIONAL SECTION

Suppose that the production process exhibits CRTS. In this event, there is no unique plant size that minimizes per-unit production cost in the long run. As shown in Figures 11.15C and 11.15D, multiple plant sizes produce output at minimum long-run average cost.

Figure 14.7 depicts a short-run equilibrium in a competitive market subject to CRTS. Focus initially on the long-run cost diagram on the left. The starting point for this figure is Figure 11.15 (the largest plant size has been removed, since the point can easily be made with four short-run plant sizes). All four plants can be analyzed in one diagram or in separate diagrams. Separate diagrams were used in the U-shaped long-run per-unit cost curves in Section 14.2 (except for Figure 14.4) because the U shape adds extra complexity, relative to a flat LAC = LMC line produced under CRTS.

The value of using a single diagram is that the diagram can be a bit larger, and the interrelations between plant sizes can be more readily seen. As a result, this single diagram is used (like Figure 14.4, as opposed to Figures 14.2, 14.3, 14.5, and 14.6). A table of output and profit values and two additional graphic features have been added to the diagram. One feature is a green diamond on each short-run marginal cost curve at the point of minimum average variable cost. These diamonds are shown, rather than four SAVC curves, because the diagram is already complex enough and the only "information" attained from a given SAVC curve is the price level where that firm would decide to shut down rather than produce in the short run. This occurs at the (x, \$/x) points on the SMC curve (3, \$27) for the K4 plant, at (6, \$18) for the K8 plant, at (9, \$15.75) for the K12 plant, and at (12, \$14.40) for the K16 plant.[1] The supply curve for each firm starts at this point and moves up the SMC curve, as discussed in Section 13.3. The second diagrammatic addition is a blue horizontal price line that depicts the short-run demand curve facing individual firms in

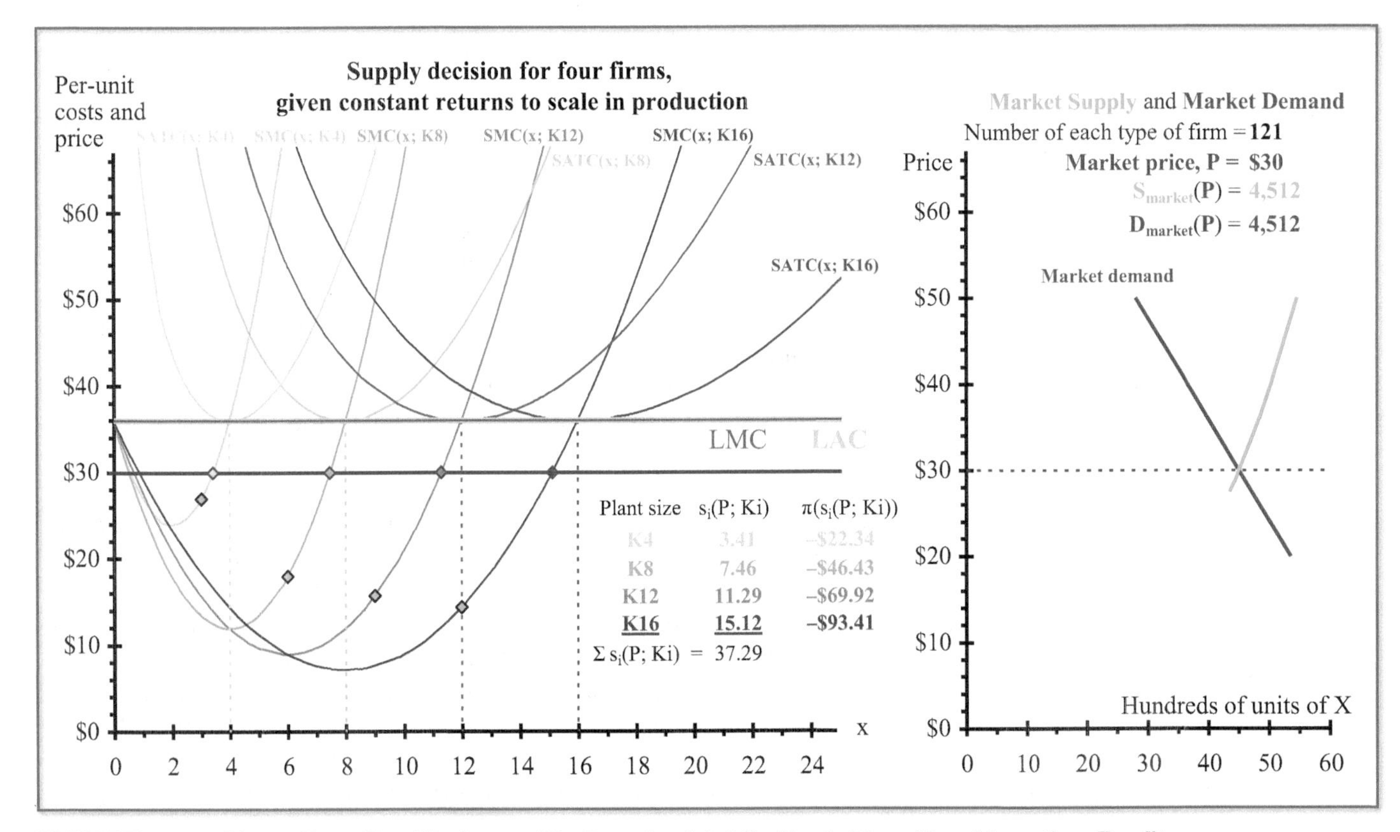

FIGURE 14.7 Short-Run Equilibrium with Constant LAC; Each Firm Has Negative Profits

this market. The diamond at the intersection of an SMC(x; Ki) curve with this P = MR line denotes points on the individual firm's supply curve associated with this price, s_i(P; Ki).

Given the four sets of short-run cost curves in Figure 14.7, all four plants will continue to produce in the short run if P ≥ \$27, three plants will produce if \$27 > P ≥ \$18, two plants will produce if \$18 > P ≥ \$15.75, and one plant will produce if \$15.75 > P ≥ \$14.40. Therefore, we see that there is a range of prices in which one or more of the firms will shut down in the short run.

Q7 and Q8. Is it possible, given CRTS, that some firms will shut down and other firms will operate at a profit in the same short run (as was depicted, given variable returns to scale, in Figures 13.10 and 14.2)?*

CRTS leads to a situation where all firms are operating at either a profit or a loss in the short run. Firms operate at a profit as long as P > \$36, and they operate at a loss as long as P < \$36, given LAC = LMC = \$36 in Figure 14.7. Therefore, we cannot see some firms operating at a profit and some at a loss in the same short run (as seen in Figures 14.2 and 14.5).

The market supply curve depends critically on how many of each type of firm are in the market. To simplify the discussion, suppose that there are the same number of each of the four types of firms in the market in all situations. The portion of the market supply curve shown starts at the price of \$27 so that all four plant sizes produce output. Were the price less than \$27, then some firms would shut down in the short run, as discussed earlier. The extended supply curve would have horizontal segments at the minimum SAVC prices listed previously (\$27, \$18, \$15.75, and \$14.40), just as in the previous section. Market demand is 4,512 units at a price of \$30. The market clearing price is \$30 in this instance because market supply, given 121 firms of each of the four plant sizes, is 4,512 = 121 · 37.29 (as noted in the table, Σs_i(\$30; Ki) = 37.29 units [Σ is the shorthand symbol for sum]). Since P < \$36 = LAC = LMC, each firm operates at a loss, ranging from –\$22.34 to –\$93.41. There are too many firms in the market, given the size distribution of firms and market demand. Some firms must exit as we move from the short to the long run.

Figure 14.8 depicts the reverse situation. With 88 firms of each type, market supply of 3,660 = 88 · 41.60 matches market demand at the short-run equilibrium price of \$40. Each firm earns positive profits, ranging from \$16.63 to \$65.09. There are too few firms in the market, given the size distribution of firms and market demand. Some firms must enter as we move from the short to the long run.

Somewhere between 88 and 121 firms of each of the four plant sizes will produce long-run equilibrium. The long-run equilibrium will occur at \$36 = $LAC_{minimum}$, but unlike the varying returns to scale case discussed in Figures 14.2–14.6, this does not occur at a unique plant size. Indeed, the four plant sizes shown are only four out of a continuum of plant sizes that could produce output at minimum long-run average cost. Figure 14.9 depicts one such long-run equilibrium. One hundred firms of each of the four plant sizes produce a total of 4,000 = 100 · 40.00 units of output. Each firm produces at a profit-maximizing profit level of \$0, given the market clearing price of \$36.

The long-run equilibrium in Figure 14.9 is described as "one such" long-run equilibrium because we could equally easily have produced this equilibrium via 200 K4 and 200 K16 firms (since 200 · (4 + 16) = 4,000). And it also could have occurred with 200 K8 and 200 K12 firms, or 1,000 K4 firms, or 500 K8 firms, or 250 K16 firms, or 333 K12 firms and one K4 firm for similar reasons. Each of these equilibria would produce 4,000 units from a large number of firms in which each firm would have average total cost and marginal cost of \$36 per unit, so each firm would attain a profit-maximizing profit level of zero. Put another way, each firm in the industry would earn a normal return on its assets, so each firm would have no incentive to exit. And since no firm earns positive profits, entry does not look profitable. Finally, the *three conditions* required for long-run

***Q7 and Q8 answer:** No, price must be below \$27 for the first firm to shut down, but price must be above \$36 to achieve positive profits, given these cost conditions. Both price conditions cannot hold at the same time.

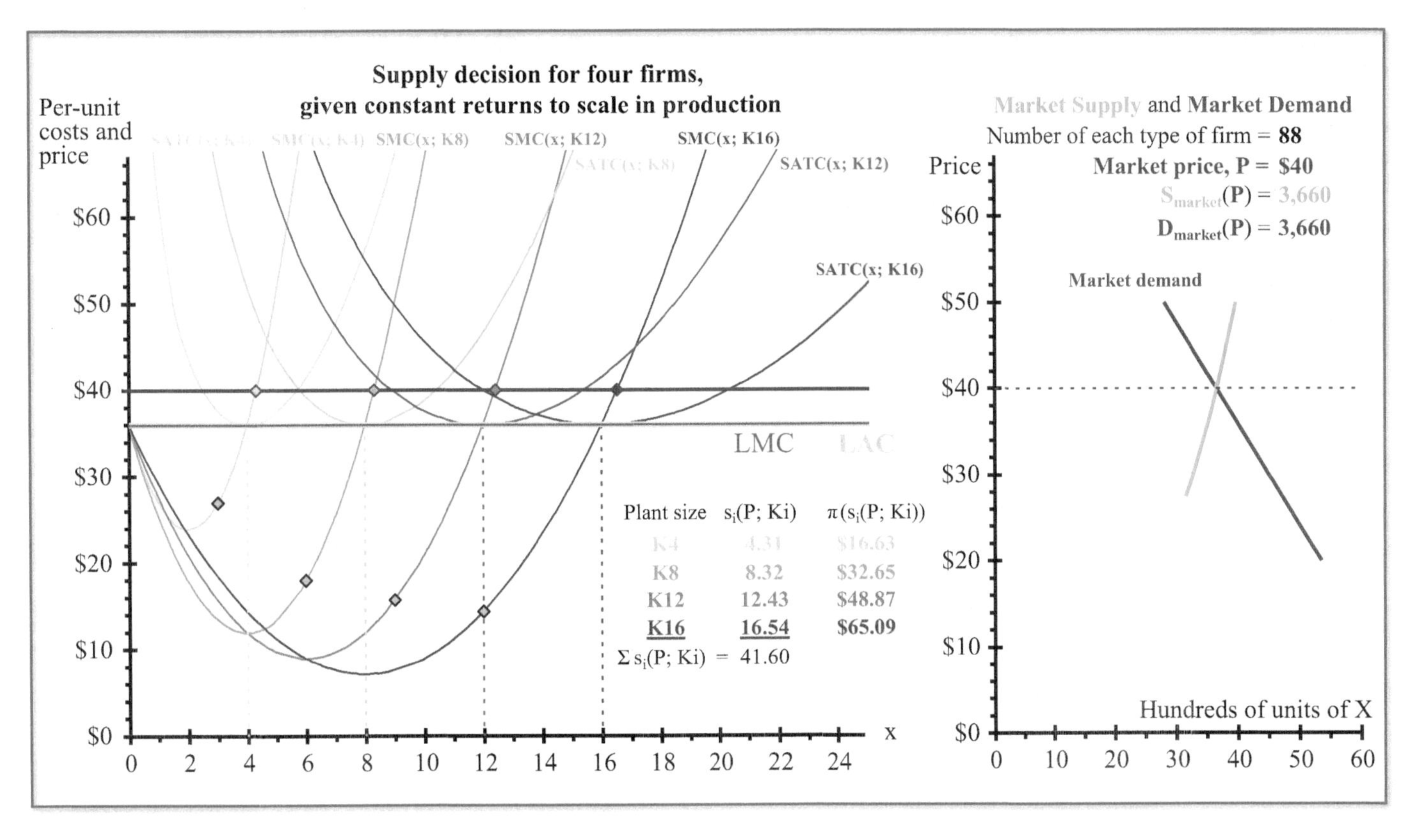

FIGURE 14.8 Short-Run Equilibrium with Constant LAC; Each Firm Has Positive Profits

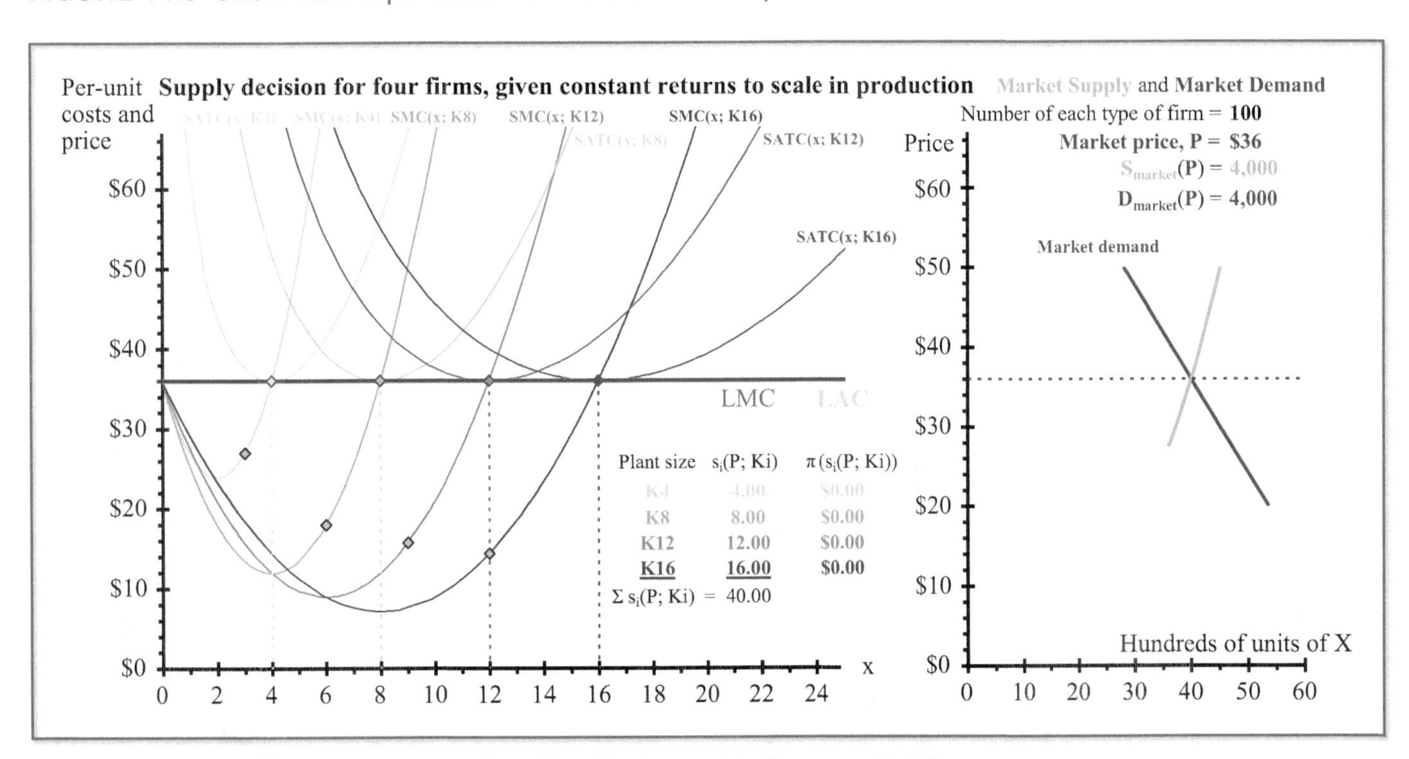

FIGURE 14.9 One Possible Long-Run Equilibrium with Constant LAC

competitive equilibrium (S = D at P*, $\pi = 0$, and P* = $LAC_{minimum}$) are satisfied by each of these scenarios.

One final point should be made regarding returns to scale in production processes. Production processes often exhibit initial increasing returns to scale, followed by a range of output for which production exhibits constant returns to scale, followed by eventual decreasing returns to scale. Economists call the output level where production first

minimum efficient scale (MES): Minimum efficient scale is the smallest level of output for which production achieves minimum long-run average cost of production.

maximum efficient scale (MaxES): Maximum efficient scale is the largest level of output for which production achieves minimum long-run average cost of production.

exhibits minimum LAC **minimum efficient scale (MES)** and the largest output level that exhibits minimum LAC **maximum efficient scale (MaxES)**. In Section 14.2, minimum and maximum efficient scale coincide at a single efficient scale of production. In Figures 14.7–14.9, MES is x = 0, and MaxES is larger than x = 25 (the largest output level shown in these figures).

When MES and MaxES are different output levels, and MES is greater than zero, the LAC curve is still U shaped (as with Section 14.2). The bottom of the U occurs over a range of outputs (as with the analysis in this section), rather than for a single LAC-minimizing output level. Figure 14.10 provides an example of long-run cost curves consistent with LAC having distinct output levels, where maximum and minimum efficient scale occurs. Numbers have been removed from both axes so that you can focus on the qualitative relation between curves that arises in this setting. The marginal cost curve in this situation coincides with LAC over the range of outputs from MES to MaxES. This same range of outputs can be seen in the total cost diagram by the coincidence of the LTC curve and the dashed minimum-sloping chord connecting the origin to the LTC curve. Over this range of outputs, production exhibits CRTS. The output levels associated with MES and MaxES are based on a visual inspection of when the curves diverge from one another. Exact values require knowledge of the function that produced these curves (and these functions are unimportant in the present context). Below MES, LMC is below LAC; therefore, LAC is declining. For output levels above MaxES, LMC is above LAC; thus, LAC is increasing. The same relation holds between average and marginal as usual: Marginal pulls average up or down, depending on whether it is above or below average.

FIGURE 14.10 Long-Run Cost Curves, Given Varying Returns to Scale: Minimum LAC Occurs Over a Range of Output

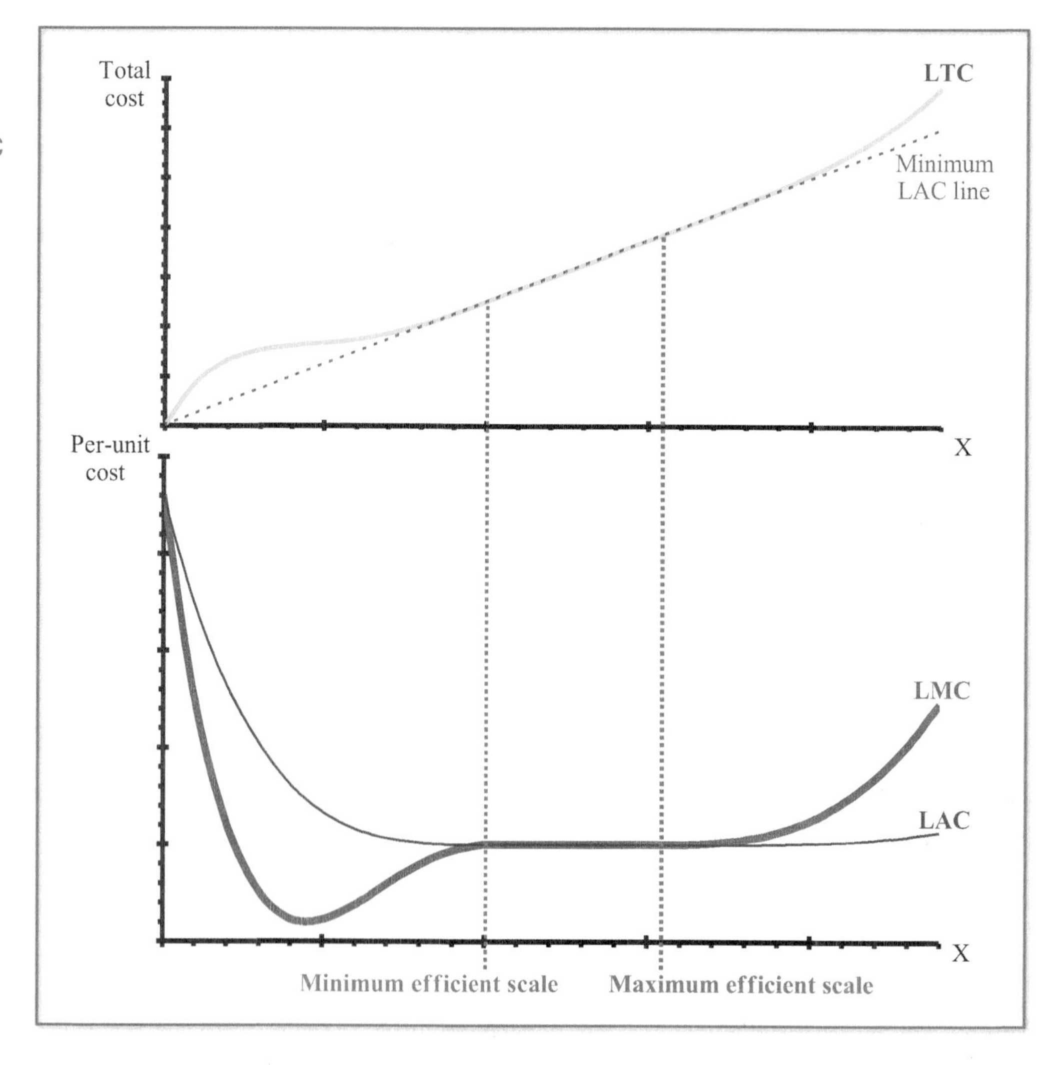

Cost curves such as these lead to indeterminate plant size in long-run competitive equilibrium. Each firm in long-run equilibrium in this instance will have a plant size somewhere between MES and MaxES, and the market clearing price P* will support each of these firms at zero economic profit, since $P^* = LAC_{minimum}$.

The analysis presented in the last two sections can be conceptualized as the adjustment of short-run competitive equilibria over time, due to profit-and-loss signals. A long-run equilibrium is achieved when all firms operate at zero economic profit and when market supply equals market demand. This adjustment occurs as the number of firms in the market changes in response to short-run profit-and-loss signals. The long-run equilibrium is characterized by each firm producing at an output level where $P^* = LAC_{minimum}$, regardless of plant size.

14.4 Long-Run Supply: What Happens When Demand Changes?

The analysis of long-run equilibrium produces a price level at which supply equals demand and each firm maximizes profits by producing at zero economic profit. This analysis is based on a fixed demand for the product. Put differently, the analysis that achieved long-run equilibrium out of a series of short-run equilibria did so by shifting short-run market supply along a fixed market demand curve. We now turn to the analysis of how long-run equilibrium adjusts to changes in demand; this is the analysis that determines a curve called the long-run supply curve. The **long-run supply (LS) curve** maps the set of long-run equilibrium (x, \$/x) points for different levels of demand. Since a point on the LS curve is a long-run equilibrium, it is a point at which there is no incentive for change (i.e., entry or exit). It is also a point at which each firm earns a normal rate of return on its capital (i.e., each firm attains zero profit).

long-run supply (LS) curve: The long-run supply curve maps the set of long-run equilibrium (x, \$/x) points for different levels of demand.

Students often confuse the LS curve with the supply curve that helps describe a long-run equilibrium. A short-run supply curve achieves a long-run equilibrium. It is not, however, a long-run supply curve because it is predicated on a fixed number of firms' SMC curves. Examples of such short-run supply curves were shown in both Sections 14.2 and 14.3. Figure 14.6 described a short-run supply curve with 276 identical firms that achieved a long-run equilibrium, given the market demand shown in Figures 14.2–14.6. This analysis was based on a varying returns to scale production technology involving a unique efficient scale of production. Figure 14.9 described a short-run supply curve with 100 firms, each of four different plant sizes that achieved a long-run equilibrium, given the market demand shown in Figures 14.7–14.9. This analysis was based on a CRTS production technology. Figures 14.6 and 14.9 are both long-run equilibria because market supply equals fixed market demand with 276 or 400 firms, and each of these firms produces output at minimum LAC and at zero profit (as required by the *three conditions* at the start of the chapter). *Had demand been different, then a different short-run equilibrium would have been required to achieve the requirements of long-run equilibrium.*

The analysis in the previous two sections produced a *single* point on the long-run supply curve. (More accurately, each section produced a single point on each of two long-run supply curves; as noted earlier, separate analyses were shown for varying returns to scale in Figures 14.2–14.6 and CRTS production technologies in Figures 14.7–14.9.) The question examined in this section is: *What happens to the long-run competitive equilibrium as demand changes?* The analysis involved in answering this question is long run in nature; each point on the long-run supply curve satisfies the requirements for long-run equilibrium. Before examining this question, we begin by describing what happens when a competitive market in long-run equilibrium faces a change in demand. While this analysis can be performed in a CRTS setting (as we examined in Section 14.3), we will find it useful to employ the varying returns to scale analysis of Section 14.2 so that we can describe the effect of different levels of demand on a representative efficient firm of determinate plant size (to mirror the discussion in that section, we call this efficient plant size C).

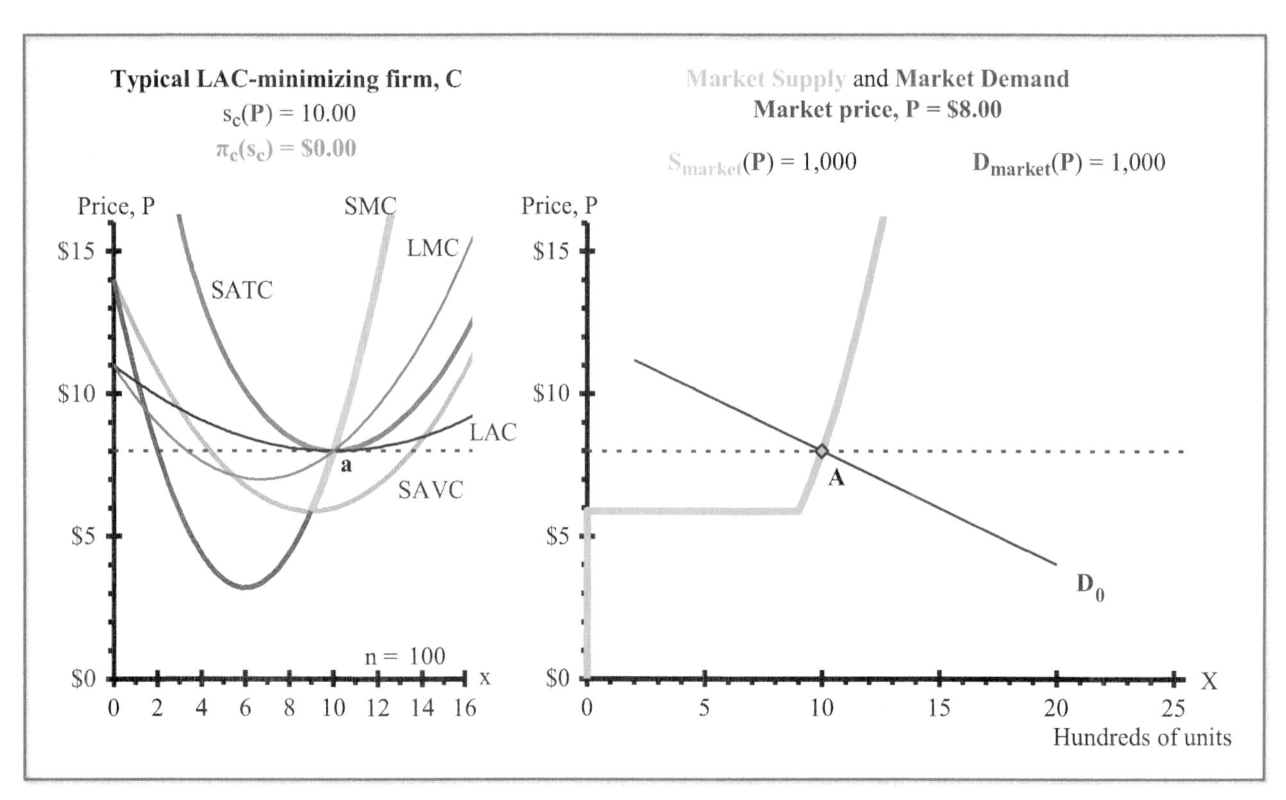

FIGURE 14.11 Each Long-Run Equilibrium Is a Point on the Long-Run Supply Curve

Suppose that a competitive market is in an initial long-run equilibrium based on demand D_0. To simplify the discussion as much as possible, assume that each C-style firm achieves minimum LAC production at (x, \$/x) = (s_c(P), P) = (10, \$8). Initial market demand at this price is depicted by point **A** in the right-hand diagram of Figure 14.11. D_0(\$8) = 1,000 units, so n = 100, according to Equation 14.5. Each of the 100 firms produces at point ***a*** = (10, \$8) in the individual firm diagram on the left in Figure 14.11. Point ***a*** produces output at minimum LAC (where LAC, LMC, SATC, and SMC coincide, as described in Equation 11.5), so that each firm earns normal profits at minimum LAC, as required by being a long-run equilibrium.

What happens when demand changes? The first factor to consider is that if market demand rotates around the initial equilibrium point (in Figure 14.11, point **A**), then the long-run competitive equilibrium does not change. (We have not provided a figure to depict this scenario; you should do this for yourself.) Market supply still equals market demand at point **A**. Further, market supply is provided by the same number of firms, each producing at minimum LAC (at point ***a***), so that each firm earns zero profits. The *three conditions* for long-run equilibrium are still satisfied if demand pivots around point **A**.

More interesting is what happens when demand shifts as shown in Figure 14.12. Demand increases at each price in moving from D_0 to D_1. The long-run per-unit cost curves have been removed from the figure because short-run output decisions are based on SMC, and short-run profits are based on a comparison of P and SATC. Further, as shown in Section 14.2, given a U-shaped LAC curve, there is an LAC-minimizing plant size, C, that is efficient and will be employed in the long run in any event.[2] One hundred such firms were in the long-run equilibrium in Figure 14.11; each of these same 100 firms produces along its short-run supply curve, s_c(P), as the market price changes due to a change in demand. The increase in demand causes the market clearing price to increase to \$10.61, as shown at **B** = (1097, \$10.61) in the right-hand diagram in Figure 14.12. The representative firm responds by producing at **b** = (10.97, \$10.61) in the left-hand diagram in Figure 14.12. (Note that this is a short-run equilibrium price, since market supply at this price S(\$10.61) = 1,097 = n · s_c(\$10.61) = 100 · 10.97 equals market demand.) Since P = \$10.61 > SATC(10.97) = \$8.11, positive short-term profits result. These profits are

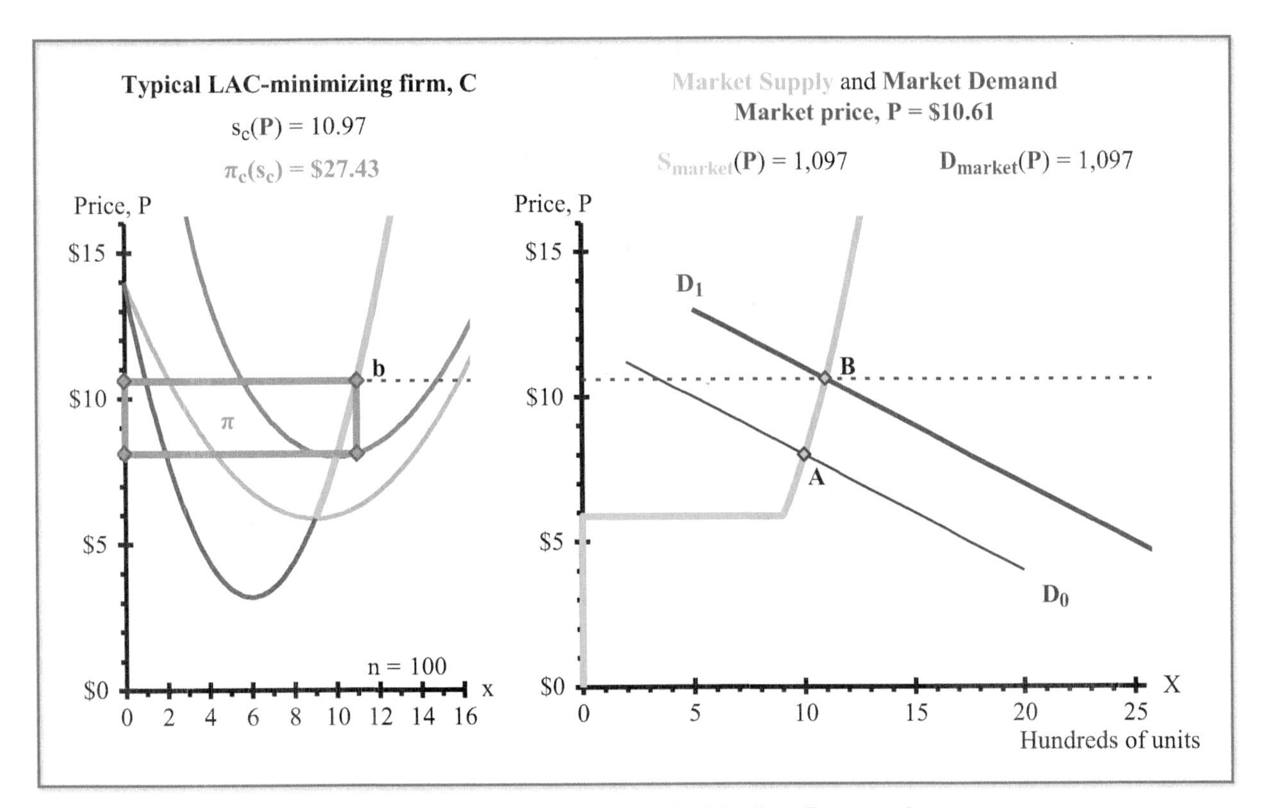

FIGURE 14.12 The Short-Run Response to a Change in Market Demand

seen as the green $s_c(P) = 10.97$ wide by $(P - SATC(s_c(P))) = (\$10.61 - \$8.11)$ high profit rectangle labeled π in the left-hand diagram:

$$\pi = \$27.43 = (P - SATC(s_c(P))) \cdot s_c(P) = \$2.50 \cdot 10.97. \quad \textbf{(14.6)}$$

Short-run profits induce entry. Entry ultimately leads to a new long-run equilibrium somewhere along demand curve D_1. This new long-run equilibrium provides us with a second point on the long-run supply curve. The location of this second point depends critically on how entry affects the market for *inputs* in the production process. Categorically, three possibilities are clear: Factor costs might increase, decrease, or remain fixed. We analyze each of these possibilities in its own subsection. Each analysis uses the demand change scenario begun in Figures 14.11 and 14.12 as the short-run springboard on which each long-run analysis is built. We begin our discussion with the third of these possibilities.

Long-Run Supply, Given Constant Factor Costs

A firm produces output based on factors of production. As noted in Chapter 9, we typically describe these factors of production as land, labor, capital, and raw materials. Suppose that the factors of production used are competitively supplied, and suppose further that this industry is one of many using these factors of production. In particular, suppose that this *industry's* demand for each factor of production is "small," relative to the size of each factor market. An increase in demand for each factor of production by that industry will have no effect on the market clearing price of that input. We say that factor costs are constant in this instance. **Factor costs are constant** if the prices of factors in the production process are not dependent on how much is demanded of those factors of production by the industry. This is also called the *constant-cost* case.

It might sound a bit unrealistic to expect that factor prices are not dependent on demand for those factors. After all, an increase in demand should increase price, according to the supply/demand model. But that model only applies when demand appreciably changes or when supply cannot be easily expanded.

factor costs are constant: Factor costs are constant if the prices of factors in the production process are not dependent on how much is demanded of those factors of production by the industry. This is also called the *constant-cost* case.

Beer as a Constant-Cost Market

Although the beer market does not completely fit the competitive model (due to the presence of large firms within the industry and because beer is viewed as a heterogeneous product), it nonetheless provides us with a useful market to consider in this instance. As a result, consider only that part of the beer market that produces low-end mass-market beer. This segment is populated by small regional producers that arguably compete on a more perfectly competitive basis. Put in the context of Figures 14.11 and 14.12, suppose that this market was originally in long-run equilibrium at a price of $8/case. Each of the 100 firms earns zero profits as a result.[3] Suppose that an American Heart Association study links beer consumption to improved cardiovascular health. This could shift demand for beer from D_0 to D_1. Price increases in the short run to $10.61/case, and individual firms produce at a short-run profit. Such profits will encourage entry, and that entry will continue until short-run profits are beaten back to zero. The price where this occurs is the subject of the current discussion.

Consider the inputs used in the production process of beer. The main ingredients are grain, water, yeast, and barley. Packaging in this segment of the market is predominately aluminum cans. Capital used in the production process is mostly stainless steel tanks, pumps, and tubing. Labor used in the production process is not highly skilled. The beer industry could double the use of each of these factors of production without affecting the market price of each factor because this industry's demand is "small," relative to the size of each of the factor markets. Total grain usage devoted to the beer industry is a miniscule part of the total grain market, so dramatic changes in grain demand by the beer industry would not have a significant effect on the price of grain. The same can be said of other factors of production used in the beer production process.

In a constant-cost industry, the per-unit cost curves in Figures 14.11 and 14.12 do not change as entry or exit occurs. The only effect that entry or exit has in this market is on market supply. Market supply shifts out as firms enter the market in response to an increase in demand. And conversely, market supply shifts in as firms exit the market in response to a decrease in demand. As entry or exit occurs, the price of the product adjusts in the direction of the unchanged long-run equilibrium price $P^* = LAC_{minimum}$. Profits will decline (as will losses) until a new long-run equilibrium is achieved in which each firm earns a normal return (of zero profits) by producing once again at minimum long-run average cost.

In this event, the long-run equilibrium with expanded demand will simply have more firms of the same size producing at minimum LAC = P*. The number of firms in the market will satisfy Equation 14.5, $n = D(P^*)/x^*$. The only remaining question is how large is demand at P*? Given the long-run equilibrium information in Figure 14.11, P* = $8/case and x* = 10 (at point ***a*** in the left-hand diagram). As shown in Figure 14.13, $D_1(P^*) = 1{,}750$, so the point **C** = (1750, $8) is a second point on the long-run supply curve, LS. This point is associated with 175 efficient firms, each producing at zero profit in long-run equilibrium (at point ***a*** = **c** in the left-hand diagram), given demand D_1. The rest of the long-run supply curve can be obtained by varying demand and following the re-equilibration process described previously. In each case, the long-run equilibrium will settle on a price of $8/case because the per-unit cost curves do not change, given constant factor costs. Long-run supply is flat in this instance, as shown by the yellow LS line through **A** and **C** in Figure 14.13.

Long-Run Supply, Given Increasing Factor Costs

Return once again to the beginning of the change in demand analysis described in Figures 14.11 and 14.12. The per-unit cost curves described in the left-hand diagram of each figure are based on a fixed number of firms in the market (n = 100). These curves are based on fixed factor costs, as described in Section 11.2. If factor costs change, then so will the cost curves.

As we described in the constant-cost discussion earlier, if an industry's demand for a factor of production represents an insignificant portion of total demand for that factor of

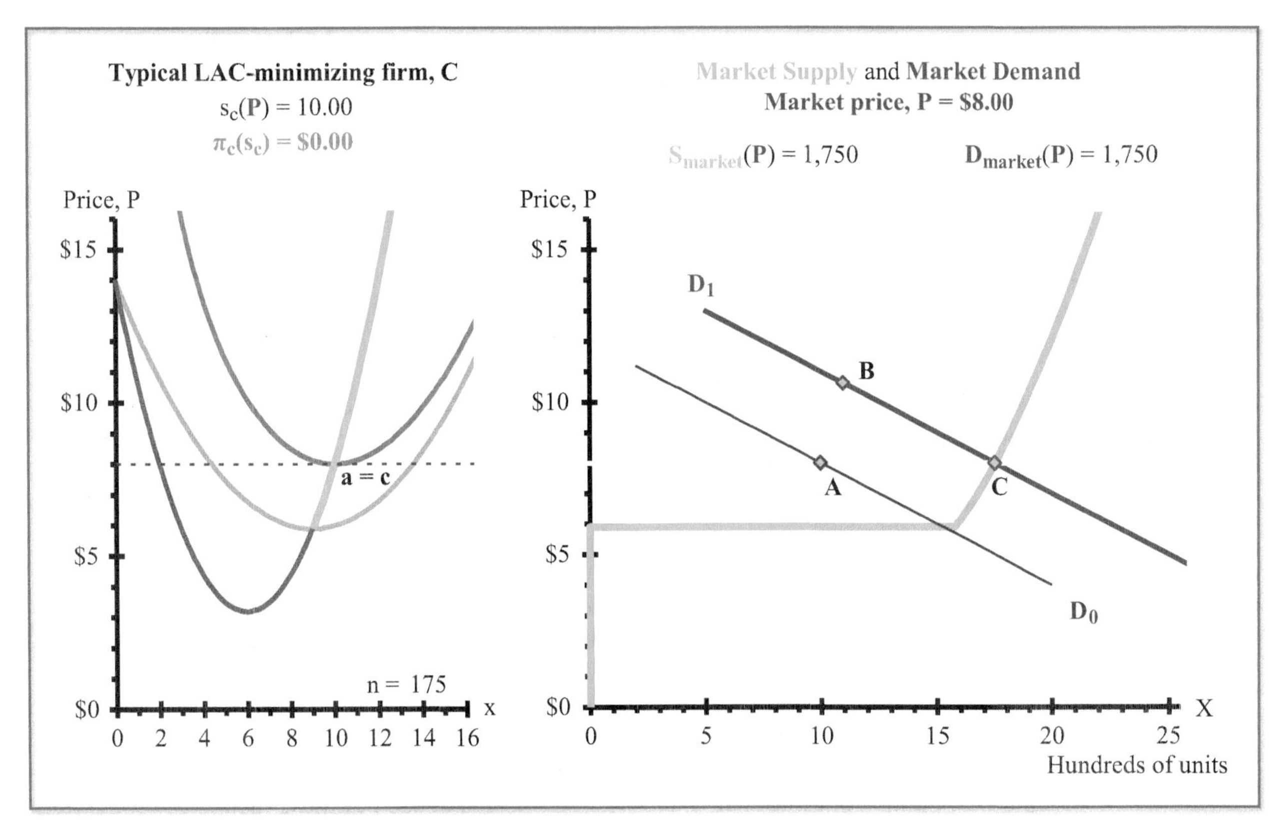

FIGURE 14.13 Long-Run Supply in a Constant-Cost Industry

production, then changes in that industry's demand for the factor will not have a noticeable effect on the market price of the factor of production.

Even if an industry's demand for a factor of production is a significant portion of total demand for that factor, changes in that industry's demand for that factor will not appreciably change the price of that factor if factor supply is readily expandable. Take, for instance, the yeast used in the production of beer. Suppose that special strains of yeast are "best" at beer production.[4] Other strains are used for wine production, bread production, and so on. An increase in demand for various strains of brewer's yeast will not increase the price of that yeast because supply of that yeast can be readily expanded at constant cost.

Unfortunately, it is not always possible to obtain increased supplies of certain factors of production without bidding up the price of those factors. In this instance, we say that factor costs are increasing. **Factor costs are increasing** if the prices of factors in the production process increase as demand for those factors increases. This is also called the *increasing-cost* case.

factor costs are increasing: Factor costs are increasing if the prices of factors in the production process increase as demand for those factors increases. This is also called the *increasing-cost* case.

If some factors of production face restricted supply, then an increase in demand for these factors of production will bid up the price of the factor. The easiest factors of production to see this with are various raw materials, such as iron ore, coal, or crude oil.

As factor demand increases, less-productive sources of these factors will be utilized. These sources are only profitable when the price of the factor increases. If these factors are an appreciable part of the production process, then this will filter through to increased factor costs.

Wine as an Increasing-Cost Market

Although wine is a highly differentiated product market, certain parts of this market have more of an undifferentiated "commodity" feel. This segment of the wine market is called the "fighting varietals" segment. Brand name is less important in this segment; price is the predominant way that the various brands "fight" with each other. We can use Figures 14.11 and 14.12 to begin our analysis of long-run supply in this market segment. It is not unreasonable to consider an initial equilibrium in the fighting varietals segment at a price of $8/bottle as depicted in Figure 14.11. Figure 14.12 describes an increase in demand from D_0 to D_1 that causes the short-run equilibrium price to rise from $8 to $10.61/bottle. Interestingly, as mentioned in Chapter 2, the wine industry had just such a demand increase in the early 1990s. This increase in demand was precipitated by a November 1991 *60 Minutes* report by Morley Safer, entitled "The French Paradox," that linked red wine consumption to reduced risk of cardiovascular disease. Demand for red wine increased substantially in the wake of this report.

The most important factor of production in the wine market is, not surprisingly, wine grapes. Wine grapes (*vinifera*) are different from table grapes, such as Thompson Seedless, which are sold as fresh produce in the grocery store and used to produce raisins. Wine grapes are typically more difficult to grow and have more-restrictive geographic and climatic requirements than other grapes (and many other types of produce for that matter). Consider the distinction between the beer and wine market. If beer producers need more grain, then the grain can be grown on farmland in much of the United States. By contrast, if wine producers need more wine grapes, expanding production is difficult, due to climatic restrictions that limit large-scale production to some parts of California (where more than 90% of the wine in the United States is produced), together with a few other parts of the United States. These restrictions mean that as demand for wine grapes increases, so will the market clearing price of wine grapes.

Other factors of production in the wine market need not respond in the same way. The other factors of production in this market include containers for the finished product (wine bottles, cork, labels, etc.), wooden barrels and stainless steel storage containers, labor, and various machines used in the production process (such as crusher/de-stemmers, presses, pumps, bottling machines, etc.). Suppose that each of these factors of production is subject to constant-cost conditions, but that wine grapes are subject to increasing cost. This means that wine is an increasing-cost industry. The easiest way to see this is to make a simple "back of the envelope" calculation. Suppose that the wine grape cost at point ***a*** in Figure 14.11 comprises 50% of the average total cost of $8 and that demand for wine increases, causing grape costs to double.

Q. What will happen to average cost if no other factors of production are affected by the increase in demand for these factors of production?*

Entry in an increasing-cost market causes increased demand for factors of production. This puts upward pressure on factor prices, as discussed earlier. Quite simply, the price of wine grapes will increase as the number of firms bidding for wine grapes increases. The easiest way to model this increase in cost is to simply shift the cost curves up or down, depending on the overall number of firms in the market.

As noted previously, the increase in demand moves us from an initial long-run equilibrium at **A**, where 100 firms cumulatively produce 1,000 units at a price of $8 per unit, to a short-run equilibrium at **B**, where the same 100 firms produce 1,097 units at a price of $10.61. Each firm earns positive short-run profits as a result. These short-run profits encourage entry into the market, and entry will move out the short-run market supply curve, causing the short-run equilibrium to begin moving to the southeast along D_1 from point **B**. All of this is the same as in the constant-cost case analyzed earlier, except for one change. As firms enter the market, grape costs increase, and per-unit cost curves begin to float upward. In a truly competitive market, this would be imperceptible for individual firm entry, but to simplify the presentation, we assume here that each firm that enters causes MC(0) to increase by $0.02, due to increases in grape cost.[5] Since the other parts of

---

***Q answer:** Cost will increase by 50% in this instance. Fifty percent of $8 is $4, and a 100% increase in grape cost implies that grape cost increases to $8. Other factors remain fixed, so total cost increases from $8 to $12. Implicit in this analysis is the assumption that production is Leontief in grapes: You cannot substitute away from grapes if you wish to produce wine. This is a reasonable assumption, since you need grapes to produce wine; there is no input substitutability with regard to this factor of production.

the cubic cost function are fixed (i.e., FC, and the coefficients of the quadratic and cubic terms), the quantities where each curve achieves its minimum will not change. In particular, minimum ATC will continue to occur at x = 10, but the \$/x value associated with this output level will simply depend on how many firms are in the market.[6]

As firms enter the market, the (P – SATC) by x profit rectangle initially described by Equation 14.6 and shown in Figure 14.12 begins to shrink. This is due to three reasons in the increasing-cost case. First, the market clearing price declines as the short-run supply curve shifts out due to the new entry. Second, average total cost increases as the cost curves shift upward. Third, profit-maximizing output produced by the firm declines. Each of these factors causes the profit rectangle to decline. This process will continue until a new long-run equilibrium is achieved along D_1, in which each firm earns zero profits while producing at minimum average total cost. Given demand curve D_1, this expansion process stops when there are 150 firms in the industry. The additional 50 firms have raised the minimum average cost of production by \$1 to \$9/unit (when each firm produces 10 units of output). At the price of \$9, market demand is 1,500 units, a number that matches market supply (since $1{,}500 = 150 \cdot 10$). This new long-run equilibrium is shown in Figure 14.14 as point **C** = (1500, \$9) in the right-hand diagram and as point **c** = (10, \$9) in the left-hand diagram. The dynamics of this change can be seen using the Excel version of Figure 14.14. Set the number of firms slider in E21:I21 to 100, and simulate entry by adjusting the number of firms from 100 to 150. As you do this, you will see a simultaneous increase in market supply and a rise in the horizontal (shutdown) segment in the right-hand diagram and the floating upward of the per-unit cost curves in the left-hand diagram.

Since Figures 14.11, 14.13, and 14.14 depict long-run competitive equilibria, each of the individual firm diagrams on the left in each figure depicts production at minimum LAC. But the individual firm diagram in Figure 14.14 differs from the other two because the minimum LAC equilibrium has floated up by \$1 to \$9.

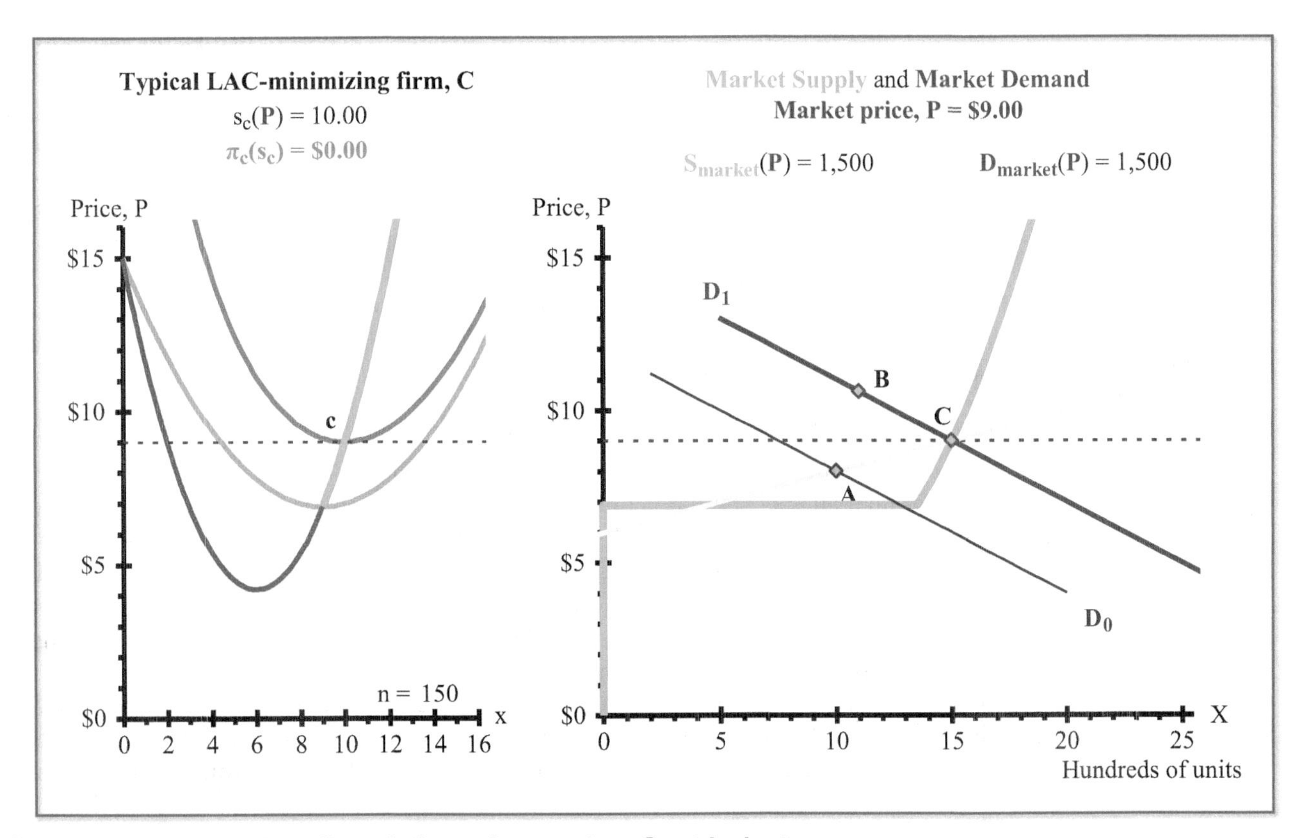

FIGURE 14.14 Long-Run Supply in an Increasing-Cost Industry

Q14. If we imagine that grape cost was 50% of the cost of production prior to the demand increase, what percentage increase in the price of wine grapes is implied by the new equilibrium (assuming that the prices of all other factors in the production process have not changed in this instance)?*

If demand increased even further, then the new long-run equilibrium production point would continue to increase in cost. Conversely, if demand declined, then the new long-run equilibrium cost level would decline. As demand varies, so would the price level associated with long-run equilibrium, unlike the constant-cost case described earlier. As a result, the yellow long-run supply curve is upward sloping in Figure 14.14.

Notice that grape costs increase even if the firm owns its own vineyards (and does not have to purchase grapes on the open market). The reason is that we should value resources according to their next best alternative use; a firm should use the notion of opportunity cost. If grape prices have risen, then the next best alternative use would be to sell grapes at this new higher price. As a result, it is inappropriate to imagine that a firm owning its own vineyards will act differently in this situation. Whether or not the winery owns vineyards, it should impute the market-defined price for all resources owned when making production decisions.

Long-Run Supply, Given Decreasing Factor Costs

The preceding two subsections have made the case for constant and increasing factor costs as a function of demand. Long-run supply responds in the same way that factor costs respond to changes in demand. If factor costs are not affected by changes in demand, then long-run supply is flat. If factor costs increase as demand increases, then long-run supply is upward sloping. The third theoretical possibility is that long-run supply is downward sloping—an outcome that would occur if an increase in demand for factors of production leads to a decrease in factor prices.

Given the supply/demand model, it is difficult to conceptualize how an increase in demand for a factor of production can lead to a decrease in cost of that factor. Nonetheless, there are circumstances where this occurs. When it occurs, we say that factor costs are decreasing. **Factor costs are decreasing** if the prices of factors in the production process decrease as demand for those factors increases. This is also called the *decreasing-cost* case.

factor costs are decreasing: Factor costs are decreasing if the prices of factors in the production process decrease as demand for those factors increases. This is also called the *decreasing-cost* case.

This scenario is, admittedly, counterintuitive. It is not as common as the constant-cost and increasing-cost cases. Nonetheless, there are markets where factor costs do act this way.[7] The reason has to do with the effect that increasing demand has on production costs within a market. If increases in demand allow large-scale methods of production to be employed that are not economically efficient for small-scale production, then increases in demand for a factor can lead to decreases in the cost of that factor. Again, the best way to make this point is by considering a concrete example.

Electronic Toys as a Decreasing-Cost Market

One of the hallmarks of the consumer electronics industry in the past 40 years has been the continual and substantial decline in cost of those products. Calculators that have the same calculating power as ones that sold for $150 in the mid-1970s are now sold in dollar stores or are given away in cereal boxes. Similar statements can be made for digital watches. Part of this, of course, is due to technological change in the semiconductor and microprocessor industry, but part is also due to increasing sales, leading to decreasing unit cost in the market. Consider the market for electronic toys, such as a talking teddy bear or a motorized toy car. Suppose that the electronic components for these toys cost $4 at the level of production implied by the initial equilibrium in Figure 14.11. Each of the 100 firms initially in the market spends half of its cost on these electronic components. An

*__Q14 answer:__ This is a 25% increase in the price of wine grapes. If 50% of the cost in Figure 14.11 is grape cost, then grape cost is $4/bottle at ***a*** in Figure 14.11. Since total cost per unit at **c** is $9, the entire $1 increase is due to grape cost. This is a 25% increase in grape cost, or viewed from the other side of the coin, this is a 25% increase in the price of grapes.

increase in demand in the market for electronic toys leads to a short-run increase in price charged by the 100 firms and short-run profits, as shown in Figure 14.12.

The short-run profits encourage entry into the market. As entry occurs, overall demand for the electronic components used in this market increases, causing the suppliers to decrease the price charged because these components are produced under a production process exhibiting economies of scale. We can model the decline in cost in a symmetric fashion to the cost-increase model developed earlier. As firms enter the market, electronic component costs decrease, and short-run per-unit cost curves begin to float downward. In a truly competitive market, this would be imperceptible for individual firm entry. To simplify the presentation, however, we assume here that each firm that enters causes MC(0) to decrease by \$0.01, due to decreases in component costs. Since the other parts of the cubic cost function are fixed (i.e., FC, and the coefficients of the quadratic and cubic terms), the quantities where each curve achieves its minimum will not change. In particular, minimum ATC will continue to occur at $x = 10$, but the \$/x value associated with this output level will simply depend on how many firms are in the market.

As firms enter the market, the profit rectangle will begin to shrink. Unlike the decreasing-cost case, the various components that comprise short-run profits do not all move so as to decrease profits. Recall that the profit rectangle is $\pi = (P - SATC(x)) \cdot x$. With decreasing cost, entry causes price and SATC(x) to decline. Since both decline, it is not clear without further information whether x increases or decreases in this instance. If price declines at the same rate as SATC, then x will not change, since the firm supplies along $P = SMC(x)$, and the SMC declines at the same rate as SATC (both decline at a rate of \$0.01 per extra firm in the market, according to our previous assumption). But the market clearing price declines more rapidly, according to the demand curve D_1. This can be seen by examining an intermediate short-run equilibrium in this instance. Suppose that 20 firms have entered the market. As a result, the per-unit cost curves have declined by \$0.20 at each output level, according to our initial assumption. As shown in Figure 14.15, the intermediate short-run equilibrium is at **I**. The price in this instance is \$9.83, down \$0.78 from the initial short-run equilibrium **B** depicted in Figure 14.12. Price has declined

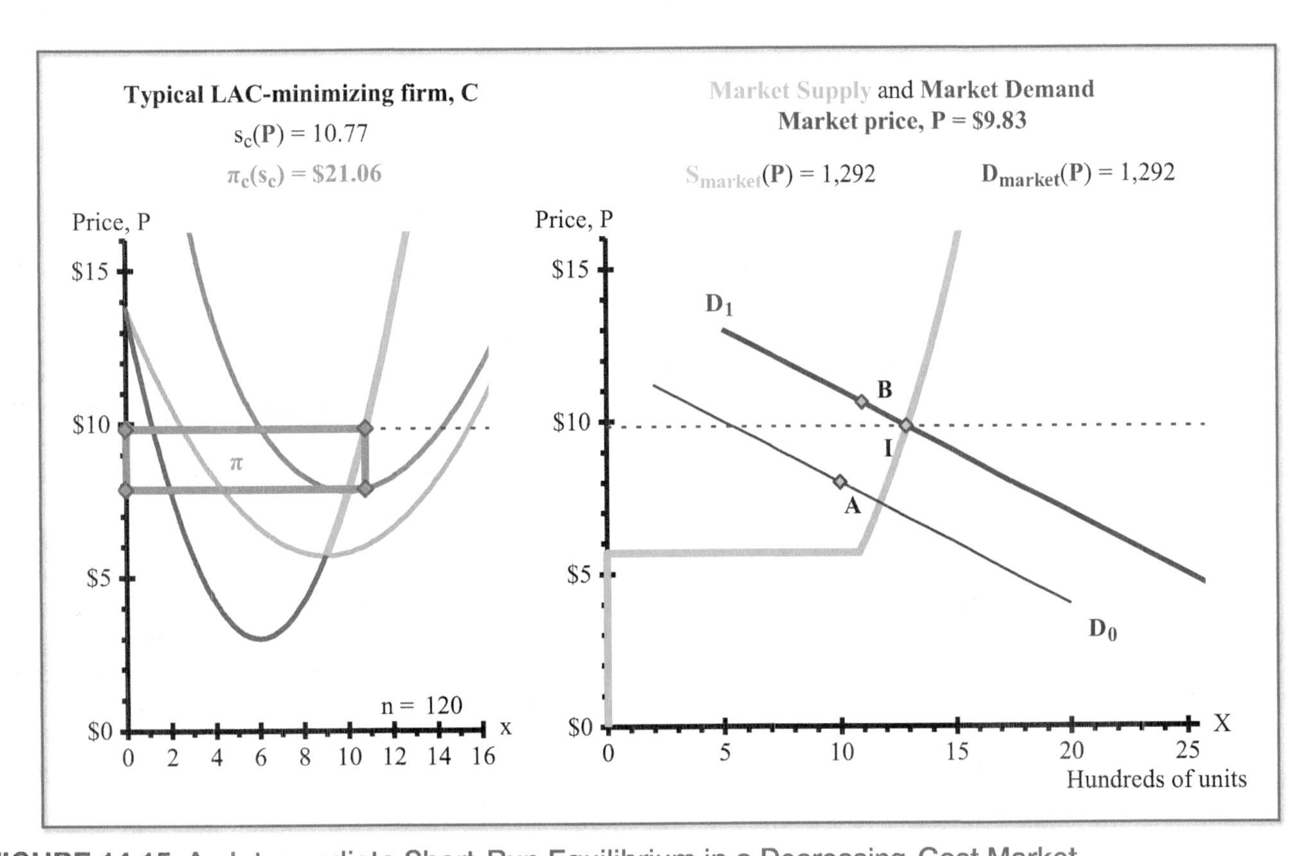

FIGURE 14.15 An Intermediate Short-Run Equilibrium in a Decreasing-Cost Market

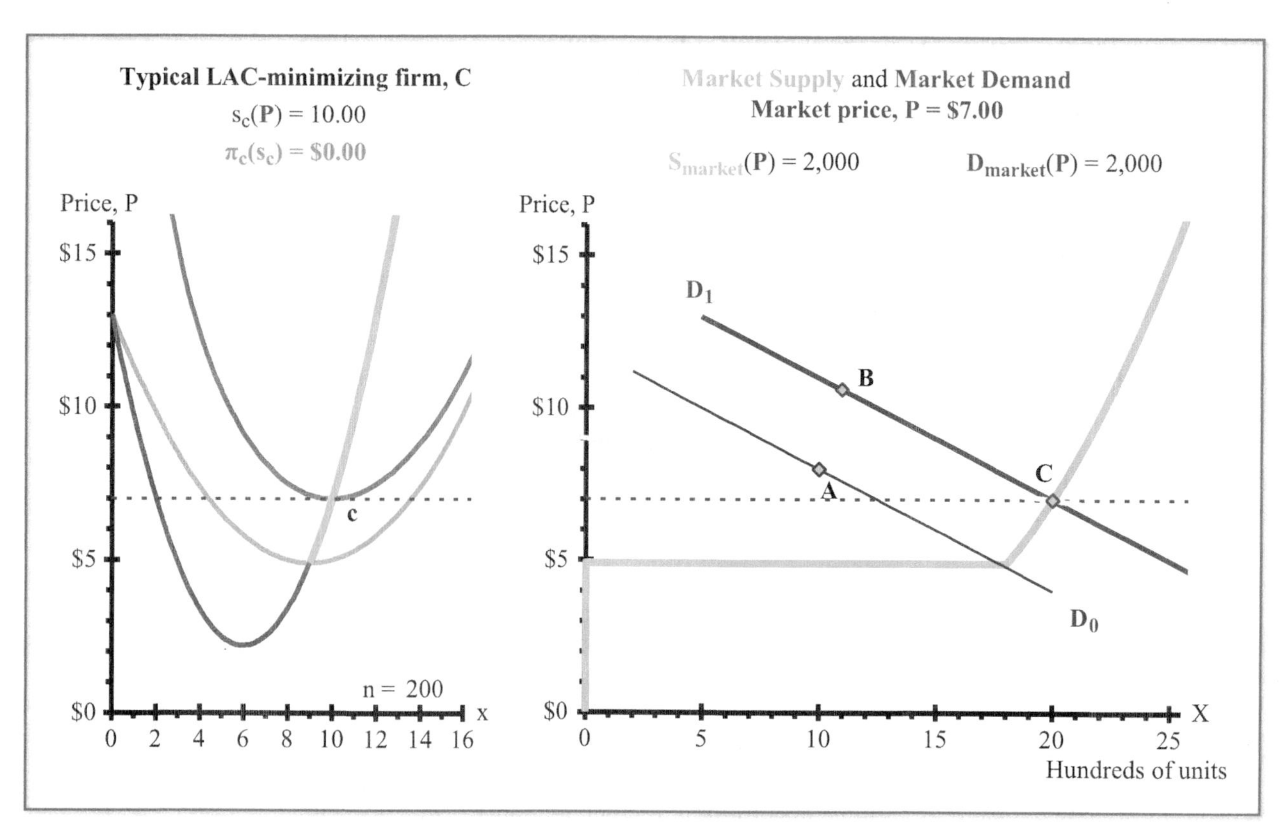

FIGURE 14.16 Long-Run Supply in a Decreasing-Cost Industry

by more than SATC, so quantity declines (from 10.97 to 10.77 units), as do profits (from \$27.43 to \$21.06), as a result of the entry of 20 firms.

The process of entry will continue until a new long-run equilibrium emerges in which profits are once again driven to zero. Given demand curve D_1, this expansion process stops when there are 200 firms in the industry. The additional 100 firms have lowered the minimum average cost of production by \$1 to \$7/unit (when each firm produces 10 units of output). At the price of \$7, market demand is 2,000 units, a number that matches market supply (since $2{,}000 = 200 \cdot 10$). This new long-run equilibrium is shown in Figure 14.16 as point **C** = (2000, \$7) in the right-hand diagram and as point **c** = (10, \$7) in the left-hand diagram. And as earlier, if demand shifted once again, then a new long-run equilibrium could be achieved by adjusting the number of firms in the market. In this instance, the set of long-run equilibria is the yellow downward-sloping LS curve shown.

We have just shown that the long-run supply curve may be upward sloping, flat, or downward sloping. Each of these possible outcomes depends on how the prices of factors used in the production process respond to changes in demand for those factors of production. With constant costs, we have a flat long-run supply curve; with increasing costs, the long-run supply curve is upward sloping; and with decreasing costs, the long-run supply curve is downward sloping.

The numbers used to create the increasing-cost, decreasing-cost, and constant-cost scenarios are not unique or special. They were chosen to highlight the qualitative relation involved in each scenario by creating an outcome that is as simple as possible, using round number solutions. The increasing-costs case involved an increase in the long-run equilibrium price of \$1 by the addition of 50 firms. The constant-cost case involved no change in the long-run equilibrium price by the addition of 75 firms. The decreasing-cost case involved a decrease in the long-run equilibrium price of \$1 by the addition of 100 firms. These solutions occur because D_1 was chosen to "hit" these outcomes and because cost changes were chosen to "hit" these outcomes as well.[8]

Had factor cost increases been more moderate, the long-run supply curve would have increased at a slower rate (in Figure 14.14). Price would increase by less than a dollar by having more than 50 firms enter the market to achieve a new long-run equilibrium along D_1. Had factor cost decreases been more moderate, the long-run supply curve would have decreased at a slower rate (in Figure 14.16). Price would decrease by less than a dollar by having fewer than 100 firms enter the market to achieve a new long-run equilibrium along D_1. Both of these outcomes are explored in Workbook problems using the Excel file for the long-run supply Figures 14.11 to 14.16.

The analysis in Section 14.4 is based on an increase in demand. The same conclusions, however, could have been just as readily derived based on a decrease in demand going from D_0 to D_1. In this event, Figure 14.12 would show short-run losses. These losses would lead to exit by some firms. Exit would reduce cost curves in an increasing-costs industry, increase cost curves in a decreasing-costs industry, and have no effect on cost curves in a constant-costs industry.

A Caution about CRTS versus Constant Costs

Because of the similarity of the words used to describe the various cost situations, students often confuse constant returns to scale and constant costs. Both use the word *constant*, and both concepts lead to flat-line outcomes, but the outcomes are conceptually quite different. *Constant returns to scale* describes the properties of the technology of production and, hence, the shape of LAC and LMC for an individual firm. As shown in Chapter 11, these individual firm LAC and LMC curves are equal and are flat lines, given CRTS. By contrast, *constant cost* refers not to the returns to scale in the production process, but to how factor costs change in response to changes in demand for those factors. When factor costs are constant, then the long-run supply curve is a flat line; this is a market phenomenon, albeit one that is predicated on individual firm behavior. As we stated at the start of this section, all cost curves in this section are based on varying returns to scale that achieve efficient scale of production at a single level of output ($x^* = 10$ throughout Figures 14.11–14.16). Therefore, varying returns in production technology are consistent with constant, increasing, and decreasing factor costs.

Conversely, we equally easily could produce an example of long-run supply being upward or downward sloping, based on CRTS production technologies. All we would need to do is to float the flat LAC = LMC curve up or down, just as the U-shaped long-run cost curves floated up or down based on changes in the cost of factors of production. The two concepts are distinct. Returns to scale describes technological imperatives for individual firms. By contrast, the question of whether costs are increasing, decreasing, or constant describes how factor market prices respond to changes in factor demand.

Summary

In a perfectly competitive market, the long run occurs when the market is in short-run equilibrium. Additionally, all firms are producing at minimum long-run average cost and earning zero economic profit. This situation provides each firm a competitive return on its assets so that no firm wishes to exit the market. It also provides no hint of further profit opportunities, so firms outside the market do not find it profitable to attempt entry. A long-run equilibrium represents a steady-state situation for a competitive market because there is no incentive for the market outcome to change.

The short-run market outcome allows the possibility that some producers will be profitable, while, at the same time, others will not. These differences are possible in the short run due to differences in the capital stock of various firms. The adjustment from the short run to the long run involves exit or capital stock adjustment by firms that are producing at a loss, and outside entry by firms that perceive profit opportunities upon entry. The ultimate result of this adjustment is a final market outcome in which each firm is producing at minimum long-run average cost. This cost must match the price for which market supply and market demand are in equilibrium.

If the production process exhibits varying returns to scale, then there may only be one plant size that produces output at minimum long-run average cost. In that event, all firms producing in the long run are forced to use this efficient plant size to remain in the market. Efficient operation occurs at the output level where production exhibits constant returns to scale. Competition produces an outcome where only those firms that are operating efficiently will survive; all others will not be able to achieve a normal rate of return and will therefore be forced to exit in the long run.

Production might also exhibit constant returns to scale over a range of outputs. In this event, the long-run equilibrium will still occur, with each firm producing at minimum long-run average cost, but firms are not forced to choose among efficient alternatives. Multiple plant sizes may exist in the long run in this instance.

The long-run analysis presented in the first part of the chapter is based on fixed market demand. The equilibrium that is achieved represents a market setting in which no change occurs unless market conditions change. The most obvious way that the market might change is that market demand changes. When this occurs, there will be an initial short-run equilibrium in which firms are no longer earning zero profits. As a result, entry or exit will occur until a new long-run equilibrium is achieved in which all firms once again produce at minimum long-run average cost that matches the market clearing price.

If a competitive market is in long-run equilibrium and demand changes, a new long-run equilibrium will eventually be achieved. This new equilibrium need not occur at the same price as the initial equilibrium. Indeed, it will only occur at the same price if output is also the same, or if changes in demand for factors of production have no effect on the price of those factors of production. When factor costs are constant, cost curves are not affected by entry or exit, and the new equilibrium will occur at the same long-run average cost-minimizing price as prior to the demand change. Otherwise, the new equilibrium will occur at a different price level.

Two possibilities exist when the long-run equilibrium changes in response to factor price changes. The most common alternative is an increase in demand for the product that causes an increase in demand for factors of production. This increase in factor demand bids up the price of factors of production, thereby causing each firm's cost curves to shift upward. The new long-run average cost-minimizing cost level will occur at a higher cost. Therefore, the new long-run equilibrium price must be higher as well (since $P^* = LAC_{minimum}$ at any long-run competitive equilibrium). This is called the increasing-cost case, and it leads to a long-run supply curve that is upward sloping. The reverse situation can also occur if increases in factor demand allow producers in the factor market to achieve efficiencies in production that allow them to reduce price. In this setting, an increase in demand leads to a new long-run equilibrium at a lower price, due to lower factor costs.

Review Questions

Define the following terms:

normal profits	minimum efficient scale (MES)	factor costs are constant
long-run perfectly competitive equilibrium	maximum efficient scale (MaxES)	factor costs are increasing
efficient scale of production	long-run supply curve (LS)	factor costs are decreasing

Match the following statements:

a. Short-run profits signal
b. Short-run losses signal
c. Normal profits signal
d. Increasing-cost case
e. Decreasing-cost case

1. Exit and consequent increase in price
2. Factor prices increase as demand for the factor increases.
3. Entry and consequent decline in price
4. Factor prices increase as demand for the factor decreases.
5. No incentive to change

Provide short answers to the following:

a. Why is the long-run supply curve for a firm the upward-sloping part of the long-run marginal cost curve above minimum long-run average (*total*) cost, while at the same time, the short-run supply curve is the upward-sloping part of the short-run marginal cost curve above minimum average *variable* cost?
b. What are the *three conditions* required for a long-run perfectly competitive equilibrium?
c. If production exhibits constant returns to scale over some range of outputs, is there a unique plant size that minimizes average total cost of production in the long run?
d. Provide examples of decreasing-, constant-, and increasing-cost markets.

Check your answers to the *matching* and *short-answer* exercises in the Answers Appendix at the end of the book.

Notes

1. Recall that the plant sizes are denoted K#, where the number after K denotes the short-run average total cost-minimizing method of producing that level of output.

2. This conclusion holds as long as cost curves do not change with entry and exit. We will discuss this in Section 14.4.

3. Do not get bogged down trying to make sense of the numerical scale on the horizontal axis. Suppose that efficient scale of production is 10,000 cases per month; in this case, simply relabel the horizontal axis in both diagrams. The left-hand diagram will be in thousands of cases per month; the right-hand diagram will be in hundreds of thousands of cases per month.

4. A quick Google search using the key words *yeast* and *beer* produces more information than you can possibly use on this topic. The general type of yeast used in beer production is called "brewer's yeast."

5. You have seen this style of move in cost curve before. Figure 13.9 examined per-unit cost functions in which FC and MC(0) vary. The present analysis holds FC constant and only varies MC(0) to model this situation.

6. Had cost increased due to fixed rather than variable factors of production (for example, due to scarce managerial talent), the change in cost would have been different. AVC and MC would not change, but ATC would increase, as would the minimum ATC output and cost level, due to a fixed cost increase.

7. In "Do Supply Curves Slope Up?" *Quarterly Journal of Economics*, 108(1) February 1993, pp. 1–32, John Shea examined 26 manufacturing industries to determine how common each type of long-run supply curve is. He found that 16 were increasing cost, 7 were constant cost, and 3 were decreasing cost. (The decreasing-cost industries were prepared foods, construction equipment, and aircraft.)

8. In slope-intercept form, market demand D_1 is given by $P = 15 - 0.004 \cdot X$. This includes the points **B** = (1097, $10.61) in Figures 14.12–14.16 and the various new long-run equilibrium points **C** associated with the three-factor cost situations. In Figure 14.13, **C** = (1750, $8); in Figure 14.14, **C** = (1500, $9); and in Figure 14.16, **C** = (2000, $7).

Monopoly and Monopolistic Competition

CHAPTER 15

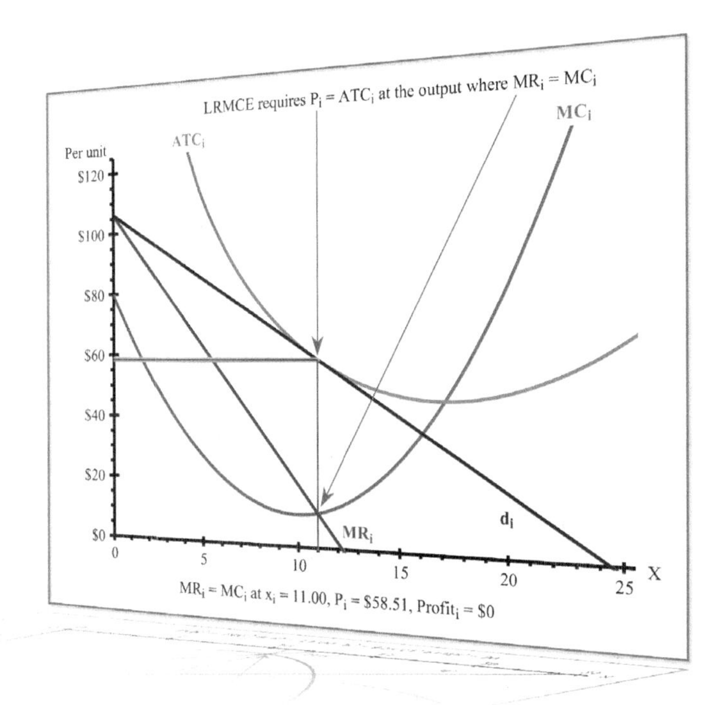

Chapter Outline

The model developed in Chapters 13 and 14 provides one end of the competitive spectrum. At the other end is monopoly, and in between are monopolistic competition and another market structure called oligopoly. This chapter deals with monopoly and monopolistic competition, and Chapter 20 examines oligopolistic markets.

Before examining a specific market structure, we begin the chapter with an acknowledgment that perfect competition leads to a unique outcome: The firm in a perfectly competitive market produces to equate marginal cost with price. In all other market structures, firms price above marginal cost. The rationale for this statement is developed in Section 15.1. Section 15.2 examines monopoly in the short run, and Section 15.3 examines how a monopolist might maintain its monopoly control over the long run. Central to this analysis is the concept of barriers to entry. Section 15.4 examines differentiated product markets. When products are differentiated, firms have some price-making ability, due to the distinctness inherent in each firm's product. Section 15.5 examines monopolistic competition, a market structure in which firms produce differentiated products under conditions of free entry and exit. This market structure has aspects of both monopoly and perfect competition. Monopolistic competition is examined both in the short run and in the long run. Section 15.6 explores how entry affects individual firm demand in differentiated product markets. This leads to a more general view of the long-run monopolistically competitive equilibrium than that posed in Section 15.5.

15.1 All Market Structures Except Perfect Competition Have P > MC

If a market is perfectly competitive, the firm perceives a flat demand at the market clearing price. This conclusion derives from the basic tenets of the competitive model: Firms produce a homogeneous product under conditions of perfect information in a setting where each firm is "small," relative to the size of the market. In this setting, a single price "clears" the market in the sense that market demand equals market supply at that price. At the same time, no firm can sell at higher than that price, and the firm can sell as much as it wishes of the product at that price. As we noted in Chapter 13, economists say that firms in a competitive market are price takers. Firms (and consumers) view price as exogenously given in a competitive market. By contrast, firms in *any* other market setting are price makers in the sense that they do not face a flat demand at a given price. A firm is a **price maker** if it has some price-setting ability for the product it produces.

price maker: A firm is a price maker if it has some price-setting ability for the product it produces.

If a firm does not face flat demand for its product, then it has *some* choice as to the price it can charge for that product. Economists also describe this situation by saying that price is an endogenous variable in this situation. The elasticity of demand that a firm faces determines how *much* choice the firm has in setting price. The more inelastic its demand, the more price-making power the firm has because there is a smaller loss in demand from an increase in price. Economists often describe all market structures where the firm has some price-making ability as **imperfectly competitive markets**. A market that fails to satisfy the requirements of perfect competition is said to be imperfectly competitive. All markets except perfectly competitive ones are imperfectly competitive. The name is not meant to have pejorative connotations; it simply provides economists with a quick way to describe market structures that are not perfectly competitive.

imperfectly competitive market: A market that fails to satisfy the requirements of perfect competition is said to be imperfectly competitive.

One of the focal points of analysis in Chapter 12 is how marginal revenue relates to demand. In Chapter 13, we argue that perfect competition leads to flat demand for the firm's product. As a result, marginal revenue equals demand, since demand is horizontal at the market clearing price in perfect competition, according to Equation 13.1. The end result is that P = MR in perfect competition. In all other market structures, P > MR, according to the geometric analysis in Section 12.2. That analysis is based on the fact that if demand is downward sloping, additional sales can only be obtained by lowering the price on all units. Selling Δx more units of x produces a change in total revenue of $\Delta TR = P \cdot \Delta x + x \cdot \Delta P$, according to Figures 12.6 and 12.7 for general changes in x, Δx ($P \cdot \Delta x$ is area **C**, and $x \cdot \Delta P$ is area **A** in those figures).[1] Dividing by Δx, we obtain estimated marginal revenue per unit, according to Equation 12.9b:

$$MR = \Delta TR/\Delta x = P + x \cdot (\Delta P/\Delta x). \qquad \textbf{(15.1a)}$$

This is labeled MR, rather than MR_e, because as Δx becomes smaller, estimated marginal revenue turns into its limiting value of marginal revenue (as shown in Equations 12.10 and 12.11). Since demand is downward sloping, $\Delta P/\Delta x < 0$, so:

$$MR = \Delta TR/\Delta x = P + x \cdot (\Delta P/\Delta x) < P. \qquad \textbf{(15.1b)}$$

The equation for marginal revenue can be rewritten in terms of elasticity, using the equation $\varepsilon = (\Delta x/\Delta P) \cdot (P/x)$. By regrouping Equation 15.1a, we obtain:

$$MR = P + P \cdot [(x/P) \cdot (\Delta P/\Delta x)] = P + P/\varepsilon = P \cdot (1 + 1/\varepsilon). \qquad \textbf{(15.1c)}$$

There is one algebraic instance in which $1 + 1/\varepsilon = 1$, and that is when $\varepsilon = -\infty$, the condition required by competitive markets. We therefore see algebraically why P = MR in competitive markets, using Equation 15.1c. Otherwise, $-\infty < \varepsilon < 0$ and $1 + 1/\varepsilon < 1$, so P > MR, as noted in Equation 15.1b.

The profit-maximizing output level is shown in Chapter 12 to occur when MR = MC. Given P = MR in perfect competition, this condition is recast as set output so as to have P = MC to maximize profits. As we saw in Chapter 13, not all output levels where P = MC maximize profits. In a competitive setting, we saw that if P = MC and MC is declining, then profits are minimized, and if $P < AVC_{minimum}$, then it is better to shut down rather than produce in the short run. This leads to the final description of a competitive firm's supply function shown in Figure 13.8 as the positively sloped part of the marginal cost curve above minimum average variable cost. The crispness of this statement turns on the equality between price and marginal revenue in perfect competition. In all other market settings, price is not equal to marginal revenue, and therefore, price will not be equal to marginal cost for a firm in an imperfectly competitive market setting. More specifically, in imperfectly competitive markets, $P > MC$, since $MR = MC$ and $P > MR$.

Inverse Elasticity Pricing Rule

The relation between marginal revenue, elasticity, and price described in Equation 15.1c helps provide us with a more explicit description of how price relates to marginal cost in imperfectly competitive markets. Given Equation 15.1c, $MR = MC$ implies:

$$MC = P \cdot (1 + 1/\varepsilon) = P \cdot (1 - 1/|\varepsilon|). \quad \textbf{(15.2a)}$$

Both versions of this equation are provided because both are commonly seen. The difference is based on whether price elasticity of demand is defined with or without the minus sign stripped from the equation. This equation allows us to confirm an assertion from Chapter 12: A profit-maximizing firm will price in the elastic range of its demand curve, $\varepsilon < -1$; since $MC > 0$ and $P > 0$, Equation 15.2a requires $|\varepsilon| > 1$.

A firm wishing to maximize profits can use Equation 15.2a to help achieve its goal. A firm with price-making ability wants to set price so as to maximize profit. Suppose the firm believes that its marginal cost of production is MC and that the elasticity of demand it faces is ε. In this event, the firm would wish to set price at:

$$P = MC/(1 + 1/\varepsilon) = MC \cdot \varepsilon/(\varepsilon + 1). \quad \textbf{(15.2b)}$$

$$P = MC/(1 - 1/|\varepsilon|) = MC \cdot |\varepsilon|/(|\varepsilon| - 1).$$

(As with Equation 15.2a, elasticity is shown both with and without absolute values, but we focus on the definition utilized in this text, the one without absolute values.) In Equation 15.2b, it is worth noting that, given elastic demand, $\varepsilon < -1$, the fraction $\varepsilon/(\varepsilon + 1) > 0$. (From a purely mathematical point of view, this is the ratio of two negative numbers, and this ratio is larger than one.) This is once again an acknowledgment that $P > MC$. In fact, it is an acknowledgment of how much larger price is than marginal cost. Equation 15.2b can be thought of as providing a rule of thumb for pricing; this equation tells us how much price should be marked up over marginal cost to maximize profits.

The price-cost margin offers a glimpse of how much *pricing power* the firm has in its market. The more pricing power the firm has over its market, the larger is the price-cost margin. Of course, the price-cost margin requires a more explicit explanation of what we mean by cost. If we view cost as marginal cost, then we know that, in the short run, a firm in a competitive market has a zero price-cost margin (since $P = MC$ in competitive markets, according to Chapter 12). If we view cost as average total cost, then we know that, in the long run, a firm in a competitive market also has a zero price-cost margin (since $P = LAC_{minimum}$ in competitive markets in the long run, according to Chapter 13). Therefore, in both of these views, competitive firms have no pricing power.

The price-cost margin can be derived from Equation 15.2a if we view cost as marginal cost. In particular, consider how much price is marked up above marginal cost by a profit-maximizing firm. By rearranging Equation 15.2a, we obtain the *inverse elasticity rule*:

$$-1/\varepsilon = 1/|\varepsilon| = (P - MC)/P. \quad \text{Lerner Index} \quad \textbf{(15.2c)}$$

The right-hand side of this equation is a price-cost margin known as the **Lerner Index** of monopoly power. Equation 15.2c shows that a profit-maximizing firm's price-cost margin is inversely proportional to the elasticity of demand the firm faces. This price-cost margin is also sometimes described as the *markup ratio of price over marginal cost.*[2]

Lerner Index: The Lerner Index is named after Abba Lerner, who first proposed $L = (P - MC)/P$ as a measure of monopoly power in the 1930s.

Claim: *Firms with greater pricing power are able to sustain greater price-cost margins. Pricing power is inversely related to the elasticity of demand the firm faces.*

Each version of Equation 15.2 provides a different glimpse of how firms with market power price to maximize profits. The three views focus on the three pieces of economic data embedded in the equations. Not surprisingly, any two of these pieces of data provide information about the third via these equations. Price is typically observable, while marginal cost and elasticity are not immediately observable. Nonetheless, both are calculable using empirical estimation techniques that are outside the scope of this textbook. These equations can help us examine firms with market power, even if they do not have complete market power—that is, even if they are not monopolists.

15.2 Monopoly Markets in the Short Run

The opposite end of the competitive spectrum from perfect competition is monopoly, the market setting in which a single firm controls the entire market for a product. As with perfect competition, true monopoly occurs in few markets. The analysis of monopoly is worthwhile nonetheless because it provides a deterministic counterpoint to the competitive norm whose short-run behavior is described in Chapter 13 and whose long-run behavior is the focus of Chapter 14. This section examines the short-run behavior of monopolists, and Section 15.3 examines monopoly in the long run.

Profit Maximization in Monopoly Markets

At one level, we have already discussed the monopoly solution, since Chapter 12 examines profit maximization for a firm facing a general downward-sloping demand curve. The MR = MC solution from that chapter applies in this defined market setting; the only change is that the firm's perceived demand (from Chapter 12) is market demand. The analysis of profit maximization as a geometric comparison of total revenue and total cost forms the basis of Section 12.4. Chapters 13 and 14 provide a per-unit interpretation of the total analysis, given a perfectly competitive market structure. We begin by providing a per-unit interpretation of the total analysis for a monopolist. These two per-unit interpretations provide bookends to the analyses of all market structures, since they represent opposite ends of the competitive spectrum.

The distinguishing difference between the competitive geometry and the monopoly geometry is that demand is downward sloping in monopoly markets. (Of course, as we argued in Section 15.1, demand is downward sloping for all imperfectly competitive markets, not just monopoly.) As a result, price and marginal revenue no longer coincide; as argued in Section 15.1, P > MR in this instance. Therefore MR = MC occurs at a different point than P = MC.

The most heuristic way to view the monopolist's decision process is to imagine it first determining quantity, then determining price. Consider the per-unit diagram in Figure 15.1. The profit-maximizing quantity is determined by finding the quantity where MR = MC at point **a** in the per-unit diagram. In this instance, x = 15 is the profit-maximizing quantity. Price is determined by finding the point on the (inverse) demand curve associated with x = 15; P(15) = $62.50 at point **b**. Although choosing points **a** and **b** is described as a sequential process, it is actually a simultaneous process because the first part requires information about demand (to obtain marginal revenue). The profits attained in this situation can be seen both in the upper total diagram and the lower per-unit diagram in Figure 15.1. The monopolist's profit-maximizing profit level is roughly equal to $275, using the profit hill in the upper diagram.

Q1. What are the monopolist's profits at x = 15 to the nearest $0.01? (Put another way, fill in the "Profits" cell in the table associated with Figure 15.1.)*

***Q1 answer:** $\pi(15) = (P - ATC) \cdot x = (\$62.50 - \$45.00) \cdot 15 = \$17.50 \cdot 15 = \$262.50$.

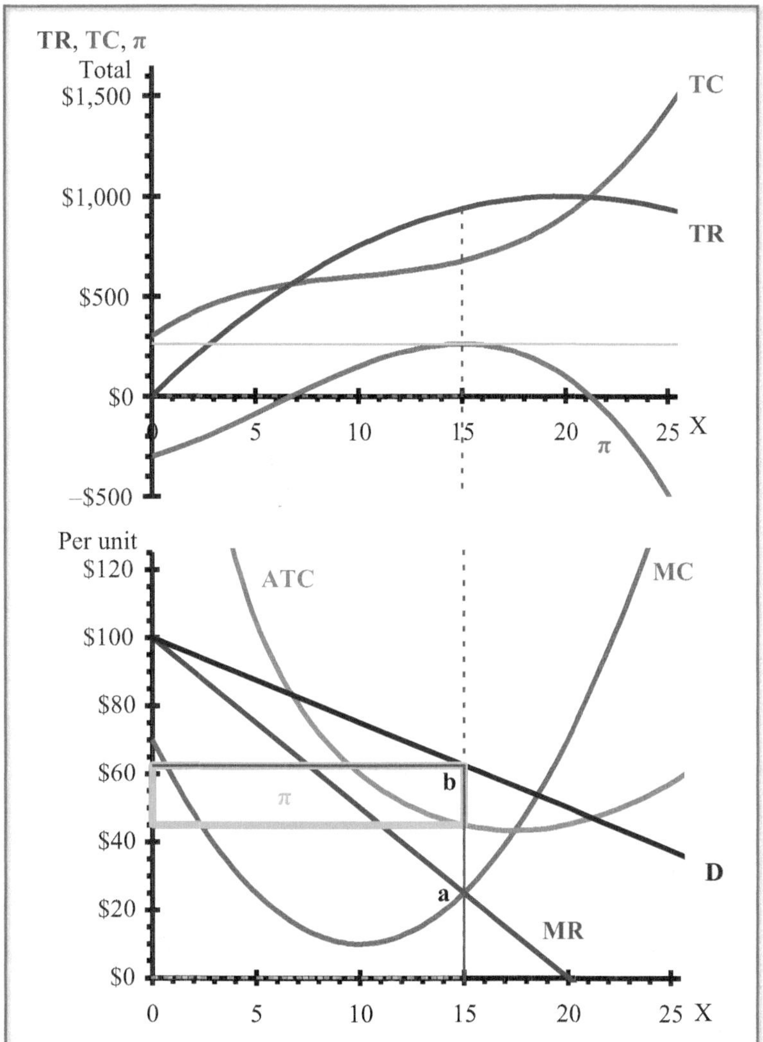

x	MR = MC	ATC	Price	Profits
15.00	$25.00	$45.00	$62.50	

FIGURE 15.1 Profit-Maximizing Output in a Monopoly Market

The green profit rectangle in the per-unit diagram is described by its two sides—quantity and the difference between price and average total cost, $\pi = (P - ATC) \cdot x$. As long as demand intersects ATC, the monopolist will earn positive profits, since demand covers cost in this instance.

Marginal profits are defined as $M\pi(x) = MR(x) - MC(x)$, and profits are maximized when marginal profits are zero. Algebraically, this means that profits are as large as possible when MR = MC. Figure 12.14 provides a total diagram analysis of this point; Figure 15.2 provides the same analysis, using a per-unit diagram. Consider the production and sale from 13 to 15 units in Figure 15.2A. The incremental revenue on these units is represented by the area under the marginal revenue curve on those units, **cade**. Incremental cost on those units is represented by the area under marginal cost on those units, **bade**. The difference is incremental profit on those units, **abc**.

Q2a. Give a dollar estimate of the loss in profit if the monopolist decides to produce 13 units rather than 15 units of output.*

*__Q2a answer:__ The loss in profits is area **abc**. Since marginal cost is a curve, the triangle estimate is not exact, but it is easy to calculate. Area **abc** ≐ 1/2 · base · height = 1/2 · ($35.00 – $15.40) · 2 = $19.60. This is close to the actual loss in profit due to underproduction of $20.40 that can be obtained using the Excel file for Figure 15.2.

FIGURE 15.2 Loss in Profits When MR ≠ MC

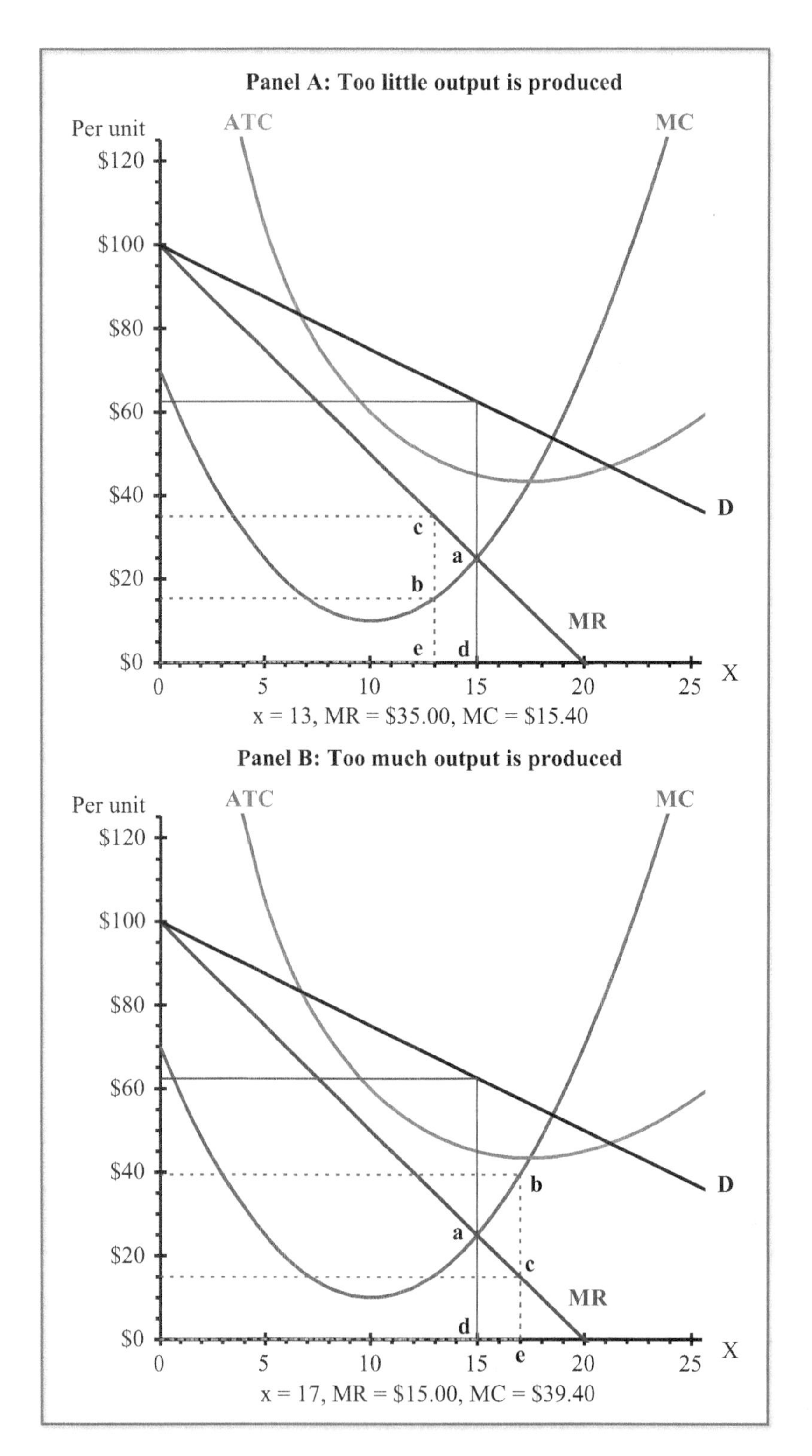

Conversely, if the monopolist produces too much, it will incur incremental costs that exceed incremental revenues, as seen in Figure 15.2B, which examines an increase in production and sale from 15 to 17 units. Incremental revenue is still **cade**, and incremental cost is **bade**. If the monopolist increases output from 15 to 17, incremental cost exceeds incremental revenue by **abc**, an amount that represents the loss in profit due to too much production.

Q2b. Give a dollar estimate of the loss in profit if the monopolist decides to produce 17 units rather than 15 units of output.*

***Q2b answer:** Area **abc** ≐ 1/2 · base · height = 1/2 · ($39.40 – $15.00) · 2 = $24.40, an amount that is close to the actual loss in profit due to underproduction of $23.60.

This diagram is the imperfect competition analog to the diagrammatic analysis for perfect competition provided in Figure 13.6. The difference between the two analyses is that marginal revenue is downward sloping in imperfectly competitive markets and is flat in perfectly competitive markets.

There Is No Supply Curve in Monopoly Markets

A firm's supply curve is a relation that connects the market price to the quantity the firm wishes to supply, given that price. For a firm in a perfectly competitive market, a unique answer is provided for each price level to the question: What is the profit-maximizing output level that the firm wishes to supply in the short run, given that price? The profit-maximizing firm in a competitive market answers that question by supplying along its marginal cost curve. Specifically, we show in Section 13.3 that the firm's supply curve is the positively sloped part of its marginal cost curve above minimum average variable cost. For prices below minimum average variable cost, the firm shuts down and supplies no output in the short run. Similarly, the market supply curve is the horizontal sum of individual firm supply curves.

A similar one-to-one description of (quantity, price) combinations cannot be determined for a monopolist; that is, there is no supply curve in monopoly markets. Of course, this does not mean that the monopolist cannot determine the optimal output level and price level, given market demand and production imperatives. It simply means that we cannot describe that relation using a single curve, as was the case in competitive markets. The reason we cannot do this in monopoly markets is that price and marginal revenue have been decoupled in imperfectly competitive markets, and this leads to a situation where we cannot uniquely describe a price level associated with any given quantity level, or vice versa.

As with competitive markets, marginal cost and marginal revenue are of primary importance in determining the monopolist's profit-maximizing production level. Consider, for instance, the cost and demand conditions shown in Figures 15.1 and 15.2. Given demand and cost conditions, the profit-maximizing monopolist sets $x = 15$ because, at this output level, $MR(x) = MC(x)$. The profit-maximizing monopolist sets price at $P = P(15) = \$62.50$, where $P(x)$ is the inverse market demand curve. The (quantity, price) combination (15, \$62.50) is certainly a point on the monopolist's endogenously determined "supply curve" if the monopolist has a supply curve. But instead, it is more appropriate to simply consider this (quantity, price) combination *a point* of monopolist supply.

If a monopolist had a supply curve, then the set of supply points that are mapped as demand changes should create a one-to-one relation between price and quantity. Figure 15.3 provides two demand changes (relative to Figure 15.1), based on a fixed set of cost curves, to show that a one-to-one relation does not hold. The shift in demand depicted in Figure 15.3A produces another $MR(x) = MC(x)$ solution at $x = 15$, since price and intercept have adjusted so that MR rotates about the point (15, \$25) because $\$25 = MC(15)$. This shows two price levels (\$62.50 and \$55.00) associated with the same profit-maximizing production level, based on a change in demand. Comparing Figure 15.1 and Figure 15.3B, we see the reverse situation. Demand changes so that $MR(x) = MC(x)$ at $x = 12.89$; the quantity the monopolist wishes to supply has changed as a result of the change in demand (from 15 to 12.89), but price remains fixed at \$62.50. We therefore see that a one-to-one relation does not necessarily hold for the profit-maximizing monopolist. We can see both multiple quantities for the same price and multiple prices for the same quantity. Put another way, *the monopolist does not have a supply curve.*

Caveats to MR = MC in Monopoly Markets

In Section 13.3, there are two caveats to supplying along the marginal cost curve in competitive markets. One caveat requires that production be along the positively sloped part of the marginal cost curve. The other caveat requires that production only occur at points where $MC(x) \geq AVC_{minimum}$. We now turn to whether each caveat applies in imperfect competition.

FIGURE 15.3 The Monopolist Has No Supply Curve

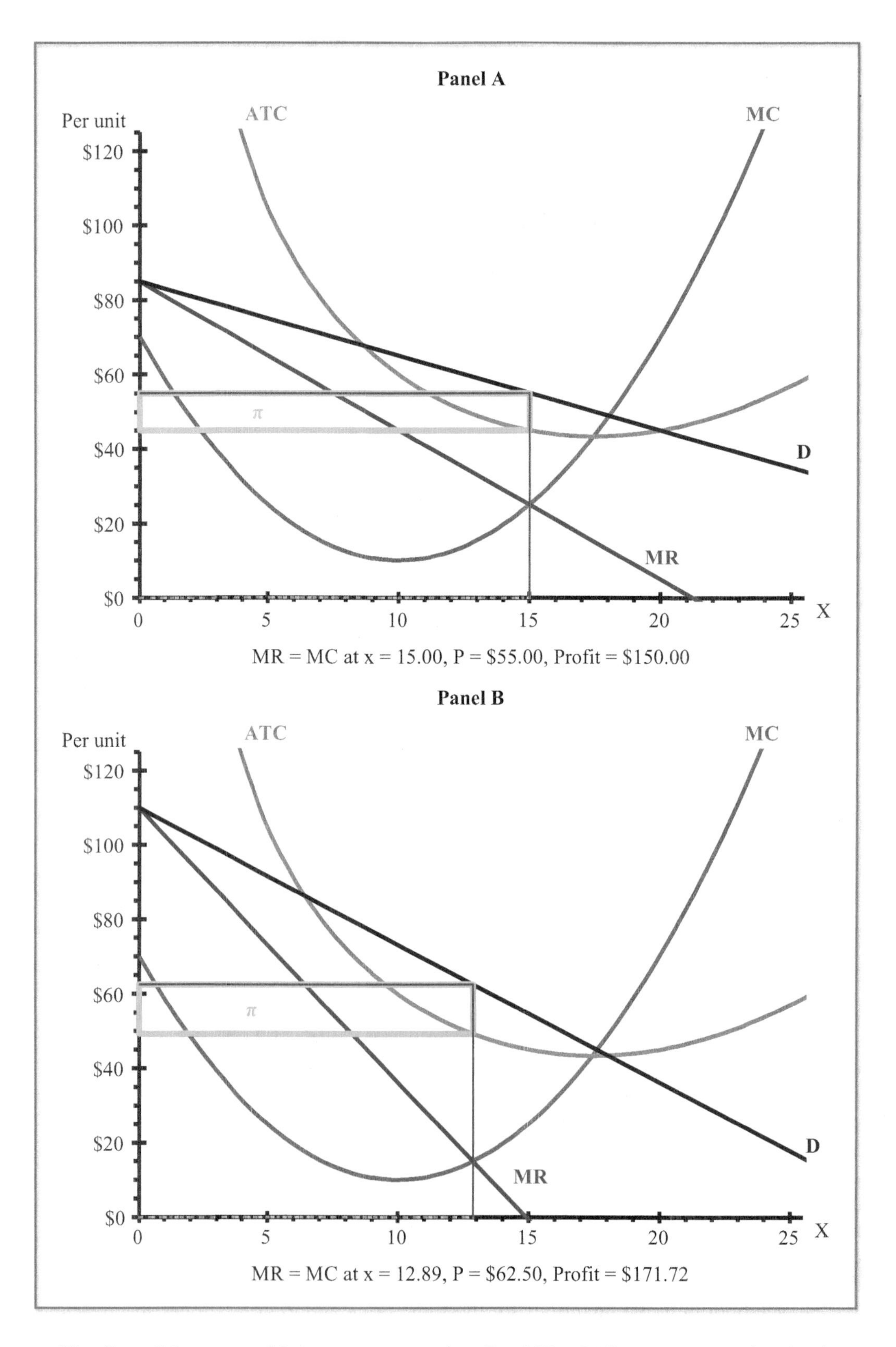

The first of the competitive caveats was when P = MR = MC at two output levels; then the output where MC was positively sloped produced the profit maximum, while the output where MC was negatively sloped produced a profit minimum. Figure 15.4 proves that the same cannot be said in imperfectly competitive markets.

Figure 15.4 shows two output levels where MR = MC; x = 1 and x = 9 are both on the downward-sloping part of the marginal cost curve. These are points **A** and **B** in the lower diagram. The smaller output level produces a profit minimum, $\pi(1) = -\$54.98$, and the

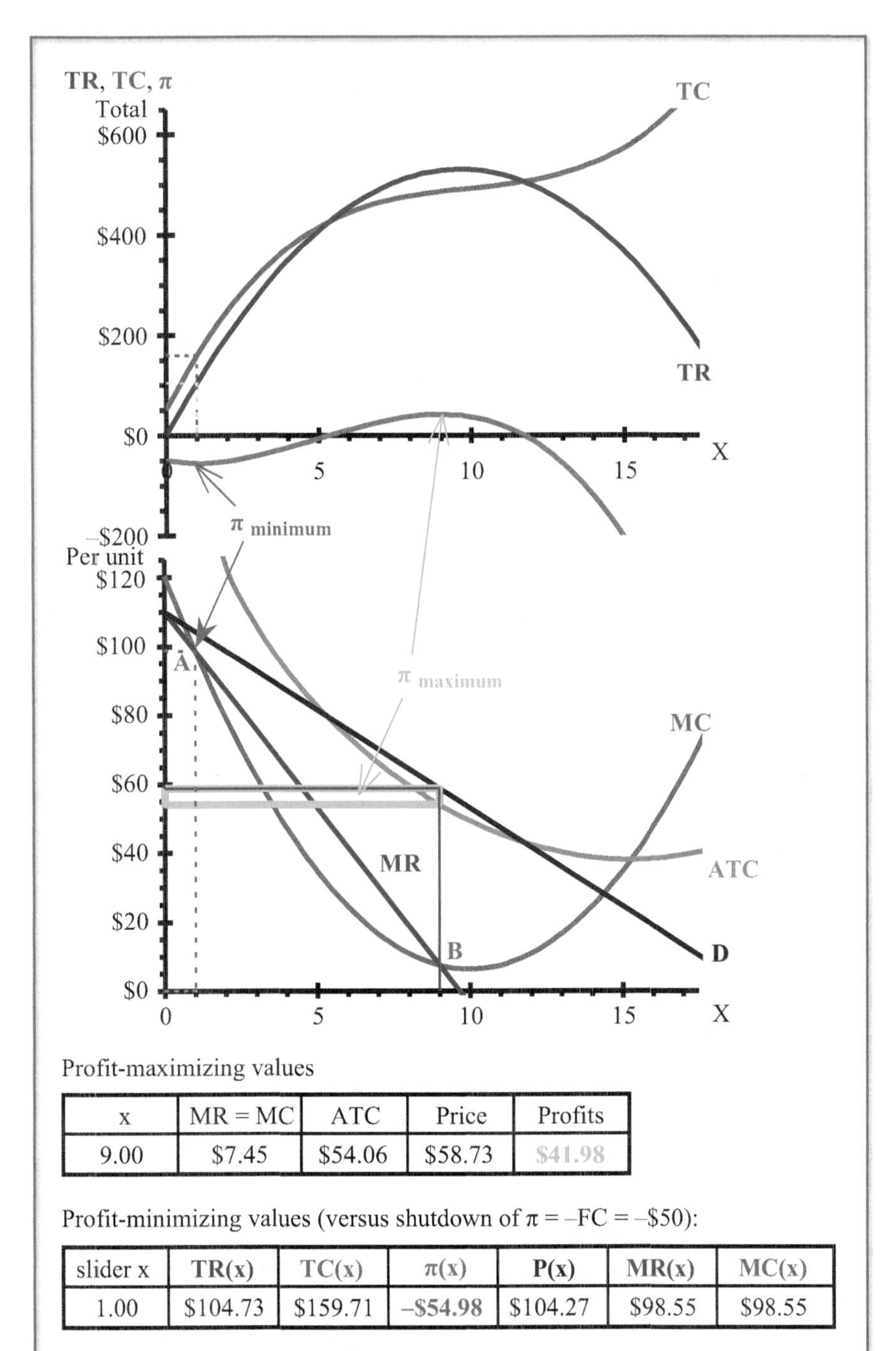

Profit-maximizing values

x	MR = MC	ATC	Price	Profits
9.00	$7.45	$54.06	$58.73	$41.98

Profit-minimizing values (versus shutdown of $\pi = -FC = -\$50$):

slider x	TR(x)	TC(x)	π(x)	P(x)	MR(x)	MC(x)
1.00	$104.73	$159.71	–$54.98	$104.27	$98.55	$98.55

FIGURE 15.4 Maximizing versus Minimizing Profits by Setting MR = MC

larger output level produces the profit maximum, $\pi(9) = \$41.98$, according to the tabular information provided with the figure. Visually, we can see that $x = 1$ is the trough of the $\pi(x)$ function, but this fact is confirmed by noting that the firm would do better in this instance by shutting down and incurring a loss in profit of $\pi(0) = -FC = -\$50$.

The qualitative relation that exists between MR and MC is the same as shown in Figure 13.5 in the competitive case. Both per-unit figures have **A** as the minimum and **B** as the maximum, and both are based on the same orientation of MR versus MC in moving through points **A** and **B**. The easiest way to understand this relation is to consider walking down the marginal cost curve from $x = 0$. For $x < 1$, $MR(x) < MC(x)$, according to the per-unit diagram; then MR = MC at point **A** in Figure 15.4. (In Figure 13.5, this occurs at $x = 3$.) In both figures, MC approaches MR from above at **A**. In both figures, MC approaches MR from below for point **B**. When marginal cost exceeds marginal revenue, an increase in output decreases profits (approaching **A** from smaller output levels).

FIGURE 15.5 When Will a Monopolist Shut Down?

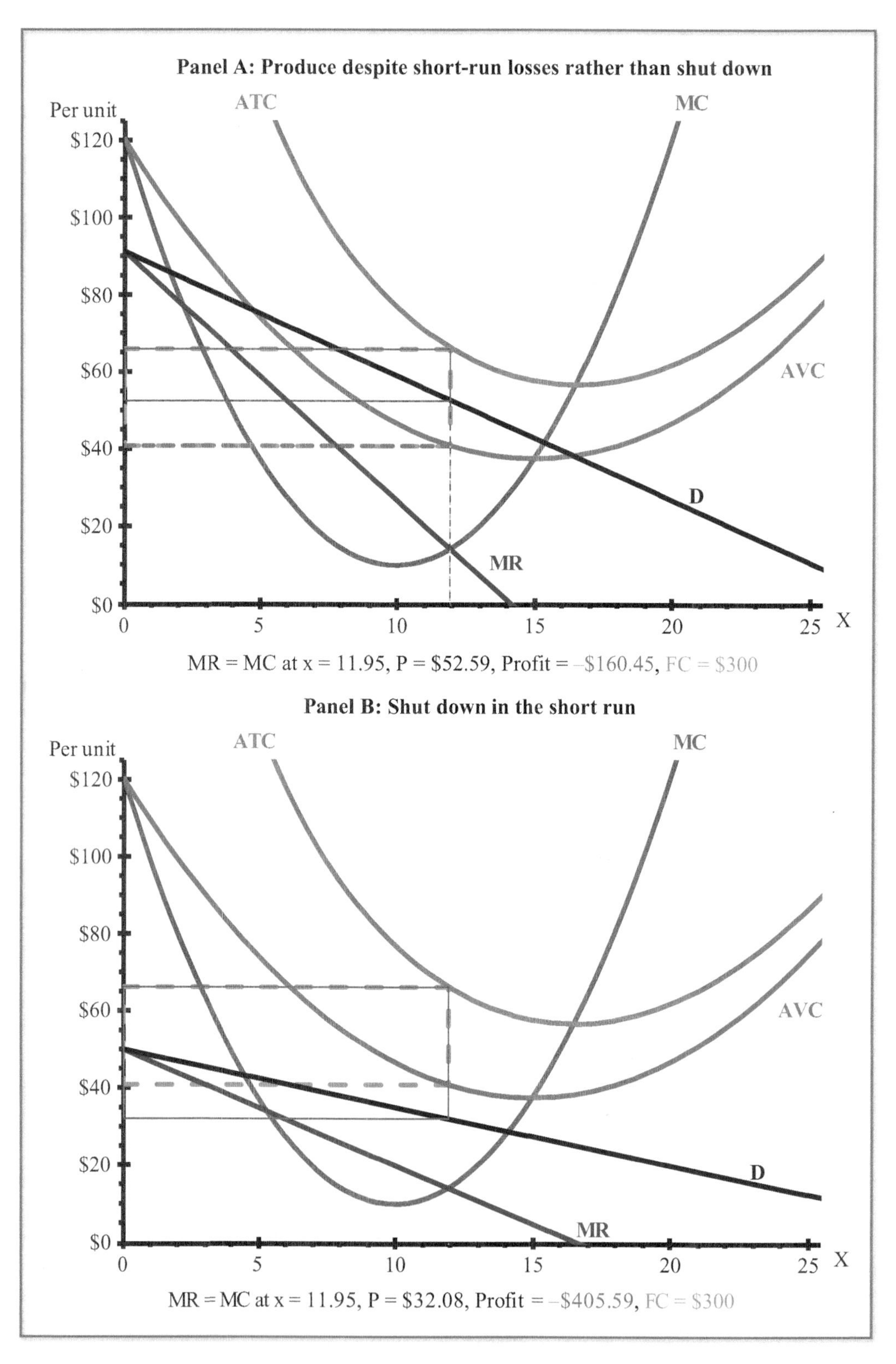

When marginal cost is smaller than marginal revenue, an increase in output increases profits (approaching **B** from smaller output levels). The relative orientation, rather than the absolute slope of MR and MC, determines whether an MR = MC intersection is a local maximum or a local minimum. The distinguishing characteristic that separates local minimums from local maximums is not whether MC is upward or downward sloping. It is, instead, that as x increases, MC(x) approaches MR(x) from below at a maximum. This is point **B** in Figure 13.5 *and* Figure 15.4. MC being positively sloped means that MC must approach a horizontal MR line from below if the MR = MC point is a maximum (i.e., MC is upward sloping at a maximum in the competitive case). This also describes, however, any situation in which MC is simply below MR as it approaches the MR = MC output level. Point **B** in Figure 15.4 is the most radical version of this maximum; both MR and MC are downward sloping, but MR is steeper than MC. MC approaches MR from below; therefore, point **B** is a maximum. The reverse holds true at **A** in Figures 13.5 and 15.4; point **A** represents a minimum because MC approaches MR from above in both instances.

Each of the figures thus far in the chapter has depicted the monopolist as earning positive profits in the short run. Certainly, the layperson's view of monopoly is that the monopolist will use its monopoly power to be profitable; the noneconomist expects a monopolist to gouge its customers and generate profits by charging high prices. From a geometric point of view, positive profits will occur as long as the demand curve intersects the average total cost curve (since this implies that there are output levels for which $P(x) > ATC(x)$, as required to have a positive profit rectangle). This need not occur. For example, the product might be perishable, and demand might exhibit seasonal differences. Demand may not cover cost in the short run. When demand does not cover cost, the firm will continue to produce in the short run as long as variable costs are covered. If variable costs are not covered, then the firm will do better to shut down in the short run.

The shutdown condition gives rise to the second caveat to the perfectly competitive firm's supply curve as its marginal cost curve—that a profit-maximizing competitive firm will supply output along its marginal cost curve only when output is at or above the minimum AVC output level. Given the discussion of Figure 15.4, it is clear that the second caveat no longer holds, at least not in its same form. Given cubic short-run cost functions, if marginal cost is minimized at $x = 10$, then average variable cost is minimized at $x = 15$ (according to Equations 11.7a and 11.7b). But $x = 9$ is a profit maximum in Figure 15.4, an outcome that would never occur had the market been competitive (because it violates both competitive caveats). The problem once again is that imperfect competition implies that P and MR are decoupled; therefore, $MR(x') = MC(x')$ at an output level, $x' < x_{minAVC}$, and yet at the same time, $P(x') > AVC(x')$ so that the firm's short-run variable costs are covered. Only if $P(x') < AVC(x')$ would the firm wish to shut down in the short run.

Figure 15.5 depicts two demand scenarios in which the monopolist cannot cover costs and, hence, operates at a loss in the short run. A monopolist, like a firm in a competitive market, will continue to produce in the short run as long as variable costs are covered. In a competitive market, this is seen by having $P \geq AVC_{minimum}$, but in an imperfectly competitive context, this occurs as long as the demand curve intersects the average variable cost curve. Both Figures 15.5a and 15.5b have $MR = MC$ at $x = 11.95 < 15 = x_{AVCminimum}$. Losses involved in producing at $x = 11.95$ are shown as the red (P – ATC) high by x wide rectangle in both panels: $\pi(11.95) = 11.95 \cdot (P(11.95) - ATC(11.95))$. This loss must be compared with the loss incurred if the firm shuts down. If the firm shuts down, it must still pay its fixed cost; geometrically, this is the (dashed pink) rectangle that is x wide by $(ATC(x) - AVC(x))$ high. In Figure 15.5A, *demand intersects AVC*, and as a result, producing at MR = MC maximizes profits by minimizing short-run losses. This is seen geometrically by having the dashed AVC(11.95) line segment that forms the bottom of the fixed cost rectangle below the bottom of the red loss if production occurs rectangle at $x = 11.95$ (whose bottom is the P(11.95) line segment). Numerically, in Figure 15.5A, $\pi_{produce} = -\$160.45 > \pi_{shut\ down} = -\$300$. By contrast, in Figure 15.5B, *demand does not intersect AVC*, and as a result, shutting down minimizes short-run losses. This is seen geometrically by having the dashed AVC(11.95) line segment that forms the bottom of the fixed cost rectangle inside the loss if production at $x = 11.95$ occurs rectangle. Numerically, $\pi_{produce} = -\$405.59 < \pi_{shut\ down} = -\$300$ in Figure 15.5B.

The distinguishing difference between Figures 15.5A and 15.5B is that in Figure 15.5A, demand intersects AVC for some levels of output so that $P(x) > AVC(x)$; the firm covers all of its variable cost and part of its fixed cost by producing at a loss in the short run. In Figure 15.5B, demand lies below AVC for all output levels; the firm is not able to cover its variable cost, regardless of production level; therefore, the firm minimizes losses by shutting down in the short run.

15.3 Monopoly Markets in the Long Run

Monopoly is simply a description of a market structure in which a single firm controls the entire market. That description does not explain why this market structure exists and whether it is likely to change in response to short-run profit or loss signals by the monopolist. All firms would like to have price-making ability, and all firms would, of course, be interested in maintaining that price-making ability over the long run. All firms would also like to maintain positive profits in the long run. To maintain profits in the long run, a monopolist must face (or create) a situation in which entry of new firms does not occur, despite positive short-run profits.

Why Won't Entry Occur?

barrier to entry (BTE): If a going firm in a market has an economic advantage over a potential entrant to that market, then the market is subject to barriers to entry.

monopoly rent: Monopoly rent is the profit that accrues due to the monopolist's sheltered market position.

Any reason that places an established (going) firm at an economic advantage, relative to a potential entrant, is called a **barrier to entry (BTE)**. It is useful to think of BTEs much like a fence. Some barriers are very high, and others are more moderate. For simplicity, the height of the BTE can be thought of as the cost disadvantage faced by the entering firm. Some of the reasons why entry is precluded apply to markets that are not strict monopolies as well; that is, they often apply to oligopoly markets, but we discuss them here in the context of monopoly. Cumulatively, BTEs emanate from three sources: *structural*, *legal*, and *strategic*.[3] These barriers create a situation where the monopolist is able to maintain profits without incurring entry. The monopoly profit that results from this sheltered market position is sometimes called **monopoly rent**.

Structural barriers exist when the technology of production places potential entrants at an economic disadvantage, relative to going firms. For example, if economies of scale in the production process are such that minimum efficient scale is large, relative to the size of the market, then entry may be precluded. Each of the per-unit cost curves in Figures 15.1–15.4 supports one rather than two firms in the market, based on demand as shown. The easiest way to see this is to note that if two firms split this market equally, then each faces a demand curve that is half the size of market demand at any price. (Attaining half the market certainly would be a reasonable upper bound on what we might expect an entrant to attain.) If we call this curve d_{50} (meaning 50% to each firm), then d_{50} is exactly the same geometric set of points as the marginal revenue curve in each of these diagrams, but the meanings of the two curves are entirely different. MR is marginal revenue relative to market demand D, and d_{50} is demand faced by two equally sized firms in a duopoly (two-firm) market. These figures are not reproduced here, since only one curve must be relabeled (as d_{50}) to make the current point. The d_{50} curve is not profitable, since it does not intersect ATC; if each firm had 50% of this market, then neither would be profitable. Each of the markets depicted in Figures 15.1–15.4 supports one profitable firm, but not two. Of course, were market demand larger, then the same analysis might lead to the conclusion that the market would support two profitable firms, but not three, and so on.

Legal barriers to entry exist for a variety of reasons. The government might impose an outright ban on entry. For example, the monopolist might have monopoly control over the market due to a patent or copyright. Patents spur innovation by giving patent holders control over what they have discovered. Patents allow patent holders to maintain a monopoly hold on their technology for a specified period of time. In the United States, patents provide this benefit for 17 years. Such monopoly control can be very valuable, as Pfizer, the owner of the patent on Viagra, can attest. Copyrights work in a similar fashion to help spur creative activity.

natural monopoly: A market is a natural monopoly if average cost of production is declining at the point where demand and average cost intersect.

Sometimes, legal barriers are imposed on markets due to the structural attributes of that market. Cost conditions within a market may suggest that a single firm will produce output more efficiently than more than one firm. Such a market is called a natural monopoly. A market is a **natural monopoly** if average cost of production is declining at the point where demand and average cost intersect. Natural monopoly has to do with cost structures, not with price structures. That is, natural monopoly is concerned with producing

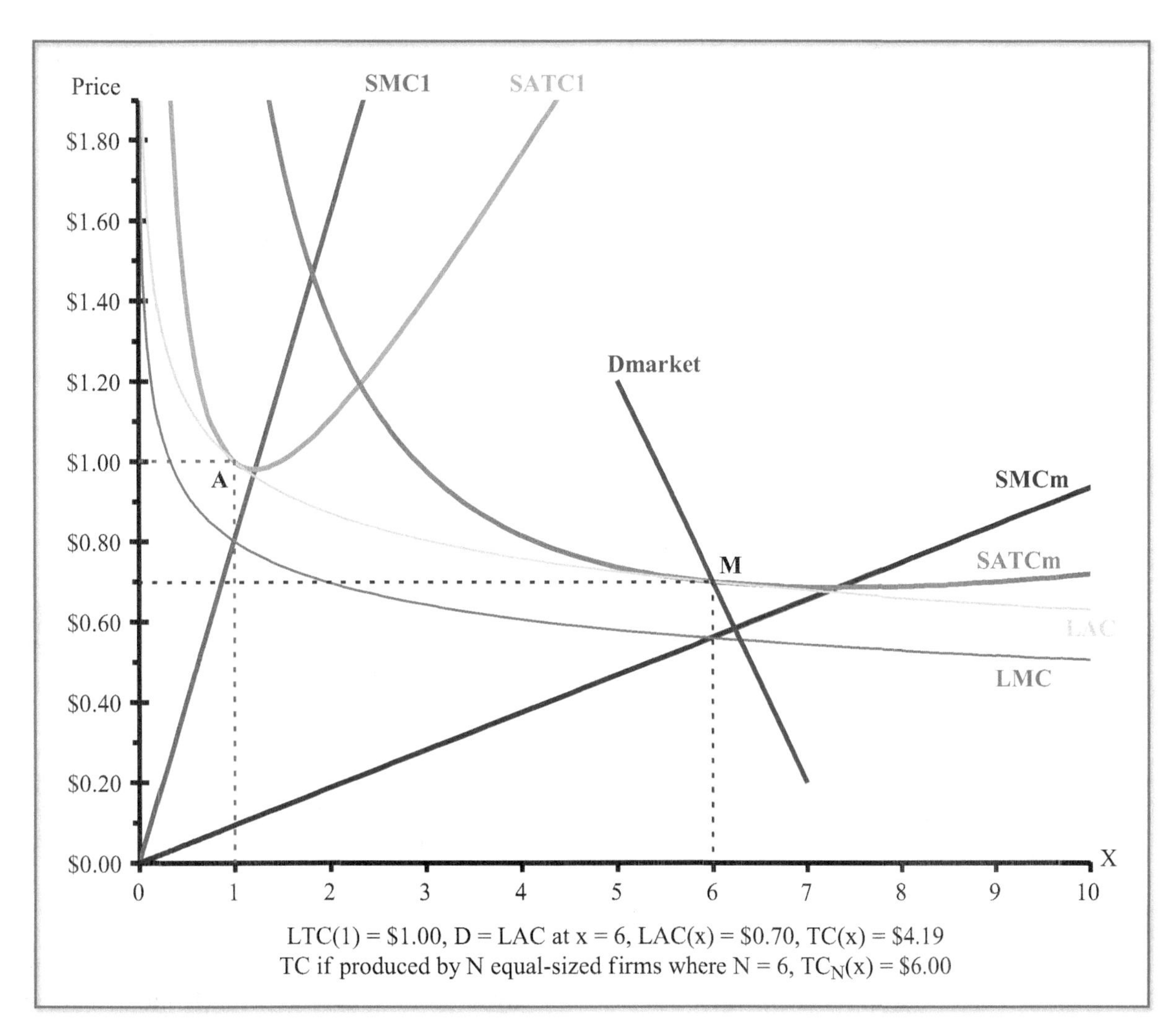

FIGURE 15.6 Natural Monopoly

output at the lowest cost; if average cost is declining, then one firm will be more efficient at producing output than more than one firm.

The Cobb-Douglas cost function associated with an increasing returns to scale production technology shown in Figure 11.19 provides an example of a natural monopoly market. Factor costs have been adjusted so that LAC(1) = $1.00 in Figure 15.6 (this makes it easy to compare a "unitary" plant size with larger plants). Market demand intersects on the downward-sloping part of the LAC, since the entire LAC is downward sloping in this instance. An example is given in Figure 15.6 where x* = 6 at point **M**. This output will optimally be served by a single plant sized k* (where k* satisfies Equation 11.4a, LAC(x*) = SATC(x*; k*)), rather than more than one plant. Since LAC is downward sloping and SATC is tangent to LAC at output level x*, average total cost is declining at this output level; therefore, this would be a natural monopoly market. It is more cost effective to produce with one plant than with more than one in this instance. For example, producing x* = 6 at LAC(6) = $0.70 represents a 30% cost savings, relative to having six unitary plants at **A** produce the same output at a cost of $6.00.

Although it was not used to introduce the notion of natural monopoly, Figure 15.4 also depicts a natural monopoly market because market demand intersects ATC on the downward-sloping part of the ATC curve. In this setting, producing the same amount of output by two firms would cost both firms more.[4]

Many local utilities are natural monopoly markets. It does not make economic sense, for example, to have two sets of electric power lines or natural gas lines in a given community because this duplication of capital is costly and wasteful. In such markets, it makes economic sense to have only one set of lines in a given community. Exclusive monopoly rights to provide service to a community are often bestowed on a firm by the local governmental authority. Of course, government-sanctioned monopoly control has its own inherent problems, the most obvious of which is that the monopolist can restrict output and increase price to take advantage of its monopoly position.[5] As a result, such monopolies are often regulated (by public utility commissions).

Finally, there are strategic barriers to entry. Firms may undertake strategic actions that will create or heighten barriers to entry. Economists describe this in two ways: One is to say that firms are *investing in rent-seeking activities*. The other is to say that firms are *investing in barriers to entry*. For example, a monopolist might seek to control access to critical raw materials used in the production process. Another common strategy is to add capacity well in advance of demand increases. This excess capacity can be used if entry occurs and provides a credible threat to those considering entry into the industry, thereby acting to heighten barriers to entry.

When Will Exit Occur?

Just because a product *can* be produced does not mean that it *should* be produced. Simply having a monopoly position in a market is not enough; sufficient demand is required to have production make economic sense, even for a monopolist. If demand cannot cover all costs of production, including opportunity costs, then exit will occur in the long run, and the market will no longer exist.

The easiest way to see this is to consider products that have fallen out of widespread usage. This often occurs due to technological change overtaking a market. For example, go to an office supply store and try to find a portable typewriter or a box of carbon paper; the personal computer and copying machine have largely supplanted these markets. As a product falls out of favor and demand declines, profits decline. As profits turn into losses, there is exit from the market in the long run. Eventually, the market may be so thin that there is only one surviving firm; the surviving firm is now a monopolist. The monopolist faces the question of whether it should it stay in business or whether it should exit the market.

In Section 15.2, we examined the short-run question of when a firm should shut down. The answer derived there is that the firm should continue producing in the short run as long as variable costs of production are being covered. As noted in Section 14.1, long-run analysis requires that firms cover average cost to remain in the market. In the present context, this simply means that demand intersects the monopolist's long-run average cost curve. If this occurs, the firm will be able to cover its cost by appropriate choice of its plant size and output level. Such a situation is depicted in Figure 15.7A. Profit-maximizing output is $x^* = 8.99$ units at the point where $MR = LMC = SMC(x^*; k^*)$.[6] Capital stock k^* is that amount of capital that produces this output level at minimum average total cost. Since the market clearing price $P(x^*)$ is greater than $LAC(x^*) = SATC(x^*; k^*)$, the firm operates at a short-run profit (in Figure 15.7A, $P(x^*) = \$60.56$, $LAC(x^*) = SATC(x^*; k^*) = \$50.75$, so $\pi = \$88.20$).

When demand does not intersect the long-run average cost curve, there is no output level for which costs of production are covered. In this instance, it makes sense for the firm to exit the market. This is the situation described in Figure 15.7B. The short-run cost curves leading to the exit decision may suggest that the firm produce at a loss in the short run (as was the case in Figure 15.5A) or shut down in the short run (as was the case in Figure 15.5B). Both short-run possibilities are consistent with the long-run outcome shown in Figure 15.7B (and the short-run curves are not shown in Figure 15.7). Producing at a short-run loss would be profit maximizing in the short run if $SAVC(x^*; k^*) \le P(x^*) = \$35.30$, and shutting down prior to exit would occur if $SAVC(x^*; k^*) > P(x^*) = \$35.30$. The short-run decision could also be described in terms of the size of fixed cost, $FC = r \cdot k^*$, inherent in this short-run production process. If $FC > \$95.11$, then the firm should produce in the short run but shut down if $FC < \$95.11$ (since $\pi(x^*) = -95.11$ in Figure 15.7B and $\pi_{\text{shut down}} = -FC$).

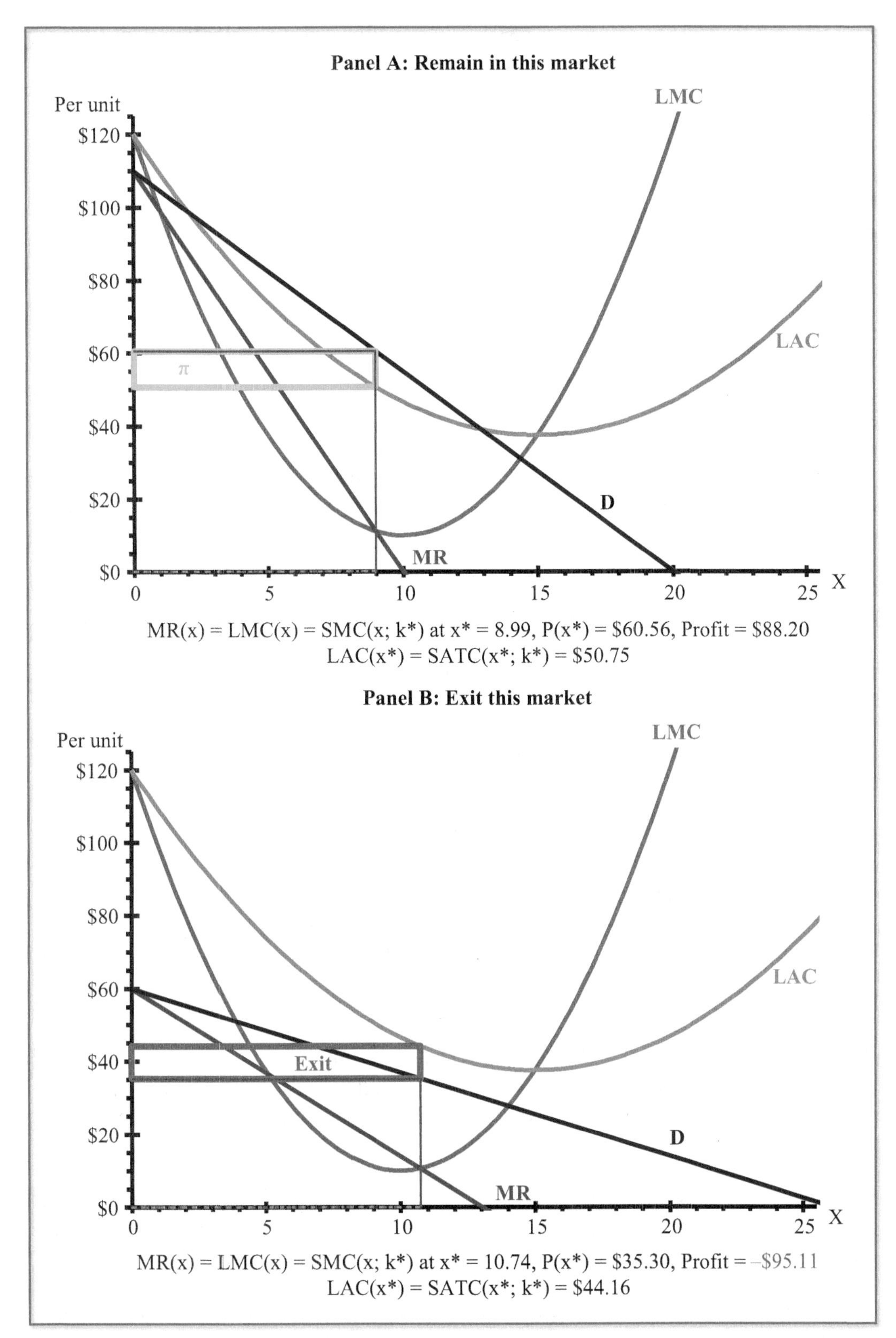

FIGURE 15.7 When Will a Monopolist Exit?

Before leaving our discussion of monopoly, it is worth noting the distinction between pricing power and the ability to generate profits. Simply having a monopoly position in a market does not guarantee monopoly rent (positive profit due to a sheltered market position). The inverse elasticity pricing rule detailed in Equation 15.2c, $-1/\varepsilon = 1/|\varepsilon| = (P - MC)/P$, provides a measure of monopoly power. Each of the markets depicted in Figures 15.1–15.7 exhibits market power, since, as noted in Section 15.1, when demand is downward sloping,

$P > MC$. The elasticities of demand at each of the profit-maximizing (x, P) points depicted in these figures range from $-1.83 \leq \varepsilon \leq -1.15$, but there is no necessary relation between more inelastic demand and more profitability, despite more inelastic demand implying a higher Lerner Index of monopoly power. The short-run loss situation depicted by Figure 15.5A has a higher Lerner Index of monopoly power than that depicted by Figure 15.3A, despite positive profits in that figure. Profitability requires price above average total cost, but monopoly pricing power depends instead on price and marginal cost. In short, *profitability relates price to average cost; power relates price to marginal cost.*

15.4 Differentiated Product Markets

Perfect competition and monopoly are the two bookends of the competitive spectrum. We noted in our discussion of perfect competition and monopoly that "pure" examples of each of these market structures are rare. Markets that are close to these competitive extremes behave like the extremes, and both of these competitive bookends have deterministic outcomes. The final market structure we examine in Part 4 is monopolistic competition, a structure that, as the name suggests, has aspects of both monopoly and perfect competition. Unlike pure monopoly and perfect competition, monopolistic competition is a very common market structure. Before we examine this market structure in detail, we must examine one of monopolistic competition's main attributes. Products are differentiated in monopolistically competitive markets. A product is **differentiated** if there are perceived differences among various firms' offerings. Differentiated products are also often described as *heterogeneous* products.

differentiated product: A product is differentiated if there are perceived differences among various firms' offerings.

An individual firm can also produce more than one differentiated product, but it is convenient to simply imagine that each firm produces a single variety. This allows us to talk about brands, varieties, and firms interchangeably. Notice that perceptual differences are sufficient to create product differentiation; actual physical differences are not required. Generic aspirin and Bayer aspirin are both based on the same chemical compound ($C_9H_8O_4$, according to the dictionary), but perceptual differences have helped Bayer maintain dominance in this market. Sometimes, the brand name itself can create such differentiation; for example, RealLemon commands a premium over generic forms of bottled lemon juice, despite being just that—bottled lemon juice!

In discussing monopoly, we have not spent much time defining the market boundary; we have simply asserted that the market has a single seller. In a world of branded products, such as Coke and Pepsi, a given firm often has some pricing power over its own brand. Some might argue that Coke and Pepsi are each monopolists in their own market. Economists would not go this far; they would place both firms in a single market that they would describe as a differentiated oligopoly. It is an oligopoly because there are a small number of large producers, and it is differentiated because each firm has some independent pricing ability. The easiest way to prove this is to simply go to the grocery store and note that, from week to week, one soft-drink brand is typically priced lower than the other. The one that is on sale in a given week has a larger volume of sales in that week. Nonetheless, if you stand in the soft-drink aisle for a couple of minutes, you will find some individuals picking up the more expensive alternative. In such situations, interdependent firms must act strategically to maximize profits. We examine such oligopolistic interdependence in Chapter 20.

When products are differentiated, the definition of *market boundary* is hazy. Economists use cross-price elasticities of demand to describe how close two goods are to being substitutes. Unfortunately, there is no "magic" numerical answer to the question: How high must the cross-price elasticity of demand between two goods be before we consider them to both be in the same market, rather than simply close substitutes in different markets? Indeed, some of the most spirited arguments in antitrust cases are based specifically on the issue of defining the market boundary.

One basic difficulty when talking about differentiated product markets has to do with how to discuss *market* demand in this setting. Describing demand for an individual brand is straightforward, but it makes less sense to describe demand across brands, due to the heterogeneity of the product under consideration. Consider, for example, automobiles. The automotive market is classically heterogeneous but is not monopolistically competitive, due to barriers to entry. We can easily imagine describing demand curves for Ford Escort and Lexus automobiles. Few would argue, however, that the two demand curves should be added horizontally to describe demand for the two automobiles. What would this demand curve signify—which cars are included and at what price? As a result, we typically describe monopolistically competitive markets using a "representative" or "typical" firm in the market and use this representative firm's cost, demand, and profits when analyzing monopolistically competitive markets.

15.5 Monopolistic Competition

The essence of monopolistic competition involves two attributes: The product market is differentiated so that each firm has some pricing power, but the market is subject to free entry and exit, so positive profits cannot be maintained in the long run. The first attribute provides the "monopoly" in monopolistic competition, and the second attribute provides the "competition."

Monopolistically competitive markets come in many shapes and sizes. There are large-scale as well as small-scale examples of this market structure. Many of the branded products sold in grocery and department stores fit the requirements of monopolistic competition. Take, for example, the market for shirts or pants. Individual producers have some price-making ability; some consumers prefer L.L.Bean while others prefer Patagonia. The technology of production is well known, and international sources of supply are readily available, so entry is free.

As noted in the discussion of competitive markets in Chapter 14, both beer and wine are heterogeneous product markets. The super-premium segment of the wine industry is populated by a large number of small firms, each of which produces a highly differentiated product. Wine lovers routinely spend $40–$100 for a bottle of Napa Valley cabernet sauvignon produced by firms whose annual production quantities range from 500 to 10,000 cases per year. The goal for all of these firms is to become the next cult vintner, such as Harlan Estates, Colgin, or Screaming Eagle, whose bottles command more than $200 upon release, a price that is willingly paid by collectors who are on these producers' allocation lists. New producers crop up and old producers go out of business when market conditions change. Start-up costs are not prohibitive, and certainly, the technology of production is well known. You need not even own vineyards or a physical winery to start a brand; bulk wine is available, as are consulting winemakers, and space is available for winery operations from various cooperatives in the Napa Valley. Microbreweries offer a similar story. The scale of production is small (as the name implies), the product is highly differentiated, and entry is easy. The goal for microbreweries is to become the next Pete's Wicked Ale or Samuel Adams.

Another set of monopolistically competitive markets exists at the local level. Many local retail establishments fit the monopolistically competitive norm. Consider hair salons, used bookstores, pizza shops, or restaurants. Each has some price-making ability: Compare the price of Kung Pao chicken at the two nearest Chinese restaurants to where you live. One restaurant is likely charging a higher price (for Kung Pao or some other item common to both menus) without completely losing its customers. All of the markets just discussed define ease of entry.

Monopolistic Competition in the Short Run

Figure 15.8 depicts two possible short-run situations for a representative firm, *i*, in the market. Both Figures 15.8A and 15.8B have the same basic curves that describe the short-run situation facing the monopolistic firms earlier in this chapter. Average total cost, ATC_i, and marginal cost, MC_i, are shown for the firm (AVC_i has been suppressed to

FIGURE 15.8 Two Views of Monopolistic Competition in the Short Run for Representative Firm *i*

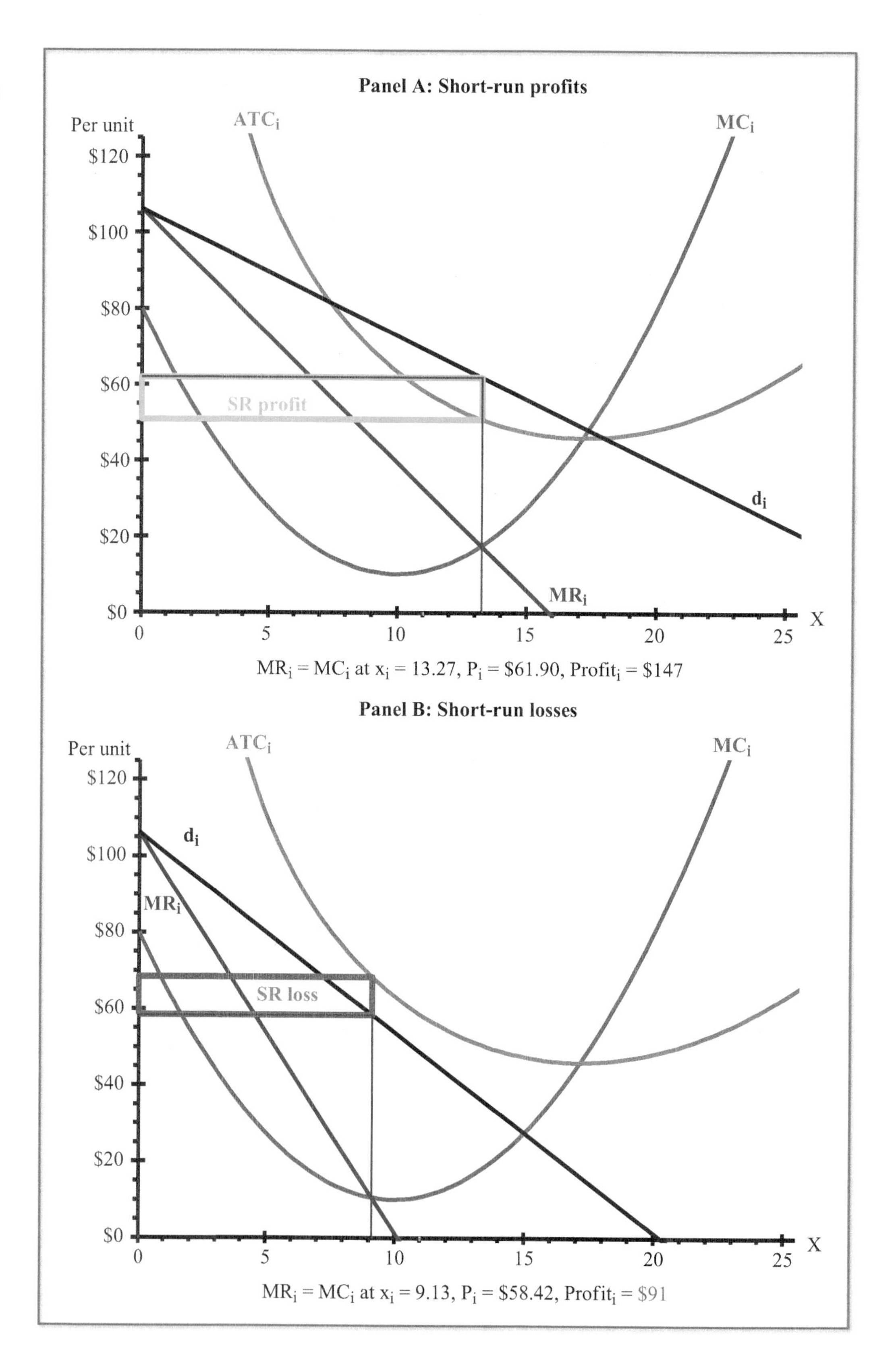

reduce clutter). Notice that demand is signified by d_i; the lowercase letter is specifically used to remind you that this represents the demand facing a single firm embedded in a market (just as the horizontal line dd represented individual firm demand in Figure 13.1 for competitive markets). (Note the contrast with earlier in this chapter, where we used D to represent the demand curve facing the monopolist. D was the demand facing a single firm, but this demand also represented the entire market demand curve.)

The representative firm has some price-making ability—that is, some pricing power—as signified by the downward-sloping demand curve. As a result, the firm's marginal revenue, MR_i, is beneath its demand curve, as noted in Section 15.1. The only difference between Figures 15.8A and 15.8B is that demand is more expansive in Figure 15.8A. In particular, demand covers cost, and profits result in the first instance, while in the second instance, the reverse holds true. These curves appear quite similar to the short-run monopoly diagrams from Section 15.2, except that the diagrams in Figure 15.8 are for a representative firm, rather than for the market as a whole. In Figure 15.8B, the absence of AVC_i suggests that the one remaining question is whether the firm should shut down in the short run, rather than sustain a loss of \$91 by producing at $x_i = 9.13$ units. In the present instance, the representative firm should continue producing at a loss in the short run because FC = \$300 (or to say the same thing, $AVC_i(9.13) < P_i = \$58.42$). Therefore, monopolistic competition Figure 15.8B is qualitatively similar to monopoly Figure 15.5A.

Both Figures 15.8A and 15.8B could easily depict the same market with one distinguishing difference: If there are N_a firms associated with Figure 15.8A and N_b associated with Figure 15.8B, then $N_a < N_b$. The reason is straightforward: If more firms compete for consumers, then each firm will have fewer consumers on average when there are more firms than when there are less. We could try to be exact about how many more firms there are in one figure than the other, but to do so would impute a degree of comparability across varieties that we wish to avoid in this setting. In Section 15.6, we examine in greater detail how demand changes as the number of monopolistic competitors sharing the market changes. Before we undertake this discussion, however, we need to move the monopolistic competitor from the short run to the long run.

One of the assumptions implicit in analyzing both Figures 15.8A and 15.8B as part of the same market, where the only difference is the number of firms sharing the market, is that, as shown, the number of firms in the market does not affect factor costs. Put another way, the markets exhibit constant cost, as described in Section 14.4. For certain monopolistically competitive markets, this may well be true; fewer or more pizza parlors or ethnic restaurants in a town should not materially affect input costs in these markets. But for other markets, this may not be true. For example, as the number of used bookstores in an area increase, so will the price paid by owners for the main input in their business: used books. This is an example of an increasing-cost industry. As noted in Section 14.4, microbrewery beers are likely to be a constant-cost market, while the boutique wine market is likely to be an increasing-cost market. Since the demand-side issues are of more interest in the present context, we simply assume that cost curves are independent of the number of firms in the appropriately defined monopolistically competitive market.

Monopolistic Competition in the Long Run

Firms in monopolistically competitive markets differentiate their products in a variety of ways. One strategy to analyze monopolistic competition is to imagine a "perceptual map" of various brands within the market. Different markets have different perceptual maps. For cereal, the dimensions might include grain base, sweetness level, shape, fruit and nut content, the presence of nutritional additives, types of advertising and spokespersons used to shape the product's image, and the presence of "free" toys or cards included in the package. For local retailers (like a corner store), the dimensions might include the physical location of the store and store hours, whether specialized services are also provided (such as a deli counter where customers can order a freshly made sandwich), availability of alternative forms of payment (whether established customers can have signature accounts; if credit cards, debit cards, ATM cards, or checks are allowed), and range of products carried.

Individual consumers have different desires with regard to offerings located at points within these perceptual maps of the market. The goal for a potential entrant is to determine a niche or position within this map where there is a significant pocket of "unsatisfied" (or weakly satisfied) demand and locate at this "point." By doing so, the entrant will take away some consumers from existing firms that are "close" to the entrant's position, as well as satisfy some consumers who were previously unsatisfied by existing offerings. If an existing brand is located at a position that is too sparsely "populated" by consumers, then the brand will not be profitable, and exit will occur. If this happens, the remaining firms that are "nearby" will see an increase in demand for their product.

Although the individual entrant's entry decision is based on a careful choice of how and where it is profitable to enter, the market analysis does not require a *specific* description of the effect on surrounding firms. It is sufficient to talk in terms of what happens to the "average" firm as entry and exit occurs. If there are too many firms in the market, the average firm will operate at a loss in the short run. If there are too few firms in the market, the average firm will operate at a profit in the short run. These profit or loss signals will encourage entry or exit as we move from the short to the long run. Exactly "where" entry or exit occurs within the perceptual map is less important for our market analysis than the effect on the average firm of that entry or exit.

Consider the short-run monopolistically competitive market described in Figure 15.8. With N_a brands (firms), the average firm attains positive profits. These profits encourage entry into the market. Entry will shift the demand curve facing the "representative" firm to the left. Conversely, the market cannot support N_b brands, so exit will occur as we move from the short to the long run. Exit will shift the demand curve facing the remaining "representative" firm to the right. Somewhere between N_a and N_b, there will be an appropriate number of firms, N*, such that each earns only normal profits ($N_a < N^* < N_b$). When this occurs, the representative firm will look like Figure 15.9. The firm's demand curve will be tangent to its average total cost curve, signifying that, given N* firms in the market, each firm maximizes profit by finding output x_i* where $MR_i(x_i^*) = MC_i(x_i^*)$, while at the same time, the firm earns a normal rate of return since $P_i(x_i^*) = ATC_i(x_i^*)$. Put another way, Figure 15.9 depicts monopolistic competition in long-run equilibrium.

Note: *To simplify later discussion, we describe the long-run monopolistically competitive equilibrium using the acronym* LRMCE.

FIGURE 15.9
Monopolistic Competition in the Long Run for Representative Firm *i*

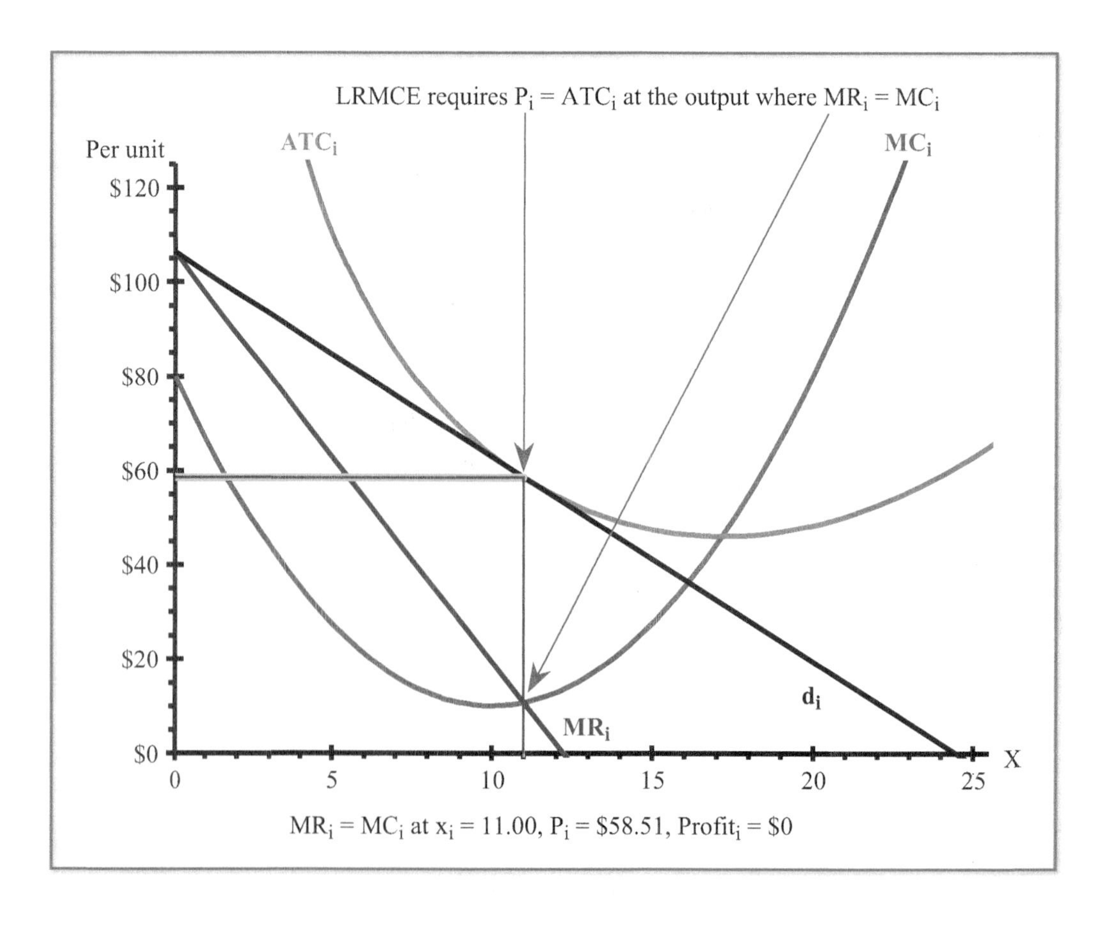

The attributes of this equilibrium are that each firm has some price-making ability (so $P_i > MC_i$), but each firm operates at zero economic profit so that there is no incentive for further entry into or exit from the market. The Chapter 15 Appendix provides an algebraic approach to monopolistic competition in the short run and in the long run.

Perfectly competitive and monopolistically competitive firms both maximize profits by setting MR = MC and earn zero profits in the long run. Perfect competitors do this by producing at minimum average total cost, but monopolistic competitors produce above minimum average total cost. Monopolistic competitors do not produce at minimum average total cost because they are only able to earn zero profits by producing at the point of tangency between the firm's downward-sloping demand curve and its average total cost curve. Therefore, the firm produces at an output level below minimum average total cost. Interestingly, the firm could produce at a lower cost, but the revenues it would generate from this production level would not support the more efficient increased scale of production. Put another way, consumers value the variety produced by different products and are willing to support price above minimum average total cost to achieve that variety. These welfare aspects of differentiated product markets are discussed in Chapter 16. A final way that producing below minimum average total cost is sometimes viewed is that firms in monopolistic competition operate with excess capacity in the LRMCE. Excess capacity simply means that the production process chosen could support a higher level of production without incurring higher per-unit costs. If a firm produces output below minimum average total cost, then it has excess capacity in its production process.

15.6 How Entry Affects Demand in Differentiated Product Markets *OPTIONAL SECTION*

One of the implicit conclusions derived in the monopolistically competitive analysis in Section 15.5 is that, as entry occurs in moving from the short run to the long run, the average price in the market declines (in moving from Figures 15.8A to 15.9). The reverse also holds true: Exit causes price to increase in moving from Figures 15.8B to 15.9. In both comparisons, the inverse relation between average price and the number of firms in the market comes through in the analysis, albeit at an implicit level. One of the reasons we did not focus on this relation between average price and number of firms is that this relation may occur, but it does not *have* to occur. Whether or not it occurs has to do with what happens in term of "differentiatedness" as a result of entry. We examine a typology of possible differentiatedness outcomes in this section.

Before we embark on the differentiated market analysis, consider what we would expect to happen to average demand with entry in an undifferentiated product market. Suppose that market demand is given by X(P). If a monopolist controls this market, it faces the entire market demand. If entry occurs and we have two equal-sized firms, then each will end up with demand of $x_i(P) = X(P)/2$ where $i = 1, 2$. More generally, if there are N firms, then demand faced by a representative firm i is given by:

$$x_i(P) = X(P)/N. \qquad \textbf{(15.3)}$$

The representative or average firm's demand is N times as small as market demand at any given price. Put in terms of slope and intercept, average demand is N times as steep as market demand with the same P intercept if there are N firms in the market. This parsing off of demand into segments that add up the monopolistic (or market) whole works in homogeneous product markets because the addition of further firms does not alter market demand; it only alters the distribution of who satisfies that demand.

A Typology of Differentiatedness

If a product is differentiated, then we cannot as easily describe how individual demand relates to market demand. Indeed, as argued earlier, it is somewhat inappropriate to talk about market demand at all in this instance because of the difficulty in determining what we mean by the market as a whole. Nonetheless, it is useful to consider what happens to the average demand curve as the number of brands (or varieties or firms) increases. Three generic possibilities seem apparent with regard to elasticity of demand at the profit-maximizing (x, P) point: Elasticity may decrease, remain fixed, or increase. These elasticity outcomes are mirrored by change in pricing power outcomes according to the Lerner Index, Equation 15.2c. Among these three elasticity outcomes, various quantitative output outcomes seem possible. These outcomes will be denoted by a letter from A to F.

Individuals like variety; therefore, we would expect consumers interested in this market to view additional varieties as a good development. If the additional brands increase the contrast between brands and sharpen the values inherent in each brand, then it is not unreasonable to assume that the average pricing power attained by a representative firm would increase as variety increases, even as the amount sold by an individual firm declines. Put in terms of elasticity of demand (using the Lerner Index rule in Equation 15.2c), if additional varieties increase the inherent differentiatedness of brands within the market, then average firm elasticity of demand is likely to become more inelastic as brands sharpen the market niches that they serve.

The best-case scenario, given a decline in demand elasticity based on increased variety, would be if this additional differentiatedness brings new consumer demand into the market as well (denote this by Outcome A). Put another way, demand does not decline in proportion to the number of firms in the market (as was the case with Equation 15.3). For example, college towns seem to attract ethnic restaurants; therefore, consider ethnic restaurants in a college town. If there is a smaller number of ethnic restaurants, then each restaurant must offer a wider range of cuisines to cover demand. Suppose that there are two ethnic restaurants in town; one offers "continental" cuisine, and the other offers Asian fare. If instead there were eight ethnic restaurants in this market, then we might have restaurants with Spanish, Swiss, Italian, French, Vietnamese, Thai, Mongolian, and Hunan offerings. It is reasonable to believe that two things might occur in this instance: (1) The average price per check might increase with greater differentiation, and (2) the average restaurant might do better than one-fourth as good in terms of overall number of meals sold, relative to when there was only a continental restaurant and an Asian restaurant in town.

Another possible outcome due to additional varieties is that average elasticity does not change (so that the average price-cost margin does not change according to Equation 15.2c), but the market is more effectively covered. As a result, demand declines less than proportionately with the increase in number of firms (Outcome B). Increased variety might decrease the differentiatedness of the average brand but allow demand to decline less than proportionately. In this instance, overall demand increases as variety increases, given more elastic demand and lower price-cost margin (Outcome C).

There need not be an overall increase in "demand" with the entry of additional firms. Another alternative, D, is that consumers consume the same number of meals but view those alternatives as more differentiated (and hence more inelastic). If there is no change in pricing power and demand changes proportionately, then this is what we would expect of homogeneous demand, as modeled by Equation 15.3 (Outcome E). Finally, the consumer might be willing to accept a higher price-cost margin due to increased differentiatedness but not purchase as many units, so that demand changes more than proportionately with increased variety (Outcome F).

Table 15.1 provides a typology of these outcomes based on the two dimensions discussed earlier: overall size of the market (rows) and pricing power (columns). Outcomes A–F populate six of the nine cells in the three-by-three table. The other three cells are labeled "na." If we assume that potential entrants are able to accurately analyze and determine the most densely "populated" unfulfilled point in the perceptual map, then the cells labeled "na" represent entry that would not occur. Each of these cells represents an outcome that is worse than would be available to homogeneous entry (cell E), and homogeneous entry simply divides demand proportionally, as noted in Equation 15.3.

TABLE 15.1 Possible Outcomes Based on Entry in a Monopolistically Competitive Market

What happens to the "typical" firm as the number of firms in the market increases?

		Change in elasticity at profit-maximizing outcome:	More inelastic	No change	More elastic
		Change in pricing power (Lerner Index):	Increase	No change	Decrease
		Implied change in price, *given* constant MC:	Increase	No change	Decrease
Less-than-proportionate*	and	increase in market demand	A	B	C
Proportionate*	and	no change in market demand	D	E	na
More-than-proportionate*	and	decrease in market demand	F	na	na

*Decrease in "typical" firm demand

The Geometry of Differentiated Entry

The clearest way to visually describe the possibilities delineated in Table 15.1 is to imagine the effect of entry going from one firm to two in the market. As with the previous section, we can derive a number of conclusions without resorting to nonlinear demand curves. Therefore, we continue to base our analysis in this section on linear demand.

One of the reasons why there were differences in price in the previous section was that there were differences in marginal cost in that analysis. This is due to the cubic functional form chosen for cost curves used to show the general attributes of the monopolistically competitive model. To focus on demand issues in this section, we reverse course and assume the simplest functional form possible for a cost function: constant marginal cost plus fixed cost. In this instance, $AVC(x) = MC(x)$, and ATC is a rectangular hyperbola that is asymptotic to the vertical axis and to the line $AVC = MC$. This simplifying assumption allows us to focus on demand issues for a very simple reason: In this instance, $MR = MC$ occurs at a constant MC. We need not examine price-cost margins to describe pricing power; we can describe pricing power by directly examining price alone. That is, *if marginal cost is constant, then changes in the profit-maximizing price are due to changes in pricing power caused by entry.* As the number of firms in the market increases, and hence, as individual firm demand declines, we can see how much smaller output is where $MR = MC$ due to extra firms in the market.

The starting point for each of the entry scenarios in the typology is a common monopoly outcome. We assume that marginal cost is \$10 and that $MR = MC$ at $x = 200$ units of output. Inverse market demand at this output level is $P(x) = \$20$. (Unlike when $N > 1$, we can talk about demand as a market demand curve in this setting.) Profits in this instance are \$1,750. This information is shown in Figure 15.10.

Q10a. What is the elasticity of demand at the profit-maximizing outcome?

Q10b. What is fixed cost in this instance?*

Entry may have disparate effects on price and quantity facing the representative firm, as discussed earlier and as described by the typology in Table 15.1. The six outcomes A–F are shown as Panels A–F in Figures 15.11–15.13. Figures 15.11A–15.11F depict the demand facing the "representative" firm for each of the six outcomes described in Table 15.1 upon entry of a *second* firm. The profit rectangles and ATC curves are suppressed in Figures 15.11A–15.11F to focus on differences in demand caused by entry.

***Q10 answer:** The Lerner Index, Equation 15.2c, tells us that the elasticity of demand is –2 in this instance: $-1/\varepsilon = 1/|\varepsilon| = (P - MC)/P = (\$20 - \$10)/\$20 = 1/2$. Fixed cost is \$250, since $\pi = TR - VC - FC$ implies that $FC = TR - VC - \pi = \$4{,}000 - \$2{,}000 - \$1{,}750$, since $VC = x \cdot AVC = 200 \cdot \$10$.

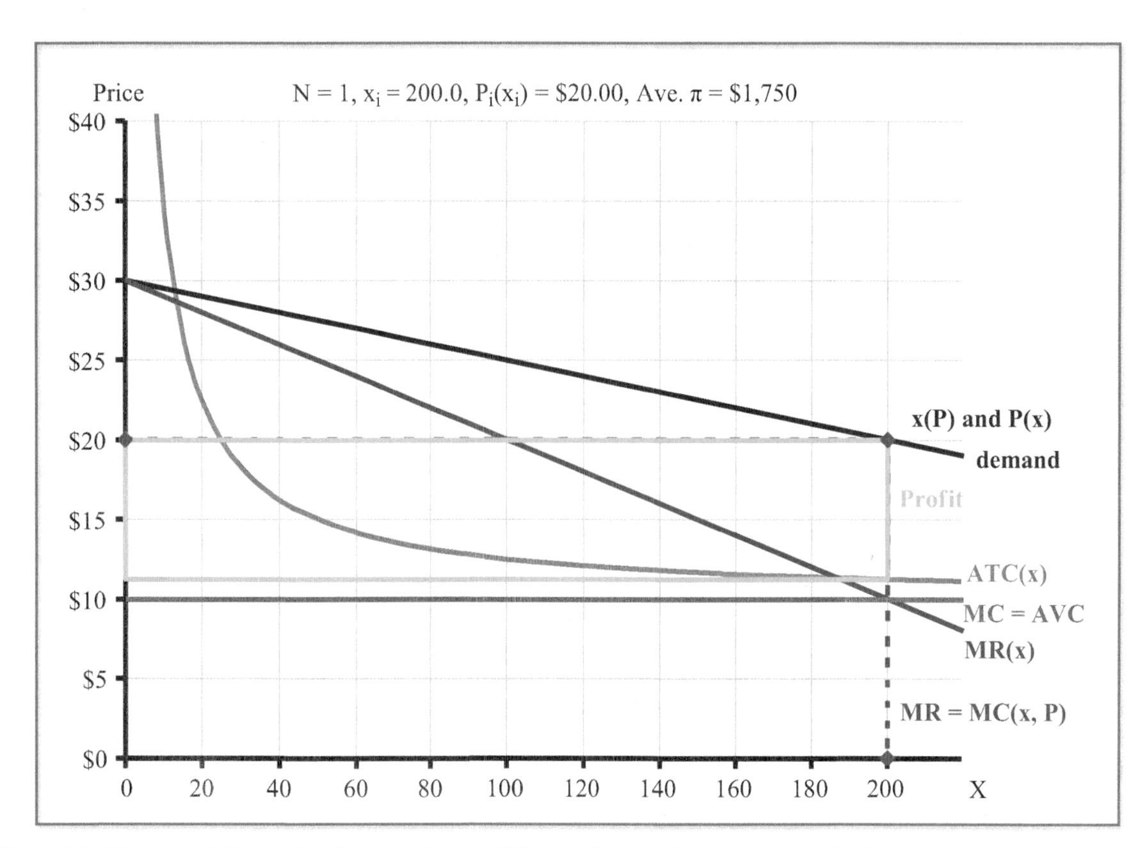

FIGURE 15.10 Demand Prior to Entry into a Differentiated Product Market

This figure is a starting point for Figures 15.11–15.13.

It is worthwhile verifying the relations described in Table 15.1. Note, for instance, that demand has decreased less than proportionately with entry in Figures 15.11A–15.11C because output $x_i > 100 = 200/2$. By contrast, Figures 15.11D and 15.11E depict proportionate change in demand, since $x_i = 100$, while Figure 15.11F depicts more-than-proportionate change, since $x_i < 100$. Pricing power increases as price increases, since marginal cost is constant. The first column in Table 15.1 (A, D, and F) is associated with an increase in pricing power. This is confirmed by price being greater than $20 in each of Figures 15.11A, 15.11D, and 15.11F upon entry. With linear demand and constant marginal cost, price will increase if the P intercept of demand increases due to entry. In Figure 15.10, the P intercept was $30. In Figures 15.11A, 15.11D, and 15.11F, it is greater than $30. By contrast, in Figures 15.11B and 15.11E, there is no change in price (because there is no change in the P intercept). Pricing power declines in Figure 15.11C, since price declines to $19.35 (due to the P intercept being less than $30 in Figure 15.11C). One final point to note about this analysis is that Figure 15.11E is what we would expect in a homogeneous product market. If entry causes proportionate change in demand and no change in differentiability, then the result is the same as that algebraically described in Equation 15.3.[7]

The discussion thus far in this section has not relied on the market being monopolistically competitive. Instead, it has focused more generally on how entry might affect demand in differentiated product markets. If the market has barriers to entry, then entry will stop short of removing all profit; the size of the BTE determines how much profit remains before entry is blockaded.

Entry will continue as long as potential entrants perceive profitable niches. Entry will cause the demand curve facing the representative firm to change once again, and if further entry occurs, there will be additional change in demand. If the market is monopolistically competitive, the ultimate result will look qualitatively like Figure 15.9.

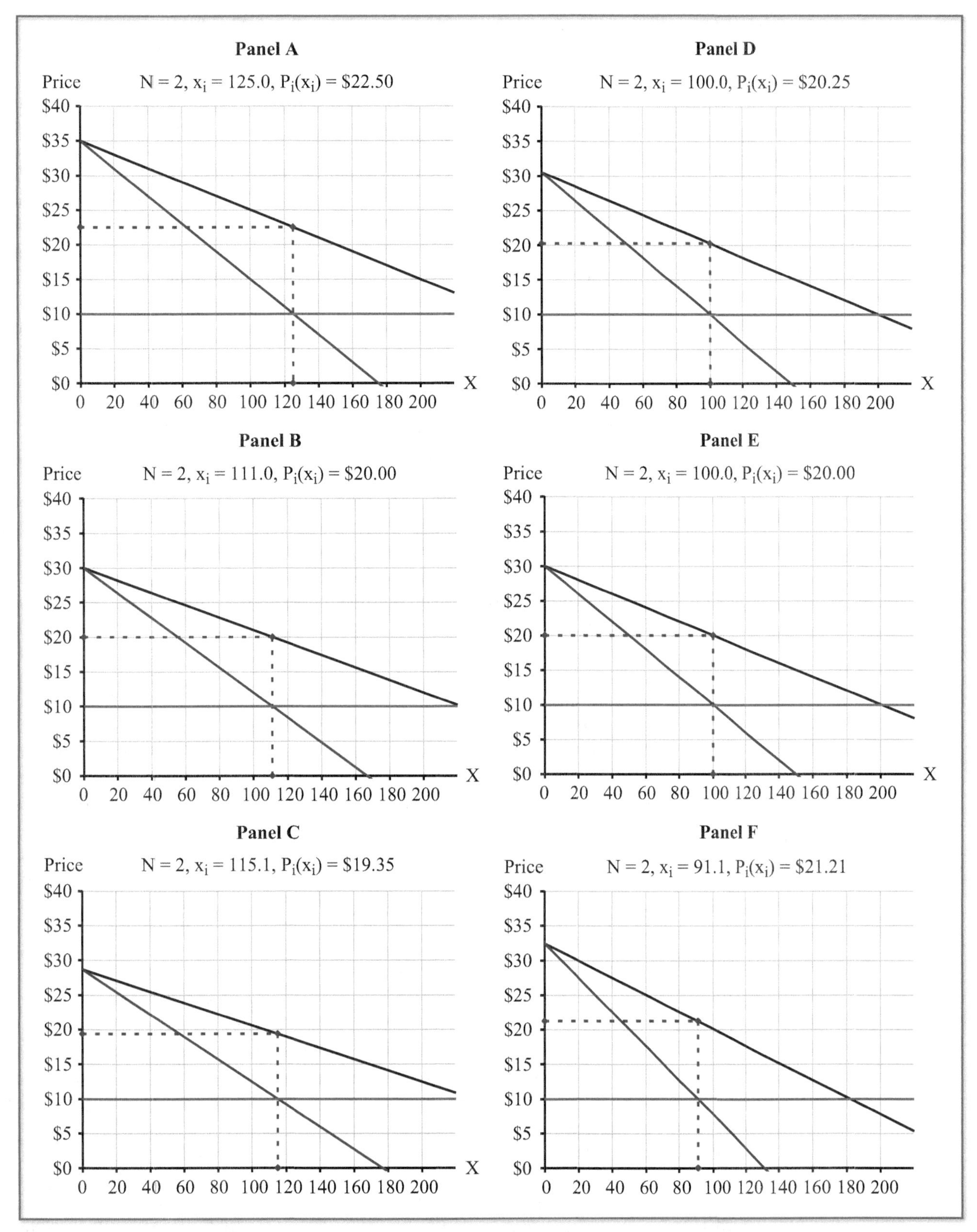

FIGURE 15.11 Possible Demand Response to Second Firm Entry into a Differentiated Product Market

The panels are based on the typology in Table 15.1. In all panels, red is MC_i, dark blue is $demand_i$, and medium blue is MR_i.

The tangency between downward-sloping demand and ATC for the representative firm in the LRMCE is a theoretical ideal. As a practical matter, we should not expect such precision for several reasons. First, and perhaps most important, potential entrants into differentiated product markets do so after careful analysis of the market and by determining the niche that they can effectively and profitably fill. As outsiders, they might well have somewhat limited information about actual demand at the perceptual map "location" at which they decide to enter. Consumer surveys and information gleaned from other sources can only tell so much of the story of what will actually happen upon entry. Second, potential entrants may well be "wearing rose-colored glasses" with regard to how well they will do—and how quickly they will be able to do it. After all, potential entrants have done the analysis and have come to believe that their idea is the best solution; otherwise, they would be doing something else. Third, existing firms will not typically share cost and demand information with outsiders. Therefore, existing market profitability can only be guessed; it cannot be ascertained with precision. Each of these reasons suggests that an actual tangency with zero profits in long-run equilibrium is not necessary to describe the LRMCE.

As a practical matter, we can describe the LRMCE in terms of the number of firms that can profitably fit in the market. To go back to our example of monopolistically competitive ethnic restaurants, a small college town may be able to support nine ethnic restaurants but not ten. We could see this graphically if the representative firm has zero profits or a small amount of positive profits when there are nine ethnic restaurants in town but not when there are ten.

Each of the six scenarios in Figure 15.11 describes a possible demand response to entry in a differentiated product market. We continue to see entry as long as the representative firm is profitable upon entry. This is the situation depicted in Figures 15.12 and 15.13. In each scenario, the profit rectangles and ATC curves have been reintroduced. When profits are positive or zero, the profit rectangle is green, and when profits are negative, the profit rectangle turns red (just like monopoly profits earlier in this chapter). Figure 15.12 depicts the largest number of firms for which the representative firm earns positive or zero profits. Figure 15.13 shows what happens when one more firm enters and the representative firm becomes unprofitable. Put another way, Figure 15.12 depicts the six monopolistically competitive equilibria, given the change in demand scenarios that were begun in Figure 15.11.

It is worthwhile to begin by examining the homogeneous market norm provided by Outcome E (in Table 15.1 and in each of the figures). Figure 15.12E shows an exact monopolistic competitive equilibrium tangency with eight firms in the market. This could have been predicted from the monopoly starting point shown in Figure 15.10. Given constant marginal cost and price, total quantity demanded will not vary based on the number of firms sharing the market under Outcome E. Therefore, total revenue will remain \$4,000 and variable cost will remain \$2,000 to produce a total of 200 units of output. This suggests an excess of revenue over variable cost of \$2,000, an amount that represents fixed cost plus profits. Aggregate fixed cost depends on how many firms are in the market; if each has a fixed cost of \$250, then the market can support eight firms before profits are zero (8 = \$2,000/\$250). Indeed, this is why fixed cost was chosen to be \$250 for the discussion of Figures 15.10–15.13.

The monopolistically competitive equilibrium depends on how entry affects differentiatedness of firms within the market. If firm entry expands overall demand for the product at a given price due to more effective focus on individual niche markets, then the market will sustain more firms than if this is less true. Similarly, if firm entry allows firms to charge more for a given amount of output because consumers value the product more, then the market will sustain more firms than if the opposite is true. Although a casual reading of these two aspects of demand might suggest that these are descriptions of the same phenomenon, we have shown previously that they are, in fact, independent effects. The former has to do with less-than-proportionate change versus more-than-proportionate change in demand, while the latter has to do with more versus less pricing power.[8]

The numbers confirm these expectations. Figure 15.12A shows that if entry causes increased pricing power and expanding market coverage, many firms result in LRMCE (N = 17). As pricing power declines, so does the number of firms supporting LRMCE, as we see in Figures 15.12B (where N = 11) and 15.12C (N = 10). The actual number of firms in each LRMCE lines up as you would expect with regard to expanding market as well. Perhaps the best comparison here is between Figures 15.12B and 15.12E because, in this instance, price remains at $20 so that the only differentiating difference is how entry affects total market coverage. Eleven firms cover the expanding market scenario in Figure 15.12B, versus the eight firms discussed earlier in the homogeneous market scenario in Figure 15.12E.

A quick comparison of Figures 15.12A–15.12F and 15.13A–15.13F shows that the patterns described in Table 15.1 continue with further entry but that entry creates a situation where the representative firm is no longer profitable. As noted previously, we should not place too much emphasis on the exact numerical values in this instance; firms do not have as precise a view of demand or cost as is implied by the model (and as a result, we have placed little emphasis on actual price or quantity outcomes in this instance). It is not unreasonable to expect that entry will sometimes place the representative firm in a loss situation, such as described in Figure 15.13. This is indeed a common market phenomenon in differentiated product markets, where entry is easy. There tends to be jostling over time as new firms come into the market with the belief that they can better serve the market than can existing firms. Sometimes, they are right; sometimes, they are wrong. Think about pizza shops in your town: There is not a huge amount of stability in this or other monopolistically competitive markets with regard to actual players, but over time, there is stability with regard to overall number of firms covering the market (assuming the size of your town has remained stable).

If the algebraic function that controls how demand changes as entry occurs changed, then we would likely end up with different numbers in all but Figure 15.12E (which, as discussed earlier, is based on Equation 15.3). The sliders in the Excel file for Figure 15.12 allow you to create your own scenario and determine how many firms ultimately result in LRMCE. Of course, the answers would change dramatically, were you to change cost conditions (either fixed cost or variable cost).

The long-run monopolistically competitive equilibria shown in Figures 15.9 and 15.12 are all predicated on reasonably inelastic demand outcomes to open up the diagrams by separating price from marginal cost in the graphic presentations. The most elastic of the seven long-run equilibria is Figure 15.12C, which, based on inverting the Lerner Index in Equation 15.2c, has an elasticity of only $-2.23 = \varepsilon = -P/(P - MC) = -\$18.15/(\$18.15 - \$10)$. Often, monopolistically competitive markets have very elastic demand for individual varieties. Highly elastic demand means that other close substitutes are available, so an individual variety has little pricing power. An example is provided in Figure 15.14, in which the Lerner Index is 10%, implying that the elasticity of demand is –10. Notice that this example is based on a quadratic cost function. You can use the Excel file for Figure 15.14 to adjust the parameters of both demand and cost function to create your own scenario.

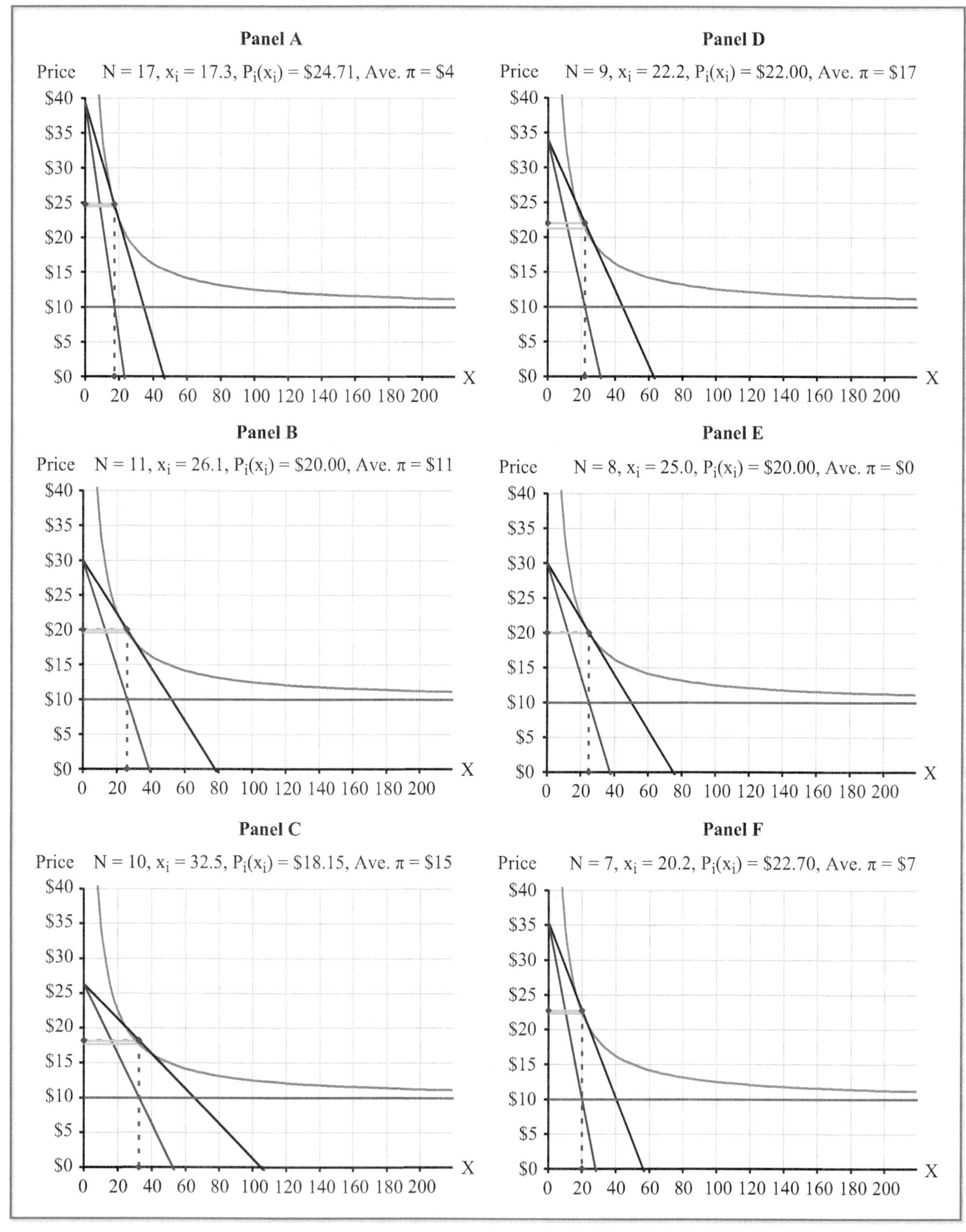

FIGURE 15.12 Monopolistically Competitive Equilibrium Number of Firms, Given Six Views of How Entry Affects Differentiatedness

The panels are based on the typology in Table 15.1. In all panels, the green rectangle is $\pi_i \geq 0$, red is MC_i, orange is ATC_i, dark blue is demand_i, and medium blue is MR_i.

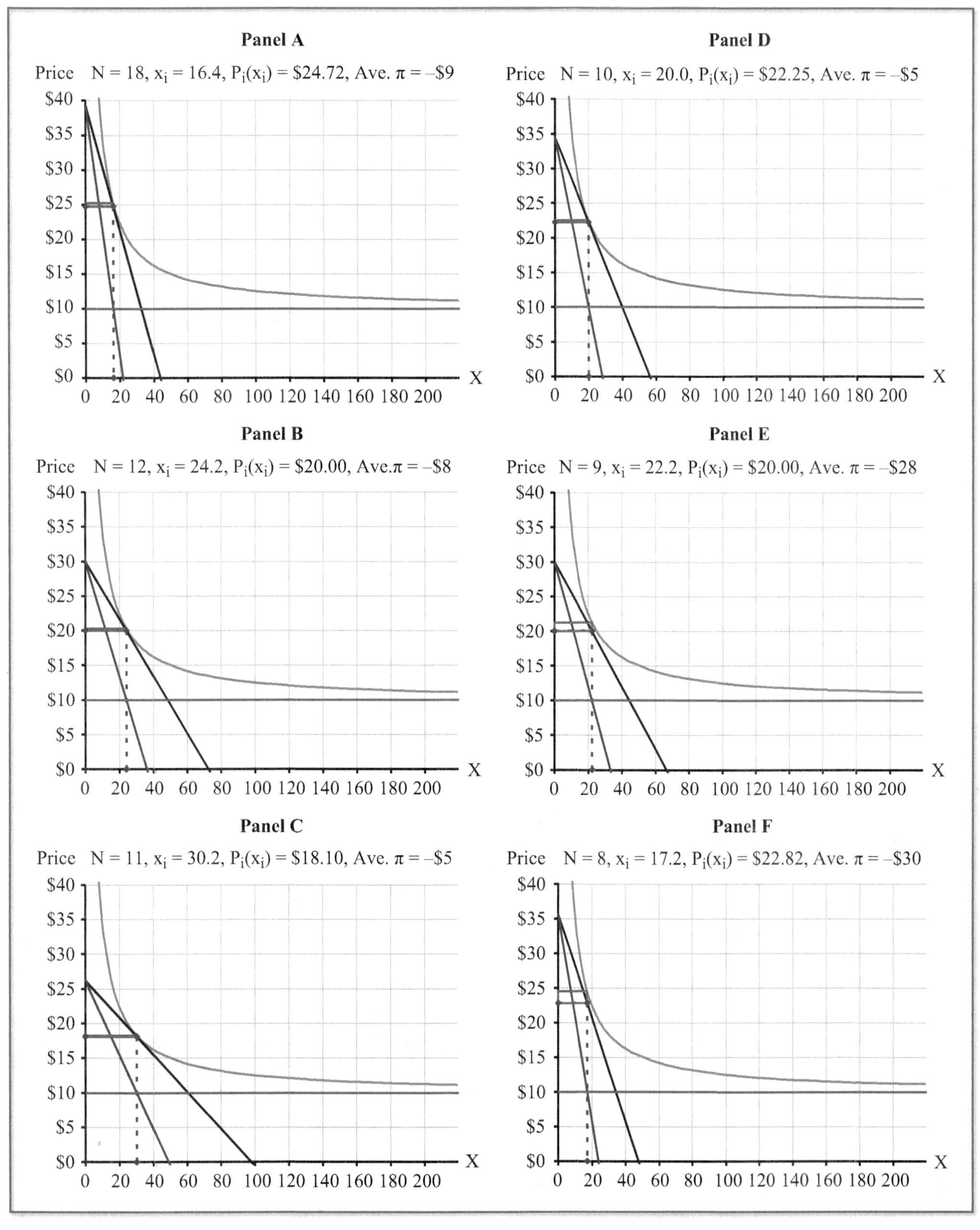

FIGURE 15.13 One Too Many Firms in Each of Six Monopolistically Competitive Markets

The panels are based on the typology in Table 15.1. In all panels, the red rectangle is $\pi_i < 0$, the red line is MC_i, orange is ATC_i, dark blue is $demand_i$, and medium blue is MR_i.

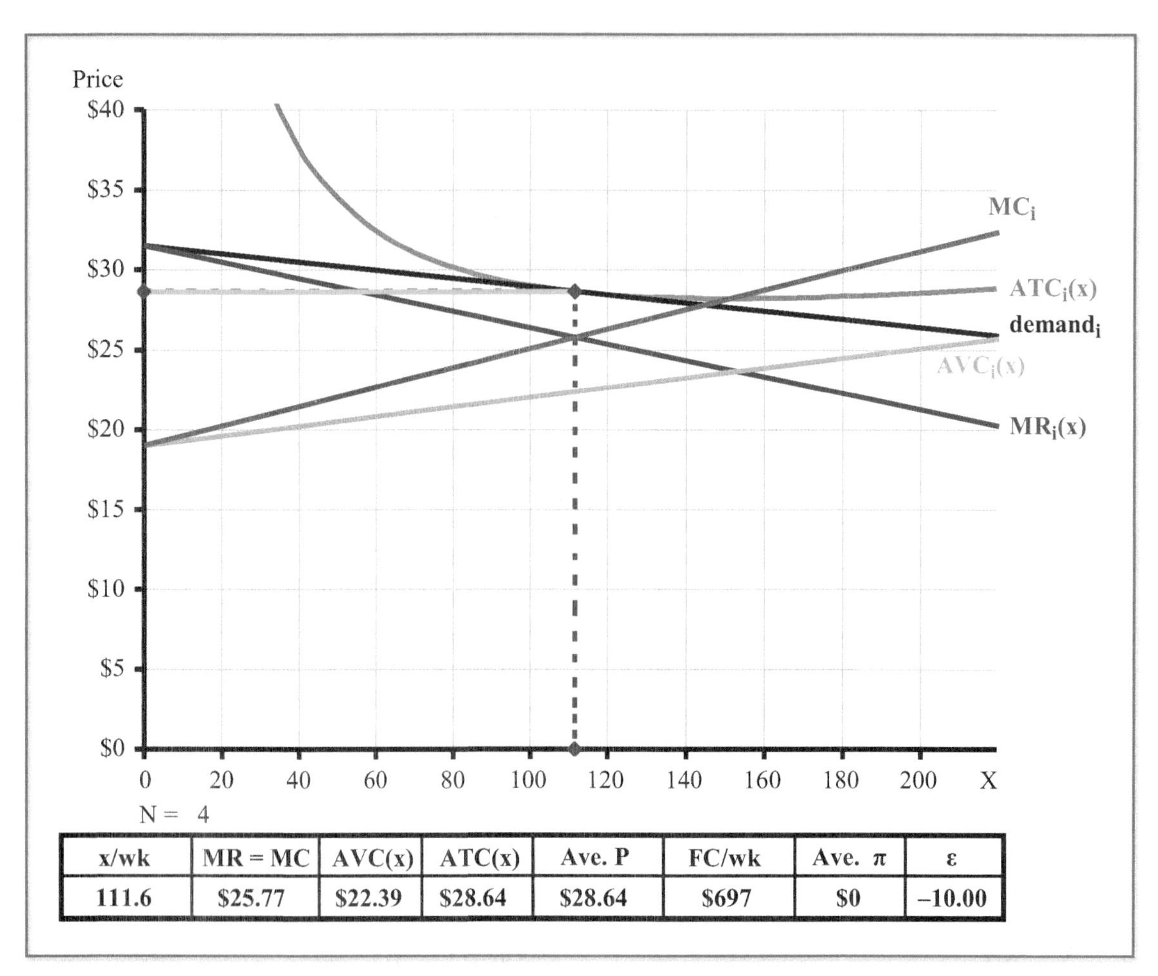

x/wk	MR = MC	AVC(x)	ATC(x)	Ave. P	FC/wk	Ave. π	ε
111.6	$25.77	$22.39	$28.64	$28.64	$697	$0	−10.00

FIGURE 15.14 Often, a Monopolistically Competitive Equilibrium Will Be Highly Elastic

Summary

Any firm wishing to maximize profits will set marginal revenue equal to marginal cost. The geometry of maximizing profits is based on a comparison of total revenue and total cost, as highlighted in the discussion in Chapter 12. That discussion was predicated on being able to identify the demand curve the firm faced. In competitive markets, the demand curve is flat; in *all* other markets, it is downward sloping.

Downward-sloping demand means that a firm has some price-making ability. That is, it has some ability to set price for its product, rather than simply taking the existing market price as given. Price is an endogenous variable for the firm in this instance; the amount of price-making ability the firm has is determined by how inelastic the market for its product is. The Lerner Index of monopoly power summarizes the amount of pricing power the firm is able to bring to the market. Pricing power is inversely related to elasticity of demand; the more inelastic is demand, the more pricing power the firm exhibits. Perfect competition has no pricing power because individual firms face perfectly elastic demand. All other market structures have some pricing power because the profit-maximizing firm sets the price above marginal cost.

The monopolist determines how much to produce by setting MR = MC. As noted previously, price exceeds marginal cost for all imperfectly competitive market structures, and monopoly is the most imperfectly competitive structure of all. Therefore, the monopolist supplies at a point, X*, where MR(X*) = MC(X*) by pricing at P* = P(X*) where P(X) is the inverse market demand for the good. Although we can describe this point (X*, P*) as a point of market supply, we cannot describe a market supply curve for the monopolist. The monopolist does not have a supply curve.

As with perfectly competitive markets, there are two caveats to the profit-maximizing rule of setting output X* so that MR(X*) = MC(X*). The first caveat has to do with how MR approaches MC. If as X approaches X* from below and MR(X) < MC(X), then X* is a profit minimum. If as X approaches X* from below and MR(X) > MC(X), then X* is a profit maximum. The second caveat has to do with when the monopolist should shut down in the short run. If $AVC(X^*) > P(X^*)$, then market demand is sufficiently thin that the firm would be better off shutting down in the short run because by producing at X^*, the firm is not even covering its variable cost of production.

Monopolies can maintain short-run profits over the long run only if there is some impediment to entry in the market. Barriers to entry may emanate from three sources: structural, legal, and strategic. Structural barriers to entry exist due to technological aspects of the production process. An example of a structural barrier to entry is when economies of scale are sufficiently large that the market is best served by a single firm. Such a situation is called a natural monopoly. For example, local utilities such as electricity and residential trash collection are most efficiently served by a single provider to avoid duplicating capital costs of distribution. In such instances, legal barriers are often introduced that bestow the right to be the legal monopolist on a single firm. (Often, this is done in conjunction with regulation of the market.) The government also bestows monopoly rights on firms in the form of patents and copyrights. This is done to spur innovative activity. Strategic barriers to entry involve actions by firms within a market that make it harder for outsiders to enter the market. Investing in excess capacity well in advance of demand is one such strategic barrier.

If different producers of a product have some price-making ability due to perceived differences between the various producers' offerings, then we say that the product is differentiated. Differentiated product markets are more difficult to examine because there are no clear dividing lines between what is inside and what is outside the market. Even if you know what is inside the market, you should not simply add across firms to describe market demand because of the heterogeneity of the varieties being added in this instance. The easiest way to remind yourself of this is to consider a luxury car and an economy car. Both move you from point A to point B, but you would not want to add the demand curves for each to get "market" demand. A strategy for discussing firms within differentiated product markets that avoids this problem is to talk in terms of a "representative" or "average" firm. In this setting, we can examine how demand facing the representative firm changes when other firms enter or leave the market.

Monopolistically competitive markets are differentiated product markets where there is free entry and exit. The differentiatedness of the product provides the monopoly element to this market structure, while the free entry and exit provides the competition. In this setting, the representative firm may earn short-run losses or profits, but in the long run, it will only earn a normal rate of return. As a result, firms in long-run monopolistically competitive equilibrium (LRMCE) produce on the downward-sloping part of their average total cost curve; they produce at a point of excess capacity. Consumers in monopolistically competitive markets value the variety that results from having more firms in the market and are willing to pay extra for it.

Entry into differentiated product markets can affect the representative firm's demand in a variety of ways. Entry may increase the average price in the market, or it may cause that price to not change or to decline. Similarly, differentiated product entry may expand the overall size of the market if new producers are able to satisfy the demand of previously unsatisfied consumers. But entry can lead to a reduction in overall market size as well if it leads to differentiated product producers becoming more specialized in their niches in a way that cuts out some of the more generalist consumers. Consider a market with one Mediterranean restaurant (one that has Greek, Italian, and Spanish cuisines but not quite as full a line of each of those cuisines as would be the case if those same cuisines were covered by three separate restaurants). Imagine that the market moves from having one Mediterranean restaurant to one each of Greek, Italian, and Spanish restaurants. Each of the three might face demand that is less than one-third the size of the Mediterranean restaurant, but each might be able to support a higher average price per meal than was the case with the single Mediterranean restaurant. Overall size and the degree of differentiatedness of the market are independent aspects of a market, and there is no determinate answer regarding how entry will affect both of these aspects of the market. A typology of entry outcomes is proposed that allows you to systematically consider what will happen with entry in differentiated product markets. This leads to a more general view of the "look" of differentiated product markets with free entry and exit, as they move toward LRMCE.

Review Questions

Define the following terms:

price maker
imperfectly competitive market
Lerner Index
monopoly
barriers to entry (BTE)
monopoly rent
natural monopoly
differentiated product
monopolistic competition
LRMCE

Match the following statements:

a. Lerner Index
b. Legal BTE
c. Structural BTE
d. Strategic BTE

1. Economies of scale are large, relative to the size of the market.
2. Excess capacity
3. (P – MC)/P
4. Patents

Provide short answers to the following:

a. Why is there no supply curve in monopoly markets?
b. Is it possible to have a monopoly market in which marginal cost is declining at the profit-maximizing output level?
c. Does a monopoly position in a market necessarily ensure positive profits?
d. Does choosing an output level where MR = MC assure that the firm maximizes profits?
e. What are the three sources of barriers to entry typically delineated by economists?
f. What are the two major attributes of monopolistic competition, and which attribute relates to the "monopoly" and which relates to the "competition" aspect of monopolistic competition?
g. Geometrically describe the long-run monopolistically competitive equilibrium. In particular, describe the position of price and marginal cost in this situation as it relates to minimum average total cost.

Check your answers to the *matching* and *short-answer* exercises in the Answers Appendix at the end of the book.

Notes

1. Note that $\Delta P < 0$, since $\Delta x > 0$ and demand slopes downward. More generally, ΔP and Δx must be of opposite signs, given downward-sloping demand.

2. The Lerner Index is named after Abba Lerner, who first proposed L = (P – MC)/P as a measure of monopoly power in the 1930s. The term *markup ratio* is often used in describing how much price is marked up over cost. As with any price-cost margin, this ratio depends on whether cost is marginal or average cost. Calculating the markup ratio also requires deciding whether price or cost is placed in the denominator of the ratio. In the present context, we use marginal cost in the numerator and price in the denominator in calculating this markup ratio.

3. We only examine barriers to entry in a passing fashion here. They are examined at length in industrial organization and regulation texts.

4. The x slider in the Excel version of Figure 15.4 allows you to vary x and see what happens to cost and revenue. ATC hits demand when x = 11.74. In this instance, TC(11.74) = \$506. If the same output is produced by two firms, each producing at x = 11.74/2 = 5.87, each firm has TC(5.87) = \$440, so having two equal-sized firms serve this market causes an increase in total cost of \$374 (\$374 = 2 · \$440 – \$506). The numerical analysis in this endnote assumes that the plant size shown produces each output level at minimum LAC, given that output level. If the plant size that produces 5.87 units at lowest cost is smaller, then there still would be a cost disadvantage from two firms, but it would be smaller than just calculated. To accomplish this more exact analysis, we would need the LAC curve as well as the SATC curves appropriate for both output levels (x = 11.74 and x = 5.87). This would produce an analysis similar to that shown in Figure 15.6.

5. For example, if the government-sanctioned monopolist at **M** in Figure 15.6 is allowed to set its own price, it would certainly exceed \$2/unit. This assertion is just a ballpark guess based on assuming that demand remains linear. If so, MR would have the same intercept and twice the slope, so it should intersect SMC at about x = 3.5. From here, go up to the extended demand curve to see that the price would be above \$2. Profits in this instance would be more than 100% of cost (since ATC would be less than \$1 in this instance). This is the kind of profit margin that would incur the regulatory wrath of public utility commissions. In Figure 15.6, MR and extended market demand are not shown in order to focus attention on cost curves. In the long run, such an unfettered monopolist would adjust plant size so as to equate MR = LMC (at about x = 3.25), thereby lowering total cost and raising price even further.

6. The short-run cost curves have not been included in this situation; qualitatively, they would look like the K4 plant size in Figure 11.14, since LAC is downward sloping at x = 4 in that figure.

7. The algebraic description of the demand curve that created Figures 15.11A–15.11F is unimportant to our discussion. The Excel file for Figures 15.10–15.13 provides qualitative sliders that can be adjusted to create your own scenario. (Equations and numbers controlling the sliders have been suppressed to maintain the geometric focus of this analysis.)

8. From a purely geometric point of view based on these figures, the former has to do with whether demand at MR = MC changes at less than the rate implied by the proportional change in Equation 15.3. If MR = MC at x > 200/N, the market is expanding (Outcomes A, B, and C); if the reverse holds true, the market is contracting (Outcome F). By contrast, given flat MC and linear demand, pricing power is completely controlled by whether the price intercept increases or decreases as N increases. If it increases, then pricing power increases (Outcomes A, D, and F); if the reverse holds true, pricing power declines (Outcome C).

Appendix:

An Algebraic Approach to Monopolistic Competition

In Chapter 15, we presented a geometric approach to monopolistic competition. A firm maximizes profit by setting MR = MC. At that output, profit is either positive or negative, depending on whether P > ATC or P < ATC at that output level in the short run. In the long run, these profit signals encourage entry or exit until zero profits remain because P = ATC at the same output level where MR = MC. Demand is tangent to ATC in this instance.

In the event that representative firm demand is linear and cost is quadratic, we can easily extend this geometric solution to an algebraic one. If demand is linear, then so is inverse demand, and inverse demand shows price (or marginal value) as a function of quantity sold. The only difference from inverse demand in Equation 15A.1 and Equation 12.7a is that p is lowercase as a reminder that this is price as viewed by an individual firm within the market. In the analysis to follow, we suppress the subscripts from various cost and demand functions that were present in the geometric analysis:

$$p(x) = b - m \cdot x. \quad \textbf{(15A.1)}$$

As shown in Section 12.2, given linear demand, then marginal revenue in this instance has the same intercept and twice the slope as inverse demand (Equation 12.11):

$$MR(x) = b - 2 \cdot m \cdot x. \quad \textbf{(15A.2)}$$

Quadratic cost is examined in Section 13.5, and the necessary equations are reproduced here (with different lettering):

$$ATC(x) = F/x + a + c \cdot x. \quad \textbf{(15A.3)}$$

$$MC(x) = a + 2 \cdot c \cdot x. \quad \textbf{(15A.4)}$$

Profit maximization requires finding the output level where MR = MC. Setting Equation 15A.2 equal to 15A.4 and solving for x, we obtain:

$$x^* = (b - a)/(2 \cdot m + 2 \cdot c). \quad \textbf{(15A.5)}$$

The profit rectangle in this instance is given by:

$$\pi^* = \pi(x^*) = (p(x^*) - ATC(x^*)) \cdot x^*. \quad \textbf{(15A.6)}$$

If $\pi^* > 0$, entry will occur, and if $\pi^* < 0$, exit will occur. This adjustment will alter demand as perceived by the representative firm. As noted in Section 15.6, the way that demand shifts is difficult to quantify due to the "differentiatedness" of the market. Entry makes representative firm demand more restrictive, and exit makes it expand.

Of course, two simple adjustments are possible, given linear demand. We could imagine entry or exit as shifting the intercept, b, down or up for fixed m. This would make demand more restrictive on entry or more expansive on exit. The same would happen if we adjust the slope, m, for fixed intercept. Both possibilities are examined in the examples that follow.

For each of the following examples, suppose that costs are given by:

$$TC(x) = 1200 + 12 \cdot x + 0.2 \cdot x^2. \quad \textbf{(15A.7)}$$

Two Short-Run Scenarios with Common Demand Intercept

Suppose further that inverse demand is given by:

$$p(x) = 72 - 0.4 \cdot x, \text{ based on } N_a \text{ firms in the market.} \quad \textbf{(15A.8a)}$$

Here, $x^* = 50$, according to Equation 15A.5, and $\pi^* = \pi(50) = (52 - 46) \cdot 50 = \$300$, so entry would occur. This scenario is shown in Panel A of Figure 15A.1.

Alternatively, suppose that demand is given by:

$p(x) = 72 - x$, based on N_b firms in the market. **(15A.8b)**

Here, $x^* = 25$, according to Equation 15A.5, and $\pi^* = \pi(25) = (47 - 65) \cdot 25 = -\$450$, so exit would occur. This scenario is shown in Panel B of Figure 15A.1.

Rotating Slope to Achieve LRMCE The only difference between these two short-run scenarios is the slope of inverse demand (based on $N_b > N_a$ firms in the market). There should be an intermediate number of firms in the market where profits are zero and the market is in LRMCE.

Suppose that entry or exit affects slope but not intercept of demand in this market. Assume that costs are unaffected by entry or exit. This intermediate inverse demand is given by:

$p(x) = 72 - m \cdot x$, based on N_{LRMCE} firms in the market. **(15A.8c)**

LRMCE would require two conditions (using Equation 15A.8c):

$72 - 2 \cdot m \cdot x = 12 + 0.4 \cdot x$ $\quad MR(x) = MC(x)$ **(15A.9a)**

$72 - m \cdot x = 1200/x + 12 + 0.2 \cdot x$ $\quad p(x) = ATC(x)$ **(15A.9b)**

Two equations in two unknowns can, in general, be solved. Solving for x and m, we obtain $x = 40$ and $m = 0.55$.[1] Checking our work, we see that, given these values of x and m, we have $MR(40) = MC(40) = \$28$, and $p(40) = ATC(40) = \$50$, as required by LRMCE. This is the scenario shown in Panel C of Figure 15A.1.

Two Short-Run Scenarios with Common Demand Slope

Had we instead assumed that entry or exit affects intercept but not slope, we could still solve for LRMCE. For example, suppose that short-run inverse demand was given by:

$p(x) = 87 - 0.55 \cdot x$, based on N_a firms in the market. **(15A.10a)**

Here, $x^* = 50$, according to Equation 15A.5, and $\pi^* = \pi(50) = (59.5 - 46) \cdot 50 = \$675$, so entry would occur. This is the scenario shown in Panel D of Figure 15A.1.

Alternatively, demand is given by:

$p(x) = 57 - 0.55 \cdot x$, based on N_b firms in the market. **(15A.10b)**

Here, $x^* = 30$, according to Equation 15A.5, and $\pi^* = \pi(30) = (40.5 - 58) \cdot 30 = -\$525$, so exit would occur. This scenario is shown in Panel E of Figure 15A.1.

Changing Intercept to Achieve LRMCE The only difference between these two short-run scenarios is the intercept of inverse demand (based on $N_e > N_d$ firms in the market). There should be an intermediate number of firms in the market where profits are zero and the market is in LRMCE. Suppose that entry or exit affects intercept but not slope of demand in this market. Assume that costs are unaffected by entry or exit. This intermediate inverse demand is given by:

$p(x) = b - 0.55 \cdot x$, based on N_{LRMCE} firms in the market. **(15A.10c)**

As before, LRMCE would require two conditions (using Equation 15A.10c):

$b - 1.1 \cdot x = 12 + 0.4 \cdot x$ $\quad MR(x) = MC(x)$ **(15A.11a)**

$b - 0.55 \cdot x = 1200/x + 12 + 0.2 \cdot x$ $\quad p(x) = ATC(x)$ **(15A.11b)**

Two equations in two unknowns can, in general, be solved. Solving for x and b, we obtain $x = 40$ and $b = 72$. Checking, we see that, given these values of x and m, we have $MR(40) = MC(40) = \$28$, and $p(40) = ATC(40) = \$50$. Once again, we have the scenario depicted by Panel C of Figure 15A.1.

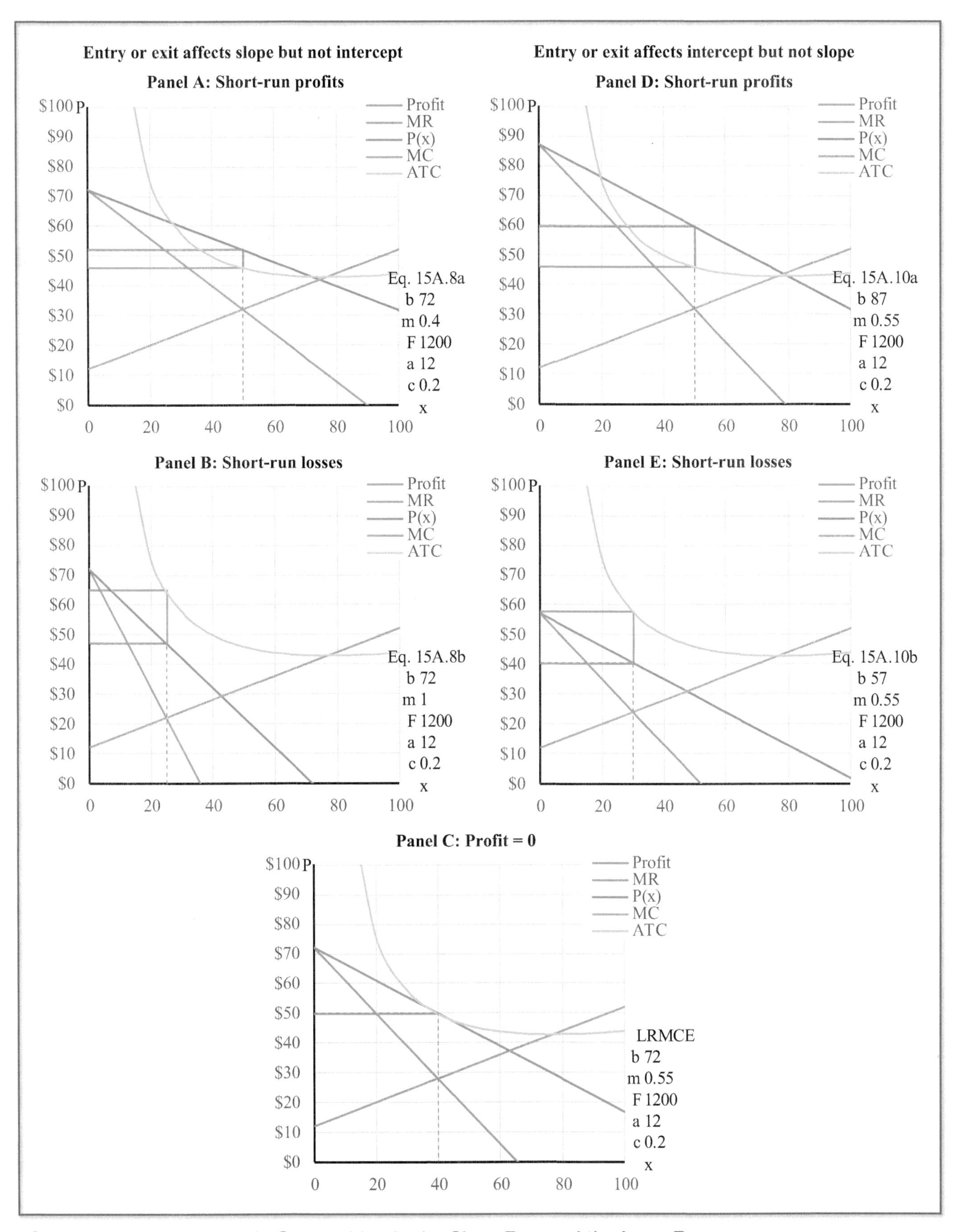

FIGURE 15A.1 Monopolistic Competition in the Short Run and the Long Run

Inverse demand: $p(x) = b - m \cdot x$, $TC(x) = F + a \cdot x + c \cdot x^2$

It is worth noting that the solutions obtained from the two ways that entry or exit affects demand (changing slope, using Equation 15A.8, and changing intercept, using Equation 15A.10) produced the same solution (shown in Panel C of Figure 15A.1). That is simply due to using the LRMCE slope of $m = 0.55$ that was the solution to Equation 15A.9 in Equation 15A.10 (or using the LRMCE intercept of $b = 72$ that was the solution to Equation 15A.11 in Equation 15A.8). Had we chosen a different slope in Equation 15A.10 or a different intercept in Equation 15A.8, the resulting solutions would not have x and p coincide in the two LRMCE situations.

Appendix Note

1. Algebra and Geometry Example 5 in the Mathematical Appendix (available in the online version of this text) describes one method of obtaining this solution if you are having difficulty solving for x and m yourself.

Welfare Economics

CHAPTER 16

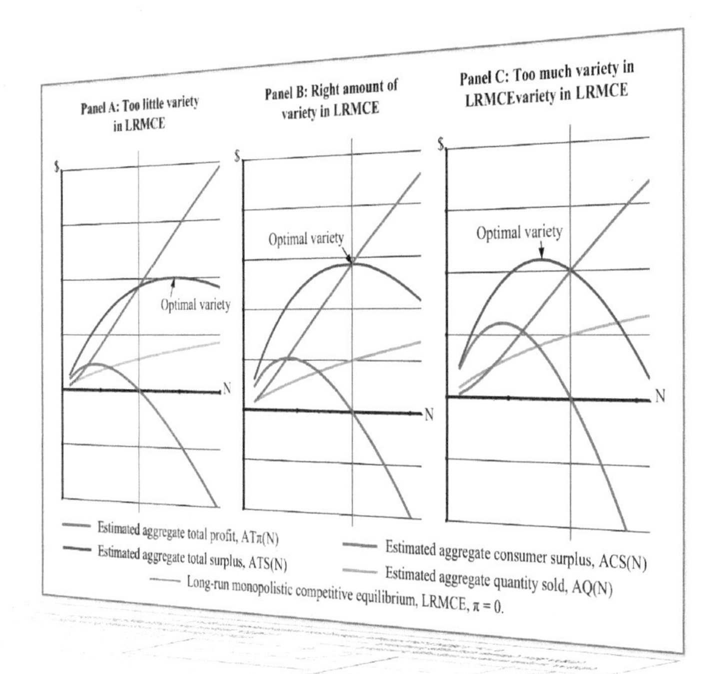

Chapter Outline

We now turn to the issue of measuring the benefits and costs associated with various market outcomes. Welfare economics involves measuring the net benefits involved when consumers and producers interact via the market. Consumers purchase goods and services because they perceive that the value of those goods and services exceeds what those goods and services cost. Similarly, firms produce units of output because they perceive that the revenue they will receive on sales of those units exceeds the cost of producing those units. In each case, there is an excess of benefit over cost that is created due to the voluntary action embodied in the market system. This chapter examines how these net benefits are measured and how they vary by market structure.

We start by examining the consumer side of the market interaction. In general, consumers purchase goods that provide more value than the price of the good. Consumer surplus—the excess of benefit over cost to the consumer—is the focus of Section 16.1. A similar measure on the producer side is examined in Section 16.2. Producer surplus is related to, but not the same as, profits because producer surplus does not include fixed cost. If we posit that consumer benefits and producer benefits should be treated equally, we can describe the total surplus to society as the sum of producer surplus and consumer surplus. Section 16.3 compares the total surplus to society from competition and monopoly. There are distributional differences between these two market structures, but monopoly also produces a deadweight loss (or allocative inefficiency) due to the output restrictiveness inherent in that market structure. Section 16.4 examines the problems that are introduced in measuring the welfare impact of entry in differentiated product markets. Consumers value variety, but variety or product heterogeneity comes at a price, and monopolistic competition does not necessarily produce the optimal mix of variety. The long-run monopolistically competitive equilibrium may have too much variety, too little variety, or the right amount of variety.

The first four sections of the chapter describe consumer welfare based on the demand diagram, but the demand diagram is not the starting place for consumer analysis; consumers most basically have preferences, and they choose bundles of goods based on the income they have and the prices they face. In Section 16.5, we examine the welfare impact on consumers of a price change, using preferences and consumption bundles. This allows us to consider two theoretically determined alternatives to change in consumer surplus on the basis of the demand decomposition examined in Chapter 8. Compensating variation holds welfare constant at the initial utility level, and equivalent variation holds welfare constant at the final utility level. In Section 16.6, we use Hicksian and Marshallian demand functions to tie together the concepts of compensating variation, equivalent variation, and change in consumer surplus. The demand diagram allows us to describe conditions under which all three measures are the same, as well as what happens when this is not the case. We conclude with an analysis of the three measures, given Cobb-Douglas preferences. In this setting, we are able to describe conditions for which consumer surplus can be used as a proxy for compensating variation or equivalent variation.

16.1 Measuring Consumer Surplus from Using the Market System

Benefits accrue to both consumers and producers, due to the voluntary exchange that occurs via the market system. A consumer buys goods for a price that, in general, is below what the good is worth to that consumer. Similarly, a firm sells goods for a benefit that, in general, is above what the good cost the firm to produce. Were this not the case, one side or the other (or both) would not voluntarily enter into the exchange. Voluntary behavior is the cornerstone of market exchange; coercion is not part of the interaction (despite protestations to the contrary when you think your local gasoline station is charging too much). The value generated by market exchange is the subject of our current analysis.

The individual consumer demand curve provides information about a consumer's valuation of various numbers of units of a good. Demand is conceived as quantity as a function of price, but if we take the reverse orientation, then we can describe price as a function of quantity. As noted in Chapters 2 and 12, the price as a function of quantity orientation of demand is called inverse demand, as well as a marginal valuation schedule. *Inverse demand tells us the value in dollar terms that an individual places on the* x*th unit of output.* Since demand is downward sloping, the consumer need not pay the entire marginal valuation on each unit consumed; the consumer only needs to pay the price of the product on each unit consumed. Indeed, the individual consumer determines how many units to demand by finding that output level where marginal valuation matches market price, P_0. This consumption choice can be described in two ways. If the consumer decides to purchase x_0 units of output, that is because

$x(P_0) = x_0$, where $x(P)$ is the individual's demand for the good, and **(16.1a)**

$P(x_0) = P_0$, where $P(x)$ is the individual's inverse demand for the good. **(16.1b)**

As a result, only the marginal unit consumed (the x_0th unit) is valued at P_0. All prior units are valued more highly. This excess of benefit attained from consumption over cost of that consumption is called **consumer surplus (CS)**. (Some authors emphasize the possessive nature of the surplus by calling this *consumer's surplus*. We refrain from adding the "'s" to the term.)

consumer surplus (CS): The excess of what the consumer would have paid over what the consumer had to pay for a good is the consumer surplus of that good.

Consumer Surplus for Discrete Goods

Consumer surplus simply provides a dollar measure of the gain from using the market system. The easiest way to understand consumer surplus is to consider a good that is consumed in discrete numbers of units. As a result, consider your demand for coffee during finals. (If you are one of those rare individuals who does not use coffee during finals, then bear with this example; just like peanut butter and jelly sandwiches, sometimes you just have to pretend.)

That first cup of coffee is worth a lot during finals. Suppose you would have been willing to pay $5 for it, but you are able to obtain it for $2.50 at your favorite coffee bar. The excess of benefit over cost is $2.50; that is, the consumer surplus on that first cup is $2.50. At that price, you might even buy a second cup, and a third. To describe your actual behavior, we need a more general description of your demand for coffee. Assume that your demand for coffee can be given by the equation:

$N(P) = \text{Integer}(25/P^2)$, where N is the number of cups you demand. **(16.2a)**

The integer function is used in Section 5.6 during our discussion of discrete goods. The N should remind you that this is a discrete good. Inverse demand is given by:

$P(N) = 5/N^{0.5}$. **(16.2b)**

Inverse demand provides the marginal valuation of each cup of coffee. As noted earlier, P(1) = $5. Since you probably cannot take square roots and invert them in your head, a table of values of P(N) is provided with Figure 16.1 for the first 27 cups of coffee you drink in a day. (If you drink more than 27 cups of coffee, you should have your head, and certainly your stomach, examined!)

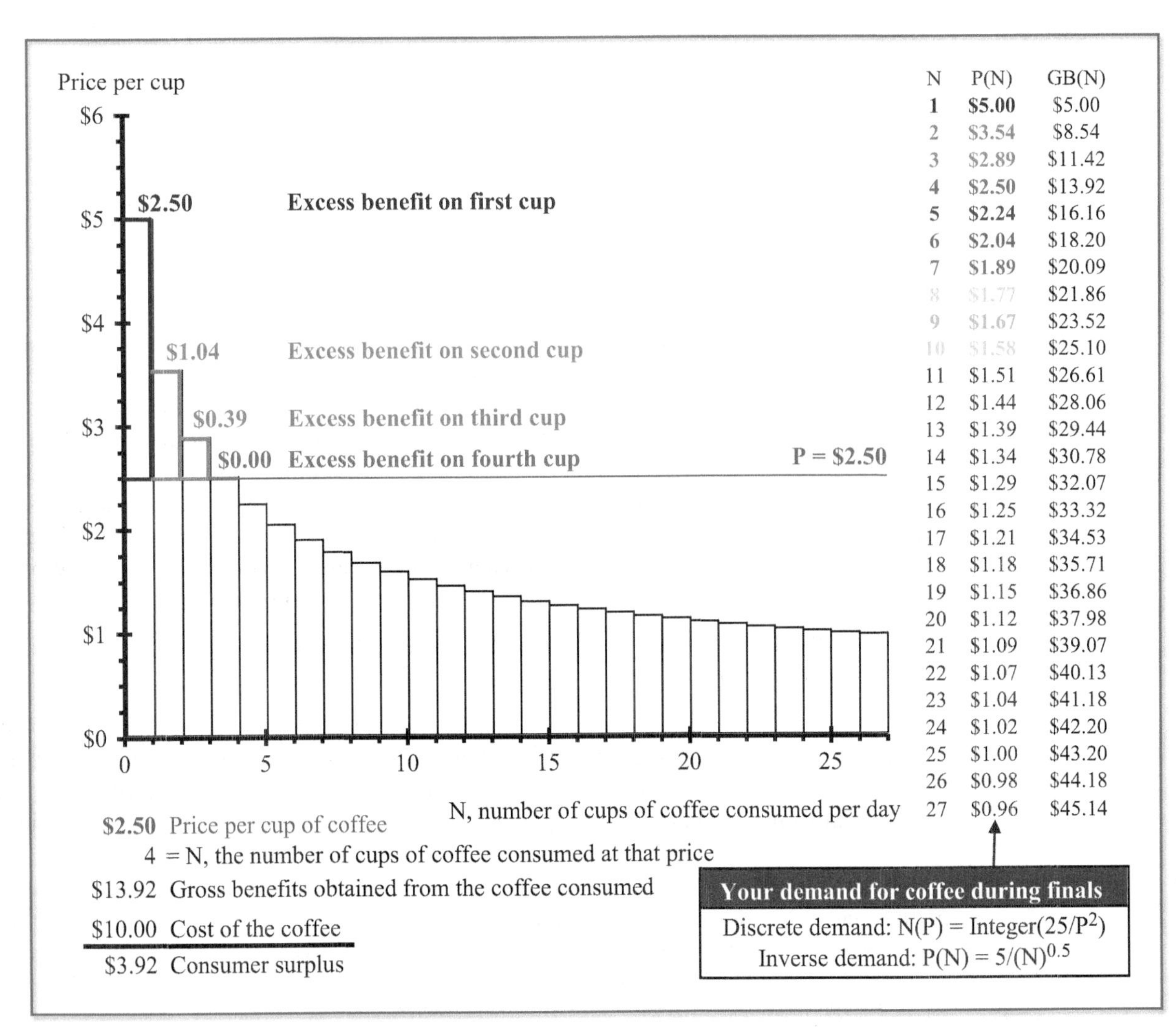

N	P(N)	GB(N)
1	$5.00	$5.00
2	$3.54	$8.54
3	$2.89	$11.42
4	$2.50	$13.92
5	$2.24	$16.16
6	$2.04	$18.20
7	$1.89	$20.09
8	$1.77	$21.86
9	$1.67	$23.52
10	$1.58	$25.10
11	$1.51	$26.61
12	$1.44	$28.06
13	$1.39	$29.44
14	$1.34	$30.78
15	$1.29	$32.07
16	$1.25	$33.32
17	$1.21	$34.53
18	$1.18	$35.71
19	$1.15	$36.86
20	$1.12	$37.98
21	$1.09	$39.07
22	$1.07	$40.13
23	$1.04	$41.18
24	$1.02	$42.20
25	$1.00	$43.20
26	$0.98	$44.18
27	$0.96	$45.14

FIGURE 16.1 Calculating Consumer Surplus for a Discrete Good

Given demand described in Equation 16.2 and depicted in Figure 16.1, you would consume four cups of coffee per day when P = \$2.50. The daily consumer surplus you attain in this instance is CS(\$2.50) = \$3.92 = \$2.50 + \$1.04 + \$0.39 + \$0.00. (The sum appears to be one penny off, due to rounding of intermediate surpluses.) Each of the first three cups provides an excess of benefit over cost, and the fourth has benefit equaling cost (since $P(4) = 5/(4)^{0.5} = 2.5$, using Equation 16.2b). Notice that we have discussed consumer surplus as the surplus involved in consuming multiple units of the good. This surplus is simply the sum of individual surpluses on each of the units consumed. Consumer surplus can also be obtained from the gross benefit column in the table as well. The **gross benefit of consuming N units of output (GB(N))** is the sum of marginal valuations of the first N units of output. Algebraically, the gross benefit is given by the equation:

gross benefit of consuming N units of output (GB(N)): The gross benefit of consuming N units of output is the sum of marginal valuations of the first N units of output.

$$GB(N) = P(1) + \ldots + P(N). \quad \textbf{(16.3)}$$

Consumer surplus is the excess of gross benefits over the cost of the goods consumed. If the N = N(P) units consumed cost P per unit, then consumer surplus at a price of P is given by:

$$CS(P) = GB(N(P)) - P \cdot N(P). \quad \textbf{(16.4)}$$

Applying this equation to the four cups of coffee consumed when the price is \$2.50 per cup is CS(\$2.50) = \$3.92 = \$13.92 – 4 · \$2.50, the same number determined earlier, based on the sum of your individual surpluses on each of the four units.

To crystallize your understanding of consumer surplus, consider what would happen to consumer surplus if price had been one cent more or less than \$2.50.

Q1a. What is the consumer surplus if the price is \$2.51 or \$2.49?*

Although Q1a asked for a consumer surplus answer, the calculation of that answer (in the footnote) used the change in consumer surplus caused by the price change. Economists find this information particularly useful because it avoids placing emphasis on valuing the initial units of output. (One has an intuitive feeling that the marginal valuation on initial units of output is subject to more speculation than is marginal valuation closer to the amount actually consumed.) For coffee drinkers, coffee provides a good example of such a first-unit issue. But the same could be said of movie aficionados: What is the value of the *first* movie to a person who goes to 15 movies a month (that is, if the person is restricted to only one movie per month)? Most moviegoers would have more difficulty describing the value of the first movie than describing the value of the thirteenth, fourteenth, fifteenth, or sixteenth movie in a month.[1] The change in consumer surplus for coffee from the one-cent price increase was a loss of three cents, and from the one-cent price decrease was a gain in consumer surplus of four cents. Of course, changes of one cent are not very interesting to coffee drinkers. Consider instead what would happen if your favorite coffee bar took pity on students during finals and dropped the price to \$2.00 per cup.

Q1b. What is the change in consumer surplus, ΔCS, if the price drops from \$2.50 to \$2.00 per cup?†

The change in consumer surplus can be calculated in a number of ways, given the available information. Equation 16.2a tells us that N = 6, given P = \$2.00 (since 6 = Integer(25/4)). This can also be seen using the P(N) column in Figure 16.1. The lowest marginal valuation that is at least \$2.00 is the sixth cup of coffee. The first four cups have

---

***Q1a answer:** If price increases to \$2.51, then consumer surplus declines by three cents to \$3.89; this represents a loss of one cent on each of the three cups that would be consumed in this instance. By contrast, if the price declines to \$2.49, then consumer surplus increases by four cents to \$3.96, since there is a gain of one cent on each of the four cups consumed in this instance.

†**Q1b answer:** The change in consumer surplus is ΔCS = \$2.28 in this instance (see next paragraph for details). The Excel file for Figure 16.1 allows you to move price in \$0.01 increments from \$6 to \$1.

an increase in consumer surplus of \$0.50 per cup, the fifth cup has an excess benefit over cost of \$0.24, and the sixth cup has an excess benefit over cost of \$0.04. Therefore, the change in consumer surplus is

$$\Delta CS = \$2.28 = 4 \cdot \$0.50 + \$0.24 + \$0.04. \quad \textbf{(16.5a)}$$

This answer could also have been attained using Equation 16.4, since the consumer surplus at a price of \$2.00 is CS(\$2.00) = GB(6) – 6 · \$2.00 = \$18.20 – \$12.00 = \$6.20. But CS at a price of \$2.50 was calculated previously to be \$3.92; therefore, the change in consumer surplus implied by the price decrease is:

$$\Delta CS = \$2.28 = CS(\$2.00) - CS(\$2.50) = \$6.20 - \$3.92. \quad \textbf{(16.5b)}$$

Consumer Surplus for Continuous Goods

Although consumer surplus has a more heuristic basis when viewed from the discrete demand perspective, the same concept applies to continuous goods. With continuous demand, the calculations are easier because we can calculate areas without having to add vertical pieces one unit at a time. And, of course, the continuous version acts as an approximation for the discrete version, even if demand can only be purchased in discrete quantities. For example, we obtain a continuous version of demand by removing the integer function from Equation 16.2a. The result is the demand function:

$$x(P) = 25/P^2. \quad \textbf{(16.6a)}$$

Inverse demand is the same as in the discrete case, with N replaced by x:

$$P(x) = 5/x^{0.5}. \quad \textbf{(16.6b)}$$

Consumer surplus can be calculated in two ways. One utilizes the definition of consumer surplus as the area underneath demand but above price. This method takes a quantity orientation (although it is formally a function of price, since the number of units consumed depends on the price the consumer faces).

$$CS(P) = GB(x(P)) - P \cdot x(P). \quad \textbf{(16.7a)}$$

This is the continuous function analog to Equation 16.4. An alternative method calculates consumer surplus using a price orientation in more direct fashion by noting that this same area can be described as the area behind the demand curve above price:

$$CS(P^*) = \text{Area behind the demand function } x(P) \text{ from } P = \infty \text{ to } P = P^*. \quad \textbf{(16.7b)}$$

When demand is linear, the consumer surplus calculation is easy because it simply requires that we calculate the area of a triangle. For nonlinear demand functions, we cannot provide a more explicit description of consumer surplus without resorting to calculus.[2]

Given a demand function, we can calculate consumer surplus using both of these methodologies. Given the demand function in Equation 16.6, Equation 16.7b leads to a functional description of consumer surplus as:[3]

$$CS(P) = 25/P. \quad \textbf{(16.7c)}$$

Given this demand function, we also know that the gross benefit of x units of the good is:[4]

$$GB(x) = 10 \cdot x^{0.5}. \quad \textbf{(16.7d)}$$

Figure 16.2 shows this demand function and suggests that at a price of \$2.00 per cup, the individual will consume $25/2^2 = 25/4 = 6.25$ cups of coffee; if partial cups can be purchased, then the individual will consume at the red diamond point (6.25, \$2.00) in the figure. These 6.25 cups cost \$12.50 = 6.25 · \$2.00 but produce a gross benefit of \$25.00 (using Equation 16.7d), so Equation 16.7a suggests that the consumer surplus associated with this consumption bundle is:

$$CS(\$2.00) = \$12.50 = GB(x(\$2.00)) - \$2.00 \cdot x(\$2.00) = \$25.00 - \$12.50. \quad \textbf{(16.8a)}$$

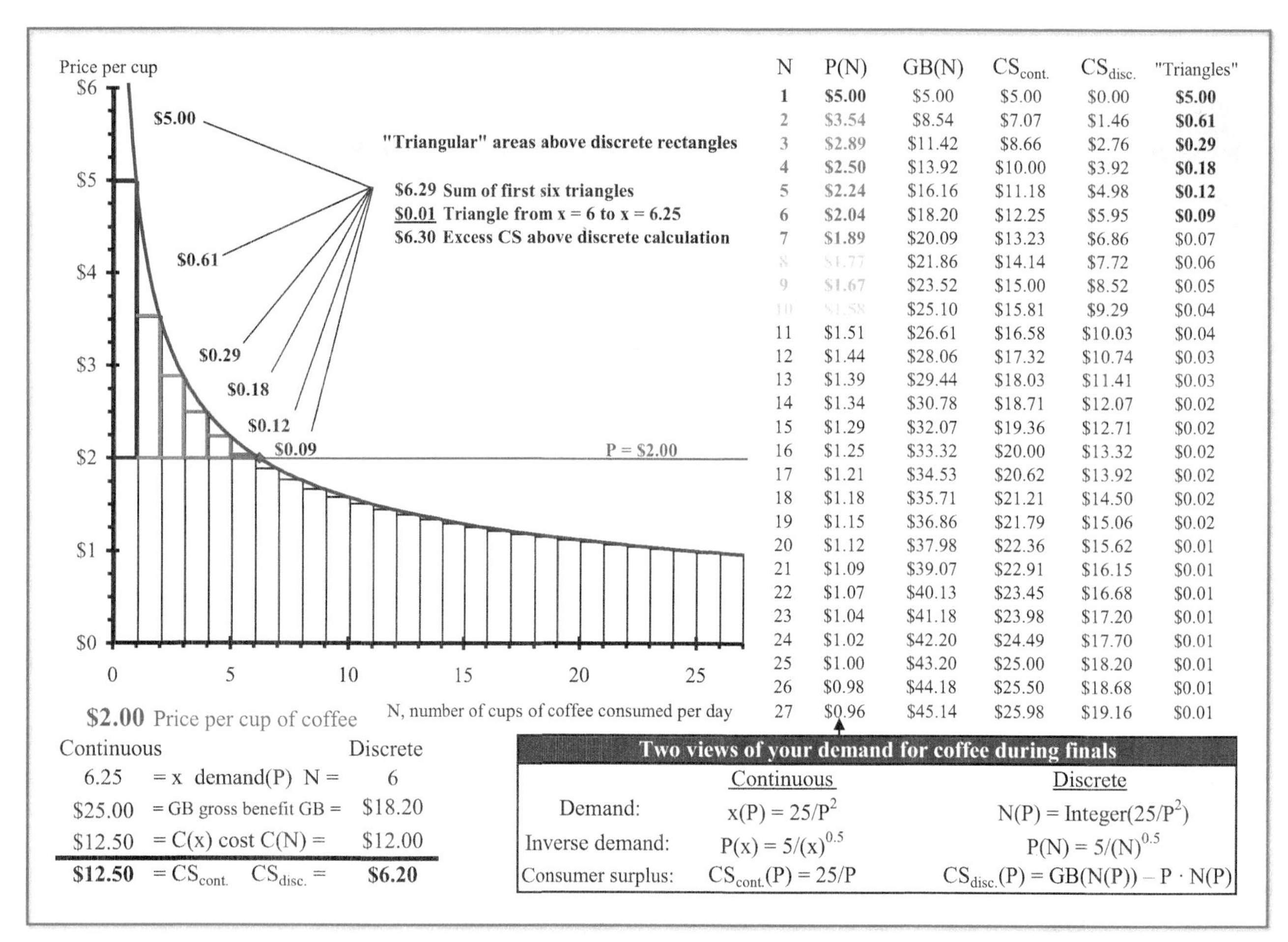

N	P(N)	GB(N)	$CS_{cont.}$	$CS_{disc.}$	"Triangles"
1	**$5.00**	$5.00	$5.00	$0.00	**$5.00**
2	$3.54	$8.54	$7.07	$1.46	**$0.61**
3	$2.89	$11.42	$8.66	$2.76	**$0.29**
4	$2.50	$13.92	$10.00	$3.92	**$0.18**
5	$2.24	$16.16	$11.18	$4.98	**$0.12**
6	$2.04	$18.20	$12.25	$5.95	**$0.09**
7	$1.89	$20.09	$13.23	$6.86	$0.07
8	$1.77	$21.86	$14.14	$7.72	$0.06
9	$1.67	$23.52	$15.00	$8.52	$0.05
10	$1.58	$25.10	$15.81	$9.29	$0.04
11	$1.51	$26.61	$16.58	$10.03	$0.04
12	$1.44	$28.06	$17.32	$10.74	$0.03
13	$1.39	$29.44	$18.03	$11.41	$0.03
14	$1.34	$30.78	$18.71	$12.07	$0.02
15	$1.29	$32.07	$19.36	$12.71	$0.02
16	$1.25	$33.32	$20.00	$13.32	$0.02
17	$1.21	$34.53	$20.62	$13.92	$0.02
18	$1.18	$35.71	$21.21	$14.50	$0.02
19	$1.15	$36.86	$21.79	$15.06	$0.02
20	$1.12	$37.98	$22.36	$15.62	$0.01
21	$1.09	$39.07	$22.91	$16.15	$0.01
22	$1.07	$40.13	$23.45	$16.68	$0.01
23	$1.04	$41.18	$23.98	$17.20	$0.01
24	$1.02	$42.20	$24.49	$17.70	$0.01
25	$1.00	$43.20	$25.00	$18.20	$0.01
26	$0.98	$44.18	$25.50	$18.68	$0.01
27	$0.96	$45.14	$25.98	$19.16	$0.01

Continuous		Discrete
6.25	= x demand(P) N =	6
$25.00	= GB gross benefit GB =	$18.20
$12.50	= C(x) cost C(N) =	$12.00
$12.50	= $CS_{cont.}$ $CS_{disc.}$ =	**$6.20**

	Continuous	Discrete
Demand:	$x(P) = 25/P^2$	$N(P) = \text{Integer}(25/P^2)$
Inverse demand:	$P(x) = 5/(x)^{0.5}$	$P(N) = 5/(N)^{0.5}$
Consumer surplus:	$CS_{cont.}(P) = 25/P$	$CS_{disc.}(P) = GB(N(P)) - P \cdot N(P)$

FIGURE 16.2 Comparing Continuous Consumer Surplus with Discrete Consumer Surplus

Alternatively, we can use the demand function in Equation 16.6 and calculate consumer surplus as the area behind the demand curve, as suggested by Equation 16.7c:

$$CS(\$2.00) = 25/\$2.00 = \$12.50. \quad \textbf{(16.8b)}$$

Not surprisingly, both calculations provide the same dollar answer to the consumer surplus at a price of $2.00.

The continuous demand curve coincides with the discrete version at each integer output level. If x is not an integer, the discrete demand step function lies beneath the continuous demand curve. As a result, continuous consumer surplus at a given price will be greater than the discrete version because of a series of right "triangle" areas in Figure 16.2 where the hypotenuse in each triangle is a curve, rather than a line. The size of each area is separately provided for each triangle to show the location of the "extra" surplus. We calculated earlier that $CS_{discrete}(\$2.00) = \$6.20$. Equation 16.8 shows that $CS_{continuous}(\$2.00) = \$12.50$, so it is worthwhile to note where the extra $6.30 is distributed. Five dollars of it is the "infinitely high triangle" above the first unit of the discrete demand step function (the base of this triangle starts at a height of P(1) = $5.00). The remaining $1.30 is distributed as shown in Figure 16.2. Notice that these triangles become more and more insignificant in size as x increases (and as P decreases). This can be seen both visually and using the "triangle" column in the table (the first six entries have been highlighted in green, since they form $6.29 of the $6.30 difference between the two measures of consumer surplus). A moment's reflection should provide an answer to why the yellow highlighted CS values in Figure 16.2 differ from the values $12.50 and $6.20 we have been discussing. The values $12.25 and $5.95 are based on a price of P(6) = $2.04, rather than $2.00.

Change in consumer surplus is easy to calculate, based on the continuous demand function. Consider a change from P = $2.50 to $2.00, the same change in price examined in Q1b earlier. We saw that $\Delta CS_{discrete} = \$2.28$ for the reasons we outlined in discussing Equation 16.5. Given a general consumer surplus equation, we can calculate the change in consumer surplus implied by a price change as:

$$\Delta CS_{continuous} = CS(P_1) - CS(P_0). \tag{16.9a}$$

Given the specific demand function in Equation 16.6 and the consumer surplus equation for this demand function described in Equation 16.7c, we see the change in consumer surplus implied by changing price from $P_0 = \$2.50$ to $P_1 = \$2.00$:

$$\Delta CS_{continuous} = 25/\$2.00 - 25/\$2.50 = \$12.50 - \$10.00 = \$2.50. \tag{16.9b}$$

These estimates differ by twenty-two cents. Twelve cents of this is the size of the fifth "triangle," nine cents of this is the size of the sixth "triangle," and one cent is the "triangle" from x = 6.00 to x = 6.25.

Consumer Surplus with Linear Demand

One goal of this chapter is to compare market structures in terms of social net benefits—benefits that cumulatively accrue to consumers and producers under various market settings. These comparisons can be accomplished with nonlinear demand and cost curves, but they are more easily made with linear demand and cost curves. The qualitative results do not change, and the geometry and algebra are much simpler, since the areas involved are rectangles and triangles, rather than nonlinear forms. As a result, it is worthwhile to focus on CS and ΔCS, given linear demand.

Figure 16.3 examines consumer surplus, given linear demand. This figure focuses on two prices: \$5 and \$2. Figure 16.3A depicts the change in consumer surplus, ΔCS, inherent in moving between these two prices. Quantities demanded at those two prices are denoted by **s** and **t** in both Figures 16.3A and 16.3B. Figure 16.3B relabels the ΔCS trapezoid as a rectangle and a triangle, **B** + **C**, and adds other area markers so that we can more easily discuss the meaning of various areas below. Neither \$5 nor \$2 should be considered first and the other second on an *a priori* basis. If \$5 is first, then ΔCS is positive, since a price decrease is being analyzed, and if \$2 is first, then ΔCS is negative, since a price increase is being analyzed. Consider the following questions:

Q3a. What is the slope and intercept of the demand curve depicted in Figure 16.3?

Q3b. What is the dollar size of ΔCS?*

Consider a price decrease from \$5 to \$2. The \$51 ΔCS area was geometrically split into two parts, **B** and **C**, as noted earlier. This separation into a rectangle and triangle occurs for theoretical as well as practical reasons. Areas **B** and **C** represent different aspects of the gain to the consumer due to the price decrease. Area **B** represents the gain on units that the consumer was willing to purchase at a price of \$5. At a price of \$5, the consumer was already buying 14 units of output because each of those units had marginal valuation that was at least \$5. Area **B** represents pure windfall gain to the consumer, since the consumer continues to purchase those units, albeit at a lower price. The noneconomist might well use this as a measure of the net benefit of the price decrease. As we see graphically, the consumer actually gains more; that is, the consumer also gains area **C**. Area **C** represents the gain on units of the good that the individual did not value highly enough to purchase at \$5 but that the person would purchase at a price of \$2. These are the units from $14 < x \leq 20$ that have $\$5 < P(x) \leq \$2$. The gross benefit on these units is **C** + **E**, but the cost of these units is **E**, so **C** represents the excess of benefit over cost—that is, the consumer surplus on those units when the price is \$2. Consumers gain in two ways due to a price decrease. First, they gain on units they were willing to purchase at the higher price. Second, they gain on units whose value was not high enough that they were willing to purchase at the higher price but are willing to purchase at the lower price.

***Q3 answer:** The slope is –0.5, and the P intercept is \$12. ΔCS = \$51, a quantity that can be most easily attained by separately calculating the area **B** = \$42 = \$3 · 14, and area **C** = \$9 = \$3 · 6/2.

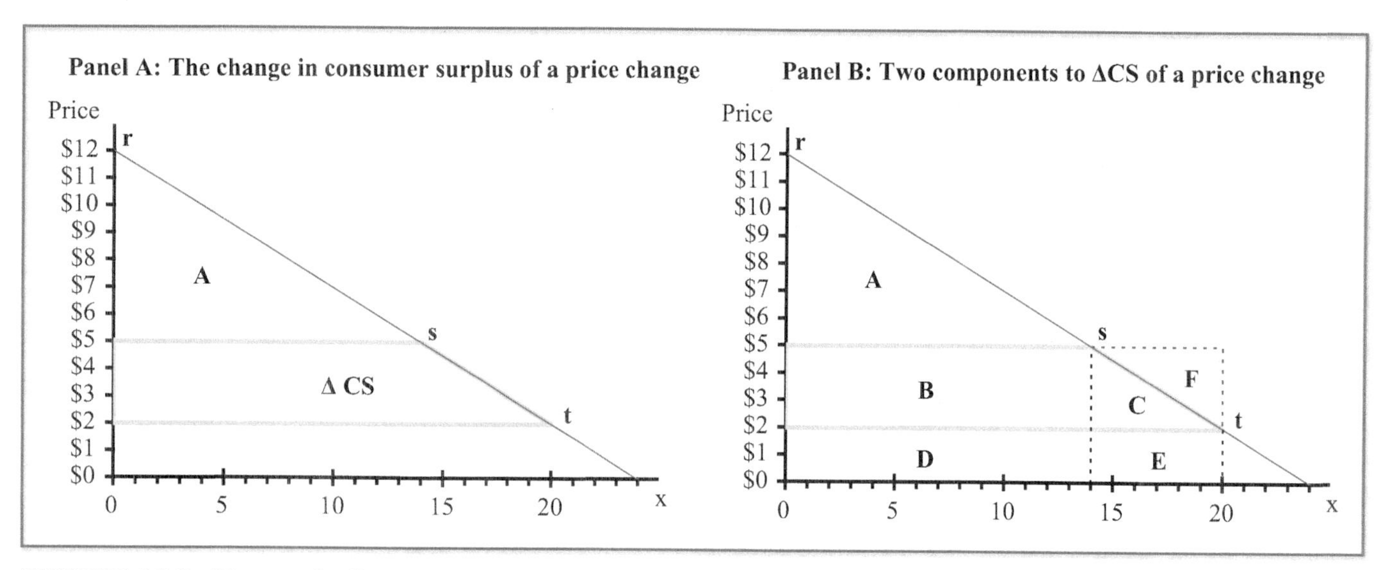

FIGURE 16.3 Change in Consumer Surplus, Given Linear Demand

The change in consumer surplus of a price increase from \$2 to \$5 is simply –ΔCS in Figure 16.3A. This loss also can be thought of in terms of the areas depicted in Figure 16.3B. If the individual maintained consumption of x = 20 in the face of the \$3 price increase, the cost incurred would be represented by area **B** + **C** + **F** = \$60. This is not a measure of the net consumer loss because some of the 20 units of consumption the consumer willingly consumed at a price of \$2 would not be consumed at a price of \$5.[5] These are the units from **t** to **s** on the demand curve whose marginal valuations do not match the new higher price of \$5. In terms of areas, these 6 units (whose x values are $14 < x \leq 20$) have gross benefit of areas **C** + **E**, but at a price of \$5 per unit, they would cost **F** + **C** + **E**. Therefore, these units would not be purchased, given the increase in price. The loss in consumer surplus on these units due to the price increase is the excess of value over cost that was incurred at the price of \$2 (represented by area **C**). We must add to this the loss of \$3 per unit on those units that will still be purchased at the higher price. This is represented by a loss of area **B**. Consumers lose in two ways due to a price increase. First, consumers lose on units they are still willing to purchase at the higher price. Second, consumers lose on units they did not value highly enough to purchase at the higher price, although they are willing to purchase them at the lower price.

As the slope or intercept of the demand curve changes, or as initial or final price changes, so will the numerical values associated with ΔCS. Nonetheless, the same calculation will produce the ΔCS dollar value. If demand is nonlinear, then the calculation becomes more complex, but the same qualitative relation holds. The change in consumer surplus is composed of two parts. The first net benefit accrues on units that will be purchased under both prices (area **B**). The second net benefit accrues on units that will be purchased under the lower price but not under the higher (area **C**).

The analysis of consumer surplus thus far has focused on the net benefit to an individual consumer. As we aggregate across consumers, we can simply add consumer surpluses to obtain an aggregate measure of consumer surplus. The reason this works is simple and is based on the area behind the demand curve conceptualization of consumer surplus described by Equation 16.7b. Market demand is simply the horizontal sum of individual consumer demands, and therefore, the area behind market demand is simply the sum of areas behind individual demand curves. Simply put, aggregate consumer surplus is the sum of individual consumer surpluses. Similarly, change in consumer surplus can be summed across consumers to determine aggregate change in consumer surplus. We could formally call this consumer*s* surplus, but we refrain from adding the "*s*" to distinguish the aggregate CS from individual CS because the context will make clear whether a market or individual CS is being determined.[6]

16.2 Measuring Producer Surplus from Using the Market System

Consumer surplus is a dollar-based measure of consumer net benefit from using a market system. The remarkable aspect of this measure is that consumer behavior is predicated on doing as well as possible, given the individual's preferences and subject to that individual's budget constraint. The *only* part of the consumer optimization process that is based on dollars is the budget constraint. Nonetheless, the consumer optimization process leads to demand curves that can be used to provide a dollar-denominated measure of consumer net benefits. On the firm side, the analysis is more direct because we have assumed from the start that the goal for firms is to maximize profits, and profits are already delineated in dollars.

Producer Surplus versus Profits

Profits are the gold-star measure of the firm's health. Producer surplus is an even easier dollar measure of how well a firm is doing in the market. **Producer surplus (PS)** is the excess of revenue over the variable cost of producing a given level of output. Algebraically,

producer surplus (PS): Producer surplus is the excess of revenue over the variable cost of producing a given level of output.

$$PS = TR - VC. \quad \textbf{(16.10a)}$$

Producer surplus is the excess of benefit over the cost of producing the good. The cost involved in this definition is variable rather than total because producer surplus focuses attention on those aspects of firm behavior that the firm can adjust over the short run. Obviously, producer surplus is related to profits, since $\pi = TR - TC = TR - VC - FC$. Regrouping results in an alternative definition of producer surplus:

$$PS = \pi + FC. \quad \textbf{(16.10b)}$$

Equation 16.10b provides the direct relation between producer surplus and profits. These two measures of producer welfare differ by fixed cost, an amount of money that is fixed in the short run. Put another way, if we maximize producer surplus, we also maximize profits, and if we maximize profits, then we maximize producer surplus. Each can act as a proxy for the other.

Students often wonder why we need two definitions of firm net benefit. Since we already know profits, why not simply work from this version of firm net benefit? There are both practical and theoretical reasons for considering PS rather than π. At a practical level, producer surplus is easier to visualize than profits (since it does not require information about ATC or FC). At a theoretical level, the only decision variables the firm should consider in the short run are those that it can affect. Therefore, there is no need to focus on fixed cost in the short run. The short-run question concerns whether revenues cover variable cost: *If revenues cover variable cost, $PS \geq 0$, and the firm should not shut down.* As we argue in Section 13.3 (and in Section 15.2), the firm should produce at a loss in the short run as long as variable costs are covered because, to the extent that $PS > 0$, fixed costs are also being at least partially covered. To not produce in this instance causes greater loss, since the firm must continue to pay its fixed cost in the short run. As a result, producer surplus is the appropriate measure of firm net benefit in the short run.

Three Views of Producer Surplus

The producer surplus attained by producing x units of output and selling them for a price of P per unit can be seen in three ways, based on average variable cost and marginal cost curves. Figure 16.4 shows one such possibility, where (x, P) = (9, \$40). At this output level, we have two further pieces of information: MC(9) = \$29, and AVC(9) = \$11. Given this, answer the following four questions:

Q4a. If this represents a profit-maximizing output level, what kind of market structure is it—perfectly competitive or imperfectly competitive?

Q4b. Will the firm shut down in the short run, regardless of market structure and size of fixed cost in this situation?

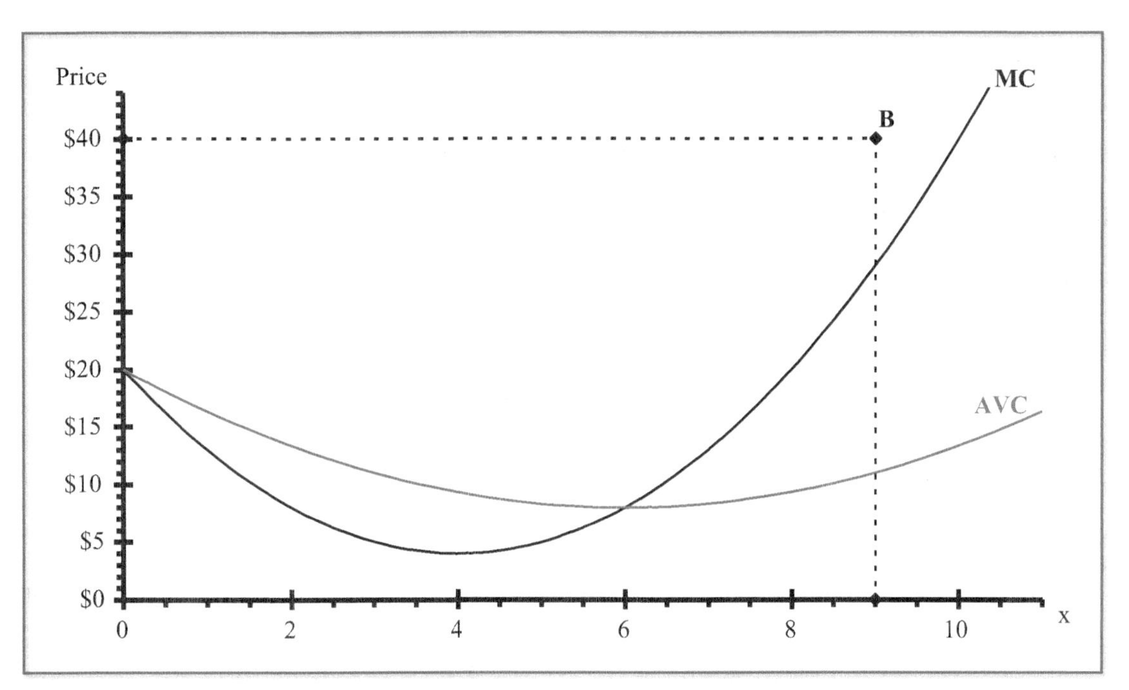

FIGURE 16.4 Calculating Producer Surplus from a Diagram: Given (x, P) = (9, \$40), MC(9) = \$29, and AVC(9) = \$11

Q4c. What is the dollar value of producer surplus implied by this figure?

Q4d. What are the profits implied by this figure?*

The diagrammatic setup in Figure 16.4 does not explicitly describe the market structure in which the firm is embedded. If this outcome is profit maximizing, then we know that it is imperfectly competitive because $P > MC$ (the condition that holds for all imperfectly competitive structures, according to Section 15.1). Were the market perfectly competitive, then this situation would imply that the firm is not producing the profit-maximizing level of output (indeed, the marginal cost curve shown has MC(10) = \$40).

Without further information about the marginal cost function (and knowledge of calculus), if you answered Q4c without looking at the answer, you did it by calculating variable cost as $x \cdot AVC(x)$. This is only one of three methods to accomplish this calculation, but it is not the one that provides a geometric interpretation of PS that is analogous to the CS described in the previous section. Before we examine the other two versions of PS, it is worth noting why we need not worry about whether profits are positive or negative in this situation. Here, PS = \$261, signifying that revenue exceeds short-run variable cost of production by \$261. If fixed cost is less than \$261, then the firm earns a short-run profit; if the reverse holds true, the firm earns a short-run loss. In either event, the firm will continue to produce in the short run because doing so produces \$261 more than not doing so (*\$261 is the producer surplus of producing*). All that matters in the short run is whether variable costs are covered, and in this situation, they are covered. They always will be as long as $P \geq AVC$ at the output level chosen. Certainly this will occur whenever $P \geq MC$ and $MC \geq AVC$, the condition that is shown in Figure 16.4.

Producer surplus is total revenue minus variable cost. Given a (quantity, price) combination, total revenue is the quantity (x) by price (P) rectangle whose opposing vertices are **B** and the origin (or **ABJo** in Figure 16.5). There are three ways to describe variable cost. Figure 16.5A depicts the AVC(x) by x rectangle method of calculating VC used to

***Q4 answer:** If x = 9 is profit maximizing, then we know that $P > MC$. As a result, we know that the market is imperfectly competitive. Regardless of market structure, the firm will produce in the short run because $P > AVC$, so variable costs are covered. $PS = TR - VC = 9 \cdot \$40 - 9 \cdot \$11 = \$261$. Profits cannot be determined, since we do not know the size of fixed cost in this instance.

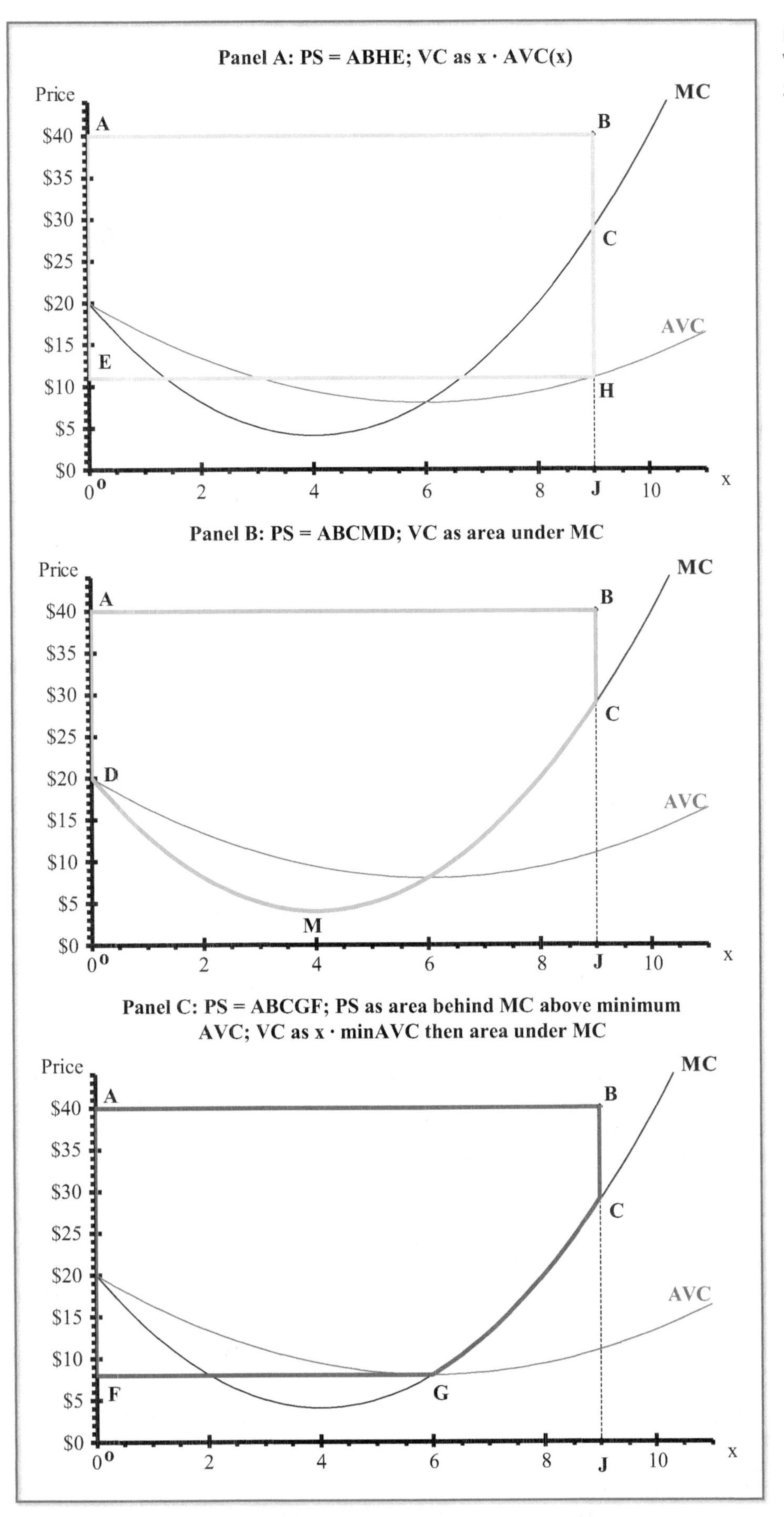

FIGURE 16.5 Three Views of Producer Surplus

FIGURE 16.6 Three Views of Producer Surplus for a Competitive Firm

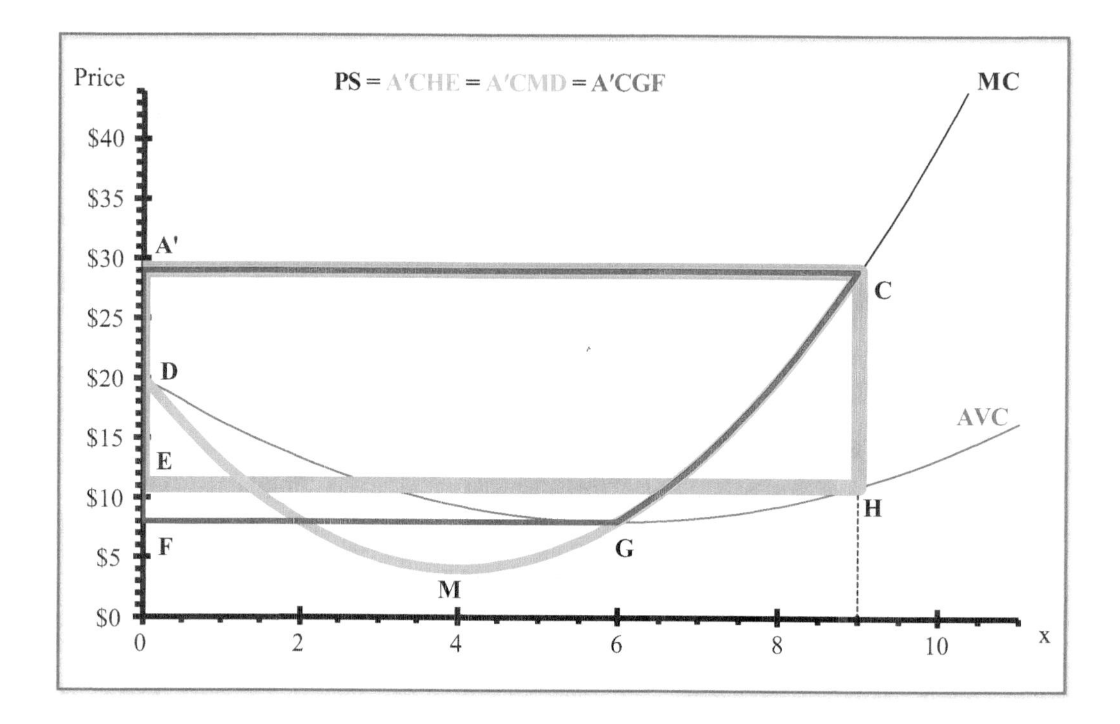

answer Q4c. Variable cost is AVC times Q, or area **EHJo**; therefore, the producer surplus rectangle is **ABHE**. The second method, shown in Figure 16.5B, focuses on the marginal cost curve. The marginal cost curve describes incremental cost of production. If we sum incremental cost across units, we obtain variable cost. That is, the area under the marginal cost curve, **DMCJo**, is variable cost.[7] Given this view of variable cost, producer surplus is the area **ABCMD**. (Point **M** has no specific significance here; it is simply provided to ensure that marginal cost is followed on the entire lower border of the area.)

The third method uses a combination of the methods used in Figures 16.5A and 16.5B. The units of output are considered in two parts: the units from zero to the minimum AVC output level use a calculation similar to Figure 16.5A; the units after minimum AVC use a calculation similar to Figure 16.5B. Using the numbers in Figure 16.5C, the variable cost of the first 6 units is VC(6) = 6 · AVC(6), or the area under **FG**. (More generally, the variable cost of the units from zero to the point of minimum average variable cost, x_G, is $VC(x_G) = x_G \cdot AVC(x_G)$.) The variable cost of the units from 6 to 9 is the area under the marginal cost curve from 6 to 9 (the area under **GC**). Total variable cost is area **FGCJo**. Therefore, producer surplus is area **ABCGF**. Put another way, *producer surplus is the area behind the marginal cost curve above minimum average variable cost*. Each of these methods produces the same dollar measure of producer surplus—in this instance, PS = $261, as noted in the earlier discussion of Figure 16.4. Were price or quantity to change, then, of course, so would producer surplus. The Excel file for Figures 16.4–16.6 allows you to vary both price and quantity and see what happens to producer surplus as a result.

A production point **B** was chosen that implies an imperfectly competitive market because P > MC in Figures 16.4 and 16.5. The only change if the market is perfectly competitive is that P = MC so that **B** and **C** must coincide. One way to show this is to simply drop the price to P = $29. Figure 16.6 depicts this situation and shows all three methods of geometrically describing PS at once. In this instance, **B** = **C**, and **A** has shifted down to **A′** = (0, $29). When P = MC, there is no longer the rectangular box that is **AB** wide by **BC** high at the top of each PS area. Each method of calculating producer surplus still yields the same dollar answer.

Q6. What is the dollar value of producer surplus implied by Figure 16.6?*

***Q6 answer:** PS = TR − VC = 9 · $29 − 9 · $11 = $162, using PS = **A′CHE**. The other methods would require the actual marginal cost function to calculate producer surplus.

Each of the three producer surplus areas, **A′CHE**, **A′CMD**, and **A′CGF**, in Figure 16.6 shares the **A′C** border and the **A′D** border. The red area behind the MC curve above minimum AVC method (PS = **A′CGF**) is shown on top because it is the preferred method from an economic point of view. This version of producer surplus is the producer-side analog to consumer surplus as the area behind the demand curve.

Producer Surplus with Linear Marginal Cost

As noted earlier, one of the goals of the welfare analysis in this chapter is to allow comparison of the welfare impact of the various market structures we have studied in Chapters 13, 14, and 15. Just as we argued in the previous section—that linear demand suffices to represent demand for this analysis—so will linear marginal cost suffice to represent the cost conditions inherent in the market. By restricting ourselves to linear demand and marginal cost, we are able to calculate welfare impacts using triangles and rectangles, rather than nonlinear geometric forms. In doing this, we follow a strategy used earlier in Chapter 13 to analyze the properties of market supply based on quadratic cost functions (which produce linear marginal cost functions).

As noted in Section 13.5, when marginal cost is linear, then minimum average variable cost occurs at $x = 0$. As a result, producer surplus is calculated as a triangle when $P = MC$ and as a triangle plus a rectangle when $P > MC$. Figure 16.7 focuses on the perfectly competitive situation in which $P = MC$. Answer the following:

Q7a. At a price of $6, should the firm produce in the short run?

Q7b. What is the change in producer surplus if the price moves from $6 to $9 per unit?

Q7c. What is the average variable cost of producing 8 units of output?

Q7d. What is a geometric representation of VC(8)?*

Producer surplus is the excess of revenue over variable cost. The area under the marginal cost curve is incremental cost of production, and the (x, P) to (0, 0) rectangle is total revenue. In the example shown in Figure 16.7B, **A** + **D** is the total revenue of producing 8 units at a price of $6, and **D** is variable cost, so **A** is the producer surplus. If price increases to $9, the firm's producer surplus increases by $33 = ΔPS in Figure 16.7A. Just as we did with the analysis of ΔCS in Figure 16.3B, it is worthwhile to split this trapezoid into two components, **B** and **C**, as shown in Figure 16.7B. At a price of $6, the producer is willing to supply 8 units of output; therefore, at a higher price, the producer will still willingly supply these 8 units (since marginal cost on these units continues to be covered as price increases). Area **B** therefore represents the windfall on these units. By contrast, area **C** represents the producer surplus on incremental units, due to the price increase. The units from $8 < x \leq 14$ would not be supplied at a price of $6 because the marginal cost of production on each of these units exceeds $6. These units are willingly supplied at a price of $9, however, because their marginal cost of production does not exceed $9. Area **E** represents the incremental cost of these units, and area **C** + **E** represents the incremental revenue attained from these units. Therefore, area **C** represents the incremental producer surplus on these units. When the price increases, the firm benefits in two ways: There is a windfall gain on units that are already under production at the lower price (area **B**), and there is an incremental surplus on units that were not profitable at the lower price (area **C**).

The analysis of producer surplus thus far has focused on the net benefit to an individual producer. As we aggregate across producers, we can simply add producer surpluses to obtain an aggregate measure of producer surplus. In perfectly competitive markets, this summation occurs for a common price, just as industry supply is the horizontal sum of individual firm supply curves. In this context, we see a graphic rationale for summing

---

***Q7 answer:** Yes, the firm should produce for all prices above $2, since $2 is minimum AVC. The change in producer surplus is ΔPS = PS($9) – PS($6) = 14 · $7/2 – 8 · $4/2 = $49 – $16 = $33. This can also be calculated as the sum of areas **B** and **C**. AVC(8) = VC(8)/8 = $32/8 = $4. Area **D** is VC(8), but it also could be represented by the rectangle whose diagonal vertices are (8, AVC(8)) = (8, $4) and (0, 0).

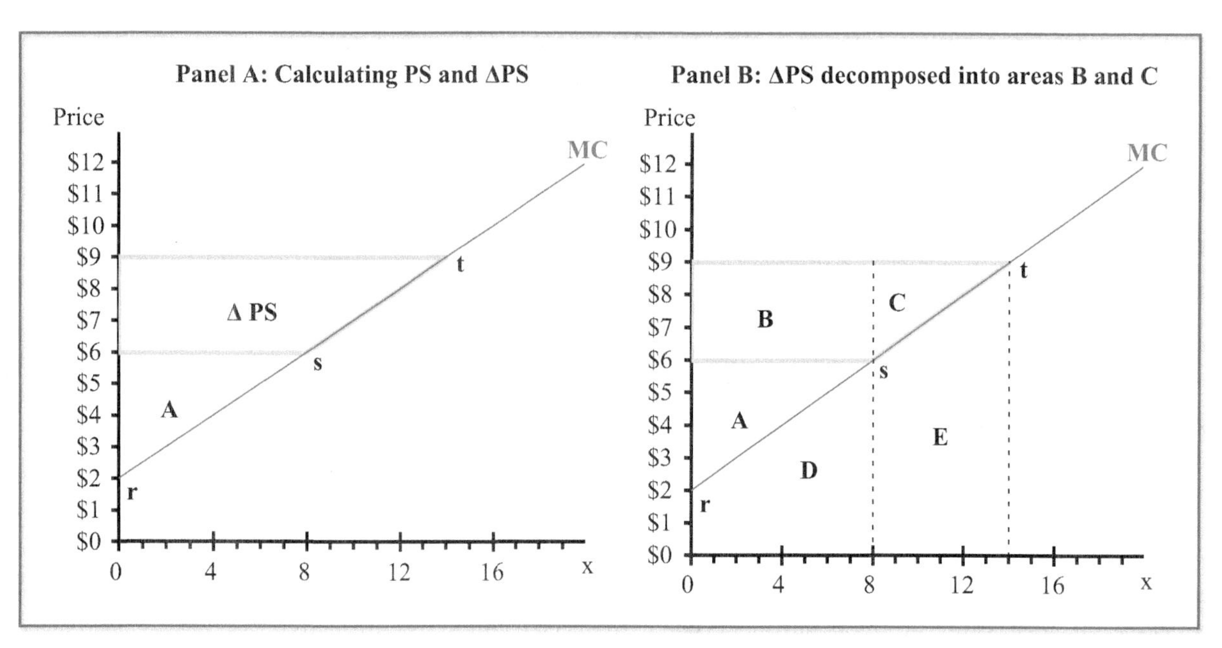

FIGURE 16.7 Change in Producer Surplus, Given Linear Supply

producer surpluses across firms, using the area behind the supply curve interpretation of producer surplus described previously ("trapezoid" **ACGF** in Figure 16.6 or area **A** in Figure 16.7). Market supply is simply the horizontal sum of individual producer supplies, and therefore, the area behind market supply is simply the sum of areas behind individual supply curves. Similarly, change in producer surplus can be summed across producers to determine aggregate change in producer surplus.

16.3 Comparing the Total Surplus of Perfect Competition and Monopoly

total surplus (TS): Total surplus is the sum of consumer surplus and producer surplus.

In Sections 16.1 and 16.2, we examine how consumers and producers gain from using the market system. Consumers gain consumer surplus because the goods they purchase have a value that exceeds what they must pay for the goods. Producers gain producer surplus because they obtain revenues that exceed the variable cost of producing the goods they sell. These surpluses represent dollar-denominated gains to society at large that accrue due to market interaction. The sum of these two surpluses is **total surplus (TS)**. Consumers and producers are two of the three types of "economic actors" delineated at the beginning of this text. The other significant economic actor is the government, and in the present context, this actor has no overt role in the market.[8]

The definition of total surplus treats surplus that accrues to consumers and producers equally. That is, total surplus makes no value judgments regarding who attains the surplus. The natural question to which we now turn is whether one market structure dominates in terms of total surplus to society. We have seen in Chapters 13, 14, and 15 that perfectly competitive markets lead to P = MC, but imperfectly competitive markets have P > MC. Therefore, perfectly competitive markets will have higher consumer surplus, *ceteris paribus*, but producer surplus is higher in imperfectly competitive markets. We now turn to a comparison of total surplus attainable at both ends of the competitive spectrum. We begin by describing the competitive end of that spectrum.

If a market is perfectly competitive, the market clearing price is determined by the intersection of market supply and market demand. Market supply is the sum of individual firm supply curves. Each individual firm supply curve is based on that firm's marginal cost curve. Therefore, supply equals demand implies that P = MC in perfect competition. More specifically, the output chosen by the market will equate the marginal value of that

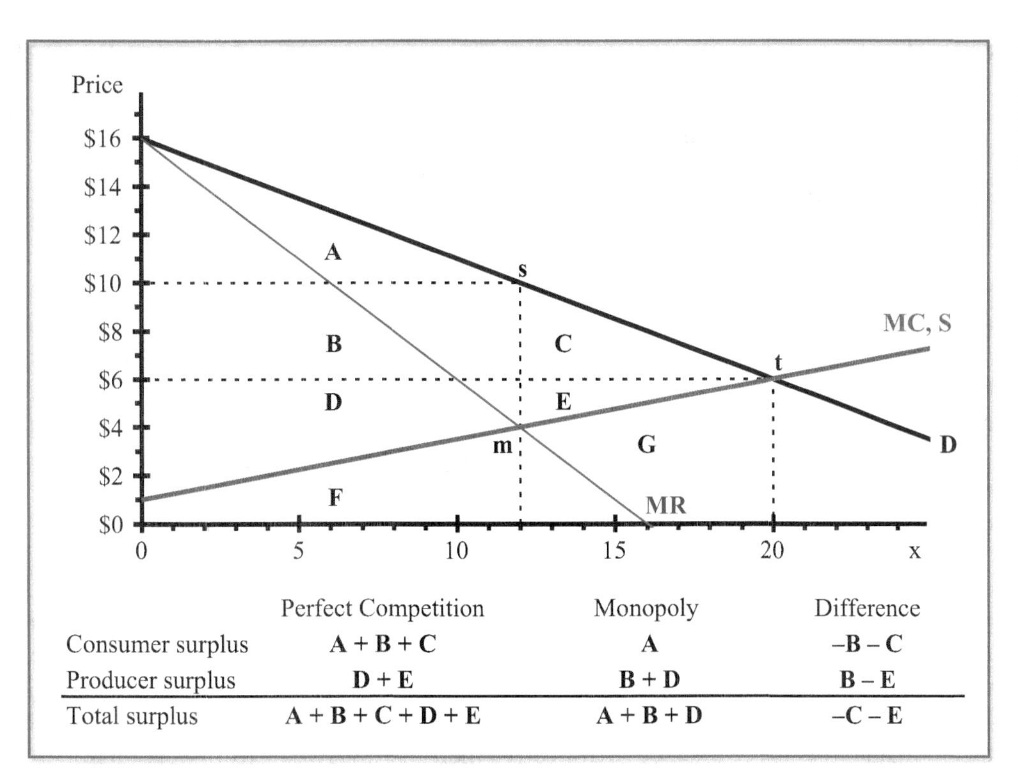

	Perfect Competition	Monopoly	Difference
Consumer surplus	A + B + C	A	–B – C
Producer surplus	D + E	B + D	B – E
Total surplus	A + B + C + D + E	A + B + D	–C – E

FIGURE 16.8 Comparing the Welfare Impact of Competition and Monopoly

unit of output, P(x), to the marginal cost of production, MC(x). The height of the demand curve at a given output level (also called inverse demand or marginal valuation of that output level) is the concept that we used in Figure 16.1 to motivate our discussion of consumer surplus. This is the situation depicted in Figure 16.8. In the competitive interpretation of the market equilibrium, the red curve is a market supply curve (i.e., it is the horizontal sum of individual firm marginal cost above minimum average variable cost curves). Market supply intersects market demand at **t** = (20, \$6). The welfare impact of this outcome is described in terms of the triangles, rectangles, and trapezoids labeled in the figure. Gross benefit to consumers of these 20 units is **A** + **B** + **C** + **D** + **E** + **F** + **G**, but consumers pay **D** + **E** + **F** + **G**, so $CS_{competition}$ = **A** + **B** + **C**. Gross benefit to firms is **D** + **E** + **F** + **G**, but the variable cost of producing these units is the area under supply (i.e., marginal cost) or **F** + **G**. Therefore, the excess of benefits over cost to producers is $PS_{competition}$ = **D** + **E**. The total surplus produced by the competitive market outcome is $TS_{competition}$ = **A** + **B** + **C** + **D** + **E**.

Q8a. What are the dollar sizes of $CS_{competition}$, $PS_{competition}$, and $TS_{competition}$?*

Suppose instead that a monopolist controls this market. In this conceptualization, the red curve in Figure 16.8 is a marginal cost curve (rather than the horizontal sum of marginal cost curves). The monopolist faces the entire market demand curve, and hence, encounters a downward-sloping demand for its product. It can only increase output by reducing price; therefore, marginal revenue is below price for any output above zero. In the present instance, profits are maximized by finding the output level where MR = MC. This occurs at **m** = (12, \$4). The profit-maximizing monopoly price is simply P(12) = \$10 at **s** = (12, \$10). As noted previously, relative to perfect competition, price is higher and output is lower under monopoly. Gross benefit to consumers of these 12 units is **A** + **B** + **D** + **F**, but consumers pay **B** + **D** + **F**, so $CS_{monopoly}$ = **A**. Gross benefit to firms is **B** + **D** + **F**, but the variable cost of producing these units is the area under marginal cost,

---

***Q8a answer:** $CS_{competition}$ = \$100 = 10 · \$20/2, $PS_{competition}$ = \$50 = 20 · \$5/2, and $TS_{competition}$ = \$150 = 20 · \$15/2, using the formula for the area of a triangle.

or **F**. Therefore, the excess of benefits over cost to producers is $PS_{monopoly}$ = **B** + **D**. The total surplus produced by the monopoly is $TS_{monopoly}$ = **A** + **B** + **D**.

Q8b. What are the dollar sizes of $CS_{monopoly}$, $PS_{monopoly}$, and $TS_{monopoly}$?*

The Deadweight Loss of Monopoly

Total surplus is lower under monopoly than under competition. There is a net loss to society, due to the output restrictiveness inherent in monopoly. The difference between perfect competition and monopoly is not just that consumers cede consumer surplus of area **B** to the monopolist in the form of higher price for the product. This is a distributional issue that is not considered by the total surplus measure because total surplus treats all dollars equally. The problem is that there are fewer dollars of surplus under monopoly than under perfect competition. The size of the inefficiency created due to the sheltered monopoly position is called the deadweight loss of monopoly. The **deadweight loss of monopoly (DWL_m)** is the loss in total surplus due to monopolistic output distortion. It is a specific example of a more general problem called deadweight loss. **Deadweight loss (DWL)** is the loss in total surplus whenever price and marginal cost do not coincide. This is also often called a loss due to *allocative inefficiency*. It is an example of a *Pareto inefficiency*. DWL arises at a given allocation of resources when the cost to produce an extra unit (marginal cost) does not coincide with the marginal valuation of that unit (price). When this occurs, society does not allocate the correct amount of resources to producing the good, and this is the essence of allocative inefficiency. Recall from Section 3.5 that an allocation of resources is Pareto efficient if no possible reallocation of resources makes at least one economic agent better off without making another agent worse off. We will describe how DWL is a form of Pareto inefficiency shortly.

deadweight loss of monopoly (DWL_m): The loss in total surplus due to monopolistic output distortion is called the deadweight loss of monopoly.

deadweight loss (DWL): Deadweight loss is the loss in total surplus whenever price and marginal cost do not coincide.

DWL occurs whenever $P \neq MC$, so monopoly is only one example of a situation involving DWL. Any imperfectly competitive market is subject to allocative inefficiency. Geometrically, DWL_m is triangle **stm** or area **C** + **E**; in dollar terms, DWL_m = \$24 in Figure 16.8. Separating DWL into the two component parts **C** and **E** is useful because both parts have a different economic interpretation and both can be conceptualized in two ways. We can start with competition and consider the change to monopoly, or we can start with monopoly and consider the change to competition. Both interpretations provide useful insights and are therefore considered in turn. The tabular description of difference areas in Figure 16.8 shows the change from competition to monopoly; therefore, that is where we begin.

The main losers in moving from competition to monopoly are, of course, consumers who lose **B** + **C**. **B** is transferred from consumers to producers, but **C** represents the consumer-side DWL due to monopolistic underproduction. **C** is a net loss to society, since it does not accrue to either side under monopoly (in this case, **C** = \$16). The main winner is the producer who becomes the monopolist (and who has net gains of **B** – **E**). **B** is a gain to producers (in this case, **B** = \$48); to the noneconomist, this might be considered the benefit from attaining monopoly status. **B** overstates the gain to the monopolist. If the monopolist must sell at a single price, then it will sell where $P > MR = MC$ to maximize profits. But to gain **B**, the monopolist must give up sales on the units from 12 to 20 that produced a surplus of **E** at the competitive price (in this case, **E** = \$8). **E** represents the producer-side DWL due to monopolistic underproduction. Both **C** and **E** are lost to society as a whole, due to the output restrictiveness that is inherent in monopoly. **C** is the consumer-side DWL, and **E** is the producer-side DWL.

If we start with monopoly and consider the change to perfect competition, we see the reverse effects. Consumers gain **B** + **C** if this change occurs. **B** is transferred from pro-

---

***Q8b answer:** $CS_{monopoly}$ = \$36 = 12 · \$6/2, $PS_{monopoly}$ = \$90 = 12 · \$4 + 12 · (\$5 + \$2)/2, and $TS_{monopoly}$ = \$126. The only part of this calculation that may cause you to pause is calculating area **D**. Do this one of two ways: Imagine that **D** is a triangle plus a rectangle (\$42 = 12 · \$2 + 12 · \$3/2), or use the formula (that you may have forgotten) from geometry for the area of a trapezoid. If a trapezoid is w units wide and has heights of h_1 and h_2 on its two parallel sides, then the area of the trapezoid = $w \cdot (h_1 + h_2)/2$.

ducers to consumers in the form of lower prices on the units that the consumers would have purchased at the monopoly price. **C** represents the net benefit on units of output that consumers did not value highly enough to purchase at the monopoly price but that are valued at or above the lower competitive price (these are the units of output from $12 < x \leq 20$ whose value along **st** exceeds \$6 per unit). Revenues of **B** are lost on the units of output the monopolist would have sold at the monopoly price (but these revenues are not a net loss; they are a transfer to consumers as noted earlier). But revenues exceed cost on the units of output from **m** to **t**. Revenue on these units is **E** + **G**, but the resource cost of this production is **G**, so **E** is the producer surplus on these units. Therefore, the net gain in moving from monopoly to competition is **C** + **E**, due to the increased production that results under competition.

Monopolists produce too little output because they wish to restrict output to increase price and maximize profits. This represents a Pareto inefficient allocation of resources because we can describe a reallocation of resources that leaves both consumers and the monopolist better off than they were under the monopoly outcome of producing at x_m and pricing at P_m (at point **s** = (12, \$10) in Figure 16.8). Consider the following alternative *sequential scenario* (based on Figure 16.8):

Step 1—First, sell 12 units of output at a price of \$10 per unit. The consumer surplus of this situation is described by **A**, and the monopolist has a producer surplus of **B** + **D**.

Step 2—Next, offer for sale $8 = x_t - x_m$ units of output at a price of $P_c = \$6$. This produces a consumer surplus of **C** and a producer surplus of **E**.

This sequential scenario is a Pareto improvement on the monopoly situation (which was to do Step 1 alone) because both parties are better off and no one is worse off. This scenario is offered as a way of showing that the monopoly outcome is Pareto inefficient. It is not offered as a strategy that a monopolist might actually be able to follow because consumers would quickly learn that if they do not buy in the first round (during Step 1), then a later round of sales will occur at a lower price (during Step 2). On the other hand, it does offer insights into why we often see firms with market power making individualized deals.

Capturing Surplus

Firms with market power use a variety of strategies to exercise that power to gain extra profits. The broad array of strategies firms with market power use to capture surplus are too numerous to fully discuss here. Nonetheless, one of those strategies should be touched upon in the current context because it offers insights into why monopolists create inefficiency. The two-step sequential scenario discussed earlier hints at one of the ways that firms with market power can capture further surplus. Firms can price discriminate. **Price discrimination** is selling the same good at different prices.

price discrimination: Price discrimination is selling the same good at different prices.

The difficulty with price discrimination is that it is difficult to determine what the consumer's marginal valuation is, *and* it is difficult to keep consumers from reselling the good. If this cannot be done, then consumers with low value will have an incentive to purchase at low prices and resell to consumers with high value: They will engage in arbitrage. Sometimes, arbitrage is formally outlawed; for example, an individual with a wine cellar cannot simply advertise to sell bottles from the cellar; reselling alcoholic beverages is illegal. Another example of price discrimination with barriers to resale is the market for prescription drugs. The same drug is sold in Canada and the United States at different prices because the manufacturers perceive that they can capture additional surplus by pricing differently in different markets and because resale is formally illegal (although, of course, there is significant debate on the wisdom of this ban).

You can see price discrimination in consumer product markets where a store caters to multiple customer groups. A good example is a local paint store (but this applies equally well to plumbing and electrical supply stores, for example). Such stores often sell to painting professionals, as well as to average homeowners who simply want to paint the interior or exterior of their home. Often, such stores will have products on the shelves without prices but only with SKU (stock keeping unit) markings. Prices are not posted for a reason: Different customers are charged different prices for the same product. The first question paint-store employees ask customers if they do not recognize them is: Do you have an account with us? This tells employees the "class" of customer with whom they are dealing. If you are simply a homeowner, you probably do not have an account. Different classes of customers receive different discounts off list price. A homeowner is typically charged a higher price than a painter because the painter has a standing account with the store and buys in much greater volume. Of course, major home improvement stores such as Home Depot have cut into specialty-store markets in recent years. Nonetheless, this remains a common phenomenon.

We see price discrimination in situations where reselling is difficult and where prices are not posted or are subject to individual negotiation (so they are individually determined). A car dealership can sell identical new cars to two individuals at different prices. Similarly, two people in need of legal services might obtain different rates from the same lawyer, or two people walking into a plastic surgeon's office for a facelift might obtain that service at different prices. The producers in each of these instances have some latitude in price setting, and resale is expensive in the first instance and impossible in the other two.

We do not dwell on price discrimination here but simply note that if a monopolist were able to perfectly price discriminate, then we would no longer have a Pareto inefficient allocation of resources. Put another way, the perfectly price-discriminating monopolist produces no deadweight loss! Consider once again Figure 16.8. If each unit can be sold for its marginal valuation, and if resale is precluded, then the perfectly price-discriminating monopolist would sell x_t units of output, but each unit would be sold for the marginal valuation of that unit, P(x). Total producer revenue and consumer cost in this instance would be **A** + **B** + **C** + **D** + **E** + **F** + **G**, the same as gross consumer benefits, so there would be no consumer surplus, $CS_{PPDM} = 0$. The variable cost of producing those units would be **F** + **G**; therefore, the excess of benefits over cost to the perfectly price-discriminating monopolist is PS_{PPDM} = **A** + **B** + **C** + **D** + **E**. Perfect price discrimination allows the monopolist to capture the surplus **A** from consumers *and* to capture **C** and **E** as well. As noted previously, **C** + **E** is the $DWL_{monopoly}$. But it is only a DWL if that monopolist is not able to price discriminate.

Perfect price discrimination is Pareto efficient because P = MC for the last unit sold; this market is allocatively efficient. The same amount is produced as in perfect competition; the difference is how much it costs consumers. Total surplus is the same as under perfect competition, but the distributional consequences are, of course, dramatically different. Even when price discrimination is not perfect, the producer's goal is the same: Try to capture more than **B** + **D** in surplus. **B** + **D** offers a "lower bound" that the monopolist can attain using a single price strategy. Such strategies for capturing additional surplus are discussed at length in industrial organization and strategy courses.

16.4 Analyzing Welfare Economics in Differentiated Product Markets *OPTIONAL SECTION*

Whenever price and marginal cost are not equal, allocative inefficiency results because additional units can be sold for more than the resource cost involved in their production. This occurs in all imperfectly competitive market structures, since P = MC only holds in perfect competition. Monopolistic competition is a market structure in which P > MC, but profits are zero in the long run, due to free entry and exit. This dual result occurs because the monopolistically competitive products are differentiated in nature, there is free entry and exit in the market, and the consumer values the diversity of products produced by firms within the market.

There are two sources of inefficiency in monopolistic competition in long-run equilibrium. Both sources emanate from the tangency of downward-sloping demand to the ATC curve condition that is the hallmark of long-run monopolistically competitive equilibrium (LRMCE). The first has to do with the monopolistic competitor producing at an

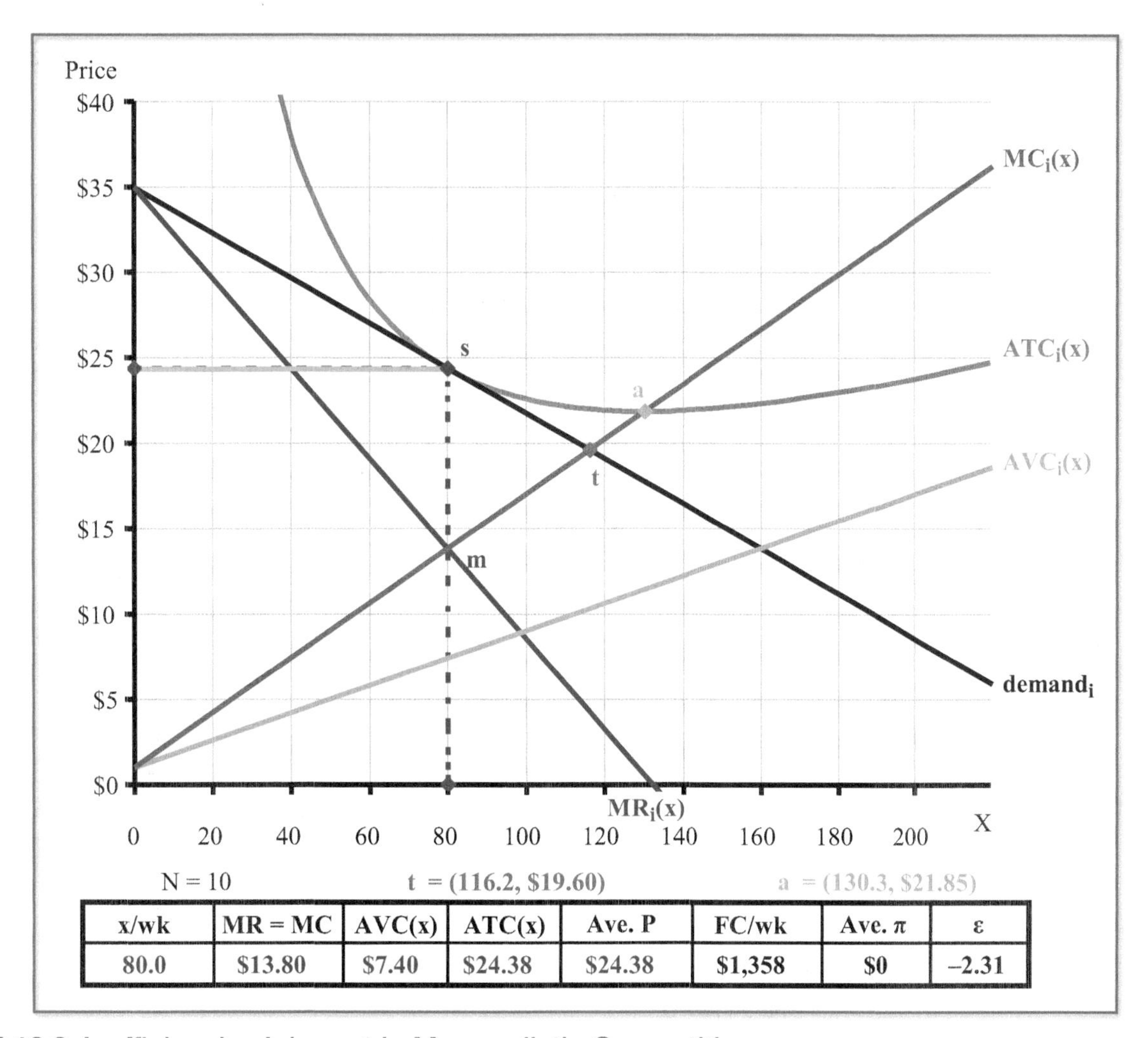

x/wk	MR = MC	AVC(x)	ATC(x)	Ave. P	FC/wk	Ave. π	ε
80.0	$13.80	$7.40	$24.38	$24.38	$1,358	$0	–2.31

FIGURE 16.9 Inefficiencies Inherent in Monopolistic Competition

allocatively inefficient point (where P > MC). The second has to do with the firm producing above minimum average total cost. Both sources of inefficiency are depicted in Figure 16.9. As in Section 15.5, the curves are for a representative firm *i* when there are N firms in the market. The monopolistic competitor maximizes profits by finding the output level x_i where $MR_i(x_i) = MC_i(x_i)$ at point **m**. Price is set by going to the (inverse) demand curve at this output level, $P_i(x_i)$ at point **s**. This is an LRMCE because of the tangency between the representative firm's demand and average total cost curves at this output level.

The deadweight loss inherent in this situation is depicted by the DWL triangle **stm**. This loss in efficiency is due to valuation (along **st**) being above the real resource cost of production (along **mt**). The other inherent inefficiency in LRMCE is that the firm is not producing at minimum average total cost. Production costs on a per-unit basis are minimized at point **a**, but the monopolistic competitor will not produce there because the firm cannot sustain that level of production without sustaining losses. The firm's only way to break even is to restrict output and to produce above minimum average total cost (at **s** rather than **a**). This leads to a steady state in which the representative firm operates with excess capacity (using the numbers in Figure 16.9, at $x_m = x_s = 80$, rather than at $x_a = 130$).

As we noted in Chapter 15, the consumer accepts a higher price in exchange for greater variety in differentiated product markets. This is why the market supports a number of firms producing and selling at **s**, rather than a smaller number of firms producing and selling at **a** in Figure 16.9. Consumers make this choice despite the price at **s** being more than 10% above the minimum ATC price in that figure (and, of course, had we used a point of tangency further up the ATC curve, we could have induced a higher premium, due to the differentiatedness inherent in the market).

Valuing Variety *OPTIONAL SECTION* **(Prerequisite: Section 15.6)**

The value to consumers of the varieties in a monopolistically competitive market is the sum across varieties of the consumer surplus of each variety. Some varieties will have more demand, and some will have less, due to the inherent nature of each variety. Rather than try to model such disparities, economists describe the behavior of the "representative" or "average" firm in the market. The analysis in Section 15.6 provides a generalized description of how the representative firm responds to entry in differentiated product markets. We then can use that analysis to describe how different responses to entry result in different qualitative outcomes in a monopolistically competitive market. The analysis presented in Section 15.6 is not exhaustive but, rather, suggestive of what might happen as firms enter and exit in differentiated product markets subject to free entry.

We can use this representative firm to estimate the welfare impact of entry and exit on the market. It must be noted that calculations of consumer surplus based on a representative firm cannot provide exact answers because a representative firm cannot fully incorporate disparities in demand across varieties. As noted in Section 15.4, care should be taken in differentiated product markets when considering market demand. It is not formally appropriate to sum demand across firms to obtain a well-defined market demand, due to the heterogeneity of the product being summed. Nonetheless, we can obtain rough aggregates, using the representative firm analysis, and we can obtain monopolistic competition's main welfare result using this analysis.

If we consider the representative firm as depicting the average firm in this market, then we can aggregate across firms by simply multiplying the individual values of the various parameters by N. Given N firms in the market, aggregate quantity sold (AQ(N)), aggregate consumer surplus (ACS(N)), aggregate profit (Aπ(N)), and aggregate total surplus (ATS(N)) are calculated as:

$$AQ(N) = N \cdot x_i, \text{ where } x_i \text{ is the output level where } MR_i(x_i) = MC_i(x_i). \quad \textbf{(16.11a)}$$

$$ACS(N) = N \cdot CS(x_i, P_i), \text{ where } P_i = P_i(x_i) \text{ is inverse demand.} \quad \textbf{(16.11b)}$$

$$A\pi(N) = N \cdot \pi_i(x_i, P_i). \quad \textbf{(16.11c)}$$

$$ATS(N) = ACS(N) + A\pi(N). \quad \textbf{(16.11d)}$$

A common expectation is that differentiated product market entry will increase overall aggregate quantity sold in the market, even though each individual firm sells less, because the market is better served by greater variety. Using the parameters in Equation 16.11a, x_i decreases, but $N \cdot x_i$ increases as N increases (although, as noted in the discussion of Table 15.1, aggregate quantity could remain fixed (Outcomes D and E) or decline (Outcome F)). Similarly, we expect that a market with greater variety will increase aggregate consumer surplus, despite the consumer surplus generated per variety declining. Individual firm profitability is a declining function of N, but aggregate profits may initially increase but must then decrease as the market eventually becomes saturated. Aggregate total surplus is the sum of an increasing function and a function that may first increase but then decrease. As a result, aggregate total surplus may first increase and then decrease as a function of N.

You may have noticed that total surplus is defined here as consumer surplus plus profits, rather than as consumer surplus plus producer surplus. As noted in Equation 16.10b, profits include fixed cost as well as variable cost, but producer surplus only includes variable cost. The reason fixed cost must be incorporated in this instance is that the addition of varieties comes at a cost; part of that cost is the fixed cost of each additional firm (or variety). As the number of firms in the market varies, so does the amount of real resources devoted to their collective production.

The easiest way to rationalize the inclusion of fixed cost is to consider the limiting case of homogeneous product entry in Outcome E in Table 15.1 and Figures 15.11–15.13. We saw that, regardless of the number of firms in the market, the price remained at \$20, and a total of 200 units was sold (the monopoly version of this is shown in Figure 15.10).

With one firm covering this market, aggregate profits are \$1,750 and consumer surplus is \$1,000.[9] With eight firms in the market, aggregate profits are \$0 (according to Figure 15.12E), but otherwise, the market situations are the same in terms of output and consumer surplus. Aggregate output, according to Equations 15.3 and 16.11a, is:

$$AQ(N) = N \cdot 200/N = 200. \quad \textbf{(16.12a)}$$

Aggregate consumer surplus remains the same, given constant aggregate demand for the homogeneous product, based on Equations 15.3 and 16.11b:

$$ACS(N) = N \cdot CS_i(x_i) = N \cdot [1/2 \cdot \text{base} \cdot \text{height}] = N \cdot [1/2 \cdot 200/N \cdot \$10] = \$1{,}000. \quad \textbf{(16.12b)}$$

In this instance, total profit based on Equation 16.11c is:

$$A\pi(N) = N \cdot (TR_i - VC_i - FC_i).$$

$$A\pi(N) = N \cdot ((200/N) \cdot \$20 - (200/N) \cdot \$10 - \$250) = \$2{,}000 - \$250 \cdot N. \quad \textbf{(16.12c)}$$

Finally, aggregate total surplus based on Equations 16.11d, 16.12b, and 16.12c is:

$$ATS(N) = ACS(N) + A\pi(N) = \$3{,}000 - \$250 \cdot N. \quad \textbf{(16.12d)}$$

From the point of view of using scarce resources, having one firm satisfy this market is preferable to having more than one firm. This statement is true even though the monopolist prices at \$20, produces a monopoly profit of \$1,750, and induces a DWL_m. If this same market is serviced by eight equally sized firms, then each will still price at \$20, aggregate quantity remains at 200, and the market will have the same aggregate DWL. The only difference between the two situations is that the aggregate profits will have been completely consumed by the seven additional plants (at FC = \$250 per plant). This is a natural monopoly market; a single firm covers this market more efficiently than more than one firm. Had we used producer surplus instead of profits, then aggregate total surplus would be independent of how many firms are in the market (as we see in Equation 16.12, PS = TR – VC = \$2,000, so that CS + PS = \$3,000, and the sum is independent of how many firms are in the market).

Does Monopolistic Competition Produce the Optimal Mix of Variety?

Consumers value variety and are willing to pay for the ability to purchase products that more closely match their preferences. The natural question to consider is whether monopolistic competition produces the optimal amount of variety. That is the question to which we now turn.

Firms' choices of which differentiated products to produce are based on the marginal valuations of those products, but the welfare effect of those products is based on the average valuation of those products. These two valuations need not coincide, and as a result, we need not attain an optimal product mix in LRMCE. We may end up with a socially optimal mix, but this need not be the case. Three possibilities are apparent: The market may produce too few, the right number, or too many varieties. We can see this using the representative firm analysis described earlier.

To focus on the question of optimal variety, Figures 16.10A–16.10C show three monopolistically competitive market scenarios based on the same cost curves. Each scenario has 10 firms in the market (N = 10) in LRMCE. Therefore, each equilibrium (x, P) point is a point of tangency on the downward-sloping part of the representative firm's average total cost curve, atc(x) (subscripts have been removed but the curves are lowercase to remind the reader that these curves are for a representative individual firm). Rather than get bogged down in the details of each scenario, look for the broad patterns that emerge from these scenarios.

Note: *The dynamic Excel file for Figure 16.10 provides a more effective understanding of this material than the static images shown in Figure 16.10.*

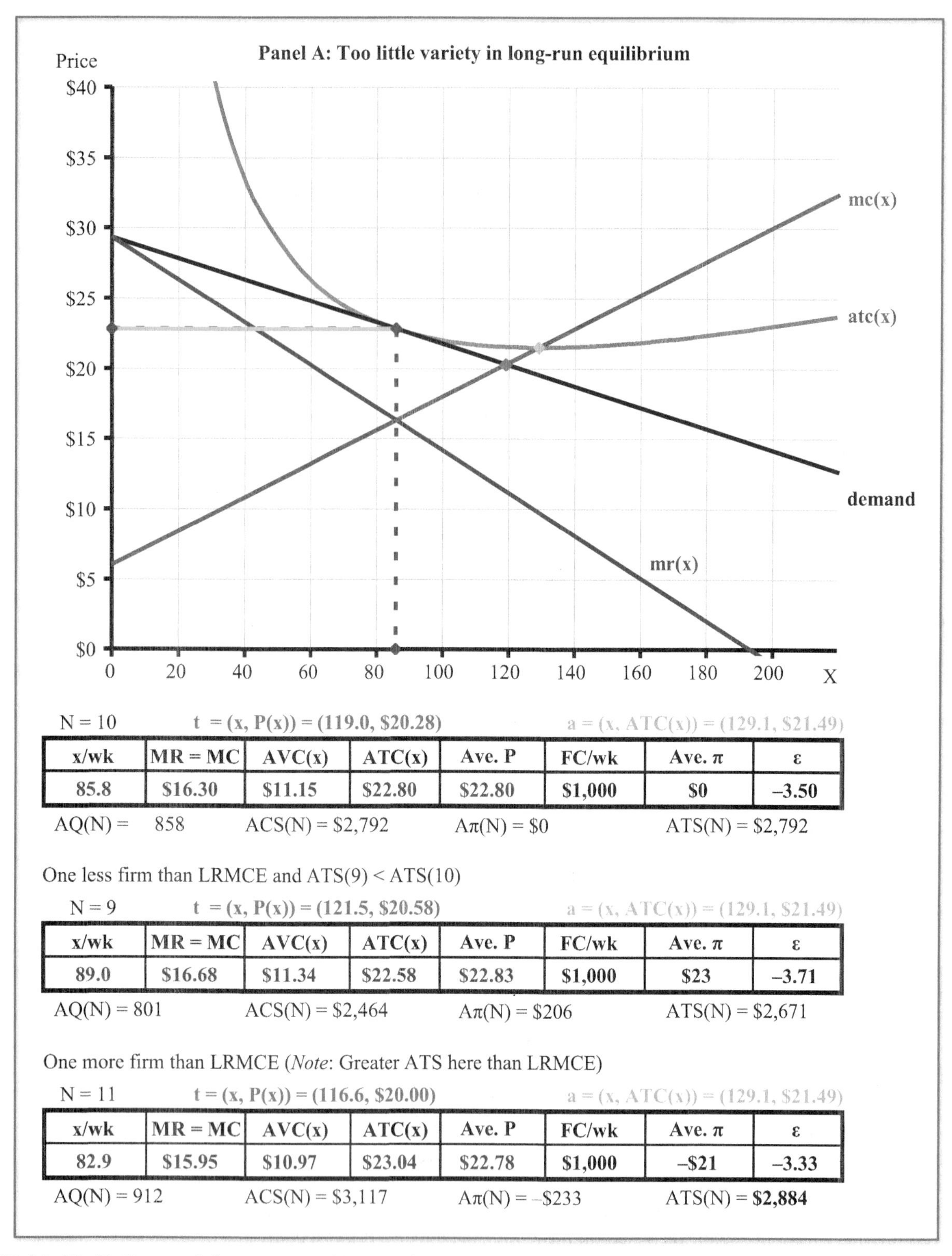

N = 10 t = (x, P(x)) = (119.0, $20.28) a = (x, ATC(x)) = (129.1, $21.49)

x/wk	MR = MC	AVC(x)	ATC(x)	Ave. P	FC/wk	Ave. π	ε
85.8	$16.30	$11.15	$22.80	$22.80	$1,000	$0	–3.50

AQ(N) = 858 ACS(N) = $2,792 Aπ(N) = $0 ATS(N) = $2,792

One less firm than LRMCE and ATS(9) < ATS(10)

N = 9 t = (x, P(x)) = (121.5, $20.58) a = (x, ATC(x)) = (129.1, $21.49)

x/wk	MR = MC	AVC(x)	ATC(x)	Ave. P	FC/wk	Ave. π	ε
89.0	$16.68	$11.34	$22.58	$22.83	$1,000	$23	–3.71

AQ(N) = 801 ACS(N) = $2,464 Aπ(N) = $206 ATS(N) = $2,671

One more firm than LRMCE (*Note*: Greater ATS here than LRMCE)

N = 11 t = (x, P(x)) = (116.6, $20.00) a = (x, ATC(x)) = (129.1, $21.49)

x/wk	MR = MC	AVC(x)	ATC(x)	Ave. P	FC/wk	Ave. π	ε
82.9	$15.95	$10.97	$23.04	$22.78	$1,000	–$21	–3.33

AQ(N) = 912 ACS(N) = $3,117 Aπ(N) = –$233 ATS(N) = **$2,884**

FIGURE 16.10 Estimated Aggregate Welfare Impact of Monopolistic Competition

Beneath each graph in Figure 16.10 are three sets of numerical information. The top set is associated with the graph showing LRMCE (N = 10), the middle set is for one fewer firms in the market (N = 9), and the bottom set is for one more firm than LRMCE (N = 11).[10] The representative firm information for each part is the boxed data plus the **t** and **a** points that are in green and lavender, respectively, as they are in Figure 16.9. (Notice that since cost curves are fixed across scenarios and numbers of firms, the point

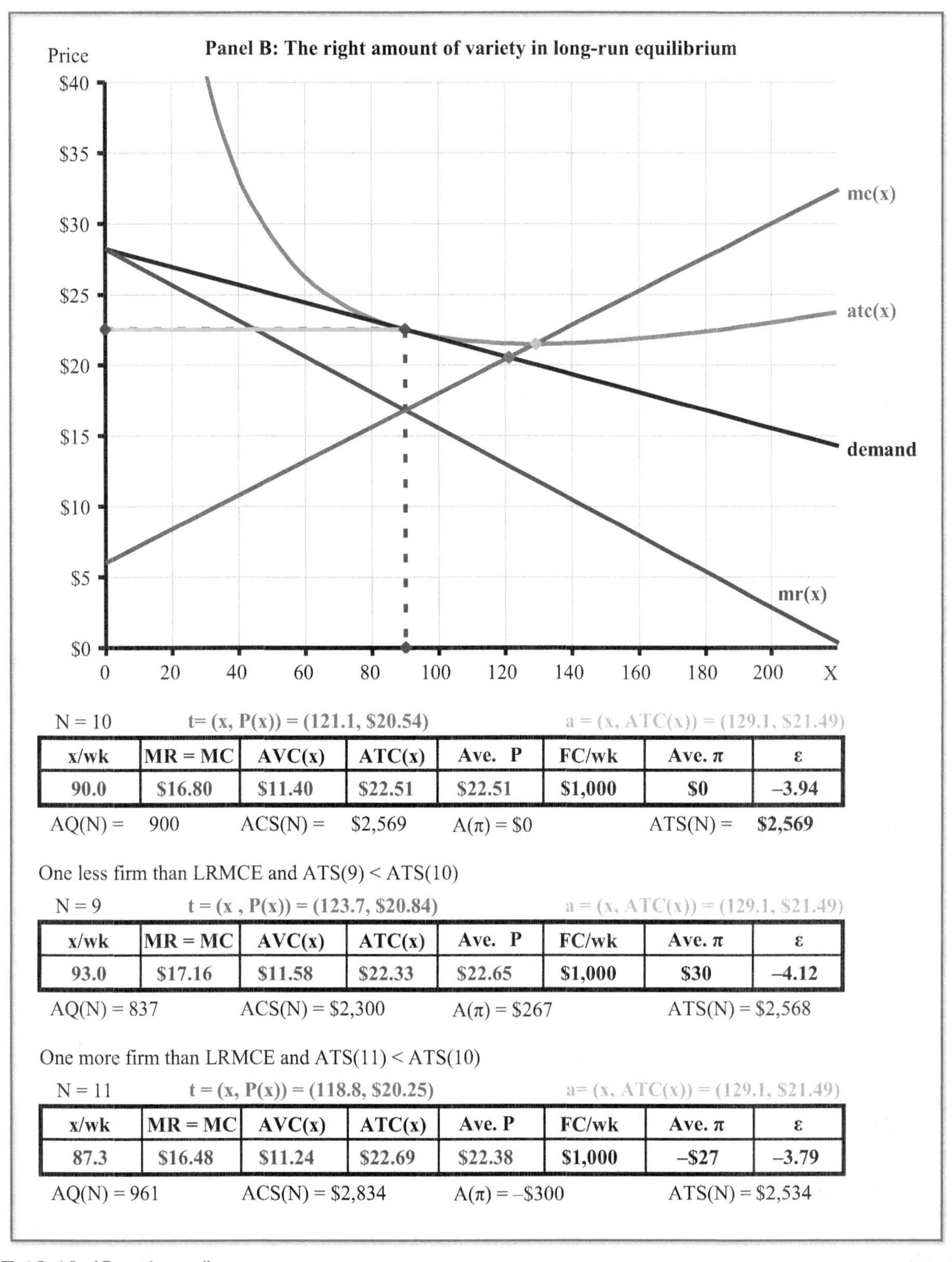

N = 10 t= (x, P(x)) = (121.1, $20.54) a = (x, ATC(x)) = (129.1, $21.49)

x/wk	MR = MC	AVC(x)	ATC(x)	Ave. P	FC/wk	Ave. π	ε
90.0	**$16.80**	**$11.40**	**$22.51**	**$22.51**	**$1,000**	**$0**	**–3.94**

AQ(N) = 900 ACS(N) = $2,569 A(π) = $0 ATS(N) = **$2,569**

One less firm than LRMCE and ATS(9) < ATS(10)

N = 9 t = (x , P(x)) = (123.7, $20.84) a = (x, ATC(x)) = (129.1, $21.49)

x/wk	MR = MC	AVC(x)	ATC(x)	Ave. P	FC/wk	Ave. π	ε
93.0	**$17.16**	**$11.58**	**$22.33**	**$22.65**	**$1,000**	**$30**	**–4.12**

AQ(N) = 837 ACS(N) = $2,300 A(π) = $267 ATS(N) = $2,568

One more firm than LRMCE and ATS(11) < ATS(10)

N = 11 t = (x, P(x)) = (118.8, $20.25) a= (x, ATC(x)) = (129.1, $21.49)

x/wk	MR = MC	AVC(x)	ATC(x)	Ave. P	FC/wk	Ave. π	ε
87.3	**$16.48**	**$11.24**	**$22.69**	**$22.38**	**$1,000**	**–$27**	**–3.79**

AQ(N) = 961 ACS(N) = $2,834 A(π) = –$300 ATS(N) = $2,534

FIGURE 16.10 (Continued)

of minimum average total cost is fixed, **a** = (129.1, $21.49).) The final row of each part provides aggregate information based on Equations 16.11a–16.11d. The final number—aggregate total surplus—is highlighted to focus on this number.

In Figure 16.10A, there is too little variety from a social welfare point of view. The market-determined optimum has aggregate total surplus of $2,792 when 10 firms are in the market. This is market determined because π = 0 in LRMCE (the graphed situation,

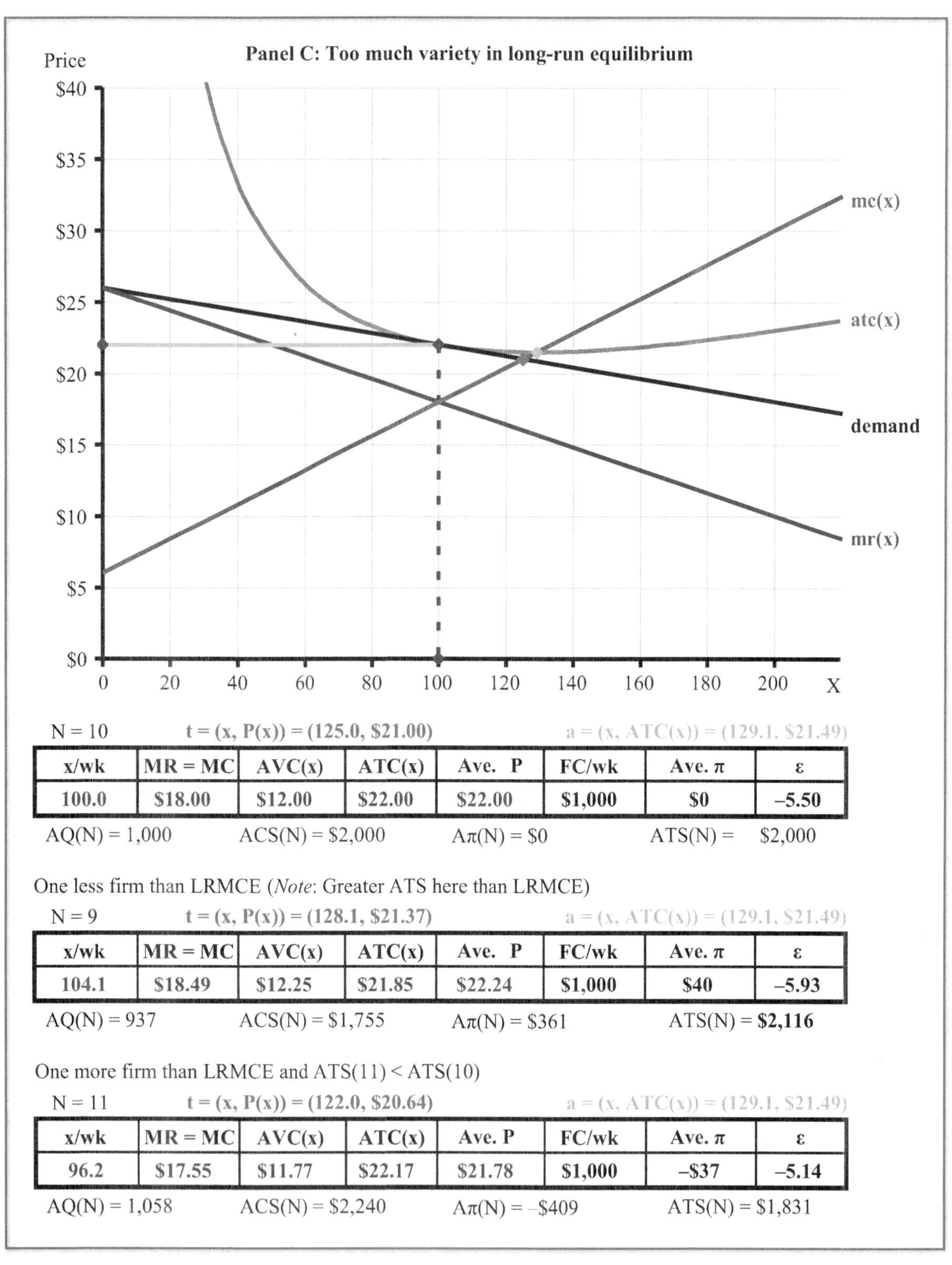

N = 10 t = (x, P(x)) = (125.0, $21.00) a = (x, ATC(x)) = (129.1, $21.49)

x/wk	MR = MC	AVC(x)	ATC(x)	Ave. P	FC/wk	Ave. π	ε
100.0	$18.00	$12.00	$22.00	$22.00	$1,000	$0	–5.50

AQ(N) = 1,000 ACS(N) = $2,000 Aπ(N) = $0 ATS(N) = $2,000

One less firm than LRMCE (*Note*: Greater ATS here than LRMCE)

N = 9 t = (x, P(x)) = (128.1, $21.37) a = (x, ATC(x)) = (129.1, $21.49)

x/wk	MR = MC	AVC(x)	ATC(x)	Ave. P	FC/wk	Ave. π	ε
104.1	$18.49	$12.25	$21.85	$22.24	$1,000	$40	–5.93

AQ(N) = 937 ACS(N) = $1,755 Aπ(N) = $361 ATS(N) = **$2,116**

One more firm than LRMCE and ATS(11) < ATS(10)

N = 11 t = (x, P(x)) = (122.0, $20.64) a = (x, ATC(x)) = (129.1, $21.49)

x/wk	MR = MC	AVC(x)	ATC(x)	Ave. P	FC/wk	Ave. π	ε
96.2	$17.55	$11.77	$22.17	$21.78	$1,000	–$37	–5.14

AQ(N) = 1,058 ACS(N) = $2,240 Aπ(N) = –$409 ATS(N) = $1,831

FIGURE 16.10 (Continued)

as well as the upper set of tabular information). But note that one more firm produces greater total surplus (ATS(11) increases to $2,884), despite not being sustainable from the point of view of the average firm in the market. Indeed, a quick check of the Figure 16.10 Excel file of this scenario shows that total surplus is maximized when there are 14 firms in this market (ATS(14) = $3,010, based on the scenario in Figure 16.10A). In Figure 16.10B, the right amount of variety exists in LRMCE because ATS(10) > ATS(9), and ATS(10) > ATS(11). And in Figure 16.10C, too much variety is produced by LRMCE

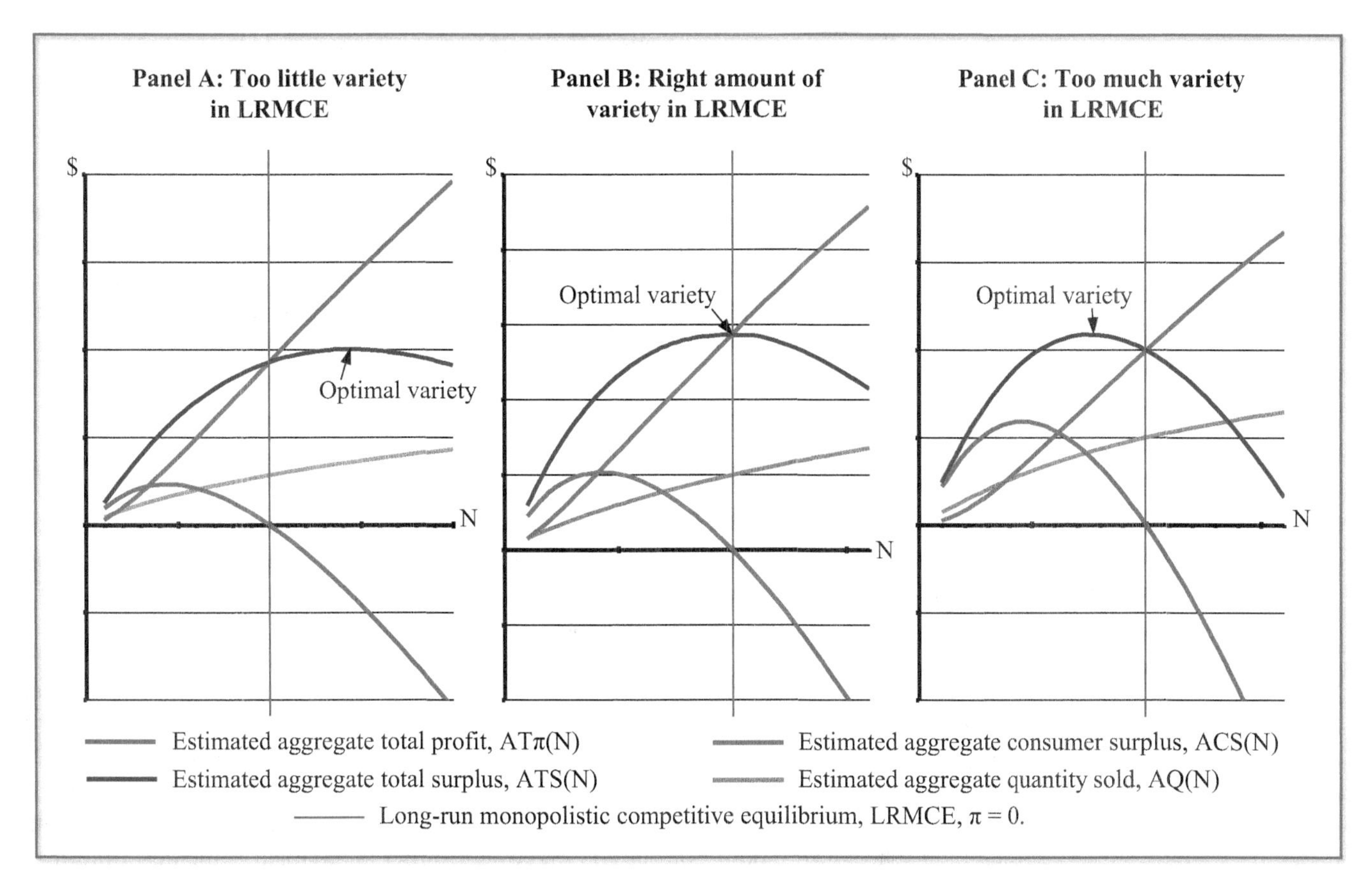

FIGURE 16.11 Optimal Variety versus Market-Determined Variety in Long-Run Monopolistic Competitive Equilibrium (LRMCE)

Data are based on the scenarios described in Figure 16.10.

because ATS(10) < ATS(9) and the Excel file for Figure 16.10 shows that eight firms maximize total surplus in this instance (ATS(8) = \$2,174, based on the scenario in Figure 16.10C). Each of the theoretically possible outcomes may occur in long-run monopolistically competitive markets. It depends on how entry affects demand, and as we have seen both in this chapter and in Chapter 15, there is no single description of how entry affects demand in differentiated product markets.

The aggregate information can be graphed as a function of the number of firms in the market to provide an alternative description of this point. Figure 16.11 depicts the four aggregate series from Equations 16.11a–16.11d for the three scenarios shown in Figure 16.10. The horizontal axis in each panel is the number of varieties in the market (in Figure 16.11A, the maximum N is 20; in the other two panels, it is 16), and the vertical axis is dollars (except for aggregate quantity sold). Numbers have been suppressed because numerical values are less important than the qualitative relations shown in each graph. As we described earlier, each scenario was created so that N = 10 is the LRMCE for this market. This is seen by $A\pi(N) = 0$ when N = 10 in each panel. This is highlighted by placing a red vertical line on each graph at this market-determined value of N. In each graph, the general expectations discussed previously are shown: Aggregate quantity and aggregate consumer surplus are both increasing functions of variety, while aggregate profits and total surplus first increase and then decrease.

Total surplus is maximized when the increase in aggregate consumer surplus due to an additional variety equals the decrease in profits due to the additional variety. In terms of the slopes of these curves, *this occurs where the slope of the pink aggregate consumer surplus curve is the same as the slope of the green profit curve* (with opposing signs). This need not occur when profits are zero (the condition required by LRMCE). In Figure 16.11A, this occurs when $\pi < 0$; indeed, we noted earlier that this occurs when N = 14.

Therefore, there is too little variety in this LRMCE. In Figure 16.11B, this occurs when $\pi = 0$, and the LRMCE exhibits the right amount of variety. Finally, optimal variety in Figure 16.11C is N = 8, so there is too much variety in this LRMCE.

The market may produce too much or too little variety in differentiated product markets subject to free entry and exit. The choice of how many varieties to produce is based on adding varieties up to the point where each variety earns only normal profits. But as we have just seen, this amount of variety does not necessarily maximize social net benefits. We cannot say that too little or too much variety is being produced without further information about how highly consumers value the diversity produced by the market, relative to how costly it is to produce that degree of diversity.

16.5 Examining Consumer Net Benefit Using the Consumption Diagram *OPTIONAL SECTION*

The net economic position of consumers within the economic system changes when economic circumstances change. For example, when the price of a good changes, so does the net benefit from consuming that good. The measure of this change in net benefit, developed in Section 16.1, was based on demand curves. Specifically, the change in consumer surplus from a price change is the area behind the individual consumer's demand curve between the two prices. We now examine the change in net benefit of a price change, using the consumption diagram. In the process, we will sharpen our understanding of what the change in consumer surplus measure actually signifies for the consumer.

We return to the consumption diagram because it formed the basis for our consumer maximization model. Consumers wish to do as well as possible, subject to the constraints they face. The starting point for our analysis of consumer behavior was the description of an individual's preferences using indifference curves (Chapter 3). From here, we introduced utility functions as a convenient artificial construct to algebraically describe preferences (Chapter 4). Budget constraints provide a simple description of the constraints posed by the market (Chapter 5). The utility-maximizing model allows us to examine how an individual responds to a price change in consumption space (Chapters 5 and 6), as well as with the demand curves that were derived from the optimal choices in the consumption diagram in Chapters 7 and 8.

We can easily answer how valuable a price change is within the consumer choice model, using the demand decomposition that was the focus of Chapter 8. Since this decomposition has not been used formally since Chapter 8, it may be worthwhile to quickly skim that chapter prior to reading further here.

Two Exact Measures: Compensating Variation and Equivalent Variation

compensating variation (CV): Compensating variation is the amount of income that may be taken from the individual to maintain the initial utility level in the face of new prices.

equivalent variation (EV): Equivalent variation is the amount of income that must be given to the individual to be as well off with old prices as that individual is in the face of new prices.

In Section 16.1, we did not delineate that the demand curve was Marshallian; we just called it demand. As noted in Section 8.4, when the nature of the individual demand curve is not specified, it is undoubtedly Marshallian. Change in consumer surplus provides an observable, albeit inexact, measure of the welfare effect of a price change. It is inexact because utility varies along the Marshallian demand curve. Indeed, we noted that Marshallian demand might be called "utility-compensated demand" because utility is compensated (adjusted) to maintain income along Marshallian demand. As a result, the welfare measure based on this demand curve suffers from what some have called a "rubber yardstick."

An exact measure of the welfare effect of a price change would base that calculation on holding welfare (or utility) constant, while varying price. Two natural choices exist regarding the welfare level to hold constant: the initial utility level or the final utility level. The former leads to a measure called **compensating variation (CV)**, and the latter leads to a measure called **equivalent variation (EV)**. CV and EV both examine the welfare effect of a price change; the difference is based on the utility level chosen as the point of reference.

TABLE 16.1 Comparing Two Exact Welfare Measures

Measure	Utility Basis for Comparison	Price Basis for Comparison
Compensating variation	Initial (old) utility level	Final (new) prices
Equivalent variation	Final (new) utility level	Initial (old) prices

CV examines the income required to maintain initial utility, while EV examines the income required to maintain final utility. *CV answers the prospective question:* "What would you require to maintain the level of welfare you currently enjoy if you face a new economic circumstance?" By contrast, if the final utility level is the point of reference, then *EV answers the retrospective question:* "How much better off are you now than you were prior to the change in economic circumstance?"

Compensating variation examines how much compensation is required to maintain the initial (or old) utility level. Economists have a variety of ways of saying this, but the basic point is simple:

Use CV if you wish to maintain old utility in the face of new prices.

The following definition has the virtue that it produces the right "signs" in its answer (i.e., price decreases are positive, and price increases are negative): Compensating variation is the amount of income that may be taken from the individual to maintain the initial utility level in the face of new prices. This will be negative for price increases but is positive for price decreases.

Equivalent variation examines how much compensation is required to maintain the final (or new) utility level. As with CV, authors have a variety of ways of saying this, but the basic point is simple:

Use EV if you wish to maintain new utility in the face of old prices.

The following definition has the virtue that it also produces the right signs: Equivalent variation is the amount of income that must be given to the individual to be as well off with old prices as that individual is in the face of new prices. This will be negative for price increases but is positive for price decreases. The difference between these measures is summarized in Table 16.1. Algebraic interpretations of both measures are provided shortly.

CV and EV of a Price Decrease from Consumption Bundles

The CV and EV definitions are made operational, using the demand decomposition from Chapter 8. Specifically, these definitions require finding substitution points on the initial and final indifference curves. Both measures are calculated as a change in income required to purchase the substitution bundle. This allows the individual to maintain a level of utility, given a change in price.

CV is based on the initial indifference curve but final prices:

$$CV = I_{final} - (P_x^{final} \cdot x_{sub}^{initial} + P_y \cdot y_{sub}^{initial}) = I_{final} - (P_x^{final} \cdot x_s + P_y \cdot y_s). \qquad \textbf{(16.13a)}$$

where $(x_{sub}^{initial}, y_{sub}^{initial}) = (x_s, y_s) = \mathbf{S}$ is the point on the initial indifference curve where the MRS equals the new price ratio. Using the price decrease described in Figure 16.12, this substitution bundle is **S** in Figure 16.12A. *Bundles **C**, **D**, and **S** are the same initial, final, and substitution bundles examined in Chapter 8.* (Indeed, these preferences are exactly the same as used to introduce Hicksian versus Marshallian demands in Figure 8.10.) In terms of the consumption bundles in Figure 16.12A,

$$\begin{aligned} CV &= I_{final} - (P_x^{final} \cdot x_s + P_y \cdot y_s) = \$10 - (\$0.25 \cdot 16.21 + \$1 \cdot 2.80) \\ &= \$10 - \$6.86 = \$3.14. \end{aligned} \qquad \textbf{(16.13b)}$$

CV is the difference in income required to support the red final budget constraint and the green substitution budget constraint, as both of these constraints are based on final prices. The green budget constraint supports the initial utility level at minimum cost, given the new lower price for x of $P_1 = \$0.25$. Given the coordinates of bundle **S**, we have the substitution budget constraint intercept at **F** = (0, 6.86), and we see CV = \$3.14 as the green vertical segment between **A** and **F**, multiplied by the price of y:

$$CV = P_y \cdot (\mathbf{A} - \mathbf{F}) = \$1 \cdot (10 - 6.86) = \$3.14. \qquad \textbf{(16.13c)}$$

Given that y is a numeraire ($P_y = 1$), the vertical axis intercept, I/P_y, acts as a measure of income required to support each budget constraint. In this instance, we can describe compensating variation as the line segment **A** – **F**. (Were $P_y \neq \$1$, we would have to multiply this length by P_y to describe CV, as noted in Equation 16.13c.)

EV examines the reverse combination of utility level and prices. EV is based on the final indifference curve and initial prices:

$$EV = (P_x^{initial} \cdot x_{sub}^{final} + P_y \cdot y_{sub}^{final}) - I_{initial} = (P_x^{initial} \cdot x_e + P_y \cdot y_e) - I_{initial}. \qquad \textbf{(16.14a)}$$

where $(x_{sub}^{final}, y_{sub}^{final}) = (x_e, y_e) = \mathbf{E}$ is the point on the final indifference curve in Figure 16.12B where the MRS = $P_x^{initial}/P_y$, the initial price ratio. This substitution point was not discussed in Chapter 8 but is determined in exactly the same way as **S**. The roll is simply in the opposite direction (to the original price ratio) along the final indifference curve, U_1. EV is the difference between the gold budget constraint tangent to the substitution bundle **E** on U_1 and the blue initial budget constraint because both of these budget constraints are based on initial prices. (Note that $I_{initial} = I_{final}$. In both instances, this income level is associated with bundle **A**.) Given the coordinates of bundle **E**, we have:

$$EV = (P_x^{initial} \cdot x_e + P_y \cdot y_e) - I_{initial} = (\$0.50 \cdot 14.45 + \$1 \cdot 7.22) - \$10$$
$$= \$14.45 - \$10 = \$4.45. \qquad \textbf{(16.14b)}$$

As with CV, the EV calculation is easy to see as lengths along the Y axis in the consumption bundle diagram, using the substitution budget constraint intercept at **G** = (0, 14.45). In this instance:

$$EV = P_y \cdot (\mathbf{G} - \mathbf{A}) = \$1 \cdot (14.45 - 10) = \$4.45. \qquad \textbf{(16.14c)}$$

EV = \$4.45 = **G** – **A**, the vertical distance between the gold and blue budget constraints (since $P_y = 1$). (You may well have noticed that CV ≠ EV in this instance. We postpone our discussion of why this is the case in order to show CV and EV of a price increase.)

CV and EV of a Price Increase from Consumption Bundles

A price increase harms consumers; therefore, each welfare measure should be negative. Figure 16.13 depicts the effect of an increase in price from $P_0 = \$0.50$ to $P_1 = \$1.25$, given the same preferences used to create Figure 16.12. Note in particular that initial budget constraint **AB** and optimal bundle **C** are the same in Figures 16.12 and 16.13. The P_1 slider in the Excel file for Figure 16.13 allows you to adjust the final price to examine how both figures may be seen as part of a dynamic continuum.

The welfare measures are calculated exactly the same as for a price decrease. As noted previously, the definitions provided produce negative answers for price increases. For example, CV is the amount of income that may be *taken* from the individual to maintain the initial utility level in the face of new prices. If the new prices are higher than the old, then a negative "taken" must be "given" to maintain the initial utility level in the face of higher prices. For a price increase, the initial indifference curve is the higher indifference curve because, in the end, the consumer is worse off because of the price increase. CV is one measure of how much worse off the individual is in this instance. This measure is based on Equation 16.13a and on the income required to support bundle **S**, given the new higher price (of \$1.25):

$$CV = I_{final} - (P_x^{final} \cdot x_s + P_y \cdot y_s) = \$10 - (\$1.25 \cdot 4.49 + \$1 \cdot 9.36)$$
$$= \$10 - \$14.97 = -\$4.97. \qquad \textbf{(16.15a)}$$

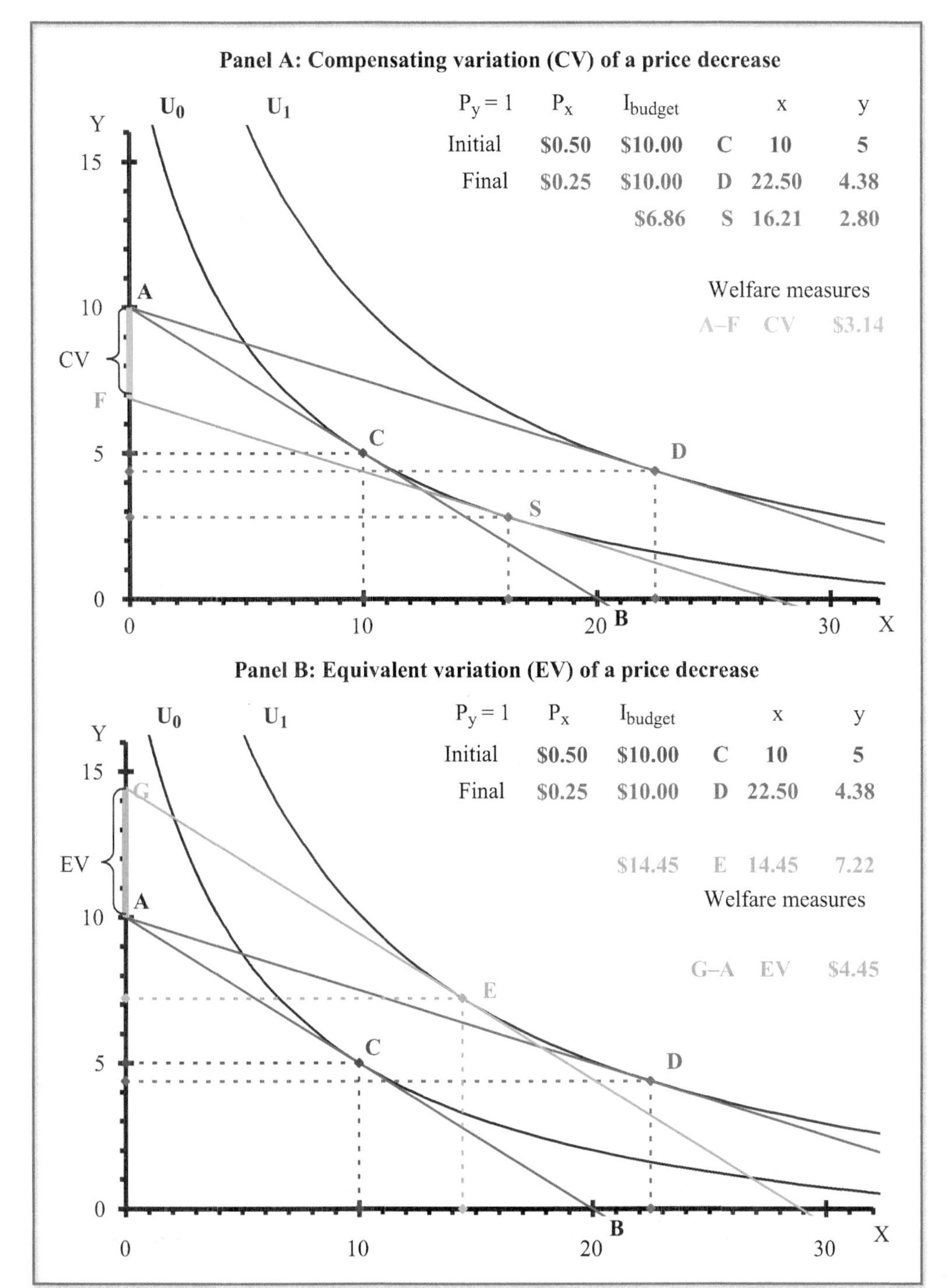

FIGURE 16.12 Measuring the Welfare Impact of a Price Decrease in a Consumption Diagram

CV is the length **A** – **F**, but it is a negative number, since the equation actually calculates CV = **A** – **F** ($10 represents the cost of **A**, and $14.97 represents the cost of **F**). The sign can be seen by **A** being below the intercept bundle **F** whenever a price increase is being considered. Similarly, EV is the amount of income that must be *given* to the individual to be as well off with old prices as the individual is in the face of new prices. If the new prices are higher, then a negative amount must be "given to" (i.e., an amount must be "taken from") the individual to achieve the new (lower) utility level, using the old (lower) prices. The final utility level is achieved at bundle **D** but is most cheaply achieved given the initial prices at the substitution bundle **E** on U_1. The EV of the price increase based on Equation 16.14a is:

$$EV = (P_x^{initial} \cdot x_e + P_y \cdot y_e) - I_{initial} = (\$0.50 \cdot 6.86 + \$1 \cdot 3.43) - \$10$$
$$= \$6.86 - \$10 = -\$3.14. \qquad \textbf{(16.15b)}$$

FIGURE 16.13 Measuring the Welfare Impact of a Price Increase in a Consumption Diagram

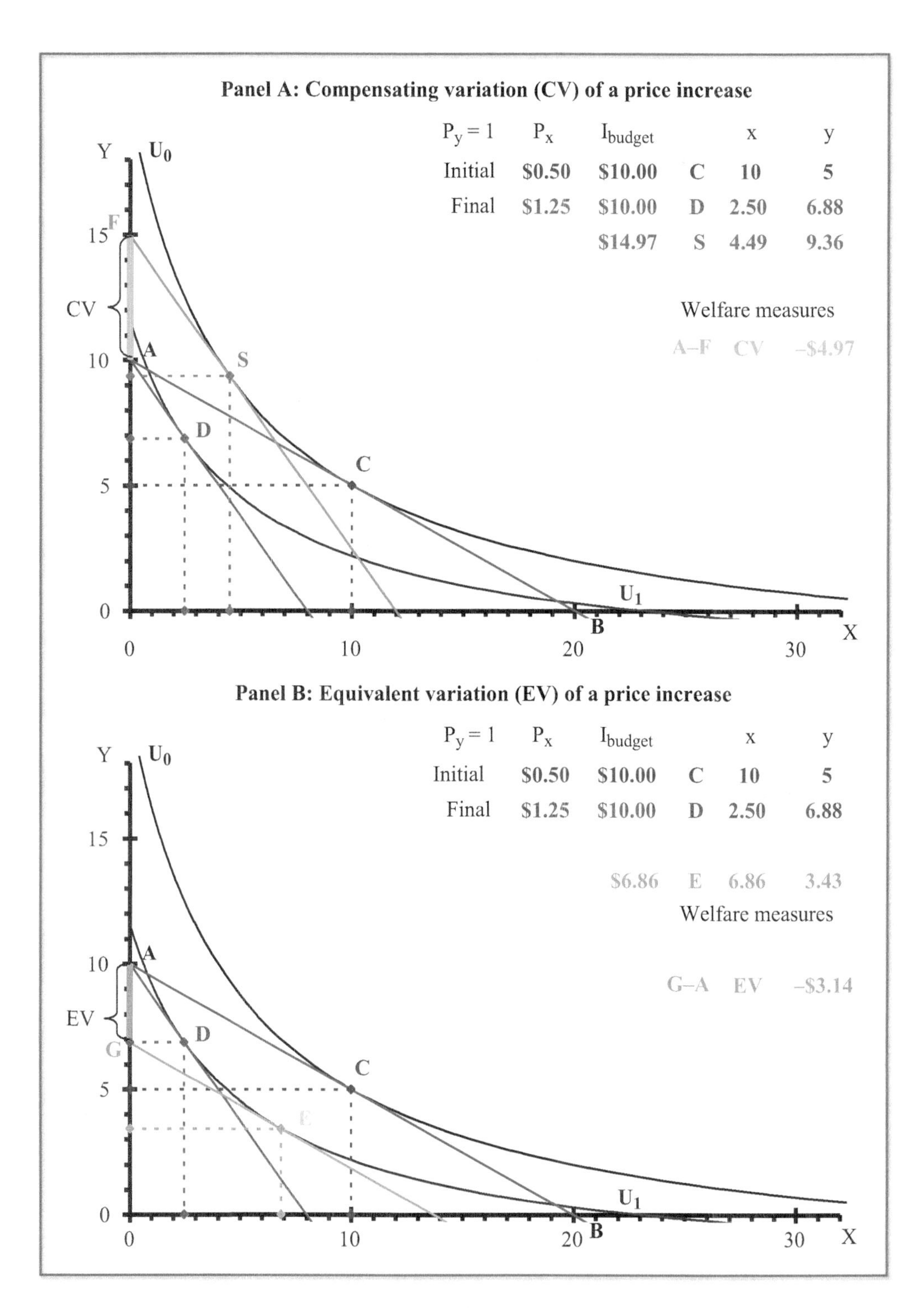

This is seen as the vertical distance **G** – **A** in Figure 16.13B, since $P_y = 1$ (the same as in Figure 16.12B). And just as in Figure 16.13A, we see that the sign is negative because **G** is below **A** on the vertical axis for price increases.

The consumption bundles **S** and **E** are derived by minimizing the expenditure required to achieve a given utility level. These bundles are points on the Hicksian demand curves associated with utility levels U_0 and U_1. Given a specific utility function, we could obtain Hicksian demand curves, using the optimization described in Equation 8.3. From here, we can obtain CV and EV for a price change based on Equations 16.13a and 16.14a.

16.6 Comparing CV, EV, and CS by Tying Consumption to Demand *OPTIONAL SECTION* ***(Prerequisite: Section 8.4)***

We have seen from the two examples shown in Figures 16.12 and 16.13 that CV and EV need not produce the same dollar measure of the change in welfare associated with a price change. Most basically, a change in welfare describes how different the initial indifference curve is from the final indifference curve. We learned in Chapter 4 that utility answers to that question are not unique because utility functions do not uniquely describe preferences. (You may recall that we stated this by noting that if you have a utility function that represents a given set of preferences, then any monotonic transformation of that function represents the same preferences.) The present situation is different in a concrete way from the monotonicity issue described in Section 4.3 because both measures are denominated in the same units of measurement; both are denominated in dollars.

Consider CV and EV in Figures 16.12 and 16.13 from a geometric perspective. Both can be seen as describing how far "apart" the initial and final indifference curves are when viewed from two parallel tangent lines to the indifference curves. These parallel lines have slope $-P_1/P_y$ for the CV measure and $-P_0/P_y$ for the EV measure. In general, these parallel lines need not remain equidistant in the face of price changes, but there is one instance in which this is the case. If preferences are quasilinear, then CV and EV always produce the same answer, and, in this instance, $CV = EV = \Delta CS$. The formal proof of this assertion requires calculus, but even without calculus, we can see the essence of why this is true. In the process, we will obtain insights into what happens more generally when CV and EV are not equal.

The Special Case of Quasilinear Preferences

The assertion that quasilinear preferences produce welfare measures in which $CV = EV = \Delta CS$ is actually two assertions. The first assertion has to do with the first equality, and the second assertion has to do with tying CV and EV to (Δ)CS.

> **Note:** *We will now drop the* Δ *and simply acknowledge that we are considering change in consumer surplus whenever we say CS in the current discussion.*

The first assertion may be proven by reexamining the properties of quasilinear functions. The formal proof of the second assertion is beyond the scope of this text. Nonetheless, we can see the heuristic basis for this assertion by a careful examination of demand.

In Chapter 4, we noted that if preferences can be represented by a utility function of the form $U(x, y) = f(x) + y$, then indifference curves are vertical translates of one another. As a result, the vertical distance between any two indifference curves does not depend on which parallel tangent lines are used to determine that distance. In terms of the substitution points that form the key to understanding CV and EV, this simply means that the substitution point and the point on the actual budget constraint are vertically aligned if preferences are quasilinear. The MRS of any bundle is determined entirely by the quantity of x in the consumption bundle; therefore, tangencies of parallel budget constraints must occur at the same quantity of x, given quasilinear preferences. In particular, the CV substitution point **S** always has the same amount of x as the final point **D**, and the EV substitution point **E** always has the same amount of x as the initial point **C**.

To examine this in greater depth, we must consider a specific quasilinear utility function:

$$U(x, y) = 5 \cdot \ln(x) + y. \quad \textbf{(16.16a)}$$

There is nothing special about this quasilinear function. As noted in Equation 7.11, this produces Marshallian demand functions:

$$x(P_x, P_y, I) = 5 \cdot P_y/P_x, \text{ and} \quad \textbf{(16.16b)}$$

$$y(P_x, P_y, I) = I/P_y - 5. \quad \textbf{(16.16c)}$$

As noted in Section 8.3, there is no income effect on demand for x, given quasilinear demand, so Hicksian demand for x is the same as Marshallian:

$$h_x(P_x, P_y, U) = 5 \cdot P_y/P_x. \quad \textbf{(16.16d)}$$

To obtain Hicksian demand for y, we simply solve for y, using the utility function given this Hicksian demand for x. This produces Hicksian demand for y of:

$$h_y(P_x, P_y, U) = U - 5 \cdot \ln(5 \cdot P_y/P_x). \quad \textbf{(16.16e)}$$

We can use this Hicksian demand information to calculate CV and EV. Hicksian demand for y requires that the utility level be specified. These utility levels are based on the change in price of x under consideration. Suppose that the initial price of x is P_0, and the final price is P_1. The initial and final utility levels, given Equations 16.16a–16.16c, are, respectively:

$$U_0 = 5 \cdot \ln(5 \cdot P_y/P_0) + I/P_y - 5, \text{ and}$$

$$U_1 = 5 \cdot \ln(5 \cdot P_y/P_1) + I/P_y - 5 \quad \textbf{(16.16f)}$$

As noted earlier, $I_{initial} = I_{final} = I$; the only difference is their geometric interpretation. The blue budget constraint represents initial price, and the red budget constraint represents final price in Figures 16.12 and 16.13. They are both equal at **A** in each graph because **A** represents spending all income on the good whose price has not changed, y. Therefore, CV, based on Equations 16.13a and 16.16d–16.16f, is:

$$CV = I_{final} - (P_1 \cdot x_s + P_y \cdot y_s)$$

$$CV = I - (P_1 \cdot (5 \cdot P_y/P_1) + P_y \cdot (5 \cdot \ln(5 \cdot P_y/P_0) + I/P_y - 5 - 5 \cdot \ln(5 \cdot P_y/P_1))$$

$$CV = 5 \cdot P_y \cdot \ln(5 \cdot P_y/P_1) - 5 \cdot P_y \cdot \ln(5 \cdot P_y/P_0)$$

$$CV = 5 \cdot P_y \cdot (\ln(P_0) - \ln(P_1)) \quad \textbf{(16.17a)}$$

Similarly, EV, based on Equations 16.14a and 16.16d–16.16f, is:

$$EV= (P_0 \cdot x_{sub}{}^{final} + P_y \cdot y_{sub}{}^{final}) - I_{initial}$$

$$EV = P_0 \cdot 5 \cdot P_y/P_0 + P_y \cdot (5 \cdot \ln(5 \cdot P_y/P_1) + I/P_y - 5 - 5 \cdot \ln(5 \cdot P_y/P_0)) - I$$

$$EV = 5 \cdot P_y \cdot \ln(5 \cdot P_y/P_1) - 5 \cdot P_y \cdot \ln(5 \cdot P_y/P_0)$$

$$EV = 5 \cdot P_y \cdot (\ln(P_0) - \ln(P_1)) \quad \textbf{(16.17b)}$$

We see algebraically that EV and CV equal each other, regardless of values P_0 and P_1. This is simply an algebraic acknowledgment of the vertical translation property discussed earlier. When these functions are evaluated at $I = \$10$, $P_y = \$1$, $P_0 = \$1$, and $P_1 = \$0.50$, we obtain the results shown in Figure 16.14. A decline in the price of x from \$1.00 to \$0.50 causes demand for x to increase from 5 to 10 (from **C** to **D**). The value of this price decrease is \$3.47, regardless of whether that value is being measured as CV = **A** – **F** or EV = **G** – **A** in Figure 16.14. Both distances are the same because both are simply examples of the vertical translate property measured along the vertical axis. The vertical translate property simply notes that the line segments **EC** = **DS** because these two vertical distances between the two indifference curves are simply two examples of the continuum of other possibilities that could have been chosen. The two indifference curves are vertical translates of each other; therefore, they are the same distance apart, regardless of x value used to check the vertical distance.

The final assertion regarding welfare measures with quasilinear preferences is that CV and EV coincide with the change in consumer surplus in this instance. To see why this is the case, return once more to our initial conceptualization of consumer surplus for coffee. Imagine purchasing espresso shots by the ounce. At \$1.00 per ounce, you buy five 1-ounce shots, but more generally, suppose that your demand for espresso shots is given by:

$$x(P) = 5/P. \quad \textbf{(16.18a)}$$

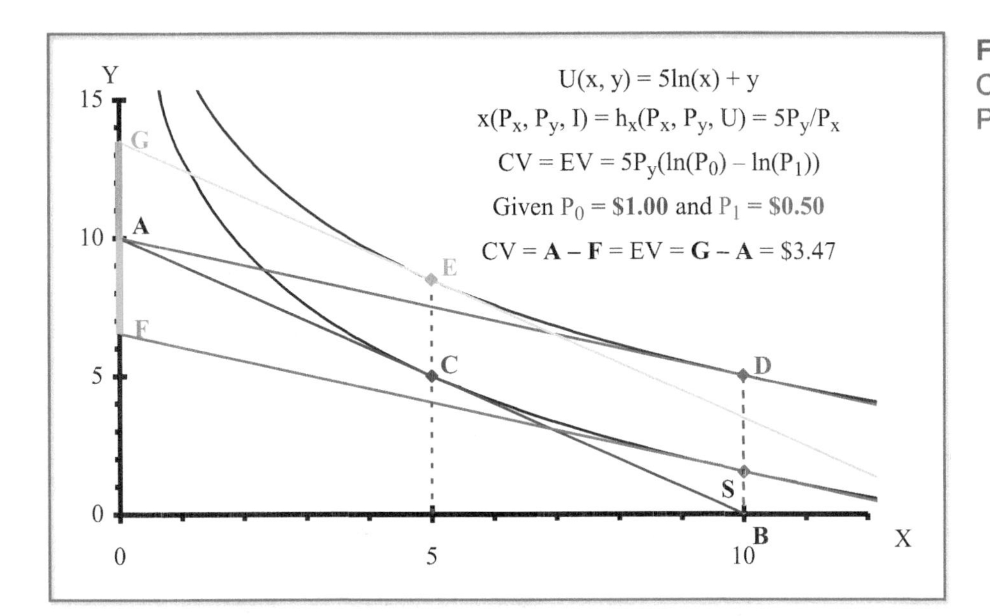

FIGURE 16.14
CV = EV for Quasilinear Preferences

This can be inverted to describe inverse demand (marginal valuation) as a function of number of shots of espresso as:

$$P(x) = 5/x. \qquad \textbf{(16.18b)}$$

This demand function is independent of income; therefore, this demand function emanates from quasilinear preferences. (Quasilinear preferences are the only kind of preferences examined in Chapter 4 for which demand is independent of income.) Indeed, this demand function is exactly the one we would derive using the preferences shown in Figure 16.14. (Note, in particular, that Equation 16.18a coincides with Marshallian and Hicksian demands in Equations 16.16b and 16.16d, given $P_y = 1$). According to Equation 16.16b, the marginal valuations of the sixth through tenth shots are \$0.83, \$0.71, \$0.63, \$0.56, and \$0.50, respectively. *These can be thought of as steps down the discrete version of a marginal valuation (inverse demand) schedule; these steps are depicted in the bottom graph of Figure 16.15.* If we consider the drop in price from \$1.00 per shot to \$0.50 per shot, we increase demand from five to ten shots. The change in consumer surplus due to this price change is approximated by the excess benefit on the first five shots of \$0.50/shot (■ $x_c \cdot \Delta P_x = 5 \cdot \$0.50 = \$2.50$ in both panels), plus an excess of \$0.33, 0.\$21, \$0.13, and \$0.06 on the sixth through the ninth shots, respectively. That is, the discrete change in consumer surplus due to the price decline is the 5 by \$0.50 rectangle, plus the "jagged" triangle from 5 to 10 above the $P_1 = \$0.50$ line in Figure 16.15. Discrete change in CS, ΔCS_d, is therefore estimated as \$3.23 in the demand panel of that figure. Discrete consumer surplus does not incorporate the "triangular" areas above each of the steps; these triangles are labeled with small numbers 6–10 above each ounce's discrete marginal valuation. The sum of these areas using 1/2 base times height is \$0.25, so our "estimation" of the area behind the demand curve, ΔCS, is \$3.48. This estimate is only one cent off the \$3.47 we obtain by applying the CV or EV calculation in Equation 16.17.

This can also be seen in the consumption diagram. We know that the slope of an indifference curve is always MRS = MU_x/MU_y. But, as we noted in Chapter 4, the marginal utility of y is constant for quasilinear functions; indeed, it is unitary: $MU_y \equiv 1$.[11]

Claim: *The height of the demand curve is marginal valuation, but in this instance, it is also the slope of the indifference curve (because MRS = MU_x, given $MU_y \equiv 1$).*

These slopes are shown in the top graph of Figure 16.15, based on the marginal valuation schedule we obtained from the demand schedule in Equation 16.18b. (Each of the separately colored L-shaped parts has a horizontal segment 1 unit wide. The height of each vertical segment is given by 5/x, the height of the marginal valuation of that unit

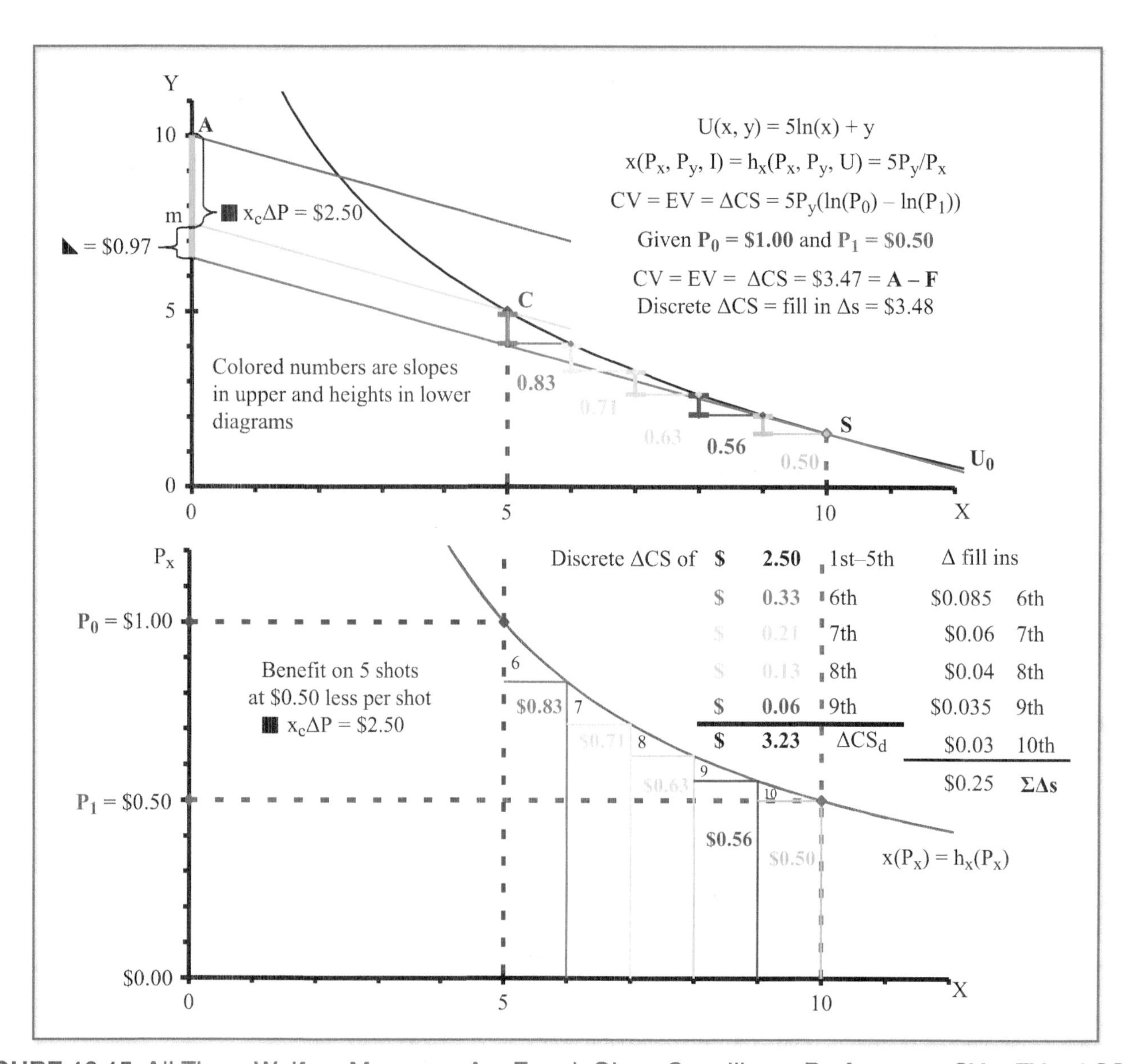

FIGURE 16.15 All Three Welfare Measures Are Equal, Given Quasilinear Preferences CV = EV = ΔCS

in the bottom graph.) This was constructed with each horizontal segment starting on the indifference curve. Due to the curvature of the indifference curve, the sum of the discrete slopes does not move us exactly from bundle **S** to bundle **C** (indeed, this is where the triangular areas in the lower diagram come into play).[12] The cumulative sum of the surpluses from shots 5 to 10 is the $0.97 vertical distance between the green substitution budget constraint tangent to **S** and the light green "fixed-basket" budget constraint that passes through **C**. This is the distance **m** – **F** on the vertical axis. The rest of the change in consumer surplus is the 5 by $0.50 rectangle in the bottom graph that is seen in the top graph as the difference between initial income (at **A**) and income required to maintain the fixed bundle **C** ($x_c \cdot \Delta P_x = 5 \cdot \$0.50 = \$2.50$) at **m**. *Therefore, the change in consumer surplus is the same amount as CV and EV in the top graph.* Each can be seen as **A** – **F**, given quasilinear preferences.

The discussion of Figure 16.15 attempts to provide a heuristic basis for seeing how the consumption and demand diagrams can both be used to calculate the welfare effect of a price change. The best case can be made for quasilinear functions because here CV, EV, and CS all coincide. They coincide in this instance for a very good reason: Hicksian and Marshallian demand are the same for quasilinear functions (as noted in Chapter 8).

When Hicksian and Marshallian demands do not coincide, we can use Hicksian demand to calculate CV and EV, and we always use Marshallian demand to calculate CS. Specifically, CV and EV are also visible in the bottom graph of Figure 16.15 as the area behind the appropriate Hicksian demand curves between the initial and the final price levels.[13] At one level, this should not be surprising because Hicksian demand is based on substitution bundles, and so are the CV and EV calculations described algebraically in Equations 16.13 and 16.14 and shown in Figures 16.12 and 16.13. We did not calculate CV and EV as areas behind demand in Equations 16.13 and 16.14. Both of those calculations are based on comparisons of income required to achieve a substitution bundle with actual income in the consumption diagram; they are not based on areas behind Hicksian demand curves.

On the Relative Sizes of CV, EV, and CS

When there are no wealth effects on demand, then CV, EV, and CS will coincide. There are no wealth effects on demand for x, given quasilinear preferences, because the demand function does not include income. But quasilinear is the only class of preferences examined in our analysis of consumer theory for which this is true. In general, demand depends on income. If a good is normal, an increase in income increases demand for the good, and if the good is inferior, the reverse holds true. When demand depends on income, the three measures of the welfare impact of a price change will not, in general, coincide. Interestingly, by viewing these measures as areas behind demand curves, we can determine the relative sizes of these measures, based on the preferences under consideration.

You may have noticed that CV was smaller than EV for a price decrease but that CV was larger (in magnitude) than EV for a price increase in Section 16.5. We can quickly show that this is normally the case, using the demand diagrams to describe CV and EV. Figure 16.16 describes the price decrease scenario. This shows exactly the same preferences and price change examined in Figure 16.12, except that a demand diagram (bottom graph) has been added, and the current consumption diagram includes both CV and EV on the same diagram. EV > CV is represented by the vertical line segments in the top graph; **G** – **A** > **A** – **F**. The bottom graph provides a quick understanding of *why* this is true. The area behind the green Hicksian demand associated with U_0 is smaller than the area behind the gold Hicksian demand associated with U_1 because $H_0 = h_x(P_x, P_y, U_0) < h_x(P_x, P_y, U_1) = H_1$, given $U_1 > U_0$. The area behind H_0 is CV; the green "trapezoid" **CSTR** = CV = \$3.14, since CV asks us to roll along U_0 from **C** to **S**. Similarly, the area behind H_1 is EV; the gold "trapezoid" **EDTR** = EV = \$4.45, since EV asks us to roll along U_1 from **D** to **E**. (Δ)CS is seen to be sandwiched between these two values because the lavender CS "trapezoid" **CDTR** starts at **C** (on the inner Hicksian) and ends at **D** (on the outer Hicksian) because CS is calculated as the area behind Marshallian demand. We see geometrically that:

$$\text{CV} < \text{CS} < \text{EV for a price decrease.} \qquad \textbf{(16.19a)}$$

Numerically, in Figure 16.16, we see this as: \$3.14 < \$3.71 < \$4.45.

The assertion that the CV and EV lengths in the consumption diagram represent the same quantities as the areas behind Hicksian demand curves in the demand diagram is often quite surprising to students. We have shown in the quasilinear case that they are quite close by numerically estimating the area behind the demand curve (which is actually all three demand curves: Marshallian, H_0, and H_1). You should note that these areas are roughly correct in the more general situation shown in Figure 16.16. Consider CV as the area behind the green initial Hicksian, H_0, in the bottom graph. This is the sum of a 10 by \$0.25 rectangle and a "triangle" that is approximately 6 wide by \$0.25 high. Therefore, this approximation of CV is $\text{CV} \doteq \$3.25 = 10 \cdot \$0.25 + 6 \cdot \$0.25/2$, close to its actual value of \$3.14.

Exactly the opposite inequality holds for a price increase in terms of magnitude (but it is important to remember that these magnitudes now represent losses). Figure 16.17

FIGURE 16.16 The Welfare Impact of a Price Decrease, as Viewed by Consumption and Demand: CV < CS < EV When x Is a Normal Good

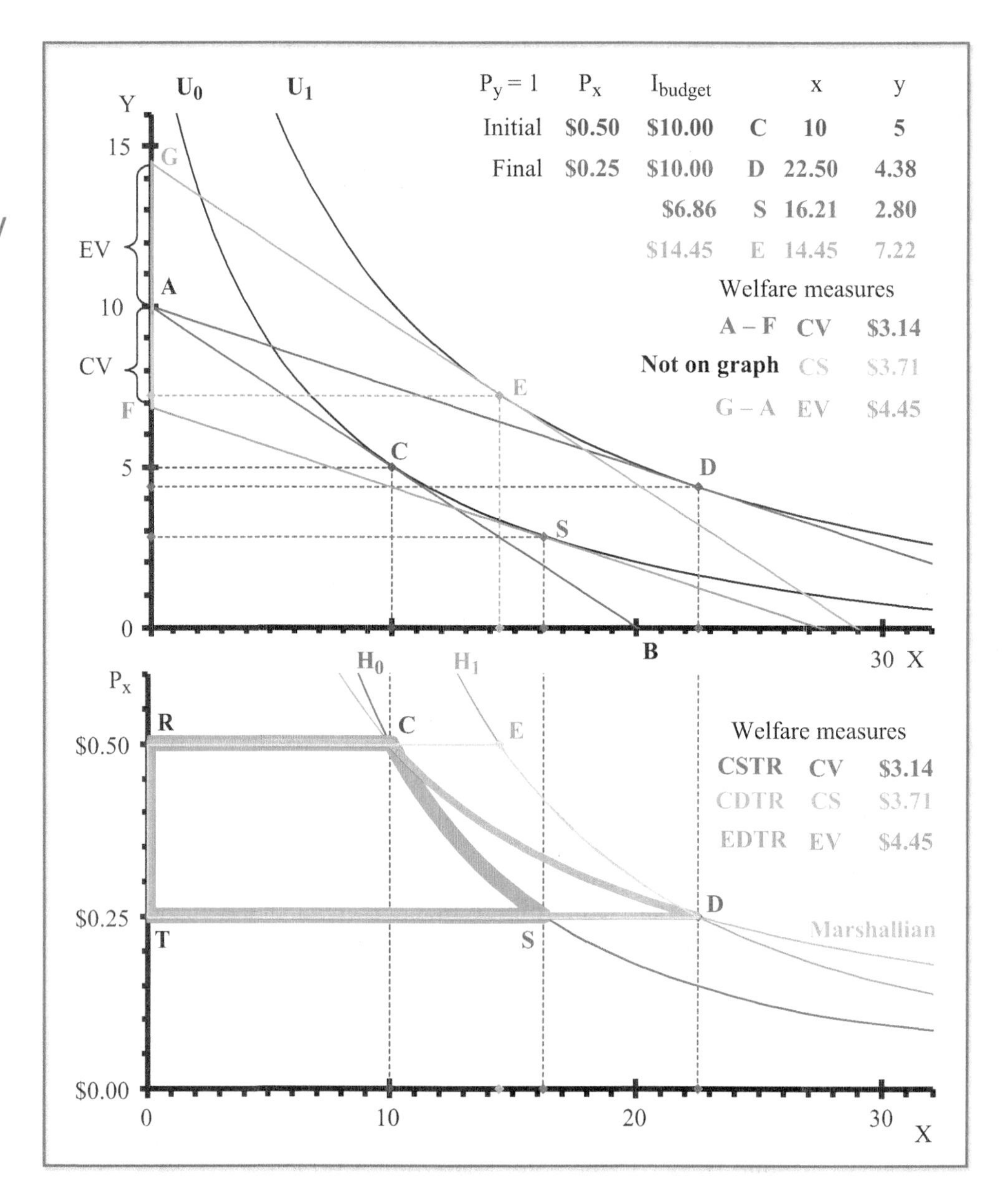

continues with the same preferences and initial price used in Figures 16.12, 16.13, and 16.16. CV is now the largest magnitude because U_0 is the highest indifference curve (and, more important, H_0 is the highest Hicksian). The next highest is CS, and the smallest is EV.

$$|CV| > |CS| > |EV| \text{ for a price increase.} \quad \textbf{(16.19b)}$$

Actual magnitudes for CV and EV are the same as in Figure 16.13, and as expected, based on the bottom graph in Figure 16.17, CS is sandwiched between these two values: $|CV| = \$4.97 > |CS| = \$3.85 > |EV| = \$3.14$.

CV and EV can be seen both in the consumption diagram and in the demand diagram, while CS can only be seen in the demand diagram, but CS can be easily derived from observed behavior. For both price increases and price decreases, we can see the theoretically correct measures of the welfare impact of a price change sandwich the empirically observable, but theoretically suspect, estimate of the welfare impact of that change. *CV and EV place bounds on CS.*

The relative orientations described in Equations 16.19a and 16.19b exist for the preferences shown in Figures 16.16 and 16.17, but the same relative orientation occurs whenever x is a normal good. (Recall that a normal good is one in which an increase in income increases demand for the good. A normal good is also described as one that has a positive income elasticity of demand, $\eta_x > 0$.) The reason for the relative magnitude of each mea-

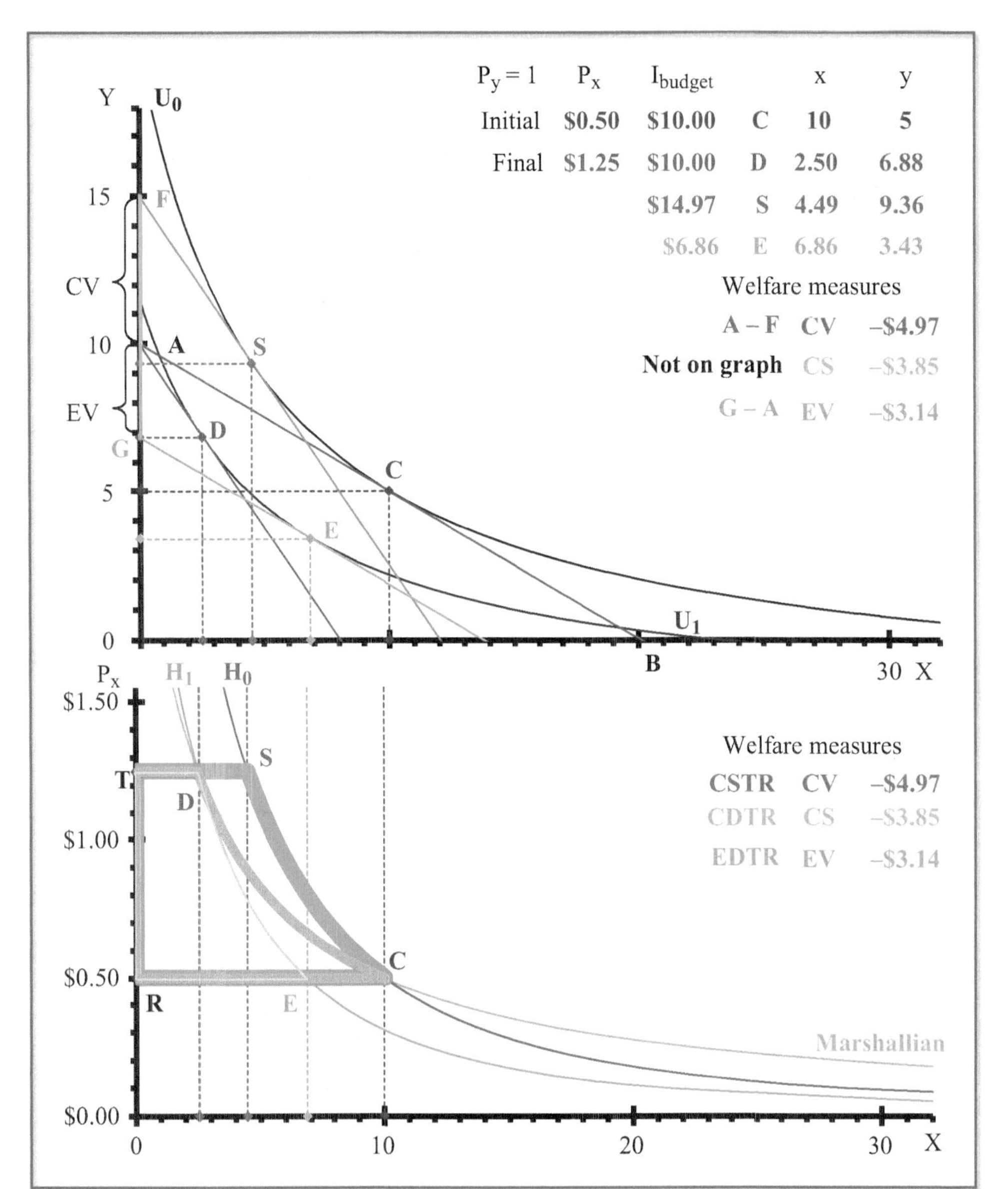

FIGURE 16.17 The Welfare Impact of a Price Increase as Viewed by Consumption and Demand: |CV| > |CS| > |EV| When x Is a Normal Good

sure is straightforward, once we consider the orientation of Hicksian and Marshallian demand curves. When x is a normal good, the income and substitution effect of a price change move in the same direction. As a result, Hicksian demand is steeper than Marshallian as long as $\eta_x > 0$ (because Hicksian demand describes only the substitution effect). If Hicksian is steeper than Marshallian, we know that the Hicksian through the lower of the two prices will always be outside the Hicksian through the upper of the two prices. Whichever utility level this is associated with, the lower price provides the larger welfare measure of the change in price. If a price increases, then the initial price produces the outer Hicksian, and as a result, |CV| is larger than |EV| for a price increase. If a price decreases, then the final price produces the outer Hicksian, and as a result, EV is larger than CV for price decreases.

We can also view normal goods in consumption space. This was most explicitly examined in the typology of goods analysis presented in Figure 8.6. The basic point in the current context is that x is a normal good if the x coordinate of **C** is less than the x coordinate of **E** and if the same can be said of **S** and **D** for a price decrease. This is true in Figure 16.16 because x is normal, $\eta_x > 0$. The limiting case is when **C** and **E** share the same x coordinate (as do **S** and **D**). This is the case of quasilinear preferences discussed earlier. In terms of income elasticity, x has zero income elasticity, since demand for x is independent of income, $\eta_x = 0$. As we saw in Figure 16.15, in this situation, all three measures

FIGURE 16.18 The Welfare Impact of a Price Decrease as Viewed by Consumption and Demand: CV > CS > EV When x Is an Inferior Good

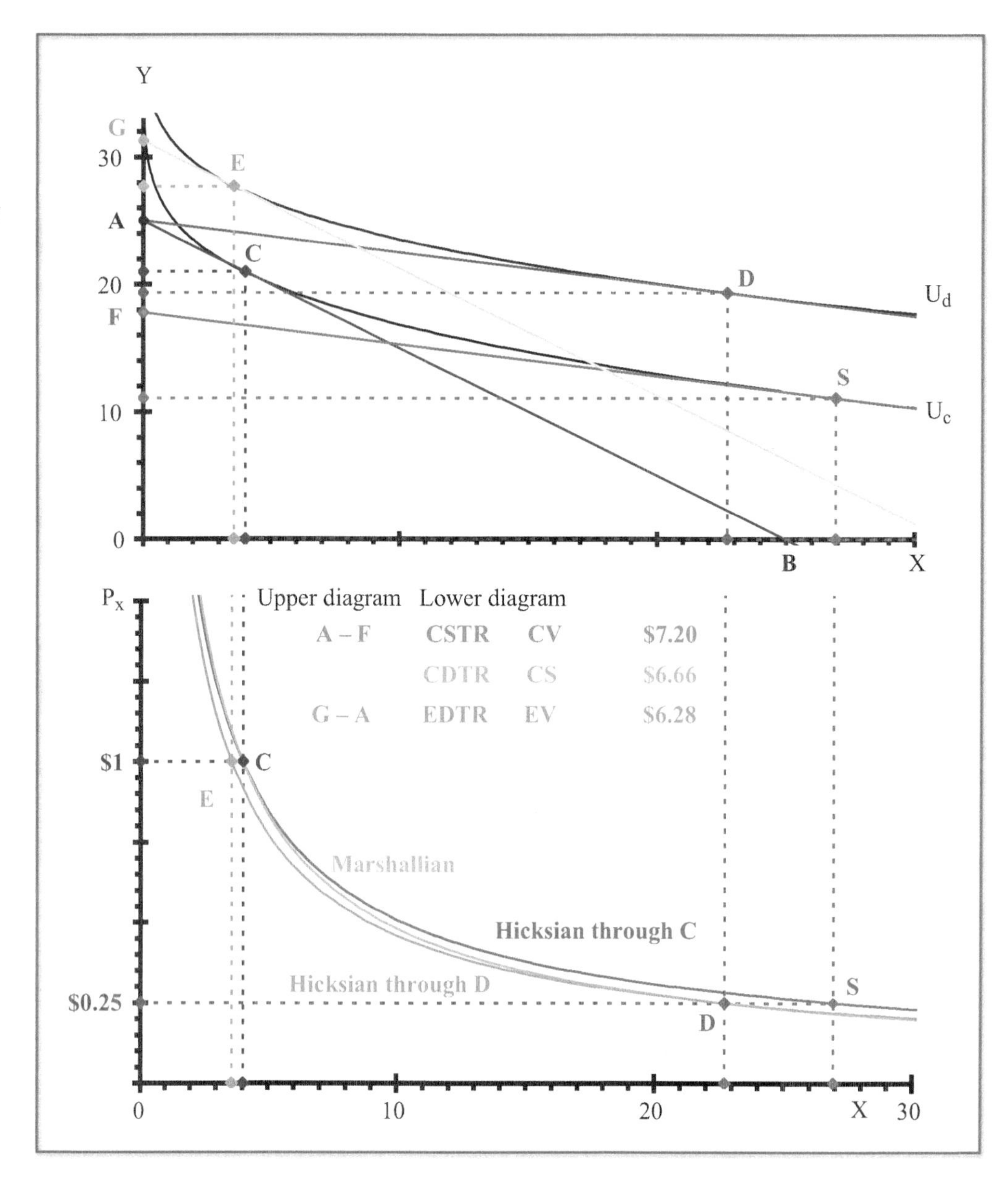

are identical. And finally, when x is inferior ($\eta_x < 0$), Marshallian demand is steeper than Hicksian. In this setting, the inequalities laid out in Equation 16.19 reverse because higher income levels are associated with smaller use of the good. The outer Hicksian in this setting is the one with higher price, so CV of a price decrease, for example, is larger than CS is larger than EV. This is the situation shown in Figure 16.18 for the preferences depicted in Figure 8.11, in which x is an inferior good. Note that the relative dollar values of CV, CS, and EV match as suggested (CV > CS > EV for a price decrease) because the Hicksian through the higher price outcome, H_0, is the outer Hicksian. This leads to the largest measure of the welfare impact of the price decrease.

We can summarize the relation between the three measures of the welfare impact of a price change, using linear Hicksian and Marshallian demand curves. We also can show both a price increase and a price decrease on the same diagram by simply not stating which Hicksian is associated with the initial or final situation. If we simply reverse initial and final prices, then CV and EV switch (and change sign). *The Hicksian demand curves in Figure 16.19 are colored light blue and dark blue, where light blue is associated with the higher price, and dark blue is associated with the lower price.* If we consider a price decrease, then the light blue Hicksian is H_0, and if we consider a price increase, then the dark blue Hicksian is H_0. Each of the three possibilities discussed previously is shown in a separate figure (although the quasilinear case is not formally shown, since in this

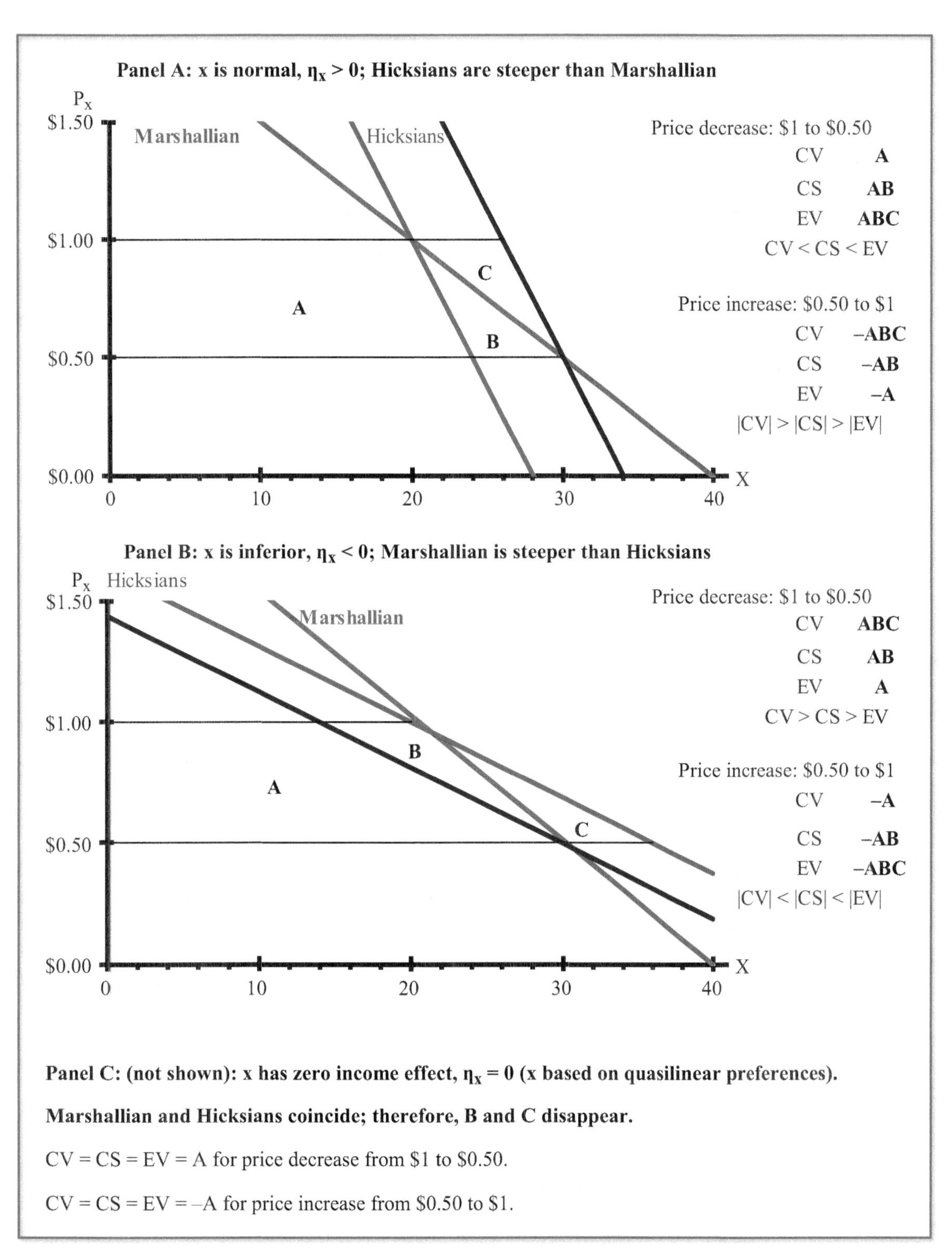

FIGURE 16.19 The Relative Size of CV, EV, and CS Depends on Income Elasticity of Demand

instance, CV = EV = CS = ± **A** (+ for price decrease, – for price increase) because **B** and **C** disappear when $x(P) = H_0(P) = H_1(P)$).

Consumer Surplus without Apology

A natural question arises, given three measures of the welfare impact of a price change: Which should you choose? Two of the three can be defended on a theoretical basis, but the third is easiest to calculate based on market data. In most situations, the practical answer is it does not matter. Only if the good in question has strong income effects, the price change is large, and if the good represents a substantial portion of spending will the differences be significant. The graphic analysis of the normal goods case (Figures 16.12, 16.13, 16.15, and 16.16) and the inferior goods case in Figure 16.18 used strong income effects, large price changes, and a substantial portion of income spent on the good to clearly show the differences between the three measures. As a result, the differences look substantial, but for a more realistic set of assumptions, these differences become much less significant. As a result, consumer surplus can be used "without apology," to reuse the wording of a famous article on this topic by Robert Willig.[14]

We can use the Hicksian and Marshallian demand information for Cobb-Douglas (CD) preferences to examine the amount of divergence between these measures of the welfare impact of a price change. These equations are reproduced here for quick reference.

Utility function

$$U(x, y) = x^r \cdot y^{(1-r)}. \tag{4.4}$$

Marshallian demands

$$x = r \cdot I/P_x. \tag{7.3a}$$

$$y = (1 - r) \cdot I/P_y. \tag{7.3b}$$

Hicksian substitution bundles

$$x_s = U \cdot ((r/(1 - r)) \cdot (P_y/P_x))^{(1-r)}. \tag{8.5a}$$

$$y_s = U \cdot (((1 - r)/r) \cdot (P_x/P_y))^r. \tag{8.5b}$$

The two Hicksian demand for x functions are simply determined by appropriate choice of utility level U, using Equation 8.5a. The two utility levels are obtained by substituting Marshallian demand solutions from Equations 7.3a and 7.3b back into the utility function (graphically, these solutions provide Marshallian bundles **C** and **D** in the diagrams in this instance).

Individuals with CD preferences (Equation 4.4) spend a constant percentage of income on each good (the percentage devoted to x is r, and the rest (1 – r) is devoted to y); the income elasticity of demand for both goods is unitary. If we describe the welfare measures in terms of percentage of income, then we obtain the same proportional results, regardless of actual income level chosen. Therefore, we can simplify our analysis by setting $P_x^0 = 1$, $P_y = 1$, and $I = 1$. If the new price of x is denoted $P_x^1 = P$, the two utility levels are given by Equations 16.20 and 16.21. (*Note:* Equations 16.20–16.26 have two versions per equation. The first (a) is the general CD solution, and the second (b) is the specific solution attained, given $P_x^0 = 1$, $P_x^1 = P$, $P_y = 1$, and $I = 1$.)

$$U_0 = x^r \cdot y^{(1-r)} = (r \cdot I/P_x^0)^r \cdot ((1 - r) \cdot I/P_y)^{(1-r)}. \tag{16.20a}$$

$$U_0 = r^r \cdot (1 - r)^{(1-r)}. \tag{16.20b}$$

$$U_1 = x^r \cdot y^{(1-r)} = (r \cdot I/P_x^1)^r \cdot ((1 - r) \cdot I/P_y)^{(1-r)}. \tag{16.21a}$$

$$U_1 = x^r \cdot y^{(1-r)} = (r/P)^r \cdot (1 - r)^{(1-r)}. \tag{16.21b}$$

By evaluating the substitution bundle described by Equations 8.5a and 8.5b at U_0, we obtain the coordinates of the CV bundle **S**, and if we use U_1, we obtain the coordinates of EV bundle **E**. Bundle **S** occurs if we use old utility at new price, so the coordinates of **S** using Equations 8.5a and 8.5b and Equation 16.20 are:

$$x_s = U_0 \cdot ((r/(1 - r)) \cdot (P_y/P_x^1))^{(1-r)} \quad \text{and} \quad y_s = U_0 \cdot (((1 - r)/r) \cdot (P_x^1/P_y))^r. \tag{16.22a}$$

$$x_s = r/P^{(1-r)} \quad \text{and} \quad y_s = (1 - r) \cdot P^r. \tag{16.22b}$$

Similarly, **E** occurs if we use new utility at old price, so the coordinates of bundle **E** are:

$$x_e = U_1 \cdot ((r/(1 - r)) \cdot (P_y/P_x^0))^{(1-r)} \quad \text{and} \quad y_e = U_1 \cdot (((1 - r)/r) \cdot (P_x^0/P_y))^r. \tag{16.23a}$$

$$x_e = r/P^r \quad \text{and} \quad y_e = (1 - r)/P^r. \tag{16.23b}$$

Compensating variation is obtained by substituting bundle **S** (Equation 16.22) into Equation 16.13:

$$CV = I - (P_x^{1} \cdot U_0 \cdot ((r/(1 - r)) \cdot (P_y/P_x^{1}))^{(1-r)} + P_y \cdot U_0 \cdot (((1 - r)/r) \cdot (P_x^{1}/P_y))^{r}). \quad \textbf{(16.24a)}$$

$$CV = 1 - P^{r}. \quad \textbf{(16.24b)}$$

Equivalent variation is obtained by substituting bundle **E** (Equation 16.23) into Equation 16.14:

$$EV = (P_x^{0} \cdot U_1 \cdot ((r/(1 - r)) \cdot (P_y/P_x^{0}))^{(1-r)} + P_y \cdot U_1 \cdot (((1 - r)/r) \cdot (P_x^{0}/P_y))^{r}) - I. \quad \textbf{(16.25a)}$$

$$EV = P^{-r} - 1. \quad \textbf{(16.25b)}$$

The change in consumer surplus implied by a change in price from P_x^0 to P_x^1 is the area behind Marshallian demand between these two prices. Given the general Marshallian demand for x from Equation 7.3a, we have:[15]

$$CS = r \cdot I \cdot (\ln(P_x^{0}) - \ln(P_x^{1})). \quad \textbf{(16.26a)}$$

Given $I = 1$, $P_x^0 = 1$, and $P_x^1 = P$, this simplifies to:

$$CS = -r \cdot \ln(P). \quad \textbf{(16.26b)}$$

The CV, EV, and CS solutions based on unitary initial price of x, price of y, and income in each "b" equation are surprisingly elegant. Given $P_x^0 = 1$, we expect that each of the welfare measures in Equations 16.24b, 16.25b, and 16.26b should produce a positive number when $P < 1$, zero when $P = 1$, and a negative number when $P > 1$. This is confirmed by each equation.

Although each measure appears straightforward, it is not immediately clear how closely the measures track one another. Can CS be used as a proxy for CV or EV "without apology," as suggested earlier? This question is examined in Figure 16.20. The graphs are based on CV, EV, and CS Equations 16.24–16.26. In both panels, CV is green, EV is gold, and CS is lavender. Price changes between a 50% decrease and a 100% increase are shown on the vertical axis. The horizontal axis describes the percentage of income required to compensate for the price change, according to each measure. The red curve describes the difference between the CV and EV measure of the welfare impact of the price change. Their general orientation is exactly as expected, based on the earlier discussion: CS is sandwiched between CV and EV, EV is larger for price decreases, and $|CV|$ is larger for price increases, just as predicted by Equation 16.19.

When the proportion of income devoted to the good is small, then all three measures track each other closely. For example, if the individual spends 15% of income on good x, $r = 0.15$ in Figure 16.20A. If the price of x doubles, then the extra income required to compensate for a 100% increase in price is about 10–11% (all three curves are tightly bunched near (–10%, 200%) in Figure 16.20A). This is exactly the result derived in the home heating oil example in Section 8.5. The compensation required to compensate for a 100% price spike, according to Figure 8.14, is 10.96% ($1,096 is 10.96% of $10,000). Note that this differs substantially from the 15% that would result from a fixed-market-basket calculation (because individuals substitute away from the good that has become more expensive). The spread between EV and CV in this scenario is only 1.1% of income (this is how the point (1.1%, 200%) on the red curve is interpreted).

Only when the proportion of income spent on the good is large and the good has a large price change do the measures diverge appreciably from one another. When 50% of income is spent on x ($r = 0.5$), a 100% increase in price for the good requires a 29–41% income response, according to Figure 16.20B. In this instance, the spread between CV and EV is 12.1%, but CS splits the difference between the two at approximately 35%. The Excel file for Figure 16.20 allows you to vary the proportion of income devoted to x between 0.05 and 0.60. As you do, you will find that the three measures track each other throughout the range of values of r. When r is small, the three measures are virtually identical. Even when r is large, if the price change is not substantial, then the differences are

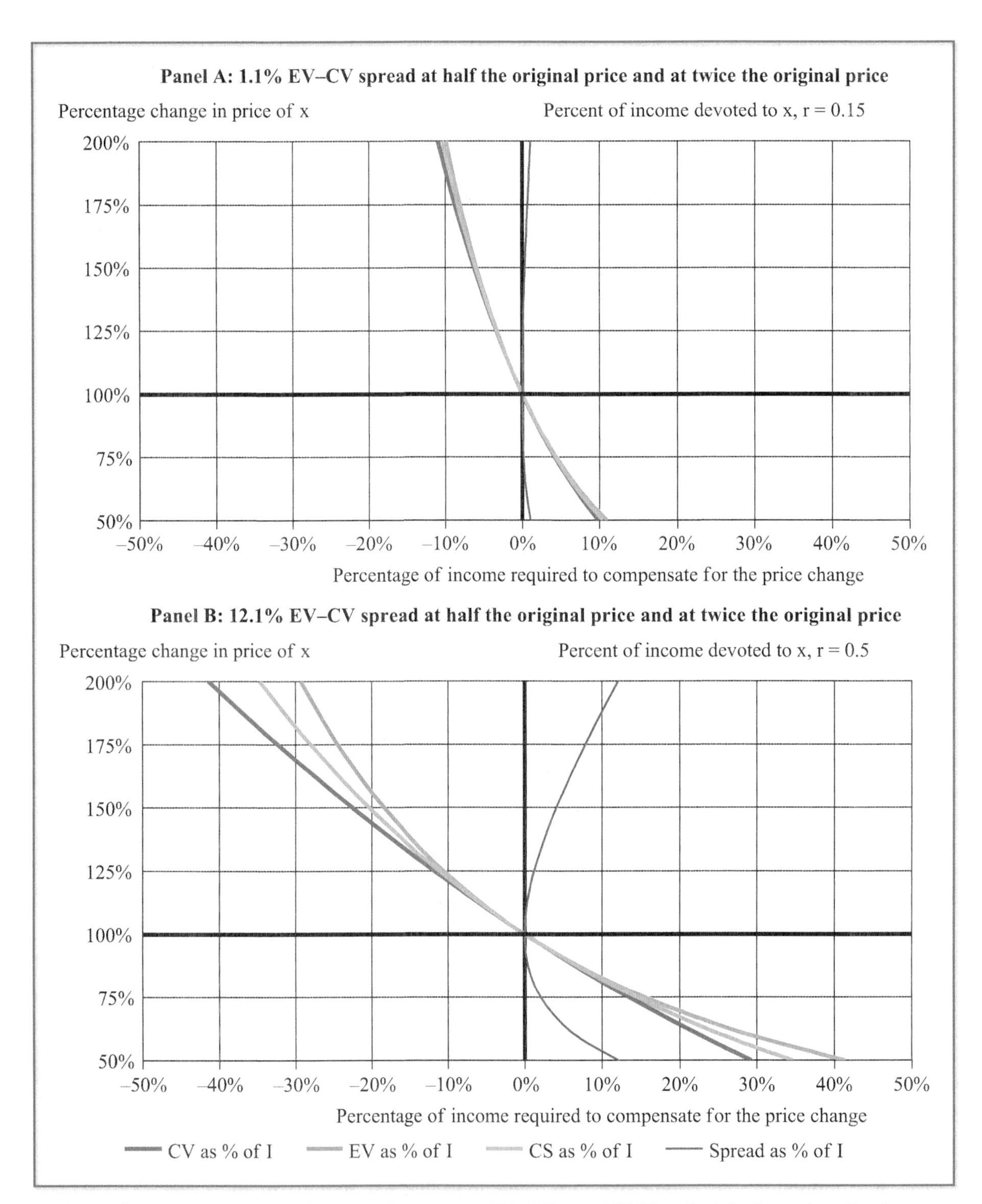

FIGURE 16.20 Comparing the Difference between CV, CS, and EV for Cobb-Douglas Preferences

not very large. For example, with r = 0.5, the difference between CV and EV is less than 2% for price changes of less than 25% (as can be seen by the position of the red curve in Figure 16.20B for prices between 75% and 125% of the initial price). Most price changes are not substantial, and most individuals do not devote a substantial portion of income to a single good. As a result, consumer surplus can, indeed, be used without apology.

Summary

This chapter has examined the welfare economics of various market structures. Consumers gain, since the benefit from consumption exceeds the price paid. Similarly, producers gain because the revenues received from consumers exceed the real resource cost of production. The market exchange process is voluntary in nature; consumers and producers interact via the market only when such action does not diminish the net welfare of the individual economic agent.

Much welfare analysis can be accomplished using supply and demand curves. The area behind the demand curve above the price charged is known as consumer surplus. This represents the excess of gross benefit from consumption over what the consumption costs. Although consumer surplus is initially developed for an individual consumer, we can readily sum across consumers to talk about the consumer surplus produced by the market as a whole because market demand is the horizontal sum of individual demand.

Economists are less interested in total consumer surplus than they are in the change in consumer surplus implied by some change in the market. A common example of such a market change is a change in price. If the price of a product decreases, the consumer gains for two reasons. First, the consumer gains a windfall on those units that would have been purchased at the higher price. Second, the consumer gains surplus on units that have value below the initial high price but above the new low price. These units of output were not sufficiently valuable that they would be purchased at the high price but are sufficiently valuable that they would be purchased at the low price. Conversely, when a price increases, the consumer loses surplus for two reasons. First, the consumer loses surplus on those units of output that would have been purchased at the higher price. Second, the consumer loses surplus on units that were previously purchased at the lower price but that are not valued enough to purchase at the new higher price.

Producer surplus is total revenue less variable cost. Producer surplus can be seen in a variety of ways, based on the individual firm's cost curves, but the most useful geometric interpretation of producer surplus is as a mirror image of consumer surplus. Producer surplus is the area behind the marginal cost curve above minimum average variable cost but below price.

Total surplus is consumer plus producer surplus. This provides a measure of the net gains to society from market interaction. This measure of social net benefit explicitly treats a dollar's worth of benefit to consumers the same as a dollar's worth of benefit to producers. In this setting, we see that monopoly leads to deadweight loss because greater total surplus can be attained under competition than under monopoly. Monopolists restrict output to generate greater profits. This output restrictiveness causes allocative inefficiency and deadweight loss. Had the monopolist been able to price discriminate, it would be able to reduce the deadweight loss to society. Price discrimination reduces deadweight loss at a distributional cost to consumers.

Consumers value the variety associated with differentiated products. When products are differentiated and entry is easy, the resulting long-run equilibrium has individual firms producing on the downward-sloping part of their average total cost curves. A firm could produce output at lower average cost if it increased production but could not support that increased output with increased revenues. Profits are maximized when firms exhibit excess capacity. Firms also produce at a point where price exceeds marginal cost. This implies that monopolistic competitors necessarily exhibit deadweight loss. But these losses are not the entire story in differentiated product markets because consumers value the diversity of product choices available when firms provide a wider variety of alternative brands. The determination of whether an additional variety is successfully introduced has to do with the valuation of that variety by the marginal consumers of that variety (those who are "on the fence" between this brand and a competing brand). By contrast, the social value of that additional variety has to do with the average valuation of consumers. There is no necessary relation that can be determined regarding which of these two valuations is higher. As a result, in differentiated product markets subject to free entry and exit, the resulting long-run equilibrium may have too little, too much, or just the right amount of variety when viewed from the perspective of total benefits to society. Aggregate total surplus is maximized when the increase in aggregate consumer surplus due to the additional variety equals the decrease in profits due to the additional variety. This need not occur when profits are zero, as required by monopolistic competition in long-run equilibrium.

Change in consumer surplus is a measure of the welfare impact of a price change derived from the Marshallian demand curve. Welfare varies along a Marshallian demand curve. As a result, the change in consumer surplus measure of the welfare impact of a price change is predicated on a moving welfare target. A more theoretically justifiable measure of the welfare impact of a price change is one that leaves the individual indifferent between the two states of nature. The two logical welfare levels to consider are the initial and final utility levels. When the initial utility level is chosen, the welfare measure is called compensating variation (CV). When the final utility level is chosen, the welfare measure is called equivalent variation (EV). In general, these two measures of the welfare impact of a price change are not equal.

There is one instance in which CV and EV are equal. They are equal when there is no income effect on demand, CV = EV. As we argue in Chapter 7, demand is independent of income when preferences are quasilinear. In this instance, once demand for the good is determined based on prices alone, the rest of income is spent on all other goods. In this situation, these two measures are also equal to change in consumer surplus. The coincidence of all three measures only occurs when there are no wealth effects on demand for the good whose price has changed.

In the more typical case, CV and EV are not equal. In this instance, change in consumer surplus will be between the two theoretically determined measures. The typical case is when an increase in income is associated with greater consumption of the good. Less common is the situation in which an increase in income leads to a decrease in demand for the good. In Chapter 7, we defined the former as a normal good and the latter as an inferior good. When the good is normal, $CV < \Delta CS < EV$ for a price decrease, but $|CV| > |\Delta CS| > |EV|$ for a price increase. When the good is inferior, each of the inequalities in the previous sentence reverses.

In most circumstances, it does not matter which of the three welfare measures is used to describe the impact of a price change. Only if the good in question has strong income effects, the price change is large, and if the good represents a substantial portion of spending will the differences be significant. In all other instances, consumer surplus can be used without apology as a proxy for CV or EV.

Review Questions

Define the following terms:

consumer surplus (CS)
gross benefit of consuming N units of output (GB(N))
producer surplus (PS)
total surplus (TS)
deadweight loss (DWL)
deadweight loss of monopoly (DWL_m)
allocative inefficiency
price discrimination
compensating variation (CV)
equivalent variation (EV)

Match the following phrases to best complete the sentence:

a. Deadweight loss is a form of
b. Total surplus is maximized by
c. Compensating variation is based on
d. Equivalent variation is based on
e. CV = EV if preferences are
f. CV > EV of a price decrease if goods are
g. CV < EV of a price decrease if goods are

1. initial prices and final utility level.
2. inferior.
3. quasilinear.
4. normal.
5. allocative inefficiency.
6. final prices and initial utility level.
7. perfect price discrimination.

Provide short answers to the following:

a. Does the social strategy of maximizing total surplus place greater emphasis on consumer or producer surpluses?
b. Why does aggregate consumer surplus differ from the gross benefit achieved by consuming a given amount of output?
c. Why does aggregate producer surplus differ from the gross benefit achieved by selling a given amount of output?
d. What is the gross benefit to producers from the point of view of consumers?
e. What restrictions can be made regarding the sign of producer surplus?
f. Describe the three geometric methods of visualizing producer surplus, and explain which version is symmetric to the geometric view of consumer surplus as the area behind the demand curve.
g. What is the consumer surplus if a monopolist is able to perfectly price discriminate?
h. Does monopolistic competition in long-run equilibrium exhibit the socially optimal amount of product variety?
i. If a good is normal, are Hicksian or Marshallian demand curves steeper?
j. If a good is normal, what are the relative sizes of CS, CV, and EV of a price decrease?
k. If a good is inferior, what are the relative sizes of CS, CV, and EV of a price decrease?
l. When are CS, CV, and EV identical?
m. What do economists mean when they say that consumer surplus can be used "without apology"?

Check your answers to the *matching* and *short-answer* exercises in the Answers Appendix at the end of the book.

1. Water provides an even more extreme example. Consider for a moment what the first ounce of water is worth to you on a given day. We scarcely consider the value of water because its price is so low, but certainly, here is a good that has an extremely high consumer surplus. Consumer surplus is at the basis of the *paradox of value* (also called the *diamonds and water paradox*) discussed in introductory textbooks.

2. Using calculus, we see consumer surplus as the integral of the demand curve but above price. This area is described as:

$$CS(P) = \int_P^{\infty} x(S)dS.$$

This integral takes a price orientation by calculating CS across values of price (from P to ∞), using demand. This is a formal version of Equation 16.7b.

The other method calculates CS across values of quantity (from 0 to x(P)), using inverse demand. The formal version of Equation 16.7a is:

$$CS(P) = GB(x(P)) - P \cdot x(P) = \int_0^{x(P)} P(s)ds - P \cdot x(P).$$

As with derivatives, you are not expected to take integrals. Answers will be provided if you need to take an integral. (Integrals are not as commonly used as derivatives in microeconomics, but one use has already occurred in the discussion of Figure 13.6, in which we showed that the area under a marginal cost curve is variable cost.)

3. Consumer surplus is the area behind the demand curve, according to Equation 16.7b. Formally, this requires calculus:

$$CS(P) = \int_P^{\infty} x(S)dS = \int_P^{\infty} 25/S^2 dS = -25/S \,\Big|_P^{\infty} = 25/P.$$

4. Integral calculus is required to formally prove that this is the gross benefit of x cups of coffee:

$$GB = \int_0^{x} P(s)ds = \int_0^{x} 5/s^{0.5} ds = 10 \cdot s^{0.5} \,\Big|_0^{x} = 10 \cdot x^{0.5}.$$

5. It is, however, the measure of loss calculated by the fixed-market-basket analysis in Section 8.5, since that calculation required the change in income to be $x \cdot \Delta P$.

6. Those authors who emphasize the possessive nature of the surplus describe this aggregate consumer surplus as consumers' surplus. Similar use of the possessive case, of course, could be made on the producer side but is avoided here.

7. Integral calculus is required to formally prove this assertion. Recall that $dVC(Q)/dQ = MC(Q)$, so

$$\int_0^{x} MC(Q)dQ = \int_0^{x} \frac{dVC}{dQ} dQ = VC(Q) \,\Big|_0^{x} = VC(x).$$

This calculation of incremental cost was seen earlier in the discussion of Figures 13.6 and 15.2.

8. For example, had we assumed that the government taxed the product, then the tax revenues generated would have to be included as *government surplus* in our calculation of total surplus.

9. Profit = TR – FC – VC = 200 · \$20 – \$250 – 200 · \$10 = \$1,750. CS = 1/2 · base · height = 1/2 · 200 · \$10 = \$1,000.

10. Graphs for N = 9 and N = 11 are suppressed but may be seen using the Excel file for Figure 16.10. Their qualitative character is all that is necessary to make our point. In each instance, the N = 9 figure shows short-run profits (and has the qualitative look of Figure 15.8A), and the N = 11 figure shows short-run losses (and looks like Figure 15.8B).

11. This means that an extra dollar in income will lead to an extra util of utility, given quasilinear preferences. Recall that the easiest way to think about demand based on quasilinear preferences is to imagine demand for x as being fulfilled "first"; then y is filled in as income allows. Once demand for x is satisfied, all extra income is spent on y in this instance. Income *meters* utility in this instance because an extra dollar purchases 1 unit of y (since $P_y = \$1$), which is worth one util, since U(x, y) = f(x) + y for quasilinear preferences.

12. These differences are difficult to see because the vertical segment in each part has a fairly thick end to the "I" used to create it. The one that is easiest to see is the \$0.085-cent triangle on top of the sixth shot that ends at bundle **C**. The actual value for the top is \$0.4922, close to the \$0.4915 = \$0.50 – \$0.085 we would have approximated using triangles.

13. The proof of this assertion is beyond the scope of intermediate-level microeconomics texts but is readily shown using the expenditure function. Varian's graduate microeconomics text (Hal R. Varian, *Microeconomic Analysis*, 3d ed., 1992, W. W. Norton, New York) provides an elegant discussion of this topic on pages 167–168. The reason the area behind Hicksian demand is the change in expenditure required to maintain a utility level is that Hicksian demand is the derivative of the expenditure function. Therefore, the area behind Hicksian demand is simply obtained by evaluating the expenditure function at starting and ending values of price. We have not formally discussed the expenditure function in this text, but it is an outgrowth of the expenditure minimization problem posed as Equation 8.3.

14. Robert Willig, "Consumer's Surplus without Apology," *American Economic Review*, 66 (1976), pp. 589–597.

15. This is obtained by taking the integral of Marshallian demand from Equation 7.3a, $x(P_x)$, between P_x^0 and P_x^1.

PART 5

APPLICATIONS

Part 5 of the text provides a series of applications chapters. Microeconomic theory is analyzed, using a small number of powerful tools developed in Parts 2–4. The tools can be recast and reused to analyze a wide range of seemingly disparate topics. The six chapters in Part 5 examine a variety of extensions of the basic models developed in Parts 2–4. These chapters are presented in a modular fashion so that they may be interleaved into the text at various points, depending on the instructor's preferences. A list of prerequisites provided at the start of each section allows you to quickly understand the intellectual dependencies required to attack this material.

Chapter 17 extends the analysis of Part 2 by examining other consumer theory topics. Chapters 18 and 19 examine factor markets. Factors of production are discussed in a cursory fashion in Part 3, but the basic supply and demand constructs developed in Parts 2–4 apply to factor markets as well. Chapter 20 extends Part 4 by examining market structures beyond perfect competition, monopoly, and monopolistic competition. Chapter 21 examines the role of information in market interactions. Information is itself a good that has nonzero cost; therefore, markets tend to have imperfect information. One especially interesting form of imperfect information occurs when one side in the market interaction has more information than the other side. This is known as asymmetric information, and it is the central focus of Chapter 21. Finally, Chapter 22 examines two other sources of market failure: externalities and public goods.

One point in particular should be noted about Chapter 19, Capital Markets. Each of the other applications chapters requires material from Parts 2–4; each of these chapters has prerequisites, ranging from Chapter 3 through Chapter 16. But Chapter 19 does not formally require any of that material, at least for a first reading. Chapter 19 is itself layered because it was written with multiple purposes in mind. One of the purposes is to provide a quick introduction to Excel. Since this text leverages Excel's power to create an active learning environment, it makes sense to provide an introduction to using Excel, and the present-value problems in Chapter 19 provide a natural place to begin. You can read Chapter 19 prior to any of the core chapters if you wish to incorporate Excel into your study (indeed, Section 19.2 provides an introduction). However, on first reading, you should ignore many of the endnotes (which create ties to various parts of the text). A second quick reading of the chapter late in the course is a valuable way to solidify some of the more subtle points in the chapter and should focus on the cross-references that link this material to other chapters.

Consumer Theory Applications

CHAPTER 17

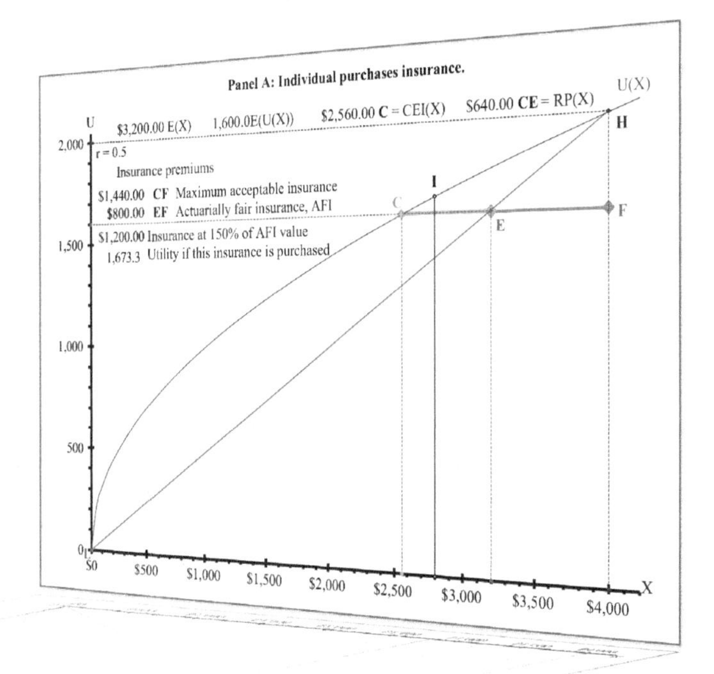

Chapter Outline

The consumer theory model developed in Part 2 of the text can be modified and extended in a variety of ways. If you have already read Part 3 of the text, you will realize that many of the analytical constructs developed in Part 2 were useful (sometimes with minor modification) in examining producer behavior. We will learn in later chapters that we can also apply the consumer-side toolkit in other ways (this is especially true with regard to labor markets in Chapter 18). Before we undertake that analysis, we examine some consumer applications of the consumer model presented in Part 2. Two substantive topic areas are discussed in Chapter 17: intertemporal choice and decisions under uncertainty.

Intertemporal choice examines how individuals allocate consumption across time to maximize intertemporal utility. We would typically expect individuals to balance consumption across time periods, rather than consume all in one period or the other. Individuals who have limited current resources but who expect that more substantial resources will be available in their future typically borrow based on those future expectations (college students take out educational loans, for example). Conversely, individuals who have high current resources but who expect lower resources in the future tend to save for the future (for example, working individuals save for retirement). Section 17.1 examines how individuals compare consumption across time periods, how they change their consumption patterns based on changes in market conditions, and how we can measure the value derived from our ability to adjust consumption across time periods by borrowing or saving.

The model developed in Part 2 is based on consumption with certainty, but not all choices available to consumers are certain in nature. Section 17.2 shows how to incorporate uncertainty into the consumer choice paradigm. This section begins by examining how to describe contingent outcomes (outcomes that do not occur with certainty). Core concepts include illustrating the set of possible outcomes or contingencies inherent in the uncertain choice, and the idea of measuring the expected outcome and riskiness inherent in the uncertain choice. These measures allow us to quantify the trade-off between risk and return of various uncertain options. Two methods of making this comparison are examined. One explicitly describes the trade-off between risk and return, using indifference curves. This allows us to study the basic attributes of portfolio choice theory. The other method considers utility as a function of income and describes expected utility as a counterpart to expected income when describing an uncertain choice. These expected values allow us to compare choices with different degrees of uncertainty and central tendency. The expected utility model allows us to examine issues such as job choice, as well as why some individuals choose to purchase insurance, while others chose to forego using this market.

Section 17.1 Outline

17.1 Intertemporal Choice

Individuals consume goods across many time periods, but the consumer model developed in Part 2 is a single-period model. We can modify the model developed in Part 2 to include consumption across multiple time periods. This allows us to examine the notions of borrowing and saving, and to see how each is affected by changes in the interest rate. The interest rate determines the terms of trade between now and the future. In Section 17.1A, we examine the basic notions of intertemporal choice, including present value, future value, and interest rate differentials. Section 17.1B examines what happens to an individual's optimal choice bundle when interest rates change. This is the intertemporal analog of examining a price change. In Section 17.1C, we determine the value inherent in being able to borrow or lend, using the demand decomposition notions proposed in Chapter 8. In Section 17.1D, we place the measure of this value in the context of compensating variation and equivalent variation of a change in economic condition, developed in Section 16.4.

17.1A Introduction to Intertemporal Choice *Prerequisite: Chapter 6*

The model developed in Part 2 can be easily adapted to examine multiple time periods. We can readily imagine N time periods, but just as we can obtain the essence of choice among goods using a two-good model, so can we obtain the essence of choice across time periods by restricting our analysis to two time periods—now and the future.

Consider a simple two-period model. The current time period is period 0, and the future is period 1. A consumer has an endowment of resources in each of two time periods, $\mathbf{E} = (e_0, e_1)$. The first coordinate describes current consumption, and the second coordinate describes future consumption. If the consumer cannot trade between time periods and if storage is impossible, then the consumer is stuck at the initial endowment point. However, if a consumer can trade across time periods, then that consumer might be made better off by either consuming more in the current time period and less in the future, or vice versa. The answer depends on three things: (1) the location of the endowment bundle, (2) the consumer's preferences across time periods, and (3) the terms of trade between time periods.

The location of the endowment bundle depends on where the individual is in life. For example, a senior in college is likely to have an endowment bundle in which the current component is substantially smaller than the future component. Conversely, an individual who is close to retirement is likely to have an endowment bundle in which the current component is large, relative to the future component.

An individual is likely to wish to have balanced consumption across time periods but is unlikely to have a rigid view of this balance (so, for example, we should not expect perfect complements preferences to hold across time periods). We will initially assume that the individual has equal-weighted Cobb-Douglas (CD) preferences (although this could easily be altered). The equal-weighted CD preferences require that equal spending occurs across time periods at the utility-maximizing intertemporal consumption bundle. To make the mathematics as simple as possible, suppose that the utility level of any bundle is given by:

$$U(x_0, x_1) = (x_0 \cdot x_1)^{0.5}. \quad \textbf{(17.1a)}$$

The marginal rate of substitution (MRS) in this situation is:

$$MRS(x_0, x_1) = x_1/x_0. \quad \textbf{(17.1b)}$$

We assume that there is no inflation, so a dollar spent in either time period purchases the same number of units of the composite commodity called "consumption." As a result, it is convenient to use dollars on each axis. The only difference between axes is that the horizontal axis is current dollars and the vertical axis is future dollars. If storage of the physical commodity purchased by these dollars is impossible across time periods, then the budget constraint depends on the interest rate, r. The interest rate describes the terms of trade between now and the future. If you borrow \$1 in the current period, then you must repay $\$1 \cdot (1 + r)$ in the future. Conversely, if you lend \$1 in the current period, then you will be repaid $\$1 \cdot (1 + r)$ in the future. This is shown in Figure 17.1A. Consider the units on both axes as thousands of dollars. The endowment bundle is **E** = (\$15, \$21). Based on this bundle and the interest rate, the budget constraint is **AB**. Consider movements along **AB** away from **E**. One direction describes lending current dollars, and the other direction describes borrowing current dollars.

Q1a. Describe the economic interpretation of bundle **A**.

Q1b. Describe the economic interpretation of bundle **B**.

Q1c. What is the interest rate implied by Figure 17.1A?*

First, note that the interest rate implied by **AB** is quite high. This was chosen so that the relations within the diagram are easy to discern, but these relations would work equally well for more moderate interest rates (and this can be accomplished with the Excel file for Figure 17.1). Figure 17.1B shows an indifference curve tangent to the budget constraint at the endowment bundle. This indifference curve is consistent with equal-weighted CD preferences because MRS(**E**) = e_1/e_0 = \$21/\$15 = 1.4, according to Equation 17.1b.

Bundle **A** represents the future value of the endowment bundle. Future value measures all amounts in future dollars.[1] This is calculated as:

$$FV(\mathbf{E}) = e_0 \cdot (1 + r) + e_1 = \$15 \cdot (1.4) + \$21 = \$42. \quad \textbf{(17.2a)}$$

The first term is the amount of money received in the future if all of the current endowment is lent at an interest rate of r per dollar. The reason e_0 must be multiplied by 1 + r is because repayment in the future involves repaying the principal (the 1 in 1 + r), plus interest on the principal (the r in 1 + r). Endowment received in the future, e_1, should not be multiplied by (1 + r) because it is received in the future, not invested in the present for the future. In contrast, bundle **B** represents the present value of the endowment bundle:

$$PV(\mathbf{E}) = e_0 + e_1/(1 + r) = \$15 + \$21/1.4 = \$30. \quad \textbf{(17.2b)}$$

In this calculation, the future endowment of \$21 must be divided by (1 + r) because only e_1 dollars will be available in the future to repay the debt incurred if the future endowment is borrowed against to consume both the current endowment and the future endowment in the current time period. Any amount borrowed must be repaid with interest, so the present

---

***Q1 answer:** Bundle **A** represents lending all of current consumption to consume all resources in the future. Bundle **B** represents borrowing all future consumption to consume all resources in the present. The interest rate is 40%, r = 0.4. This is obtained by calculating slope, m = \$42/\$30 = 1.4 = 1 + r (ignoring the minus sign); therefore, r = 0.4.

FIGURE 17.1 Intertemporal Choice Is Based on the Endowment of Resources (E), Preferences, and the Interest Rate between Time Periods, r.

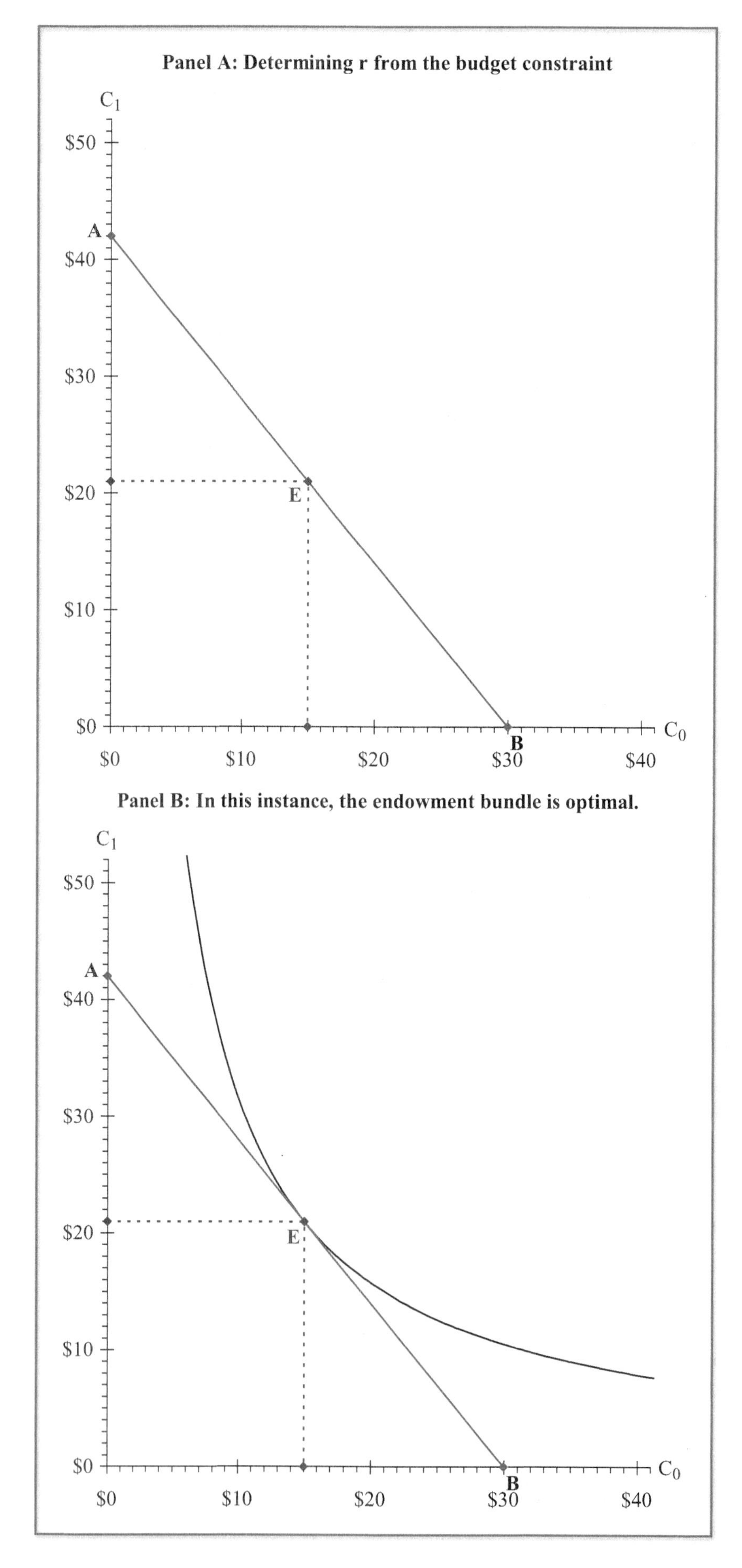

value of the future endowment is $e_1/(1+r)$ because $e_1 = (1+r)\cdot e_1/(1+r)$. Both measures accurately represent the value of the endowment bundle; they simply describe that value in different time periods.

Interestingly, the set of equal-weighted CD preferences does not require equal consumption in both time periods. Rather, it requires that half of the value of the endowment be devoted to each time period, and that is exactly the case. This can be seen using the present and future value calculations in Equations 17.2a and 17.2b. Half of each of these numbers represents the utility-maximizing consumption bundle, **C** = (c_0, c_1), given the budget constraint **AB** (c_0 = PV(**E**)/2 = \$15, and c_1 = FV(**E**)/2 = \$21). **C** coincides with the endowment bundle **E**, but this need not be the case. Consider, for example, an alternative endowment **E′** = (\$10, \$28). This bundle is also on **AB**, but it would not represent the utility-maximizing choice, given preferences and interest rate. Given **E′** and an interest rate of 40%, the utility-maximizing consumer would return to **C** = (\$15, \$21).

Q1d. If the individual is endowed with **E′** = (\$10, \$28) and wishes to consume at **C**, what must that individual do to accomplish this reallocation of consumption?*

Given equal-weighted CD preferences, the endowment point **E** = (\$15, \$21) is utility maximizing at an interest rate of 40% (as noted in Figure 17.1B). But at *any* other interest rate, it is not utility maximizing. This is shown based on two other interest rates: 0% in Figure 17.2A and 100% in Figure 17.2B (as with 40%, these numbers are extreme but are used so that the diagrammatic differences are easy to see). When the interest rate is zero, the individual increases utility by borrowing from future consumption to pay for an increase in current consumption. The utility-maximizing bundle in this instance is **C** = (\$18, \$18), a balanced result that is consistent with the interest rate of zero. (Of course, such an interest rate is not plausible, but it provides a natural boundary for analysis.) By contrast, the consumer who faces an interest rate higher than 40% will forgo current consumption to attain higher consumption in the future. At r = 100%, the future value of the endowment bundle is \$51, and the current value is \$25.50, according to Equations 17.2a and 17.2b. As a result, the utility-maximizing consumption bundle **C** = (\$12.75, \$25.50). In both instances, **C** is preferred to **E** because it is on a higher indifference curve.

Interest Rate Differentials

One common attribute of interest rates is that there is a difference between the rate an individual can attain when lending money and the rate an individual must pay to borrow money. For example, if you go to the bank and ask to borrow some money, the bank charges you more than what it would give you if you lent it some money (by putting money in a savings account). If we call this difference d, then $r_{borrow} = r_{lend} + d$. In this instance, the budget constraint is nonlinear, much like the food-stamps constraint discussed in Section 5.4. In actual capital markets, this differential is modest. When the interest rate differential is small, however, the budget constraint appears linear because the kink is modest. As a result, a more stark contrast is provided in Figure 17.3. In this instance, a consumer receives r_{lend} = 0% when lending, but faces an interest rate of r_{borrow} = 100% when borrowing. Imagine that this individual lends by storing current consumption goods under a mattress until the future and borrows by going to a loan shark. In this instance, the slope on **AE** is –1, and the slope on **EB** is –2 because slope = $-(1 + r)$.

Even a consumer who does not have equal-weighted CD preferences may stay put at **E**. The general CD utility function $U(x, y) = x_0^s \cdot x_1^{(1-s)}$ has MRS = $(s/(1-s))\cdot(x_1/x_0)$, according to Equation 4.4 (note that the CD exponent "r" in Equation 4.4 has been changed to s because, in the current context, r denotes interest rate). Given the coordinates of bundle **E**, we see that the individual will remain at **E** as long as:

$$1 \leq \text{MRS}(\mathbf{E}) \leq 2$$

$$1 \leq (s/(1-s))\cdot(21/15) = 1.4\cdot(s/(1-s)) \leq 2. \qquad \textbf{(17.3a)}$$

***Q1d answer:** The individual will have to borrow \$5 in the current period and repay \$7 in the future.

FIGURE 17.2
Borrowing and Lending (assuming preferences and endowment as in Figure 17.1)

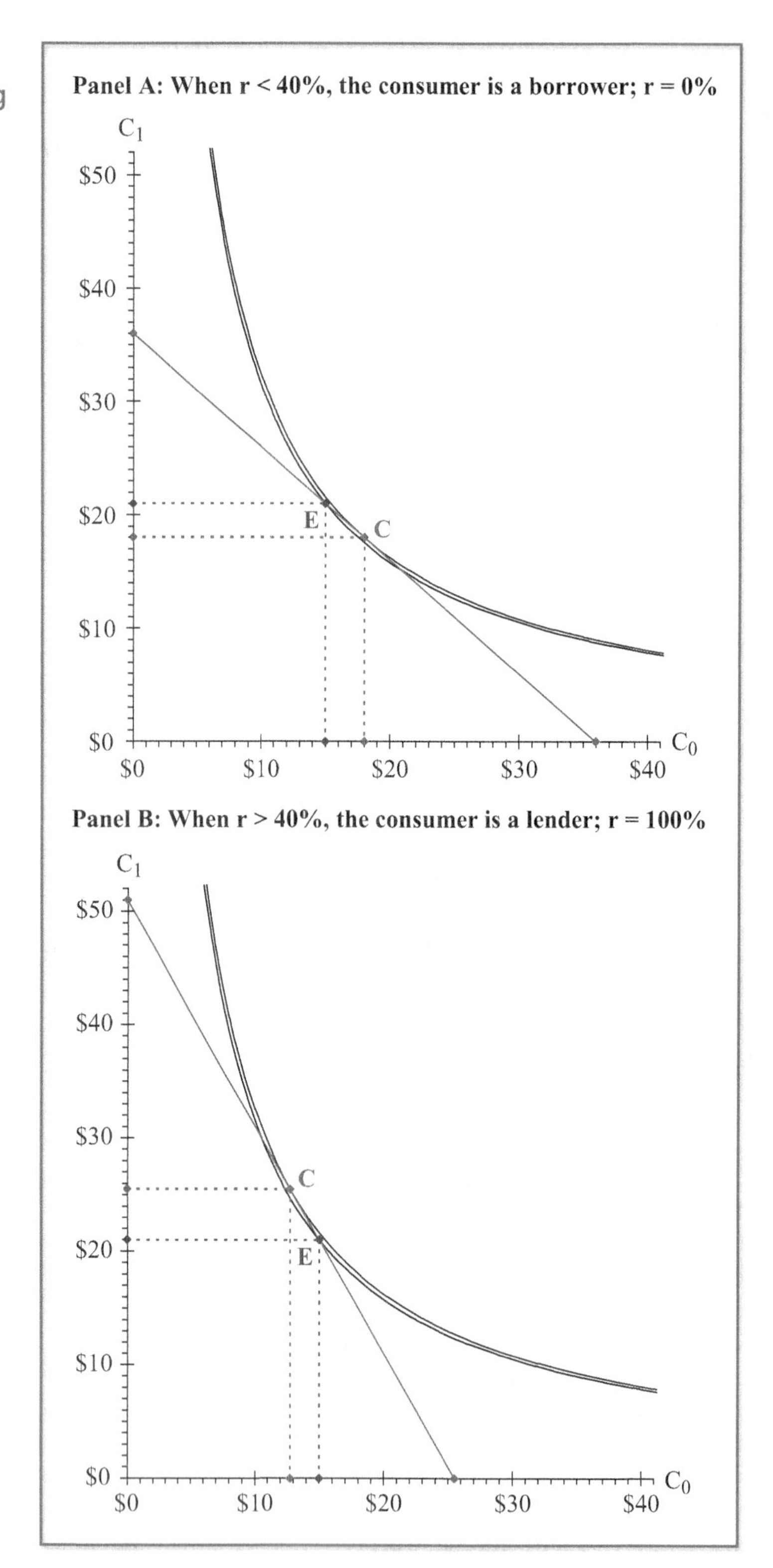

Solving for s using each of these inequalities provides bounds on s:

$$0.417 = 1/(2.4) \leq s \leq 2/(3.4) = 0.588. \qquad \textbf{(17.3b)}$$

As s varies between these bounds, the indifference curve through **E** would rotate about **E**, maintaining a slope of between –1 and –2, as required for **E** to remain the optimal bundle. Recall that s represents the proportion of income devoted to current consumption. As long as this is between 41.7% and 58.8%, the individual will remain at **E**, rather than put off some current consumption to the future, or borrow based on future consumption

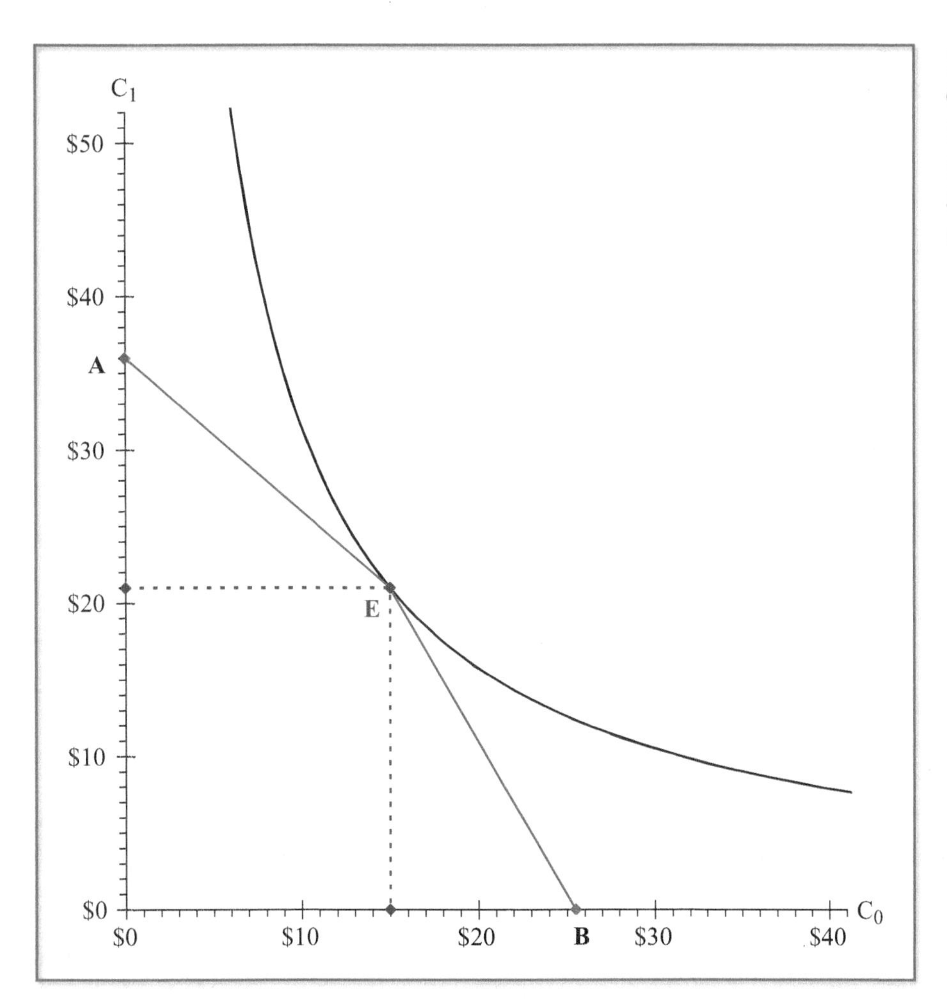

FIGURE 17.3 Optimality When the Individual Cannot Borrow and Lend at the Same Rate ($r_{lend} = 0\%$, $r_{borrow} = 100\%$)

to consume more in the present. Beyond these bounds, the individual would either lend (put off current consumption to the future despite $r_{lend} = 0\%$) if $s < 0.417$, or borrow (at a rate of $r_{borrow} = 100\%$) if $s > 0.588$.

Figure 17.4 depicts a more modest but still substantial differential of 10% between lending and borrowing. In particular, $r_{lend} = 10\%$ and $r_{borrow} = 20\%$ in both Figures 17.4A and 17.4B. The kink at **E** is no longer discernible visually, but it is easy to see by manually calculating slopes. There is a slope of –1.1 on **AE** and a slope of –1.2 on **EB**. Two scenarios are shown: Figure 17.4A depicts an equal-weighted CD student with endowment of (10, 36), who is looking forward to higher income in the future. Figure 17.4B describes an equal-weighted CD individual who is looking forward to retirement in the future. The student borrows $10 (thousand), despite the 20% interest rate that requires repaying $12 (thousand) in the future. The student's utility-maximizing consumption bundle is **C** = ($20, $24). The individual who is close to retirement saves (lends) $12.27 of the current consumption endowment of e_0 = $30. This allows the individual to receive 1.1 · $12.27 = $13.50 in the future, in addition to the future endowment of $6, to achieve a utility-maximizing consumption bundle of **C** = ($17.73, $19.50). Both of the slopes can be seen in the final consumption bundles, according to Equation 17.1b. In Figure 17.4A, we see MRS(**C**) = $24/$20 = 1.2, as expected based on **C** being on the **EB** part of the multi-period budget constraint. In Figure 17.4B, we see MRS(**C**) = $19.50/$17.73 = 1.1, as expected based on **C** being on **AE**.

An Aside on Buying and Selling

One final point should be made regarding the model of intertemporal choice developed thus far. The intertemporal endowment bundle and differential interest rates on borrowing and lending lead to a nonlinear budget constraint. This same model could be used to

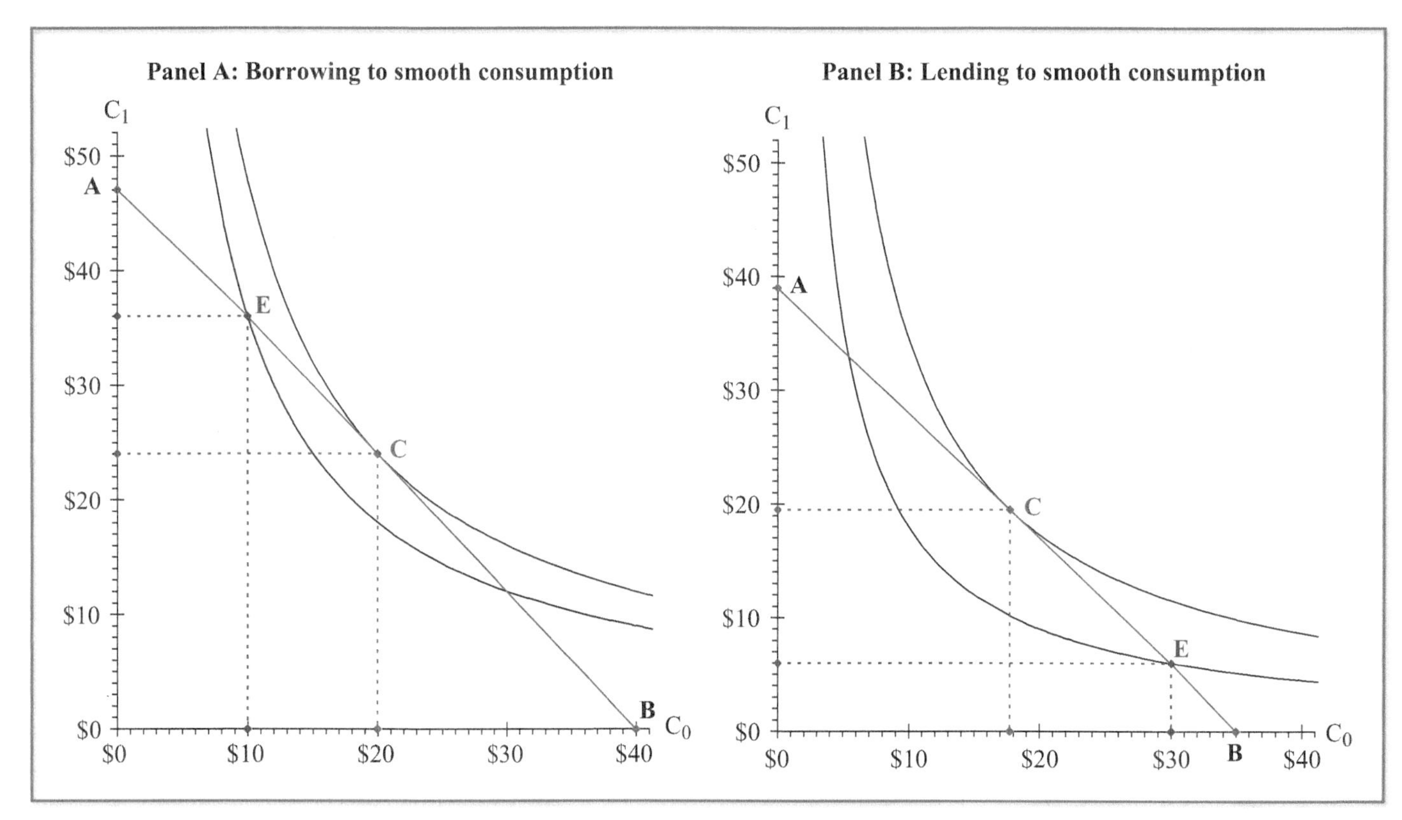

FIGURE 17.4 Borrowing and Lending to Smooth Consumption, Given $r_{lend} = 10\%$ and $r_{borrow} = 20\%$

examine buying and selling a good. Consider a single-period two-good model, (x, y). The good under consideration is x, and y is all other goods ($P_y = \$1$ as a result). You have an endowment x_e of good x and a certain amount of income you can use to buy other goods, y_e. Suppose you can buy extra x for \$1 per unit. In this event, your "income" is $y_e + x_e$, as long as you wish to consume $x_c \geq x_e$ because the slope of the budget constraint to the right of the endowment bundle is $-1 = -P_x/P_y$ (since we have assumed that both prices are unitary). To the left of the endowment bundle, the story is different. An individual who would prefer more other goods can only get them by selling some of the individual's endowment of x. To do this, the person will have to sell x at a discount, $P < \$1$.[2] This produces an "income" of $y_e + P \cdot x_e$ to the left of the endowment bundle. Units of y still cost \$1, but even if the individual wishes to sell the entire endowment of x, x_e units of x produce less than x_e dollars in this instance (because you only receive $P < \$1$ per unit). The slope on this segment of the budget constraint is $-P$. The slopes are different in the earlier intertemporal choice analysis, but the qualitative relation of buying and selling is identical to that described in Figure 17.3. Both have a budget constraint with a kink at the endowment point. To the right of the endowment bundle, the constraint is steeper than it is to the left. This produces the same "sticky" result in which there is a range of MRS values for which the individual will remain at the endowment bundle, rather than trade in either direction.

17.1B Interest Rate Changes *Prerequisites: Sections 7.2 and 17.1A*

The prices in the intertemporal model described in Section 17.1A are the rates of exchange that connect consumption between now and the future. When prices change, so do optimal consumption choices. These changes were the focus of Chapter 7. The price consumption curve (PCC) describes how the optimal consumption bundle varies as price varies. The optimal consumption bundle varies because the budget constraint varies when prices change. The same holds in the intertemporal choice setting, with the interest rate providing the intertemporal price.

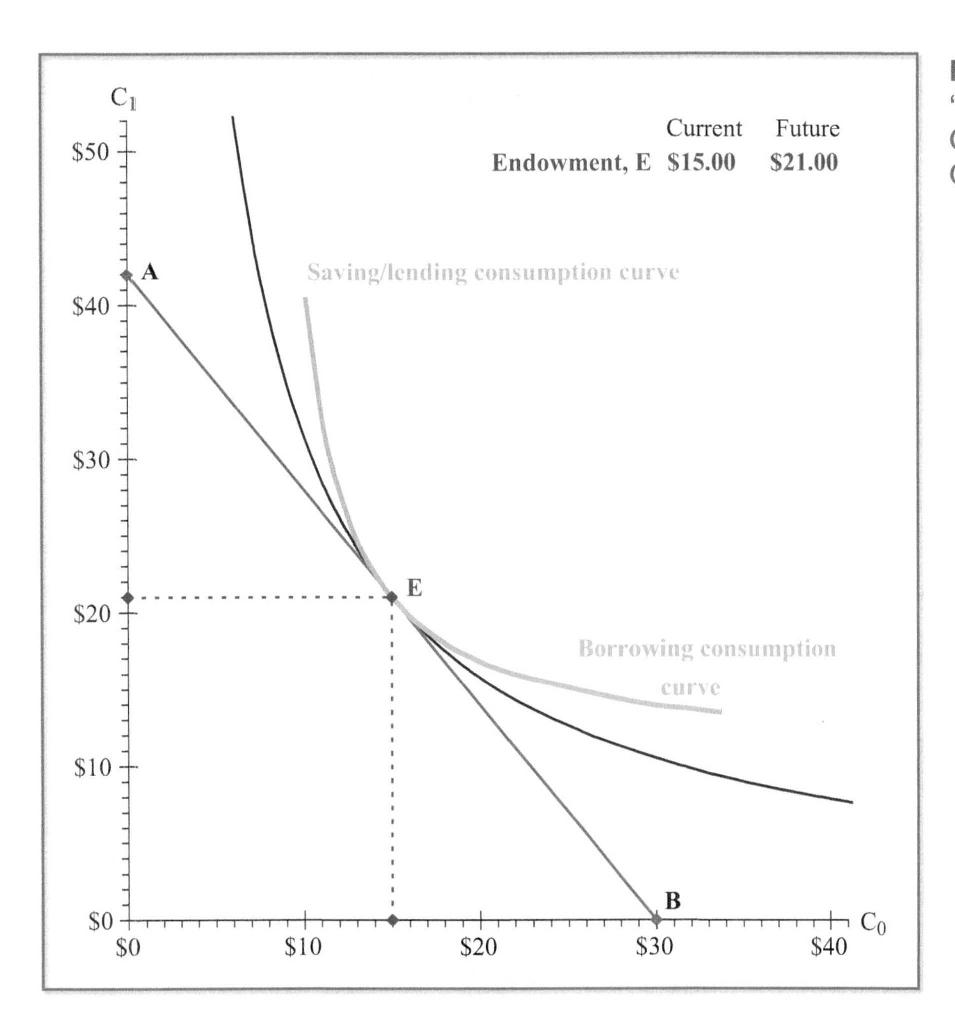

FIGURE 17.5 The "Price" Consumption Curve in Intertemporal Choice

Consider first the single-interest-rate scenario described in Figures 17.1 and 17.2 (i.e., there is no differential between borrowing and lending interest rates). Given the endowment bundle **E** = ($15, $21) and equal-weighted CD preferences, the individual would maximize utility by remaining at **E** if the interest rate on borrowing and lending was 40%. If the terms of trade between now and the future suggest an interest rate of less than 40%, the consumer will borrow against future consumption to increase current consumption. This is the scenario shown as bundle **C** = ($18, $18), given an interest rate of 0% in Figure 17.2A. This bundle is part of the green borrowing consumption curve in Figure 17.5. Conversely, if the interest rate is more than 40%, the consumer will choose to put off current consumption and save for the future. The point **C** = ($12.75, $25.50) in Figure 17.2B depicts this for an interest rate of 100%. This is a point on the lavender saving/lending consumption curve. The curves are shown as distinct colors, but they are both parts of the intertemporal analog to the PCC from Section 7.2. The interest rate slider allows you to vary the interest rate and watch as C moves along the PCC in this instance. For very low interest rates, the consumption bundle starts on the borrowing part of the consumption curve. For interest rates above 40%, the consumption bundle becomes a point on the lending consumption curve.

When lending and borrowing interest rates differ from one another, there will be a range of interest rates for which neither borrowing nor lending occurs. This was initially discussed in Figure 17.3 but was examined for more asymmetric intertemporal bundles in Figure 17.4. Figure 17.6 reexamines the asymmetric bundles from Figure 17.4. In each panel, only one of the consumption curves is shown, but the other is theoretically possible, given a high enough or low enough interest rate.

Consider first the student scenario shown in Figure 17.6A. Given the endowment of **E** = ($10, $36), the student borrows for any interest rate below 260%. This (absurdly

FIGURE 17.6 The Borrowing and Saving/Lending Consumption Curves

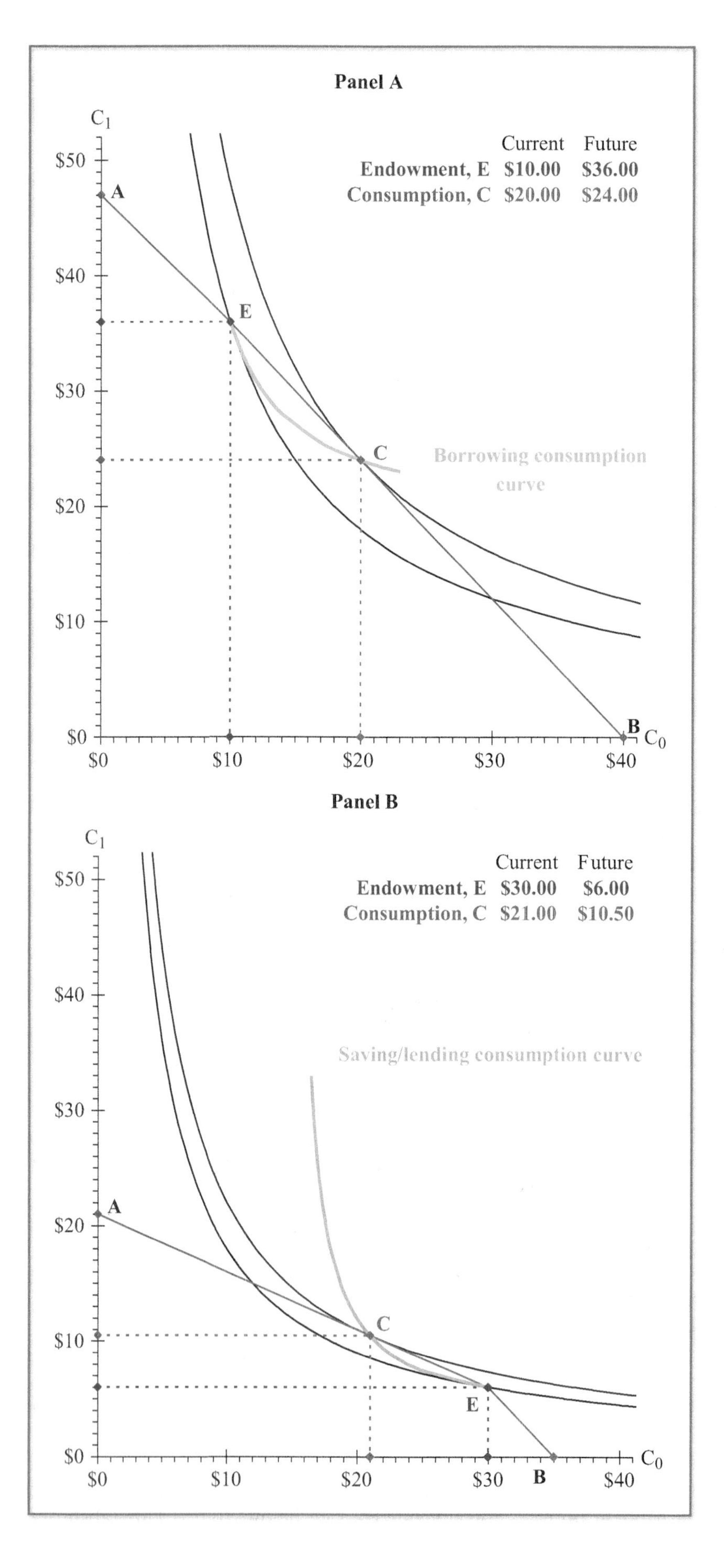

high) answer is an outgrowth of MRS(**E**) = \$36/\$10 = 3.6. This bundle is chosen if MRS(**E**) = 1 + r. For any borrowing interest rate r_{borrow} below 260%, the student borrows. Lower and lower borrowing interest rates produce larger and larger levels of borrowing. The borrowing budget constraint **EB** rotates out as r_{borrow} declines. As this occurs, the optimal consumption bundle increases in current consumption and decreases in future consumption along the green borrowing consumption curve. Bundle **C** shows the situation associated with a borrowing interest rate of 20%, and the end of the borrowing consumption curve is the bundle (\$23, \$23) associated with an interest rate of 0%.

Conversely, the worker who is saving for retirement, depicted in Figures 17.4B and 17.6B, saves along the saving/lending consumption curve in Figure 17.6B. Higher and higher lending interest rates produce larger and larger savings as the lending budget constraint **AE** becomes steeper as r_{lend} increases. As this occurs, the optimal consumption bundle will increase in future consumption and decrease in current consumption along the lavender saving/lending consumption curve.

Even in the absence of specific preferences (such as the equal-weighted CD), as long as the individual has well-behaved preferences, we can use Figure 17.6 to make general statements about borrowing and lending in the face of interest rate changes. Suppose that the utility-maximizing consumption bundle involves the individual borrowing from the future at a given interest rate (as depicted by bundle **C** in Figure 17.6A).

Claim: *If the borrowing interest rate* declines, *the borrower will continue to be a borrower.*

As the borrowing budget constraint **EB** rotates flatter through the endowment bundle **E**, new feasible bundles preferable to **C** become available (to the southeast of **C** along the borrowing consumption curve in Figure 17.6A). These new bundles all share one attribute: They all have current consumption more than the endowment bundle. The individual will remain a borrower in this instance.

Conversely, suppose the individual is currently lending at a given lending interest rate (such as at bundle **C** in Figure 17.6B).

Claim: *If the lending interest rate* increases, *the lending individual will continue to lend.*

The reasoning is symmetric to that used in the borrowing context. An increase in the lending interest rate rotates the lending budget constraint **AE** steeper through the endowment bundle **E**, causing new feasible bundles preferable to **C** to become available (to the northwest of **C** along the lending consumption curve in Figure 17.6B). These bundles all share one attribute: They all have current consumption less than the endowment bundle. The individual will remain a lender in this instance.

An Aside on Storage Losses

An individual who has more in the current period than in the future will wish to save for the future to smooth consumption across time periods. This was the scenario initially discussed in Figure 17.4B, based on a lending interest rate of 10%. In that setting, the consumer chose bundle **C** = (\$17.73, \$19.50) on the budget constraint (and on the lavender saving/lending consumption curve in Figure 17.6B). At 0%, the consumer would choose a utility-maximizing bundle of (\$18, \$18) that would also be on the lavender curve. But what is the interpretation of the bundle **C** shown in Figure 17.6B? More specifically, what is the interest rate implicit on **AE** in this instance? The slope of **AE** is –0.5, implying that the interest rate is –0.5. Because we do not expect negative interest rates when we lend, something else must be going on here. The situation depicted in Figure 17.6B allows us to reinterpret our intertemporal choice model to obtain further insights.

Suppose that there are no capital markets for lending, and the consumption good is food. Imagine that you can store current food for consumption in the future but that some of the food goes bad. The magnitude of the slope of **AE** describes the proportion of stored food that is good in the future. In the scenario shown, the slope of **AE** is –0.5. This means that 50% of any food stored from the current period will be consumable in the future period. (Or to put it another way, the loss rate is 50%.) Were the loss rate 25%, then the slope of **AE** would be –0.75. More generally, if the loss rate is –100r%, then the slope of **AE** would be –(1 + r), just as it was earlier for positive interest rates. The only difference here is that r is negative. In this interpretation, a consumer faced with intertemporal endowment of **E** in Figure 17.6B would store some current consumption for the future as long as the loss rate is less than 80%. The reason is straightforward, given **E** = ($30, $6), MRS(**E**) = $6/$30 = 0.2. This bundle would be chosen if MRS(**E**) = 1 + r when r = –0.8. For any smaller loss rate, the consumer would save for the future along the saving/lending consumption curve, as shown in Figure 17.6B.

17.1C Decomposing Intertemporal Choice

Prerequisites: Sections 8.3 and 17.1A

A simple question is examined in this extension of Section 17.1A: What is the value of being able to borrow or lend? We can answer this question using the substitution bundle examined in Sections 8.1–8.3. The substitution bundle **S** = (x_s, y_s) for the equal-weighted CD utility function in Equation 17.1a is given by Equations 8.5a and 8.5b, reproduced here:

$$x_s = U_0 \cdot (P_y/P_x)^{0.5} \quad \textbf{(8.5a)} \qquad\qquad y_s = U_0 \cdot (P_x/P_y)^{0.5} \quad \textbf{(8.5b)}$$

These equations are put in the context of the goods x and y as current consumption, C_0, and future consumption, C_1, with a price ratio $P_x/P_y = 1 + r$. Given endowment, **E**, the indifference curve U_0 through **E** has utility level $U_0 = (e_0 \cdot e_1)^{0.5}$. Therefore, the least-cost method of producing utility level U_0 involves using bundle **S** = (s_0, s_1):

$$s_0 = (e_0 \cdot e_1)^{0.5}/(1 + r)^{0.5}. \qquad \textbf{(17.4a)}$$

$$s_1 = (e_0 \cdot e_1)^{0.5} \cdot (1 + r)^{0.5}. \qquad \textbf{(17.4b)}$$

The substitution bundle, **S**, can be compared to the chosen consumption bundle, **C**, to determine the gains available from being able to borrow or lend. If we sum the differences between coordinates of **C** and **S** across time periods, we obtain the value from being able to borrow or lend. If **C** = (c_0, c_1), then a natural description of the gains attained by moving from the initial endowment bundle **E** to **C** involves summing extra consumption in each time period, relative to a bundle that produces the same utility as **E**, given the market exchange rate between time periods of 1 + r (the bundle **S**). To put the two time periods into a single unit of measure, we must either calculate a present value or a future value (just as was done in Equation 17.2). Care must be taken when doing this to compare "apples with apples" by appropriately discounting to the present or compounding to the future. The present-value calculation is given by:

$$PV_{exchange} = (c_0 - s_0) + (c_1 - s_1)/(1 + r). \qquad \textbf{(17.5a)}$$

The one remaining question in determining the net benefit of exchange is what value of r should be used for the calculations in Equations 17.4 and 17.5? We note in Section 17.1A that the lending and borrowing interest rates may well be different from one another. This was examined in Figures 17.3 and 17.4. When this happens, the budget constraint has a different slope on each side of the endowment bundle. If the utility-maximizing consumption bundle is to the northwest of **E**, the appropriate interest rate is the lending rate because **AE** represents lending in those figures. By contrast, if the utility-maximizing consumption bundle is to the southeast of **E**, the appropriate interest rate is the borrowing rate because **EB** represents borrowing.

Examples of both situations were provided in Figure 17.4. Figure 17.7 starts with Figure 17.4, but incorporates the substitution bundle described in Equations 17.4a and 17.4b and the present value of exchange described in Equation 17.5a. Figures 17.4A and 17.7A depict a student who wishes to borrow from future earnings. Figures 17.4B and 17.7B depict a worker who wishes to save for retirement. The MRS = 1.2 at **S** and **C** in Figure 17.7A, since the borrowing rate is 20% ($1 + r_{borrow} = 1.2$). The present-value

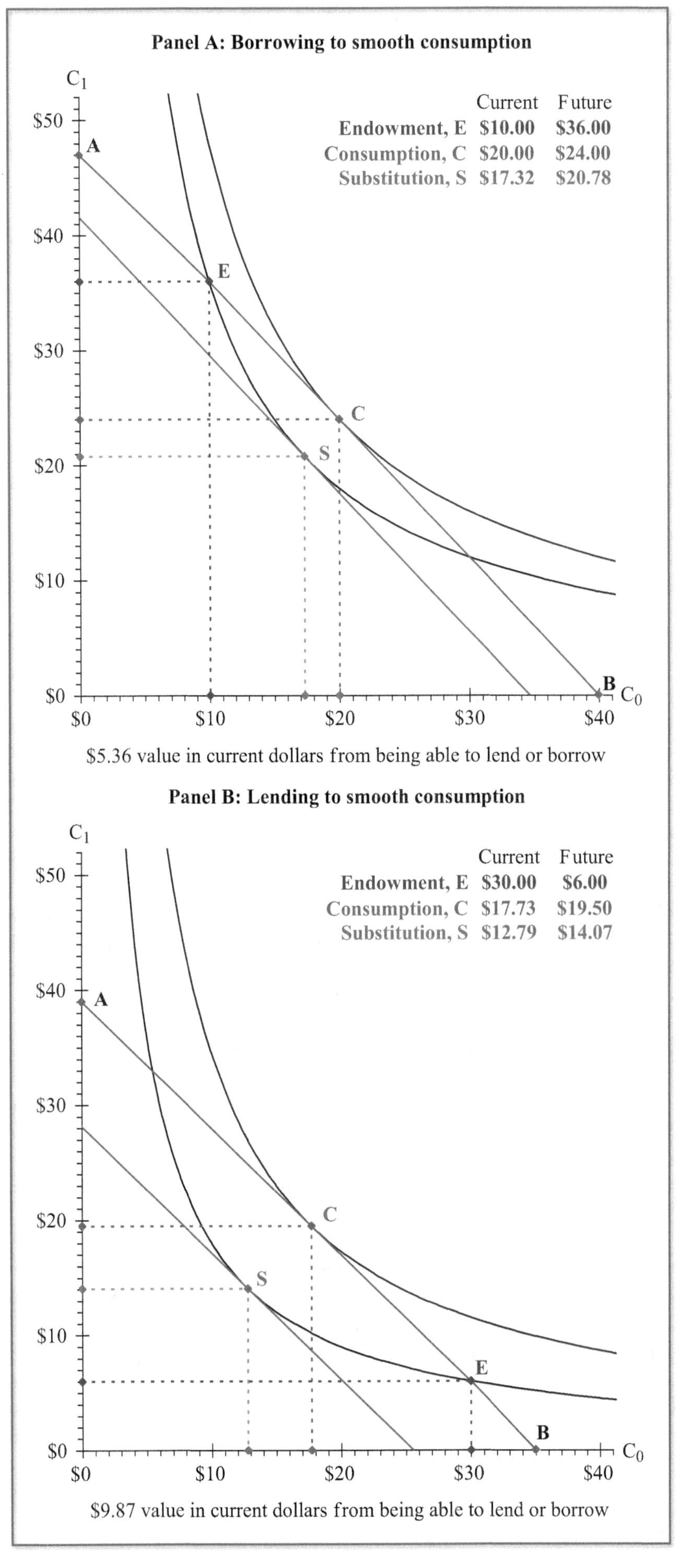

FIGURE 17.7
Estimating the Value of Borrowing and Lending

calculation shows that being able to borrow produces a net value to the student of more than \$5 (thousand), given the assumptions in Figure 17.7A:

$$PV_{exchange} = (c_0 - s_0) + (c_1 - s_1)/(1 + r_{borrow}) = (20 - 17.32) + (24 - 20.78)/1.2 = \$5.36. \quad \textbf{(17.5b)}$$

By contrast, the MRS = 1.1 at **S** and **C** in Figure 17.7B, since the lending rate is 10%. The present-value calculation shows that being able to save for retirement is worth almost \$10 (thousand) to the worker in Figure 17.7B:

$$PV_{exchange} = (c_0 - s_0) + (c_1 - s_1)/(1 + r_{lend}) = (17.73 - 12.79) + (19.50 - 14.07)/1.1 = \$9.87. \quad \textbf{(17.5c)}$$

17.1D The CV or EV of Intertemporal Exchange

Prerequisites: Sections 16.5 and 17.1C

One final point should be made regarding the calculation proposed in Section 17.1C: These calculations compare being able to use financial markets to borrow or lend with not being able use financial markets for this intertemporal exchange. The change in market condition under consideration is not a price change, but the presence or absence of a market. Compensating variation (CV) and equivalent variation (EV) were defined for price changes in Section 16.5, but the same concepts can be modified to examine the presence or absence of a market. The graphical analysis and calculations in Section 17.1C describe the value of the introduction of intertemporal markets. This is a CV-style calculation because the initial indifference curve is being used as the point of reference (the roll to the substitution bundle **S** occurs along the initial indifference curve). An EV-style measure is intractable in this instance because EV uses the new indifference curve *with original prices* (in the price change conceptualization of EV in Section 16.5). The new indifference curve is easy to determine, but the analog to "original prices" is more problematic because the initial scenario is the absence of a market. The absence of a market provides no unique signal regarding where the substitution bundle **E** should be on the final indifference curve. The same problem does not occur with respect to the CV-style measure derived in Section 17.1C.

Of course, had we proposed the following alternative question at the start of Section 17.1—"What is the cost to an individual who had previously been able to borrow or lend if that individual is no longer able to borrow and lend?"—instead of "What is the value of being able to borrow or lend?" we would have come to a different CV/EV conclusion in the previous paragraph. The measure developed in Section 17.1C *also* answers this alternative question. It does so by providing an EV-style measure because the only unique "prices" connecting the present and future are those that allow exchange between time periods. Based on this alternative wording of the welfare question, this is the old set of prices (since the individual was initially able to borrow or lend). In the alternative conceptualization of the welfare question, the CV-style measure is intractable. Regardless of how the welfare question is worded, the appropriate indifference curve to use for welfare calculations is the one going through the intertemporal endowment bundle because the appropriate price ratio to consider is one that is based on working markets.

Summary of Section 17.1

The intertemporal choice model developed in Section 17.1 allows us to examine how individuals allocate consumption across time to maximize utility. Individuals typically wish to smooth consumption across time periods. As a result, they typically wish to borrow in lean times and save in plentiful times. These general observations are confirmed based upon a simple model of intertemporal consumption, using an equal-weighted CD utility function applied to consumption in two time periods—now and the future. Roughly speaking, the individual chooses to consume half of the value of the endowment in each time period to maximize intertemporal utility. If the individual's current endowment is higher than what it will be in the future, the individual will save for the future (for example, employed people tend to save for retirement). This act of saving for the future can also be viewed as lending out some current consumption with repayment in the future. By contrast, if the individual's current endowment is lower than what it will be in the future, the individual will borrow against future earnings to consume more in the current period (for example, college students typically take out loans).

Both borrowing and lending involve exchanging consumption across time periods. This is not typically done with physical goods; rather, it is done with dollars because dollars purchase physical goods in each time period. The interest rate determines the terms of trade between time periods. One dollar lent (saved) in the current time period produces $1 · (1 + r) in the future. One dollar borrowed in the current time period must be repaid with $1 · (1 + r) in the future. The slope of the intertemporal budget constraint is therefore $-(1 + r)$.

Typically, the interest rate depends on whether the individual is borrowing or lending. The rate you pay to borrow money is higher than the rate you receive on money you save. This produces a kinked budget constraint that is steeper on the borrowing segment than on the lending segment. As a result, there are a range of MRS values for which the individual will neither act as a borrower or a lender.

When interest rates change, individuals adjust their consumption behavior. The interest rate analog to the price consumption curve in Chapter 7 describes how intertemporal consumption changes as the terms of trade across time change. If an individual is a borrower and the borrowing interest rate declines, the individual will remain a borrower. Similarly, if the individual currently saves at a given lending interest rate, the individual will remain a saver if the lending interest rate increases. Finally, the intertemporal gains from being able to borrow or lend can be measured, using the intertemporal analog of the substitution bundle described in Chapter 8 and further analyzed in Chapter 16.

17.2. Decisions under Uncertainty

Section 17.2 Outline

The model of consumer behavior developed in Part 2 is predicated on certain choice. But not all choices available to individuals are certain in nature. If you have ever bought a lottery ticket or a used car, invested in stock, or bet on a sporting event, you have directly participated in a market in which the outcome is uncertain.[3] Even if you cannot recall participating in a market in which the outcome is uncertain, you have preferences over uncertain outcomes that are offered to you as choices.

The discussion of decision making under uncertainty is divided into three parts. In Section 17.2A, we lay out some basic descriptive statistics that allow us to describe in a systematic fashion the possible alternative outcomes that may occur when outcomes are not certain. We explore both the idea of the expected value attached to an uncertain situation, as well as how much variability there is with regard to that expectation. In Section 17.2B, we examine a utility function that explicitly compares the risk of a choice with the expected return from that choice. This allows us to derive some of the basic results of portfolio choice theory. In Section 17.2C, we study the trade-offs inherent in uncertain situations, using a utility function that allows us to compare the dollar outcomes of various contingencies with the utility levels achieved under those contingencies. This model allows us to understand why individuals might purchase insurance, even when that insurance is not actuarially fair.

17.2A Describing Uncertain Situations — *Prerequisite: Chapter 3*

If an outcome is uncertain, there is some possibility that the outcome will not occur. The first task when considering uncertain situations is to simply list all possible outcomes. Each outcome involves both the resources associated with that outcome occurring and the likelihood that the outcome will occur. The resources associated with each contingency need not be monetary, but monetary outcomes are especially easy to describe and are the focus here.[4] The likelihood of an outcome occurring can be described by the probability attached to that outcome (we use the terms *likelihood* and *probability* interchangeably). Economists use the term *lottery* to describe the complete list of contingencies. A **lottery** is simply a list of possible outcomes, together with the probabilities of each of the outcomes. The list must contain all possibilities. A lottery can be as simple as a 50/50 chance at paying or receiving $1. This would be described as:

lottery: A lottery is a list of all possible outcomes, together with the probabilities of each of the outcomes.

Win outcome:	$1 with probability 0.5
Loss outcome:	–$1 with probability 0.5

Although we often think of probabilities in percentage terms, we have not multiplied by 100. If instead there were n possible outcomes in Lottery X, then it could be described using 2n numbers (n payouts and n probabilities) as:

$$\text{Payout of } X_i \text{ with probability } p_i > 0 \text{ for } i = 1, \ldots, n, \text{ and } p_1 + \ldots + p_n = 1. \quad \textbf{(17.6)}$$

Notice the two conditions associated with the probabilities: Each must be greater than 0, and they must sum to 1. The first condition simply signifies that the *i*th outcome is a possibility. Were $p_i = 0$, then the *i*th contingency would not be possible. The second condition implies that all possibilities have been covered.

Equation 17.6 assumes that the individual is able to determine the probabilities associated with each contingent outcome. This need not be the case; you might be uncertain about the amount of uncertainty you face. Some authors make the distinction between risk (which involves knowing the probabilities attached to each contingent outcome) and uncertainty (which involves not knowing the probabilities attached to contingent outcomes or not knowing that a contingency exists). All uncertain outcomes examined in this chapter involve risky, rather than uncertain, situations, according to this distinction, but we use the two terms interchangeably.

Although Equation 17.6 describes an n-possibility lottery, we most commonly restrict our discussion to n = 2 because of the ease with which we can visually and numerically describe this situation. A deeper knowledge of probability and statistics and calculus allows us to examine lotteries involving a continuum of possible alternatives but we do not spend time on that here. The essence of decision making under uncertainty can be described in this more restricted setting, without resorting to a formal analysis of probability distributions.

Table 17.1 describes a certain outcome A and 10 two-contingency lotteries B–K. Each has a low payout X_L and a high payout X_H. (B–K are lotteries because $p_L + p_H = 1$ in each instance. Although A is not formally a lottery, it can be called a lottery for simplicity.) The basic point regarding choices under uncertainty is the following: If offered the choice of one of these 11 lotteries by your rich Uncle Lotto, you would be able to describe which you prefer. Indeed, if asked, you would be able to rank-order these 11 lotteries. Different individuals may well have different rankings of these bundles, but the simple fact is that individuals can evaluate alternatives involving multiple contingencies. Even if you have never had a course in probability and statistics, you are able to provide an answer to such

TABLE 17.1 Describing Lotteries as Probability-Weighted Outcomes

	Low Payout		High Payout	
Lottery	X_L	p_L	X_H	p_H
A			$1,000	100%
B	$400	25%	$1,200	75%
C	$500	50%	$1,500	50%
D	$600	75%	$2,200	25%
E	$700	90%	$3,700	10%
F	$100	25%	$1,300	75%
G	$300	50%	$1,700	50%
H	$200	60%	$2,200	40%
I	$0	50%	$2,000	50%
J	$0	75%	$4,000	25%
K	$0	99%	$100,000	1%

a question. Even without formal training in these topics, you probably can describe some lotteries as being more risky than others. We now turn to a discussion of commonly used terms to describe value and variability.

Consider once again the 50/50 chance at paying or receiving \$1. You may not know why this is true, but you are likely to understand at an intuitive level that this lottery has an expected payout of \$0. Similarly, if you faced a 50/50 chance at paying or receiving \$10, you are likely to know that it has the same expected payout but is a much riskier lottery than the first lottery. Finally, if you faced a 2/3 chance to lose \$1 and a 1/3 chance to win \$2, then you probably would intuitively understand that the expected payout remains \$0 (if you play this game often, you will be likely to lose \$1 twice as often as you are likely to win \$2). Each of these intuitive beliefs is an example of the concept of expected value. The **expected value** of an outcome is the probability-weighted sum of possible outcomes. This is often called a *weighted average* or *mean*.[5] Algebraically, this is given by the equation:

expected value: The expected value of an outcome is the probability-weighted sum of possible outcomes.

$$E(X) = p_1 \cdot X_1 + \ldots + p_n \cdot X_n. \quad \textbf{(17.7)}$$

Expected value is a measure of central tendency. It does not imply that you expect the outcome to actually occur. Each of the lotteries used to motivate this definition has an expected value of \$0, despite none of the contingent outcomes being \$0.

The lotteries in Table 17.1 were chosen because they each have the same expected value of \$1,000. Without formally doing the calculations, this is easy to see with the equal-weighted (symmetric) lotteries (C, G, and I) but is less obvious for the asymmetric lotteries.

A basic expectation about most individuals' preferences over lotteries is that a higher expected value is good and a higher degree of risk is bad, *ceteris paribus*. If two lotteries have the same expected value, then the one with lower risk is likely to be preferred to the one with higher risk. But to make this more formal, we need a definition of *risk*.

In the context of numerical outcomes, risk occurs if there is a divergence in numerical outcomes across contingencies. The expected payout is somewhere between the high and low payouts. You might initially imagine that the deviation of a payout from the expected payout, $D_i = X_i - E(X)$, summed across contingencies, is a measure of the overall variability of a lottery. The problem with this interpretation is that positive deviations balance negative deviations, and the sum of deviations will be zero (at least in the equal-weighted circumstance). To deal with this problem, we could simply count positive and negative deviations stripped of their signs as divergence from the expected outcome. This measure of variability might be called the sum of absolute deviations measure, Sum|D|:

$$\text{Sum}|D| = \Sigma\,|X_i - E(X)| = |X_1 - E(X)| + \ldots + |X_n - E(X)|. \quad \textbf{(17.8a)}$$

In the context of a two-alternative lottery, this simply measures the spread of values between the high and low alternatives. If there are only two possible alternatives, one is the low payout, X_L, and the other is the high payout, X_H; then:

$$\text{Sum}|D| = X_H - X_L. \quad \textbf{(17.8b)}$$

Since each of the lotteries described in Table 17.1 has the same expected value, they only differ on the amount of riskiness inherent in each lottery. If you looked at risk in this fashion, you would have the following rank ordering of preferences over these 11 alternative lotteries (the risk of each lottery is beneath the respective letter):

$$\begin{array}{ccccccccccccccccccccc} A & \succ & B & \succ & C & \succ & F & \succ & G & \succ & D & \succ & H & \sim & I & \succ & E & \succ & J & \succ & K \\ 0 & & 800 & & 1{,}000 & & 1{,}200 & & 1{,}400 & & 1{,}600 & & 2{,}000 & & 2{,}000 & & 3{,}000 & & 4{,}000 & & 100{,}000 \end{array} \quad \textbf{(17.8c)}$$

by Sum|D|.

A more sophisticated individual might realize that some of the alternatives are truly long shots and that these long shots should not be provided with as much weight as a more likely alternative. The measure of variability posed in Equation 17.8 treats all alternatives as being equally likely. If an alternative is not very likely to occur, it should be given less weight than an alternative that is very likely to occur. This is exactly the sort of reasoning that led to the expected value calculation in Equation 17.7. In the context of deviations from the mean, we can sum absolute deviations across alternatives weighted by the likelihood that each alternative (and hence each deviation) is going to occur. The resulting measure is a weighted average of absolute deviation, denoted W.Ave.|D|:

$$\text{W.Ave.}|D| = \Sigma\, p_i \cdot |X_i - E(X)| = p_1 \cdot |X_1 - E(X)| + \ldots + p_n \cdot |X_n - E(X)|. \qquad \textbf{(17.9a)}$$

An individual using this measure of riskiness would have the following rank ordering of preferences over the 11 alternative lotteries in Table 17.1:

$$\begin{matrix} A & \succ & B & \succ & F & \succ & C & \succ & E & \succ & D & \succ & G & \succ & H & \succ & I & \succ & J & \succ & K \\ 0 & & 300 & & 450 & & 500 & & 540 & & 600 & & 700 & & 960 & & 1{,}000 & & 1{,}500 & & 1{,}980 \end{matrix} \qquad \textbf{(17.9b)}$$

by W.Ave.|D|.

Notice in particular that Lottery E has moved up substantially in the rankings according to this measure. The reason is straightforward and instructive: The low payout in E is \$700, an outcome that is deemed very likely to occur, since $p_L = 90\%$. This payout is balanced by a much larger payout of \$3,700 that only has a 10% probability of occurring. The absolute spread on this lottery is large (\$3,000, according to Equation 17.8b), but the weighted-average spread is much smaller (\$540, according to Equation 17.9a) because the likely outcome is close to the expected outcome, and the unlikely outcome is far away.

Note: *Different individuals might well view the same choices in different ways because they perceive the risk inherent in those choices in different ways. No single measure of variability can be designated the appropriate measure. The appropriate measure simply depends on how the individual perceives risk.*

One final measure—standard deviation—should be discussed because it is widely used by statisticians. This measure is based on squaring the deviations (this is an alternative way to remove the minus signs, rather than taking absolute value). By squaring deviations and taking the weighted-average sum of squared deviations, we obtain a measure called variance. Formally, *variance* is defined as:

$$\text{Variance} = \Sigma\, p_i \cdot (X_i - E(X))^2 = p_1 \cdot (X_1 - E(X))^2 + \ldots + p_n \cdot (X_n - E(X))^2. \qquad \textbf{(17.10)}$$

Notice the similarity between Equations 17.10 and 17.9a. The only difference is the squaring, rather than taking absolute value. Variance is a measure of variability, but the square root of variance is even more commonly used. This measure is called *standard deviation (SD)*:

$$SD = (\Sigma\, p_i \cdot (X_i - E(X))^2)^{0.5} = (p_1 \cdot (X_1 - E(X))^2 + \ldots + p_n \cdot (X_n - E(X))^2)^{0.5}. \qquad \textbf{(17.11a)}$$

For symmetric two-way lotteries, this measure of deviation is identical to the weighted-average deviation. For asymmetric lotteries, however, this no longer holds. An individual who perceives risk according to this measure of riskiness will have the following rank ordering of the 11 lotteries in Table 17.1:

$$\begin{matrix} A & \succ & B & \succ & C & \succ & F & \succ & D & \succ & G & \succ & E & \succ & H & \succ & I & \succ & J & \succ & K \\ 0 & & 346 & & 500 & & 520 & & 693 & & 700 & & 900 & & 980 & & 1{,}000 & & 1{,}732 & & 9{,}950 \end{matrix} \qquad \textbf{(17.11b)}$$

by SD.

Notice that this same preference ordering of these alternatives would occur if the individual used variance, rather than standard deviation, as the measure of risk.[6]

Figure 17.8 provides a visual summary of lotteries A though J. Lottery K is substantially more risky than the other lotteries (according to two of the three measures); therefore, Lottery K is omitted from Figure 17.8 because its inclusion compresses the scale and makes the other lotteries appear less distinct. Each two-way lottery can be described by four pieces of information: low payout, high payout, expected payout, and a measure of risk inherent in the lottery. The graphical construct used in Figure 17.8 allows us to show these four pieces of information in a convenient way. (This construct is not typically used for this purpose; this is actually Excel's "Chart Wizard" format for showing

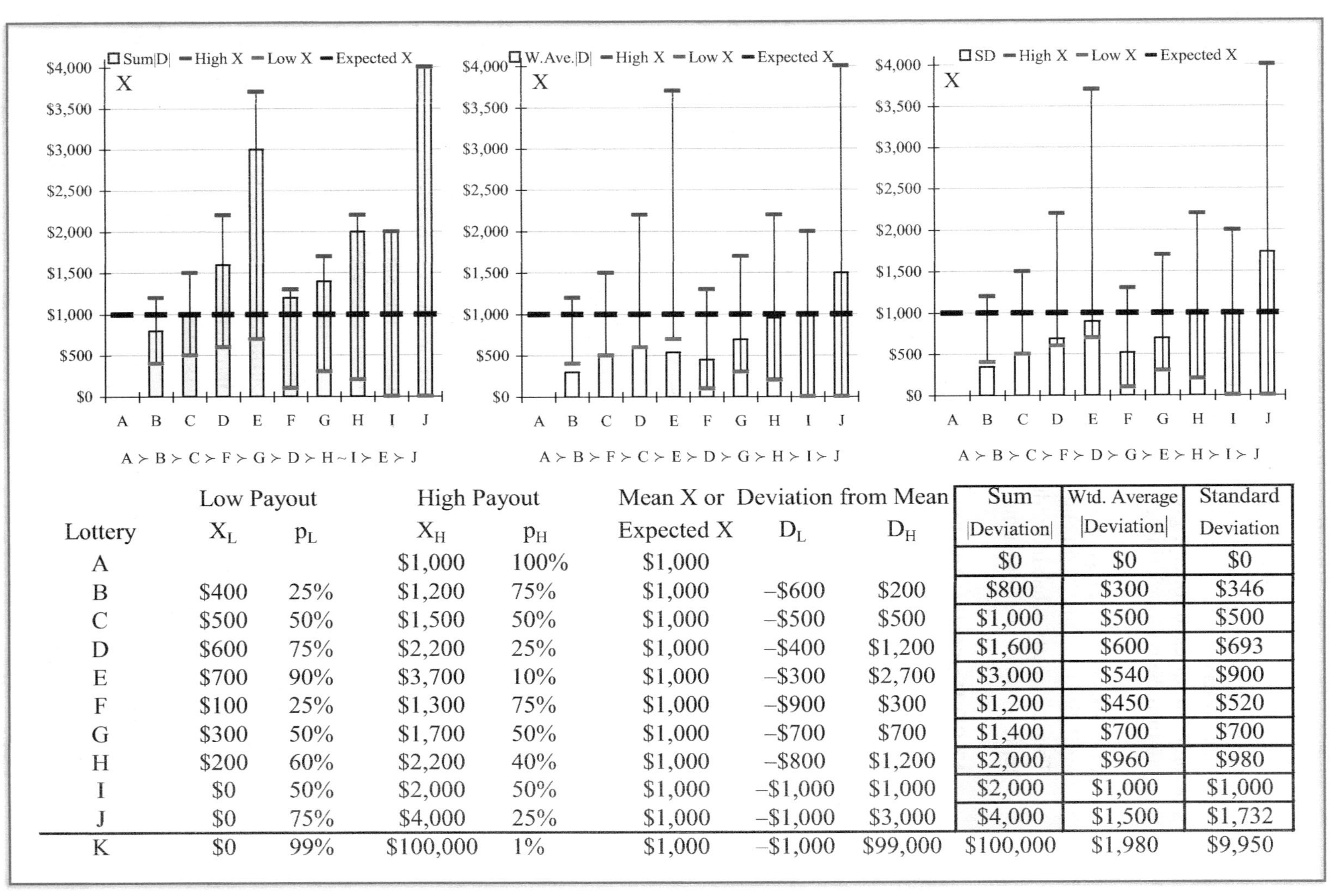

	Low Payout		High Payout		Mean X or	Deviation from Mean		Sum	Wtd. Average	Standard
Lottery	X_L	p_L	X_H	p_H	Expected X	D_L	D_H	|Deviation|	|Deviation|	Deviation
A			$1,000	100%	$1,000			$0	$0	$0
B	$400	25%	$1,200	75%	$1,000	–$600	$200	$800	$300	$346
C	$500	50%	$1,500	50%	$1,000	–$500	$500	$1,000	$500	$500
D	$600	75%	$2,200	25%	$1,000	–$400	$1,200	$1,600	$600	$693
E	$700	90%	$3,700	10%	$1,000	–$300	$2,700	$3,000	$540	$900
F	$100	25%	$1,300	75%	$1,000	–$900	$300	$1,200	$450	$520
G	$300	50%	$1,700	50%	$1,000	–$700	$700	$1,400	$700	$700
H	$200	60%	$2,200	40%	$1,000	–$800	$1,200	$2,000	$960	$980
I	$0	50%	$2,000	50%	$1,000	–$1,000	$1,000	$2,000	$1,000	$1,000
J	$0	75%	$4,000	25%	$1,000	–$1,000	$3,000	$4,000	$1,500	$1,732
K	$0	99%	$100,000	1%	$1,000	–$1,000	$99,000	$100,000	$1,980	$9,950

FIGURE 17.8 Depicting Lotteries Using "Stock" Diagrams: Expected Outcome, X_{high}, X_{low}, and Three Measures of Risk

stock market data. The four pieces of information about a stock are: high, low, close, and volume for a stock.) In the present context, the black dash is the expected payout (which by construction of the lotteries is $1,000 in each instance), the red dash is the low payout, the blue dash is the high payout, and the colored rectangle describes the risk inherent in the lottery. We have described three measures of risk in Equations 17.8, 17.9, and 17.11; therefore, each graph depicts one of these measures of risk (these measures are calculated in the final three columns of the table beneath the graphs).[7] A quick comparison across the graphs confirms that the other three pieces of information are the same in each. Since each lottery has the same expected value, the height of the colored box tells us the rank ordering of each lottery, given the measure of risk. The graphs provide a quick way to confirm the rank ordering given in Equations 17.8c, 17.9b, and 17.11b.

When lotteries have different expected values, individuals must compare the inherent trade-offs between risk and return. They must be able to compare the costs and benefits available from uncertain choices that have different expected values and degrees of risk. This is exactly what individuals do when they consider various investment options, a topic to which we now turn.

17.2B Portfolio Analysis and the Risk/Return Trade-off

Prerequisites: Chapter 6 and Section 17.2A

We can describe an individual's preferences over risk and return using indifference curves that describe the trade-offs between expected outcome and the risk inherent in that option. Higher-risk options should also have higher expected returns. We restrict our focus here to rates of return on various investment options, and we use standard deviation as our measure of risk.

Risky assets can be described in terms of their risk and return. An asset can be described as a point in (s, r) space, where s denotes standard deviation, and r denotes expected rate of return. Consider a bundle such as **C** = (8%, 4.2%) in Figure 17.9. An indifference curve, U*(s), passes through **C**. This indifference curve is convex but is not monotonic because risk is an economic bad rather than an economic good (using the terminology of Chapter 3). This individual is willing to accept greater risk to attain greater expected return (for example, the bundle (s, r) = (16%, 9%) is also on this indifference curve). Conversely, this individual would also be indifferent with lower expected return and lower risk (for example, the bundle (s, r) = (4%, 3%) is also on this indifference curve). The functional form of this utility function is not of critical importance for our current analysis, but it is the same form used to show x satiation in Chapter 3.[8] The critical point for our analysis is that the trade-off produces upward-sloping indifference curves in which better is in the northwest direction. The steepness of the indifference curve at any point is determined by the individual's willingness to accept risk. If the individual is more risk averse, then the indifference curve will be steeper than if the individual is more tolerant of risk. A slider allows you to adjust the degree of risk tolerance in the Excel version of Figure 17.9.

The utility level associated with an indifference curve can be described by reference to the risk-free return associated with this indifference curve. In standard utility theory, the numbers attached to the indifference curve lack cardinal meaning. In the present circumstance, we can attach a cardinal number to the indifference curve because we can pull that number off the vertical axis, and we understand what it means. All (s, r) bundles on the vertical axis are risk free since s = 0; therefore, the return r is a certain return. The risk-free return associated with an indifference curve is simply the intersection of the indifference curve with the vertical axis. This is called the *certainty equivalent rate of return*. In Figure 17.9, we can see that the certainty equivalent return is 2.60% at the point labeled U*(0) on the vertical axis. This individual is indifferent between 2.60% with certainty and an expected return of 4.2%, with standard deviation of 8% (bundle **C**), as well as the other bundles, including those noted in the previous paragraph. Put another way, each of these points has a certainty equivalent rate of return of 2.60%.

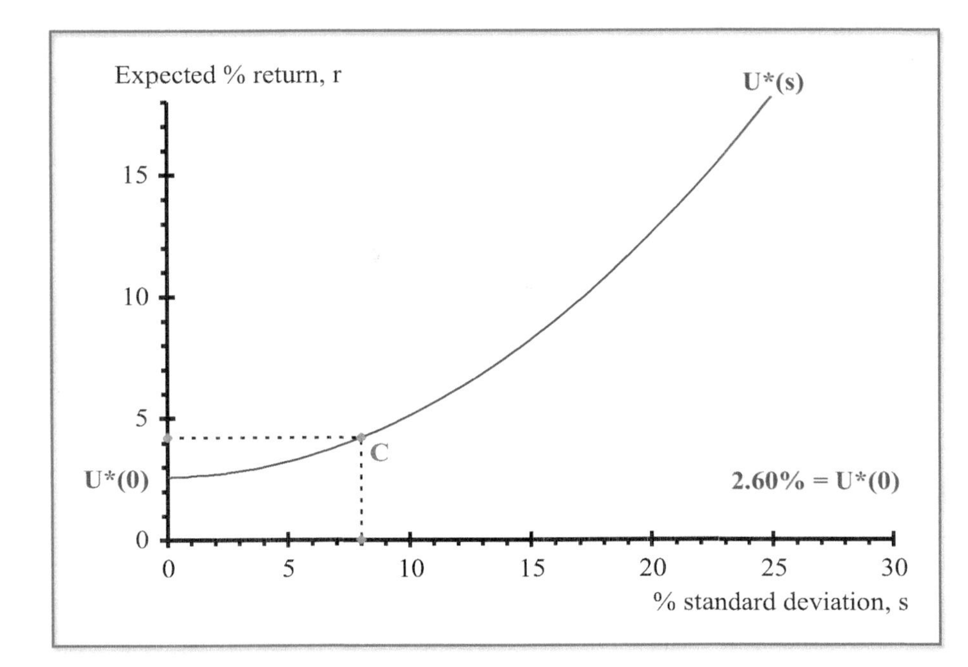

FIGURE 17.9 The Risk/Return Trade-off

One of the main ways individuals invest in the future is by investing in various asset markets. The easiest way to do this is to invest in a mutual fund. A full treatment of portfolio analysis is beyond the scope of this text, but we can examine basic issues of asset allocation across different classes of risk, using the risk/return trade-off discussed in Figure 17.9.

The question we wish to examine is how an individual should decide to allocate wealth across risk-free versus risky assets. To simplify our discussion, assume that we have two assets from which to choose: Treasury bills (T-bills) are essentially risk free but have a low yield; investing in stocks has a higher yield but is a riskier alternative. Consider the time period from 1928–2014. Table 17.2 shows annual rates of return on common stock (Standard & Poor's 500) in two ways (this table is actually a chart and a frequency distribution). The upper chart shows that the returns vary significantly across time. The lower part of the table is a frequency distribution of this data. This shows that annual stock returns were most commonly in the range of –10% to 40% (in 71 of the 87 years listed). Common stock had an average return of 11.53% with a standard deviation of 19.90% over this time period. During this same time period, inflation averaged 3.13%, and T-bills had an average return of 3.54%. We must subtract inflation from nominal returns to obtain real returns.

Feasible Allocations of Risk and Return

Consider the decision to allocate wealth between T-bills and a portfolio of stocks; the former has no risk but a lower return, while the latter has high risk but also a more substantial return. If all wealth had to be placed in one or the other, then a simple comparison of utility levels associated with T-bills and stocks determines which alternative to choose. Of course, individuals need not invest completely in one or the other. Most individual investors choose to spend some fraction on stocks and the rest on T-bills. The proportion spent on each depends critically on how the individual views risk. We can show this graphically, using indifference curves such as that shown in Figure 17.9, together with a "budget constraint" that describes the feasible (risk, return) bundles allowable, given the options provided by the market.

In terms of (risk, return) bundles, the risk-free rate is $\mathbf{F} = (0, f)$, and the stock market portfolio is $\mathbf{M} = (s_m, m)$. Recall that the second coordinate refers to an expected return, and the first coordinate is the standard deviation of that expectation. The set of bundles between **F** and **M** is the *capital allocation line (CAL)*. The most intuitive way to describe

TABLE 17.2

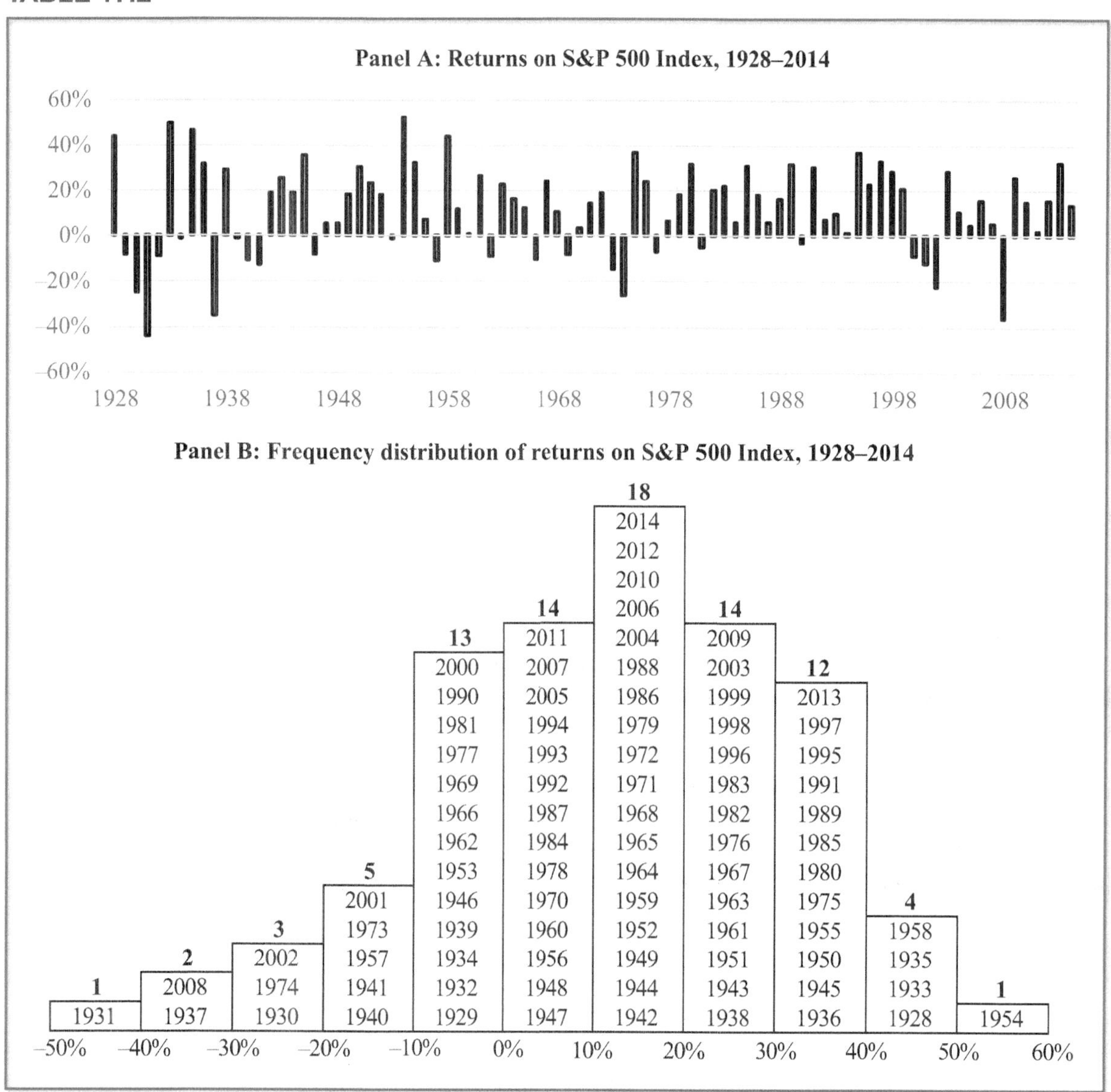

Source: Data taken from Aswath Damodaran, Historical Returns: Stocks, T. Bonds, and T. Bills with Premiums, Stern School of Business website: http://www.stern.nyu.edu/∞adamodar/New_Home_Page/data.html

this line is using the parametric representation described in Equation 5.1b. The CAL is the set of bundles **C** = (risk$_c$, return$_c$) where:

$$\mathbf{C} = (t \cdot s_m,\ f + t \cdot (m - f)), \text{ or } \mathbf{C} = t \cdot \mathbf{M} + (1 - t) \cdot \mathbf{F}, \text{ with } 0 \le t \le 1. \quad \textbf{(17.12a)}$$

The parameter t represents the proportion of wealth devoted to the risky asset, **M**. The rest, (1 – t), is devoted to the risk-free asset, **F**. Some students prefer to view the risk and return components of the bundle separately. The risk of the combined portfolio (of risk-free and risky assets) is directly related to the proportion of the risky asset in the combined portfolio. A portfolio with 25% of wealth devoted to the risky asset will be 25% as risky as a portfolio with 100% of wealth devoted to the risky asset. If that proportion is t, then the risk attached to that combined portfolio is:

$$\text{risk}_c = t \cdot s_m. \quad \textbf{(17.12b)}$$

The risk premium of the market portfolio is the difference between the risky and risk-free rate, m – f. The expected return on a complete portfolio with a proportion t devoted to the risky asset is:

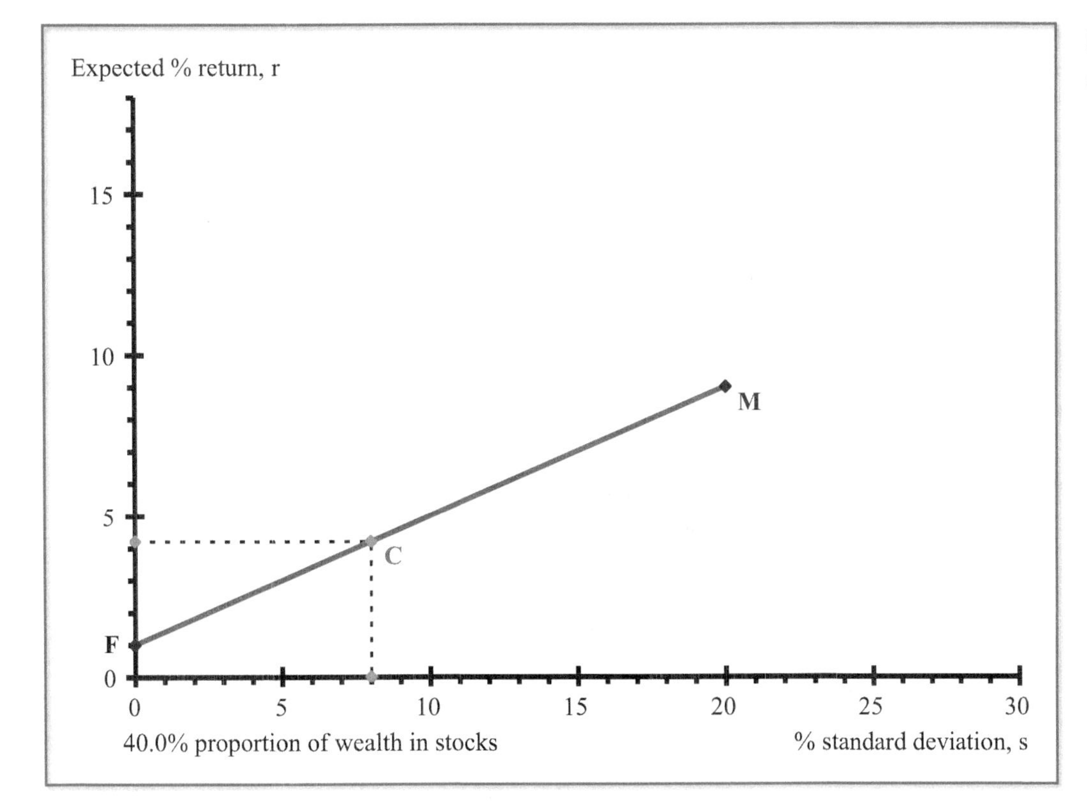

FIGURE 17.10 Capital Allocation Line

$$\text{return}_c = f + t \cdot (m - f). \quad \textbf{(17.12c)}$$

The expected return on the combined portfolio is directly related to the proportion of the risky asset in the combined portfolio (as is risk of the combined portfolio).[9] The bundle **C** on the capital allocation line **FM** in Figure 17.10 represents investing 40% on the risky asset **M** and 60% on the risk-free asset **F**. If $t > 40\%$, the (risk, return) bundle will be closer to **M**, and if $t < 40\%$, the bundle will be closer to **F**. The values for **F** = (0%, 1%) and **M** = (20%, 9%) are reasonably close to those described earlier based on T-bill, stock, and inflation information from 1928–2014. They have been adjusted slightly so that numerical solutions (which we will discuss shortly) are easy to see. The sliders in the Excel file for Figure 17.10 allow you to adjust risk and return to more accurately reflect the numerical values discussed earlier.

The Optimal Allocation of Risk and Return

By allocating different proportions of spending toward the two goods, an individual is able to adjust the risk/return profile in a portfolio. Not surprisingly, an individual with less risk tolerance will devote a larger percentage of wealth to the risk-free asset and a smaller percentage to the risky asset than will an individual with more risk tolerance. Individual A (Figure 17.11A) is more averse to risk than Individual B because A's indifference curve is flatter at any bundle than B's would be at the same bundle. As a result, A devotes 40% of wealth to stocks, while B devotes 80% to stocks. Despite this difference in overall behavior, both individuals face the same marginal trade-off between risk and return. Each continues to increase the amount of the risky asset in their portfolio up to the point where their MRS equals the slope of the CAL. This is not a surprising result; the slope of the CAL is simply a "price ratio" describing the terms of trade between risk and return. More specifically, the slope of the CAL is:

$$\text{Slope}_{CAL} = \Delta\text{return}/\Delta\text{risk} = (m - f)/s_m. \quad \textbf{(17.13a)}$$

The slope of the capital allocation line describes the incremental expected return per unit of standard deviation. In Figures 17.10 and 17.11, this ratio is:

$$\text{Slope}_{CAL} = (m - f)/s_m = (9 - 1)/20 = 0.4. \quad \textbf{(17.13b)}$$

FIGURE 17.11 Optimal Asset Allocation

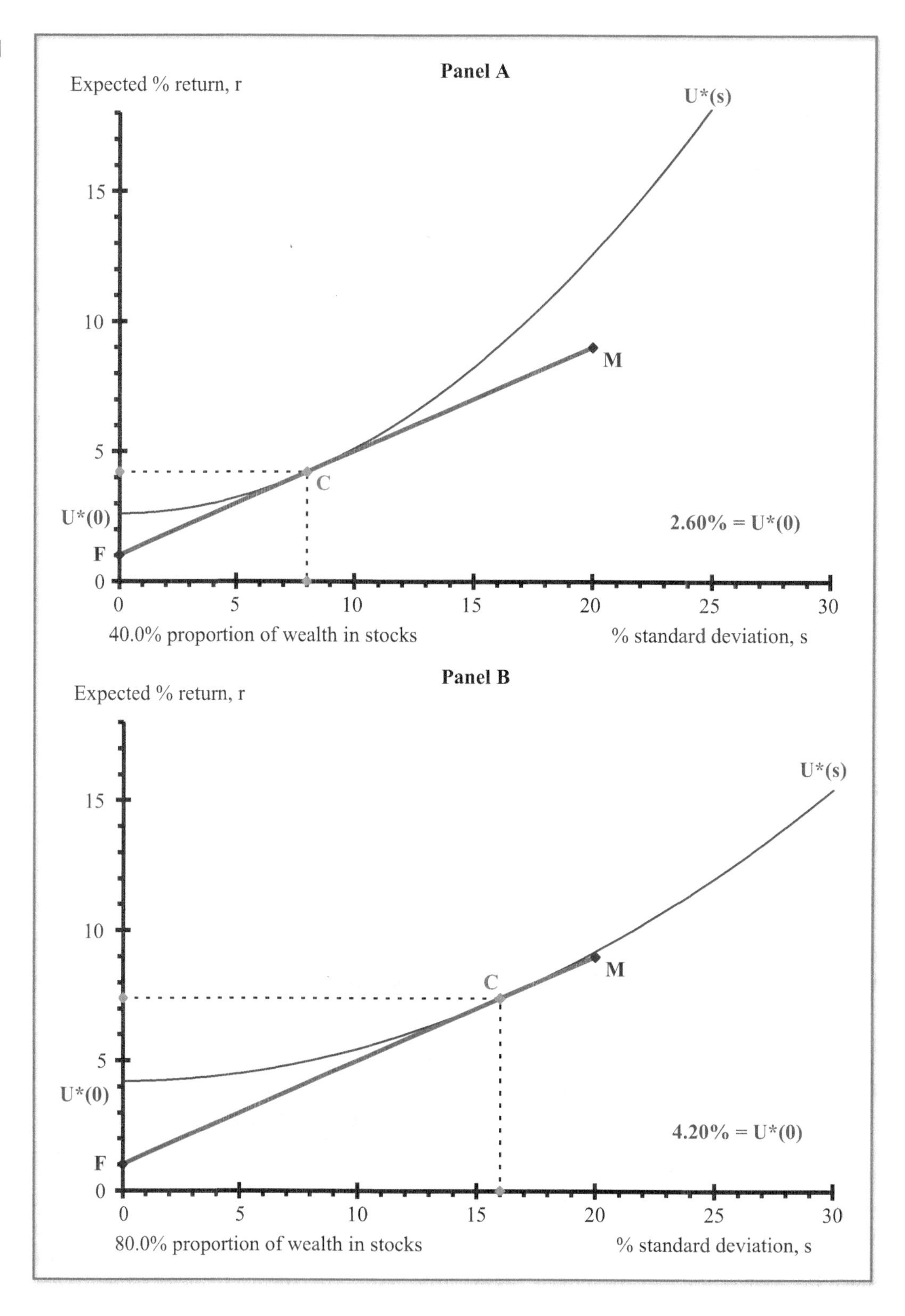

Investment analysts call this the *reward-to-variability ratio*. Each 0.4% increase in expected return of the complete portfolio comes with a price tag of a 1% increase in standard deviation on that return. Just as in Chapter 6, the tangency condition forces different individuals to have the same marginal behavior, despite differences in overall behavior.

Both of the individuals depicted in Figure 17.11 chose to invest some in the risky asset and some in the risk-free asset. Geometrically, both are on the interior of the capital allocation line **FM**. This need not be the case. Individuals with a very low degree of risk aversion will have reasonably flat indifference curves. If MRS(**M**) $\leq$ Slope_{CAL},

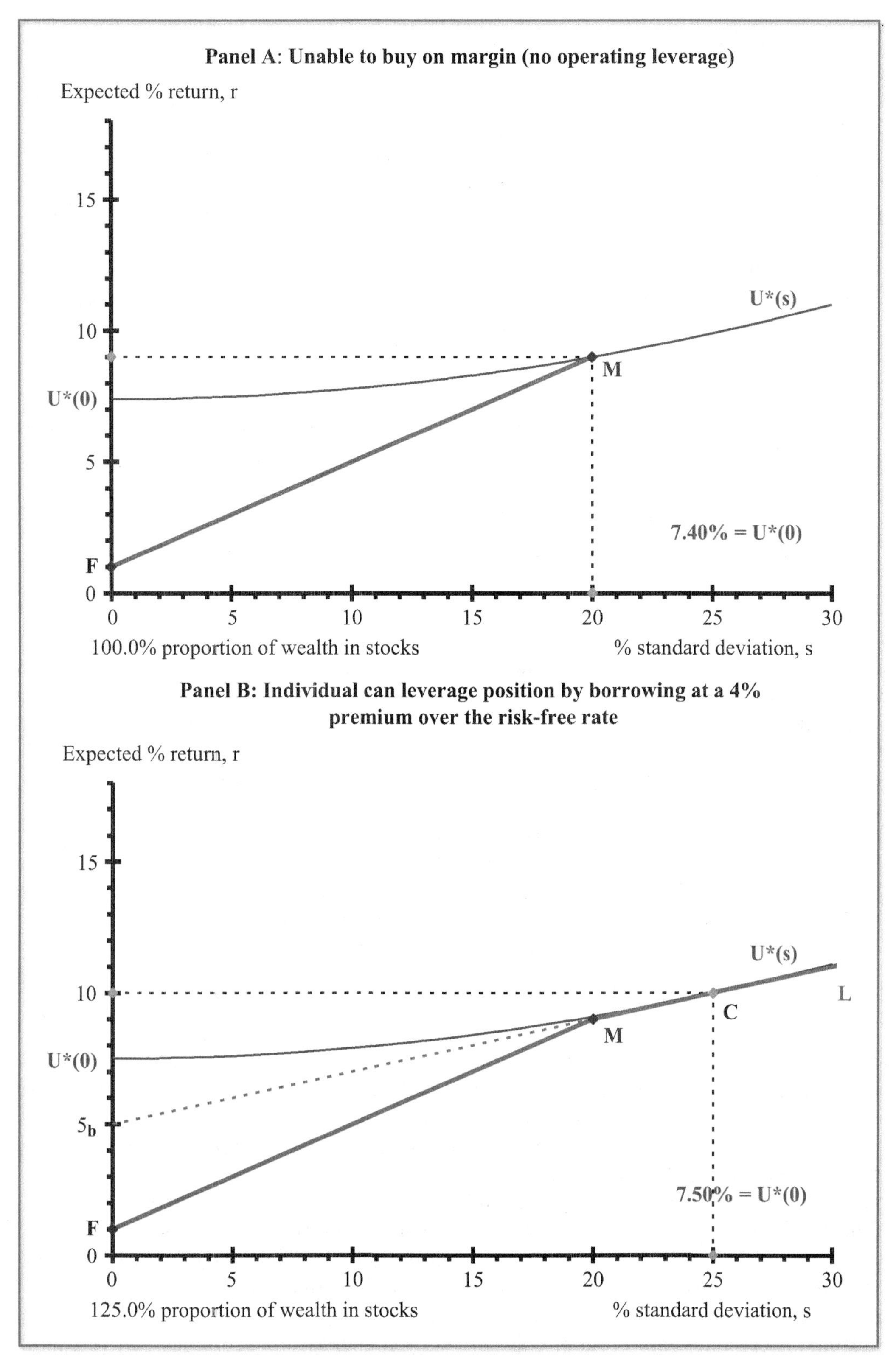

FIGURE 17.12 Optimal Asset Allocation for an Individual with Minimal Risk Aversion

they will choose to invest 100% of their wealth in the stock portfolio.[10] This is the situation depicted in Figure 17.12A. The certainty equivalent utility level associated with this portfolio is 7.40%, according to the diagram. If MRS(**M**) < Slope_{CAL}, these individuals would prefer to invest even more heavily in stocks if they were not constrained by already investing all of their wealth in the market. Such individuals do typically have the ability to leverage their position and invest even more heavily in risky asset markets. They do this by buying on the margin.

Using Leverage

If individuals borrow money to invest in the market, they can effectively increase the amount of wealth that they devote to risky investments. Such individuals take a *leveraged position* in the risky asset. If these individuals were able to borrow at the risk-free rate, then they could construct portfolios that extend the set of feasible risk/return bundles beyond **M** in a straight line. Such portfolios would, of course, have a higher expected return but also a higher level of risk. The capital allocation line would then contain **M** as an interior point, and these individuals could allocate more than 100% of their wealth to the risky asset.

In practice, investors cannot borrow at the risk-free rate because the activity they are considering is innately risky. As a result, they must pay a higher interest rate on loans, $r_b > f$.[11] If investors set up a margin account with their brokers, they will be able to buy stock "on margin" at an interest rate of r_b:

$r_b = f + d$, where f is the risk-free rate and d is the interest rate differential. **(17.14)**

If individuals borrow on margin and invest the proceeds in the risky asset, then they are able to increase the expected return on their overall portfolio past the market portfolio's expected return of m. The cost of that increase in expected return is an increase in risk. The incremental return per unit of risk, the reward-to-variability ratio on this leveraged investment, is:

$$\text{Slope}_{\text{LeveragedCAL}} = \Delta\text{return}/\Delta\text{risk} = (m - r_b)/s_m. \quad \textbf{(17.15a)}$$

The numerator in this fraction is the increment in expected return from the market over the cost of capital to the investor, and the denominator is the riskiness of the market portfolio.

The capital allocation line is now kinked. To the left of **M**, the investor need not borrow (and indeed the investor is acting as a lender at the risk-free rate of f). Equation 17.13 describes the slope of the CAL on **FM**. To the right of **M**, the investor must borrow at the borrowing interest rate of r_b in order to make *leveraged purchases*. Equation 17.15 describes the slope of the CAL on **ML**. Both parts of the kinked CAL are shown in Figure 17.12B, based on an interest rate differential of d = 4%. The borrowing interest rate is therefore $r_b = f + d = 1 + 4 = 5\%$. The borrowing interest rate is seen as point **b** = (0%, 5%) in Figure 17.12B (and the interest rate differential d is the vertical difference between **b** and **F**). Given this borrowing interest rate, the reward-to-variability ratio on the leveraged investment is:

$$\text{Slope}_{\text{LeveragedCAL}} = (m - r_b)/s_m = (9 - 5)/20 = 0.2. \quad \textbf{(17.15b)}$$

The slope is flatter on the borrowing segment of the CAL because of the interest rate differential, d. If this differential was smaller, then the kink would be smaller, but the same qualitative results would apply (i.e., the kink would remain as long as $d > 0$).

The investor whose risk preferences are described by the indifference curves in Figure 17.12 would choose to leverage the investment and invest an additional 25% of wealth in stocks. This leveraged investment would allow the expected return on the chosen portfolio to increase from the 9% associated with investing 100% of wealth in the stock portfolio (at **M**) to 10% (at **C**). The chosen portfolio is not worth the entire extra 1% in incremental expected return because this incremental return comes at a cost of increased risk. Specifically, the risk at **C** is 25% higher than at **M** (25% is 25% higher than 20%). Indeed, the certainty equivalent of **C** is only 0.1% higher than the certainty equivalent of **M**, as can be seen by comparing Figures 17.12A and 17.12B (7.5% is 0.1% above 7.4%).

The kink at **M** means that a range of individuals would be willing to invest all wealth in stocks without resorting to margin purchases. Any individual whose MRS(**M**) is in the range $\text{Slope}_{\text{LeveragedCAL}} \leq \text{MRS}(\mathbf{M}) \leq \text{Slope}_{\text{CAL}}$ will find **M** to be the utility-maximizing (risk, return) bundle. These individuals cover a range of degrees of risk aversion. Using the CAL in Figure 17.12B, **M** would be utility maximizing as long as $0.2 \leq \text{MRS}(\mathbf{M}) \leq 0.4$. Figure 17.13A depicts the most risk-averse individual who would choose **M** (this individual's MRS(**M**) = 0.4). This individual's certainty equivalent rate of return is 5%. Any

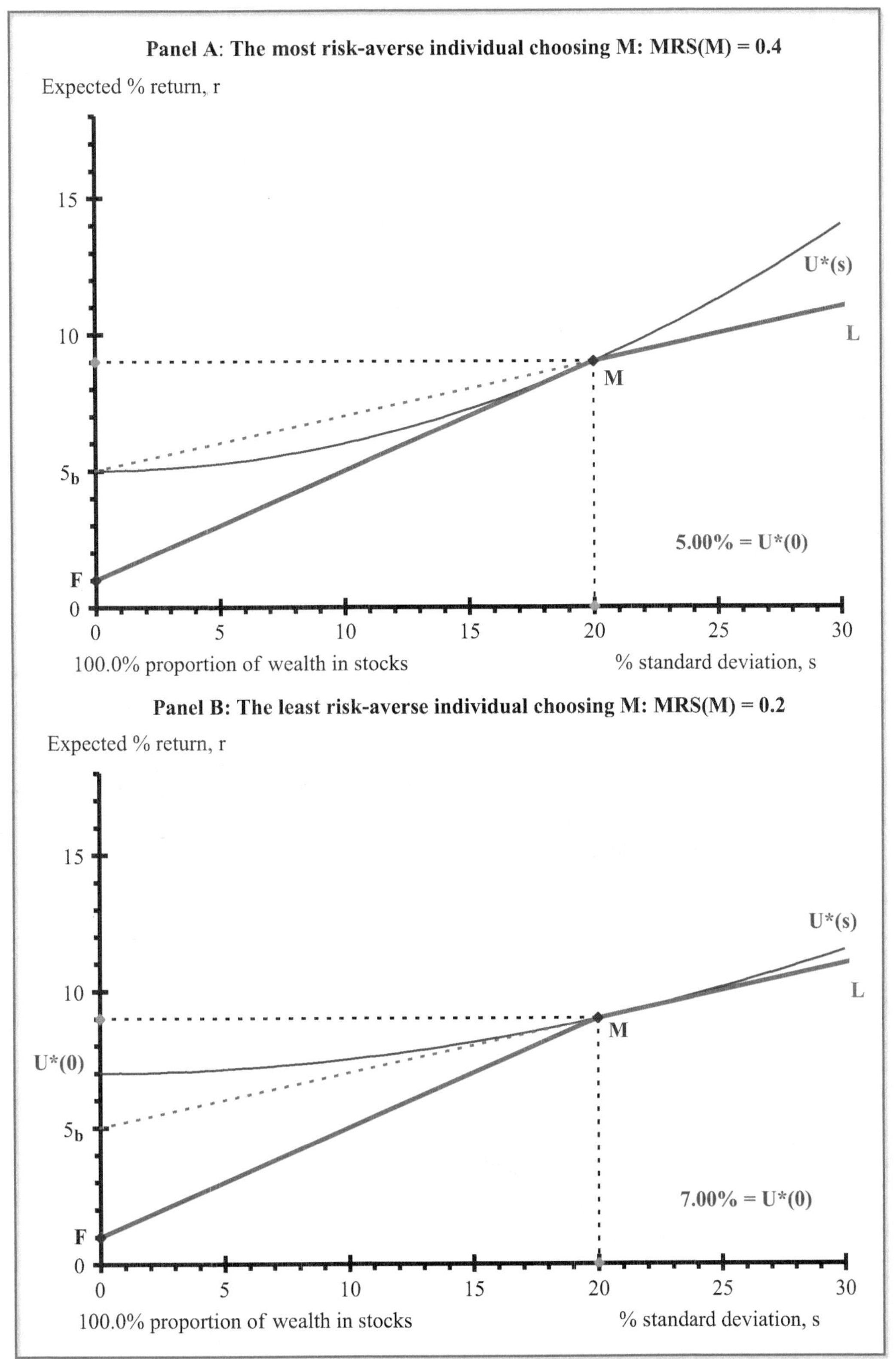

FIGURE 17.13 Consuming at the Kink: The Range of Risk-Averse Individuals Who Will Spend 100% of Wealth on Stocks

degree of risk aversion greater than this would produce an optimal complete portfolio in which some portion of wealth is devoted to the risk-free asset (because in this instance the individual's MRS(**M**) > 0.4, implying that there are complete portfolios on **FM** that are preferred to **M**). Such individuals would also have a certainty equivalent rate of return on the complete portfolio of less than 5% (Figures 17.11A and 17.11B are examples of this situation). Figure 17.13B depicts the least risk-averse individual who would choose **M** (this individual's MRS(**M**) = 0.2). This individual's certainty equivalent rate of return is 7%. Any degree of risk aversion less than this would produce an optimal complete portfolio in which some leveraged purchases would occur (because in this instance the individual's MRS(**M**) < 0.2, implying that there are complete (leveraged) portfolios on **ML** that are preferred to **M**). Such individuals would also have a certainty equivalent rate of return of more than 7% (Figure 17.12B depicts this situation). These results mirror those found elsewhere when consumers are faced with nonlinear constraints.[12] Such constraints cause a vertex bundle to be chosen by consumers with a range of preferences because the MRS no longer needs to hold with equality for the bundle to be the best feasible option.

Constraining Leverage Via Regulation T

Individuals who have little risk aversion and who therefore wish to heavily leverage their wealth cannot borrow unlimited amounts for this purpose. Federal Reserve Board Regulation T sets margin requirements. The investor must provide at least 50% of the value of the investment. This means that you can purchase a maximum of 200% of your wealth, regardless of your willingness to tolerate risk. Given the numbers used to create Figures 17.12 and 17.13, this would occur on the extension of **ML** at the (risk, return) point **T** = (40%, 13%), which is outside the range of risk values shown in those figures. To show the impact of Regulation T, an alternative scenario is shown in Figure 17.14. The individual depicted in Figure 17.14 has the same risk aversion as the one shown in Figure 17.13B. All other parameters are the same with one exception: The market risk level s_m = 10%, rather than 20%. This creates a capital allocation line of **FMT**. Reducing risk by 50% has doubled the reward-to-variability ratio on both segments of the CAL to $\text{Slope}_{\text{CAL}} = 0.8$ and $\text{Slope}_{\text{LeveragedCAL}} = 0.4$. The maximum leverage the individual is able to achieve without violating Regulation T is to invest at **T** = (20%, 13%). In the current setting, the investor would wish to operate at a point of even greater leverage because MRS(**T**) = 0.2 in this instance.[13] Indeed, if free of this requirement, the individual shown in Figure 17.14 would end up investing 400% of wealth in the risky asset. Viewed in terms of margins, this amount of leverage would imply that the individual's wealth represents only 25% of the total investment in the risky asset (half the size of Regulation T's minimum wealth requirement).

FIGURE 17.14
Operating at Maximum Leverage

Individuals cannot borrow more than 100% of their wealth for margin purchases. Margin purchases may not exceed 50% of purchase value.

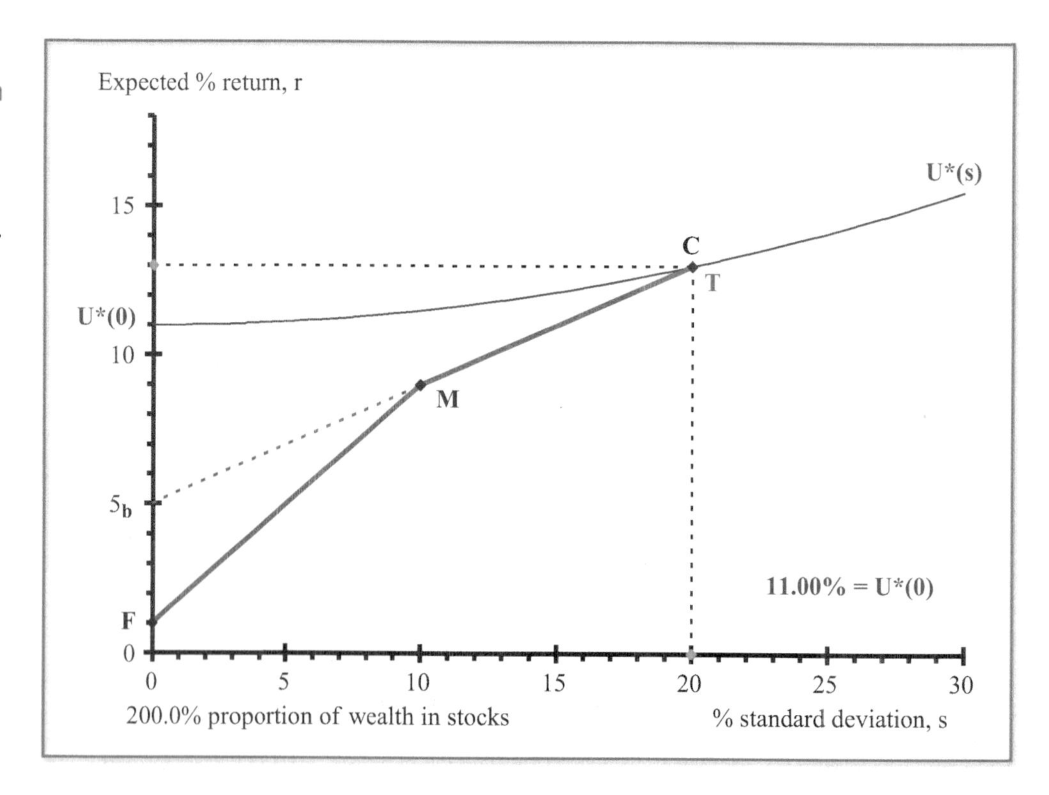

17.2C Expected Utility and Insurance

Prerequisites: Chapter 6 and Section 17.2A

We now turn to an alternative way to visualize lotteries from that proposed in Figure 17.8. That figure provided a way to visualize both expected outcome and various descriptions of the variability in that outcome (via maximum, minimum, and the measure of risk). Each contingency is denominated both in dollars and in the likelihood that the outcome will occur. From this information, we are able to describe the expected dollar value of the lottery, using Equation 17.7. Dollar value of a lottery, however, is only one way to measure the value of the lottery.

Expected Utility and Risk Aversion

Since dollars create buying power, each contingency implies a certain amount of buying power. Of course, dollars are used to purchase goods, and these goods produce utility, so we can imagine dollars as producing utility (via the goods that those dollars purchase). Therefore, we can consider the utility associated with each contingency as a function of income, $U = U(X)$. Different contingencies have different incomes, X_i, and hence, different utility levels associated with that contingency, $U(X_i)$. Just as we can consider the expected dollar value of a lottery, so can we consider the expected utility of a lottery in a symmetric calculation to Equation 17.7:

$$E(U(X)) = p_1 \cdot U(X_1) + \ldots + p_n \cdot U(X_n). \qquad \textbf{(17.16)}$$

Claim: *If we posit that expected utility describes the utility level associated with a lottery, then the lottery has two expected values: One is an expected dollar value (E(X) in Equation 17.7), and the other is an expected utility value (E(U(X)) in Equation 17.16).*

The central question we now address is how expected utility relates to the utility of the expected outcome. Algebraically, this question is: How does E(U(X)) relate to U(E(X))? If we return to the lotteries examined in Table 17.1 and Figure 17.8, we know that each of the lotteries had the same expected income value, E(X) = \$1,000. We also know, based on each measure of risk in Equations 17.8, 17.9, and 17.11, that each of the Lotteries B–K is worse than "Lottery" A, which offered \$1,000 with certainty. This is only true because we assumed that the individual viewed risk as an economic bad rather than as an economic neutral or economic good (to use the terminology of Chapter 3). Put another way, each of these individuals was risk averse. We used the term *risk averse* in the previous section to describe the positive slope of the individual's risk/return indifference curves. We can make this concept more explicit, using the concept of expected utility:

- An individual is **risk averse** if the utility associated with the expected income level derived from the lottery exceeds the expected utility of the lottery. Algebraically, $U(E(X)) > E(U(X))$ if the individual is risk averse.
- An individual is **risk neutral** if the utility associated with the expected income level derived from the lottery equals the expected utility of the lottery. Algebraically, $U(E(X)) = E(U(X))$ if the individual is risk neutral.
- An individual is **risk loving** if the utility associated with the expected income level derived from the lottery is less than the expected utility of the lottery. Algebraically, $U(E(X)) < E(U(X))$ if the individual is risk loving.

In each definition, U(E(X)) signifies the utility level associated with the expected income level. Whether an individual is risk averse, risk neutral, or risk loving depends on how U(E(X)) compares to the expected utility level achieved by the lottery, E(U(X)). If the utility from the lottery exceeds the utility achieved with certainty by the expected income from the lottery, the individual is risk loving. If the reverse holds true, the individual is risk averse. The individual who is indifferent in this regard is risk neutral.

risk averse: An individual is risk averse if the utility associated with the expected income level derived from the lottery exceeds the expected utility of the lottery.

risk neutral: An individual is risk neutral if the utility associated with the expected income level derived from the lottery equals the expected utility of the lottery.

risk loving: An individual is risk loving if the utility associated with the expected income level derived from the lottery is less than the expected utility of the lottery.

These definitions are most easily understood by considering a specific example. Consider Lottery F from Table 17.1, the 25/75 chance at either \$100 or \$1,300. Suppose that we fix the utility level associated with income of \$1,000 attained with certainty at U(\$1,000) = 1,000.[14] If we map utility, U, as a function of income, X, we obtain an upward-sloping function passing through the (X, U) certainty bundle **A** = (\$1,000, 1,000); in Figure 17.15, this is the blue diamond in each panel. Each contingency has both an income level and a utility level attached to it; each contingency can be mapped as a point in (X, U) space on the curve U(X). The expected income of a lottery is the weighted average of contingent income levels (Equation 17.7), and the expected utility of a lottery is the weighted average of the contingent utility levels (Equation 17.16). Therefore, the (expected income, expected utility) bundle associated with a lottery is the expected value of the lottery viewed in both dimensions. *This expected value bundle can be visualized for a two-way lottery as a point on the line segment connecting the contingent choices.*[15] The location of the expected value bundle along the line segment is determined by the probabilities attached to each contingency. In the case of Lottery F, the expected outcome, **E**, is the red diamond bundle three-quarters of the way along the red line segment connecting **L** to **H**, where **L** = $(X_L, U(X_L))$ is the pink low contingent outcome, and **H** = $(X_H, U(X_H))$ is the dark red high contingent outcome. The description of the lottery as a point on the line segment between contingent outcomes holds, regardless of the individual's attitude toward risk.

If the individual is risk averse, then **E** will be below **A** because both (X, U) bundles have a common X value, but U(E(X)) > E(U(X)) by definition. This is the situation shown in Figure 17.15A. In terms of expected utility level,

$$\begin{aligned} U(E(X)) &= 1{,}000 > 950 = 0.25 \cdot 200 + 0.75 \cdot 1{,}200 \\ &= p_L \cdot U(X_L) + p_H \cdot U(X_H) = E(U(X)). \end{aligned} \qquad \textbf{(17.17a)}$$

This means that the risk-averse individual will prefer the utility associated with expected income attained with certainty, rather than the expected utility of the lottery. More generally, this would occur if U(X) is increasing but is convex downward, or stated a different way, U(X) increases at a decreasing rate. If the individual is risk neutral, then U(E(X)) = E(U(X)), and the individual is indifferent between the expected utility of the lottery and the utility of the expected income. In this instance, **E** and **A** coincide in Figure 17.15B. This is seen algebraically as:

$$\begin{aligned} U(E(X)) &= 1{,}000 = 1{,}000 = 0.25 \cdot 100 + 0.75 \cdot 1{,}300 \\ &= p_L \cdot U(X_L) + p_H \cdot U(X_H) = E(U(X)). \end{aligned} \qquad \textbf{(17.17b)}$$

This occurs if U(X) is linear in X. Finally, if the individual prefers the expected utility of the lottery to the utility of the expected income from the lottery, then the individual is risk loving. This occurs when **E** is above **A**, as shown in Figure 17.14C. Algebraically, we see in this instance:

$$\begin{aligned} U(E(X)) &= 1{,}000 < 1{,}063 = 0.25 \cdot 50 + 0.75 \cdot 1{,}400 \\ &= p_L \cdot U(X_L) + p_H \cdot U(X_H) = E(U(X)). \end{aligned} \qquad \textbf{(17.17c)}$$

More generally, this occurs if U(X) is increasing and is convex upward, or stated a different way, U(X) increases at an increasing rate.

The key to determining the individual's risk aversion in this geometric conceptualization is to establish the convexity of utility as a function of income, U(X). Utility is an increasing function of income, but the key issue is how utility changes as income changes. Put more directly, what happens to the slope of the utility function as income increases? If it increases, the individual is risk loving, and if it declines, the individual is risk averse. This can be put in economic rather than mathematical terms by noting that the slope of this function is the marginal utility of income, $MU_{income} = \Delta U/\Delta X$ (since X represents dollar income). If MU_{income} is an increasing function of income, extra dollars are worth more and more in incremental utility. By contrast, if MU_{income} is a decreasing function of income, extra dollars are worth less and less in incremental utility.

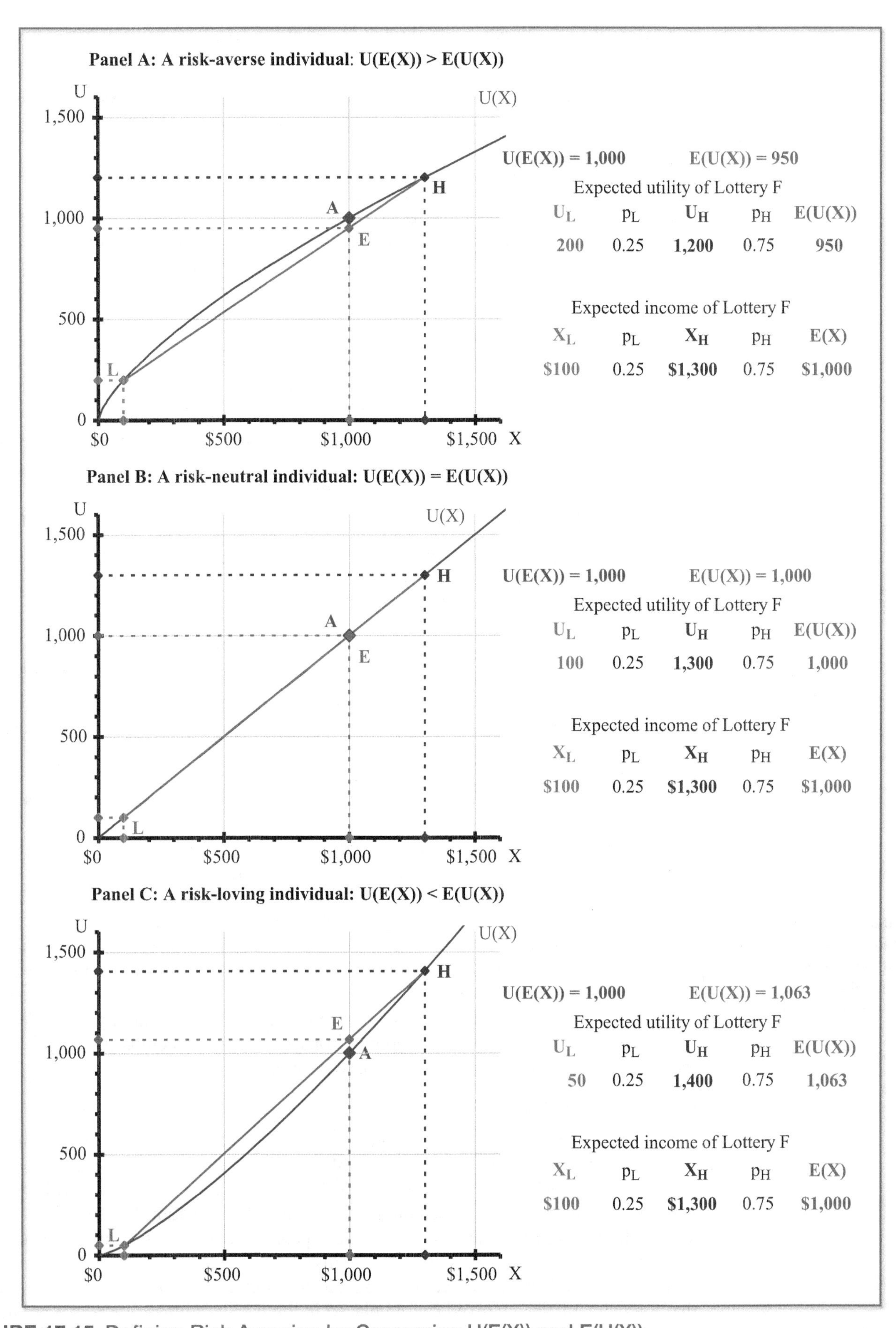

FIGURE 17.15 Defining Risk Aversion by Comparing U(E(X)) and E(U(X))

Claim: *If an individual's marginal utility of income declines as income increases, the individual is risk averse. If the opposite occurs, the individual is risk loving.*

Our general expectation is that most individuals find greater utility from an extra dollar when they do not have many dollars than when they have many dollars. That is, most individuals are risk averse.

Of course, risk-averse individuals differ in their degree of risk aversion. The risk-averse individual shown in Figure 17.15C is based on a specific utility function, but other utility functions can show a greater or lesser degree of risk aversion. Various functional forms are possible to depict such functions. An especially convenient form, and the one used to create Figures 17.15A–17.15C, is the power function:

$$U(X) = A \cdot X^r. \qquad \textbf{(17.18a)}$$

As noted earlier, we fixed U($1,000) = 1,000 to simplify the graphic presentation. To fix this utility level, we simply need to set $A = 1{,}000^{(1-r)}$ in Equation 17.18a. When $r < 1$, the individual is risk averse; when $r = 1$, the individual is risk neutral; and when $r > 1$, the individual is risk loving. We can use the U(X) function to create additional rank orderings of the options in Table 17.1. The rankings depend on how risk averse the individual is. In the current context, this depends on the curvature of the utility function (which is controlled by the size of r). When $r = 0.5$, the utility function is:

$$U(X) = (1{,}000 \cdot X)^{0.5}. \qquad \textbf{(17.18b)}$$

The rank ordering of expected utility levels of the lotteries in Table 17.1, using Equation 17.18b, is simply the alphabetical order:

$$\begin{matrix} A & \succ & B & \succ & C & \succ & D & \succ & E & \succ & F & \succ & G & \succ & H & \succ & I & \succ & J & \succ & K \\ 1{,}000 & & 980 & & 966 & & 952 & & 945 & & 934 & & 926 & & 862 & & 707 & & 500 & & 100 \end{matrix} \qquad \textbf{(17.19)}$$

by expected utility.

Equation 17.19 provides a fourth rank ordering of these lotteries (in addition to those provided in Equations17.8c, 17.9b, and 17.11b). But if we changed r, we could create a fifth, and a sixth, and so on. This is not problematic; it is simply an acknowledgment that people differ in how they perceive risk. As noted earlier, each of these lotteries has the same expected dollar value and differs only in its level of riskiness (and how that riskiness is viewed).

An especially useful attribute of expected utility is that it implicitly incorporates both risk and return into a single number—the expected utility of the lottery. If we posit that an individual chooses lotteries based on the highest expected utility, then the individual is acting based on the **expected utility criterion**, and we can compare lotteries using this criterion. An expected utility-maximizing consumer will choose the lottery with the highest expected utility level. This allows comparison across lotteries with different expected return outcomes and riskiness outcomes. The preferred lottery may well be one with lower expected income if the risk inherent in the lottery is substantially lower. We now turn to an examination of two such comparisons. One involves comparing job offers, and the other examines the decision to purchase insurance.

expected utility criterion: If an individual chooses lotteries based on the highest expected utility, then that individual is acting based on the expected utility criterion.

Considering a Risky Job Offer

We can describe how much the risk inherent in a lottery costs the individual using the expected utility criterion. One measure of this risk is the *vertical* distance between U(E(X)) and E(U(X)) (so that Lottery B costs 20 utils, Lottery C costs 34 utils, Lottery D costs 48 utils, and so on, based on the utility values in Equation 17.19). A better measure is the *horizontal* distance between the expected bundle and the curve because this distance is metered in dollars (rather than utils).

To examine this measure, we focus on a new lottery that has round dollar answers so that the mathematics involved can be placed in the background as much as possible. As you work through the calculations, try to create your own diagram that visually describes your results. We postpone discussion of that graph until after we have analyzed the problem numerically.

To make this as concrete as possible, suppose that you have graduated with an MBA and have a job offer where commissions are an important part of the compensation package. For simplicity, assume that half of the weeks are good weeks, and the other half are bad weeks. On good weeks, you earn \$4,000, and on bad weeks, you earn \$1,000. (The numbers have been chosen to make the point with round numbers, so bear with the artificiality of the scenario under consideration.) Assume that your utility function is:

$$U(X) = (1{,}000 \cdot X)^{0.5}.$$

(Note that this is the same as Equation 17.18b, which produced the utility levels in Equation 17.19.) *Try answering the following questions before looking at the answers in the paragraph that follows* (you may need a calculator to take square roots):

1. What is the expected income and expected utility associated with a job offer where you have a 50/50 chance to earn \$1,000 or \$4,000?
2. Which would you prefer—the lottery examined in Question 1 or \$2,000 with certainty?
3. Which would you prefer—the lottery examined in Question 1 or \$2,400 with certainty?
4. How much compensation would you require with certainty to be indifferent with the lottery in Question 1?

Questions 1–4 are straightforward. Expected values are easily calculated in this instance, using Equation 17.7 and the utility function $U(X) = (1{,}000 \cdot X)^{0.5}$:

$$E(X) = 0.5 \cdot \$1{,}000 + 0.5 \cdot \$4{,}000 = \$2{,}500. \quad \textbf{(17.20a)}$$

$$E(U(X)) = 0.5 \cdot (1{,}000 \cdot 1{,}000)^{0.5} + 0.5 \cdot (1{,}000 \cdot 4{,}000)^{0.5} = 500 + 1{,}000 = 1{,}500. \quad \textbf{(17.20b)}$$

When considering such a job offer, a natural question to consider is how this offer compares to alternative offers. Two thousand dollars with certainty produces utility of:

$$U(\$2{,}000) = (1{,}000 \cdot 2{,}000)^{0.5} = 1{,}000 \cdot 2^{0.5} = 1{,}414. \quad \textbf{(17.20c)}$$

Similarly, \$2,400 with certainty produces utility of:

$$U(\$2{,}400) = (1{,}000 \cdot 2{,}400)^{0.5} = 1{,}000 \cdot 2.4^{0.5} = 1{,}549. \quad \textbf{(17.20d)}$$

You prefer the lottery to \$2,000 with certainty because $U(\$2{,}000) < E(U(X))$, but you prefer \$2,400 to the lottery because $U(\$2{,}400) > E(U(X))$, according to Equations 17.20b–17.20d.[16] Some level of income between \$2,000 and \$2,400, achieved with certainty, will produce an alternative that is considered indifferent to the lottery, according to the expected utility criterion. This level of income is called the certainty equivalent income.[17] The **certainty equivalent income (CEI(X))** is the amount of income that produces the same utility level as the expected utility level of the lottery. Given the utility function, the certainty equivalent income is found by solving for X. Using the general form expected utility function in Equation 17.18a, we have:

certainty equivalent income (CEI(X)): The certainty equivalent income is the amount of income that produces the same utility level as the expected utility level of the lottery.

$$CEI(X) = (E(U(X))/A)^{(1/r)}. \quad \textbf{(17.21a)}$$

Given the specific values of r and A from Equations 17.18a and 17.18b for this problem, we have

$$CEI(X) = (1{,}500/(1{,}000)^{0.5})^2 = 1{,}500^2/1{,}000 = \$2{,}250. \quad \textbf{(17.21b)}$$

Therefore, the answer to Question 4 is that you are indifferent between \$2,250 with certainty and a 50/50 shot at either \$1,000 or \$4,000.[18]

A final way to look at the risk of a lottery is to determine the risk premium associated with the lottery. The **risk premium (RP(X))** of a lottery is the amount of income an

risk premium (RP(X)): The risk premium of a lottery is the amount of income an individual would be willing to pay to avoid the risk.

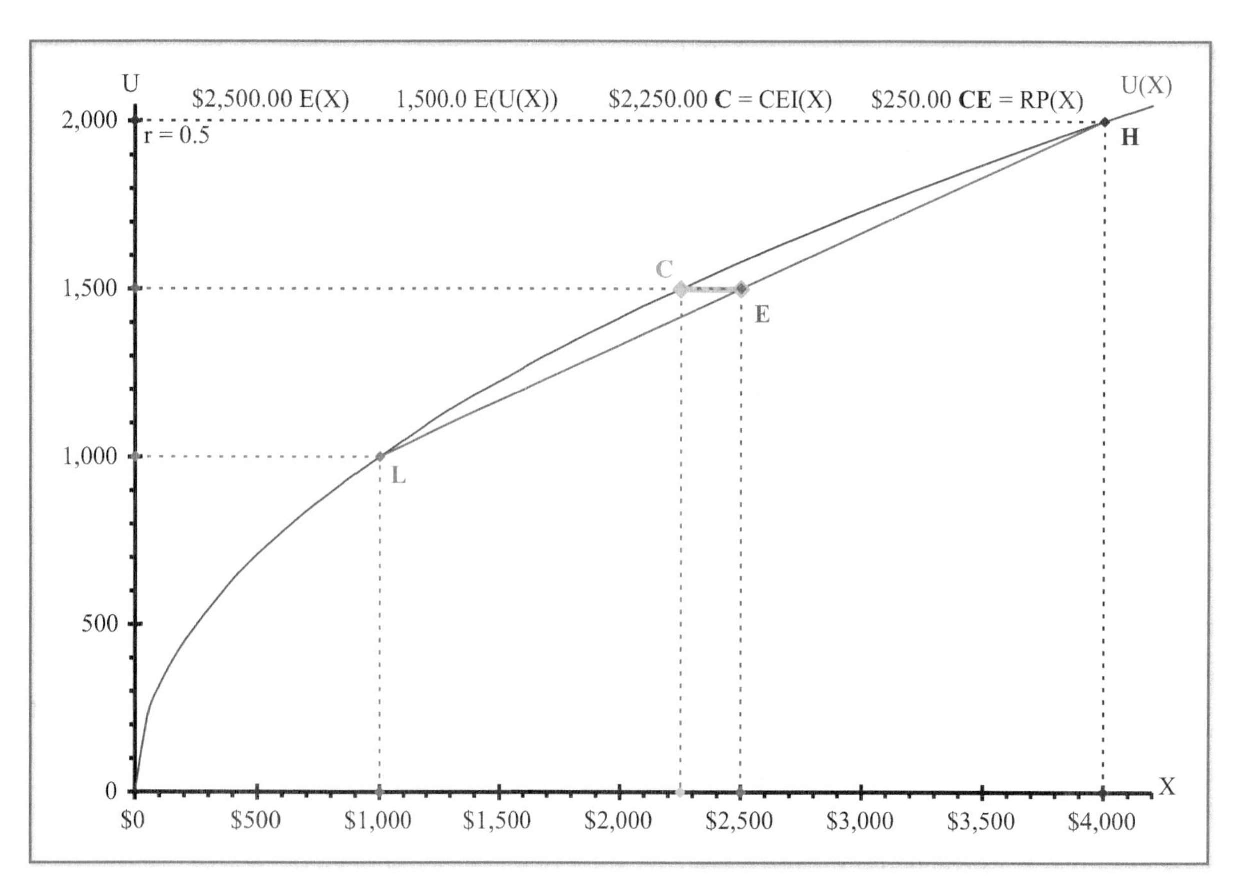

FIGURE 17.16 The Certainty Equivalent Income, CEI(X), and Risk Premium, RP(X), of a Lottery

individual would be willing to pay to avoid the risk. Algebraically, the risk premium is given by the difference between the expected income from the lottery and the certainty equivalent income of the lottery:

$$RP(X) = E(X) - CEI(X). \tag{17.22}$$

With the job offer analysis just described, the risk premium of the 50/50 shot at either $1,000 or $4,000 is $250 (based on Equations 17.20a and 17.21b). The risk premium provides a second way to answer Questions 2 and 3 from earlier. Question 2 requires a $500 discount to avoid the risk. This amount exceeds the risk premium associated with the lottery; therefore, the option in Question 2 ($2,000 with certainty) would not be chosen. By contrast, Question 3 requires a $100 discount to avoid the risk. This amount is less than the risk premium associated with the lottery; therefore, the option in Question 3 ($2,400 with certainty) is preferred to the risky alternative.

These results can be seen in Figure 17.16. The lottery in this instance is midway between **L** and **H** at **E**. The height at **E** is 1,500 utils; all other alternatives need to be compared to this expected outcome. The certainty equivalent income is found by going over to the U(X) curve at that U level (bundle **C**) and dropping down to the X axis to determine the income level that produces this utility level with certainty (this is simply a geometric description of the calculation in Equation 17.21). In this instance, CEI(X) = $2,250 because U($2,250) = 1,500, the same utility level as the lottery. The difference between **E** and **C** is the risk premium of the lottery. This is shown as the lavender line segment between **C** and **E**.

Buying Auto Insurance

People buy insurance to be compensated in the event that an adverse outcome occurs. This compensation reduces the risk inherent in uncertain situations. Health, property, and automobile insurance are just three common examples of such insurance. We can use the model developed previously to analyze why some people choose to purchase insurance and others choose to forgo purchasing insurance. To make this specific, we consider automobile insurance, and as before, we choose numbers that provide easy numerical solutions to focus on the general attributes of the insurance market. The sliders in the Excel file for Figure 17.17 allow you to adjust the scenario as you wish.

Basic insurance can be understood by establishing several simple assumptions.

Assumption 1: Suppose that you live in a state that does not require collision insurance on your own automobile. Buying this insurance is voluntary.

Assumption 2: You own a used car. If you have an accident, you will "total" the car. In this event, you lose the car worth \$4,000 but do not face further losses. If you do not have an accident, the car is worth \$4,000 to you.

Assumption 3: You have a 10% chance of "totaling" your car within the next year.

Assumption 4: You can purchase full-coverage collision insurance for a premium of $P_{insurance}$ = \$600. The insurance will pay you \$4,000 in the event that you total your car.

Based on this information, should you purchase insurance? To answer this question, we require one further piece of information: We need to know how you view risk. We argued earlier that the utility function described in Equation 17.18 provides a convenient method of describing an individual's view of utility as a function of income (and consequently, the individual's attitude toward risk). Suppose in particular that we have two individuals, A and B, who face the scenario just described and whose utility function is based on this equation. The only distinguishing factors are that $r_A = 0.5$, and $r_B = 0.75$. Specifically, A and B face the following utility function:

$$U(X) = 2{,}000 \cdot (X/4{,}000)^r. \qquad \textbf{(17.23)}$$

This function includes the bundle (X, U) = (\$4,000, 2,000) and (\$0, 0), regardless of r.[19] Expected income and expected utility for both individuals is **E** = (\$3,600, 1,800). The certainty equivalent income and risk premium for both individuals is shown at the top of both Figures 17.17A and 17.17B.

Full-coverage insurance works in the following fashion: You pay the premium, regardless of whether you "use" the insurance or not. Consider the two possible states of nature that occur if you purchase insurance for \$600. First, you might not total your car. If this happens, your net wealth is the value of the car less the cost of the insurance, an amount that comes to \$3,400 = \$4,000 – \$600. Second, you might total your car. If this happens, your car has no value, and you have to pay for the insurance, but the insurance company pays you for your loss. Your net wealth in this instance is \$3,400 = \$0 – \$600 + \$4,000. The insurance has completely removed the risk inherent in the risky situation for a price, and that price is the cost of the policy. In both instances, you have a net wealth of $X_H - P_{insurance}$. We now examine whether that price is too high.

Insurance companies sell policies because they can pool risk across a large number of policyholders. From the point of view of the insurance company, the first question to consider is: What is the actuarially fair value of the insurance? The premium of **actuarially fair insurance** is the expected payout of the policy. From the insurance company's point of view, the answer is straightforward: It faces a 10% chance of paying \$4,000 and a 90% chance of paying \$0, based on the previous assumptions. This has an actuarially fair cost of:

actuarially fair insurance: The premium of actuarially fair insurance is the expected payout of the policy.

$$\$400 = 0.9 \cdot \$0 + 0.1 \cdot \$4{,}000 = \textbf{EF} = \text{Actuarially fair cost of insurance.} \qquad \textbf{(17.24a)}$$

Insurance companies wish to cover overhead costs and make a profit, so they will not sell at the actuarially fair rate; they will charge more. How much more determines whether or not the individual will purchase insurance.

A risk-neutral individual will never purchase insurance for more than the actuarially fair price. A risk-averse individual, however, may purchase the insurance for more than the actuarially fair price because of a willingness to accept smaller wealth in exchange for

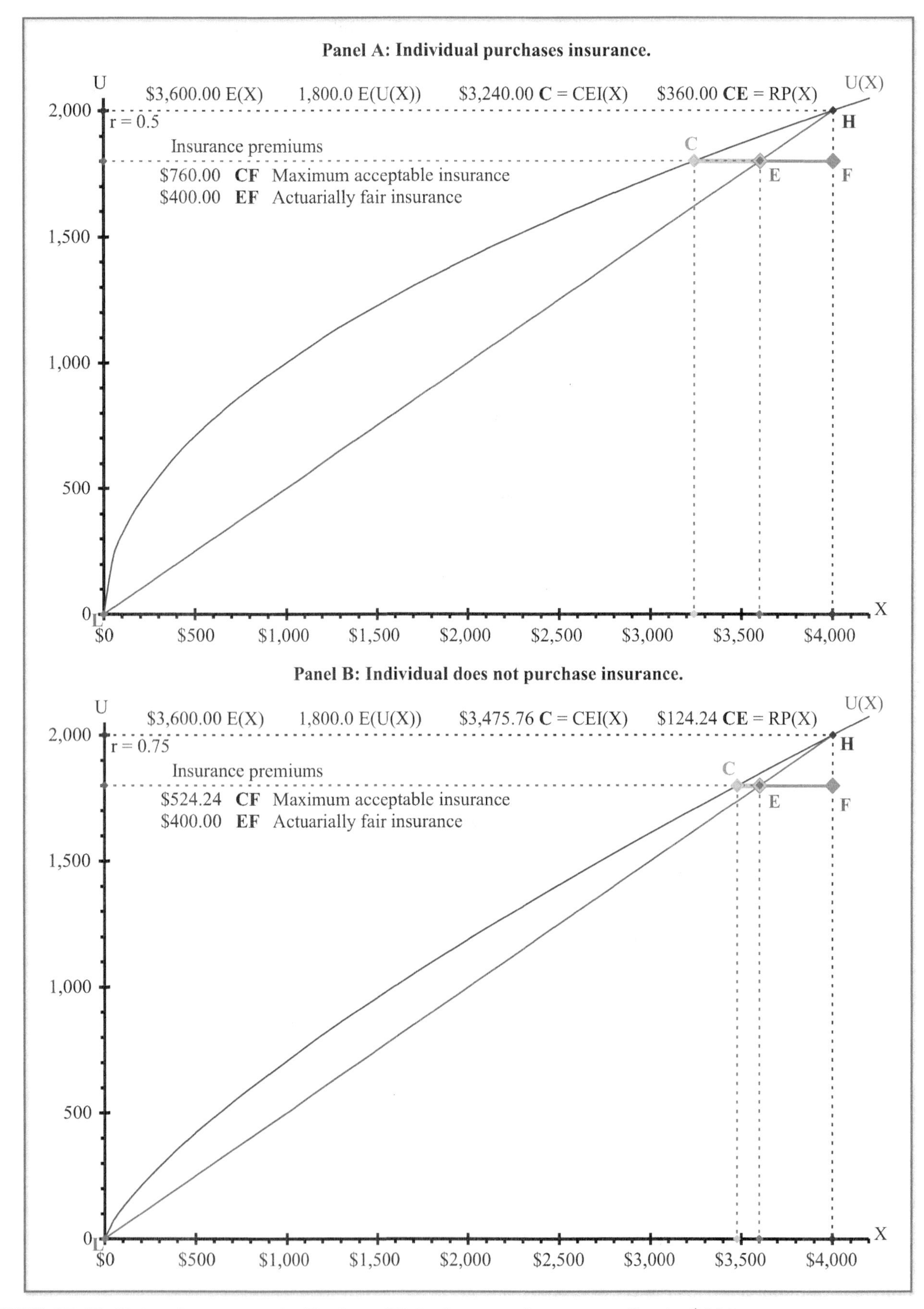

FIGURE 17.17 Using Insurance to Reduce Risk: Assume Insurance Costs $600

greater certainty about that wealth. The excess of the price of the policy above its actuarially fair cost is effectively the price the insurance company charges to remove the risk inherent in the risky situation. Denote this RR, for *risk removal*. In the previous example, RR is:

$$RR = P_{insurance} - \text{Actuarially fair cost} = \$600 - \$400 = \$200. \quad \textbf{(17.24b)}$$

The individual need only compare RR with the risk premium placed on the risky situation—RP in Equation 17.22. If RR < RP, the individual will purchase insurance because the certain outcome with insurance achieves a higher utility level than that associated with the risky situation:

$$\text{Buy insurance if } RR < RP \text{ because } U(X_H - P_{insurance}) > E(U(X)). \quad \textbf{(17.25a)}$$

If the reverse holds true, the individual would prefer not to purchase insurance:

$$\text{Do not buy insurance if } RR > RP \text{ because } U(X_H - P_{insurance}) < E(U(X)). \quad \textbf{(17.25b)}$$

Figure 17.17A depicts the former, since RR = \$200 < \$360 = RP, and Figure 17.17B depicts the latter, since RR = \$200 > \$124.24 = RP. The only difference between Figures 17.17A and 17.17B, as noted previously, is the degree of risk aversion associated with each individual. A is more risk averse than B, so A decides to purchase insurance, and B does not.

We can use the length **CF** in Figure 17.17 to provide an alternative geometric interpretation to the buy/no-buy decision described in Equation 17.25. **CF** represents the maximum an individual is willing to pay to remove the risk and be fully insured. Given that the price of insurance is \$600, we need only determine if **CF** is larger or smaller than \$600. In Figure 17.17A, **CF** = \$760 > \$600 = $P_{insurance}$, and the individual should purchase the insurance. In Figure 17.17B, **CF** = \$524.24 < $P_{insurance}$, and the individual should not purchase the insurance.

Figure 17.18 takes this one step further by showing the location of the purchase insurance solution on the utility function. One change has been made in Assumptions 1–4 so that the geometry of the situation is clearer. Assumption 3 has been changed to 3′:

3′: You have a 20% chance of "totaling" your car within the next year.

(Yes, this makes you an even worse driver than you were before!) Insurance is shown with a premium of 150% of the actuarially fair value. Given the assumptions of the model, the price of insurance is \$1,200 or a risk removal cost of \$400. Buying insurance leaves the individual at bundle **I** = (\$2,800, U(\$2,800)) with certainty. In Figure 17.18A, the individual buys insurance because U(\$2,800) =1,673 > 1,600 = E(U(X)). (**I** is higher than **E** in Figure 17.18A.) The reverse holds true in Figure 17.18B, so the individual does not buy insurance: U(\$2,800) = 1,531 < 1,600 = E(U(X)). (**I** is lower than **E** in Figure 17.18B.) The height of bundle **I**, relative to **E**, provides a geometric alternative to Equations 17.25a and 17.25b. As with Figure 17.17, the only difference between Figures 17.18A and 17.18B is the degree of risk aversion associated with each individual. A is more risk averse than B, so A decides to purchase insurance, and B does not.

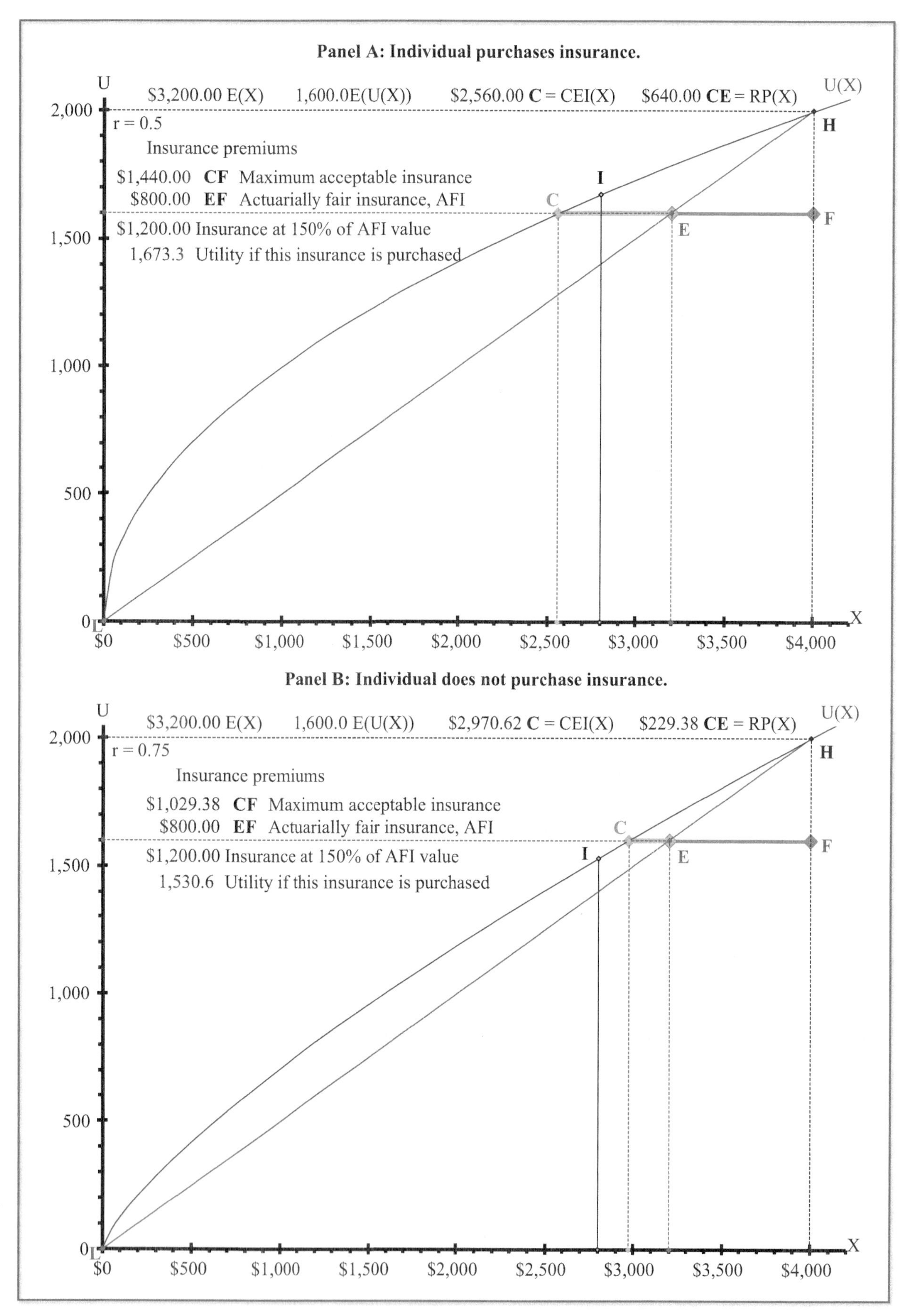

FIGURE 17.18 Using Insurance to Reduce Risk: Assume Insurance Costs 150% of Fair Insurance

Summary of Section 17.2

Many choices that consumers face are not certain in nature. The most obvious such choice is the decision to purchase a lottery ticket, but many other goods also provide an uncertain stream of benefits. The first task is simply to be able to describe uncertain situations. Economists use the term *lottery* to describe the set of possible outcomes. To economists, a lottery involves more than simply buying a lottery ticket. A lottery is a listing of all contingencies, together with the probabilities attached to each of the contingent outcomes. This list must include *all* possibilities to be a lottery (meaning that the sum of probabilities must be 1). We restrict our discussion to lotteries involving monetary contingencies.

Individuals typically prefer certainty to uncertainty, but of course, there is a trade-off between the risk and return inherent in goods providing contingent outcomes. To describe these trade-offs, we must be able to describe both the expected outcome and the degree of certainty associated with that expectation. Different individuals may well have different perceptions of the risk inherent in lotteries. As a result, different individuals may well come to different conclusions regarding how to rank-order lotteries.

An individual who believes that there is a trade-off between risk and return is risk averse. A risk-neutral individual is indifferent between two lotteries with the same expected return, even if one of those lotteries has higher risk than the other. A risk-loving individual prefers a lottery with greater variability to a more certain outcome with the same expected return (such an individual may act on this preference by playing the lottery, for example).

We examine two ways to incorporate uncertainty into our model of consumer choice. One method compares expected outcome versus the risk associated with that outcome, using indifference curves that directly describe the trade-off between risk and return. This allows us to examine some of the basic properties of portfolio analysis. Different individuals will invest in different portfolios because of differences in risk aversion. Individuals with minimal risk aversion will invest in risky assets beyond their total wealth by leveraging their purchases in those assets.

The second way to incorporate uncertainty into a utility-maximizing model is to treat utility in the same way we treat income. The income associated with various contingencies has an expected value, but so does the utility associated with the various contingencies. If individuals wish to maximize expected utility, then we can compare lotteries according to this criterion. This model allows us to understand why some individuals will accept risky jobs, while others choose jobs that provide a more certain compensation package. Similarly, some individuals will not purchase insurance, and others will voluntarily purchase insurance. Both differences can be seen as a consequence of different degrees of risk aversion. Those who are more risk averse will trade greater certainty for smaller expected returns.

Review Questions

Define the following terms:

Section 17.1

intertemporal choice

interest rate

present value

future value

interest rate differential

storage loss

Section 17.2A

lottery

expected value

weighted average

variance

standard deviation

Section 17.2B

certainty equivalent rate of return

capital allocation line (CAL)

leveraged purchases

Regulation T

certainty equivalent rate of return

Section 17.2C

risk averse

risk neutral

risk loving

expected utility criterion

certainty equivalent income

risk premium

actuarially fair insurance

Provide short answers to the following:

Section 17.1

a. How does the slope of the intertemporal budget constraint relate to the interest rate between time periods?
b. Why do we typically expect to have a kink at the intertemporal endowment point in the intertemporal choice diagram?
c. Explain the difference between present value and future value in a two-period model.
d. Will a borrower continue to borrow if the borrowing interest rate declines?
e. Will a borrower continue to borrow if the borrowing interest rate increases?
f. Will a lender continue to lend if the lending interest rate declines?
g. Will a lender continue to lend if the lending interest rate increases?

Section 17.2A

a. If two lotteries, A and B, have the same expected value, will two risk-averse individuals necessarily agree about whether A is better than B?
b. Why does the sum of deviations from the mean not offer a good measure of the risk inherent in a lottery?
c. Why is there no unique measure of risk proposed in Section 17.2A?

Section 17.2B

a. How are assets described in a risk/return diagram? In particular, what are the two axes in figures in Section 17.2B?
b. What is the shape of an indifference curve for a risk-neutral individual in this model?
c. You are risk averse and currently own a portfolio **A** = (s_a, r_a) and are considering a second portfolio **B** ≠ **A**. In which quadrants might **B** reside, relative to **A**, if you are indifferent between **A** and **B**?
d. What does the slope of the capital allocation line represent in the portfolio choice model?
e. Why do leveraged borrowers typically face a premium over the risk-free interest rate?

Section 17.2C

a. In the expected utility model in Section 17.2C, what does X signify in the utility function U(X)?
b. What is the shape of U(X) if the individual is risk averse?
c. What is the shape of U(X) if the individual is risk neutral?
d. What is the shape of U(X) if the individual is risk loving?
e. How is a two-way lottery depicted, using the expected utility model?
f. If an individual compares the expected values of two lotteries, **A** and **B**, and finds that E(U(**A**)) > E(U(**B**)), but E(X(**A**)) < E(X(**B**)). What do the two expectations signify, and can this individual choose between Lottery **A** and Lottery **B**, based on this information?
g. Given the setup described in Question f, which lottery has a higher risk premium—**A** or **B**?
h. Given the setup described in Question f, which lottery has a higher certainty equivalent income—**A** or **B**?
i. If two individuals face the same cost of insurance, why might one individual choose to purchase the insurance, while the other chooses not to?

Check your answers to the *short-answer* exercises in the Answers Appendix at the end of the book.

Notes

1. Present value and future value are discussed in greater detail in Chapter 19.

2. If you do not believe that you will have to sell at a discount, try to sell your textbooks for full price and see what happens!

3. You may wonder why a used car is an uncertain investment. Not all used cars are created equal (indeed, not all used cars of the same make, model, and mileage are created equal). There is a quality aspect to used cars that is unobservable prior to purchase; the seller knows more about the quality of the automobile than the buyer. This is called the "lemons" problem and is a result of asymmetric information. Asymmetric information is the central focus of Chapter 21.

4. An example of a nonmonetary uncertain outcome is playing a sport or going fishing.

5. By contrast, $(X_1 + \ldots + X_n)/n$ is an unweighted average. The unweighted average implicitly assumes that each of the possible outcomes is equally likely to occur.

6. The reason is straightforward. If $y < z$ are the standard deviations of two lotteries Y and Z with E(Y) = E(Z) then $Y \succ Z$. This holds with variance as well because $y^2 < z^2$ given that both y and z are nonnegative. The same cannot be said once we no longer have the same expected values across lotteries. In this instance the trade-off between risk and return will be perceived differently according to the measure of risk chosen.

7. These calculations are easy to accomplish within Excel, and they are a worthwhile exercise. A separate worksheet is provided with the Excel version of Figure 17.8 that has the payout information from Table 17.1. You can use this information as a starting point for such an analysis.

8. See most specifically the Excel file for Figure 3.8. Move the x satiation level to x = 0. The function shown here is $U(s, r) = r - A \cdot s^2$. The parameter A describes the degree of risk aversion the individual perceives. Notice that this function is quasilinear.

9. Linearity of portfolios that combine a risk-free and risky asset occurs because there is no covariance possible between the two assets when one of the assets is risk free. When deciding on portfolios of risky assets, we can no longer model portfolios of those assets as a linear combination of the individual assets because there may be covariance between assets. A complete discussion of this topic requires a deeper knowledge of statistical concepts than is assumed here, but the basic point can be made by example: Suppose that you are considering investing equal amounts in two stocks; each has some expected return and degree of risk attached. If there is no covariance between these stocks, then the risk involved is the average of the two levels of risk (the linear outcome). If there is positive covariance between the two stocks (both are procyclical, for example), then the combined risk will be greater than the average of the two individual risks. If there is negative covariance between the two stocks (one is procyclical; the other is countercyclical), then the combined risk will be less than the average of the two individual risks. This is why investors should diversify their portfolios. The important issue is the level of nondiversifiable risk. Our risky asset is a stock portfolio that has a certain level of nondiversifiable risk. The current discussion does not require that we deal with this problem because all we are interested in is the choice between a risky asset and a risk-free asset.

10. Note that the MRS should be thought of here as slope (rather than minus slope) because we want to discuss the trade-off between risk and return as a positive number. In our discussion of MRS in Part 2, we calculated the MRS as the ratio of marginal utilities. Because r is an economic good but s is an economic bad, in the present context, we calculate the MRS as $MRS = -MU_s/MU_r > 0$.

11. This is the same notion of an interest rate differential examined in Section 17.1. For a further discussion of risk premiums, see Section 19.1.

12. The food-stamp program examined in Sections 5.4 and 6.3, and the intertemporal choice analysis with interest rate differentials in Section 17.1, described similar results.

13. If you have been following closely, this MRS will not surprise you because the preferences depicted in this analysis are quasilinear, and bundle **T** has the same amount of risk as bundle **M** in Figure 17.13B (s = 20%). In Chapter 4, we found that the hallmark of quasilinear preferences is that indifference curves are vertical translates. Since the individuals depicted in Figures 17.13B and 17.14 had the same risk aversion, and because they face the same risk at these two bundles (both have a standard deviation of 20%), both have the same MRS.

14. This need not be the case but is done to provide a fixed point for our discussion. As we have seen in Section 4.3, utility is an ordinal concept; therefore, we should not attach too much weight to the specific numbers associated with utility functions. In the present situation, we will assume we can aggregate across uncertain outcome, using a utlity function of income. Expected utility functions are not the same with respect to *all* monotonic transformations, but they are with respect to all positive linear transformations. A positive linear transformation is a function $f(x) = a \cdot x + b$, where $a > 0$. Nonlinear monotonic transformations produce the same preferences over certain outcomes (in particular, more income is still preferred to less), but do not maintain the expected utility property described by Equation 17.16.

15. If the lottery is a three-choice lottery, then it is a point inside the triangle containing the three contingencies as vertices; if the lottery is a four-choice lottery, then it is a point inside the quadrangle, and so on. A more mathematically sophisticated way to describe a lottery is as the convex combination of contingencies. You may recall that we used convex combinations to describe convex preferences in Chapter 3, and we used convex combinations to provide a parametric representation of the budget constraint in Chapter 5 and the capital allocation line in Equation 17.12a.

16. Some students may object at this point and say: "I would take the $2,000 with certainty rather than the risky job." That is fine; it just means that these students are more risk averse than we have assumed. Their expected utility function (Equation 17.18a) has a smaller r (than the r = 0.5 assumed in this instance). If other students object and say that they would prefer the lottery to $2,400 with certainty, it simply means these students are less risk averse than we have assumed (and their r > 0.5).

17. This same concept emerged as part of the analysis of risk and return in Section 17.2B, where the certainty equivalent rate of return provided an unambiguous way to describe the utility level associated with a (risk, return) indifference curve.

18. It is worth noting that E(U(X)) = U(CEI(X)), based on this definition of certainty equivalent income. This is simply a restatement of Equations 17.21a and 17.21b obtained by raising both sides to the power r and multiplying both sides by r. (In Equation 17.21b, $A = 1000^{0.5}$, and r = 0.5.)

19. The scaling parameter "A" from Equation 17.18 has changed in this instance so that the (X, U) bundle ($4000, 2000) is the "fixed point" rather than ($1,000, 1,000) used in Figures 17.15 and 17.16. Nonetheless, when r = 0.5, U($1,000) = 1,000, given this utility function.

Topics in Factor Markets

CHAPTER 18

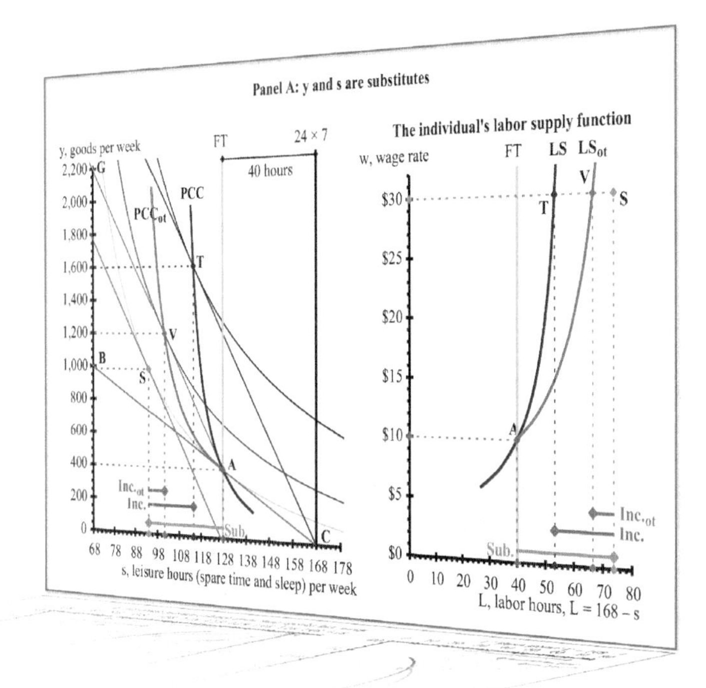

Chapter Outline

Factor markets have many of the same attributes as product markets, but some of those attributes are "turned on their head." For example, firms are the consumers of factors of production, while consumers are often the suppliers of factors of production. The most important factor that consumers supply is, of course, labor.

We can examine factor markets from both the supply and demand sides. Labor stands out on the supply side of the market because individuals provide labor, and they provide it by giving up their time. Time is a scarce resource for which individuals have an alternative use; they can sleep or read or goof off if they are not working. (Sometimes, they do that while they are working, but that issue is discussed in Chapter 21.) The labor/leisure trade-off is the focus of Section 18.1. Factors of production have been explicitly examined earlier in the text, especially in Chapter 9. The demands for factors of production are derived demands, and we examine this demand in Sections 18.2 and 18.3.

18.1 Individual Labor Supply

Section 18.1 Outline

Individuals purchase goods from firms, but firms also purchase the services of individuals in the form of labor services. This duality between consumers and producers is described in introductory economics texts, using the circular flow diagram. The presentation in Part 2 is predicated on thinking of individuals as consumers. In this section, we focus on the reverse side of this coin (or the "other" side of the circular flow diagram) by examining individuals as suppliers of labor services. Section 18.1A examines the labor/leisure trade-off, using the model of consumer theory developed in Part 2. Section 18.1B applies the price change analysis from Chapter 7 to describe wage rate changes. Section 18.1C uses the labor/leisure trade-off to examine whether overtime versus a straight pay raise is likely to result in a greater willingness to work longer hours. Section 18.1D decomposes wage rage change into income and substitution components.

18.1A The Labor/Leisure Trade-off **Prerequisite: Chapter 6**

Labor as a factor of production differs from other factors in an important aspect: Labor has an alternative to work in that individuals value their leisure time. We might argue that pieces of machinery value leisure time because if a machine stands idle, the machine has not incurred the physical wear and tear of a machine hour's use; that is, physical depreciation has not occurred. Nonetheless, the basic point is that we typically do not worry about a machine's feelings (unless we are reading Isaac Asimov's *Robot* series).[1] We can examine the labor/leisure trade-off using the consumer model developed in Part 2 of the text. It is not surprising that the analysis of labor market supply uses consumer tools; after all, laborers are, first and foremost, consumers. Individuals typically work to make money so they can act as consumers; most would not work were this incentive not present. The aphorism "After all, that's why they call it work" applies.

Suppose that an individual has an hourly job (rather than receiving a salary with quasi-flexible hours) and is considering the choice of how many hours to work. Each dollar of income allows the individual to purchase a dollar's worth of consumption goods, y. To make the analysis as straightforward as possible, assume that $P_y = \$1$. If an individual has an hourly wage of w per hour, then that individual earns an income of $I = w \cdot L$ if L hours per week are worked. In this event, $168 - L = s$ hours of leisure per week remain ($168 = 24$ hours $\cdot$ 7 days per week). (Unfortunately, *leisure*, like *labor*, starts with the letter L; therefore, imagine that s stands for "spare time and sleep.") An individual who works an extra hour has 1 hour less leisure available. Put another way, the price of leisure is the wage rate, since labor is leisure's next-best alternative use. *The opportunity cost of an hour of leisure is the wage rate.*

The individual values both leisure, s, and goods, y. Given that the utility function over goods and leisure, U(s, y), the marginal utilities for s and y are positive (i.e., both goods are economic goods, according to the definition in Chapter 3). If a worker has complete flexibility in the number of hours worked, the worker will balance the gains from the extra income produced by extra labor with the loss in leisure time. More explicitly, the individual will choose to work a number of hours where the loss in utility from the last hour worked (and, therefore, the gain in utility had that hour been spent doing leisure activities) equals the increment to utility from the goods that may be purchased with the additional income produced by working that extra hour. If ΔL in extra labor supplied produces $\Delta I/\Delta L$ in extra income, and if each dollar of income produces $(\Delta U/\Delta y)/P_y$ in incremental utility, then the utility-maximizing labor supply condition may be described algebraically as:

$$\Delta U/\Delta s = (\Delta I/\Delta L) \cdot [(\Delta U/\Delta y)/P_y]. \quad \textbf{(18.1a)}$$

We saw earlier that $I = w \cdot L$, so the rate of increase in income as labor changes by 1 unit is w; $w = \Delta I/\Delta L$. We have also assumed that $P_y = 1$, so the utility-maximizing condition in Equation 18.1a may be rewritten as:

$$\Delta U/\Delta s = w \cdot \Delta U/\Delta y. \quad \textbf{(18.1b)}$$

By regrouping, we can recast this equality in terms of the $MRS_{y,s}$:

$$MRS_{y,s} = MU_s/MU_y = \Delta U/\Delta s/\Delta U/\Delta y = w. \quad \textbf{(18.1c)}$$

For simplicity, we assume that the individual has no alternative sources of income other than labor. Given a fixed wage rate, as the number of hours worked changes, so does income, according to the equation that connects hours worked to wage income received:

$$I = w \cdot L. \quad \textbf{(18.2a)}$$

Although this equation offers the most direct view of the relation between labor hours and income, it is more useful to describe consumption possibilities in (s, y) space. We assumed earlier that goods y cost \$1 per unit, so $y = I$ units of y can be consumed, given income I. But $L = 168 - s$ because, within this model, time is divided between labor and leisure. By substituting $y = I$ and $L = 168 - s$ into Equation 18.2a, we obtain

$$y = w \cdot (168 - s). \tag{18.2b}$$

This is a budget constraint for the individual because it describes the combinations of leisure hours and goods that the individual can purchase, given a fixed number of hours in a week. These hours can be allocated toward either labor or leisure, given the wage rate of w per hour.

Figure 18.1 depicts the trade-offs just discussed. This figure consists of two interrelated diagrams; the one on the left is a consumption diagram, and the one on the right is a labor market diagram. Focus initially on the red and black lines in the consumption diagram on the left. The black vertical line depicts the constraint imposed by having 168 hours in a week. The bottom of that line is the point **C** = (168, 0) on the individual's red budget constraint. The budget constraint is described algebraically by Equation 18.2b. To place this in the context of models developed earlier in the text, point **C** on this constraint can be conceptualized as the individual's endowment bundle (the individual has a week's worth of time and no income at the start of the week). The question is: How much of that time does the individual wish to devote to work, and how much should be devoted to leisure?

Bundle **C** would occur if the individual devotes the entire week to leisure, $s = 168$ and $y = 0$, since the individual has generated no income with which to purchase goods.[2] If an individual works 100 hours in a week (which, of course is unlikely), that person would receive an income of $100 \cdot w$ and would have 68 hours of leisure. This is point **B** = (68, 1,000) on the red budget constraint in the consumption diagram in Figure 18.1. The starting point for the horizontal axis is 68 so that wage rates are easily inferred using the vertical axis.[3] The wage rate is the (absolute value of the) slope of the budget constraint. Given an $s = 68$ starting point for the vertical axis, *the wage rate is obtained by moving the "intercept" number over two decimal places* ($w = \Delta y/\Delta s = 1{,}000/100 = 10$ between **B** and **C**). Although students often view this slope with skepticism, it is consistent with our

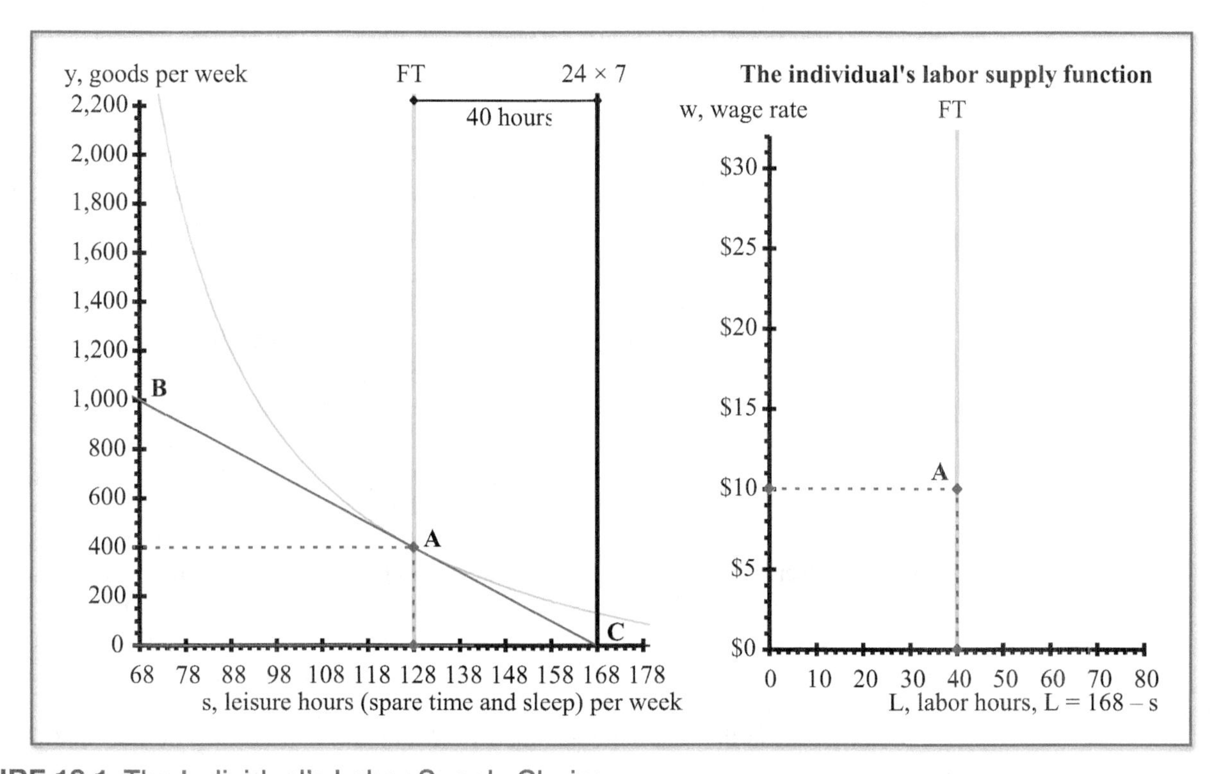

FIGURE 18.1 The Individual's Labor Supply Choice

earlier understanding of the slope of budget constraints. The magnitude of the slope of the budget constraint from Chapter 5 is $|m| = P_x/P_y$. We have assumed $P_y = \$1$, so $|m| = P_x$, the price of the good on the horizontal axis in a consumption diagram. In Figure 18.1, that good is not a physical commodity but, rather, leisure time. As noted previously, the price of leisure is simply the opportunity cost forgone by not working for that hour but instead using that time as leisure. *The price of leisure is the wage rate.*

The indifference curve shown in Figure 18.1 depicts an individual who maximizes utility by working 40 hours a week and thereby has 128 hours of free time. This individual earns an income for the week of $I = \$400 = 40 \cdot \$10$, but each unit of consumption goods y costs \$1, so $y = 400$ is consumed by this individual. The individual consumes at **A** = (128, 400) in Figure 18.1. This point is on the budget constraint given by Equation 18.2b, and it has MRS(**A**) = w, the utility-maximizing condition described by Equation 18.1c. These are the same conditions described in the utility maximization problem in Equation 6.1. There was a two-part solution to that problem: First, the individual should spend all income (i.e., be on the budget constraint), and second, the individual should have MRS = price ratio. Both conditions hold at **A** in Figure 18.1. In this diagram, the individual wishes to work 40 hours per week. $L_a = 40$ was chosen because we commonly view this as full-time employment, FT. This is shown as the blue vertical line FT in the consumption diagram. This tangency need not occur at 40 hours per week of labor; that number was chosen because it is a common solution seen in the market. We could easily imagine alternative scenarios in which the utility-maximizing consumer, given a wage rate of w = \$10, would choose to work more or fewer than 40 hours. The former would occur if the tangency between the indifference curve and the budget constraint occurred along the **BA** segment of the budget constraint and MRS(**A**) < w. The latter would have the tangency occur along the **AC** segment and MRS(**A**) > w.

The chosen bundle is shown in a different way in the diagram on the right in Figure 18.1. This diagram depicts the individual's labor supply as a function of wage rage. The point **A** in that diagram depicts the labor supply of the individual whose preferences are shown in the left diagram; at a wage rate of \$10 per hour, the individual chooses a utility-maximizing amount of leisure as 128 hours per week. This individual therefore willingly supplies 40 hours of labor at this wage rate. The bundle **A** = (40, \$10) is a point on the individual's labor supply curve. To determine other points on this supply curve, we must vary the wage rate and determine what happens to the utility-maximizing consumption bundle.

18.1B How an Individual Responds to Wage Rate Changes

Prerequisites: Chapter 7 and Section 18.1A

In Chapter 7, we saw how a change in one good's price causes changes in consumption of that good as well as other goods. The price consumption curve (PCC) summarizes this information in the consumption diagram. In the current context, we can see that the demand for goods, y, and the demand for leisure, s, are jointly affected by changes in the price of leisure. Because labor and leisure directly compete as possible uses for the individual's time, the price of labor is also the price of leisure; the opportunity cost of leisure is the wage rate.

The demand curve also summarizes this information by directly plotting how quantity demanded changes as the price of the good changes. In the current context, we could graph the demand for leisure as a function of the wage rate, using the vertical stack of diagrams described in Section 7.2. A better strategy is to focus on the dual-use nature of time in this context and note that *by deriving an individual's demand curve for leisure, we have also derived that individual's supply curve for labor*. This dual result occurs because, within this model, anything that is not labor is leisure, and vice versa.

In the standard analysis, a change in the price of one good has no effect on the amount of the other good that can be consumed if all income is used to purchase that good. In Chapter 7, we saw that a change in the price of x had no effect on the amount of y that could be consumed if all income is spent on y. The y-intercept bundle $(x, y) = (0, I/P_y)$ acts as the fulcrum on which the budget constraint pivots as the price of x changes. In the present context, this no longer holds. Leisure is the good on the horizontal axis in Figure 18.1, and at a price of leisure (wage rate) of $10 per hour, we see that the budget constraint is **BC**. If the wage rate changes, the budget constraint rotates on the endowment bundle **C**. If the wage rate doubles to $20, then the new budget constraint will allow purchase of 2,000 units of y if the individual is willing to work for 100 hours. The bundle **G** = (68, 2,000) is on the new budget constraint in this instance. This is shown in Figure 18.2A. The budget constraint becomes twice as steep as **BC** in this instance. Figure 18.2B shows a tripling of wage rate to $30 per hour (in which case the new budget constraint is three times as steep as **BC**). The pivot occurs on the axis whose price is changing because the endowment bundle can be consumed regardless of wage rate, since the individual can always decide not to work any hours during the week. As the wage rate changes, so does the amount of income the individual receives for a given number of hours of work. In particular, the budget constraint bundle on the y "axis" is $(68, 100 \cdot w)$; the y coordinate of this bundle depends on the wage rate w.

A common expectation from production theory is that an increase in the price of a good will increase the number of units of that good that a firm is willing to supply. This is most explicitly seen in the perfectly competitive context by noting that a firm supplies along the upward-sloping part of its marginal cost curve. If a firm produces a factor of production (i.e., it produces intermediate products in the production chain), then we should have the same expectation: Factor supply should be upward sloping. This expectation need not occur in labor markets. Whether this occurs depends on if goods and leisure are considered consumption substitutes or complements, or if a more complex relation holds between goods and leisure. Figures 18.2–18.4 examine each of these possibilities.

Figure 18.2 provides an example of preferences that *produce* the result seen for other factors: An increase in the price of labor increases labor supply. This occurs because the individual chooses to consume smaller and smaller quantities of leisure as the price of leisure increases. In the consumption diagram in Figure 18.2A, leisure hours decline by 10 when the wage rate increases to $20 (at bundle **D** for double) and by another 3 hours and 20 minutes at a wage rate of $30 (at bundle **T** for triple), as shown in Figure 18.2B (exact numerical values are available from the Excel version of Figure 18.2). Because this individual's leisure demand involves consumption bundles oriented along a downward-sloping PCC, this same individual's labor supply curve will be upward sloping. This information is shown at points **D** and **T** on the labor supply function, LS, in the right diagram of each panel in Figure 18.2. *Individual labor supply is upward sloping because leisure and goods are consumption substitutes*, according to the preferences shown in Figure 18.2. Preferences over leisure and goods need not, however, be consumption substitutes.

If leisure and goods are consumption complements then an increase in wage rate leads to an increase in demand for leisure. This is the situation depicted in Figure 18.3. The geometric setup for each of the figures is the same; **D** and **T** represent the impact of doubling and tripling the wage rate, respectively. In this instance, leisure (s) and goods (y) are complements (so that indifference curves are more L-shaped). As a result, the PCC is upward sloping, and the labor supply function, LS, is downward sloping. This unusual situation—a downward-sloping supply curve—makes sense in the context of the good in question. The individual in this situation values goods and leisure in conjunction with one another. An increase in wage rate in this setting allows greater purchases of goods, given fixed labor supply, but the individual depicted wishes to have more leisure time to play with the extra goods purchased. (Such individuals would argue that free time is more fun if you have more toys to play with. The bumper sticker "He who dies with the most toys wins" may be on this individual's SUV.) This individual would back off on hours worked to enjoy the fruits of labor more fully. (An intermediate to these two outcomes is also possible. The demand for leisure may be independent of wage rate. In this instance, the PCC is vertical, and the labor supply function LS will be vertical. This graph is easily obtained using the Excel version of Figure 18.3.)

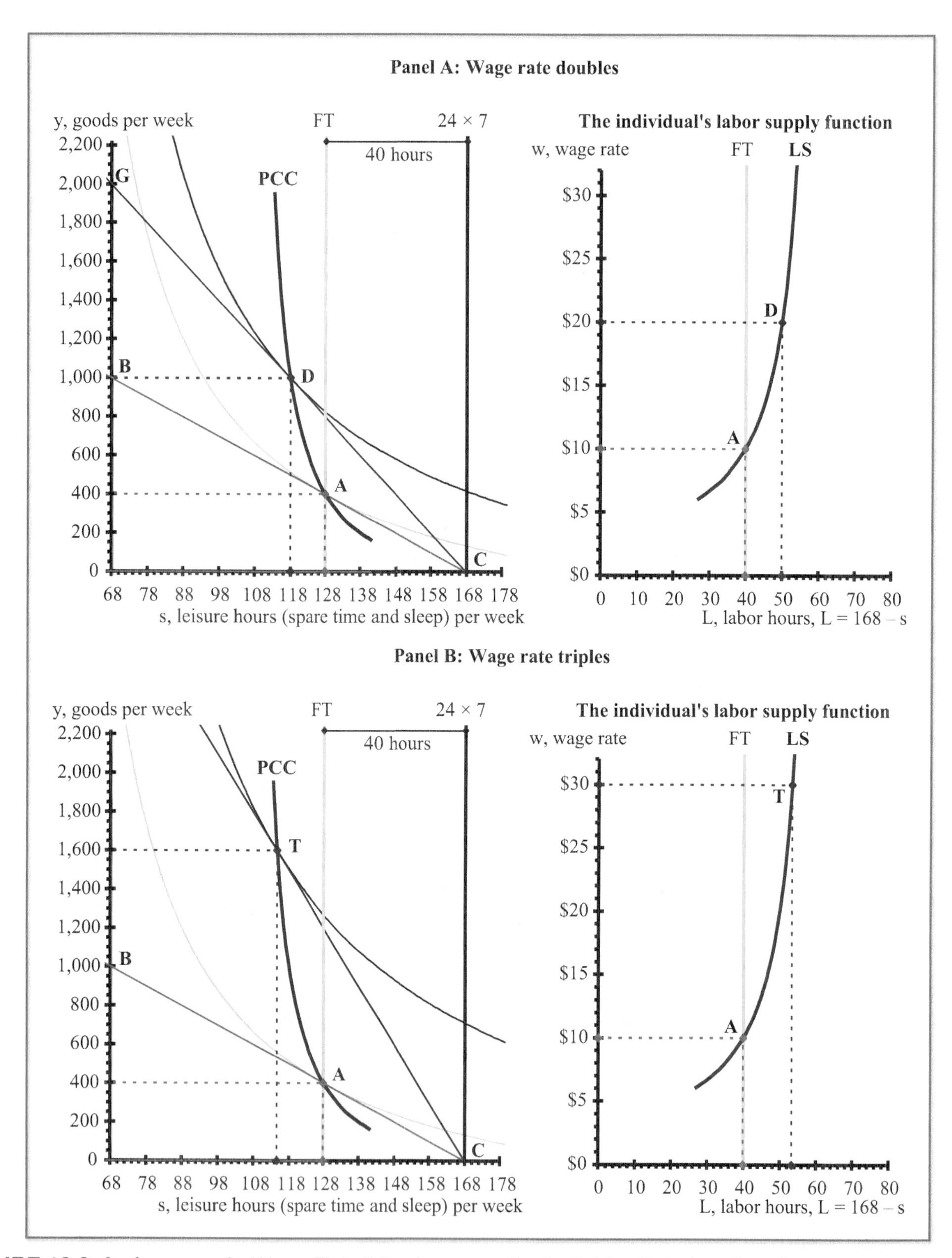

FIGURE 18.2 An Increase in Wage Rate May Increase the Individual's Labor Supply

When Will Labor Supply Be Backward Bending?

Leisure and consumption goods need not be substitutes or complements over all wage rates. We might expect that when wages are low, an increase in wage rate would increase the individual's incentive to substitute consumption goods for leisure and thereby increase

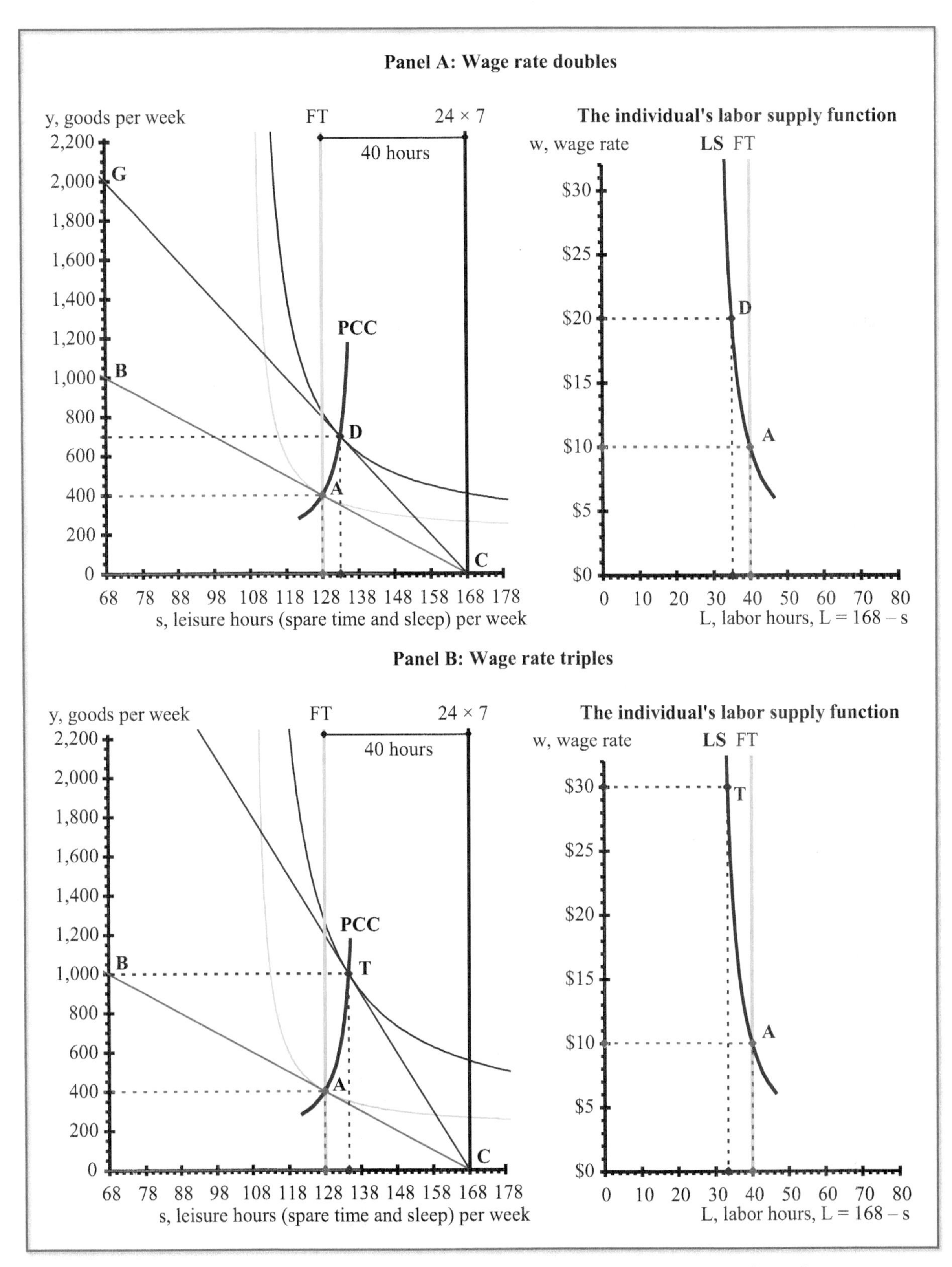

FIGURE 18.3 An Increase in Wage Rate May Decrease the Individual's Labor Supply

labor supply. Past a point, however, the reverse should hold true. Now the individual has "enough" income to purchase goods, and further increases in wage rate will lead to a greater incentive to have leisure time. One classic group exemplifying this phenomenon is doctors. Doctors who are in practices with more modest hourly wage rates tend to work longer hours, while those charging much higher rates may work fewer hours and take Wednesdays off for golf. Of course, wage rates need not be in the hourly range that doctors receive for this to occur. After all, individuals with higher incomes typically have higher fixed obligations than individuals with lower incomes. Suppose that an individual facing an initial wage of w_0 = $10/hour wishes to work 40 hours per week. This is shown as point **A** in Figure 18.4. This individual might initially substitute away from leisure

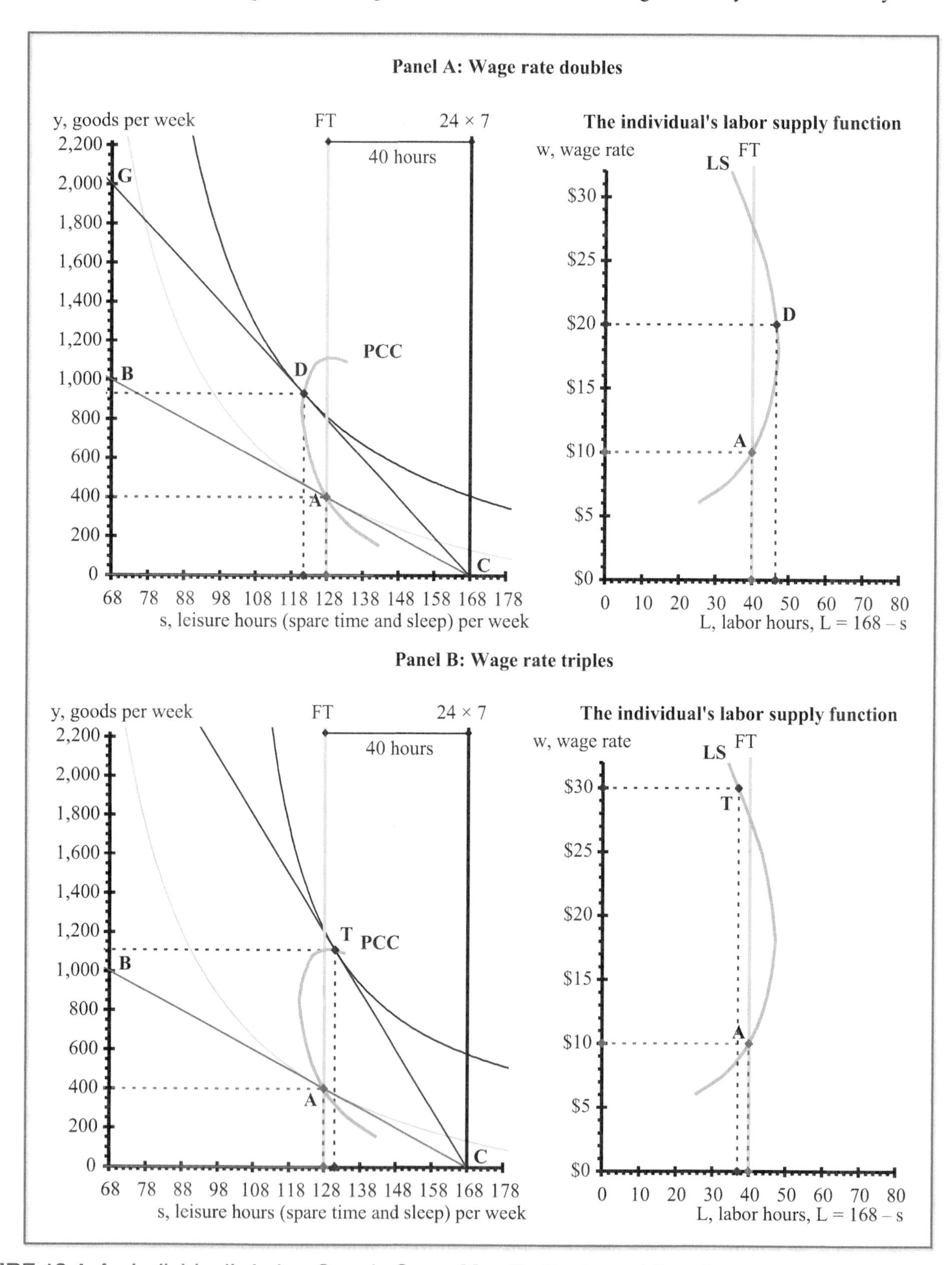

FIGURE 18.4 An Individual's Labor Supply Curve May Be Backward Bending

and toward greater labor supply for initial wage increases but reverse this substitution past a point. In Figure 18.4A, the individual has increased labor supply to 46.5 hours in response to wages doubling at **D**. This same individual works fewer hours if the wage triples (37 hours of labor at w = $30), as indicated by point **T** in Figure 18.4B. The individual's PCC and labor supply curves both reverse direction as a result. *The labor supply function is backward bending as a result of this individual's changing willingness to substitute leisure time for consumption goods.*

The PCC and LS curves can be analyzed further, using the income and substitution effects described in Chapter 8. Before we turn to that discussion, we examine the use of overtime pay, a common strategy that firms use to increase the number of hours that workers are willing to work. This analysis uses the labor/leisure trade-off developed earlier.

18.1C Will Overtime Pay Increase Labor Supply?

Prerequisites: Chapter 7 and Section 18.1B

The discussion in Section 18.1B helps us to understand why wage increases do not necessarily produce workers who are willing to work longer hours. While workers value the increased income that they can attain from higher wages, they also value having free time. Sometimes, the net effect of a wage increase is to produce workers who wish to work fewer hours for more pay. Put in terms of the consumption and labor supply diagrams in Figures 18.3 and 18.4, a positively sloped price consumption curve creates a negatively sloped labor supply curve.

A firm wishing to create an incentive structure that produces individuals who are willing to work more hours is better served by using a nonlinear wage structure, such as overtime pay. If a firm pays one wage rate for all hours worked up to a certain number of hours per time period, and a higher wage for hours worked above this number, the higher wage rate is called the **overtime** wage rate. Workers might be paid time-and-a-half if they work more than 8 hours in a day, or double time if they work more than 40 hours per week. We typically describe the cutoff point between the standard wage rate and the overtime wage rate as the full-time level of employment. Workers are therefore paid a standard wage rate if they work full time or less, but receive a higher wage rate for work beyond full time.

overtime: If a firm pays one wage rate for all hours worked up to a certain number of hours per time period and a higher wage for hours worked above this number, the higher wage rate is called the overtime wage rate.

Suppose the firm offers to pay workers a higher wage rate if they work more than the full-time level of 40 hours per week.

Claim: *If the worker has smooth preferences over goods and leisure, and if the worker previously wished to work 40 hours per week, then introducing such an incentive structure will necessarily increase labor supply.*

This is true even if the individual would reduce labor supply in the face of a general wage increase. Figures 18.5A–18.5C show the three generic possibilities. Each panel is based on an offer by the firm to pay triple time for overtime. (This admittedly high overtime rate is used to separate the various parts of the consumption diagram so it is more easily visualized. The qualitative relations shown in Figure 18.5 hold for more modest overtime rates as well. The overtime wage rate slider in the Excel file for Figure 18.5 allows you to model more modest overtime rates.) Figures 18.5A–18.5C include the budget constraint and utility-maximizing consumption point **T** associated with a tripling of the wage rate, as well as the PCC and labor supply functions (LS) for comparison. Figure 18.5A expands on the analysis from Figure 18.2 and shows the results when consumption goods are substitutable for leisure. Figure 18.5C expands on the analysis from Figure 18.3 and shows the results when consumption goods are complementary with leisure. Figure 18.5B depicts the middle ground mentioned earlier as a separate figure in which the individual's response to a straight wage increase (if overtime is not offered) is simply to maintain the same level of labor supply. This occurs if leisure and consumption goods are independent; in this event, the PCC and LS curves are vertical.

The proposed overtime pay scheme creates a nonlinear budget constraint with a kink at the full-time employment level, **A**. The pink budget constraint has a slope of –10 when s > 128 (since w = $10 when L < 40) and a slope of –30 when s < 128 (since w = $30

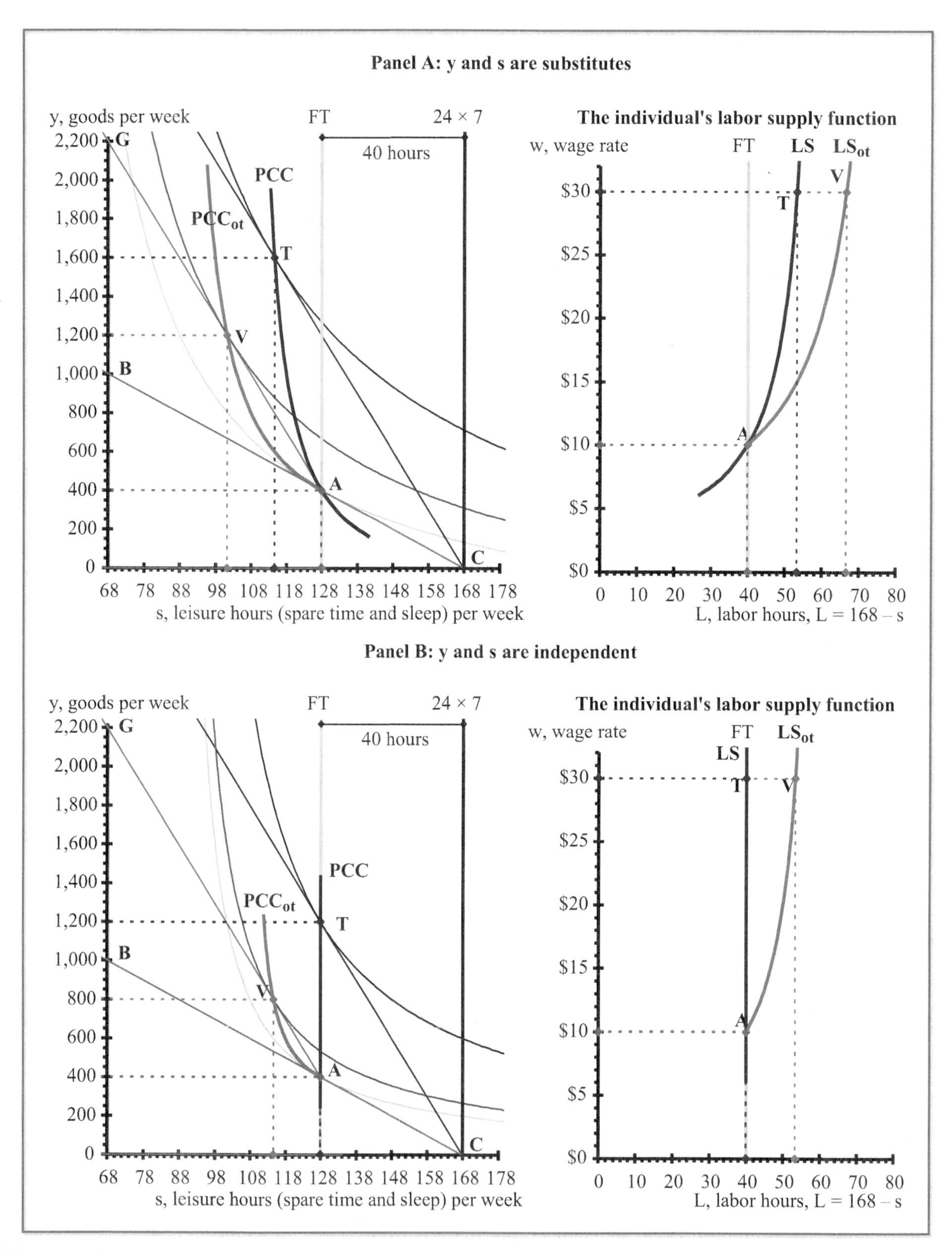

FIGURE 18.5 Overtime Always Produces a Greater Labor Supply Increase Than a Straight Wage Increase

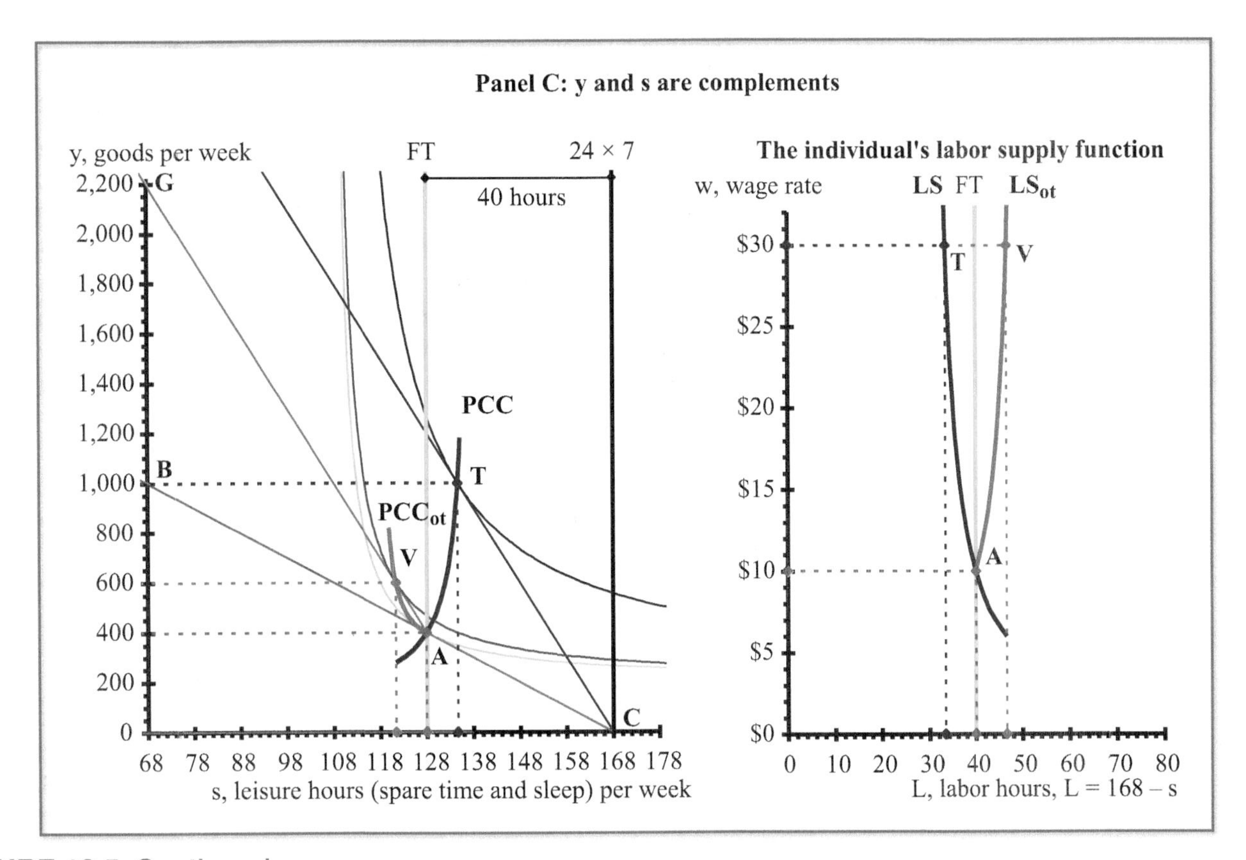

FIGURE 18.5 Continued

when L > 40). The budget constraint is therefore **GAC**. The bundle **G** = (68, 2,200) can be readily seen as resulting from working 100 hours: 40 hours at \$10 per hour and 60 hours at \$30 per hour. The resulting wage income of \$2,200 purchases 2,200 units of y, given $P_y = \$1$.

Any individual who optimally chooses to supply 40 hours of work at an hourly wage rate of \$10 will *necessarily* supply some overtime if offered an overtime wage rate higher than the standard wage rate. The reasoning is straightforward: The institution of overtime produces feasible consumption bundles along the overtime portion of the budget constraint, **GA**, some of which must be preferred to **A** (given the initial assumed tangency at **A**). Each of these bundles has one thing in common: They all have s < 128 (and consequently L > 40). For triple time, the chosen bundle is at the point of tangency between the nonlinear budget constraint and the utility-maximizing indifference curve at **V** in each panel. **V** is on the pink overtime PCC curve, PCC_{ot}, in each panel. PCC_{ot} describes how the individual responds to different overtime wages. If the overtime wage is less than three times the standard wage rate, then the kink at **A** will be less severe, and the individual will consume along the PCC_{ot} between **V** and **A**. Notice that, unlike the straight wage PCC (which passes through **T** and **A**), the overtime PCC is not defined for prices below the standard wage rate (of \$10 in these figures). For wages above \$10, the overtime consumption choice is a point on the PCC_{ot} curve, and this curve is negatively sloped, regardless of preferences. In particular, note that, even if the straight wage PCC is positively sloped (as in Figure 18.5C), the PCC_{ot} remains negatively sloped. Higher overtime wages necessarily increase labor supply, as seen in the right-side diagram in each panel, even if the straight wage labor supply curve is downward sloping (as in Figure 18.5C). The amount of overtime varies according to the size of the overtime wage rate and the individual's willingness to trade leisure for other goods. Figures 18.5A–18.5C depict three examples from a continuum of possibilities. The triple-time overtime wage at **V** produces an increase in labor supply of 26 hours and 40 minutes in Figure 18.5A, 13 hours and 20 minutes in Figure 18.5B, and 6 hours and 40 minutes in Figure 18.5C.

18.1D Decomposing Wage Rate Changes

Prerequisites: Chapter 8 and Section 18.1C

The demand decomposition described in Chapter 8 allows us to quickly understand the net effect of a wage change on labor supply. The total effect of a price change on demand is decomposed into two components: the substitution effect and the income effect. As noted in Section 8.2, both effects can be viewed from three perspectives. The "own-price" perspective is the most instructive view in the current context.

The total effect of the wage increase can be decomposed into an income and a substitution effect. A wage increase means that leisure is more "expensive" because the opportunity cost of leisure has increased; in a relative sense, other goods have become cheaper. As a result, the individual substitutes consumption goods for leisure along the indifference curve; **S** is to the left of the initial optimum bundle **A** along the initial indifference curve. The substitution effect of a wage increase on the demand for leisure is unambiguously negative. A wage increase boosts the income produced from any amount of labor supplied; therefore, a wage increase has a positive income effect as long as the good is a normal good. Certainly, most individuals would consider leisure a normal good; free time is more fun to have if you have money to spend on activities than if you do not have spending money.

The net (or total) effect of the wage increase depends on whether the own-price income or substitution effect dominates. Three possibilities exist, and each is shown separately in Figures 18.6A–18.6C, based on a tripling of wage rate. The substitution effect may be larger than, equal to, or smaller than, the income effect. Figures 18.6A and 18.6C use Figures 18.2B and 18.3B as a starting point for the analysis and include own-price substitution and income effects at the bottom of each diagram.

If the substitution effect dominates the income effect, then leisure and consumption goods are substitutable. The net effect of the wage increase is to increase consumption of the good whose price has not changed (consumption goods, y) at the expense of the good

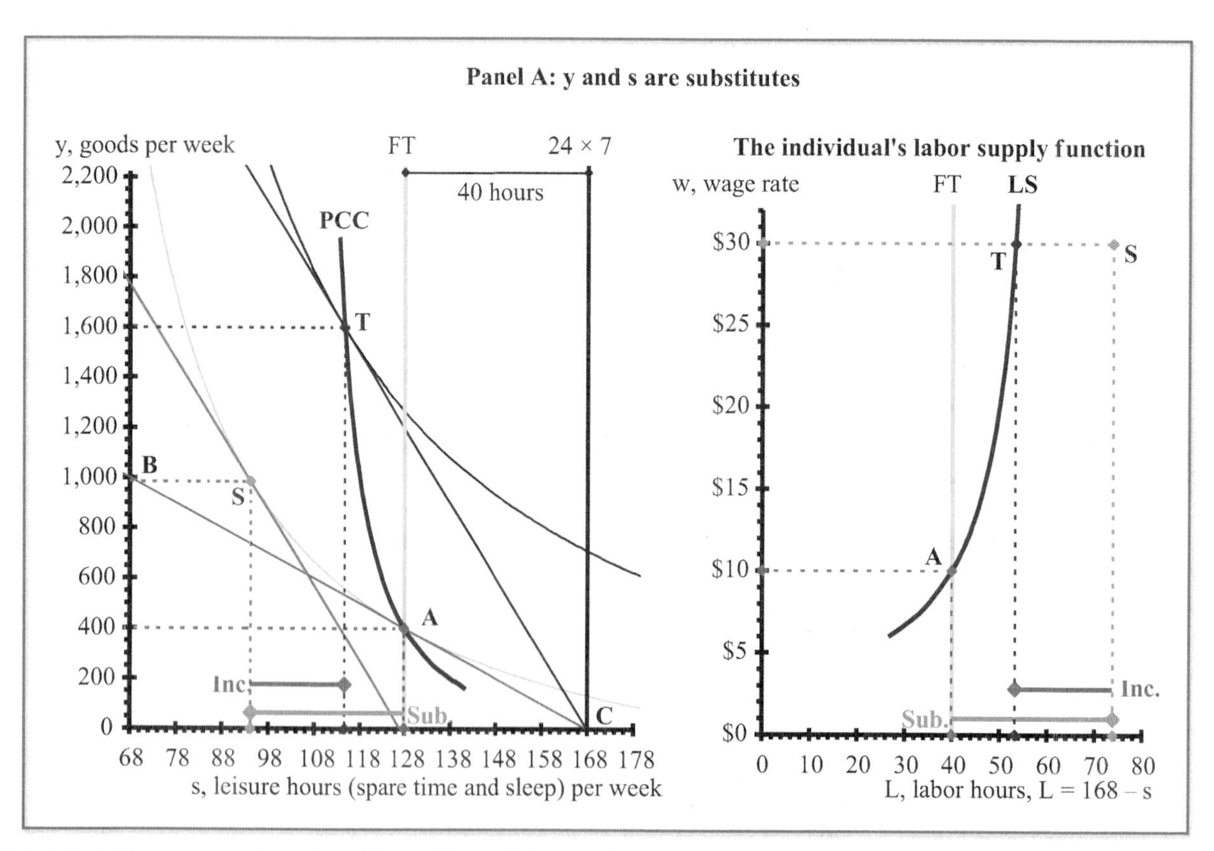

FIGURE 18.6 Decomposing the Wage Rate Change into Income and Substitution Effects

whose price has increased (leisure, s). The net effect is to decrease the demand for leisure *and therefore simultaneously* to increase the supply of labor, as shown by the location of **T** in both diagrams in Figure 18.6A.

If the substitution and income effect cancel each other, the net effect is no change in leisure demand or labor supply. In Figure 18.6B, **T** is on the vertical PCC and LS curves

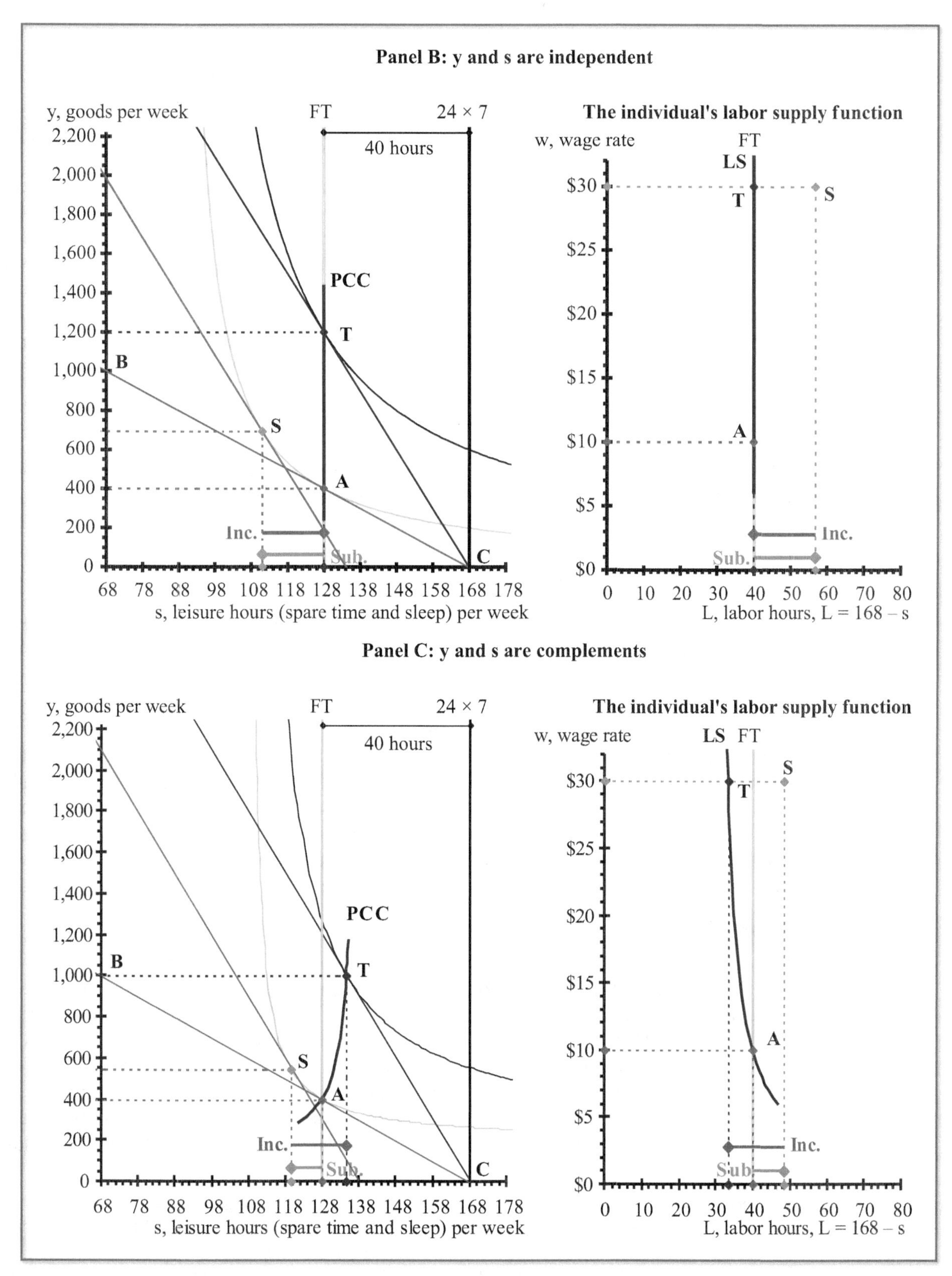

FIGURE 18.6 Continued

in this instance. This outcome is associated with consumption goods and leisure being independent goods.

If the income effect dominates the substitution effect, then leisure and consumption goods are complementary. The net effect of the wage increase is to increase the demand for leisure and decrease the supply of labor in this instance. In Figure 18.6C, **T** is on the upward-sloping PCC and downward-sloping LS as a result.

Backward-Bending Labor Supply Decomposed

We can use the substitution and income effect of a wage change to reexamine backward-bending labor supply. This was initially examined in Figure 18.4, which showed that at a wage rate of \$20, the individual is willing to supply more labor than at a wage rate of \$10, but that at a wage rate of \$30, the individual is willing to supply less labor than at a wage rate of \$10. In Section 18.1B, we argued that this seemingly paradoxical result is explained by noting that the individual might consider leisure and consumption goods to be substitutable for low wage rates, but for higher wage rates, leisure and consumption goods may be considered complementary. Figure 18.7 returns to the preferences described in Figure 18.4 but now depicts the wage rate at which this individual supplies the maximum amount of labor. For wage rates above and below this level, the individual chooses to supply less labor (and thereby to consume more leisure). At **E**, the income and substitution effects cancel each other, leaving the PCC and LS vertical.

Q7. What is the wage rate associated with consumption at **E** in the consumption diagram in Figure 18.7?*

The leisure-minimizing consumption level is at bundle **E** in the consumption diagram in Figure 18.7, and the maximum labor supply level is at **E** in the right diagram in Figure 18.7.

Consider a wage rate $w_0 < \$18$. The utility-maximizing consumption bundle is on the PCC below **E** in this instance. Consider an increase in wage rate to $w_1 = \$18$. The substitution effect dominates the income effect of the wage increase so that the net effect is to decrease demand for leisure and increase the supply of labor. Put another way, the PCC is negatively sloped, and consequently, the labor supply function is upward sloping for wages below \$18.

Conversely, consider a wage increase from $w_0 = \$18$ to a larger wage $w_1 > \$18$. Over this range of wages, the income effect dominates the substitution effect of the wage increase, so the net effect is to increase demand for leisure and decrease the supply of labor. In this event, the leisure component of the PCC increases as the wage rate increases, and the labor supply function is negatively sloped. The labor supply function is backward bending if the substitution effect of a wage increase on leisure dominates the income effect for low wages and if the reverse holds true once wages are "high enough." Where this occurs depends, of course, on the individual's preferences over goods and leisure. Some individuals will have this "turnaround" at a lower wage rate than others.

Overtime Pay Decomposed

In Section 18.1C, we argue that if an individual chooses to work full time, given the ability to choose any level of employment and straight wages, then instituting a nonlinear wage structure involving overtime pay for hours worked above full time will necessarily increase the number of hours the individual will willingly work. In terms of the substitution and income effects of the wage increase, the income effect can never match the magnitude of the substitution effect because the optimal bundle **V** must be to the left of **A** along the overtime portion of the budget constraint **GA**. We can examine the overtime/straight-time pay distinction, using substitution and income effects. Figure 18.8 adds

*__Q7 answer:__ The wage rate $w = \$18$ in this instance. This is easy to see using point **F** on the vertical axis. We noted earlier that for straight-line budget constraints the wage rate is simply the number on the vertical axis divided by 100 (because this bundle would occur if the individual worked for 100 hours), given $P_y = \$1$. It is also readily seen as the wage-rate coordinate of point **E** in the individual labor supply function.

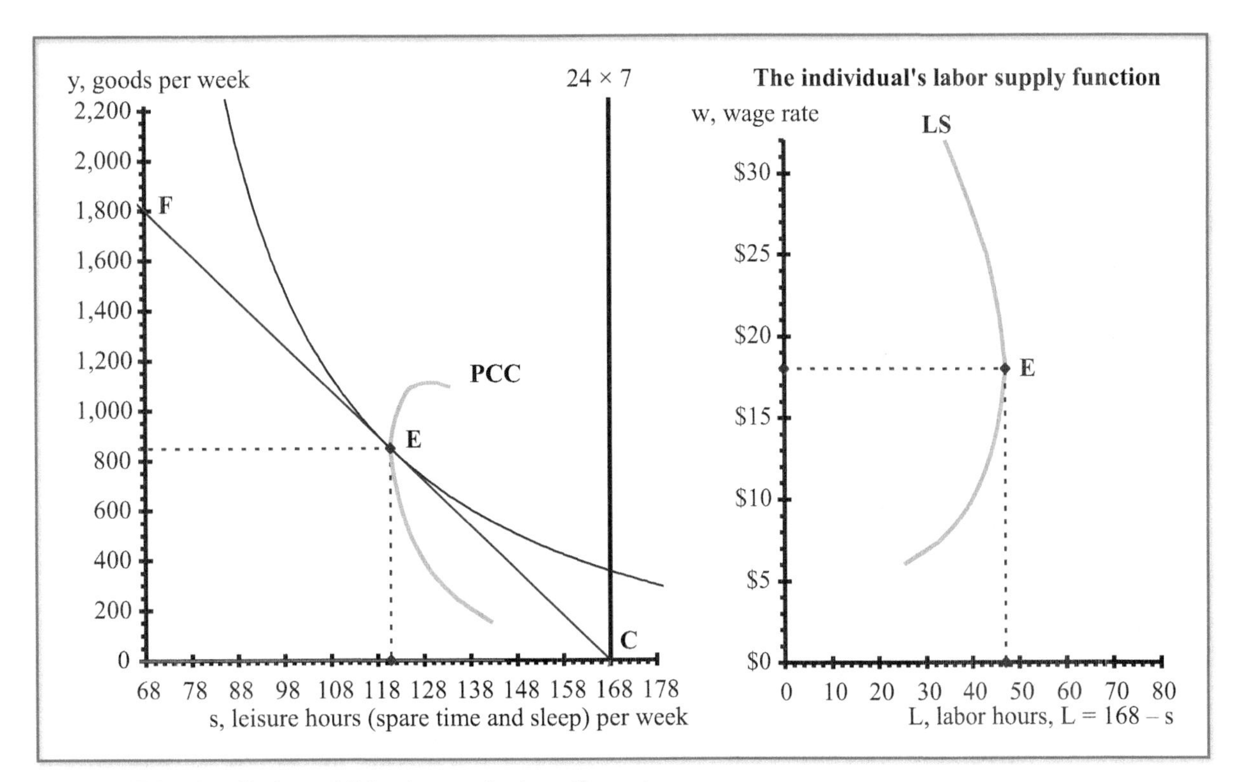

FIGURE 18.7 E Is the Point of Maximum Labor Supply

E splits the price consumption curve and labor supply curve into two parts: Below **E**, the substitution effect dominates the income effect (the net effect is qualitatively the same as in Figure 18.6A); above **E**, the income effect dominates the substitution effect (the net effect is qualitatively the same as in Figure 18.6C).

income and substitution effects to Figure 18.5. The move from **S** to **T** is the income effect of a (straight) wage increase, and the move from **S** to **V** is the income effect of an overtime wage increase. The budget constraint indifference curve tangencies at **S**, **V**, and **T** are each based on the same wage rate. *The only difference between **V** and **T** is the size of the income effect caused by overtime versus a straight wage increase (since both a wage increase and the institution of overtime at the higher wage rate have the same substitution effect from **A** to **S**).*

We can numerically describe the size of the income effect difference caused by overtime versus a straight wage increase. For hours of labor above the full-time number of hours worked, both wage schemes are the same, but for hours below full-time employment, the wage differential is:

$$\Delta w = w_1 - w_0 = \$20. \quad \textbf{(18.3a)}$$

By assumption, **A** is the full-time level of employment (and therefore the point at which overtime pay takes effect). The size of the income difference between a straight wage increase and the introduction of overtime is therefore easy to estimate; the difference is:

$$\Delta I = L_a \cdot \Delta w = 40 \cdot \$20 = \$800. \quad \textbf{(18.3b)}$$

The income difference, ΔI, can be seen as length **TA** in Figure 18.8b, but it is more generally the vertical distance between the **CT** and **GA** budget constraints, given wage rate w_1. The overtime portion of the budget constraint **GA** is always ΔI below the straight wage budget constraint, regardless of the location of the tangencies **T** and **V** along each constraint. That is, *the income difference is independent of the individual's preferences*. If the individual's indifference curve is tangent to the initial budget constraint at **A**, then the new consumption bundle associated with instituting an overtime wage will be along the overtime portion of the budget constraint. This constraint is ΔI below the straight wage constraint, even though the optimal bundles associated with those two constraints are not vertically aligned. Put in terms of bundles in Figure 18.8, if **V** = (s_v, y_v) and **T** = (s_t, y_t),

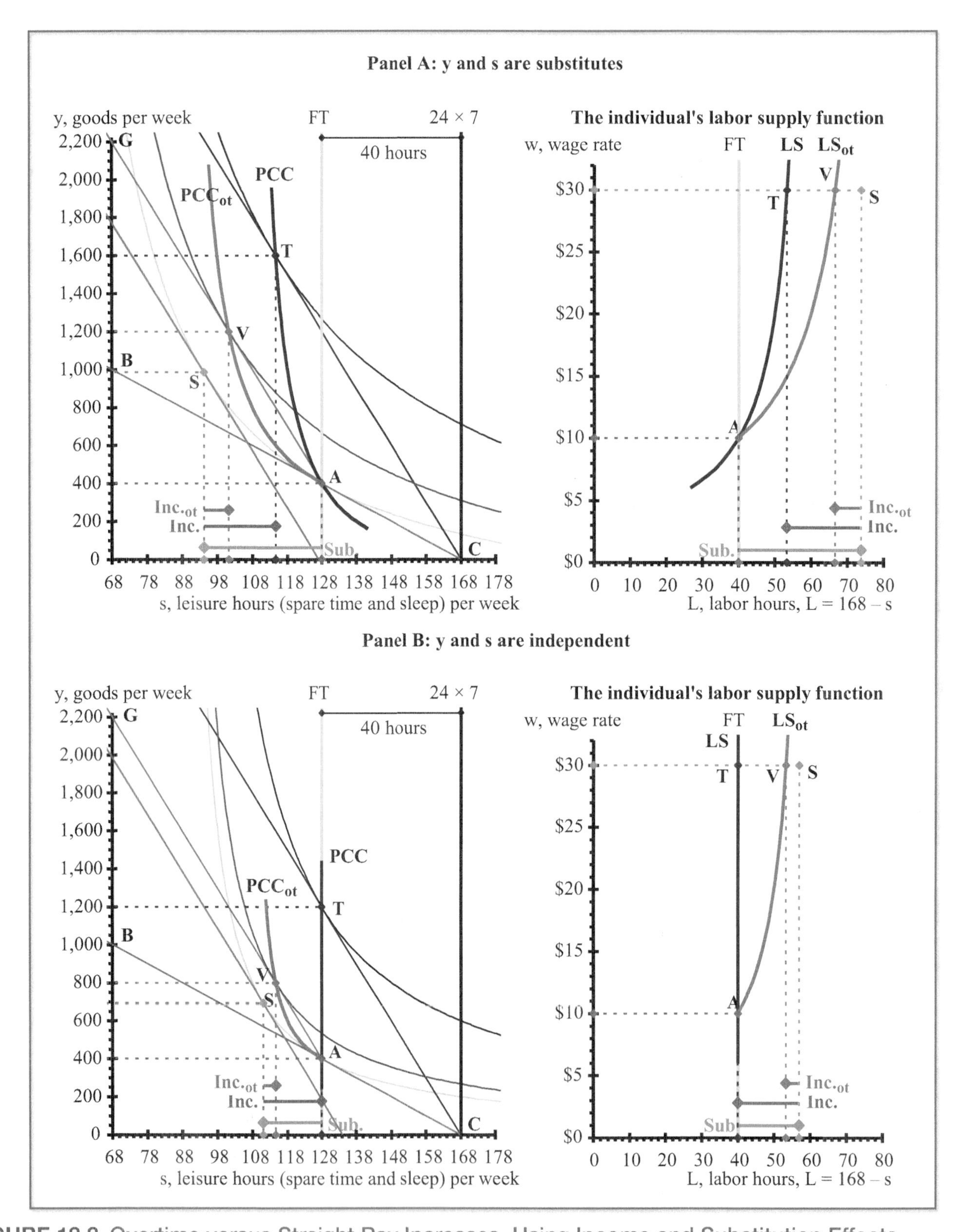

FIGURE 18.8 Overtime versus Straight Pay Increases, Using Income and Substitution Effects

then the income difference between these bundles does not depend on the location of the bundles **V** and **T** along the two constraints. Given the initial equilibrium at **A**, the income differential is the same, regardless of where the preferences produce actual tangencies at **V** and **T**. Algebraically, we have:

$$\Delta I = L_a \cdot \Delta w = (s_t - s_v) \cdot w_1 + (y_t - y_v) = \$800. \quad \textbf{(18.3c)}$$

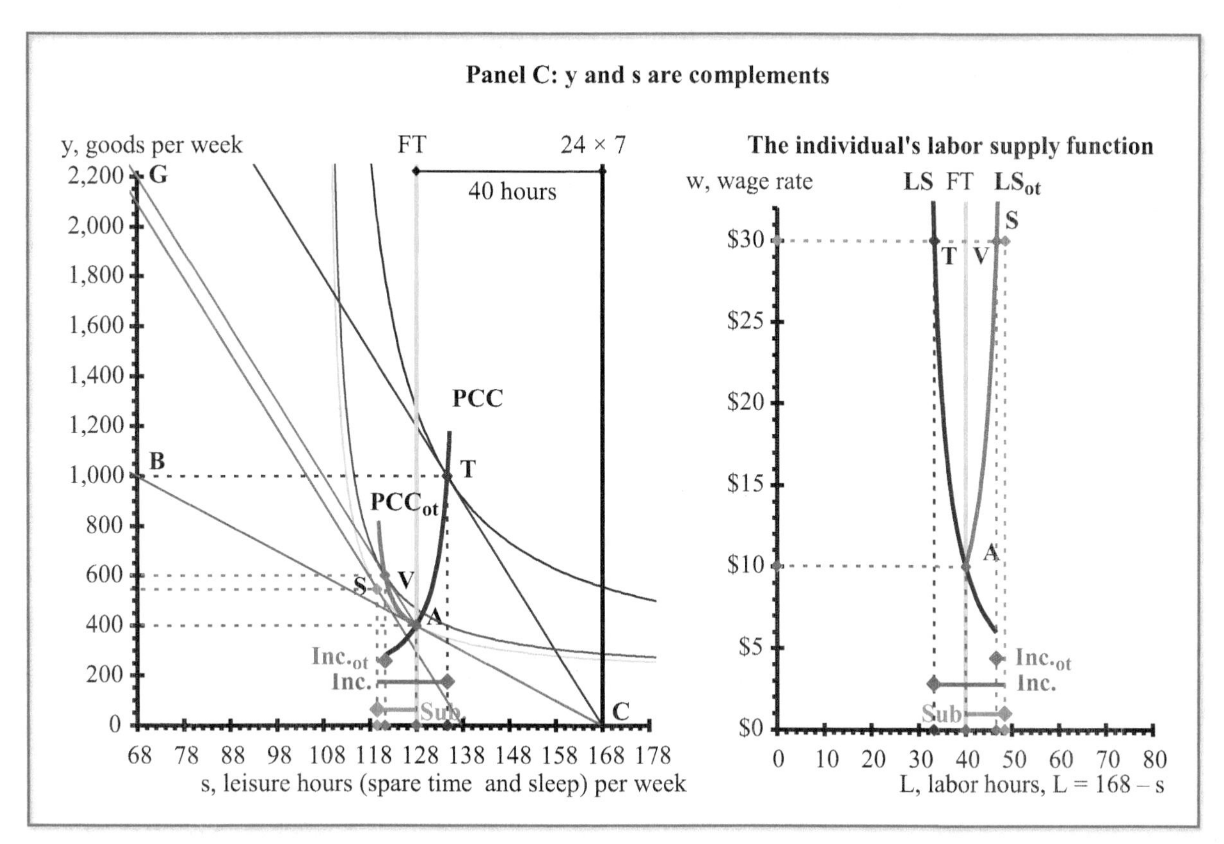

FIGURE 18.8 Continued

This same equality holds for all wage rates $w_1 > w_0$ but is only shown for $w_1 = \$30$ (were w_1 different, then the income differential would no longer be \$800 but would instead be $L_a\Delta w$). This says that the bundles **T** and **V** are always the same "distance" apart; the distance is measured vertically, but **T** need not involve having ΔI units more "income" because part of that income is used to "purchase" more leisure. In Figure 18.8, half of the distance between the two budget constraints, given $w_1 = \$30$ (\$800 in Equation 18.3c), is consumed by increased purchases of leisure (by not working as many hours) at **T** over **V** (because $(s_t - s_v) \cdot \$30 = \$400$ in each panel in Figure 18.8). The net gain in income due to a straight wage increase to \$30, relative to an overtime-only wage increase to \$30, is seen to be \$400 in each panel.

The difference described in Equation 18.3c may seem familiar in the context of Section 8.5. This is the Slutsky equation fixed-market-basket approximation of the income effect described in Equation 8.10b and shown in Figure 8.12.[4] In the context of the argument put forward in Section 8.5, overtime wages have an unambiguous effect on labor supply because, as a first approximation, overtime wages induce a pure substitution effect. Of course, "first approximations" are only approximations, and they are necessarily better for small changes in price. The change in wage rate shown is very large (wages triple) to make the difference between the approximation and the actual income effect noticeable.[5]

Summary of Section 18.1

Labor differs from other factors of production because individuals "rent" themselves out (supply labor) in exchange for receiving a wage. Individuals own other factors of production, such as financial capital, that they also rent out at a price. But labor differs from other factors that individuals own in that the alternative to work has an innate alternative value to the individual: People value leisure time.

The fixity of time produces an exact trade-off between hours devoted to work and hours that can be devoted to all other activities. The hours devoted to work are called labor, and the hours devoted to everything else are called leisure. Although leisure is not directly purchased in the market, it is indirectly purchased by forgoing labor. This is a classic example of the notion of opportunity cost: An hour of leisure costs an hour's worth of labor forgone. As a result, the price of leisure is the wage rate.

Factor market supply, in general, works like traditional product market supply. The supply of a factor of production is an increasing function of the price of the factor of production, just as firms typically are willing to increase supply when the price of the product increases. By contrast, an increase in wage rate may increase, not change, or decrease the amount of labor that the individual is willing to supply. The determining factor in this instance is how the individual views leisure in relation to other goods. If leisure is substitutable for other goods in producing utility, then labor supply will increase as the wage rate increases. If leisure is independent of other goods in producing utility, then labor supply will not change as the wage rate increases. If leisure is complementary with other goods in producing utility, then labor supply will decrease as the wage rate increases. These patterns need not exist over all wage rates. We might expect that, for low wages, the individual will consider leisure to be substitutable for consumption goods, but beyond a point, the opposite will hold true, and the individual will view leisure and consumption goods as complementary. This pattern of preferences leads to a backward-bending labor supply curve.

Firms wishing to increase the number of hours their workers are willing to supply do not necessarily attain this result by increasing the wage rate. A firm can produce this result with overtime pay. If in the absence of overtime pay, a worker chooses to work full time, then that worker will willingly work overtime if offered higher wages for overtime work.

The labor/leisure trade-off can be examined in light of the substitution and income effects analyzed in Chapter 8. Labor supply will increase as the wage rate increases if the substitution effect of a wage increase on leisure demand exceeds the income effect of a wage increase on leisure demand. Labor supply will decrease as the wage rate increases if the reverse holds true. Labor supply is backward bending if, for low wage rates, the substitution effect dominates the income effect, and if for high wage rates, the relative importance of these two effects switches.

Section 18.2 Outline

18.2 Factor Demand with Competitive Factor Markets

Prerequisites: Chapters 9–15

Since demands for factors of production are derived demands, they can only be analyzed in the context of market interaction. The labor supply analysis in Section 18.1 was based on the theoretical apparatus developed in Part 2 of the text. The only market interaction that was necessary was an understanding of the wage rate (which, of course, is determined by the interaction of supply and demand in the labor market). By contrast, the factor demand analysis developed in this section and in Section 18.3 depends much more heavily on the market interaction developed in Part 4 of the text, and as a result, both Sections 18.2 and 18.3 have the same prerequisites.

Consumer choice theory is based on the constrained optimization process that balances the individual's preferences for goods and services with the individual's income and the market-determined prices for those goods and services. Utility maximization subject to a budget constraint provides the basis for consumer demand. Producers face a different "end game," and that game is profit maximization. As a result, a producer's demands for factors of production emanate from profit maximization.

The producer analysis in Parts 3 and 4 of the text focuses on the output side of the producer's decision calculus. (The profit-maximizing decision rule MR = MC was developed as an output phenomenon.) Producers also act as purchasers of inputs in the production process. That is, firms are "consumers" of factors of production (and as we noted at the beginning of this chapter, consumers also reverse roles and act as sellers for many of these factors of production).

The factor market analysis requires "unpeeling," much as the output market analysis is unpeeled in Chapters 9–15. Of course, this unpeeling can be accomplished much more quickly, partly because the superstructure provided by Chapters 9–15 has been developed and partly because we have already discussed factor markets in those chapters. The production function analysis in Chapter 9 includes a basic discussion of factors of production. Producing a given level of output at minimum cost requires the comparison of marginal factor productivity with factor cost to choose the production point that equates the bang for the buck across all variable factors of production.[6] In Chapter 10, we developed conditional factor demands, which are functions of input prices and the quantity of output the firm wishes to produce. These conditional demand curves also require an understanding of the time frame inherent in the analysis—that is, which factors are fixed and which are variable in the analysis. Factors of production are part of the discussion beyond Chapter 10, but they are placed in the background as the analytical focus shifts to more directly confront the output side of the firm's market interaction. This process begins in Chapter 11, where cost is considered as a function of units of output produced, rather than as a function of the inputs used to produce the output. Chapters 12–15 continue the output market focus by examining the profit-maximizing output choice both in a general setting and under the assumption that the output market is competitive, monopolistic, or monopolistically competitive.

In this section, we begin to unpeel the factor market "onion" by assuming that input markets are competitive. In Section 18.3, we examine what happens if factor markets are themselves imperfectly competitive. Even if input markets are competitive, the output produced by that input need not be sold in competitive markets. The demand for factors of production depends on the value of the output being produced, and as we have seen in Part 4 of the text, that value depends on the market structure in which the firm is embedded. We begin as we did in Chapter 12—by describing the general requirement for profit-maximizing input choice, and then we restrict that analysis by considering how this requirement is modified as we impose various market structures or time frames on the analysis. Although this input market analysis applies to all factors of production, we often consider labor as our input of choice.

18.2A Profit-Maximizing Input Choice *Prerequisites: Chapters 9–15*

The general requirement for profit maximization laid out in Chapter 12 is to produce output at the point where MR = MC. This concise conclusion is analyzed in detail in that chapter, and it stands as the hallmark of a profit-maximizing firm's decision calculus. That analysis considers a single dimension: The firm decides how much output to produce. Price is determined by the market, based on that output decision. For perfectly competitive markets, that price is independent of output level chosen by an individual firm, and for imperfectly competitive markets, it is based on the downward-sloping demand curve faced by the firm. If the firm has more dimensions on which it can compete, then we should expect the same marginal decision calculus to hold along each dimension. For example, if the firm competes in a differentiated product market and wishes to further differentiate its product via advertising, then it will choose that level of advertising where the marginal revenue generated by a bit more advertising equals the marginal cost incurred as a result (this is examined more formally in Section 21.7).

In coming to a profit-maximizing output decision, the firm implicitly uses the same decision criterion on the input side of the market. Factors of production that may be adjusted are used up to the point where the incremental revenue attained by a bit more of the factor equals the incremental cost associated with using a bit more of the factor. It is useful to have formal terms for the concepts described in the last sentence. The **marginal revenue product of factor F, MRP(F)**, is the incremental revenue generated by using a bit more F, MRP(F) = ΔTR/ΔF, *ceteris paribus*. The **marginal factor cost of factor F, MFC(F)**, is the incremental cost incurred when the firm uses a bit more F, MFC(F) = ΔTC/ΔF, *ceteris paribus*. Profit-maximizing behavior on the input side requires that all variable factors be adjusted so that:

marginal revenue product of factor F, MRP(F): The marginal revenue product of factor F is the incremental revenue generated by using a bit more F, MRP(F) = ΔTR/ΔF, *ceteris paribus*.

$$\text{MRP(F)} = \text{MFC(F)}. \quad \textbf{(18.4)}$$

marginal factor cost of factor F, MFC(F): The marginal factor cost of factor F is the incremental cost incurred when the firm uses a bit more F, MFC(F) = ΔTC/ΔF, *ceteris paribus*.

MRP = MFC is the input market equivalent to MR = MC.

The profit-maximizing input decision rule in Equation 18.4 can be further explored by more carefully examining each side of the equation. The marginal revenue product of a factor of production, MRP(F) = ΔTR/ΔF, is the incremental revenue generated by an incremental amount of input F. *Incremental input F generates revenue by generating extra output that is sold.* The amount of output generated by an incremental amount of a factor of production is one of the most important concepts discussed in Chapter 9; this is the marginal product of the factor of production. For a general factor of production, F, we often write this as MP_F, but in the present context, it is worthwhile to more explicitly acknowledge that the marginal product of F is a function of F by writing it as $MP(F) = \Delta Q/\Delta F$. This is sometimes described as the marginal *physical* product of a factor of production. It measures physical units of incremental output produced by an incremental amount of factor F (and hence, some texts label this MPP(F)).

The firm only cares about producing more output to the extent that the additional output can increase revenue. Economists describe the incremental revenue generated by an incremental amount of output as marginal revenue, $MR(Q) = \Delta TR/\Delta Q$ (and, of course, much of Part 4 is based on MR). Since each unit of output produces MR dollars in incremental revenue, then MP units of incremental output will produce $MR \cdot MP$ dollars in incremental revenue. Put more explicitly, we can rewrite the marginal revenue product of a factor of production as the product of the marginal (physical) product of that factor times the marginal revenue generated by incremental output:

$$MRP(F) = MR(Q) \cdot MP(F). \quad \textbf{(18.5)}$$

$$\Delta TR/\Delta F = (\Delta TR/\Delta Q) \cdot (\Delta Q/\Delta F).$$

The second line in Equation 18.5 shows why the product on the right side of the equation describes the marginal revenue product of the factor of production. The change in revenue due to an incremental change in a factor of production is the product of the output increase caused by this change in the factor and the increment to revenue of an increase in output.

Equations 18.4 and 18.5 hold, regardless of input or output market structure. As we impose specific structures on either side of the market, we can begin to simplify the profit-maximizing condition further. As noted earlier, we assume in this section that factor markets are competitive. When the factor market is competitive, the marginal factor cost is simply the price of the factor, $MFC(F) = P_f$. This allows us to rewrite the profit-maximizing condition as:

$$MR(Q) \cdot MP(F) = P_f, \text{ for } \pi \text{ maximum, given a competitive factor market F.} \quad \textbf{(18.6a)}$$

We can make one final adjustment to this equation if we face competitive output markets as well as competitive input markets. In this event, marginal revenue equals price of the good produced, $MR = P$, as noted in Chapter 13, so:

$$P \cdot MP(F) = P_f, \text{ for } \pi \text{ maximum, given competitive factor and output markets.} \quad \textbf{(18.6b)}$$

The profit-maximizing rule provided in Equation 18.6 must hold for each factor that the firm is able to adjust. Depending on the time frame, the firm may not be able to adjust some factors of production. We begin by examining the short run, in which the firm is only able to adjust one factor of production.

18.2B Input Choice with One Variable Factor of Production

Prerequisite: Section 18.2A

With competitive input and output markets, we can show the marginal revenue product curve graphically, using Figure 18.9. Two of the curves shown in Figure 18.9 were the focus of much of Chapter 9: the dark red univariate production function (total product curve), Q(L), and the slope of this curve, the pink marginal product of labor curve, MP(L). These two curves are shown in a single diagram here, rather than in separate panels, as was done in Chapter 9.[7] (These curves are shown in separate diagrams in Chapter 9 because they are based on different units of measure: Q is measured as total output, and MP is measured on a per-unit (Q/L) basis. The other curves in Figure 18.9 are measured in dollars per unit of labor, rather than units of output.) The competitive output market is seen by the horizontal line denoting the output price, $P = \$10$. As noted in Section 13.2 (and Equation 13.2), $P = MR$ for competitive output markets. The final curve, the downward-sloping blue curve labeled $MRP(L) = P \cdot MP(L)$, is a graphical representation of the left-hand side of Equation 18.6b.[8]

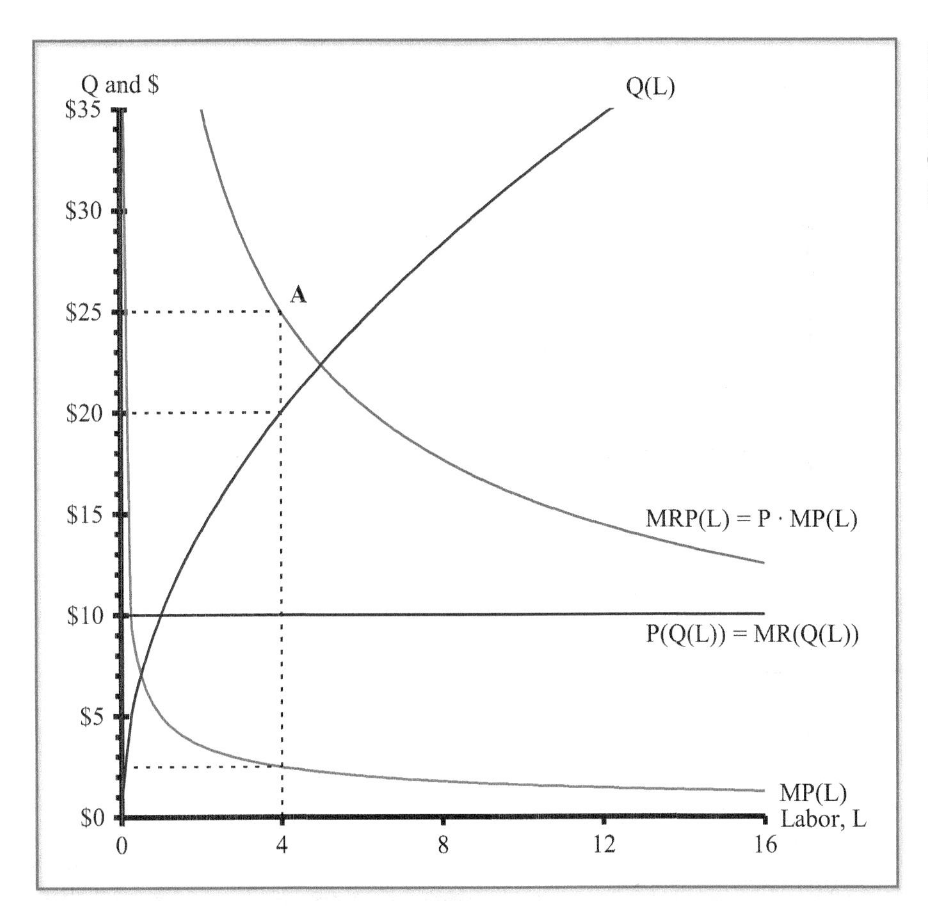

FIGURE 18.9
Determining Factor Demand, Given Competitive Factor and Product Markets

Before we consider the interpretation of MRP, we should see how it is constructed. To do this, L = 4 has been noted on each of the four curves in Figure 18.9. When L = 4, 20 units of output are produced, Q(4) = 20. The slope of the total product curve is the marginal product of labor, and at L = 4, we see that MP(4) = 2.5; this is the point (4, 2.5) on the marginal product of labor curve. Given P = $10 and MP(4) = 2.5, we see that MRP(4) = $25, according to Equation 18.6b. This is point **A** on the MRP(L) curve.

Since the input market is competitive, the price of labor, w, is used in conjunction with the marginal revenue product curve to determine the demand for labor. For example, at a wage rate of w = $25, the profit-maximizing firm would choose L = 4. This is point **A** on the firm's labor demand curve in Figure 18.9. If the wage rate were a different amount, then the firm would simply move to the corresponding point on the MRP(L) curve to determine the new quantity of labor to demand.

Claim: *The MRP(L) curve is the firm's derived demand for labor function.*

This is a symmetric result to the competitive firm's profit-maximizing output choice of producing along the marginal cost curve because, at this point, P = MR = MC. In both instances, the orientation on which the curve is interpreted changes, but MRP and MC both act to delineate the profit-maximizing production decision.[9]

When we relax the assumption that the output market is competitive, we no longer have P = MR. (Indeed, as noted in Section 15.1, P > MR for all imperfectly competitive product markets because demand is downward sloping.) One particularly useful downward-sloping demand curve is the constant elasticity demand curve initially explored in Section 12.3. As noted in that section, this demand curve has a marginal revenue curve that is a constant proportion "below" the demand curve. The dark blue demand for labor curve shown in Figure 18.10 has $\varepsilon_x = -2$, the same as shown in Figure 12.10A. In this instance, the dark green marginal revenue curve, MR(Q), is half the height of inverse demand P(Q) for any output level.[10] Q(L) and MP(L) are unchanged from Figure 18.9. Given the separation of price and marginal revenue in this instance, P · MP(L) differs from MRP(L).

FIGURE 18.10 Comparing Factor Demand in Perfectly and Imperfectly Competitive Output Markets

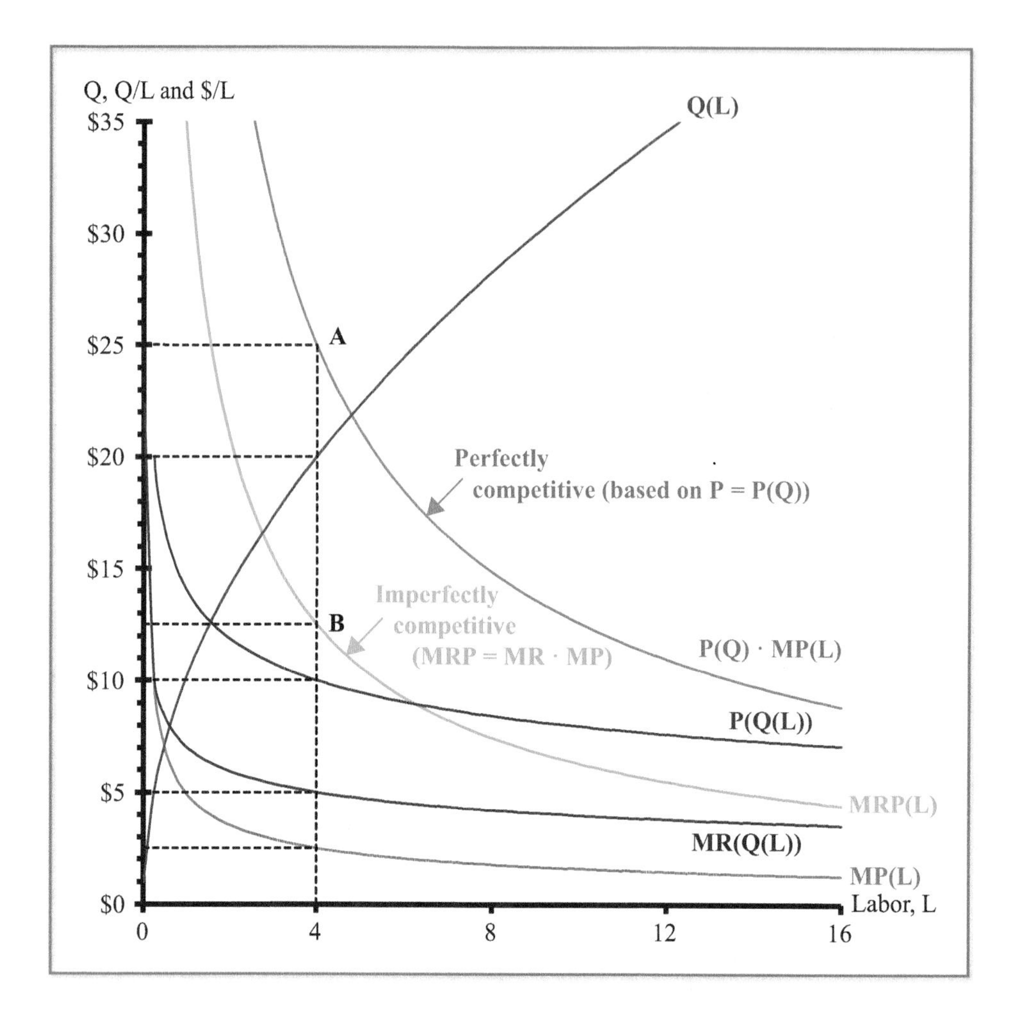

With $\varepsilon_x = -2$, MRP(L) is half the height of P · MP(L) for every level of labor, L. In particular, labor demand would be L = 4 when w = \$12.50 = \$5 · 2.5 = MR(Q(4)) · MP(4), not at \$25 = \$10 · 2.5 = P(Q(4)) · MP(4) (at **B** rather than **A** in Figure 18.10). Different elasticities would produce different MRP curves (since elasticity changes the marginal revenue curve, according to Equation 12.12d), and different amounts of other factors (that are held fixed in our *ceteris paribus* analysis) would produce different MRP curves (since they would change the marginal product of labor). But as long as the factor market remains competitive, we can use the marginal revenue product curve to meter factor demand. Different wage rates would be associated with different quantities of labor demanded; each would be along the schedule MRP(L), just like the competitive firm's profit-maximizing output choice of producing along the marginal cost curve.

Demand for a factor of production is downward sloping because the marginal revenue product schedule is downward sloping. Equation 18.5 shows that MRP is the product of marginal revenue and the marginal product of the factor. Therefore, when the output market is competitive, MRP is downward sloping as a result of the law of diminishing marginal product. When the output market is imperfectly competitive, there are two reasons why MRP is downward sloping. In addition to MP being a declining function of the factor of production (holding all other factors constant), marginal revenue is a declining function of output because demand is downward sloping, and output is an increasing function of the factor of production.

18.2C Input Choice with Multiple Variable Factors of Production

Prerequisite: Section 18.2B

In the cost-minimizing discussion in Chapter 10, we argue that for production to occur at the cost-minimizing input bundle, each factor of production that may be adjusted should be used up to the point where there is equal "bang for the buck" across factors: $MP_i/P_i = MP_j/P_j$ for input factors i and j that are allowed to vary in the time frame under consideration. This condition is equivalent to having a tangency between the isocost line whose slope is $-P_i/P_j$ and the isoquant whose slope is $MRTS_{j,i}$, as described by Equation 10.6Bi. As noted in Exhibit 10.1, cost minimization is a more general concept than profit maximization; if the input bundle maximizes profit, it must necessarily minimize cost. We can obtain the cost-minimizing condition as a byproduct of the profit-maximizing condition shown in Equation 18.6b by noting that Equation 18.6b applies to multiple variable factors.

Suppose that two factors i and j are variable and that output and input markets are competitive. In this event, Equation 18.6b holds for both factors. By cross-multiplying, we obtain the following:

$MP_i/P_i = 1/P = MP_j/P_j$,
where P is the price of the output produced using i and j. **(18.7a)**

Both equalities are regrouped versions of Equation 18.6b, and both are equal to the common value, the inverse of output price. Since they are both equal to a common value, they are equal to each other; this equality is simply a restatement of the cost-minimizing input choice described in Equation 10.6B′i.

The difference between the cost-minimizing input choice and the profit-maximizing input choice is instructive. Cost minimization simply requires that the input bundle be on the lowest isocost line producing that level of output. This is not necessarily profit maximizing because the firm may be producing the wrong level of output. The right level of output is the one where the output bang for the input buck equals one over the price of the good being produced. We can rewrite Equation 18.7a in a different order to highlight the relation between profit maximization and cost minimization:

$$MP_i/P_i \quad \underset{\uparrow}{=} \quad MP_j/P_j \quad \underset{\uparrow}{=} \quad 1/P. \qquad \textbf{(18.7b)}$$

All cost-minimizing bundles — Bundles that are also π maximizing

The first equality occurs at all cost-minimizing input bundles; the second *only* occurs when profits are maximized. If the second equality were replaced by ">," then the profit-maximizing firm would increase demand for both factors of production (because by cross-multiplying, we see in this instance that $MRP_i > P_i$ so that the incremental revenue from factor usage exceeds the incremental cost of the factor). If the reverse were true, then both factor demands should decline.

One way to consider multiple variable inputs is to note that there can be multiple variable inputs in the short run. Raw materials, m, and labor, L, are both commonly described as factors that are variable in the short run. In this context, the multiple-input requirement described in Equation 18.7b involves finding, among the cost-minimizing points, that point which is also profit maximizing. This is geometrically seen as choosing among the points of tangency between the isoquant and the isocost line (first equality in Equation 18.7b) that point of tangency where the output bang for the buck for labor and materials also equals the inverse of the product's price (second equality in Equation 18.7b). This makes economic sense; a higher-priced product needs less of an output increase due to an increase in a factor of production to make it worthwhile to increase usage of that factor of production.

The intuition of the situation is stronger, however, if we cross-multiply and return to the $MRP_i = P_i$ across variable factors of production form of Equation 18.7b (which is not formally written as a single chain of equalities but instead considers each factor market separately). Upon cross-multiplication, Equation 18.7b requires that MRP(L) = w, and MRP(m) = P_m, given competitive factor and output markets. Profit-maximizing input choice in this instance simply requires that the marginal revenue product of each factor equals the price of that factor. If this is not the case, then either the firm is not cost minimizing (the first equality in Equation 18.7b is violated), or the firm is cost minimizing but is producing the wrong level of output (the second equality in Equation 18.7b is violated).

FIGURE 18.11 Long-Run versus Short-Run Labor Demand, $K_0 < K_1$

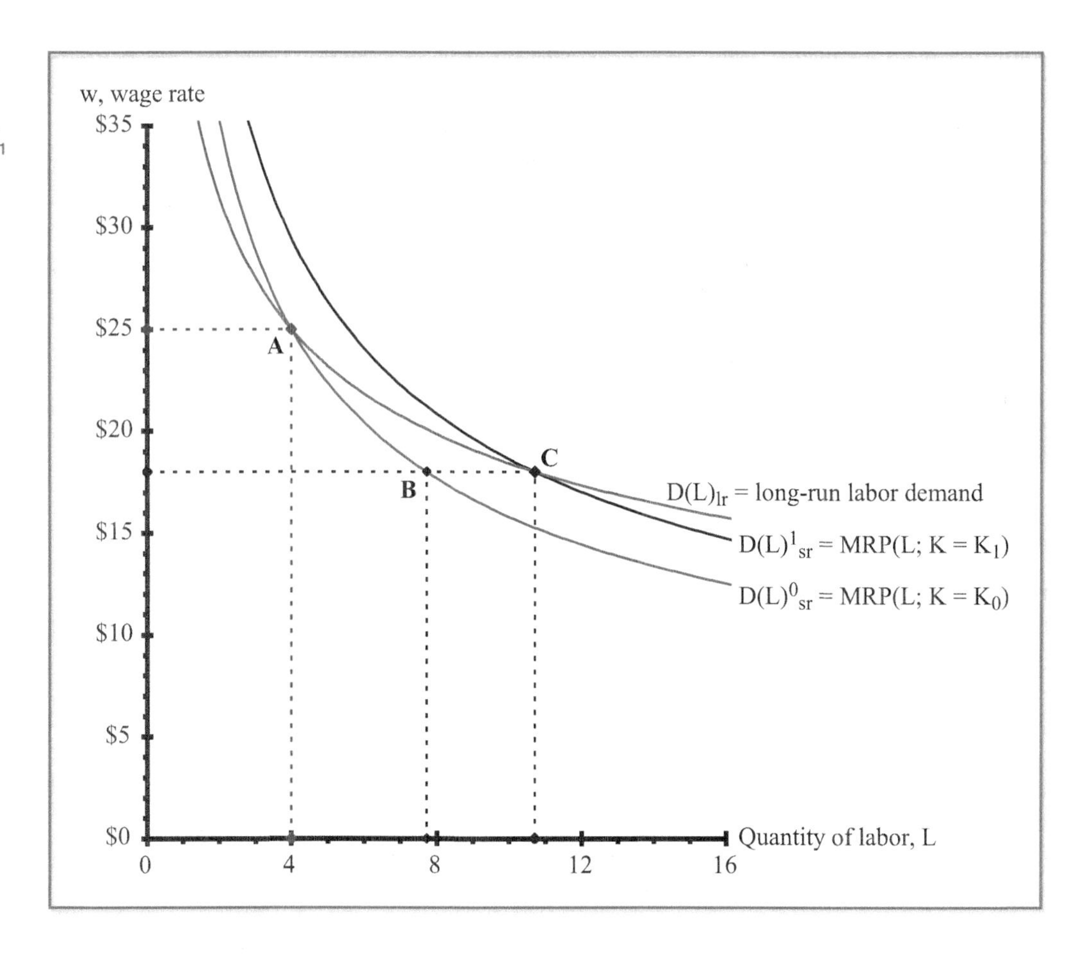

The other way to consider multiple variable inputs is to change the time frame involved in the analysis. Capital is fixed in the short run but is allowed to vary in the long run, while labor is allowed to vary in both time frames. Recall that the marginal revenue product function describes how revenue varies as the use of the factor varies, holding all other factors of production constant. The marginal revenue product of labor function describes the short-run demand for labor; this function holds capital fixed, so we can write this more explicitly as MRP(L; $K = K_0$), where the semicolon denotes that capital is fixed (at K_0). Consider an initial short-run equilibrium at point **A** on the blue MRP(L; $K = K_0$) curve in Figure 18.11. Suppose that this is also a point on the firm's long-run labor demand curve. (This would be the case if the firm would not change capital, even if it had the option to adjust capital.) In this event, both labor and capital would satisfy Equation 18.7b.

If the firm faces a drop in the wage rate from $w_0 = \$25$ to $w_1 = \$18$, it will maximize profit in the short run by almost doubling the use of labor to point **B** along MRP(L; $K = K_0$), given the initial fixed short-run capital level $K = K_0$. An increase in labor usage, given fixed capital, typically increases the marginal productivity of capital so that $MP_K/P_K > MP_L/P_L$. If the firm is able to adjust capital as it moves from the short to the long run, it will increase capital to $K_1 > K_0$. The capital level K_1 is that capital level for which capital as well as labor once again satisfies Equation 18.7b. As capital increases, the marginal revenue product *of labor* increases because labor now has more capital with which to produce output (and hence, MP_L increases). The change in capital therefore shifts the marginal revenue product of labor curve. This is shown geometrically as point **C** on the new (dark blue) short-run marginal revenue product curve, MRP(L; $K = K_1$).

The drop in wage has two effects on labor demand: First, there is the short-run adjustment to a drop in wage rate, since bang for the labor buck increases as wage decreases (from **A** to **B**). Second, there is an increase in labor demand because an increase in capital stock increases labor productivity (from **B** to **C**). Were the change in wage rate a different amount, then the long-run adjustment to a new capital stock would change as well. The red long-run labor demand curve, $D(L)_{lr}$, in Figure 18.11 describes the set of (L, w) bundles for which both labor and capital satisfy Equation 18.7b. *The long run labor demand curve is the set of points on short-run labor demand curves where marginal product per dollar spent on labor and capital are equal, and are equal to the inverse of output price,* as required by Equation 18.7b. As the wage rate changes from $25, the capital stock adjusts as well: For example, if the new wage rate is between $18 and $25, the capital stock producing a new long-run equilibrium adjusts to an amount between K_0 and K_1 (and the Excel file for Figure 18.11 allows you to see this adjustment). The long-run demand for factors is therefore more elastic than the short-run demand.

18.2D Industry Demand for Labor **Prerequisite: Section 18.2C**

The analysis thus far in this section has been based on an individual firm. To determine market demand for a factor of production, we must horizontally sum across industries, much as we aggregated individual demand across consumers to determine market demand for goods. The summation across industries is straightforward, but obtaining industry demand requires a bit more care. As a result, we focus on how we obtain industry demand from individual firm demand. When a monopolist controls an industry, industry demand for the factor of production is the monopolist's marginal revenue product of the factor. We focus on the opposite end of the competitive spectrum by examining the industry demand for a factor of production in a perfectly competitive market. This analysis examines the industry demand for labor, but it applies to other factor markets as well.

The starting point for the industry analysis is the individual firm discussion in Figure 18.9. The marginal revenue product curve was labeled as $MRP(L) = P \cdot MP(L)$ in that figure to acknowledge that an individual firm faces a horizontal demand for its product (so that MR = P). In Figure 18.9, the price of the good produced was $10 so that the marginal revenue product curve was 10 times as large as marginal product for any level of labor employed. The marginal revenue product of labor curve is reproduced in Figure 18.12A as di(L; P = $10), and the other curves from Figure 18.9 have been suppressed so that we can focus on how moving from a single firm to the industry affects labor demand (ignore for the moment Figure 18.12B). The curve is labeled *di*, using a lowercase *d* to denote demand for labor by individual firm *i* (if the graph were static, it would be denoted d_i, but subscripting is not possible with click-boxes). The semicolon followed by P = $10 is provided to explicitly acknowledge that price is fixed at $10 along this curve. If only one firm faced a change in wage rate, then this is the appropriate marginal revenue product curve to consider when describing individual firm demand for labor. Two points are noted on this curve: **A** is associated with a wage rate of $25, and **B** is associated with a wage rate of $15.

Consider a decrease in wage from $25 to $15. If only one firm is affected by the wage decrease, then it will simply increase labor demand from **A** to **B** in Figure 18.12A. But if all firms in the industry face the same wage decrease, the wage decrease will have an effect on the market clearing price of the product produced. The lower wage allows firms to expand their output, and as output expands, the market clearing price declines (lower wages shift supply out for fixed demand, causing the price in the output market to decline). The size of the decline depends on the elasticity of demand in the output market. Figure 18.12B depicts industry demand for the factor, based on the assumption of 100 similarly situated firms in the industry (note that the numbers on the horizontal axis are in hundreds of units of labor in this panel). The example shown in Figure 18.12B *assumes* that the net effect will be a decline in output price from $10 to $8. This causes the marginal revenue product to decline by 20% for any quantity of labor (according to Equation 18.6). The resulting curve is the representative firm's dark blue demand for labor curve, di(L; P=$8), in Figure 18.12A. The sum of individual firm demand curves is therefore 20% lower, given a price of $8 (this is seen by noting that the (L, w) points (4, $20) and (11.1, $12) are on the dark blue di and Σdi (Sum di) curves, 20% below points **A** and **B** in both panels). Point **A** represents industry demand for labor at a price of $25, and Point **C** represents industry demand for labor at a price of $15. The set of all such points is the red industry demand for labor curve denoted D_{labor}. (The Excel file for Figure 18.12 allows

FIGURE 18.12 Demand for Labor in a Competitive Industry

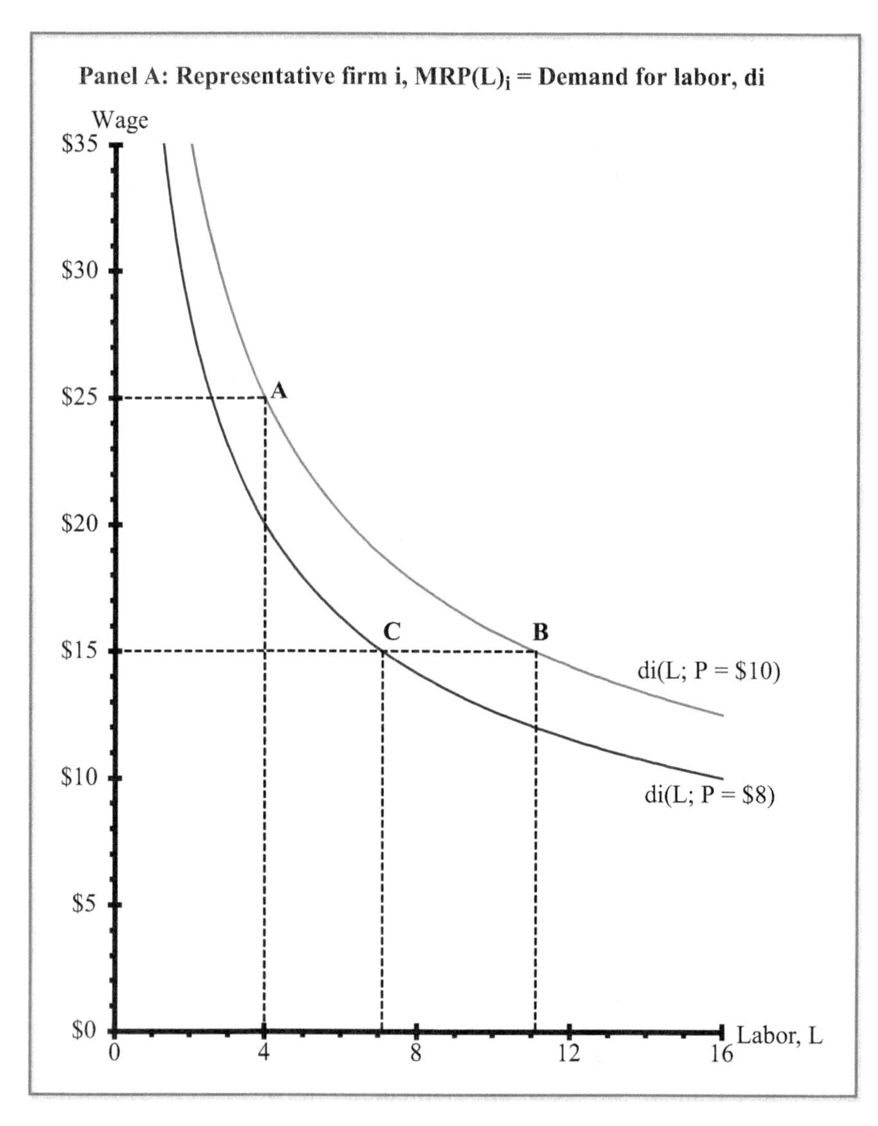

you to vary the wage rate to see other points on this curve that are produced as the dark blue Σdi curve floats up or down as the wage rate changes.) It is important to note that point **B** is *not* a point on the industry demand for labor curve because the market clearing price of the good being produced does not support this level of labor demand (price has declined as a result of the output increase produced with the extra labor). **B** would be supported in this instance only if the output market demand was perfectly elastic (so that the price would remain at $10 in the face of increased supply).

The difference between **B** and **C** depends on the output market elasticity of demand. Points **A** and **C** on the labor demand curve determine two output market points (via the production function).[11] The output market information provided in Figure 18.12B allows you to estimate the output elasticity of demand implicit in the diagram.

> **Q12.** Estimate output market elasticity of demand, using the initial situation as the point of reference, based on the market information provided.*

The Excel file for Figure 18.12 allows you to adjust the output elasticity of demand. More elastic demand produces industry demand that is closer to the "no price change" curve through **A** and **B**, while less elastic market demand produces a labor demand curve that is more inelastic than the one through **A** and **C**.

***Q12 answer:** Elasticity is $\varepsilon = \%\Delta Q/\%\Delta P$. Using the initial situation as the point of reference, $\%\Delta Q = (2{,}000 - 2{,}667)/2{,}000 = -1/3$ and $\%\Delta P = (\$10 - \$8)/\$10 = 1/5$, so $\varepsilon = (-1/3)/(1/5) = -5/3 = -1.67$.

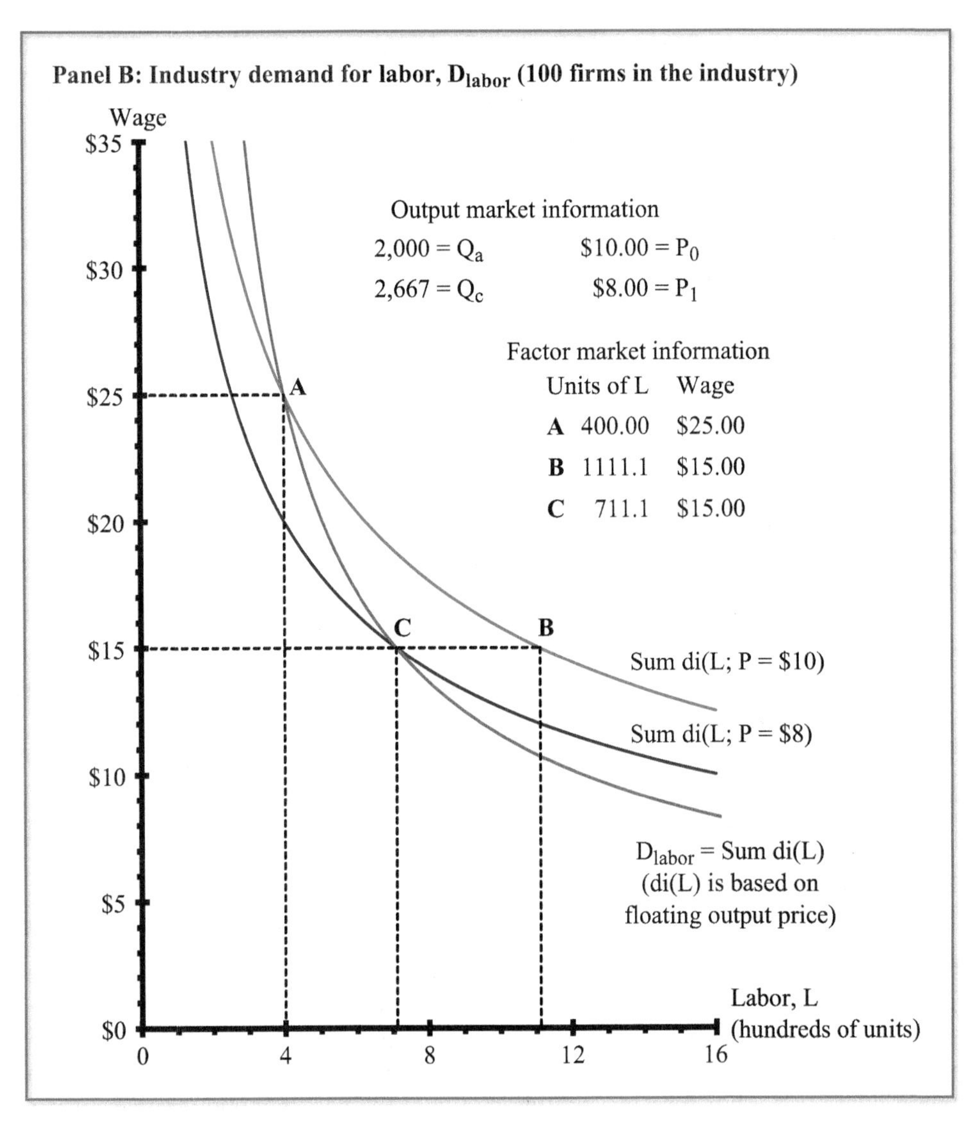

FIGURE 18.12
Continued

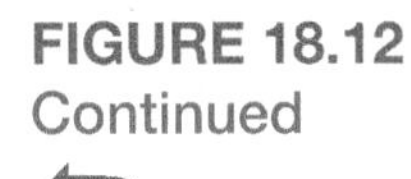

Summary of Section 18.2

Firms demand factors of production because those factors further the firm's goal of maximizing profits. The firm will choose to employ factors of production up to the point where the marginal revenue generated by the use of a bit more of the factor equals the marginal cost of that factor's incremental usage. This is the input market analog to the profit-maximizing decision rule to set output where MR = MC. Factor markets are assumed competitive throughout this section, and as a result, the firm's incremental cost is simply the price of the factor.

The revenue generated by incremental usage of a factor of production exists because the factor produces incremental output that can be sold. The incremental output produced is the marginal product of the factor of production, MP(F). These additional units of the good can be sold to produce incremental revenue. Incremental revenue per unit of output is marginal revenue, MR, so that the marginal revenue product of a factor of production is the product of marginal revenue and marginal product, $MRP(F) = MR \cdot MP(F)$.

When the output being produced is sold in a competitive market, P = MR, so marginal revenue product is simply $MRP(F) = P \cdot MP(F)$. The marginal revenue product curve is a declining function of factor usage because marginal productivity declines as the factor of production increases, due to the law of diminishing marginal product. If the output market is imperfectly competitive, marginal revenue is a declining function of output so that the MRP function is the product of two declining functions.

The marginal revenue product curve acts as the demand function for the factor of production, just as the marginal cost curve acts as the supply function for a competitive firm. The firm will demand along its MRP(F) curve for each factor it can adjust to maximize profits. With multiple factors that the firm is able to adjust, the profit-maximizing solution will not only be profit maximizing but also cost minimizing. This analysis works for multiple variable factors in the short run, as well as with capital and labor in the long run.

As factors adjust, the firm's marginal revenue product curves will adjust as well. For example, as capital increases, the marginal product of labor schedule will shift outward because extra capital creates extra marginal productivity for labor. The long-run demand for factors is therefore more elastic than the short-run demand.

Market demand for a factor of production is the sum of factor demands from those industries using the factor. Factor demand for an industry is the sum of demands across firms in the industry. As demand for the factor increases, the market price of the good being produced using that factor will decline, even if the industry is competitive. When this happens, the marginal revenue product curves will decline (because marginal revenue declines). Put another way, the demand for labor by an industry is less elastic than is the horizontal sum of individual firm marginal revenue product curves.

Section 18.3 Outline

18.3 Imperfectly Competitive Factor Demand

Prerequisites: Chapters 9–15 and Section 18.2

In Section 18.2, we consider how perfectly competitive and imperfectly competitive output markets affect factor demand. That analysis assumes that factor markets are perfectly competitive. When factor markets are imperfectly competitive, the analysis in Section 18.2 must be modified.

A market is an interaction in which a buyer buys from a seller. The discussion of imperfectly competitive output markets in Chapter 15 only examines imperfectly competitive sellers because the buyers are assumed to be too numerous and "small," relative to the size of the market, to individually affect the market outcome. We relax this assumption in factor markets because buyers as well as sellers can be "large enough" to alter the market outcome.[12] Before examining imperfectly competitive buyers, we turn to imperfectly competitive sellers of inputs.

18.3A Monopoly Power on the Seller Side of a Factor Market

Prerequisite: Section 18.2

Suppose that the factor under consideration is provided by a single supplier—that is, suppose that the factor market is supplied by a monopolist. This would be the case if, for example, a raw material or component part is only available from a single source. The most important factor market where seller monopoly power sometimes exists is when a union controls a labor market. If a union is able to exert monopoly power, it is able to affect the market outcome. As you might expect, the union will attempt to increase the wage paid its members. We can see how this occurs, using a model that looks virtually identical to the monopoly model in Chapter 15.

To focus on how monopoly power enters the model, we assume that demand and supply of labor are linear and that the output market is competitive. Specifically, suppose that S_{labor} represents the amount of labor that union members will willingly supply at different wage rates. Similarly, D_{labor} represents the demand for labor services by firms that employ these unionized workers. This curve is the aggregate of marginal revenue product schedules, as discussed in Section 18.2.

An output market monopolist is able to set its price, but it does not have "complete" control over its price in other than a superficial sense because it understands that the higher the price charged for the product, the more restricted unit sales will be. The monopolist realizes that it faces a downward-sloping demand for its product, and it sets output accordingly by choosing the output level Q_m where MR = MC. By choosing this output level, the monopolist implicitly chooses the price $P_m = P(Q_m)$, where P(Q) is the market's inverse demand curve for the product. (Alternatively, we could conceptualize the monopolist's decision as choosing price, and then the market implicitly chooses output based on that price. In either event, the same price and quantity are chosen because they are jointly determined according to market demand for the product.) An input market monopolist faces the same joint decision.

Claim: *If a union has monopoly control over a labor market, it has price-setting power with respect to wages.*

What Will the Union Do with Its Market Power?

The monopolist input seller can choose what it wishes to do with its monopoly power, just as on the output side. On the output side, we did not explore alternatives to profit maximization, but in the present instance, it makes sense to acknowledge that the union may wish to pursue goals other than "profit" maximization.[13] In particular, we might imagine three competing goals.

Goal 1: The union wishes to maximize the number of workers hired.

Goal 2: The union wishes to set a wage rate to maximize wage receipts of its members.

Goal 3: The union wishes to maximize the net dollar benefits to its members.

We can describe how the union might achieve each of these outcomes, using Figure 18.13.

If the union wishes to maximize the number of workers hired (Goal 1), it should choose the lowest possible wage rate. This occurs at the point where $S_{labor} = D_{labor}$, point **t** in Figure 18.13. The union will set the union wage rate at $12 per hour, where 20 units of labor are employed (this could be 20,000 worker hours if the horizontal axis is metered in thousands of worker hours, but to simplify the discussion, imagine that each unit is an hour). If, instead, the union considers Goal 2 to be more appropriate, it would set a higher wage rate and accept that fewer union jobs would result. In Figure 18.13, this occurs when the marginal (wage) revenue generated by an additional worker is zero. The MR_{labor} curve describes how incremental wage revenues vary as the number of worker hours varies. $MR_{labor} = 0$ when there are 16 hours of labor (at **z**), and the corresponding wage rate is $\$16 = D_{labor}(16)$ (at **r**). Those who are lucky enough to have the union jobs benefit from this policy (since they receive $4 more per hour than they would have under the $12 wage solution provided by a union following Goal 1). The cost of this policy to union workers is, of course, that not as many union workers are able to find union jobs at this higher wage rate.

If the union considers Goal 3 to be more appropriate, it would bargain for an even higher wage and, consequently, accept that even fewer union jobs would result than with Goal 2. Remember that the supply of labor curve represents the opportunity cost schedule for workers. Workers would be willing to supply labor along this curve. The area under the supply curve up to a given level of labor is the resource cost of that much labor. Since we assume union workers are paid a common wage rate, some workers obtain excess

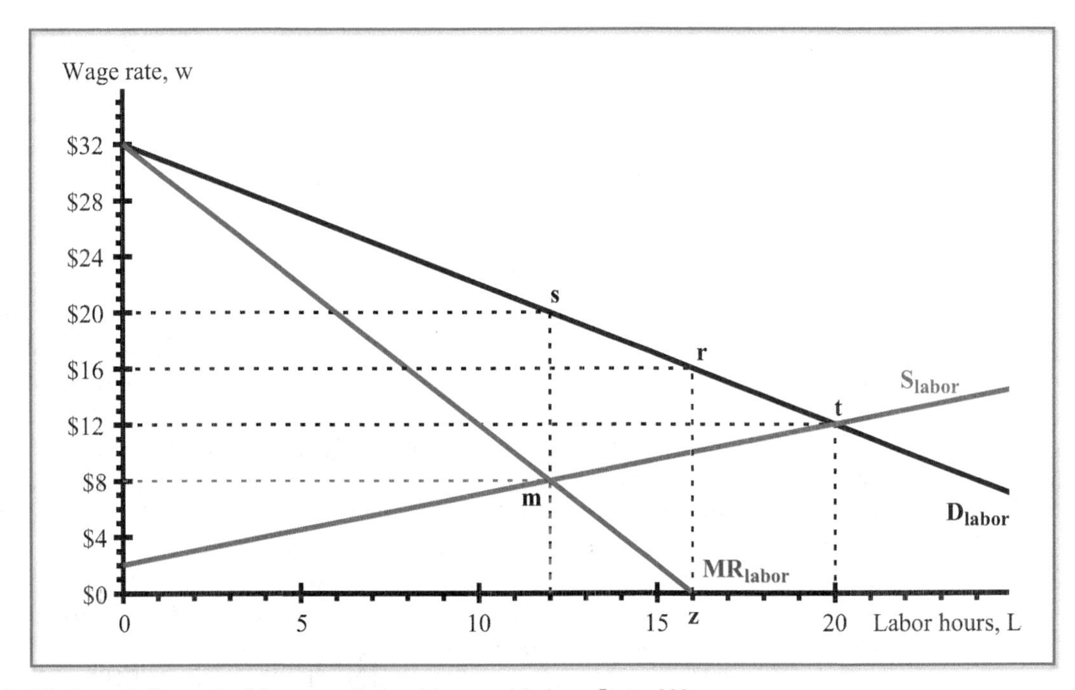

FIGURE 18.13 Input Supply Monopolist—How a Union Sets Wages

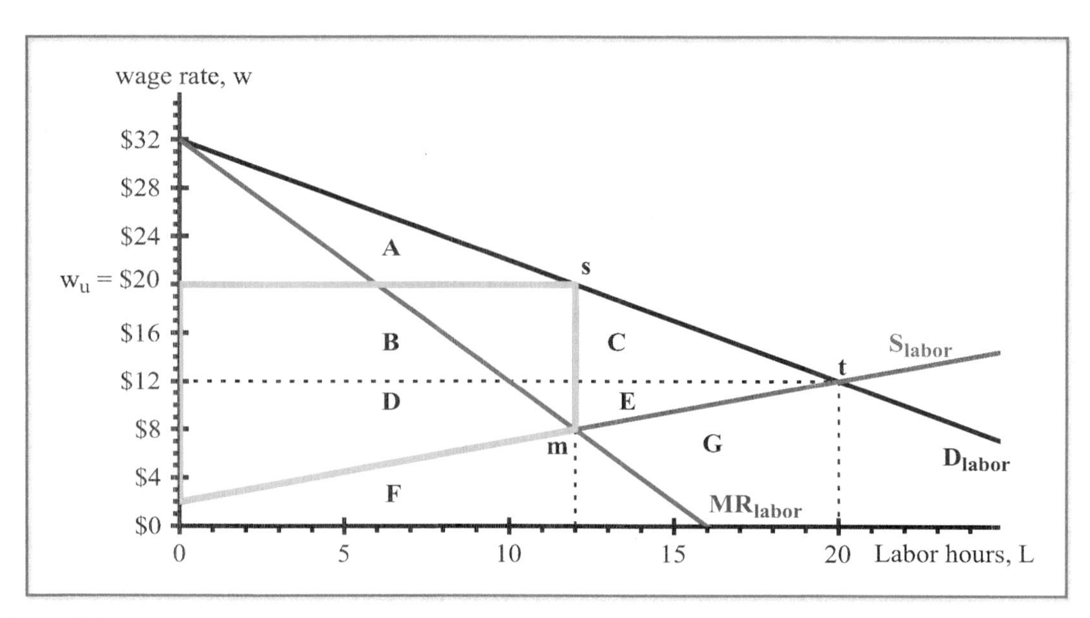

FIGURE 18.14 Maximizing Net Benefits to Union Members

benefits because the labor supply curve is upward sloping. The excess of benefit (wage received) over resource cost (the wage the worker would have been willing to accept) is the net dollar benefit to workers hired at any given wage rate. (This is strictly analogous to a profit-maximizing firm wishing to choose output so as to maximize the excess of benefit over cost of production.) Suppose that the union wishes to set the wage rate so as to maximize this net benefit. It pays for the union to set a wage so that the marginal wage receipts received by using an incremental amount of labor equals the marginal cost of that incremental labor. This occurs where $MR_{labor} = S_{labor}$ (at point **m**) because, as we argued earlier, S_{labor} represents the opportunity cost schedule of union workers. The wage rate associated with this output level is the height of labor demand at this output level, $w_u = \$20 = D_{labor}(12)$ (at **s**). The cost of this policy to union workers is that there is less work available for union workers under this union contract than under the other two contracts (that were based on points **t** and **r**).

Figure 18.14 provides a second view of Goal 3, net benefit maximization. The revenue-maximizing bundle and (L, w) dashed markers have been removed so we can more readily see the trade-offs inherent in net benefit maximization. The gross benefits (wage receipts) of striking a union bargain at **m** and **s** for a wage rate of w_u is area **B** + **D** + **F**, but the real resource cost of supplying this labor is area **F**. Therefore, the net benefit is **B** + **D**, an area that has been traced out in light green.[14] This is larger than any other wage choice (for the same reason that MR = MC is the profit-maximizing level of output, as shown in Chapter 15).

A Union's Choices Can Affect Nonunion Workers

The union's wage choice can affect nonunion workers as well as union workers. The easiest way to show this is to consider a simple model in which total labor supply is fixed, $S_{labor} = 100$. There are two types of workers, union workers and nonunion workers. Suppose that $D_u(w_u)$ represents demand for union workers and that $D_n(w_n)$ represents demand for nonunion workers. Since labor supply is fixed at 100, the employment in each sector can be conceptualized as a percentage of the workforce employed in a given sector. This depends, of course, on the wage rate in each sector. In the absence of any wage discrepancy between sectors (so $w_u = w_n = w$), the market clearing competitive wage rate, w*, will simply be at the point where $D_{total} = D_u(w^*) + D_n(w^*) = S_{labor}$. Suppose that this occurs at a wage rate of $10 per hour. This is seen as point **C** = (100, $10) in Figure 18.15. Employment is distributed among union and nonunion jobs at points **A** = (D_u($10), $10) and **B** = ($D_n$($10), $10), where market clearing implies that $D_u(\$10) + D_n(\$10) = 100$.

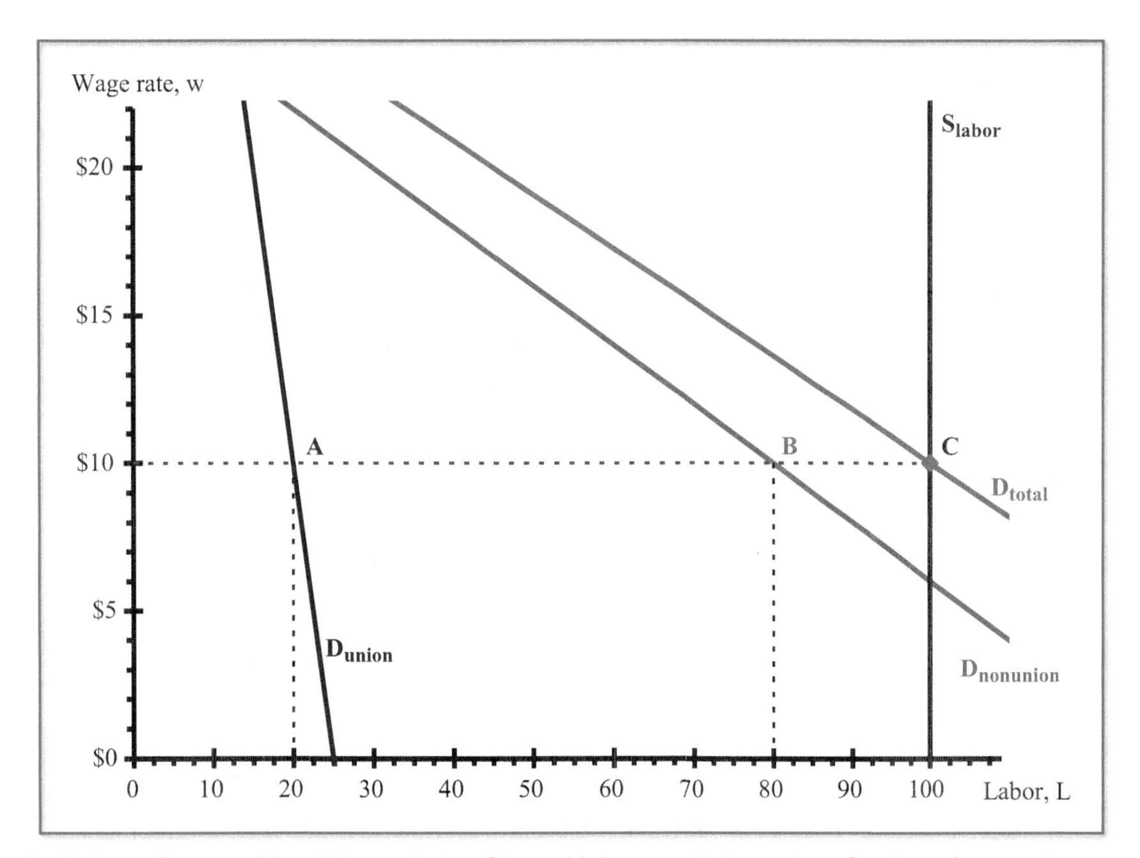

FIGURE 18.15 The Competitive Wage Rate, Given Union and Nonunion Sectors (assuming no wage disparity between sectors)

The size of D_u and D_n depends on how important union shops are in the total mix of labor demand. As shown in Figure 18.15, in the absence of wage differences, 20% of the jobs are union jobs, and 80% are nonunion at this common wage rate.

If the union settles on a wage contract for more than the competitive wage, then some of the union workers who would have been employed in union jobs at the common wage will have to move from a union shop to a nonunion shop. Since total labor supply is (assumed to be) fixed, any worker who does not work in the union sector will find employment in the nonunion sector. This increase in nonunion labor supply will tend to depress wages in the nonunion sector. The extent to which nonunion wages are depressed depends on the elasticity of demand for labor in the nonunion sector and on how large the union sector is, relative to the nonunion sector. Three scenarios are shown in Figure 18.16 to explore this interdependence. Before examining these issues, it is worthwhile to understand the general effects of a union wage increase. The following descriptions are appropriate for Figures 18.16A–18.16C, since each is based on an increase in union wage from $10 to $20. Union employment falls as a result of the wage increase. These workers must move to the nonunion sector (since labor supply is assumed fixed), so nonunion employment must increase. This increase in supply of nonunion laborers can only be accommodated by dropping the nonunion wage rate (since the demand for nonunion labor is downward sloping). In terms of Figures 18.16A–18.16C, the increase in union wage from $10 to $20 causes union employment to fall from **A** to **U** and nonunion employment to increase from **B** to **N**.

> **Claim:** *The union wage increase (**UD**) causes a decline in union employment (**DA**) that equals the increase in nonunion employment (**FN**) and a decline in nonunion wages (**BF**).*

As noted earlier, the size of these effects (**DA** = **FN** and **BF**) depends on labor demand elasticity and union participation rates.

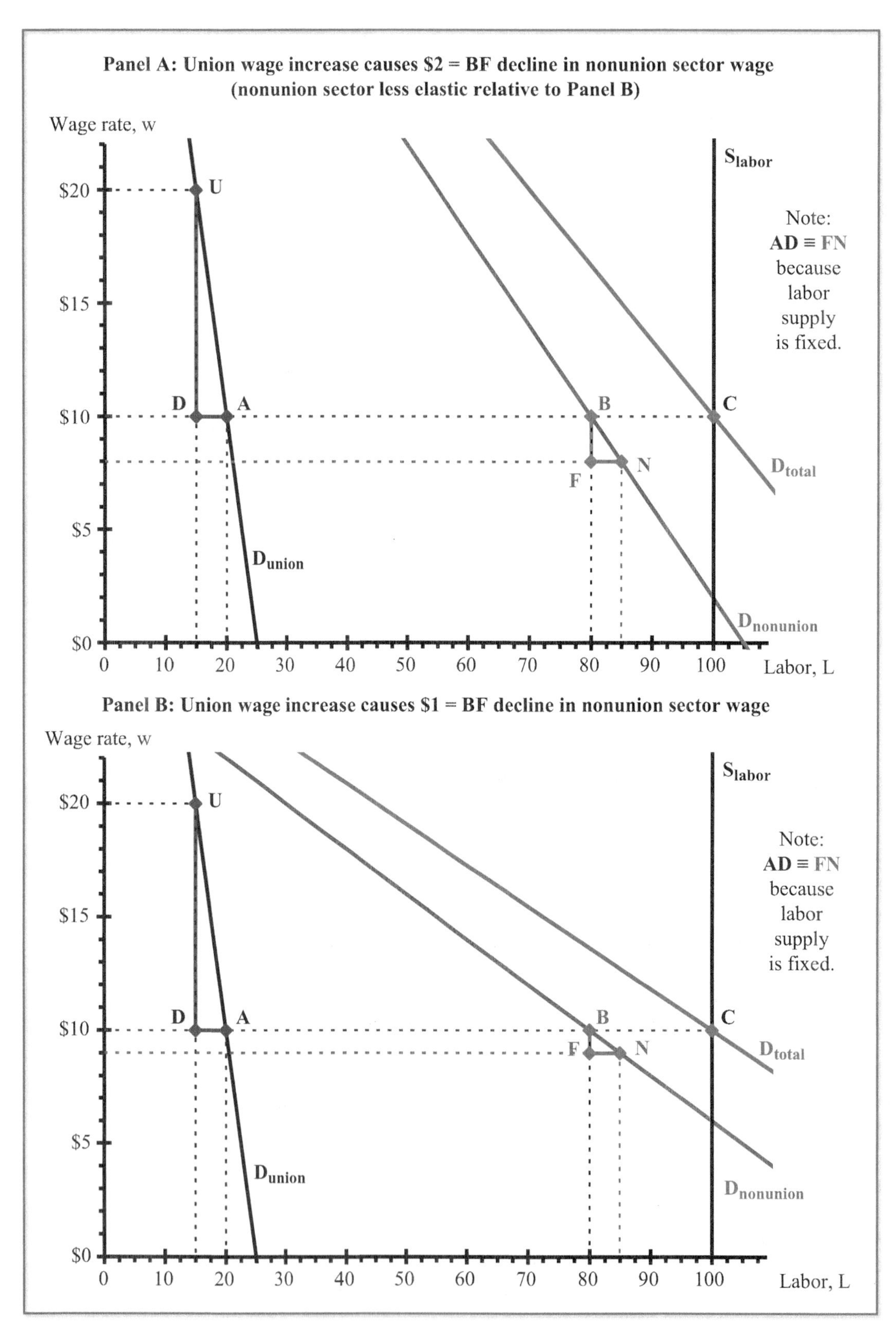

FIGURE 18.16 The Effect of Union Wages on Union and Nonunion Sectors

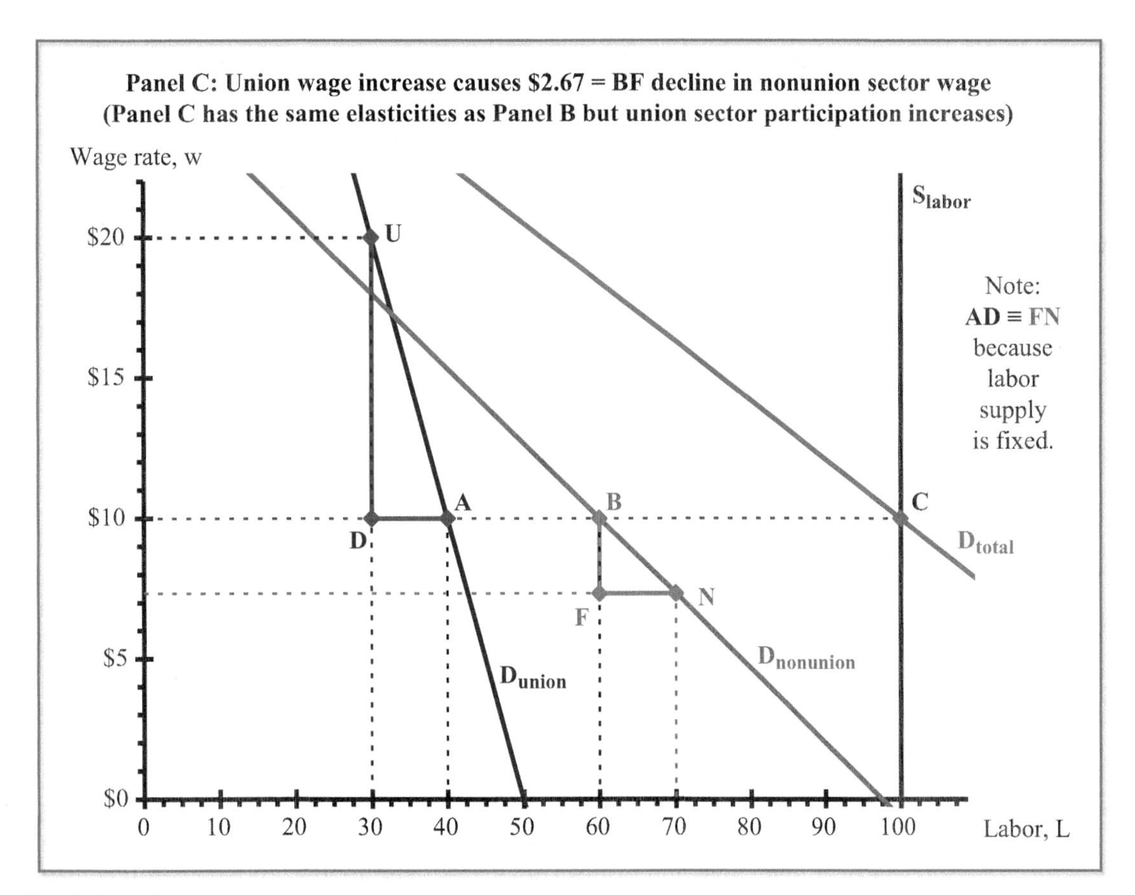

FIGURE 18.16 Continued

Figure 18.16B starts with the sector demands from Figure 18.15 but assumes that the union decides to set a union wage of $20, twice the competitive level. As noted earlier, labor supply has been fixed at 100, so labor quantities can be viewed as percentages. Given the union labor demand shown in Figures 18.16A and 18.16B, the increase in union wages causes a decline in union employment of 5% (from 20 to 15). This means that nonunion employment must increase by 5% (from 80 to 85). In Figures 18.16A and 18.16B, this shift in sectoral employment is seen by **DA** = **FN** = 5. The change in nonunion wage rate that supports this increase in nonunion labor supply depends on the elasticity of nonunion demand for labor. The more elastic is nonunion demand, the smaller is the loss in wages in the nonunion sector. Figure 18.16A depicts a less elastic nonunion labor demand and, consequently, a larger nonunion wage decline (of $2 rather than $1).

The other factor determining the magnitude of the nonunion wage change is the size of the union versus nonunion sectors. The appropriate comparison is between Figures 18.16B and 18.16C, which maintain the elasticities of demand in both sectors but double the initial union participation depicted by bundle A from 20 to 40. Given twice as many union jobs at any wage rate, there will be twice the size of decline in union jobs, due to a doubling of the union wage rate. (Put another way, **AD** is 10 in Figure 18.16C, rather than 5 in Figure 18.16B.) This means that final employment in the union sector will be 30 and in the nonunion sector will be 70. The cost of this increase in nonunion labor supply on nonunion wages is that the wage decrease is $2.67, rather than $1 (given constant elasticities across Figures 18.16B and 18.16C). Both results make solid economic sense: *The flight from the union sector to the nonunion sector from a given union wage increase will have a greater impact on nonunion wages: (1) the less elastic is nonunion labor demand, and (2) the larger is the size of the flight from the union sector to the nonunion sector caused by that wage increase.*

18.3B Monopsony: Monopoly on the Buyer Side of a Market

Prerequisite: Section 18.3A

When buyers are "large," they can use their buying power to extract special concessions from the economic agents who sell them goods. The most extreme example of such buying power is when there is one buyer of the good. Such a market is called a **monopsony** market. Actual monopsony markets are rare, but markets with monopsony power are more common. Buyers have **monopsony power** if they have the ability to affect the price of a good via their purchase decisions.

monopsony: A monopsony is a market that has only one buyer.

monopsony power: Buyers have monopsony power if they have the ability to affect the price of a good via their purchase decisions.

Examples of Monopsony Power

A classic example of a monopsony market is the market for weapons systems. Even in an open market, there are not a lot of potential buyers for expensive weapons systems, so individual purchasers have monopsony power. In addition, U.S. manufacturers are restricted by federal law from selling weapons systems to anyone but the federal government.[15] As a result, the government acts as a legally sanctioned monopsonist in this market. As noted earlier, examples of monopsony in consumer goods markets are rare because the end-users are individual consumers, and consumers by their very nature are "small," relative to the market. Individual consumers have no ability to affect prices.

The federal government has monopsony power in purchases of consumer goods such as prescription drugs. Similarly, state and local governments can exert monopsony power over the purchase of some consumer goods. The Pennsylvania Liquor Control Board (PLCB), for example, is one of the largest single buyers of wine and spirits in the United States. This provides the PLCB with significant monopsony power in its interactions with wine and spirits producers. Pricing concessions are a standard result of this power.[16]

Local municipal authorities sometimes exert monopsony power in consumer markets. In the borough of Carlisle, Pennsylvania, for example, property owners are required to maintain the sidewalks in front of their properties by fixing cracks and potential hazards posed by uneven sidewalks and curbs. Sidewalks in need of repair are marked in the early spring each year by borough employees. If the property owner does not address the problem by a certain date, it is fixed by a masonry contractor hired by the borough. The borough then bills the individual property owner for the services performed. Interestingly, if an individual property owner privately hires the same contractor to perform the service, the owner is likely to be charged a *higher* price for the same service. The borough is able to extract preferable rates due to its monopsony power.

Walmart provides a private market example of monopsony power. This retailer has such reach and purchasing power that it has been able to achieve substantial discounts in the goods it purchases.[17] Walmart does not purchase goods to consume; it purchases goods to turn around and sell to consumers. Put in terms of the production model developed in Part 3 of the text, Walmart purchases goods from manufacturers as inputs in the production process and produces output by selling those goods to consumers at retail.

If a single buyer dominates a labor market, then the labor market is monopsonistically controlled. A factory or mine that is the sole employer in a town takes advantage of its monopsony power by setting wages so that profits are maximized. Another classic labor market example involves major league baseball. Prior to 1975, major league baseball operated under a *reserve clause* that effectively allowed team owners to control the destiny of players who had been drafted by a team for life. If a player had been under contract with a team, that player could not market himself to other teams, even though his contract had expired; he could not act as a "free agent." As a result, owners had monopsony control in negotiating new contracts with players. The result of such monopsony power is lower wage rates than would occur under competitive conditions.[18]

The Monopsonist's Marginal Expenditure Function

The analysis of monopsony is a mirror image of the monopoly analysis of Chapter 15. The only difference is that now the "marginal" curve is marginal to supply, rather than demand, because a monopsonist purchaser affects the price of the good being purchased by the purchase decision. This is true whether the good is a factor of production or an output. If supply is upward sloping, then more can be purchased only by increasing the market price for the good. The marginal expenditure, therefore, is greater than the price paid for the product. The **marginal expenditure, ME(x)**, is the incremental expenditure required to purchase a bit more x. Let TE(x) denote the total expenditure required to purchase x units of a good; $TE(x) = x \cdot P_s(x)$, where $P_s(x)$ is the inverse supply of x (i.e., the height of the supply curve for the *x*th unit purchased). Given this, marginal expenditure is:

marginal expenditure, ME(x): The marginal expenditure is the incremental expenditure required to purchase a bit more x.

$$ME(x) = \Delta TE/\Delta x = (P_s(x_1) \cdot x_1 - P_s(x_0) \cdot x_0)/(x_1 - x_0). \quad \textbf{(18.8)}$$

If the buyer is a price taker, then $P_s(x_0) = P_s(x_1) = P$, and ME = P (just as if sellers are price takers, then P = MR, a point that was noted at length in Section 13.1). For discrete changes in x, this is an estimate (just as with estimated marginal revenue in Equation 12.9). More generally, it is simply the slope of the total expenditure hill.

Since we are analyzing monopsony in the context of factor markets, the discussion that follows is based on a labor market monopsony. The same analysis would apply to other factor markets or to output markets that are monopsonistic.

Just as on the revenue side, if the supply curve is linear, then the marginal expenditure schedule has a straightforward geometric interpretation. Section 12.2 laid out in detail the relation between inverse demand and marginal revenue, given linear demand. Since the only difference is the sign of the slope, there is no need to provide the same level of detail here. The conclusions are straightforward and strictly analogous to those laid out in Chapter 12.

A monopsonistic purchaser of labor understands that as more labor is purchased, the price of labor is bid up; the monopsonist faces an upward-sloping labor supply curve. Given linear labor supply, we can write this in slope-intercept form as:

$$w = c + d \cdot L. \quad \textbf{(18.9a)}$$

This inverse labor supply equation is strictly analogous to the linear inverse demand curve in Equation 12.7a. Just as the (inverse) demand curve can be conceptualized as an average revenue curve (since it describes price as a function of quantity), so can the (inverse) labor supply curve be conceptualized as an average expenditure curve (since it describes what wage rates support various levels of labor employment). As noted earlier, marginal revenue based on linear demand has the same intercept and twice the slope, according to Equation 12.11. The same is true in this instance:

$$ME(L) = c + 2 \cdot d \cdot L. \quad \textbf{(18.9b)}$$

Marginal expenditure has the same intercept and twice the slope as the supply schedule. The change in sign (of the slope) causes marginal expenditure to be above supply, while marginal revenue is below demand.

Figure 18.17 shows the geometry behind Equations 18.9a and 18.9b. Figure 18.17A lays out the change in expenditure, given an increase in labor from 6 to 7. If the firm wants to employ L_0 units of labor, it can do so for a wage rate of w_0 per unit, according to the S_{labor} curve. Total expenditure on labor is $w_0 \cdot L_0$ (or area **B**). However, if the firm wishes to employ $L_1 > L_0$ units of labor, it must pay a higher wage of w_1 to entice this many workers to work. Total expenditure in this instance is $w_1 \cdot L_1$ (or area **A** + **B** + **C**). Not only does incremental labor cost the wages paid on that incremental labor ($w \cdot \Delta L$, or area **C**), but the monopsonist must also pay the higher wage to laborers who would have worked at the lower wage ($\Delta w \cdot L$, or area **A**). Just as we subtracted area **A** from area **C** to determine marginal revenue in Figure 12.7A, so we must add area **A** to area **C** to determine marginal expenditure in Figure 18.17A. To show the marginal expenditure on ΔL units as the height of a ΔL-wide rectangle, we must stack an area **A′** = area **A** on top of the ΔL-wide area **C** rectangle in Figure 18.17A. Marginal expenditure is above the labor supply curve facing the monopsonist. The marginal expenditure on labor (using Equation 18.8) is therefore represented for the linear supply case, using areas in Figure 18.17A:

$$\begin{aligned} ME(L) &= (w_1 \cdot L_1 - w_0 \cdot L_0)/(L_1 - L_0) = (\mathbf{A} + \mathbf{B} + \mathbf{C} - \mathbf{B})/\Delta L \\ &= (\mathbf{A} + \mathbf{C})/\Delta L = (\mathbf{A'} + \mathbf{C})/\Delta L. \end{aligned} \quad \textbf{(18.9c)}$$

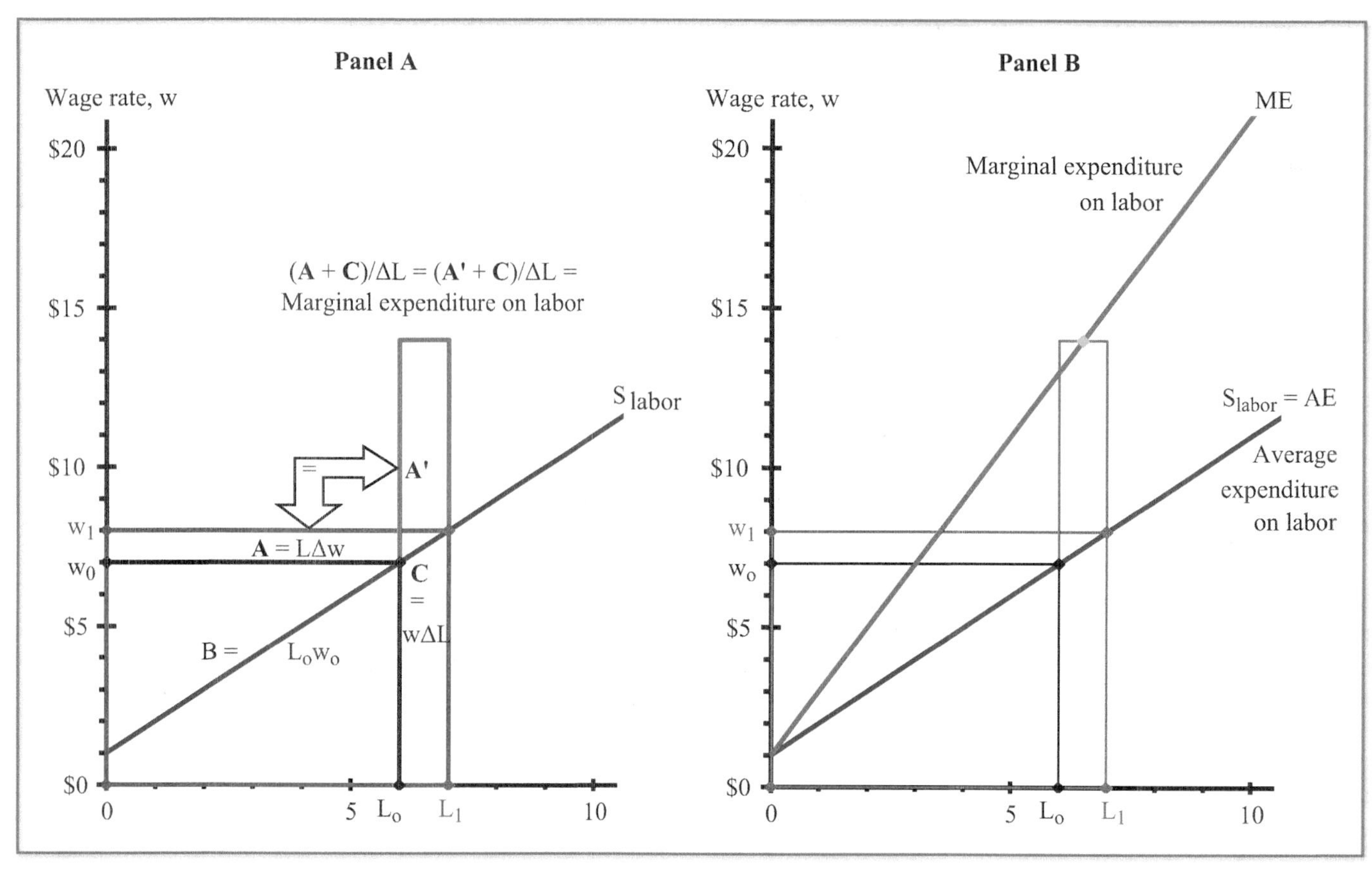

FIGURE 18.17 The Marginal Expenditure Faced by a Monopsonist

Equation 18.9c is a geometric interpretation of Equation 18.9b. Figure 18.17B simply provides the green marginal expenditure schedule based on this analysis. With this groundwork, answer the following questions (these are especially easy to answer if you have skimmed Section 12.2):

Q17a. If $S_{labor} = c + d \cdot L$, what are c and d?

Q17b. What is the height of **A′** + **C**?

Q17c. If ME(L) is the marginal expenditure schedule, then what level of labor L is associated with **A′** + **C**?

Q17d. What is the equation for ME(L) in this instance, and what is ME(6)?*

The Monopsonist's Profit-Maximizing Purchase Decision

The universal rule for profit maximization, MR = MC, applies to the monopsonist wishing to choose the optimal input mix. As a monopsonistic purchaser of labor, the monopsonist realizes that it can only purchase more labor by offering a higher price of labor. This higher price means that marginal expenditure on a unit of labor is more than the wage rate for that unit of labor. As we argued earlier, the marginal expenditure on labor exceeds the wage rate required to support a given level of hiring (this wage rate can be read off of the labor supply schedule). Marginal factor cost for the monopsonist is the marginal expenditure schedule, and marginal revenue is marginal revenue product (or the labor

***Q17 answer:** The intercept is c = 1 (because this is where the blue labor supply curve intersects the w axis). Since $w_0 = \$7$ when $L_0 = 6$, the slope of the labor supply function is d = 1. The height of **A′** + **C** = $\$1 \cdot 6 + \$7 \cdot 1 = \$14$. This is the marginal expenditure associated with the midpoint of L_0 and L_1's worth of labor, ME(6.5) = \$14. Given c and d, Equation 18.9b suggests that $ME(L) = 1 + 2 \cdot L$. ME(6) = \$13. (Students often assume that the height of **A′** + **C** is the marginal expenditure of the lower amount of labor. We have just seen that this is not true. The rationale for this being the midpoint is discussed in Section 12.2.)

demand schedule, as discussed in Section 18.2). The monopsonist's profit-maximizing rule described by Equation 18.4 becomes:

$$MRP(F) = MFC(F) = ME(F). \quad \textbf{(18.10)}$$

This leads to the profit-maximizing monopsony solution depicted in Figure 18.18. Focus initially on Figure 18.18A. To maximize profits, the monopsonist restricts labor purchases to point **s**, where $ME(L) = D_{labor}$, consistent with Equation 18.10. If we denote this amount of labor L*, then we obtain the market clearing monopsony wage rate, w_m, by noting the height of the labor supply function at L* (point **m**); $S_{labor}(w_m) = L^*$. Given the curves depicted, this occurs at a market clearing monopsony wage rate of $w_m = \$9.50$.

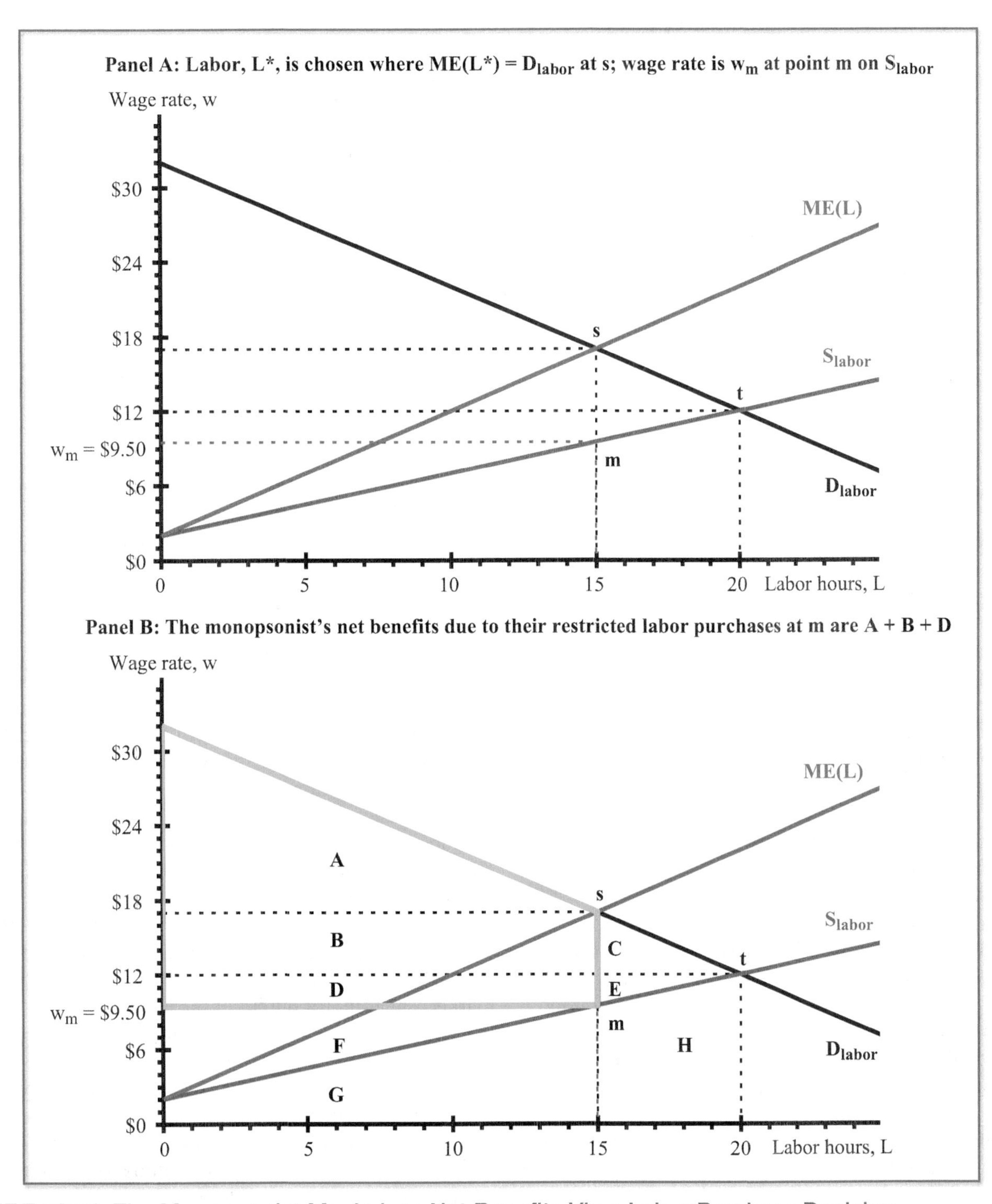

FIGURE 18.18 The Monopsonist Maximizes Net Benefits Via a Labor Purchase Decision

Q18. If $S_{labor} = c + d \cdot L$, what are c and d in Figure 18.18A?*

Figure 18.18B provides a second view of the monopsonist's profit-maximizing decision. The gross benefit of hiring L workers is the area under the MRP (demand for labor) schedule, but cost is $w \cdot L$. The net benefit is the area above the wage but below the demand curve. The monopsonist chooses to purchase at **m** and **s** for a wage rate of w_m. The gross benefit to the monopsonistic buyer is area **A** + **B** + **D** + **F** + **G**, but the cost of purchasing this labor is area **F** + **G**, so the net benefit is **A** + **B** + **D**, an area that has been outlined in light green. This is the maximum net benefit available to the monopsonist because ME = MRP.

Figures 18.18B and 18.14 offer interesting counterpoints to one another. Both examine the net benefit to the holder of market power in the labor market. The difference is who has the power. When sellers of labor services have pricing power, they can take advantage of this to *raise* the wage rate to increase net benefits to the sellers of those services (union members). When buyers of labor services have pricing power, they can take advantage of this to *lower* the wage rate to increase net benefits to the buyer of those services (the firm). The former produces an outcome that is higher than the competitive wage rate; the latter produces an outcome that is lower than the competitive wage rate. Both outcomes reduce labor employment to a level below the competitive level of employment (employment is at **m** and **s**, rather than at **t** in both diagrams). To put this in terms of the welfare discussion in Chapter 16, both markets create a deadweight loss of areas **C** + **E**, but they do so with very different distributional implications. Those distributional implications form the basis for the labor supply and labor demand decisions discussed previously.

***Q18 answer:** The w intercept is c = 2, and the slope is d = 10/20 = 0.5. You can verify these values by noting that S($9.50) = 15, using the slope-intercept version of the labor supply function: $w = c + d \cdot L = 2 + 0.5 \cdot 15$.

Summary of Section 18.3

When a factor market is imperfectly competitive, the factor will not be used up to the point where marginal valuation equals marginal cost, as required by economic efficiency. Marginal valuation in this context is the height of the factor demand curve. In Section 18.2, factor demand is shown to be the marginal revenue product of the factor of production. Marginal cost is the opportunity cost of the factor of production. This is the height of the supply curve for the factor of production. Imperfectly competitive factor markets can be imperfectly competitive on both the buyer and seller sides of the market interface.

When an input is sold by a single seller, there is an input market monopoly. The seller is able to exercise its monopoly power by doing the same thing that a monopolist on the output side does: The monopolist raises price and lowers production as a result. We expect most input market monopolists to maximize profits, but we can imagine other goals if the factor market in which the seller monopoly exists is a labor market.

Monopoly power in the provision of labor services can be a result of a labor union acting as the sole bargaining agent in labor market negotiations. If a union has monopoly control over a specific labor market, it can use that market power to pursue a variety of goals, subject to the constraint imposed by the demand for labor in that market. Three goals are examined: employment maximization, gross wage receipt maximization, and net wage receipt maximization. One way to describe how a union exercises its monopoly power is by the wage/employment level package the union bargains to attain. The most expansive level of union employment is, of course, also the one with the lowest wage rate. The least expansive level of union employment is the one with the highest wage rate; this is the outcome that results if the union's goal is net wage receipt maximization. In this instance, the input market monopolist acts in a symmetric fashion to an output market monopolist. This input market monopolist sets the wage/employment level at the point where the incremental wage receipts it can attain for members by lowering wage and increasing employment level just equals the opportunity cost to the marginal union member. This is the input market analog to a profit-maximizing monopolist in the output market. Quantity (of output or the factor) is restricted, and the price (of the output or the factor) is higher under this market than under competition.

When unions bargain for higher wages, they affect employment in their sector, but they also affect employment conditions in the nonunion sector as well. Since higher wages reduce demand for union labor, unemployed union workers must switch to the nonunion sector to gain employment. This increases nonunion labor supply and thereby reduces wages in the nonunion sector.

The reverse side of the coin is market power on the buyer side of the market. This situation does not typically occur with consumer goods because, almost by definition, consumers are too numerous, and their purchases are too insignificant individually to affect the market price of the product. Factors of production, by contrast, may well be sold to buyers who are large enough to affect the market price of the factor. Large purchasers can bargain for better deals, and in doing so, the purchasers are employing monopsony power. When a single purchaser of the product exists, the market is a monopsony. Monopsonistic purchasers of inputs understand that their actions drive the price of the input. Greater quantities of a factor of production typically can only be obtained by paying a higher price for the factor; factor supply is upward sloping. In this instance, the marginal expenditure exceeds the price of the factor. Marginal expenditure is marginal to the factor supply curve facing a monopsonist, just as marginal revenue is marginal to the demand curve facing a monopolist. Profits are maximized when the monopsonist chooses that factor price and factor employment level for which the marginal expenditure on the factor equals the marginal revenue product of the factor. Quantity of the factor is restricted to keep the factor price below the competitive level.

Review Questions

Define the following terms:

Section 18.1

individual labor supply

individual leisure demand

overtime pay

Section 18.2

marginal revenue product of factor F, MRP(F)

marginal factor cost of factor F, MFC(F)

derived demand for a factor of production

Section 18.3

labor union

monopsony

monopsony power

marginal expenditure function

Provide short answers to the following:

Sections 18.1A–18.1C

a. What can we say about the magnitude of the sum: Labor supply + Leisure demand?
b. What is the price of leisure?
c. If leisure and other goods are substitutes, then an increase in wage rate causes what change in labor supply?
d. If leisure and other goods are independent, then an increase in wage rate causes what change in labor supply?
e. If leisure and other goods are complements, then an increase in wage rate causes what change in labor supply?
f. If the individual's labor supply function is backward bending, does this mean that higher wages eventually lead to increased leisure or decreased leisure?
g. Suppose that the firm's goal is to increase the amount of labor that individuals are willing to supply to the firm. Would a firm that previously only offered a flat pay of w per hour be better served by increasing the overall wage rate to $1.5 \cdot w$ or by maintaining nonovertime pay at w and instituting a policy of paying $1.5 \cdot w$ for overtime?

Section 18.1D

a. What must be true about the substitution and income effect of a wage increase if labor supply increases as a result of this wage change?
b. What must be true about the substitution and income effect of a wage increase if labor supply does not change as a result of this wage change?
c. What must be true about the substitution and income effect of a wage increase if labor supply decreases as a result of this wage change?
d. Why do overtime wages have an unambiguous effect on labor supply as a first approximation (using substitution and income effect analysis)?

Section 18.2

a. How is the marginal revenue product of a factor of production related to the marginal physical product of that factor?
b. Why is the demand for a factor of production described as a "derived" demand?
c. Is the demand for a factor of production typically more elastic in the short run or the long run?
d. Why must care be taken when determining the demand for a factor of production by an industry?

Section 18.3

a. Why might a union have multiple competing goals? What three goals were delineated in Section 18.3?
b. Why might a union's choices affect nonunion workers?
c. What is the likely effect on nonunion wages of an increase in union wages?
d. What is the monopsonist's marginal expenditure function analogous to in the monopoly model?

Check your answers to the *short-answer* exercises in the Answers Appendix at the end of the book.

Notes

1. We also rarely see machines form unions (or at least we do not think that they have).

2. For simplicity, we have assumed that individuals are paid by the hour only for those hours worked. They are not paid wages for vacation days, for example. They also have no nonwage income. We could easily modify the analysis to incorporate more complex payment schemes, but such modifications would not appreciably change the results obtained from our more streamlined model.

3. Had s = 0 been chosen instead, the tangency would have been crowded along the far right side of the diagram. By adjusting the starting value for the horizontal axis, we are able to examine only the relevant range of values for leisure. Starting at s = 68 means that we believe that labor supply per week is likely to be less than 100 hours; this seems like a reasonable assumption, and it allows slope to be easily calculated.

4. The fixed market basket in this instance is the full-time bundle **A**.

5. In terms of the bundles in Figures 18.8A–18.8C, the income effect is **ST**, while the approximation of the income effect is **VT**.

6. This is formally described by Equation 10.4a.

7. The geometry is more important here than the algebra that got us to the geometry. Nonetheless, it is worth noting that this is the short-run Cobb-Douglas production function $Q(L) = 10 \cdot L^{0.5}$. The marginal product of labor in this instance is $MP(L) = 5/L^{0.5}$, according to Equations 9.8a and 9.8b.

8. You may have seen $P \cdot MP(F)$ called the *value of the marginal product of factor F* in your introductory microeconomics text. We do not have a separate term for this concept but note that when the output market is competitive, this is simply the marginal revenue product of factor F.

9. The competitive firm's supply curve derived in Chapter 13 takes a price orientation, while MC takes a quantity orientation. In the present context, the labor demand curve takes an input price (wage) orientation, while the MRP(L) curve takes a quantity (of labor) orientation. In actuality, MRP is a derived *inverse* demand because it shows marginal value of labor as a function of quantity of labor.

10. As with the production function, the geometry is more important than the algebra of the demand curve. Nonetheless, the demand curve in this instance is $Q(P) = 2{,}000 \cdot P^{-2}$. The Excel file for Figure 18.10 allows you to vary the elasticity, but it adjusts the number 2,000 so that the point (Q, P) = (20, \$10) remains on the demand curve. We should also note that this demand curve is drawn with L as the horizontal axis. This is only indirectly the case because additional L produces additional output, according to the production function noted earlier. This is why the inverse demand function, P(Q), and marginal revenue function, MR(Q), are noted as composite functions (of Q(L) in Figure 18.10).

11. Given the production function noted in endnote 6, $Q(L) = 10 \cdot L^{0.5}$, we see that industry demand is $N \cdot Q(L_i)$, where N is the number of firms in the industry. Given that N = 100 and industry demand for labor is 711.1 at **C**, according to the factor information in Figure 18.12B, $Q_c = N \cdot Q(L_i) = 100 \cdot ((10 \cdot (711.1/100)^{0.5})) = 2{,}667$.

12. Buyer power can also occur in output markets. The U.S. government is the sole purchaser of many goods used by the U.S. Department of Defense, for example. Although such purchases are (obviously) important, they are sufficiently uncommon that a separate analysis of monopsony markets is not provided in Chapter 15. The monopsony analysis in Section 18.3B applies equally well to output markets. Defense is also a classic example of a public good. Section 22.2 examines public goods.

13. This is not because firms *must* maximize profits. We have simply assumed that this is the most likely goal of firms. Industrial organization and strategy classes explore this goal and alternatives to this goal. We also touch upon this topic in Section 21.6.

14. If you have read Chapter 16, you will note that this is the input market analog to the output market monopolist's producer surplus rectangle in Figure 16.8.

15. A number of statutes control sales. See, for example, the Arms Export Control Act of 1976 and the Export Administration Act of 1979.

16. These pricing concessions do not necessarily lead to lower prices in PLCB stores. Liquor and wine are subject to an 18% liquor tax, in addition to the Pennsylvania sales tax. Also, PLCB stores are the only source for retail wine and liquor in the state. The high liquor tax rate, together with the state-imposed monopoly on sales of liquor, are the reasons why, despite PLCB's purchasing power, its prices are substantially higher than prices for the same products in surrounding states. We examined this market in another context in Section 7.5. To learn more about PLCB policies and prices, go to the wine and liquor part of the PLCB website: http://www.lcb.state.pa.us/Retail/Direct_Shippers.asp.

17. The Harvard Business School case "Wal-Mart Stories in 2003" by Pankaj Bhemawat, Ken Mark, and Stephen Bradley provides an extensive analysis of this topic.

18. See Gerald W. Scully, "Pay and Performance in Major League Baseball," *American Economic Review*, Vol. 64, No. 6 (December 1974), pp. 915–930.

Capital Markets

CHAPTER 19

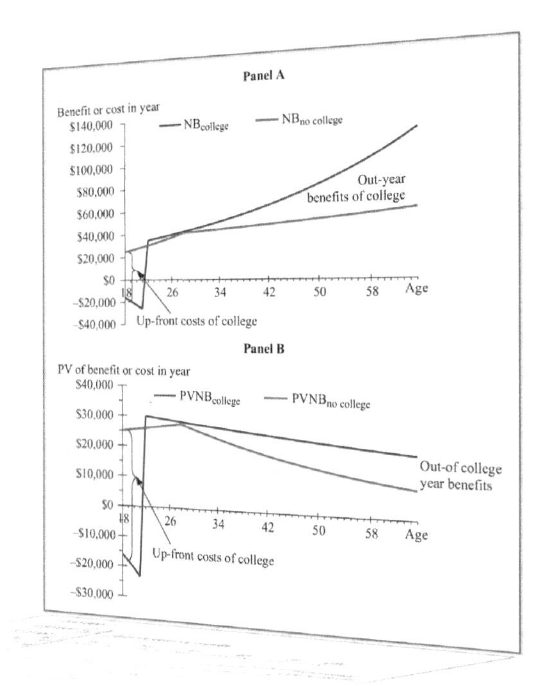

Chapter Outline

Capital takes on a number of meanings in economics. At one level, capital is simply a factor of production, but capital also describes the market for loanable funds. Loanable funds allow money to be exchanged across time periods for a price, and this price sets up the terms of trade across time. All capital investment decisions that firms consider, as well as many decisions that consumers must make, involve a comparison of costs and benefits occurring in many time periods. To analyze such decisions, we need to compare apples with apples. Present value allows such a comparison.

Chapter 19 comprises four sections. Section 19.1 examines capital market basics, including a discussion of present value. Since present value calculations are repetitive, Excel is a natural choice for present value analysis. As a result, Section 19.2 provides an introduction to doing repetitive calculations in Excel. Section 19.3 examines present value in the consumer context. Finally, Section 19.4 examines capital investment decisions. This discussion includes a comparison of the payback method, the net present value method, and the internal rate of return method for evaluating investments.

For those who wish to incorporate Excel more heavily into their course, this is a natural chapter to read early in the semester. If this chapter is put off until later in the semester, then some of the topics (and especially some of the endnotes) will be more transparent. Put another way, this chapter has been written in a layered fashion. If you read this chapter early in the semester, you may wish to simply skim the endnotes (or ignore them altogether), but if you read this chapter after having read most of the earlier chapters, you will be able to incorporate the insights of those chapters into your reading (via a more careful reading of the endnotes).

Section 19.1 Outline

19.1A The Basics of Present Value

19.1B What Discount Rate Should You Use?

19.1 Basics of Capital Markets

Prerequisite: Chapter 2

When economists talk about factors of production, they typically highlight two factors: capital and labor. Economists distinguish between capital and labor by noting that firms typically have more flexibility in their use of labor than in their use of capital. This long-run/short-run distinction is central to much of Parts 3 and 4 of the text. Most basically, capital is a factor of production. But the term *capital* is also used to denote a wide array of concepts within microeconomics. Capital goods are goods that are used to produce other goods. Buildings and machines are examples of capital goods. Firms often purchase capital goods by borrowing money from those who are willing to supply loanable funds. Much of the confusion that students have in understanding the market for loanable funds has to do with the nature of the market price of this product. The interest rate at which the supply of loanable funds equals the demand for loanable funds is the market price for exchanging money between time periods. Economists often call this rate of exchange the "*time value of money*."

Individuals supply loanable funds by putting money in the bank or by investing in securities markets; the supply of loanable funds comes, in large part, from consumers. At a given point in time, some individuals will wish to save, and some will wish to borrow.[1] The amount that individuals wish to save and borrow depends, of course, on how expensive it is to borrow (and how valuable it is to save). Put another way, it depends on the interest rate. Although it is theoretically possible that the supply of loanable funds is vertical or negatively sloped, most empirical estimates suggest that it has a positive slope.[2]

Demand for capital goods is basically a demand for a factor of production. It is therefore a derived demand based on what that factor of production can do to increase the firm's profitability.[3] Firms invest in projects for which the incremental benefits exceed the cost of capital. If a firm must go to external capital markets for financing, then the cost of capital is simply the interest rate the firm is charged for a loan. Firms face different costs of capital, depending on the risk of the project under consideration. This is why a firm requesting funds must often provide the lender with a prospectus showing the cost and benefit streams that the firm expects as a result of the project. Individual firms face a continuum of possible projects (at least theoretically), and they typically try to organize them in descending profitability (within a given risk class). We explicitly examine how firms evaluate possible projects according to such a profitability scale in Section 19.4.

19.1A The Basics of Present Value

When examining multiperiod models, we need a method of connecting time periods so that comparisons of costs and benefits occurring in different time periods can be consistent. Present value and future value are two methods used to describe dollars occurring in different time periods. These concepts are examined in the two-period context in Section 17.1, but they are discussed more generally in this chapter. Section 17.1 is not a prerequisite for this chapter.

The main equation used in present value calculations turns a dollar amount paid in year t into the present value equivalent of that amount. This calculation requires three pieces of information: the year, t; the amount paid in year t, X_t; and the (annual) **discount rate**, r. The **discount rate** is the rate at which consumers and firms are willing to trade dollars across time periods. This is also sometimes called the *rate of time preference* or the *time value of money* because it delineates the terms of trade between now and the future. The formula for present value (PV) is:

discount rate: The discount rate is the rate at which consumers and firms are willing to trade dollars across time periods.

$$PV(X_t) = X_t/(1 + r)^t. \quad \textbf{(19.1a)}$$

For example, \$100 received 4 years from today is worth \$82.27 if the discount rate is 5% per annum ($82.27 = 100/1.05^4$). One common modification on present value occurs when payments are not made annually. Suppose that there are n time periods during the year when payments are made (for example, quarterly payments would have n = 4 and monthly would have n = 12). The present value of a payment of X_k, paid k periods from now, given an annual discount rate of r, is:

$$PV(X_k) = X_k/(1 + r/n)^k. \quad \textbf{(19.1b)}$$

The quantity r/n is called the *periodic rate*. If we are considering quarterly payments and the discount rate is 5% per annum, the periodic rate is 1.25% per quarter. For example, $100 received 7 quarters from today is worth $91.67 if the discount rate is 5% per annum ($91.67 = 100/(1.0125)^7$).

A symmetric equation allows us to convert money paid in the current time period to an equivalent amount of money at some time in the future. If you wish to know how much X_0 paid now is worth t years from now, you simply replace the division sign by a multiplication sign in Equation 19.1a:

$$FV(X_0)_t = X_0 \cdot (1 + r)^t. \quad \textbf{(19.1c)}$$

Future value (FV) increases nonlinearly over time. This is the value of **compounding**. If X earns r in interest per dollar per period for t periods, the amount of interest earned exceeds $X \cdot r \cdot t$ because the principal increases each time an interest payment occurs (as long as the interest is allowed to accrue to the principal). This excess occurs because of compounding. A simple example should clarify this point. Suppose that you receive an unexpected $1,000 from your great aunt, and suppose that you decide to put the money in the bank, where it earns 5% per annum.[4] If you leave this alone for 20 years (and it continues to earn 5% per year), your ending balance will *not* be $\$2,000 = \$1,000 + \$1,000 \cdot 0.05 \cdot 20$, the amount that would occur if the future value changed linearly over time. Rather, it equals $\$2,652 = \$1,000 \cdot (1 + 0.05)^{20}$. You earn r in interest on a dollar of principal each year, but each year, the principal increases by the amount of interest from the previous year. In this example, you earn $50 in interest in the first year, but in the second year, you earn $52.50, rather than $50, because you earn interest on last year's interest as well as on the original principal. This continues in year three, and so on. The surprising result for most students is how powerful such compounding can be over a period of years ($2.50 does not sound like very much, but over time, these small amounts are compounded into a much larger whole).

compounding: If X earns r in interest per dollar per period for t periods, the amount of interest earned exceeds $X \cdot r \cdot t$ because the principal increases each time an interest payment occurs (as long as the interest is allowed to accrue to the principal). This excess occurs because of compounding.

Comparing APR and APY

Financial investments, as well as credit card companies, often quote two rates rather than one. Compounding is at the core of the difference between the two rates. The two rates are the *annual percentage rate* (APR) and the *annual percentage yield* (APY). These rates differ because the APR (also sometimes called the interest rate) does not take into account any intrayear compounding that may occur. The APY, by contrast, does take compounding into account. To determine how large the APY is, relative to the APR, we must know how often compounding occurs. Suppose that compounding occurs n times per year; then the formula for the APY is:

$$APY = (1 + r/n)^n - 1, \text{ where } r = APR. \quad \textbf{(19.2a)}$$

The specifications of the financial instrument under consideration determine how often compounding occurs (this is usually described in the fine print). Obviously, lenders are looking for a high rate, and borrowers are looking for a low rate, so it is important that you recognize which rate is being quoted if you only see one.

The difference between the APR and the APY depends on how often interest is compounded and on how large the APR is. Larger APR rates and more frequent intrayear compounding cause larger differences between the APR and the APY. Table 19.1 shows two examples. The first is a high interest rate, much like those commonly charged by credit card companies: APR = 18%. The other is one-tenth the size to make the relative comparison as easy as possible: APR = 1.8%. This rate is on the order of magnitude offered by banks for savings accounts. The simple or uncompounded APR is listed in the

TABLE 19.1 Comparing APR and APY

	APY Given Different Numbers of Compounding Periods per Year					
	2	4	12	365	∞	= n, periods per year
APR = r	Semiannual	Quarterly	Monthly	Daily	Continuous	Formulas (Equations 19.2a, 19.2b)
18.0%	18.810%	19.252%	19.562%	19.7164%	19.7217%	$APY = (1+r/n)^n - 1$
1.8%	1.808%	1.812%	1.815%	1.81625%	1.81630%	$APY_{continuous} = e^r - 1$

first column of Table 19.1, and APY values, given different versions of intrayear compounding, are listed in subsequent columns. For example, an APR of 18% implies that the monthly (or periodic) rate is 1.5% per month (1.5% = 18%/12). Compounding results in an extra yield of 1.562% per year, given monthly compounding (19.562% – 18%). (We are not suggesting that you evaluate percentages at 1/1000th of a percent; the percentages are shown at this number of digits simply to show differences between the various forms of discounting.) At lower interest rates, the effect of compounding is less than proportionate (at an APR of 1.8%, monthly compounding produces an extra yield of 0.015%, much less than one-tenth of 1.562%). As the number of time periods per year increases, the APY increases, but it increases at a decreasing rate. Indeed, it reaches a limit as the number of subintervals to the year approaches infinity. It can be shown mathematically that the limiting value of the APY is:

$$APY_{continuous} = e^r - 1, \text{ where } r = APR. \quad \textbf{(19.2b)}$$

Often, economists assume continuous compounding because it produces APYs that are close to the discrete APY values, and it avoids the need to consider how often compounding occurs. (The difference between monthly and continuous APYs is 0.16%, given an APR of 18% and 0.001% for an APR of 1.8%.) Compounding has nonlinear effects both in time periods per year and as a function of the APR.

19.1B What Discount Rate Should You Use?

When there is a common rate at which borrowing and lending occurs, then this same rate should be used as the discount rate for present value calculations. When a firm is able to borrow capital freely, then the discount rate is the firm's cost of capital.

The firm's cost of capital is composed of three components: (1) a pure rate of time preference, (2) an expected inflation rate, and (3) a risk premium. The pure rate of time preference component has to do with the general notion that individuals and firms will typically prefer to have access to financial or real resources for more time periods, rather than fewer. This can be explained by a simple example: Suppose that there is no inflation and that you are assured that you will receive the money offered either now or in the future—that is, there is no risk inherent in the offer (therefore, the second and third components no longer apply). In this event, an individual is still likely to prefer $100 now, rather than $100 a year from now, because access to the money now provides the ability to purchase goods either now *or* in the future. Under these conditions, we could determine an amount of money X received 1 year from today that the individual or the firm would consider to be worth the current offer of $100. Once X is found, the pure time value of money is also determined for this individual or firm: r = X/100 – 1.

Claim: *If an individual or firm faces no inflation or risk and is indifferent between $100, now, and X, 1 year from now, then the pure rate of time preference is:*

$r = X/100 - 1.$

The second component of the cost of capital is the expected inflation rate. In this text, we use single-period models with few exceptions, so we have not needed to talk about inflation.[5] Inflation is the general change in price level from year to year (and this can be calculated using a number of indices, such as the Consumer Price Index [CPI] or Producer Price Index [PPI]). Our interest in the current setting is on how many goods can be purchased in various time periods with the dollars from those time periods. Therefore, we must adjust our calculations to take into consideration that a dollar buys less next year if inflation has occurred than if inflation has not occurred. Inflation changes a dollar's purchasing power. Ex-post we are able to determine the real rate of interest, given the nominal rate of interest and the actual inflation rate over the time period. Unfortunately, investments are forward looking, and we do not have actual inflation information for the future. Therefore, we must be satisfied with an expected rate of inflation. In this event, we have an expected real interest rate based on two expected values: an expected nominal interest rate and an expected rate of inflation. Whether we are talking actual inflation or expected inflation, the real and nominal interest rates are related according to the formula:

$$\text{Real interest rate} = \text{Nominal interest rate} - \text{Inflation}. \quad \textbf{(19.3a)}$$

We can also describe the nominal rate as a function of the real rate and inflation:[6]

$$\text{Nominal interest rate} = \text{Real interest rate} + \text{Inflation}. \quad \textbf{(19.3b)}$$

Given the distinction between real and nominal rates, it is important to make sure that any investment model you build is consistent in its usage of interest and growth rates. A typical project will have an up-front investment that produces a stream of revenues (cash flows) over time. If you expect this revenue stream to grow at 5% per year based on the investment, then it is important to understand explicitly whether that expected growth rate is a real or a nominal growth rate. Suppose that you think it is a real growth rate. In this event, the nominal growth rate will similarly be related to the real growth rate by the formulas:[7]

$$\text{Real growth rate} = \text{Nominal growth rate} - \text{Inflation}. \quad \textbf{(19.3c)}$$

$$\text{Nominal growth rate} = \text{Real growth rate} + \text{Inflation}. \quad \textbf{(19.3d)}$$

If your expected growth rate is real and your discount rate is nominal, then you must change one or the other for your investment model to be appropriately specified.

Nominal rates are easier to work with, at least initially, because they are the rates that are seen in the market. The interest rates quoted by banks and financial institutions are nominal; only by subtracting inflation (or expected inflation) are we able to obtain a real (or expected real) rate. Despite this ease in working with nominal rates, economists often find it convenient to work with real interest rates and real growth rates when creating an investment model because growth rates are easier to conceptualize on a real basis. As long as parameters are appropriately adjusted to either be all real or all nominal, there is no difference in the present value outcome, depending on which form of analysis you choose (obviously, the nominal dollar outcomes depend on whether you include or exclude inflation). Therefore, each of the present value calculations shown here is real rather than nominal in nature.[8]

The third component of the firm's cost of capital mentioned earlier is risk. At a given point in time, a going firm confronts many opportunities for investment. Not all proposed projects are equally risky; some are substantially more risky than others. Risky projects should not be judged on the same "scale" as nonrisky projects. As a result, a risk premium typically is assigned to a project, based on its perceived level of risk. Firms often place projects into groups with comparable risk. For example, a capital replacement project that is required to maintain an existing product line faces a smaller degree of market risk than a project whose goal is to start a new product line. A pure research and development project is riskier still. If the firm is large enough that it does not need to justify individual decisions to fund projects, it should nonetheless adjust its required return to take into account the degree of risk associated with a given project. (If the firm does not do this, then it will eventually increase the perceived risk of the firm in the eyes of investors.) Small firms often need to provide specific information to the lender (in the form of a prospectus) that lays out the expected costs, benefits, and risks associated with the project. The lender then makes its own decision as to the risk of the project, and consequently, the required return it will charge to finance the project.

Even if you do not formally use capital markets, you can still conceptualize the discount rate by answering a simple question. Suppose that you are offered two options: (1) Receive $100 today, or (2) receive nothing today but receive X 1 year from today. There must be some value of X for which you are indifferent between the two alternatives. Once you have this indifferent value of X, you have also implicitly obtained your discount rate, $r = X/100 - 1$, as noted earlier.[9] Individuals have different implicit rates of time preference at different points in their lives. Students typically have a high rate of time preference because money in the future is (theoretically) much more plentiful than money today, due to lack of earning (and borrowing) power during the school years. (Of course, this is moderated by the ability to obtain college loans; to the extent that you are able to obtain such loans, you have a market reference point for an interest rate by using the rate on the loan. If you borrow the maximum allowable and still want to borrow more, you once again face no formal capital market for marginal consumption.)

One final point should be made regarding present value calculations. Investment decisions are inherently speculative in nature because they attempt to predict benefit streams into the future. Even under the best of circumstances, there is uncertainty regarding the future. As a result, we should not place too much weight on small differences among projects. Your present value estimates are only as good as your data, and your data, by necessity, are somewhat speculative. This is a perfect place to perform sensitivity analysis on the parameters used to create the model.

This same admonition concerns trying to be overly precise in interpreting the results of the model. We often present the results as a precise answer, but we only do so for a pedagogical reason (as we did previously with the discussion of the difference between the APR and the APY). If we are precise in our answers, we can often help students avoid algebraic mistakes made in their own models. (If you do as we suggest and try to create your own Excel model based on a given set of assumptions, you should get *exactly* the same answer [except for differences in formatting]; if you do not, something is wrong somewhere within your model.) But that precision should not be interpreted as suggesting that we should choose projects based on differences that are only visible in the third decimal place. A manager would look at such data and say that the projects are equally valid, rather than try to choose based on unreasonably precise answers. A manager would also look at the projects using multiple evaluative methods, as we discuss in Section 19.4. Even if projects look virtually identical using one method, an alternative evaluative method may provide a reason for choosing among projects.

Section 19.2 Outline

19.2A Creating Patterns
19.2B Writing Equations
19.2C Writing Equations That Drag by Using Relative and Absolute Referencing

19.2 Using Excel for Repetitive Calculations

Prerequisite: Chapter 2

This chapter benefits substantially from Excel and has few prerequisites, so it may be examined early on, partly as a way to learn Excel. Those who already have used Excel can quickly skim this section, which provides some basic Excel instruction. Excel, however, is so complex that you are always likely to learn new Excel techniques and tricks.

Excel is basically a large calculator that does repetitive calculations very well. To harness Excel's power, there are a few simple rules to follow. If you have not used Excel before, you will benefit most from this discussion if you have Excel open and replicate what is being shown in the text. The tables shown are available in Excel (each table is on a different worksheet within the file; simply click on the tab at the bottom of the screen to go to the table you wish to examine). But you will retain more if you create the Excel files yourself. (Start from your own blank worksheet or add a blank worksheet to the file. In Excel 2007, click the **Insert Worksheet** tab to the right of the existing worksheet tabs at the bottom of the worksheet. If you are still using Excel 2003, click **Insert, Worksheet**.)

Note: *Keys and commands in Excel are in bold type in this chapter.*

The focus here will be on getting Excel to answer a question; we will not spend time on formatting issues that are centered on making that answer "look good." Therefore, do not worry if your end result has a different "look" from those in the text. Worry only if the numbers are different. (Remember that 0.1 is 10%; do not expect whole numbers for percent values unless you format a cell that way.)

A useful starting point for solving problems in Excel is to consider the general architecture of the problem. If the data used in the calculations are put in a single location, they can be easily referenced and changed as necessary to perform comparative statics analysis.

Excel tactic: *Placing the data in the upper left corner of a worksheet with the calculations elsewhere is typically the best general architecture for mapping a problem.*

This architecture makes it easy for you to examine how sensitive the conclusions are to the assumptions that underlie the analysis. Economists often perform such comparative statics analysis. Before we examine complex present value problems, we need to discuss several preliminary issues, such as creating runners and entering equations.

19.2A Creating Patterns

Excel's most powerful feature is its ability to do repetitive actions. Excel has built-in routines that attempt to replicate patterns that have been started. Table 19.2 has data entered into 10 cells in six columns. These are provided to show you how easy it is to create runners (patterns). The runner often used in present value problems is started in column A. Columns B and C show that the increments need not be unitary. If you enter nonnumeric information, Excel will try to create a pattern from that data. Three examples are shown in columns D through F. (Notice that even without formatting the cells, the numbers are right-justified within a cell, and the nonnumeric data are left-justified. This can be changed by manually formatting cells using the **Home** ribbon.)

To create a runner, you must highlight the cells you wish to run. This is shown in Table 19.2 for cells A1:A2. (A colon is used to describe blocks of Excel cells. Each cell has a letter and number reference; columns are letters, and rows are numbers.) Cells A1 and A2 are highlighted by left-clicking on cell A1 and then holding down the left-click button, moving the mouse down to cell A2, and then releasing the left-click button. As you move your mouse over the cell, you initially will see an open white plus sign. Move the mouse to the lower right corner of the cell (in this instance, A2), and you will see a black plus sign. Once you see the black plus sign, hold down the left-click and drag in the direction you wish to create the runner. (You can also create multiple runners at once. If you highlight A1:C2, you can create three runners at once; alternatively, you can create each runner individually, as just described.)

TABLE 19.2 Screenshot of Excel Worksheet That Creates Patterns (Compare with Table 19.3)

	A	B	C	D	E	F	G	H
1	0	2	5	Mon	Mon	Feb		
2	1	2.5	7		Wed			
3								
4								
5								

TABLE 19.3 Patterns Created in Excel by Dragging Cells from Table 19.2

	A	B	C	D	E	F	G	H
1	0	2	5	Mon	Mon	Feb	Mar	Apr
2	1	2.5	7	Tue	Wed	Mar		
3	2	3	9	Wed	Fri	Apr		
4	3	3.5	11	Thu	Sun	May		
5	4	4	13	Fri	Tue	Jun		

Table 19.3 shows the result of this dragging process. No manual data entry has occurred; the cells have been filled as a result of dragging the patterns that were begun in Table 19.2. The runner in column A increases by 1 and starts from 0; B increases by 0.5, starting at 2; C increases by 2, starting at 5; D gives days of the week, E skips days, and F gives months of the year, starting with February. The entries in G1:H1 show that if you drag cell F1 sideways, you can create horizontal, rather than vertical, runners.

19.2B Writing Equations

The same strategy used to create runners allows you to create equations that do repetitive calculations. To accomplish this, you need to know how to enter equations. *Entering equations is straightforward: Excel follows the same rules you learned in algebra.*

Excel tactic: *The most difficult part of entering equations is to remember* never *to type in a number that is part of the data for the problem. Instead, use a cell reference to refer to that data within the equation.*

If you do not do this, you will get the correct answer to the question you are calculating, but you will lose much of Excel's power to do comparative statics analysis.

To make this specific, suppose that you expect to receive $10,000 4 years from today. Suppose further that the discount rate you use for present value calculations is 10%.

Q4a. What is $10,000 received 4 years from now worth to you today?

The answer is:

$\$6{,}830 = \$10{,}000/(1.1)^4$, using Equation 19.1a. **(19.4a)**

This answer can be obtained easily in Excel in a number of ways. The most obvious strategy is to simply type the equation =10000/1.1^4 into a cell (all Excel equations start with an equal sign and ^ means exponentiate in Excel). The problem with this strategy is that it does not allow sensitivity analysis. In this context, for example, we might ask:

Q4b. What happens if your discount rate is 9% or 11% instead of 10%?

Q4c. What happens if you receive the $10,000 3 or 5 years from today instead of 4 years from today?

(You will have a chance to answer these questions in a minute.) These are the kinds of questions economists ask when performing a comparative statics (or sensitivity) analysis. If you simply type in the equation using numbers, you have to retype the equation four more times to answer Q4b and Q4c.

The preferred strategy is to put the data in cells in the upper left corner of the worksheet and do the calculations in another part of the worksheet. (Cell A1 is always easy to return to in Excel.)

Excel hint: *The* **Control** *and* **Home** *keys pressed simultaneously always return you to cell A1 on a worksheet, even if A1 is not visible at the time you press* **Ctrl Home**.

TABLE 19.4 Using Data from Excel Cells to Calculate an Answer

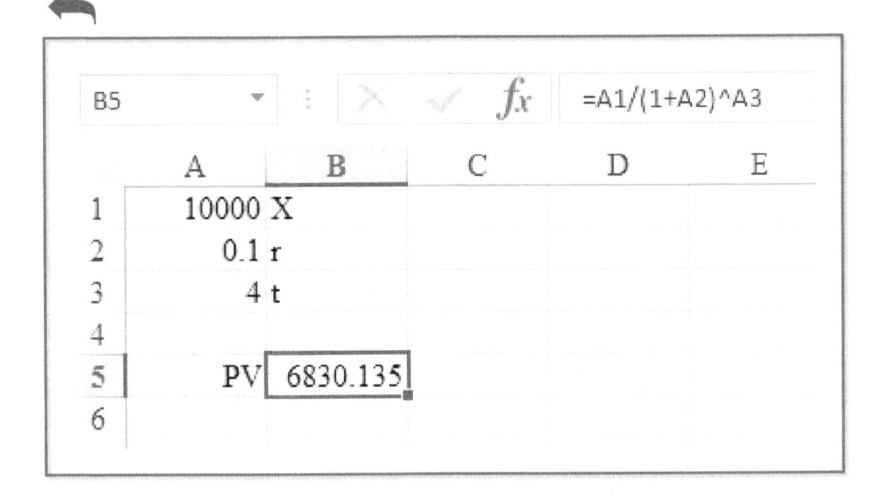

This strategy for setting up the data and entering equations is shown in Table 19.4. In cell B5, it looks like the number 6830.135 has been typed into the file, but in fact, it is the result of an equation. You can find the underlying equation for any cell by clicking on the cell (the chosen cell will be outlined in black, and the row and column labels will be darkened as a result). This is shown in Table 19.4; the location of the cell is in the **Name Bar** (the white area above the A and B labels), and the content of that cell is seen in the **Formula Bar** (the white area above the D and E labels next to the *fx* sign). In this instance, we see that Equation 19.4a is entered in Excel in cell B5 as:

=A1/(1+A2)^A3 **(19.4b)**

Notice that the equation in B5 references the data, rather than puts in numbers (such as 10000, 0.1, or 4). This allows you to change the data for comparative statics analysis. In particular, use Excel to answer Q4b and Q4c from earlier.*

Excel hint: *When typing equations that reference cells, you can either type in the cell location or you can click on the cell as you type. Typing and clicking can be mixed in writing an equation.*

If we denote an underscored cell reference as being entered via a mouse click, the equation in cell B5 could be typed as: =<u>A1</u>/(1+a2)^<u>A3</u>↵ (↵ signifies the **Enter** key). A1 and A3 have been entered via mouse click, and a2 has been typed in without being capitalized. Once you hit ↵ and return to cell B5, you will notice that Excel has capitalized this reference as A2.

Excel hint: *Entering equations via mouse clicks often decreases the likelihood that an incorrect cell is being referenced.*

19.2C Writing Equations That Drag by Using Relative and Absolute Referencing

We have discussed how to create runners by dragging a pattern that had been established. You can also drag equations in Excel (as opposed to numbers). We argued earlier that when you have data that you may wish to change, you should use a cell reference to the data, rather than type in numbers, to allow for comparative statics analysis.

Whenever you drag an equation, you must consider what you want to change and what you want to keep fixed. Excel has a way to fix some parts of the equation and allow other

***Q4 answer:** The answers are: \$7,084 for r = 9%, \$6,587 for r = 11%, \$7,513 for t = 3, and \$6,209 for t = 5. These values are obtained by changing the numbers in cells A2 and A3. As you change one number, you obtain the result without having to reenter the formula, given the new value of r or t.

parts to vary. If you master the difference between absolute and relative cell referencing, you can save yourself time and create more elegant solutions to problems done in Excel. Suppose that an equation references a cell with data. If you do not want a referenced cell to change as you drag the equation, you need to make your data reference *absolute*; if you want it to change, you need to make your data reference *relative*.

> **Excel rule:** *If you put a dollar sign ($) in front of a letter, it creates an absolute column reference, and if you put a $ sign in front of a number, it creates an absolute row reference.*

There are four possibilities as a result (regarding the presence or absence of $ signs); these are examined in Table 19.5. (This table has nothing to do with present value; it simply provides an array of numbers to help clarify how the $ signs are used to create different versions of referencing.) The data for this example are in cells A1:C3. The four possible $-sign placements are labeled 1–4 in E1:L11. In each of the four parts, the upper left corner cell is highlighted in gray and has one of the four possible versions of the simple equation =A1 in the cell. This equation has been dragged sideways and down to complete the 3 × 3 array in each area. (You can do this for yourself in the Excel file for Table 19.5.) The resulting arrays are distinctively different from one another. It is worth taking time to consider how each array relates to the original array in A1:C3.

If you wish to replicate this array in a different location, you can use an equation with relative referencing. You simply need to create an equation that references the upper left corner (such as =A1) and then drag over and down. The result is shown in E2:G4 in Table 19.5. If you want to fix the reference as you drag, then use double $ signs, as shown in the **Formula Bar** (which shows the equation in cell J2). These two versions of referencing are "pure" forms in that either they adjust completely or they are completely fixed as the equation is dragged horizontally or vertically. The other two are mixed versions of absolute and relative referencing, where only one direction is absolute. The $ sign in the equation in cell E9 (=A$1) means that row 1 is fixed (absolute reference), but the column is allowed to float as the equation is dragged sideways. The final version (=$A1) holds the column fixed in column A but allows the row to vary as the equation is dragged vertically.

Entering $ signs in equations tends to be a bit tedious. As a result, Excel has a special function key that helps in this regard.

TABLE 19.5 Using Excel's Absolute versus Relative Cell Referencing in Equations

J2 | fx | =$A$1

	A	B	C	E	F	G	J	K	L
1	1	3	5	1. Relative referencing (=A1)			2. Absolute referencing (=$A$1)		
2	2	5	8	1	3	5	1	1	1
3	3	7	11	2	5	8	1	1	1
4				3	7	11	1	1	1
6	Note: You can cycle			Mixed referencing					
8	through the four			3. Absolute row (=A$1)			4. Absolute column (=$A1)		
9	versions of relative			1	3	5	1	1	1
10	versus absolute			1	3	5	2	2	2
11	referencing with **F4**.			1	3	5	3	3	3
12									

Excel hint: *The* **F4** *special function key allows you to cycle through the four possible absolute versus relative referencing options shown in Table 19.5.*

Relative referencing allows a second way to create a runner. Put the starting value in a cell (such as 0 in cell A1). In cell A2, type =A1+1. This equation can be dragged to create a column that increases one per row. When the equation in A2 is pulled down to A3, the A1 turns into an A2 (which has the value of 2).

With simple equations, the type of referencing is typically easy to see, but with more complex equations, it is often useful to mix the types of referencing in a single equation. In this instance, it is often best to enter the equation (and make sure the equation is producing results that seem appropriate) first, and then go back and consider how you wish each part of the equation to respond to being dragged.

Excel hint: *When entering a complex equation, it sometimes is worthwhile to enter the equation first without referencing; then go back and add $ signs as necessary, using the* **F4** *special function key (above the 4 and 5 keys on most keyboards).*

To do this, click on the cell reference you wish to add $ signs to in the **Formula Bar**, and then click **F4** until the appropriate version of $ signs appears in the **Formula Bar**. The four versions *cycle* in the order shown in Table 19.5 (A1, $A$1, A$1, $A1). Relative referencing is the default; when a cell is clicked during the creation of an equation, the relative version is assumed.

Relative referencing and absolute referencing are easier to visualize than the mixed referencing options, so we begin by examining a problem that uses relative and absolute referencing. The current example extends the PV problem examined in Table 19.4 to a comparison of PV and FV based on Equations 19.1a and 19.1c. Table 19.6 describes the present value of X = $10,000 paid t years from now in E8:E15. With the exception of time period 0 (the current time period), each PV is less than X. By contrast, if you have X in the current time period and want to know its future value in year t, you can obtain this in B8:B15. Both series change nonlinearly: FV increases more than linearly, and PV decreases less than linearly. The numbers are not as important for our present purpose as are the equations used to obtain the numbers. In all, 19 cells have numbers displayed in them. The five gray cells are the only ones in which numbers were entered; all other cells are based on equations. Focus on the equation for future value in cell B8 shown in the **Formula Bar**. As years change, the initial amount and interest rate should not change, but the year should. Therefore, B1 and B2 should be held fixed, and A8 should be allowed to vary. This is why the equation in cell B8, =$B$1*(1+$B$2)^A8, is the appropriate equation to drag down the B column.[10] Row 15 has been added (as has the general future year t in B3) so that the nonlinear nature of PV and FV is more obvious. The equation in cells B15 and E15 must have the exponent changed from A15 to B3. Otherwise, both columns of numbers are easily obtained from two equations: one written in B8 and the other in E8 (that equation is shown in F8 but, of course, column F is only provided for expositional purposes). *The important point is that if you did not use the $ signs, you would have to write equations for each cell in B8:B15 and E8:E15, rather than simply two equations.* By adjusting r, we can perform a comparative statics analysis on present value, much like we were asked to do in Q4b earlier. (The answer to Q4a is in cell E12, and the answer to Q4c is provided in cells E11 and E13.)

We can see the answers to both Q4b and Q4c by filling in a 3 × 3 comparative statics table with our best guess of time and discount rate in the center cell. Such a table allows us to compare variations along one dimension with variations along another. It also allows us to show the value of using the mixed referencing $ signs shown in parts 3 and 4 of Table 19.5. Rather than simply replicate the comparative statics analysis from earlier in the section, we have opted to show alternative deviations for both r and t (that are half the size of the ones used for Q4b and Q4c). Table 19.7 has added two new data parameters to perform this analysis. The new parameters are Δr, the deviation in best-guess discount rate being examined, and Δt, the deviation in best-guess time being examined ($\Delta r = 0.5\%$, and $\Delta t = 0.5$ in the table). Values of r and t based on the parameters B2:B5 are shown in cells B7:D7 and A8:A10.

TABLE 19.6 Calculating Present Value and Future Value in Excel

B8 | fx | =$B$1*(1+$B$2)^A8

	A	B	C	D	E	F
1	X	$10,000	Principal in time period zero			
2	r	10%	Rate at which you could borrow or lend			
3	t	10	General future year			
5		The future value in year t			The present value of a payment of	
6		of X paid today			X in period t, $PV(X_t) = X/(1+r)^t$	
7	Time	FV(X) in year			$PV(X_t)$	Excel equation
8	0	$10,000	$= X\cdot(1+r)^0$	$FV(X)_0$	$10,000	=$B$1/(1+$B$2)^A8
9	1	$11,000	$= X\cdot(1+r)^1$	$FV(X)_1$	$9,091	=$B$1/(1+$B$2)^A9
10	2	$12,100	$= X\cdot(1+r)^2$	$FV(X)_2$	$8,264	=$B$1/(1+$B$2)^A10
11	3	$13,310	$= X\cdot(1+r)^3$	$FV(X)_3$	$7,513	=$B$1/(1+$B$2)^A11
12	4	$14,641	$= X\cdot(1+r)^4$	$FV(X)_4$	$6,830	=$B$1/(1+$B$2)^A12
13	5	$16,105	$= X\cdot(1+r)^5$	$FV(X)_5$	$6,209	=$B$1/(1+$B$2)^A13
14	⋮	⋮	⋮	⋮	⋮	⋮
15	t	$25,937	$= X\cdot(1+r)^t$	$FV(X)_t$	$3,855	=$B$1/(1+$B$2)^B3

Q7. Describe equations you would use to obtain B7:D7 and A8:A10.*

The equation in cell B8 shown in the **Formula Bar**, =$B$1/(1+B$7)^$A8, allows you to fill in the other eight cells in the table by dragging. The key to being able to use a single equation for this task is the appropriate use of various forms of cell referencing in the equation.

Excel tactic: *For each reference to a piece of data in an equation, ask yourself: Do you want the reference to change if you drag the equation horizontally and vertically?*

The present value equation $PV = X/(1 + r)^t$ is based on three pieces of data: X, r, and t. This question must be asked with regard to each piece of data in the equation.

The principal amount X in B1 should be held fixed to dragging in both directions. Therefore, double $ signs should be used on the principal reference, $B$1 (this is *absolute* referencing, as shown in part 2 of Table 19.5, or one click of the **F4** special function key).

The interest rate r varies by column in going from column B to C to D. No longer should the interest rate refer to B2 because we want interest rates to vary. The interest rate to reference in the equation is in row 7. When the formula in B8 is pulled sideways, we want the interest rate to change, so the column reference should be relative (no $ sign on

*__Q7 answer:__ It is important to use a cell reference, rather than simply type in numbers in these cells. As a result, the equation in cell A8, for example, should be either =B3-B5 or =A9-B5. If you do not use a cell reference, then the table will not adjust as you change the data in cells B1:B5. Try to set this up yourself, and then check your results by setting $\Delta r = 1\%$, and $\Delta t = 1$. Your answers should match those noted in the **Q4 answer**. You can also check your answers by going to the Excel worksheet for Table 19.7 and putting these values into cells B4 and B5.

TABLE 19.7 Using Mixed Referencing to Perform a Two-Way Comparative Statics Analysis

B8 | fx | =$B$1/(1+B$7)^$A8

	A	B	C	D	E	F	G
1	X	$10,000	Principal in time period t				
2	r	10%	Best-guess rate at which you could borrow or lend				
3	t	4	Best-guess time				
4	Δr	0.5%	Deviation from best-guess value of r				
5	Δt	0.5	Deviation from best-guess value of t				
7	PV(X)	9.5%	10.0%	10.5%	r		
8	3.5	$7,279	$7,164	$7,051			
9	4	$6,956	$6,830	$6,707			
10	4.5	$6,647	$6,512	$6,381			
11	t	A two-way comparative statics analysis					

letters). But when the formula in B8 is pulled vertically down, we want the interest rate to remain fixed, so the row reference should be fixed ($ sign on numbers). The reference to interest rate should therefore be B$7, which allows the column to float but holds the row fixed at row 7 (this is *absolute row* referencing, as shown in part 3 of Table 19.5, or two clicks of the **F4** special function key).

Time t varies by row in going from row 8 to 9 to 10. No longer should time refer to B3; rather, the time parameter to reference is in A8:A10. When the formula in B8 is pulled down, we want the time reference to change, so the row reference should be relative (no $ sign on numbers). But when the formula in B8 is pulled sideways, we want the time reference to remain fixed, so the column reference should be fixed ($ sign on letters). The reference to time should therefore be $A8, which allows the row to float, but holds the column fixed at column A (this is *absolute column* referencing, as shown in part 4 of Table 19.5, or three clicks of the **F4** special function key).

19.3 Applying Present Value in the Consumer Setting

Prerequisites: Chapter 2 and Section 19.2

Future value (FV) and present value (PV) are simply two ways to put dollars occurring in different time periods into a common unit of measurement. The value of present value is that the time period is understood to be *now*; with future value, one final piece of information is required: How far in the future is future value to be evaluated? As a result, we typically use present value when comparing costs and benefits that accrue at different points in time. If you compare two possible benefit streams having payouts in a number of time periods, you arrive at the same conclusion regarding which has the highest net value. The only difference is that future value in period t will be $(1 + r)^t$ times larger than present value (a result that is obvious, given Equation 19.1c, which relates present and future values).

Section 19.3 Outline

19.3A Comparing Alternative Payments if You Win the Lottery

State lotteries often advertise the amount that lottery winners win, using the sum of the stream of payments that occur over a period of years. For example, if the winner is to receive $1 million for each of the next 20 years, the state lottery commission says that the lottery was worth $20 million. Different states use different payment schemes (and even different schemes for different lottery games within a state). For our purposes, it is sufficient to simply consider one example. The following was taken from the Illinois Lottery website:[11]

> **Do I receive my prize in a one-time cash payment?**
> This depends on how you want to claim your prize. For the Mega Millions and Lotto, winners have 60 days from the date of the drawing to decide whether to claim a one-time lump sum or a 26-year annuity. The lump-sum payment is approximately 51% of the advertised jackpot amount.

annuity: An annuity is a stream of equal-sized payments paid at regular intervals.

perpetuity: A perpetuity is a perpetual annuity.

Notice that the Illinois Lottery explicitly states that its *advertised jackpot* is virtually twice as large as its lump-sum payment. The advertised jackpot is $26 \cdot X$, where X is the annuity payment per year. An **annuity** is a stream of equal-sized payments paid at regular intervals. The most common interval is annual, but other intervals are possible. Similarly, the number of payments can be a well-defined finite amount of time (such as 26 years), but it also can be more flexibly defined (such as a lifetime annuity). If the stream of payments is infinite, the annuity is called a **perpetuity**.

To calculate the value of an annuity or perpetuity, we need to know when the payments start, when they end, how much is paid each period, and the discount rate. The value of a perpetuity paying X per period and starting 1 year from today is a particularly easy formula to remember:[12]

$PV_{Perpetuity} = X/r$, assuming that the initial payment is in period 1. **(19.5a)**

If the perpetuity begins with a payment today, then X must be added to the amount in Equation 19.5a:

$PV_{Perpetuity} = X \cdot (1 + 1/r)$, assuming that the initial payment is in period 0. **(19.5b)**

If the annuity is not perpetual, the present value calculation is a bit more complex (but is based on the same algebraic manipulation used to derive Equation 19.5a). Given the ease with which we can analyze the problem using Excel, it is not as important to remember. Nonetheless, we can readily use a single equation to analyze finite annuities. As earlier, there are two versions, based on when the initial payment is made. Suppose that there are n payments, and the discount rate is r. If the annuity pays X per period, beginning 1 year from today, the annuity is worth:

$$PV_{Annuity} = (X/r) \cdot (1 - (1/(1 + r)^n)). \quad \textbf{(19.6a)}$$

If the first payment is in the current period, the annuity is worth:[13]

$$PV_{Annuity} = X \cdot (1 + 1/r) \cdot (1 - (1/(1 + r)^n)). \quad \textbf{(19.6b)}$$

We can use this equation to analyze the Illinois Lottery discussed earlier.

To analyze the choice faced by a winner of the Illinois Lottery, we must describe what the winner wins. Consider the following assumptions:

1. The winner wins a lottery with an advertised jackpot of $26 million.
2. The lottery pays out this money as a 26-year annuity. The first payment of $1 million is paid immediately.
3. The individual has a discount rate of 5%.
4. If the winnings are paid out as a lump sum, the winner would receive $13,260,000 immediately ($13,260,000 = 0.51 · $26,000,000).

Should the lottery winner choose the annuity or the lump sum? This question can be answered using Equation 19.6b, and this equation can be easily programmed into Excel. But using Excel's repetitive equations discussed previously produces the same solution, and it provides a more transparent guide to how this value is obtained. Both solutions (and one more) are shown in Table 19.8A. (Ignore for now Table 19.8B, which provides an

TABLE 19.8 Evaluating Lottery Options Using Present Value

Panel A, r = 5%

	A	B	C
1	$ 1,000,000	Payout per year	
2	26	Number of annual payments	
3	$13,260,000	Lump sum offered	
4	0.05	Discount rate	
5			
6	Payment #	Time	PV payout
7	1	0	$ 1,000,000
8	2	1	$ 952,381
31	25	24	$ 310,068
32	26	25	$ 295,303
33		NPV = Σ PV	$ 15,093,945
34	NPV using annuity formula		$ 15,093,945
35		NPV using Excel's f_x	$15,093,945
36	Formulas used to create the table		
37	Cell C7: =$A$1/(1+$A$4)^B7		
38	Cell C33: =SUM(C7:C32)		
39	NPV using alternative methods		
40	Cell C34: =A1*(1+1/A4)*(1-1/(1+A4)^A2)		
41	Cell C35: =-PV(A4,A2,A1,,1)		

Panel B, r = 10%

	A	B	C
1	$ 1,000,000	Payout per year	
2	26	Number of annual payments	
3	$13,260,000	Lump sum offered	
4	0.1	Discount rate	
5			
6	Payment #	Time	PV payout
7	1	0	$ 1,000,000
8	2	1	$ 909,091
31	25	24	$ 101,526
32	26	25	$ 92,296
33		NPV = Σ PV	$ 10,077,040
34	NPV using annuity formula		$ 10,077,040
35		NPV using Excel's f_x	$10,077,040
36	Formulas used to create the table		
37	Cell C7: =$A$1/(1+$A$4)^B7		
38	Cell C33: =SUM(C7:C32)		
39	NPV using alternative methods		
40	Cell C34: =A1*(1+1/A4)*(1-1/(1+A4)^A2)		
41	Cell C35: =-PV(A4,A2,A1,,1)		

alternative version based on a different Assumption 3.) Rows 9–30 have been reduced in height to conserve space.[14] The value of the annuity is the present value of the payment in each period summed across periods. The present value of each payment is calculated in C7:C32, and the sum is calculated in C33. Two alternative (single-equation) versions of this calculation are presented in cells C34 and C35 (with the corresponding Excel equation noted in rows 40 and 41). Each says the same thing: Given the assumptions stated earlier, the individual should take the annuity because it has a higher present value than $13,260,000.

If the individual's discount rate is 10%, rather than 5%, the answer reverses, as can be seen in Table 19.8B. The lump-sum payment exceeds the value of the annuity, given the higher discount rate. One way to think about this is to consider different kinds of individuals. Those who have a more "long-term" view might well prefer the annuity. Their "long-term" view can be modeled as having a low discount rate. Those who prefer to "take the money and run" have a higher discount rate. (As noted earlier, economists sometimes use the term *rate of time preference* for discount rate. Those who more equally value different time periods have a lower rate of time preference.)

What if an individual has a discount rate that makes the person indifferent between the two options? This discount rate would be the rate that makes the present value of the annuity equal to the present value of the lump-sum payment. Table 19.8 tells us that this rate must be somewhere between 5% and 10%.

Using Goal Seek to Solve Problems

net present value (NPV) Net present value is the sum of present values.

If we imagine that there is a continuum of individuals with regard to how they view the future, then we could use Excel to search for the discount rate associated with an individual who is indifferent between the two options. We could do this manually by changing the discount rate in cell A4 and noting what happens to the **net present value (NPV)**, which is simply the sum of present values, in C33. Each time, you would adjust up or down to try to zero in on an NPV of $13,260,000. Excel has a built-in function called **Goal Seek** that offers a faster solution to this problem.[15] **Goal Seek** is a choice from **What If Analysis** on the **Data** ribbon in Excel 2007 (or on the **Tools** pulldown menu in Excel 2003). This function allows you to obtain any answer you wish by changing one of the parameters that underlie the model. In this instance, you wish to **Goal Seek** on cell C33 by changing the discount rate in cell A4 so that the answer in cell C33 is $13,260,000. The results are shown in Table 19.9.

Table 19.9 starts with the information from Table 19.8B but provides a screenshot that is in the *middle* of using **Goal Seek**. This screenshot shows how **Goal Seek** is set up to answer the question. (You may find it less confusing to try **Goal Seek** yourself, using the Table 19.8 worksheet rather than Table 19.9. Table 19.9 adds information in the gray cells D6:F34 that you would not have to include in doing the problem yourself. These are provided to avoid having a separate screenshot once the **Goal Seek** process has been concluded.)

Start by clicking on the cell you wish to change (in this instance, C33 is the clicked cell). (The equation in this cell is in the **Formula Bar**, and its border is darkened.) Next, click **Data, What If Analysis** if using Excel 2007 (or **Tools** if using Excel 2003), **Goal Seek**. From here, you obtain the **Goal Seek Menu**, shown in D1:F5. The menu will have C33 in the **Set cell** area. The other two areas must be filled in as shown. (13260000 is placed in the **To value** area because the annuity would then have the same value as the lump sum, and the discount rate A4 is typed into the **By changing cell** area because the

TABLE 19.9 Using **Goal Seek** to Do Break-Even Analysis

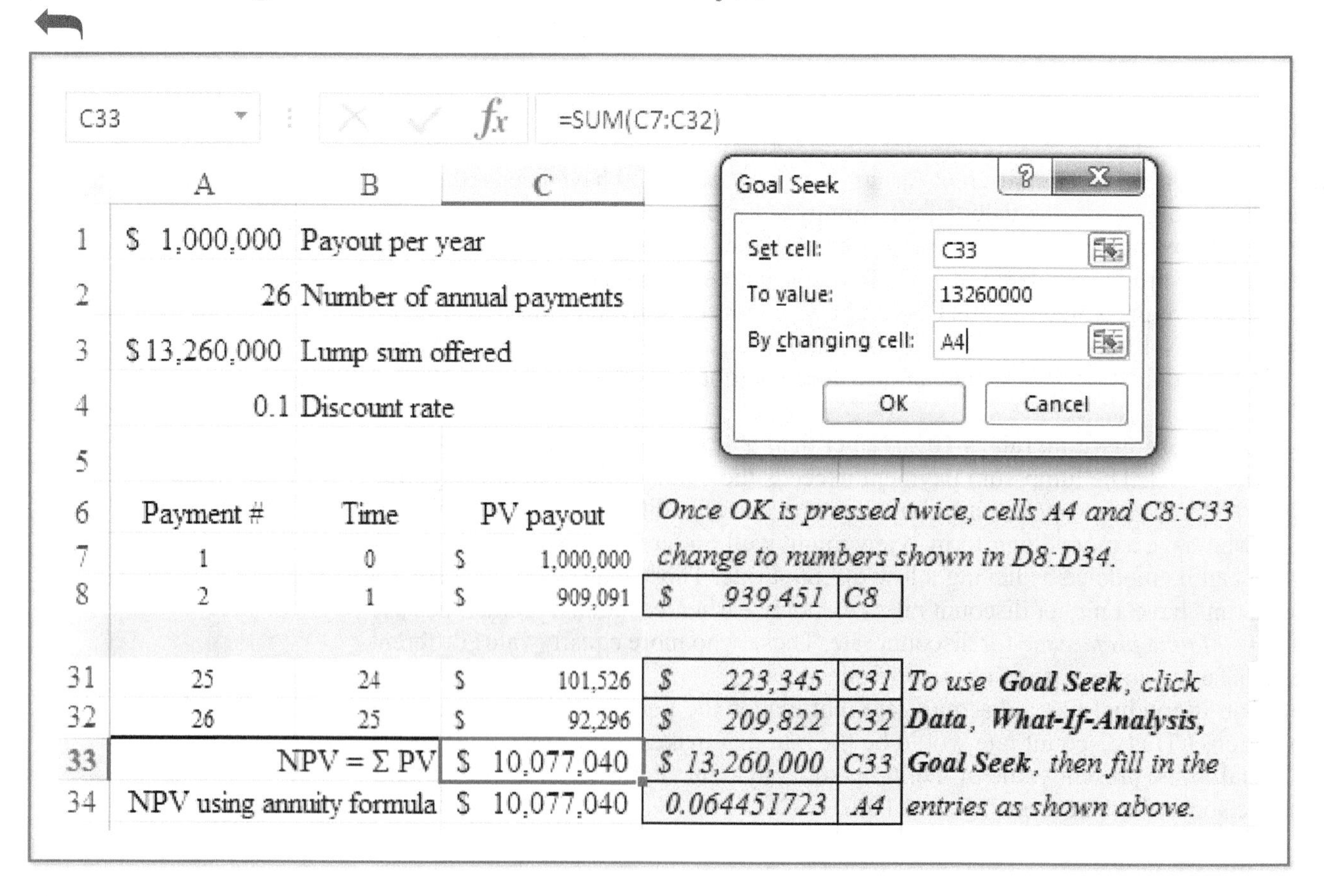
C33 | fx =SUM(C7:C32)

	A	B	C	D	E	F
1	$ 1,000,000	Payout per year				
2	26	Number of annual payments				
3	$ 13,260,000	Lump sum offered				
4	0.1	Discount rate				
5						
6	Payment #	Time	PV payout	*Once OK is pressed twice, cells A4 and C8:C33*		
7	1	0	$ 1,000,000	*change to numbers shown in D8:D34.*		
8	2	1	$ 909,091	*$ 939,451*	*C8*	
31	25	24	$ 101,526	*$ 223,345*	*C31*	*To use **Goal Seek**, click*
32	26	25	$ 92,296	*$ 209,822*	*C32*	***Data, What-If-Analysis,***
33		NPV = Σ PV	$ 10,077,040	*$ 13,260,000*	*C33*	***Goal Seek**, then fill in the*
34	NPV using annuity formula		$ 10,077,040	*0.064451723*	*A4*	*entries as shown above.*

question asks: At what discount rate will you be indifferent between the two options?) Once this is accomplished, click **OK** twice to see the solution provided by **Goal Seek**. (These steps have not been taken because the **Goal Seek** menu would no longer be visible, but the answers have been manually reproduced in cells D8:D34.) The key cells to look at are D33, which indeed equals $13,260,000 as requested, and D34, which provides the discount rate that produces this result (which would be in A4). We see that an individual who has a rate of time preference of 6.45% is indifferent between the annuity and the lump-sum payout. If the discount rate were higher, the individual would prefer the lump-sum payout, and if the discount rate were lower, the individual would prefer the annuity (we saw examples of both outcomes in Table 19.8).

Given the two single-equation methods of calculating the value of the annuity in C34 and C35 in Tables 19.8 and 19.9, the question naturally arises: Why should we concern ourselves with the calculation in A7:C33? One answer is that present value problems often involve varying amounts of money in various time periods, and in this event, the equations no longer apply. The method shown allows more complex analysis as a result. However, even on simple problems such as that shown in Table 19.8, the more complex the equations being employed, the more likely that a mistake will be made in entering the equation. Although there are more equations in A7:C33, each equation is simple (and only two equations need to be entered; the rest were created via dragging). By contrast, even the "canned" PV equation provided using the *fx* key requires care to make sure that the appropriate choices are made in working through this function.[16] These versions are shown to allow you to see alternative methods of attacking the problem. The preferred method of understanding present value is to lay out the PV problem in an array, rather than work from a single PV equation. This allows you to see the flow of costs and benefits across time. This strategy allows you to see why the answer is what it is; the single-equation strategy is more like putting data into a black box and hoping that the result is the correct answer. Once you are comfortable with the array calculation, you should feel more comfortable with the *fx* version as well (and you may also have gained enough of an intuitive feel about PV problems that you will be able to recognize when the "black box" answer seems incorrect).

19.3B Calculating the Net Benefit of College

Many people wonder whether college is worth the money. College costs have skyrocketed in the past quarter century, far outstripping inflation. The cost of an undergraduate degree varies substantially, depending on whether the school is public or private, and how much financial aid is available, but this is only one of the costs involved in obtaining an education. Individuals typically cannot hold down a full-time job if they are full-time students. Therefore, there is also an opportunity cost to going to school. Of course, these costs are balanced by the higher-paying jobs typically available to college graduates. There are also many nonmonetary benefits from going to college (indeed, most academics think that these benefits are far more important than are the monetary benefits), but we wish to look simply at the monetary costs and benefits involved in the decision to go to college.

Certainly, this is a complex decision and one that is subject to a great deal of speculation. How much higher paying is the college graduate's job, and how do the lifetime trajectories of the wage profiles compare? The five assumptions that follow are only suggestive; they allow you to see how to attack a complex problem by breaking it into pieces and then putting those pieces together into a unified answer. Excel allows you to easily modify the assumptions to model a situation closer to your own. Specific numerical values for the five assumptions are presented in 10 gray cells B1:H4 and C5 of Table 19.10. Before focusing on the calculations and their interpretation, it is worthwhile to consider the assumptions on which the calculations are based (the final assumption is made to simplify the analysis as much as possible).

Assumption 1: College costs increase substantially from year to year (row 1).

Assumption 2: Students earn some money during summers and during the academic year. This increases modestly from year to year (row 2).

TABLE 19.10 Using Present Value to Calculate the Net Benefit of Going to College

	A	B	C	D	E	F	G	H
1		$20,000	College costs first year, t = 0			15.0%	%Δ per year college cost	
2		$4,000	Summer and part-time job, t = 0			2.0%	%Δ per year summer job	
3		$35,000	Starting salary upon graduation			3.0%	%Δ per year salary	
4	High school starting salary		$25,000	%Δ 1-10 5.0%			%Δ 11-47 1.0%	
5	Discount rate 4.0%			Net benefit from going to college		$98,264		
6	Copy answer in top area.				$NPV_{college}$	$999,477	$NPV_{no\ college}$	$901,213
7	Age	t = age-18	Gross benefit	Gross cost	$N.B._{college}$	$PVNB_{college}$	$N.B._{no\ college}$	$PVNB_{no\ college}$
8	18	0	$ 4,000	$ 20,000	$ (16,000)	$ (16,000)	$ 25,000	$ 25,000
9	19	1	$ 4,080	$ 23,000	$ (18,920)	$ (18,192)	$ 26,250	$ 25,240
10	20	2	$ 4,162	$ 26,450	$ (22,288)	$ (20,607)	$ 27,563	$ 25,483
11	21	3	$ 4,245	$ 30,418	$ (26,173)	$ (23,267)	$ 28,941	$ 25,728
12	22	4	$ 35,000		$ 35,000	$ 29,918	$ 30,388	$ 25,975
13	23	5	$ 36,050		$ 36,050	$ 29,630	$ 31,907	$ 26,225
17	27	9	$ 40,575		$ 40,575	$ 28,507	$ 38,783	$ 27,249
18	28	10	$ 41,792		$ 41,792	$ 28,233	$ 40,722	$ 27,511
19	29	11	$ 43,046		$ 43,046	$ 27,962	$ 41,130	$ 26,717
20	30	12	$ 44,337		$ 44,337	$ 27,693	$ 41,541	$ 25,946
55	65	47	$ 124,758		$ 124,758	$ 19,747	$ 58,847	$ 9,314
56		PV lifetime earnings			$NPV_{college}$	$999,477	$NPV_{no\ college}$	$901,213
57		Students often compare Σ net benefits:			$3,033,313	Ignoring PV	$2,185,751	Never ignore PV.

Table 19.10 equations in yellow cells using data from gray cells (*Note:* Column widths differ from Table 19.10; widths of rows without equations have been minimized.)

	A	B	C	D	E	F	G	H
1		$20,000	College costs first year, t = 0			15.0%	%Δ per year college cost	
2		$4,000	Summer and part time job, t = 0			2.0%	%Δ per year summer job	
3		$35,000	Starting salary upon graduation			3.0%	%Δ per year salary	
4	High school starting salary			$25,000	%Δ1-10 5.0%		%Δ 11-47 1.0%	
5	Discount rate 4.0%			Net benefit from going to college =F6-H6				
6	Copy answer in top area.				$NPV_{college}$ =F56		$NPV_{no\ college}$ =H56	
7	Age	t=Age-18	Gross benefit	Gross cost	Net benefit	$PVNB_{college}$	Net benefit	$PVNB_{no\ college}$
8	18	=A8-18	=$B$2*(1+$F$2)^B8	=$B$1*(1+$F$1)^B8	=C8-D8	=E8/(1+$C$5)^B8	=$D$4*(1+$F$4)^B8	=G8/(1+$C$5)^B8
12			=$B$3*(1+$F$3)^B8					
19							=G18*(1+$H$4)	
56		PV lifetime earnings			$NPV_{college}$ =SUM(F8:F55)		$NPV_{no\ college}$ =SUM(G8:G55)	

Assumption 3: The initial salary for the college graduate is higher than the salary for the noncollege individual (B3 versus D4).

Assumption 4: A noncollege career has a higher initial growth rate in salary, but it plateaus after a period of time. By contrast, a college-graduate career has a more steady growth in salary from year to year (F4 and H4 versus F3).

Assumption 5: Inflation is zero (all growth rates and the discount rate are real rates, rather than nominal rates), and all annual payments are at the start of each year.

This is a complex problem because you must be careful to keep track of the six different percentage rates of change. (A new heading area has been inserted at row 60 of the worksheet. This area of the worksheet is not protected, so you can replicate the analysis by adding equations beneath row 60.) Each of the six rates differs from one another in Table 19.10; therefore, you will get the wrong answer if you reference the wrong rate. In all, ten parameters are used to create this model—six percentage rates and four initial dollar amounts.

The only equations that need to be entered to create Table 19.10 are those with a highlighted yellow background. The rest of the equations are obtained by dragging these equations. These highlighted equations are shown separately, below Table 19.10. The only "surprises" that emerge from these equations are in cells C12 and G19. C12, the first-year salary for a college graduate, references B8 in the exponent because B3 is the starting salary at the age of 22 for a college graduate (therefore, the growth factor (1+$F$3) should be raised to the 0th power, rather than the 4th power in that cell). The equation in G19 describes the point where the noncollege individual's annual salary trajectory flattens out from a 5% annual increase to a 1% annual increase (G17 to G18 is an increase of about $2,000, but G18 to G19 is an increase of about $400). The algebraic problem involved in changing the growth rate is that students are often conditioned to use exponents for series showing constant growth (such as in cells C8, D8, G8, and C12). If a similar equation is used in cell G19, it should not start from the starting salary; rather, it should start from the previous year's salary (in G18). This is why the more simplistic solution of multiplying the previous year's salary by (1+$H$4) works here (notice that G18 is relative referenced as a result in cell G19, unlike the absolute referenced dollar amounts in the salary and cost calculations in C8, D8, G8, and C12).[17]

Before we discuss the results, it is worthwhile to note the general structure shown in Table 19.10. We mentioned earlier that when creating models for comparative statics analysis within Excel, you should put the data at the top of the sheet with the analysis beneath. One new tactic is shown in cells D5:H6: The answers are brought up to the top of the analysis area to make comparative statics analysis easier. This tactic is especially useful when the problem is so long that the answer cannot be seen without moving the screen. (One final point has to do with the lack of "open space" in Table 19.10. A typical worksheet should not be as compact as shown here; there should be more space between areas. The "compactness" of Table 19.10 is for presentation purposes only.)

Not surprisingly (given that a college professor wrote this text), going to college is worthwhile, given the assumptions of the model. The net benefit of going to college is about $100,000 more than not going to college. First, examine the basic information derived from these assumptions. Individuals who are economically naïve sometimes ignore present value considerations and simply consider the option producing the highest sum of net benefits as being the best option. These sums have been calculated in cells E57 (=SUM(E8:E55)) and G57 (=SUM(G8:G55)), but *both sums make no economic sense.*[18] Individuals looking at these numbers would choose the right option for the wrong reason. If you adjust the out-year salary increase for the noncollege job in H4 from 1% to 2%, the noncollege undiscounted sum in G57 increases to about $2.6 million, so G57 is still smaller than E57. But this change causes the net present value of not going to college to be about $8,000 higher than going to college. That is, the appropriate economic choice, given this new scenario, is *not* to go to college, despite the undiscounted net benefit being approximately $400,000 higher for going to college. These differences point to the value of discounting for making long-range decisions.

Graphing Present Value Problems

As should be clear by this point in the chapter, present value problems are best analyzed via spreadsheets. Some flow aspects of present value problems are more heuristically understood by depicting the information from the spreadsheets graphically. As a result, Figure 19.1 provides a time-series view of the decision to go to college, based on the data in Table 19.10. Figure 19.1A shows the undiscounted dollar comparison described in columns E (blue) and G (red). Figure 19.1B shows the same comparison on a present value basis, based on columns F (blue) and H (red). Consider first the broad outlines of the comparison. In both Figures 19.1A and 19.1B, note that red depicts the net benefit stream for an individual who goes to work directly out of high school and that blue depicts the college graduate's net benefit stream (note also that there is a different scale on the two vertical axes).

College is an investment, as noted earlier. Not only is there the up-front cost of college itself; there is also the opportunity cost lost by only being able to hold down part-time and summer employment during college. During the first 4 years, the red stream is above the blue. The difference between the red and blue curves is the "net" cost of going to college (this includes both the direct cost of going to college and the net loss in opportunity cost inherent in not being able to maintain a full-time job). The "up-front" investment is paid to obtain higher wages in later out-years. This is shown by the blue curve being above the red curve once the college graduate starts working full time.

FIGURE 19.1
Comparing Costs and Benefits of Going to College

NB = Net benefit;
PV = Present value;
PVNB = Present value net benefit

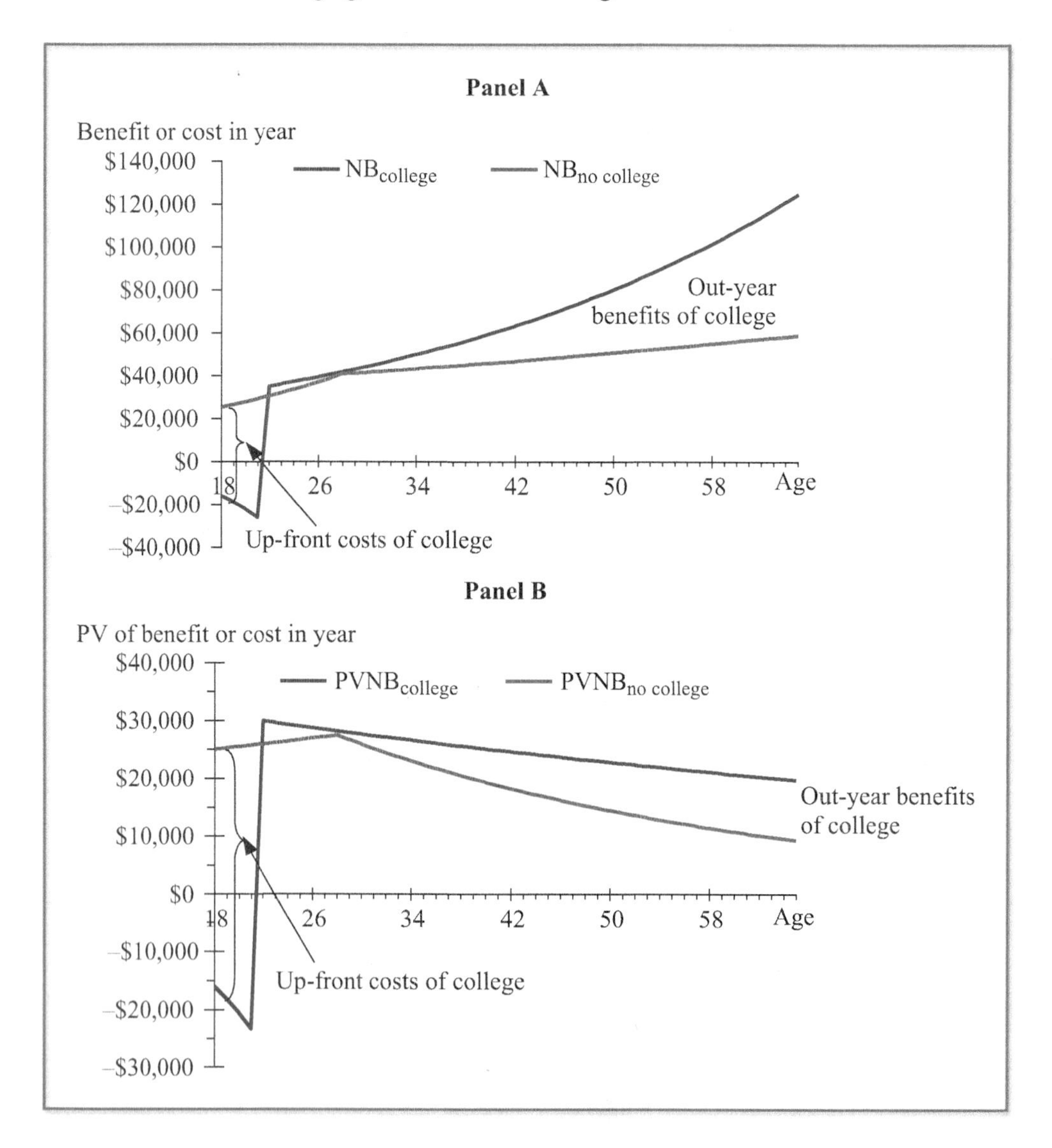

The trajectories of the various curves are worth considering in light of the parameters of the model. College costs increase at a rate of 15%, according to cell F1 in Table 19.10. The part-time job is smaller and has a smaller growth rate, so in net, college costs increase (since costs are negative numbers on the vertical axis, this means that the college net benefit curve declines for the first 4 years). The initial growth in salary for the noncollege job is faster than for the college job, so by age 28, the college graduate's salary is only about $1,000 higher than that of the noncollege individual (compare cells E18 with G18). The blue salary is only slightly above the red salary as a result in both Figures 19.1A and 19.1B. Past age 28, the salary paths diverge, as the college graduate continues to have 3% raises, compared with the 1% raises for the noncollege individual.

The final point concerns why the undiscounted salary schedules are generally upward sloping (with the exception of the 4 years of college discussed earlier), but only the initial part of the noncollege salary schedule is upward sloping in Figure 19.1B. The reason for this is straightforward: Each of the salary growth rates except the first 10 years of noncollege salary are smaller than 4%, the discount rate used for calculating present value. Therefore, the only series that is increasing over time on a present value basis is the first 10 years of the noncollege job. The net growth during that period is approximately 1% (5% – 4%).[19] The same reasoning suggests that the present value of the college salary series declines by about 1% per year (3% – 4%) and that noncollege salary in the out-years declines by about 3% per year (1% – 4%). (This is why the "out-year benefits of college" area in Figure 19.1B gets larger over time.)

The geometric interpretation of net present value (F56 = F6 for college and H56 = H6 for noncollege) is simply the area "under" the present value net benefit schedules in Figure 19.1B. The quotes surrounding *under* are there to remind you that it is only under when the present value in a given year is positive; when the reverse is true (i.e., during the college years), the area is between the horizontal axis and the curve (in which case, the area represents a net present value loss in those years). Similarly, the geometric interpretation of the net benefit of going to college from cell G5 is simply the net size difference between the two curves in Figure 19.1B. The area labeled "up-front costs of college" must be subtracted from "out-year benefits of college" to determine the present value net benefit of going to college in Figure 19.1B. In the scenario numerically shown in Table 19.10 and graphically shown in Figure 19.1B, the excess of benefit over cost is approximately $100,000 according to cell G5 in Table 19.10.

Comparative Statics Analysis

This model can be used for comparative statics analysis to examine how sensitive the decisions are to the various assumptions used to create the model. For example, suppose that you are relatively confident about the salary information but are less confident about what is going to happen to college costs in the next 4 years. A quick check (via **Goal Seek**) shows that the annual growth rate in college costs that produces equal net present value of going to college and not going to college is 69.3% (clearly higher than is likely to occur) in Table 19.10. (To see this, click on cell G5 and, using **Goal Seek**, set to 0 by changing F1.) *Similar break-even calculations can be done with respect to any of the parameters of the model.* When a break-even calculation is done in **Goal Seek**, the geometric interpretation of breakeven is that the PV of out-year benefits exactly offsets the PV of up-front costs. This is represented as the areas between the PV curves in Figure 19.1B.

The value of doing **Goal Seek** on the difference between net present values of the two options is that this effectively ties the two alternatives to one another. **Goal Seek** therefore nudges one value toward the other if a parameter only affects one side or the other. (All but one of the parameters used to create the comparison [the 10 gray data cells] affect only one side or the other. The six parameters in rows 1 to 3 affect only the college calculation, and the three parameters in row 4 affect only the noncollege calculation.) When a parameter affects both calculations, **Goal Seek** adjusts the parameter to create equilibrium between sides. The only parameter to affect both sides in the present problem is the discount rate in C5. At a discount rate of 4%, college is a good deal. But college is a good deal because the value in higher wages later in life more than make up for the up-front costs of college. These costs are substantial: The undiscounted sum of gross college costs is about $100,000, and these costs are "front-loaded," meaning that they occur early in the investment (and added to these costs is the opportunity cost of the full-time wage income not received). This is an investment in the same way a firm invests in plant or equipment (i.e., physical capital). Indeed, economists often describe investing in education as investing in human capital. **Human capital** comprises the skills, talents, experiences, and capacities that allow individuals to contribute to the production of goods and services. An important aspect of human capital is the knowledge that is gained through education. By going to college, you are undoubtedly creating human capital.[20] Firms also invest in "firm-specific human capital" by providing on-the-job training.

human capital: Human capital comprises the skills, talents, experiences, and capacities that allow individuals to contribute to the production of goods and services.

The time pattern of costs and benefits involved in investing in college is very much the typical pattern. Given this pattern of costs and benefits, higher discount rates will unambiguously reduce the net present value of going to college.[21] To determine at what discount rate both net benefit streams have equal net present value, simply **Goal Seek** on G5 to 0 by changing C5. The result is a rate of time preference of 5.6% (in which case, both NPVs equal $687,746).

We can also use **Goal Seek** for more sophisticated searches that tie together parameters. For example, suppose that you expect the trajectories of costs and benefits to have the growth rates shown and that you expect the starting salary differential between college and high school jobs to remain $10,000. We might ask: How high would the high school starting salary have to be before going to college is a break-even alternative to not going to college? The idea being examined here is that the $10,000 wage differential becomes less and less significant, relative to the up-front costs of college, the larger the forgone wage income is in the 4 college years. This can be easily tested by tying the two starting salaries (in B3 and D4) to one another. For example, start with the Table 19.10 scenario. (If you have adjusted the parameters of the model, you can return to this scenario easily by using the **Scenarios** function [from **What If Analysis** on the **Data** ribbon in Excel 2007, or the **Tools** pulldown menu in Excel 2003].) Click **Scenarios, 19.10, Show, Close**. From here, click on cell B3 and type =D4+10000. The number in B3 still looks the same as in Table 19.10, but now if D4 changes, so will B3. To find the break-even starting salary, click on G5 and **Goal Seek** on G5 to 0 by changing D4.[22] The required high school starting salary is $43,676 (and consequently, the college starting salary is $53,676). Since it is unlikely that a high school graduate will get this starting salary, going to college is once again confirmed as the dominant option.

Before leaving this analysis, it is worthwhile to consider the effect of Assumption 5—that inflation is zero. Clearly, we do not expect inflation to be zero, but this assumption allows us to create an analysis that is completely based on real growth and discount rates, and the dollars involved are constant dollars. (This does not mean that there is no rate of time preference; it just means that a dollar has the same purchasing power in each time period.) We could obtain the same NPV results discussed with nominal rates, as long as we are careful to turn all rates into nominal rates based on an expected inflation rate, π. The only tricky part of the adjustment is that the starting salary for the individual going to college must be inflated by $(1 + \pi)^4$ to turn this value into a nominal value in the fourth year of the model. (Of course, the undiscounted results would change as inflation is introduced into out-year salaries.) The scenario shown had a net benefit of college of approximately $100,000 ($98,264 to be exact). If we assume instead that expected inflation is 3% and we use Equations 19.3b and 19.3d to adjust discount and growth rates by 3%, the result is still an approximate $100,000 net benefit of going to college ($103,376 is the exact value). But if we use the exact versions of these equations (provided in endnotes 6 and 7), we return to the exact result (of $98,264). Both versions are provided as separate worksheets in the Excel file for this chapter (and these worksheets allow you to adjust the expected inflation rate to examine how this affects the results of the model).

19.4 Evaluating Capital Investment Decisions

Prerequisites: Chapter 2 and Section 19.3

Firms use a variety of methods to examine capital investment decisions (indeed, entire courses are taught on this subject in business school). No one method is dominant, and many of the methods are beyond the scope of this text. We examine three methods of analyzing a capital investment decision in this section: the *payback* method, the *net present value* method, and the *internal rate of return* method. We have already calculated net present value in the context of consumer decisions in Section 19.3, but the other two methods are yet to be discussed. The first method may be disposed of in short order.

19.4A Payback as a Decision Criterion

Managers often examine investments based on a determination of how long it takes to recover the up-front investment. If the recovery period is "too long," the firm chooses not to undertake the project. If payback of the investment occurs further in the future than the cutoff date, the investment will not be undertaken. This method of evaluating investments can be illustrated by means of a simple example.

Suppose that the firm chooses to fund all investments having a payback period of 3 years or less. Consider the four investments in Table 19.11; each has an up-front cost of $10.[23] By this method, A is the best investment because costs are recovered after only 2 years. B and C are next best because each will have a payback in 2.5 years ($8 after 2 years and $12 after 3 years means $10 in 2.5 years). Finally, D is recovered in 3 years and 3 months. If the firm accepts all projects that have a payback period of less than 3 years, then the firm would accept A–C and reject D. If the firm were cash constrained and could only choose one project, then it would choose A because A has the quickest payback period.

Despite managers' common usage of this criterion, it suffers from a number of problems. First and foremost, this criterion treats all dollar benefits as being equally valuable, regardless of the timing of those benefits; present value considerations are ignored. A is the most preferred project by this criterion, but it should never be accepted because it has a negative net present value for *all* discount rates (greater than zero). This method does not distinguish the timing of payments that occur in the years prior to the cutoff time. B and C are equally worthwhile, according to the payback criterion, despite the payback stream being closer to the present in B than in C. On present value grounds, B should dominate C. A second problem concerns how to set the cutoff time. This is arbitrary and can lead to projects being incorrectly discarded. A final problem with this criterion is that it ignores benefits occurring outside the cutoff period. These problems can be seen by

TABLE 19.11 Comparing Four Investment Projects via the Payback Criterion

Year	A	B	C	D	Project
0	-$10	-$10	-$10	-$10	
1	$1	$5	$3	$5	
2	$9	$3	$5	$4	
3	$0	$4	$4	$0	
4	$0	$0	$0	$4	
Years to break-even point:	2	2.5	2.5	3.25	Payback method
Decision:	Invest	Invest	Invest	Do not invest	Given cutoff is 3 years

calculating NPVs for each project. Suppose that the discount rate is 10%. In this event, the net present value calculations for Table 19.11 are:

A	B	C	D	Project
–$1.65	$0.03	–$0.14	$0.58	NPV at r = 10%

The only investment that was rejected by the payback method was D, but D is the one with the highest NPV. As noted earlier, the "best" project on a payback basis has a negative NPV. Further, B and C were equally attractive on a payback basis, but on an NPV basis, C should be rejected, while B should be undertaken. *Despite the ease with which the payback method is calculated, it does not provide a solid basis for decision making.*

One modified version of the payback method calculates cash flows on a present value basis and sets a cutoff based on PV of paybacks, rather than on the undiscounted sum of paybacks. Under this method, only B would be chosen, since NPV > 0 by year 3, using r = 10%. (NPV = 0 is required for the present value of benefits to be equal to the up-front costs, or put another way, the PV of the payout would have occurred by the cutoff time.) This ameliorates the present value problems with the payback method, but the other problems remain. In particular, to use the previous example, D would still be discarded based on a 3-year cutoff, despite being the most profitable on an NPV basis.

Before discussing the internal rate of return method, we should say a few more words about the net present value method.

19.4B Net Present Value as a Decision Criterion

Net present value sums the present value of cash flows in different time periods to obtain a net present value for the project. This allows dollars occurring in different time periods to be compared on a consistent basis. The firm should pursue any project for which NPV ≥ 0 because the discounted sum of costs is smaller than or equal to the discounted sum of benefits.

When a firm is not cash constrained (i.e., it can undertake as many projects as it wishes), the NPV suggests that all projects in which NPV ≥ 0 should be undertaken. As noted in Section 19.2, however, care must be taken to apply the appropriate discount rate in calculating the NPV because the firm faces a continuum of potential projects in terms of the riskiness of the project. Higher-risk projects should be evaluated on an NPV basis using a higher discount rate.[24]

When the firm is cash constrained and does not have sufficient funds to undertake all worthwhile projects, it must choose among projects for which NPV ≥ 0. Unfortunately, the NPV criterion does not provide a method for evaluating which project should be pursued in this setting. The NPV criterion allows us to distinguish among projects that should be pursued and those that should not be pursued, but it does not provide a ranking of projects that should be pursued. The problem can be understood by a simple comparison. Consider two projects, E and F, that are equally risky and that are evaluated based on a 10% cost of capital. These projects are described in Table 19.12. If the firm can only undertake one project, then a comparison of E and F via the NPV criterion suggests that E should be pursued rather than F (because it returns $0.04 more in NPV than F). But consider more closely the difference between E and F. F has an up-front investment of $10 and produces a discounted net gain of $0.86. By contrast, E produces only $0.04 more in net value, despite having an up-front cost that is five times the size of F's up-front cost. Most business managers would prefer F to E, despite E's higher net present value.

19.4C Internal Rate of Return as a Decision Criterion

One difficulty in using the NPV criterion is knowing the appropriate discount rate to use for the project under consideration. Once a discount rate is determined, the decision to undertake the project depends on whether NPV ≥ 0. For the typical project, costs tend to

TABLE 19.12 Comparing Two Investment Projects via the NPV Criterion

year	E	F	Project
0	-$50	-$10	
1	$25	$5	
2	$25	$4	
3	$10	$4	
	$0.90	$0.86	NPV at r = 10%

TABLE 19.13 Net Present Value Is Typically a Declining Function of the Discount Rate, r

Year	E	10.0%	10.2%	10.4%	10.6%	10.8%	11.0%	11.2%	11.4% = r
0	-$50	-$50	-$50	-$50	-$50	-$50	-$50	-$50	-$50
1	$25	$22.73	$22.69	$22.64	$22.60	$22.56	$22.52	$22.48	$22.44
2	$25	$20.66	$20.59	$20.51	$20.44	$20.36	$20.29	$20.22	$20.15
3	$10	$7.51	$7.47	$7.43	$7.39	$7.35	$7.31	$7.27	$7.23
	NPV	$0.90	$0.74	$0.59	$0.43	$0.28	$0.12	-$0.03	-$0.18

occur early on, and benefits occur later in the life of the project. If at a given discount rate, we have NPV > 0, then at a higher discount rate, the NPV will decline. At a high enough discount rate, the NPV will become negative. This is shown for investment E from Table 19.12, given different discount rates in Table 19.13. For this project, the discount rate for which NPV = 0 is slightly less than 11.2%. This rate is called the internal rate of return. The **internal rate of return (IRR)** on an investment is that discount rate for which the NPV of that investment equals zero.

internal rate of return (IRR): The internal rate of return on an investment is that discount rate for which the NPV of that investment equals zero.

The IRR may be calculated using **Goal Seek** (by setting NPV = 0 by changing the discount rate). There is also an IRR function available within Excel's ***fx*** menu. Figure 19.2 provides a graphical description of the internal rate of return based on project E in Table 19.12. The IRR of a project can be seen visually by graphing net present value as a function of discount rate to produce the blue net present value profile. As noted earlier, since costs are front-loaded, and benefits occur later in the life of the project, an increase in the discount rate decreases the NPV. The NPV(r) starts at $10 when r = 0% (the sum of the undiscounted cash flows is $10) for project E. The IRR for the project is that discount rate for which NPV = $0. In Figure 19.2, this occurs at slightly more than 11%. As long as the project is "typical" (meaning costs occur earlier than benefits), and the undiscounted gross benefit stream exceeds the undiscounted gross cost scheme, then the NPV(r) may have a different slope or intercept, but it will have the same general shape and the same general conclusion shown in Figure 19.2: NPV(0) > 0, and there will be a discount rate r* for which NPV(r*) = 0. This value of r is the IRR for the project.

The IRR for a project is internally generated by the cash flows in that project. The IRR does not depend on the cost of capital for the firm (meaning that the cost of capital is not used as the discount rate). Rather, the IRR is compared against the cost of capital of the firm to determine whether the project should be pursued. Those projects whose IRR exceeds the cost of capital are profitable investments that should be pursued, and those projects whose IRR is less than the cost of capital are not profitable. Therefore, IRR = cost of capital acts like NPV = 0 as a separating condition determining which projects

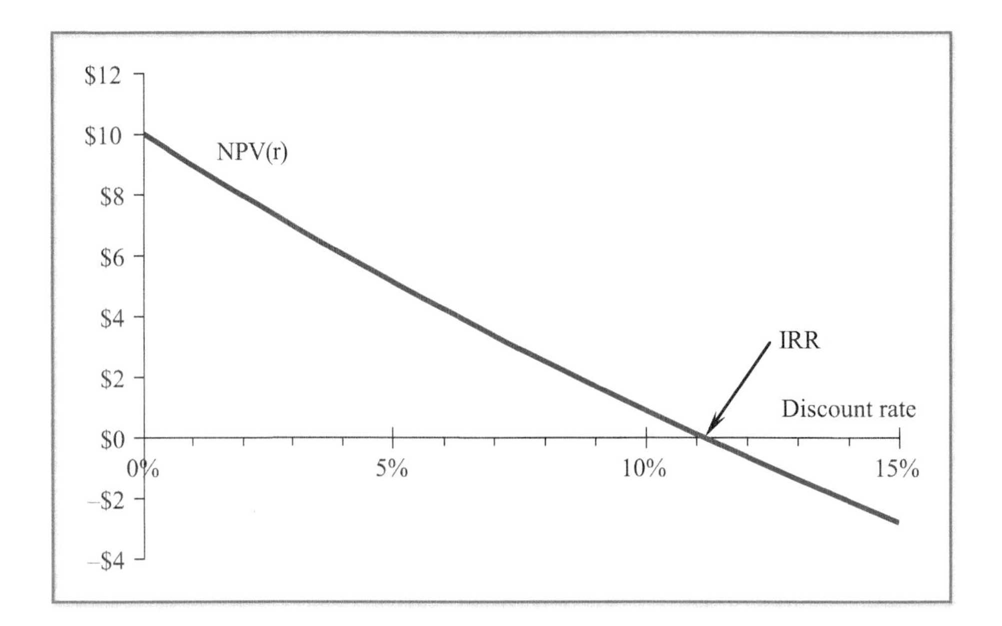

FIGURE 19.2 Net Present Value as a Function of Discount Rate for a Typical Investment

are profitable and which are not. Both conditions separate projects into two groups: those that will increase the profitability of the firm and therefore that should be pursued and those that are not profitable. But as described in the discussion of Table 19.12, the NPV criterion does not provide a reliable method for ranking worthwhile projects. One benefit of the IRR is that it provides a ranking of investments. Table 19.14 revisits the investments in Tables 19.11 and 19.12, and shows all three methods of evaluating the projects. As noted previously, the payback method does not provide an economically sound rank ordering. The IRR provides a more solid basis for ordering projects (as long as each project is in the same risk class and as long as the cash flow is typical).

If the firm faces capital constraints and cannot undertake all projects for which the IRR is greater than the cost of capital, then the IRR decision rule is to rank projects according to the IRR.

> **IRR decision criterion:** *Fund first the project with the highest IRR, then the next highest, and the next highest, and so on until the capital constraint is reached or until the IRR is less than the cost of capital, whichever comes first.*

Consider how this rule would be applied if the firm faced the possible projects A–F, all of which are equally risky. Suppose further that the cost of capital is 10% and that the firm faces a capital constraint of $50 (i.e., the bank would not loan the firm more than this amount). The firm is best served by borrowing $30 and funding F, D, and B. Total net benefits are $1.47 = $0.86 + $0.58 + $0.03 in this instance. By contrast, had the firm

TABLE 19.14 Comparing Three Measures of Profitability

Year	A	B	C	D	E	F	Project
0	-$10	-$10	-$10	-$10	-$50	-$10	
1	$1	$5	$3	$5	$25	$5	
2	$9	$3	$5	$4	$25	$4	
3	$0	$4	$4	$0	$10	$4	
4	$0	$0	$0	$4	$0	$0	
	2	2.5	2.5	3.25	2	2.25	Payback method
	-$1.65	$0.03	-$0.14	$0.58	$0.90	$0.86	NPV at r = 10%
	0.00%	10.18%	9.26%	13.06%	11.16%	15.02%	IRR

simply funded according to the highest NPV, it would have chosen E and attained a net benefit of \$0.90, and its cash constraint would be binding, meaning that if a new \$10 project cropped up, it could not be pursued.

The IRR provides a demand curve for loanable funds for the firm (to the extent that the firm requires external financing to fund its projects). The IRR would, as a result, appear to be the dominant method for evaluating investment projects. Unfortunately, the IRR is not a panacea that allows the firm an easy mechanistic solution to the its capital investment decision calculus.

The IRR cannot be used mechanically because not all projects are typical. If costs do not all occur at the start of the project, there can be multiple IRR values, and there can be singular IRR solutions that are not supported by lower discount rates. More specifically, if the cash-flow series has more than one sign change, there may be multiple discount rates for which the present value of inflows and outflows are equal—that is, there may be multiple discount rates that formally satisfy the definition of the IRR. To understand why this works, we first need to understand the implicit assumption that the IRR criterion and the NPV criterion make regarding reinvestment of cash flows that occur over the life of the investment. The IRR is a discount rate for which the present value of inflows equals the present value of outflows.

> **IRR's assumption:** *The IRR calculation implicitly assumes that inflows occurring during the life of the project are reinvested at the IRR rate of return.*

By contrast,

> **NPV's assumption:** *The NPV calculation implicitly assumes that inflows occurring during the life of the project are reinvested at the capital cost rate of return.*

The latter assumption is more reasonable than the former because inflows can either be used to invest in other projects or returned to shareholders as dividends. In either event, the opportunity cost of the capital is the required rate of return. It makes no sense to expect that a firm will be able to maintain the IRR rate attained on one project on subsequent projects. The examples that follow should help to clarify this point.

Consider an investment in which there is an initial investment, and then a large payout, followed by another large investment at the end of the project with no subsequent payouts. This is decidedly atypical because costs occur early *and* late in the stream of cash flows. Nonetheless, this is not unheard of; a mining operation may have to restore the surface of the strip-mined land to its former contours at the end of mining operations, for example. Figure 19.3 shows what might happen in this instance. In Figure 19.3A, we see a project whose IRR is 100%, clearly higher than we can expect on typical investments. (Students often have difficulty conceptualizing a 100% return; it simply means that a nominal dollar amount 1 year from today is worth only half as much today: \$40 1 year out is worth \$20 today, and \$40 2 years out is worth \$10 today, as noted in the table that accompanies Figure 19.3A.) Despite having a 100% IRR, this investment should not be undertaken. The reason is that the IRR of 100% only makes sense if we are able to invest the cash flows at 100%, and this is an unlikely proposition, as noted earlier.[25] If we follow the more reasonable strategy of valuing cash flows at the cost of capital, we will *inevitably* lose money on this project (because, as the graph of NPV(r) in Figure 19.3A suggests, NPV < 0 for all $r \neq 100\%$). One example is shown in the table; the NPV at 10% is a loss of \$6.69. Figure 19.3B suggests that similar problems occur when we have multiple discount rates at which the discounted costs and benefits coincide. (Figure 19.3B is easily obtained from Figure 19.3A by increasing the \$40s in periods 1 and 2 to \$45.) The mathematical results suggest IRRs at 50% and 200%, but, just like in Figure 19.3A, these IRRs are problematic because we cannot sustain these rates of return on cash flows occurring during the investment. While it is true that the NPV is positive for discount rates between 50% and 200%, such discount rates are well above the cost of capital for firms. The cost of capital provides a market indication of the discount rate we might expect on alternative projects.

FIGURE 19.3 The IRR May Have Multiple Solutions if the Cash-Flow Stream Switches Sign More Than Once: Both Curves Are NPV(r), Based on a (−, +, −) Investment

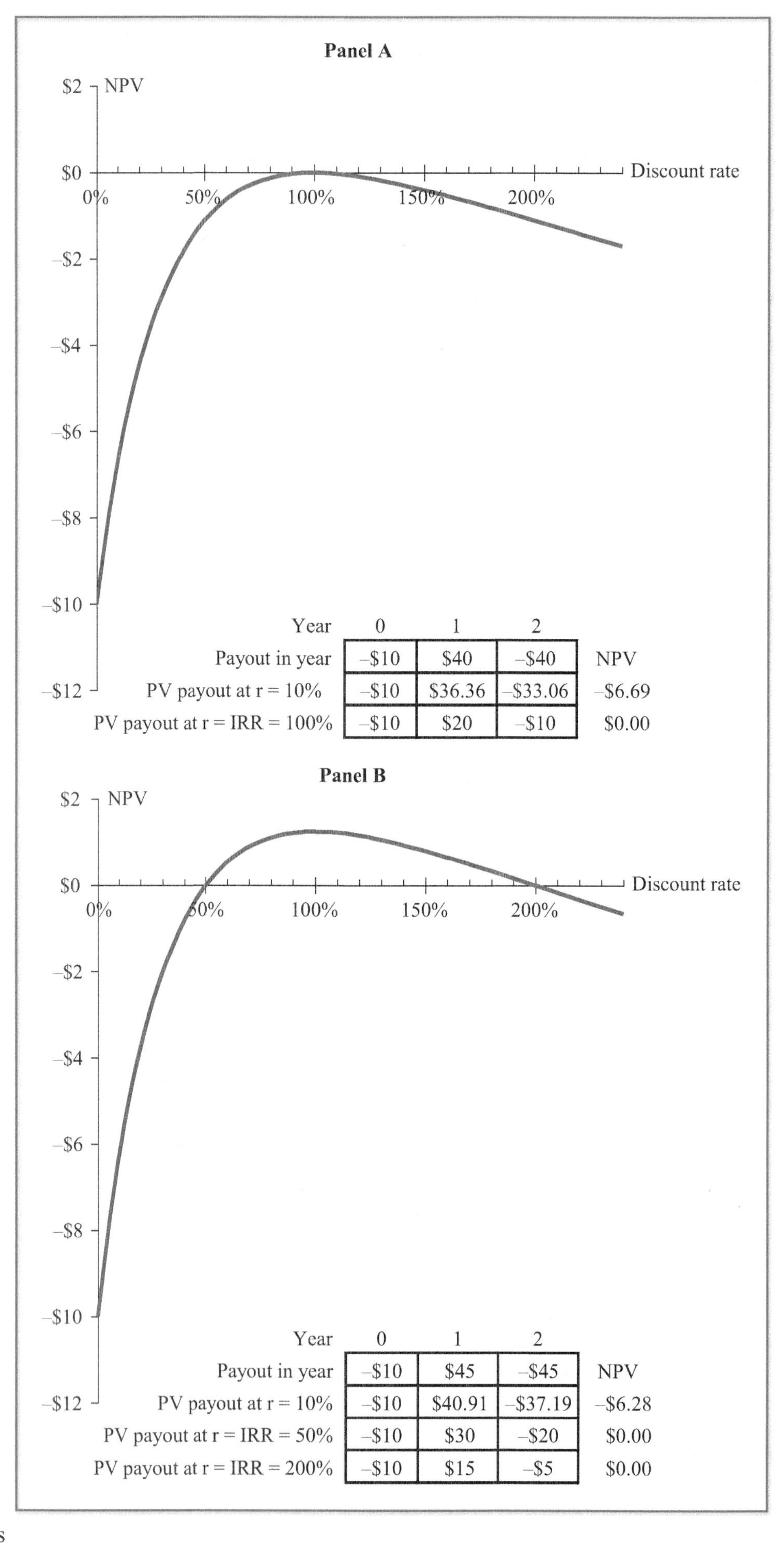

Year	0	1	2	
Payout in year	−$10	$40	−$40	NPV
PV payout at r = 10%	−$10	$36.36	−$33.06	−$6.69
PV payout at r = IRR = 100%	−$10	$20	−$10	$0.00

Year	0	1	2	
Payout in year	−$10	$45	−$45	NPV
PV payout at r = 10%	−$10	$40.91	−$37.19	−$6.28
PV payout at r = IRR = 50%	−$10	$30	−$20	$0.00
PV payout at r = IRR = 200%	−$10	$15	−$5	$0.00

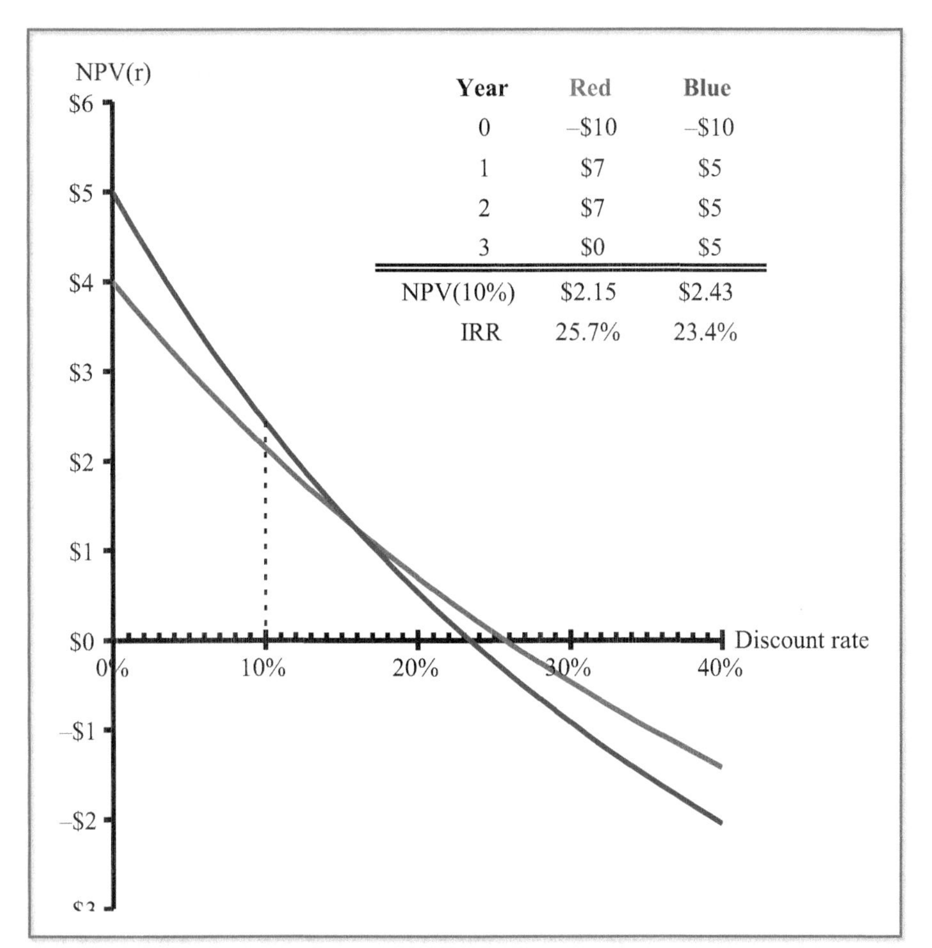

Year	Red	Blue
0	–$10	–$10
1	$7	$5
2	$7	$5
3	$0	$5
NPV(10%)	$2.15	$2.43
IRR	25.7%	23.4%

FIGURE 19.4 Comparing Two Typical Investments via the IRR Criterion and the NPV Criterion

The implicit assumption associated with the IRR criterion (that interim cash flows are reinvested at the internal rate of return) creates problems even for typical investments. Consider two equally risky simple investments, Red and Blue, shown in the table embedded in Figure 19.4. The figure provides NPV profiles for each investment as a function of the discount rate. Suppose that the cost of capital is 10% for the firm. In this event, Blue is the preferred investment, since it has the highest net present value ($2.43 > $2.15), but Red has the highest IRR (25.7% > 23.4%).[26] Therefore, these two investment criteria provide conflicting advice regarding which is the better investment. When this happens, the NPV is typically considered the superior decision rule because it values cash flows at the cost of capital, rather than the IRR. Of course, we still have the problem described earlier that the NPV has difficulty ranking alternatives.

There is no simple rule that firms can always rely on for choosing among investment projects. Potential investments are inherently heterogeneous, and as a result, no single decision rule provides the "best" answer. Both the IRR criterion and the NPV criterion are based on discounting cash flows occurring in different time periods. Both are likely to provide a more reasoned recommendation than payback period, but both are more difficult to implement (since they require knowledge about cash flows occurring outside the payback cutoff time period). The IRR and NPV criteria both require knowledge of the cost of capital, and this cost must be risk adjusted, as noted in Section 19.1. The NPV criterion is generally considered superior to the IRR criterion but suffers from an inability to rank alternatives. As a result of this lack of a unified conclusion, managers often use more than one decision criterion to compare across multiple dimensions. Many other decision rules are also used in capital investment analysis, but they are beyond the scope of this text.

Summary

This chapter focuses on the intertemporal exchange of money both to smooth consumption and to act as an investment vehicle for individuals and firms. Capital markets are the markets in which loanable funds are traded. Loanable funds are, in large part, supplied by individuals for a price, and that price is the interest earned on the money that has been loaned. Loanable funds are demanded by individuals and firms based on the price of those funds. The interest rate is therefore determined by the supply and demand for loanable funds.

Dollars occurring in different time periods are not "worth" the same "amount" as each other. One reason why a dollar a year from now is not worth as much as a dollar today is that there may be inflation. If inflation occurs, the dollar will have diminished purchasing power; it will not buy as many physical units of goods and services as it will today. Another reason this is true is that the future is inherently uncertain (relative to the present). But even without inflation and uncertainty, there is a pure rate of time preference because control of a dollar today means that it can be used today *or* tomorrow, while control of a dollar tomorrow only means that it can be used tomorrow. Having the money today provides the holder of the money with more options because, even in the absence of capital markets, money can be saved for use in the future. Money today is worth more than money tomorrow, *ceteris paribus*. How much more it is worth today than in the future is determined by three factors: the pure rate of time preference, the expected rate of inflation, and the risk premium attached to the future. These factors combine to determine the nominal interest rate. The real interest rate subtracts out the inflation rate. Sometimes, economists are explicit in noting that this is a risk-adjusted real interest rate.

The reverse side of the coin is that money in the future is worth less than money in the present, so money in the future must be discounted to the present to compare dollars occurring in different time periods. The discount rate is simply the interest rate at which borrowing and lending occurs. Put another way, this is the cost of capital. The main formula used in the chapter is $X_{PV} = X_t/(1 + r)^t$. Algebraically, this states that the present value of X_t dollars received in year t is worth X_{PV} dollars today, given an annual discount rate of r. Future value works in the opposite direction (and consequently, replaces the division sign in the previous formula with a multiplication sign).

Present value calculations are easily accomplished using Excel. Excel has canned financial formulas that may be used, but the emphasis in this chapter is on creating an architecture for doing present value calculations that assists in comparative statics analysis. We suggest placing the parameters of the model in a central location and placing the calculations elsewhere. It is often worthwhile to provide a copy of the results of these calculations close to the parameters so that sensitivity analysis is readily accomplished. Comparative statics analysis is especially important in investment analyses because the future is inherently uncertain.

This chapter integrates Excel more centrally into the content because present value calculations are repetitive in nature, and Excel does repetitive calculations with very little effort. This chapter explores only a few of Excel's capabilities, including creating runners, using equations by referencing data, and creating equations that can be repeated. Two powerful Excel tools are the idea of absolute versus relative cell referencing (using $ signs in front of the row and/or column reference) and the use of **Goal Seek**.

An understanding of present value helps individuals to make intertemporal decisions. Individuals often face the choice of how they receive or spend money. Two examples are provided on the consumer side: One involves winning the lottery, and the other involves whether or not to go to college. The decision to go to college is complex and provides a natural place to perform comparative statics analysis.

Firms use a variety of methods to evaluate capital investments, and the chapter examines three of them. The payback method accepts all projects where the gross stream of cash inflows recovers the up-front cost prior to a predetermined cutoff date. The payback method suffers from a variety of problems: It ignores present value considerations, the cutoff date is arbitrary, and it disregards benefits that occur outside the cutoff period. Despite these problems, it is widely used because it is easy to calculate.

Both the internal rate of return (IRR) criterion and the net present value (NPV) criterion explicitly consider present value issues. Net present value sums the present value of cash flows in different time periods to obtain a net value for the project. The internal rate of return is that discount rate where the net present value of cash flows equals zero. The NPV criterion suggests that a firm should fund all projects for which the NPV is nonnegative. The IRR criterion suggests that a firm should fund all projects if the IRR is at least as large as the cost of capital. Both criteria choose the same projects if the projects are typical (meaning that investment costs are up-front and the benefits occur later in the life of the project). For typical projects, if a project satisfies one of these conditions, it satisfies the other as well. (Mathematically, we can show that as long as the project is typical, IRR $\geq$ cost of capital if and only if NPV ≥ 0.) A profit-maximizing firm without cash constraints should choose all such projects.

Firms are often cash constrained and cannot undertake all worthwhile projects. As a result, it is important to be able to rank projects. Unfortunately, each of the criteria has problems. The NPV criterion does not effectively rank worthwhile projects in the event that the firm is cash constrained. The IRR criterion ranks worthwhile projects, but the ranking is not without problems. The IRR ranking of projects is particularly problematic if costs exceed benefits in later years of the cash flow (that is, if the project is not typical). As a result, no single decision rule can always be relied on for choosing among projects.

Review Questions

Define the following terms:

Section 19.1

discount rate
rate of time preference
time value of money
present value (PV)
compounding
annual percentage rate (APR)
annual percentage yield (APY)
cost of capital
real interest rate
nominal interest rate

Section 19.3

annuity
perpetuity
net present value (NPV)
human capital

Section 19.4

payback criterion
present value of payback criterion
net present value criterion
internal rate of return (IRR) criterion

Know how to do the following Excel tasks (or understand these Excel concepts):

Sections 19.2–19.3

Creating runners
Writing an equation in a cell
Formula bar
Dragging an equation
Absolute referencing
Relative referencing
Mixed referencing
Absolute row referencing
Absolute column referencing

Goal Seek

Creating a two-way comparative statics matrix similar to Table 19.7

Provide short answers to the following economics questions:

Section 19.1

a. What are the three components of a firm's cost of capital?
b. How is the real interest rate related to the nominal interest rate?
c. Why do economists often work with real interest rates and real growth rates, rather than their nominal counterparts?

Section 19.3

a. Are advertised lottery winnings based on a lump-sum payment?
b. Why are the nominal trajectories of salary over time upward sloping, but the real trajectories of salary over time downward sloping in Figure 19.1?
c. When would the real trajectory of salary over time be constant? (You can check your answer by using the Excel file and changing the data in the problem to be consistent with your answer.)

Section 19.4

a. What are the main problems with the payback criterion as an investment decision rule?
b. What is the main difficulty with the NPV criterion when capital is scarce?
c. When is the IRR criterion problematic?
d. Does any single investment decision rule dominate from an economic perspective?

Provide short answers to the following Excel questions:

Sections 19.2–19.3

a. Why is it worthwhile to use a cell reference to data that have been typed into a data area, rather than to type the data directly into an equation?
b. Why is it useful to have a data area in a central location within the Excel file?
c. How can you obtain a day-of-the-week column using a runner?
d. How do you undertake a comparative statics analysis using Excel?
e. Why is it useful when entering complex equations to first enter the equation and then deal with referencing issues, using the **F4** key?
f. Why is **Goal Seek** especially useful for break-even analysis?

Check your answers to the *short-answer* exercises in the Answers Appendix at the end of the book.

1. This aspect of intertemporal choice by consumers is examined in Section 17.1, using the consumer optimization model developed in Part 2.

2. This theoretical possibility has to do with the income and substitution effects of a price change initially examined in Chapter 8. An increase in interest rate rotates the intertemporal budget constraint (from Section 17.1) and causes a new utility-maximizing consumption bundle to occur. This bundle may have more or less savings. It will have more savings if the substitution effect on savings dominates the income effect on savings. This view of an individual's saving decision is analogous to the analysis in Section 18.1 that examines the labor supply curve via the labor/leisure trade-off. (Let the horizontal axis be current consumption and the vertical axis be future consumption. Consider the endowment bundle to be a given income level in the current time period, with no income endowment for the future [i.e., the endowment bundle is on the horizontal axis]. The capital market analog to an increase in wage rate is an increase in interest rate. In Section 18.1, we see why the net effect of an increase in price is ambiguous in this instance.)

3. Derived demand for a factor of production is examined in Section 18.2.

4. As discussed in Section 17.1, this is counter to most students' reality.

5. In Section 17.1, we examined intertemporal choice, but we assumed in that instance that there was no inflation because we wished to focus on the choice to allocate consumption of goods across time periods.

6. These equations are only approximately correct. If the real rate of interest r is defined in terms of the inflation rate π (note: this is one place within the text where π does not mean profit) and the nominal interest rate ρ (rho), then the exact relation connecting real and nominal rate is:

$r = (\rho - \pi)/(1 + \pi)$. **(Exact version of Equation 19.3a)**

This is close to Equation 19.3a ($r = \rho - \pi$) as long as inflation is modest (so that π is close to zero). Solving for the nominal rate of interest, we obtain the exact version of Equation 19.3b:

$\rho = r + \pi + r \cdot \pi$. **(Exact version of Equation 19.3b)**

This is close to Equation 19.3b because $r \cdot \pi$ is the product of two small numbers.

The exact equations are based on the intertemporal analysis in Section 17.1 (therefore, the rest of this endnote will not make sense if you have not read that material). The slope of the intertemporal budget constraint must be adjusted if there is inflation. This slope is:

$$1 + r = (1 + \rho)/(1 + \pi).$$

This equation holds because the slope of the intertemporal budget constraint changes as the general price level changes (inflation), since the intertemporal axes are the consumption goods that may be purchased in a given period. From this starting point, we can solve for the real interest rate r by subtracting 1 from both sides of the equation. This yields:

$$r = (1 + \rho)/(1 + \pi) - 1 = ((1 + \rho) - (1 + \pi))/(1 + \pi) = (\rho - \pi)/(1 + \pi).$$

The relation between nominal interest, real interest, and inflation is known as the *Fisher effect* in the finance literature.

7. These are approximations, just like Equations 19.3a and 19.3b discussed in endnote 6. Let g be the real growth rate and γ (gamma) be the nominal growth rate. The true relations connecting g and γ are:

$g = (\gamma - \pi)/(1 + \pi)$. **(Exact version of Equation 19.3c)**

$\gamma = g + \pi + g \cdot \pi$. **(Exact version of Equation 19.3d)**

Both relations follow from the equation $1 + \gamma = (1 + g) \cdot (1 + \pi)$, which says that nominal growth is real growth marked up by inflation.

8. We followed the same strategy of focusing only on real returns in our analysis of risk and return in Section 17.2. We provide an example in Section 19.3 where we look at the decision to go to college. The same present value answers result, whether nominal or real values are used in the calculation. Worksheets for the exact nominal (based on the previous two endnotes) and the rough nominal values (based on Equations 19.3a–19.3c) are provided along with the real worksheet that is the main focus of the text discussion.

9. In this instance, the rate is nominal because inflation has not been explicitly excluded from the problem.

10. You may have wondered why this equation is used when $t = 0$. For all numbers z, $z^0 = 1$, so a separate equation is not required for the current time period. As a result, using the general equation in the current time period saves the entry of a separate equation in this cell.

11. *Source:* http://www.illinoislottery.com/subsections/news03.htm#num11

12. The proof is elegant but not essential to our discussion (therefore, do not bother with it unless you are interested). Let P denote the value of the perpetuity:

$$P = X/(1 + r) + X/(1 + r)^2 + X/(1 + r)^3 + \ldots.$$

We can rewrite this as:

$$P = X/(1 + r) + (1/(1 + r)) \cdot [X/(1 + r) + X/(1 + r)^2 + X/(1 + r)^3 + \ldots].$$

But the amount inside the brackets is, by definition, P; therefore, we can rewrite the equation as:

$$P = X/(1 + r) + (1/(1 + r)) \cdot P.$$

Solving for P, we obtain Equation 19.5a.

13. Both Equations 19.6a and 19.6b are derived using the same algebraic trick used to derive Equation 19.5a (as discussed in endnote 12). As a result, only the second is shown. If P is the value of the perpetuity, then the value of the annuity, A, is:

$$P = \{X + \ldots + X/(1+r)^{n-1}\} + (1/(1+r)^n) \cdot [X + X/(1+r) + X/(1+r)^2 + X/(1+r)^3 + \ldots] = A + (1/(1+r)^n) \cdot P$$

because the term inside the { } is A, and the term inside the [ ] is P. Solving for A, we obtain Equation 19.6b, using Equation 19.5b.

14. If you want to see these full height, just place your mouse over the row 8 number at the far right, then hold down the left-clicker, and move down to the row 31 number. Next move to the row 31/32 border until a symbol with a horizontal line and an up-and-down arrow appears (this is the row height symbol). Double-click and the rows will resume being full height. To return to the reduced height rows, simply use the undo arrow above the **Home** ribbon in Excel 2007 or the **Standard** toolbar in Excel 2003.

15. If you have read Section 7.5, you have already seen an introduction to **Goal Seek**.

16. There are a number of "canned" financial functions available within Excel. To access these functions, click on the down arrow next to the Σ (AutoSum) button on the **Home** ribbon in Excel 2007 (or the **Standard** toolbar in Excel 2003).

17. Had you wanted to use an exponential growth equation in this cell as well, you could have done so. The following would also work in cell G19 (but is more complex): =$G$18*(1+$H$4)^B9. In this event, the starting salary for the lower growth rate is absolute referenced, but the exponent is allowed to float. Both equations yield the same answer.

18. Nonetheless, this is exactly how the Illinois Lottery calculates its value of the winning lottery; it ignores present value considerations when it states that the lottery is worth the (undiscounted) sum of the annuity stream.

19. It is approximately correct to subtract growth rates in this instance. The exact growth rate is 0.96% ≐ 1% = 5% – 4%. The exact relation is easy to obtain. Let α be the actual growth rate in this instance. If X grows at g percent per year, but future values are discounted at the rate of r, the following must hold:

$$X \cdot (1+\alpha)^n = X \cdot (1+g)^n/(1+r)^n.$$

Simplifying, we obtain:

$$1 + \alpha = (1+g)/(1+r) = ((1+r) + (g-r))/(1+r) = 1 + (g-r)/(1+r).$$

Solving for α we obtain: $\alpha = (g-r)/(1+r) \doteq g - r$, as long as the discount rate r is "small." Applying this to the above, we see that $\alpha = 0.01/1.04 = 0.0096$. If you think you have seen these calculations before, you have. This is the same analysis used to tie real and nominal growth rates to one another in Equation 19.3c (and the exact version is labeled "Exact version of Equation 19.3c" in endnote 7).

20. You are also undoubtedly creating an informational signal; such signals are the focus of Section 21.3.

21. Only if the cost stream in out-years is greater than the benefits in those years will an increase in discount rate increase the NPV of a stream of net benefits. This is not a commonly observed investment pattern, but it is the commonly observed pattern for loan repayment.

22. You must use D4 because **Goal Seek** only works when the **By changing cell** reference is to a number; it does not work on equations (so you would not get an answer in this situation had you tried to adjust B3 in this **Goal Seek**).

23. If you are bothered by the size of the investment, think of this in thousands or tens of thousands of dollars. There are enough issues to consider in Section 19.4 that we will focus less on the "realism" of the investment than we did in Section 19.3. As a result, the calculations are less complex than those developed in that section. As in earlier sections of this chapter, you should try to do these yourself in Excel, and then check your answers against those provided in the text.

24. We saw a similar conclusion in Section 17.2 with respect to portfolio risk. Portfolios with a greater degree of risk require a greater return as a result.

25. It may help to consider what you would need to do to pay off this investment: The $10 outlay in period 0 can be settled by paying $20 of the $40 in year 1. The remaining $20 would then need to be invested at 100% to obtain the $40 necessary to retire the $40 year 2 outlay. These are clearly unreasonable assumptions.

26. The reason this occurs is straightforward. Both have identical up-front costs. Blue's payment stream is larger than Red's but it also extends farther into the future than Red's. Therefore, at low discount rates, Blue's NPV dominates, but for high discount rates, Red's dominates.

Strategic Rivalry

CHAPTER 20

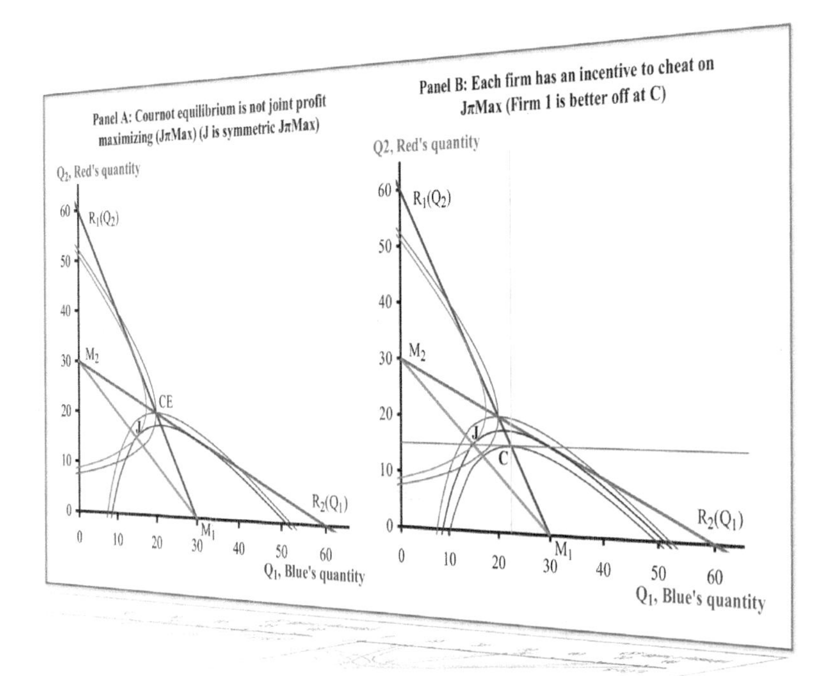

Chapter Outline

This chapter scratches the surface of an active area of economic research: the study of oligopolistic interdependence. Unlike the deterministic models of perfect competition, monopoly, and monopolistic competition, the market outcome when there are a "few" firms is inherently uncertain. This lack of well-defined outcome provides a richness to oligopolistic models that is the centerpiece of an area of economics known as industrial organization. This entire chapter requires Chapter 15 as a prerequisite.

20.1 An Introduction to Oligopoly Markets

Prerequisite: Chapter 15

Section 20.1 Outline

Perfect competition and monopolistic competition are market structures in which the actions of individual firms in the market have no effect on the market as a whole. Firms are said to be atomistic in this setting. Monopoly, of course, is the opposite end of the spectrum, since a monopolist controls the entire market. In between these extremes are markets in which there are a small number of firms. Economists use the general term *oligopoly* to describe this market structure. **Oligopoly** is a market structure in which a few firms dominate the market. Oligopolistic markets need not have a small number of firms in an absolute sense; they only need to have a small number of firms in the core of the market. In this event, the rest of the firms are considered a competitive fringe. Firms in the **competitive fringe** have little independent market power.

oligopoly: Oligopoly is a market structure in which a few firms dominate the market.

competitive fringe: Firms in the competitive fringe have little independent market power.

In an oligopolistic market, each firm in the core has some effect on other firms in the industry. Coke's actions affect Pepsi, and vice versa. There are other firms in the soft-drink market, but Coke and Pepsi are the main players in the cola segment of this market. There is a variety of regional brands (as well as firms that produce private-label products). These firms only have marginal market power, relative to Coke or Pepsi.

Oligopoly involves competition among a small number of firms. An oligopolistic market may be homogenous or differentiated. A special case is a **duopoly** market—a market in which there are two sellers.

duopoly: A duopoly is a market in which there are two sellers.

20.1A Oligopolistic Interdependence

Interdependence is the key to understanding oligopolistic behavior. The difference between oligopoly and perfect competition, monopoly, and monopolistic competition can be summarized with a simple equation that describes an oligopolist's profit function. The point is most easily made in a homogeneous duopoly market. Consider the market from the perspective of Firm 1. Profit for Firm 1 is total revenue less total cost, $\pi_1 = TR_1 - TC_1$. The total cost of producing x_1 units of output is straightforward, given the total cost function derived in Chapter 11. We write total cost as $TC(x_1)$. Total revenue is price times quantity produced, but this product depends on the actions of Firm 2 as well as Firm 1. The market price of the product is based on market inverse demand, $P(X)$, where X is market quantity. Given a duopoly market, $X = x_1 + x_2$. We can therefore write Firm 1's profit function as:

$$\pi(x_1) = x_1 \cdot P(x_1 + x_2) - TC(x_1). \quad \textbf{(20.1)}$$

Of course, a similar equation could be written for Firm 2.

The distinguishing point for each firm is that the firm's profits depend on the other firm's behavior, as well as its own behavior. In Equation 20.1, this is seen in the market inverse demand curve. As Firm 2 increases output, the market clearing price declines, *ceteris paribus*. This, of course, decreases the profits for Firm 1, *ceteris paribus*. Similarly, for Firm 2, an increase in output by Firm 1 decreases Firm 2's profits, *ceteris paribus*. There is a behavioral interdependence inherent in oligopoly that is not present in other market structures.

If there were n firms rather than two in the oligopolistic core, then we would simply need to adjust the equation to take this into consideration. Similarly, if we were discussing differentiated products, rather than homogeneous products, the same interdependence would hold. In this instance, we would not discuss that interdependence using a market inverse demand curve because each variety has its own demand curve. Nonetheless, each firm's demand for its variety depends on the actions of other firms in the differentiated product market.

Each time a firm acts, it has a belief about how its rivals will react. These beliefs are called **behavioral assumptions**. For example, you might expect your rival to match your price changes. Alternatively, you might expect your rival to hold output fixed in the face of changes in your output. These are two different alternative behavioral assumptions; each would lead to a different model of firm behavior. Both guesses are simply that; they are your best guess as to what you expect your rival will do.

behavioral assumptions: Each time a firm acts, it has a belief about how its rivals will react. These beliefs are called behavioral assumptions.

Behavioral assumptions are guesses about how other players will act in response to your actions. These assumptions form the basis for any oligopolistic model, due to the interdependent nature of the firms in this setting. We model the behavior of each firm predicated on each firm's belief about what other firms will do in response to its actions. A different set of behavioral assumptions will produce a different oligopolistic reaction.

Oligopolistic models may well appear to provide definitive answers for how firms act in oligopolistic markets, but this appearance is deceptive. Each definitive model is based on a set of assumed behavior patterns. Not surprisingly, it is all but impossible to be completely accurate regarding such assumptions: Neither firms nor individuals are completely predictable. This can be stated another way: There is no single oligopolistic model that works in all situations. Oligopoly is inherently uncertain due to oligopolistic interdependence.

In an interdependent market, a firm may well attempt to signal via its actions behavior patterns that lead to particularly positive outcomes for that firm. That is, firms may undertake **strategic behavior** to gain an advantage over their rivals. For example, firms may undertake a strategy of adding capacity in advance of need. A firm with excess capacity can easily increase output whenever it is deemed necessary. This ability acts as an effective signal (read: *threat*) to existing as well as potential rivals that hostile actions will be met with hostile reactions.

strategic behavior: A firm engages in strategic behavior if it undertakes actions with the expectation that those actions will signal future actions that are favorable to the firm.

Game theory is an important tool for examining strategic behavior. Before we examine game theory in Section 20.5, we consider a geometric introduction to oligopolistic interdependence, using the notion of reaction functions.

20.2 Reaction Functions

Section 20.2 Outline

Reaction functions offer a way to describe graphically firms' actions, based on assumed behavior patterns of rivals. Reaction functions can be examined with more than two firms, but if we restrict our analysis to a duopoly, we can obtain much of the flavor of the more general oligopolistic setting and still work with two-dimensional graphs. To examine the interdependence between two firms, we model the cost and demand structure, using three simple assumptions:

1. Both firms have zero marginal cost of production, but each faces a fixed cost of $200.
2. The good is homogeneous.
3. Market demand for the product is linear: $P(Q) = 60 - Q$.

The first assumption is simply made for convenience. We examine what happens when we relax these assumptions in Section 20.3.

Consider the competitive and monopoly prices and outputs that would occur in this market. The competitive firm will set $P = MR = MC$; since $MC = 0$, $P = 0$, and 60 units of output will be produced in the short run. The monopolist will set $MR = MC$ and price along the demand curve. We know from Equation 12.11 that the monopolist's marginal revenue curve will have the same intercept and twice the slope as inverse demand: $MR = 60 - 2 \cdot Q$. Given this, $MR = MC$ at $Q = 30$, causing the monopolist's price to be $30. Total revenue in this instance is $900, and profit for the monopolist is $700 (given fixed costs of $200).

Of course, having two firms in the market means that neither the competitive nor monopolistic outcomes would prevail, but they provide us with bounds on what will prevail under the duopoly. In particular, we would expect the duopoly solution to have between 30 and 60 units of output sold. Suppose that we start by splitting the market in two, with both firms producing 30 units of output. This can be shown on a figure in which the axes are the quantities produced by each firm as the point (30, 30). Figure 20.1 shows this point and provides horizontal and vertical lines through this point. The horizontal axis is output by Firm 1 (which we can also call Blue), and the vertical axis is output by Firm 2 (which we can also call Red). Using colors in addition to firm numbers will help you keep track of "who is who" in the graphical analysis to come.

Q1a. Relative to point **A**, which direction (north, south, east, or west) is unambiguously better for Blue?

Q1b. What are Blue's profits at **A**?

Q1c. Which direction (north, south, east, or west) is unambiguously better for Red, relative to point **A**?

Q1d. What are Red's profits at **A**?*

***Q1 answer:** Less output by Red is better for Blue, so south of **A** is higher profits for Blue. $\pi_{A,Blue} = -\$200$ because TR = $0, and TC = FC + VC = $200. Less output by Blue is better for Red, so west of **A** is higher profits for Red. $\pi_{A,Red} = -\$200$ because TR = $0, and TC = FC + VC = $200.

FIGURE 20.1
Determining Higher Profits in a Duopoly Market

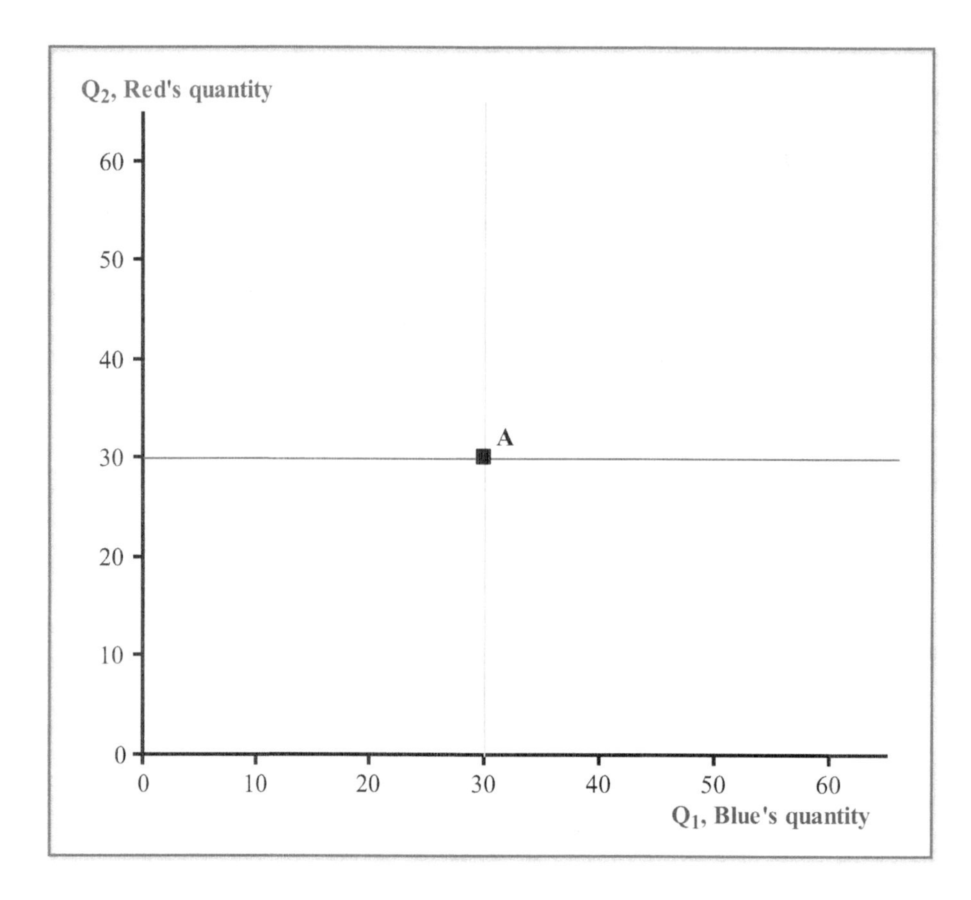

Consider, in particular, Firm 1. Any output by Firm 2 less than 30 is better for Firm 1 than 30. The *best* outcome for Firm 1 would be if Firm 2 produced nothing; in this instance, Firm 1 is a monopolist. This is represented by the point (30, 0) in the figure. Similarly, the point (0, 30) represents Firm 2 as a monopolist.

We can use profits at any joint production point to examine how firms might react to one another. Consider Blue's profits. Blue's monopoly outcome is certainly its highest profit solution (this profit level is \$700 = TR – TC = \$900 – \$200). Other points have lower profits than this. Figure 20.2 shows four isoprofit contours for Blue, although the monopoly isoprofit contour is simply the (dark blue) point (30, 0). Higher isoprofit contours are the ones closer to the monopoly outcome. The least-profitable isoprofit contour is the diagonal line connecting (60, 0) and (0, 60), since total output is 60 along this contour. Given this, price is zero, as noted earlier, so that $\pi_{Blue} = -200$ along this contour (because MC = 0). The next two isoprofit contours shown pass through the points (15, 30) and (20, 20)—the triangle and the diamond, respectively.

Q2. What are Blue's profits associated with these two isoprofit contours?*

Firm 1 will choose different output levels, based on what it expects Firm 2 to produce. If Firm 1 expects Firm 2 to produce 20 units of output, for example, it will maximize profits, subject to Firm 2's production of 20 units, by producing 20 units itself. This is the diamond at the point (20, 20) at the top of the third isoprofit contour in Figure 20.2. But if Firm 1 expects Firm 2 to produce 30 units of output, Firm 1's optimal reaction is to produce 15 units of output (and produce at the triangle that is at the top of the second isoprofit contour in Figure 20.2). Both of these points represent optimal reactions by Firm 1 to different outputs by Firm 2. If Firm 1 expects that Firm 2 will produce a different output level, then Firm 1 will have a different optimal reaction. We can describe Firm

*__Q2 answer:__ The isoprofit contour through the triangle $\pi_{Blue}(15, 30) = Q \cdot P - TC = 15 \cdot \$15 - \$200 = \$25$, and the one passing through the diamond is $\pi_{Blue}(20, 20) = 20 \cdot \$20 - \$200 = \$200$. The only part of this calculation that is not immediately clear is how price is determined. Price is simply inverse demand evaluated at $Q_1 + Q_2$, so $P = 60 - (Q_1 + Q_2)$, according to Assumption 3 above.

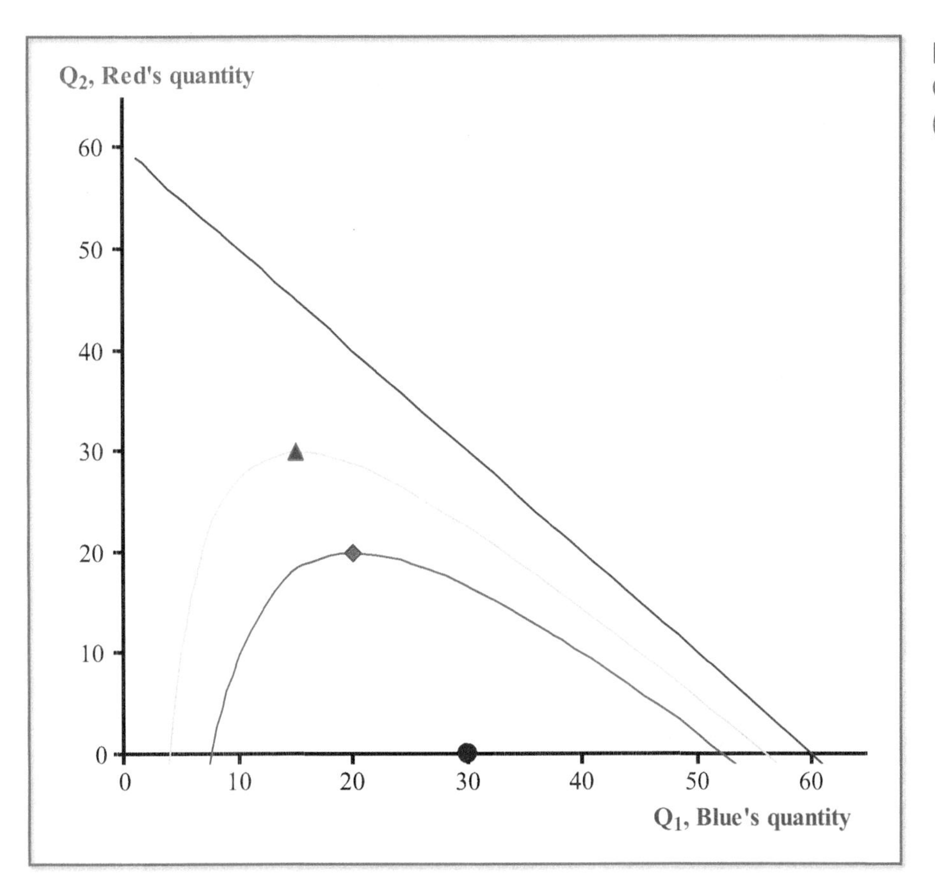

FIGURE 20.2 Isoprofit Contours for Firm 1 (Blue)

1's reaction to Firm 2's various production levels using a reaction function. A **reaction function** describes how one firm reacts to another firm's actions.

reaction function: A reaction function describes how one firm reacts to another firm's actions.

Figure 20.3A describes Firm 1's reaction function to various output levels produced by Firm 2, $R_1(Q_2)$. The pink horizontal line at $Q_2 = 20$ represents Firm 2 producing 20 units of output. Given this level of production by Firm 2, Firm 1's profit-maximizing decision is to produce 20 units of output (as noted earlier). This is a point on the reaction function. Other points on the reaction function are similarly situated at the top of each isoprofit contour. These points represent Firm 1 doing as well as possible, given different output levels by Firm 2. Note, in particular, the two endpoints of $R_1(Q_2)$. If Firm 2 produces no output, then Firm 1 acts as a monopolist and produces 30 units; if Firm 2 produces 60 units, then $P = 0$, and it does not make sense for Firm 1 to produce any output.

Figure 20.3B reverses the orientation and examines profit maximization from the point of view of Firm 2. As noted in Figure 20.1, higher profits for Firm 2 are toward the left. Since both firms have the same marginal cost structure, they face the same best outcome for any level of output by their rival. The best outcome from the point of view of Firm 2 is for Firm 1 to produce nothing; in this event, Firm 2 produces the monopoly output of 30 units. If Firm 1 produces 60 units of output, Firm 2 will produce nothing. And if Firm 1 produces 20 units of output (the blue vertical line at $Q_1 = 20$), Firm 2's optimal response will be to produce 20 units of output as well. (This is the point on the highest isoprofit contour for Firm 2, given $Q_1 = 20$.)

20.2A The Cournot Assumption

Figures 20.3A and 20.3B examine an individual firm's reaction function. These reaction functions represent how each firm would react to various output levels by the other firm. *Each of these reaction functions represents the optimal response function if each firm believes that the other firm will maintain its output.* This behavioral assumption is called the **Cournot quantity assumption**. If a firm has Cournot quantity beliefs, it reacts along its reaction function. In a duopoly market, if both firms have Cournot quantity beliefs

Cournot quantity assumption: If a firm believes that rival firms will maintain their output level, regardless of what it does, the firm assumes Cournot quantity behavior by rival firms.

FIGURE 20.3 Reaction Functions for Firms 1 and 2

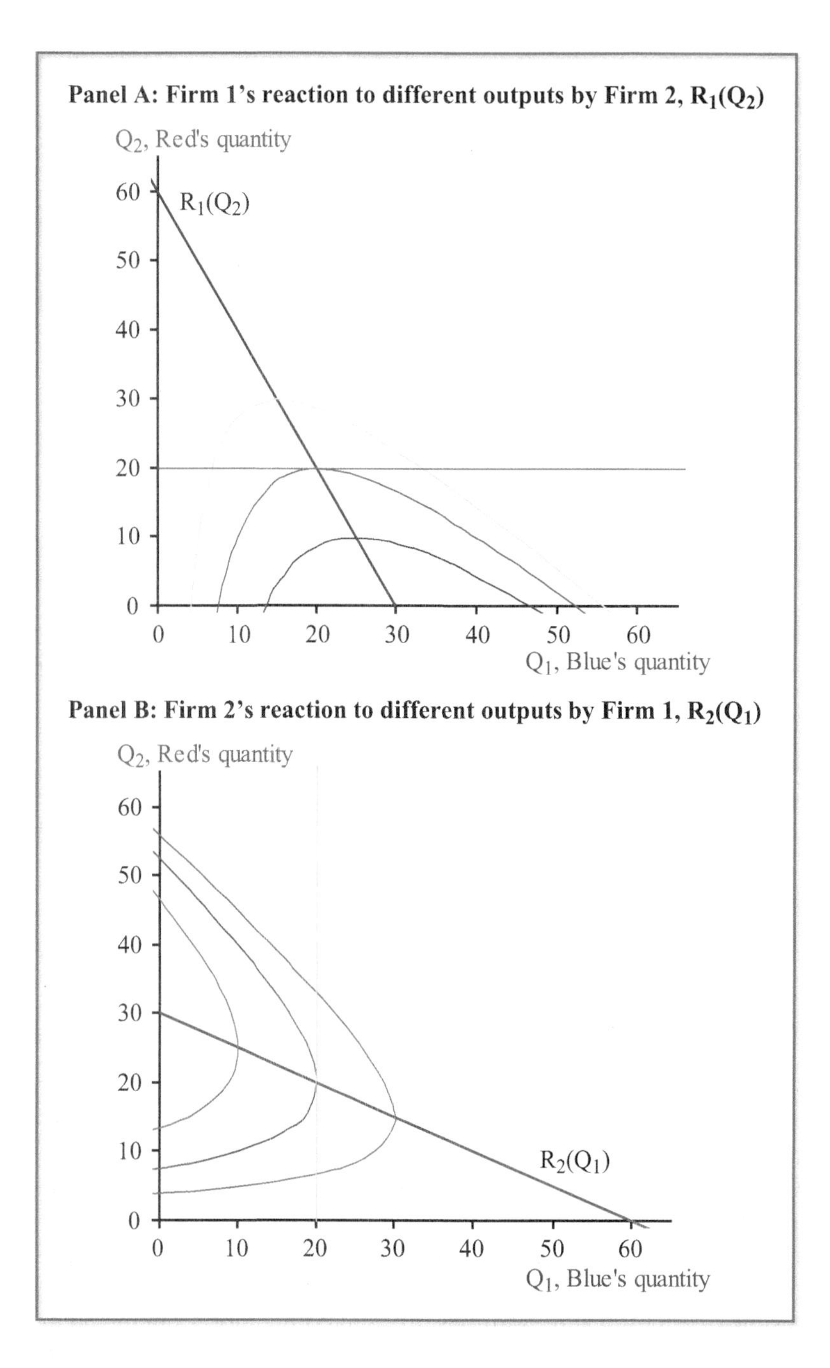

about their rivals, then the point where their reaction functions intersect represents the best that each firm can do, given what the other firm is doing. It further represents a point where each firm's beliefs about its rivals' behaviors are realized. This point is called the **Cournot equilibrium (CE)**.

Cournot equilibrium (CE): A Cournot equilibrium is the intersection of each firm's reaction functions.

The Cournot equilibrium is shown in Figure 20.4. If both firms have Cournot quantity beliefs about their rivals, then each firm will choose the CE output level in response to its rival choosing the CE output level. Each firm's behavioral assumption is realized in this instance. In particular, let CE = $(Q_{1,CE}, Q_{2,CE})$. Firm 1 produces $Q_{1,CE}$ units of output, based on its expectation that Firm 2 will not change its production from $Q_{2,CE}$. Similarly, Firm 2 produces $Q_{2,CE}$ units of output, based on its expectation that Firm 1 will not change its production from $Q_{1,CE}$. Both firms' expectations about their rivals' behavior are realized at this joint production point. This is the essence of the intersection point being in equilibrium.

The Cournot equilibrium is a special example of the more general game theoretic concept of a Nash equilibrium, named after the Princeton mathematician/economist John

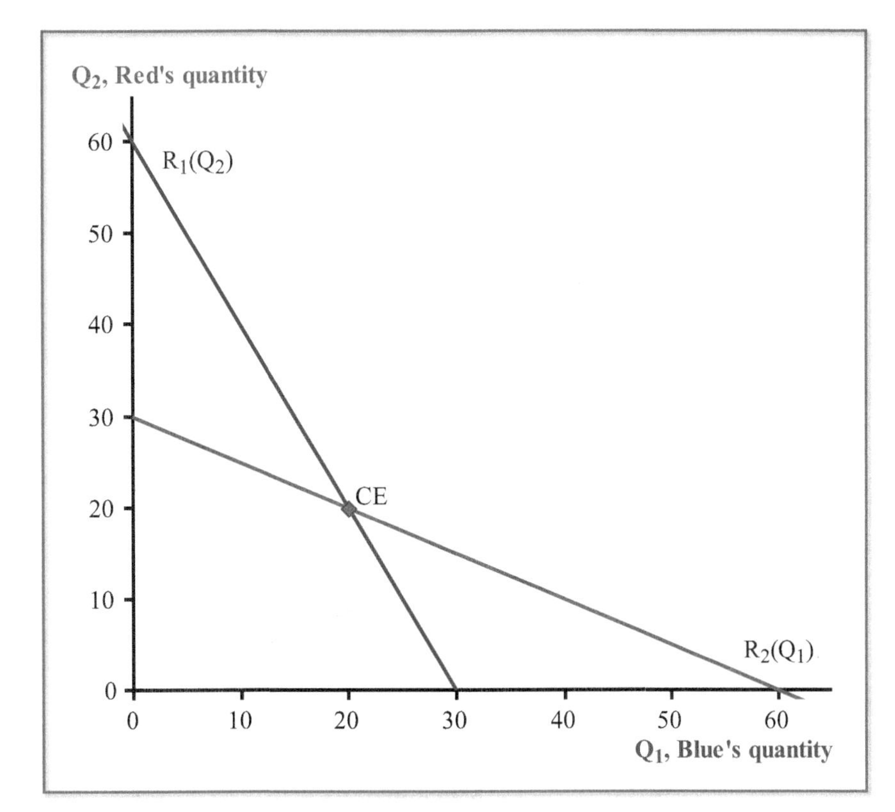

FIGURE 20.4 The Cournot Equilibrium

Nash, who first codified this concept in 1951.[1] A **Nash equilibrium** occurs if every player's strategy is optimal, given competitors' strategies.

Nash equilibrium: A Nash equilibrium occurs if every player's strategy is optimal, given competitors' strategies.

A set of strategies is a Nash equilibrium if all of the individual players are doing the best they can, given the strategies of all opponents. In the present instance, if each firm has Cournot quantity beliefs, then each firm will react along its reaction function. The Cournot quantity assumption is that rival firms maintain output, regardless of what the firm does. *If each firm has Cournot quantity beliefs, then the CE is the* only *point for which these beliefs are realized.* At this point, each firm's beliefs about the action (or inaction) of other firms are confirmed. At any other point, these beliefs are not confirmed.

Is Cournot Joint Profit Maximizing?

The question naturally arises, is the Cournot equilibrium the best the industry as a whole can do? Is the CE joint profit maximizing? Interestingly, the answer is an unambiguous *no*. Although the Cournot equilibrium represents the profit-maximizing solution for each firm in the industry, given what each firm believes its rivals will do (in this case, maintain output), it is not profit maximizing in the more global sense.

Once each firm's isoprofit contours through CE are shown, then the reason the Cournot equilibrium is not joint profit maximizing becomes clear. All isoprofit contours for Firm 1 are horizontal at $R_1(Q_2)$ (according to Figure 20.3A), and all isoprofit contours for Firm 2 are vertical at $R_2(Q_1)$ (according to Figure 20.3B). Both firms' isoprofit contours through CE are shown in Figure 20.5A. *All* points in the football-shaped area to the southwest of CE are more profitable for *both* firms than is the intersection point. The same will be true as long as there is a "positive football," just as was the case with the Edgeworth Box diagrams in Chapters 3 and 7. To put it in the language of that discussion, all points inside the football are Pareto superior to points on the border of the football.

Consider the Cournot equilibrium in terms of the dollar values calculated earlier. We know that each firm has profits of \$200 in CE (since $\pi = TR - TC = 20 \cdot \$20 - \$200 = \$200$). Given this, joint profit for the industry is \$400 at CE. By contrast, profits at each of the monopoly positions are \$500, given the assumptions of this model (because the monopolist's profits are \$700 and the firm that shuts down in the short run faces a loss of

FIGURE 20.5
Profitability in Cournot Equilibrium

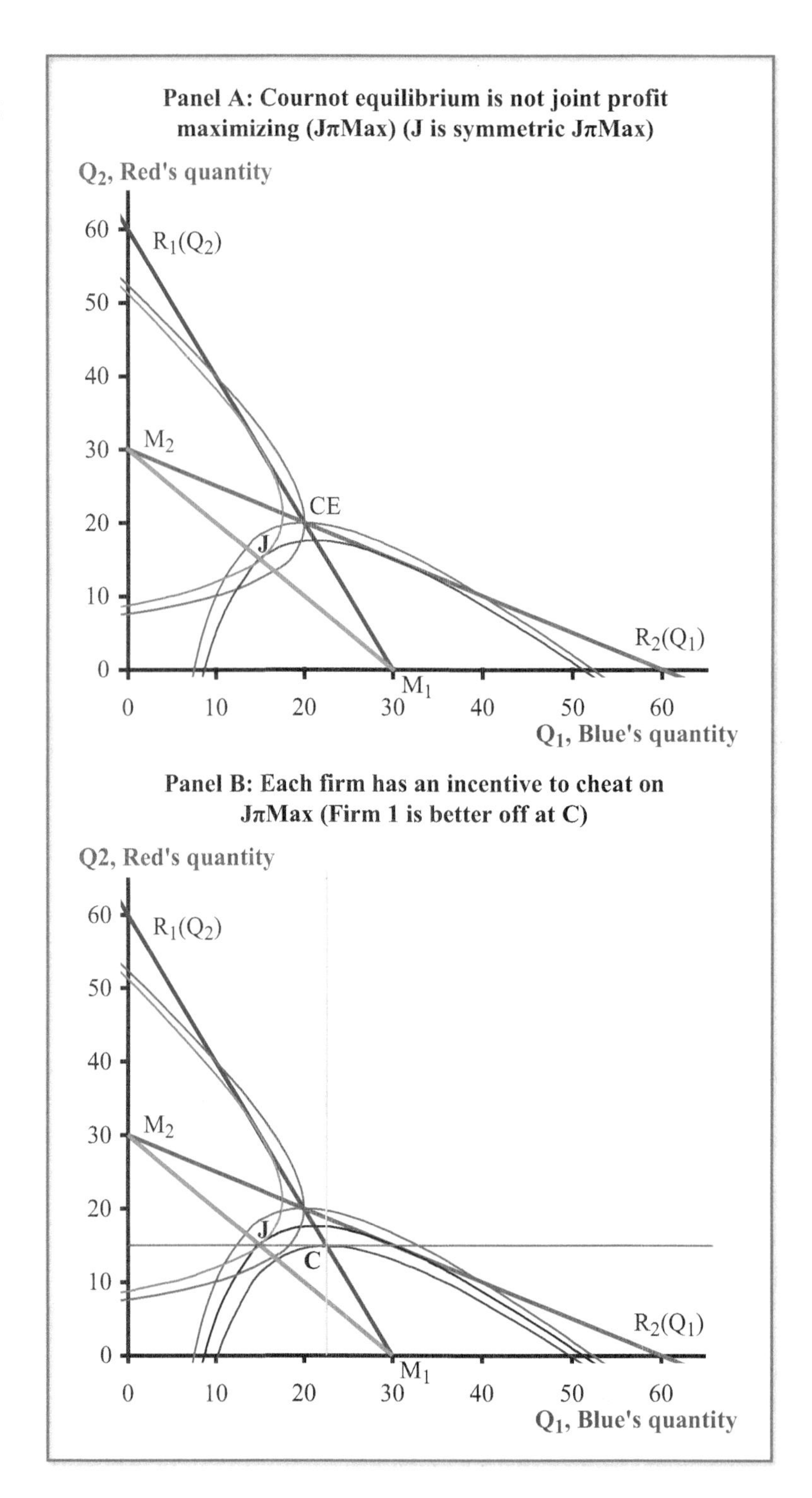

\$200 = FC in this instance). These are the points M_1 and M_2 in Figure 20.5A. Given equal constant marginal costs across firms, it does not matter which firm produces the 30 units of output from the point of view of total profits. It also does not matter how much each firm produces, as long as total production is restricted to 30 units of output, because all points where total output is 30 maintain joint profits of \$500. The green line segment connecting M_1 and M_2 in Figure 20.5A therefore represents the set of joint profit-maximizing outcomes.

Although total profits are constant along M_1M_2, the distribution of those profits depends critically upon the individual production levels. Points closer to M_1 are better for Firm 1 and worse for Firm 2, and vice versa. Point **J** in Figure 20.5A represents the symmetric joint profit-maximizing outcome.

Q5. What are each firm's profits at point **J**?*

Point **J** dominates the Cournot equilibrium for each firm because each attains $50 more in profits. We see this visually because each firm's isoprofit contour through **J** is higher than the respective isoprofit contour passing through CE.

All points on the line segment M_1M_2 are points of tangency between isoprofit contours. One firm cannot make more profits without the other firm making less at these points. Economists often call this set of "zero footballs" the *contract curve* (just as was the case for consumers in the Edgeworth Box).

If firms were able to collude effectively, they could therefore do better than the Cournot equilibrium. This is not, however, that easy to accomplish because each firm has an incentive to cheat on the collusive bargain. Suppose that each firm has agreed (perhaps only tacitly) to produce at **J**. (Tacit coordination is discussed in Section 20.5. It involves no direct communication or agreement. Such direct communication violates the antitrust laws.) This joint profit-maximizing outcome is difficult to maintain because each firm has an incentive to cheat. Consider the joint production at **J** from the perspective of Firm 1. If Firm 2 produces 15 units of output, Firm 1 can achieve even higher profits by cheating on the tacit bargain and producing 22.5 units of output ($\pi_1 = \$306.25 = 22.5 \cdot \$22.50 - \$200$ as a result). This is shown as point **C** in Figure 20.5B. Of course, the same reasoning applies to Firm 2. If both firms cheat on their tacit bargain, the tacit bargain breaks down. Profits for both firms are lower than profits at CE if both firms cheat and produce 22.5 units of output (indeed, $\pi_1 = \pi_2 = \$137.50 = 22.5 \cdot \$15 - \$200$ as a result).

The Cournot model is a useful starting point for oligopolistic analysis because it provides a simple way to see that the oligopolistic bargain is between the competitive outcome and the bargain achieved by a perfect cartel. (A perfect cartel is a group of firms that act in a joint profit-maximizing fashion. Perfect cartels are difficult to maintain because, as noted earlier, there is always an incentive to cheat. If you do not believe this, consider how difficult it has been for OPEC [Organization of Petroleum Exporting Countries] to maintain production discipline over the years, despite being a *legal* entity.) In the context of our diagrams, CE = (20, 20), and total production of 40 is between the competitive level of 60 and the perfect cartel level of 30 units of output. The Cournot model also provides useful insights into how firms might try to do better than CE and the difficulty involved in achieving and maintaining such preferable outcomes.

One serious limitation of the Cournot model is that it only models equilibrium behavior. Each firm's belief about the other's actions is *only* confirmed at CE. At all other points, each firm's belief about the other firm's inaction is not realized. Put another way, the Cournot model does not provide insights into the dynamics of the disequilibrium adjustment process.

20.2B Stackelberg Leadership

The Cournot model is based on firms having symmetric behavioral assumptions about rival behavior. Each firm believes that its rivals will not change output, regardless of what the firm does. *Firms need not have symmetric beliefs about their rivals.* If one firm acts as a dominant firm, then it can take advantage of its dominance to increase profits. The dominant firm will not be able to force rivals out of the market completely, but it will be able to assert its dominance by choosing an output level that produces higher profits than it could achieve under Cournot. Such a firm will choose to maximize profits, subject to what it expects its rivals to do in response to its actions. We call such a firm a **Stackelberg leader**. A Stackelberg leader believes that its rivals will choose their output based on what the Stackelberg leader chooses to produce. By contrast, the Stackelberg follower takes the actions of the Stackelberg leader as given and reacts accordingly. In the context of

Stackelberg leader: A Stackelberg leader believes that its rivals will choose their output based on what the Stackelberg leader chooses to produce.

***Q5 answer:** The easy answer is $250 because we know that the solution is symmetric, and we know that total profits are $500 along M_1M_2. This is confirmed by noting that at the symmetric joint profit-maximizing point **J** = (15, 15), we have $\pi = TR - TC = 15 \cdot \$30 - \$200 = \$450 - \$200 = \$250$ for each firm.

FIGURE 20.6 Stackelberg Leadership

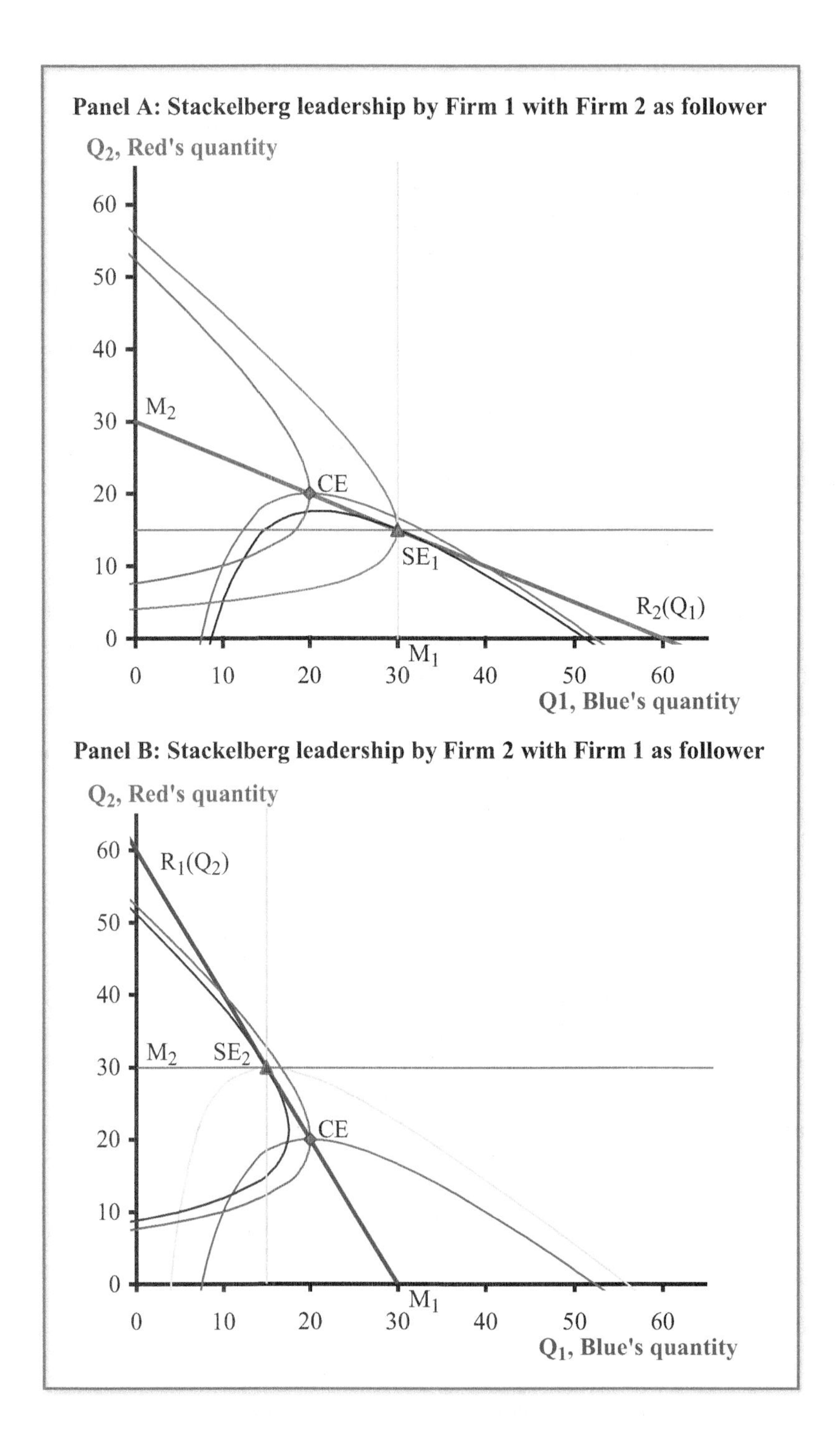

the quantity-based model, this means that the Stackelberg follower has Cournot quantity assumptions about the leader.

If the follower believes that the leader will maintain its quantity, the leader will take that belief into consideration in determining how much to produce. We can model how this is done, using the reaction functions we derived earlier. Suppose that Firm 1 is the Stackelberg leader. In this instance, Firm 1 will wish to maximize profits, subject to Firm 2 reacting along its reaction function, $R_2(Q_1)$. Firm 1 will choose that output level where its isoprofit contour is tangent to $R_2(Q_1)$. This is the point labeled SE_1 in Figure 20.6A. *The leader no longer chooses to produce along its reaction function because it does not believe that its rival will maintain output. Instead, the leader believes that the rival will believe that the leader will maintain output.* A comparison of the geometry of the figures is worthwhile. Firm 1's tangency at $SE_1 = (30, 15)$ is to Firm 2's reaction function in Figure 20.6A, as opposed to the horizontal line $Q_2 = 20$ at CE = (20, 20) in Figures 20.4 and

20.5. This difference is due to the difference in Firm 1's behavioral assumption in the two models. By contrast, Firm 2 has Cournot quantity beliefs about Firm 1 in *both* models. Hence, Firm 2 reacts along $R_2(Q_1)$ at CE in Figures 20.4 and 20.5, and at SE_1 in Figure 20.6A. In both instances, Firm 2's isoprofit contour is vertical at the equilibrium.

Q6. What are profits for Firm 1 and Firm 2 if each firm acts as expected in Figure 20.6A?*

If both firms have the beliefs described, then SE_1 is a Nash equilibrium. Firm 1 takes advantage of its leadership position and does better in SE_1 than in CE. Firm 2 maximizes profits subject to Firm 1's output choice and has lower profits in SE_1 than in CE. It has higher profits in SE_1 than at any other output level for Firm 2 (subject to Firm 1 producing 30 units of output). Each firm does the best it can, given what it believes the other firm will do, and each firm's beliefs are confirmed by the behavior of the other firm. In particular, Firm 2 reacts along R_2, as expected by Firm 1, and Firm 1 maintains output, as expected by Firm 2. One final point to notice about the *Stackelberg equilibrium* is that industry profits decline, relative to the Cournot equilibrium. A comparison of the two situations suggests that Firm 2 loses more than Firm 1 gains in profits in this situation.

If Firm 2 acts as the Stackelberg leader and if Firm 1 acts as a Stackelberg follower (i.e., has Cournot quantity beliefs), we obtain a symmetric Nash equilibrium along $R_1(Q_2)$. Given the symmetry of our cost assumptions, it is not surprising that the results are a mirror-image equilibrium at SE_2 in Figure 20.6B. Firm 2 now has higher profits (of $250), and Firm 1 has lower profits (of $25) than attained in Cournot equilibrium.

Of course, firms are not identified as leaders or followers within an industry on an *a priori* basis. Figure 20.6 clearly shows that there are benefits to leadership, so it makes sense that firms would wish to be the industry leader. Firms must assert their leadership by virtue of their actions. And if both firms in a duopoly attempt to assert their leadership over the industry, each will attempt to expand output. The result is that too much output will be produced within the duopoly. This can be modeled, using the Stackelberg analysis provided earlier. Suppose that both firms have Stackelberg leader beliefs: Each firm believes that it is the leader, and that as a result, its rival will predicate its actions based on the actions of the leader. Firm 1 chooses the output level that maximizes Firm 1's profits subject to R_2 by producing at $Q_{1,SE1}$. Firm 2 chooses the output level that maximizes Firm 2's profits subject to R_1 by producing at $Q_{2,SE2}$. This joint choice produces an outcome known as *Stackelberg disequilibrium*, SD = $(Q_{1,SE1}, Q_{2,SE2})$. This is shown in Figure 20.7. Given the simplifying assumptions in our model, the Stackelberg disequilibrium produces the competitive level of output.

Stackelberg disequilibrium is not a Nash equilibrium. Each firm's belief about its rival's behavior is not realized, and each firm's behavior is not optimal, given the behavior of its rival. In particular, Firm 1 believed that Firm 2 would produce 15 units in response to Firm 1's production of 30 units. Similarly, Firm 2 believed that Firm 1 would produce 15 units in response to Firm 2's production of 30 units. Neither of these expectations is realized. And given the actions of each firm, each would be better off it reduced output to 15 units (by reacting along its reaction function). Of course, if both did that, then they would achieve the joint profit-maximizing solution **J** examined in Figure 20.5 (and each firm would also have the incentive to cheat, based on that outcome discussed in Figure 20.5B).

20.3 What Happens as We Relax the Assumptions of the Model?

Section 20.3 Outline

20.3A Asymmetric Costs

20.3B More Than Two Firms in the Market

The assumptions used to examine oligopolistic behavior can be relaxed to examine more general economic circumstances. Demand was assumed to be linear with an intercept of 60 and a slope of –1 so that we could easily calculate price based on production (as $P = 60 - Q$). We can easily adjust this to a more general linear (inverse) demand function:

$$P(Q) = a - b \cdot Q. \quad \textbf{(20.2)}$$

***Q6 answer:** $\pi_{1,SE1} = 30 \cdot \$15 - \$200 = \$250$, and $\pi_{2,SE1} = 15 \cdot \$15 - \$200 = \$25$.

FIGURE 20.7
Stackelberg Disequilibrium

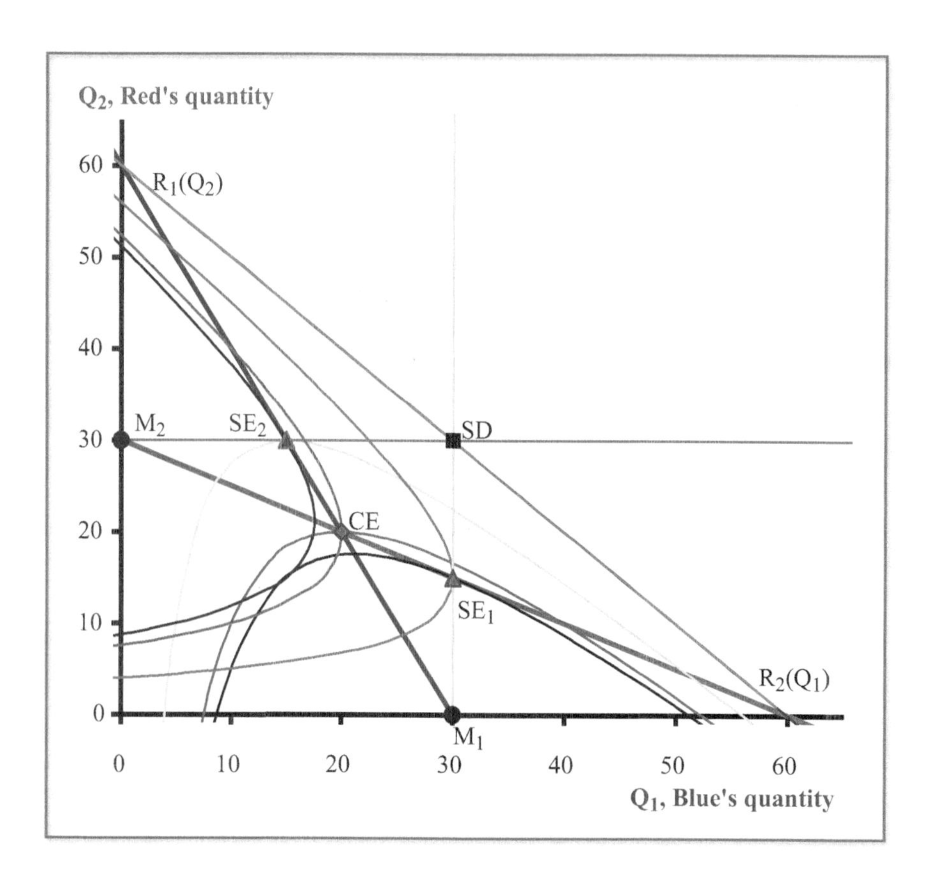

Nonlinear forms produce reaction functions that are nonlinear as well (as a result, we restrict our analysis to linear demand). Equation 12.11 tells us that in this instance the monopolist's marginal revenue curve will be $MR_{monop}(Q) = a - 2 \cdot b \cdot Q$.

If both firms have identical marginal costs, $MC_1 = MC_2 = c$, then this will have little effect on the analysis provided previously, even if $c > 0$. To see why, notice that the profit-maximizing monopoly solution is MR = MC or:

$$a - 2 \cdot b \cdot Q = c. \tag{20.3a}$$

Solving for quantity, we obtain the monopoly solution:

$$Q_{monopoly} = (a - c)/(2 \cdot b). \tag{20.3b}$$

At the opposite end of the spectrum, the competitive market requires P = MC. Given Equation 20.2, we see that the competitive market requires $(a - b \cdot Q = c)$. Solving for Q, we see that the competitive market will produce twice as much output as the monopolist:

$$Q_{competition} = (a - c)/b. \tag{20.3c}$$

Equations 20.3b and 20.3c provide the two intercepts for each reaction function in this instance, just as was the case earlier. For example, if b = 1 and c = \$5, then if a = \$65, both reaction functions *are identical* to those derived previously. The reason for this is straightforward: Given marginal cost of \$5, the competitive market will require a competitive price of \$5. This means that 60 units will be sold, given Equation 20.3c. (This is the vertical intercept of $R_1(Q_2)$ and the horizontal intercept of $R_2(Q_1)$ in Figure 20.4.) By contrast, a monopolist facing these cost and output conditions would produce 30 units of output, according to Equation 20.3b. (This is the horizontal intercept of $R_1(Q_2)$ and the vertical intercept of $R_2(Q_1)$ in Figure 20.4.) Between these boundary points, we can show (via calculus) that R_1 will maintain a slope of –2 and that R_2 will maintain a slope of –1/2.

Interestingly, the slope of the market demand curve does not affect the slopes of the reaction function. When $b \neq 1$, the same reaction function slopes are maintained for a simple reason. The magnitude of b determines how many units of output are sold in the competitive and monopoly solutions (since b is in the denominator of Equations 20.3b and 20.3c), but the ratio of these two equations describes the slopes of the two reaction functions, and this slope is independent of the size of b.[2]

Since each firm's cost structure is the same in the previous discussion, the Cournot and Stackelberg solutions are symmetric about the 45° line. For example, the Cournot equilibrium is the intersection of $R_1(Q_2)$ and $R_2(Q_1)$. The equations for these reaction functions are:

$$R_1(Q_2) = (a - c)/(2 \cdot b) - 1/2 \cdot Q_2. \qquad \textbf{(20.4a)}$$

$$R_2(Q_1) = (a - c)/(2 \cdot b) - 1/2 \cdot Q_1. \qquad \textbf{(20.4b)}$$

The first term in each equation is the monopoly solution for that firm, and the second term suggests that the firm reduces output by 1/2 unit for each unit produced by the other firm.[3] The intersection of these reaction functions is easily derived by setting $Q_1 = R_1(Q_2)$ and $Q_2 = R_2(Q_1)$. The two curves intersect where Equations 20.4a and 20.4b are jointly equal:

$$Q_1 = (a - c)/(2 \cdot b) - 1/2 \cdot [(a - c)/(2 \cdot b) - 1/2 \cdot Q_1]. \qquad \textbf{(20.5a)}$$

Solving for quantity as a function of a, b, and c, we obtain the Cournot quantity for Firm 1:

$$Q_1 = (a - c)/(3 \cdot b). \qquad \textbf{(20.5b)}$$

Substituting this back into Equation 20.4b produces the same quantity for Firm 2 in Cournot equilibrium.[4] The reaction function Excel file allows you to vary a, b, and c to see what happens to each of the resulting equilibria.

20.3A Asymmetric Costs

If firms have different cost structures, we will no longer see a symmetric Cournot equilibrium. Return once again to the demand curve used earlier in this section: $P(Q) = 60 - Q$. Suppose that Firm 1 has no variable cost (i.e., $MC = 0$), but $FC = \$400$. Firm 2 has no fixed cost, but variable cost is \$12 per unit (a number chosen to produce whole-number solutions). Firm 1's reaction function is the same as earlier, $Q_1 = 30 - 1/2 \cdot Q_2$ (the only difference is that profits are \$200 less, due to the \$200 increase in FC). Firm 2, on the other hand, will not produce output if total output is greater than 48 units because then price is below marginal cost (of \$12). This means that the horizontal axis intercept for $R_2(Q_1)$ is (48, 0). Using Equation 20.3b, we see that Firm 2's monopoly output (point M_2, the vertical axis intercept of $R_2(Q_1)$) is 24 units. Once again, $R_2(Q_1)$ has slope –1/2. The difference is that $R_2(Q_1)$ is no longer symmetric with $R_1(Q_2)$. These two reaction functions intersect at CE = (24, 12), as shown in Figure 20.8. Rather than show a series of panels, this figure includes M_1, M_2, SE_1, SE_2, SD, and the contract curve.

When marginal costs are not symmetric, neither is the Cournot equilibrium. It is worthwhile to consider the profits attained by both firms in this instance. Consider first Firm 1. Profits for Firm 1 are given by:

$$\pi_{1,CE} = TR - TC = 24 \cdot \$24 - (24 \cdot \$0 + \$400) = \$176. \qquad \textbf{(20.6a)}$$

Similarly, profits for Firm 2 are given by:

$$\pi_{2,CE} = TR - TC = 12 \cdot \$24 - (12 \cdot \$12 + \$0) = \$144. \qquad \textbf{(20.6b)}$$

Firm 2 has lower profits, even though it has lower costs of production. The reason, of course, is that Firm 2 also has lower total revenues because of its reduced production level.

It is worthwhile considering what would be required to attain the joint profit-maximizing solution, given asymmetric costs. You can determine the perfect cartel solution by answering the following questions:

Q8a. Which firm is the most profitable if it acts as a monopolist?*

***Q8a answer:** If Firm 1 acts as a monopolist, it attains a profit of $\pi_1 = \$500 = 30 \cdot \$30 - \$400$. If Firm 2 acts as a monopolist, it attains a profit of $\pi_2 = \$576 = 24 \cdot \$36 - 24 \cdot \$12$. Therefore, Firm 2 is more profitable as a monopolist.

FIGURE 20.8 Reaction Function Equilibria, Given Asymmetric Costs

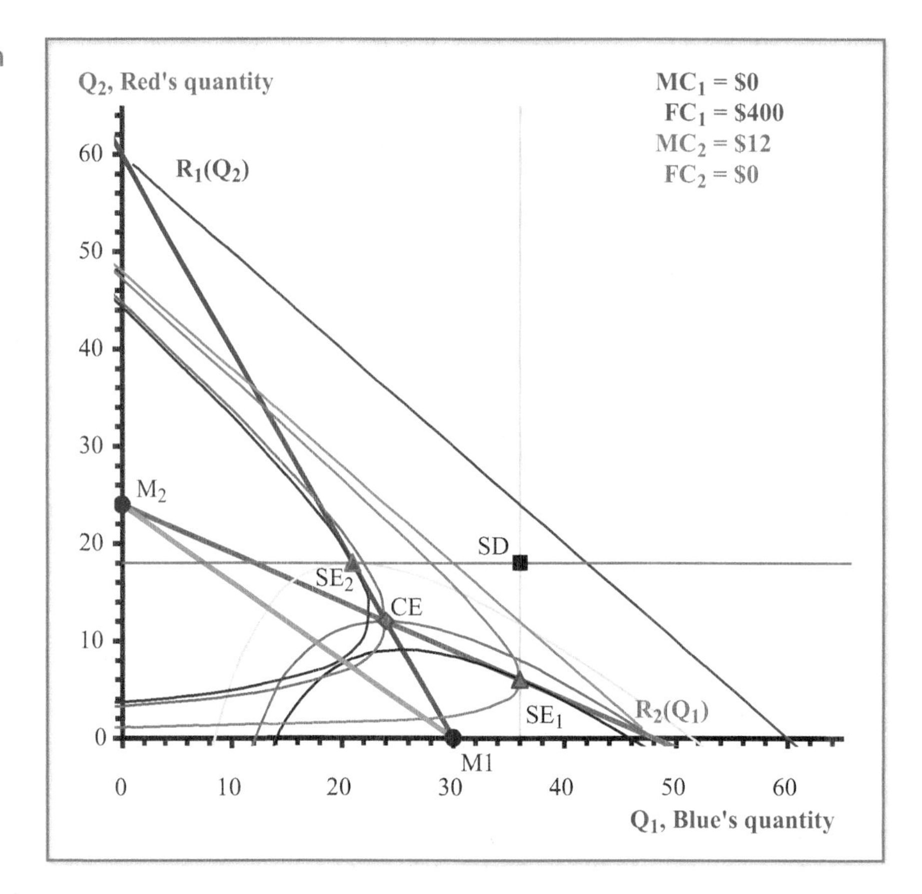

Q8b. Where are joint profits maximized?

Q8c. What are profits in this instance?

Q8d. How do your answers to Q8a and Q8b relate to one another?*

When costs are not symmetric, the joint profit-maximizing outcome no longer occurs over the entire contract curve. The contract curve still represents "zero footballs" or tangencies of isoprofit contours. These points represent joint production levels for which profits for one firm cannot be increased without decreasing profits for the other firm. But unlike when marginal costs are equal across firms, when marginal costs are different, the joint production point location along M_1M_2 determines overall profitability. The reason is straightforward: As we move along M_1M_2, starting at M_2, notice the following: Each time Firm 2 produces one fewer units, total production costs decline by $12 (Firm 2's marginal cost of production). Part of the increase in profits in moving from M_2 to M_1 is the reduction in cost of producing the 24 units (the total reduction in variable cost due to this move is $\$288 = 24 \cdot \$12$). The rest of the difference in profit is due to the higher total revenue when 30 units of output are sold than when 24 units are sold ($\Delta TR = 30 \cdot \$30 - 24 \cdot \$36 = \$36$).[5]

Not surprisingly, the Stackelberg equilibria are not symmetric in this instance either. It is worth noting that Stackelberg disequilibrium will not occur here because Firm 2 is better off shutting down than producing at the joint production point SD = (36, 18). The reason Firm 2 would prefer to shut down in this instance is that this production point

*__Q8b–8d answer:__ b. Joint profits are maximized when Firm 1 acts as a monopolist. Cost minimization is a prerequisite for profit maximization, so you always want to produce output at minimum variable cost. Firm 1 does so at zero variable cost. (Fixed cost is irrelevant because it is fixed in the short run.)
c. Joint profits in this instance are $\text{Joint}\pi(M_1) = \$500$, since there are no fixed costs for Firm 2. By contrast, $\text{Joint}\pi(M_2) = \$176 = \$576 - \$400$, since Firm 1's fixed cost must be included in joint profits, despite Firm 1 shutting down in this instance.
d. The individual profit-maximizing solution does not include the loss to the other firm. Therefore, answers a and b can both hold at the same time.

produces a price of \$6 = 60 – (36 + 24) beneath marginal cost of \$12. As noted earlier, Firm 2 would prefer to produce nothing when more than 48 units of output are produced.[6] Of course, at the time the production decision is made, Firm 2 does not know that Firm 1 will produce 36 units of output. Firm 2's decision to produce 18 units is based on the (erroneous) belief that Firm 1 will react to Firm 2's output along $R_1(Q_2)$. Put another way, Firm 2's decision is predicated on the belief that it is the Stackelberg leader in this market.

20.3B More Than Two Firms in the Market

The other restrictive assumption in the Cournot model in Section 20.2 involves the number of firms in the oligopoly. Cournot behavior need not be restricted to a duopoly setting (but a duopoly setting allows us to provide a geometric interpretation of the oligopolistic interaction). As we increase the number of firms in the oligopoly, the resulting equilibrium becomes more and more competitive (in terms of the number of units of output produced), just as you might expect.

Suppose that each of the n firms faces constant marginal cost of c and has fixed cost of F, and suppose that each has Cournot quantity beliefs about the other n – 1 firms. Suppose further that demand is given by Equation 20.2 ($P = a - b \cdot Q$). Given symmetric costs, each firm will produce the same amount of output in Cournot equilibrium. The goal is to determine how much output is produced by each firm as a function of *a*, b, c, and n. Let d be the amount of output produced by each of the other n – 1 firms in the market, and let x be the amount produced by the last firm (the *n*th firm). The market clearing price is therefore a function of the amount produced by the *n*th firm (given that the other n – 1 firms each produces d units of output):

$$P(x) = a - b \cdot ((n - 1) \cdot d + x). \qquad \textbf{(20.7a)}$$

Total revenue is $P \cdot x$, and total cost is $c \cdot x + F$, so profits are:

$$\pi(x) = (a - b \cdot ((n - 1) \cdot d + x)) \cdot x - (c \cdot x + F). \qquad \textbf{(20.7b)}$$

Regrouping, we have profits as the following quadratic function of x:

$$\pi(x) = -b \cdot x^2 + (a - b \cdot d \cdot (n - 1) - c) \cdot x - F. \qquad \textbf{(20.7c)}$$

The reaction function output level x for the *n*th firm is based on the amount produced by each of the other n – 1 firms, d, and on the demand and cost parameters *a*, b, and c. The reaction function is:[7]

$$x = R_n(d) = (a - c - b \cdot d \cdot (n - 1))/(2 \cdot b). \qquad \textbf{(20.8)}$$

The Cournot equilibrium, given symmetric cost conditions, will have all firms producing the same output. The level of output x will be profit maximizing, given that the other firms produce d (and given the expectation that the other firms will not change their production levels from d). The Cournot equilibrium can therefore be represented algebraically by the point where d = x in Equation 20.8. Substituting d = x into this equation, we obtain:

$$x = (a - c - b \cdot x \cdot (n - 1))/(2 \cdot b). \qquad \textbf{(20.9)}$$

Solving for x, we obtain the Cournot equilibrium quantity produced by a given firm:

$$x_{CE} = (a - c)/(b \cdot (n + 1)). \qquad \textbf{(20.10a)}$$

A more intuitive version of this equation occurs if we consider industry output in Cournot equilibrium as a function of the number of oligopolists in the market, n. Industry output is $Q_{CE}(n) = n \cdot x_{CE}$; therefore:

$$Q_{CE}(n) = (n/(n + 1)) \cdot (a - c)/b. \qquad \textbf{(20.10b)}$$

How do Equations 20.10a and 20.10b relate to those derived earlier? The monopoly outcome from Equation 20.3a is obtained by setting n = 1 in Equation 20.10a (this is geometrically seen as points M_1 or M_2 in the figures). As n increases, the total output produced in the oligopoly approaches the competitive output described in Equation 20.3b

($Q_{competition} = (a - c)/b$) because as n increases, n/(n + 1) approaches 1 This means that the total Cournot quantity approaches $(a - c)/b$, according to Equation 20.10b. Finally, the n = 2 Cournot duopoly production level described in Equation 20.5b is obtained by setting n = 2 in Equation 20.10a. The results are exactly what you would expect and as we saw in our earlier example in Section 20.2: Monopoly output is half the size of competitive output (30 versus 60), aggregate symmetric Cournot duopoly output is two-thirds the size of competitive output (40 versus 60), aggregate symmetric Cournot "tri-opoly" output is three-fourths the size of competitive output, and so on. As the number of firms in the market increases, each firm produces a smaller amount, but the total production increases and approaches the competitive level of production. As the number of oligopolists increases, the tightness of the resulting oligopolistic bargain decreases.

Section 20.4 Outline

20.4A Asymmetric Demands

20.4 A Differentiated Product Oligopoly Model

The simplicity of the model of oligopolistic interaction examined in Sections 20.2 and 20.3 is based, in part, on the ability to describe market (inverse) demand as a linear function of total industry output. As we discussed in Section 15.4, when products are differentiated, we can no longer describe market demand in such a unified fashion. We resort to discussion of a "typical" monopolistically competitive firm in Sections 15.5, 15.6, and 16.4. In the current situation, we instead assume that we can separately describe the demand curves for each duopolist. The analysis in this section has strong similarities to that described previously. As a result, we will not show as many figures, and we will be able to move more quickly through the analysis.

The key feature of a differentiated product market is that firms can charge different prices without completely losing their market to rival producers. The ability to have different prices is why we perform the analysis in price space as opposed to quantity space (as was done earlier). The axes are therefore Firm 1's price and Firm 2's price. Rather than focus on the algebra in this situation, it is sufficient to note that each firm's demand curve depends not only on the price charged by that firm, but also on the price charged by the other firm. In particular, we should expect the following (the signs beneath each price signify the direction of change in quantity for an increase in that price):

$$Q_1(P_1, P_2) = f(\underset{-}{P_1}, \underset{+}{P_2}). \qquad \textbf{(20.11a)}$$

$$Q_2(P_1, P_2) = f(\underset{+}{P_1}, \underset{-}{P_2}). \qquad \textbf{(20.11b)}$$

The plus sign on the cross price means that an increase in your rival's price increases demand for your good. (Put in terms of elasticities, the two goods are substitutes, since $\varepsilon_{x,y} > 0$.) Therefore, an increase in a rival's price increases your profits because the rival's price increase shifts demand in the direction of your firm, *ceteris paribus*. Higher profit for Firm 1 is north, and higher profit for Firm 2 is east in the (P_1, P_2) diagram (exactly the opposite of the quantity diagram depicted in Figure 20.1).

Before examining the specifics of the reaction function diagrams, consider a general description of what we should expect in a differentiated product market. We begin by assuming that the firms share the market equally when they charge equal prices. Put another way, each firm controls 50% of the market along the 45° line $P_1 = P_2$. Of course, the size of the market depends on the price charged (since each firm's demand is a negative function of its own price, as noted in Equation 20.11). More interesting is what happens when the two firms charge different prices.

From the point of view of Firm 1, if Firm 2 charges a very low price, then Firm 1 may well wish to price above Firm 2, even though Firm 1 will lose market share. Firm 2 has higher market share than Firm 1 beneath the 45° line because Firm 1 is willing to give up market share to avoid competing with a "bottom-feeder." On the other hand, if Firm 2 charges a very high price, then Firm 1 may well wish to price below Firm 2 to take away market share from Firm 2. These two observations signify that Firm 1's reaction function should be steeper than the 45° line. A symmetric argument for Firm 2 suggests that Firm 2 should have a reaction function that is flatter than the 45° line.

The steepness of each reaction function depends on how substitutable the two varieties are. If the two varieties are considered close substitutes, then there will be little divergence between the prices of the two varieties. In this instance, both reaction functions will be close to the 45° line (R_1 will be steeper, and R_2 will be flatter). The less dependent the two varieties are on one another, the smaller will be the loss in market share from a given amount of divergence in price.

Consider now the reaction functions shown in Figure 20.9A. As with the quantity analysis, Firm 1's reaction function and isoprofit contours are shades of blue, and Firm 2's are shades of red. As noted earlier, $R_1(P_2)$ is steeper than the 45° line. Each point on the reaction function represents the profit-maximizing price for Firm 1, given the price charged by Firm 2. This is seen by having $R_1(P_2)$ intersect each isoprofit contour for Firm 1 at the point where the contour is flat. By contrast, the reaction function for Firm 2, $R_2(P_1)$, is flatter than the 45° line, and each point on this reaction function intersects Firm 2's isoprofit contour at the point where that contour is vertical (because this represents the profit-maximizing price choice by Firm 2, given a fixed price by Firm 1). These reaction functions are based on linear demand equations. If nonlinear equations had been assumed instead, then the reaction functions would be nonlinear as well.[8]

If each firm believes that its rival will not change price, no matter what the firm does, then it has *Cournot price beliefs*. If a firm has Cournot price beliefs, it prices along its reaction function to maximize profits, given what it believes its rival will do. If both firms have Cournot price beliefs, then the intersection of the two reaction functions is the Cournot equilibrium, **CE**. Price is $3 and profit is $20 for each firm in **CE**.

Although the two Cournot models have obvious differences, they contain many similarities as well. The Cournot equilibrium is a Nash equilibrium in both models because it represents the optimal choice, given the choice of its rival. The Cournot equilibrium is not joint profit maximizing. The reason is the same as with the quantity model: In both instances, there is an entire "football" of joint price combinations to the northeast of **CE** that produce higher profits for both firms than **CE**. The joint profit-maximizing solution in this instance is at **J** = ($7.50, $7.50) in Figure 20.9A. **J** is that point on the contract curve where the sum of profits is maximized ($\pi_1 + \pi_2 = \$80.50$). In this instance, the contract curve is indeed a curve.[9] (As it turns out, the joint profit-maximizing price bundle is unique; by contrast in Figure 20.5, joint profits are constant and maximized on the entire contract curve.)

The difficulty with the joint profit-maximizing solution is that, once again, it is difficult to maintain. Consider the situation from the point of view of Firm 1. If Firm 1 believes that Firm 2 will price at $7.50, it makes sense to undercut Firm 2 and price at $4.69, as represented by point **A** in Figure 20.9A (since **A** is profit maximizing, given a price of $7.50 by Firm 2). Firm 2 faces the same incentive to cheat by pricing at $4.69 in response to Firm 1's price of $7.50, as shown by point **B**. If both cheat on the joint profit-maximizing bargain, that solution breaks down.

This discussion points to the value of being the *follower* in setting price. If a firm acts as a leader in setting price, then the follower can gain at the expense of the leader by undercutting the leader's price. Figure 20.9B depicts the case of Firm 1 acting as Stackelberg leader. *The behavioral assumptions that produce this equilibrium are that Firm 1 believes that Firm 2 believes that Firm 1 will maintain price,* and *that Firm 2 believes that Firm 1 will maintain price.* Put in terms of reaction functions, Firm 2 will react along $R_2(P_1)$ to whatever price Firm 1 sets. Firm 1 maximizes profits subject to this constraint by setting a price of $3.55 (as opposed to $3 in Cournot). Firm 1's profits increase slightly over Cournot (from $20 to $21).[10] Firm 2 maximizes profits subject to Firm 1's price of $3.55 by undercutting Firm 1 and setting a price of $3.20. Firm 2's profits increase more dramatically as a result of the increase in market share attained in this situation (from $20 to $25).

FIGURE 20.9
Differentiated Product Reaction Functions

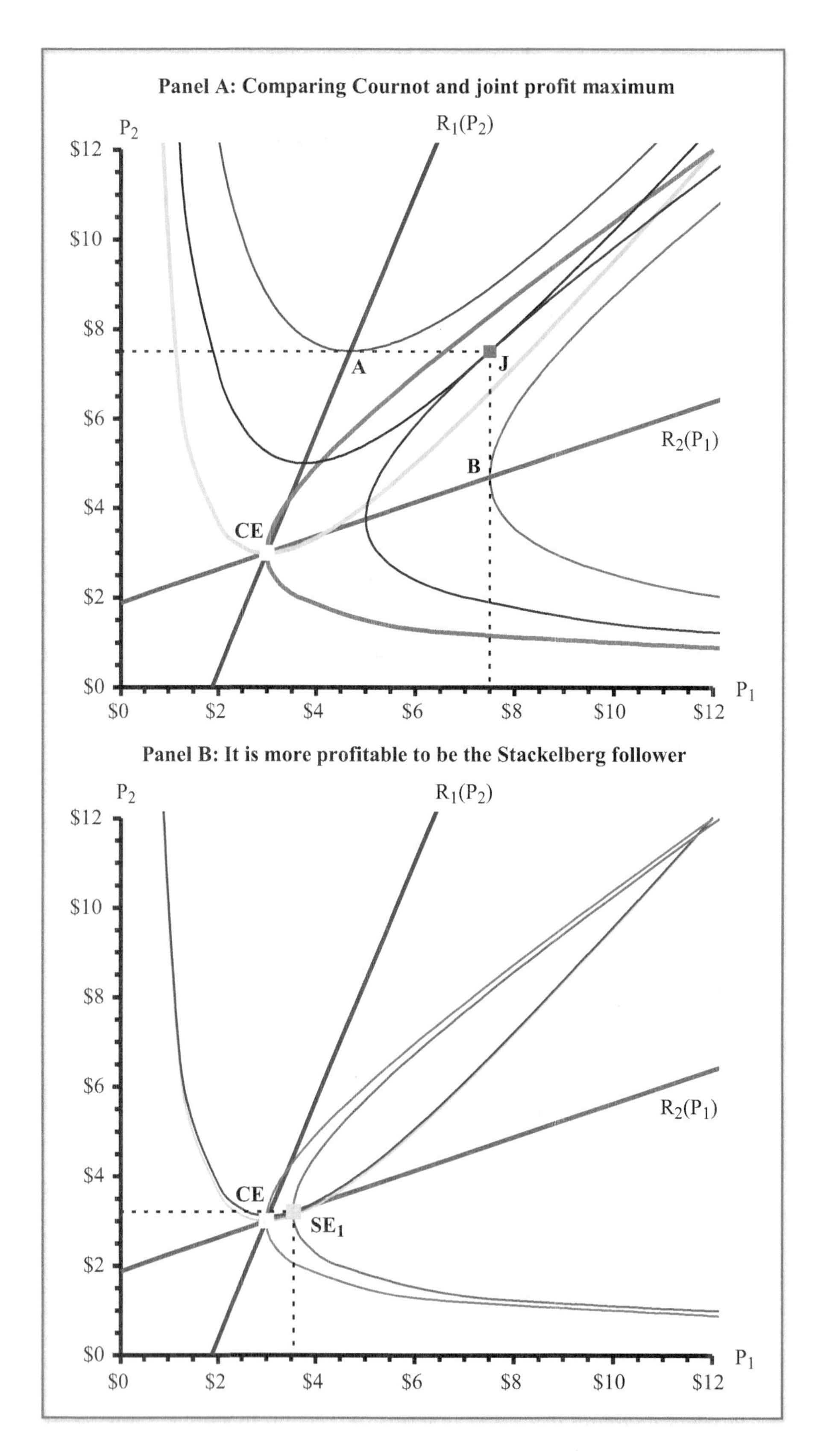

The Stackelberg price leader model provides an interesting contrast to the Stackelberg quantity leader model described in Figure 20.6. In both versions, the leader does better than in Cournot. But in the quantity version, the leader does so by forcing the follower to have reduced market share. In the price version, the leader does so by allowing the follower to increase market share (by undercutting the leader's price).

20.4A Asymmetric Demands

We used differences in cost structure across firms to examine asymmetric equilibria in Section 20.3. With differentiated products, we can achieve asymmetric equilibria, even if costs are constant across firms. If individual varieties have asymmetric demand curves, then the duopoly solution need not be symmetric, even in the Cournot equilibrium. This is easily modeled, using the model of pricing rivalry developed earlier.

Suppose that Firm 2 has the more dominant market niche and that Firm 1 has a smaller niche. Three possible qualitative relations can occur in Cournot equilibrium: The dominant firm could have a higher, equal, or lower price than its rival. Examples of each outcome are shown in Figure 20.10. The Cournot equilibrium shifts from ($3, $4) to ($4, $4) to ($4, $3) in moving from Figure 20.10A to 20.10B to 20.10C. The tabular information beneath each panel lays out the demand functions on which each panel is based. Also included are price, quantity, and profit information for each firm at the Cournot equilibrium, **CE**; joint profit maximum, **J**; and the two "cheat on joint profit maximum" points **A**

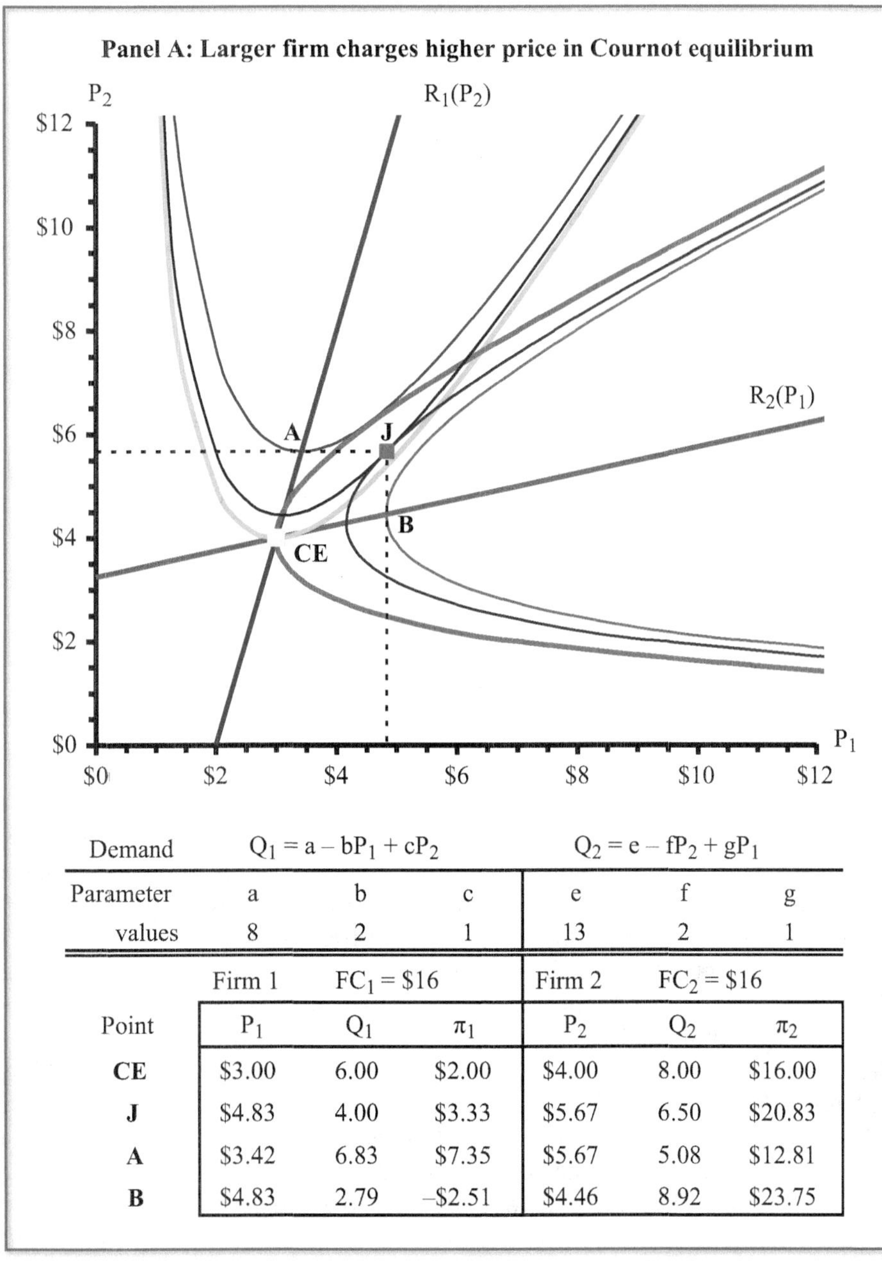

Demand	$Q_1 = a - bP_1 + cP_2$			$Q_2 = e - fP_2 + gP_1$		
Parameter	a	b	c	e	f	g
values	8	2	1	13	2	1

	Firm 1	$FC_1 = \$16$		Firm 2	$FC_2 = \$16$	
Point	P_1	Q_1	π_1	P_2	Q_2	π_2
CE	$3.00	6.00	$2.00	$4.00	8.00	$16.00
J	$4.83	4.00	$3.33	$5.67	6.50	$20.83
A	$3.42	6.83	$7.35	$5.67	5.08	$12.81
B	$4.83	2.79	–$2.51	$4.46	8.92	$23.75

FIGURE 20.10 Differentiated Product Duopoly with Asymmetric Demand for Each Variety

Continued on next page

FIGURE 20.10
Continued

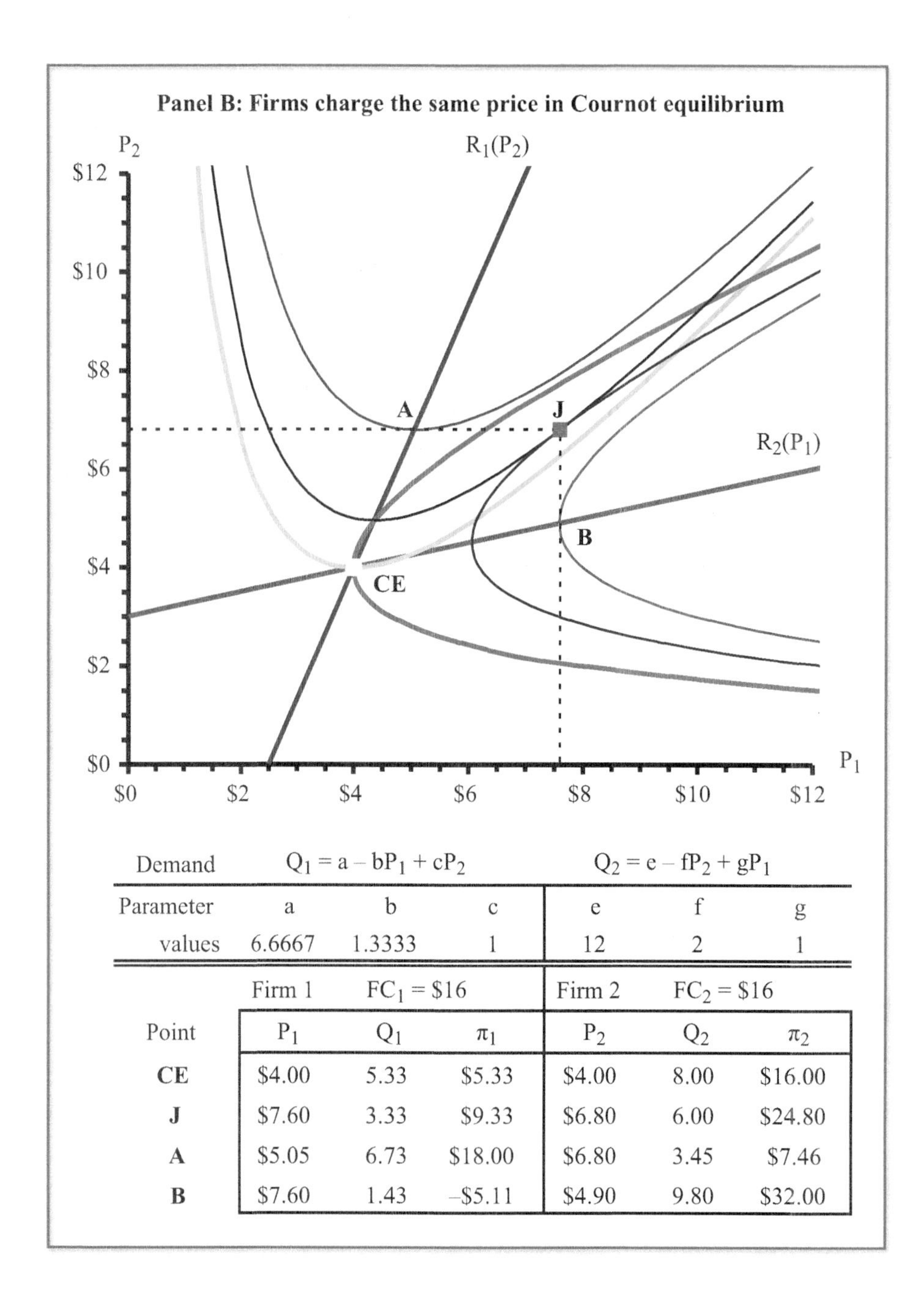

Demand	$Q_1 = a - bP_1 + cP_2$			$Q_2 = e - fP_2 + gP_1$		
Parameter	a	b	c	e	f	g
values	6.6667	1.3333	1	12	2	1

	Firm 1	FC_1 = $16		Firm 2	FC_2 = $16	
Point	P_1	Q_1	π_1	P_2	Q_2	π_2
CE	$4.00	5.33	$5.33	$4.00	8.00	$16.00
J	$7.60	3.33	$9.33	$6.80	6.00	$24.80
A	$5.05	6.73	$18.00	$6.80	3.45	$7.46
B	$7.60	1.43	–$5.11	$4.90	9.80	$32.00

and **B**. This numeric information was not systematically provided in Figure 20.9 to focus on the geometric properties of the various points, rather than on numerical outcomes.[11]

The structure of a differentiated product market duopoly equilibrium depends on the underlying demands for the varieties provided by the firms. A quick comparison of the profit levels for each firm in Figures 20.10A–20.10C confirms that Firm 2 is more profitable than Firm 1 in Cournot and at the joint profit-maximizing pricing point. Further evidence of Firm 2's dominance is seen in comparing the two cheating options. If Firm 1 cheats on the joint profit-maximizing bargain, then Firm 1's profits are lower (at **A**) than Firm 2's profits that accrue if Firm 2 cheats on the joint profit-maximizing bargain (at **B**). Of course, these differences are driven by the quantity dominance of Firm 2 over Firm 1 (and this quantity difference cannot be seen directly in the figures, but must be inferred from demand).

One caution should be noted about reading too much into the models developed in the last three sections. These models were developed based on linear demand curves to derive reaction functions that are also linear. Such linearity is unlikely to occur in actual markets. Consider, for example, the cross-price effects assumed in the price model developed in this section. The reaction functions are predicated on a cross-price effect that assumes

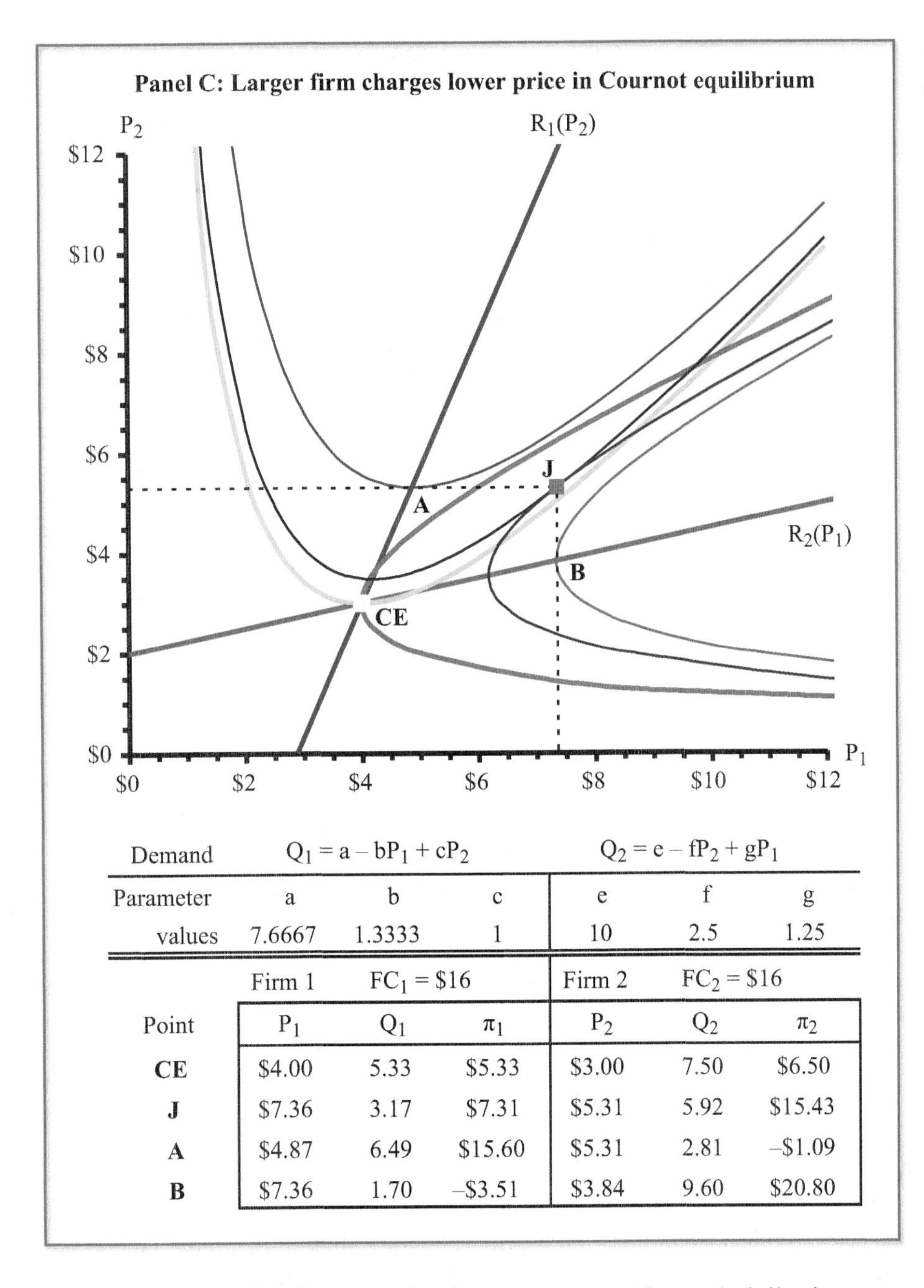

Demand	$Q_1 = a - bP_1 + cP_2$			$Q_2 = e - fP_2 + gP_1$		
Parameter values	a	b	c	e	f	g
	7.6667	1.3333	1	10	2.5	1.25

	Firm 1	FC_1 = $16		Firm 2	FC_2 = $16	
Point	P_1	Q_1	π_1	P_2	Q_2	π_2
CE	$4.00	5.33	$5.33	$3.00	7.50	$6.50
J	$7.36	3.17	$7.31	$5.31	5.92	$15.43
A	$4.87	6.49	$15.60	$5.31	2.81	–$1.09
B	$7.36	1.70	–$3.51	$3.84	9.60	$20.80

FIGURE 20.10
Continued

that demand for Firm 1's product increases by the same amount for each dollar increase in Firm 2's price. A more sophisticated graphical analysis would note that if Firm 2 prices itself out of the market (by charging too high a price), it should no longer have any effect on Firm 1's demand (after all, all of Firm 2's consumers would by that point have switched to Firm 1).[12] If such assumptions are incorporated via a nonlinear assumption on the cross-price effect on demand, the resulting reaction function is nonlinear. These refinements do not change the qualitative results derived in this section.

20.5 Game Theory

[Section 20.5 was contributed by J. Kerry Waller of Piedmont College.]

20.5A An Introduction to Static versus Dynamic Analysis

In this chapter, we move from static analysis, where the other elements of the systems we explore are held constant (*ceteris paribus*), and add dynamic elements to our system. In a dynamic system, an individual or firm is again faced with choices regarding the best strategy for the situation at hand, but this actor recognizes that other individuals or firms

Section 20.5 Outline

are also making decisions about their best strategy—and these decisions help determine which choice ends up being the optimal choice.

Analysis of this sort often relies on a set of tools known as *game theory*. Believe it or not, you have been participating in game theoretic analysis for years. Think of all of the decisions that you make in your life—from work to play to your relationships with your loved ones—where your best option depends on the behavior of the others you are interacting with. I recently played a game of hide-and-seek with my nieces, and my seven-year-old niece found an amazing hiding place in her parents' closet. I looked and looked (even in that closet!) without finding her. I eventually gave up and called for her to come out. She was obviously very proud to have outsmarted her uncle and showed me where she had hidden. In future rounds, however, she never returned to that same spot. But why not? It was obviously an excellent hiding spot. If she wanted to win the next round, why not return to that spot?

Even a seven-year-old intuitively understood that I would now be certain to check that spot in the next rounds of the game. My change in behavior impacted the potential reward to her of using that spot, so understanding that my behavior was going to change, she changed her own. And I'm sure you can think of countless examples of playing with your siblings or cousins or friends where you did something similar. You never realized what a good game theorist you were.

Other examples abound. During the 2014 football season, the Denver Broncos averaged 4 yards every time they ran the ball, but gained 7.4 yards per passing play. Given how relatively successful the pass plays were, we could argue that they should always pass the ball. Yet, they still opted to run on a little more than 40% of their offensive plays! Why would they do that? Do they need a new coach?

The answer again lies in game theory. If the Broncos always passed the ball, opposing defenses could opt for defensive plays that are better suited to stop the pass. Pass plays would then be less rewarding, decreasing the Broncos' chances of winning the game. The Denver coaches recognized this and chose the less-productive play on 4 of every 10 snaps to ensure that the defense could not effectively predict what was coming next and alter its plans accordingly. The Broncos' best strategy was to ensure that there was enough uncertainty in their opponents' minds to allow both types of plays to have success—even if that meant pursuing a strategy with a lower expected reward in the short run.

In the business world, the choices made by your rivals are an essential consideration. The choice to raise or lower prices must be undertaken with the recognition that rival companies also have the ability to change their prices. The choice to enter a new geographic market or a new line of business is impacted by the number of competitors and their potential responses to this entry. Using the structure of some game theoretical models can provide a framework for a better understanding of the potential outcomes of making choices in a dynamic system, as well as of the potential risks and rewards of the choices that are made.

Each dynamic scenario is broken down into a structure known as a **game**. Every game is defined by the number of **players**, the choices they face (**strategies**), and the potential **payoffs**, given each strategy and the action of the other player(s). The simplest game theory models involve just two players, each facing two possible strategies to undertake. But additional players and additional choices can be considered, each increasing the complexity of the game exponentially.

game: A game involves players making strategic decisions from an available set of options.

players: Players are the decision-making units that play games. Each player chooses among various strategies or options.

strategy: A strategy is an option available to a player.

payoffs: Payoffs are the outcomes associated with a set of strategies. Each player will have a payoff for each set of alternatives.

By considering all of the possible strategies, a game theorist identifies the potential reward, or payoff, from each strategy. In a game with two players, with two strategies each, there would be four (2×2) possible payoffs. These payoffs could be profits from entering a line of business, the joy of besting your uncle at a game of hide-and-seek, or the first down gained from fooling the rival defense with a running play when they anticipated a pass. Of course, the rewards could be negative, too, if the wrong strategy is pursued. Companies lose money by competing against a more well-established rival product, children are found quickly when they hide in an obvious spot, and running backs are thrown for a loss when they run into the arms of a waiting defensive player.

To best understand the potential payoffs faced in a dynamic game, it is often helpful to build a payoff matrix. A **payoff matrix** is a table that details each possible combination of strategies and the payoffs associated with each combination. For example, imagine a market with two players who face the choice to increase their price, decrease their price, or leave their price the same. With two players and three strategies, there are now nine (3×3) possible payoffs. If Player 1 raises its price, but Player 2 maintains the existing price, Player 1 will likely lose a few customers to Player 2, but will receive a higher price from those customers who stay. The actual rewards will be based on own- and cross-price elasticities of the good in question, but if we assume that we have a good estimate of those elasticities, we can make a reasonable guess as to the potential gains (or losses) from this combination of strategies for *both* Players 1 and 2. We then consider what happens if both Players 1 and 2 increase their price, and what happens if Player 1 increases its price and Player 2 decreases its price. After recording the rewards to both players, we repeat the process for price decreases, and then again for keeping the price the same. By placing all of these payouts in a payoff matrix, we can try to determine the most lucrative path to follow. We examine how to read a payoff matrix by considering a classic game, the prisoners' dilemma.

payoff matrix: A payoff matrix is a table that details each possible combination of strategies and the payoffs associated with each combination.

20.5B The Prisoners' Dilemma

The most widely known and commonly cited example of game theory is what is known as the *prisoners' dilemma.* If you have ever watched any of the numerous crime dramas on television, you have seen the police put this model put into action. In this game, there are typically two players, and they are partners in a crime that has been at least partially detected. The police suspect that the crime has been committed by these two suspects and bring them in for questioning, but at present, they do not have enough proof to convict both suspects of the entire crime. Rather than question the suspects together, the police put them in separate rooms to question them individually. Why do you think this is so?

Most of us have an intuitive understanding of the advantage that the police gain by separating the two suspects. Put another way, it is worthwhile for police to thwart communications. We can use game theory and a payoff matrix to better understand the choices the two suspects (players) of this game face. To make this easier to follow, let's call the suspects Fred and Barney. Fred and Barney have been brought in, and regardless of what happens next, the police will be able to convict them on a smaller crime (like possession of stolen goods). This crime alone will put both Fred and Barney in jail for 2 years. But if the police can prove that Fred and Barney actually broke in and stole the goods in question, the penalty will be 10 years in jail.

To get enough proof to prosecute the burglary, the police offer both Fred and Barney a deal. If one of them talks, that person will be released and not even prosecuted for the possession of stolen goods. He will escape with no jail time at all, but his partner will get the full 10 years in jail. If both Fred and Barney decide to cooperate with the police (i.e., talk), they will both go to jail with a reduced sentence of 4 years in recognition of their willingness to cooperate. Table 20.1 details these outcomes in a payoff matrix. *Fred's payoffs are the first number inside the parenthesis, and Barney's payoffs are the second.*

First, put yourself in Fred's shoes. Fred listens to what the police have to say and realizes that he can talk and get either 0 or 4 years (depending on what Barney does), or

TABLE 20.1 The Prisoners' Dilemma Game

Payoffs to (Fred, Barney)

		Barney	
		Talk	*Stay quiet*
Fred	*Talk*	(–4, –4)	(0, –10)
	Stay quiet	(–10, 0)	(–2, –2)

stay quiet and get either 2 or 10 years (again, reliant on Barney's strategy). Obviously, he would rather avoid any jail time, but depending on what Barney does, that might not be an option. If Fred has studied game theory, he realizes that he alone does not determine his fate. His fate is a combination of both his actions and those of Barney. To decide what he should do, Fred should consider what Barney is likely to do. Therefore, Fred should think about what he should do, assuming a specific strategy from his former partner. In this instance, Barney can do one of two things.

If Barney stays quiet, what is the best thing for Fred to do? If Fred talks, he walks away without penalty. But if Fred stays quiet, he will go to jail for 2 years. Given that choice, the best thing for Fred to do is to *talk*.

But what if Barney talks? If Barney talks and Fred stays quiet, Fred will go to jail for 10 years. But if Barney talks and Fred also talks, that 10 years is reduced to 4. Again, Fred's best decision is to *talk*. *Talking* is Fred's dominant strategy. A player's **dominant strategy** is the strategy that provides a preferable outcome, regardless of a rival's behavior.

dominant strategy: A player's dominant strategy is the strategy that provides a preferable outcome, regardless of a rival's behavior.

Now put yourself in Barney's shoes. His payoffs are exactly the same as Fred's, so he will quickly arrive at the same conclusion: Barney's dominant strategy—his best option, *regardless of Fred's strategy*—is to talk. If the payoffs remain constant, this combination of dominant strategies gives us an equilibrium result that will occur with every playing of the game, known as a dominant strategy equilibrium. A **dominant strategy equilibrium** occurs if each player in a game has a dominant strategy and chooses it.

dominant strategy equilibrium: A dominant strategy equilibrium occurs if each player in a game has a dominant strategy and chooses it.

If we take this analysis a little further, we see exactly how treacherous this trap is. If Barney tries to anticipate what Fred will do, he will quickly realize that Fred's best play is to talk. With the expectation that Fred is going to talk, Barney is even more compelled to talk, and Fred will come to the same conclusion when considering Barney's best option. Considering what outcome is best in each scenario and anticipating what your rival will do yield the same result in this scenario.

In terms of total time spent in jail for the partners, the best scenario would be for both to stay quiet and receive a total of 4 years. But the dominant strategy pushes both players to talk, resulting in 8 total years spent in jail.

Models of oligopoly often rely on a prisoners' dilemma type analysis. In oligopoly, the presence of a limited number of competitors presents a situation where collusion can restrict output, increase price, and consequently improve profits for the firms in the industry. But in reality, we rarely see this type of behavior successfully implemented. Game theory gives us an explanation as to why this is true.

In the interest of simplicity, we again limit the scenario to just two players, and we give them the options of working together (colluding) or competing (cheating on the proposed cooperation). If the firms compete for the available customers in the markets, profits tend to be low, so let us assume that they exist in a world of zero economic profit. Payoff to both firms of a compete/compete strategy are zero. Given this, there is a high incentive to set up a cooperative scheme where they agree to limit output and raise prices. If the cooperation is maintained, profits for both firms jump to $500 each. The complication arises when we consider what happens when one firm cheats on the agreement. If Firm A increases its price to the agreed-upon price (colludes) and Firm B undercuts that price (cheats), Firm B is stealing business from Firm A. In such a situation, Firm A loses $300, and Firm B gains $1,200.

The payoffs are simply reversed if Firm A is the cheater and Firm B is the colluder. Firm A then collects the large profits ($1,200) and Firm B incurs the losses (–$300). Table 20.2 details these payoffs.

The oligopolists face the same choices that Fred and Barney did. If they work together, they can improve their situation significantly. But once Firm A considers its best strategy, given a particular strategy from Firm B, Firm A discovers that its best option is to cheat. Firm B faces the exact same calculation and also decides to cheat. The dominant strategy equilibrium in this example is again for both firms to cheat. Price fixing in oligopolistic markets is a concern, but in market after market, we see that these types of schemes are not common because the temptation to cheat is so strong. (Of course, price-fixing is also

TABLE 20.2 Payouts for a Collusive Bargain

Payoffs to (A, B)

		Firm B	
		Cheat	***Collude***
Firm A	***Cheat***	(0, 0)	(1,200, –300)
	Collude	(–300, 1,200)	(500, 500)

illegal in many settings. For example, Section I of the Sherman Act outlaws "every contract, combination . . . or conspiracy in restraint of trade.")

20.5C External Authority

Let's return to our original prisoners' dilemma. Acting alone, Fred and Barney are in a situation where the dominant strategy is to talk. The police know this and therefore try to put suspects into this dilemma as often as possible. Confessions are a lot easier to manage than trials. But is there a way for the suspects to avoid the trap associated with this game? In the real world (and on TV crime dramas), the criminals don't always talk. But why not? Game theory tells us that this is not an optimal strategy. If the payoffs are exactly as described in our payoff matrix, we would expect the criminals to follow the dominant strategy and always talk. Because this strategy is dominant, criminals recognize that the only way to alter the result is to alter the payoffs.

They do this through a variety of methods. One method is to create a stigma associated with talking to the police. People who talk to the police are called "rats," and are held in low esteem by their peers once they are released. This type of shaming device can be used to alter the perceived costs of a particular behavior, altering the optimal strategy. Of course, shame alone may not be a strong enough device when facing a long stretch in prison, so criminal organizations have found other ways to exert pressure, such as threatening harm to anyone who talks as well as their loved ones. Such threats can be a strong deterrent.

How does this translate to the business world? Imagine a decision to enter a particular market. This market has some high start-up costs and an existing competitor (Firm B), whose product is widely accepted, allowing it to make a $150-million profit. If you (Firm A) enter the market, you will have to spend $50 million just to get up and running. If Firm B stays in, the resulting competition will reduce industry profits to $70 million, which you will split equally. But given your initial investment, this still leaves you $15 million in the hole. Of course, if you could somehow convince your rival to leave the industry, the whole $150 million is available to you, which leaves you $100 million ahead, given your start-up costs. Given these payoffs (detailed in Table 20.3), do you have any incentive to enter?

Firm A does not have a dominant strategy in this instance. Consider your best strategy if Firm B stays in the market. You could either lose $15 million by entering or lose nothing by staying out. Most people would rather have $0 than –$15 million. So the best play is to stay out. If Firm B could be convinced to leave, however, you would have $100 million in profits coming your way! Your strategy depends on what Firm B does. So do you

TABLE 20.3 Payoffs with High Start-Up Costs

Payouts to (A, B)

		Firm B	
		Stay in	***Leave***
Firm A	***Enter***	(–15, 35)	(100, 0)
	Stay out	(0, 150)	(0, 0)

TABLE 20.4 Payoffs after Subsidy Applied

Payouts to (A, B)

		Firm B	
		Stay in	***Leave***
Firm A	***Enter***	(15, 35)	(130, 0)
	Stay out	(0, 100)	(0, 0)

enter in the hopes that Firm B will leave? The smart thing to do would be to put yourself in Firm B's shoes to see if you can figure out what it will do.

Obviously, the best-case scenario for Firm B is for you to stay out because it will still make monopoly profits of $150 million. If you enter, Firm B still makes $35 million if it stays and $0 if it leaves. Firm B's dominant strategy is to stay, so you must act with the understanding that Firm B is not going anywhere.

The issue is those start-up costs. If you could get some outside influence—an *external authority* like the government—to pay for some or all of these costs, the payoff matrix is altered. Table 20.4 shows what happens if an effective lobbying campaign nets $30 million to defray your start-up costs. Now Firm A's dominant strategy is to enter, regardless of what Firm B does. The action of the external authority has altered the structure of the game.

20.5D Nash Equilibrium, Take 2

If every game resulted in a dominant strategy equilibrium, game theory would be a much more limited tool in the economist's arsenal. However, most games do not result in such an equilibrium and require a return to the Nash equilibrium concept detailed earlier in this chapter. *A Nash equilibrium is defined in Section 20.1 as being a set of strategies where every player's strategy is optimal, given its competitors' strategies.* When attempting to determine a Nash equilibrium, it is important to recognize that the best alternative for one player is often based on what the opponent does. In our game of hide-and-seek, the closet hiding space was the best strategy in the first game, but my niece anticipated that I would now check that spot more carefully, so in future games, that spot was no longer her best option.

If we refer back to a firm's decision to increase, decrease, or maintain price from earlier, it is possible to imagine a world where, sometimes, increasing the price is the correct call; other times, maintaining the existing price is the best path, and sometimes, the best call is to decrease the price—all depending on what your rival does. Firms weigh the potential gains and losses and plan their strategies, based on their expectations of what their rivals will do. Once both firms refine their strategies to a point where they cannot change their strategy without making themselves worse off, the resulting equilibrium is a Nash equilibrium, with both parties doing as well as they can, given their rival's strategy.

20.5E Zero-Sum Games and Variable-Sum Games

zero-sum game: In a zero-sum game (or constant-sum game), the gains and losses of the parties exactly offset one another.

In a **zero-sum game** (or *constant-sum game*), the gains and losses of the parties exactly offset one another. Poker is an excellent example of a zero-sum game. For anyone to walk out with more money than he entered with, others need to have losses that exactly match those gains. There is a fixed pool of money on the table. If you take $1 more than you put in, then someone else has to end up with $1 less. But to go through the game theory of poker could fill (and has filled) several books. Another simple example of a zero-sum game is the negotiation over the price of a good. If you are buying a used car and haggling over a price, for every dollar that you gain through a reduction in price, the seller loses that same dollar. The key aspect of these games is that for someone to win, a rival must lose. (We will have more to say about used cars in Chapter 21.)

In a **variable-sum game**, the total value of the payoffs varies, based on the strategies that the players pursue. One set of strategies might allow for cooperation that makes both players better off than another set (a win-win outcome). Win-win outcomes are a key component of any functioning economic system. If you have a painting that is worth $500 to you but that a collector values at $2,000, the collector can offer you $1,000 for it, and you can both be better off. You end up with $1,000 instead of a painting that was only worth $500 to you. The collector owns a painting that she perceived to be worth $2,000 but for which she only gave up $1,000 to acquire.

However, both parties could also made choices that put them into a highly competitive environment, reducing the gains available to both parties (a lose-lose outcome). A firm's decision to lower a price could force other firms to compete with lower prices of their own, reducing the pie of profits available to the entire industry and leaving all parties with lower profits than before.

variable-sum game: In a variable-sum game, the total value of the payoffs varies, based on the strategies that the players pursue.

20.5F Bargaining

Bargaining is a common phenomenon in an individual's life. Children bargain with their parents over bedtimes and how many vegetables they need to eat. Teenagers argue curfews and access to the car. Young couples bargain over all of the decisions that need to be made as they establish a life together—from who does the dishes on a given night to where they will spend next Christmas. Employers and employees bargain over wages and benefits and working conditions. Customers and salespeople bargain over price and maintenance and warranties.

The extensive universe of interactions involving bargaining provides an increasingly complex group of games to investigate. In the games described previously, we assumed that communication, signaling, and interaction among players was limited or nonexistent. By relaxing this assumption and allowing for direct communication and or indirect communication among players, the opportunity to bargain exists.

bargaining: Bargaining is negotiating over the terms of an agreement.

Cooperative and Noncooperative Games

The ability to communicate with a rival to reach a mutually beneficial conclusion changes the nature of games. Examples of cooperative games include buying a car or a house. A **cooperative game** is a game in which the players can negotiate explicit binding contracts over various states of nature. Cooperative games are often zero-sum games. Such bargaining can be conducted directly between players or indirectly, using intermediaries if there are concerns about asymmetric information. We focus on problems of asymmetric information in Chapter 21. But the key component of these types of games is that communication is allowed, and explicit bargains, sometime even involving written contracts, are a likely outcome of this bargaining.

When the level of communication is limited or prohibited, uncertainty increases dramatically, and the complexity of these games increases with this uncertainty. We typically think of the interactions among firms as a noncooperative game. A **noncooperative game** is a game in which formal negotiation and entering into a legally binding contract are not possible. While firms might like to coordinate their decisions on production and prices to generate higher profits, many governments do not permit explicit agreements of this type. In situations where the actions of firms are easily observable and the number of firms is limited, tacit bargaining can occur. **Tacit bargaining** is bargaining that is not openly expressed but that is implied by actions.

With tacit bargaining, no explicit agreement is made, but all parties infer future behavior from the current choices made by their rivals. In our earlier example, attempts to collude in an oligopolistic industry are undermined by the dynamics of the prisoners' dilemma. This model was designed as a **one-shot game**, where all players make their choices just once. If we expand the model to make it a **multiple-shot game**, we allow for multiple opportunities to play the game, and the dominant strategy of cheating can be undermined, leading to an unstated, but profitable, collusion.

cooperative game: A cooperative game is a game in which the players can negotiate explicit binding contracts over various states of nature.

noncooperative game: A noncooperative game is a game in which formal negotiation and entering into a legally binding contract is not possible.

tacit bargaining: Tacit bargaining is bargaining that is not openly expressed but that is implied by actions.

one-shot games: One-shot games are games in which each player chooses strategy once, and payoffs are determined as a result of that choice.

multiple-shot games: Multiple-shot games are games in which strategies are chosen and payoffs determined in repeated plays of the game.

When a firm has just one chance to maximize its profits, the resulting equilibrium must be the cheat-cheat equilibrium of the prisoners' dilemma. But if each day represents a new chance to play the game, a different strategy could emerge. If instead of cheating, all of the firms decide to trust one another and set higher prices, they would all reap greater benefits than they would by cheating. And most importantly, they would send a signal to the other firms that they are willing to avoid a destructive price war. The agreement is never explicitly stated, since that would be illegal. But if all of the players can trust each other once, it creates a greater incentive to trust each other the next day, and the next day, and so on. This type of tacit bargaining relies on all players valuing the long-term profits of cooperation more highly than the short-term benefits of conflict.

limited war: A limited war is a contest in which each player opts to eliminate potential strategies in an effort to preserve resources or avoid undesirable outcomes resulting from escalation in future iterations of the game. The eliminated strategies are *qualitative*, rather than *quantitative*, in nature.

Another form of tacit bargaining is known as a limited war. A **limited war** is a contest in which each player opts to eliminate potential strategies in an effort to preserve resources or avoid undesirable outcomes resulting from escalation in future iterations of the game. The eliminated strategies are *qualitative*, rather than *quantitative*, in nature—for example, no chemical weapons, no nuclear weapons—not how many of these types of weapons. In a business context, there are many dimensions to compete over in an effort to differentiate yourself to your potential customers. The most obvious is price, but firms compete on quality, style, brand, convenience, and many other dimensions. In a limited war, firms reach an equilibrium where certain dimensions of possible competition are ignored. With the advent of price aggregators in the airline industry, customers can see all prices for flights from Cleveland to Denver, for example. One possibility for the airlines is to battle to try to offer the lowest price. But this obviously undermines profits and is easily discovered by rivals, allowing those rivals to respond and lower the price even further. Instead of engaging in this type of destructive price competition, airlines could choose to attract your business with other desirable features, such as free checked bags, more leg room, or friendly customer-service agents. (I can only hope that an executive from the airline industry reads this text and is inspired, as this clearly is not the path most airlines have chosen.)

threat: A threat involves undertaking an action that harms yourself if your rivals do something you do not want them to do. You also harm them, but the key attribute of a threat is that you make *yourself* worse off.

promise: A promise is a commitment made to a second party in a bargain.

In noncooperative games that are unable to rely on tacit bargaining, threats and promises can be used. A **threat** involves undertaking an action that harms yourself if your rival does something you do not want them to do. You also harm them, but the key attribute of a threat is that you make *yourself* worse off. A **promise** is a commitment made to a second party in a bargain. Both threats and promises are means to limit options for one of the players. With a threat, Player A communicates a willingness to punish Player B if Player B follows a particular strategy. With a promise, Player A willingly limits behavior to convince Player B to pursue a particular strategy (or to avoid a strategy that might be particularly harmful to Player A).

Consider two firms (A and B). Firm A currently sells its product in North Dakota only, and Firm B sells in South Dakota only. Because of a lack of competition, both firms are doing fairly well, as described in Table 20.5. With both firms working in a single state, Firm A makes 100, and Firm B makes 150. A consultant tells management at Firm A that Firm A could make more (130) by expanding its market into South Dakota. Is this consultant correct?

The consultant is correct only if Firm B fails to retaliate and enter North Dakota in response to Firm A's expansion. Management at Firm A is smart enough to consider this

TABLE 20.5 Two Firms Considering Expansion into a Neighboring Market

Payouts to (A, B)

		Firm B	
		South Dakota only	***Both***
Firm A	***North Dakota only***	(100, 150)	(60, 180)
	Both	(130, 100)	(50, 120)

possibility, and in doing so, they realize exactly how much worse off they are if Firm B decides to enter their territory. So they reach out to Firm B with the following:

Firm A's threat: If you enter North Dakota, we will enter South Dakota.

Firm A's promise: If you stay in South Dakota, we will remain exclusively in North Dakota.

Firm A is committing to its strategies in advance of Firm B's decision in an effort to ensure a particular result. Firm A is better off entering South Dakota *only if* Firm B does not react. The first statement is a threat because Firm A would be better off staying out of South Dakota if Firm B enters North Dakota. Similarly, the second statement is a promise because if Firm B does not expand, then it is profitable for A to expand into South Dakota. But Firm A is universally worse off if Firm B enters its territory. So in an effort to convince Firm B not to expand, Firm A restricts its own behavior with both a threat and a promise.

For threats and promises to be effective, they need to be believable. Put another way, they need to pose a **credible threat**. Threats require a willingness to reduce your own reward, so by their very nature, they are often suspect. If you signal that you will reduce price in response to a rival's action, you are indicating a willingness to reduce your own profits or even to take a loss because this behavior also reduces profits for the rival. A threat that causes too great a harm to yourself will not be believable. If in negotiations for a raise, you tell your boss that you will quit unless you get a 10% increase in your salary, but the national economy is in a recession and jobs are not easy to find, your boss is not likely to believe you and will be in a position to reject your request. This puts you in the position of accepting the salary that is offered or leaving your job in pursuit of another. If it is not reasonable that you would take that risk, your threat will not be credible, and your boss will ignore it. Credible threats are a large part of poker strategy, but as indicated earlier, a thorough poker discussion would take a lot more space than we have here.

credible threat: A credible threat is a threat that is realistic enough to be believable.

Is Firm A's threat from earlier credible? Absolutely. Firm A does better if both firms remain in their original states than if both expand into the other's state. The credibility of a promise is also critical to its effectiveness. The promise that Firm A issued to stay out of South Dakota is not credible on its own in a one-shot game. Firm A would do better entering South Dakota if it believed that Firm B was not planning to expand. But by offering to forgo that opportunity, Firm A is able to convince Firm B to stand pat, eliminating the possibility of increased competition and lower profits for both firms if each decides to expand. The effectiveness of threats and promises depends on the level of communication. In business where such coordination is not allowed, it can be difficult to deliver your message, and it can also be hard to enforce penalties on a broken promise. Despite this, a Nash equilibrium may well emerge even in games when direct communication is not possible.

Focal Points

When communication is not possible and there are multiple Nash equilibria available, players seek to coordinate their strategies in some way to reach a Nash equilibrium. In his 1960 book *The Strategies of Conflict*, Nobel Laureate Thomas Schelling explores these types of situations. Schelling asks the reader to consider the following situation: You are supposed to meet a friend in New York City tomorrow, but you do not know where or when the meeting is supposed to occur, and communication between you and your friend is impossible. Where would you go and at what time?

Take a moment and consider your options if you were faced with this dilemma. While there are many good choices, a few locations may stand out among your guesses. The Empire State Building, the ice-skating rink at 30 Rockefeller Plaza, and Grand Central Station all seem like reasonable guesses. When Schelling asked his class this question, his students' most common response was Grand Central Station. If he was supposed to meet one of his students and decided to go to Grand Central Station, he would have a fighting chance. But at what time? Well, very early in the morning or very late at night don't make much sense. And picking a time like 4:32 in the afternoon seems unlikely. Schelling's students' most commonly chosen time was noon. So in a city of hundreds of thousands of locations and out of all the possible times in a given day, why is it that certain locations and certain times won out?

Both parties have an incentive to try to find one another. The Nash equilibria of this game all involved times and places that both parties choose, allowing them to "win" the game and reap the reward of spending time together. So both players put themselves into the shoes of the other and try to predict what the other will do. The most predictable places are the most famous places in the city. The most predictable times are the times on the hour and in the heart of the day. Schelling calls these choices focal points. **Focal points** are points chosen due to their prominence or conspicuousness. Focal points are unique choices in a game that offer hints to the players as to where the positive outcomes can be found. According to Schelling, focal points are "each person's expectation of what others expect him to do." Players choose them because they are obvious and because there are rewards to selecting the obvious choice.

focal points: Focal points are points chosen due to their prominence or conspicuousness.

Simultaneous or Sequential Choices

In the previous examples, parties choose their positions simultaneously. When communication is possible, it is easier to find strategies that yield positive results for both players, but when communication is limited, other methods are needed to find the best outcomes. Some games allow for the strategy of one player to be observed before the next player's strategy is set. Picture a chess game. Moves are made in turn, and the choice that you make is typically impacted by the choice that comes before it. In effect, this is a form of communication that can help you more easily discover the optimal paths. A time consistency problem arises, however, when there is an advantage to going either first or second. A **time consistency problem** exists when a player's best strategy changes as rivals make observable choices ahead of that player's choice. If making the first move conveys a disadvantage to the player who moves first, a battle can arise over making that first move. One classic axiom in negotiation is "never make the first offer." In any bargaining situation, the act of making an offer conveys some information to your rival. Your rival's next offer then can be made with a better understanding of what you might accept in your half of the bargain.

time consistency problem: A time consistency problem exists when a player's best strategy changes as rivals make observable choices ahead of that player's choice.

In the model of duopoly behavior developed in Section 20.2, for example, it is in Firm 1's interest to be able to send the message: I intend to produce 30 units of output, and I will not change from that, no matter what you plan to do. If Firm 1 can persuasively provide this message and Firm 2 receives it, then Firm 2 is stuck with a best option of producing 15 units of output and acting as the Stackelberg follower. Of course, Firm 2 would like to send a symmetric message to Firm 1. If, for some reason or other, Firm 1 is unable to *receive* messages, then the bargain will be struck in Firm 1's favor, and SE_1 will result.

Summary

Outcomes in oligopolistic markets are uncertain because of the interdependent nature of the players in these markets. Each deterministic model of oligopolistic rivalry is based on a set of behavioral assumptions. Common behavioral assumptions include: Rival firms will match price changes; rival firms will maintain their current prices; rival firms will maintain their current output; rival firms will match price decreases but not price increases; and rival firms will always choose that option that produces the worst outcome for their rivals. Each of these (and many other) behavioral assumptions lead to different deterministic models of oligopoly interaction. Each implies different market outcomes because each is based on different presumed behavior patterns: Different presumed behavior leads to different outcomes.

A reaction function describes how one firm reacts to another firm's actions. Reaction functions can be used to examine oligopolistic rivalry in a geometric fashion. They are based on assumed behavior patterns of rivals. The simplest reaction function model is based on the Cournot quantity assumption: Each firm believes that its rival will maintain output. If both firms in a duopoly market have Cournot quantity beliefs about their rivals, then the intersection of their reaction functions is a Cournot equilibrium. This point represents the best that each can do, based on what it expects others to do. The Cournot equilibrium is a special case of a more general concept called Nash equilibrium. A Nash equilibrium occurs if every player's strategy is optimal, given competitors' strategies. An alternative version of the Cournot model can be built on which rivals compete in a differentiated product market environment, based on the assumption that the rivals will maintain price. In this event, a Cournot pricing model results.

Although the Cournot-Nash outcome is the best that each firm can do, given what it expects of its rivals, it is not the best that the industry could do, were the industry to act as a perfect cartel. Put another way, the Cournot equilibrium is not joint profit maximizing. Nonetheless, the joint profit-maximizing outcome is not stable in the sense that each firm has an incentive to cheat on this solution. Of course, if each firm cheats, the outcome breaks down.

An alternative to the symmetry of the Cournot model is when one firm acts as a leader and assumes that the other firms will simply follow the leader. In this event, the leader maximizes profits, subject to followers reacting along their reaction functions. The resulting equilibrium is called a Stackelberg leadership model. Of course, this is only an equilibrium if the follower acts like a follower. Stackelberg disequilibrium results if both firms attempt to lead.

Oligopolistic interaction can also be modeled using game theory. Game theory allows us to mathematically model strategic behavior. As with reaction functions, games are most easily examined if we restrict our analysis to two players. Models of game theory assess the strategies available to two or more players and the payoffs that result from the interaction of their strategic choices. When your best strategy is a function of the choices made by rivals, an understanding of game theory can help you understand the possible outcomes, anticipate the best outcomes for your rivals, and react accordingly.

The simplest models of game theory often yield a dominant strategy equilibrium where your best strategy is clear, regardless of the behavior of your rival. The *prisoners' dilemma* leads to a destructive equilibrium where the players make a choice that does not yield the best possible outcome to avoid an outcome that is significantly worse. A Nash equilibrium emerges where your best move is a function of the choices your rivals made. The presence (or lack) of communication and the ability to play multiple iterations of a game (or not) can also have dramatic impacts on the ultimate determination of the best combination of strategies in a game.

Bargaining is negotiating the terms of an agreement, and models of bargaining also rely on game theoretic models. The bargaining may be overt if communication is allowed between parties or tacit if communication is limited or forbidden. The use of credible threats and promises can help a mutually beneficially bargain to be struck, and focal points can provide a convenient set of strategies to emerge in games in which there is little sharing of information.

Review Questions

Define the following terms:

Sections 20.1–20.4

oligopoly
competitive fringe
duopoly
behavioral assumptions
strategic behavior
reaction function
Cournot quantity assumption
Cournot equilibrium (CE)
Nash equilibrium
Stackelberg leader
Stackelberg follower
Stackelberg equilibrium
Stackelberg disequilibrium
Cournot price beliefs

Section 20.5

game
player
strategies available to players
payoffs
payoff matrix
prisoners' dilemma
dominant strategy
dominant strategy equilibrium
external authority
zero-sum game
constant-sum game
variable-sum game
bargaining
cooperative game
noncooperative game
tacit bargaining
one-shot games
multiple-shot games
limited war
threat
promise
credible threats
focal points
time consistency problem

Provide short answers to the following:

Sections 20.1–20.4

a. If two firms share a market and each has Cournot quantity assumptions, will the resulting Cournot equilibrium be joint profit maximizing?
b. What is true about the isoprofit contours for each firm at the joint profit-maximizing output point?

c. What happens as the number of firms in the market increases if each firm acts in a Cournot fashion?
d. If an economist models a market using the Cournot pricing model, is the product homogeneous or heterogeneous?
e. In the Stackelberg pricing model, is it more profitable to be a leader or a follower?

Section 20.5

a. Would you expect the same result from a prisoners' dilemma game played as a multiple-shot game as from the prisoners' dilemma as a single-shot game? Why or why not?
b. Why do the police guarantee that the prisoners' dilemma is played as a noncooperative game?
c. What can the government do to limit collusion and ensure that pricing decisions in an oligopolistic market mirror the prisoners' dilemma?
d. Which is more credible—a threat from a 5-year-old or a 25-year-old? Explain.
e. What is tacit bargaining? Is tacit bargaining more effective in the short run or the long run? Explain.
f. In bargaining, why is it often a bad move to make the first offer? What advantage do you confer to your rival when you act first?
g. What is a limited war? How does the concept of limited war relate to the discussion of oligopolistic market?
h. You and a friend are challenged to select a square in the table that follows. If you select the same square, you will each win \$20. Which square will you select? Why?

i. What concept from this chapter suggests that you might be about to win \$20?

For problems j, k, and l, consult the following table of payoffs to (Jack, Jill):

		Jill	
		Movies	***Mini-golf***
Jack	***Movies***	(40, 40)	(20, 60)
	Mini-golf	(50, 10)	(80, 50)

j. Jack and Jill are friends who have a couple of options for entertainment this afternoon. Given the payoffs shown in the table, what will they do?
k. Does this game have a dominant strategy equilibrium?
l. Is this an example of a prisoners' dilemma?

Check your answers to the *short-answer* exercises in the Answers Appendix at the end of the book.

Notes

1. Many of you will recognize John Nash as the person who was made famous not by winning the Nobel Prize in Economics in 1994, but by Russell Crowe's portrayal of John Nash in the 2001 movie *A Beautiful Mind* that received four Oscars, including Best Picture and Best Director (Ron Howard).

2. The magnitude of slope of R_1 is $Q_{competition}/Q_{monopoly} = ((a - c)/b)/((a - c)/(2 \cdot b)) = 2$, and the magnitude of slope of R_2 is $Q_{monopoly}/Q_{competition} = ((a - c)/(2 \cdot b))/((a - c)/b) = 1/2$.

3. A common mistake is to look at Equation 20.4a and think that the slope is –1/2, the coefficient of Q_2 in the equation. But the slope is the coefficient of Q_1 once a linear equation is put in slope-intercept form. If this is done with Equation 20.4a, we obtain: $Q_2 = (a - c)/b - 2 \cdot Q_1$. Although this is mathematically identical to Equation 20.4a, this does not have the same behavioral interpretation, since Firm 1's reaction to output by Firm 2 should be written as a function of Q_2, not Q_1.

4. You can quickly check your work by noting that $Q_1 = 20$ when $a = 60$, $b = 1$, and $c = 0$, using Equation 20.5b.

5. The difference in joint profits between M_1 and M_2 can be seen in two ways. One is as the sum of reduced variable cost and increased revenue: $\Delta J\pi = \$288 + \$36 = \$324$, the same amount seen by directly taking the difference from the footnote answer for Q8c: $\Delta J\pi = \text{Joint}\pi(M_1) - \text{Joint}\pi(M_2) = \$500 - \$176 = \$324$.

6. This is seen by the red isoprofit contour for Firm 2, $\pi_2 = \$0$, connecting the points (0, 48) and (48, 0). SD is outside this isoprofit contour for Firm 2. By contrast, Firm 1 would wish to produce at SD because \$216 of the fixed costs of production

are covered in this instance ($216 = 36 · $6), leaving Firm 1 with a short-run loss at the SD joint production point of –$184. Therefore, SD is inside the isoprofit contour, $\pi_1 = -\$400$, connecting the points (0, 60) and (60, 0).

7. The proof requires calculus. Take the derivative of profits, $d\pi(x)/dx = -2 \cdot b \cdot x + (a - b \cdot d \cdot (n-1) - c)$, and set it equal to zero; then solve for x to obtain the reaction function. Solving for x, we obtain the reaction function in Equation 20.8. Notice that, as with the other market structures, the production decision does not depend on fixed costs F.

8. As noted earlier, we wish to focus on the geometry of the situation, rather than the algebra (the algebra is quite similar to that provided earlier for the quantity-based Cournot model). Nonetheless, it is worth noting the demand and cost functions that form the basis for these reaction functions:

Demand for Firm 1's variety: $Q_1 = 15 - 4 \cdot P_1 + 3 \cdot P_2$.

Demand for Firm 2's variety: $Q_2 = 15 - 4 \cdot P_2 + 3 \cdot P_1$.

Note that these equations satisfy the requirements of Equation 20.11. As with the earlier model, we assume symmetric cost conditions: Marginal cost is zero, and fixed cost is $16 for each firm. The resulting reaction functions are:

$R_1(P_2) = 15/8 + 3/8 \cdot P_2$ and $R_2(P_1) = 15/8 + 3/8 \cdot P_1$.

9. The contract curve is the set of tangencies between both firms' isoprofit contours. Each tangency must be upward sloping. This will only occur in the area to the right of R_1 and above R_2. The actual point of maximum profits is derived by adding each firm's profit functions together, taking the partial derivative in the P_1 and P_2 directions, and setting these partial derivatives equal to zero. Joint profit-maximizing price levels are then obtained by solving for P_1 and P_2 from these equations.

10. Actual dollar values for price and profits are obtained by using the demand functions in endnote 8. The algebra involved is not important for our purposes; the essence of the model exists in the tangencies of the isoprofit contours to the various lines in the figure (such as at **A**, **B**, **J**, and **SE**$_1$).

11. Reaction functions based on these demand and cost conditions are:

Figure 20.10A: $R_1(P_2) = 2 + 1/4 \cdot P_2$ and $R_2(P_1) = 13/4 + 1/4 \cdot P_1$.

Figure 20.10B: $R_1(P_2) = 5/2 + 3/8 \cdot P_2$ and $R_2(P_1) = 3 + 1/4 \cdot P_1$.

Figure 20.10C: $R_1(P_2) = 23/8 + 3/8 \cdot P_2$ and $R_2(P_1) = 2 + 1/4 \cdot P_1$.

The derivation of these reaction functions requires the use of calculus and is examined in the workbook.

12. If Firm 2 prices itself out of the market, then Firm 1's isoprofit contours are only a function of Firm 1's price. Therefore, each of Firm 1's isoprofit contours is vertical when the demand for Firm 2's product is zero. Similarly, if Firm 1 prices itself out of the market, then Firm 2's isoprofit contours are only a function of Firm 2's price. Therefore, each of Firm 2's isoprofit contours is horizontal when the demand for Firm 1's product is zero. The same can be said of the reaction functions in this instance. $R_1(P_2)$ is vertical once Firm 2 prices itself out of the market, and $R_2(P_1)$ is horizontal once Firm 1 prices itself out of the market.

CHAPTER 21

Informational Issues

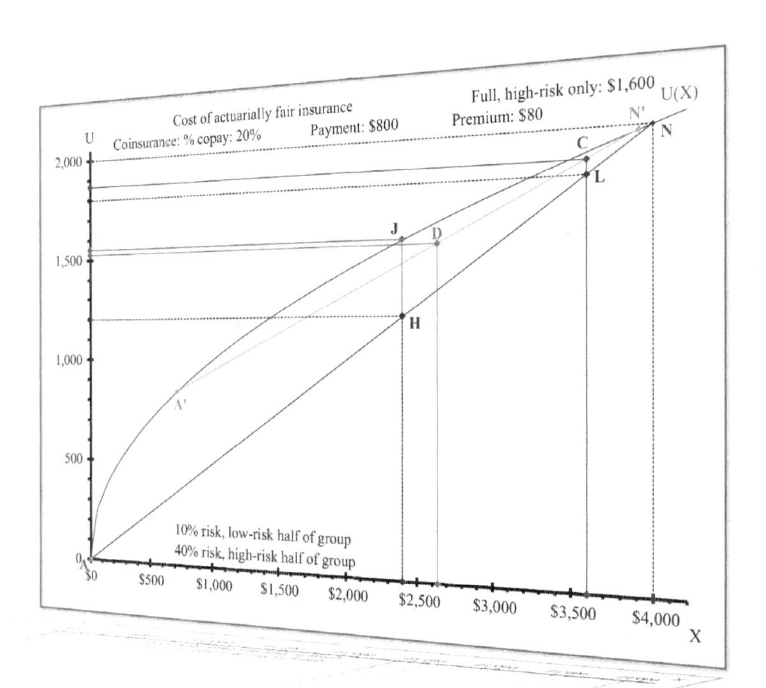

Chapter Outline

For much of the text, we have assumed that consumers and producers have perfect information. In reality, this is not the case. In this chapter, we initially examine what happens to the market equilibrium if we assume that information is imperfect. Then the main part of the chapter examines asymmetric information—a specific form of imperfect information that leads to market failures. The chapter concludes with a discussion of advertising in theory and in practice.

21.1 Imperfect Information versus Asymmetric Information ***Prerequisite: Chapter 2***

[Sections 21.1–21.4 were contributed by Jue Wang, University of California, San Diego.]

Perfect information, where all agents involved in economic activities have full access to all information necessary to make optimal decisions, has been an underlying assumption of most of our discussions so far. In reality, however, information is usually costly to obtain or is simply unavailable to some or all agents. In this chapter, we incorporate *imperfect information* into economic analysis and discuss how this can change the implications derived from basic economic models.

To broadly see how the lack of information, as a form of market failure, changes previous conclusions of economic models, let us consider the process of price making in a competitive market. When all buyers and sellers have perfect information, all sellers will price at the equilibrium price, which clears the market. Any seller who prices even slightly above this price will lose all its buyers. When it is costly for buyers to gain access to all prices available in the market (e.g., some stores are too far away), they likely will end up purchasing at a price level higher than the lowest price. This results in price dispersion, and we no longer have a single market clearing price. Even though we do not have a perfectly competitive market in this example, the demand and supply curves are still in place on a local level, and the sellers do not have full control over pricing. The amount of price dispersion depends on a number of factors.

Advertising is one way that firms typically let consumers know about the price of their product. Certainly, advertising attempts to affect consumer demand by talking about much more than price, but price is a common product attribute that is highlighted via advertising. The weekly grocery store advertisements in the local newspaper are a simple way that consumers can obtain information about price for a variety of products at various stores. Consumers can use these ads to become more informed about prices at stores where they do not typically shop. Becoming informed requires that consumers take the time to peruse the ads. Such behavior is itself costly (in time and energy that could be devoted to other activities). The ads tend to reduce the price dispersion for products, but not all products are typically advertised on a price basis in this way. And the ads do not ensure that all individuals seek out and process that information.

The size of relative price dispersion should decline as the price of the product increases. The reason is straightforward: A product that has a higher price deserves a greater amount of search because the cost of the price search is largely independent of the price range of the product under consideration. Consider calling around to determine the price of an automobile versus the price of a small, flat-screen television. It may take longer to get price information from an auto dealership than from a big-box or discount store, but it certainly will not take 10 times as long. The price difference is about 100 times as large ($250 versus $25,000). If a few phone calls can help distinguish a 1% price dispersion, then these calls are much more likely to occur for an automobile than for a flat-screen television (because many consumers would be willing to make several phone calls if it saves them $250, but not if it only saves them $2.50).

We would expect price search to continue as long as the marginal benefit from that search exceeds the marginal cost of that search. The more expensive the product, the higher the benefits of better information tend to be. But even if two individuals face the same benefit from search, they might not respond with the same level of search activity because they may each perceive a different marginal cost of additional search. In plain terms, some people are "born shoppers," and others are not, and this fact helps to explain why price dispersion exists for a homogeneous good.

More generally, if consumers have different packets of information, then varieties of a product might sell for different prices, even if the varieties do not have appreciable differences. Assume that consumers would like the varieties equally well if they were fully informed. In the absence of full information, different consumers will have different "bundles" of information; therefore, different consumers will have different preferences over the varieties.

The perfect information assumption can be violated under many circumstances. In this chapter, we focus on a specific one in which the buyers/consumers and the sellers/producers have different information about the product in a systematic pattern. We usually refer to this type of imperfect information as asymmetric information. A market is subject to **asymmetric information** if one party or the other tends to have a systematic informational advantage, relative to the other party in the market interaction. Since the asymmetry is systematic, it usually gives advantage to one party over another in economic transactions. This makes the situation of special interest to economists and policymakers. In the sections that follow, we discuss some classic examples of asymmetric information, based on the work of three economists—George Akerlof, Michael Spence, and Joseph Stiglitz, who jointly shared the Nobel Prize for their work on asymmetric information in 2001.

asymmetric information: A market is subject to asymmetric information if one party or the other tends to have a systematic informational advantage, relative to the other party in the market interaction.

21.2 The "Lemons" Model

Prerequisite: Section 21.1

One of the more prominent markets where asymmetric information has a big presence is the used-car market. In the used-car market, sellers inevitably know more about the quality of the car than buyers. George Akerlof argued that this is the reason why used cars sell for significantly less than new cars, even if they are only a few months old with minimal mileage.[1]

To understand how asymmetric information leads to this situation, let us consider a simple model where the commodity—a car—is described by its condition (new and used) and quality (good [or "cherry"] and bad [or "lemon"]). Once out of the factory, the quality of the car is fixed, yet unobservable until the car has been used for some time. Both sellers and buyers are aware that some cars are *lemons*. In the new-car market, neither sellers nor buyers know the quality of a particular car, so there is no asymmetric information, and the buyer purchases the car at the market price for a new car. In the used-car market, however, the seller has used the car and knows whether the car is a cherry or a lemon, while the buyer does not. This uncertainty of quality for the buyer causes the price of a used car to decrease because the buyer must consider the possibility that the used car is a lemon, even if it is in almost-new condition. We now prove this statement with a simple numeric example.

First, consider what happens when buyers have perfect information in the used-car market. Assume that, under perfect information, there are 1,000 cars sold in the used-car market, and a quarter of them (250) are lemons. Perfect information means that both seller and buyer are perfectly aware of the quality of each car when making the trade. This is equivalent to having two markets, each with a different product to sell: the cherry market and the lemon market. These two markets are now perfectly competitive, as we studied in previous chapters, so we know that an equilibrium price exists to clear both the cherry market and the lemon market. We can identify these prices through the supply and demand curves for these markets. Suppose that under this scenario, the price for a cherry is \$12,000, and the price for a lemon is \$5,000.

What happens when a buyer can no longer tell if a given used car is a cherry or a lemon? In this case, used cars become a homogenous good, and all used cars are sold at the same price. At the same time, buyers are aware that a fourth of the cars are lemons, which means that there is a 25% probability that a given used car is a lemon. The expected value of a used car can be calculated as following:

$$\$10{,}250 = p_L \cdot P_L + p_c \cdot P_c = 0.25 \cdot \$5{,}000 + 0.75 \cdot \$12{,}000. \qquad \textbf{(21.1)}$$

However, this expected value will not be the price of used cars because sellers will use asymmetric information to their advantage. Out of the 1,000 used-car sellers, 750 of them are aware that their cars are cherries, and each of them is willing to sell their cherry at a price of \$12,000. Some cherry owners will choose not to accept the \$10,250 offer (because supply is upward sloping). On the other hand, there are 250 lemon owners who are willing to sell at a price of \$5,000. And because supply is upward sloping, there are other lemon owners who value their lemon at more than \$5,000 but less than \$10,250 and who will want to sell their cars at a price of \$10,250 (the price made possible because asymmetric information makes it possible for buyers to offer a higher price for a lemon when mistaking it as a cherry). With fewer cherry owners willing to sell and more lemon owners willing to sell, buyers face an increased likelihood of obtaining a lemon instead of cherry. This further lowers the expected value of a used car and lowers buyers' willingness to pay. This lower offer drives away more cherry owners, increasing the probability of buying a lemon even further. What does market equilibrium look like in this case? That depends on how quickly both types of used-car owners react to selling their cars at the common price. The final percentage of lemons in the market is less important for our purposes than recognizing that the market will have a higher proportion of lemons sold than in the absence of the information asymmetry. Because cherry owners cannot be distinguished from lemon owners, some of the cherry owners will hold onto their cherries at the lower blended price.

Let us abstract from the numeric example and think about how equilibrium is pinned down conceptually. We can revisit the basic supply and demand model, and use it to describe what is happening in this market. We know that demand is a function of price, P. It is downward sloping with regard to price: The higher the price, the lower the quantity demanded, *ceteris paribus*. This is the law of demand. In the used-car market, since we have essentially two different goods, cherries and lemons, the quality of the car must also factor into buyers' demand. So now, demand is function of both price and quality. If we let A be the average quality of used cars in the market, demand will be a positive function of A (different levels of A would be represented as a shift in demand). We can write this in multivariate fashion as: Demand = f(P, A).

As we discussed earlier, higher price means that there are more cherries in the market, so A is also higher, A = A(P) with $\Delta A/\Delta P > 0$. Higher price leads to higher quality, thus resulting in higher demand. There are two competing component parts—demand as a function of price and demand as a function of average quality, which is itself a function of price:

$$\text{Demand(P)} = f(\text{P, A}) = f(\text{P, A(P)}). \quad \textbf{(21.2a)}$$

To sum up, in this market, when we consider how demand responds to a change in price, we need to consider both the direct response to the price change and the response to quality change as the result of the price change. In symbols:[2]

$$\begin{array}{llllllll} \Delta\text{Demand(P)}/\Delta\text{P} & = \Delta f(\text{P,A})/\Delta\text{P} & + \{[\Delta f(\text{P,A})/\Delta\text{A}] & \cdot & [(\Delta\text{A(P)}/\Delta\text{P}]\}. & & & \textbf{(21.2b)} \\ ? & = \quad - & + \{ \quad [+] & \cdot & [+] \quad \} & & & \\ \text{Total effect (of price } \Delta) & = \text{Price effect} & + \quad \text{Quality effect} & & & & & \end{array}$$

Much of the analysis in Part 2 of the text can be used to verify the law of downward-sloping demand and to establish conditions under which this does not hold. (Demand is upward sloping only if the good is "super inferior," as shown in Section 8.2; this is the case of a Giffen good used to describe consumption of potatoes during the Irish potato famine. The current situation is not one of a Giffen good; it is one in which demand varies because quality varies as price varies.)

The first factor is negative, according to the law of demand. The second factor is the product of the effect of quality on demand and the effect of price on quality. As discussed earlier, both of these components are positive. The sign of the total effect is ambiguous; we do not know if the first term dominates the second, or the other way around. Despite this ambiguity, we can posit which effect dominates in different price ranges.

If the price of used cars is relatively high, compared to new cars, we know that many cherries are being traded in the market. A marginal increase or decrease in price should not affect the average quality of used cars by too much; thus, the (second part of the) second term, $\Delta A(P)/\Delta P$, is likely to be small. In this situation, the first term dominates, and demand over this price range is downward sloping. Following the same logic, when prices are low, a marginal change in price leads to a more substantial change in the average quality of used cars in the market. Now the second term dominates, and demand over this price range is upward sloping. Step back and consider what happens over a range of prices: For high prices, demand is downward sloping, but for low prices, it bends backward on itself and is upward sloping. This unintuitive behavior is the result of asymmetric information.

21.3 Signaling

Prerequisite: Section 21.2

The "lemons" model of asymmetric information is, of course, not limited to the used-car market. We can use it to describe any markets in which buyers have less information than sellers about the quality of the goods traded. We do know that asymmetric information can cause inefficiency, so an important question for economists to ask is: How can we avoid the problem?

One answer is to use signals. *Signals* can help buyers observe the quality of the goods and thus, ideally, give buyers the same information that sellers have. What kind of signals can sellers send, and what signals allow buyers to interpret quality with confidence? Let us think back to the used-car example. Owners of both cherries and lemons want to signal that their cars are cherries. So a seller telling a potential buyer that "my car is good quality" really cannot serve as a credible signal. This is why we look for signals, such as repair and maintenance records, when we buy used cars. Lemon owners are not willing to provide these documents because the documents show the quality of the car. If buying from a used-car dealership, we look for *warranties* or *guarantees*. Another widely used signal is *reputation*. Think about *brand names*. When a brand is established in a market, people consider the brand as a signal that product quality is good. This is why companies work hard to establish a brand name, and why big brands work hard to keep their reputation as "number one" or "best" in the market. Firms use brand names to tell consumers that the firm's reputation is on the line.

In this section, we focus on one of the most studied signaling mechanisms—job market signaling. It is crucial that this signaling works because it applies to every participant in the labor market, and the cost associated with firing and hiring is high. Prior to hiring, employers would find it useful to ascertain the productivity of a potential employee, but productivity is not observable until after the potential employee starts working. Meanwhile, potential employees have significantly more information about their own productivity than employers. How can productive potential employees signal their high ability, and how can employers encourage this type of signaling?

Again, let us begin by thinking about the scenario where asymmetric information is not present in the labor market; that is, productivity of a potential employee is directly observable prior to hiring. In this case, we have the classic firm problem. To optimize profit, firms use their production functions to determine the demand for labor at each productivity level. High-productivity workers are assigned to posts requiring high skills, and low-productivity workers are assigned to less-substantial posts. Firms pay workers their competitive wage, which is also their marginal revenue product of labor (as noted in Section 18.2).

Now assume that asymmetric information is present in the labor market. In particular, suppose that firms have no knowledge of a worker's productivity, prior to hiring. In this scenario, rather than being paid based on marginal productivity of labor, wages will be based on the average productivity. This will result in low-productivity workers being paid more than they are worth, while high-productivity workers receive less than they are worth.

Fortunately, firms have a way to separate high-productivity workers from low-productivity workers in the hiring process, even if productivity levels of potential employees are not observable. Michael Spence argued that employers can use the educational attainment of a potential employee as a signal of productivity level.[3] How can education level be linked to productivity level? In his model, Spence made the connection by imposing a simple and reasonable assumption: Education costs are different for people of different productivity levels. More specifically, achieving a given level of education is more costly to a low-productivity worker than to a high-productivity worker.

Productivity affects the cost of education for two reasons. First, attaining a certain degree is more expensive for a low-productivity worker. Costs associated with a longer time span to graduate and more repeated classes all add to the expense of tuition and fees. Second, opportunity cost is higher for a low-productivity worker. Each year of schooling means the loss of a year's wage. For every individual, at a certain point in education, one extra year of schooling is simply worth less than a year's wage. Very likely, the lower one's productivity, the earlier this threshold comes in one's career. Both reasons point to the fact that education is more costly to low-productivity workers. This means that they are likely to choose to enter the labor market earlier, instead of continuing schooling.

Workers exhibit many different levels of productivity in an economy. To explore the mechanism in greater detail, we assume that there are just two productivity levels—low and high. For the purposes of this model, we assume that education does not add to the skill level of a worker (we discuss this assumption later). For this signaling mechanism to work, we also need a wage scheme that incentivizes the signaling of education by linking education to wage. For a worker with E years of education, the firm will pay a lifetime wage W_E, with W_E an increasing function of years of education.

How do workers decide how many years of education to attain, given that firms link the wage rate to education level? Consider how a high school graduate ($E = 12$) decides whether to continue schooling for 4 more years to get a college degree. The student has two options: Stop getting education to receive wage W_{12}, or go to college to receive wage W_{12+4}. Meanwhile, the cost of college is P_L for the low-productivity worker and P_H for the high-productivity worker. If a low-productivity worker chooses to go to work instead of school, it means that:

$$W_{12} > W_{12+4} - P_L. \quad \textbf{(21.3a)}$$

On the other hand, if a high-productivity worker chooses to continue with schooling instead of going to work, it means that:

$$W_{12} < W_{12+4} - P_H. \quad \textbf{(21.3b)}$$

The twin conditions in Equations 21.3a and 21.3b are at least theoretically possible because $P_H < P_L$. Put another way, offering a choice of wage schemes based on educational attainment may lead to a situation where low-productivity workers voluntarily choose the low-wage option, while high-productivity workers voluntarily choose the high-wage option.

More generally, if we assume that the cost of a year of education is C_L for a low-productivity worker and C_H for a high-productivity worker and that $C_L > C_H$, we should observe the following inequality:

$$(W_{k+x} - W_k)/C_L < x < (W_{k+x} - W_k)/C_H. \quad \textbf{(21.3c)}$$

The differences in compensation and costs of education affect the level of education attainment the workers choose, represented here by x. Potential employees face two options: a wage offer of W_{k+x} for those with $k + x$ years of education, or a wage offer of W_k for those with k years of education. The left-hand inequality of Equation 21.3c says (upon multiplying both sides by C_L): $W_{k+x} - W_k < x \cdot C_L$. The low-productivity worker is better off choosing the less education and lower wage combination because the difference in lifetime wage is less than the cost of x years of education. On the other hand, the right-hand inequality of Equation 21.3c says: $x \cdot C_H < W_{k+x} - W_k$. The high-productivity worker is better off choosing the more education and higher wage combination because the difference in lifetime wage exceeds the cost of x years of education. This is called a separating equilibrium. In a **separating equilibrium**, high-productivity and low-productivity segments are separated by workers choosing to use a signal.

separating equilibrium: A separating equilibrium is one in which high-productivity and low-productivity segments are separated by workers choosing to use a signal.

This mechanism allows workers of different productivity levels to voluntarily separate themselves into different education levels, thus making something unobservable (i.e., productivity) observable (via education). This is why education is an ideal signal to deal with asymmetric information. Notice that under the assumptions in this model, we are not asserting that education increases productivity; *education simply signals productivity.* While education as a signal oversimplifies the role of education in shaping workers, its value as a signal in the labor market presented in this model makes education a worthwhile investment.

While Spence's analysis focused on education as a job-market signal, the seminal point is this: *Sellers can signal quality through actions, but only if those actions (i.e., signals) are differentially costly to provide.* A signal is *only* effective if the signal cost for a high-quality seller is relatively less expensive than it is for a low-quality seller. Much like Akerlof's lemons model discussed earlier, this analysis is widely applicable outside the job market. A perfect example of this type of signaling device is a warranty. A *warranty* acts as a signaling device because the presence of a warranty on a product is relatively more expensive to a seller of a low-quality product than to a seller of a high-quality product. The low-quality product is more likely to fail and result in the buyer "cashing in" the warranty; this is less likely the case for a high-quality product. Therefore, the presence and type of warranty provided is a useful signaling device to buyers.

21.4 Insurance Markets

Prerequisite: Section 21.3

Section 21.4 Outline

With the basic toolbox to understand and deal with asymmetric information developed in Sections 21.2–21.3, we can start analyzing more complicated problems. In this section, we look at several problems analyzed by Joseph Stiglitz and colleagues that occur most notably in insurance markets.[4]

21.4A Adverse Selection

When pricing a policy, an insurance company needs to calculate the expected expense of the policy, which depends largely on the riskiness of the policyholders. This resembles the lemons problem; however, the difference is that buyers of insurance have information (about their riskiness) that sellers of insurance desire but cannot observe. Recall that in the lemons problem with asymmetric information and no signal, some cherry owners exit the market because the price is too low for the value of their cars. The proportion of lemons in the market for trade is likely to be higher than the overall proportion of lemons on the road. In the insurance market, the "cherry" buyers are the less-risky buyers. When an insurance company determines the price of a policy by factoring in both the "cherry" and the "lemon" (or riskier) buyers, the resulting price may well be higher than the premium that "cherry" buyers are willing to pay. The result is the adverse selection problem: High-risk individuals are more likely to buy insurance than low-risk individuals. The **adverse selection problem** occurs if the market is skewed because of asymmetric information.

adverse selection problem: The adverse selection problem occurs if the market is skewed because of asymmetric information.

To see the problem inherent here, consider the following example: Suppose that three potential buyers—A, B, and C—want to purchase insurance to cover their potential \$10,000 loss. Each of them has a positive probability of generating this loss. More specifically, the probability is 0.1 for A, 0.5 for B, and 0.6 for C. If an actuarially fair insurance company can observe the probabilities, it will price each policy at its expected loss on an individual level:

$$\text{Price of A's policy} = \text{A's expected loss} = \$10{,}000 \cdot 0.1 = \$1{,}000. \quad \textbf{(21.4a)}$$

$$\text{Price of B's policy} = \text{B's expected loss} = \$10{,}000 \cdot 0.5 = \$5{,}000. \quad \textbf{(21.4b)}$$

$$\text{Price of C's policy} = \text{C's expected loss} = \$10{,}000 \cdot 0.6 = \$6{,}000. \quad \textbf{(21.4c)}$$

At these price points, the insurance company breaks even by offering policies based on the probability with each individual policyholder. What happens when the insurance company cannot observe each individual's probability and has to set one price for A, B, and C? Assume that the insurance company knows that the average probability of a \$10,000 loss is currently $(0.1 + 0.5 + 0.6)/3 = 0.4$ in the market but not which individuals are attached to each probability. So the actuarially fair price will be set at:

$$\text{Actuarially fair price} = \text{Expected loss} = \$10{,}000 \cdot 0.4 = \$4{,}000. \quad \textbf{(21.4d)}$$

Given this price, A will not buy the insurance (unless A is strongly risk averse, as described in Section 17.2C), and B and C will purchase at \$4,000. This means that the insurance company is charging $\$4{,}000 \cdot 2 = \$8{,}000$ to cover the expected loss of $\$5{,}000 + \$6{,}000 = \$11{,}000$. To fill this gap between price and expected loss, the insurance company would have to charge $\$11{,}000/2 = \$5{,}500$ for each policy. What will happen now? Since B's expected loss is lower than the updated price, B may also choose not to buy the policy (depending on B's degree of risk aversion). If this happens, the only person buying insurance is C, the riskiest buyer.

To sum up the previous process, we know that at a given price level, those who are the least-risky members of the group an insurance company is trying to cover may well decide to forgo purchasing the policy. Adverse selection occurs. If this happens, the insurance company will need to raise its price to cover the cost, and further adverse selection occurs. Insurance companies can deal with the adverse selection problem in a number of ways.

Institutional Intervention

A government can require all individuals to purchase insurance. For example, in California, all cars operating on the road are required to be covered by insurance. A government or an institution can also intervene by purchasing insurance for designated groups with universal coverage. Examples of this type of intervention are medical care for the elderly (Medicare) and insurance that comes with employment benefits. By avoiding people's self-selection process, less-risky buyers are policyholders who pay a price higher than their expected loss, making it possible for the insurance company to cover riskier policyholders (who pay a price below their expected loss).

Screening

An insurance company can issue policies with different prices and different coverages to allow policyholders to self-select into their respective risk groups. Stiglitz argues that if appropriately priced, such policies can create conditions where individuals sort themselves into risk classes and avoid the adverse selection problem, in much the same way that employees sorted themselves into productivity groups via the education signal.[5] This is called **screening**. One example of screening is by using coinsurance as well as full-coverage policies (full-coverage policies are discussed in Section 17.2C). **Coinsurance** is insurance that provides less-than-full coverage to the insured party. That part not covered by the insurance company must be provided by the insured party. This means that the buyer is responsible for a certain portion of the claim, and the insurance company pays the rest. Since less-risky buyers are less likely to suffer a loss, they are willing to accept coinsurance rather than full-coverage insurance. Insurance companies also offer lower-priced policies with higher deductibles—again, so that less-risky buyers will purchase the policies. If offered in conjunction with full-coverage insurance for the more-risky buyers, these policies may well screen individuals (as we will see in Section 21.5).

screening: A set of insurance policies screens individuals if the individuals self-select into different risk classes.

coinsurance: Coinsurance is insurance that provides less-than-full coverage to the insured party. That part not covered by the insurance company must be provided by the insured party.

21.4B Moral Hazard

For the insurance market, the problem of asymmetric information does not stop at the screening process. Once a contract is established, the insurance company is financially responsible for the actions of policyholders. Meanwhile, the insurance company cannot directly observe the intention behind policyholders' actions. What if policyholders take riskier actions than they would otherwise take because they know that the insurance company will pay for their actions? For example, suppose that the insurance company has a policy that covers a potential loss of \$100 for the price of \$5. Consider a policyholder with a 5% probability of generating this loss. For the insurance company, this contract breaks even:

$$\text{Expected loss} = \$100 \cdot 5\% = \$5 = \text{Price of contract.}$$

Knowing that when \$100 is lost, the insurance company will cover it, the policyholder might take risker actions, increasing the probability of generating a \$100 loss to 8%:

$$\text{Expected loss} = \$100 \cdot 8\% = \$8 > \$5.$$

With the current contract price, the insurance company is now facing an expected loss of \$3. If the insurance company can observe this change in risk taking and if updating the price of the contract is free, a simple solution is for the insurance company to immediately change the price of the contract to \$8 when the policyholder's riskiness changes, making this, again, a break-even contract. However, because of asymmetrc information, when a loss occurs, the insurance company cannot be sure if it is the result of higher risk-taking behavior or not. And updating a contract is financially costly and cannot happen instantaneously. So now the insurance company has to bear the risk of this policyholder not acting at the original risk-taking level assumed when the policy was purchased. This is commonly known as the **moral hazard problem**, and it occurs when the insured party undertakes actions that the party would not undertake in the absence of insurance.

The moral hazard problem is an example of a more general problem caused by information asymmetry—the principal-agent problem. The **principal-agent problem** occurs when the principal cannot monitor the actions of the agent (either a person or an institution) who is charged with making decisions on behalf of the principal. This is also often called the *agency issue*. For example, the board of directors and the management team of a company are usually two different groups of people. The board members, along with shareholders, are the owners of the firm, so they are the principals. The management team members are the agents, and they make decisions about the firm on behalf of the principals. The principal-agent problem comes into play because the owners cannot observe all the actions of the management team, and it becomes especially troublesome if the two groups do not share the same goals or visions for the firm.

moral hazard problem: The moral hazard problem occurs when the insured party undertakes actions that the party would not undertake in the absence of insurance.

principal-agent problem: The principal-agent problem occurs when the principal cannot monitor the actions of the agent who is charged with making decisions on behalf of the principal.

Of course, there are limits to managers' ability to pursue objectives not shared by owners. These limits emanate from the product market, as well as from the market for corporate control. If the market for the firm's product is competitive, then this competition forces managers to act in the owners' interest to survive.

In imperfectly competitive markets, managers have some latitude to pursue their own objectives, but if they stray too far from the owners' goals, they may find themselves without a job. They can be removed from their positions by the board of directors or due to a corporate takeover. To solve this problem, owners may use a managerial compensation package that ensures that the owners' interests are shared by the managers. Profit-sharing and stock-option plans are common ways to create such *incentive-compatible mechanisms*.

21.5 A Geometric Analysis of Screening

Prerequisites: Sections 17.2C and 21.4

Section 21.5 Outline

- **21.5A** The Geometry of Adverse Selection
- **21.5B** The Geometry of Coinsurance
- **21.5C** Using Multiple Policies to Screen Individuals into Risk Classes

The starting point for this analysis of screening is the model of automobile insurance provided in Section 17.2C. The model presented there was that you own a used car worth \$4,000. If you are in an accident, you "total" the car and it is worth zero, but you face no further losses. Individuals are risk averse, and their preferences over risky bundles (lotteries) are given by Equation 17.23, reproduced here:[6]

$$U(X) = 2{,}000 \cdot (X/4{,}000)^r. \quad \textbf{(21.5)}$$

In the absence of insurance, the individual's expected outcome depends solely on the likelihood of an accident. Here, we assume even worse drivers than in Chapter 17 to show the geometry of screening more clearly. In particular, we assume that the average driver faces a 25% chance of totaling the car within a year. Given this, the average driver achieves an expected utility level of 1,500 in the absence of insurance. This is represented by the vertical axis coordinate of point **P** in Figure 21.1 (ignore for the moment points **H**, **I**, and **L**). Point **P** is the lottery associated with not having an accident with probability 0.75 (and being at the no-accident point **N** = (\$4,000, 2,000) as a result) and having an accident with probability 0.25 (and being at the accident point **A** = (\$0, 0) as a result). Using the parametric representation of a line segment, the coordinates of **P** are:

$$\mathbf{P} = 0.25 \cdot \mathbf{A} + 0.75 \cdot \mathbf{N} = 0.25 \cdot (\$0, 0) + 0.75 \cdot (\$4{,}000, 2{,}000) = (\$3{,}000, 1{,}500). \quad \textbf{(21.6)}$$

The horizontal coordinate is an expected dollar value, and the vertical coordinate is an expected utility level. As discussed in Section 17.2C, individuals who choose among lotteries based on the highest expected utility level are acting based on the expected utility criterion. The present analysis is based on the expected utility criterion.

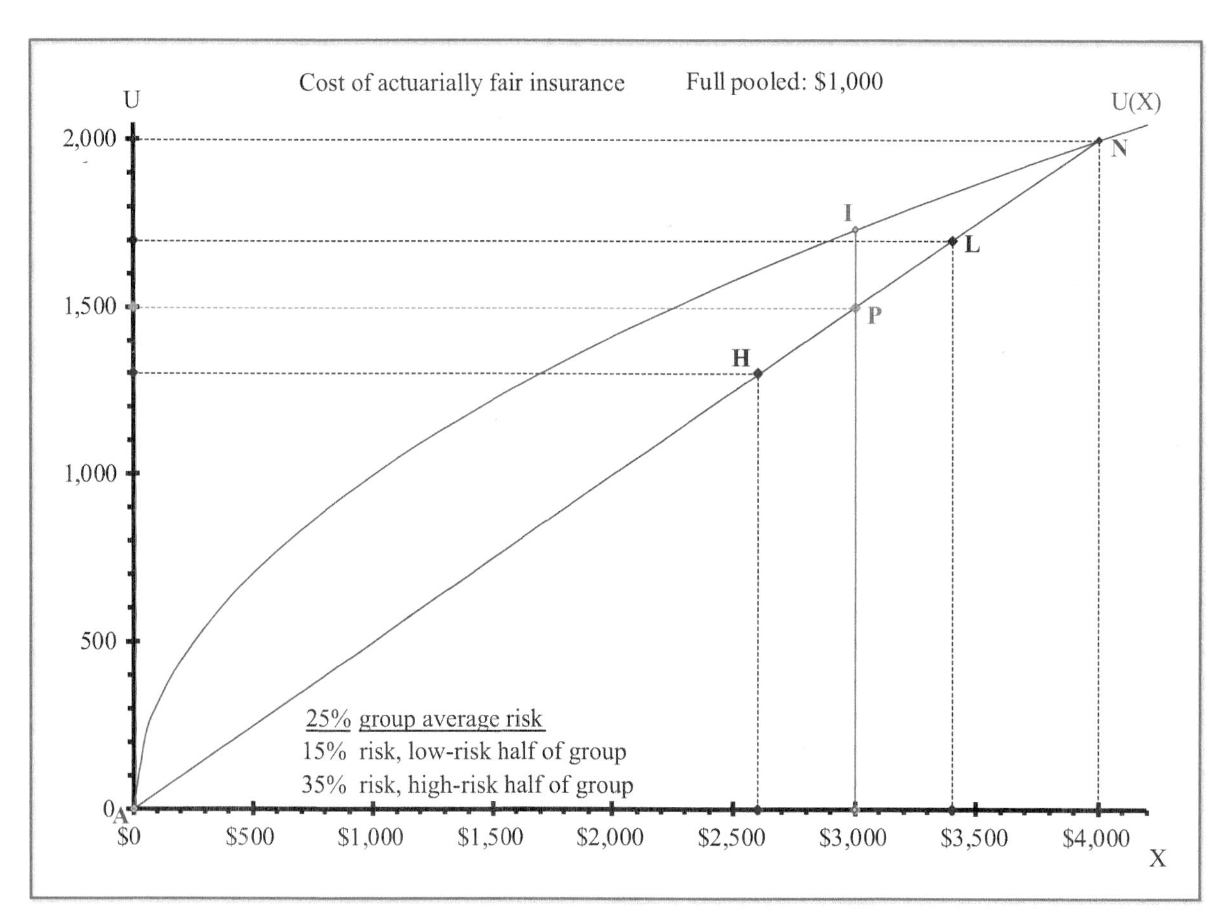

FIGURE 21.1 An Insurance Market without the Adverse Selection Problem

To focus on screening, we assume that the insurance offered is actuarially fair. Given these assumptions, full-coverage insurance will cost $1,000. This insurance provides the individual with $3,000, regardless of whether the individual gets in an accident. (The reason is straightforward: If there is no accident, the individual pays $1,000 for the insurance but has a used car worth $4,000; if there is an accident, the individual pays $1,000 for the insurance and has a totaled car worth $0 but also has a check from the insurance company for the amount lost—$4,000.) There is *no* risk with full-coverage insurance, so the utility achieved by purchasing this actuarially fair insurance, based on Equation 21.5, is:

$$U(\text{full-coverage insurance}) = 2{,}000 \cdot (3{,}000/4{,}000)^{0.5} = 1{,}000 \cdot 3^{0.5} = 1{,}732. \qquad \textbf{(21.7)}$$

This is depicted as point **I** = ($3,000, 1,732) in Figure 21.1. Notice that **I** is on the U(X) curve, meaning that there is no risk involved in this outcome.

21.5A The Geometry of Adverse Selection

We can introduce the possibility of adverse selection into the analysis by assuming that some drivers are better than average, and some are worse than average. Specifically, assume that we have equal numbers of less-risky and more-risky individuals who have been offered this insurance. Given equal numbers of low-risk and high-risk individuals, the average risk is simply the average of the two risk levels.[7] Suppose that low-risk individuals have a 15% probability of totaling the car and that high-risk individuals have a 35% probability of totaling the car. Low-risk individuals are at **L**, and high-risk individuals are at **H** in Figure 21.1. The expected utility level for each type is lower than that achieved by purchasing insurance, so both low-risk and high-risk drivers purchase full-coverage insurance. This is called a *pooled equilibrium* because both risk classes act the same way in this instance. Unfortunately, this need not be the case.

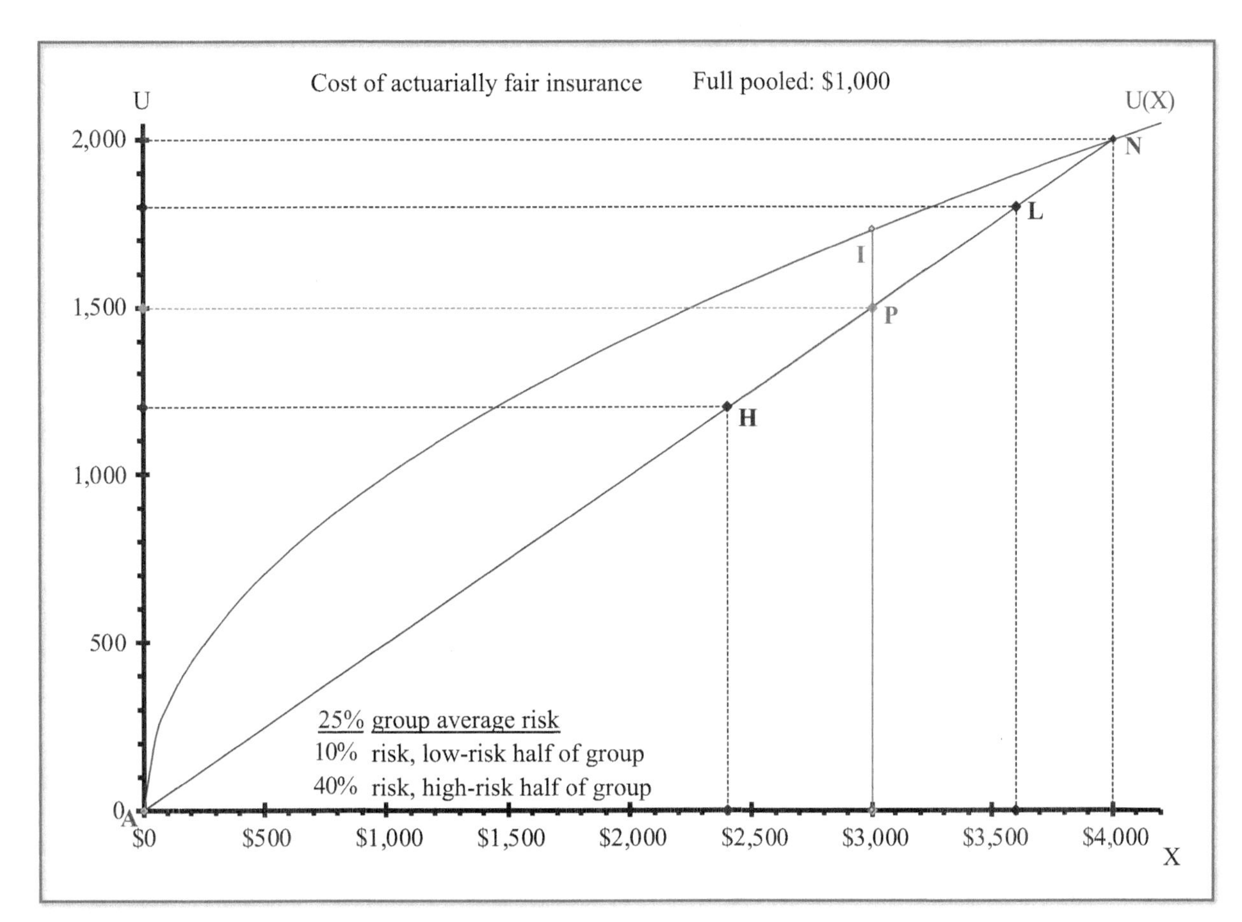

FIGURE 21.2 An Insurance Market with the Adverse Selection Problem

If the difference between high-risk and low-risk individuals who are grouped together and are offered insurance is large enough, the low-risk individuals will choose to avoid purchasing insurance. Figure 21.2 shows that, given the previous assumptions, if we increase the difference from 15%/35% to 10%/40%, we can no longer sustain a pooled equilibrium full-coverage insurance policy. The reason is straightforward: In this instance, the low-risk individual is better off by not purchasing insurance. Consider the expected income and expected utility achieved if low-risk individuals do not purchase insurance. This is described geometrically by point **L**:

$$\mathbf{L} = 0.1 \cdot \mathbf{A} + 0.9 \cdot \mathbf{N} = 0.1 \cdot (\$0, 0) + 0.9 \cdot (\$4{,}000, 2{,}000) = (\$3{,}600, 1{,}800). \quad \textbf{(21.8a)}$$

Low-risk individuals choose to not purchase insurance for $1,000, since the expected utility from facing the lottery, E(U(**L**)), exceeds the certain utility achieved by purchasing full-coverage insurance, U(**I**) ($E(U(\mathbf{L})) = 1{,}800 > 1{,}732 = U(\mathbf{I})$). *This is the essence of the adverse selection problem.*

If insurance companies offer a full-coverage policy with a premium of $1,000, only the high-risk individuals will purchase the insurance, due to the adverse selection problem. Actuarially fair insurance in this instance is $1,600, rather than $1,000, because the insurance company must only consider the riskiness of those who purchase insurance ($1,600 = 0.4 · $4,000). If the insurance company only offers a full-coverage policy, given the dispersion in risk between risk classes shown in Figure 21.2, the policy will look like that depicted in Figure 21.3, rather than Figure 21.2. The result is that high-risk individuals purchase insurance and achieve a utility level of U($2,400) = 1,549 with certainty:

$$U(\$2{,}400) = 2{,}000 \cdot (2{,}400/4{,}000)^{0.5} = 1{,}000 \cdot (2.4)^{0.5} = 1{,}549. \quad \textbf{(21.8b)}$$

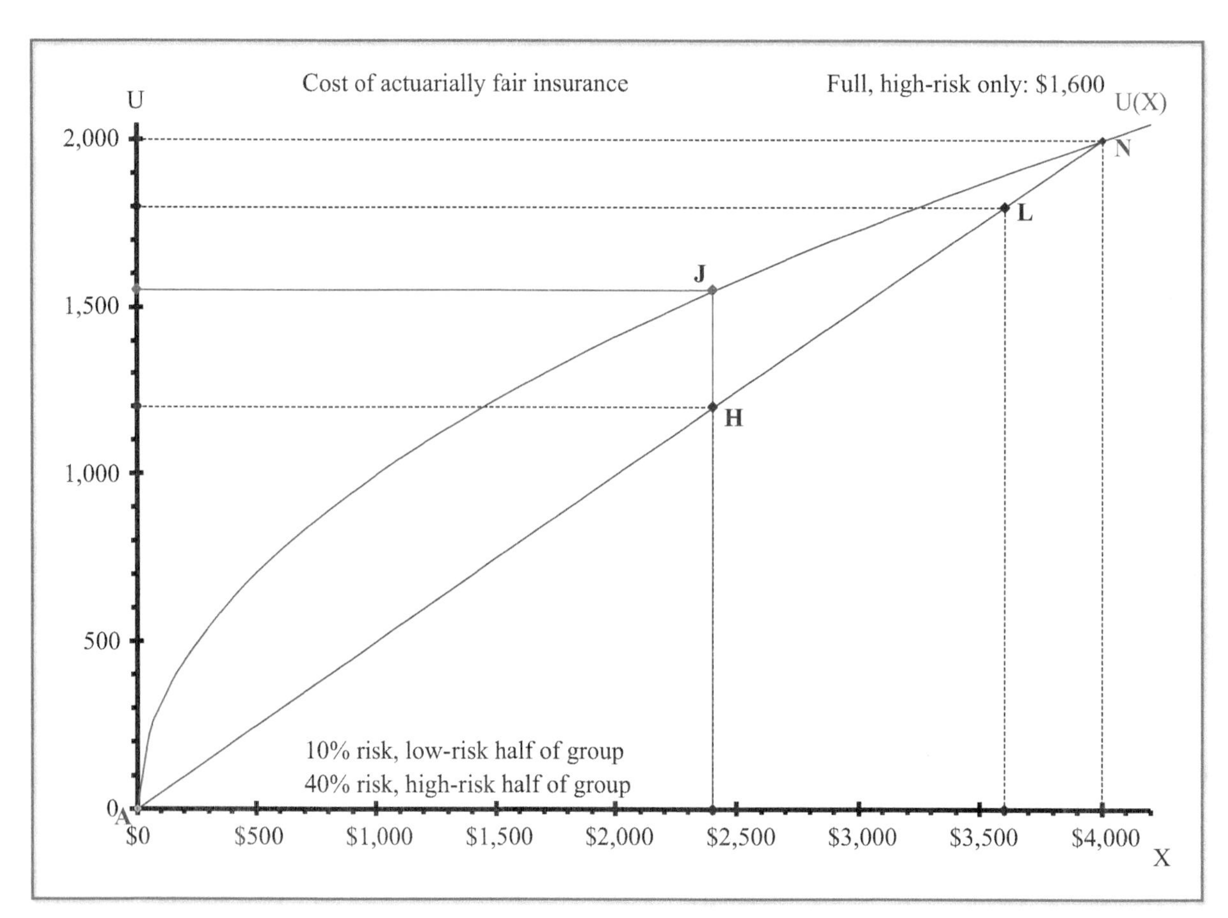

FIGURE 21.3 The Result of Adverse Selection if Only Full Coverage Is Available in an Insurance Market with the Adverse Selection Problem

This is point **J** = ($2400, 1549) in Figure 21.3. As argued earlier, low-risk individuals would not purchase full-coverage insurance for $1,000; therefore, they certainly would not purchase full-coverage insurance for $1,600 (E(U(**L**)) = 1,800 > 1,549 = U(**J**)).

21.5B The Geometry of Coinsurance

Full-coverage insurance effectively captures the high-risk subset, but the low-risk subset of the market remains uninsured. Coinsurance can help the low-risk segment of the market achieve a higher expected utility level by reducing the risk that segment faces, while at the same time not appealing to the high-risk segment of the market. To see this, first consider what coinsurance does.

Suppose that the insurance company offers 20% coinsurance that sells for $80. (Ignore for a moment why we chose 20% or $80 and focus instead on what this insurance offers.) For a price of $80, the insured individual receives 20% of the loss in the event that the accident occurs. Given the numbers in this example, the insurance payout for an accident is $800 = 0.2 · $4,000. This leads to two possible outcomes:

	Accident	**No Accident**
Net income, X	$720 = $800 – $80	$3,920 = $4,000 – $80
Utility level, U	U($720) = 849	U($3,920) = 1,980
(X, U) bundle	**A′**	**N′**

With no insurance coverage, the lottery is seen as the line segment **AN** in Figure 21.4. With 20% coinsurance, the lottery is seen as the line segment **A′N′**. Individuals with

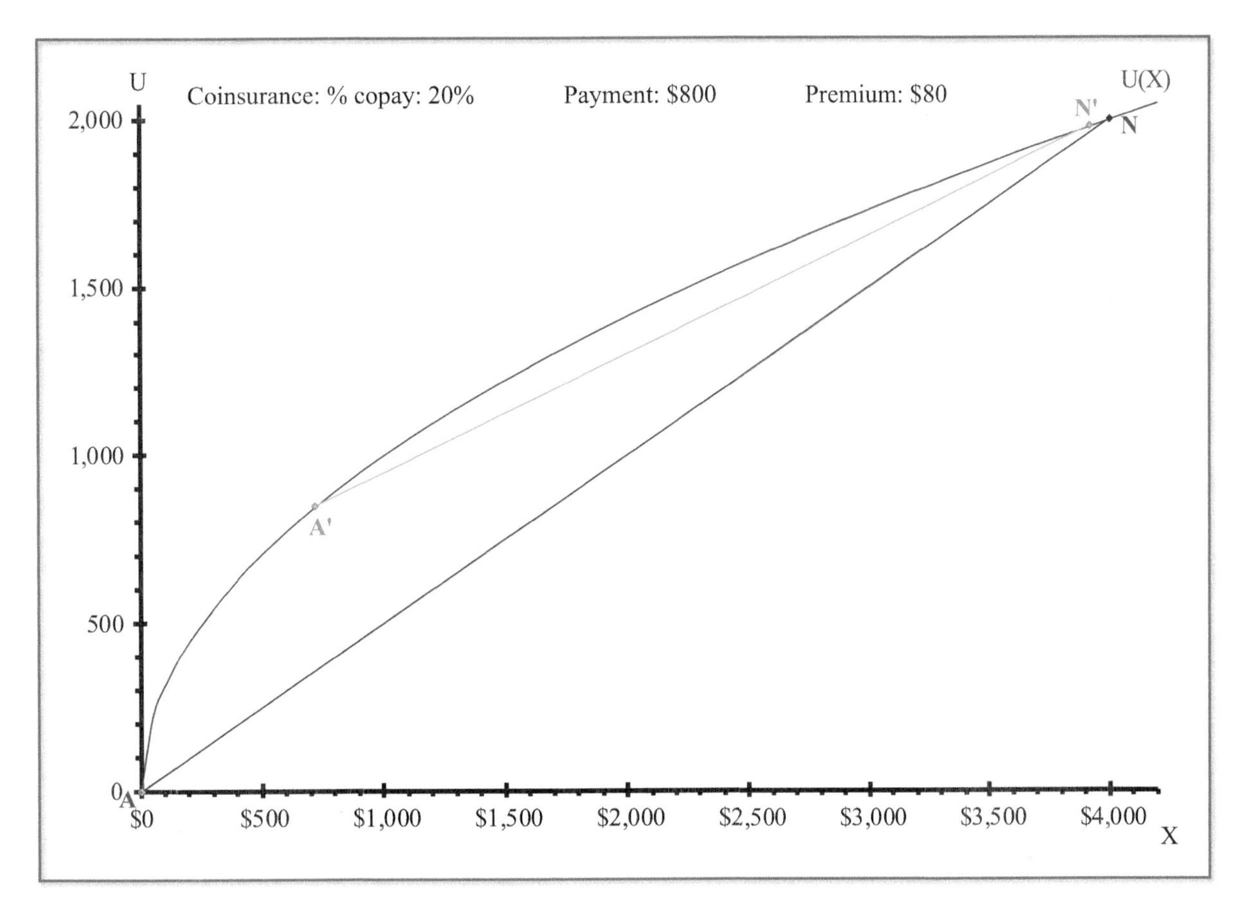

FIGURE 21.4 A Market in Which Coinsurance Is Offered

different risk are represented as different percentages from the "no accident" end of each lottery line segment, **N′**, to the "accident" end, **A′**. Coinsurance has reduced the riskiness of the lottery by making **A′N′** closer to U(X) than **AN**.

21.5C Using Multiple Policies to Screen Individuals into Risk Classes

The remaining issue is how the premium was chosen for this insurance policy. *This price was chosen because it is actuarially fair, given an assumption that only low-risk individuals purchase the coinsurance policy.* The actuarially fair price for this policy for a low-risk individual is $80 = 0.1 · $800 because low-risk individuals have an accident 10% of the time. The low-risk individual will always purchase actuarially fair coinsurance because it allows the low-risk individual to increase expected utility from **L** to **C** in Figure 21.5.[8]

The pair of insurance policies—full coverage for a premium of $1,600 at **J** and 20% coinsurance for a premium of $80 at **A′N′**—screens high- and low-risk individuals. These policies create an incentive structure in which different risk classes of individuals reveal their risk class via their insurance choice. Each individual faces three choices: no insurance, full coverage, or partial coverage. We know from the discussion of Figure 21.3 that the low-risk individual will prefer no coverage at **L** to full coverage at a premium of $1,600 at **J** (E(U(**L**)) = 1,800 > 1,549 = U(**J**)). The low-risk individual will face an expected outcome with coinsurance of **C**, 10% of the way to **A′** from **N′**:

$$\begin{aligned}\mathbf{C} &= 0.1 \cdot \mathbf{A'} + 0.9 \cdot \mathbf{N'} = 0.1 \cdot (\$720,\ 849) + 0.9 \cdot (\$3{,}920,\ 1{,}980) \\ &= (\$3{,}600,\ 1{,}867). \end{aligned} \qquad \textbf{(21.8c)}$$

The expected utility level associated with coinsurance for the low-risk individual exceeds the expected utility level associated with no insurance: E(U(**C**)) = 1,867 > 1,800 = E(U(**L**)), according to Equations 21.8a and 21.8c.

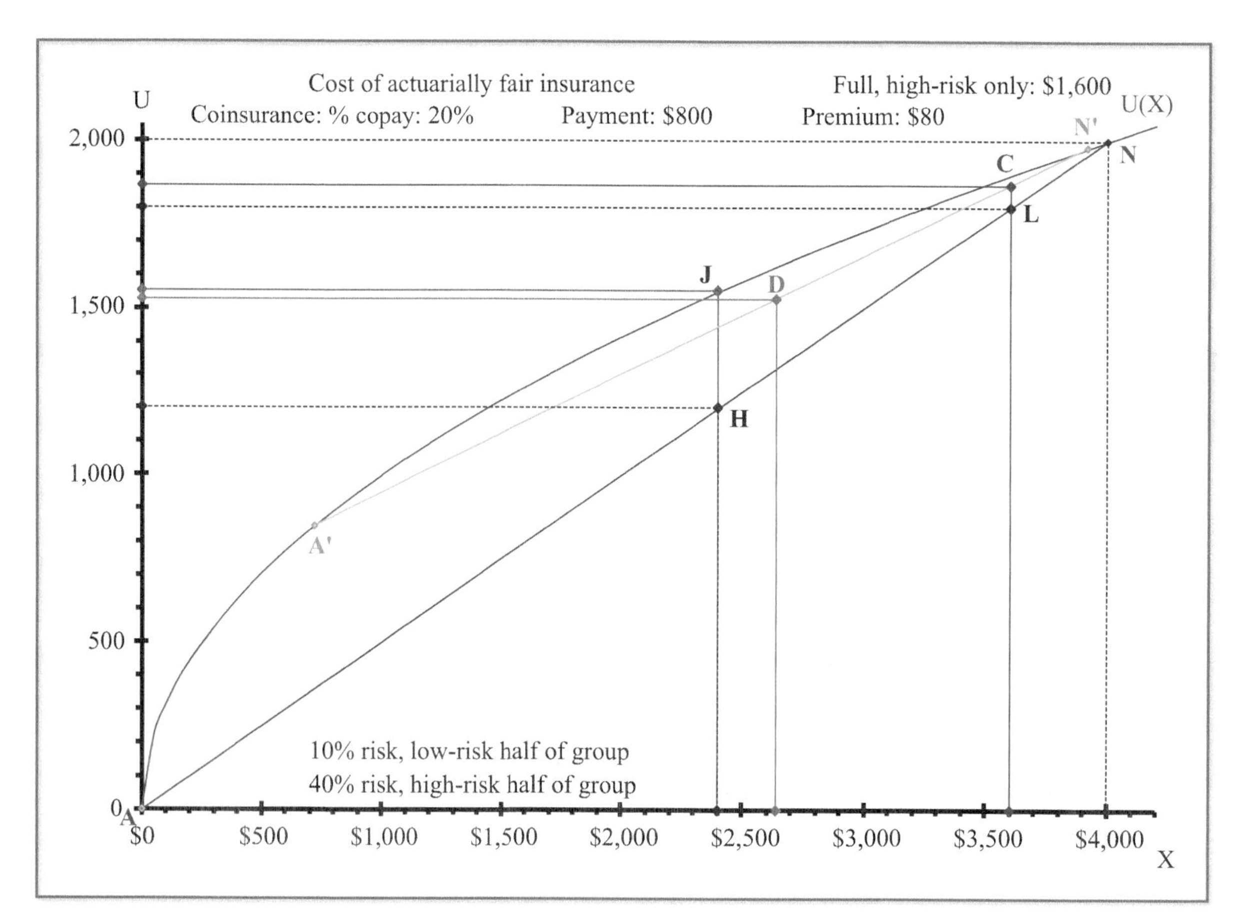

FIGURE 21.5 Offering Coinsurance and Full Coverage Screens Individuals into Risk Classes

Full coverage is at **J**; coinsurance is at **D** for high-risk individuals and at **C** for low-risk individuals. Low-risk consumers choose coinsurance, and high-risk consumers choose full coverage.

By contrast, the high-risk individual achieves an expected outcome of **D**, 40% of the way to **A′** from **N′**, with coinsurance:

$$\mathbf{D} = 0.4 \cdot \mathbf{A'} + 0.6 \cdot \mathbf{N'} = 0.4 \cdot (\$720, 849) + 0.6 \cdot (\$3{,}920, 1{,}980) = (\$2{,}640, 1{,}527). \quad \textbf{(21.8d)}$$

This outcome is dominated by full coverage at **J** because $U(\mathbf{J}) = 1{,}549 > 1{,}527 = E(U(\mathbf{D}))$, according to Equations 21.8b and 21.8d. Finally, both types of insurance dominate no insurance for high-risk individuals (since $E(U(\mathbf{H})) = 1{,}200$).

Offering a choice of policies does not always effectively screen individuals into risk classes. Suppose that 40% (rather than 20%) coinsurance based on low-risk individuals is offered, together with full coverage for high-risk individuals. The choice is shown in Figure 21.6; once again, full-coverage insurance is at **J**, and coinsurance is at **A′N′**. (Due to the higher coinsurance rate in this instance, **A′N′** is smaller in Figure 21.6 than in Figure 21.5.) Suppose that the insurance company provided these choices with the goal of allowing the insured individuals to screen themselves via their insurance choice.

Claim: *This choice of policies no longer screens individuals into risk classes, given the same assumptions about risk of loss (i.e., an equal number of individuals at 10% and 40% risk) and degree of risk aversion.*

Coinsurance now dominates full coverage for the high-risk individual as well as the low-risk individual (since **D** is above **J** in Figure 21.6), *but this choice is unsustainable for the insurance company.* The insurance company charges a premium for the coinsurance of $160, predicated on a payment of $1,600 = 0.4 · $4,000 and an average loss rate of 10% for those choosing coinsurance. If both high- and low-risk individuals choose coinsur-

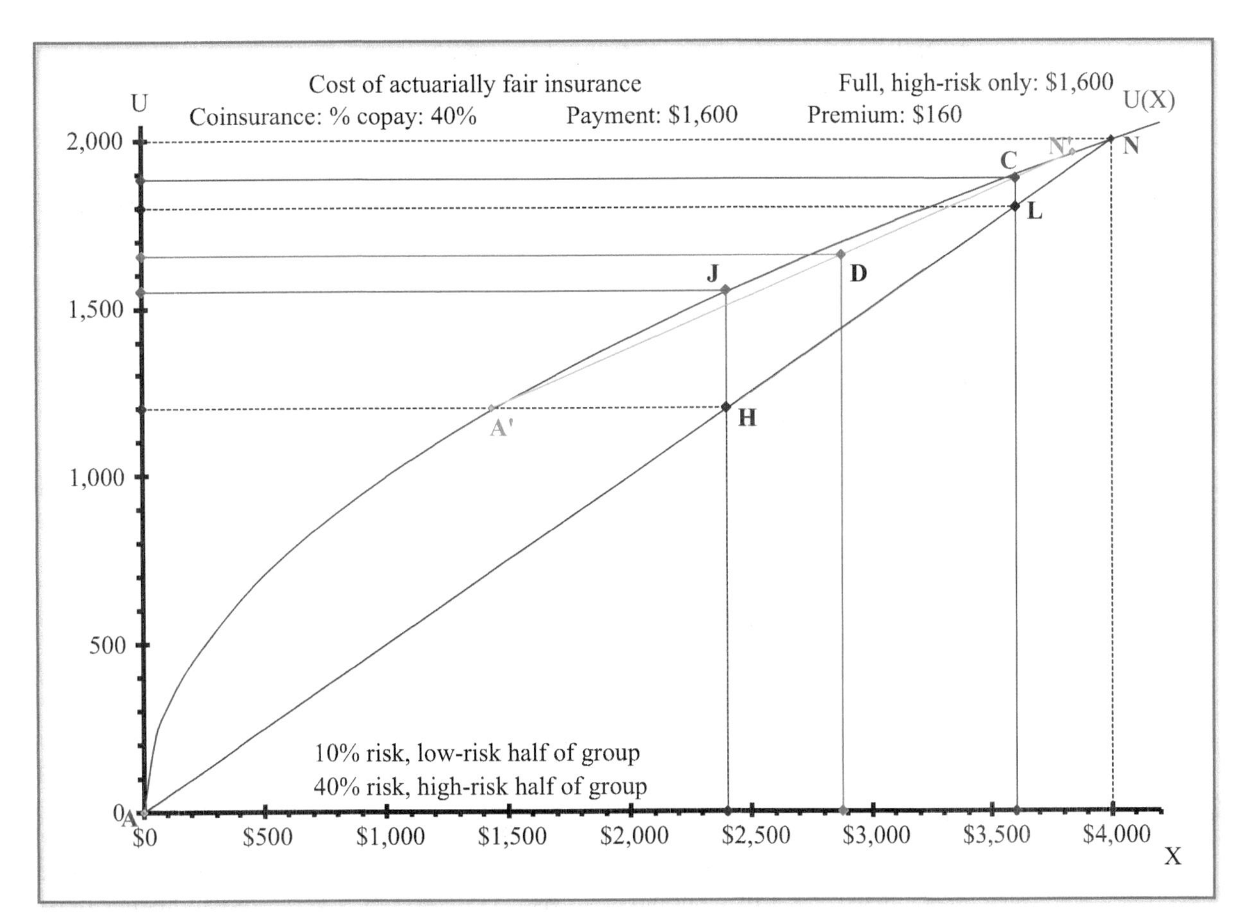

FIGURE 21.6 Insurance Offers That Fail to Screen Customers into Risk Classes

Full coverage is at **J**; coinsurance is at **D** for high-risk individuals and at **C** for low-risk individuals. Both low-risk and high-risk consumers choose coinsurance.

ance, the actuarially fair coinsurance premium is $400 (the fair premium is the expected payout: $\$400 = 0.4 \cdot 0.5 \cdot \$1{,}600 + 0.1 \cdot 0.5 \cdot \$1{,}600 = 0.25 \cdot \$1{,}600$). Offering a variety of policies with different levels of risk bearing can act as a screening device, but it need not do so.

21.6 Advertising

Prerequisite: Chapter 15

Section 21.6 Outline

Advertising is ubiquitous. We are constantly bombarded by television, radio, newspaper, magazine, Internet, and billboard advertising demanding our attention. Madison Avenue has developed creative ways to advertise. Did you ever notice how many times a bottle of Sterling Vineyards wine is shown in the movie *The American President*? How important was the candy Reese's Pieces to the movie *ET*? These product placements did not happen by accident.

Firms advertise to increase demand for their product. This much is clear. How this occurs is much more heavily debated within the economics community. Does advertising increase demand by changing tastes or by informing customers of the product's existence and attributes? Put another way, does advertising simply inform, or does it persuade? Can advertising increase desires for a good, or can it only awaken latent desires by focusing on product attributes that the consumer already finds desirable? These topics are beyond the scope of what we can deal with here, but they provide an indication of some of the debates economists engage in with regard to advertising. We can only brush the surface of this topic area.

Some economists argue that *all* advertising is informative in nature. Nelson (1974) attempts to fit persuasive advertising into the informative advertising mold. According to Nelson, even advertisements that have no obvious informative role may be considered indirectly informative:

> . . . the miniscule amount of direct information from advertising for experience qualities gives the consumer an incentive to extract any conceivable indirect information that would help. Such indirect information is available from advertising. The consumer can learn that the brand advertises. . . . The consumer believes that the more the brand advertises, the more likely it is to be a better buy.[9]

Essentially, Nelson argues that advertising acts as a meter of product quality. Others, including Schmalensee (1978), dispute this view. Their argument is based, in large part, on the notion that if low-quality firms believe that consumers view advertising as a meter of product quality, then they will simply advertise more heavily themselves. Low-quality producers can advertise at the same cost as high-quality producers, and even if they do not receive repeat business, they may well find it advantageous to "take the money and run."[10] In this view, advertising does not have signaling value (using Spence's notion of signaling) because it is not differentially costly to produce.

21.6A Optimal Advertising

Advertising can increase demand for a product, regardless of how or why this works. The question naturally arises: How much advertising should the firm undertake if it wishes to maximize profits? In an oligopolistic market setting, the answer depends significantly on how rivals react to your actions. Coke and Pepsi might both benefit from decreasing their advertising, but only if they are certain that their rivals will do the same. This is an example of the prisoners' dilemma discussed in Section 20.5. If the firm does not face the conjectural variations associated with oligopoly, we can derive a simple rule that describes how intensively a firm should advertise. More-complex versions can also be derived that include cross-advertising elasticities, but the present version provides an elegant way to conclude the discussion of optimal behavior by firms if they are able to adjust advertising as well as price in their search for maximum profits.

Consider a firm that wishes to maximize profits by setting the optimal level of advertising. Such a firm would increase advertising up to the point where the marginal revenue produced from an additional dollar spent on advertising equals the marginal cost of an additional dollar spent on advertising. This is just the MR = MC rule examined in Section 12.4, applied to another decision variable. Consider more carefully what is entailed in the marginal revenue of an additional dollar of advertising and the marginal cost of an additional dollar of advertising.

The marginal revenue of an additional dollar of advertising is the incremental revenue generated by extra output sold due to the incremental advertising. Algebraically, we can describe this as:

$$MR_{\text{advertising}} = \Delta TR/\Delta A. \tag{21.9a}$$

The extra revenue generated is due to the increase in demand caused by an increase in advertising, holding all else, including price, constant. We therefore can rewrite ΔTR as $P \cdot \Delta Q$ and the marginal revenue of advertising is:

$$MR_{\text{advertising}} = P \cdot (\Delta Q/\Delta A). \tag{21.9b}$$

The marginal cost of a dollar's worth of advertising is, interestingly, more than a dollar. If an incremental dollar of advertising induces incremental output, then that output must be produced, and the production cost of incremental output is MC per unit of output (where MC is the marginal cost of production examined in Chapter 11). Therefore, the marginal cost of advertising has two components:

$$MC_{\text{advertising}} = 1 + MC \cdot (\Delta Q/\Delta A). \tag{21.10}$$

The first component is the cost of the incremental dollar of advertising, and the second component is the incremental cost of production required because the incremental advertising increases demand by $\Delta Q/\Delta A$.

Setting the marginal revenue of the activity equal to the marginal cost of that activity, we have (from Equations 21.9b and 21.10):

$$P \cdot \Delta Q/\Delta A = 1 + MC \cdot (\Delta Q/\Delta A). \quad \textbf{(21.11a)}$$

Regrouping, we obtain:

$$1 = (P - MC) \cdot (\Delta Q/\Delta A). \quad \textbf{(21.11b)}$$

Multiplying through by $A/S = A/(P \cdot Q)$ and regrouping, we obtain the advertising-to-sales (A/S) ratio for the profit-maximizing firm:

$$A/S = A/(P \cdot Q) = [(P - MC)/P] \cdot [(\Delta Q/\Delta A) \cdot (A/Q)]. \quad \textbf{(21.12a)}$$

The first bracketed term is the price-cost margin, and the second is the advertising elasticity of demand (since it satisfies the general equation for elasticity from Equation 2.1). We can therefore rewrite Equation 21.12a as:

$$A/S = [(P - MC)/P] \cdot \varepsilon_{advertising}. \quad \textbf{(21.12b)}$$

The firm will have a higher A/S ratio if the price-cost margin is higher or if the advertising elasticity of demand is higher. This is an interesting result in its own right, but we can push this result even further by noting that the price-cost margin is inversely related to the price elasticity of demand. This is the pricing rule known as the Lerner Index of monopoly power. The Lerner Index, derived as Equation 15.2c, notes that the price-cost margin is inversely related to the price elasticity of demand for a profit-maximizing firm. This equation is reproduced here as Equation 21.13:

$$-1/\varepsilon_{demand} = 1/|\varepsilon_{demand}| = (P - MC)/P. \quad \textit{Lerner Index} \quad \textbf{(21.13)}$$

The profit-maximizing firm that faces two decision variables (price and advertising) will choose price and advertising levels so that Equations 21.12b and 21.13 hold simultaneously. Substituting Equation 21.13 into Equation 21.12b, we obtain the Dorfman-Steiner rule:[11]

$$A/S = \varepsilon_{advertising}/|\varepsilon_{demand}|. \quad \textit{Dorfman-Steiner rule} \quad \textbf{(21.14)}$$

The *Dorfman-Steiner rule* described in Equation 21.14 applies to monopoly as well as to monopolistic competition. Equations 21.13 and 21.14 jointly describe how a profit-maximizing firm should set price and advertising. The price-cost margin is higher the more inelastic is demand, according to Equation 21.13. The Dorfman-Steiner rule implies that advertising intensity will be greater if advertising is more effective (higher advertising elasticity) *or* if demand is more price inelastic. A higher advertising elasticity means that there is a greater output response due to an increase in advertising. A lower price elasticity of demand means that each unit sold will be more profitable because there is less loss in demand due to a price increase. Both factors produce a market setting in which more advertising is warranted.

A more complex version of the Dorfman-Steiner rule based on oligopolistic rivalry can also be derived, but this derivation is beyond the scope of this text. This version allows an oligopolistic firm to estimate optimal advertising strategy in the face of rivalrous reactions. As noted earlier, the analysis of oligopolistic pricing and advertising can be modeled as a prisoners' dilemma game (see Section 20.5). This more general form shows that the larger the A/S ratio is, the smaller is the expected advertising reaction of rivals and the loss suffered due to rival reaction. The less tight the oligopoly structure is, the smaller the rival reaction is likely to be. The lower the perceived substitutability between rival brands is, the smaller is the loss in sales due to a given rival's reaction.

21.6B Advertising in Practice

The Dorfman-Steiner model of optimal advertising provides a rule of thumb for firms regarding advertising expenditures. Firms should advertise more heavily when they have more market power (as measured by the elasticity of demand) and when advertising is more effective (as measured by the advertising elasticity of demand). Of course, market power tends to be higher when the oligopolistic structure is tighter. Tight oligopolies are the ones most likely to face the prisoners' dilemma, in that there is an incentive for each oligopolistic rival to "cheat" and advertise more heavily than is warranted by the market. Therefore, we expect to see higher advertising in heavily differentiated oligopolistic markets. Whether the product differentiation is due to effective advertising or the product's innate characteristics is less relevant to the discussion than the fact that product differentiation is high.

Advertising Age annually publishes the top 200 national advertisers. The data are provided for the company as a whole, and most of the companies in the top 200 have brands in multiple industrial segments. Pure measures would examine A/S ratios for specific brands. Nonetheless, these impure measures offer interesting, and entirely reasonable, patterns. Sixty percent of the top 200 are publicly traded domestic corporations for which sales data are readily available. These companies have been grouped into categories in Table 21.1, and average A/S ratios for each category are noted beneath category labels. Categories have been organized from lowest to highest average A/S ratio in Table 21.1.

Although individual entries are interesting, the most important point to take away from Table 21.1 is that there is less variation in A/S ratios within a category than across categories. Companies in the logistics, technology, home improvement, automotive, and travel categories tend to have low A/S ratios ($A/S < 2\%$). At the opposite end of the spectrum, companies in the online enterprises, cosmetics, and for-profit education categories tend to have high A/S ratios ($A/S > 10\%$). These results are entirely consistent with our expectations derived earlier. Companies tend to advertise more heavily when the product is more differentiable or when the product market is more inelastic.

The highest A/S of the top advertisers is IAC, an online enterprise whose brands include chemistry.com, delightful.com, match.com, and tinder.com, with $A/S = 21.6\%$. This implies that \$1 out of every \$4.64 received is being devoted to advertising ($4.64 = 1/0.216$). The second-highest A/S is the cosmetics firm Elizabeth Arden with $A/S = 18.0\%$. This implies that \$1 out of every \$5.56 received is being devoted to advertising ($5.56 = 1/0.18$). These outliers are certainly in highly differentiated product markets in which at least part of the differentiatedness is due to advertising.

At the opposite end of the spectrum are several low A/S outliers of note. Amazon and Walmart both have an A/S ratio that is one-seventh the size of the average A/S within their category. These behemoths dwarf their rivals in sales and are able to remain profitable in their segment with a much smaller advertising budget (relative to sales) than their smaller rivals. Ebay is perhaps the closest product market rival to Amazon among online enterprises, and its A/S ratio is more than twice the size of Amazon's ($2.5 = 0.034/0.014$). Walmart, the largest retailer in the United States, spends comparatively little on advertising. Walmart's A/S of 0.4% is among the lowest of all companies in the sample. Discount retailers work on smaller margins, and we would expect to see relatively low A/S ratios as a result. Target, another discount retailer, has an A/S ratio that is more than five times that of Walmart's ($5.7 = 0.023/0.004$). And Sears Holding Corporation, whose holdings include Sears and Kmart, has an A/S ratio that is more than seven times that of Walmart's ($7.8 = 0.031/0.004$). Both Amazon and Walmart are able to achieve success without advertising heavily, at least by the standards of their rivals.

TABLE 21.1 Advertising-to-Sales Ratios for Publicly Traded U.S. Companies, 2014

Category (average A/S)	Company	*Ad Age* Rank	Advertising $millions	Sales $millions	A/S
Logistics (0.5%)	FedEx Corp.	138	$ 293.9	$ 47,453	0.6%
	United Parcel Service, Inc.	187	$ 203.2	$ 58,232	0.3%
Tech (0.8%)	Microsoft Corp.	27	$ 1,407.6	$ 90,207	1.6%
	Google	32	$ 1,280.7	$ 66,001	1.9%
	Apple	55	$ 794.9	$ 182,795	0.4%
	IBM Corp.	89	$ 451.0	$ 92,793	0.5%
	General Electric	102	$ 393.2	$ 148,589	0.3%
	Intel Corp.	105	$ 387.0	$ 55,870	0.7%
	Hewlett-Packard	150	$ 273.0	$ 111,876	0.2%
Home improvement (1.5%)	Lowe's Cos.	54	$ 797.5	$ 56,223	1.4%
	Home Depot	56	$ 793.7	$ 83,176	1.0%
	Sherwin-Williams Co.	162	$ 239.3	$ 11,130	2.2%
Auto (1.9%)	General Motors Co.	3	$ 3,120.0	$ 155,929	2.0%
	Ford Motor Co.	6	$ 2,467.1	$ 144,077	1.7%
Travel (1.9%)	Carnival Corp.	153	$ 267.9	$ 15,884	1.7%
	Caesars Entertainment	164	$ 235.7	$ 8,516	2.8%
	Southwest Airlines Co.	182	$ 207.0	$ 18,605	1.1%
	Hilton Worldwide Holdings	194	$ 188.9	$ 10,502	1.8%
	Royal Caribbean Cruises	198	$ 181.2	$ 8,074	2.2%
Pharmaceutical (2.1%)	Pfizer	17	$ 1,673.2	$ 49,605	3.4%
	Eli Lilly & Co.	57	$ 777.1	$ 19,616	4.0%
	Merck & Co.	73	$ 604.4	$ 42,237	1.4%
	AbbVie	78	$ 565.5	$ 19,960	2.8%
	Bristol-Myers Squibb Co.	124	$ 356.7	$ 15,879	2.2%
	Gilead Sciences	143	$ 287.0	$ 54,890	0.5%
	Abbott Laboratories	165	$ 234.9	$ 20,247	1.2%
	Amgen	167	$ 231.8	$ 20,063	1.2%
Banks (2.2%)	JP Morgan Chase	14	$ 1,896.5	$ 91,066	2.1%
	Bank of America Corp.	20	$ 1,584.0	$ 95,181	1.7%
	Capital One Financial Corp.	25	$ 1,464.4	$ 23,869	6.1%
	Wells Fargo & Co.	66	$ 635.0	$ 88,372	0.7%
	Citigroup	58	$ 767.3	$ 69,269	1.1%
	US Bancorp	108	$ 382.0	$ 21,392	1.8%
	PNC Financial Services	155	$ 253.0	$ 16,251	1.6%

Continued on next page

TABLE 21.1 Continued

Category (average A/S)	Company	*Ad Age* Rank	Advertising $millions	Sales $millions	A/S
Retailer (2.8%)	Walmart Stores	13	$ 1,940.1	$ 485,651	0.4%
	Target Corp.	18	$ 1,647.0	$ 72,618	2.3%
	Macy's	19	$ 1,602.0	$ 28,105	5.7%
	Kohl's Corp.	34	$ 1,189.0	$ 19,023	6.3%
	Sears Holding Corp.	40	$ 974.4	$ 31,198	3.1%
	J.C. Penney Co.	46	$ 887.0	$ 12,257	7.2%
	Kroger Co.	67	$ 648.0	$ 22,953	2.8%
	Best Buy Co.	69	$ 635.5	$ 40,339	1.6%
	Walgreens Boots Alliance	82	$ 521.0	$ 76,392	0.7%
	L Brands, Inc.	106	$ 384.6	$ 11,454	3.4%
	CVS Health	112	$ 375.9	$ 139,367	0.3%
	Staples	125	$ 353.3	$ 22,492	1.6%
	Office Depot	129	$ 336.9	$ 16,096	2.1%
	TJX Cos.	146	$ 282.2	$ 29,078	1.0%
	Dick's Sporting Group	159	$ 248.7	$ 6,814	3.6%
Communication (2.9%)	AT&T	2	$ 3,272.0	$ 132,447	2.5%
	Verizon Communications	5	$ 2,526.0	$ 127,079	2.0%
	Softbank Corp. (Sprint)	24	$ 1,500.0	$ 34,532	4.3%
	Deutsche Telekom	28	$ 1,400.0	$ 29,564	4.7%
	CenturyLink	177	$ 214.0	$ 18,031	1.2%
Insurance (2.9%)	Allstate Corp.	44	$ 893.4	$ 35,239	2.5%
	Progressive Corp.	68	$ 646.8	$ 19,391	3.3%
Financial services (3.4%)	Berkshire Hathaway	23	$ 1,539.2	$ 194,673	0.8%
	BlackRock, Inc.	168	$ 233.2	$ 10,849	2.1%
	H&R Block	176	$ 219.0	$ 2,986	7.3%
	Realogy Holdings	196	$ 183.5	$ 5,328	3.4%
Food (3.8%)	PepsiCo	35	$ 1,180.3	$ 66,683	1.8%
	General Mills	47	$ 866.4	$ 17,770	4.9%
	The Hershey Co.	60	$ 744.9	$ 7,422	10.0%
	Kellogg Co.	64	$ 666.0	$ 14,580	4.6%
	Coca-Cola Co.	65	$ 663.5	$ 45,998	1.4%
	Dr Pepper Snapple Group	94	$ 414.3	$ 6,121	6.8%
	ConAgra Foods Inc.	103	$ 392.4	$ 15,838	2.5%
	Campbell Soup Co.	132	$ 319.7	$ 8,268	3.9%
	Mondelez International	147	$ 278.4	$ 34,244	0.8%
	Tyson Foods	151	$ 271.9	$ 37,580	0.7%
	The J.M. Smucker Co.	154	$ 257.2	$ 5,693	4.5%

TABLE 21.1 Continued

Category (average A/S)	Company	*Ad Age* Rank	Advertising $millions	Sales $millions	A/S
Clothing (4.5%)	Nike	31	$ 1,307.4	$ 29,200	4.5%
	The Gap Inc.	84	$ 492.7	$ 16,435	3.0%
	VF Corp.	98	$ 401.5	$ 12,282	3.3%
	Under Armor	142	$ 288.3	$ 3,084	9.3%
	PVH Corp.	184	$ 205.6	$ 8,241	2.5%
Alcohol (5.0%)	Anheuser-Busch InBev	22	$ 1,568.3	$ 47,063	3.3%
	Constellation Brands	119	$ 361.1	$ 5,448	6.6%
Media (5.1%)	Comcast Corp.	4	$ 3,028.0	$ 68,775	4.4%
	Walt Disney Co.	10	$ 2,109.1	$ 48,813	4.3%
	Time Warner	16	$ 1,696.6	$ 27,359	6.2%
	21st Century Fox	21	$ 1,583.5	$ 31,867	5.0%
	Viacom	59	$ 758.7	$ 13,783	5.5%
	Time Warner Cable	62	$ 684.0	$ 22,812	3.0%
	Dish Network Corp.	77	$ 566.7	$ 14,643	3.9%
	Netflix	96	$ 406.4	$ 5,505	7.4%
	CBS Corp.	123	$ 356.8	$ 13,806	2.6%
	Lions Gate Entertainment	145	$ 285.4	$ 2,515	11.3%
	Activision Blizzard	163	$ 237.6	$ 4,408	5.4%
	Liberty Media Corp.	173	$ 226.0	$ 4,450	5.1%
	News Corp.	197	$ 182.1	$ 8,574	2.1%
Credit cards (5.4%)	American Express Co.	7	$ 2,364.3	$ 35,999	6.6%
	Discover Financial Services	61	$ 735.0	$ 9,611	7.6%
	Visa	87	$ 485.1	$ 12,702	3.8%
	MasterCard Inc.	131	$ 336.2	$ 9,473	3.5%
Personal care (5.5%)	Proctor & Gamble Co.	1	$ 4,607.0	$ 83,026	5.5%
	Johnson & Johnson	12	$ 1,967.8	$ 74,331	2.6%
	The Clorox Co.	88	$ 469.0	$ 5,591	8.4%
	Colgate-Palmolive Co.	95	$ 411.4	$ 17,277	2.4%
	Church & Dwight	100	$ 396.6	$ 3,298	12.0%
	Kimberly-Clark Corp.	115	$ 365.5	$ 19,724	1.9%
Toys (5.8%)	Mattel	93	$ 415.1	$ 6,024	6.9%
	Hasbro Inc.	190	$ 198.7	$ 4,277	4.6%
Brokerage (6.1%)	TD Ameritrade Holdings	157	$ 250.0	$ 3,098	8.1%
	Charles Schwab Corp.	161	$ 245.0	$ 6,058	4.0%

Continued on next page

TABLE 21.1 Continued

Category (average A/S)	Company	*Ad Age* Rank	Advertising $millions	Sales $millions	A/S
Online enterprises (9.8%*)	Amazon*	33	$ 1,231.7	$ 88,988	1.4%
	Expedia	48	$ 845.7	$ 5,763	14.7%
	IAC (online dating)	63	$ 670.7	$ 3,110	21.6%
	Ebay	70	$ 616.9	$ 17,902	3.4%
	The Priceline Group	130	$ 336.3	$ 8,442	4.0%
	Liberty TripAdvisor Hold.	200	$ 180.0	$ 1,329	13.5%
Cosmetics (11.1%)	Estée Lauder	41	$ 954.6	$ 10,968	8.7%
	Coty	133	$ 314.7	$ 4,552	6.9%
	Revlon, Inc.	178	$ 210.8	$ 1,941	10.9%
	Elizabeth Arden, Inc.	180	$ 209.3	$ 1,164	18.0%
For-profit education (11.6%)	Apollo Education Group	101	$ 394.4	$ 3,024	13.0%
	DeVry Education Group	191	$ 196.3	$ 1,923	10.2%
Miscellaneous	UnitedHealth Group	139	$ 293.7	$ 130,474	0.2%
	Tempur Sealy International	181	$ 209.1	$ 2,990	7.0%

*Average A/S for **Online enterprises** category is 11.4% without Amazon.

Source: Advertising Age, July 15, 2015, for advertising ranking and dollar advertising among top 200 advertisers. Sales data pulled from Yahoo Finance.

Summary

Information is often taken for granted in most classic economics models, even though it is actually costly to obtain and process. Although this chapter touches briefly on imperfect information in general, as well as on advertising, the central focus is on what happens when there is an informational asymmetry between buyers and sellers in a market.

Economists often assume that information is widely available to both buyers and sellers; yet, this is generally not the case. Information is usually costly to obtain. This results in individuals having different bundles of information. When the market's reaction to these information imperfections is explicitly examined, many concepts that are touchstones of economics suddenly fall into question.

Three economists jointly shared the Nobel Prize for their work in asymmetric information. At its core, asymmetric information exists when one side knows more than the other during a transaction. Sellers may have more information than buyers, or buyers may have more information than sellers.

The first situation, in which sellers have more information than buyers, is modeled by George Akerlof in the "lemons" model. Akerlof's model examines the market for used cars, some of which are high quality, or "cherries," while others are low quality, or "lemons." With perfect information, lemons would sell for a lower price than cherries. Asymmetric information exists since buyers do not know if a specific car is a lemon or cherry prior to buying it, but the seller knows if the car is a lemon or a cherry. As a result, a single price clears the market. More lemons and fewer cherries are sold than would be the case if buyers had the same information as sellers. Adverse selection results. Another implication is that demand for used cars may bend backward as price declines, since lower prices are associated with lower quality; purchasing a used car at a low price increases the likelihood of purchasing a lemon.

Akerlof argues that sellers can take measures to prove to buyers that their cars are not lemons. A used-car company can, for example, provide a warranty for some, but not all, of the cars on its lot. Such a tactic is a signal because it provides buyers with the assurance that the dealership stands behind this car. Put another way, the dealership has signaled that the specific car is of high-enough quality that the dealership is willing to stand behind it.

Michael Spence takes signaling in a different direction by applying it to job markets. He argues that firms have no way of distinguishing high-productivity workers from low-productivity workers prior to hiring them. This results in loss of productivity for the firm and loss in pay for the high-productivity workers. It is in high-productivity workers' self-interest to signal to firms that they are high-productivity workers or to separate themselves from workers of lower productivity. Spence argues that a separating device—in this case, educational attainment—is a way to do this. Education is differentially costly for high-productivity workers to obtain, relative to low-productivity workers. Therefore, high-productivity workers are more likely to put off working to achieve some level of education, while low-productivity workers are more likely to enter the workforce as soon as possible. Firms offer a palette of job possibilities, some which require a certain level of education but offer higher pay, and others that pay less but do not require extended education. This allows high- and low-productivity workers to self-select into the jobs that are suited for their level of productivity.

The reverse asymmetry occurs when buyers have more information than sellers. Joseph Stiglitz analyzes this situation, using the insurance industry. Insurance companies do not know if individuals are high risk or low risk, prior to buying insurance. Stiglitz argues that, to compensate for this, insurance companies offer multiple insurance policies. These policies allow high- and low-risk individuals to screen themselves into the different risk categories. Low-risk individuals choose policies that are less expensive and that may involve aspects such as a copay. High-risk individuals are likely to choose the more expensive options that offer more inclusive or full coverage. The difficulty is that offering multiple policies does not guarantee that individuals are screened into risk classes via these choices.

Another issue in insurance markets is the moral hazard problem, which occurs when individuals alter behavior as a result of purchasing insurance. For example, they may begin to engage in more risky activities because they know that their insurance will cover their expenses. This increases the risk of claims to the insurance company and is due to the altered behavior created by becoming insured.

This moral hazard problem is an example of a broader category of problems called the principal-agent problem. When principals (e.g., a board of directors) cannot monitor the actions of agents (e.g., a management team) who are charged with making decisions on behalf of the principals, a principal-agent problem may occur. The agents may put their interests or objectives before those of the principals. The most common example of this problem is a firm that is owned by one individual but managed by another who pursues personal objectives over those of the owner. There is not total freedom in this instance, however; if managers deviate too far from owners' goals, they risk termination from the position. To solve this problem, owners may use managerial compensation packages, such as profit-sharing and stock-option plans, that ensure that managers share owners' interests

The final topic discussed in this chapter is advertising. Advertising can be informative, but it can also be persuasive. However it works, advertising acts to increase demand for the advertised good. The amount that firms advertise depends on how effective the advertising is and how important it is to increase demand. Advertising can simply be thought of as another decision variable available to the firm. In this view, the optimal amount of advertising is that amount where the marginal revenue from a bit more advertising equals the marginal cost of a bit more advertising. This leads to the Dorfman-Steiner rule: The profit-maximizing firm will choose an advertising-to-sales ratio that is proportional to the advertising elasticity of demand and inversely proportional to the price elasticity of demand, $A/S = \varepsilon_A/|\varepsilon_D|$. A firm embedded in an oligopolistic market, especially if that market is differentiated, may well advertise past the optimal level, due to the prisoners' dilemma.

Review Questions

Define the following terms:

imperfect information	brand name	moral hazard problem
asymmetric information	separating equilibrium	incentive compatibility
"lemons" model	adverse selection problem	pooled equilibrium
signals	screening	Dorfman-Steiner rule
warranty	coinsurance	
guarantee	principal-agent problem	

Provide short answers to the following:

Sections 21.1–21.5

a. Do new-car sellers know more about the quality of a specific new car than new-car buyers?
b. What information asymmetry is the key to the lemons model?
c. Why might a car with very few miles on it sell at a substantial discount, relative to a new car?
d. True or false and explain: The portion of bad used cars (lemons) that are sold is likely to be higher than the portion of lemons on the road.

e. Why could demand be upward sloping in the used-car market?
f. If demand is upward sloping, then which effect dominates—the price effect or the quality effect of a price change?
g. When is a signal effective?
h. Does obtaining an education increase the productivity of the job seeker in Spence's model?
i. How can education separate productive job seekers from nonproductive ones?
j. Does the job seeker or the potential employer have more information in Spence's model?
k. Are warranties and guarantees signals?
l. Does the insurance buyer or insurance seller typically have better information?
m. How is the menu of insurance choices available to a buyer of insurance similar to the menu of wage choices available to individuals considering employment by a company?
n. Is a full-coverage insurance policy aimed at low-risk or high-risk individuals?
o. Is the lemons model an example of the adverse selection problem?
p. Is the principal-agent problem an example of the moral hazard problem?

Section 21.6

a. Does advertising have signaling value?
b. If a firm wishes to maximize profits, what advertising-to-sales ratio should the firm pursue?
c. The result described in the previous question is based on what basic result regarding profit maximization from earlier in the text?

Check your answers to the *short-answer* exercises in the Answers Appendix at the end of the book.

Notes

1. George Akerlof, "The Market for 'Lemons': Quality Uncertainty and the Market Mechanism," *Quarterly Journal of Economics* 84 (1970): 353–374.

2. Those who have had multivariate calculus will note that this is the total derivative of demand with respect to price:

$$dDemand/dP = \partial f/\partial P + \partial f/\partial A \cdot dA/dP.$$

3. Michael Spence, "Job Market Signaling," *Quarterly Journal of Economics* 87 (1973): 355–374.

4. Michael Rothschild and Joseph Stiglitz, "Equilibrium in Competitive Insurance Markets: An Essay on the Economics of Imperfect Information," *Quarterly Journal of Economics* 90 (1976): 629–649.

5. Ibid.

6. The figures shown in this section assume that r = 0.5. The Excel file for Figure 21.1 allows you to vary r to model different degrees of risk aversion.

7. Given unequal weights, we would need to calculate a weighted average instead. This would not appreciably change the analysis (although **L** and **H** would no longer be located equal distances from **P** in Figure 21.1).

8. Formally, $\mathbf{C} = r_L \cdot \mathbf{A'} + (1 - r_L) \cdot \mathbf{N'}$, where r_L is the risk of an accident for a low-risk individual (r_L = 10% in Figure 21.5). **L** and **C** have the same expected income levels (because the insurance is actuarially fair), but the coinsurance reduces the risk involved in the lottery. The proof that **L** and **C** have the same expected income level is a workbook exercise.

9. Philip Nelson, "Advertising as Information," *Journal of Political Economy* 82 (1974): 732. Contrast this with Stephen Erfle, "Persuasive Advertising and Consumer Welfare," *Pennsylvania Economic Review* 2 (1992): 14–30.

10. Richard Schmalensee, "A Model of Advertising and Product Quality," *Journal of Political Economy* 86 (1978): 485–503. The number of "infomercials" on cable TV for "miracle" weight-loss products and "no-risk" wealth creation schemes suggests that there are profit opportunities available to firms selling products where the probability of repeat purchases is low.

11. Robert Dorfman and Peter O. Steiner, "Optimal Advertising and Optimal Quality," *American Economic Review* 44 (1954): 826–836.

Externalities and Public Goods

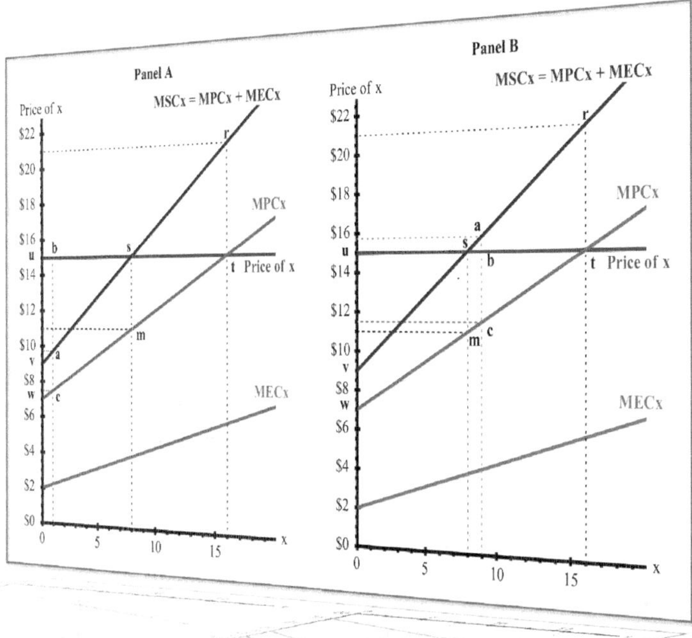

Chapter Outline

22.1 Externalities

22.2 Public Goods

Chapter 16 describes imperfectly competitive markets as one source of market failure. Monopoly power distorts the allocation of resources and thereby reduces social welfare. But monopoly is only one source of market failure. Chapter 21 discusses one nonmonopoly source of market failure—imperfect information. This chapter discusses two more—externalities and public goods.

22.1 Externalities

Prerequisite: Chapter 16

Externalities refer to interactions of actors within the economic system that are not reflected in markets. Externalities are economic effects that are not internalized via the market system. The classic example of an externality is air or water pollution. Smokestack pollution caused by a steel mill damages surrounding neighborhoods. This damage is not incorporated into the cost of steel production; it is *external* to the market system. Section 22.1A examines the nature and scope of externalities, and Section 22.1B examines the market failure that results from externalities. Section 22.1C focuses on public policy responses to externalities. The concept of an externality is intimately related to the notion of property rights. Externalities can be internalized via bargaining under certain conditions. Sections 22.1D and 22.1E examine conditions under which bargaining can lead to Pareto optimal outcomes. Section 22.1F discusses externalities involving common property resources.

Section 22.1 Outline

22.1A The Nature and Scope of Externalities

22.1B Externalities and Economic Efficiency

22.1C Public Policy Responses to Externalities

22.1D Property Rights and the Coase Theorem

22.1E A Graphical Analysis of the Coase Theorem

22.1F Common Property Resources and the Tragedy of the Commons

22.1A The Nature and Scope of Externalities

externality: An externality exists if a consumer or producer does not capture the full benefit or face the full cost of an economic action.

negative externality: A negative externality occurs if an economic actor does not face the full cost of an economic action.

positive externality: A positive externality occurs if an economic actor does not capture the full benefit of an economic action.

Externalities occur when the effect of an action by an economic actor is not fully incorporated into the market system. An **externality** exists if a consumer or producer does not capture the full benefit or face the full cost of an economic action. Quite simply, externalities are external to the system. The classic example of an externality is pollution caused by a production process, but this is only one possibility. Producers need not cause the externality, and the externality need not be negative. A **negative externality** occurs if an economic actor does not face the full cost of an economic action. This is often called an *external diseconomy*. The extra cost induced by the external diseconomy is called an *external cost*. A **positive externality** occurs if an economic actor does not capture the full benefit of an economic action. This is often called an *external economy*. The extra benefit induced by the external economy is called an *external benefit*.

Table 22.1 provides eight examples of externalities based on the consumer/producer dichotomy for positive and negative externalities. These examples do not exhaust the range of possible externalities that may exist within markets, but they do provide an idea of the scope of external effects. The typology provided in the table should not be considered as strict; certainly, water pollution produced by a firm may affect individual consumers, and air pollution produced by a firm may affect other firms. You should try to come up with your own examples of each of the eight types of externalities listed in the table.

The scope of external effect depends on the externality under consideration. A home with lavish landscaping provides an external economy (and a trash-strewn property causes an external diseconomy) to others in the neighborhood. By contrast, an individual who is immunized against a disease creates benefits for society at large because the higher the proportion of the population that is immunized against a disease, the lower is the likelihood that *anyone* will contract the disease (including those who are not immunized). Similarly, society at large benefits from the technological progress brought about by research and development efforts. Certainly, some of the benefits of research and development are internalized via the patent system, but some benefits are not internalized because it is often possible to create a new design that closely imitates the patented product. This same line of reasoning suggests that education has external benefits for society at large. Similarly, air pollution is wide ranging because it affects the environment of anyone who wishes to use the affected air.

TABLE 22.1 Examples of Positive and Negative Externalities

		Party Causing the Externality	
Negative Externalities		***Producer***	***Consumer***
Affected Party	***Producer***	Two firms use a stream, and one firm is upstream from the other.	Automobile emissions harm orange growers along the 405 freeway.
	Consumer	Smokestack pollution harms a nearby town.	A property owner paints his house hot pink.
Positive Externalities		***Producer***	***Consumer***
Affected Party	***Producer***	A beekeeper helps a nearby apple grower.	A beach volleyball tournament increases business for beachfront merchants.
	Consumer	A college provides performances for students that also benefit neighbors in town.	A property owner invests in extensive landscaping.

Network Externalities

Prerequisite: Chapter 7

In Part 2 of the text, we implicitly assumed that an individual consumer's demand for a good does not depend on other consumers' demands for the good. My demand for a hamburger is not affected by your demand for a hamburger. For most goods, this is quite reasonable, but this is not always the case. Sometimes, the value of a good to a consumer is based on how many other consumers own the good. A classic example is the landline telephone. Back in the early 1900s, when landline telephones were first introduced, the telephone was only useful to the owner if the intended recipients of calls also had telephones. Indeed, the value of having a telephone was an increasing function of the number of telephones in use. In this instance, there is a network externality associated with the good. A **network externality** exists if one consumer's demand for a good depends on other individuals' demands for the good. Network externalities can be positive or negative, just like the externalities discussed earlier. The old landline telephone was a good that exhibited a positive network externality. Economists often call this a bandwagon effect. If a consumer's demand for a good increases as more consumers demand the good, then the good has a **bandwagon effect**.

network externality: A network externality exists if one consumer's demand for a good depends on other individuals' demands for the good.

bandwagon effect: If a consumer's demand for a good increases as more consumers demand the good, then the good has a bandwagon effect.

Online gaming access provides a prime example of a good that has a bandwagon effect. The value attached to this service—the height of inverse demand—depends on the number of subscribers. Figure 22.1 shows the bandwagon effect. Suppose that at a price of $15 per month, 20 million subscribers choose to have online gaming services. Suppose also that the price declines to $10 per month. The net effect of this decline in price is composed of two parts—the pure price effect and the bandwagon effect. Suppose that demand would increase by 10 million subscribers, based on the $5 price decline, in the absence of a positive network externality associated with gaming services. This pure price effect is the move from **A** to **B** in Figure 22.1. Given a strong positive external economy to gaming services, the increase in demand may well be more. If the bandwagon effect causes an additional 20 million subscriptions (from **B** to **C**), the net effect of the decline in price is an increase of 30 million customers (from **A** to **C**).

Some goods may be subject to a negative network externality. A given consumer's demand for a good may be inversely related to the number of other individuals who purchase the product. The greater the number of other individuals using the good, the lower is the value of that good to a given individual. Prom dresses are a simple example.[1] Economists describe this as a **snob effect**. Designer watches, works of fine art, and expensive automobiles are other examples of goods that may exhibit a snob effect.

snob effect: If a consumer's demand for a good decreases as more consumers demand the good, then the good has a snob effect.

Consider membership to an exclusive club. At a price of $15,000 per year, 200 memberships are sold. In the absence of a negative network externality, suppose that there would be 500 memberships sold at a price of $10,000 per year. Were this to happen,

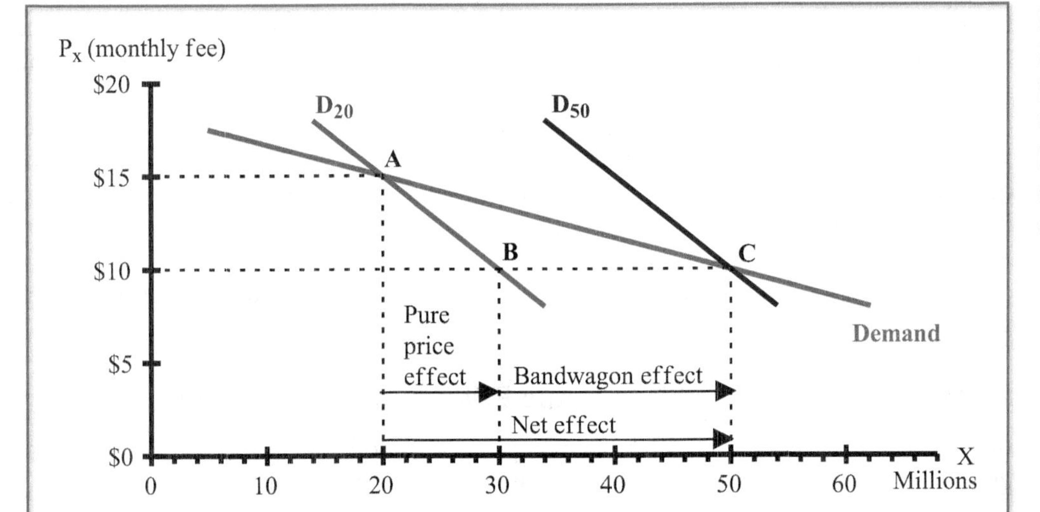

FIGURE 22.1 The Effect of a Decrease in Price of an Online Gaming Service: The Bandwagon Effect (positive network externality)

FIGURE 22.2 The Effect of a Decrease in Price of Club Membership: The Snob Effect (negative network externality)

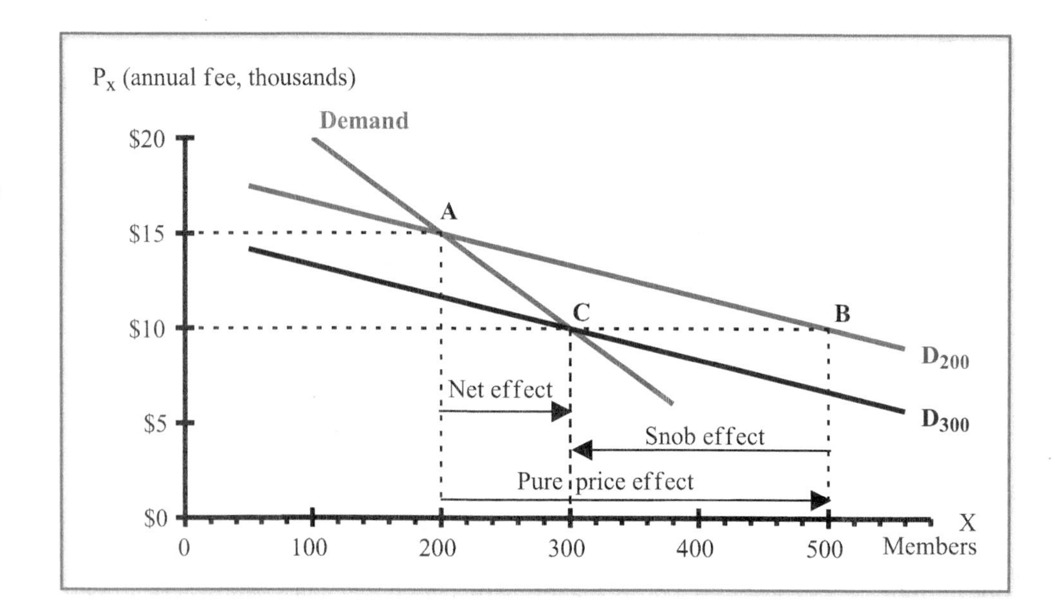

however, the snob appeal of the club would decline. The net effect is an increase of fewer than 300 memberships. This is shown in Figure 22.2. Point **A** depicts demand at a price of $15,000, and **C** denotes demand at a price of $10,000. The net effect of the change in price (from **A** to **C**) is the sum of two effects: The pure price effect is the increase from 200 to 500 members (from **A** to **B**), and the snob effect moves demand back to 300 at this lower price (from **B** to **C**).

Another example of a negative network externality is congestion. Commuters on streets create an external diseconomy for other commuters during peak travel times. Each individual commuter faces only part of the cost of his or her actions; each also creates costs in terms of additional congestion for other commuters.

Many network externalities are associated with physical networks, such as telephones, the Internet, and roadways. But network externalities are also present in less-tangible settings. These are called virtual networks. Take, for example, the positive network externality created by a widely used computer software program such as Microsoft Windows or Microsoft Office. Such programs are more valuable because of their dominance, which creates a situation in which applications are written using this software as a platform. *This textbook is an example: Excel was chosen as the spreadsheet program, rather than a more specialized graphing program, specifically because most computers already have Excel.*

Finally, network externalities can be associated with networks of individuals. Fads are examples of the bandwagon effect; individuals find that they "have to have" a product because others in their circle have it. Consider the phenomena of Beanie Babies and Pokemon cards. Part of the value inherent in these products was certainly due to your friends collecting them, too.

The scope of the network externality depends on the size of the network. Some networks are large, and others are much more local in nature. The Internet and personal computer users provide examples of large networks. The transportation network is quite large, but the appropriate network from the point of view of congestion is local in nature. A commuter in Los Angeles is not interested in congestion in San Francisco, for example. And the network of individuals who matter to a girl ordering a prom dress is other girls going to her prom.

22.1B Externalities and Economic Efficiency *Prerequisite: Chapter 16*

In the absence of market failure, the market price of a good conveys the entire social marginal cost and social marginal benefit of an economic interaction. As shown in Section 16.3, social net benefits are maximized when markets are competitive. This is not true if there are side effects in the production or consumption of the good that are not incorporated in the market exchange. When externalities are present, there are costs and benefits that are not accounted for by the market system. These costs and benefits must be incorporated into the analysis to determine the socially optimal outcome.

Although externalities can occur under a variety of market structures, we focus on the effect of externalities in a market that is otherwise competitive. We also restrict our discussion to linear demand and cost to simplify the analysis as much as possible. (The analysis would not appreciably change if we used nonlinear cost and demand curves.)

Negative Externalities

External diseconomies create costs that are not incorporated into the private market decision. We now must distinguish between the marginal cost perceived by the individual economic agent and the marginal cost perceived by society at large. These marginal costs differ, due to the marginal cost that is external to the market decision. Put another way, the sum of marginal private cost and marginal external cost is marginal social cost:[2]

$$MPC + MEC = MSC. \quad \textbf{(22.1)}$$

The **marginal private cost (MPC)** is the increment in cost imposed on producers who produce one more unit of output. This is the notion of marginal cost examined in Chapter 11. The **marginal external cost (MEC)** is the increment in external cost imposed by producing one more unit of output. The **marginal social cost (MSC)** is the increment in cost imposed by producing one more unit of output. This is the sum of private and external marginal cost.

In Figure 22.3, marginal external cost is upward sloping because marginal external damages increase for many forms of pollution. This means that not only do total (external) damages increase, but these damages increase at an increasing rate. As noted in Equation 22.1, marginal social cost is the sum of private and external marginal cost. For

marginal private cost (MPC): The marginal private cost is the increment in cost imposed on producers who produce one more unit of output. This is the notion of marginal cost examined in Chapter 11.

marginal external cost (MEC): The marginal external cost is the increment in external cost imposed by producing one more unit of output.

marginal social cost (MSC): The marginal social cost is the increment in cost imposed by producing one more unit of output.

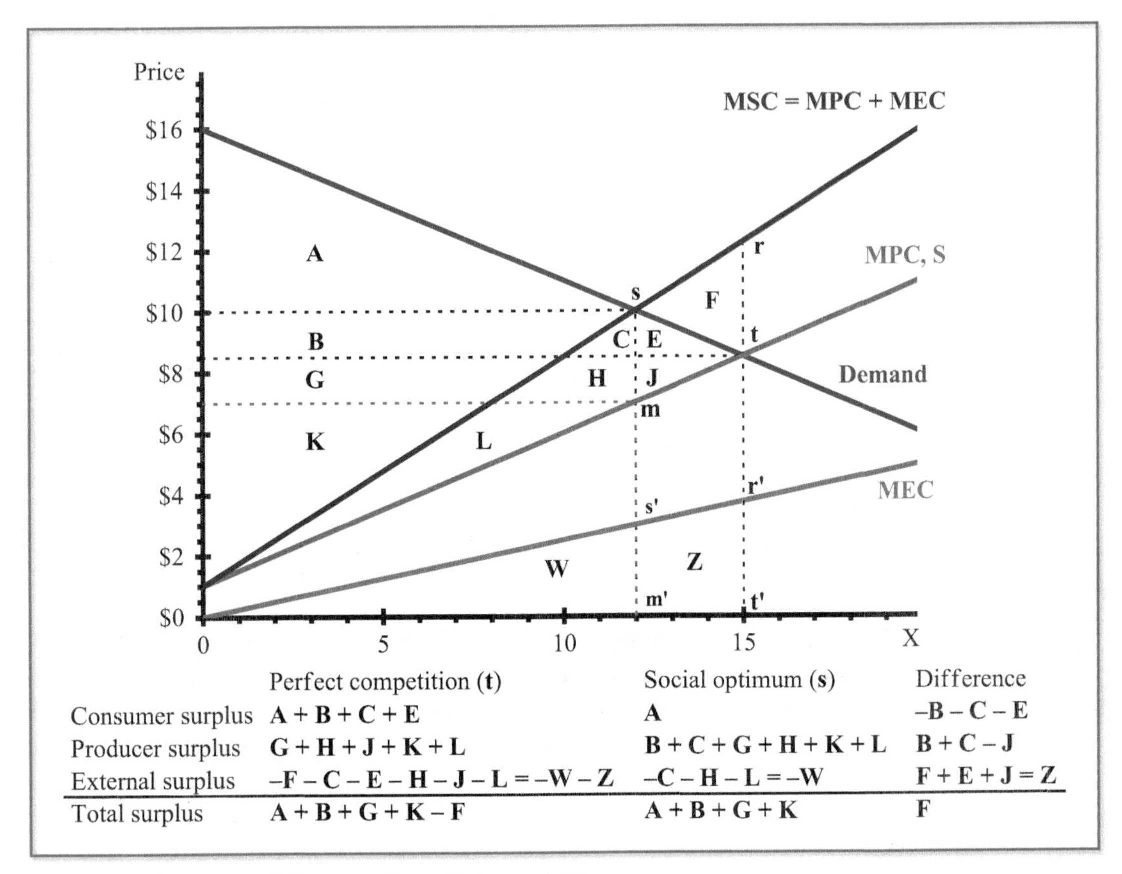

	Perfect competition (t)	Social optimum (s)	Difference
Consumer surplus	A + B + C + E	A	–B – C – E
Producer surplus	G + H + J + K + L	B + C + G + H + K + L	B + C – J
External surplus	–F – C – E – H – J – L = –W – Z	–C – H – L = –W	F + E + J = Z
Total surplus	A + B + G + K – F	A + B + G + K	F

FIGURE 22.3 The Allocative Effects of an External Diseconomy

each output level, MEC must be added to MPC to obtain MSC. Therefore, marginal social cost is the vertical sum of marginal private cost and marginal social cost. By construction, therefore, **sm** = **s′m′**, and **rt** = **r′t′**.

Q3a. What is the MEC at 12 units of output (to the nearest $0.10)?

Q3b. What is the dollar increase in the MEC per unit of output produced (assuming that the MEC is linear)?*

The welfare economics of an external diseconomy are displayed in the table at the bottom of Figure 22.3. Total surplus now includes external surplus, in addition to consumer and producer surplus (and external surplus is negative because this is an external diseconomy). The external cost associated with production must be incorporated into the measure of social net benefit. The area under the marginal external cost curve represents the external cost of producing a given number of units of output. This must be added to the area under the marginal private cost curve to obtain the social cost of producing a given number of units of output. The sum of these costs represents the real resource cost of production. Society is best served if the market produces **s** units of output ($x_s = 12$ in Figure 22.3). Unfortunately, an unfettered competitive market will produce more output, since the externality is not internalized, and the private market will achieve an equilibrium at **t** ($x_t = 15$ in Figure 22.3). The net loss to society, relative to the social optimum, is a deadweight loss due to competition, $DWL_{competition}$, of area **F**. A competitive market will overproduce goods that have negative externalities, *ceteris paribus*.

As noted earlier, many (but not all) forms of pollution have an increasing MEC as a function of output produced. If the marginal external damage caused by increased production is not an increasing function of output produced, the MEC schedule will not increase. If MEC is constant, then marginal social cost is simply a vertical translate of marginal private cost (the shift factor is MEC). If MEC is a declining function of output, then MSC remains above MPC but gets closer as output increases. In any event, the same welfare conclusion holds: Too much production occurs because the marginal external cost is not internalized into the production and consumption decision produced by the competitive market.

We explore the range of policy responses used to internalize externalities in Section 22.1C. The most obvious response is to use a tax, but other strategies can also achieve a socially optimal outcome. Before examining these responses, it is worthwhile to examine external economies.

Positive Externalities

marginal private benefit (MPB): The marginal private benefit is the increment in internal benefit achieved by consuming one more unit of output. This is an alternative name for the inverse market demand curve discussed in Chapter 12.

marginal external benefit (MEB): The marginal external benefit is the increment in external benefit achieved when consumers consume one more unit of output.

External economies create benefits that are not incorporated into the private market decision. When viewed as a function of quantity, the (inverse) demand curve can be conceptualized as a marginal valuation (or benefit) schedule. But inverse demand is only the marginal benefit schedule associated with purchasers of the good. This schedule does not include benefits that accrue to nonpurchasers of the product. We now must distinguish between the marginal benefit perceived by consumers of the product and the marginal benefit perceived by society at large. These differ due to the marginal benefit that is external to the market decision. Put another way, the sum of marginal private benefit and marginal external benefit is marginal social benefit:[3]

$$MPB + MEB = MSB. \quad \textbf{(22.2)}$$

The **marginal private benefit (MPB)** is the increment in internal benefit achieved by consuming one more unit of output. This is an alternative name for the inverse market demand curve discussed in Chapter 12. The **marginal external benefit (MEB)** is the increment in external benefit achieved when consumers consume one more unit of output.

***Q3 answer:** The MEC at x = 12 is $3, the distance **sm** = **s′m′**. The increase in the MEC is $0.25 per unit of output. This is most easily calculated as the slope of the MEC curve. Given $3 = **s′m′** at x = 12, $slope_{MEC}$ = $3/12 = $0.25 per unit of output.

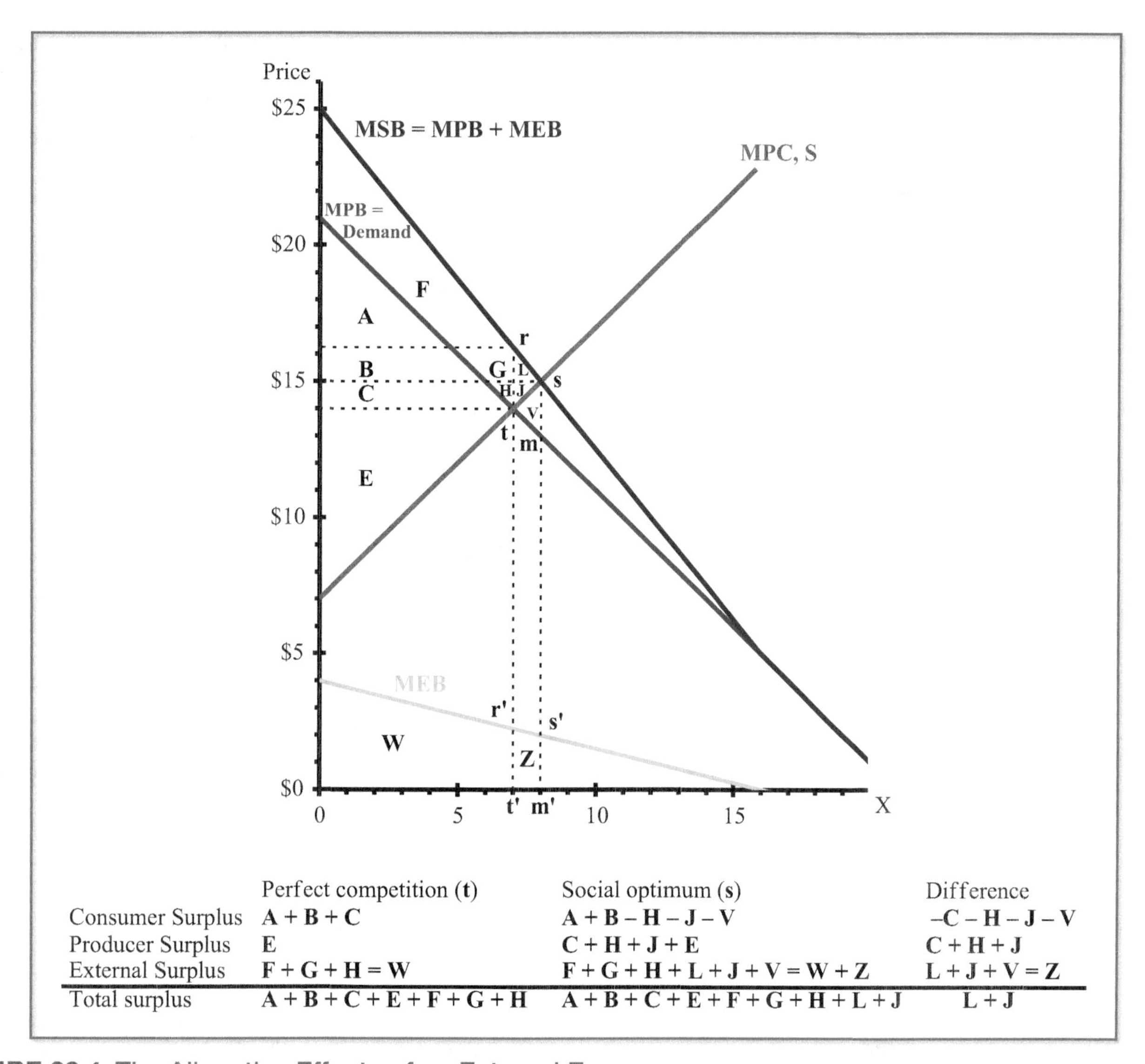

	Perfect competition (t)	Social optimum (s)	Difference
Consumer Surplus	A + B + C	A + B – H – J – V	–C – H – J – V
Producer Surplus	E	C + H + J + E	C + H + J
External Surplus	F + G + H = W	F + G + H + L + J + V = W + Z	L + J + V = Z
Total surplus	A + B + C + E + F + G + H	A + B + C + E + F + G + H + L + J	L + J

FIGURE 22.4 The Allocative Effects of an External Economy

The **marginal social benefit (MSB)** is the increment in benefit achieved by consuming one more unit of output. This is the sum of private and external marginal benefits.

marginal social benefit (MSB): The marginal social benefit is the increment in benefit achieved by consuming one more unit of output. This is the sum of private and external marginal benefits.

External economies produce a symmetric decomposition on the demand side to those produced on the supply side by external diseconomies. The reason is straightforward: Supply deals with cost, and demand deals with benefits, so it is natural to incorporate external costs to the supply side and external benefits to the demand side.

We model external economies as a declining function of output. Consider a neighbor's landscaped yard. The first $100 that the neighbor spends on landscaping is likely to have greater external benefits than the second hundred or the third. Total external benefits increase, but they increase at a decreasing rate. As noted in Equation 22.2, marginal social benefit is the (vertical) sum of private and external marginal benefit; therefore, by construction, **sm** = **s′m′**, and **rt** = **r′t′** in Figure 22.4.

Q4a. What is the MEB at 8 units of output (to the nearest $0.10)?

Q4b. What is the dollar decrease in the MEB per unit of output produced (assuming that the MEB is linear)?*

***Q4 answer:** The MEB at x = 8 is $2, the distance **sm** = **s′m′**. The MEB at x = 7 is perhaps easier to see as approximately $2.25 = **rt** = **r′t′**. The decrease in the MEB is $0.25 per unit of output. This is most easily calculated as the slope of the MEB curve. Slope is rise/run = –$4/16 = –$0.25.

Too little of the good is produced by competitive markets subject to an external economy, *ceteris paribus*. This is a reverse of the market failure from an external diseconomy. The market produces an outcome of **t**, but the socially optimal outcome is **s** in Figure 22.4. As shown in the table at the bottom of Figure 22.4, the net loss due to this underproduction is a $DWL_{competition}$ of area **L** + **J**.

Markets misallocate resources because external costs and benefits are not incorporated into the decision calculus present in the market mechanism. Private costs and benefits do not capture the entire cost or benefit in such markets. The result is allocative inefficiency. Allocative inefficiency exists whenever the marginal social cost and marginal social benefit are not equal. Competitive markets with external costs and benefits, therefore, do not produce efficient results. Goods that are associated with negative externalities are overproduced and overconsumed, while goods with positive externalities are underproduced and underconsumed. The government has created a variety of methods of intervening in the market to try to cure this market failure.

22.1C Public Policy Responses to Externalities

The private market produces inefficient results because it does not internalize external costs and benefits. The most direct response is to create a tax on goods that produce a negative externality (or a subsidy on goods that produce a positive externality). This is only one of a variety of solutions that have been used to cure the market failure created by the externality. No single method dominates from a public policy perspective; each has its own costs and benefits, and entire courses examine this topic. Suffice it to say that we only scratch the surface of this issue. We start with a discussion of the use of taxes and fees, then move to a discussion of the imposition of standards, and finally examine efforts to create markets for pollution rights.

Per-Unit Taxes and Subsidies (Pigouvian taxes)

The inefficiency can be removed if the marginal external cost (or marginal external benefit) can be internalized by designating an appropriately sized tax (or subsidy) on the externality-creating good. The appropriate size of the per-unit tax (subsidy) is the size of the MEC (MEB) at the socially optimal level of output. A per-unit subsidy is simply a negative per-unit tax, so this symmetry should not be surprising. If the size of the tax (subsidy) is appropriate, consumers and producers will adjust their behavior so that the private optimum coincides with the social optimum. Such taxes are sometimes called **Pigouvian taxes** in honor of A. C. Pigou, who argued for their use to correct market failures.

Pigouvian tax: A Pigouvian tax is a per-unit tax on the output of goods that produce externalities. The tax attempts to equate marginal social benefit with marginal social cost to internalize the externality.

A common application of supply/demand analysis in introductory microeconomics is to show that the incidence of a tax does not depend on who pays for a per-unit tax in a nominal sense. Regardless of how the tax is implemented, the allocative effects remain the same. If the firm pays the government the tax revenues, then the tax is simply an additional incremental cost of production: Marginal cost increases by the amount of the tax; therefore, supply shifts *up* by the amount of the tax. If the consumer pays the government the tax revenues, then the tax can be viewed as the demand curve shifting *down* by the amount of the tax.[4] In both events, the same allocative outcome occurs. The incidence of a tax depends on the relative elasticities of supply and demand. If demand is more inelastic than supply, consumers bear the greater burden of the tax, and if the reverse is true, firms bear the greater burden. Only when demand and supply are equally elastic will both bear an equal share of the tax burden. Since incidence does not depend on who pays the tax bill to the government, we need not be concerned with whether we model the tax as a shift up in supply or down in demand. This same point can be made for per-unit subsidies used to internalize a positive externality.

Consider first a negative externality. If a per-unit tax of **sm** in Figure 22.3 is imposed on the market, the competitive outcome will change from x_t to x_s units of output, regardless of who pays the tax in a nominal sense. Figure 22.5 shows the two possibilities.

When producers pay the tax, it simply becomes an additional marginal cost of production. In this event, the marginal private cost increases by **sm** per unit of output. Graphi-

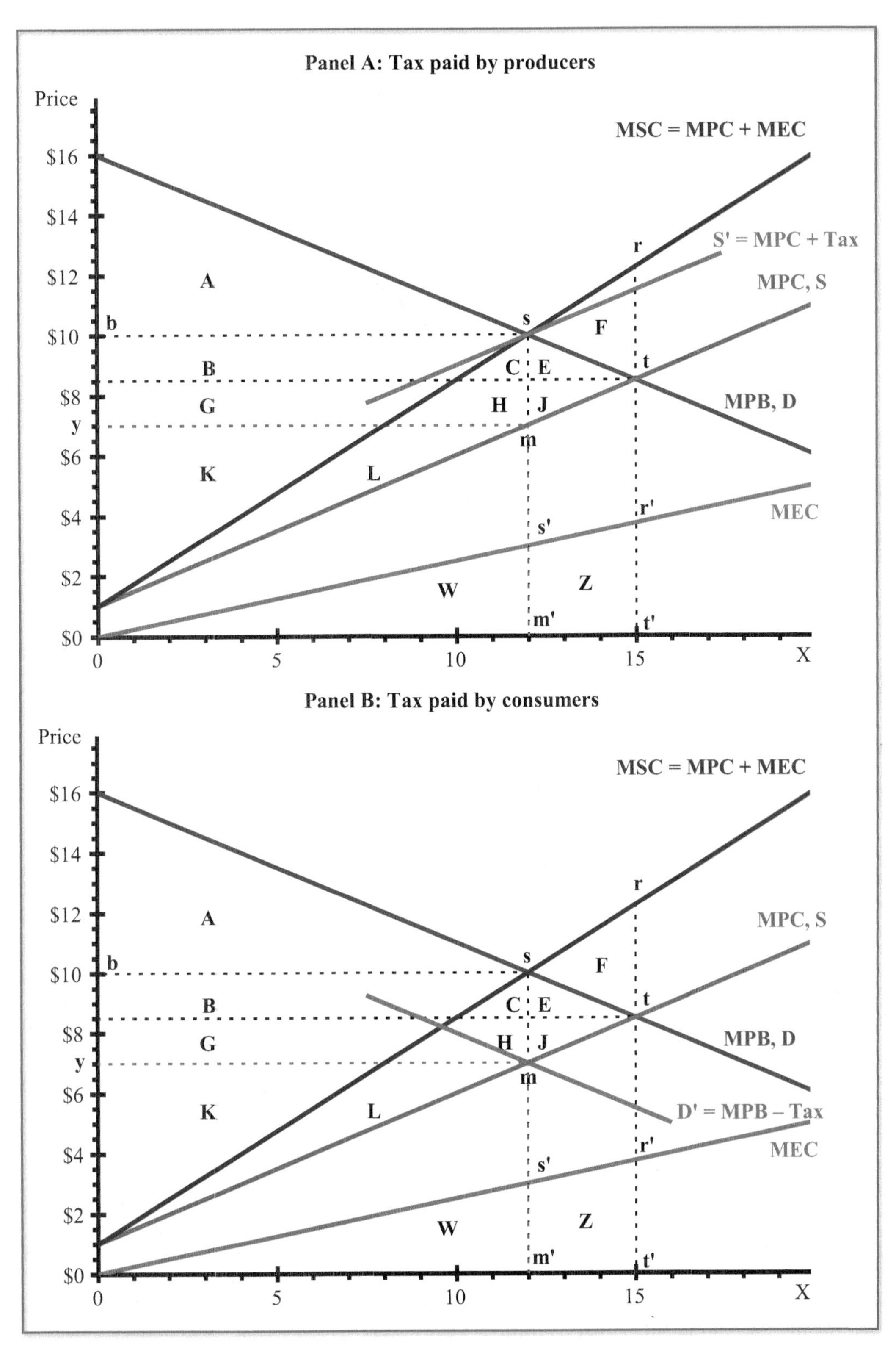

FIGURE 22.5
Internalizing an External Diseconomy via a Tax

cally, this is shown by the green post-tax supply, S′, a vertical translate of pre-tax supply, S, in Figure 22.5A. (Recall from Chapter 13 that industry supply is the horizontal sum of marginal cost curves above minimum AVC, so an increase in the private marginal cost of **sm** per unit of x translates directly to an increase in the inverse supply of **sm** per unit of x as well.) The resulting equilibrium is at x_s units of output. Tax revenues paid by the firm are **sm** per unit on **ym** units, or **B** + **C** + **G** + **H** = rectangle **bsmy**.[5]

The same quantitative result occurs if consumers pay the per-unit tax. In this instance, the demand curve shifts "down" by **sm** per unit. The green tax-paid marginal valuation

FIGURE 22.6
Internalizing an External Economy via a Subsidy

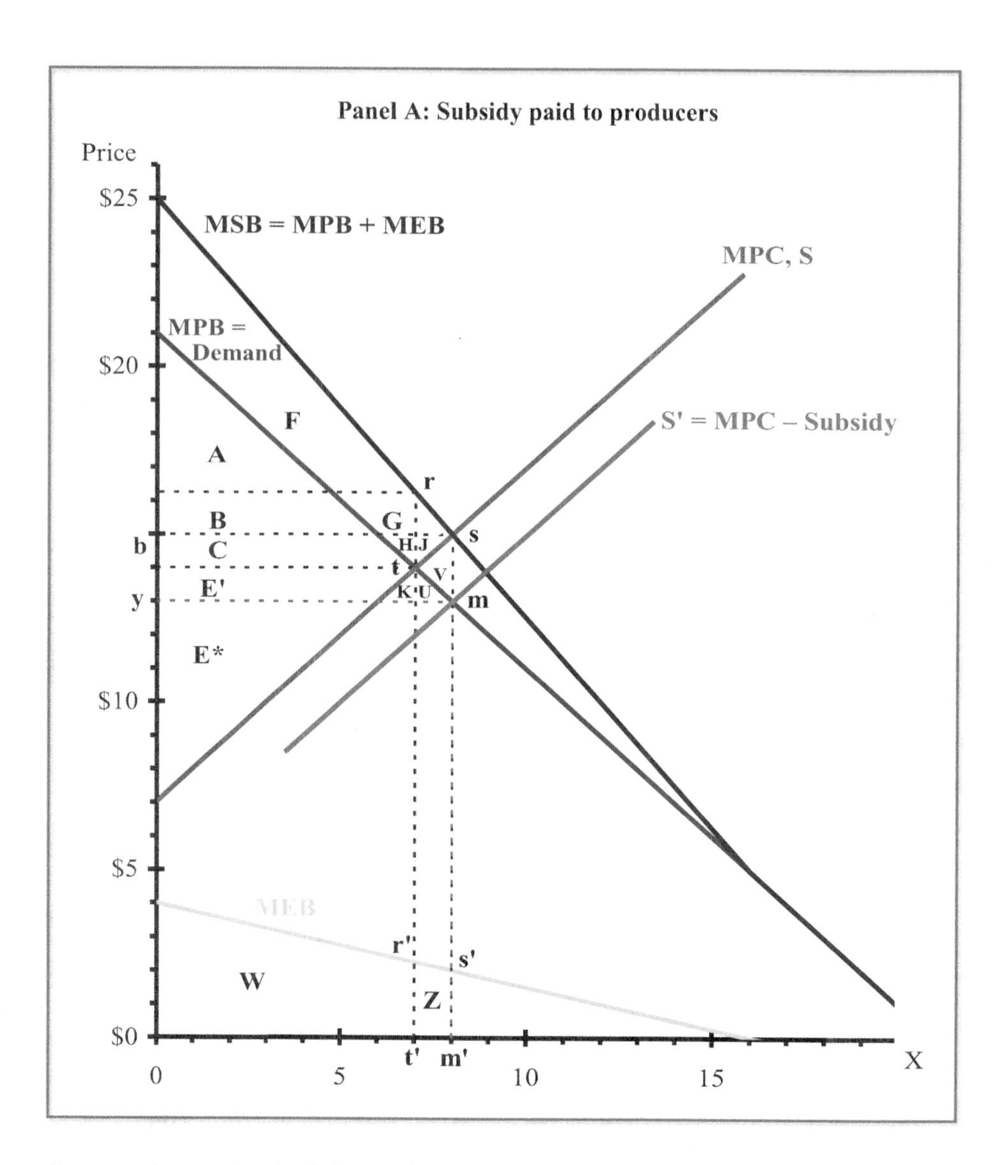

(inverse demand) schedule, D′, is **sm** units per unit of x lower than the pre-tax marginal valuation (inverse demand) schedule D because consumers do not care whether the government or firms receive the dollars paid for x. The resulting equilibrium is at x_s units of output. Tax revenues paid by consumers are **sm** per unit on **ym** units, or **B** + **C** + **G** + **H** = rectangle **bsmy**. In both instances, the externality has been internalized by an appropriate choice of Pigouvian tax.

A symmetric analysis holds for positive externalities. A subsidy is simply a negative tax, so the appropriate policy response is to provide a per-unit subsidy of **sm** per unit of x. If provided to producers, this shifts inverse supply down by **sm** at each level of output to S′, as shown in Figure 22.6A. If provided to consumers, this shifts the marginal valuation (inverse demand) schedule up by **sm** at each level of output to D′, as shown in Figure 22.6B. In both instances, the socially optimal output level, x_s, results from public subsidization. The public subsidy increases social net benefits by **L** + **J** more than the outcome that occurs without public subsidization.

Pigouvian taxes provide a socially optimal solution to the externality problem. Unfortunately, implementing such a tax requires information on marginal external costs and benefits that are often difficult to quantify. Notice, for instance, that if the government chooses a per-unit Pigouvian tax the size of the marginal externality at the private optimum (**rt** in Figures 22.3–21.6), then the resulting market "overinternalizes" the externality, resulting in too little of the negative-externality–causing good or too much of the positive-externality–causing good.[6]

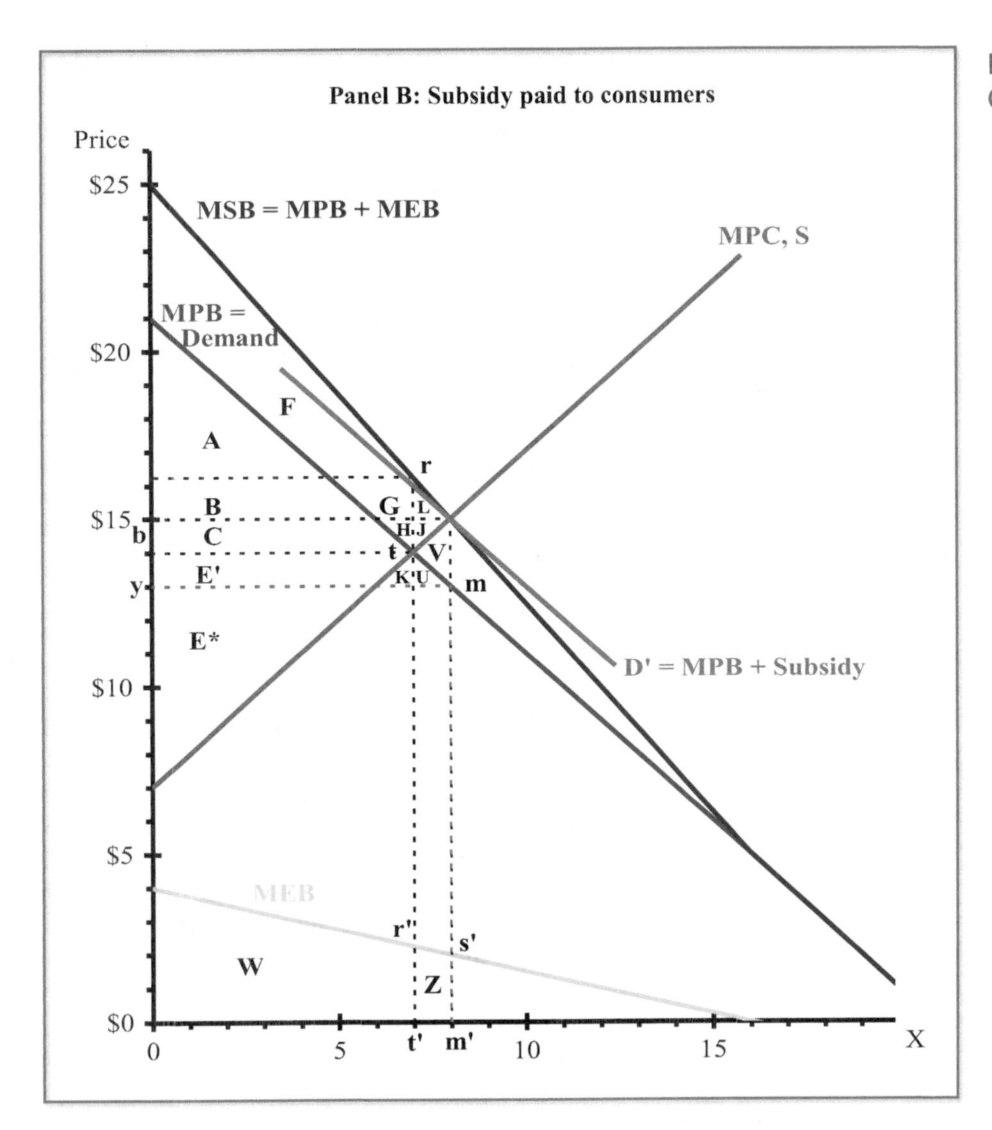

FIGURE 22.6
Continued

Even if the correct tax rate is determined, that tax rate is dependent on the level of output in the industry. To use the graphs from earlier in this section, suppose that an optimal Pigouvian tax of $3 is implemented, based on Figure 22.5. If demand for this product at any price increases, the increase in demand will require a higher Pigouvian tax than $3 per unit because more of the externality-causing good will be consumed. And if demand declines, then the reverse will hold true.

Because marginal external cost is a function of output, we have implicitly assumed that the damage caused by producing output does not depend on the production process used, but this need not be the case. Some methods of production cause more damage per unit of output produced than others. For example, a coal-fired power plant can produce electricity using low-sulfur and high-sulfur coal. The low-sulfur coal produces less external damage than the high-sulfur coal per megawatt of electricity generated. A Pigouvian tax applied equally to output (megawatts) of various producers will not optimally internalize the externality because the tax will be too high for those using low-sulfur coal and too low for those using high-sulfur coal. A preferable solution in this instance would be to directly tax sulfur emissions, rather than indirectly tax emissions by taxing output (electricity) produced.

Emissions Fees and Pollution Abatement Subsidies

Unlike a Pigouvian tax on output, an emissions fee or tax is targeted directly at the pollution itself. An **emissions fee** is a fee based on the amount of damages caused. This is also

emissions fee: An emissions fee is a fee based on the amount of damages caused.

often called an *emissions tax* and an *effluent fee*. An alternative governmental strategy is to provide subsidies based on pollution reduction activities. These are called pollution abatement subsidies. A **pollution abatement subsidy** is a government subsidy earmarked for activities that reduce pollution. We can envision the abatement subsidy as a "carrot," while the emissions fee is a "stick." Both can alter firm behavior, but firms obviously prefer receiving an abatement subsidy to paying an emissions tax.

pollution abatement subsidy: A pollution abatement subsidy is a government subsidy earmarked for activities that reduce pollution.

A firm produces a certain level of pollution as a byproduct of its production process. Any abatement activity reduces the level of pollution below this maximum level. If we denote this maximum level as "100% pollution," then we can measure abatement activities relative to this norm. (We could also perform this analysis using absolute numbers, rather than relative values. The horizontal axis would then be measured in absolute terms as the number of tons of particulates emitted from a smokestack per year or the number of parts per million of specific chemicals added to the discharge water from the plant.) The term *100% pollution* means 0% abatement, *90% pollution* means 10% abatement, and so on. Since pollution abatement is an economic good, we place the amount of pollution abated (in percentage terms) on the horizontal axis, and the vertical axis represents the cost or benefit per 1% of pollution abatement.

The question we are interested in knowing is: What is the economically efficient level of abatement activity? The theoretical answer is straightforward: The efficient level of abatement activity is that level for which the marginal benefit of an additional percent of abatement equals the marginal cost of an additional percent of abatement. Of course, we must be more explicit about what we mean by marginal cost and marginal benefit in this context. The **marginal benefit of abatement ($MB_{abatement}$)** schedule represents the external benefit when pollution is cleaned up. The $MB_{abatement}$ curve also could be called a "marginal external cost of pollution schedule." We model the $MB_{abatement}$ curve as downward sloping because we typically expect that the marginal damage increases as pollution increases. (Pollution increases and the marginal external cost of pollution schedule increases when viewed from right to left along the $MB_{abatement}$ curve; when viewed from left to right, the $MB_{abatement}$ curve declines.) We also assume that the polluting firm receives no private benefit from pollution abatement activity. If the firm did receive benefits, these would have to be added to the external benefits to obtain a marginal social benefit of abatement schedule.

marginal benefit of abatement ($MB_{abatement}$): The marginal benefit of abatement schedule represents the external benefit when pollution is cleaned up.

The **marginal cost of abatement ($MC_{abatement}$)** represents the incremental cost to the polluting entity of pollution reduction activities. This schedule is shown as upward sloping because pollution reduction activity is differentially costly. Cleaning up the first 10% of pollution is likely to be less expensive than the next 10%, or the next. And cleaning up the "last" 10% (so that the plant emits no pollutants) is likely to be extremely expensive indeed.

marginal cost of abatement ($MC_{abatement}$): The marginal cost of abatement is the incremental cost of reducing pollution.

If pollution by a given firm exhibits the marginal benefit and marginal cost of abatement schedules shown in Figure 22.7, the socially optimal amount of abatement is 40% for this firm (based on the intersection at **e**). This outcome can be achieved in a number of ways. Figure 22.7A depicts the result of an emissions fee of **f** per 1% of pollution remaining. The firm responds to this fee by undertaking 40% abatement. The cost of this 40% abatement is **C**, the area under the marginal cost of abatement schedule from 0% to 40%. After that, it is less expensive to simply pay the effluent fee of **f** per 1% pollution remaining (since $MC_{abatement} > \mathbf{f}$ above 40% abatement) than to abate pollution further. Since 60% remains, the total fee paid the government is $60 \cdot \mathbf{f} = \mathbf{D} + \mathbf{E}$ (the pink rectangle). The total cost devoted to abatement activity by the firm under this government policy is $\mathbf{C} + \mathbf{D} + \mathbf{E} = \mathbf{C} + 60 \cdot \mathbf{f}$.

As noted previously, the same result can be achieved using a carrot rather than a stick. The carrot in this instance is a pollution abatement subsidy of $\mathbf{s} = \mathbf{f}$ for each percent decrease in pollution produced by the firm. As shown in Figure 22.7B, such a subsidy will cause the firm to abate 40% of its pollution. Firms will not choose to abate more than 40% of pollution in this instance because the cost they face (along $MC_{abatement}$) exceeds the subsidy they receive, **s**. The cost to the firm of 40% abatement is area **C** (the area under

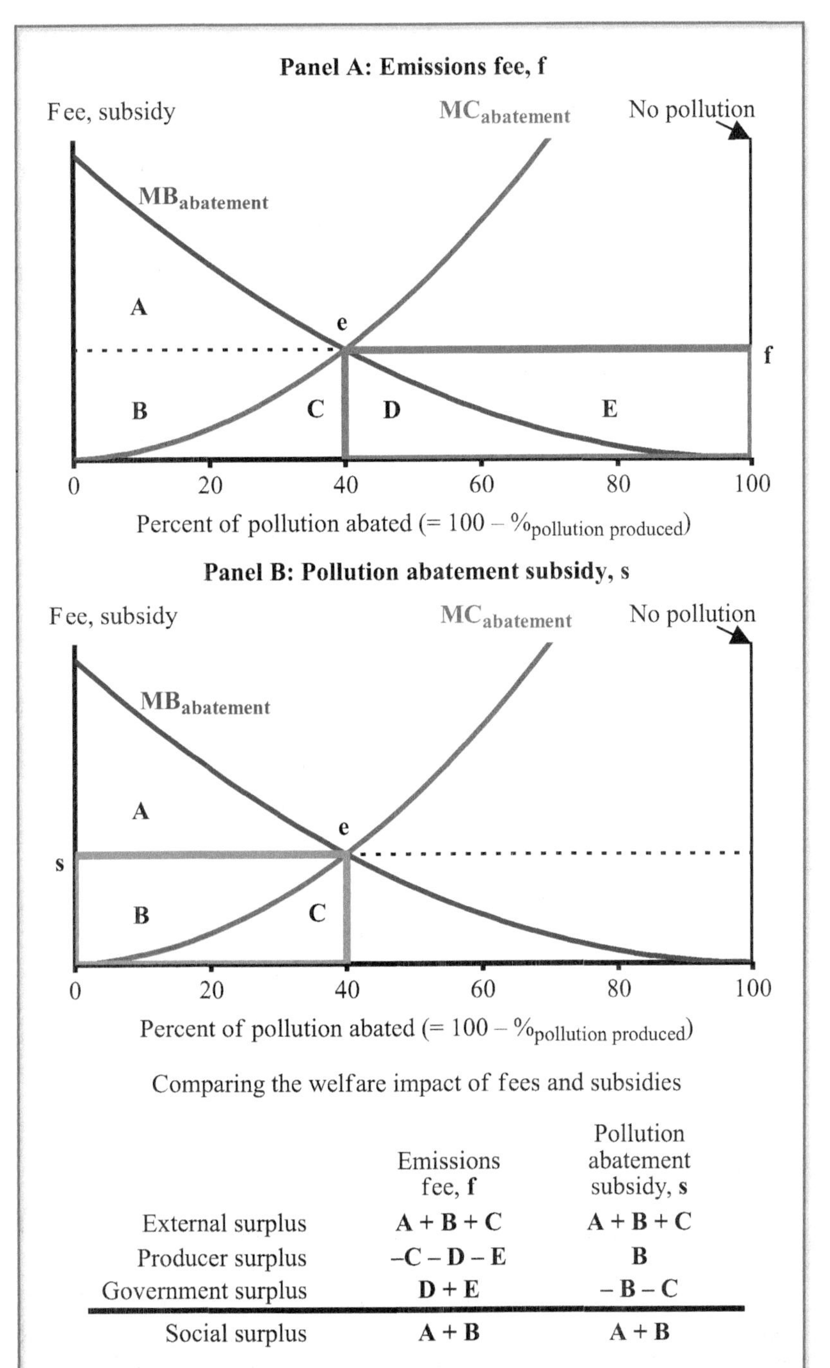

	Emissions fee, f	Pollution abatement subsidy, s
External surplus	A + B + C	A + B + C
Producer surplus	–C – D – E	B
Government surplus	D + E	– B – C
Social surplus	A + B	A + B

FIGURE 22.7 Obtaining the Optimal Level of Pollution Reduction via an Emissions Fee or Pollution Abatement Subsidy

the $MC_{abatement}$ from 0 to 40%), and the firm is paid **B** + **C** = 40 · **s** (the green rectangle), yielding a net benefit of **B** for the firm. Of course, the carrot comes at a cost, and the cost is to the government, which must pay out **B** + **C**.

As noted earlier, the same analysis could be performed with levels of pollution abatement on the horizontal axis, rather than percentage abatement. The fee or subsidy would then be the amount per unit (rather than the percent) of pollution remaining or abated. The same qualitative result emerges: The optimal amount of pollution abatement activity will emerge if the appropriate fee or subsidy is chosen. That fee equates the marginal benefit and marginal cost of abatement. This same result can be attained by imposing standards.

Standards

Another policy alternative is for the government to set a standard of behavior expected by firms. Examples of standards are: Firms cannot emit more than X per time period, or firms must reduce emissions by a given percentage, or an automobile manufacturer must meet a corporate average fuel economy (CAFE) standard of 32.5 miles per gallon in 2016. Such pollution standards can, at least theoretically, produce an efficient result.

The analysis of emissions fees versus subsidies is useful in this regard. The efficient level of abatement is 40%, at **e** in Figure 22.7. Suppose that the government simply mandates that firms undertake a 40% reduction in emissions. This will require that the firm undertake emission abatement at a cost of **C** to the firm. The firm will prefer the standard to facing the emissions fee but will prefer the subsidy to the standard. (Under an emissions fee, the cost is **C** + **D** + **E**; under a standard, the cost is **C**; but the firm receives a benefit of **B** under a subsidy.) Although there are distributional differences among policy options, the allocation of resources devoted to abatement is the same under each of the programs; each program produces a socially optimal level of pollution reduction. But this need not be the case, as we see next.

Suppose that the benefit schedule is well known but there is uncertainty about the cost of abatement schedule. This is quite reasonable for a variety of forms of pollution. The damage associated with a given amount of pollution may be well known; therefore, the benefit from pollution reduction is readily understood. Assume that, for simplicity, the marginal benefit of pollution reduction is a constant in this instance (unlike in Figure 22.7). The appropriate fee (or subsidy) is the size of this marginal benefit. Denote this by **f**. Suppose that the *typical* firm emitting this pollutant has a marginal cost of abatement schedule in which, given this fee, 40% of pollution is abated (just like at point **e** in Figure 22.7). A standard requiring 40% pollution abatement will require *all* firms to meet this standard. But some firms may have different marginal cost of abatement schedules; in particular, some firms face higher abatement costs than others. In this event, a standards approach to pollution abatement will not reduce emissions as efficiently as an effluent fee approach.

A standard will require each firm to abate the same level of pollution. Each firm must abate 40% of emissions under the standard shown in Figure 22.8. Firm 1 abates the *40*th percent of pollution at a marginal abatement cost of **m1**, but Firm 2 has a much lower abatement cost for the *40*th percent of pollution, **m2** < **m1**. The same amount of pollution will be abated if an emissions fee is employed, but it will be abated at a lower total cost of abatement.[7] Indeed, we can readily see how much more efficient the fee will be in this instance.

Under a fee approach, Firm 1 abates 25% (at **x**), and Firm 2 abates 55% (at **y**). As under the standards approach, the average abatement is 40%, but the cost is lower under a fee approach. Firm 1 avoids abatement costs of **A** + **C** + **D** because it abates 15% less, but Firm 2 incurs an extra abatement cost of **F** by undertaking a higher level of abatement. In exchange for avoiding this abatement cost, Firm 1 pays an extra fee of **C** + **D**, and at the same time, Firm 2 avoids a fee of **B** + **F**. By construction, **C** + **D** = **B** + **F** so that the net effect of a change from standards to a fee is a decline in real resources devoted to abatement of **A** + **B** (since **A** + **B** = **A** + (**C** + **D** – **F**) = **A** + **B** + **F** – **F**).[8] The reason an emissions fee is more efficient in this case is straightforward: *Emissions fees equalize marginal cost across firms*. To produce a given amount of product across firms at minimum cost, we must have all firms producing at equal marginal costs of production. The only difference here is that the good under consideration is pollution abatement.

Unfortunately, fees need not lead to a more efficient outcome. Suppose that there is uncertainty regarding both the optimal fee and the optimal standard. In this event, a misestimated standard may be more or less efficient than a misestimated fee. Once again, start from a true equilibrium level at **e** in Figure 22.7 in which there is an optimal fee, **f***, and an optimal standard of abatement, **s***. The optimal standard in Figure 22.7 and in Figure 22.9 is **s*** = 40%. Suppose that because of uncertainty regarding the market for pollution abatement, the government imposes a standard of 50% abatement. This standard is 25% higher than is optimal and will lead to too much abatement activity. Deadweight loss (DWL) results from this inefficiently strict standard. Is this DWL larger or smaller than would occur had the fee been misestimated by a similar percentage? The answer is, it depends.

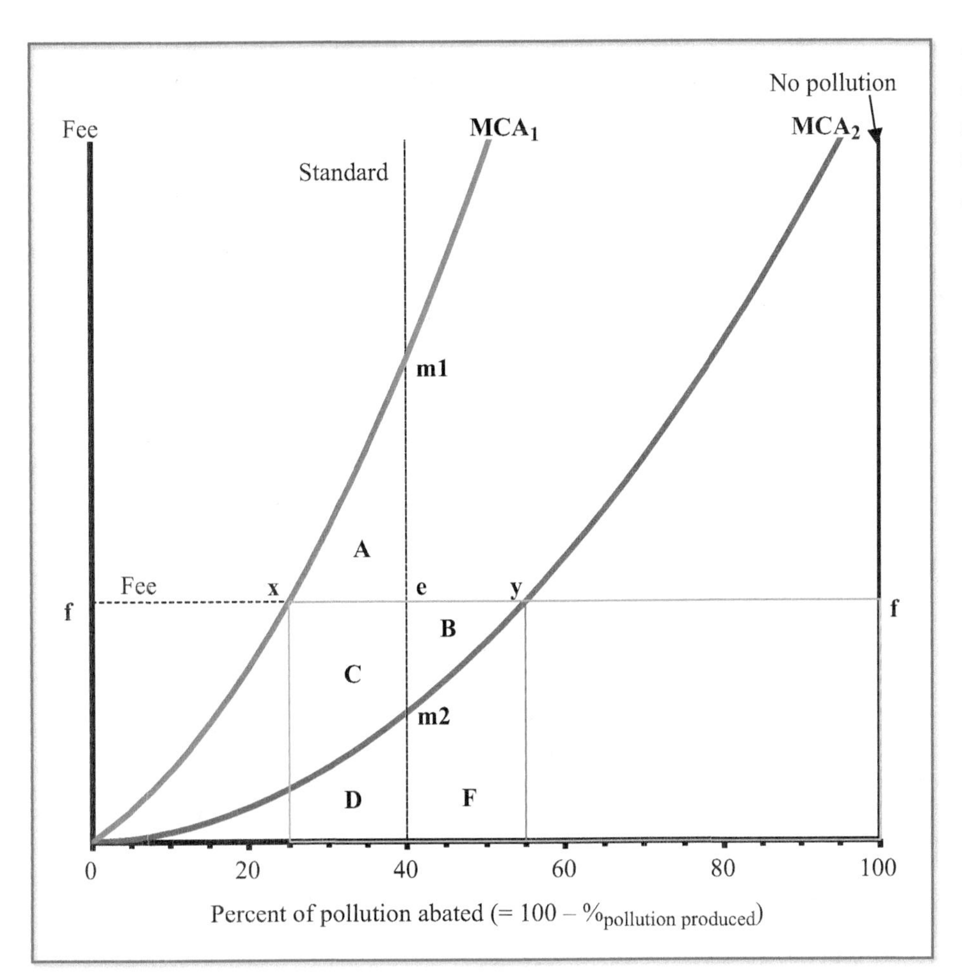

FIGURE 22.8
Comparing Standards and Emissions Fees, Given Different Cost of Abatement Structures

Figure 22.9 depicts the three possible outcomes. *The green horizontal line at* **f′** *represents a 25% higher emissions fee than is optimal, and the blue vertical line at* **s′** *represents a 25% higher standard than is optimal in each panel.* Figure 22.9A reproduces the $MB_{abatement}$ and $MC_{abatement}$ schedules from Figure 22.7. Figures 22.9B and 22.9C maintain the marginal benefit schedule but adjust the marginal cost of abatement curve to show the three possibilities. In Figure 22.9A, an overly strict fee produces less DWL than an overly strict standard, but in Figure 22.9C, the reverse is true. In Figure 22.9B, both produce an equal DWL.

The distinguishing difference between panels is the elasticity of $MC_{abatement}$ at the optimal abatement point. In Figure 22.9A, the $MC_{abatement}$ is inelastic; in Figure 22.9C, it is elastic; and in Figure 22.9B, it has unitary elasticity. This result is easy to understand by simply recalling the definition of elasticity as $\varepsilon = \%\Delta Q/\%\Delta P$. In this context, the numerator is the percentage change in standard, and the denominator is the percentage change in fee, $\varepsilon = \%\Delta s/\%\Delta f$.

If a standard is used but is misestimated by a given percentage (in Figure 22.9, we used 25%, since $\mathbf{s'} = 1.25 \cdot \mathbf{s^*}$), then this fixes the numerator of the fraction, $\%\Delta s$. If the elasticity fraction is less than 1 (as in Figure 22.9A), the denominator ($\%\Delta f$) would have to be *more than* this percentage higher ($MC_{abatement}$ at $\mathbf{s'}$ is about $1.5 \cdot \mathbf{f^*} > \mathbf{f'} = 1.25 \cdot \mathbf{f^*}$ in Figure 22.9A). Put another way, a 25% misestimated fee of **f′** represents a *smaller-than-proportional* change in standard of abatement in Figure 22.9A (since $\mathbf{s^*} = 40\%$, about $1.125 \cdot \mathbf{s^*} = 45\% < 50\% = \mathbf{s'} = 1.25 \cdot \mathbf{s^*}$). A fee is preferred to a standard in this setting since a misestimated fee will produce smaller DWL than a similarly misestimated standard (**A** + **B** versus **A** + **B** + **C** + **D** + **E** in Figure 22.9A). If $MC_{abatement}$ is elastic, then these results reverse, as shown in Figure 22.9C.

One final way to conceptualize this distinction is to note that the intersection of the misestimated fee and the misestimated standard (**s′**, **f′**) represents an equal percentage

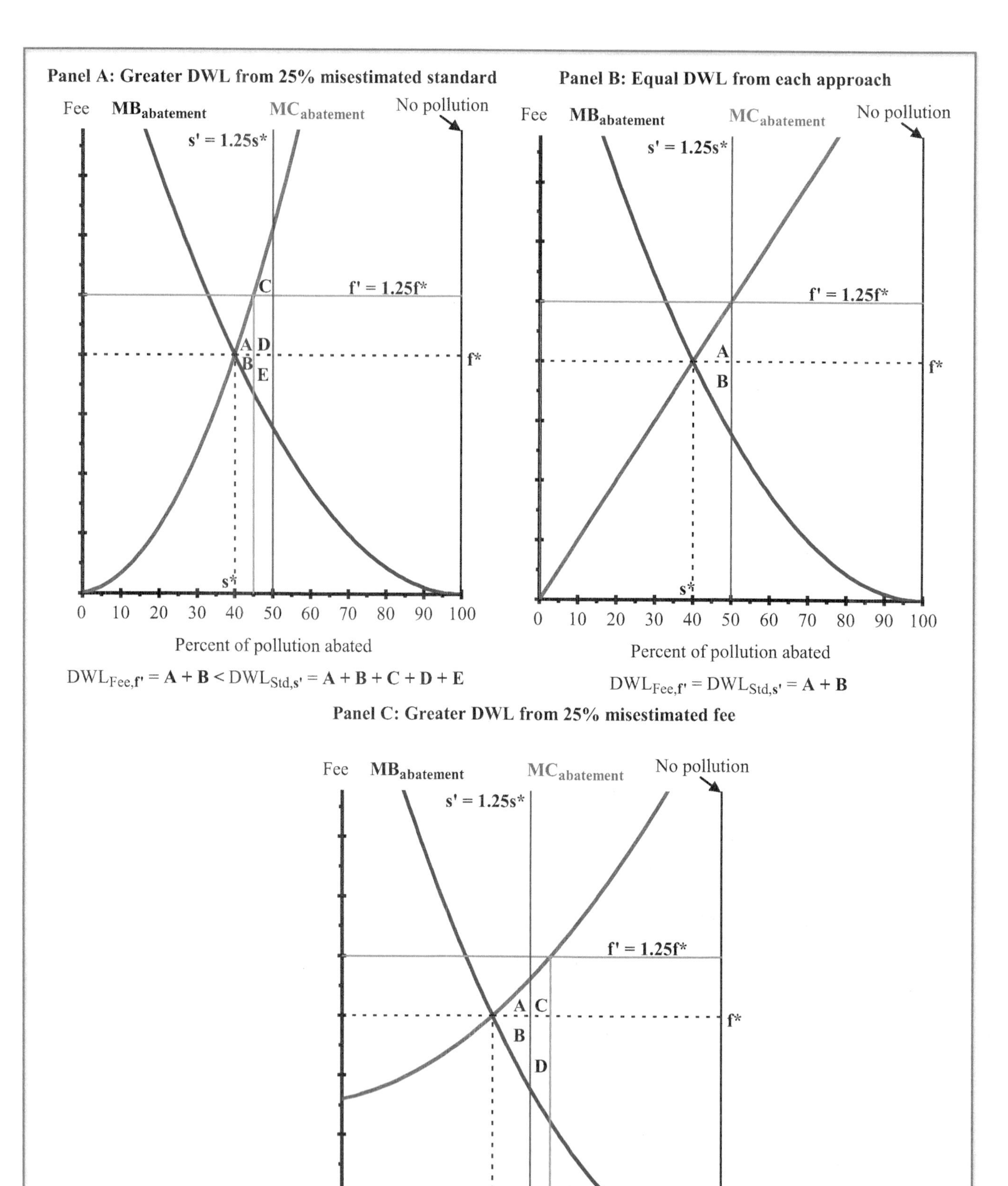

FIGURE 22.9 Comparing DWL from Misestimated Standards and Misestimated Emissions Fees

change in both quantity (standard) and price (fee), so that if the $MC_{abatement}$ schedule passes through this point, it has a unitary (arc) elasticity. This is exactly what is shown in Figure 22.9B. If the $MC_{abatement}$ schedule passes to the left of (**s′**, **f′**) (as in Figure 22.9A), the numerator is the smaller percentage, and if it passes to the right (as in Figure 22.9C), the denominator is the smaller percentage.

The government can achieve a similar outcome using an emissions fee if it creates a market for the right to pollute. Although it sounds unusual to give a right to pollute and to create a market for this right, this policy prescription has gained popularity, in part due to the policy shift signaled by President George H. W. Bush in the early 1990s.[9]

The Marketable Rights Approach: Marketing Los Angeles Smog

The marketable rights approach can best be understood by examining an actual market for which this approach has been used. Tradable discharge rights have been used to clean up smog in the Los Angeles basin.[10] The South Coast Air Quality Management District (SCAQMD) created the Regional Clean Air Incentives Market (RECLAIM) program of tradable emissions rights in 1994. This program provided pollution rights to more than 300 high-volume, stationary emissions sources of nitrogen and sulfur oxides (these sources had emissions in excess of 4 tons per year). Initial permit levels were based on existing pollution levels but were below the baseline levels. In subsequent years, the allowable levels were further restricted to increase the ambient air quality in the LA basin.

The RECLAIM program gave plants the choice of how to meet the restrictions imposed by the program. Plants could install pollution control equipment, restrict their operations, or purchase the right to pollute above their allocated level of pollution. The final option is where the marketable discharge right occurs. A **marketable discharge right** gives the plant the right to pollute at a certain level. If the plant exceeds this level, it must purchase discharge rights from other plants, and if the plant's emissions are lower than the number of permits it holds, it can sell the remaining permits to plants that are in the markets for these permits. If a plant reduces pollution below its required level, it has tradable permits, which it can sell to another plant that needs to purchase the right.

marketable discharge right: A marketable discharge right gives the plant the right to pollute at a certain level. If the plant exceeds this level, it must purchase discharge rights from other plants, and if the plant's emissions are lower than the number of permits it holds, it can sell the remaining permits to plants that are in the markets for these permits.

Marketable discharge rights produce an outcome at which a given level of pollution is achieved at minimum cost. This is easy to see within the context of Figure 22.8 if we simply imagine that the two firms have the same initial quantity of pollution (say, 100 units rather than the percent) and, hence, have the same number of permits. Suppose that each firm is given 60 permits. On the face of it, each plant must reduce emissions by 40 units. In the absence of trading permits, it will be much more expensive for Firm 1 to achieve this reduction than Firm 2 because Firm 1 has higher abatement costs than Firm 2. If Firm 2 can be convinced to clean up an extra unit of pollution, it will cost Firm 2 **m2** dollars, but in exchange, Firm 2 will have 1 unit of discharge rights that it can sell to Firm 1. Firm 1 will gladly pay more than **m2** for this right because it allows Firm 1 to avoid having to abate a unit of discharge that has a marginal cost of **m1** > **m2**. The value of the discharge right is somewhere between **m1** and **m2** (and depends on the bargaining powers of the firms). If we allow this trading to continue, Firm 1 will purchase a total of 15 units of pollution rights from Firm 2 (assuming that trading is costless). Given the marginal cost structures shown in Figure 22.8 and assuming that a competitive market for discharge rights develops, the price of the right will be **f**, the common marginal cost at points **x** and **y**.

The permits approach allowed SCAQMD to achieve pollution reduction in a cost-minimizing fashion. There has been a two-thirds reduction in total emissions and a reduction in the market cost of emissions allowances in the LA basin below national averages. Prior to the institution of the program, the marginal cost of emissions reduction in the LA basin stood at five times the national average in some categories of emissions.

22.1D Property Rights and the Coase Theorem

We saw earlier that emissions fees and pollution abatement subsidies can each lead to a socially optimal level of pollution abatement if the costs and benefits of abatement are

property right: A property right is a legal rule stating what property owners can do with their property.

transactions costs: Transactions costs are the costs involved in negotiating and enforcing an agreement between two parties.

well known. Despite their allocative similarity, they have distributive differences, and these differences are based on implicit property rights assignments. A **property right** is a legal rule stating what property owners can do with their property. The most obvious example of property rights is the set of rights attached to land ownership. Property owners can do certain things with the property they own, but they may not do other things. There are restrictions on how a given piece of property can be used. Zoning laws, for example, assign different property rights to properties located in different parts of a town or county.

Pollution abatement subsidies implicitly assign the property rights to the polluter. The polluter is offered a subsidy to encourage abatement activity. Emissions fees are implicitly based on the opposite property rights assignment: The harmed party (i.e., society at large) is compensated for pollution that is not abated. Marketable discharge rights are based on providing an intermediate property rights assignment. Each of these outcomes occurs due to government intervention.

Property rights are important for goods other than land, and well-defined property rights are the basis for a deeper understanding of externalities. This was one of the seminal insights that Ronald Coase provided in his 1960 article for which he was awarded the Nobel Prize in 1991.[11] Coase argues that government intervention is not necessary to achieve an efficient solution to the externality problem under certain conditions. Specifically, Coase argues that if property rights are well defined and if **transactions costs** (the costs involved in negotiating and enforcing an agreement between two parties) are negligible, then the parties involved will bargain among themselves and will obtain an efficient solution to the externality problem, even in the absence of government intervention. Indeed, under certain conditions, they will achieve the *same* allocative outcome, regardless of initial property rights assignment.

The Reciprocal Nature of the Problem

Externalities are not imposed by one party on the other in Coase's analysis. Coase provides a number of examples to make his point. A rancher and a farmer share a common property line, and the rancher's cattle sometimes trample the farmer's crops. A doctor's examination room is adjacent to a confectioner's noisy machinery, and the noise disrupts the doctor's ability to examine patients. The traditional economic and legal view is that the party causing the harm ought to be restrained.

Coase argues that this is a one-sided view of the externality and that this traditional view ignores *the reciprocal nature of the problem*. The farmer is only harmed because the farmer is located next to the rancher. The doctor is only harmed because the doctor's examination room is located next to the confectioner's machinery. Not restraining the rancher or confectioner causes harm to the farmer or doctor; however, restraining the confectioner or rancher causes harm to these parties. In both examples, there are two harms caused: the harm to the affected parties if the polluters create the damage, and the harm to the polluters if they are required to alter their behavior. The question of which harm is greater is empirical; the larger of the harms should be avoided.

Consider the farmer and the rancher, and suppose that the farmer has the right to a trample-free environment. The farmer can require the rancher to restrain the cattle. Suppose that this can be accomplished by building a fence at the cost of F. If the fence is not built, the cattle will trample crops and cause damage, D. Economic efficiency suggests that the fence *should* be built if $F < D$. The fence *should not* be built if $F > D$. This latter statement is true even though the farmer *could* force the rancher to erect the fence (since the farmer has a right to a trample-free environment). In this event, the preferable outcome would be to achieve a bargain in which the rancher pays the farmer an amount B, such that $F > B > D$ in exchange for being allowed to not build the fence. The rancher is better off by $F - B > 0$, and the farmer is better off by $B - D > 0$ because the payment of B exceeds the farmer's damage of D. This Coasean exchange is Pareto superior to building the fence. *In the absence of transactions costs, a bargain will be struck because both parties are better off if the larger of the two expenses is avoided.*

The same outcome will occur if the rancher is not liable for the damage caused by the rancher's errant cattle. Suppose that the crop damage is less expensive than the cost of erecting the fence, $D < F$. The farmer will prefer to incur the crop damage to paying the larger cost of erecting the fence. No fence will be erected. And if $F < D$, the farmer will erect the fence at a cost of F and avoid damages of D.

The allocative outcome is the same in both property rights assignments. If negotiation between affected parties is costless, an efficient outcome will occur, regardless of property rights assignment. The fence will be built only if it is the least costly solution to the problem, and it will not be built if less costly solutions exist. As long as the property rights assignment is clearly defined, bargaining between affected parties will lead to an efficient outcome. This is an example of a more general result called the Coase Theorem. The **Coase Theorem** states that if transactions costs are zero and property rights are clearly defined, then an efficient allocation of resources will result, regardless of who has the property rights.

Coase Theorem: The Coase Theorem states that if transactions costs are zero and property rights are clearly defined, then an efficient allocation of resources will result, regardless of who has the property rights.

Although the allocative outcome discussed earlier does not depend on who is given the property rights, the distributional outcome certainly depends on that property rights assignment. Each party would prefer to have the property rights because the bestowal of property rights is like the bestowal of wealth. When the farmer has the rights, the worst-case scenario from the farmer's perspective is no crop damage. The rancher must pay for the fence or compensate for the damage caused by the cattle. When the rancher has the rights, no compensation need be paid. The cost is now borne by the farmer.

22.1E A Graphical Analysis of the Coase Theorem

Suppose that two firms, x and y, are commonly located along a river, and Firm y is downstream from Firm x. No other individuals or firms are downstream from Firm x. Both firms compete in competitive markets for goods X and Y that have market clearing prices of P_x and P_y (as with our discussion of perfect competition in Chapters 13 and 14, lowercase letters refer to individual actors, and uppercase letters refer to the market as a whole). If Firm x pollutes the river and causes damage to Firm y, then Firm y's damage caused by Firm x can be summarized as MEC_x.[12]

Firm y incurs damage because increased Firm x production decreases Firm y production, *ceteris paribus*. Given fixed inputs in production by Firm y, we can describe this loss in production as $\Delta y/\Delta x < 0$. (This simply means that Firm y produces less output from a given bundle of inputs if Firm x production increases.) Since Firm y production has an incremental value of P_y per unit of y produced, the incremental loss to Firm y is the loss in revenues due to decreased Firm y production caused by increased Firm x production. This is also the loss in profits to Firm y because we assume, *ceteris paribus*, that Firm y has not changed its input bundle. We can summarize the external damage caused by Firm x as:

$$MEC_x = -P_y \cdot \Delta y/\Delta x = -\Delta\pi_y/\Delta x. \quad \textbf{(22.3)}$$

In the graphical analysis that follows, we assume that this marginal external damage is an increasing function of Firm x production. (This assumption is not required for the Coase Theorem to work but is consistent with the MEC curves shown in earlier figures in this chapter.)

Coasean bargaining proceeds by comparing the answer to two incremental questions. The first question is: What would it take to get the firm that has the property right to give it up? The other question relates to the firm that is trying to obtain the property right via Coasean bargaining. These questions examine maximums and minimums, so they can be called the *minimum question* and the *maximum question*:

Minimum question: What is the minimum compensation an economic agent with a property right would require to give up the right?

Maximum question: What is the maximum compensation an economic agent without a property right would pay to obtain the right?

These questions appear to be different, depending on who has the property right; therefore, we must examine each property rights assignment separately. We consider two property rights assignments: (1) Firm x has the right to pollute the river, and (2) Firm y has the right to a pollution-free river.

Property Rights Assigned to the Polluter

If Firm x has the right to pollute, then there is an *opportunity cost* associated with that right. Firm x can pollute in this instance; that much is clear. But Firm x can also decide to pollute less if it is profitable to do so. The question for Firm x is the standard economic question: *What is the value of the resource (the property right) in its next best alternative use?*

Consider the problem from the point of view of Firm x. In the absence of bargaining of any kind, Firm x would choose to produce at the point where $P_x = MPC_x$, or point **t** in Figure 22.10. $P_x - MPC_x = \$0$ at x = 16. If Firm x is offered an amount of money z to reduce production, this would make economic sense as long as z is larger than the profits that Firm x gives up by reducing production. Put another way, the *minimum* that Firm x requires as compensation to produce 1 less unit of x is the loss in profits on that unit, $\Delta\pi_x = P_x - MPC_x$.

When viewed from Firm y's perspective, given that Firm x has the right to pollute, the starting point is the private market outcome in the absence of bargaining, or point **t** in Figure 22.10. This causes marginal external damage to Firm y of $-P_y \cdot \Delta y/\Delta x$, or length **rt** = \$6 in the figure. This represents the *maximum* that Firm y (the party without the property right) would pay to have Firm x production reduced by 1 unit. In general, the maximum that Firm y would pay for a 1-unit reduction in output by Firm x is the loss in profits that Firm y incurs due to that 1 unit of Firm x production. This is the marginal external cost of Firm x. Put another way, it is the difference between the marginal social cost and the marginal private cost of Firm x production.

Since the maximum that Firm y is willing to pay is larger than the minimum that Firm x requires, the property right to this unit of production of Firm x will be traded for an

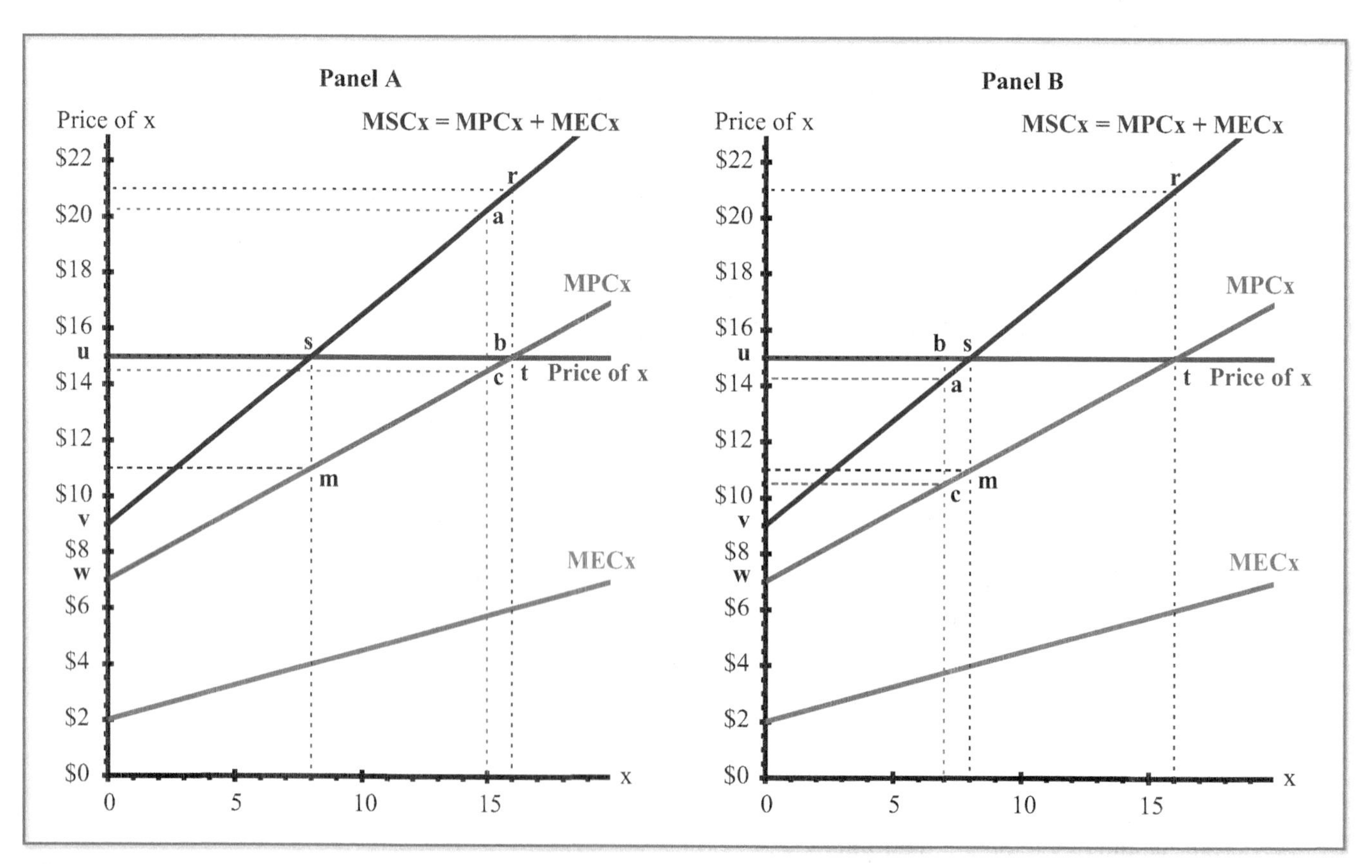

FIGURE 22.10 Coasean Bargaining, Given That Firm x Has the Right to Pollute

amount of money z, where \$0 < z < \$6. The bargaining will continue. Consider the 15th unit of output in Figure 22.10A. Firm x requires a minimum compensation of profits forgone on this unit, $P_x - MPC_x$ = \$0.50 = **bc**, substantially smaller than the maximum that Firm y would be willing to pay of $-P_y \cdot \Delta y/\Delta x$ = \$5.75 = **ac**.[13] Once again, the bargaining will continue. Indeed, it will continue as long as **ac** = $-P_y \cdot \Delta y/\Delta x > P_x - MPC_x$ = **bc**, and it will stop when the greater-than sign turns into an equals sign. This occurs at 8 units of output in Figure 22.10 (where $-P_y \cdot \Delta y/\Delta x = P_x - MPC_x$ = \$4 = **sm**).

Further bargaining will not continue in this instance, as can be seen in Figure 22.10B. Consider the seventh unit of Firm x production. Firm x requires a minimum compensation of $P_x - MPC_x$ = \$4.50 = **bc**, but the maximum that Firm y is willing to pay is $-P_y \cdot \Delta y/\Delta x$ = \$3.75 = **ac**. Since the minimum that Firm x requires exceeds the maximum that Firm y will pay, the bargain will not be made. *Coasean bargaining leads to an efficient allocation of Firm x production without any government intervention.*

Property Rights Assigned to the Harmed Party

If Firm y has the right to a pollution-free river, then there is an *opportunity cost* associated with that right. Clearly, Firm y can require that Firm x not pollute in this instance. But Firm y also can decide to allow Firm x to pollute if it is profitable for Firm y to do so. The question for Firm y is the standard economic question: What is the value of the resource (the property rights) in its next best alternative use?

Given this property rights assignment, the *minimum* compensation that Firm y requires to give up this right is the external damage caused by Firm x production. The minimum required compensation is $-P_y \cdot \Delta y/\Delta x$. At x = 0, this is length **vw** = \$2 in Figure 22.11. The *maximum* that Firm x would be willing to pay is the marginal profit on this production, or $P_x - MPC_x$ = **uw** = \$8 at x = 0. Since the maximum that Firm x is willing to pay exceeds the minimum that Firm y requires, the trade will be made for an amount of money z, where \$2 < z < \$8. The bargaining will continue. At x = 1 in Figure 22.11A, the minimum that Firm y requires as payment is \$2.25 = **ac**, which is smaller than \$7.50 = **bc**, the

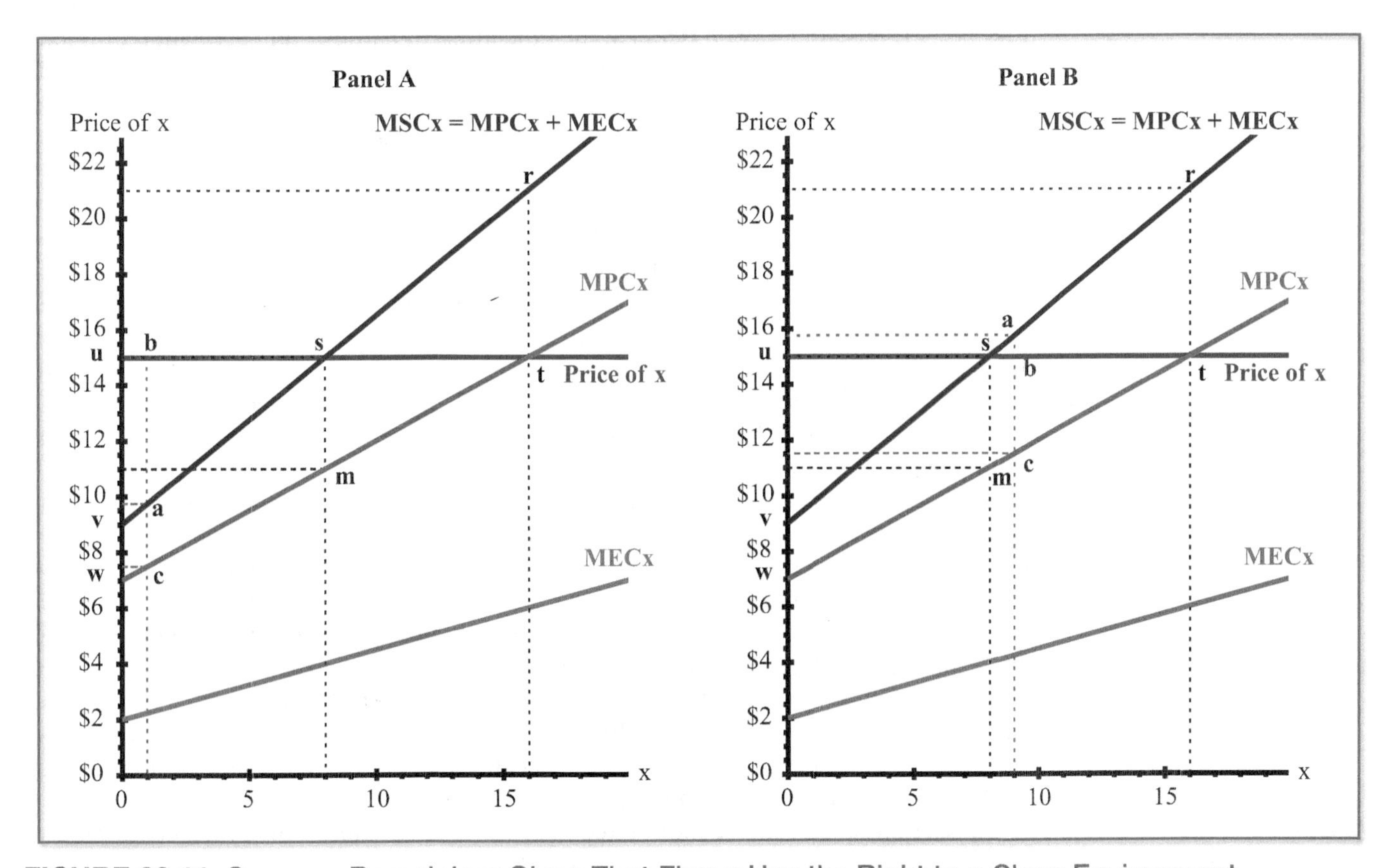

FIGURE 22.11 Coasean Bargaining, Given That Firm y Has the Right to a Clean Environment

maximum that Firm x is willing to pay to obtain the right to produce this unit of output. Bargaining will continue as long as $-P_y \cdot \Delta y/\Delta x < P_x - MPC_x$, and it will stop when the less-than sign turns into an equals sign. This occurs at 8 units of output in Figure 22.11 (where $-P_y \cdot \Delta y/\Delta x = P_x - MPC_x = \$4 =$ **sm**).

Further bargaining will not continue in this instance. Consider the ninth unit of Firm x production in Figure 22.11B. Firm y requires a minimum compensation of $-P_y \cdot \Delta y/\Delta x = \$4.25 =$ **ac**, but the maximum that Firm x is willing to pay is $P_x - MPC_x = \$3.50 =$ **bc**. Since the minimum that Firm y requires exceeds the maximum that Firm x will pay, the bargain will not be made. *Coasean bargaining leads to an efficient allocation of Firm x production at point **s** in Figure 22.11 without any government intervention.*

Indeed, both property rights assignments lead to the same efficient allocation of resources in the simple model put forward in this section. Although allocative outcomes are the same, the overall outcomes are not because the property rights assignment has distributional effects, just as there were distributional effects earlier for the farmer and rancher.

Coase's analysis suggests that we need not worry about externalities from a public policy perspective. But, of course, we do worry about externalities from a public policy perspective, and therefore, it is worthwhile to consider what makes Coasean bargaining break down.

Limits on Coasean Bargaining

The true insight provided by Coase's analysis is not that efficient outcomes *must* occur but that they *can* occur under the right conditions. Externalities need *not* inevitably lead to market failures. A substantial body of analysis has examined conditions under which Coasean bargaining will occur and what prevents that bargaining from occurring. When should the government intervene, and when can the government assume that private bargains will lead to an economically efficient allocation of resources? Much of the analysis in the area of law and economics, as well as in environmental economics, has shifted in light of Coase's insights.

The first point involves making sure that the property rights are unambiguously assigned. If property rights are not well defined, then the affected parties find negotiation difficult, since it is unclear who should pay whom. Negotiation costs escalate as lawsuits are filed. Much legal analysis is centered on defining property rights in ways that are most likely to produce an economically efficient outcome. If you own a hotel in Miami Beach and have a pool that is sunny throughout the afternoon, do you have the right to prevent a neighboring hotel from erecting an addition on its property that blocks the sun at your pool?[14]

Even when property rights are well defined, the problem of transactions costs remains. Indeed, some argue that market failure is not the externality per se, but rather that transactions costs are sufficiently high to preclude Coasean bargaining. If the magnitude of the externality is small, then it may not pay in time, effort, and legal costs to bargain for an efficient outcome. The externalities we used to introduce Coasean bargaining were purposely limited in nature; only two parties were involved, and hence, transactions costs were likely to be small. But even in this instance, transactions costs could be substantial enough to preclude Coasean bargaining.

We can use Figures 22.10 and 22.11 to see how transactions costs can preclude Coasean bargaining. *Coasean bargaining conceptually proceeds through the incremental trading of rights.* These marginal trades continue as long as the minimum amount that the party with the property right is willing to accept to give up the marginal right is smaller than the maximum amount that the party without the property right is willing to give to obtain the marginal property right. Given zero transactions costs, Coasean bargaining moves production from **t** to **s** if the polluter has the property rights or from zero to **s** if the victim has the property rights. This bargaining occurs because there is a "pie" to be bargained over; Coasean bargaining exists because there is an excess of benefit over cost that the parties in the agreement split.

Transactions costs may be more fixed than variable in nature. An agreement to reduce output by 8 units may well involve the same transactions cost as an agreement to reduce output by 6 units or 4 units. In this event, we can see how large transactions costs, T, must be to preclude Coasean bargaining. This depends on the property rights assignment.

Suppose that the polluter has the property rights. The bargaining pie in this instance is triangle **rts** = \$24, so this represents the maximum amount that transactions costs can be before Coasean bargaining is precluded. If transactions costs are smaller than **rts**, a Coasean bargain will be made, since net benefits of **rts** – T > 0 remain. The victim pays the transactions costs (since the victim does not have the property rights).

Suppose that the victim has the property rights. In this instance, the bargaining pie is **uvs** = \$24. (These two magnitudes [**rts** and **uvs**] need not be equal; they would have been different if the MEC's slope or intercept had been different from shown, for example.) If transactions costs of Coasean bargaining are smaller than **uvs**, then they will be paid by the polluter, and **uvs** – T > 0 remains to be split between the polluter and victim. If transactions costs are fixed, then an efficient bargain will be struck as long as those costs are smaller than the size of the gross gain from Coasean bargaining. If transactions costs are larger than the gross gain, then Coasean bargaining is precluded.

Suppose that transactions costs are variable, rather than fixed. For example, the lawyer hired by the party without the rights offers to accept payment based on the number of units of damage that has been abated.[15] Suppose that the lawyer charges a fee to the victim of T = \$3 per unit of x reduced (when the polluter has the property rights). The resulting Coasean solution is shown in Figure 22.12A. The green curve labeled $MSC_x - T$ represents the net social benefit schedule, once transactions costs of T = **rd** = **ab** = \$3 per unit of x reduced are imposed on victims. Coasean bargaining will lead to 12 units of x produced. At this output level, the maximum that the victim is willing to pay the polluter is **bc** = \$2 (plus **ab** = \$3 to the lawyer), which is also the minimum that the polluter is willing to accept ($P_x - MPC_x$ = **bc** = \$2 at x = 12). Coasean bargaining reduces x output from 16 to 12, leading to legal fees of **rdba** = \$12 and a net gain that is split between the polluter and victim of **dtb** = \$6. Firm x produces more than the socially optimal

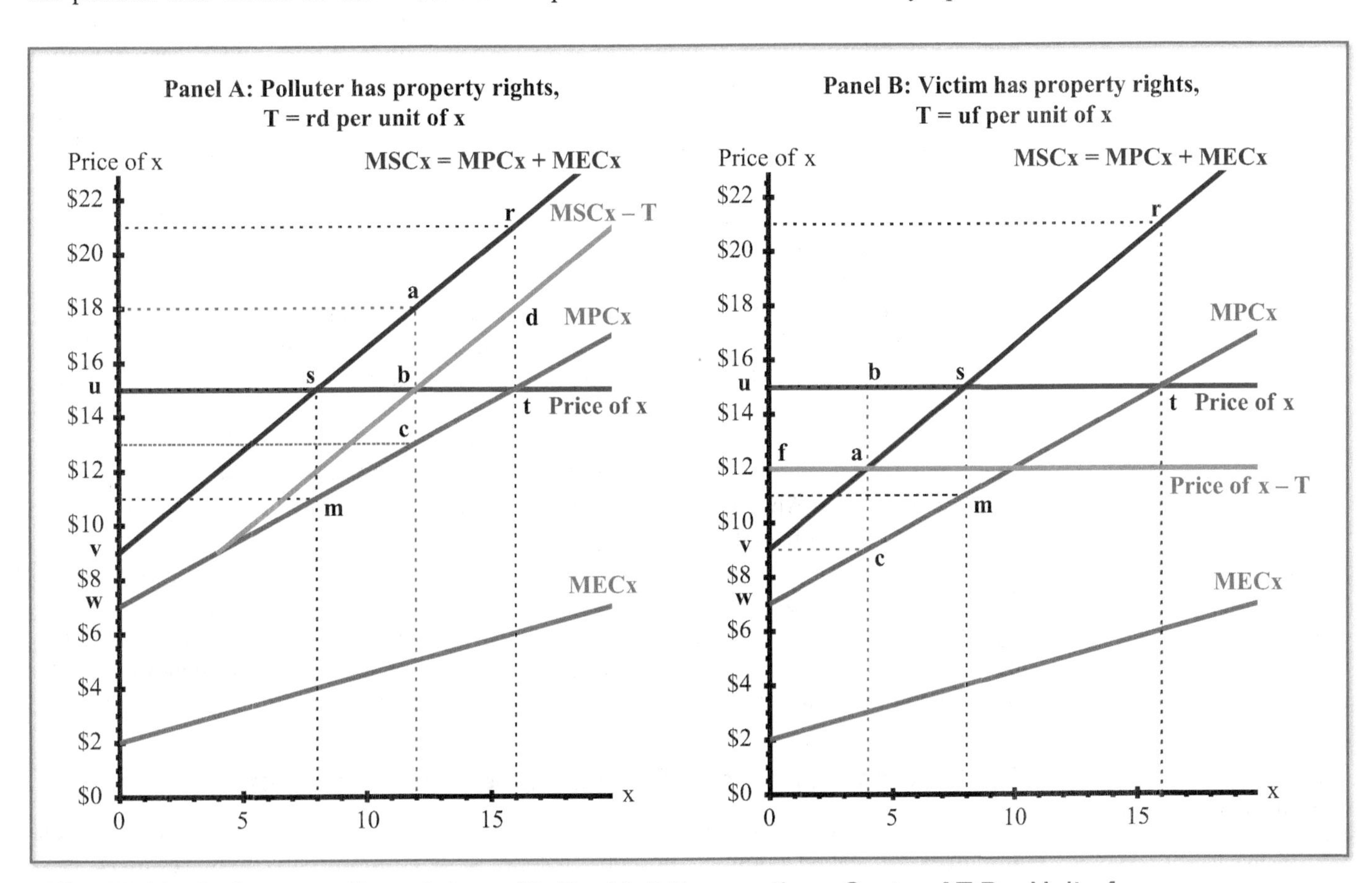

FIGURE 22.12 Coasean Bargaining with Per-Unit Transactions Costs of T Per Unit of x

output (12 at **b**, versus 8 at **s**). The market shows a deadweight loss of *over*production of **abs** = $6 even after Coasean bargaining occurs because variable transactions costs alter the marginal bargaining signal perceived by the victim.

The reverse is true if the victim has the property rights and transactions costs are variable, as depicted in Figure 22.12B. Suppose that the polluter must pay a transactions cost of T = **uf** = **ba** = $3 for every unit of x that it is allowed to produce. Since Firm x receives a gross benefit of P_x = $15, the benefit remaining after transactions costs are paid is $P_x - T$ = $12 per unit of x produced. Coasean bargaining will lead to 4 units of x produced. At this output level, the maximum that the polluter is willing to pay the victim is **ac** (plus **ba** to the lawyer), which is also the minimum that the victim is willing to accept. Coasean bargaining increases x output from 0 to 4, resulting in legal fees of **ubaf** = $12 and a net gain that is split between the polluter and victim of **fav** = $6. Firm x produces less than the socially optimal output (4 at **a**, versus 8 at **s**). The market shows a deadweight loss of *under*production, given by **abs** = $6, even after Coasean bargaining occurs because variable transactions costs alter the marginal bargaining signal perceived by the polluter.[16]

The Coasean analysis could also be done with abatement, rather than the polluting firm's output, on the horizontal axis. The qualitative results would be the same: Coasean bargaining would lead to an efficient level of abatement if transactions costs were negligible. If such transactions costs alter marginal signals (since they are variable in nature), Coasean bargaining may reduce the effect of the externality, but an efficient outcome will not occur; DWL will remain.

As noted earlier, transactions costs increase as the number of parties involved in the bargain increases. If a town is located downstream from Firm x and victims have the property rights, then Firm x must deal with many victims, rather than only one. Such situations are inherently more difficult because it makes sense for individual victims to hold out in reaching agreement because their bargaining position is enhanced if they are the last to reach a bargain with the polluter. But of course, all individuals have the same incentive to hold out and increase their bargaining position. Transactions costs may well become prohibitive, even if costs and benefits are well understood, and Coasean bargaining (with zero transactions costs) should proceed.

Coase forced economists and legal scholars to redirect their efforts toward a deeper understanding of property rights and the analysis of transactions costs as an impediment to the efficient internalization of externalities. As a simple example, note in the analysis from Figure 22.12 that the deadweight loss of overproduction and the deadweight loss from underproduction are the same size. This is based on an assumption of equal transactions costs per unit of output change, regardless of property rights assignment. This need not be the case. Suppose that the polluter has lower per-unit transactions costs (legal fees) than the victim, $T_p < T_v$. In this event, we would want to provide the victims with the initial property rights. The DWL of underproduction of **abs** that results when the polluter bargains to **a** in Figure 22.12B (where $P_x - T_p$ intersects MSC_x) is smaller than the DWL of overproduction of **abs** that results had we provided the polluter with the initial property rights and had the victims bargain toward **b** in Figure 22.12A (where $MSC_x - T_v$ intersects P_x), given $T_p < T_v$. An understanding of transactions costs allows us to make the most efficient choice of property rights assignment.

Coase single-handedly altered the analytical landscape surrounding externalities. Coase does not argue that Pigouvian taxes are never necessary to internalize an externality. He simply points to conditions under which they are not required to internalize the externality. Primary among these conditions are that property rights are unambiguously defined and that transactions costs involved in transferring those rights are negligible.

22.1F Common Property Resources and the Tragedy of the Commons

common property resource: A common property resource is a resource to which anyone has free access.

Sometimes, a resource is available to all who wish to access it without explicit cost. Such resources are called common property resources. A **common property resource** is a resource to which anyone has free access. This is sometimes called a *common pool resource*.

A classic example is a common grazing pasture. In preindustrial and early industrial societies, the typical practice was to have a pasture where anyone could graze their cattle. (Boston Commons was once such a grazing pasture.) In this example, each herdsman creates a negative externality on other herdsmen using the common resource; each one is only interested in the returns they receive from grazing cattle on the common land. They do not consider the damage that results from grazing their herd. Overgrazing results. This is an example of the "*tragedy of the commons*."[17]

Consider cattle that are raised for milk. As the number of cattle using the commons increases, the total milk production is likely to increase, but the amount of production per cow is likely to decrease, due to competition among the cows for the grass on the commons. The cow's average productivity declines, but its marginal productivity declines more quickly. An individual using the commons will add an additional cow as long as the average productivity from the cow is worth more than the real resource cost of the cow. But from a social welfare point of view, total productivity is maximized when the marginal productivity from a cow is worth the real resource cost of the cow. Since average exceeds marginal productivity in this instance, deadweight loss from overgrazing results.

This can be seen on a simple graph. Suppose that the average productivity of a cow declines linearly with the number of cows using the field. In this event, marginal product has the same intercept and twice the slope as average product (just like in Chapter 12, where MR has the same intercept and twice the slope as inverse demand). If cows were "free," then total milk production is maximized at the point where MP = 0, but instead, cows have a real resource cost, which is assumed to be constant. Suppose that this cost is measured in units of milk. Figure 22.13 depicts the situation. Cows will be added until the expected (average) productivity of the last cow equals the real resource cost of that cow. This occurs at point **c** with 80 cows, each of which produces 1,200 pounds of milk (the same as the opportunity cost of the cow). No social surplus results from this situation because milk produced (1,200 pounds per cow times 80 cows) equals the real resource cost of the cows used to produce the milk.

Society would benefit if the herdsmen could be coerced into reducing the total number of cows. The 80th cow produced a net increase of only 400 pounds of milk (at **d**), substantially below the average productivity of 1,200 pounds. It is not that the last cow produces 800 fewer pounds of milk; it is that average productivity of all cows on the commons declines by 10 pounds for each additional cow added to the commons (–10 is the slope of the average product curve). Cows should be removed from the commons as long as the marginal product of the last cow is less than its real resource cost. The socially optimal number of cows using the commons is 40 in this instance (at **s**). Each cow produces a surplus of **bs** = 400 pounds of milk per cow, so the net benefit to society of this outcome is area **abse** = 16,000 pounds of milk. This is the excess milk produced over the real resource cost of the 40 cows. If this is not done, deadweight loss represented by area **cds** = 16,000 pounds of milk results. (The DWL associated with the tragedy of the commons is the same size as the net benefit to society if the tragedy is avoided.)

How can the tragedy of the commons be avoided? One way would be to have the local government charge a user tax of 400 pounds of milk per cow. This would increase the real resource cost of a cow to 1,600 pounds of milk, in which case 40 cows will use the commons (the average product of 40 cows is 1,600 pounds of milk per cow). Alternatively, the government could sell the commons to a single person, and that person could charge a fee for use of the commons (of 400 pounds per cow). Or the owner of the (now private) commons would decide to let 40 cows graze on the land. An individual owner would view the appropriate decision in terms of marginal product, much like a monopolist would use MR rather than average revenue (inverse demand) when making profit-maximizing decisions.

The tragedy of the commons occurs in many other situations. Two other traditional examples are fishing grounds and hunting on public lands. Fishing on lakes, rivers, and the ocean exhibits the common pool problem. Consider a commercial fishing boat on the Georges Bank. Each additional boat faces a larger average catch than its marginal catch because each boat imposes a negative externality on other boats using the Georges

FIGURE 22.13 The Tragedy of the Commons

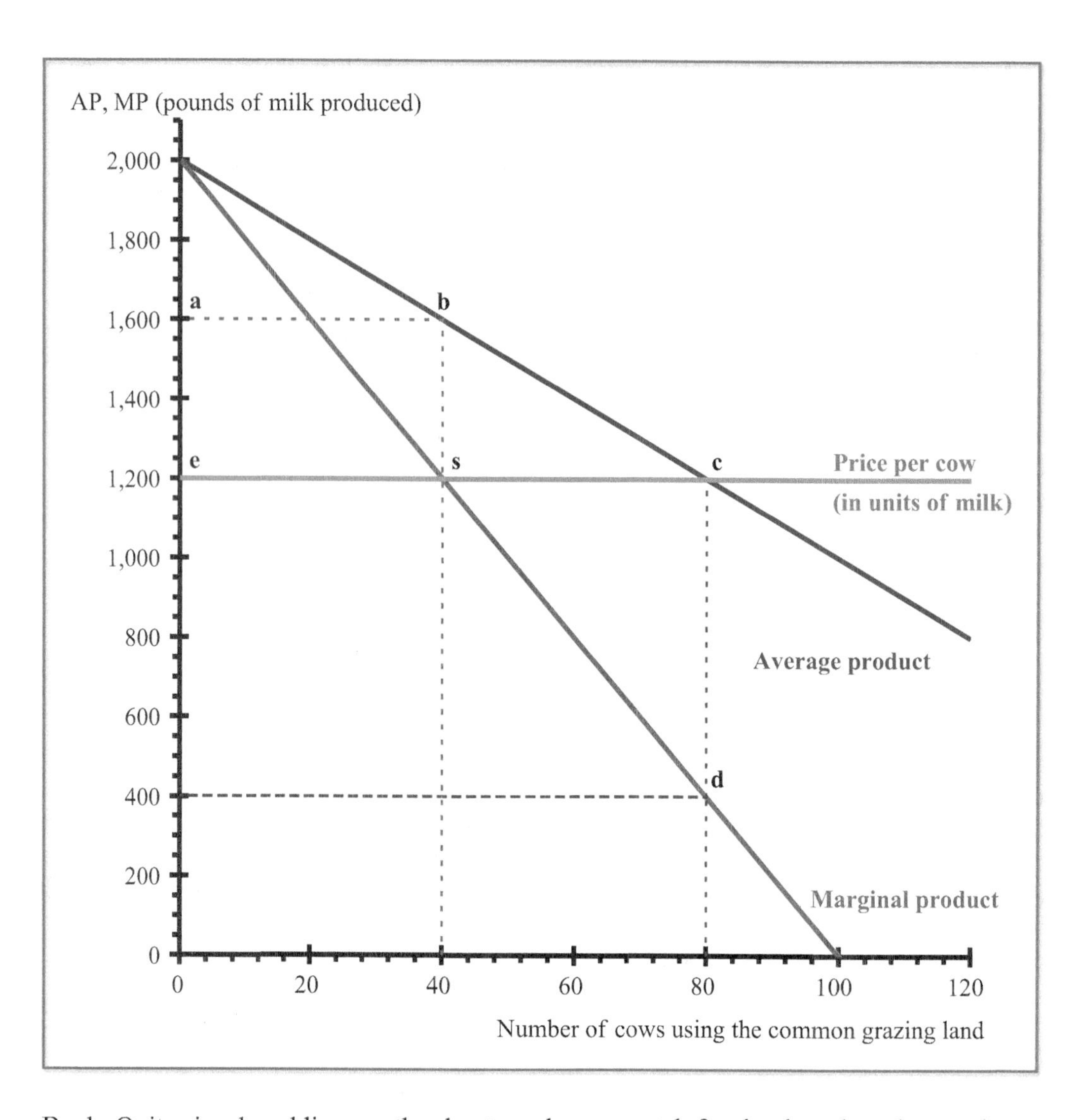

Bank. Quite simply, adding another boat produces a catch for that boat but also produces a reduced catch for other boats. The excessive fishing of the common resource causes significant damage to the stock of fish and creates problems for future harvests. Requiring hunting and fishing licenses and imposing maximum catch limits reduce the overall damage caused to the common resource.

Oil and natural-gas fields also exhibit the common pool problem if a number of independent producers have access to a single oil field. The oil exists in a common reservoir beneath the ground, but ownership of the oil coming out of the field accrues to the producer who extracts the oil. Individual producers face a different incentive structure from society in this instance. Individual producers wish to extract the oil as quickly as possible because oil will migrate and property rights are established upon extraction. The total amount of oil available from a reservoir, however, depends on how quickly the oil is extracted. If oil is extracted too quickly, total reservoir yield declines. As a result, oil fields are sometimes "unitized." Unitization delegates the property rights to a single producer but apportions net revenues among all parties. Focusing the property rights on a single party acts in the same way as giving property rights to the commons to a single person. This producer will extract oil more slowly, using a smaller number of wells, resulting in more barrels extracted, as well as smaller capital costs.

Common property rights produce a problem of overuse. Placing the right to the property in the hands of a single party can eliminate this problem. The single party will internalize the externality and produce the socially optimal outcome. Licensing and taxation can also reduce the economic inefficiency created due to the common pool problem.

Summary of Section 22.1

Externalities exist when the effect of an economic agent's actions is not fully incorporated into the market system. Consumers or producers can cause externalities, and they can affect consumers or producers. Externalities can be positive or negative in nature. Positive externalities are often called external economies, and negative externalities are often called external diseconomies. Externalities are a market failure because they result in a misallocation of resources. Too few resources are devoted to external economies, and too many are devoted to external diseconomies. Network externalities are a situation where one individual's demand for a product is based on how many other individuals demand the product. The bandwagon effect is a positive network externality, and the snob effect is a negative network externality.

The government has developed a variety of public policy programs to mitigate the problems associated with externalities. Since society requires goods producing a negative externality to have reduced production and consumption, one method to induce this behavior is to tax the production of the product. Goods exhibiting positive externalities require increased production and consumption, and as a result, subsidies offer one method to induce such behavior. Taxes or subsidies such as these are known as Pigouvian taxes.

An alternative method of reducing pollution is to directly tax emissions. Emissions fees (also called effluent fees) are taxes on pollution. If appropriately sized, these taxes can induce the socially optimal behavior. The same behavior can be produced by pollution abatement subsidies, but the distributive effect of emissions fees and pollution abatement subsidies is dramatically different. Emissions fees implicitly give the property rights to society, and pollution abatement subsidies implicitly give the property rights to the polluting entity. An intermediate property rights assignment is to impose a pollution standard on the polluting entity.

Fees are preferred to standards if there are differences in the marginal cost of abatement across firms, but the marginal benefit of abatement is common across firms. A standards approach forces all firms to comply, while a fee approach can achieve the same level of abatement at lower cost. Fees are not always preferred to standards because the deadweight loss from a misestimated fee may be larger or smaller than the deadweight loss from a similarly misestimated standard.

A major shift in the analysis of externalities came with the publication in 1960 of the article "The Problem of Social Cost" by Ronald Coase. Coase argues that externalities need not lead to resource misallocation because the parties involved will voluntarily bargain with one another to optimally internalize the externality. For this to occur, the property rights assignment needs to be well defined, and the transactions costs involved in Coasean bargaining need to be negligible. The Coase Theorem offers a theoretical norm from which to examine the effects of externalities. Coase shifted the analytical focus to a deeper discussion of property rights and transactions costs. Coase acknowledges that transactions costs are often present; the question that then arises is: Is there a property rights assignment that minimizes the costs of Coasean bargaining? If so, that is the property rights assignment to use.

One final type of externality discussed in this section is a common property resource (also called a common pool resource). A resource to which anyone has free access is called a common property resource. Examples include common grazing land, fishing and hunting grounds, and oil fields. Individual economic agents tend to overuse common property resources, and this leads to a deterioration in the common property resource. Fish at the fishing ground become scarce, or the common pasture becomes barren. Altering the property rights assignment so that a single agent is placed in charge of the common property resource can avert the problem. A single owner will internalize the negative externality created by the common pool resource. Taxes can also restrict the use of the common property resource. Another common solution is to require licenses (for example, a fishing or hunting license) and to impose maximum catch limits.

22.2 Public Goods

Prerequisite: Chapter 16

Public goods offer another situation in which there is a market failure. The private market often provides too little of public goods, and therefore, the government often intervenes and provides them. National defense is the classic example of a public good, but there are many other examples as well. In Section 22.2A, we examine the nature and scope of public goods. In Section 22.2B, we examine the market for public goods and describe the requirements for the efficient provision of a public good.

Section 22.2 Outline

22.2A The Nature and Scope of Public Goods

22.2B The Market for Public Goods

22.2A The Nature and Scope of Public Goods

One of government's most important responsibilities is to provide public goods. However, not all government-provided goods are public goods. The term *public good* tends to create confusion, and therefore, it is worthwhile to examine what economists mean by public goods.

nonexclusive good: A good is nonexclusive if it is impossible or expensive to exclude individuals from benefiting from the good.

Public goods have two properties. One is that the good is nonexclusive. A good is **nonexclusive** if it is impossible or expensive to exclude individuals from benefiting from the good. National defense and access to public lands are classic examples of nonexclusive goods. While city streets could be turned into toll roads, it would be expensive, and as a result, city streets also are nonexclusive. If a good is nonexclusive, it is not *possible* to ration its use. By contrast, toll roads such as the Pennsylvania Turnpike or the Golden Gate Bridge are exclusive. And, of course, everything you buy in your local grocery or department store is exclusive. It is possible to limit the use of these goods because you are not allowed to remove them from the store without paying for them.

nonrivalrous good: A good is nonrivalrous if consumption by one party does not diminish the ability of other parties to consume the good.

Public goods also are nonrivalrous. A good is **nonrivalrous** if consumption by one party does not diminish the ability of other parties to consume the good. Once a nonrivalrous good is produced, consumption by an additional person involves no additional cost of production. An uncongested road is nonrivalrous. You driving on the road does not affect your neighbors also driving on it. If a good is nonrivalrous, it is not *desirable* to ration its use. National defense is once again an example, as are roads during off-peak travel times. By contrast, roads during peak travel times are rivalrous because each additional driver diminishes the ability of other drivers to use the road.

pure public good: A pure public good is nonrivalrous and nonexclusive.

club good: A club good is nonrivalrous and exclusive.

private good: A private good is rivalrous and exclusive.

Goods that are both nonrivalrous and nonexclusive are called **pure public goods**. It is neither possible nor desirable to ration use of a pure public good. Impure public goods have one but not both of these attributes. We have already described nonexclusive goods that are rivalrous as *common property resources* in Section 22.1E (since these goods also can be analyzed within the rubric of externalities). Goods that are exclusive but nonrivalrous are called **club goods**. **Private goods** are rivalrous and exclusive; they are the kinds of goods that we typically encounter in everyday life. Private goods have been the central focus of most of the text.

Table 22.2 provides examples of each of these types of goods. It is worth noting that some goods move from one category to another, depending on the specific attributes of the good. A road can be a toll road or a nontoll road (exclusive versus nonexclusive), and it may also be crowded or uncrowded (rivalrous versus nonrivalrous). It should also

TABLE 22.2 A Typology of Economic Goods

		Excludability	
		Exclusive	***Nonexclusive***
Rivalry	***Rivalrous***	**Private Goods**	**Common Property Resources**
		Rock concert (sold out)	Common grazing grounds
		Food, clothing	Fishing on rivers and lakes
		Automobile	Crowded public park
		Crowded toll road	Crowded nontoll road
	Nonrivalrous	**Club Goods**	**Pure Public Goods**
		Rock concert (not sold out)	National defense
		Cable TV and pay-per-view TV	Over-the-air TV
		Restricted-access websites	Free websites
		Uncrowded toll road	Uncrowded nontoll road

be noted that rivalry and excludability are not strictly dichotomous. Although the table forces the dichotomy, some private goods are more "private" than others, and some public goods are more "public" than others.

As noted at the beginning of this section, the government provides goods that are not pure public goods. Public education is provided, for example, not because it is a pure public good but because education produces external economies. Public education is excludable (you must be accepted to a public university, and once accepted, you must still pay tuition) as well as rivalrous (since there are only a [reasonably] fixed number of spaces in each entering class). A national park has some degree of excludability (since you must pay an entry fee), and rivalry exists (because there are a limited number of campsites available at a given park). Nonetheless, both are publicly provided. (Interestingly, city parks are more nonexclusive, since it would be impractical to exclude people, due to the ease of access to most of these facilities. New York City's Central Park could be fenced in and an entry fee could be charged, but part of the utility of Central Park is due to its openness.)

22.2B The Market for Public Goods

Any amount of the public good produced provides benefits for all consumers because consumption is nonexclusive. This is in marked contrast to private goods, where the benefits of consumption are exclusionary. Before we examine the optimal provision of a public good, it is worthwhile to review what we require for the optimal provision of a private good.

With private goods, we require that each individual's marginal valuation of the good equals the marginal cost of production of that good. The individual's marginal valuation is the height of the individual's demand curve (recall from Chapter 12 that we also called this inverse demand). Marginal valuation for society (the height of market demand) is obtained as the sum of individual demands at each price. Put another way, market demand is the *horizontal sum* of individual demand curves. Mathematically, this was stated as Equation 12.1, reproduced here as Equation 22.4:

$$D(P) = d_1(P) + \ldots + d_n(P), \text{ given n individuals in the market.} \quad \textbf{(22.4)}$$

As shown in Chapter 16, the efficient outcome occurs at the intersection of supply and demand. This determines a market clearing price that is charged to each individual consumer. To find the distribution of output across consumers, we simply look at each individual consumer's demand at that price. (This just "unpacks" market demand into each of the individual demands.) With private goods, we are interested in how we distribute output across individuals. Each individual faces the same price, and that price acts as the rationing device to determine how much each individual consumes. *With private goods, price allows us to distribute output across consumers. Exactly the opposite is true with public goods because public goods are nonexclusive.*

The Demand for a Public Good

With a public good, each consumer is able to consume the entire amount of the good available. This is true because the good is nonexclusive; no consumer can be excluded from the use of the good, once it is produced. In this instance, we should include the benefits to all consumers for each unit of the good produced. To find demand for a public good, we *vertically sum* marginal valuations at each output level. If we denote the marginal valuation for the xth unit by individual i as $MV_i(x)$, then the marginal value to society of the xth unit, $MSV(x)$, given n individuals who benefit from the public good, is:

$$MSV(x) = MV_1(x) + \ldots + MV_n(x). \quad \textbf{(22.5)}$$

Since the good is also nonrivalrous, allowing multiple consumers to benefit from the good does not diminish the marginal valuation (demand) of any consumer.

Figure 22.14 compares the demand for public and private goods, based on the demand curves used in Figure 12.2. Figure 22.14A replicates the disaggregated private good information from Figure 12.2 on a single diagram. This information is also examined algebraically in Equations 12.4–12.6. The green market demand curve, D(P), is the *horizontal*

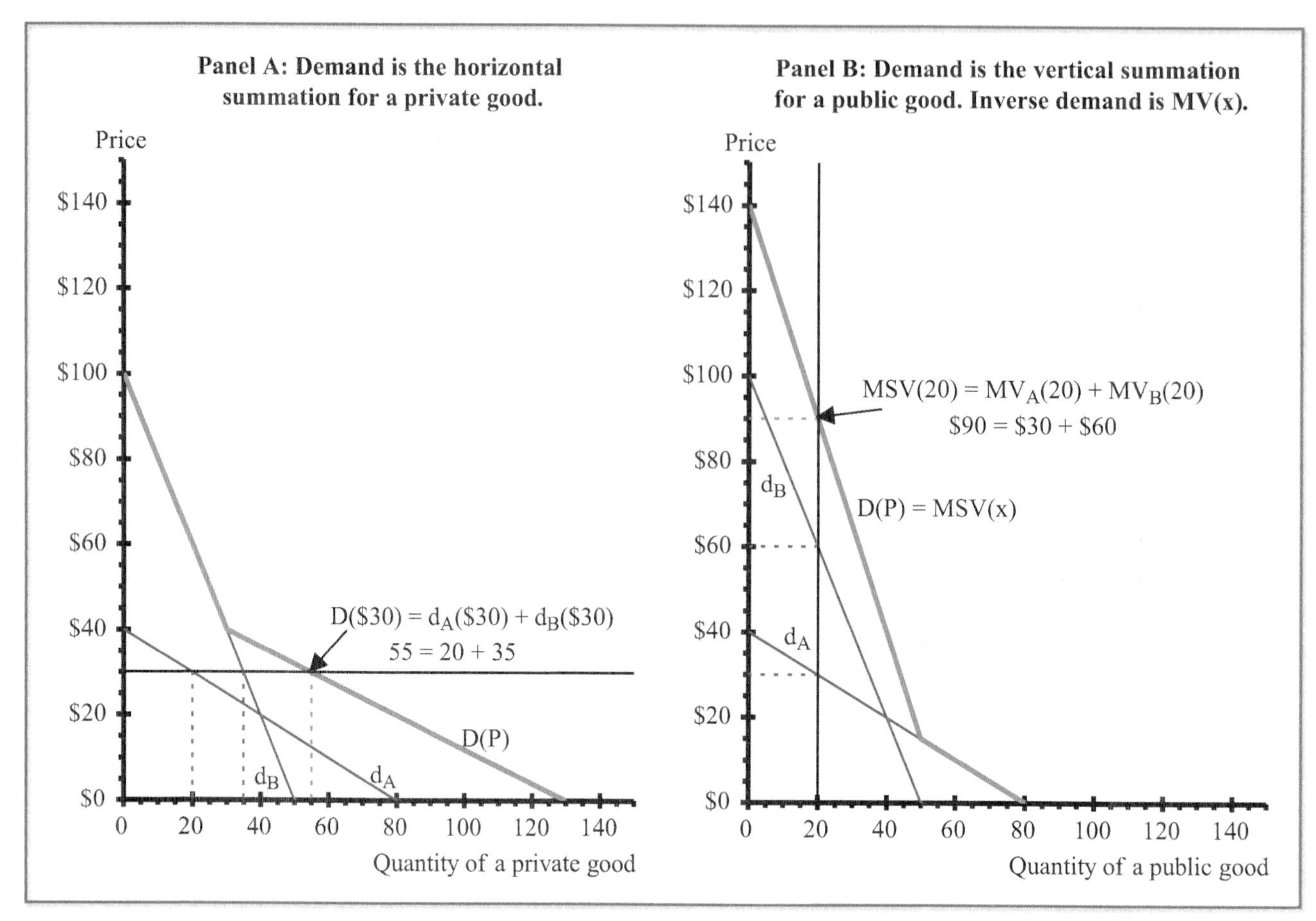

FIGURE 22.14 Comparing Demand for Public and Private Goods

sum of Andy's blue demand and Beth's red demand (Equation 12.5a: $d_A(P) = 80 - 2 \cdot P$, and Equation 12.5b: $d_B(P) = 50 - 0.5 \cdot P$), using Equation 22.4. Market demand is the sum of these individual demand curves. (Equation 12.6 describes this sum; it is reproduced here as Equation 22.6.)

Equation over Price Range, P	Individuals in the Market at This Price	
$D(P) = 0$ for $P \geq 100$.	None	
$D(P) = 50 - 0.5 \cdot P$ for $100 \geq P \geq 40$.	Beth only	**(22.6)**
$D(P) = 130 - 2.5 \cdot P$ for $40 \geq P \geq 0$.	Andy and Beth	

This is piecewise linear because, at different prices, different individuals are in the market. For example, at a price of \$50, only Beth is in the market, so that market demand $D(\$50) = d_B(\$50) = 20$. At a price of \$30, market demand is $55 = D(\$30)$. This demand is the sum of Andy's demand of $20 = d_A(\$30)$ and Beth's demand of $35 = d_B(\$30)$, as shown in Figure 22.14A.

If instead d_A and d_B represent Andy's and Beth's demands for a public good, then we vertically sum demands to find market demand because the good is nonexclusionary. This is algebraically described as the sum of inverse demands (rather than demands), using Equation 22.5, because inverse demand is marginal valuation as a function of output. Given Andy's and Beth's inverse demands (Equations 12.4a and 12.4b: $MV_A(x) = 40 - 0.5 \cdot x$, and $MV_B(x) = 100 - 2 \cdot x$), we have the green marginal social valuation (market demand) schedule in Figure 22.14B as the *vertical* sum of Andy's blue inverse demand and Beth's red inverse demand. As with the horizontal sum for the private good in Equation 22.6, we have a piecewise linear market demand for the public good, since only Andy values more than 50 units of x:

Equation over Output Range, x	Individuals with $MV(x) \geq 0$ for This x	
$MSV(x) = MV_A(x) + MV_B(x)$ $= 140 - 2.5 \cdot x$ for $x \leq 50$.	Andy and Beth	
$MSV(x) = MV_A(x) = 40 - 0.5 \cdot x$ for $50 \leq x \leq 80$.	Andy only	**(22.7)**
$MSV(x) = 0$ for $x > 80$.	None	

The marginal social value of the 20th unit of output (height of market demand) is $\$90 = MSV(20)$. This is the sum of Andy's marginal value of $\$30 = MV_A(20)$ and Beth's marginal value of $\$60 = MV_B(20)$, as shown in Figure 22.14B.

The distinction between private and public goods is seen in how we sum demand across consumers to obtain market demand. With private goods, demand is summed horizontally because all consumers respond to a single price signal and determine how many units to produce based on that signal. With public goods, demand is summed vertically because consumers respond to a single quantity, given the nonexclusive nature of the good in question.

The Efficient Provision of a Public Good

Economic efficiency requires that marginal social value equal marginal cost. Marginal social value is the vertical sum of individual consumer marginal valuations for the public good. For simplicity, we will use the same two-person model used in Figure 22.14B and described algebraically by Equation 22.7. Suppose that marginal cost is flat at a price of \$90 per unit. Given this, 20 units of the good should be provided because, as noted earlier, $MV_A(20) = \$30$, and $MV_B(20) = \$60$. The socially optimal solution occurs when $MSV(20) = MC = \$90$ at point **S** in Figure 22.15.

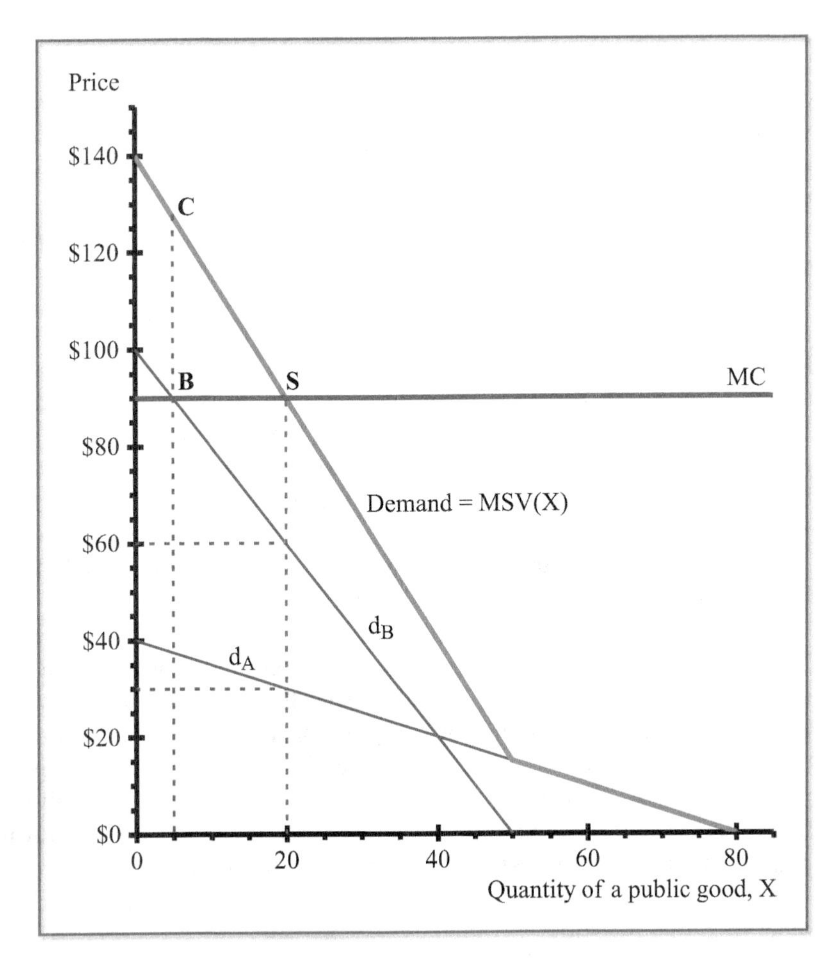

FIGURE 22.15 The Optimal Provision of a Public Good

Given the assumptions depicted in Figure 22.15, if output is more or less than 20 units, deadweight loss results. This is readily apparent in the diagram. The slope of the demand curve at **S** is –2.5, according to Equation 22.7. If 19 rather than 20 units of the public good are produced, Andy values the 19th unit at $30.50, and Beth values the 19th unit at $62.00, so total marginal valuation of the 19th unit is $92.50. This unit should be produced because total marginal valuation exceeds the marginal cost of $90 by $2.50. If this production does not occur, society faces a DWL of underproduction of $2.50. The reverse is true for the 21st unit: MSV(21) = $87.50, which is $2.50 below the marginal cost of production. If 21 units are produced, a DWL of overproduction of $2.50 occurs.

The private market will not achieve this level of production. Suppose that the government does not attempt to intervene in any way in this market. Given P = $90, Andy will not purchase any units of the good (he will only purchase this good if the price is less than $40). Beth demands 5 units at point **B**. Beth will not purchase more than 5 units because $d_B(x) < \$90$ when $x > 5$. Too little output results from private provision. Notice that even though Beth purchases 5 units, Andy receives benefits on these units (represented by the area under d_A from 0 to 5 units). Indeed, the marginal value of the fifth unit to Andy is $37.50, an amount that is, by construction, length **BC** in Figure 22.15. Since Andy's valuation is not incorporated into Beth's decision, deadweight loss due to underconsumption of the privately provided public good results. This is represented by area **CBS**.

Complications to the Efficient Provision of a Public Good

free rider: A free rider is an individual who benefits from a nonexclusive good purchased by others.

One aspect of the private provision of a public good noted previously is that once Beth purchases 5 units of output, Andy is able to benefit, despite not having to pay anything in exchange for the benefit received. Andy acts as a free rider in this instance. A **free rider** is an individual who benefits from a nonexclusive good purchased by others.

Free riders create a problem for public goods because individual economic actors realize that they can benefit from a good, even if someone else pays. An individual is better off if a public good is purchased by someone else because the individual is able to avoid the cost of purchasing the good. Individual economic actors, therefore, are reluctant to contribute voluntarily toward the purchase of a public good. Of course, all individuals will think the same way: Each will avoid paying for the public good, hoping that someone else will pay for it. Each attempts to get a free ride from the efforts of others within the community.

We can see the problem more clearly if we adjust marginal cost so that each individual purchases the good as a private good. Andy is only willing to purchase the good if the price is less than $40, so consider a price of $30. The situation is shown in Figure 22.16. Suppose that there is no public provision of the public good, but Andy and Beth know about each other's preferences for the good (this is a large assumption, as we will see later). Andy would like to purchase **A** = 20 units, and Beth would like to purchase **B** = 35 units. This does not mean, however, that they wish to purchase 55 units between them because each can utilize the units purchased by the other. We will soon see that the best-case scenario in this instance is that, together, they will purchase 35 units, 9 fewer than is socially optimal (at **S**). If this occurs, a DWL of underproduction of **CBS** results. But that best-case scenario is, perhaps, overly optimistic because both Andy and Beth are likely to try to get a free ride from the other.

Consider the situation from Andy's point of view. At a price of $30, Andy will purchase 20 units of the public good if he knows that Beth will not purchase the good. But to the extent that Andy knows Beth's preferences for this good, Andy will likely notice that Beth has a much higher consumer surplus for these units than he does.[18] Andy might try to wait to see if Beth purchases these units, in which case he could get a free ride on that purchase. But Beth is likely to realize that, if she waits, Andy will purchase more than half of the 35 units of the public good that Beth would purchase—if Andy can be made to believe that Beth will not step in and purchase those units. Beth will try to get a free ride from Andy. This is akin to a game of "chicken"; each individual tries to "out-wait" the other to gain a free-rider advantage.

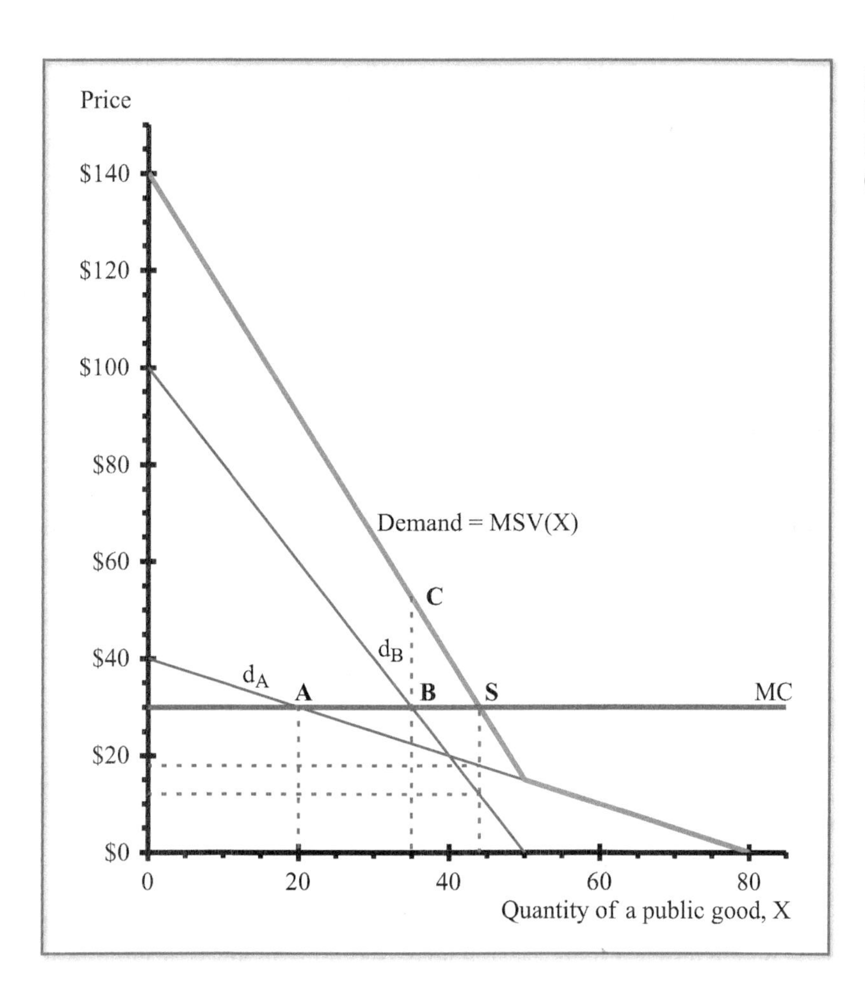

FIGURE 22.16 Free Riding, Given Private Provision of a Public Good

The *free-rider problem* becomes more severe as the number of individuals sharing the public good increases. The more local the public good, the smaller is the free-rider problem, *ceteris paribus*. If 5 farmers would benefit from a levee that reduces the probability that their land will flood, these farmers are more likely to contribute and less likely to try to get a free ride from their neighbors than if 100 farmers are affected. When there are only 4 other farmers involved, each knows that there is little ability to get a free ride from the others, but when there are 99 other farmers involved, the free-rider problem is greater.

Lindahl Pricing

The efficient provision of a public good requires that we understand the marginal costs and benefits associated with various public goods. The costs are relatively easy to determine (e.g., we should be able to estimate the cost of a 10-mile-long levee on a weak riverbank). The difficult thing to determine is the benefits of such projects, even though we have thus far assumed that we knew the marginal valuation schedules.

A socially optimal solution is to have individuals pay according to their marginal valuations, even though marginal valuations differ across individuals. This is called Lindahl pricing. **Lindahl pricing** involves having individuals who benefit from a nonexclusive good share the cost by paying different prices for the good, based on their marginal valuation schedules. Based on a marginal cost of production of $90, the Lindahl pricing solution shown in Figure 22.15 is to have Andy pay $30 and Beth pay $60 for each of the 20 units supplied at **S**. If, instead, the marginal cost of production is $30, as shown in Figure 22.16, the Lindahl solution is to have Andy pay $18 and Beth pay $12 for each of the 44 units supplied at **S**. Both solutions use individual marginal valuations rather than total valuations (i.e., consumer surplus) of those units. (Note in this example that Beth pays less under Lindahl pricing as long as MC < $40 because Andy and Beth have the same marginal valuation of 40 units of the public good ($MV_A(40) = MV_B(40) = \$20$). This

Lindahl pricing: Lindahl pricing involves having individuals who benefit from a nonexclusive good share the cost by paying different prices for the good, based on their marginal valuation schedules.

is true despite Beth having greater consumer surplus, given her more inelastic marginal valuation schedule.)

With Lindahl pricing, there is price discrimination to achieve economic efficiency. Lindahl pricing can be thought of as allocating the cost of the public good across individuals, given a common level of the good. This sharply contrasts with using the market to allocate private goods.

Note: *With private goods, the market allocates quantity using a common price, but with public goods, Lindahl pricing allocates price using a common quantity.*

Getting individuals to reveal their true preferences for public goods is inherently difficult because there is a free-rider problem associated with preference revelation. The problem with the Lindahl outcome is that if the government states that it will pursue Lindahl pricing, then each individual has an incentive to understate personal preferences, in the hope that others will bear the burden of paying for the public good. That is, each individual will misstate (lie about) personal preferences in the hope of getting a free ride from others. But, of course, the same incentive is true for all individuals. Therefore, overall willingness to pay is understated.

Suppose that the opposite is true: Suppose that individuals believe that there is *no* link between their professed preferences for a public good and what they would have to pay for that good. In this event, it would be in every individuals' interest to exaggerate their benefits derived from the good. In both instances, there is an incentive to lie about personal preferences for a public good. This is sometimes called the *preference revelation problem*. This same incentive to lie does *not* hold for private goods. With private goods, the benefits accrue entirely to the consumer, and it does not make sense for the consumer to purchase something if the item's marginal valuation is not at least as large as its price.

The free-rider problem and the preference revelation problem lead to a general underprovision of public goods by private individuals. The government often steps in to provide public goods. Of course, the level of public goods to provide is not easy to determine and is subject to much political debate.

Summary of Section 22.2

Public goods are goods that are nonrivalrous and nonexclusive. A good is nonrivalrous if, once the good is produced, additional consumers can benefit from the good without diminishing the ability of other consumers to benefit from it. An uncrowded road is nonrivalrous because additional drivers can use it at no additional cost. By contrast, a hamburger is rivalrous. If I eat a hamburger, you cannot eat the same hamburger. A good is nonexclusive if it is difficult or impossible to exclude individuals from benefiting from the good. A city street is nonexclusive; certainly, it is *possible* to imagine setting up tollbooths on city streets, but the cost would be prohibitive. A toll road, by contrast, is exclusive; it is easy to exclude nonpurchasers.

The efficient provision of public goods requires determining a marginal social valuation schedule (this is the inverse market demand for the public good). Marginal social valuation is the vertical sum of individual marginal valuations (individual inverse demand). This sharply contrasts with private goods, where market demand is the horizontal sum of individual demands. The distinction can be viewed based on what is constant in each situation: *With private goods, all consumers face the same price, so the sum of outputs is horizontal (for fixed price); with public goods, all consumers face the same output, so the sum of marginal valuations is vertical (for fixed quantity).*

The efficient level of output is where the marginal cost of production equals the marginal social value of that level of production. If the government does not intervene in public goods markets, too little of the public good is usually produced. Deadweight loss results from this private underprovision for several reasons. Private provision may not occur, since it may not be in the best interest of any individual to undertake the purchase (i.e., individual marginal value is less than marginal cost), despite social marginal value being above marginal cost. Even if individuals purchase the public good, they will only purchase up to the point where their marginal valuation equals the marginal cost of the good. Social marginal valuation will exceed this private gross benefit because other consumers benefit once the good is purchased. Nonpurchasers get a free ride from those who purchase the public good.

In general, individuals will try to get a free ride from others within society. Since a public good is nonexclusive, those who do not pay for the good still benefit from it. The free rider benefits more than another individual with identical demand who pays for the good because both receive the same marginal valuation, even though only one individual pays for it.

The free-rider problem is more significant for public goods that have a "large" public than for those that have a "small" public. Shirking is easier when the public good affects a larger number of individuals. Consider a levee used for flood control. If only a few farmers are affected by a flood-control project, they are more likely to each contribute toward that project than if many individuals are affected by a flood-control project.

Since public goods generally tend to be underproduced, the government often steps in to provide them. Unfortunately, it is not a simple matter to determine how much of a public good to provide because, unlike the demand for private goods, the demand for a public good is difficult to estimate. Estimates are difficult because it benefits individual taxpayers to lie about their preferences for public goods. If taxpayers believe that they will be held accountable for the intensity of their demands for a public good (i.e., that they will in some way be taxed based on their professed marginal valuation schedule), it is in their best interest to understate their true preferences to get a free ride from others. Of course, the same incentive holds for all taxpayers, so there will be a general understatement of preferences for a public good. On the other hand, if taxpayers do not believe that their tax bills are tied to their espoused preferences for a public good, they tend to overstate the value they attach to that good. In either event, it is difficult to determine the true marginal social valuation attached to public goods.

Review Questions

Define the following terms:

Section 22.1

externality
negative externality
external diseconomy
external cost
positive externality
external economy
external benefit
network externality
bandwagon effect
snob effect
marginal private cost (MPC)
marginal external cost (MEC)
marginal social cost (MSC)
marginal private benefit (MPB)
marginal external benefit (MEB)
marginal social benefit (MSB)
Pigouvian tax
emissions fee
effluent fee
pollution abatement subsidy
marginal benefit of abatement ($MB_{abatement}$)
marginal cost of abatement ($MC_{abatement}$)
pollution standard
marketable discharge right
property rights
transactions costs
Coase Theorem
Coasean bargaining
common property resources
tragedy of the commons

Section 22.2

nonexclusive good
nonrivalrous good
pure public good
club good
private good
free rider
free-rider problem
Lindahl pricing
preference revelation problem

Match the following terms:

a. Marginal benefit of abatement
b. Marginal cost of abatement
c. Sum of MPC and MEC
d. Bandwagon effect
e. Common property resource
f. Club good
g. Lindahl pricing
h. Competitive pricing

1. Marginal benefit of pollution
2. Positive network externality
3. Rivalrous and nonexclusive
4. Marginal cost of pollution
5. Marginal social cost of production
6. Apportions output for common price
7. Nonrivalrous and exclusive
8. Apportions price for a common output

Provide short answers to the following:

Section 22.1

a. What is the difference between the external cost of steel production and the marginal external cost of steel production?
b. Suppose that marginal external cost is a declining function of output produced. Describe how the external cost of production relates to output in this instance. Provide a production process that fits this description of external costs.

c. Suppose that marginal external cost is an increasing function of output produced. Describe how the external cost of production relates to output in this instance. Provide a production process that fits this description of external costs.
d. Suppose that marginal external benefit is a declining function of output produced. Describe how the external benefit of production relates to output in this instance. Provide a production process that fits this description of external benefits.
e. Suppose that marginal external benefit is an increasing function of output produced. Describe how the external benefit of production relates to output in this instance.
f. Suppose that a Pigouvian tax is instituted to internalize an externality. Why doesn't it matter who pays the government the tax in this instance?

Section 22.2

a. Is it nonexcludability or nonrivalry that leads to the free-rider problem?
b. Why do common areas tend to be overutilized in many situations?
c. Why is it difficult to determine how valuable public goods are to individuals?

Check your answers to the *matching* and *short-answer* exercises in the Answers Appendix at the end of the book

Notes

1. *Wall Street Journal*, "Promoting One-of-a-Kind Looks, Shops Keep Prom Dress Registries," April 1, 2015. http://www.wsj.com/articles/promoting-one-of-a-kind-looks-shops-keep-prom-dress-registries-1427937210. Trudys Brides and Special Occasions in Campbell, California, offers a dress registry so that no two shoppers buy the same dress for the same prom. This article requires subscription access, but you can check out this phenomenon yourself by typing "prom dress registry" into Google.

2. This is another point where economists have not settled on a single term for each form of marginal cost. Some authors place the qualifiers (social, private, external) in front of marginal, and others use subscripts. We choose to place marginal in front to emphasize the incremental nature of each of these cost concepts.

3. This is another point where economists have not settled on a single term for each form of marginal benefit. Many simply maintain "demand" instead of the more awkward name MPB, but we choose to use MPB to maintain symmetry with the other benefit and cost schedules.

4. This is based on viewing demand as a marginal valuation schedule. Consumers do not care whether they are paying a firm or the government; they only care about their total payment. If they must pay T per unit to the government, their willingness to pay, the marginal valuation schedule faced by the firm, is T lower at any output than if they did not have to pay the tax.

5. In describing the social net benefit of an allocation of resources, we would now need to add a fourth "surplus"—government surplus. Tax revenues represent a surplus to society that should be included in a complete accounting of social surplus.

6. It would be worthwhile to use the Excel files for Figures 22.5 and 22.6 and use the tax slider in order to verify that this is the result.

7. This is only formally true, given the use of percentages on the horizontal axis, if each firm pollutes the same absolute quantity in the absence of abatement expenditures. The analysis would not require this restriction if we were using quantity of pollution abated on the horizontal axis; however, to maintain symmetry in the discussion of Figures 22.7 and 22.8, this has not been done.

8. From a welfare point of view, we need not concern ourselves with the fees themselves because that is simply a transfer from producers to the government. This is therefore a distributional, but not an allocative, issue.

9. See Chapter 6 of the *1990 Economic Report of the President.*

10. This example is discussed in a June 1997 Joint Economic Committee Study on Tradable Emissions from the U.S. Congress. See: http://www.jec.senate.gov/reports/105th%20Congress/Tradable%20Emissions%20(1676).pdf. More recently, carbon trading has become a hotly debated method of dealing with greenhouse gas emissions under the Kyoto Protocol. This is simply another example of a marketable discharge right.

11. The article is "The Problem of Social Cost," *Journal of Law and Economics* 3 (1960): 1–44. This article acted as a springboard for the development of an entire "law and economics" field of economics analysis. For an excellent introduction to Coase's contribution to economics, see the press release provided by the Nobel Prize organization http://nobelprize.org/economics/laureates/1991/press.html. See also the essay "The Swedes Get It Right" by David Friedman, referenced in http://coase.org/coaseonline.htm.

12. If other individuals or firms are also affected by the pollution from Firm x, then the damage to these actors will have to be added to the loss to Firm y to obtain a measure of marginal external damage caused by Firm x production.

13. In all panels of Figures 22.10–22.12, point **a** is along the MSC_x schedule, **b** is along the horizontal line P_x (representing marginal revenue to Firm x), and **c** is along the MPC_x schedule. The specific location of **a**, **b**, and **c** in each panel highlights the comparison of $P_x - MPC_x =$ **bc** and $-P_y \cdot \Delta y/\Delta x =$ **ac** for different output levels.

14. This question is at the center of *Fontainebleau Hotel Corp. v. Forty-Five Twenty-Five, Inc.* (Fla. 1959).

15. Given the assumption of fixed damage per unit of output, this translates to a cost that is proportional to the number of units of x bargained over.

16. The sizes of the various areas are the same under both property rights assignments, but this is due to the numbers chosen to simplify the diagrammatic analysis. Legal fees (**rdba** and **ubaf**), the size of the Coasean "pie" (**dtb** and **fav**), and DWL (**abs**) need not be symmetric in this situation. In particular, if s is not midway between zero and **t**, this will not occur. It will also not occur if the MSC schedule is nonlinear.

17. "The Tragedy of the Commons," Garrett Hardin, *Science*, 162 (1968):1243–1248.

18. It is not necessary to be bogged down in consumer surplus calculations here, but notice that if Beth purchases the first 20 units, she attains a consumer surplus of $1,000, but Andy attains a consumer surplus of $100 on those same units if Andy purchases these 20 units. Even if Beth purchases these 20 units, then Beth's consumer surplus is larger than Andy's gross surplus (of $700) on these free-ridden units.

Answers Appendix

Chapter 1: Preliminary Issues

Matching Exercise

a. 6; b. 4; c. 1; d. 7; e. 2; f. 3; g. 5.

Answers to Questions

a. Real prices are nominal prices adjusted for the rate of inflation.
b. This is an example of a positive model. It examined what would happen under various allocations of study time. It did not examine whether the allocation was "good" or "bad."
c. It is an exogenous variable because it is not determined within the model but is taken as a given.
d. The opportunity cost of economics in units of French is 1.25. The opportunity cost of French in units of economics is 0.80 = 1/1.25.

Chapter 2: A Review of Supply and Demand

Matching Exercise

a. 4; b. 7; c. 1; d. 6; e. 2; f. 5; g. 3.

Answers to Questions

a. There is no change in price or quantity, given perfectly inelastic supply. The entire tax is borne by firms.
b. If supply is perfectly elastic, then price increases by the amount of the tax, and quantity declines. The entire tax is borne by consumers.
c. Price increases by the amount of the tax, and quantity remains constant. The entire tax is borne by consumers.
d. There is no change in price, and quantity declines. The entire tax is borne by firms.
e. The price of y increased.
f. The price of y decreased.
g. Nothing will happen because the ceiling is not binding in this situation.
h. Excess demand will result.
i. Excess supply will result.
j. Nothing will happen because the floor is not binding in this situation.

Chapter 3: Preferences

Matching Exercise

a. 4; b. 6; c. 1; d. 5; e. 7; f. 2; g. 3.

Answers to Questions

a. The MRS is minus the slope of the indifference curve.
b. One of the goods is a "good," and the other is a "bad."
c. The MRS is positive.
d. Every point represents an allocation of resources.
e. Because "zero football" points represent allocations of resources where MRSs are equal across consumers. These are allocations of resources that have the property that there are no Pareto superior reallocations available.
f. No, voluntary exchange requires both parties to be at least as well off after the exchange as they were before the exchange occurred. A Pareto optimal allocation means that no reallocations are possible in which every economic actor is at least as well off as prior to the reallocation.

Chapter 4: Utility

Matching Exercise

a. 3; b. 5; c. 1; d. 2; e. 4.

Answers to Questions

a. Yes, because this is a monotonic transformation, it maintains order.
b. No, because the order is reversed by this transformation.
c. Set the function U(x, y) equal to a series of constants (2, 4, 6, 8, . . .), and map the results in (x, y) space.
d. Indifference curves such as this can emanate from shifted CD preferences (with $a = 0$ and $b < 0$) or from quasilinear preferences, such as shown in Figure 4.13.

Chapter 5: Resource Constraints

Matching Exercise

a. 3; b. 7; c. 6; d. 4; e. 2; f. 8; g. 1; h. 5.

Answers to Questions

a. It does not change.
b. If the price of one of the commodities changes when more than a certain amount is purchased.
c. The new budget line is inside the old, and it is flatter than the old.
d. The new budget line is inside the old, and it is steeper than the old.
e. The new budget line is outside the old, and it is steeper than the old.
f. The new budget line is outside the old, and it is flatter than the old.
g. The new budget line crosses the old, and it is flatter than the old.
h. The consumer is purchasing as many units of x as possible in this instance. The consumer does not have enough money to buy another unit of x but does have some money left over that can be used to purchase y (if y is continuous or if y is discrete and $P_y \leq I - P_x \cdot \text{Integer}(I/P_x)$ so that at least 1 unit of y can be purchased).

Chapter 6: Consumer Choice

Matching Exercise

a. 4; b. 2; c. 1; d. 3; e. 5.

Answers to Questions

a. Each will have the same MRS at the utility-maximizing bundle chosen (as long as they consume both of the goods) because each responds to the same pricing signals.
b. It is required that the indifference curve through the optimal bundle does not intersect the budget constraint at more than one point. (If it does, it is qualitatively like the indifference curve through bundles **B** and **C** in Figure 6.2B.)
c. Because all income may not be spent (like at bundle **D** in Figure 6.1A). And even if all income is spent, this does not necessarily distinguish between maximums and minimums. If preferences are nonconvex, then MRS = price ratio and all income is spent could occur at a local minimum (as shown at bundle **B** in Figure 6.15).
d. Three-fourths of income is devoted to x and one-fourth to y.
e. More to y and less to x.
f. More to x and less to y.
g. The individual should remain at **A** in this instance.

Chapter 7: Deriving Demand

Matching Exercise

a. 6; b. 4; c. 2; d. 9; e. 8; f. 7; g. 1; h. 3; i. 5.

Answers to Questions

a. Demand for x is zero, and all income is spent on y.
b. Demand for y is zero, and all income is spent on x.
c. The demand curve shifts.
d. Because at MRS = P_x/P_y, the entire budget constraint provides the optimal solution.
e. Because the two goods are used in fixed proportions.
f. No, a luxury requires $\eta > 1$, and an inferior good has $\eta < 0$.
g. Yes, a necessity requires $\eta < 1$, and an inferior good has $\eta < 0$, so any inferior good is also a necessity.
h. Yes, a necessity requires $\eta < 1$, and a normal good has $\eta > 0$; the good is both as long as $1 > \eta > 0$.

Chapter 8: Decomposing Demand

Matching Exercise

a. 4; b. 9; c. 3; d. 1; e. 6; f. 8; g. 2; h. 7; i. 5.

Answers to Questions

a. There is no substitution effect in this instance. The roll along the L-shaped indifference curve leaves the consumer at the vertex.
b. The bundle view, own-price view, and cross-price view.
c. The own-price income effect is zero; the entire income effect is on the other good.
d. The bias is estimated at between 0.4% and 1.5% by various economic analysts (see endnote 16).
e. Demand is upward sloping if x is inferior and if $|s_x \cdot \eta_x| > |\varepsilon_x^{\text{Hicksian}}|$.
f. Because goods are typically normal, there is a positive income effect of the price change that is not incorporated into Hicksian demand but is incorporated into Marshallian demand.
g. The good must be inferior (negative income elasticity).

Chapter 9: Production Functions

Matching Exercise

a. 8; b. 4; c. 1; d. 6; e. 2; f. 9; g. 3; h. 5; i. 7.

Answers to Questions

a. The number attached to the isoquant means something in a cardinal sense. It is the level of production.
b. Yes, the production function $Q(L, K) = L^{0.75} \cdot K^{0.75}$ exhibits diminishing marginal product with respect to both labor and capital (since each exponent is less than 1) but also exhibits increasing returns to scale, since $1.5 = 0.75 + 0.75$.
c. A typical total product curve is initially convex upward and then changes convexity and becomes convex downward. The initial portion is due to increasing marginal productivity, and the point of inflection is the point of maximum marginal product; beyond this output level, marginal product declines.
d. Because even the most labor-intensive processes require a bit of capital to produce output and even the most capital-intensive processes require at least some labor to keep that process running.
e. To have the sum of the exponents to be greater than 1.
f. Average increases.

Questions g–i are based on:
$Q(L, K) = (c \cdot \text{Minimum}(L/a, K/b))^d$
for a, b, c, and $d > 0$.

g. $d > 1$.
h. There is no substitutability in this process. This is Leontief production.
i. The isoquant map with equal increments in output gets closer and closer together for an increasing returns to scale production function (like Figure 9.9C). The input bundle (a, b) is the vertex of an isoquant producing c^d units of output. The proportional increase input bundle $(2^{(1/d)} \cdot a, 2^{(1/d)} \cdot b)$ is less than twice as large as (a, b) since $d > 1$, but it is the vertex of the isoquant producing twice as much output ($2 \cdot c^d$ units of output).

Questions j–l are based on $Q(L, K) = (a \cdot L + b \cdot K)^c$ for a, b, and $c > 0$.

j. $c < 1$.
k. There is perfect substitutability between L and K in this instance.
l. The isoquant map with equal increments in output gets more and more spread out for a decreasing returns to scale production function (like Figure 9.9A). The input bundles (b, 0) and (0, a) are the L and K intercepts of a straight-line isoquant producing $(a \cdot b)^c$ units of output. The input bundles $(2^{(1/c)} \cdot b, 0)$ and $(0, 2^{(1/c)} \cdot a)$ are more than twice as large as (b, 0) and (0, a), since $c < 1$, but input bundles along this line are required to produce twice as much output ($2 \cdot (a \cdot b)^c$ units of output).
m. The marginal product vector is perpendicular to the isoquant, just like the marginal utility vector is perpendicular to the indifference curve.

Chapter 10: Cost Minimization

Matching Exercise

a. 3; b. 1; c. 4; d. 2.

Answers to Questions

a. They result in the same set of marginal conditions, but in actuality, they are duals of each other (reverse sides of the same coin, so to speak).
b. There is no single isocost line like there is a single budget constraint because cost must be balanced against revenues to determine how much to produce. The budget constraint is predicated on a single income level.
c. The short-run expansion path holds capital fixed (and is a horizontal line), but the long-run expansion

path allows capital and labor to vary and is the set of $MRTS_{K,L} = P_L/P_K$ points for different levels of output.

d. No.
e. Yes.
f. Increase labor and decrease capital along the isoquant.
g. Yes; yes; do nothing.
h. No; yes; increase capital and decrease labor along the isoquant.
i. No because the $MP_K > 0$ for all input bundles (L, K), given CD production.
j. Yes because there are a range of input bundles (L, K) where $MP_K < 0$. These are the bundles above the yellow $MP_K = 0$ set of bundles in Figure 10.11.
k. No value of a can be given, but $b = 2/3$, and $c = 1/3$.
l. You can no longer provide explicit values for a, b, or c, but you can state that $b = 2 \cdot c$.

Chapter 11: Cost Curves

Matching Exercise

a. 8; b. 4; c. 5; d. 7; e. 6; f. 2; g. 1; h. 3.

Answers to Questions

a. Average variable cost increases.
b. Average total cost declines.
c. Because there are no fixed costs in the long run; as a result, all costs are variable, so there is no distinction between average total cost and average variable cost (or total cost and variable cost).
d. No, if average variable cost is declining, average total cost must also be declining.
e. Yes. This is shown in Figure 11.7.
f. Marginal cost must be below average variable cost and average total cost, but it need not be declining.
g. Marginal cost must be above average variable cost and average total cost at this output level; marginal cost must be increasing.
h. The long-run total cost curve is the envelope of the short-run total cost curves.
i. The long-run average cost curve is the envelope of the short-run average total cost curves.

Chapter 12: Profit Maximization in a General Setting

Matching Exercise

a. 2; b. 4; c. 1; d. 5; e. 3.

Answers to Questions

a. Because as more and more individuals are added to the market, a smooth curve closely approximates the piecewise smooth kinked actual market demand.
b. Demand takes a price orientation, and inverse demand takes a quantity orientation of the same (Q, P) data points.
c. Marginal revenue has the same intercept and twice the slope as inverse demand.
d. Marginal revenue is a constant proportion of inverse demand.
e. When MR = MC.
f. Set output so that MR = MC.
g. Because a profit-maximizing firm wishes to set output MR = MC, but since MC > 0, MR > 0. MR > 0 occurs on the elastic portion of the demand curve.

Chapter 13: Short-Run Profit Maximization in Perfectly Competitive Markets

Matching Exercise

a. 4; b. 3; c. 1; d. 5; e. 2.

Answers to Questions

a. Set output so that MR = MC is the general rule. The specific rule in a competitive market is to set output so that P = MC.
b. The firm's supply curve is the positively sloped part of the marginal cost curve above minimum average variable cost. For prices below minimum average variable cost, the firm minimizes losses by shutting down (set output to zero in the short run).
c. Market supply is the horizontal sum of individual firms' supply curves.
d. Marginal cost is linear, given quadratic costs.
e. The four tenets are: (1) a large number of price-taking buyers and sellers; (2) the product under consideration is homogeneous; (3) there is free entry and exit in the market; and (4) there is perfect information about all relevant aspects of the market.

Chapter 14: Long-Run Profit Maximization in Perfectly Competitive Markets

Matching Exercise

a. 3; b. 1; c. 5; d. 2; e. 4.

Answers to Questions

a. Because in the long run, all costs are variable, so the two conditions that look different are, in fact, the same.
b. (1) The market is in short-run equilibrium. (2) Each firm is earning zero economic profit. (3) $P^* = LAC_{minimum}$.
c. No, the only restriction is that plants must be between minimum efficient scale and maximum efficient scale.
d. The personal computer market is likely a decreasing-cost industry. The production of many foods (carrots, corn, etc.) is likely constant cost. The production of some foods is likely to be increasing cost if the food only grows in restricted areas (wine grapes were an example in the chapter).

Chapter 15: Monopoly and Monopolistic Competition

Matching Exercise

a. 3; b. 4; c. 1; d. 2.

Answers to Questions

a. Because there is no one-to-one relation between price and quantity for monopoly markets (as there is in competitive markets). This is shown in a comparison of Figures 15.1 and 15.3A and 15.3B, where there are multiple quantities associated with a single price ($62.50) and multiple prices associated with a single quantity (15).
b. Yes, this is possible. The profit-maximizing output level in Figure 15.4 occurs along the negatively sloped part of the marginal cost curve.
c. No, the market may be too thin to support even one producer of the product.
d. No, MR = MC is necessary but not sufficient to ensure a profit maximum. X = 1 in Figure 15.4 is a profit minimum, despite being a point where MR = MC.
e. Structural, legal, and strategic.
f. The "monopoly" attribute is that the product is differentiated so that each firm faces a downward-sloping demand curve for its specific version of the product. The "competition" attribute is that there is free entry and exit in the market.
g. In long-run equilibrium, MR = MC at the profit-maximizing output level, and P = ATC > MR = MC for that output level. Profits are zero in this instance. The individual firm's demand curve is tangent to the downward-sloping part of its average total cost curve.

Chapter 16: Welfare Economics

Matching Exercise

a. 5; b. 7; c. 6; d. 1; e. 3; f. 2; g. 4.

Answers to Questions

a. It places equal emphasis on consumer and producer surpluses.
b. Because consumers must pay for the goods they consume.
c. Because producers must pay for producing the goods they sell.
d. It is the cost to consumers.
e. Producer surplus cannot be negative.
f. One method is the (P–AVC) by Q rectangle. The second is the P × Q rectangle, less the area under the marginal cost curve. The third is the area behind the marginal cost curve between P and minimum AVC. The third version is the one that is analogous to consumer surplus as the area behind demand (because marginal cost above minimum average variable cost is the firm's supply curve).
g. Zero.
h. Not necessarily.
i. Hicksian is steeper than Marshallian for normal goods.
j. CV < CS < EV.
k. CV > CS > EV.
l. When the good is quasilinear (and hence, demand for the good is independent of income).
m. They mean that, in most circumstances, the difference in size between the theoretically justifiable measures and consumer surplus is small.

Chapter 17: Consumer Theory Applications

Answers to Questions

Section 17.1

a. The slope is $-(1 + r)$, where r is the interest rate.
b. Because individuals typically face different interest rates for borrowing and lending.
c. The present value of a stream of payments is the value in the current time period of payments now and in the future. The future value of a stream of payments is the value in the future of a stream of payments now and in the future. If there is no difference between the

borrowing and lending interest rates, these two values differ by a factor of $(1 + r)$, with future value $(1 + r)$ times larger than present value.

d. Yes, a borrower will continue to borrow as the borrowing interest rate declines.
e. No, the borrower need not continue to borrow as the borrowing interest rate increases.
f. No, a lender need not continue lending if the lending interest rate declines.
g. Yes, a lender will continue lending if the lending interest rate increases.

Section 17.2A

a. No, because they may not view risk in the same fashion.
b. Because the sum of deviations from the mean is *always* zero.
c. Because individuals differ in how they perceive risk.

Section 17.2B

a. An asset is described by two attributes: its expected rate of return and the standard deviation associated with that expected value. The horizontal axis is the standard deviation of return, and the vertical axis is the expected rate of return.
b. It is horizontal in this model because all that matters in this instance is expected return.
c. **B** must be in the first or third quadrant, relative to **A**, because standard deviation of return is an economic bad, and expected return is an economic good.
d. It is the incremental expected return per unit of standard deviation. This is called the reward-to-variability ratio.
e. Because the activity that is undertaken by leveraged borrowing is innately risky.

Section 17.2C

a. Income.
b. U(x) increases at a decreasing rate; it is convex downward.
c. U(x) increases linearly.
d. U(x) increases at an increasing rate; it is convex upward.
e. As a point on the line segment connecting the two possible outcomes.
f. E(U(**A**)) > E(U(**B**)) signifies that Lottery **A** is better than Lottery **B** because it has a higher utility level. E(X(**A**)) < E(X(**B**)) signifies that Lottery **A** has a lower expected income level than Lottery **B**. **A** ≻ **B**, based on this information.
g. **B** must have the higher risk premium because it has a higher expected income, and at the same time, a lower expected utility level.
h. **A** has a higher certainty equivalent income because it has a higher expected utility level.
i. The more risk-averse individual may find it worthwhile to purchase the insurance because that person perceives a larger risk premium than the less risk-averse individual.

Chapter 18: Topics in Factor Markets

Answers to Questions

Sections 18.1A–18.1C

a. It is equal to the total amount of time available (24 hours per day, 168 hours per week).
b. The wage rate.
c. An increase in labor supply.
d. No change in labor supply.
e. A decrease in labor supply.
f. Increased leisure.
g. Overtime pay provides a greater increase in labor supply.

Section 18.1D

a. The substitution effect dominates the income effect.
b. The substitution and income effect are the same magnitude.
c. The income effect dominates the substitution effect.
d. Overtime wages have an unambiguous effect on labor supply because, as a first approximation, overtime wages induce a pure substitution effect. The substitution effect unambiguously increases labor supply (by decreasing leisure demand).

Section 18.2

a. The marginal revenue product of a factor is the marginal physical product of that factor times marginal revenue.
b. The firm is only interested in the factor because it helps the firm to increase profits via increased output produced (and then sold).
c. If all factors of production are allowed to vary, then demand for any specific factor of production will be more price sensitive (i.e., more elastic) than if some factors are fixed.
d. Because as the price of the product being produced changes, this change will shift the marginal revenue product curve for the factor (since marginal revenue changes).

Section 18.3

a. Because the union need not have a single objective. The three objectives laid out in the section are: (1) maximizing the number of workers hired, (2) maximizing wage receipts of union members, and (3) maximizing net dollar benefits of union members.

b. Because unemployed union workers will migrate to nonunion jobs, thereby shifting nonunion labor supply outward.
c. A decrease in nonunion wages.
d. Marginal revenue.

Chapter 19: Capital Markets

Answers to Economics Questions

Section 19.1

a. The pure rate of time preference, the expected rate of inflation, and a risk premium.
b. Real rate = Nominal rate – Rate of inflation.
c. Because it is easier to imagine how the various revenue and cost streams vary in the future on a real basis.

Section 19.3

a. No, they are the nominal sum of annuity payments.
b. Because the rate of time preference is higher than the growth rate in salary in this model.
c. When the rate of time preference equals the rate of growth in salary.

Section 19.4

a. It ignores present-value considerations, and it ignores timing within and outside the cutoff time.
b. It is not possible to rank investments using net present value.
c. When investments are not "typical" (a typical investment has an up-front cost, followed by a stream of net income in out years).
d. Each investment decision rule has problems; no single rule is dominant.

Answers to Excel Questions

Sections 19.2 and 19.3

a. Because if you wish to do comparative statics analysis, you need only change the data in the data area, rather than in each equation.
b. Because it makes comparative statics analysis easier to accomplish.
c. Type the starting day in a cell, and drag that cell down.
d. Change each of the parameters in the model one at a time, holding all other values at their best-guess values.
e. Because it will reduce the incidence of mistakes. First, you should focus on getting the equation right; then you should focus on how to "fix" the equation so that it can be dragged as needed.
f. Because it allows you to set two values equal to one another simply by goal seeking on the difference between the two values.

Chapter 20: Strategic Rivalry

Answers to Questions

Sections 20.1–20.4

a. No, it will not be joint profit maximizing. We can see this graphically by the isoprofit "football" going through the Cournot equilibrium. Each point in this football represents a quantity pair that produces higher profits for both firms.
b. Each firm's isoprofit contour through the point is tangent to the other firm's isoprofit contour.
c. Individual firm output declines, but total quantity increases and approaches the competitive output level as the number of firms increases.
d. It is heterogeneous.
e. It is more profitable to be the Stackelberg follower.

Section 20.5

a. No, the prisoners' dilemma is a greater problem for one-shot games. With multiple rounds, you are able to learn from your rivals and tacitly coordinate your actions.
b. Because it increases the likelihood of cheating (i.e., confessing and implicating your partner in crime).
c. Vigorously pursue antitrust actions.
d. It is easier for an irrational person to make a credible threat; therefore, the 5-year-old poses the greater threat (unless the 25-year-old is in need of psychiatric help).
e. Tacit bargaining is bargaining that is not explicit. This is more effective in the long run because you can learn from your rivals over time and have a better understanding of what a given signal means.
f. Because you learn something by seeing what your rival does in the first move. If you move first, then your rival learns something from you (simply by what you did in that move).
g. The bounds on the war need to be qualitative, not quantitative—for example, no price competition, not how much price competition.
h. The smiley-faced cell. It is the only "unique" cell out of the nine cells shown.
i. A focal point.
j. Both will choose to play mini-golf.
k. This is a dominant strategy equilibrium because it is the dominant strategy for both players.
l. It is not an example of a prisoners' dilemma because the coordinated action of both Jack and Jill choosing movies does not produce higher total payoffs than both playing mini-golf.

Chapter 21: Informational Issues

Answers to Questions

Sections 21.1–21.5

a. No. They both may know that a certain percentage of cars are lemons, but they don't know about the quality of a specific new car.
b. Sellers have better information about the used cars they are selling than do buyers.
c. If this were not true, then car owners would turn around and get rid of a car as soon as they were able to determine that it was a lemon.
d. This is likely to be true. This is the adverse selection problem. There is a lower quality of used cars sold than exist overall because some of the owners of good used cars will be unwilling to sell at an "average" used-car price.
e. As price increases, average quality increases in the used-car market. If the increase in demand due to increased quality is larger than the reduction in demand due to the pure price effect, then demand will be upward sloping.
f. The quality effect dominates.
g. When it is differentially costly to provide.
h. No, education acts purely as a signal within Spence's model.
i. Because it is differentially costly to obtain.
j. Job seekers know more about their own productivity than potential employers.
k. Yes, because they are differentially costly to provide.
l. The insurance buyer has more information in this instance.
m. Both act as a way of getting individuals to voluntarily separate themselves into groups according to their abilities or attributes.
n. It is aimed at high-risk individuals.
o. Yes, the lemons model is an example of the adverse selection problem.
p. No, the reverse is true. The moral hazard problem is an example of the principal-agent problem.

Section 21.6

a. No, because it is not differentially costly to provide.
b. $A/S = \varepsilon_A/|\varepsilon_D|$.
c. It is based on employing the profit-maximing rule, MR = MC, simultaneously on the advertising and the quantity dimensions.

Chapter 22: Externalities and Public Goods

Matching Exercise

a. 4; b. 1; c. 5; d. 2; e. 3; f. 7; g. 8; h. 6.

Answers to Questions

Section 22.1

a. The external cost of a given level of output is the sum of marginal external cost up to this amount of output, just as variable cost is the sum of marginal cost.
b. External cost increases at a decreasing rate in this instance. If you need "pure" water as part of your production process, the initial levels of water pollution may be more damaging than more-polluted water (on a marginal basis). Beer production may fit this externality pattern. Coors uses "pure Rocky Mountain spring water."
c. External cost increases at an increasing rate in this instance. Some air pollution is bad; a lot of air pollution is far worse (on a marginal basis).
d. The external benefit increases at a decreasing rate. Landscaping fits this description.
e. External benefits increase at an increasing rate. (Since I cannot think of an example of a process fitting this description, I did not ask you to provide one.)
f. Because tax incidence is independent of who pays the tax in a nominal sense. Tax incidence depends on the relative elasticities of supply and demand.

Section 22.2

a. Nonexcludability.
b. Because individual users base their behavior on the average productivity of their actions, but social optimality requires behavior to be based on marginal productivity. Average product exceeds marginal product in this instance, leading to an overutilization of the common resource.
c. Because it pays to misstate your true preferences for a public good.

Glossary

A

accounting costs: Accounting costs are the costs reported by accountants on financial reports.
actuarially fair insurance: The premium of actuarially fair insurance is the expected payout of the policy.
adverse selection problem: The adverse selection problem occurs if the market is skewed because of asymmetric information.
annuity: An annuity is a stream of equal-sized payments paid at regular intervals.
arbitrage: Arbitrage is the process of buying a good at a low price and reselling it at a higher price.
asymmetric information: A market is subject to asymmetric information if one party or the other tends to have a systematic informational advantage, relative to the other party in the market interaction.
average fixed cost (AFC): Average fixed cost is fixed cost divided by quantity, $AFC(Q) = FC(Q)/Q$.
average product of labor: The average product of labor is defined as $AP_L(L) = TP(L)/L$. It tells us the average number of units of output produced per unit of labor.
average total cost (ATC): Average total cost is total cost divided by quantity, $ATC(Q) = TC(Q)/Q$.
average variable cost (AVC): Average variable cost is variable cost divided by quantity, $AVC(Q) = VC(Q)/Q$.

B

bandwagon effect: If a consumer's demand for a good increases as more consumers demand the good, then the good has a bandwagon effect.
bargaining: Bargaining is negotiating over the terms of an agreement.
barrier to entry (BTE): If a going firm in a market has an economic advantage over a potential entrant to that market, then the market is subject to barriers to entry.
barter: Barter involves exchanging goods and services without the use of money.
behavioral assumptions: Each time a firm acts, it has a belief about how its rivals will react. These beliefs are called behavioral assumptions.
binding: A constraint is binding on a given bundle if tightening the constraint by a small amount makes the bundle infeasible.
black market: A black market is an illegal market for a good.
bliss point: A bliss point occurs at the point of x *and* y satiation.
boundary: A bundle on the boundary of the consumption set contains at least one good that is not consumed. (Alternatively, we say that consumption of that good is zero.)
budget constraint: The set of bundles $(x_1, \ldots, x_n)$ that satisfy the equality $P_1x_1 + P_2x_2 + \ldots + P_nx_n = I$ with each $x_i \geq 0$ is called the budget constraint.

C

capital or capital good: If an input is itself an output, it is called capital or a capital good. Capital goods are goods that are used to produce other goods.
cardinal: A relationship between two distinct numbers is cardinal if the magnitude of the difference matters.
certainty equivalent income (CEI(X)): The certainty equivalent income is the amount of income that produces the same utility level as the expected utility level of the lottery.
***ceteris paribus*:** *Ceteris paribus* means all else held equal.
club good: A club good is nonrivalrous and exclusive.
Coase Theorem: The Coase Theorem states that if transactions costs are zero and property rights are clearly defined, then an efficient allocation of resources will result, regardless of who has the property rights.
coinsurance: Coinsurance is insurance that provides less-than-full coverage to the insured party. That part not covered by the insurance company must be provided by the insured party.
common property resource: A common property resource is a resource to which anyone has free access.
comparative statics analysis: Comparative statics analysis involves examining the effect of a change in an exogenous economic variable on various endogenous variables. Economists often call this *sensitivity analysis*.
compensating variation (CV): Compensating variation is the amount of income that may be taken from the individual to maintain the initial utility level in the face of new prices.
competitive fringe: Firms in the competitive fringe have little independent market power.
complement: If an increase in the price of one good, y, leads to a decrease in demand for the other good, x, then y is a complement of x. In terms of elasticity, y is a complement of x if $\varepsilon_{x,y} < 0$.
complete: Preferences are complete if you are always able to answer the question: Which do you prefer?

compounding: If X earns r in interest per dollar per period for t periods, the amount of interest earned exceeds $X \cdot r \cdot t$ because the principal increases each time an interest payment occurs (as long as the interest is allowed to accrue to the principal). This excess occurs because of compounding.
constant returns to scale (CRTS): If an increase of s% in all factors of production causes an s% increase in output, the production process exhibits constant returns to scale.
consumer surplus (CS): The excess of what the consumer would have paid over what the consumer had to pay for a good is the consumer surplus of that good.
consumption diagram: The consumption diagram is consumption bundle space, (x, y).
contract curve: The contract curve is the set of all Pareto optimal allocations of resources.
convexity: A set is convex if, for any two points in the set, the set of points on the line segment between those two points is also in the set.
cooperative game: A cooperative game is a game in which the players can negotiate explicit binding contracts over various states of nature.
Cournot equilibrium (CE): A Cournot equilibrium is the intersection of each firm's reaction functions.
Cournot quantity assumption: If a firm believes that rival firms will maintain their output level, regardless of what it does, the firm assumes Cournot quantity behavior by rival firms.
credible threat: A credible threat is a threat that is realistic enough to be believable.
cross-price elasticity: A cross-price elasticity examines how a change in the price of one good affects demand for another good.

D

deadweight loss (DWL): Deadweight loss is the loss in total surplus whenever price and marginal cost do not coincide.
deadweight loss of monopoly (DWL_m): The loss in total surplus due to monopolistic output distortion is called the deadweight loss of monopoly.
decreasing returns to scale (DRTS): If an increase of s% in all factors of production causes a less than s% increase in output, the production process exhibits decreasing returns to scale.
demand curve: A demand curve describes the quantity consumers wish to purchase for various prices. Often, this is shortened to *demand.*
demand decomposition: The total effect of a price change on demand is decomposed into the substitution effect and the income effect of a price change.
demand diagram: A demand diagram is a diagram whose axes are the quantity of a good on the horizontal axis and the price of that good on the vertical axis.
differentiated product: A product is differentiated if there are perceived differences among various firms' offerings.
discount rate: The discount rate is the rate at which consumers and firms are willing to trade dollars across time periods.
dominant strategy: A player's dominant strategy is the strategy that provides a preferable outcome, regardless of a rival's behavior.
dominant strategy equilibrium: A dominant strategy equilibrium occurs if each player in a game has a dominant strategy and chooses it.
duopoly: A duopoly is a market in which there are two sellers.

E

economic neutral: An individual views a good x as an economic neutral if the individual is indifferent between the initial bundle and a new bundle with a bit more or less of x, holding all other goods constant.
economic region of production: The economic region of production is the set of input bundles where each input has positive marginal productivity.
efficient scale of production: A short-run production process is produced at an efficient scale of production if this plant size is associated with minimum long-run average cost.
elastic: When $|\varepsilon| > 1$, we say that demand is elastic.
elasticity: Elasticity is a measure of responsiveness. Specifically, $\varepsilon_{x,v} = \%\Delta x/\%\Delta v$ where v is any variable that affects x. The most common variable is P_x, in which case we remove the subscripts. Other common variables are P_y (cross-price elasticity, $\varepsilon_{x,y}$), income, or advertising. Income elasticity is written with η (eta) rather than epsilon: $\eta = \varepsilon_{x,I}$.
emissions fee: An emissions fee is a fee based on the amount of damages caused.
endogenous variable: An endogenous variable is one whose value is determined within the economic system (or model) under consideration.
Engel curve: An Engel curve maps optimal levels of a good as a function of income.
envelope: An envelope is a curve drawn by connecting least-cost points for all quantities.
equivalent variation (EV): Equivalent variation is the amount of income that must be given to the individual to be as well off with old prices as that individual is in the face of new prices.
estimated marginal revenue (MR_e): Estimated marginal revenue is calculated as the rate of change in revenue for a discrete change in output.
excess demand: A market exhibits excess demand at a given price when the amount that consumers wish to purchase exceeds the amount that firms wish to supply.
excess supply: A market exhibits excess supply at a given price when the amount that firms wish to supply exceeds the amount that consumers wish to purchase.
exit: If a firm decides to leave the market and sell its capital stock, it is said to exit the market. Once the firm exits the market, it no longer has fixed assets, and therefore, it no longer has fixed costs.
exogenous variable: An exogenous variable is one whose value is determined outside the economic system (or model) under consideration.
expansion path: An expansion path depicts the set of cost-minimizing input bundles as output varies for fixed factor prices.
expected utility criterion: If an individual chooses lotteries based on the highest expected utility, then that individual is acting based on the expected utility criterion.
expected value: The expected value of an outcome is the probability-weighted sum of possible outcomes.

explicit costs: Explicit costs are out-of-pocket expenses.
externality: An externality exists if a consumer or producer does not capture the full benefit or face the full cost of an economic action.

F

factor costs are constant: Factor costs are constant if the prices of factors in the production process are not dependent on how much is demanded of those factors of production by the industry. This is also called the *constant-cost* case.
factor costs are decreasing: Factor costs are decreasing if the prices of factors in the production process decrease as demand for those factors increases. This is also called the *decreasing-cost* case.
factor costs are increasing: Factor costs are increasing if the prices of factors in the production process increase as demand for those factors increases. This is also called the *increasing-cost* case.
feasible: The set of bundles $(x_1, \ldots, x_n)$ that satisfy the inequality $P_1x_1 + P_2x_2 + \ldots + P_nx_n \leq I$ with each $x_i \geq 0$ is called the set of feasible consumption bundles.
firm's supply curve, s(P): The firm's supply curve, s(P), is the positively sloped part of its marginal cost curve above minimum average variable cost. For prices below minimum average variable cost, the firm shuts down and supplies no output in the short run.
fixed cost (FC): Fixed cost is the opportunity cost that accrues to factors of production that are fixed in the short run.
focal points: Focal points are points chosen due to their prominence or conspicuousness.
free rider: A free rider is an individual who benefits from a nonexclusive good purchased by others.

G

game: A game involves players making strategic decisions from an available set of options.
Giffen good: A Giffen good is a good with a positively sloped demand curve.
gross benefit of consuming N units of output (GB(N)): The gross benefit of consuming N units of output is the sum of marginal valuations of the first N units of output.

H

Hicksian demand: Hicksian demand is demand for a good as a function of its price, holding all other prices and utility constant.
homogeneous of degree k: A function f(**X**) is homogeneous of degree k if $f(t \cdot \mathbf{X}) = t^k \cdot f(\mathbf{X})$.
homothetic: A function g(**X**) is homothetic if it is a positive monotonic transformation of a homogeneous function.
human capital: Human capital comprises the skills, talents, experiences, and capacities that allow individuals to contribute to the production of goods and services.

I

imperfectly competitive market: A market that fails to satisfy the requirements of perfect competition is said to be imperfectly competitive.
implicit costs: Implicit costs are costs that are not explicitly paid out but are nonetheless incurred.
income consumption curve (ICC): The income consumption curve is the set of utility-maximizing consumption bundles associated with different levels of income (for fixed prices).
income effect: The income effect of a price change is that part of the total effect that is due to the individual adjusting consumption in response to the changing purchasing power induced by the price change.
increasing returns to scale (IRTS): If an increase of s% in all factors of production causes a more than s% increase in output, the production process exhibits increasing returns to scale.
independent: If an increase in the price of one good, y, has no effect on demand for the other good, x, then y is independent of x. In terms of elasticity, y is independent of x if $\varepsilon_{x,y} = 0$.
independent of income: A good is independent of income if $\eta = 0$. Demand is independent of income.
indexing: A program is indexed to a fixed market basket if the level of payments provided by the program is adjusted to maintain the affordability of that market basket.
indifference curve: An indifference curve represents bundles that provide the same satisfaction for the consumer and between which the consumer is indifferent.
individual's demand for a good: An individual's demand for a good shows how much of the good the individual willingly consumes at various prices of the good, *ceteris paribus*. This term is often shortened to (most commonly) *individual demand, demand curve*, and *demand.*
inelastic: When $|\varepsilon| < 1$, we say that demand is inelastic.
inferior good: An inferior good is a good whose demand decreases as income increases. In terms of elasticity, the good is inferior if $\eta_x < 0$.
inflation: Inflation is the general change in the price level over time. Typically, inflation is calculated using the Consumer Price Index, CPI.
input: An input is a resource used in the production process. Another common term for an input is a *factor of production.*
interior: An interior bundle is a bundle that contains positive quantities of all goods.
internal rate of return (IRR): The internal rate of return on an investment is that discount rate for which the NPV of that investment equals zero.
inverse demand curve: An inverse demand curve describes price as a function of quantity.
isocost line: An isocost line is the set of input bundles that cost the same amount of money.
isoquant: An isoquant maps out the set of input bundles that produce the same level of output.
isoquant map: An isoquant map is a graphical display of multiple isoquants.

L

law of diminishing marginal product: The law of diminishing marginal product states that as more and more of a factor of production is used, with all other factors and technology held constant, there must eventually be a decline in the incremental output produced by extra units of the variable factor of production.
law of downward-sloping demand: The law of downward-sloping demand states that quantity demanded increases as price decreases, *ceteris paribus*. This is also often called the *law of demand.*

Leontief: A production function is Leontief if it exhibits fixed proportions.
Lerner Index: The Lerner Index is named after Abba Lerner, who first proposed $L = (P - MC)/P$ as a measure of monopoly power in the 1930s.
lexicographic: Preferences are lexicographic if $\mathbf{A} \succ \mathbf{B}$ whenever $x_a > x_b$ or if $x_a = x_b$ and $y_a > y_b$.
limited war: A limited war is a contest in which each player opts to eliminate potential strategies in an effort to preserve resources or avoid undesirable outcomes resulting from escalation in future iterations of the game. The eliminated strategies are *qualitative*, rather than *quantitative*, in nature.
Lindahl pricing: Lindahl pricing involves having individuals who benefit from a nonexclusive good share the cost by paying different prices for the good, based on their marginal valuation schedules.
long run: The long run is the time frame in which the firm is able to vary all of its inputs.
long-run average cost curve, LAC(Q): The long-run average cost curve, LAC(Q), is the curve relating the average cost of production to the level of output produced when all factors of production are allowed to vary.
long-run expansion path (LREP): The long-run expansion path is the set of cost-minimizing input bundles for different levels of output and fixed factor prices.
long-run marginal cost curve, LMC(Q): The long-run marginal cost curve, LMC(Q), is the curve relating the incremental cost of production to the level of output produced when all factors of production are allowed to vary.
long-run perfectly competitive equilibrium: A long-run perfectly competitive equilibrium exists if market supply equals market demand, and firms have no incentive to enter or exit the industry.
long-run supply (LS) curve: The long-run supply curve maps the set of long-run equilibrium (x, \$/x) points for different levels of demand.
long-run total cost curve, LTC(Q): The long-run total cost curve, LTC(Q), is the curve relating the total cost of production to the level of output produced when all factors of production are allowed to vary.
lottery: A lottery is a list of all possible outcomes, together with the probabilities of each of the outcomes.
luxury: A good is a luxury if $\eta > 1$. An increasing percentage of income is spent on the good as income increases.

M

marginal benefit of abatement ($MB_{abatement}$): The marginal benefit of abatement schedule represents the external benefit when pollution is cleaned up.
marginal cost (MC): Marginal cost is the incremental cost of producing one more unit of output.
marginal cost of abatement ($MC_{abatement}$): The marginal cost of abatement is the incremental cost of reducing pollution.
marginal expenditure, ME(x): The marginal expenditure is the incremental expenditure required to purchase a bit more x.
marginal external benefit (MEB): The marginal external benefit is the increment in external benefit achieved when consumers consume one more unit of output.
marginal external cost (MEC): The marginal external cost is the increment in external cost imposed by producing one more unit of output.
marginal factor cost of factor F, MFC(F): The marginal factor cost of factor F is the incremental cost incurred when the firm uses a bit more F, $MFC(F) = \Delta TC/\Delta F$, *ceteris paribus*.
marginal private benefit (MPB): The marginal private benefit is the increment in internal benefit achieved by consuming one more unit of output. This is an alternative name for the inverse market demand curve discussed in Chapter 12.
marginal private cost (MPC): The marginal private cost is the increment in cost imposed on producers who produce one more unit of output. This is the notion of marginal cost examined in Chapter 11.
marginal product of factor i at input bundle F, $MP_i(F)$: The marginal product of factor i at input bundle **F**, $MP_i(\mathbf{F})$ for small changes in input i, Δf_i, is calculated as $MP_i(\mathbf{F}) = (Q(\mathbf{F} + \Delta f_i) - Q(\mathbf{F}))/\Delta f_i = \Delta Q/\Delta f_i$. This is also sometimes called the *marginal physical product of factor i*.
marginal profit ($M\pi(x)$): Marginal profit is the slope of the profit hill.
marginal rate of substitution (MRS): The marginal rate of substitution is defined as $MRS = -\Delta y/\Delta x$ along an indifference curve.
marginal rate of technical substitution, $MRTS_{j,i} = -\Delta f_j/\Delta f_i$: The marginal rate of technical substitution, $MRTS_{j,i} = -\Delta f_j/\Delta f_i$, holding all other factors of production constant along the isoquant.
marginal revenue (MR): Marginal revenue at a given output level is the slope of total revenue at that output level.
marginal revenue product of factor F, MRP(F): The marginal revenue product of factor F is the incremental revenue generated by using a bit more F, $MRP(F) = \Delta TR/\Delta F$, *ceteris paribus*.
marginal social benefit (MSB): The marginal social benefit is the increment in benefit achieved by consuming one more unit of output. This is the sum of private and external marginal benefits.
marginal social cost (MSC): The marginal social cost is the increment in cost imposed by producing one more unit of output.
marginal utility: The marginal utility of good *i* at bundle **A**, $MU_i(\mathbf{A})$, is calculated as: $MU_i(\mathbf{A}) = (U(\mathbf{A} + \Delta x_i) - U(\mathbf{A}))/\Delta x_i = \Delta U/\Delta x_i$ for small changes in good *i*, Δx_i.
marketable discharge right: A marketable discharge right gives the plant the right to pollute at a certain level. If the plant exceeds this level, it must purchase discharge rights from other plants, and if the plant's emissions are lower than the number of permits it holds, it can sell the remaining permits to plants that are in the markets for these permits.
market clearing price: The market clearing price is the price at which supply equals demand. Often, this is called the *equilibrium price* or *market price*.
market supply: Market supply is the horizontal sum of individual firm supply curves.
Marshallian demand: Marshallian demand is demand for a good as a function of its price, holding all other prices and income constant.

maximum efficient scale (MaxES): Maximum efficient scale is the largest level of output for which production achieves minimum long-run average cost of production.
minimum efficient scale (MES): Minimum efficient scale is the smallest level of output for which production achieves minimum long-run average cost of production.
monopoly rent: Monopoly rent is the profit that accrues due to the monopolist's sheltered market position.
monopsony: A monopsony is a market that has only one buyer.
monopsony power: Buyers have monopsony power if they have the ability to affect the price of a good via their purchase decisions.
monotonicity: Preferences are monotonic if more of a good is at least as good as less of that good.
monotonic transformation: A monotonic transformation is a function, f(x), that preserves order. A function preserves order if whenever $x < y$, then $f(x) < f(y)$.
moral hazard problem: The moral hazard problem occurs when the insured party undertakes actions that the party would not undertake in the absence of insurance.
MP vector, (MP_L, MP_K): The MP vector, (MP_L, MP_K), points in the direction of the maximum rate of change in production, and the size of the vector represents how quickly this change occurs.
$MRS_{j,i}$: $MRS_{j,i} = -\Delta x_j/\Delta x_i$, holding all other goods constant along the indifference curve.
MU vector: The MU vector, (MU_x, MU_y), points in the direction of the maximum rate of change in utility, and the size of the vector represents how quickly this change occurs.
multiple-shot games: Multiple-shot games are games in which strategies are chosen and payoffs determined in repeated plays of the game.

N

Nash equilibrium: A Nash equilibrium occurs if every player's strategy is optimal, given competitors' strategies.
natural monopoly: A market is a natural monopoly if average cost of production is declining at the point where demand and average cost intersect.
necessity: A good is a necessity if $\eta < 1$. A decreasing percentage of income is spent on the good as income increases.
negative externality: A negative externality occurs if an economic actor does not face the full cost of an economic action.
net present value (NPV): Net present value is the sum of present values.
network externality: A network externality exists if one consumer's demand for a good depends on other individuals' demands for the good.
nominal price: The nominal price of a good is the price posted for the good. This price is not adjusted for inflation.
noncooperative game: A noncooperative game is a game in which formal negotiation and entering into a legally binding contract is not possible.
nonexclusive good: A good is nonexclusive if it is impossible or expensive to exclude individuals from benefiting from the good.
nonrivalrous good: A good is nonrivalrous if consumption by one party does not diminish the ability of other parties to consume the good.
normal good: A normal good is a good whose demand increases as income increases. In terms of elasticity, the good is normal if $\eta_x > 0$.
normal profits: A firm earns normal profits when total revenue and total cost coincide.
normative economic analysis: Normative economic analysis moves beyond the realm of descriptive and predictive analysis to examine what should be done to achieve a set of goals put forward by policymakers.
not binding: A constraint is not binding on a bundle if the bundle remains feasible when the constraint tightens by a small amount.
numeraire: A numeraire is a good whose price is fixed at $1.00.

O

oligopoly: Oligopoly is a market structure in which a few firms dominate the market.
one-shot games: One-shot games are games in which each player chooses strategy once, and payoffs are determined as a result of that choice.
opportunity cost: The opportunity cost of a resource is the value of that resource in its next-best alternative use. Another term used for opportunity cost is *economic cost*.
options contract: An options contract gives the purchaser the ability to purchase a product at a given date in the future for a fixed price.
ordinal: A relationship between two distinct numbers is ordinal if the ordering matters. Ordering means which is larger or which is smaller of the two numbers.
ordinary good: A good is an ordinary good if its demand is downward sloping.
overtime: If a firm pays one wage rate for all hours worked up to a certain number of hours per time period and a higher wage for hours worked above this number, the higher wage rate is called the overtime wage rate.

P

parametric representation: The parametric representation of the budget constraint describes the constraint in terms of the portion of the budget devoted to each good.
Pareto optimal: An allocation of resources is Pareto optimal if there are *no* reallocations of resources in which at least one is made better off and no one involved is made worse off.
Pareto superior: A reallocation of resources is Pareto superior to the initial allocation if no one involved is made worse off, and at least one is made better off.
payoff matrix: A payoff matrix is a table that details each possible combination of strategies and the payoffs associated with each combination.
payoffs: Payoffs are the outcomes associated with a set of strategies. Each player will have a payoff for each set of alternatives.
perfect complements: Two goods are perfect complements if they tend to be consumed in fixed proportions.
perfect substitutes: Two goods are perfect substitutes if you are willing to trade one good for another at a constant rate.
perpetuity: A perpetuity is a perpetual annuity.
Pigouvian tax: A Pigouvian tax is a per-unit tax on the output of goods that produce externalities. The tax attempts to equate

marginal social benefit with marginal social cost to internalize the externality.
players: Players are the decision-making units that play games. Each player chooses among various strategies or options.
pollution abatement subsidy: A pollution abatement subsidy is a government subsidy earmarked for activities that reduce pollution.
positive economic analysis: Positive economic analysis uses economic models to predict or understand the effect of a change in economic circumstance on the economic system.
positive externality: A positive externality occurs if an economic actor does not capture the full benefit of an economic action.
preferences: Preferences are an individual's valuation of goods and services, independent of budget and price.
preferences are convex: Preferences are convex if the upper contour set (the set of bundles that is at least as good as a given bundle) is a convex set.
price ceiling: A price ceiling is a legally imposed maximum price at which the good can be sold.
price consumption curve (PCC): The price consumption curve is the set of utility-maximizing consumption bundles associated with different prices for a good.
price discrimination: Price discrimination is selling the same good at different prices.
price elasticity of demand: The price elasticity of demand is the percentage change in quantity demanded for a given percentage change in price ($\varepsilon = \%\Delta Q_d/\%\Delta P$).
price elasticity of supply: The price elasticity of supply is the percentage change in quantity supplied for a given percentage change in price. It is also commonly shortened to *supply elasticity*.
price floor: A price floor is a legally imposed minimum price at which the good can be sold.
price maker: A firm is a price maker if it has some price-setting ability for the product it produces.
price taker: An economic actor is a price taker if it can buy or sell as much or as little as it wishes without affecting the market price of the product.
price vector: The price vector, (P_x, P_y), points in the direction of maximum increase in cost. Since the components of the price vector are prices, the size of this vector represents how quickly costs increase.
principal-agent problem: The principal-agent problem occurs when the principal cannot monitor the actions of the agent who is charged with making decisions on behalf of the principal.
private good: A private good is rivalrous and exclusive.
producer surplus (PS): Producer surplus is the excess of revenue over the variable cost of producing a given level of output.
production function: A production function summarizes the relation that exists between a given bundle of inputs and the maximum amount of output that can be produced from those inputs. A production function is based on a given state of technology.
production possibilities frontier (PPF): A production possibilities frontier (PPF) represents the set of alternative combinations of goods that a producer can produce, given fixed inputs and technology.
promise: A promise is a commitment made to a second party in a bargain.
property right: A property right is a legal rule stating what property owners can do with their property.
purchasing power: Purchasing power is the ability to generate utility through the purchase of goods.
pure public good: A pure public good is nonrivalrous and nonexclusive.

Q

quantity demanded: The quantity demanded is the amount consumers wish to purchase at a given price.
quantity supplied: The quantity supplied is the amount producers wish to sell at a given price.

R

reaction function: A reaction function describes how one firm reacts to another firm's actions.
real price: The real price of a good is the nominal price of the good adjusted for inflation.
relative price: If r is the relative price, $r = P_x/P_y$, r will be the price of x if y is the numeraire.
rent control: Rent control is a price ceiling applied to rental housing.
representing: A utility function, U, represents a given set of preferences, $\succ$, if the following holds for any two bundles **A** and **B**: If $\mathbf{A} \succ \mathbf{B}$, then $U(\mathbf{A}) > U(\mathbf{B})$, and if $U(\mathbf{A}) > U(\mathbf{B})$, then $\mathbf{A} \succ \mathbf{B}$.
risk averse: An individual is risk averse if the utility associated with the expected income level derived from the lottery exceeds the expected utility of the lottery.
risk loving: An individual is risk loving if the utility associated with the expected income level derived from the lottery is less than the expected utility of the lottery.
risk neutral: An individual is risk neutral if the utility associated with the expected income level derived from the lottery equals the expected utility of the lottery.
risk premium (RP(X)): The risk premium of a lottery is the amount of income an individual would be willing to pay to avoid the risk.

S

satiation point: The point where a "good" turns into a "bad" is called a satiation point.
screening: A set of insurance policies screens individuals if the individuals self-select into different risk classes.
separating equilibrium: A separating equilibrium is one in which high-productivity and low-productivity segments are separated by workers choosing to use a signal.
short run: The short run is the time period in which the firm is unable to vary some of its inputs.
short-run expansion path (SREP): The short-run expansion path is the set of cost-minimizing input bundles for different levels of output and fixed factor prices, given some fixed factors of production.
short-run perfectly competitive equilibrium: The short-run perfectly competitive equilibrium is the (Q, P) combination for which market demand and short-run market supply are equal.

shut down: If a firm decides to produce no output in the short run, economists say the firm has decided to shut down. When a firm shuts down, it still must pay its fixed costs.
slope-intercept representation: The slope-intercept representation of the budget constraint presents the constraint in $y = m \cdot x + b$ format.
Slutsky equation: The algebraic structure used to describe demand decomposition is called the Slutsky equation.
snob effect: If a consumer's demand for a good decreases as more consumers demand the good, then the good has a snob effect.
Stackelberg leader: A Stackelberg leader believes that its rivals will choose their output based on what the Stackelberg leader chooses to produce.
store method: The store method of representing a budget constraint simply adds the amount spent on each good across goods. The resulting sum is income.
strategic behavior: A firm engages in strategic behavior if it undertakes actions with the expectation that those actions will signal future actions that are favorable to the firm.
strategy: A strategy is an option available to a player.
strict convexity: Preferences are strictly convex if all bundles **C** *between* any two indifferent bundles **A** and **B** are strictly preferred to the endpoints.
strict monotonicity: Preferences are strictly monotonic if more of a good is better than less of that good.
substitute: If an increase in the price of one good, y, leads to an increase in demand for the other good, x, then y is a substitute for x. In terms of elasticity, y is a substitute for x if $\varepsilon_{x,y} > 0$.
substitution bias: The compensation required to maintain a fixed market basket overstates the true cost of living because it does not control for the substitution that occurs when relative prices change. This overstatement is called the substitution bias.
substitution effect: The substitution effect of a price change is the part of the total effect that is due to the individual adjusting consumption in response to changing relative prices of both goods induced by a price change.
sunk cost: A sunk cost is a cost that has already occurred and cannot be recovered.
supply curve: A supply curve describes the quantity firms wish to sell for various prices. Often, this is shortened to *supply*.

T

tacit bargaining: Tacit bargaining is bargaining that is not openly expressed but that is implied by actions.
threat: A threat involves undertaking an action that harms yourself if your rivals do something you do not want them to do. You also harm them, but the key attribute of a threat is that you make *yourself* worse off.
time consistency problem: A time consistency problem exists when a player's best strategy changes as rivals make observable choices ahead of that player's choice.
total cost (TC): Total cost is the sum of fixed and variable cost.
total effect: The total effect of a price change is the change in consumption of both x and y induced by a change in price.
total product curve: A total product curve is the maximum quantity produced as a function of a single factor of production, holding all other factors of production fixed.
total surplus (TS): Total surplus is the sum of consumer surplus and producer surplus.
transactions costs: Transactions costs are the costs involved in negotiating and enforcing an agreement between two parties.
transitive: Preferences are transitive if you prefer bundle **A** to **B**, and **B** to **C**, then you must prefer **A** to **C**.
two-part tariff: A two-part tariff involves two fees: One part is an entry fee; the other part is a fee for specific usage. Amusement parks often have a two-part tariff structure.

U

unitary budget constraint: A unitary budget constraint is obtained by setting all prices and income equal to one.
unitary elasticity: When $|\varepsilon| = 1$, we say that demand has unitary elasticity.
unitary income elasticity: A good has unitary income elasticity if $\eta = 1$. A constant percentage of income is spent on the good.
utility level: The utility level is the number that is assigned to a given bundle. The numbers representing utility levels are called *utils*.

V

variable cost (VC): Variable cost is the opportunity cost that accrues to factors of production that are allowed to vary in the short run.
variable-sum game: In a variable-sum game, the total value of the payoffs varies, based on the strategies that the players pursue.

W

weak convexity: Preferences are weakly convex if all bundles **C** *between* any two indifferent bundles **A** and **B** are weakly preferred (preferred or indifferent) to the endpoints.
well behaved: Preferences are well behaved when they are complete, transitive, monotonic, and convex.
well defined: Preferences are well defined if they are both complete and transitive.

Z

zero-sum game: In a zero-sum game (or constant-sum game), the gains and losses of the parties exactly offset one another.

Index

Note: f after a page number indicates material in a figure; t indicates material in a table; n indicates material in an endnote.